Breeding Bird Atlas
of Santa Clara County, California

D. Wheye 2007

Breeding Bird Atlas
of Santa Clara County, California

William G. Bousman

WITH CONTRIBUTIONS BY:

Stephen C. Rottenborn
Michael M. Rogers
Charles J. Coston
Paul L. Noble
Ann Verdi
Carl M. Wentworth (geology)
Lynne A. Trulio
David L. Suddjian

Sara Timby (plant communities)
Michael J. Mammoser
Gloria G. Heller
Roy S. Cameron
M. Clark Blake, Jr. (geology)
Cheryl M. Strong
Phyllis M. Browning

Santa Clara Valley Audubon Society
Cupertino, California
2007

Library of Congress Cataloging-in-Publication Data:
Author: Bousman, William G. 1941-
Breeding Bird Atlas of Santa Clara County, California
547 pp.
Includes bibliographic references (24 pp.)

ISBN 978-0-9796038-0-8

Library of Congress control number: 2007927672

Published 2007 by:
Santa Clara Valley Audubon Society
22221 McClellan Road
Cupertino, CA 95014

Our Breeding Bird Sponsors

In an effort to promote awareness of our *entire* breeding bird community of 177 species, the Santa Clara Valley Audubon Society sent out an invitation in September 2007 to both our dedicated members and the wider South Bay Birds online audience. The response was almost immediate, with many people offering support for their favorite species! The following parties are now recognized for their significant involvement in the publication of the landmark work you now hold in your hands, but more importantly, for demonstrating our community's interest in the full complement of its breeding bird population. Santa Clara Valley Audubon is pleased to recognize each of them for their interest in this important project, the many years of work, and the 177 breeding birds it represents. Thank you!

SPECIES (IN TAXONOMIC ORDER)	SPONSORED BY
Canada Goose	Shannon McMahon
Wood Duck	Ann Verdi
Gadwall	Anne Creevy: to my Fall 2007 Birding Basics Class
Mallard	Katy Obringer
Blue-winged Teal	Lennie Stovel
Cinnamon Teal	Janet MacDonald Ehmke
Northern Shoveler	Barbara and Win Foster
Northern Pintail	Susan D. Thomas
Green-winged Teal	Dorothy Wisler Parrine
Canvasback	Rodney Forseth
Redhead	Robert Stephens and Julie Packard
Ring-necked Duck	Minda Thomas
Lesser Scaup	In Honor of Bob Power by his PAAS birding class
Common Merganser	Debbie and Steve Thompson
Ruddy Duck	Ann Davidson and Marcia Ruotolo
Ring-necked Pheasant	Chris and Lisa Spooner
Wild Turkey	Derry and Charlene Kabcenell
Mountain Quail	David McIntyre and Antoinette Konski
California Quail	In Memory of Judith Gwynne Holmquist
Pied-billed Grebe	Joan Leighton
Eared Grebe	Lynn Tennefoss

SPECIES (IN TAXONOMIC ORDER)	SPONSORED BY
Western Grebe	In Honor of Bob Power by his PAAS birding class
Clark's Grebe	Bob Roadcap
Double-crested Cormorant	Mary Lorey
American Bittern	Bonnie Bedford-White
Great Blue Heron	Margo Tenold
Great Egret	Nancy Neal Yeend
Snowy Egret	Pati Rouzer, D.C.
Little Blue Heron	Edwin G. Ehmke
Cattle Egret	Ashutosh Sinha
Green Heron	For my brother Lance Spletzer
Black-crowned Night-Heron	James Hulseman
White-faced Ibis	Penny Howell
Turkey Vulture	Jim and Donna Meyer
Osprey	Ralph W. Schardt
White-tailed Kite	Ohlone Audubon Society
Northern Harrier	Bill and Diane Carver
Sharp-shinned Hawk	Laurie Bechtler
Cooper's Hawk	Jan Hintermeister
Red-shouldered Hawk	Casa Dos Rios
Red-tailed Hawk	Carter Jones
Golden Eagle	David McIntyre and Antoinette Konski
American Kestrel	Tate and Curtis Snyder
Peregrine Falcon	Cheesemans' Ecology Safaris
Prairie Falcon	George S. Peyton, Jr. and Lani Rumbaoa
Clapper Rail	Charles J. and Susan M. Bell
Virginia Rail	Betty Burridge
Common Moorhen	Elinor Spellman
American Coot	Bob and Hanno Lewis
Snowy Plover	Judy Rickard
Killdeer	Killdeer chicks are special—in honor of Sam Brain
Black-necked Stilt	San Francisco Bay Bird Observatory
American Avocet	Santa Clara Valley Audubon Society
Spotted Sandpiper	Mary Jane Ehmke
California Gull	Katy Obringer
Western Gull	A member of Matthew Dodder's PAAS class
Caspian Tern	Deborah Jamison and Steven Patt
Forster's Tern	Bobbie Handen
Black Skimmer	Karen DeMello
Rock Pigeon	Joanne H. Lazar
Band-tailed Pigeon	Kay Partelow
Mourning Dove	Patty McGann
Greater Roadrunner	Bob and Deborah Hirt
Barn Owl	Dotty Calabrese and Donna Clarke
Western Screech-Owl	Delores and Peter White
Great Horned Owl	Kay Matthews
Northern Pygmy-Owl	Robert Stephens and Julie Packard

SPECIES (IN TAXONOMIC ORDER)	SPONSORED BY
Burrowing Owl	Ruth and Gene Troetschler
Long-eared Owl	Jane Jordan
Northern Saw-whet Owl	David McIntyre and Antoinette Konski
Common Poorwill	Amy Lauterbach
Vaux's Swift	Madrone Audubon Society
White-throated Swift	Sam, Amy, and Bob Power
Black-chinned Hummingbird	In memory of Jane Becker-Haven, an Audubon Moment
Anna's Hummingbird	Rita R. Colwell
Costa's Hummingbird	Amy Forseth
Allen's Hummingbird	Kay and Ed Kinney
Belted Kingfisher	Eric Goodill
Lewis's Woodpecker	David McIntyre and Antoinette Konski
Acorn Woodpecker	Ruth and Gene Troetschler
Nuttall's Woodpecker	Joy L. Robinson
Downy Woodpecker	Rebecca and Everett Palmer
Hairy Woodpecker	James Yurchenco
Northern Flicker	Patty Boyle
Pileated Woodpecker	Eric Goodill
Olive-sided Flycatcher	John and Clysta McLemore
Western Wood-Pewee	David Suddjian
Pacific-slope Flycatcher	In honor of Ulistac Natural Area
Black Phoebe	Joyce Bartlett
Say's Phoebe	The Tiwari Family (Vivek, Gargi, Anika, Vayun)
Ash-throated Flycatcher	Kendric and Marion Smith
Cassin's Kingbird	Susan Bodenlos and Ashok Khosla
Western Kingbird	Margot Rawlins
Loggerhead Shrike	Mary Ann Allan
Bell's Vireo	Rosalie Lefkowitz
Cassin's Vireo	Honoring Kelly Dodder (from PAAS students)
Hutton's Vireo	Emily Allen
Warbling Vireo	Kelly Dodder
Steller's Jay	To honor Theresa Grieve for her work with the jays
Western Scrub-Jay	Jim and Kathy Johnson
Yellow-billed Magpie	Honoring Ken Himes - Good Morning Sir!
American Crow	Ronald LeCount
Common Raven	Ashok Khosla
Horned Lark	Cathy and Don Priest
Purple Martin	Kay Partelow
Tree Swallow	David Cook and Barbara Hutchings
Violet-green Swallow	Robert Stephens and Julie Packard
Northern Rough-winged Swallow	In Honor of Bob Power by his PAAS birding class
Cliff Swallow	In Honor of Bob Power by his PAAS birding class
Barn Swallow	Harry L. Elliott, Jr.
Chestnut-backed Chickadee	Debbie and Steve Thompson
Oak Titmouse	Phil Leighton
Bushtit	Larisa K. Miller

SPECIES (IN TAXONOMIC ORDER)	SPONSORED BY
Red-breasted Nuthatch	Connie West
White-breasted Nuthatch	Eric Goodill
Pygmy Nuthatch	Sequoia Audubon Society
Brown Creeper	Kirsten R. Holmquist
Rock Wren	Kirsten R. Holmquist
Canyon Wren	Eric Goodill
Bewick's Wren	Sue and Jim Liskovec
House Wren	David and Tiffany Speer
Winter Wren	Richard Page
Marsh Wren	Betty Wyatt
American Dipper	The Norton Family
Golden-crowned Kinglet	Leonie F. Batkin
Blue-gray Gnatcatcher	Leda Beth Gray and David Drake
Western Bluebird	Janna Pauser
Swainson's Thrush	Steven Patt
Hermit Thrush	John and Clysta McLemore
American Robin	Katy Obringer
Wrentit	Ashutosh Sinha
Northern Mockingbird	Katy Obringer
California Thrasher	Eric Goodill
European Starling	Chris MacIntosh
Cedar Waxwing	Lisa Myers, Let's Go Birding
Phainopepla	Lori Cuesta
Orange-crowned Warbler	Ken Schneider
Yellow Warbler	Dave Johnston, PhD.
Yellow-rumped Warbler	In Honor of Bob Power by his PAAS birding class
Black-throated Gray Warbler	David McIntyre and Antoinette Konski
Hermit Warbler	Nicholas Verdi
MacGillivray's Warbler	Robert Stephens and Julie Packard
Common Yellowthroat	Leonie F. Batkin
Wilson's Warbler	Deborah Jamison
Yellow-breasted Chat	Phil and Joan Leighton
Western Tanager	Jocelyn Khosla
Spotted Towhee	George and Lilo Miller
California Towhee	David Presotto and Caryl Carr
Rufous-crowned Sparrow	David McIntyre and Antoinette Konski
Chipping Sparrow	Honoring Matthew Dodder (from his PAAS students)
Black-chinned Sparrow	Matthew Dodder
Lark Sparrow	David McIntyre and Antoinette Konski
Sage Sparrow	Bob and Deborah Hirt
Savannah Sparrow	Luigi and Greg
Grasshopper Sparrow	Mary Wisnewski and Bill Walker
Song Sparrow	Napa-Solano Audubon Society
Dark-eyed Junco	Nancy R. Teater
Black-headed Grosbeak	The Armer Family
Blue Grosbeak	Tom Grey

SPECIES (IN TAXONOMIC ORDER)	SPONSORED BY
Lazuli Bunting	Ralph W. Schardt
Indigo Bunting	Boyce Burge and Linda Lotspeich
Red-winged Blackbird	Katy Obringer
Tricolored Blackbird	James W. Thomas
Western Meadowlark	Lisa Myers, Let's Go Birding
Brewer's Blackbird	Andrew Verdi
Great-tailed Grackle	Neil and Eldig Lukes
Brown-headed Cowbird	Leonie F. Batkin
Hooded Oriole	Barbara and Ron McDow
Bullock's Oriole	Robert Stephens and Julie Packard
Purple Finch	Ken Peterson
House Finch	Liz and Gary Nielsen
Red Crossbill	Ashutosh Sinha
Pine Siskin	Wild Bird Center of Los Gatos
Lesser Goldfinch	J. Bryson
Lawrence's Goldfinch	Bob and Deborah Hirt
American Goldfinch	Amanda Verdi
House Sparrow	Gay Katilius

TO ALL OF OUR SPONSORS, THANK YOU.

To the memory of

L. Richard Mewaldt, 1917–1990

for his steadfast encouragement of the amateur

contribution to ornithology

ACKNOWLEDGMENTS

First and foremost, I acknowledge the dedication and skill of the atlasers who conducted the fieldwork for this atlas from 1987 to 1993. This legion of careful observers is listed in full in Appendix 1, along with many other contributors who furnished individual records. The skilled and careful work of all of these observers is reflected in the breadth and accuracy of this atlas.

The financial necessities attendant upon conducting the atlas were largely borne by the dues paid by the atlasers themselves during the atlas period. In addition, generous contributions were made by Dorothy Hunt, Donald S. Starks, the Sequoia Audubon Society, the Santa Clara Valley Audubon Society, and Michael J. Mammoser.

Atlasing was conducted on both public and private land. Numerous stewards of publicly owned lands, even those normally closed to the public, granted atlasers access. Kay E. Schmidt-Robinson of the California State Parks facilitated access for atlasers in the vast Henry Coe State Park. Within Coe Park, Barry Breckling, the onsite ranger and a birder himself, was helpful to atlasers in the park. Numerous staff members of the Santa Clara County Parks and Recreation Department assisted atlasers in their surveys in local county parks, including Rebecca J. Black for Ed Levin County Park. Rangers and personnel with the Midpeninsula Regional Open Space District assisted atlasers in visits to these properties. Chris Sanger is particularly appreciated for his assistance with access to Mt. Umunhum. Brian Hartsell offered assistance for San Jose's Alum Rock Park. Edward H. Stewart and George Lester granted access to San Francisco Water Department lands in the drainage of Calaveras Reservoir.

Private landowners, ranch managers, and lessees of private lands were generous in granting access to these lands, particularly in the Diablo Range. These included: Joe Aljoe, Fanny Arnold, William H. Beeger, Chet Behen, John Covo, Marlin Gohn, Sam Halsted, James Hawley, Carmen Lomanto, Jack and Phyllis Mallison, McComb Enterprises, Katherine McGeehon, Dennis Moreno, Roy E. Naftzger, Jr., Doug Renaud, John W. Scherrer, Clyde Shearer, Garry and Ruth Stoddard, Dwight Testerman, Alan A. Wray, and Leonard W. Yates. Allyn Erickson of the Almaden-IBM Research Facility granted access to IBM land above the Almaden Valley. The Hewlett and Packard families, owners of San Felipe Ranch, provided access to these lands through Debbie Reagan, Barbara Jacobsen, and Ralph Jacobsen. The San Jose Water Company was generous in allowing access to its private lands in the Los Gatos Creek watershed and the Lake Elsman area. Stanford University allowed access to a number of areas normally closed to the public.

Taryn Lindquist of the U.S. Geological Survey in Menlo Park allowed access to maps within the San Jose 1:100,000 quadrangle where she had added property lines from Santa Clara County property records to support a Survey research project. She also provided a database of contact information. Both sets of data were used to contact private landowners in the Diablo Range.

I appreciate the tolerance and understanding of the people at my other job with the U.S. Army Aeroflightdynamics Directorate at Moffett Field, who supported this extracurricular activity. In particular I acknowledge the support and advice of Dr. William Warmbrodt of the National Aeronautics and Space Administration and Dr. Chee Tung and Thomas Maier of the U.S. Army Aeroflightdynamics Directorate.

Joy Albertson of the U.S. Fish and Wildlife Service offered Clapper Rail nesting information, from her studies in the South Bay that improved our knowledge of this rail's distribution. Similarly, Gary Page and Janet Kjelmyr of PRBO Conservation Science provided field notes from their surveys of breeding Snowy Plovers. Janet T. Hanson, Gina Barton, and Cheryl M. Strong of the San Francisco Bay Bird Observatory provided unpublished records concerning breeding birds and banding results from their various research programs in the South Bay. Alvaro Jaramillo and Debra L. Shearwater gave us useful information concerning local breeding species.

Following the atlas period, Michael M. Rogers established and maintained the postatlas database, based on the contributions of many individuals (also listed in Appendix 1). The postatlas data have augmented the atlas data, particularly for birds breeding in the Santa Clara Valley.

During and after the atlas period, a number of contributors assisted with research dealing with Santa Clara County's birds. Gloria G. Heller went through a number of references and compiled estimates of egg dates for possible breeding species. Gloria also visited the Western Foundation of Vertebrate Zoology when it was located at Brentwood, Cal., and looked up records of local breeding of species believed to be particularly rare. Phyllis M. Browning went through all issues of the *Condor*, spanning the years from 1899 to 1994, and developed a list of all articles relevant to birds within Santa Clara County or nearby. Her list also included a brief synopsis. Stephen C. Rottenborn developed a file that included extracts or summaries from the local literature. This included extracts from published materials, such as Price (1898a-f), Van Denburgh (1899b), Grinnell and Wythe (1927), Grinnell and Miller (1944), Sibley (1952), and Row (1960). Dr. Rottenborn also went through back issues of newsletters of the Santa Clara Valley Audubon Society and copies of *Bird-Lore* to obtain information concerning local birds. Rosalie Lefkowitz searched through the published records for the Middle Pacific Coast Region (now Northern California Region) in 50 volumes of *Audubon Field Notes* and *American Birds* and extracted records relevant to local birds. Joan Priest granted access to records on 3x5 file cards at the Humane Society of Santa Clara Valley that recorded information on injured and dead nesting birds. Ann Verdi then examined the file cards from 1987 to 1993 and assembled data entry records for those cases that included location information.

The development of the atlas maps benefited from the assistance of those with expertise in Geographic Information Systems (GIS). Rusty Scalf helped with general mapping information for Santa Clara County. Meredith Williams, at the Branner Geology Library at Stanford University, assisted with the GAP data that are shown in Chapter 3. Bob Patrie, a volunteer with

ACKNOWLEDGMENTS

Henry Coe State Park, furnished mapping data dealing with that park's boundaries. Matthew Sagues, Kristi Altieri, and Cindy Roessler of the Midpeninsula Regional Open Space District assisted with mapping data for the district's land holdings.

The search for historical breeding records in Santa Clara County was assisted by a number of museums, both in the United States and overseas. René Corado of the Western Foundation of Vertebrate Zoology, Camarillo, Cal., helped me in numerous ways, both on my visits to Camarillo to use the Foundation's data from their extensive egg collections and in offering answers to my many inquiries. Data for the egg and specimen collections at the Museum of Vertebrate Zoology, Berkeley, Cal., were accessible online; this extensive database was easily consulted and yielded many records. Carla Cicero was most helpful in answering specific questions about the collections. Douglas J. Long aided me in a visit to the California Academy of Sciences, San Francisco, Cal. Craig Ludwig furnished records from the egg and specimen database at the U.S. National Museum; these data are particularly useful for the records of the early collectors, before 1900. Gerald Braden of the San Bernardino Natural History Museum, Redlands, Cal., and Krista Fahy of the Santa Barbara Museum of Natural History, Santa Barbara, Cal., also supported my searches of historical records. Assistance on specific records in European collections was provided by Robert Prys-Jones of The Natural History Museum, Tring, Great Britain, and Bernd Nicolai of the Museum Heineanum, Halberstadt, Germany.

Expertise on current records was offered by the Regional Editors of the Middle Pacific Coast Region (now Northern California Region) of *North American Birds*, including Michael M. Rogers, Steven A. Glover, Luke W. Cole, and Scott B. Terrill. I have had an extensive and beneficial correspondence, dealing with local breeding records, with my counterparts for nearby atlases, including David L. Suddjian of the Santa Cruz County Breeding Bird Atlas (unpubl.), Rick Johnson and Peter J. Metropulos of the San Mateo County Breeding Bird Atlas (Sequoia Audubon Society 2001a), and Robert J. Richmond of the Alameda County Breeding Bird Atlas (unpubl.). In addition, David L. Suddjian has given me access to unpublished field notes of Edward McClintock and Leslie Hawkins that are contained in the Santa Cruz Bird Club files.

Jann Null of Golden Gate Weather Services is acknowledged for recommending a variety of information sources for rainfall and other weather data for the San Francisco Bay area.

Thomas Ryan was helpful in obtaining historical information on county reservoirs while he was working for the Santa Clara Valley Water District.

I have used or adapted a number of figures from the literature, and I appreciate the permission to use these figures. The figure on water balance in Chapter 1 is from Major (1988) with permission from Phyllis Faber, California Native Plant Society. The map of Palo Alto in the 1840s was compiled and drawn by Alan K. Brown and is used with his permission. I have adapted data from Cohen and Carlton (1998) with permission from Andrew N. Cohen.

In the long period before publication of this atlas, many libraries have furnished reference materials. The materials in the Falconer Biology Library, Stanford University, have been my main sustenance over the past decade, as well as occasional feasts of the older literature held in the Stanford Auxiliary Libraries. I have also had the opportunity to use the Menlo Park Library, the Mountain View Public Library, and the joint San Jose Public Library and San Jose State University Library, including their auxiliary library. In all cases, the staff at these libraries have been courteous and helpful. Also, I acknowledge H. T. Harvey and Associates for providing me access to their private library.

Many people have helped with the publication of this book. John Rawlings has offered advice on aspects of book publication by amateurs. People who have read through portions of the final manuscript and sought to seek out and destroy the inevitable errors, include Phyllis M. Browning, Bill Carver, Rosalie Lefkowitz, Michael J. Mammoser, and Michael M. Rogers.

Last, but not least, I appreciate the patience and support of my wife, Billie R. Bousman, who has watched the growing heaps of files and paper over the years and held her tongue. But most important, she has been my bibliographic specialist, search engine, and point woman on regular foraging trips into the Stanford University libraries.

ATLAS ORGANIZATION

Atlas Development

Project Coordinator
    William G. Bousman

Atlas Committee (* founding members)
    William G. Bousman*, chair
    Gloria G. Heller*
    Grant Hoyt
    Amy Lauterbach
    Michael J. Mammoser
    L. Richard Mewaldt*
    Paul L. Noble*
    Michael D. Rigney*
    Michael M. Rogers
    Milton L. Seibert*
    David L. Suddjian*
    James Yurchenco

Regional Coordinators
    Region 1   Paul L. Noble
    Region 2   David L. Suddjian
    Region 3   Michael J. Mammoser
    Region 4   Roy S. Cameron
    Region 5   William G. Bousman
    Region 6   Michael M. Rogers, Grant Hoyt
    Region 7   Amy Lauterbach, James Yurchenco

Database Review Committee
    Michael J. Mammoser, chair
    William G. Bousman
    Paul L. Noble
    Michael M. Rogers
    Stephen C. Rottenborn

Contributing Authors
    M. Clark Blake, Jr.
    William G. Bousman
    Phyllis M. Browning
    Roy S. Cameron
    Charles J. Coston
    Gloria G. Heller
    Michael J. Mammoser
    Paul L. Noble
    Michael M. Rogers
    Stephen C. Rottenborn
    Cheryl M. Strong
    David L. Suddjian
    Sara Timby
    Lynne A. Trulio
    Ann Verdi
    Carl M. Wentworth

Atlas Publication

Editorial Committee
    William G. Bousman, chair
    Phyllis M. Browning
    Leslie Y. Chibana
    Rosalie Lefkowitz
    Michael M. Rogers
    Stephen C. Rottenborn

Editor
    Bill Carver

Literature Cited Editor
    Phyllis M. Browning

Art Committee
    William G. Bousman, chair
    Leslie Y. Chibana
    Rita Colwell
    Michael J. Mammoser
    Michael M. Rogers

Artists
    Karen L. Allaben-Confer
    Ellen L. Armstrong
    Bonnie Bedford-White
    Rita R. Colwell
    Emélie Curtis
    Shawneen E. Finnegan
    Marni Fylling
    Keith Hansen
    Alan Hopkins
    Zev Labinger
    Michael J. Mammoser
    Tim Manolis
    Ray Nelson
    Cynthia J. Page
    Don Radovich
    Edward Rooks
    Sophie Webb
    Darryl Wheye

Production Managers
    Matthew Dodder
    Bob Power
    Brenda Torres-Barreto

ARTISTS AND THEIR ILLUSTRATIONS

Illustrations for the species accounts are arranged by artist, and, for each artist, by taxonomic order. An * indicates that the illustration is originally published here; other drawings are from previously published atlases. Illustrations that appear with the Introduction and chapter-opening pages plus the cover and title page are also listed here. All illustrations in this atlas are copyrighted by the artist and are reproduced here with their permission.

Karen L. Allaben-Confer (Brooktondale, NY): Double-crested Cormorant, American Bittern, Great Blue Heron, Great Egret, Snowy Egret, Little Blue Heron, Cattle Egret, Sharp-shinned Hawk, Red-tailed Hawk, Golden Eagle, Virginia Rail, Common Moorhen, American Coot, Black Skimmer, Downy Woodpecker, Hairy Woodpecker, Western Wood-Pewee, and Yellow-billed Magpie.

Ellen L. Armstrong (Plainwell, MI, ellen.armstrong@wmich. edu): Gadwall, Blue-winged Teal, Indigo Bunting, and Purple Finch.

Bonnie Bedford-White: White-faced Ibis*.

William G. Bousman: Bewick's Wren (Chapter 5)*.

Rita R. Colwell (rcolwell@sbcglobal.net): Wood Duck*, Mallard*, Lesser Scaup*, Eared Grebe*, Green Heron*, Cooper's Hawk*, California Gull*, Western Screech-Owl*, Anna's Hummingbird*, Lewis's Woodpecker*, Acorn Woodpecker*, Nuttall's Woodpecker*, Pacific-slope Flycatcher*, Cassin's Vireo*, Warbling Vireo*, Chestnut-backed Chickadee (Chapter 8)*, White-breasted Nuthatch*, Pygmy Nuthatch, Swainson's Thrush*, Northern Mockingbird*, California Thrasher*, Spotted Towhee*, Rufous-crowned Sparrow*, Lazuli Bunting*, Red-winged Blackbird, Western Meadowlark*, and American Goldfinch*.

Emélie Curtis: Common Merganser*, Western Grebe*, Black-crowned Night-Heron*, White-tailed Kite*, Red-tailed Hawk (Introduction)*, Peregrine Falcon*, Prairie Falcon*, Black-necked Stilt*, Spotted Sandpiper*, Great Horned Owl (Chapter 7)*, Northern Pygmy-Owl*, Burrowing Owl*, Red-breasted Nuthatch*, Marsh Wren*, and Western Bluebird*.

Shawneen E. Finnegan (Portland, OR, shawneenfinnegan@ gmail.com): Northern Shoveler, Clark's Grebe, Osprey, American Avocet, Greater Roadrunner, Ash-throated Flycatcher, Cassin's Kingbird, Western Scrub-Jay, Purple Martin, Violet-green Swallow, Barn Swallow, Rock Wren, American Robin, Yellow-rumped Warbler, California Towhee, Black-chinned Sparrow, Song Sparrow, Dark-eyed Junco, Black-headed Grosbeak, Lesser Goldfinch, and Lawrence's Goldfinch.

Marni Fylling (marni_fylling@hotmail.com): Western Gull*.

Keith Hansen (www.keithhansen.com or birdhansen@earthlink. net: Mountain Quail, California Quail, Clapper Rail, White-throated Swift, and Horned Lark.

Alan Hopkins: Phainopepla.

Zev Labinger: Turkey Vulture, Northern Harrier, Cooper's Hawk (Chapter 6), Red-shouldered Hawk, Golden Eagle (Chapter 1), American Kestrel, Killdeer, Belted Kingfisher, Steller's Jay.

Michael J. Mammoser: Snowy Plover*.

Tim Manolis (Ylightfoot@aol.com): Oak Titmouse, Orange-crowned Warbler, Blue Grosbeak, Tricolored Blackbird, Brewer's Blackbird, and Hooded Oriole.

John S. Mariani (130 Morris Drive, Lumberton TX, 77657, www.birdswest.com): Common Poorwill*, Blue-gray Gnat-catcher*, and Hermit Warbler*.

Ray Nelson (429 15th Street, Bellingham, WA 98225, raynelsonart@msn.com): Say's Phoebe, Yellow Warbler, Yellow-breasted Chat, Western Tanager, Great-tailed Grackle, and House Finch.

Cynthia J. Page (page4cba@windstream.net): Canada Goose, Cinnamon Teal, Northern Pintail, Green-winged Teal, Canvasback, Redhead, Ring-necked Duck, Ruddy Duck, Rock Pigeon, Mourning Dove, Yellow-billed Cuckoo (Chapter 4), Barn Owl, Great Horned Owl, Long-eared Owl, Northern Saw-whet Owl, American Crow, Cliff Swallow, Brown Creeper, House Wren, Golden-crowned Kinglet, Chipping Sparrow, Savannah Sparrow, and House Sparrow.

Don Radovich: Red Crossbill and Pine Siskin.

Edward Rooks: Wild Turkey, Golden Eagle (cover)*, Northern Rough-winged Swallow, and Brown-headed Cowbird.

Sophie Webb: Ring-necked Pheasant, Pied-billed Grebe, Caspian Tern, Forster's Tern, Band-tailed Pigeon, Vaux's Swift, Black-chinned Hummingbird, Costa's Hummingbird, Allen's Hummingbird, Northern Flicker, Pileated Woodpecker, Olive-sided Flycatcher, Black Phoebe, Western Kingbird, Loggerhead Shrike, Bell's Vireo, Hutton's Vireo, Tree Swallow, Chestnut-backed Chickadee, Bushtit, Rock Wren (Chapter 2), Canyon Wren, Bewick's Wren, Winter Wren, American Dipper, Hermit Thrush, Wrentit, European Starling, Cedar Waxwing, Black-throated Gray Warbler, MacGillivray's Warbler, Common Yellowthroat, Wilson's Warbler, Lark Sparrow, Sage Sparrow, Grasshopper Sparrow, Bullock's Oriole, and Pine Siskin (Chapter 3).

Darryl Wheye (birds.stanford.edu): Acorn Woodpecker (title page)* and Common Raven.

CONTENTS

CONTENTS

CONTENTS

LIST OF FIGURES

LIST OF FIGURES

LIST OF TABLES

Breeding Bird Atlas
of Santa Clara County, California

Introduction

A breeding bird atlas seeks to determine the birds that breed within a geographic area. For this purpose, the area is divided by a grid, and each block formed by that grid is monitored for breeding activity over a nominal time span. Upon completion of the atlas, the data accumulated offer a richness of detail about breeding birds that can be obtained in few other ways. But the ultimate value of the atlas is realized when the entire effort is repeated, once each 25 years, making it possible to assess the changes in breeding bird populations with each new human generation.

The *Breeding Bird Atlas of Santa Clara County, California*, which reports the results of fieldwork in Santa Clara County from 1987 to 1993, was undertaken to determine the current status of all species of birds known to be breeding in the county. These data have been augmented with additional field observations reported from 1994 to 2005.

For the purposes of this atlas, we divided the county into 168 5-km by 5-km blocks. Over the seven-year atlas period, knowledgeable volunteers attempted to survey all of these blocks, across the span of months when breeding could reasonably be expected to occur, and to determine which species were breeding within each of the blocks. Coverage was easily obtained for blocks that were publicly accessible, but was difficult in many areas in the Diablo Range, where much of the land is privately held. Nonetheless, many landowners were happy to cooperate, and atlasers were able to obtain adequate coverage of 165 of the county blocks. (Only three blocks, in the southeastern part of the county, were not accessed.) The resulting data are presented as 177 species accounts, each of which consists of one page of text and a facing graphics page. Each graphics page includes a county map indicating those blocks where breeding of that species was confirmed, probable, or possible.

The first three chapters of the atlas offer a description of Santa Clara County, so as to afford the user a better understanding of the habitats in the county that are used by birds. Chapter 1, "A Description of Santa Clara County," is an overview of the county. It discusses the general climatic regime of the west coast of North America and how the county fits into that regime. Various features of the county's geography are discussed, including its major drainage patterns, its rainfall patterns (both geographi-

cal and temporal), and the water balance that characterizes the Mediterranean California climatic pattern and its effects on vegetation growth. The major features of the urban areas of the county, and the extent and distribution of public parklands, are discussed and mapped.

Chapter 2, "Geology and Tectonic History of Santa Clara County," by M. C. Blake, Jr., and C. M. Wentworth, describes the tectonic history of Santa Clara County and central California. With this tectonic history as backdrop, they describe the various geologic formations in the county and how they influence the soils and vegetation here.

Chapter 3, "Vegetation Communities in Santa Clara County," by Sara Timby, describes the county's vegetation types. Using the current GAP analysis, 28 plant communities are grouped in six categories and mapped. The general characters of each community are described, and the dominant constituent plants are enumerated.

Chapter 4, "A Natural History of Change," describes the natural habitats in Santa Clara County at the time of European settlement, and the changes that occurred as the land was settled, agriculture developed, and a mixture of industry and residences became much of what we see today.

Chapter 5, "Atlas Organization and Methods," describes the entire atlas process, as well as the methods and protocols used, and how these accord with similar efforts elsewhere in the country and the world.

Chapter 6, "Atlas Results," gives a broad perspective on the results of the atlasing in the county. The total number of species found breeding during the atlas period (and subsequently) are described. The most and least common species found are indicated.

Chapter 7, "Species Accounts," is the core of the book, providing historical and analytical text and graphics for each of the 177 species of birds that we consider the breeding avifauna of Santa Clara County today. The introductory paragraphs of this chapter describe the general structure of the species account texts and defines the symbols that are used on the facing graphics pages.

Chapter 8, "The Once and Future County," is an essay that looks backward at what has been lost and forward to what

1

INTRODUCTION

can be preserved and restored.

A variety of appendixes supports the materials set forth in the atlas. Appendix 1 lists the volunteer atlasers and other contributors who made the book possible.

Appendix 2 presents a history of ornithological study in the local area.

Appendix 3 summarizes avifaunal changes here in the 200 years since European settlement, to the degree that this can be determined.

Appendix 4 furnishes details on the breeding season "windows" (opening and closing dates for each species) that were used in determining breeding evidence, and in that respect supports Chapter 5.

Appendix 5 provides abundance estimates for the 159 species of birds that were confirmed to be breeding during the atlas period from 1987 to 1993.

Appendix 6 lists alphabetically the scientific and common names of the plants and animals (other than birds) that are mentioned in the text.

Appendix 7 is a gazetteer of place names for various locations in Santa Clara County and nearby areas that are no longer in use. Most of these names are mentioned in the historical literature, and many of them turn up in the species accounts.

Appendix 8 presents species accounts for ten species of birds that are known to have nested in Santa Clara County in the past, but are now considered extirpated here.

Appendix 9 gives species accounts for six non-native species of birds that have been introduced into the county, some of which may currently breed here, but have not established permanent populations.

Appendix 10 reports breeding confirmations of Bald Eagle and Virginia Rail that were obtained after 2005, but before publication of the atlas.

The book concludes with Literature Cited (an alphabetic listing of all the sources cited within its eight chapters and ten appendixes), and an Index to birds treated or mentioned in the text and appendixes.

1 A Description of Santa Clara County: Geography, Drainage Basins, Rainfall, and Land Use

ZeV

From equator to pole, the Earth's atmospheric circulation patterns present four climatic zones. The equatorial zone, straddling the equator, is characterized by high temperatures and heavy rainfall. The subtropical zone, to the north, is largely dry, with moderate temperatures and little wind. In North America, this zone is associated with the desert areas of the southwestern United States and northern Mexico. The temperate zone, farther north, is an area of westerlies, wide variations in temperature, and changeable weather with cyclonic storms. Finally, the polar zone, in the far northern latitudes, is again an area of little moisture. Associated with the changing of the seasons are shifts in zonal boundaries. Here, the California high, which is associated with the subtropical zone, moves south during the winter, allowing temperate-zone storms to sweep through the state. But in the summer this high shifts north once again, precluding rainfall in much of the state.

Major (1988) identified five climatic regions in California: Northwest Pacific Coast, Mediterranean California, Sierra Nevada-Cascades, Cold Desert (in the northeast), and Hot Desert (in the southeast). Santa Clara County falls largely within the Mediterranean California climatic region, although its western edge is along the boundary of the Northwest Pacific Coast province. This overlap enhances the county's ecological diversity and increases the avian species count. Within the Northwest Pacific Coast province in California there is a sevenfold gradient in rainfall from north to south (Major 1988). In the hills and coastal canyons of this province, still covered with coniferous forests of Douglas fir and coast redwood, the coastal fog that forms over the cold currents of the Pacific Ocean yields additional water as fog drip. This bonus is particularly important in the summer months, when 7 to 8 inches of equivalent rainfall settle within these coastal forests (Major 1988). In California, the coastal forest narrows from north to south, but is more or less continuous. South of Mendocino County, however, in Sonoma and Marin counties, gaps begin to occur. At San Francisco Bay, the persistent summer fog that flows through the Golden Gate provides moisture for a small coastal forest in the western Contra Costa Hills of Alameda and Contra Costa counties. South of San Francisco Bay, the coastal slopes of the Santa Cruz Mountains once again support an extensive coniferous forest, an out-

post and a reminder of the great forests of the Pacific Northwest. Finally, south along the coast of Monterey County, these forests come to an end in the coastal canyons of the Big Sur, and the land is dominated by chaparral and other vegetation typical of the Mediterranean California climate.

The Mediterranean California climate, typical of Santa Clara County and much of the rest of California, has been described by Major (1988) as "a desert in summer, a sodden, dripping landscape in winter, a glory of wildflowers in the spring." It is characteristic of this climate that the rainfall and growing season are out of phase. The period of maximum growth in most climates, as temperature and the amount of sunshine increase, corresponds in the Mediterranean California climate, to a time of drought, when plants must rely on surface ground water, which is soon depleted as the summer heat becomes more intense.

Figure 1.1 is a map of California, its counties, and the major California river systems. The cyclonic temperate zone storms that lash the state in winter come from the west. Substantial amounts of rainfall are captured by the Coast Ranges, and the streams descend to valleys that often parallel the coast in the same orientation as the coastal ranges themselves. Far inland, the higher Cascades-Sierran mountains capture vast amounts of the rainfall from the winter storms, much of it in the form of snow, and the water thus accumulated flows into the great interior rivers of the Central Valley of California. The Sacramento River, from the north, and the San Joaquin River, from the south, join at the Sacramento delta in central California, and then cut through the Coast Ranges to the sea at the San Francisco Bay. At the south end of this great estuary is Santa Clara County, consisting of a long valley between two of the coastal mountain ranges, as shown in Fig. 1.2.

Geography

Santa Clara County, with an area of 3,408 km^2, is one of the smaller counties of the state, being 38th of 58 in size. As shown in Fig. 1.2, the topography of the county is roughly divided into three parts: the Santa Cruz Mountains to the west, the Santa Clara Valley in the center, and the Diablo Range to the east. The county's western boundary mostly follows the hydrographic crest of the Santa Cruz Mountains, so that streams

CHAPTER ONE

Figure 1.1. The state of California, showing county borders and major river systems. Santa Clara County is shown with shading.

west of the county line generally flow west to the Pacific Ocean, either through San Mateo County in the north or Santa Cruz County in the south. Streams east of this boundary flow toward the Santa Clara Valley and eventually to the San Francisco Bay in the north, or to the Pajaro River in the south. Similarly, the county's eastern boundary with Stanislaus and Merced counties more or less follows the hydrographic crest between the Diablo Range drainage basins (which flow to the San Francisco Bay or the Pajaro River) and the interior range streams that flow east (into the Central Valley).

The Santa Cruz Mountains are one of the coastal ranges of California. In the north they rise from the San Francisco peninsula and widen into sets of multiple ridges within San Mateo, Santa Cruz, and Santa Clara counties, and then narrow before reaching the southern terminus of the range at the Pajaro Riv-

er. These mountains reach their greatest height at Loma Prieta (3,791 feet), southeast of Los Gatos, and at their widest are 30 to 40 km west to east. West of Gilroy, the southern reaches of the Santa Cruz Mountains narrow to 10 to 15 km in width.

The Diablo Range, one of the interior ranges of California, extends from Mt. Diablo, in Contra Costa County, south through Alameda and Santa Clara counties, and into San Benito and Monterey counties. South of the Alameda County line the Diablo Range, 40 to 50 km wide, consists of multiple ridges dissected by northwest–southeast trending stream drainages. Farther south, at Pacheco Pass, the range narrows to 10 or 15 km, but then widens once more in northern San Benito County. The highest point of the Diablo Range in Santa Clara County is Mt. Hamilton (4,213 feet), but Eylar Mountain at 4,089 feet, adjacent to the Alameda County line, is nearly as high as Mt.

4

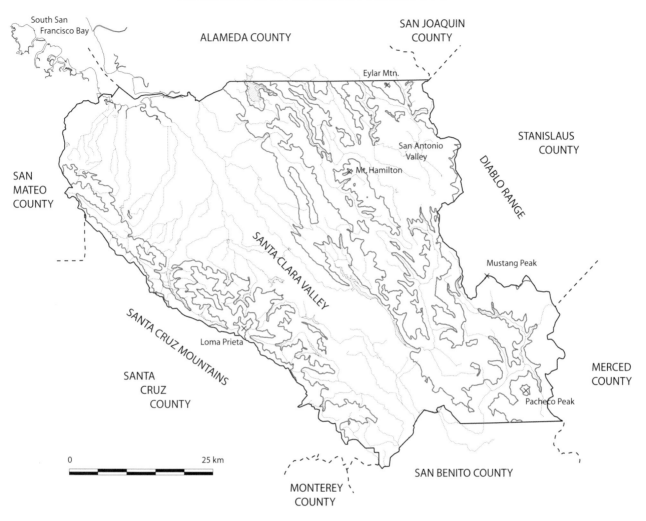

Figure 1.2. Geographic features of Santa Clara County. 1,000-foot contour intervals shown in gray.

Hamilton. To the south, the range decreases in elevation. Mustang Peak, for example, is 2,263 feet in elevation, and Pacheco Peak is 2,770 feet. Well south of Santa Clara County, the Diablo Range again rises, reaching a height of over 5,000 feet at San Benito Mountain in southern San Benito County.

The Santa Clara Valley, lying between the Santa Cruz Mountains and the Diablo Range, is a fairly level valley, its floor consisting of alluvial deposits from the two adjacent ranges. These alluvial deposits or flatlands have been mapped (Helley et al. 1979), and their boundary is illustrated by the solid interior lines in Fig. 1.3. Adjacent to South San Francisco Bay the Northern Santa Clara Valley is about 25 km wide and maintains this width to the southeast for 20 to 25 km. Here the valley narrows between the foothills of the Santa Cruz Mountains and the Diablo Range. The Santa Teresa Hills and a small outlier, Tulare Hill, constrict the Santa Clara Valley on its southwest side, whereas the hills above Thompson and Silver creeks constrain the valley on the northeast. The width of the valley decreases to only a few hundred meters north of the town of Coyote, at the appropriately named Coyote Narrows. Southeast of the Narrows

the valley widens once more. By Morgan Hill it is about 5 km in width, and at Gilroy it is 10 km wide. South of Gilroy the valley widens farther into the Bolsa de San Felipe, where the Santa Clara Valley, the valley of Pacheco Creek, and the Hollister Valley (in San Benito County) meet. Close by, to the northeast, the valley of Pacheco Creek cuts into the Diablo Range for 10 or 15 km, although nowhere is it more than a half a kilometer wide.

Drainage Basins

Helley et al. (1979) also identified the major drainage basins in the San Francisco Bay area. Figure 1.4 shows portions of the three basins that lie within Santa Clara County. The Peninsula-Coyote drainage basin extends in the northwest from the Bay side of the City of San Francisco southeast to the southernmost extent of Coyote Creek in Santa Clara County. The Alameda basin includes all of the streams that drain into Alameda Creek, including large areas of Alameda County to the north of the area shown in Fig. 1.4. The Pajaro-Pacheco basin includes the southern drainages of the Santa Cruz Mountains and the Diablo Range, as well as the Hollister Valley.

Figure 1.3. Flatland or alluvial soil boundaries (unbroken lines) in Santa Clara County (Helley et al. 1979).

Within Santa Clara County, the Peninsula-Coyote basin includes watersheds that drain portions of the Santa Cruz Mountains and the Diablo Range. In the Santa Cruz Mountains the most important of these is the Guadalupe River-Los Gatos Creek watershed, whereas in the Diablo Range the most significant is the watershed of Coyote Creek. During the period of summer drought many of the streams in these watersheds run dry, but in the winter, following periods of heavy rain, these same streams become rushing torrents bringing rocks and sediments down from the hills. Prior to American settlement only a few of these watersheds, in particular Coyote Creek and Guadalupe River, extended to the Bay.

Medium-sized watersheds, such as San Francisquito Creek and Saratoga Creek, extended nearly to the Bay, forming freshwater willow swamps or *sausals* near the marsh edge. The swamp at the end of San Francisquito Creek, for example, was close to where the Palo Alto airport is today, and the creek probably overflowed into the Bay following every winter storm.

Smaller streams descended from arroyos in the hills and flowed onto the alluvial fans, percolating into gravelly soils. In some cases the water would re-emerge at the base of the fans in swamps on the valley floor, often well away from the Bay (Grossinger et al. 2006). In winters with heavy rainfall some of these streams would follow old channels down the alluvial fans or overflow into the salt marshes ringing the Bay. With American settlement, ditches or channels were built to allow the water to move more easily to the Bay and prevent winter flooding. In many cases, the natural terminuses of these distributary creeks can be identified as the point in Fig. 1.4 where a creek's course changes from meandering to straight.

The Guadalupe River-Los Gatos Creek watershed drains a significant portion of the east side of the Santa Cruz Mountains. Los Gatos Creek and Guadalupe River come together in the center of San Jose. This confluence, with its permanent water and large stands of Fremont cottonwoods and western sycamores, is where the Spanish settled when they arrived in the valley in the late 1700s. Today, cottonwoods and sycamores still grow along the Guadalupe River and Los Gatos Creek as they thread through

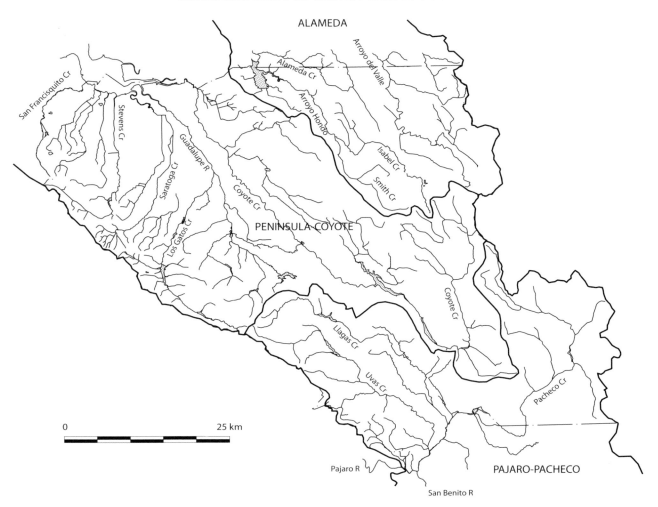

Figure 1.4. Major drainage basins in Santa Clara County (Helley et al. 1979).

the downtown area. Los Gatos Creek starts on the northwestern slopes of Loma Prieta and curves down into the valley, for much of its course next to Highway 17 as it drops from the summit. Reservoirs in this drainage include Lake Elsman, Lexington Reservoir, and Vasona Reservoir (see Table 1.1).

Above San Jose, Guadalupe River drains the northeast side of the Sierra Azul, the eastern ridges of Loma Prieta, and both sides of the Santa Teresa Hills. A number of small reservoirs—Guadalupe, Almaden, and Calero—lie at the headwaters of the river. Each of these was constructed in 1935 as part of a system of reservoirs and percolation ponds designed to provide groundwater recharge. From its confluence with Los Gatos Creek in the center of San Jose, the Guadalupe River flows northwest, to where it enters the Bay at Alviso Slough. Originally, the Guadalupe River entered the Bay at Guadalupe Slough, but it was diverted to Alviso Slough in the late nineteenth or early twentieth century (Collins and Grossinger 2004). With the construction of salt ponds at Alviso in the 1930s, Guadalupe Slough was permanently sealed off from the river.

Coyote Creek is the other major watershed in the Peninsula-Coyote basin. In its lower reach the creek flows northwest along the Santa Clara Valley floor for more than 40 km

to San Francisco Bay, and over much of this stretch it is often within a few kilometers of the adjacent Guadalupe River. Coyote Creek drains much of the central Diablo Range within Santa Clara County. The Middle Fork folds back and forth among the northwest-southeast ridges of the range, and the East Fork, starting at the southern edge of San Antonio Valley, joins the Middle Fork in the center of Henry Coe State Park. The creek then flows south, passing Gilroy Hot Springs, and makes a broad swing before flowing northwest through Coyote and Anderson lakes and onto the valley floor. Interestingly, once it reaches the valley floor, Coyote Creek's northwest course to San Francisco Bay is mirrored by the Llagas Creek system's southeast course to the Pajaro River and Monterey Bay. These two drainages are separated by a shallow hydrographic crest formed from the streams' alluvial fans. Barely discernible from Highway 101 as a slightly higher "height of land" in the center of the valley floor, this hydrographic crest runs down the middle of the Santa Clara Valley for a number of miles. Details of the Coyote Creek watershed below Anderson Dam have been reported by Grossinger et al. (2006).

The other watersheds in the Peninsula-Coyote basin, from the northwest to the southeast are: the San Francisquito, Matade-

7

Table 1.1 Santa Clara County reservoirs.

RESERVOIR	DATE BUILT	ELEV (ft)	CAPACITY (acre-ft)
Almaden Reservoir	1935	606	1,780
Anderson Lake	1948	625	91,300
Calaveras Reservoir	1925	750	100,000
Calero Reservoir	1935	480	10,500
Chesbro Reservoir	1935	525	8,952
Coyote Lake	1936	775	22,925
Guadalupe Reservoir	1935	614	3,723
Lake Elsman	1951	1,145	6,150
Lexington Reservoir	1952	645	19,834
Pacheco Lake	1939	472	6,143
Stevens Creek Reservoir	1935	536	3,465
Uvas Reservoir	1957	488	9,901
Vasona Reservoir	1935	307	400

ro, Barron, Adobe, Permanente, Stevens, Calabazas, Saratoga, and San Tomas Aquino Creek watersheds. Of these, only Saratoga Creek appears to have reached the Bay prior to settlement, the others ending in willow swamps. The only reservoir in these drainages is the Stevens Creek Reservoir.

Alameda Creek drains much of the northern Diablo Range in Santa Clara County, as well as significant areas of southern Alameda County. The creek enters San Francisco Bay just north of Coyote Hills Regional Park. The upper part of the Alameda basin in Santa Clara County consists of four portions: from west to east, these are Arroyo Hondo-Isabel Creek, Alameda Creek, Arroyo Valle, and Arroyo Mocho. A drive over Mt. Hamilton crosses Smith Creek on the west side and Isabel Creek on the eastern slope. Flowing north, both creeks join north of Mt. Hamilton and form Arroyo Hondo. Continuing the Mt. Hamilton drive east into the San Antonio Valley and then north toward Livermore, one passes the many creeks that make up the headwaters of Arroyo Valle, including Arroyo Bayo, San Antonio Creek, and Colorado Creek.

North of San Antonio Valley, Mines Road, a popular birding route, leaves the Arroyo Valle drainage beyond Colorado Creek and crosses into the drainage of Arroyo Mocho following this stream down to the Livermore Valley in Alameda County. The Alameda Creek drainage basin includes three major reservoirs. Calaveras Reservoir, owned by the City of San Francisco, is supplied by Arroyo Hondo, and lies along the northern border of the county. San Antonio Reservoir and Lake del Valle are entirely within Alameda County.

The Pajaro-Pacheco Basin consists of two major watersheds within Santa Clara County: creeks that flow from the eastern side of the Santa Cruz Mountain into the Pajaro River, and the Pacheco Creek system, which drains much of the southern Diablo Range. The Pajaro River watershed comprises primarily the Uvas-Carnadero Creek system and Llagas Creek to the northwest and the San Benito River to the southeast. Uvas Creek

drains a portion of the southeast slopes of Loma Prieta and flows southeast, joining the Pajaro River near Sargent. Llagas Creek also drains the eastern and southeastern slopes of Loma Prieta and drops onto the valley floor, where it passes through Morgan Hill and Gilroy before joining the nascent Pajaro River at the county border. Both of these creeks are used for water storage, with Uvas Reservoir along Uvas Creek and Chesbro Reservoir along Llagas Creek.

Pacheco Creek drains the southeastern portion of Santa Clara County and a little bit of northern San Benito County. The creek descends to the alluvial soils of the Bolsa de San Felipe, where much of its route parallels Highway 152. It then makes a loop south into San Benito County and finally flows northwest to drain into San Felipe Lake (often called "Soap Lake" by the local residents). The Bolsa de San Felipe is like a flat plate with slightly upcurved edges. During drier winters Pacheco Creek terminates in San Felipe Lake, the water sinking into the ground, and the "lake" is sometimes an expanse of gravel. In wet winters, however, the lake fills and overflows into canals that allow the waters to flow onward into the Pajaro River system. Originally, the Bolsa was suitable only for pasturage because of the build-up of salts (Broek 1932). Much of this basin is still used to grow forage, but with modern soil amendments the basin is also suitable for other crops. The only reservoir along Pacheco Creek is Pacheco Lake, just off Highway 152.

Rainfall Patterns

The distribution of annual rainfall in Santa Clara County largely follows topography. Figure 1.5 shows contours of annual precipitation (isohyets) in the county (Rantz 1971). Winter storms generally come from the northwest or west, and the greatest rainfall occurs on the western slopes of the Santa Cruz Mountains, mostly in San Mateo and Santa Cruz counties. Higher areas, such as Ben Lomond Mountain, receive up to 60 inches a year. Along the crest of the Santa Cruz Mountains, rainfall totals are more like 40 to 44 inches a year, and downwind or east of the crest, where a rain shadow is formed, the precipitation totals decline further. On the valley floor the rainfall is only 14 to 18 inches a year. As the land rises again at the western edge of the Diablo Range, the annual precipitation increases, some 24 to 30 inches a year falling over the higher ridges of the range. The precipitation totals then decline in the eastern Diablo Range, dropping to 12 to 16 inches a year east of the hydrographic crest.

Figure 1.5 includes a cut, or transect, across the isohyets, from the Pacific Ocean to the Central Valley. Rainfall and elevation along this transect are shown in Fig. 1.6, which illustrates the effects of both elevation and distance from the coast on rainfall.

The temporal distribution of precipitation in the county is typical of a Mediterranean climate, as shown in Fig. 1.7 for six recording stations for the period 1932 to 1996. The highest rainfall occurs in the months of December through March, whereas almost no rain falls in June through August. The temporal distribution of rainfall for the six stations is very similar, differing only by a scale factor (Rantz 1971).

Historical rainfall data are available for San Jose from 1874 to the present. The distribution of these data across time

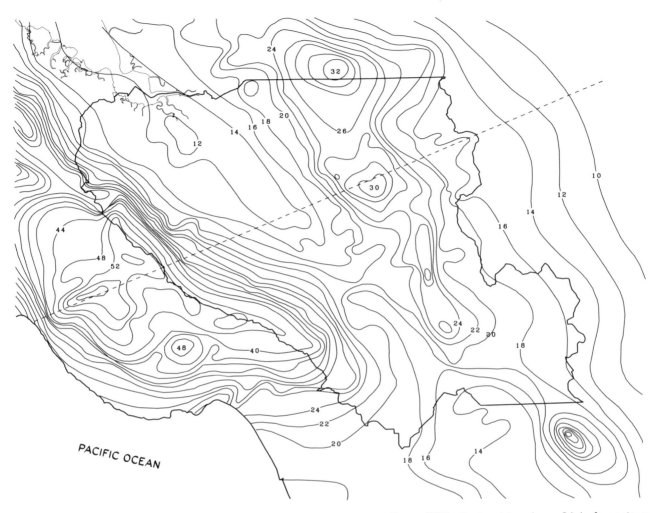

Figure 1.5. Contours of mean annual rainfall in inches for Santa Clara County (Rantz 1971). Contour intervals are 2 in/yr for contours less than 40 in/yr, and 4 in/yr above 40 in/yr. Dashed line shows transect for comparison of rainfall and elevation (Fig. 1.6).

is shown in Fig. 1.8. The precipitation is shown as a percent of normal, which for this time series is 14.27 inches. Yearly rainfall is defined as the precipitation that occurs from 1 Jul of the initial year to 30 Jun of the subsequent year. (Arbitrarily, this seasonal rainfall is associated with the second year in the figure; thus, the rainfall data from the last half of 1874 and the first half of 1875 is shown as occurring in 1875.) In addition to the scale showing percent of normal (at the left), a second scale (at the right) gives the percentile distribution of the yearly rainfall. Note that the 50th percentile scale does not correspond exactly to 100% normal precipitation, since these rainfall data are not normally distributed. The percentile scale is nonetheless useful in showing the severity of dry years. For example, the 1975–76 season, 60% below normal, was a 4th percentile year, meaning that 96% of all years had more rainfall. Similarly, the precipitation that fell in the El Niño years of 1982–83 was 100% above normal and constituted a 100th percentile event.

The seven years of atlas fieldwork are shown in Fig. 1.8 as shaded. As can be seen, the first five years of the atlas period were a time of fairly severe drought. Above normal rainfall did not occur in the atlas period until the concluding winters of

1991–92 and 1992–93.

Wet and dry periods can be identified from the San Jose precipitation data using two approaches. Long-term changes in rainfall can be calculated based on the cumulative departure from the seasonal norm (Poland and Ireland 1988), as shown in Fig. 1.9a. In this case, an excess or deficit is computed for each rainfall season and is added to the cumulative excess or deficit from prior years. Figure 1.9a shows that through the end of the 1880s, the rainfall was fairly consistent. Then, a period of increased rainfall (excess) occurred through the late teens, when the pattern reversed and years of deficit were encountered. The deficit years were particularly severe in the late 1920s. The late 1930s saw an increase in rainfall again, but only for a decade, the rainfall then decreasing into the 1960s. Only minor changes are observed until the early 1980s, at which point the excess rainfall in the 1982–83 El Niño years returned the deficit to near zero. A new drought started in the late 1980s, coincident with the first five years of the atlas period, and recovery occurred in the 1990s.

A second way to look at wet and dry cycles is to look at the short-term excess or deficit. In this approach the excess or

9

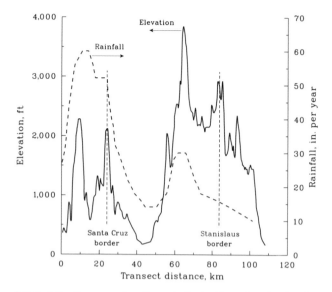

Figure 1.6. Cross section through Santa Clara County showing mean annual rainfall (Rantz 1971) and elevation. Dashed lines show the border with Santa Cruz County (on the left) and the border with Stanislaus County (on the right).

deficit in a single season is computed as before. If an excess is computed and the prior year also had an excess, then the two amounts are added to provide a cumulative excess. Likewise, if a deficit is calculated and the prior year was also in deficit, then a cumulative deficit is determined. These cumulative sums are continued until there is a reversal from excess to deficit or vice versa, at which point the cumulative sum is begun again. Figure 1.9b shows the short-term excess and deficit rainfall. The figure shows that there are few sequences of wet years occurring more than two or three years at a time, and the cumulative excess in such series rarely exceeds 100% of normal. In stark contrast, at least three significant deficit sequences are observed: 1926–34, 1943–51, and 1987–91. The last of these deficit sequences, which corresponds to the first five years of the atlas period, was clearly less severe than the first sequences of the early 1930s and late 1940s.

The Mediterranean California climatic pattern of wet winters and dry summers presents an abundance of water when temperatures are low and growing conditions are poor, and a

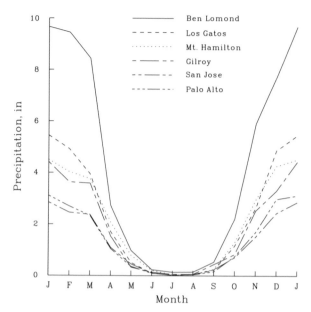

Figure 1.7. Averaged annual rainfall distribution at five stations in Santa Clara County, plus a reference station at Ben Lomond, Santa Cruz County, to indicate the rainfall amounts on the western slopes of the Santa Cruz Mountains, 1932 to 1996.

deficit of water when there are ample sun and high temperatures. Biomass production for plants tends to be maximized when water availability and temperature are in-phase, as occurs in typical temperate climates, rather than out-of-phase, as here in California. Major (1988) constructed water-balance diagrams that are useful for understanding the seasonal effects of water use by plants. Figure 1.10 is a water-balance diagram for the Hastings Reservation in Monterey County, which is a good approximation of the water balance expected in Santa Clara County. The potential evapotranspiration (PotE) curve, based on temperature, represents the amount of water or rainfall that can be used by vegetation for growth, if there were no water limitations. By November the PotE is still decreasing as the temperature drops and the initial winter rains provide more water than can be used by growing plants and this extra water recharges the groundwater system ("Soil Recharge"). By the end of the year the groundwater system has been recharged and the winter rains deliver a surplus of water, which in due course becomes runoff that

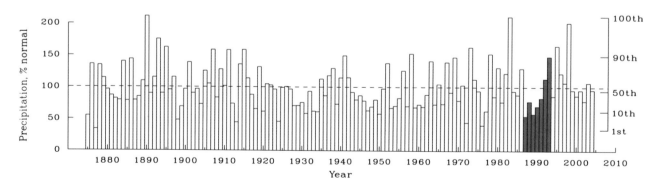

Figure 1.8. Yearly distribution of rainfall for San Jose, 1877 to 2005. The years of atlas fieldwork are shaded.

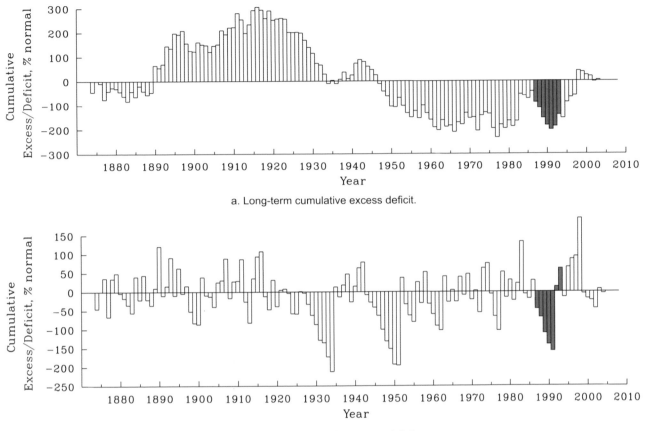

a. Long-term cumulative excess deficit.

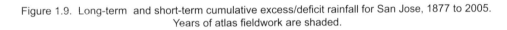

b. Short-term cumulative excess deficit.

Figure 1.9. Long-term and short-term cumulative excess/deficit rainfall for San Jose, 1877 to 2005. Years of atlas fieldwork are shaded.

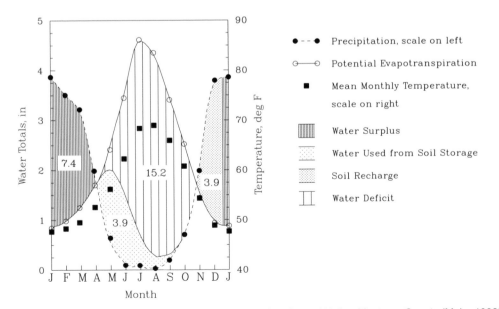

Figure 1.10. Water-balance diagram for Hastings Reservation, Carmel Valley, Monterey County (Major 1988).

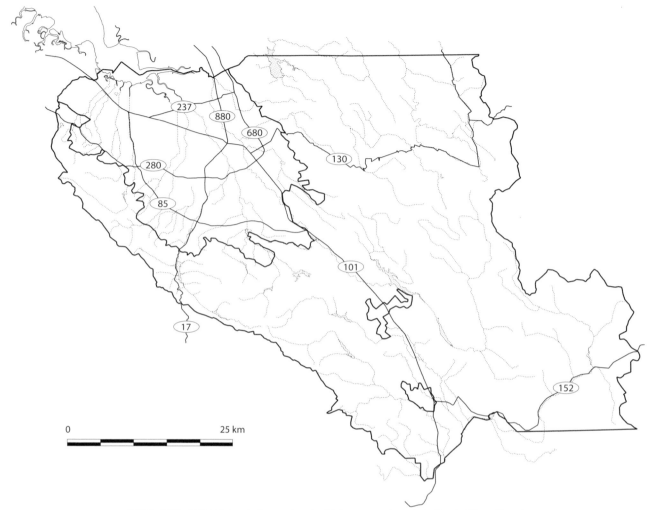

Figure 1.11. Urban boundaries and major highways and roads in Santa Clara County.

will either be captured in reservoirs or flow to the ocean. By April, temperatures are rapidly increasing and the PotE is also increasing, such that plants begin to use more water than is available from rainfall, and start to use the water in the soil for their growth. By May or June most of the groundwater resources are depleted and, even though the PotE is high, plant growth decreases and finally stops, because of the absence of available water. With declining temperatures the PotE excess declines until once again the winter rains arrive and provide a surplus of water for groundwater recharge. Although vegetation in the Northwest Pacific Coast province, where there is fog drip, can grow through the summer, the plant communities in the Mediterranean California province are adapted to growth in spring and early summer, and must have means to avoid water loss through the dry summer season.

Land Use

European settlement in Santa Clara County began on the valley floor, because of the availability of water and the excellent soils there. Farms, towns, and then cities expanded outward to essentially occupy all of the valley floor. The current bound-aries of the urban expanse of the northern Santa Clara Valley and the cities of Morgan Hill and Gilroy (both in the southern Santa Clara Valley) have been estimated by examining the density of streets on the most recent topographic maps. Areas with a high density of streets are an indicator of developed urban lands, whereas areas with only a few streets represent undeveloped land. Figure 1.11, a map of Santa Clara County, delineates those urban boundaries for the three urban zones of the Santa Clara Valley, along with the major roads and highways. Within the northern Santa Clara Valley, there is a close correspondence between the urban and flatland boundaries (see Fig. 1.3), whereas in the southern Santa Clara Valley there are still extensive, unde-veloped agricultural lands.

During the atlas period 1987–93, the total area of park-lands in Santa Clara County was approximately 436 km^2, which is about 13% of the county's area. These parklands included a single state park, Henry Coe State Park in the Diablo Range (much of which lies in Stanislaus County), many county parks, Midpeninsula Regional Open Space District parklands, and local city parks. The ten largest parklands in the county are listed in Table 1.2 with their areas. These ten areas constitute about 80%

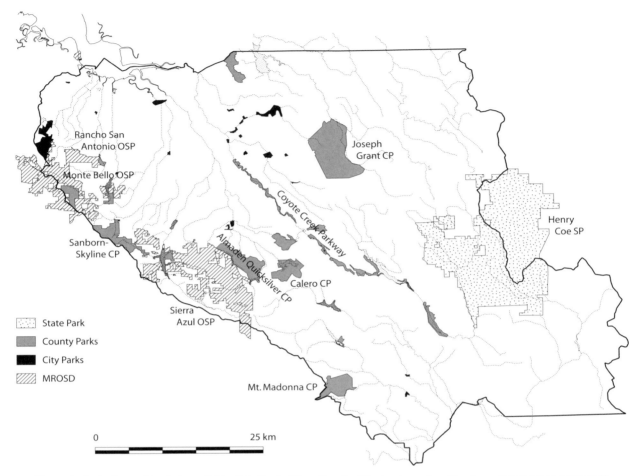

Figure 1.12. Major parklands (over 0.1 km²) in Santa Clara County. The ten largest parklands are labeled (see Table 1.2).

of all county parklands. Parklands greater in area than 0.1 km^2 are mapped in Fig. 1.12. Unmapped are the over 200 local community parks less than 0.1 km^2 in area, which together comprise less than 2% of all county parklands. Henry Coe State Park and Joseph Grant County Park, both in the Diablo Range, comprise about 46% of the county's parklands, whereas the other parks in Table 1.2, most of which are in the Santa Cruz Mountains, comprise about 34% of the county's parks.

Since the end of the atlas period in 1993, additional parkland has been purchased in Santa Clara County. A number of significant parcels have been added to Henry Coe State Park on its southern side, including the Redfern addition in 1993 and the Hunting Hollow addition in 1997. Santa Clara County has made additional purchases including the Harvey Bear Ranch (18 km^2), which was bought in 1997 and added to Coyote Lake County Park. In 1992, the formation of the Santa Clara County Open Space Authority was approved by voters, and this open space district has been purchasing lands in those parts of the county that are not covered by the Midpeninsula Regional Open Space District (MROSD).

Table 1.2. Ten largest parklands of Santa Clara County; where parcels extend beyond county borders, tabulated areas fall within county's borders.

PARK	AREA, km^2
Henry Coe State Park	157
Sierra Azul OSP	70
Joseph Grant CP	43
Almaden Quicksilver CP	16
Sanborn-Skyline CP	13
Monte Bello OSP	12
Mt. Madonna CP	11
Calero Reservoir CP	11
Rancho San Antonio OSP	9
Coyote Creek Parkway	8

2 The Geology and Tectonic History of Santa Clara County

M. Clark Blake, Jr. and Carl M. Wentworth

U.S. Geological Survey, Menlo Park

Much that distinguishes the varied habitats used by birds in Santa Clara County can be traced to the county's geologic history. The different types of vegetation in the county to which the birds respond (see Chapter 3) result from local differences in climate, topography, and soils. All three of these factors result from or are influenced by the rocks and tectonic history of the county. Local climate is greatly influenced by the locations and shapes of the mountains and valleys, which in turn result from geologic uplift, subsidence, erosion, and deposition in the county over the past several million years. Local differences in soils are largely determined by the various mineralogies, chemistries, and textures of the underlying rocks and sediments from which they are formed.

Our story of how the county geology developed is a long one, and begins about 150 million years ago, before any of the county's land had formed. At that time, sediment that had eroded from the continent began accumulating upon older oceanic rocks along the continental margin, and was later assembled into the rock collage that is now Santa Clara County. We cast this geologic history in terms of plate tectonics, the grand unifying paradigm of geology that describes the behavior of the numerous independent segments (plates) that form the outer crust of the earth. The plates, floating on the earth's mantle, are all moving, each in its own direction.

Like glacial ice, the solid rock of the mantle can flow slowly under pressure, and heat-driven convection in the mantle moves the plates at very low but perceptible rates (several centimeters per year, or about as fast as your fingernails grow).

The plate boundaries, where most of the tectonic deformation on Earth takes place, are marked by three different kinds of behaviors, depending on the relative motions of the adjacent plates (see Fig. 2.2, below). The simplest, where the plate motions are essentially parallel to their common boundary and the plates slide past each other, is a transform boundary. The San Andreas fault, which passes through the southwest side of Santa Clara County, is the transform boundary between the North American and Pacific plates, along which the Pacific plate is moving northward toward the Aleutian Islands, southwest of mainland Alaska.

A second kind of boundary is a subduction zone, where two plates converge. One plate moves toward the other, dives down beneath it, and is ultimately consumed in the mantle. In the process, the downgoing plate begins to melt and volcanoes are typically formed above, near the leading edge of the overriding plate. The northward-moving Pacific plate, for example, is subducting beneath the southern margin of the Aleutians. More relevant to our story, the Juan de Fuca plate, located north of Cape Mendocino, California, is diving eastward into the Cascadia subduction zone beneath Oregon and Washington, where it has produced the Cascades volcanic arc.

The third type of boundary, often called an oceanic ridge or spreading center, occurs at rifts where adjacent plates move away from each other and new crust is formed in the gap. Together, these three types of boundaries accommodate the disparate motions of the plates as they make their independent ways about the planet.

In the following pages we present a simplified plate tectonic history of the rocks that now form Santa Clara County. This history is summarized in Figure 2.1, which also defines the terms that we use to specify standard intervals of geologic time. We then describe the various rock types and show their distribution within the county (Figs. 2.3 and 2.4). The bedrock is concealed by soil and vegetation throughout most of the county, except along streams and in roadcuts, and we suggest places where examples of some of the various kinds of rocks and rock units can be seen.

Tectonic History of the County

The tectonic history of the rocks in Santa Clara County began about 150 million years ago (150 Ma) with the initiation of a subduction zone and associated volcanic arc along the western margin of North America. This setting was much like the one we see today along the Cascadia subduction zone, where an active volcanic arc on the overlying North American plate, above the subduction zone, extends from Mt. Lassen, in northern California, north through Mt. St. Helens and Rainier into southern British Columbia. Detritus eroded from that ancient volcanic arc in California was carried westward by rivers and

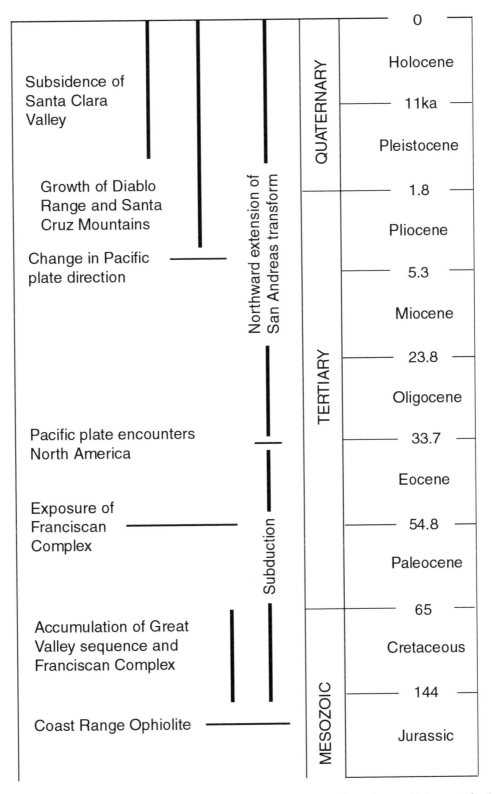

Figure 2.1. A summary of geologic events and their timing. Time boundaries are in millions of years (Ma), except for the most recent, 11ka (11,000 years). Note that although the intervals are all shown with the same graphic length, their durations are actually quite different. The Cretaceous period, for example, is 7,000 times longer than the Holocene.

deposited in a marine basin floored by still older (about 165 Ma) oceanic igneous rocks. Those older rocks, known as the Coast Range ophiolite, consist of a sequence of ultramafic rock from the upper mantle (now largely altered to serpentinite), gabbro, and oceanic basalt, rocks that are all rich in iron and magnesium. This sequence of rocks is similar to rocks that form the basement of all the world's oceans. The Coast Range ophiolite had been formed elsewhere, and was then transported and attached (accreted) to continental North America by plate tectonic processes sometime prior to about 150 Ma.

Accumulation of the arc-derived sediment atop the ophiolitic basement continued for about 85 Ma (from about 150 to 65 Ma), forming a stratigraphic sequence of sandstone, mudstone, and conglomerate thousands of feet thick that is called the Great Valley sequence (named for its extensive exposure along the west side of the Great Valley of California). During this time, much detritus from the ancient arc was also carried even farther west and deposited in a deep marine trench at a subduction zone where the east-moving oceanic Farallon plate was diving beneath the continental margin. This subduction carried the trench sediment and underlying oceanic chert and basalt to great depth (20–30 km; 12–19 miles), where high pressure and extensive shearing produced the highly deformed and metamorphosed rocks that are known as the Franciscan Complex. The deeply buried Franciscan rocks were later returned to shallow depth and ultimately exposed to erosion near the end of Paleocene time (about 55 Ma). Just how this return was accomplished is not clear, and vigorous debate amongst geologists involves several very different alternatives.

Subduction of the Farallon plate continued along what is now the California coast until about 30 Ma, when the oceanic ridge that separated the Farallon and Pacific plates arrived at the trench near Guaymas, Mexico (Fig. 2.2A). Formation of new crust at the trailing edge of the eastward-moving Farallon plate had progressively enlarged the Pacific plate until the spreading center reached the North American plate boundary. Once that happened, subduction there stopped and was replaced (transformed) by steep, lateral faults of the San Andreas transform system, along which the Pacific plate continued to move northwestward. By 10 Ma, material that had previously been accreted to the continent farther south was sliced off by the expanding transform and carried northwestward to the area that is now Santa Clara County (Fig. 2.2B). These displaced rocks, now present in the county, include several slivers of Coast Range ophiolite and Franciscan Complex as well as a large fragment of the granitic continental margin. This fragment, known as Salinia, had formed about 300 kilometers (185 miles) farther south, near what is now the Mojave Desert.

In Figure 2.2A (30 Ma), the leading edge of the Pacific plate has just encountered North America off the coast of Mexico, and subduction has begun to be replaced by lateral movement along the vertical San Andreas transform fault. By 10 Ma (2.2B), the transform boundary between the North American and Pacific plates has expanded north to San Francisco. Today (2.2C), nearly all of California is marked by transform faulting, with subduction and volcanism continuing only where small remnants of the Farallon plate remain north of Cape Mendocino (called the Juan de Fuca plate) and south of Guaymas (called the

Rivera plate).

About 4–5 Ma the direction of movement of the Pacific plate shifted slightly clockwise to a more northerly direction relative to North America, leading to compression across the San Andreas transform system (Cox and Engebretson 1985). Note the arrows that mark this change in plate direction (Fig. 2.2C). In the San Francisco Bay region the San Andreas system is quite wide and consists of several strands, including the San Andreas, Hayward, and Calaveras faults (Fig. 2.3). The slightly convergent motion continues today (Fig 2.2C), and has led to the formation of compressive thrust faults and uplift of the Santa Cruz Mountains and the Diablo Range. In the past million years, the area between these two ranges has subsided to form Santa Clara Valley and the San Francisco Bay trough, both of which were largely filled with detritus eroded from the uplifted blocks.

The Rocks and Their Distribution

In Figure 2.3, we have divided the bedrock of the county into eight structural blocks, which are distinguished from each other by different rocks and stratigraphic sequences that record different geologic histories. Also shown in the figure are the major faults that bound these blocks, and the alluvial deposits of the Santa Clara Valley. (It will often be helpful to consult Figures 2.3 and 2.4 together.)

Figure 2.4 is a generalized geologic map showing the major rock types found in Santa Clara County and vicinity, together with the principal faults. This information was taken from three more detailed maps published by the U.S. Geological Survey and the California Geological Survey (Brabb et al. 2000; Wentworth et al. 1998; and Wagner et al. 2002).

The extreme western margin of the county includes a small portion of the Santa Cruz block, which extends inland from the coast to the San Andreas fault. This block, which is part of the terrane (not terrain) called Salinia, differs from all the others in the county in having a basement that consists largely of granitic rock. None of the granite is actually exposed within the county, but it forms the crest of Ben Lomond Mountain (Fig. 2.3 and also 2.4, where it is partly obscured by the legend) and is exposed along Coast Highway 1 near Montara Mountain. This Salinian basement is overlain by Paleocene and younger marine sedimentary rocks (sandstone, mudstone, and conglomerate), which are folded, but lack the shearing seen in many of the rocks farther east.

Because these sedimentary rocks were largely derived from a granitic source, they are enriched in silica, alumina, calcium, and potassium, as are their overlying soils. This composition, coupled with the abundant coastal rainfall, has fostered a remarkable coniferous forest dominated by coast redwoods, locally interrupted by patches of chaparral and grassland on the steeper slopes.

Northeast of the San Andreas fault, a narrow slice of Coast Range ophiolite (shown as serpentinite on Fig. 2.4) is overlain by Jurassic and Cretaceous sedimentary rocks plus younger sedimentary rocks of Eocene and Miocene age. These rocks of the Sierra Azul block have been repeated in at least three superimposed slices by young thrust faults. Although most of this block lies in the rain shadow of the Santa Cruz Mountains, some elevations here are as high as or higher than those to the west.

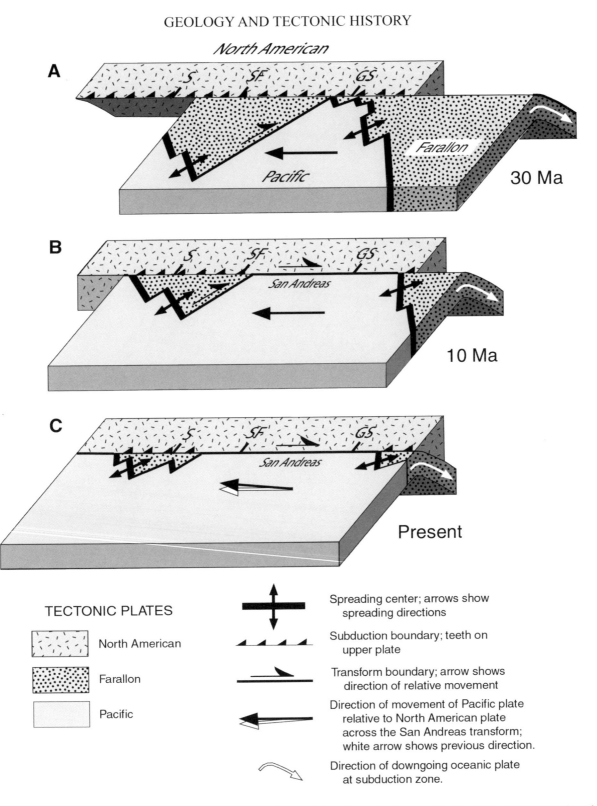

TECTONIC PLATES

North American

Farallon

Pacific

Spreading center; arrows show spreading directions

Subduction boundary; teeth on upper plate

Transform boundary; arrow shows direction of relative movement

Direction of movement of Pacific plate relative to North American plate across the San Andreas transform; white arrow shows previous direction.

Direction of downgoing oceanic plate at subduction zone.

Figure 2.2. Sequential diagrams showing interactions between the North American, Farallon, and Pacific plates and the evolution of the San Andreas transform fault (modified from Irwin, 1990, Fig. 4.1). S, Seattle; SF, San Francisco; GS, Guaymas, Mexico. (See text for details.)

17

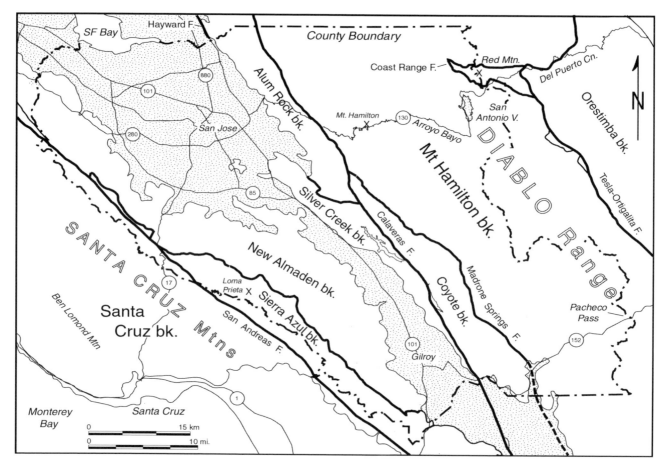

Figure 2.3. Bedrock blocks and major bounding faults within and adjacent to Santa Clara County. The stippled pattern shows the alluvial deposits of the Santa Clara Valley.

The area around Loma Prieta Peak, for example (shown on Fig. 2.3), receives much rainfall, and yet the vegetation is dominated by chaparral. This apparent anomaly is probably due to the fact that the rocks there are ophiolite, and the overlying soils thus lack critical nutrients, particularly alumina and potassium.

Farther to the northeast, the New Almaden block forms the northeastern flank of the Santa Cruz Mountains. It underlies the Sierra Azul block structurally along the previously mentioned thrust faults, and farther north is in contact with the Santa Cruz block along the San Andreas fault (Fig. 2.4). The northern and eastern margins of the block are covered by younger alluvium of the Santa Clara Valley.

The New Almaden block consists of resistant blocks and slabs of Franciscan greenstone (altered submarine basalt) as well as minor amounts of oceanic chert and limestone, all of which are tectonically mixed within an abundant matrix of highly sheared mudstone and sandstone. This combination of rocks (called mélange after the French word for mixture) forms a large part of the Franciscan Complex. The relatively soft matrix and scattered hard lumps produce a hummocky, landslide-prone topography supporting grassland and scattered deciduous trees that is typical of Franciscan mélange.

The rocks of the Silver Creek block are mostly Jurassic

Coast Range ophiolite (chiefly serpentinite) with minor overlying sedimentary rocks. The serpentinite forms a nearly continuous belt, in places more than 2 kilometers (1 mile) wide, along the eastern margin of the block between Coyote and Anderson reservoirs. Because these rocks, too, lack the nutrient elements seen in the other rock types, particularly alumina and potassium, the overlying soils are not suitable for most trees and plants, and only a sparse native grassland is supported. This area is particularly important for serpentine-endemic plants, as discussed in Chapter 3.

The Alum Rock and Coyote blocks consist almost entirely of sedimentary rocks (sandstone, mudstone, and conglomerate). Only a few small serpentinite bodies remain of the basement of Coast Range ophiolite on which the sediments were originally deposited. Overlying soils and vegetation in the two blocks are very similar. Nevertheless, the blocks are distinguished because they are separated by faults and their different stratigraphies mark different geologic histories.

The very large Mt. Hamilton block in the eastern part of the county is bounded on the west by the Calaveras and Madrone Springs faults and on the east (chiefly outside the County) by the Tesla-Ortigalita and Coast Range faults (Fig. 2.3). The block consists almost entirely of slightly schistose sandstone (meta-

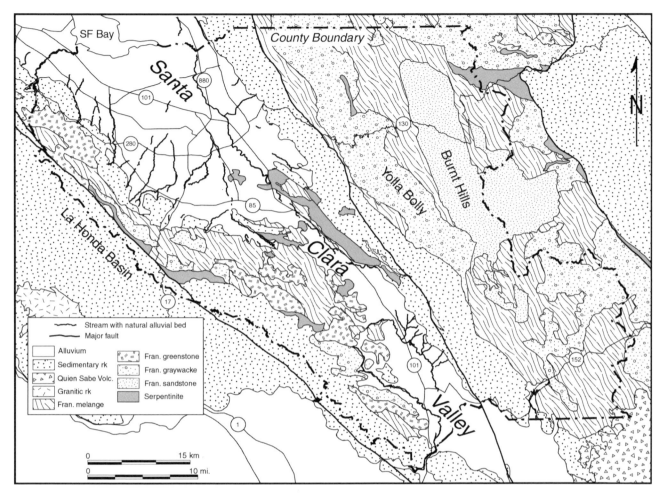

Figure 2.4. Geologic map of Santa Clara County and vicinity, showing rock types and major faults, and unmodified stream courses within Santa Clara Valley.

sandstone, or metagraywacke) and mélange, which occurs both as thin slices within the metagraywacke and as thicker slabs separating more coherent Franciscan units (see below). Also present are several small bodies of serpentinite that are considered to be faulted slices of Coast Range ophiolite. Near the southern margin of the county, these Franciscan rocks are overlain with great unconformity by Miocene marine sandstone and overlying volcanic rocks. The latter, which have been dated at 8–12 Ma, are northern outliers of the Quien Sabe volcanic field, which extends southeastward from the corner of Figure 2.4. In contrast to the rocks of the rest of the county, those of the Mt. Hamilton block lie east of the Calaveras fault and have not experienced large northward transport by the San Andreas fault system.

Detailed studies indicate that two distinctive Franciscan terranes are present in the Diablo Range (Fig. 2.4). Such terranes are defined as being fault-bounded geologic units having stratigraphies and geologic histories that differ from those of their neighbors. The Cretaceous Burnt Hills terrane consists largely of thin-bedded sandstone derived from a granitic source, whereas the Jurassic Yolla Bolly terrane consists largely of thick-bedded sandstone (metagraywacke) derived from a

mixed, granitic-volcanic-sedimentary source. Both units have been metamorphosed and contain such metamorphic minerals as lawsonite, jadeite, and aragonite. The fact that these minerals formed under high pressure indicates that the rocks were once buried to great depth beneath the Earth's surface (as great as 30 km, or 19 miles). Radiometric dating suggests that the rocks of the Yolla Bolly terrane were subducted beneath the continental margin about 110 Ma, and those of the Burnt Hills terrane about 82 Ma.

Mélange in the Mt. Hamilton block is made up chiefly of resistant blocks and slabs of greenstone and chert in a sheared matrix of mudstone and argillite. There are also numerous blocks of highly metamorphosed blueschist that are considerably older than most other Franciscan rocks (about 160 Ma on the basis of radiometric dating). Much controversy is associated with the origin of these mélanges and how the older blueschist blocks were incorporated. Unlike previous workers, we believe that the mélanges did not form during subduction, but rather during tectonic uplift of the previously subducted terranes, and that the blueschist blocks were emplaced during this uplift, perhaps by submarine landslides.

19

The landscapes and characteristic vegetations in each of these three Franciscan units are quite different. Coherent, well-bedded rocks of the Yolla Bolly terrane form resistant ridges and steep canyons. They support a cover of oak trees at lower elevations and conifers on the higher peaks. The best place to see these rocks is along the Mt. Hamilton road between Halls Valley and Isabel Creek.

Sandstone of the Burnt Hills terrane (Fig. 2.4) is less resistant than that of the Yolla Bolly terrane and is usually covered with chaparral. Good outcrops can be seen along the Mt. Hamilton road, extending eastward from Isabel Creek along the Arroyo Bayo to San Antonio Valley.

The mélange zones, with their clay-rich matrix, are by far the weakest of the three Franciscan units, and contain many landslides. Because of their low permeability, they are covered by grassland and only scattered trees. The trees locally mark blocks of more resistant rock types that are extensively fractured and thus can store groundwater.

The portion of the Orestimba block that lies within Santa Clara County consists of the small body of ophiolite near Red Mountain (Figs. 2.3 and 2.4). It lies above the Franciscan rocks of the Mt. Hamilton block along the Coast Range fault, an old structure formed during or soon after subduction. The ophiolite consists of serpentinized ultramafic rock (peridotite) that is less sheared and more resistant than the serpentinites west of the Diablo Range. Nevertheless, the rocks here are also depleted in silica, alumina, and potassium, and the sparse overlying soils support a cover of only grass and scattered foothill pines. East of the county, the Orestimba block is faulted against the Franciscan Complex of the Mt. Hamilton block by the Tesla-Ortigalita fault, which is younger than the Coast Range fault and offsets it. The Orestimba block here includes more than 7,600 meters (25,000 feet) of sandstone, mudstone, and conglomerate of the Great Valley sequence. The original depositional contact at the base of these rocks on the ophiolite is locally preserved.

The Deposits of the San Francisco Bay and Santa Clara Valley

The various unconsolidated alluvial deposits that underlie the Santa Clara Valley and the southern margin of San Francisco Bay have been described in several reports (Helley and Brabb 1971; Helley et al. 1979), as well as in the previously cited map sheets. In addition, a number of papers have been published that deal with the depositional and tectonic history of these young deposits, as well as effects related to changes in sea level (Atwater et al. 1977; Page 1992; Page et al. 1998; and more recent papers cited below).

The oldest deposits along the western margin of the Santa Clara Valley are Pliocene-Pleistocene terrestrial deposits made up of sandstone and siltstone, plus minor volcanic rocks that are all assigned to the Santa Clara Formation. Fossils and dated basalt flows and ash layers indicate an age range from about 4 Ma to 0.5 Ma. Similar deposits of about the same age are found along the eastern margin of the valley where they are known principally as the Silver Creek and Packwood gravels. These deposits have great tectonic significance, because they mark the end of marine deposition (except for the Bay itself) and the be-

ginning of uplift and erosion of the adjacent mountain ranges.

Overlying these Pliocene-Pleistocene gravels along the margins of the valley and in the mountain ranges are younger, partly consolidated alluvial fan and stream deposits. These include deposits found at Pacheco Pass, where uplifted gravels are now preserved at about 300 meters (1,100 feet) above sea level, and in San Antonio and Isabel Valleys, where similar gravels are as much as 600 meters (2,000 feet) above sea level.

But while the mountains were rising, the Santa Clara Valley has been sinking. Recent work in the northern Santa Clara Valley, based in part on records from several 1,000-foot-deep drill holes, has revealed new details about the history of this alluvial basin (Mankinen and Wentworth 2003; Wentworth and Tinsley 2005; and papers by these and other authors presented at the symposium on the Santa Clara Valley at the meeting of the Geological Society of America in San Jose, California, in May 2005). Subsidence of the Santa Clara basin has proceeded at a nearly constant rate of nearly 4 cm (1.6 inches) per century during at least the past 0.75 Ma. Alluvial sedimentation has kept pace with this elevator-like subsidence, resulting in a sequence of flat-lying alluvial sediment 300–500 meters (1,000–1,600 feet) thick that underlies the northern Santa Clara Valley. It is this alluvium that contains the principal groundwater resource in the county.

The present distribution of alluvial sediment on the valley floor is shown in considerable detail in the maps of Quaternary deposits by Knudsen et al. (2000) and Witter et al. (2006). The heads of the latest Pleistocene alluvial fans are preserved around the margins of the valley, particularly along its west side, but most of the valley is floored by Holocene deposits that supported exceptional agricultural soils prior to urbanization. Estuarine sediment accumulated in and around the southern part of San Francisco Bay when the sea once again entered the bay estuary about 5,000 years ago as glaciers melted and sea level rose following the last, Wisconsinan, glacial epoch (Atwater et al. 1977). These muds support the modern saltmarsh plant community around the Bay margin.

Three sets of streams (see also Chapter 1) flow across the northern alluvial plain today: (1) generally northeast-flowing streams draining the eastern flank of the Santa Cruz Mountains that are the latest representation of the streams that have built the large alluvial fans underlying the western part of the Valley; (2) axial streams (Coyote Creek and Guadalupe River) that flow northwestward along the toes of those fans to San Francisco Bay; and (3) the few local streams that flow out of the edge of the Diablo Range from the northeast, where only small fans have been built. Coyote Creek is a relative newcomer to the valley; in late Pleistocene time, at least, it built a large alluvial fan below the site of present-day Anderson Dam and flowed south to the Pajaro River.

All of these streams have built natural levees along their margins from sediment dropped there when flood waters slowed as they overran the stream banks, and older levees evident elsewhere on the fans mark the paths of earlier streams. The present streams are now entrenched well below fan level as part of the natural geomorphic progression of the landscape, making flooding more difficult, particularly in their upper reaches. Controlled releases on the many streams that have been dammed further limit the potential for flooding. Natural channel bottoms and riparian habitats are still preserved along many of the stream channels (Fig. 2.3), despite extensive bank modifications, but much of the rest of the valley floor has been covered by streets and buildings.

Summary

The great variety of habitats in Santa Clara County are in many ways the direct result of its remarkably involved geologic history. Subduction-driven accretion and transform-driven lateral transport assembled the present collage of rocks. Uplift of the Santa Cruz Mountains and the Diablo Range and subsidence of the intervening Santa Clara Valley were produced by compression across the San Andreas fault that began when the relative motions of the tectonic plates across the transform shifted slightly about 4–5 million years ago. The orographic effects of these mountains produce large differences in local climate. Erosion of the highlands has produced the alluvial plain of Santa Clara Valley, and details of the present climate-driven geomorphic cycle have resulted in entrenchment of the streams crossing that plain.

Differences in the slope of hillsides and character of soils are controlled by differences in the underlying rocks, which range widely from potassium-rich granite to nutrient-poor serpentinite, and from resistant sandstones supporting steep slopes to sheared, relatively impermeable mélange supporting only gentle slopes with abundant landslides. The collage of these different kinds of rocks has been formed through a 150-million-year history of sedimentation and rock formation, northward transport by drifting tectonic plates, accretion at subduction zones, and tectonic shuffling along the San Andreas transform. Large vertical transport brought rock of the earth's mantle (now serpentinite) up to be exposed at the Earth's surface, and brought rocks of the Franciscan Complex up from the great depths at which they were metamorphosed.

The rich variety of bird life in Santa Clara County is thus greatly indebted to the long plate-tectonic history of its rocks. The plates continue to move, at rates that are too slow to appreciably affect the birds, but sufficiently fast to occasionally affect those of us who observe them.

3 Vegetation Communities in Santa Clara County

Sara Timby

Driving through Santa Clara County, we see an obviously altered landscape, reflected primarily in urban, built-up land and agricultural fields. But not far off the main roads, and certainly on hikes in county parkland, we see "native" plant communities and realize that they are quite different from the vegetation we might have had in our former homelands (at least those readers who, like the majority of county residents, were born outside of California). Santa Clara County lies within the California Floristic Province, a broad region that is unusual among world vegetation patterns in being adapted to summer-dry and winter-wet conditions—a feature of a very few Mediterranean-type climates existing only in parts of California, Chile, South Africa, Australia, and of course the Mediterranean basin.

The native vegetation in Santa Clara County goes dormant in late summer from lack of water, not from an onset of cold. Our burst of growth occurs with the winter rains, leading into lengthening days and warmer weather, most growth tapering off in May and June rather than only beginning to flourish then. The exceptions to this rule here are the plant communities with summer water—the salt and freshwater marshes and the riparian zones, and of course the developed areas with home gardens and cropland. There, the bulk of biomass is produced in midsummer.

The plant communities of Santa Clara County bear more resemblance to those of the East Bay counties of Contra Costa and Alameda than to those to the west (San Mateo and Santa Cruz), which border the ocean. Contra Costa, Alameda, and Santa Clara line up on a north-south axis, their eastern boundaries forming a continuous line. Following the geographic classification system of *The Jepson Manual: Higher Plants of California* (Hickman 1993), all five counties, together with Marin, constitute a subdivision (the San Francisco Bay Area) of the Central Western California sub-region of the California Floristic Province. The sub-region is noteworthy for its unusually diverse plant communities, ranging from wet redwood forest to dry oak/pine woodland and chaparral. You see some of this remarkable heterogeneity if you drive the 72 kilometers of Highway 152 from Hecker Pass in the Santa Cruz Mountains (on the Santa Cruz County border) east to Pacheco Pass in the Mt. Hamilton Range (on the Merced County border).

The geology, climate, and human history that are taken up in our other introductory chapters explain the past events (some very ancient) and present circumstances that have determined the character of our current plant communities. Vegetation change continues, even in the relatively short term, both by seemingly isolated catastrophic events such as wildfire, flood, landslide, and disease, but also incrementally, by human activity. Humans are in fact the primary cause of vegetation change in the county today. Degradation and destruction of natural habitat by urban and agricultural development, flood control measures such as stream channelization and reservoirs, irrigation of landscaping and crops, carbon dioxide buildup in the atmosphere, fire suppression, introduction of weeds and pathogens, and nitrogen deposition from car exhaust—all have greatly increased the rates and extent of vegetation change.

We are fortunate to have two regional floras that cover Santa Clara County: John Hunter Thomas's *Flora of the Santa Cruz Mountains* (Thomas 1961), and Helen Sharsmith's *Flora of the Mount Hamilton Range* (Sharsmith 1982). Both books include good descriptions of plant communities and their indicator species.

Vegetation Classification

In this chapter, vegetation classification is based on the plant communities described by Robert Holland (1986). Mapping data come from the California Gap Analysis Project (Davis and Stoms 1999, www.biogeog.ucsb.edu). This project (CA-GAP) is part of a national effort by the U.S. Fish and Wildlife Service and The Nature Conservancy to identify gaps in the preservation of species and habitats. While numerous efforts are underway by public and private groups to assess the status of biodiversity at local to sub-regional scales, a statewide (and national) effort was needed to identify landscapes that contain unprotected vegetation types and vertebrate species that would otherwise be overlooked in the more local studies. The mapping for Santa Clara County was completed in the summer of 1996, but will be periodically updated and refined.

The Santa Clara County plant communities, as described by Holland, are shown in Table 3.1. The six primary types of vegetation in that scheme are based on height and dominant life

VEGETATION COMMUNITIES

Table 3.1. Santa Clara County vegetation types and plant communities (Holland 1986). Some of the listed plant communities are too small in area to be mapped and do not appear in the figures, but are nonetheless discussed in the text.

Vegetation type	Plant community	Cover, %	Figure
Herbaceous		15.8	
	Northern Coastal Salt Marsh		3.1
	Coastal and Valley Freshwater Marsh		
	Brackish Marsh, Vernal Pools, etc.		
	Annual, Non-native Grassland		3.1
	Serpentine Grassland		
	Coastal Prairie		3.1
Shrub		16.7	
	Buck Brush Chaparral		3.2
	Chamise Chaparral		3.2
	Upper Sonoran Manzanita Chaparral		3.2
	Mesic North Slope Chaparral		3.2
	Diablan Sage Scrub		3.3
	Central (Lucian) Coast Scrub		3.3
	Northern (Franciscan) Coast Scrub		3.3
	Leather Oak Chaparral		3.3
	Scrub Oak Chaparral		3.3
	Interior Live Oak Chaparral		3.3
Woodland		16.9	
	Black Oak Woodland		3.4
	Valley Oak Woodland		3.4
	Blue Oak Woodland		3.4
	Coast Live Oak Woodland		3.4
	Foothill Pine–Oak Woodland		3.4
	Open Foothill Pine Woodland		3.4
	Serpentine Foothill Pine–Chaparral Woodland		3.4
Forest		18.0	
	Mixed Evergreen Forest		3.5
	California Bay Forest		3.5
	Coast Live Oak Forest		3.5
	Black Oak Forest		3.5
	Ponderosa Pine Forest		
	Coulter Pine Forest		3.5
	Upland Redwood Forest		3.5
	Tan Oak Forest		3.5
Riparian and Lacustrine		0.5	
	Cottonwood–Sycamore Riparian Forest		3.6
	Central Coast Live Oak Riparian Forest		
	White Alder Riparian Forest		
	Sycamore Alluvial Woodland		
	Central Coast Riparian Scrub		
	Mule-fat Scrub		
	Lacustrine Habitat (reservoir- or lake-based)		3.6
Developed Habitats		32.1	
	Urban or Built-up Land		3.7
	Agricultural Types		3.7
	Eucalyptus Groves		3.7
	Conifer Plantations		3.7
	Quarries		3.7

form (herb, shrub, tree), canopy cover (open woodland to closed forest), proximity to water (streamside, which can have aspects of any or all dominant life forms, and lacustrine, in open fresh water), and the most extensive type, developed habitats.

These plant-community terms are ideals—they are concepts we can easily understand, recognize, and communicate—and they are useful for the particular purpose of this atlas. More specific distinctions for plant-community terms are described by protocols developed by the California Native Plant Society (Sawyer and Keeler-Wolf 1995) and, more recently, the California Department of Fish and Game's Natural Communities List (California Resources Agency 2003). These fine tunings are particularly useful in scientific research and for the description of rare plant communities that require recognition and protection. Still other vegetation-classification systems for California have been developed (Munz and Keck 1970, Cheatham and Haller 1975, and Mayer and Laudenslayer 1988), but the purposes of our particular treatment were best served by the maps available from CA-GAP, which utilize Holland's well-defined plant-community terms.

The GAP maps are based on a determination of the predominant or primary vegetation cover of each of the county's 100-hectare (240-acre) polygons. Data also exist for secondary and tertiary cover in each polygon, but we cannot illustrate that level of detail, owing to space and scale constraints. When a contiguous plant community extends beyond the county border, the full extent of the community is shown in the figures. A number of plant communities within the county are too small to be recorded with the GAP analysis but can nonetheless be of interest, and those that are significant are discussed where appropriate.

In the San Francisco Bay Area, the term "primary" vegetation can be somewhat misleading. This central, coastal part of California is known for its "interdigitation" or interfingering of vegetation types. This is manifested where a difference in slope aspect caused by small drainages (northeast- and southwest-facing slopes in particular) will host very different plant communities side by side. This pattern rarely occurs in northern and southern California, where one finds, respectively, either continuous forest cover on both slope aspects in the north, or continuous chaparral cover on both slope aspects in the south.

Another limitation of the maps is the inability to show "ecotones," the numerous habitat edges and the transitory states of vegetation change within a community. Some examples of the latter are the loss of grasslands to gradual encroachment of coyotebrush, or the successional stages of growth after a chaparral burn. According to research by Thomas Sisk (1991), some birds prefer, and even require, the "edge effect," using different permutations of plant communities for feeding, cover, and nesting. One can predict that small habitat patches with convoluted edges will increase bird abundance. Likewise, the flush of new growth in the first years after a burn increases the populations of deer, small mammals, reptiles, and birds (Wirtz 1991).

Further analysis of GAP plant-community mapping in relation to the specific spatial data presented on the maps for individual breeding bird species will be rewarding. (Clark Blake and Carl Wentworth are investigating the correlation of particular soils with their vegetation cover, and cite many examples in Chapter 2 of this volume.)

Herbaceous-Dominated Plant Communities

Figure 3.1 shows the distribution of herbaceous-dominated plant communities in the county, including Northern Coastal Salt Marsh, Annual Non-native Grasslands, and Coastal Prairie. (Again, occurrences of Freshwater Marsh, Brackish Marsh, and Serpentine Grassland here are too small in area to be mapped.) Due to year-around water availability, the three marsh communities are of significant habitat value compared with the grassland communities. At only a tiny fraction of the total herbaceous cover, they provide a tremendous habitat resource.

Northern Coastal Salt Marsh. The south end of the San Francisco Bay has been used to host our garbage dumps. As early as 1949 John Thomas Howell, a California Academy of Sciences botanist, decried the negative public attitude to the "perfect and balanced creation of oozy, smelly, insectiferous salt marshes. . . . How tragic is the present-day tendency to 'reclaim' so perfect and balanced a creation by destroying it!" (Howell 1949). Most marshes, however, were destroyed, and the bird and fish populations are now a fraction of their former numbers. Today, introduced organisms outnumber native species. But on a positive note, the outlook for the South Bay salt marsh habitat is good. The purchase in 2003 of some 15,100 acres in the South Bay (and 1,400 acres in the North Bay) by state and federal agencies—with assistance from several local private foundations—of salt evaporator ponds presents the opportunity to restore a major portion of the salt marsh habitat around the outlets of the Guadalupe River and Coyote Creek watersheds.

We now recognize that salt marsh is of tremendous ecological value. Cord grass, at the low end of the food chain, produces five to ten times as much nutrient material and oxygen per acre as wheat. Insects eat it fresh, but many more organisms make use of the decayed form. At the high end of the food chain, the number of birds supported by this habitat in the nineteenth century was staggering, especially in the fall and winter when those that nested in the far north, or on lakes in the Great Basin, arrived here either to overwinter or to rest and feed briefly before traveling on south to their wintering grounds. Even the diminished numbers supported by our remaining marshland are impressive, and make it that much more imperative that we preserve these marshes. Populations of migratory waterbirds are probably more limited by shrinking wintering areas in California than by their lack of nesting space to the north.

Wildlife use of salt marsh comes and goes with the tides. Nutrient flow through the mud flats and marsh is high because the tidal currents deliver phytoplankton, zooplankton, and oxygen. Myriad invertebrates, including worms, shrimp, and mollusks, rely on this tidal flow for food. An example is the ribbed mussel, which attaches to stems of cord grass. The phosphate-rich fecal pellets that the mussels excrete are excellent fertilizer for marsh plants (Kuenzler 1961). These mussels constituted 57 percent of the volume of prey items in the stomachs of 18 Clapper Rails from the San Francisco Bay examined in 1939 (Moffitt 1941). Other shorebirds, such as avocets, dowitchers, and willets, wait for the low-tide exposures of muddy banks and flats to hunt for worms, shrimp, and small mollusks. Terns and cormorants wait for the concentration of fish in the larger sloughs as the tide ebbs.

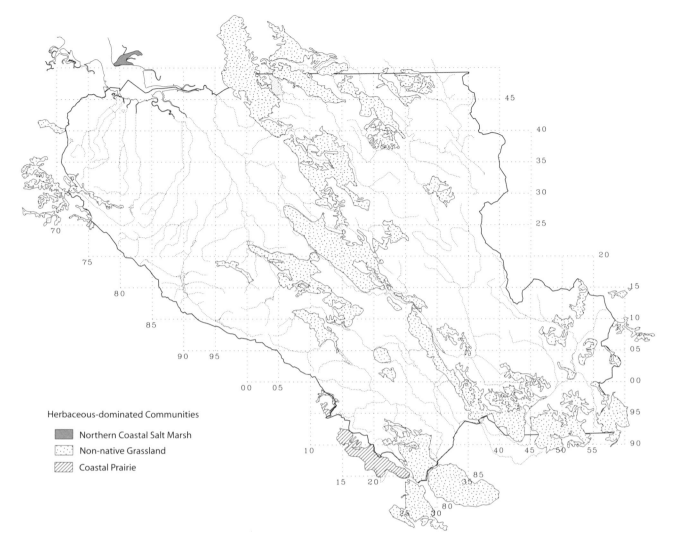

Fig. 3.1. Herbaceous-dominated plant communities.

Egrets and herons stalk their prey at any tide. High tide brings diving and fish-eating ducks, kingfishers, and terns, all competing for the high-tide fish. At the highest tides, harriers course above the marsh, searching for the mice that the high water has flushed from cover. The indicator bird species for the salt marsh in our area include the Clapper Rail, the salt marsh race of the Song Sparrow, the Savannah Sparrow, and the Marsh Wren.

The plant community in the marsh is also defined by the tides. Plants must tolerate the daily ebb and flow, as well as variations in salinity because of rain or freshwater floods at river outlets, or effluent from local sewage treatment plants. The salt marsh vegetation varies in species composition from the outer lower margin, which is covered daily by the tides, to the innermost part, which is reached only by the highest tides. All species need both inundation and exposure; different species require different amounts, which results in distinct vegetation zones.

California cord grass, in the lower zone, can tolerate a tidal flood of more than six hours, but above-water exposure is limited to the fifteen-day period between spring tides. Submer-

gence in the higher zone is often less than six hours, but exposure here may be weeks or months in duration. In this higher zone, pickleweed and other succulent plants are dominant. At still higher ground are saltmarsh dodder, saltgrass, alkali heath, arrow grass, and gum plant.

There are good access points from which to view this limited habitat (so limited that only a single Alameda County location is shown in Fig. 3.1) at the Palo Alto Baylands Nature Preserve, Shoreline Park at Mountain View, the Stevens Creek Nature Study Area (which includes some brackish-water marsh), Sunnyvale Baylands Park, and the Alviso Environmental Education Center at the south end of the Don Edwards San Francisco Bay National Wildlife Refuge. The Salt Marsh habitat shown in the upper northwest corner of Fig. 3.1 (Alameda County) is part of the Refuge at Dumbarton Point (the mouths of Newark and Mowry sloughs).

Coastal and Valley Freshwater Marsh. The ultimate birding experience could be the dawn of a spring day at a freshwater marsh, absorbing the frenetic cacophony of the morning chorus. Unfortunately, the most accessible freshwater marsh here is the Coyote Creek Parkway mitigation site, created along Coyote Creek between Silicon Valley Boulevard and Metcalf Road, where the noise of Highway 101 will interfere with the enjoyment of the avian chorus. Probably 98% of the county's original freshwater marsh is gone, an even higher percentage loss than that for our salt marshes.

Freshwater marsh habitat is defined by its lack of significant current, and by being permanently flooded with fresh rather than brackish water. Pools of open water are often present unless the marsh is silting in. Prolonged saturation permits accumulation of deep, peaty soils that support perennial bulrushes and cattails, which can form completely closed canopies. Other common plants are species of sedges, spikerushes, and grasses. Marsh plants are adapted to a paucity of oxygen in the soils. The bacteria on the floor of the marsh that decompose dead material use oxygen but release methane.

Like other aquatic habitats, freshwater marsh is rich in living things, ranging from plankton to large fish and birds. Insects, relatively more abundant than in the salt marsh, are of great importance. There are also snails, leeches, worms, and many small vertebrates, such as frogs, newts, turtles, snakes, and many varieties of fish. For birds, the habitat provides abundant food and dense cover for nesting and hiding. The concealing plant cover discourages mammalian predators and even the sharp-eyed Northern Harrier. The Pied-billed Grebe, Great Blue Heron, Wood Duck, Mallard, Ruddy Duck, Common Moorhen, American Coot, Killdeer, Belted Kingfisher, Black Phoebe, swallows, Common Yellowthroat, Song Sparrow, and Red-winged Blackbird are summer residents in these marshes.

Some freshwater marshes still remain in Santa Clara County, but none is large enough to register on the GAP maps that are the basis of Fig. 3.1. They are found near the margins of lakes and springs, and along the backwaters of creeks. The Caltrans mitigation marsh on Coyote Creek mentioned previously is 9.7 hectares in extent, but includes riparian habitat as well as true marsh. Also on Coyote Creek are bits of marsh at the south end of the borrow ponds (created usually by the need for highway fill) off the old Monterey Highway at Ogier Avenue, and on the west side of the creek at Coyote. There is a small marsh just above Gilroy on Uvas Creek; an environmental protection area in marshy land near Grant Lake in Joseph Grant County Park; and a small amount on the Bolsa de San Felipe, south of Gilroy just over the San Benito County line. There are small sag ponds and water impoundments for cattle throughout the Mt. Hamilton range (you can see some in Henry Coe State Park), but they are usually associated with very little freshwater marsh, either because they dry up in the summer or because the vegetation is grazed.

Brackish Marsh, Vernal Pools, and Other Wetlands. Brackish marsh (fresh water with occasional tidal influence) is formed near creek mouths at the Bay, where the water is almost still. These marshes are not large enough to be included in Fig. 3.1, but they are common near the Bay and exhibit the characteristic vegetation of both salt and freshwater marshes. Some examples of brackish marsh occur where Stevens Creek freshwater sits unable to drain farther; on Guadalupe River from Montague Expressway to the Alviso Slough; in the "South Coyote Slough"

between salt pond A18 and the Newby Island landfill; on Coyote Creek from below Highway 237 downstream to Coyote Slough; in Artesian Slough; and in Guadalupe Slough near the Sunnyvale Water Pollution Control Plant. All have habitat dominated by bulrushes with little cattail (Stephen C. Rottenborn, pers. comm.).

Stanford University offers several wetland sites: Lagunita and Felt Lake in Santa Clara County, and Searsville Lake and its contiguous marsh in San Mateo County. All three are manmade: Lagunita was originally created for livestock and is now only seasonally wet; Searsville and Felt lakes were created for human use and remain wet through the summer (though diminished). Stanford's Center for Conservation Biology is actively working on seasonal wetland restoration projects and their evaluation. Some small experimental seasonal wetlands can be viewed at Stanford on the southeast side of Palm Drive: one is between El Camino Real and Arboretum Road, and the other near Museum Way. Seasonal wetlands are relatively predator-free and allow frogs, salamanders, and other amphibians to breed, lay eggs, and develop in comparative safety. Most aquatic predators need year-around water. Most of those found in the county, especially largemouth bass, red swamp crawfish, and American bullfrog, are non-native species, all of them capable of consuming vast quantities of juvenile fish, amphibians, and reptiles.

Vernal pools, a rare form of habitat, existed in Santa Clara County until a few years ago when the Disk Drive and Nortech Avenue area of Alviso was developed. The Disk Drive pool played host to some uncommon spring migrants (Ruff, Pacific Golden-Plover, and White-faced Ibis) and produced a spectacular display of flat-faced downingia in late spring. These shallow ephemeral spring ponds, on hardpan soils, occur only in Mediterranean-type climates. They dry up completely in the summer. Their invertebrate populations of vernal pool fairy and vernal pool tadpole shrimp survive as eggs in the dry period, hatching only as the pools fill with water in winter. Birds are common spring visitors to the pools in search of these shrimp. The harsh conditions of inundation followed by desiccation limit the number of plant species that can survive there, and those that do are specially adapted native species that are rarely found elsewhere. The vernal pools in closest proximity to our county today are near the Bay in the Warm Springs district of Alameda County.

Annual, Non-native Grasslands. Today the predominant grassland type in all of California is annual grassland dominated by plants of Mediterranean origin. Both grasses and annual forbs (broad-leaved plants) are constituents of these grasslands. This form of plant community covers roughly 16% of the county, mostly east of the Santa Clara Valley, as shown in Fig. 3.1. The woodland (or savanna) plant communities also include annual grasslands, covering another 17% of the county (see the discussion below).

Mounting evidence suggests that there may not have been an original, prehuman-contact grassland here, as we currently envision it. This theory (Hamilton 1997, Keeley 2005) suggests that today's grassland is controlled not so much by soil or aspect as by disturbance. And this disturbance has been largely man-made. Long before the Europeans' arrival, Native Americans had been burning brush to encourage the development of open grassland, which improved the land's forage capacity for both large and small game. Missions and ranches, with their over-stocked herds of cattle and sheep, maintained the open grassland by overgrazing and further burning. The great numbers of us who have no connection to ranching are unlikely to appreciate the economic importance of grassland as opposed to shrub land, or to recognize the strong incentive the early ranchers had to convert chaparral to grassland.

The Mediterranean annual grasses and forbs that arrived from the barnyards of Spain flourished in our similar climate and outcompeted the largely perennial grasses that were native. Heavy grazing pressure, the lack of the insect controls found in their homeland, and thousands of years of adaptation to intensive grazing and agriculture favored the imports over the native grasses. Most recently, urban development rendered the coup de grace to the deep, fertile soils of the grasslands. Of the grass-lands still remaining, those that are protected from grazing and fire are subject to colonization by shrubs (particularly coyote-brush) and succession toward woodland associations. It should be noted, however, that grassland does not always revert to shrubland. Naturalized annual grass seeds germinate and grow quickly after the first rains and can outcompete the slower-ger-minating perennial seedlings for water and light, thus forming a stable climax community in central California.

The height, density, and species composition of these annual grasslands vary year-to-year, owing to dramatic differences in patterns of weather and livestock grazing, both during the year and between years. Before the arrival of fall rains the grassland appears to be mostly dead, its survival depending on the seed bank. In years of high rainfall and light stock grazing, there can be large amounts of standing dead material. The first rains are not predictable and can vary in the timing of their arrival date by many weeks. The growth, flowering, and seed-set of most annuals then follows in the short period from winter through spring.

Helen Sharsmith, in her very informative *Flora of the Mount Hamilton Range* (1982), noted a seasonal periodicity in the grassland flora, primarily in the Mt. Hamilton Range, but elements of the periodicity are visible in most grasslands, particularly those that are grazed or are on poor soils. It has two components, vernal and aestival. The vernal flora, composed of many species of short-lived annuals, usually flowers in late March or early April. The aestival flora, with a different growth habit, blooms in late August and September, during the period of highest temperatures and lowest rainfall. This aestival flora is represented by relatively few species, but the number of individuals produced, and the area covered, are great. The growth pattern often starts in spring as a flat rosette of broad leaves fed by the rapid growth of a deep taproot. Later, as the vernal competition dies back, the lower leaves also wither away and a flowering stalk with little, if any, leaves is produced. The aestival flora is dominated by such native forbs as the tarweeds, buckwheats, and dove weed. The ubiquitous, non-native yellow star thistle is gaining ground in this late-summer niche.

Introduced annual grass species usually dominate the vernal grassland community. These include wild oats, ripgut brome, soft chess, Spanish brome, Italian ryegrass, mouse barley, and foxtail fescue. Common introduced forbs include the filarees, bur clover, and black mustard. Characteristic native an-nual wildflowers include buttercups, California poppies, lupine species, owl's clover, tidytips, and goldfields.

Many county parks, including Santa Teresa, Calero, Ed Levin, and Joseph Grant, as well as Henry Coe State Park, offer hiking access in grasslands. It is worth noting that all these parks were once part of cattle ranches. The lower part of the drive up to Mt. Hamilton from the west side, and Felter Road in the Los Buellis Hills just east of Milpitas, also provide exceptional views of grasslands.

Although the original elk and pronghorn herds are gone (elk have been reintroduced in the Mt. Hamilton Range), there are still numerous small native grazers living in the grasslands. Many rodents eat either roots, leaves, or seeds, and the seeds are shared with seed-harvesting birds such as goldfinches and sparrows. Aphids, ants, grasshoppers, and slugs consume herba-ceous material, and Western Kingbirds, Western Meadowlarks, and Horned Larks eat the insects. Owls, American Kestrels, Red-tailed Hawks, and Loggerhead Shrikes prey upon rodents. Coyotes may eat birds and insects, as well as the rodents. A very few birds (Western Meadowlark, Horned Lark, and Grasshopper and Savannah sparrows) nest on the ground in the grasslands; more birds (Mourning Dove, Western Bluebird, and Yellow-billed Magpie) come from bordering habitats into the grasslands in search of food. Red-winged Blackbirds are found where mus-tards and other herbaceous weeds are abundant.

Serpentine Grassland. Native grasslands with a rich mixture of perennial bunchgrasses and wildflowers are found in a few places in the county, but all of these places are too small to be mapped and do not appear in Fig. 3.1. This community, rich in the native forbs that make spectacular spring wildflower displays, is found on soils derived from the mineral serpentine. The predominant native grasses here are purple needlegrass and big squirreltail. One of the most important native forbs is the di-minutive California plantain, which, together with owl's clover, hosts the larvae of the last remaining local population of the bay checkerspot butterfly.

The native grasslands on serpentine soils have not yet succumbed to the widespread takeover by Mediterranean an-nuals, because the latter cannot tolerate the difficult growing conditions presented by low calcium, nitrogen, and phosphorus, coupled with high magnesium, nickel, and chromium (McCarten 1993). Plants that can tolerate these unusual soils escape from competition, but it is not that they need the unusual nutrients. It is hypothesized that with ongoing nitrogen deposition from car exhaust one can expect conversion to more non-natives such as Italian ryegrass and soft chess in the serpentine grassland (Weiss 1999).

Unlike many songbirds, some grassland birds spend a lot of time on the ground. For these, the native grasslands provide important structure and diversity in their cover that are missing in the dense, limited species richness of the annual grassland. The space between perennial bunchgrasses allows grassland birds to forage for seeds and avoid predators. The high diversity of plant species ensures a continuing flowering season, with seeds produced over a long period of time. The Grasshopper Sparrow and Savannah Sparrow are examples of birds that prefer the native grassland to the annual grassland. Where flying insects provide the main diet, bird use of serpentine grasslands

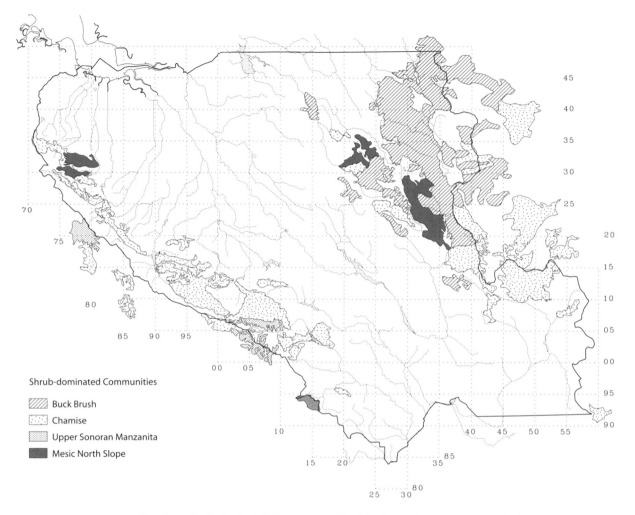

Fig. 3.2. Shrub-dominated plant communities (dominant chaparral communities).

is similar to that of the annual grasslands. And some birds, such as the Red-winged Blackbird, feed on mustards or other plants that are not found on serpentine soils.

The greatest extent of this special plant community in the county is on private land in the eastern hills above Coyote Valley, near Morgan Hill. This is the Silver Creek block discussed in Chapter 2. Small pockets of serpentine grasslands can also be found in the New Almaden and Calero county parks, and particularly along the Stile Ranch trail at Santa Teresa. There is also a 14-hectare serpentine grassland on the eastern shoulder of El Sombroso in the Sierra Azul Open Space Preserve at about 1,800 feet elevation (Hopkins 1986).

Coastal Prairie. Another native grassland, the Coastal Prairie, is found on the high ridges of the Santa Cruz Mountains just west of the Santa Clara and Santa Cruz county border (see Fig. 3.1). Primarily to the south of Hecker Pass, this area is high enough to receive additional rainfall and the cooling influence of the coastal air mass. In this habitat the grasses stay green longer and perennials predominate, particularly the native California oatgrass. But coastal prairie is far more common along the coast to the north of San Francisco Bay. It was (and is) considered one

of the best dairy farm grasslands because the long season allows grazing almost year-round. Beef cattle are usually moved off annual grasslands in late spring.

Shrub-Dominated Plant Communities

Figures 3.2 and 3.3 show the distribution of the shrub-dominated communities. Together, they constitute just under 17% of the county's area. The Chamise and Buck Brush communities, named for their dominant chaparral species, are shown with Mesic North Slope and Upper Sonoran Manzanita communities in Fig. 3.2. The six sage and scrub oak communities are patchy in their distribution and cover a relatively small percentage (Fig. 3.3). These ten different plant communities (Holland 1986) are discussed in four groups: (1) the "soft" chaparrals of Diablan Sage, Central (Lucian) Coast Scrub, and Northern (Franciscan) Coast Scrub; (2) Chamise and the Upper Sonoran Manzanita chaparrals; (3) Buck Brush, Leather Oak, Scrub Oak, and Interior Live Oak chaparrals; and (4) Mesic North Slope Chaparral. These shrub-dominated plant communities reflect differences in primary species cover, but also differences in the actual plant structure and soil structure. The so-called soft chap-

VEGETATION COMMUNITIES

arrals included in the first group are dominated by the summer-deciduous California sagebrush. The two hard chaparral communities of chamise and buck brush each have the characteristic brushy growth and dense, rigid branching that is adapted to and maintained by fire. Both have small, thick, leathery, evergreen leaves and very deep roots. Mesic North Slope Chaparral receives more moisture; it is typified by more species diversity, with larger, softer, leaves and a taller, overall greener, cover.

Occasional fire is necessary to maintain chaparral communities, be they stump sprouters or fire-obligate seeders. Most wild animal populations reach peak densities in 1 to 15 years after a chaparral fire. The plant community that immediately follows a fire includes species whose seeds have lain dormant for years—annuals, perennial herbs, and sub-shrubs such as California buckwheat and deerweed, and most species of ceanothus. After 10 to 30 years the canopy of the largest shrubs closes, and the low-growing species are shaded out. Dead material begins again to accumulate.

It appears that increased fire protection can play a role in the conversion of grasslands to shrublands. Lack of fire, coupled with a reduction in grazing during the second half of the twentieth century as ranches were transferred to public parklands, has led to coyotebrush "invasions" into grasslands. Coyotebrush, in turn, can foster the establishment of additional woody species.

In several ways, chaparral provides good animal habitat. The varieties of berries, seeds, and insects afforded there, as well as protection from predators and provision of roosting and nesting sites, are all important. Some small herbivores eat shrub species when the grasses have dried up. Shrubs also provide needed shade during hot weather. Some of the animals that find shelter in these dense thickets are nocturnal predators—owls, skunks, and ringtails. For them, mice, brush rabbits, lizards, and insects are sought-after prey. Snakes are also common in brushlands, mainly because they eat rodents, birds, and their eggs. Commonly seen birds include the Wrentit, Bewick's Wren, Western Scrub-Jay, and the ground-foragers with good running ability such as the California Thrasher, the California Quail, and the Spotted and California towhees.

The interface between chaparral and grassland often presents a "bare zone." For a long time it was postulated that chemicals in the chaparral were inhibiting the grass from growing there. It has since been shown that seed- and grass-eating animals use the chaparral as cover from predators, venturing out only a minimum distance to forage (and thus creating the bare zone) before retreating again to safety (Bartholomew 1970).

Palo Alto's Foothills Park, the Black Mountain trail from Rancho San Antonio Open Space Preserve, several trails in the Sierra Azul Open Space Preserve, and Henry Coe State Park all provide good opportunities to visit the various chaparral communities.

Diablan Sage Scrub, Central (Lucian) Coast Scrub, and Northern (Franciscan) Coast Scrub. Diablan Sage Scrub is the often-called "soft" chaparral. Sage scrub is usually coastal, but in Santa Clara County it is found well inland from coastal fog, perhaps because there is significant fog in the Santa Clara Valley itself. It grows in pockets on the inner coast ranges from Mt. Diablo south to the Cholame Hills, hence "Diablan." It is also found on the lower, rolling hills of the western side of the Santa

Clara Valley. It likes thin, rocky soils, and disturbances caused by landslides and road-cuts are often invaded by this scrub. Many of the patches are too small to be indicated on the map.

Compared with the true coastal scrubs, the interior Diablan Sage Scrub has fewer shrub species but a greater diversity of perennial herbs. The dominant plants are California sagebrush, coyotebrush, yerba santa, sticky monkeyflower, and California buckwheat. It is typically found on hot, southern exposures that receive less moisture than the "hard" chaparrals at higher elevations receive. Rather than the typical evergreen leaves of chaparral, California sagebrush is drought-deciduous. Its growth spurt comes immediately after the first rain; and by the end of summer it appears almost dead.

This community can be seen in many places, including areas near Coyote and Anderson reservoirs on the eastern side of the Santa Clara Valley, on the northern slope of Alum Rock canyon, in the upper drainages of the Pajaro River on the west side, and in the low hills of Santa Clara Valley in such county parks as Santa Teresa and Calero. During the atlas period, Santa Clara County was experiencing a prolonged drought. Coyote Reservoir dried out and revegetated with this Diablan sage scrub, which was very attractive to Song Sparrows and Lazuli Buntings. Spotted Sandpiper records came from similar habitat at Anderson Reservoir (James Yurchenco, pers. comm.). Birds associated with the sage scrub include the California Thrasher, Spotted Towhee, Bewick's Wren, and Rufous-crowned Sparrow (Stephen C. Rottenborn, pers. comm.). Anna's Hummingbirds can be seen feeding on sticky monkeyflower.

Central Coast Scrub (or Lucian Scrub) is also dominated by California sagebrush, but this community receives more moisture than the Diablan Sage Scrub, and supports more coyotebrush, poison oak, coffeeberry, and red berry, among other constituents. The community is adapted to fire by crown-sprouting. The largest site is found north of the outlet of Anderson Reservoir on south-facing slopes.

Northern Coast Scrub (or Franciscan Scrub) is rarely seen in Santa Clara County but can be found on windy, exposed sites with shallow, rocky soils in the Santa Cruz Mountains. The shrubs are low and dense, and often are broken by scattered grassy openings. Low-growing coyotebrush and Douglas iris are common. The location large enough to be mapped on Fig. 3.3 straddles the Santa Cruz–Santa Clara county line near the southern end of the Santa Cruz Mountains.

Chamise Chaparral and Upper Sonoran Manzanita Chaparral (with Knobcone Pine stands). These three communities are fire-dependent, and the knobcone pine and manzanita communities border the chamise in the upper elevations of the east side of the Santa Cruz Mountains. The knobcone pine, a lesser component of the manzanita chaparral, is not mapped in Fig. 3.2, but is described here because of its use by Red-breasted and Pygmy Nuthatches and Yellow-rumped Warblers.

Chamise Chaparral is an important component of the county's vegetation (7%). It is our most common chaparral shrub, 1–3 meters tall, occurring in almost pure stands with densely interwoven branches in the older stands. The water-conserving evergreen leaves are small and needle-like, and there is usually very little leaf litter or herbaceous understory. Chamise is found on warm, dry slopes and ridges in shallow soils, where

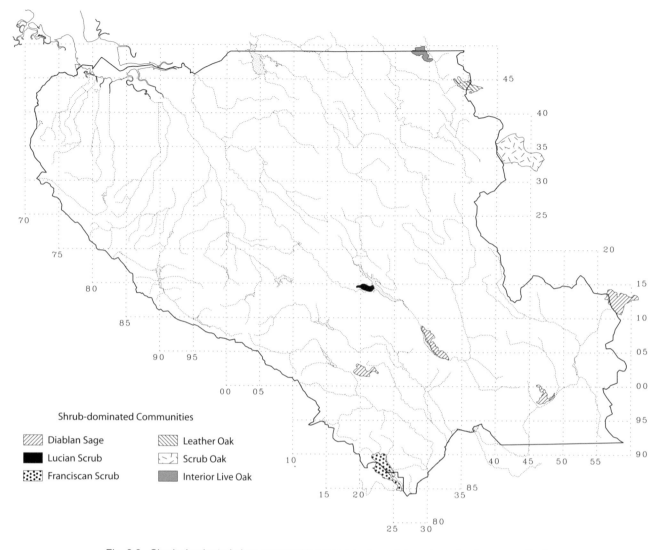

Fig. 3.3. Shrub-dominated plant communities (sage and coastal scrub, and oak communities).

the roots are able to penetrate cracks in the rock. Also known as greasewood, chamise is recognized as fire-dependent, regenerating by stump-sprouting.

The largest stands lie on the eastern slopes of the Santa Cruz Mountains and the interior of the Mt. Hamilton range, particularly in the Burnt Hills area. Both the Sage Sparrow and the Black-chinned Sparrow favor early successional growth in chamise after a fire. An effect similar to that of wildfire has been noted when ranchers drag the chaparral with a chain and/or bulldoze it, improving grazing as well as the habitat for birds (William G. Bousman, pers. comm.). Other birds in this habitat include Wrentit, California Thrasher, Spotted Towhee, and Bewick's Wren.

In our area, the Upper Sonoran Manzanita Chaparral is usually found at higher elevations than chamise, where there is more moisture and better soils. The community has a high, dense cover, reaching as high as 15 feet. Most stands appear to follow disturbance such as fire or logging. Floristically rich, it can include several varieties of manzanita, ceanothus, and scrub

oak, as well as silktassel, chaparral pea, toyon, and yerba santa.

On thin and infertile soils and steep slopes, a constituent of this manzanita chaparral may be the knobcone pine, our county's only closed-cone pine. The cone needs the heat of a fire to open. It then sheds its seeds on the ash bed and germinates in the newly available sunlight. Stands are thus usually all of one age, except on relatively "fire-proof," rocky sites. The pines occur between chamise, on their lower border, and forest, at their upper edge. On the east side of the Santa Cruz Mountains, knobcone pine is found in pockets on Mount Umunhum, Loma Prieta, and Mount Madonna. You can view a typical stand on the Knibbs Knob trail at Uvas Canyon County Park.

Buck Brush Chaparral, Leather Oak Chaparral, Scrub Oak Chaparral, and Interior Live Oak Chaparral. These chaparral types are found predominantly in the interior and eastern parts of the Mt. Hamilton range in the northeast corner of the county. Buck brush is the dominant species, covering approximately 7% of the county's area. We usually think of oaks as majestic trees. In fact, over half of California's oak species are shrubs. These have multiple trunks arising from the ground, with dense, interwoven canopies, and tough, spiny, evergreen leaves. Leather Oak and Interior Live Oak chaparrals comprise only 0.1% each. Scrub oak doesn't even warrant 0.1%, but you can see it fairly often as an occasional component of other communities. In Fig. 3.3, a fairly large stand just barely crosses into Santa Clara County from adjacent Stanislaus County, where it is found at the head of high canyons on the east side of the range.

Buck brush is dominant or codominant with chamise in this plant community. It is a dense chaparral, although less so than pure chamise, because the branches are not so tightly interwoven. The cover is slightly higher than chamise, averaging a little over 2 meters. This is an intermediary chaparral between the more typically southern California chamise and the northern California stands of pure buck brush. Found on dry slopes and alluvial fans, it borders pure stands of chamise, but at higher elevations. It can also border open foothill pine woodland. The Wrentit, the so-called "voice of the chaparral," is often heard in the buck brush stands. The Spotted Towhee is also common there.

Scrub oak and interior live oak chaparrals both require slightly more moisture than buck brush and are found adjacent to buck brush on north-facing slopes, canyons, and valley bottoms. Leather oak is found on the serpentine soil of the Red Mountain area in the remote, northeast corner of the county. All three oaks are densely branched and evergreen, and are approximately 3 meters tall. These communities can also contain mountain mahogany. Substantial leaf litter accumulates. Most of these oaks are in an area that few people visit, because they are in private holdings in the northeast corner of the county where there is little public access. You can view similar oak chaparral at the summit of Mt. Hamilton (see the discussion of the Blue Oak Woodland below).

Mesic North Slope Chaparral. A mixed chaparral with no dominant species, this community is typically on shady north- and east-facing slopes above 3,000 feet, but can also be found at lower altitudes. It covers 1.7 % of the county land area. Major constituents include toyon, hollyleaf cherry, coffeeberry, poison oak, ceanothus, manzanita, mountain mahogany, interior live oak, and scrub oak. After the breeding season in the autumn, berries of toyon, hollyleaf cherry, and poison oak attract American Robins, Hermit Thrushes, and Cedar Waxwings.

This community often interdigitates with blue oak woodlands or chamise on adjacent south-facing slopes, or on sites with shallow soils or poor drainage. On the north- and east-facing summit slopes of Mt. Hamilton there are large areas of this community, composed almost entirely of three shrubby, evergreen oaks (scrub oak and the shrubby forms of interior live oak and canyon live oak), occasionally mixed with manzanita.

Woodland-Dominated Communities (Open Canopy)

Woodlands, largely of various oak species and foothill pine communities, are shown in Fig. 3.4. Most are found in the eastern portions of the county, with the exception of the Blue Oak Woodlands, which are also found on the hills west of Santa Clara Valley.

California's iconic oak woodlands have lost ground over the years. They have been cleared for housing developments or cut for fuel, and their regeneration has been hindered by grazing and competition from non-native annual grasses. Now a new threat is recognized: climate change. A recent study (Kueppers et al. 2005) predicts that blue oak and valley oak woodlands will shift northward and to higher elevations, decreasing to nearly half their current range in all of California.

Most of our woodland consists of one of four oaks, the two predominant communities being Blue Oak Woodland (5.9% of county land) and Coast Live Oak Woodland (3.5%). Blue oaks are also part of the Foothill Pine–Oak woodland community, which is the largest woodland plant community in the county (6.2%). Taken together, woodlands occupy just under 17% of the county.

Woodlands have significant grassland cover under and between trees, but for identification purposes they are considered to have no less than 30% canopy cover. In "forest," which is essentially a closed canopy, the grassland understory is rare. Less than 30% cover is usually considered an ecotone, or edge situation, and is often called a savanna. Most likely, the savannas supported more trees at one time, and could hypothetically have more again. In most cases, the existing savanna oaks are large and old. They were probably saved by ranchers to provide shade and acorns for livestock.

The leaves of our local oaks are of three kinds—evergreen, winter-deciduous, and drought-deciduous. Each kind reflects its own adaptations to our peculiar circumstance of water being least available when it is needed the most. Evergreen leaves, such as those of coast live, canyon live, and scrub oaks, are tough and leathery, with a thick, waxy cuticle that minimizes water loss. Their stomata, moreover, can shut rapidly in response to aridity. These trees lose leaves from the previous year during August, thus concentrating water use in the current year's growth. The leaves of winter-deciduous oaks such as black and valley oaks, have a thinner cuticle and cannot adjust their stomata in the same way. These black and valley oaks occupy relatively moist environments (at higher elevations and in deep valley soils, respectively). Blue oaks have a third kind of leaf, drought-deciduous. These oaks have many of the drought-tolerant characteristics of the evergreen oaks, but they go them one better by shedding their leaves in late summer and autumn to further avoid desiccation of woody tissue (Pavlik et al. 1991).

Oak communities are of profound significance to both vertebrate and invertebrate wildlife species. Acorns, leaves, wood, and sap are sustenance for insects, birds, and mammals. Reptiles and amphibians do not eat oak products but rely on the myriad insects that do. Acorns are consumed by at least 30 species of birds. The Acorn Woodpecker relies on them for over half of its diet, and acorns make up 25 to 50% of the yearly intake of Wood Ducks, Wild Turkeys, Band-tailed Pigeons, and jays. But for most birds, the invertebrates found in oak communities are of more importance than acorns. Bushtits, wrens, and warblers glean bugs directly from leaves; flycatchers, such as Western Kingbird and Black Phoebe, catch them in the air; and thrashers, towhees, and thrushes forage on the ground. Finally, at least as important as food, is the significance of shelter for nesting and cover. Many kinds of birds build nests in the canopies of

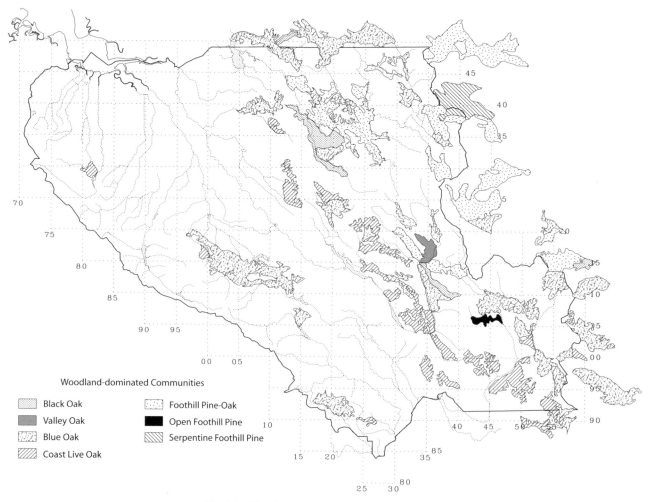

Fig. 3.4. Woodland-dominated plant communities.

oak trees; others are cavity nesters, and among their numbers are woodpeckers, swallows, White-breasted Nuthatches, House Wrens, Western Bluebirds, Western Screech-Owls, and Northern Pygmy-Owls (Pavlik et al. 1991).

Although some bird species are broadly distributed in oak savanna, woodland, and even forest, others are more specific in their preferences. Those broadly distributed among oaks include Western Screech-Owl, Western Scrub-Jay, Oak Titmouse, and White-breasted Nuthatch. The Western Bluebird and Yellow–billed Magpie seem to prefer the more open oak woodlands, and the Chestnut-backed Chickadee prefers the closed canopy of the mixed evergreen forest.

Black Oak Woodland and Valley Oak Woodland. Black Oak Woodland covers 0.9% of the county; Valley Oak Woodland, 0.2%. The two have some similarities: both communities are found predominantly in the Mt. Hamilton Range, and both oaks are deciduous, requiring the most moisture of all of our oaks. Their particular habitats, however, are quite distinct, and they rarely overlap in their distribution. Black oaks are generally found between 2,500 and 4,000 feet, often on ridges or north-eastern exposures. Valley oaks are usually below 2,000 feet, and usually in valleys!

Black Oak Woodland is found on northerly slopes of the western and eastern crests of the Mt. Hamilton Range. One drives through it approaching the summit area of Mt. Hamilton from the west, and again after leaving the summit area driving east. Black Oak Woodland also occurs in suitable habitat of the Santa Cruz Mountains, although not dominant enough there to show up in Fig. 3.4. Associates can include ponderosa pine and madrone. There can be a shrubby understory, often with mountain mahogany. The ground cover is usually well-developed, and there is generally a good litter layer. Most stands are even-aged (all trees are of the same age) because of past burns, and are generally younger than 125 years. Although black oak is a stump-sprouter, stands less than 60 years old are not very resistant to fire.

The open country of Valley Oak Woodland resembles more a grassy savanna than a true woodland, rarely exceeding 30-40% absolute cover. Valley oak is often the only species of tree present in the community, though one can also find a significant blue oak component in places. The fact that the understory is such a homogeneous grassland is likely the result of repeated human-caused management burns and grazing. This form of woodland is found on deep, well-drained alluvial soils, usually in valley bottoms, or at least along drainages, and these alluvial soils provide excellent grassland forage for livestock. Because the community occupies fairly small drainages, the stands are underrepresented on the map. Good examples can be viewed in the San Antonio and Isabel valleys in the Mt. Hamilton Range, and on the east fork of the Coyote Creek drainage in Henry Coe State Park (this is the single location that appears in Fig. 3.4—it is a full-day's roundtrip walk from headquarters). Associated birds may include Lewis's Woodpecker, Western Kingbird, and Western Bluebird (Stephen C. Rottenborn, pers. comm.).

Valley oak is California's largest broad-leaved tree; it can achieve a maximum age of 500 years. George Vancouver, traveling from San Francisco to San Jose in 1792, marveled at this "park-like" woodland (Vancouver 1798). Some of the trees he saw still survive in the deep alluvial soils of the Peninsula towns of Palo Alto, Menlo Park, and Atherton.

Blue Oak Woodland. Blue Oak Woodland is a relatively large constituent of Santa Clara County, at 5.9%. It can include scrub oaks and interior live oaks as well as foothill pines. Stands vary from open savanna with a grassy understory (usually at lower elevations) to fairly dense woodland with a shrubby understory. Components in the shrubby understory include California buckeye, red berry, coffeeberry, hollyleaf cherry, and yerba santa.

Blue oaks require well-drained soils. The high die-off rate of mature trees after the unusually big rainfalls of the 1998-99 El Niño years was attributed to the back-to-back seasons of water-logged soils. Frequent fire favors blue oak (a long-lived stump sprouter) over its common associate, foothill pine. Blue Oak Woodland is supplanted at higher elevations and in cooler sites by Black Oak Woodland or Foothill Pine–Oak Woodland. At lower elevations it borders annual, non-native grassland; there, the blue oaks are largely confined to north slopes and canyons. Associated birds include Oak Titmouse, Ash-throated Flycatcher, White-breasted Nuthatch, and Western Bluebird.

All three deciduous oak woodlands are found throughout the Mt. Hamilton Range, and particularly to the west and south of Calero Reservoir in the Santa Cruz Mountains.

Coast Live Oak Woodland. Coast live oak is usually the only dominant tree in this woodland, which comprises 3.5% of the county. Evergreen, the aptly named live oak ranges from 30 to 80 feet in height. Other trees in the community may include California buckeye, madrone, and California bay. The understory is dominated by grassland, including ripgut brome and wild oats in the sunnier areas and miner's lettuce, common chickweed, bedstraw, and hedge parsley in the shade. The shrub layer is poorly developed, but may support toyon, currants, poison oak, California sagebrush, and elderberry.

Coast Live Oak Woodland is found typically on north-facing slopes and in shaded ravines. It intergrades with grasslands and Diablan Sage Scrub on lower or drier sites, and with Coast Live Oak Forest or Mixed Evergreen Forest on higher or wetter sites. Large stretches of the woodland are more dominant on the eastern side of Santa Clara Valley, but there are many small patches on the western side as well. This is another good example of a plant community that doesn't map well because of occurring so often in sites of limited size. Oak Titmouse, White-breasted Nuthatch, Hutton's Vireo, and Chestnut-backed Chickadee all use this evergreen oak woodland habitat.

Foothill Pine–Oak Woodland, Open Foothill Pine Woodland, and Serpentine Foothill Pine–Chaparral Woodland. These three woodland communities are similar in their predominant constituent, the foothill pine (a.k.a gray pine, formerly digger pine). They differ in their relative composition of species. The foothill pine is deep-rooted and drought-resistant; it is able to live on as little as 10 inches of rain a year, surviving five summer months of heat hovering near 100°. The cones, large and heavy, contain tasty pine nuts. Foothill Pine Woodlands typically occur at elevations between 1,000 and 3,000 feet, intergrading at lower elevations with chamise, buck brush, or Blue Oak Woodland, and at higher elevations, or on more mesic (cooler and more moist) sites, with Black Oak Woodland. Foothill pine mingles with the closely related Coulter pine at the latter species' lower levels (see the discussion of Forests, next), and occasionally the two will occupy the higher ridge tops together.

The Foothill Pine–Oak Woodland, the most common of the three communities, is an open, savanna-like woodland dominated by foothill pine and blue oak, in various combinations. It constitutes 6.2% of the county and is found primarily in the northeastern section of the Mt. Hamilton Range. The understory of this open woodland is typically composed of annual grasses and forbs, the areas under the deciduous oaks being a bit richer in growth and species composition than the nearby open grassland due to the accumulation of leaf litter. The added shade of the oaks in late spring and summer also protects the understory from the heat of the day.

Open Foothill Pine Woodland is found throughout the interior of the Mt. Hamilton Range on rocky, exposed slopes, ridge tops, gravelly flats, or the flood beds of intermittent streams. The understory is more sparse than that found in combination with blue oaks. The one occurrence shown on Fig. 3.4 is in the southern section of Henry Coe State Park near Rock Springs Peak.

The Serpentine Foothill Pine–Chaparral Woodland (0.1%) is on serpentine soils near Red Mountain in the north-east corner of the county. A much larger contiguous section extends into Stanislaus County. In these serpentine substrates the foothill pine usually has an understory of shrubby cover, including chamise, manzanita, buck brush, and leather oak.

Bird life among the foothill pines is rather sparse, at least in the hot summer months. The oaks, however, attract many flying insects in the spring, and the leaves can often be badly infested with caterpillars—good foraging for insectivorous birds. In the fall, pine nuts and acorns provide food for Band-tailed Pigeons, Western Scrub-Jays, and Acorn and Lewis's Woodpeckers. The grassy understory provides food and cover for California Quail, Western Meadowlarks, and Lark Sparrows.

Forest-Dominated Communities (Closed Canopy)

The forests in Santa Clara County, shown in Fig. 3.5, constitute 18% of the county and are found along the crest of the Santa Cruz Mountains, at higher elevations in the Mt. Hamilton Range, and in the upper Pacheco Creek drainage. Forests, as contrasted with woodlands, have a closed canopy, and usually occur in cooler, more mesic sites, often at higher altitudes or

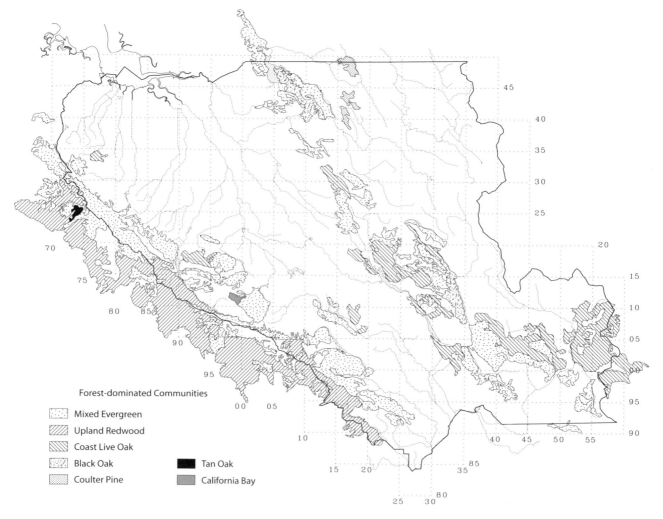

Fig. 3.5. Forest-dominated plant communities.

on steeper, north- and east-facing slopes. There is less under-story because less sunlight reaches the ground. The diversity of both plant and animal species is therefore not as great as in woodlands.

Mixed Evergreen Forest, California Bay Forest, and Upland Douglas Fir Forest. The closed-canopy Mixed Evergreen Forest is dominated by a great diversity of broadleaved evergreen trees, mostly 30 to 100 feet tall. Some winter-deciduous species also occur, including bigleaf maple, black oak, hazelnut, and dogwood; a drought-deciduous tree, the California buckeye, also occurs here. The richness of this vegetation type is mainly in its trees; relatively little understory can grow under the dense canopy. Comprising 10% of the county, the Mixed Evergreen Forest often occurs in small, mosaic-like patches, which are not visible in Fig. 3.5. The species composition of the forest in the Mt. Hamilton Range differs significantly from that in the Santa Cruz Mountains; it is only in the latter that one finds Douglas fir, tan oak, and chinquapin. Moreover, both madrone and bigleaf maple, common in the Santa Cruz Mountains, are rather rare in the Mt. Hamilton Range. The most common species in both ranges include canyon live oak, coast live oak, black oak, and California bay.

These three forest types occur on moist, well-drained, coarse soils, usually on slopes, and often around rock outcrops in heavier soils. The California Bay Forest and Upland Douglas Fir Forest need slightly moister conditions than the Mixed Evergreen Forest. The latter intergrades with Chamise Chaparral and Upland Redwood Forest in the Santa Cruz Mountains, and with Coast Live Oak Woodland, Coast Live Oak Forest, and Non-Native Grassland in the Mt. Hamilton Range.

One can see the Mixed Evergreen Forest in many places: Sanborn-Skyline County Park, the Fern Loop and Steep Hollow trails in Palo Alto's Foothills Park (both include patches of California Bay Forest), and the trail to Black Mountain in Monte Bello Open Space Preserve. Fallen limbs and trees on the ground (sometimes up to 20% of the forest floor surface) provide a rich habitat for invertebrates, particularly ants and beetles, including the Douglas-fir beetle. These insects, in turn, are a good source of food for vertebrates and, together with seeds, berries, and other fruits from the trees, provide for many, including the Brown Creeper, Golden-crowned Kinglet, Steller's Jay, American shrew-mole, western gray squirrel, and dusky-footed woodrat.

The plant community more exactly defined as California Bay Forest is found occasionally in the Santa Cruz Mountains. It constitutes only 0.1% of the county, and typically consists of dense stands of California bay with almost no other associates. Evergreen, to 95 feet tall, it often has no understory, although occasionally one sees an extensive cover of coastal wood fern. The stands of bay are probably formed by crown-sprouting clones after fires. A good example is a grove along the Wildcat Trail above Deer Hollow Farm in Rancho San Antonio Open Space Preserve, and in Palo Alto's Foothills Park near Los Trancos Creek.

Although Douglas fir is rarely encountered as a distinct forest in Santa Clara County, it is an important component of the Mixed Evergreen Forest in the Santa Cruz Mountains. It is associated with redwoods, tan oaks, madrone, and California bay. Good examples in the county are at the crest of the mountains, including Saratoga Summit and Mount Madonna. This species appears to be increasing (Alan K. Brown, pers. comm. to William G. Bousman), perhaps because fire kills Douglas fir and we have been suppressing fires in the Santa Cruz Mountains.

Coast Live Oak Forest. In many ways, this community is similar to the Mixed Evergreen Forest and the Coast Live Oak Woodland, although not quite so dense and with fewer tree species than the former, and more dense than the latter. Coast live oak is a broad-crowned, sclerophyllous (hard-leaved) evergreen tree to 80 feet tall. Common associates include madrone, California bay, and poison oak. Comprising 4.9% of the county, it is found on drier sites than the Mixed Evergreen Forest and on moister sites than the Coast Live Oak Woodland. It may intergrade with both, and is found on valley bottoms as well as on slopes.

Most acreage in the county is found on the west side of the Mt. Hamilton Range, and can best be seen on Calaveras Road above the reservoir, and in the upper western sections of the Pacheco Pass Road. It is also found on the lower eastern slopes of the Santa Cruz Mountains.

Black Oak Forest and Ponderosa Pine Forest. As with Black Oak Woodland, most stands of Black Oak Forest are even-aged, reflecting past burns. Occasional pockets of Ponderosa Pine Forest occur with black oaks. Other constituent tree species can include California bay, madrone, California buckeye, and canyon live oak. Not common (1% of the county), the only substantial stretches of black oak forest occur in the Mt. Hamilton Range southeast of the Calaveras Reservoir (on Oak Ridge) and in Henry Coe State Park. Smaller patches occur elsewhere.

There are areas of closed-canopy Ponderosa Pine Forest in Henry Coe State Park on Pine Ridge and Blue Ridge, as well as in portions of the San Felipe Ranch (parts of Bollinger Ridge). It is in these areas of Henry Coe where Olive-sided Flycatchers and Western Tanagers are most often found (James Yurchenco, pers. comm.). One can easily hike (1/2 hour) above park headquarters to the 3,000-foot-high Pine Ridge Overlook to view the fine stand of ponderosa pine.

Coulter Pine Forest. Coulter pines can best be seen with the shrubby forms of two evergreen oaks (canyon live oak and interior live oak) on the summit of Mt. Hamilton. The community is subject to fairly frequent fires. As with foothill pine, fire kills the closely related Coulter pine, but the oaks resprout, forming shrubby colonies with multiple trunks. Occupying 0.3% of the county land, Coulter pines are typically found on the dry, rocky soils of summit ridges at elevations of 3,000 to 4,000 feet. They grow most abundantly on the eastern slopes of the western crest of the Mt. Hamilton Range.

This species, mainly of southern California, reaches its northernmost extension in the Mt. Hamilton Range, except for two colonies in the vicinity of Mt. Diablo. The only units large enough to appear on our map are on private property in the northeast extremity of the county. Coulter pine is rare in the Santa Cruz Mountains, but can be found occasionally in Santa Cruz County. You can view scattered trees at the parking lot of Lick Observatory on top of Mt. Hamilton, and if you continue to drive east of the summit approximately 3 km, you will see that the road crosses a ridge with a fine stand of Coulter pines.

The cone of Coulter pine is impressive; it is the most massive of any pine cone in the world and bears strong, incurved hooks. These cones, weighing up to 9 pounds and reaching 14 inches in length, open in midwinter, well after a fire would have burned. If a fire had occurred, the seed would drop onto a nourishing mineral ash bed, sending down deep roots the first year, the tree quickly maturing to bear its own cones within 10 to 15 years.

A digression on the four pines of Santa Clara County is warranted. Pines are rather specialized conifers, being well-adapted to sunlight and resistant to long periods of drought. Both the foothill pine and the Coulter pine are restricted to the California floristic province, although they formerly had a larger and more southerly distribution. They are closely related one to another and are considered to be relicts of the Tertiary geologic period, still clinging to parts of their former range. Foothill pine is not a forest-building tree. As discussed above, it occurs in open woodland with blue oak and chaparral. Coulter pine grows only in a few groves where a relatively mild climate with moderate precipitation prevails. Knobcone is a relatively scarce pine in the county, growing in scattered stands in the chaparral zone of the Santa Cruz Mountains, but nowhere in the Mt. Hamilton Range. In contrast to these three, ponderosa pine is found throughout the American west in a multitude of habitats, and yet within our county it is very restricted in range.

Upland Redwood Forest and Tan Oak Forest. The Upland Redwood Forest is a dense forest dominated by coast redwoods, usually 220 to 250 feet tall. The understory is very sparse, typical species including sword fern, redwood oxalis, trilliums, thimbleberry, and huckleberry. In drier areas it is associated with Douglas fir and tan oak. Much of the original Upland Redwood Forest in the Santa Cruz Mountains has of course been cut, and in our county all stands are second growth. The trees respond to fire and cutting by crown-sprouting, often becoming multitrunked as a result.

The Upland Redwood Forest constitutes 1.7% of the county. It is found along the higher ridges and deeper canyons and ravines of the Santa Cruz Mountains, the greater distribution lying to the west in Santa Cruz County. Where redwood occurs in our county it is moistened by summer fog, which condenses on the needles and drips to the ground, forming significant precipitation. Several of the higher trails in Mt. Madonna County

35

Park provide good access to second-growth redwood habitat, as does the Sanborn trail to the Todd Creek redwoods in Sanborn-Skyline County Park.

The Upland Redwood Forest in Santa Clara County is often interspersed by grasslands, oak woodlands, chaparral, or riparian corridors, and wildlife makes good use of this added vegetation diversity. But where forests are thick and extensive, the number of bird species sharply declines. The Winter Wren is a good indicator of redwood forest in our area. Summer visitors in this habitat include Pacific-slope Flycatchers, American Robins, Hermit and Swainson's thrushes, Wilson's Warblers, and Dark-eyed Juncos.

The Tan Oak Forest, sometimes accompanied by madrone, often borders the redwood forest in the Santa Cruz Mountains. The occurrence shown on Fig. 3.5 is outside the county, slightly to the west of the crest of the range, but smaller patches are also found on steep slopes within the county. The forest has a very dense canopy, and as with redwoods it has a similar lack of understory vegetation. Also like the redwoods, it is on deep soils, in contrast to adjacent chaparral and woodland communities. Much of the tan oak forest in our area is successional, following the redwood forests after logging and fire. Birds that rely on tan oak acorns as a source of food include the Steller's Jay, Band-tailed Pigeon, Varied Thrush, and Acorn Woodpecker. Deer and squirrels also relish them, and in the past they were enjoyed by humans and grizzly bears. The bark has high tannin content and was once used extensively in California for curing leather.

Riparian Plant Communities and Lacustrine Habitat

The riparian plant communities here range from closed-canopy forest to scrublands. Representative communities in Santa Clara County include Central Coast Cottonwood–Sycamore Riparian Forest, Central Coast Live Oak Riparian Forest, White Alder Riparian Forest, Sycamore Alluvial Woodland, Central Coast Riparian Scrub, and Mule-fat Scrub (Holland 1986). These communities generally occur only as narrow corridors bounding permanent or intermittent streams, and as a consequence they are not mapped in Fig. 3.6, which uses the GAP criteria. The one exception is a 5-km stretch of Central Coast Cottonwood–Sycamore Riparian Forest that occurs along the Pajaro River as it flows downstream from the edge of Santa Clara County. (Figure 3.6 also includes permanently flooded Lacustrine Habitat.)

The loss of riparian habitat in California may exceed 95% of its presettlement extent (Barnes 1993). The figures for Santa Clara County are unavailable, but the figure has to be high, particularly in our developed urban and agricultural habitats. Many of the surviving riparian ecosystems are in unsatisfactory condition, and are dominated by human activities. Because of the unusually high biomass productivity in riparian corridors, they support a wealth of insect life that feeds amphibians, fish, and birds. In California, over 135 species of native birds are either completely dependent on riparian woodland or use it during some stage of their life cycle. Riparian habitat provides food, water, shelter, shade, and cover, and serves as a wildlife corridor, or linkage, to other habitats. The need to protect this resource

in Santa Clara County is obvious, as is the need to restore what can still be restored.

Riparian tree communities are, with few exceptions, winter-deciduous. Many are related to well-established broadleaved species of the east coast. Furthering the contrast with our other woodlands and forests, most of these trees and shrubs have distributions throughout the west—few California endemics here. Why? The main clue is the habitat. Permanent water makes an evergreen adaptation less useful. Decaying leaf litter can benefit plants by increased soil fertility. And above all, water is not a problem in these stream courses in the hot summer months.

Among the factors determining the biotic composition of the stream environment are water temperature, seasonal fluctuation, rate of flow, and degree of pollution. Santa Clara County creeks present variants of all these conditions. They cover about 0.5% of the county.

Discussed below are three types of riparian forest, one riparian woodland, and two riparian scrub communities. The forest communities exist on well-established stream banks, protected from major flooding that would alter the bed of the creek. The Sycamore Alluvial Woodland is subject to occasional violent flooding, but the trees are well-rooted, and the large cobbles and boulders of the stream bed cannot support much understory. The two scrub communities are transitional; if no further flooding occurs they will eventually become woodland or forest types.

Cottonwood–Sycamore Riparian Forest. This community has a moderately closed canopy of broadleaved trees. The most extensive forest occurs along the Pajaro River just downstream of the county line, as shown in Fig. 3.6. But along valley streams there are many stands of this forest community that are too small to be mapped. On the flat valley floor, this forest is dominated by Fremont cottonwood and high willows in the lower reaches of the South Bay streams (Guadalupe River, Los Gatos Creek, and Coyote Creek). Western sycamore, oaks, and California buckeye become more common above Willow Glen and Coyote. Other common components of the lower reaches include box elder and blue elderberry. There is a fairly clear zone of transition from the lower-elevation cottonwood/willow zone to the higher-elevation sycamore zone (Stephen C. Rottenborn, pers. comm.). The lower elevations produce flat stream reaches with fine-textured sediment and fairly constant water-table depth. Higher, the bed load (the larger rocks and gravels that are at the bottom of a stream) is fairly coarse, and the water table has a seasonably variable depth.

Central Coast Live Oak Riparian Forest. This closed-canopy forest is found along perennial streams, often in the flatter canyon bottoms of the foothills. It is often part of a mixed-evergreen forest environment in both the Mt. Hamilton Range and in Santa Cruz Mountains. Characteristic understory plants include poison oak, honeysuckle, the native blackberry, and snowberry.

White Alder Riparian Forest. Above the valley floor the streams change character, with a medium-tall forest of white alder and bigleaf maple becoming major components. The understory is typically shrubby and deciduous. This community is best developed along rapidly flowing, well-aerated perennial streams with coarse bed loads that reflect high stream power during the rainy season. These streams typically flow in bed-

VEGETATION COMMUNITIES

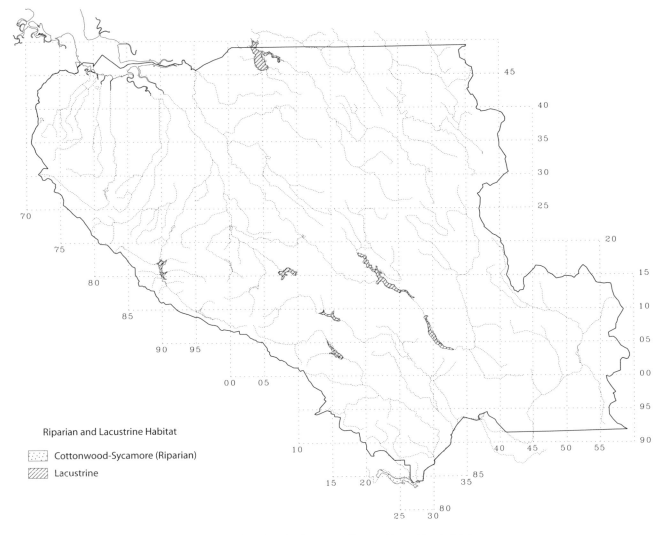

Riparian and Lacustrine Habitat

Cottonwood-Sycamore (Riparian)

Lacustrine

Fig. 3.6. Riparian plant communities and lacustrine habitat.

rock-constrained, steep-sided canyons, and the riparian corridor is therefore narrow. In the Santa Cruz Mountains, Uvas Canyon County Park and parts of Croy Road that lead into the park present good examples. Mature stands of white alder border the Pajaro River near Sargent. On the western side of the Mt. Hamilton Range, along Arroyo Hondo and its tributaries, Smith Creek and Isabel Creek, there are thick canopies of alder, bigleaf maple, madrone, western sycamore, and California bay.

Sycamore Alluvial Woodland. This open, winter-deciduous broadleaved woodland is overwhelmingly dominated by well-spaced sycamores. They are located on broad floodplains and terraces along low-gradient streams, usually with a cobble or boulder substrate covering deep alluvial deposits. Flowing water usually occurs for only brief periods after winter storms, but these flows may be quite violent, damaging or even uprooting the trees. Sycamores have well-developed vegetative reproduction, giving the woodland a clumped appearance. Good sites for viewing this community include Coyote Creek in Morgan Hill and along Pacheco Creek near Casa de Fruta. Henry Coe State Park has a lovely stretch on the upper reaches of Coyote Creek,

between China Hole and Poverty Flat. On intermittent streams of the interior and eastern side of the Mt. Hamilton Range, one finds only scattered trees of sycamore, Fremont cottonwood, and arroyo and red willows. On the western side of the Santa Clara Valley, the Los Gatos Creek Trail from Vasona Lake County Park to the town of Los Gatos offers fine views of sycamores.

Central Coast Riparian Scrub. This community constitutes a scrubby streamside thicket, varying from open to impenetrable, and dominated by any of several willows, including arroyo, red, and narrow-leaved, as well as the shining and Scouler willows that are found only on the west side of the county in the Santa Cruz Mountains. The willows germinate after major disturbance, and the community may transition to any of several other riparian woodland or forest types if no further severe flooding occurs. The community is usually found on relatively fine-grained sand and gravel bars. You can see good examples on the Coyote Creek Trail near the borrow ponds near Ogier Avenue and around the borders of the freshwater marsh upstream from Silicon Valley Boulevard. Many neotropical migrants have used these streamside thickets in the past, including Willow

37

Flycatcher, Swainson's Thrush, Wilson's Warbler, and Yellow-breasted Chat, but few are found here now, perhaps owing to habitat degradation and Brown-headed Cowbird parasitism.

Mule-fat Scrub. Like the riparian scrub just described, the Mule-fat Scrub is a transitory community resulting from disturbance. Fairly coarse substrates differentiate the environment from that of riparian scrub. This scrub frequently occurs on intermittent stream channels with moderate water-table depth, and in openings in the Sycamore Alluvial Woodland, especially under heavy grazing. Lacking floods, the stands would transition to cottonwood or sycamore-dominated riparian forests or woodlands. Other characteristic species include sedge and hoary nettle. A good site from which to view this community is on Coyote Creek just north of the Coyote Creek Golf Course in southern San Jose. Before the Coyote and Anderson reservoirs were completed on Coyote Creek in 1936 and 1948, respectively, the area near Coyote flooded and scoured every year, and Lesser Nighthawks nested in the gravel flood plain there. None have been seen in that location since the late 1930s (William G. Bousman, pers. comm.).

Permanently Flooded Lacustrine Habitat. In our county the larger bodies of these waters are, without exception, reservoirs. The relatively calm water contrasts sharply with the flow of creeks and rivers, and the organisms supported are quite different. Temperatures vary seasonally and with depth; light penetration is dependent on turbidity; and oxygen content is relatively low compared with that of running water. Phytoplankton are the dominant organisms, and are the base on which the rest of life depends. Plants and animals vary with water depth; duckweed and other floating vegetation may cover the surface of shallow water. It is the fish population here that attracts such birds as the Bald Eagle, Belted Kingfisher, Double-crested Cormorant, and Great Blue Heron. Some locally breeding birds found on the reservoirs include the Pied-billed Grebe, Wood Duck, Mallard, Ruddy Duck, and American Coot.

Shoreline vegetation varies depending on the steepness of the slope and the aspect (south-facing vs. north-facing, etc.). The fluctuation of the waterline ensures a problematic situation for plants: most are submerged during part of the year and desiccated during low water (and sometimes there will be several dry years in a row). In some situations a limited freshwater marsh-plant community can be found with scattered stands of bulrushes. On reservoirs used for recreational boating, trees and large shrubs on the shoreline have had to be cut for safety reasons. Nevertheless, the year-round water availability and the muddy shoreline host insects and invertebrates and the wildlife that feed on them. Birds consuming bugs either above the water or on the shoreline include various swallows and blackbirds, as well as the Western Bluebird, Black Phoebe, and Killdeer.

Developed Habitats

Developed habitats include all those that have been significantly altered by man; in Santa Clara County they total some 32.1% of the land area. Most of these habitats, as shown in Fig. 3.7, are found on the Santa Clara Valley floor. The northern Santa Clara Valley, including the highly modified South Bay salt marshes, is classified as urban or built-up habitat. A small amount of the Pacheco Valley, along Highway 152, is also con-

sidered developed. The Santa Clara Valley south of the Coyote Narrows, the Bolsa de San Felipe and the San Benito River Valley, both in northern San Benito County, and flatlands in Santa Cruz County are all classified as agricultural land. There are also a few areas of agricultural land in the Santa Cruz Mountains and the Diablo Range, including the alluvial soils in the San Antonio Valley, where alfalfa is generally grown.

Urban or Built-up Land. The effect of urbanization on bird communities in Santa Clara County is the subject of an article (Blair 1996) that looked at sites within a 3-km radius of Stanford University that had historically been oak woodland. Today, the sites form a gradient that runs from the Jasper Ridge Biological Preserve through the Stanford University Academic Reserve ("The Dish," a combination of grassland and oak woodland), a golf course, a residential area, the Stanford office park, and the downtown business district of Palo Alto. Blair examined the responses of bird species to urbanization by estimating summer resident bird densities, and found that the composition of species shifted from predominantly native in the preserve to invasive and exotic species in the business district. The "pre-development" species, presumably those at the least developed site, dropped out gradually as the sites became more urban. Interestingly, species richness peaked in the moderately disturbed sites.

The actual species composition in Blair's study is worth recording here. At the time there were seven urban avoiders: Dark-eyed Junco (this is now found throughout the urban area; Michael M. Rogers, pers. comm.), Blue-gray Gnatcatcher, Ash-throated Flycatcher, Steller's Jay, Wrentit, Western Wood-Pewee, and Hutton's Vireo. These absences probably have a lot to do with the absence of oaks in the urban area. Blair found thirty species to be suburban-adaptable, birds that exploited additional resources such as the ornamental vegetation that can be grown with increased water, fertilizers, pruning, etc.: Oak Titmouse, Bewick's Wren, European Starling, Cliff Swallow, Nuttall's Woodpecker, Violet-green Swallow, Brewer's Blackbird, Western Scrub-Jay, California Thrasher, Mallard, Pacific-slope Flycatcher, Barn Swallow, Western Bluebird, Black Phoebe, Spotted Towhee, Acorn Woodpecker, Red-winged Blackbird, California Quail, White-breasted Nuthatch, American Robin, Brown-headed Cowbird, Mourning Dove, Anna's Hummingbird, California Towhee, House Finch, Bullock's Oriole, Lesser Goldfinch, Northern Mockingbird, Chestnut-backed Chickadee, and Bushtit. In the business district were three urban exploiters: Rock Pigeon, White-throated Swift, and House Sparrow. But if a wider geographic scope is considered, as embraced by this atlas, Blair's conclusions may be less valid. As shown in the species accounts, Dark-eyed Junco and possibly Steller's Jays are now found widely in urban areas, particularly those areas with established trees. Many of the listed suburban-adaptable species, as can be seen from the atlas maps, are generalists that succeed in suburban, rural, and wild areas of Santa Clara County.

The fact that both species richness (the total number of species) and species density (numbers of individuals) were found to be highest at the golf course, and that species diversity (the evenness, or relative abundance with which each species is represented in an area) was highest at the Stanford Academic Reserve (the grassland and oak woodland), deserves further

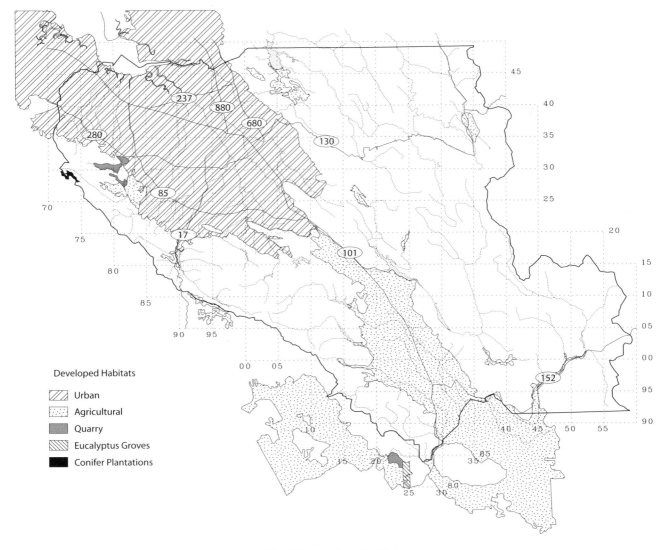

Fig. 3.7. Developed habitats.

comment. That "diversity" reflects both richness and density and differs from "richness" can be illustrated by an analogy with a university dorm that has succeeded in housing representative numbers of perhaps eight ethnic groups (diversity, with eight groups) versus a dorm that might have more ethnic groups overall, but only one or two individuals representing 15 groups and 80% representing one group (richness, with sixteen groups). In summary, moderate levels of development increased overall bird species richness at the expense of native bird diversity. And increasingly dense development lowered both total diversity and native diversity.

Santa Clara County suburban and urban areas benefit from a relatively mild climate, resulting in an unusual "richness" of exotic trees, shrubs, and nectar-producing flowers. Lawns are beneficial to bug-eating birds; pruned hedges provide excellent dense cover. Bird feeders, bird baths, sprinklers, wood piles, and bird boxes improve habitat. Even annual weedy growth in vacant urban areas is beneficial to seed eaters. On the negative side are outdoor cats, reflective windows, automobiles, the

spraying of insecticides, stream channelization, the removal of dead trees and tree limbs, and a paucity of the brush piles that elsewhere host invertebrates.

Stephen C. Rottenborn (1997) studied the impacts of urbanization on the riparian bird communities in Santa Clara County. As discussed above, mature riparian woodland supports much higher avian species richness and density than are found in the surrounding developed areas. Unfortunately, riparian corridors in urban areas are at particular risk from flood-control measures (destruction of native vegetation, damming, diversion, channelization, and weedy invasions in the disturbed habitats). They are also subjected to detrimental adjacent land use (bridge crossings that fragment riparian corridors, and inadequate setbacks for buildings, roads, and agricultural fields).

Agricultural Types, Eucalyptus Groves, Conifer Plantations, and Quarries. Croplands, now some 9.5% of the county land, have greatly reduced wildlife diversity and populations in California. They are established on the richest alluvial soils of the valley floors, which once supported a very different wildlife

39

community. Some birds have adapted to the change, but in so doing, they are now considered agricultural pests, feeding on fruit and nuts. These include Northern Flicker, Western Scrub-Jay, American Crow, Oak Titmouse, Brewer's Blackbird, House Finch, Band-tailed Pigeon, American Robin, and Cedar Waxwing. Both rodents and birds are controlled by fencing, trapping, and poisoning, to prevent crop losses. Some wildlife that use waste grains after harvest are not discouraged, and in those cases where croplands are flooded for weed control, leaching, and irrigation, a variety of associated wetland wildlife can make use of the habitat.

As with urban and suburban habitats, there are structures in agricultural areas that benefit birds: barns and animal shelters, with their concentration of droppings, bugs, and feed, provide a special habitat, as do fenceposts, which provide survey opportunities in pasture land. Here, as elsewhere in developed habitats, utility poles and wires also are favored viewing perches.

Eucalyptus groves, evergreen orchards, Christmas tree farms, and other conifer plantations often have little or no understory and limited habitat value, but they can be beneficial to wildlife for nesting, foraging, and roosting during cold weather in winter, or in hot summer periods for their water and shade. Among the birding community, eucalyptus, in particular, have their defenders and their enemies. Much of the disagreement over their value, or lack thereof, rests on what they are replac-ing, and depends considerably on the density and age of the trees in question. Dense stands of young, spindly trees with no understory are poor habitat compared with the occasional, large specimen trees with a well-developed branching structure. Cavity-nesting species and foliage-gleaning insectivores rarely are found in eucalyptus groves. On the other hand, there is evidence that eucalyptus are selected preferentially by nesting raptors (Rottenborn 2000; David L. Suddjian, pers. comm.).

Stands of eucalyptus are common in Santa Clara County, but only one is large enough to be shown in Fig, 3.7. It is along Highway 101 in Monterey County and just touches the edge of Block 2580. Christmas tree farms large enough to be mapped (Block 7025) can be seen along Skyline Boulevard near Monte Bello Open Space Preserve in Fig. 3.7.

There are three significant quarries in Santa Clara County, the 529-acre Hanson Permanente limestone quarry in the Cupertino foothills being the largest. The Stevens Creek quarry (62 acres) is near Cupertino on county land, and the Lexington rock quarry (54 acres) is just off Alma Bridge Road above Los Gatos. Another large quarry is south of the Pajaro River in Monterey County. Quarries associated with dam construction in the 1930s through the 1950s, and now inactive, are too small to be mapped. In addition to the obvious loss of vegetation entailed, factors including blasting, high dust levels, creek siltation, and groundwater contamination add up to a detrimental effect on wildlife.

4 A Natural History of Change: Landscape Changes in Santa Clara County

Broadly speaking, the history of Santa Clara County can be seen as falling into four periods, here referred to as the Costanoan, Spanish-Mexican, Agricultural, and Urban periods. Local Indian groups, for which the Costanoan Period is named (Donley et al. 1979), had little effect on the environment, and natural ecosystems remained largely intact. Over the subsequent periods, there has been a transition to cattle raising and small-scale farming, then to intensive agriculture and urban development, and finally to the establishment of protected recreational lands, a pattern that mirrors land development over much of the Earth (Foley et al. 2005).

The Costanoan Period is defined as the era before the Spanish expeditions of exploration first entered the Santa Clara Valley in 1769. This period is characterized by a low population density and limited disturbance of the environment by the hunters and gatherers who lived in the valley. In terms of our natural history, this period represents a baseline from which we can attempt to compare subsequent changes, and although we have the writings of early explorers to draw on, considerable guesswork is required to characterize this period.

The Spanish-Mexican Period extended from the first expedition of exploration in this area, in 1769, to 1848, when the Treaty of Guadalupe Hidalgo conveyed California to the United States. The nonindigenous population of the Bay area increased gradually through this period, to about 24,000 people by 1850. Initially, this local population required subsidies from Spain for support, but later they were largely self-sufficient, trading in cattle tallow and hides for necessities that they could not produce locally. They made only limited modifications to local streams, for purposes of irrigation. At the start of the period, the prairie on the valley floor and the grasslands in the hills consisted of native grasses and forbs, but by the period's end non-native invasive annual grasses from Europe had almost completely displaced the native grasses and forbs (Burcham 1957). The major elements of the California megafauna—grizzly bear, elk, pronghorn, and sea otter—were affected differently: the grizzlies increased, but the elk and pronghorn declined, and the sea otters were eliminated from the Bay area.

The Agricultural Period extended from 1848 to 1920. This was a period of rapid growth, such that Santa Clara County

increased from about 7,000 people in 1852 to over 100,000 in 1920. At the outset of the period, valley lands were still used primarily for grazing cattle, but within one or two decades, wheat and hay had become the primary crops. By the late 1800s, orchards replaced wheat and became the primary use of agricultural land. Wells were dug to tap the vast aquifer beneath the Santa Clara Valley, but the increasing demand for water through the period had the effect of dropping the water table, eventually causing ground subsidence in the northern part of the valley. Other environmental changes followed the cutting of the old-growth timber on the eastern side of the Santa Cruz Mountains. The cinnabar mines that were developed south of the Almaden Valley produced most of the mercury used in California for the separation of gold from ore during the refining process in the latter half of the nineteenth century. The tailings from these long-closed mines continue to affect the streams that flow into the Bay today. Such elements of the megafauna as remained in the 1850s, i.e., grizzlies, elk, and pronghorn, were eliminated within two or three decades by hunting and population pressure.

The Urban Period, starting in 1920 and continuing to the present, began with a recognition that continuing development in the county was dependent upon increasing its water supplies. The Tibbetts and Kieffer report, published in 1921, proposed the construction of 17 reservoirs and associated plumbing and percolation ponds (Rickman 1981). Although the Tibbetts and Kieffer plan was never fully carried out, a period of reservoir construction did occur, from the early 1930s through the 1950s. Orchards dominated agricultural production during the first years of the Urban Period, but by the end of World War II, the orchards, laid out where there had once been wheatfields, were in turn razed in favor of housing and light industry. The salt marshes, relatively intact at the beginning of the period, were graded or leveled, and levees were built to form salt evaporator ponds through 1960. With the loss of these marshes, there was an associated reduction of the marsh specialists, such as the Clapper Rail and the salt marsh harvest mouse. Just as in the earlier periods, land-use decisions were made for economic reasons. Other land uses, such as recreation and preservation, were also considered, and in time began to be effected.

Each of the four periods we will be examining is characterized by how people lived on the land, how they modified it for their immediate benefit, and how they manipulated water resources to solve the imbalance of water availability in our Mediterranean California climate. Humans, in each of these periods, impacted the vegetation and animal communities, and these impacts sometimes had unintended and irreversible consequences. In other cases, however, the impacts, although great, were not necessarily permanent. It is the purpose of this chapter to encourage an understanding of the human influence in the county in its historical context, and to provide a basis for sound judgments in the future.

The Costanoan Period

Estimates of the number of Indians living in California at the time of Spanish settlement vary, from the 200,000 proffered by Heizer (1958) to 350,000 by Baumhoff (1963). For the entire state, their population density ranged from fewer than 10 people per 100 km^2 (Great Basin and southeastern deserts) to over 70 people per 100 km^2 (northwestern California and portions of the Central Valley). Along the central coast, population densities were from 45 to 69 people per 100 km^2 (Donley et al. 1979). These people were hunters and gatherers in small villages near the Bay or along streams at higher elevations. To judge from middens excavated near Coyote Hills, the mammals most commonly hunted locally were sea otters and mule deer (Harvey et al. 1992). The deer were probably the more important food species. Ninety percent of the birds excavated from the Coyote Hills midden were geese and ducks, likely captured during the winter months. Father Font indicated that the local Indians also harvested shellfish from the Bay (Bolton 1930c), and acorns were gathered from the local oak woodlands, the mast then processed for food. Father Crespí described the Indians as using the seeds of various grasses and other plants for food (Brown 2001); and rhizomes and tubers of various native plants were also dug up for food.

The Indians who lived in the Santa Clara Valley made few changes to the local environment (Broek 1932). Sea otters, deer, geese, and ducks were all plentiful in the South Bay region when the first Europeans arrived, and there is no evidence that the Indians had had any impact on these local animal populations. Crespí, describing extensive burning of local grasslands, stated that the Indians did this to improve food production (Brown 2001). Keeley (2005) has studied the current pattern of grassland fires in the San Francisco Bay area and has concluded that lightning-caused fires would have been too infrequent to have produced the extensive grasslands that were encountered by the first Spanish explorers. Instead, it seems likely that the Indians regularly burned areas of grasslands, chaparral, shrublands, and even woodlands, all of which would have increased the extent of the grasslands. Cooper (1926) believed that the Indians also regularly burned the understory of the woodlands, so as to enhance acorn mast production. The digging of rhizomes and tubers on a regular basis may have improved the production of these underground foodstuffs (Anderson and Rowney 1998). Hypersaline ponds, formed at the upper boundary of the salt marsh, were filled by the high tides in June and July, and when the water evaporated in August and September, salt deposits remained. The local Indians harvested this salt for their own use, as well as

for trade. In some cases they made minor modifications to the ponds to enhance salt production (Ver Planck 1958).

After two centuries of change in what is now Santa Clara County, it is difficult to describe accurately the primeval countryside and the pristine vegetation seen by the Spanish exploration parties when they first arrived. Descriptions from the early explorers and settlers, particularly the Franciscan friars who set up the missions, can be helpful, as can inferences and deductions made from the composition of the present plant communities. A number of authors have made substantial efforts to assess the original plant communities, including Broek (1932), who discussed the Santa Clara Valley; Burcham (1957), who focused on California grasslands; Clarke (1959), who examined the southern half of the San Francisco Bay area; Barbour and Major and their contributing authors (1988), who looked at all of California's plant communities; and Grossinger et al. (2006), who have made detailed historical studies of the Coyote Creek watershed from Anderson Dam to the Bay.

The Franciscan friars who visited the Bay area in the 1760s and 1770s, such as Juan Crespí, Francisco Palóu, and Pedro Font, and soldiers, such as Pedro Fages, had been educated in Spain and were diligent in recording many details of the countryside as they traveled ever farther north in California to find appropriate locations for the California missions. To a substantial degree they focused on issues of importance for settlement, such as the availability of water (for the settlers as well as for irrigation), firewood, wood for construction, pasturage for horses and cattle, and land for raising crops. Nonetheless, their diaries (Bolton 1930a, Bolton 1930c, Priestley 1937, Brown 2001) provide useful details of the local country through which they traveled.

South Bay Habitats. Thus, we have a general idea of the appearance of the South Bay prior to Spanish settlement. Early maps and observers' descriptions have been combined in the development of the EcoAtlas (Goals Project 1999). Figure 4.1 shows the portion of the EcoAtlas that covers the South Bay area. (The South Bay, at the top of the figure, connects to San Francisco Bay through the Dumbarton Narrows, between Ravenswood and Dumbarton points.) At the left of the figure, San Francisquito Creek flows in from the west, and, on the opposite side, Coyote Creek flows in from the east, showing the characteristic "thumb" shape where the creek flows north around where the Newby Island landfill is today. The Guadalupe River, seen flowing from the eastern margin of the figure, meanders through the tidal marsh that surrounds the South Bay, joining the Bay at its southern edge.

Today, tidal flats are found at the edge of the Bay, but in presettlement times meandering channels and large tidal-flat islands were exposed at low tide. Olympia oysters formed extensive beds, and long windrows of oyster shells were found along the western edge of the Bay (Townsend 1893). The salt marsh bordering the Bay covered a broad area, roughly corresponding to where the salt evaporation ponds lie today. Most of the meandering sloughs in the South Bay salt marshes ended at the upper edge of the marsh, but a few merged with streams that regularly flowed into the Bay, such as Guadalupe River and Coyote Creek, or streams that connected to the tidal sloughs following winter storms, such as San Francisquito Creek. At the upper edge of

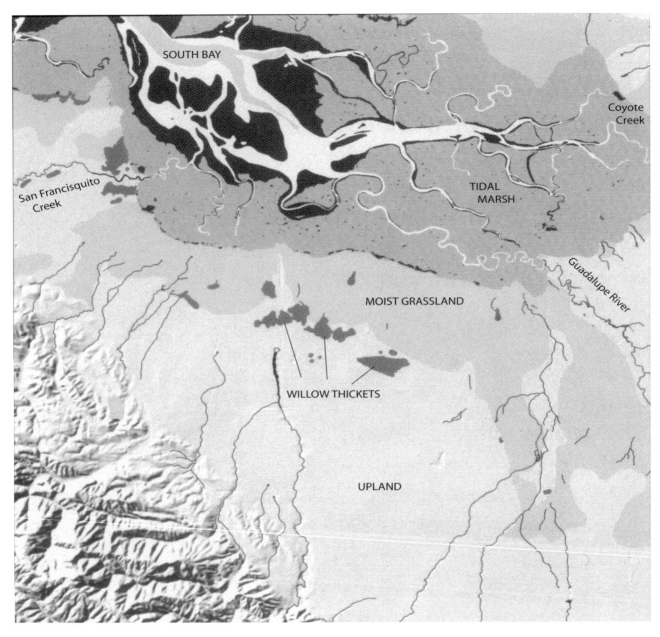

Figure 4.1. The South Bay in presettlement times (adapted from Goals Project 1999).

the marsh, particularly along its southern edge, *salinas* formed. These *salinas*, or ponds, were independent of the tidal sloughs and normally filled with salt water only during the summer and winter high tides. At other times of the year they lost water to evaporation and generally became highly saline. A particularly large *salina* is visible in Fig. 4.1 south of where San Francisquito Creek enters the salt marsh. This *salina* was about 6.5 ha in area and straddled the present Highway 101 about a hundred meters south of Embarcadero Road.

Sloughs within the tidal marsh formed intricate, meandering channels. In a dendritic pattern, the sloughs divided into channels, which then formed smaller channels, and then even smaller channels. The pattern of channels is illustrated in Fig.

4.2, which shows the entrance of the Palo Alto estuary as mapped by the U.S. Coast Survey in 1857 (http://maps.sfei.org/tSheets/viewer.htm). This map shows many features that are recognizable today. The estuary entrance divides into two major sloughs, with Mayfield Slough to the west and Charleston Slough to the east. Hook's Isle, east of the estuary entrance, was connected to the remainder of the marsh at this time, but that connecting neck has now eroded away. Sand Point, west of the entrance, is much smaller in extent than it is today. West of the entrance, Mayfield Slough divides into two parts. The southern portion is the May-field Slough on present topographic maps, but now contained within the Palo Alto Flood Control Basin. The northern portion forms a large loop that corresponds to the muted tidal lagoon

Figure 4.2. Palo Alto estuary entrance from U.S. Coast Survey sheet 28, 1857 (courtesy of San Francisco Estuary Institute).

immediately north of the Palo Alto Duck Pond. At the left edge of the figure is the end of San Francisquito Creek as it enters the salt marsh. At the time of the survey, there were already a number of small buildings, probably small warehouse and storage facilities, where the creek connected to the tidal sloughs.

San Francisquito Creek probably ponded where the Palo Alto Municipal Airport is today, and there were dense willow thickets or groves (*sausals*) there. Winter floods would break through the willow groves and extensive ponds would form at the edges of the salt marsh (Snyder 1904). Eventually, much of the San Francisquito Creek outflow would find its way to the meandering slough that joined the Bay at the estuary entrance between Sand Point and Hook's Isle (Fig. 4.2). Guadalupe River and Coyote Creek appear to have had more permanent flows during the summer time, at least in their lower reaches (Grossinger et al. 2006). Along their upper stretches, above San Jose, portions of these riverbeds were dry, and the movement of water was beneath the ground as described by Palóu (Bolton 1930a). Very near where the Guadalupe River entered the salt marsh in Fig. 4.1 is where Alviso is located today. The Alviso

Slough is north of the Guadalupe Slough and they were not connected in presettlement times. Sometime in the late nineteenth or early twentieth century, the Guadalupe was connected to Alviso Slough (Grossinger et al. 2006), and now the meandering channels of the original Guadalupe Slough are hidden beneath the salt ponds.

A number of the Spanish explorers commented on the intricate patterns of sloughs and ponds within the tidal marsh (Clarke 1959), but there is little mention of specific plants within the marsh community. Father Palóu (Bolton 1930a) reported on the beds of tule (likely hardstem bulrush or California bulrush) along the edge of the tidal marsh in San Mateo County. Langsdorff (1927), in his visit to the Palo Alto area in 1806, described the shore as a low boggy plain overgrown with pickleweed and intersected with many little channels. The plant communities of that time were probably similar to those of the remnant salt marsh that exists in the South Bay today. It is likely that California cord grass dominated the lower marsh; pickleweed and salt-marsh dodder grew in the middle and high marsh; and saltgrass, fathen, alkali heath, and gum plant were found in the high marsh and the upland border.

Santa Clara Valley Habitats. Beyond the upland edge of the salt marsh was an extensive area of moist grasslands, which in turn, transitioned to upland areas. Grossinger et al. (2006) have examined historical maps, soils reports, and other records from the nineteenth century for the Coyote Creek watershed, and have described the most important features of the valley's geomorphology. Alluvial fans of loose, gravelly materials extend from the mouths of canyons and arroyos along the sides of the valley. Similar loose gravels, deposited by floods, form natural levees along the Coyote Creek and the Guadalupe River as they flow north through the valley, creating rich soils. However, away from the fans and streamside flood plains are flat bottomlands of fine clays with poor drainage. These poorly drained soils tend to concentrate salts, even away from the Bay edge, and were rarely suitable for anything more than pasturage. The distributary creeks from the hills generally flowed out onto the fans and disappeared into the gravelly soil. The smaller streams disappeared within a few hundred meters of the alluvial soil boundary, whereas some of the larger streams extended for a considerable distance down the fans and sometimes to the bottomlands. Often, the water that disappeared into the alluvial fans would reappear at the juncture of the fans and the poorly drained bottomlands, as shown in Fig. 4.1. Here, the water created swamps, often with thickets of willows.

Near the Bay, the bottomlands (moist grassland on Fig. 4.1) were largely treeless except for occasional willow groves. The water table was close to the surface in these grasslands, and the soils tended to be saturated. Cooper (1926) considered the area between the marsh edge and the oak parklands growing on the alluvial fans to be a willow-composite community. He noted that this plant group was almost completely eradicated by the early twentieth century, being replaced by pasturage and sometimes wheatfields. He believed that the bulk of the community was made up of herbaceous plants, of which common spikeweed was the most common. In scattered locations, where water came to the surface, there were thickets of arroyo willow and other trees. In Fig. 4.1, these *sausals* are shown as darker areas at the borders of the moist grasslands. Old-time residents told Cooper that they could remember the clearing of the willow thickets in the latter half of the nineteenth century. Clarke (1959) believed that there was some transitional vegetation in this area, but questioned whether there was adequate evidence to support Cooper's description.

Freshwater willow swamps also occurred at higher elevations along the stream courses, where water was trapped between alluvial fans and natural levees. There was a sizeable marsh with extensive willows on the Guadalupe River, south of San Jose, not far from where Willow Glen is today. This willow swamp is probably the one described by Father Palóu (Bolton 1930a) when, in November 1774, his party traveled northwest from a campsite near Coyote and encountered a swamp of tules that was so miry that they could not cross it, but had to detour to the south to bypass it. On the opposite side of the valley was an area of poor drainage known as Laguna Socayre that formed a large lake in wet years with inflows from distributary creeks such as Norwood and Thompson (Grossinger et al. 2006). This *laguna* or marsh occupied the land where Lake Cunningham and

Reid-Hillview Airport are today. This marsh was still present at the end of the nineteenth century, as described by Schneider (1893): "In the center and deepest part, tall tules rise many feet above one's head . . . where the water is quite shallow rushes grow luxuriantly . . . [and] along the shore in many places, where the water is very shallow or the ground merely damp, coarse marsh grass grows, and along the edges of this thick clusters of clover thrive." Farther to the south, and west of Coyote, between Santa Teresa Boulevard north of Bailey Road and the hills to the west, was a lake known as Laguna Seca. This lake, shown on the Thompson and West 1876 atlas, was about three-quarters of a mile long and was filled with tules, undoubtedly the source of the name Tulare Hill, which is immediately to the east.

Admiral George Vancouver, while visiting San Francisco in November 1792, traveled from San Francisco to the Santa Clara Mission on horseback (Vancouver 1798). He wrote that over the last 6 miles of their trip they had to travel over low, swampy country, and that their horses were knee-deep in mud. It is possible that their route took them through the moist grasslands adjacent to the Bay, which were saturated with water from the sinks of the various streams, such as Permanente and Stevens creeks.

The streams of the Pacheco Creek-Pajaro River system appear to have formed swamps and lakes where they flowed onto the flatlands of the Bolsa de San Felipe. In 1774, Rivera, along with Father Palóu, explored the San Francisco Bay area to look for mission sites, traveling from Monterey in November. They crossed the Pajaro River probably not far from where the Highway 101 bridge is today. After crossing the Pajaro, Palóu wrote (Bolton 1930a):

> Having crossed the river we ascended some hills of land very thickly grown with grass, although with no other trees than now and then a live oak which grows in the canyons of the hills. We spent about half an hour in crossing the range of hills, from which we saw a large lake with plentiful water, two dry lakes, and a pond with plentiful water from a spring.

Font, taking approximately the same route in March 1776, on De Anza's expedition, wrote of the country south of Gilroy that "This valley is very miry and when it rains heavily it is for the most part a lake" (Bolton 1930c). Font also commented that in this valley they saw many pronghorn and "white and gray geese." At the end of the expedition, De Anza crossed through the center of the Diablo Range, entering near Bethany and coming out at the Cañada de los Osos (Cañada Road) on Easter Sunday. Font commented that marshes and lakes were normally found in the valley near Gilroy, "but since it had not rained much this year it was quite dry and we were able to cross it without difficulty." Despite the dryness of that winter, an extensive lake was still present, and the Indians who were camped beside that lake provided fish for the Spaniards. It seems likely that much of the Bolsa de San Felipe flooded during the winter and formed a large lake, much larger than the present San Felipe Lake. The Thompson and West 1876 atlas shows an unnamed swamp where San Felipe Lake is today. To the west, on lower Uvas Creek, the atlas shows a large swamp just above the Pajaro

River named "Willow Swamp." This swamp was entirely east of the present railroad tracks and was 2 to 3 miles in length from north to south.

The grasslands near the Bay appeared as a prairie, and the few large streams that passed through these grasslands flowed in deep arroyos with eroded, steep banks. In the stream beds, however, grew trees and shrubs, including Fremont cottonwood, western sycamore, and California bay. Pedro Font described the Guadalupe River near Agnew as being difficult to cross, as the banks were so high and ". . . so grown with trees. . ." The area around the river was ". . . one of very level land well covered with pasturage, but it is lacking in firewood for there is no other timber than the growth along the river" (Bolton 1930c).

It appears that major streams on the valley floor were sometimes narrow riparian corridors with a thick growth of Fremont cottonwood, box elder, coast live oak, and California bay along the banks and in the stream beds, but elsewhere there were open sections with braided streams and western sycamores, not unlike the section of Pacheco Creek above Casa de Fruta today. From a distance, the riparian vegetation provided the traveler with a good idea of the paths taken by the various stream courses. Father Palóu describes looking north in the Santa Clara Valley in November 1774, probably from the hill where the county's communication center is located now, south of Oak Hill Memorial Park (Bolton 1930a). He observed that a long line of trees marked the course of Coyote Creek as it flowed toward the Bay.

The moist grasslands near the Bay transitioned to drier valley grasslands and oak savanna farther south in the Santa Clara Valley (Heady 1988, Grossinger et al. 2006). The plant composition of these grasslands will probably never be known (Hamilton 1997). A number of early investigators believed that these grasslands were dominated by perennial bunchgrasses, of which purple needlegrass was the most common (Burcham 1957, Heady 1988), although more recently Hamilton (1997) has concluded that annual grasses and forbs may have been dominant in these grasslands, and that the species composition depended to some extent on rainfall and the amount of ground moisture. The grasslands extended into the oak savanna, oak woodlands, and chaparral with relatively little change in species composition. Similar grasslands occurred in the foothills, in meadows in the Santa Cruz Mountains, and widely throughout the Diablo Range. Although the native grasses that made up the once pristine grasslands that covered the Santa Clara Valley have been replaced by non-native annual grasses, the mosaic of grasslands, chaparral, and oak woodland that is found today in undeveloped areas of the Santa Cruz Mountains and Diablo Range is probably little changed since the beginning of Spanish settlement (Burcham 1957, Heady 1988).

The valley grasslands extended from the marsh edge of the Bay south through the Coyote Narrows to the Bolsa de San Felipe at the southern edge of the Santa Clara Valley. On either side of the valley was an oak savanna and the density of the oaks increased toward the edge of the alluvial soils at the foothill boundary (Cooper 1926, Broek 1932). On the west side of the valley, Font described these bands of oaks as extending from near San Martin to north of Redwood City (Bolton 1930c). South of San Martin, however, Font described the valley as an open plain with few oaks. Admiral Vancouver (1798) commented in traveling from San Mateo to Palo Alto, that

> For almost twenty miles it could be compared to a park which had originally been planted with the true old English oak; the underwood, that had probably attained its early growth, had the appearance of having been cleared away and had left the stately lords of the forest in complete possession of the soil, which was covered with luxuriant herbage and beautifully diversified with pleasing eminences and valleys.

On the east side of the valley, the oak parklands probably ended near Milpitas, leaving only grasslands farther north (Clarke 1959).

The extent to which the Indians burned the grasslands and chaparral for their own purposes is debated (Frenkel 1970, Keeley 2005). Although there is agreement that fire was used to facilitate hunting and to aid the growth of native plant foods, the extent of its use is unclear. It is also unclear whether the use of fire changed the basic pattern of grasslands, savanna, woodlands, and forest that is seen today. Some authors have suggested that the chaparral originally extended farther into the grasslands under a regime of regular burning, whereas others believed that the grasslands and woodlands had increased as a consequence of the Indians' use of fire (Frenkel 1970). Keeley (2005) has concluded that the extent of the grasslands in the Bay area at the time of Spanish settlement was largely a result of Indian use of fire, but the boundaries between grasslands, chaparral, and woodlands seen today are largely unchanged from settlement times (Heady 1988).

In any case, there appear to have been extensive areas of chaparral on the valley floor prior to settlement (Cooper 1926). Much of Cooper's information on early plant communities in the northern Santa Clara Valley was obtained from G. F. Beardsley, who lived near Mountain View in the 1860s and 1870s. At that time there was an "unbroken" area of chaparral extending from Mountain View to Saratoga and Los Gatos, with patches along the Saratoga Road to within a mile or two of San Jose. Within the chaparral were occasional small islands of coast live oaks, but the areas of chaparral may have been patchier and less extensive than as described by Beardsley. In November 1774, Francisco Palóu described traveling from a campsite on what was probably Calabazas Creek to Palo Alto (Bolton 1930a). He noted that the group's travel "has been heavy, for although it has all been over level ground, yet it has been troublesome on account of the thick groves of junipers and madrones that I spoke of yesterday, although the woods were interspersed with good spots of land covered with grass, oaks and live oaks." Rivera also described that day's journey, noting that there was a level plain grown over with many live oaks and patches or bands of brush of a kind of juniper chaparral. It is likely that the junipers Palóu described were chamise, and that what he called madrones were manzanitas (Clarke 1959).

Santa Cruz Mountain Habitats. The Santa Cruz Mountains were well wooded when the first Spanish expeditions entered the Santa Clara Valley. The soldiers and Franciscan brothers, long familiar with the deserts of Sonora and Baja California, as well as the tropical forests of Nayarit, must have found it very strange to encounter the ancient coast redwoods, which Crespí and his fellow explorers called *palo colorado*, and the Douglas firs, which were nearly as massive (Brown 2001). There is little mention in the Spanish accounts, however, of the composition of the forested areas of the Santa Cruz Mountains. In passing over this range in February 1846, General John Frémont (1848) described it as a "... grassy and timbered mountain, watered with small streams, and wooded on both sides with many varieties of trees and shrubbery, the heavier forests of pine and cypress occupying the western slope." He also mentioned the presence here of coast redwood, interior live oak, and madrone.

The second-growth coniferous forests seen today on the eastern side of the Santa Cruz Mountains were originally logged from about 1850 to 1872 (Jensen 1939). These forests were probably a mixture of coast redwood and Douglas fir, although coast redwood likely occurred with greater frequency than today, and the redwood stands would have occurred lower down along the various streams flowing east from the Santa Cruz Mountains (Clarke 1959). Tan oak, which is a common understory tree in the coniferous-broadleaved evergreen forest, was not mentioned by early observers, but it must have been common, since its harvest for tanneries was noted in the 1840s (Clarke 1959).

Diablo Range Habitats. On their early explorations, the Spanish noted that the west side of the Diablo Range was largely grasslands. In March 1776, De Anza described the foothills near Milpitas as "a small range completely bare of trees, for none are seen except some which grow in the canyons" (Bolton 1930b). During this exploratory trip, De Anza, Font, and their party rode around the northern end of the Diablo Range and then cut back through its center. Their route took them south from Corral Hollow across Crane Ridge, and up Arroyo Mocho. They reached the height of land between Arroyo Mocho and Colorado Creek, probably not far from where Mines Road crosses that same height of land today. Font described the view as "extended and very rough ranges, and all the distance traversed and that was seen on all sides, thickly grown with oaks, pines, and brush" (Bolton 1930c). They then descended into the Colorado Creek and noted the red serpentine soils on the slopes of Red Mountain. Font wrote

> At the beginning of this valley, . . . we saw sierras or hills which attracted the attention of all of us because of their appearance; for while the others are very thickly covered with brush and trees, these have no trees but only a very open, scrubby growth, so that on the ridges and at intervals there are seen some strips and pieces of very white gravel. And that range, along whose base flows an arroyo, . . . is red in color. For this reason all said that it had excellent signs of minerals, and to me it appeared very much like the sierras of the mines of Guanajuato.

This area along Red Mountain looks much the same today as it did when De Anza and Font passed through, except for the tailings from the old magnesite mines that never came close to matching the wealth of Guanajuato (Cutler 2001). All that is left from the mining era are these tailings and the name of the road

that passes through.

From San Antonio Valley, De Anza and Font had a hard descent along Coyote Creek, eventually cutting across where Cañada Road is today. Font wrote

> All this country which we crossed this day and the next is very broken, and is the haunt of many bears, judging from the tracks which we saw. Although seen from the outside this range appears to be bare on all sides and without trees, yet in the center it is very tangled and full of brush, pines, live oaks, oaks, spruce, and other trees. Among them there is a plant like a fig tree, but with smaller leaves, and though on the outside its fruit is like figs, on the inside it is somewhat more like a chestnut, more like it in the shell and the color than in the form. The heathen eat it, judging from the piles of its shells which we saw in the abandoned huts.

The figlike tree was California buckeye, and although there were no Indians living in the range at this season, it was apparent that they traveled regularly into the Diablo Range to harvest buckeyes and other nuts.

By and large, it appears that habitats in the Diablo Range at the time of Spanish settlement were similar to what is seen today, except, of course, that the original perennial grasslands have largely been replaced with non-native annual grasses.

The Spanish-Mexican Period

During the seventeenth and eighteenth centuries, the colonial development of northwestern Mexico was a protracted process, largely because of the costs of pacifying native tribes and settling new country where there were few resources. By the middle of the eighteenth century, there were chains of missions in northern Mexico extending into the present states of Arizona, New Mexico, and Texas, as well as in lower California. The process of settlement was often awkward, in that there were two lines of authority, civil and religious. The civil authority in each new settlement was normally invested in a Spanish garrison or presidio. This presidio was funded and supplied by the government in Mexico City. The religious authority was normally invested in one or more fathers from one of the orders of the Catholic Church. Often, these missionaries had their own sources of funding and were responsible primarily to their own order. Disputes developed between the civil and religious authorities and continued until the secularization of the missions in Upper California in the 1830s.

Spain had made some limited exploration of the Pacific Coast of North America in the sixteenth and seventeenth centuries, but had not attempted to settle there. In the latter 1700s, however, the colonial government became concerned about the increasing activity of English and Russian explorers. They therefore initiated a new plan of exploration and settlement to ensure their claim to Upper California (Brown 2001). In 1769, Gaspar de Portolá led an expedition that included the Franciscan fathers Junípero Serra and Juan Crespí setting forth from Velicatá in Baja California Norte. They arrived in San Diego and founded the Mission San Diego de Alcala, the first of the California missions, in July. Father Serra remained in San Diego, but Juan Crespí continued north with Portolá, with the purpose of establishing a settlement at Monterey Bay. But Portolá and his party did not recognize Monterey Bay as the site that had been described to them from the earlier explorations by sea. The party then continued north, following the coast, until they crossed the Santa Cruz Mountains at San Andreas Lake. They then moved south along the west side of San Francisco Bay, making their final camp in early November at San Francisquito Creek, where the present-day Middlefield Road crosses the creek (Brown 2001). Although the main party had not gone as far north as San Francisco, its scouts had seen the entrance to the Bay. Pedro Fages, an officer under Portolá, then led a party that went east toward Milpitas and then north along the eastern side of the Bay, in an unsuccessful attempt to encircle it. With supplies low, Portolá retraced his route, arriving back in San Diego in early February 1770.

In April 1770 Portolá once again traveled north to Monterey Bay, and this time realized that this was indeed the harbor described by earlier sailors. At Monterey he established a presidio, and the fathers who had accompanied him founded the Mission San Carlos Borromeo de Carmelo, the second of the California missions. Pedro Fages was made the commandant of the presidio at Monterey. In November of 1770, he and a small party pioneered a route up the Santa Clara Valley, not far from where Highway 101 proceeds today (Bolton 1911). Subsequent explorations to the San Francisco Bay area followed in 1772 and 1774. In March and April 1776, Juan Bautista de Anza and Pedro Font again traveled to the Bay area and chose a site for a mission and presidio in San Francisco. The following year, 1777, a mission was established by Father Serra at Santa Clara, near the Guadalupe River. A presidio was established at San Jose in the same year.

The mission fathers recruited Indians to labor at the new missions. The fathers saw this work as one of salvation and civilization, although others considered it no better than servitude. Cattle, horses, and sheep had been brought from lower California along with grapevines, seeds for fruit trees, wheat, corn, olives, and other plants. Guadalupe Vallejo (1890) described agriculture at the missions in these early days. Field crops, such as wheat, were grown on flat lands near the mission, and these fields were surrounded by a ditch, often filled with chaparral, to keep the cattle out. Orchards of various fruiting trees were planted near the missions and were often enclosed by adobe walls or extensive hedges of prickly pear cactus. Varieties of pears and apples, ripening at various times, were planted, so there would be an extended period of fresh fruit. At the Santa Clara Mission, an irrigation ditch 3 km long brought water from the Guadalupe River. The mission garden provided French and kidney beans, carrots, peas, corn, pumpkins, melons, and red peppers, and the orchards and vineyards provided apples, pears, apricots, peaches, figs, olives, and grapes (Broek 1932).

In time, the missions became largely self-supporting. Extra fruits, vegetables, grain, and beef were traded with ships or hunters and trappers, but the primary source of trade was the barter in tallow and hides from cattle and sometimes from elk. The *matanza*, or killing season, was in early summer, following the fattening of the cattle on the annual grasses from the winter rains. There were two kinds of fat, the *manteca*, which

was nearest the hide, and the *sebo*, which was nearest the body (Davis 1889). Generally, the *manteca*, which was of better quality, was used locally or traded to the Russians at Fort Ross. The *sebo* was used in general trade. Both fats were rendered in large pots and then stored in hide bags. At this season, each bullock slaughtered would supply from three to four *arrobas* (an *arroba* is about 25 pounds) of tallow. The tallow would be shipped to South America, where there was generally a good market in Peru and Chile. The hides, which were less valuable, were shipped around Cape Horn to Boston.

The missions would also trade with trappers or hunters for the skins of sea otter, river otter, and beaver (Davis 1889). The sea otter pelts, in particular, were greatly desired in China (Ogden 1941). As early as 1787, the Spanish government had seen the value of developing trade with China in sea otter skins. Initially, the missions were the agency for the collection of otter skins, but this responsibility was later transferred to the secular authorities. At the time, the Spanish already had a controlled market in Canton, through their Philippine Company. Friction between new world entrepreneurs in Mexico and the established Philippine Company developed, eventually destroying a Spanish market for sea otter skins, and the trade was abandoned to the Russians and the American smugglers (Ogden 1941).

Once the Spanish plans for the new sea otter trade failed, the small presidios along the coast of California had great difficulty in stopping the illegal hunting of sea otters (Ogden 1941). Both the Russians and the American smugglers employed Aleuts from the Alaskan islands to harvest otters. Initially, preventing the illegal harvest was a losing battle, since the Spanish had only foot patrols. In time, however, the Spanish learned to post guards at freshwater sources on land, and were then able to hamper the smuggling.

When the Mexican revolution erupted in 1810, the supply ships from San Blas no longer sailed to Upper California. There was then little reluctance among the Spanish to trade otter skins with the Russians and Americans. Governor José Darío Arguello said "Necessity makes licit what is not licit by the law" (Ogden 1941). Following the revolution the new Mexican government did regain some control of the otter trade, by allowing Mexican citizens to contract with outsiders for the otter harvest, but *contrabandistas* continued to operate along the coast. The otter trade ended not because of any resolution between the Californios and the foreigners, but because the otters were extirpated. The peak of the harvest occurred about 1815, and the last otters taken in San Francisco Bay were 20 or so shot near the Petaluma River mouth in 1846 (Ogden 1941).

Although the missions had become largely self-supporting by the end of the eighteenth century, the presidios still relied heavily on transports from the west coast of Mexico. With the revolution in Mexico in 1810, and an end to the regular supply ships, the presidios found it difficult to maintain themselves. In 1814, the central government in Mexico City required the missions to support the presidios with food and clothing for the soldiers there, and for their families (Geary 1934). The new government agreed to reimburse the missions for their support of the garrisons, but these debts were never paid, and underlying friction between secular and religious authorities only increased.

The process of secularization, that is, converting the missions into parish churches, and the Christianized natives into a new yeomanry that could pay taxes to the government, had been the long-term objective of Spain, and under Mexican authorities, continued to be of major importance (Geary 1934). Whereas the policy of secularization in Mexico City seemed rational, its implementation in California was corrupted by local politicians and landowners. By law, the mission properties were to be divided among the mission Indians, who were then expected to support the new parish church. Commissioners were appointed to oversee this process, but most simply took the mission resources as their own, or gave them to their cronies, and by 1840 the missions had been destroyed as an economic force in California.

The economic basis of the Spanish-Mexican Period was ranching and the export of tallow and hides. Farming was limited to the agricultural products that supported the local populace. Efforts at extractive industries were limited. The few small lumber operations that came to be established, normally by gringos, supplied enough lumber for the limited uses of the Californios (Wilson 1937, Brown 1966). Salt extraction from saline marsh ponds continued under Spanish and Mexican rule, but harvest techniques were little changed from those that had been used by the Indians for thousands of years (Ver Planck 1958). In the 1820s, two Californios had explored a cave near Almaden where the Indians had extracted a red pigment which they used to paint their bodies. The Californios had been intent on finding gold or silver, but the mineral cinnabar at the site produced neither. In 1845, they showed the Indian diggings to Andres Castillero, a Mexican officer traveling with General Castro. Castillero, who had some knowledge of mining, filed a claim for rights to the diggings, and after some experimentation determined that the cinnabar was rich in mercury (Schneider 1992). Mercury was particularly valued in the New World for its use in the reduction of gold and silver ore, and Castillero began mining the cinnabar in 1846.

At the start of the Spanish-Mexican Period, settlers had accompanied De Anza on his second overland trip to California. The process of colonization was slow under Spanish rule, but increased under the Mexican government, which was willing to provide land grants to settlers. Initially, in the Santa Clara Valley, the Californios lived mostly in the Pueblo of San Jose, but ranchos developed under Mexican rule, and there were 40 or so in the valley by the end of the period (Broek 1932). By 1848, there were approximately 14,000 non-Indians in California, of which nearly half were considered foreigners (Storer and Tevis 1955). But as the European populations increased, the number of natives declined. Baumhoff (1963) believed that 350,000 Indians had lived in California in 1769, but by 1850 these numbers had declined to 75,000. Although some Indian lives were lost in intertribal warfare—a common practice, as described by Crespí and Fages (Priestley 1937, Brown 2001)—the major losses were from the many European diseases brought into California for which the Indians had no resistance. Father Crespí, who lived out his life at the mission in Carmel, buried half as many converts as he was able to baptize (Brown 2001). By 1782, the year Juan Crespí died, Spanish soldiers estimated that the large Indian towns along the El Camino Real beside the Santa Barbara Channel had declined to half the numbers that Crespí had

first encountered when Portolá's expedition passed that way in 1769.

The land around Palo Alto, near where Portolá camped in late 1769, had changed little by the 1840s. A map drawn by Alan K. Brown in 1963, based on historical *diseños* (maps of local ranches that were used to show extents of ownership), is shown in Fig. 4.3. The map shows San Francisquito Creek flowing from south to north along the left edge of the map and into the salt marsh at the top. A point of land projects into the marsh where the creek has deposited sediment during winter floods. A number of *salinas*, or highly saline ponds, are seen along the edge of the marsh (Brown refers to these as "hotponds"), including a large one about 5,000 or 6,000 feet east of San Francisquito Creek. This is the 6.4-ha *salina* mentioned above that was located along the present Highway 101, a few hundred meters south of Embarcadero Road.

Near where San Francisquito Creek enters the marsh are two extensive areas of willows, one on each side of the creek. These willow groves were still present in the early 1900s, when Joseph Grinnell was a student at Stanford University. Grinnell (1901a) commented, "San Francisquito Creek at its mouth forms a slightly elevated delta sloping away gently into the surrounding salt marsh." Within the willows and upstream, Grinnell collected Song Sparrows of subspecies typical of upland habitats, *Melospiza melodia gouldii*, whereas immediately adjacent in the salt marsh he found the salt marsh race, *M. m. pusillula*. Grinnell noted that, "near the foot of the Embarcadero Road, where a salt slough, its banks matted with *Salicornia*, winds along a willow thicket," he found the two subspecies within a stone's throw of each other, *gouldii* always within the willows, and *pusillula* in the salt marsh.

Upstream on San Francisquito Creek, Brown shows redwoods growing along the edge of the creek. Nearby, on both sides of the creek were extensive groves of live and deciduous oaks. Farther to the south and east, the groves open and the land becomes a parkland. To the southwest, toward the hills, the oak groves transition to chaparral, mostly chamise.

A number of smaller streams are shown on the map, flowing from the foothills to the flatlands, but ending well short of the Bay marshes. The creek Brown has labeled *Arroyo de las Yeguas* is what we now call Adobe Creek. To its left, the unnamed minor creek is now called Barron Creek. Farther left is Matadero Creek. Then a series of small streams is seen, where Stanford University is located today. The largest of these streams drains into the present Lake Lagunita on the campus. A few wagon roads and ranch houses were present in the 1840s, as shown on the map.

South Bay Habitats. Changes to the South Bay during the Spanish-Mexican Period were slight by comparison with the changes one sees today. There was limited use of the Bay for fishing under Spanish and Mexican rule. Small embarcaderos were constructed where tallow and hides from the ranches could be loaded onto the small schooners that sailed to Yerba Buena (now San Francisco), and were then transshipped to larger vessels for transport to South America and the East Coast. Broek (1932) estimated that by the end of the period there were perhaps four of these small embarcaderos in the South Bay, none of them including warehouses or similar structures. The non-native

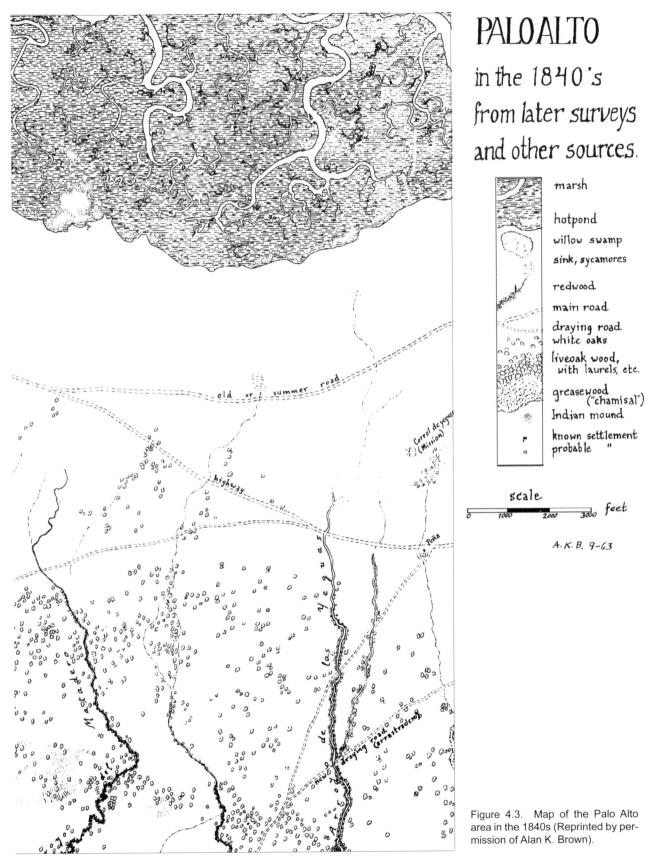

PALOALTO

in the 1840's
from later surveys
and other sources.

marsh

hotpond
willow swamp
sink, sycamores

redwood
main road
draying road
white oaks
liveoak wood,
    with laurels, etc.

greasewood
    ("chamisal")
Indian mound

known settlement
probable   "

scale   feet
0   1000   2000   3000

A.K.B. 9-63

Figure 4.3. Map of the Palo Alto
area in the 1840s (Reprinted by permission of Alan K. Brown).

Norway rat generally prefers marshes adjacent to urban areas, rather than extensive open marsh (Breaux 2000), but with the movement of cargoes into the South Bay they may have become established even prior to the construction of warehouses that ensued in the 1850s. Today, this rat is a major predator of Clapper Rail eggs and nestlings (Albertson and Evens 2000).

The most significant change in the South Bay fauna during this period was the extinction of the sea otter throughout the Bay (Ogden 1941). At the start of the period "San Francisco Bay abounded in otters. Apparently they not only swam around in the bay but frequented the numerous estuaries and even hauled up on the shore. The animals were found on Point San Quentin, around the mouths of Petaluma and Sonoma creeks, and in the estuaries of San Jose, San Mateo, and San Bruno" (Ogden 1941).

Santa Clara Valley Habitats. The Santa Clara Valley was originally a prairie transitioning from the salt marsh edge into oak savanna, oak woodlands, and chaparral. The herbaceous vegetation of this prairie was mostly saltgrass and other salt-tolerant plants near the marsh edge, becoming a mixture of perennial bunchgrasses and native annuals on the better soils. Adobes from some of the earliest buildings, such as the mission of San Antonio de Padua near Jolon, include significant amounts of such non-natives as filaree, curly dock, and prickly sowthistle (Hendry 1931). Hendry concluded that these non-native species arrived before 1769 when Portolá passed this way, borne either by waste from ships at sea or by the earlier Spanish expeditions to the Colorado River. Non-native plant seeds were in any case introduced inadvertently with the first Spanish settlers, either mixed in with cultivated plant seeds that they purposefully carried or attached to equipment, furnishings, and the like. Although early botanists tended to focus on new plant species, rather than non-native plants from the Old World, it is possible to estimate the rate of introduction of non-native species. On the basis of a variety of summaries, Frenkel (1970) showed the increase in non-natives since the first Spanish expedition, as adapted here in Fig. 4.4. As of 1959, there were 839 non-native or introduced plant species in California, which represents an increase of about 2.9% a year and constitutes about 11% of the California flora.

Burcham (1957) discussed the displacement of native perennials and annuals in the California rangelands by the non-native annual grasses that accompanied the first Spanish settlers. He identified between three and four major grassland successions, each one resulting in reduced value of the range for forage. The first succession was dominated by wild oats over much of the range, with wild mustard flourishing in the fertile valleys. This first succession reached its peak from 1845 to 1855, at the end of the Spanish-Mexican Period and the beginning of the Agricultural Period. In this era, ranchers noted that one could ride for days through wild oats that were tall enough that one could tie them over the saddle. In 1846, Edwin Bryant (1848), in describing traveling in the bottomlands of the Mokelumne River, said, "We passed through large tracts of wild oats during the day; the stalks are generally three to five feet in length."

Wild mustard was found widely in the Santa Clara Valley at this time and was a significant pest species. Bryant (1848), in traveling from Fremont through the Santa Clara Valley to San

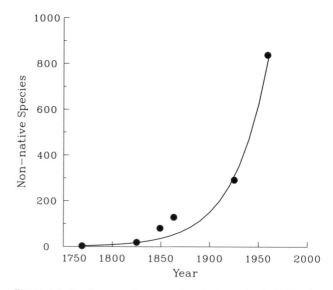

Figure 4.4. The increase in non-native plant species in California, 1769 to 1959 (from Frenkel 1970).

Jose and Palo Alto in September 1846, noted that north of Santa Clara, "We traveled fifteen miles over a flat plain, timbered with groves and parks of evergreen oaks, and covered with a great variety of grasses, wild oats, and mustard. So rank is the growth of mustard in many places, that it is with difficulty that a horse can penetrate through it." Bryant stated that the wild mustard stalks were 6 to 10 feet in height. John Frémont also passed through the Santa Clara Valley in 1846 and wrote that places in the valley were ". . . overgrown with wild mustard, growing ten or twelve feet high, in almost impenetrable fields, through which roads are made like lanes." Cleland (1941) recounts that cattle would hide within the mustard. When the stalks died in early summer, the ranchers would gather herds of other cattle for "runs through the mustard" to break down the stalks and eliminate the hiding places.

There were occasional droughts during the Spanish-Mexican Period, as is the case now. Burcham (1957) records that the period from 1820 to 1832 was particularly dry, and that from 1828 to 1830 there were 22 months in which no rain fell. How much these droughts affected the local plant and animal communities is unknown, but there was a massive loss of cattle and horses at this time.

The Santa Clara Valley prairie originally supported pronghorn, elk, and mule deer. The Californios did little hunting, but they did lasso the elk during the *matanza* for their fat, which was superior to that of cattle (Davis 1889). It is likely that pronghorns declined slightly during this period, from the loss of range and the declining value of forage, but mule deer may have been less affected, particularly those animals living away from the valley floor. The grizzlies, on the other hand, likely increased, as the extensive butchering of cattle provided a significant new food resource (Storer and Tevis 1955). Davis (1889) describes how the grizzlies would come down from the Santa Cruz Mountains to the *matanza* at night to feed on the carcasses and offal. At one *matanza* in what is Mountain View today, Davis's father-in-law and ten soldiers from the Yerba Buena presidio killed forty grizzlies in one night. The bears were captured from horseback with *reatas* and then killed. This sport, requiring great skill and courage, was a favorite of the Californios (Storer and Tevis 1955). During this period both horses and cattle escaped from the ranchos and became feral. Travelers in the 1830s commented that wild horses and cattle were abundant, and were wilder than the deer and elk (Burcham 1957).

Little is known of the avifauna present in the Santa Clara Valley during the Spanish-Mexican Period. It seems likely that the replacement of native grasslands with non-native species reduced some bird populations while increasing others. At Monterey, Pedro Fages (Priestley 1937) described some of the larger birds found in that area, including white pelicans, "cranes," geese, ducks, and quail, as well as "countless small birds." Early voyages of exploration, such as those of Jean François de Galaup, the Compte de la Pérouse, in 1786, George Vancouver from 1792 to 1794, Duhaut-Cilly from 1827 to 1828, and Frederick Beechey from 1825 to 1828, all collected plant and animal specimens along the coast. David Douglas traveled in California from 1830 to 1832, Thomas Nuttall in 1834, and William Gambel in 1841. These early explorers and naturalists collected specimens that were later described in museums (see Appendix 2), but little or no information was obtained on the life histories of these California birds.

The Santa Cruz Mountains and Diablo Range Habitats. Changes to the native grasslands in the Santa Cruz Mountains and the Diablo Range during the Spanish-Mexican Period likely paralleled those that occurred on the valley floor. Typically, the Californios grazed their cattle in bottomlands during the summer and later moved them into the hills (Broek 1932). This practice undoubtedly assisted the replacement of the native perennial and annual grasses with non-natives, particularly in drought years. There was some timber harvest (Brown 1966) in the forest along creeks, but the local market for timber was slight. Some forest animals, such as grizzlies, benefited from the harvest of cattle at the *matanzas* in the valley. A water-powered lumber mill built at Alma on Los Gatos Creek (now beneath Lexington Reservoir) in 1845 began the harvest of the old-growth forests on the eastern side of the Santa Cruz Mountains (Wilson 1937). The mercury mining undertaken at New Almaden at the end of the period resulted in limited development in the Almaden Valley foothills.

The Agricultural Period

Broek (1932) wrote that at the end of the Spanish-Mexican Period, Santa Clara County was a remote borderland:

> As a borderland, the Santa Clara Valley necessarily was a closed economic region, almost isolated from the world—self sufficient. Moreover, each occupance unit within the valley had to rely on its own products and manufactures, for division of labor and trade were yet in their beginnings. . . . Agriculture was for local need, with some export to presidios and occasional supplies for ships. The cultivated fields were almost negligible in size when compared with the immense, oak-dotted, natural pastures, extending over the valley and far into the mountains—a clear areal reflection of the production process that characterized the time.

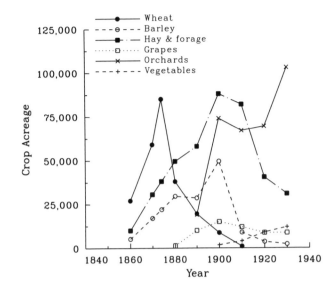

Figure 4.5. Acreage in agricultural products, Santa Clara County, 1860 to 1930 (from Broek 1932).

Although the area was remote, there was nonetheless political turmoil in Upper California in the late 1840s, which did not end until the signing of the Treaty of Guadalupe Hidalgo on 2 February 1848. This treaty marked the end of the Mexican War, a war that was fought over Texas, not California. As part of the treaty settlement, Upper California was ceded to the United States. The discovery of gold at Sutter's mill only a few weeks before the treaty took effect caused a different kind of turmoil, one that brought massive changes to California and the Santa Clara Valley and guaranteed that neither would continue to be a remote borderland.

Development of farming in the Santa Clara Valley during the Agricultural Period advanced steadily through three eras (Broek 1932). The first, from 1850 to 1865, was devoted to cattle ranching and wheat farming. As demonstrated by Fig. 4.5, the second era, from 1865 to 1875, was dominated by the raising of wheat. The third era, from 1875 to the end of the period, in 1920, accentuated new agricultural products, with both forage crops (for cattle and horses) and orchards supplanting wheat.

In the first of these eras, the ranching economy, which had thrived on producing tallow and hides, was permanently transformed by the markets created by the influx of miners to the Sierra foothills and the consequent rapid growth of San Francisco, Sacramento, and Stockton (Burcham 1957). Local ranchers found a ready and valuable market in the foothills for their beef. Ranches in southern California brought their cattle north in large cattle drives, as did ranches from Texas and northern Mexico. Pioneer parties brought extra cattle overland from the Midwest for sale in the mining areas.

As with many boom economies, the initially high price for cattle caused overstocking of the range, and the demand for beef declined (Burcham 1957). The period from 1853 to 1865 was one of very low precipitation, which, combined with overstocking, brought about a decline in the range resource and significant losses in cattle. In November 1855, early in this drought period, James G. Cooper visited the Santa Clara Valley and remarked on "the great numbers of cattle dying on those plains" (Cooper and Suckley 1860). Almost a decade later, in 1864, William H. Brewer traveled in the same area and wrote: "May 27 we came up the San José Valley. The drought is terrible. In this fertile valley there will not be over a quarter crop, and during the past four days' ride we have seen dead cattle by the hundreds" (Brewer 1966). In Monterey County, the assessor wrote, "Two successive years of drought have almost swept the country clean of livestock. . . . The total absence of rain during the greater part of 1863 and 1864, made pasture last year exceedingly scarce" (McGarvey 1866). Although the average precipitation over this period was low, the winter of 1861–62 had had extraordinary rainfall, and there was tremendous flooding, particularly in the Central Valley. But that excess rainfall had done little to help the range and, moreover, many thousands of cattle were drowned. The struggles of the 1860s dampened speculation in cattle and there was a shift to sheep, which were thought more suitable for a semi-arid climate (Burcham 1957). In Santa Clara County, 35,648 cattle were censused in 1860 and by 1870 the number had dropped to 14,569 (Broek 1932).

The cattle industry in California was supported from the beginning by open-range laws, which required agriculturists to protect their crops by fencing out the cattle. A lawful fence was expensive, however, and was generally used only on smaller plots of land. The terrible droughts of the 1850s and 1860s reduced the power of the cattlemen (Broek 1932) and increased pressure for "No Fence" laws, that is, laws that would place the burden of fence construction on the cattleman and not the farmer. Trial "No Fence" laws were introduced in 1866 and became final in 1870 (Burcham 1957). The invention of barbed wire about 1873 aided in the transition from an open-range economy to a new era of more broadly based agriculture.

In Santa Clara County, wheat became the primary crop in the 1860s and 1870s, with production peaking in 1874 (Broek 1932). Most of the wheat was shipped to San Francisco by boat from Alviso (Jacobson 1984). At first, wheat was produced for the new California markets, but by 1855 a surplus was being exported to England and China. Although wheat continued to be an important crop in California through the end of the nineteenth century, in Santa Clara County its production declined. These declines came about partly because of drops in the yield as the fertility of the land was reduced, but also because other agricultural areas in California became more competitive (Broek 1932).

The railroad from San Francisco to San Jose was completed in 1864 and soon offered a new means of transport for agricultural products, although the high rates and poor schedules often frustrated local farmers (Jacobson 1984). Additional markets were opened when the transcontinental railroad was completed in 1869. Prior to completion of the new rail line to San Francisco, most freight had gone through the port at Alviso, but with the loss of this traffic "Alviso sunk into insignificance" (Thompson and West 1876). Unhappy with the freight rates on the San Francisco–San Jose line, vegetable growers in Santa Clara attempted to revive the freight route via the port at Alviso by building their own narrow-gauge line from Santa Clara to Alviso. Completed in 1878, this alternate route was unsuccessful, for the operators of the main line from San Francisco simply lowered their freight rates (Broek 1932).

The third era of the Agricultural Period in the Santa Clara Valley was the replacement of wheat with more valuable agricultural products, in particular, fruits. In 1870, at the height of the wheat period, orchard fruits had been grown here and there in the valley, largely for local markets. But in the following decade, various new production techniques, primarily commercial drying and canning, began to allow the export of fruit (Broek 1932). Henry W. Coe (whose son would later develop the Pine Ridge Ranch in the Diablo Range, now Henry Coe State Park) was the first of the local orchardists to experiment with fumigating cut fruit with sulfur as a means of preservation (Jacobson 1984). The completion of the new rail lines permitted the shipping of both dried and canned fruit. By 1890, the acreage in commercial orchards had come to equal that in wheat production (Broek 1932), and by the end of the 1890s, Santa Clara County was the world's largest center for the canning of fresh fruit and the processing of dried fruit (Jacobson 1984). Twenty years later, in 1920, there were 40 canneries and 30 packing houses in the county, and by 1930, 103,000 acres were in orchards, almost none in wheat (Broek 1932).

In the 1880s and 1890s, Santa Clara County had come to be the primary source of hay and forage for horses in San Francisco (Jacobson 1984). An area from Sunnyvale to Mayfield was extensively planted in hay, a crop that remained important into the early 'teens, when the increasing numbers of automobiles and trucks eliminated the need for horse transport.

Agriculture, then, largely defined the development of Santa Clara County during the Agricultural Period, but four other areas of commerce were important, and each impacted the natural environment: (1) oyster farming, (2) salt extraction, (3) lumbering, and (4) mercury mining.

At the time of European settlement, there were extensive beds of Olympia oysters in the shallow waters all along the western side of San Francisco Bay (Skinner 1962). Fishing for these native oysters was limited during the Spanish-Mexican Period, but at the start of the Agricultural Period, Olympia oysters from Shoalwater Bay, Washington, were brought to San Francisco, some for immediate sale, and others were held in storage beds off Sausalito (Postel 1988). Significant production of oysters, however, did not occur until after the completion of the transcontinental railroad in 1869 (Skinner 1962, Postel 1988). Starting in the 1870s, seed of eastern oysters were brought by railroad from the east coast and planted in oyster beds. The best of these new oyster beds were in the Central Bay, off Millbrae and San Mateo, and in the South Bay, south of Dumbarton Point. The eastern oysters were found to grow much faster in the cold bay waters than they did in the east, but they did not spawn, which meant that railroad carloads of oyster seed were required each year during the spring and fall planting seasons (Postel 1988). Still, from 1895 to 1904, the oyster fishery was the most valuable fishery on the west coast (Skinner 1962, Postel 1988). Around 1900, however, this fishery began to decline. The oysters took much longer to reach maturity, and the meat was thin and watery. By 1908, the eastern oyster seed would no longer set in the beds, and it was necessary to import more developed oysters. Bonnot (1935) wrote that the cause of this decline was uncertain, although Skinner (1962) suggested that pollution was the primary reason. Postel (1988) noted that the lack of natural flushing from freshwater inflows during the rainy season may have harmed the oysters growing in the South Bay, and the destruction of salt marshes may also have had deleterious effects. In any case, by 1915, oyster production had declined by over 90%.

Long before the development of an oyster fishery, windrows of native oyster shell had formed on the western side of the Bay, from about San Mateo to 12 miles to the south (Skinner 1962). These windrows completely covered the shore and formed bars that extended into the Bay. Townsend (1893) wrote that schooners came along the edge of the Bay and loaded quantities of these shells for garden walks and other purposes. According to Townsend, "[t]he supply is unfailing."

The Indians, and later the Spanish and Mexicans, had harvested salt from natural saline ponds at the edge of the salt marshes along San Francisco Bay. Ver Planck (1958) described the early history of the salt industry in the Bay area. The first attempts at controlling the salt evaporation process by building levees were undertaken about 1854 in the East Bay. The first salt works to employ the modern techniques of successive intake, evaporation, and crystallizing ponds were established near Barron's Landing in the vicinity of Alvarado in 1862. Removal of the bittern (the solution that remains after removal of sodium chloride) from the crystallizing ponds left highly pure salt deposits, but the bittern dumped into the Bay was a serious pollutant. By the end of the nineteenth century, the salt industry extended from San Leandro Creek to just south of Alvarado. At the beginning, most of the salt works were small, family-owned businesses, but over time these businesses consolidated, and by the start of the twentieth century many of the salt works had been combined into just three companies. By 1936, all were part of the Leslie Salt Company.

Prior to the Agricultural Period, there were few lumbering operations in the Santa Cruz Mountains. As mentioned previously, a lumber mill was built on Los Gatos Creek at Alma as early as 1845 (Wilson 1937), but many of the operations were just two-man saw pits operating at the edge of the coniferous forests (Stanger 1967). The gold rush brought a tremendous demand for lumber, which initially was met with fir imported from Oregon and pine from the east coast. But powered mills developed rapidly on the eastern slopes of the Santa Cruz Mountains, from the Spring Valley Lakes (now Crystal Springs Reservoir) south to Mt. Madonna. Most of the redwood forests on the eastern side in San Mateo County were cut out by the 1860s, and most of the lumber was shipped through the appropriately named Redwood City for construction in San Francisco, Stockton, and Sacramento (Stanger 1967). Farther south, the mills worked their way up the Los Gatos Creek and other drainages, and by the 1870s most of the timber had been removed (Jensen 1939). Mills were in operation on Bodfish Creek as early as the 1860s, and the redwoods in the Mt. Madonna area were logged in the 1870s and 1880s to supply Gilroy (Wilson 1937). As the forests on the eastern side of the Santa Cruz Mountains were logged, the mills shifted to the western slopes. Page Mill No. 2, for example, was built on Peters Creek on the western side of the Santa Cruz Mountains, and in 1867 a road was built over the crest and down to Mayfield (now part of Palo Alto), a road still known as Page Mill Road (Stanger 1967). Santa

Cruz and Boulder Creek became the major lumber centers on the west side, since transport costs there were less. Farther north, the old-growth forests in the Butano and Pescadero drainages survived, because of the higher transportation costs there. By the first decade of the twentieth century, most of the timber was gone (Wilson 1937). By the 1930s, only about 8% of the original forest was left, and a third of that was protected in state and county parks.

Stanger (1967) tallied the lumber shipments through Redwood City for a typical midsummer week in 1862. Thirty-two ships left the port that week, carrying 50,000 board feet of lumber, 1,730,000 shingles, 108,700 fence posts, and 152 cords of firewood. These numbers are probably representative of the lumber demand at the time the forests on the eastern side of the Santa Cruz Mountains were being logged. In the Santa Clara Valley, there was a demand for construction lumber, shingles, and fence posts and rails. Prior to the passage of the "No Fence" laws, the farmers had been required to provide a "hog-tight" fence to protect their farms from depredation by cattle and horses. Typically, these were made using closely spaced redwood fence posts held together with pine or fir boards (Broek 1932). Following the passage of the "No Fence" laws, it became necessary for ranchers to build similar fences to keep their cattle in. Although barbed wire first came into use in the United States in the 1870s, it appears that many ranchers continued to build redwood fences, and some were remarkably extensive, even as late as 1880 (Broek 1932). Additional wood products also became important when Santa Clara County was becoming a center of fruit processing, and a box and crate industry developed. A photograph in Jacobson (1984), taken in 1866, shows a box factory that apparently supplied boxes for the local fruit industry, just off First Street in San Jose. The mercury mines at New Almaden and along the Guadalupe Creek required an extensive supply of timber for shoring up the ceiling and walls of the tunnels in the expanding mines in the foothills there (Schneider 1992).

In the Santa Clara County atlas published by Thompson and West (1876), the authors describe the supply of lumber from the Santa Cruz Mountains as inexhaustible. But even factoring in the normal optimism that is required of the publishers of a subscribed book, this statement seems particularly wide of the mark, since by the 1870s, shipments through Redwood City were already declining, and by the 1890s lumber was once again being imported to the region from Oregon and Washington (Stanger 1967).

Andres Castillero had formed a stock company to mine cinnabar in New Almaden in 1845, and by 1846, near the end of the Spanish-Mexican Period, the mines were extracting mercury from the ore (Sawyer 1922, Schneider 1992). Mostly, the mercury was exported via the various embarcaderos in the South Bay, but later, when a railroad spur was extended to New Almaden, the mercury was shipped by rail (Broek 1932). These mines were a major supplier of mercury for the California gold mines, as well as elsewhere in the world. Up to 1887, half the world's supply was from California, the greatest portion of it from the New Almaden mines. In 1886, 1,400 employees lived at the New Almaden site, but by 1922, the ore had given out and only a few miners were left, still looking for new sources of ore. Today, the mines are closed, and what is left of the abandoned mining towns is part of the Almaden Quicksilver County Park.

The data from the first census in Santa Clara County, in 1850, were lost, but a recount in 1852 tallied 6,764 people (Broek 1932). During the Agricultural Period, the population increased about 3.9% per year, as shown in Fig. 4.6, and at the end of the period, in the 1920 census, 100,676 people were recorded. Most of the increase was from immigration. For the most part, the original Californio families saw their ranchos broken up and the source of their wealth lost (Broek 1932). The Indians, who had been the sole occupiers of these lands a century before, had almost all died. In 1858, Chief Lupe Yñigo, who lived near Mountain View, told Alfred Doten that "when he was a little boy his tribe was numerous about here—but all have died, and he is the only one left" (Clark 1973).

The mission fathers had built ditches to divert water to their crops. Some of the Mexican land grantees also constructed irrigation canals. Alvirez, who held the Laguna Seca land grant, built a canal from Laguna Seca in the 1830s to irrigate lands north of the Coyote Narrows (Grossinger et al. 2006). Irrigation, to a degree, was still used at the start of the Agricultural Period. It was soon discovered, however, that an artesian aquifer lay beneath the valley lands, and successful artesian wells were drilled as early as the 1850s. Thompson and West (1876), who had considered the lumber supply in the Santa Cruz Mountain to be unlimited, were even more certain of the artesian well water: "This supply is inexhaustible, and would, with the inauguration of the proper system, be sufficient to irrigate the entire valley." Eugene T. Sawyer (1922) was just as sanguine, claiming that "there can be no doubt that artesian water can be found at any point in the valley, not excepting the higher ground near the foothills." The reality of the ground-water supply in Santa Clara County was far different from what its boosters suggested, and changes would become necessary by the end of the period.

The intensive development of irrigated agriculture in the Santa Clara Valley started about 1900 (Poland and Ireland 1988). In the northern Santa Clara Valley, the number of irrigation wells for agricultural use increased from 115 in 1890 to 1,590 by 1920. The average well depth, about 35 feet in 1910, increased to 65 feet by 1920 (Broek 1932). As more wells were drilled, the water table dropped, and more and more farmers saw their pumping costs increasing. By the 1920s, it was clear to most thoughtful observers that the valley's water supplies were not "inexhaustible," and actions to correct the problem were essential (Rickman 1981). In 1920, the Santa Clara Valley Water Conservation Committee was formed to study the problem and propose solutions. In many ways, the composition of this committee marked a turning point between the old agricultural interests and the urban development that has taken over the valley in recent times. Although the conservation committee was initiated by valley farmers, they were joined by the county Chamber of Commerce. The latter organization saw that the overuse of water was not just a farm problem, but one affecting all businesses (Rickman 1981). The committee hired Fred H. Tibbetts and his associate Stephen E. Kieffer to examine the water supply problems and propose solutions. Funding was about 25% from the county, the balance split between farm organizations and the San Jose Chamber of Commerce. The need for control of the valley's water supply ended a period of unfettered agricultural

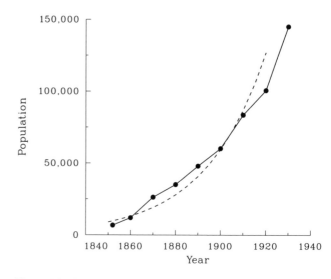

Figure 4.6. Population census data for Santa Clara County, 1852 to 1930. The exponential fit added for the years 1852 to 1920 indicates an increase of 3.9% per year.

development.

Figure 4.7 shows a map of the Palo Alto area surveyed in 1899, toward the end of the Agricultural Period. This section of the topographic sheet includes all of Brown's 1840 map (shown in Fig. 4.3), but true north in Brown's map is offset by about 40° from that of Fig. 4.7, and Brown's map is therefore a smaller quadrilateral, angled at 40°, contained within the larger quadrilateral of Fig. 4.7. San Francisquito Creek flows from left to right across Fig. 4.7 and, where it enters the Bay, exhibits little difference from how it is shown on Brown's 1840s map. The topography delineated in Fig. 4.7 provides no details of the willow thickets that were still near the mouth of the San Francisquito Creek at the time, nor is there the wealth of detail showing the live oak forest and chamisal present during the 1840s. Palo Alto is at this point a town of roughly seven by 11 blocks that sits between San Francisquito Creek, the railroad, and Embarcadero Road. Fisher (1940) described Palo Alto in 1900 as "a small spread-eagle town with board sidewalks, unpaved streets very muddy in the winter, dim street lights, and stores with false-fronts." The newly formed Stanford University is under construction southwest of Palo Alto, across the railroad tracks and El Camino Real. Matadero Creek's terminus on the valley floor is seen just northeast of the railroad tracks. Adobe and Permanente creeks, however, have been extended to the Bay with ditches. Few changes from Brown's map of the 1840s are observed in the Bay marshes.

South Bay Habitats. During the Agricultural Period, massive changes occurred throughout the San Francisco Bay estuary (Cohen and Carlton 1998), as well as in South Bay habitats. Figure 4.8 shows the cumulative number of alien organisms found in the estuary from 1850 to 1920. These invading species include plants, invertebrates (such as worms and mollusks), and vertebrates. The increase over this period is 5.6% per year (using Cohen and Carlton's modified data). Cohen and Carlton (1998) have concluded that there are three primary reasons for the large numbers of invading species. First, multiple

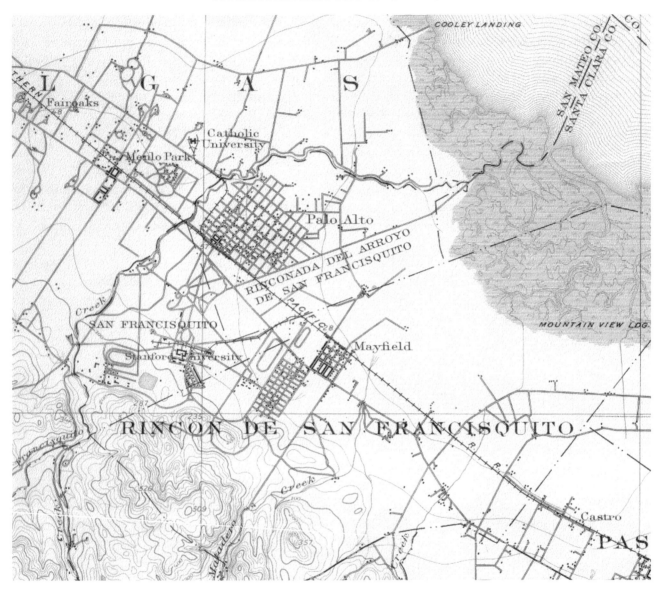

Figure 4.7. The Palo Alto area in 1899, from U.S. Geological Survey 15′ Palo Alto topographic sheet.

transport vectors brought in exotic organisms. The San Francisco Bay was a major port of entry and had been so since the discovery of gold in 1848. Alien species were able to arrive on ships' hulls, as part of their cargo, or in their ballast. Other species, including the eastern oyster and striped bass from the East Coast, and the Pacific oyster from Japan, were purposely introduced. With these purposeful introductions came other alien species, such as the Atlantic oyster drill, a snail that is a serious predator of oysters, and the ribbed mussel. Second, the original biota of the Bay was depauperate; as a relatively young estuary it had had less time for the development of a more diverse biota. Third, the extensive modifications to the estuary created a disturbance environment that benefited introduced species, just as disturbance on the land allowed invading weed species to thrive. The Bay communities most strongly affected were those living in bottom sediments, the fouling communities (species found on

ships' hulls and wharves), the brackish-water zooplankton, and the freshwater fish (Cohen and Carlton 1998). In these communities, alien species typically account for 40 to 100% of the common species present today.

Early observers in San Francisco Bay had noticed how plentiful salmon had been at the time of American settlement, yet by the 1860s the salmon and other fisheries were in decline for a variety of reasons, including overfishing and pollution. On 2 April 1870, the state legislature passed a law for the restoration and preservation of the state fisheries and formed a commission to oversee the new law (Skinner 1962). In the commission's fifth biennial report (California State Commissioners of Fisheries 1879), W. N. Lockington wrote:

> Already the fishery carried on in the Bay of San Francisco is much less productive than it was in

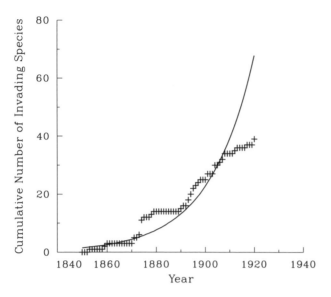

Figure 4.8. Invasion of exotic species in San Francisco Bay, 1850 to 1920 (from Cohen and Carlton 1998).

the early days of the American occupation; species that were abundant fail to attain their full dimensions. Nor is over-fishing the sole cause of this. The constant hurrying to and fro of the numerous ferry-boats and other steamers, indispensable to our comfort, tends to drive away the timid finny tribes, whilst the ashes and cinders let fall injure the character of the bottom.

But the injury from this source is small compared with that inflicted by the constant fouling of the waters by the foetid inpourings of our sewers . . . into the waters to pollute them for the destruction of creatures of which human beings are largely dependent for the means of life.

In the early 1850s, when oysters had been shipped from Washington's Shoalwater Bay for sale in San Francisco, the oyster beds off Sausalito had been used for their temporary storage and fattening (Postel 1988). But in the winter of 1861–62, nearly the entire supply was smothered by silt that filled the beds, most of the silt coming from the hydraulic mining debris of the Sierra Nevada mines. New oyster beds, established in the Central and South bays, were considered protected from storms and mine debris, and oyster farming was successful in the South Bay until the end of the nineteenth century, despite Lockington's warning of the fetid output from the sewers of South Bay cities. Eventually, though, the oyster industry collapsed, probably from a number of factors, including pollution, the destruction of salt marshes at the Bay's periphery, and the diversion of freshwater for agriculture in the Santa Clara Valley (Postel 1988). It is ironic that agricultural interests in the Santa Clara Valley considered the fresh water that flowed to the Bay as lost or wasted (Broek 1932), whereas for the oyster fishery it was necessary for cleansing of the South Bay waters.

The South Bay marshes were left largely intact dur-

ing the Agricultural Period, although conversion of marshes to salt evaporator ponds had got under way in the East Bay at this time (Ver Planck 1958). Walter R. Welch (1931), born in Marin County, moved with his family to a fruit orchard near Mayfield in 1872. He wrote:

During the early seventies the marshes surrounding the Bay of San Francisco were practically in their virgin condition. No attempt had been made to reclaim them, and from Alameda, on the east side of the bay, and Hunter's Point on the west side, to the head of the bay at Alviso, the marshes were in their natural condition, and during the fall and winter months were inhabited by millions of ducks, geese, shore birds and other waterfowl of every variety.

This was in the era when wheat and hay were grown along the Bay. Alfred Doten, who worked on a farm near Mountain View, wrote of the immense numbers of geese seen in October 1856, "[m]ore geese about here than I ever saw in my life—at times the sky is almost darkened with them" (Clark 1973). Doten also described large flocks of Sandhill Cranes that used the same farm fields. Both the geese and the cranes were attracted by the waste grain. Despite their great numbers, these waterfowl were wary of hunters. Doten described how, in the 1850s, some hunters would use an ox as a moving blind so that they could approach the flocks of geese. This tactic was also used in a later period by the market hunters in the Central Valley (Wilson 1931). Welch (1931) described how hunters in the 1870s would wait at the edge of the grainfields each night and shoot the geese and ducks as they flew from the marshes to the fields to feed on the waste grain. It is possible, though, that the number of waterfowl wintering in the South Bay nonetheless increased as agriculture in the 1850s afforded them a new food resource.

In the 1860s, hunting in the South Bay was limited by transportation. The San Francisco–San Jose line scheduled trains in the morning and afternoon, but these times were not convenient for hunting. In the late 1880s, the railroad put together a "Hunter's train" for the marshes south of San Francisco. Welch (1931) wrote:

As soon as these trains were put on hunters flocked in from San Francisco and other large cities, and where formerly one could see but a dozen hunters on Sunday one could now see hundreds in every direction, and as there was no bag limit on ducks, geese, shore birds or quail, the hunters shot them indiscriminately. I have seen hunters come off the marsh in the vicinity of Belmont, with all the rail and ducks they could carry, and it was not unusual for a hunter to kill from 50 to 150 rail during a day's shoot in that locality.

In our present day, it is difficult to imagine the quantities of ducks, rails, and shorebirds that lived on and along San Francisco Bay. Chase Littlejohn, an avid naturalist and hunter who was raised in Redwood City, described the quantities of ducks that used the marshes in the 1860s (Ellsworth 1931):

We had more ducks in San Mateo County up to the time I was 10 years old [1865] than we have in this whole state at present. This seems like an exaggerated statement, but you could go any time during the winter months, look up and down the sloughs or over the marshes and see masses of ducks rafted everywhere.

When only a little fellow, barely able to handle a gun, I went out with my brother. We turned a bend and ahead was an immense flock of teal duck. Something frightened them, but they flew out only a little way and then began to swim back. My brother made one shot with his big gun. The numbers of birds rising up so surprised him that he failed to fire the second barrel. I picked up 75 ducks. It is hard to believe that so many teal could be killed with one shot.

Littlejohn also described the masses of shorebirds that were found: "In the early days waders were so abundant in the tide flats and water of San Francisco Bay that a stone thrown among them would result in many casualties. When a boy, I sometimes remember going out with a pocketful of stones and killing any number. They were so thick that it was possible to hit them without much skill."

Walter E. Bryant (1890) wrote of his father's experience along the Bay in 1850, where near San Bruno he saw thousands of gray and white geese (probably Greater White-fronted, Snow, and Ross's geese) grazing beside the roadside. These geese had no fear of man, but in a few years they became much more wary as the new settlers hunted them in the fall and winter.

The plentiful numbers of waterfowl and shorebirds in the Bay did not decline until the 1880s and 1890s, when market hunting began to affect their populations. Welch (1931), a market-hunter himself, did not notice the decline until 1892. Grinnell et al. (1918) concluded that the major decrease occurred between 1890 and 1910. Laws were eventually passed prohibiting the sale of game birds in the markets, but by this time the damage was done and none of these game species ever recovered their former numbers.

Clapper Rails, as well as ducks, were hunted extensively in the Bay area during this period. Observers in the 1890s noted the decline in this species, largely from overhunting and from predation by the Norway rat (Barlow 1894b, Taylor 1894a, Taylor 1894b, Cohen 1899), although Ernest Adams (1900) felt there had been no change in the population. Predation pressure from Norway rats undoubtedly dated from the development of the port at Alviso and other landings along the Bay edge in the 1850s. This rat was notably abundant in San Francisco at the time, according to Alfred Doten (Clark 1973). The hunting pressure on Clapper Rails had built rapidly in the 1860s and 1870s, particularly because the railroad provided improved access to these marshes. However, overhunting and Norway rats were not the only problem faced by this species. With the introduction of eastern oyster seed, the ribbed mussel from the East Coast also invaded the South Bay. This mussel expanded quickly in the marshes and sloughs. In a presentation to a meeting of the Audubon Association of the Pacific, Chase Littlejohn (*Gull 4*:2 1922) was quoted as saying:

There is no open season on clapper rail now, but their numbers are diminishing, nevertheless. Their feeding flats have been taken up by leveeing for cattle and industries. The levees are infested with rats, which destroy the rail's eggs. The planting of oysters has also resulted in establishing mussels, beds of which form a pavement over the feeding grounds of the rail. In contrast with the oyster, which opens its shell when dying, a mussel shell shuts tightly under such circumstances. A rail starting to eat a mussel while its shell is open, will mortally wound the shell-fish, and the shell will snap shut, catching the bill of the bird, which then slowly starves to death. Mr. Littlejohn exhibited a stuffed specimen of clapper rail with its bill still clamped between the valves of the mussel shell, as he found the bird dying on the flats. The birds also suffer greatly from having their toes caught, and finally amputated, by the same process. In one locality on the marshes, of quite limited area, where there are no mussels yet, the nests of the clapper rail still abound, but they are never found in those portions where the mussels have become established.

Santa Clara Valley Habitats. The rangeland economy was completely changed at the outset of the Agricultural Period as ranchers moved from the production of tallow and hides to the production of beef for the mines and the growing cities. Cattle ranching increased greatly in the Santa Clara Valley in the 1850s, and the range was overstocked during the severe drought of 1853–65. This overstocking increased in the 1860s as the beef market declined and ranchers chose to keep their cattle on the range. The consequent overgrazing of the range accentuated the transition from native grasses to the non-natives seen today. Burcham (1957) described between three and four stages in this transition. The first stage of wild oats and wild mustard was over by about 1855. The second stage, which included filaree (storksbill), mouse barley, and nitgrass, extended to 1865 or 1870, with decreasing forage value for cattle. The third stage, dominated by introduced barleys, red brome, and silver hairgrass, is largely what appears on the range in Santa Clara County today. The acreage required to support cattle at the present time is twice that needed on the pristine range present when the Spanish expeditions first arrived (Burcham 1957).

The deterioration of the range in California was already apparent to some of the early ranchers. Bidwell (1866) wrote,

It cannot have escaped the observation of those engaged in rearing stock in California that the indigenous grasses, once so abundant as to pasture thousands of animals where only hundreds are able to subsist now, are fast disappearing from the plains. This is attributable no doubt to excessive grazing, especially by sheep and horses. . . . Weeds spring up and encumber the ground, and stock disappears.

Burcham (1957) comments that "Few places on earth, if any, have had such a rapid wholesale replacement of native plants by introduced species. It has not progressed to a comparable degree on our range lands at higher elevations or under greater rainfall, which suggests an intimate relationship between the process and local climate, as well as with intensity of use and other factors."

The changes in California's grasslands during the Agricultural Period must have affected wildlife as well. Mule deer, elk, and pronghorn were all common in local grasslands at the start of the period. With American settlement, hunting pressure became severe. Deer and, to some degree, pronghorn withdrew to more forested areas, whereas elk moved into marshlands. By the late 1850s, elk and pronghorn had largely been killed off near the growing towns (Evermann 1915). Deer were more successful, but the reduced quality of the forage and, in particular, the reduced period of green forage, were detrimental to their populations (Burcham 1957). Smaller animals, such as California ground squirrels, black-tailed jackrabbits, and desert cottontails, increased in numbers on overgrazed lands (Burcham 1957).

Almost nothing is known of population changes of the avian grassland specialists, such as Horned Larks, Savannah and Grasshopper sparrows, and Western Meadowlarks, nor species such as Rufous-crowned and Lark sparrows, that are sometimes found at the grassland edge. Today, a few of these birds, particularly Horned Larks and Grasshopper Sparrows, are more plentiful on serpentine grasslands than they are in rangelands dominated by non-native annual grasses. These serpentine grasslands are in many ways similar to the pristine grasslands in their mixture of native forbs and grasses that are tolerant of the serpentine soils.

Wheat became an important agricultural crop in the Santa Clara Valley in the 1850s (Broek 1932), and local residents raised vegetables, poultry, and other food crops for their own use in small plots. Beal (1907) pointed out that for some species agriculture provides improved food resources, some species gain the protection of man, but others decline because of the loss of presettlement foods, and still others suffer from the depredations of man. In the Santa Clara Valley these depredations included the indiscriminate shooting of both game birds and raptors, as well as the extensive killing of California ground squirrels, coyotes, and striped skunks with broad-scale poisons such as strychnine (Clark 1973). The significant changes brought about early in the agricultural period must have impacted many local populations, but there were few who commented on avifauna at this early stage. Even after the orchards began to replace the wheat fields later in the century, only a few of the early naturalists noted these changes. John Van Denburgh (1899b) wrote about the Western Meadowlark that "[t]his was formerly a very common resident in all parts of the valley, but of late years the converting of grain fields into orchards has resulted in a great restriction of its territory."

In the northern end of the Santa Clara Valley, near San Francisco Bay, Cooper (1926) described a mesic community of willows and composites. Many of the smaller streams ended on the alluvial fans or on valley bottomlands and small ponds or swamps thick with willows formed at the termini of these streams or at the edges of the fans where the water returned to the surface. By 1876, when the Thompson and West atlas was published, almost all the stream termini were connected to the Bay by ditches. Early settlers told Cooper that most of the willow thickets had been cut down, and that the area was then used for pasturage or planted in small crops. Cooper described the willow and composite community as "nearly eradicated" when he made his studies in the 1920s.

The cutting of the coniferous and broad-leaved evergreen forests on the eastern side of the Santa Cruz Mountains in the 1860s and 1870s was apparent to those who had settled in the Santa Clara Valley (Broek 1932), and the oak savanna and woodlands were also cleared, for agricultural purposes. All of this deforestation, so readily visible, in time led to reforestation efforts on the valley floor (Broek 1932). Typical farmyard plants at this time were Australian eucalyptus, especially the bluegum eucalyptus, pepper trees from Chile, and California fan palms from southern California. Many conifers, including pines and cypresses, were also planted in farmyards and in lots in town. Broek (1932) wrote

> From a landscape point of view, the eucalyptus was by far the most dominant tree of the Valley because of its frequency as well as its height. This tree was extensively planted about 1870 as a result of the anxiety aroused by the rapid destruction of trees during the sixties. Not only were the mountains denuded of trees, but the Valley also: the groves of oak were rapidly vanishing, the wood generally used for fuel and the bark of the live oak for tanning purposes.

Grainfields were still common in the Valley through the 1890s, particularly in the southern Santa Clara Valley. W. E. Unglish commented in a 1913 letter to Joseph Grinnell (Grinnell et al. 1918) that geese were once abundant on the lands between Gilroy and Hollister, but although the country was still sown to grain, the number of geese had declined dramatically.

At the start of the Agricultural Period, the higher lands on the alluvial fans, from Los Altos to southern San Jose, were covered with extensive stands of chaparral and oaks (Cooper 1926, Brown 2002). Early in the period the oaks were cut for firewood and charcoal (Brown 2002), but the chaparral, with no economic value, was left. In 1873–74, the San Francisco–San Jose railroad began paying for chaparral roots as a fireplace fuel, and this led to the clearing of these lands. Both fruit trees and grapevines did well on the cleared lands, and within a few years there was nothing left of the original chaparral (Cooper 1926).

The Santa Cruz Mountains and Diablo Range Habitats. In February 1863, James G. Cooper wrote to his sister Fan about his explorations in the Santa Cruz Mountains (Coan 1982):

> I have been two weeks visiting my old hunting grounds at Mountain View, and hunting along the Coast Range west of there along Arroyo Quito. There I found the most lovely scenery I have yet met with in California or anywhere else, and am only sorry that I could not afford to stay longer. It is not as magnificent as that of Yosemite Valley. . . but the details are more beautiful. I should

think—groves of tropical looking *Arbutus* with orange-like leaves and red berries, mingled with firs eight feet in diameter and 300 high, redwoods like gigantic yew trees, and many beautiful flowers beneath—altogether make it a most charming picture. Birds were swarming, rich in song and plumage.

Arroyo Quito was present-day Saratoga Creek. Timber cutting started in the 1850s or 1860s in the Los Gatos and Saratoga creek drainages. The great trees that Cooper saw along Saratoga Creek were gone by the 1870s as the mills moved up the creeks and all the large timber was harvested (Jensen 1939).

In the early years of lumbering operations there was a tendency to leave young trees standing, to provide a head start for the second-growth forests that followed (Jensen 1939). Later, fire used to burn bark and debris often resulted in the logged areas regrowing as chaparral and oak woodlands. Wilson (1937) estimated that of the 400,000 acres logged in the Santa Cruz Mountains, about half was regrowing as redwood forest, the other half as brush and woodlands. Although redwood was the primary interest of the lumbermen, they also used Douglas fir for boxes, crates, and fences. More selective logging used madrone for the manufacture of charcoal and tan oak for its bark for the tanning industry. Broek (1932) wrote, "While the slopes on the Valley side of the Santa Cruz Mountains have been almost stripped of their former fir stand, the ocean side still has—though not unbroken—splendid forests with Redwood and Douglas fir as the predominating species." It is hard to envision the old-growth forests that once ranged along the creeks that dropped down the eastern side of the Santa Cruz Mountains. Cooper's short description hints at a magnificent world that once existed along these creeks. In some areas on the eastern slopes, second-growth forests are now maturing, providing a hint of what once was there.

In the hills between Guadalupe and Alamitos creeks, where the Almaden Quicksilver County Park is located today, the initial effect of mining at New Almaden was the cutting of much of the oak woodlands and forests on these hills, to power the reduction furnaces for the processing of the cinnabar ore. By the 1870s and 1880s, most of the hills around the mines and furnaces were open grasslands, where once they had been woodlands and forest. But as with the coniferous forests in the Los Gatos Creek watershed, some of this grassland has reverted to oak woodland and forest, thick in the wetter gulches with California bay and poison oak. A few eucalyptus and other exotics that were planted around Englishtown and other settlements on the hill are a reminder that people lived on these hills a century ago, but little else remains.

Although forests and woodlands have returned to the foothills near New Almaden, mercury contamination from the mining has continued to the present. The New Almaden mining district was the largest in North America at the end of the nineteenth century (Conaway et al. 2004) and was the primary source of mercury, which was used for the refining of gold. In the early days of mining, crushed slag and tailings from the mercury reduction process were dumped at the edges of Los Alamitos and Guadalupe creeks and were then washed away by the winter rains (Schneider 1992). The early refining process

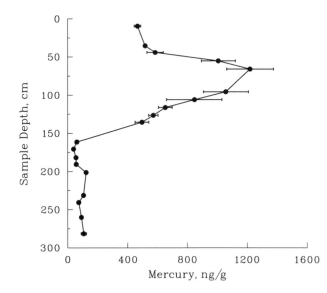

Figure 4.9. Mercury in a core sample near Triangle Marsh (from Collins and Grossinger 2004). Sample depth is representative of time.

was inefficient, and the slag contained significant quantities of mercury. Later, when the mining was largely over, many of the remaining mine tailings and dumps were reworked for the mercury that was still there, but even these processes remained inefficient and tons of cinnabar ore with its mercury were flushed into the creeks (Schneider 1992). The mercury from the mine tailings has passed down the Guadalupe River and into the Bay, where it has been deposited in the Bay sediments. Figure 4.9 shows measurements of the mercury content in a core sample from Triangle Marsh (Conaway et al. 2004, Collins and Grossinger 2004). The sample depth is related to time, but because the deposition of sediments is episodic, depending upon rainfall and flooding, it is difficult to relate the sample depths to time periods. At 240 cm, a cord grass rhizome was dated to about 1570±70 years (Conaway et al. 2004). The core samples from depths greater than about 160 cm apparently represent a background level of mercury of 80 nanograms per gram (ng/g). Pollen from eucalyptus and English plantain, ascribed to 1870±10 years, was found at 140 cm, at which time, there was already an increase in mercury in these sediments. The mercury deposition peaked at 1,220 ng/g, probably in the middle part of the twentieth century. Evidence of the 1982-83 El Niño event is apparent at about 35 cm, with a peak in the deposition of pollen and seeds of sedges. The current amounts of mercury that are being deposited are much reduced from the peak, but the sediment contamination remains in place. The mercury deposition at Triangle Marsh is representative of a number of sites in the South Bay (San Francisco Estuary Institute 2005). Bacteria in these sediments have converted the mercury to methylmercury, which is more easily absorbed by fish and benthic organisms and becomes toxic in high concentrations. Although miners at New Almaden occasionally suffered from mercury poisoning (Schneider 1992), the problem of mercury contamination of the environment went unnoticed during the Agricultural Period. But it left a legacy that significantly affects us today.

Throughout the Agricultural Period, ranchers moved away from the valley floor and into the foothills, particularly in the Diablo Range. Along the wetter, western side of the Diablo Range, the range, although degraded, provided reasonable grazing. Farther east, in the drier interior parts of the range, more land was required for each head of cattle, and ranchers found making a living more difficult.

Under pressure from hunters, mule deer and grizzly bears withdrew from the valley floor into the mountain and foothill areas of the Santa Cruz Mountains and the Diablo Range. There, the mule deer found suitable forage and browse, and their numbers have remained steady in the following century (Dasmann and Dasmann 1963). The grizzly, however, failed to find a balance with the increasing numbers of people in foothill and mountain areas. Welch (1931) recounts stories of John Lucas Greer of Palo Alto, who was raised in Woodside. He told of raids by grizzlies in the 1850s on beef that had been slaughtered and hung, as well as their coming into his family's yard to kill a sow and pigs. The last grizzly bear in Santa Clara County was killed on 15 July 1879 in the Diablo Range, near the Merced County line, by Walter King. *The Daily Alta California* (31 Jul 1879) reported that

> King got on a bear track on Tuesday, and went out early yesterday morning. Not returning in time, his companion went out to search for him, and found him unconscious, but still alive, with his skull fractured and his left side torn. The grizzly lay dead about 60 yards away. King was restored to consciousness and carried back to the camp, and assistance was given by a couple of men who were camping a few miles distant. King tells that he followed the bear's tracks to a sort of a cave in the hillside, heavily bordered with chapparal [sic], and, supposing that the animal was inside, was on the watch, when a rustling of a bush caused him to turn and discover Bruin only thirty or forty feet away. He raised his Spencer and fired, and the bear came for him. He shot three times, dropped his gun, and pulled his hunting-knife, just as the beast reached him. He cut frantically but was struck on the head by the animal's paw, and remembered no more until carried back to camp. The place where this occurred was literally alive with bears ten or twelve years ago, but most of them have been killed off. King will recover.

The last grizzly in San Mateo County was also killed in 1879 (Storer and Tevis 1955), while in Santa Cruz County, at least one remained until 1886, when killed by O. S. Blodgett. Blodgett, who had a ranch on Ben Lomond Mountain, described in a letter to Walter R. Welch (1931) how he killed this last grizzly:

> This bear had been killing stock, principally hogs, around the neighborhood, and finally came one night and took a 300 pound hog out of our pen— one we had been fattening. The dogs annoyed the bear so it was compelled to leave the hog, and we

found it covered with leaves and brush a short distance from the pen. Thinking the bear would eventually come back for the hog, we tied up the dogs and watched for three or four nights without success. On the night the bear returned we had given up watching and were about to go to bed, when the dogs commenced to bark, and thinking they had scented the bear, I took my gun—an old muzzle-loading shotgun—and went out. As I approached the spot where the hog was buried, I heard the bear coming though the brush, and in an effort to get a better shot I crawled to the corner of the fence and we met. The bear reared up and I aimed for the head and fired. I was lucky enough to hit the bear in the left eye, and the slug went clear through and killed it instantly. I was so close to the bear that the powder burned the hair around the eye. It was an old female, gray around the muzzle, and weighed just 642 pounds dressed. I sold the meat to the Chase Market at Santa Cruz for 10 cents a pound, and the hide for $25.

The Urban Period

By the 1920s, it was clear that action was needed to improve the supply of water in the valley. With settlement, agriculture had gone through stages of cattle raising, wheat, and now orchards. Broek (1932) wrote: "No form of agriculture has so completely transformed the appearance of the Santa Clara Valley as has the cultivation of fruit trees. Once a grassland dotted with evergreen oaks, a large portion of the Valley is now covered by a veritable forest of deciduous trees." The increasing number of fruit trees in the valley, the canning and packing houses in San Jose, and a growing infrastructure all needed water.

The Santa Clara Valley Water Conservation Committee, formed in 1920, funded a study by Fred H. Tibbetts and Stephen E. Kieffer to determine the best way to recharge the groundwater in the valley (Rickman 1981). Their report (Tibbetts and Kieffer 1921) recommended a system of 17 large reservoirs and percolation ponds. But when the committee attempted to carry through these plans by forming a district with taxing and bond authority, in September 1921, the electorate failed to support the committee (Rickman 1981). The committee tried once again to form a district, this time without Morgan Hill or Palo Alto, but it was again disapproved by the voters in April 1924 (Rickman 1981). The committee then disbanded.

A new committee was formed in 1926, as the Santa Clara Valley Water Conservation Association (Fish 1981). In the previous decade, the average depth of wells in the valley had dropped from 60 to 140 feet, and the need for change had become clearer. This time, a vote in November 1929 provided overwhelming support for a new district, which was named the Santa Clara Valley Water Conservation District.

The new district made plans to carry out much of the original Tibbetts and Kieffer plans. A 1931 bond issue for new construction failed, but the district continued to work on obtaining land for reservoirs (Fish 1981). A new bond issue in 1934 finally passed, and with the help of federal money, major construction got under way (Dickey 1981). The dams for Almaden, Calero, Guadalupe, Stevens Creek, and Vasona reservoirs were completed in 1935, and the Coyote dam was finished in 1936. Anderson Reservoir was constructed in 1948 and Lexington Reservoir in 1952.

By 1930, it was clear that even if the Tibbetts and Kieffer recommendations were fully implemented, the growing demands on water could not be met by local sources alone (Broek 1932). Poland and Ireland (1988) have estimated the amounts of groundwater pumping and water imports in the northern Santa Clara Valley over time, and the effects of these flows on the artesian head and ground subsidence during the Urban Period. Figure 4.10 shows the drop in the artesian head (well height) and ground subsidence with regional rainfall, groundwater pumping, and water imports. The regional rainfall is based on seasonal measurements at San Jose from 1874–75 to 1995–96. The rainfall amount is the cumulative departure from the seasonal mean. The cumulative departure is calculated by first computing the seasonal rainfall excess or deficit relative to the mean for each July to June season. Then, for each season, the excess or deficit is added to, or subtracted from, that from the previous year (this is the long-term cumulative excess deficit described in Chapter 1). As shown in Fig. 4.10, the cumulative departure was positive and quite large from 1910 to about 1925, indicating a period of above-average rainfall. The cumulative departure then declined, approaching zero in the mid-1930s. The cumulative departure became more positive during a wet period in the early 1940s, before becoming negative again about 1947. The departure remained negative through the 1980s, indicating a period of relatively less rainfall.

Groundwater pumping, both for agricultural and municipal purposes, is shown in Fig. 4.10 as a negative value, to allow comparison with the change in artesian head, since one expects increased groundwater pumping to be reflected in a dropping of the artesian head. Groundwater extraction increased rapidly from 1915 to the early 1930s, but in the mid-1930s there was a roughly 40% drop in groundwater pumping occasioned by reduced extraction by agricultural users during the Great Depression. Groundwater pumping increased again in the late 1930s and continued to increase into the 1960s, but the pumping was now driven by municipal water users. Then, with the addition of imported water from the Hetch Hetchy Aqueduct in 1956, and particularly the South Bay Aqueduct in 1965, groundwater pumping was reduced.

The effects of all these factors on a typical artesian well are shown at the top of the figure. In 1915, the head at this well was slightly positive, but as the excess in rainfall (positive cumulative departure) declined in the next 20 years and the groundwater pumping increased, the well depth fell to –103 feet by 1935. Increasing rainfall and decreasing pumping allowed the well height to recover to about –35 feet in the early 1940s. But in the late 1940s, as the cumulative departure in rainfall became negative and groundwater pumping continued to increase, the well height became more negative, reaching a minimum of about –175 feet in the 1960s. As imported water reduced the need for groundwater pumping in the late 1960s, the artesian well height recovered to about –100 feet in 1982, the last year in which data were recorded by Poland and Ireland (1988). Ground

subsidence, measured in a borehole near the artesian head measurements, generally follows the downward trend with artesian well height, but it is an irreversible process. That is, when the well height recovers, as it did in the period from 1935 to 1950, the level of ground subsidence remains unchanged. Then, when groundwater pumping increases and the well height starts to sink again, the ground subsidence follows right along.

Water imports from the Hetch Hetchy and South Bay aqueducts were substantially augmented when the San Felipe Project was completed in 1987 and water from the Central Valley Project was imported via the San Luis Reservoir and the Pacheco Tunnel. In 2004, 100,000 acre-feet were imported through the South Bay Aqueduct, and 152,500 acre-feet by the San Felipe Project. These amounts represent roughly 57% of all water use in Santa Clara County.

The end of the Agricultural Period and the start of the Urban Period have been defined by the necessity of finding new water resources, to support, first, a thriving agricultural area and, second, the needs of an increasing urban population. The groundwater pumping estimates from Poland and Ireland (1988) illustrate the transition from an agricultural economy to an urban one when the water consumed by the two groups are shown separately, as in Fig. 4.11. Agriculture was the dominant user of groundwater through the late 1950s, but near the end of World War II, municipal uses began to increase rapidly. The crossover of the two sectors occurred from 1957 to 1959. By the end of the period shown, municipal uses accounted for 94% of all the groundwater consumed.

The transition from an agricultural to an urban or industrial economy is also illustrated by the changes in agricultural acreage over the same period. In Fig. 4.12, which shows changes in crop acreage by decade, the data through 1930 are from Broek (1932) and county agricultural crop reports are used for the remainder of the years. The figure shows that hay and forage began to decline in 1910 as automobiles and trucks became the dominant forms of transportation. Orchard acreage reached its peak from 1930 to 1940 and then declined as orchards were replaced by housing tracts and light industrial parks. The acreage in vegetables, because of their higher value per acre, continued to increase as orchards declined, but peaked in 1950. As of 2000, vegetables remained the major agricultural crop by acreage. Rangeland, which has not been included in this analysis, has remained fairly constant at about 200,000 acres over the last 40 to 50 years.

As an agricultural economy transitioned to an industrial one, the population continued to increase, as shown in Fig. 4.13. From 1920 to 1970 the rate of increase was about 4.4% per year, the most rapid growth occurring in the 1950s and 1960s. Although the county's population has continued to increase through the end of the twentieth century, it has done so at a decreasing rate.

The transition from agriculture to an industrial and urban mix took place over a fairly long period. The canneries and packing houses in San Jose and Santa Clara, many dating to the 1890s, were an early example of an industrial base within the county, and the canning and fruit packing industry maintained its dominance into the 1960s (Jacobson 1984). At the same time, as farmers moved to crops with a higher value per acre, there was a

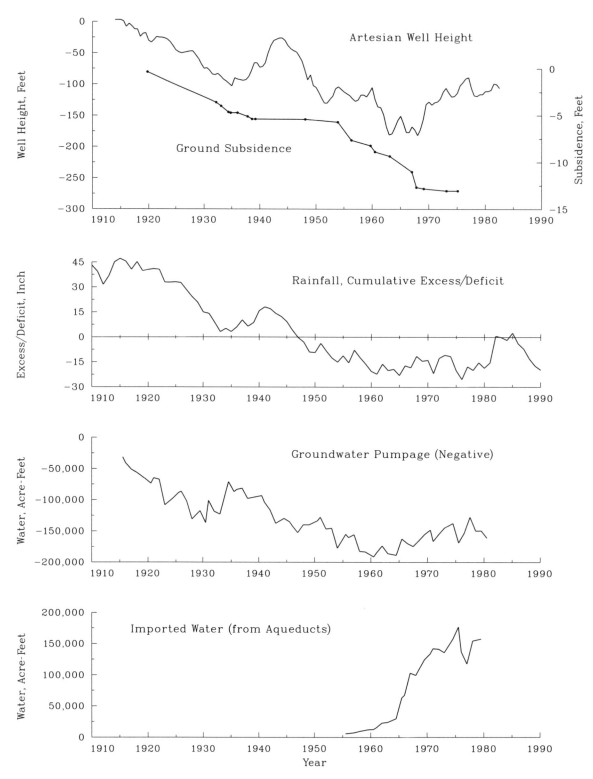

Figure 4.10. Drop in artesian head in response to rainfall, ground-water pumping (negative), and water imports in the northern Santa Clara Valley, 1915 to 1981 (adapted from Poland and Ireland 1988).

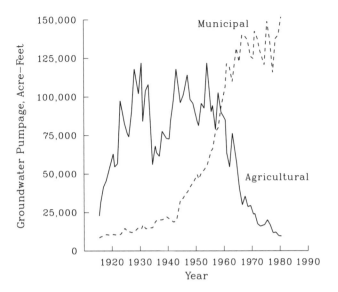

Figure 4.11. Groundwater usage in Santa Clara County by agricultural and municipal sectors, 1915 to 1981 (Poland and Ireland 1988).

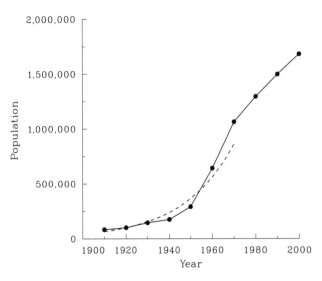

Figure 4.13. Population census data for Santa Clara County, 1910 to 2000. The dashed line shows the exponential fit of population data from 1910 to 1970 (4.4% per year growth).

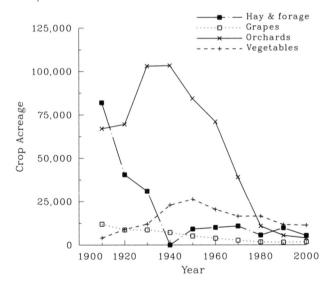

Figure 4.12. Acreage in agricultural products, Santa Clara County, 1910 to 2000 (from Broek 1932; Santa Clara County Agricultural Crop Reports, available at Santa Clara County Division of Agriculture).

decrease in the size of their farms. Broek (1932) examined the distribution of farm size over the period from 1880 to 1930. In 1880, about half the farms were on less than 100 acres, but by 1930 this had increased to 90%. In 1880, the greatest number of farms were between 100 and 500 acres in size, but by 1930, most were between 10 and 19 acres. The demographics of farming also changed during this period, as urban workers purchased small orchard plots that they could work on weekends, or when not at work in seasonal industries. The attractiveness of semirural life led to the development of home sites "in the country." Broek (1932) wrote

More and more this undulating foothill region is being taken for residential settlement. The strip south of the railroad Monte Vista–Los Altos is almost entirely occupied by or destined for home sites. The reason for the increasing populous settlement here is obviously the scenic attractions—grassy knolls, wooded canyons, and beautiful views over the Valley—combined with a very agreeable climate and easy access to urban centers. This foothill district has a distinctive pattern as a landscape unit, its numerous country houses and educational, social and civic institutions, all with well-planned gardens, situated amidst wild oat grazing tracts, vineyards, orchards, and wooded groves. At the foot of this belt, the orchards stretch across the Valley in almost unbroken formation, and above it rises the mountain-country.

Later, in the 1950s, as the pressure for homes and development became stronger, local cities started leapfrog annexation of farmland and orchards, putting pressure on holdout farmers with increased taxes. This pattern of urban versus rural development led directly to the Williamson Act, which provided farmers with some protection from nearby cities (Jacobson 1984).

Palo Alto in 1940, from the U.S.G.S topographical sheet, is shown in Fig. 4.14. Except for San Francisquito Creek, there are almost no similarities to Brown's map of 1840. The city itself has expanded south of Embarcadero Road and enveloped the former town of Mayfield. El Camino Real is still Highway 101, but the new Bay Shore Boulevard has been constructed and will eventually become the present freeway. Extensive dikes have been built out into the marshlands, and the Bay has been driven back before the expanding community. Where the willow thickets were once found, on the flood plain of San Francisquito Creek, an airport has been built. The creek still follows

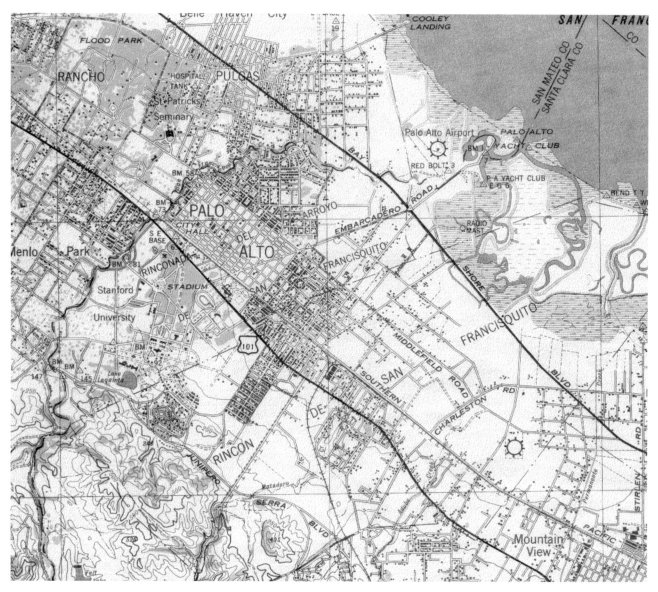

Figure 4.14. The Palo Alto area in 1940 from U.S. Geological Survey 15′ Palo Alto topographic sheet.

its passage out past the yacht harbor in Fig. 4.14, but in a few years it will be diverted to the north and the county lines will be shifted as well. Although this map does not have the level of detail of Brown's 1840 map, the oak forest he showed north of San Francisquito Creek was still intact to some degree. Even future development in Menlo Park and Atherton would allow some of these "stately lords of the forest," as Vancouver (1798) called them, to remain.

Some of the extractive industries of the Agricultural Period were played out by the start of the Urban Period. Logging in the hills above Saratoga, Los Gatos, and Gilroy was largely over by the late 1800s. The Urban Period marked the renewal of second-growth forest in some areas on the east side of the Santa Cruz Mountains, whereas in others the land was given over to oaks, scrub, brush, and new homesites. The era of mercury mining at New Almaden was largely over, although a few individu-

als continued to make a living from residual ore as late as the 1920s.

Mining in the Diablo Range, however, followed a later path. In 1776, when the De Anza party crossed the Diablo Range, they came up Colorado Creek beside Red Mountain and noticed there "strips and pieces of very white gravel," which reminded Father Font of "the mines of Guanajuato" (Bolton 1930c). The white strips Font noted were outcrops of magnesite. In December 1900, at the end of the Agricultural Period, James Merchant, a longtime resident of Livermore, staked claims to the magnesite veins in Red Mountain (Cutler 2001). The wagon road from San Antonio Valley to Livermore, which followed Crane Ridge, was not suitable for the transport of ore, and a new road (Mines Road) was constructed in 1904. The market for magnesite, either for the manufacture of refractory bricks or oxychloride cement, was rarely favorable in the first decades of the twentieth century, largely because of transportation costs. There was a boom during World War I, followed by a crash afterwards, and significant mining did not get underway until a new tariff was enacted that raised the costs of Austrian and Greek magnesite. Following the tariff, 20,000 to 40,000 tons of magnesite were mined each year, calcined on site, and hauled to Livermore until the mines were exhausted in the 1940s (Cutler 2001).

Along the Bay, older deposits of oyster shells were dredged for the making of cement at Redwood City, from 1924 to 1971 (Smith 1925; Tim F. Orazem, pers. comm.). The Kaiser Permanente Quarry (now the Hanson Quarry), on the edge of Cupertino, began the manufacture of cement in 1939 and continues to this day. As useful as a cement quarry is in an urban area, its presence remains an irritant to the local community.

The one area of Santa Clara County largely untouched by commerce at the start of the Urban Period was the salt marsh that extended from Alviso to Mountain View. At the edge of the marshes, farmers had built dikes and used the wet fields for grazing. But as agricultural pumping lowered the water table and as rainfall decreased, during the 1920s, these lands became saltier and eventually useless for pasturage (Broek 1932). The sloughs that had been used by schooners and steamers 50 years earlier were silting up. Yet some visionaries foresaw a deepwater port for San Jose near the confluence of the Guadalupe and Alviso sloughs. Dredging would be used to open the South Bay and reclaim the salt marshes. Broek (1932) supported these new plans, writing, "At present the Bay forms a swampy back wash, not a door to the world's commerce." These grandiose plans never went forward. Rather, salt evaporation ponds replaced the salt marshes.

Prior to the Urban Period, most salt production had taken place in Alameda and San Mateo counties (Ver Planck 1958), but in the 1930s, new salt ponds were created in the former salt marshes from Alviso to Mountain View, and by the 1960s, the original marsh was nearly entirely eliminated. The consolidation in the saltmaking industry that had been underway since the turn of the century continued, and by 1936 all the South Bay production was under the ownership of the Leslie Salt Company.

South Bay Habitats. The changes to the San Francisco estuary that had begun during the Agricultural Period (Cohen and Carlton 1998) continued during the Urban Period. Figure 4.15 shows the continuing increase in alien or exotic species from 1910 to 1995 (see Fig. 4.8 above for the period from 1850 to 1910). The data for this period show an exponential increase in the number of foreign organisms, with a growth rate of 1.9% per year, using Cohen and Carlton's modified data.

By the end of the Agricultural Period, many sloughs in the South Bay that had been used for landings had silted up, as sediments were transported and deposited. Broek (1932) wrote, "Where once ships came to the landings [embarcaderos] one finds but shallow, mud-filled channels; the harbor of Alviso, once the main port of the Valley, now only serves as a yachting harbor and for this it is hardly deep enough." Eventually, it became too costly to maintain even the yacht harbor and today it is the Alviso Marina County Park. A boardwalk crosses the old harbor, now filled with bulrushes, Marsh Wrens, Song Sparrows, and (in the winter) Virginia Rails and Soras.

Along with the increasing number of foreign organisms

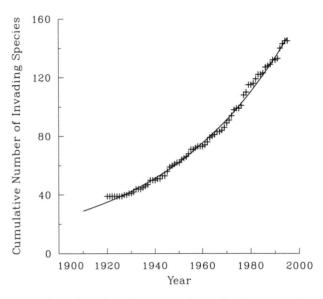

Figure 4.15. Invasion of exotic species in San Francisco Bay, 1910 to 1995 (from Cohen and Carlton 1998).

in the estuary, and of sedimentation in the sloughs, came two other changes that affected the South Bay. First, the increase in the amount of groundwater pumping resulted in land subsidence at the edge of the Bay in the northern reaches of Santa Clara County and, second, the conversion of salt marshes to salt evaporator ponds significantly influenced the avian species living beside the Bay.

The effect of groundwater pumping in northern Santa Clara Valley was to remove water from interstices in beds of gravel far below the surface of the ground, which allowed the beds to compact, causing subsidence (Poland and Ireland 1988). Figure 4.16 shows subsidence contours for the northern Santa Clara Valley over the period 1934 to 1967. The greatest subsidence for this time period, in excess of 8 feet, occurred near the center of the valley beneath the cities of Santa Clara and San Jose. To the south, the subsidence in the alluvial soils was prevented by the outcropping where the county communications center is presently located. The subsidence was greater than 6 feet at Alviso, lessening north of Alviso and on nearby flatlands in Alameda County. The effect of this irreversible subsidence is readily visible at Alviso, where one can stand on the levee beside the Guadalupe River and see the buildings of the town beneath river level.

Originally, the salt marshes in the South Bay transitioned to upland vegetation of native grasses and forbs that could tolerate the wet and sometimes salty soils. These areas of transition were important as refugia for salt marsh resident species during winter and summer high tides. With the construction of levees for pasture along the Bay edge, these refugia were degraded. Because of the land subsidence it was necessary to construct new levees for flood protection, and the entire transition zone was lost. The loss of the high-tide refugia in the salt marsh transition to uplands resulted in excessive predation of many of the salt marsh residents, such as Black and Clapper rails and salt marsh harvest mice, during high tides.

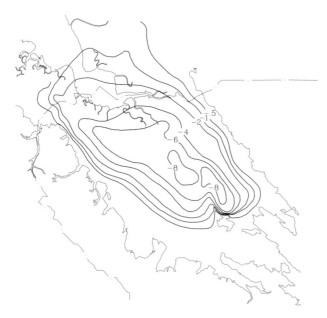

Figure 4.16. Subsidence contours (in feet) in northern Santa Clara Valley, 1934 to 1967 (Poland and Ireland 1988).

The second major change in the Urban Period was the conversion of the South Bay salt marshes to salt evaporator ponds. In the East Bay, construction of these ponds started in the 1850s, and by the start of the urban period there were salt ponds in the East Bay from San Leandro Creek to Alvarado (Ver Planck 1958). In San Mateo County, salt evaporator ponds were developed at the beginning of the twentieth century, in an area from south of San Mateo to Redwood City. Salt works were established in Santa Clara County in the 1930s, when evaporator ponds were built from Mountain View to Alviso.

The immediate effect of the South Bay salt ponds built in the 1930s and 1940s was the elimination of the salt marsh habitat used by Clapper Rails and salt marsh harvest mice, and the decline of these species has continued. Other species, however, including Snowy Plover, American Avocet, and Caspian and Forster's terns, were attracted by these new habitats. Snowy Plovers were first noted breeding at the Alvarado salt works by L. R. Reynolds in 1914 (Grinnell et al. 1918). It was noted that they foraged along the salt pond edges in preference to nearby mud flats in the salt marshes. Chase Littlejohn found a nest with one egg on a pond levee in the Redwood City salt works on 15 Mar 1919 (WFVZ #38544). The first evidence of American Avocets nesting in the Bay area was a downy young collected at Alvarado by Ralph E. Ellis, Jr. on 11 May 1926 (MVZ #145184). Dudley S. De Groot found Caspian Terns nesting on salt ponds near the east end of the Dumbarton Bridge in 1922, although this colony may have formed as early as 1916 (De Groot 1931, Grinnell and Miller 1944). Milton L. Seibert found Forster's Terns nesting near the east end of the San Mateo Bridge in 1948 (*Audubon Field Notes 2*:187 1948). In this respect, salt ponds benefited some species, either as a nest substrate or for foraging, just as they eliminated breeding habitat for others.

Santa Clara Valley Habitats. Most of the major landscape changes in Santa Clara Valley had been made by the close of the Agricultural Period. The oak savanna and woodlands that extended north from San Martin, which the Spanish had called the *Llano des Robles* (Plain of Oaks), were cut in the 1850s and sold for firewood, and the land was then planted in wheat. The chaparral fields on the west side of the valley were cleared after completion of the San Francisco–San Jose railroad, which engendered a market for fuel wood in San Francisco. Many of the streams that drained the Santa Cruz Mountains and the Diablo Range had originally ended in the alluvial fans or freshwater swamps on the valley floor, but by the 1920s almost all of these swamps had been drained and ditches extending to the edge of the Bay had been constructed.

The larger streams on the Santa Clara Valley floor, such as the Guadalupe River and Coyote Creek, were largely unaffected by these landscape changes. These streams followed a seasonal pattern of winter floods with minor scouring, and the rivers dried out in many areas during the summer drought. During the rainy season, when a storm moved across the Santa Clara Valley, farmers in the lower section of Coyote Creek checked the amount of rainfall, for if it was much over an inch, the creek would come over its banks a day later. In some reaches of the valley streams, the creeks in flood would spread out over rough cobbles, and the riverbed vegetation would come to be dominated by species that flourished following periods of scouring and flood. Pickwell and Smith (1938) described a section of Coyote Creek, where the Parkway Lakes are today, that at that time was made of gravelly overflow channels where Lesser Nighthawks nested. These channels included sparse vegetation, plants like mule-fat, Oregon false goldenaster, Douglas groundsel, blazing star, California brickellbush, and wild mustard. Once the new dams (the Coyote Dam in 1936 and the Anderson Dam in 1948) were built, the Coyote Creek was tamed and the scoured channels were either buried beneath minor percolation ponds or covered by new vegetation that replaced those plants adapted to periodic flooding. Figure 4.17 shows measurements from a streamflow gauge on Coyote Creek between Anderson Dam and Highway 101 for the periods before and after dam construction. Prior to dam construction, the summer flow rate, from June through November, was close to zero. During the rainy months, flow rates increased to over 250 ft^3/sec. Following dam construction, flow rates have been evened out, with flow rates now between 40 and 120 ft^3/sec. These changes have largely eliminated plant communities historically associated with flooding, and have increased riparian communities that require summer water to flourish (Grossinger et al. 2006).

Historically, during periods of winter flood and high water, steelhead moved up the valley creeks to spawn (Snyder 1934), but the new dams rendered these streams no longer suitable for steelhead. The construction of dams and the rapid urbanization on the valley floor changed the character of the urban streams. Figure 4.18 shows that fish assemblages in the major drainage basins remained largely intact into the 1940s (Leidy 1984). Then progressively more exotic fishes were introduced and became established in these basins. For the most part, the replacement of native fish occurred in lower- and middle-elevation stream sections, which were subject to the greatest disturbance. Native fish assemblages remained unchanged in undisturbed intermediate and headwater stream sections (Leidy 1984).

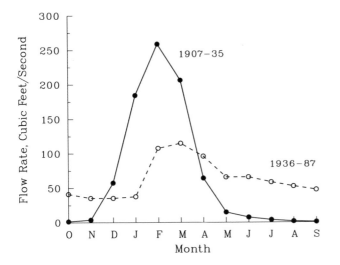

Figure 4.17. Comparison of flow rates in Coyote Creek before and after dam construction. Flow gauge 1.2 mi. downstream of Anderson Dam (Grossinger et al. 2006).

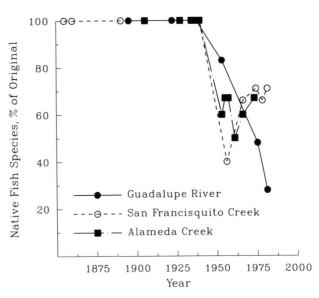

Figure 4.18. Reduction of native fish species in Santa Clara County drainage basins (Leidy 1984).

The continuing development of orchards in the Santa Clara Valley in the Urban Period probably had mixed effects on the local birds. Some appear to have benefited, at least in the short term. Chestnut-backed Chickadees, which were largely absent from the Diablo Range in presettlement times, likely used the orchards and new urban trees to move across the valley and expand into the Diablo Range as well (Dixon 1954). Data from egg collections suggest that Chipping and Lark sparrows both favored local orchards as nest sites, but as housing tracts and light industry replaced orchards these two sparrows disappeared from the valley floor.

The 1950s were marked by rapid growth in new housing and light industry. Prior to this period, outdoor watering was largely limited to irrigation for gardens, orchards, and agricultural fields. Outdoor landscaping that required extensive summer watering became the norm in new municipal buildings, schools, light industry, and homes. Rantz (1972) has estimated that 75% of the water supplied within municipal areas was used for outside watering, whereas about 50% of water for home use went to outside watering. As discussed in Chapter 1, our Mediterranean climate yields a deficit of water in the summer. The impact of outdoor watering is to increase substantially the biomass that is produced during the summer period, when there are high temperatures and ample sun. This also increases insects and other invertebrates dependent upon the additional vegetative growth. The increased plant biomass and invertebrate numbers produced by this pattern have likely benefited many avian species that had always lived on the valley floor and have adapted well to the new watering regime. Urban watering has also benefited a number of species, such as the American Robin and Northern Mockingbird, which were not present here as breeding species in presettlement times.

Urbanization and light industry may have benefited a number of species by providing water during the normal summer drought period, but a downside for the environment from increasing development has been the contamination of streams and groundwater from pollution. Some of this has been at small

scale, that is individuals have dumped normal household supplies, used oil, and other contaminants on the ground or in storm drains that flow to the Bay. In more rural areas, similar contamination has occurred as residents use their local stream as a landfill, expecting the winter storms to transport the debris downstream, just as the owners of the New Almaden mines disposed of their mine residues in Los Alamitos and Guadalupe creeks.

But the contamination problem in this valley from the new industries associated with electronics and chip manufacture has been far more severe (Byster and Smith 2006). Groundwater contamination was discovered at the IBM and Fairchild plants in the early 1980s from the improper handling of toxic chemicals and leaking underground storage. This problem was not limited to just a few sites, but was widespread. Eventually, the U.S. Environmental Protection Agency identified 29 sites in the Santa Clara Valley that qualified as "Superfund" sites, the greatest concentration in the country (Byster and Smith 2006). A great deal has been learned in the last few decades about these contaminants, and special programs to treat these hazardous wastes have been put in place. Nonetheless, contaminants remain in our environment and we will have to deal with these poisons for generations.

The Santa Cruz Mountains Habitats. Logging in the Santa Cruz Mountains has continued to the present, but only on the western side of the mountains, in Santa Cruz and San Mateo counties. Some second-growth forests on the eastern side of the range may be logged in the future, but much of the forested lands have been purchased with public funds and are expected to remain in public hands for the foreseeable future. Santa Clara County obtained its first park lands in 1924, when 400 acres near Cupertino were purchased and are now part of Stevens Creek County Park. Establishment of the county's Parks and Recreation Department, in 1956, led to further acquisitions in the 1960s and 1970s, often in cooperation with the Santa Clara Valley Water District. Figure 4.19 shows the increase in acreage

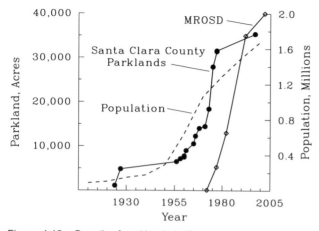

Figure 4.19. Growth of parklands in Santa Clara County during the Urban Period, compared with population growth. Santa Clara County park data obtained from park brochures; Midpeninsula Regional Open Space District (MROSD) data taken from news releases.

in the county parklands during the Urban Period and compares this increase with the corresponding increase in population. In 1972, the Midpeninsula Regional Open Space District, originally formed in northwestern Santa Clara County, initiated land purchases both in the Santa Cruz Mountains and along the Bay. In 1976, the district expanded to include parts of southern San Mateo County, and today the district includes lands west of the Santa Cruz Mountains crest.

Homesites have been developed in the Santa Cruz Mountains throughout the Urban Period, but because of the steepness of the terrain, housing there has generally been of low density. The logging roads of the Agricultural Period were mostly paved during the Urban Period, but except for Highway 17, which crosses the range from Los Gatos to Santa Cruz, these roads tend to be narrow and winding. Many of the high-gradient streams that drain the Santa Cruz Mountains on the east side still appear healthy, and a number of these streams still support nesting American Dippers, as they did a century ago.

The Diablo Range Habitats. Throughout the Agricultur-

al Period, the raising of cattle was the only significant economic activity in the Diablo Range. Ranching as a way of life has continued through the Urban Period, but it is often difficult now to make a suitable living. A number of ranches within the Diablo Range are now owned by people whose wealth has come from other endeavors, and they continue to operate these ranches not so much to produce income, but to maintain a way of life that they find attractive.

In the Diablo Range, the creation of public parklands has taken place in the Urban Period, just as it has in the Santa Cruz Mountains. In 1953, Sada Coe Robinson, the daughter of the pioneer rancher Henry W. Coe, Jr., donated the Coe Ranch properties to Santa Clara County. Five years later, these lands were transferred to the state, and became Henry Coe State Park. Since 1958, the state has acquired adjacent lands, and the park is now the second largest in California, after Anza-Borrego Desert State Park in San Diego County. Other parklands have also been obtained in the Diablo Range in recent years, notably the Joseph Grant ranch lands, which were made a county park in 1975. In 1993, the Santa Clara County Open Space Authority was formed to purchase additional parklands, both in the Santa Cruz Mountains (areas not covered by the Midpeninsula Regional Open Space District) and in the Diablo Range.

This chapter opened by discussing how the environment in Santa Clara County underwent a transition from natural ecosystems to frontier clearing and small-scale farming. Farming became more intensive in the 1850s, and areas of rural settlement grew into great urban expanses. The county is now largely urban, as industry has replaced agriculture. At the same time, during this last phase, society has purchased lands for protection and recreation. These societal transitions in land use have been seen throughout the world (Foley et al. 2005), and have generally been accompanied by environmental degradation in the earlier stages. As societal wealth has increased, there have been attempts to reverse some of the environmental damage of the past. The notion that portions of these increases in per capita income will be directed toward environmental restoration, sometimes referred to as the environmental Kuznets curve, is still actively debated by economists (Barbier 1997). Only time will tell.

5 Atlas Organization and Methods

During their 1985 annual meeting in Sacramento, the Western Field Ornithologists held a seminar on breeding bird atlases. At that time, atlas fieldwork had already been completed in Marin County, and a number of atlas efforts had been undertaken in other California counties, including Orange, Riverside, San Bernardino, and Sonoma. The presentations at the meeting recounted the history and goals of atlasing, offered recommendations for the conduct of an atlas, and noted useful sources of information.

In the United States, atlasing began in the East, and the first published state atlas was that for Vermont, in 1985 (Laughlin and Kibbe 1985). Regional meetings sponsored by the North American Ornithological Atlas Committee (NORAC) were held in the northeastern United States in 1981 and 1986, and the first national meeting was held in San Francisco in 1989. These meetings encouraged information exchange between ongoing atlas projects, which eventually resulted in uniform NORAC protocols.

Founding of the Santa Clara County Breeding Bird Atlas

In early 1987, the writer prepared a detailed plan for a breeding bird atlas for Santa Clara County and distributed the plan to active birders within the county. A meeting of interested participants in the spring resulted in the formation of the Atlas Committee, which has carried out the work of preparing the atlas. Because the 1987 breeding season was already underway, it was decided that 1987 would be treated as a "pilot" year, and members of the committee would select a limited number of county blocks to atlas. Then, drawing on the experience of the pilot year, we would begin a full program of atlasing in 1988 and continue that effort through 1992.

The Atlas Committee organized the atlas project as an independent affiliate of the nonprofit Coyote Creek Riparian Station (CCRS). Affiliation with the riparian station afforded us a number of benefits, including tax-exempt status for fund raising, some limited insurance for field observers, and the basic support of a science-based organization. Atlas finances were kept separate from those of CCRS.

Initial expenses for the atlas included the printing of forms used by atlasers for their fieldwork and the purchase of topographic maps that could be cut up to create individual maps of the 5-km atlas blocks. For the first few years of the atlas, a newsletter was sent to all participants, but this was eventually discontinued because of the time and expense it required. Atlas costs were covered largely by $5 annual dues and by donations.

Atlas Organization and Conduct

The atlas effort was initially defined as a six-year period, from 1987 to 1992, although only limited fieldwork was performed in the 1987 pilot year. At the end of the 1992 year, however, we decided to extend the atlas by one year to include the 1993 field season. The primary reason for the extension was that by 1992, atlasers had obtained access to private lands in the northern Diablo Range, but the coverage in that vast, uneven terrain was still considered incomplete. Coincidentally, limited access was also gained in the southern Diablo Range in a few blocks. Further work in both areas offered promise of significant rewards. Including the pilot year and the one-year (later) extension, the atlas period covered the seven years from 1987 to 1993.

We selected the Universal Transverse Mercator (UTM) grid as a reference for atlas records. This UTM grid was based on the 1927 North American datum (NAD). Since Santa Clara County lies completely within zone 10 of the UTM grid, we knew we would not be confronted with partial blocks near zonal boundaries.

The block size we selected, 5 kilometers square, resulted in 168 blocks completely covering the county. A map of the county overlaid with the UTM grid is shown in Fig. 5.1. We designated blocks by the coordinates of their southwest corner, the "easting" coordinate given first and the "northing" second. Under this definition, the block at the upper left corner of Fig. 5.1 initially was referred to as 570 east, 4145 north, because the blue tick marks on the edges of the U.S. Geological Survey topographic maps designate this block as $^{5}70$ east and $^{41}45$ north. But because the grid for Santa Clara County is less than 100 blocks from west to east and less than 100 blocks from south to north, we dropped the prefix numbers from the block designa-

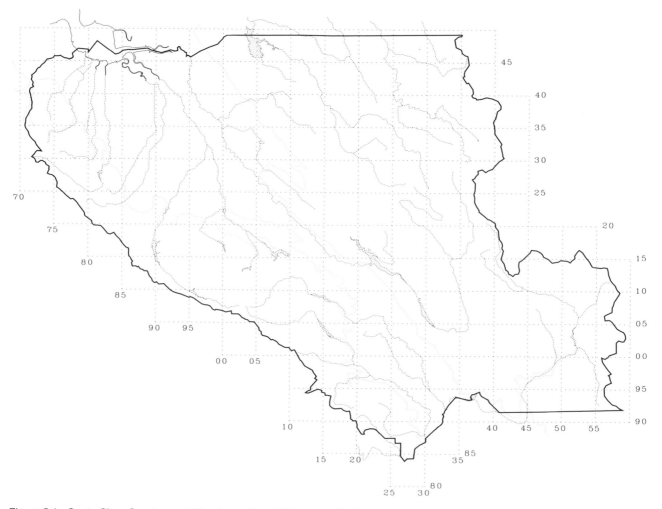

Figure 5.1. Santa Clara County overlaid with the 5-km UTM atlas grid. Darker dotted lines indicate watercourses; lighter dotted lines show the alluvial soil boundary of the Santa Clara Valley.

tions. Thus, the block at the upper left of the figure became simply Block 7045. Using these definitions, the block immediately east of Block 9545 is Block 0045, not 10045. Similarly, the block north of Block 1095 is Block 1000.

The blocks on the county's borders, referred to as edge blocks, were covered in their entirety, even when a significant fraction of a block was in an adjacent county. Data records for edge blocks from adjacent atlases in Santa Cruz County (1987–93), San Mateo County (1991–97), and Alameda County (1993–97) are included in the atlas database for those years that coincided with the Santa Clara County atlas period. Coverage across these edge blocks was fairly uniform, but for edge blocks in which no atlasing was ongoing in the adjacent county, there was a tendency for atlasers to focus on the lands within Santa Clara County. When edge blocks were mostly within Santa Clara County, the coverage tended to be quite good. But when edge blocks lay mostly in an adjacent county, the coverage was sometimes less complete.

Maps for individual blocks were prepared by cutting up a set of 7.5′ topographic maps that covered the entire county. Many such maps could be cut from the topographic sheets as

single 5-km blocks, but in other cases a block map required either two segments from adjacent sheets or, in a few cases, four segments from adjacent sheets. An acetate overlay at the same scale as the atlas block map, provided to each atlaser, could be used to locate the UTM coordinates of confirmation records.

The protocols we used for the atlas were those developed by NORAC, but by drawing on the experiences of other atlas projects, we could include additional protocols for the Santa Clara County atlas. In particular: (1) atlasers added the dates of breeding evidence to the field card to enhance later development of phenology data, (2) a record of field hours was included as a means of tracking the level of effort, (3) abundance codes were added to the field cards (see below), but their use was considered optional, (4) coordinates of confirmations or other significant records, accurate to 50 m, were added as an option, and (5) we encouraged atlasers to provide data on additional confirmations, rather than limiting themselves to a single confirmation per species per block (see the Block Supplementary List, below).

Two forms were of primary use by atlasers covering a block. The first, the Field Card, was the primary source of breeding records for the block. The Field Card was augmented

B1040.92A

SPECIES	O	PO	PR	CO	A
LEsser GOldfinch		i	2 P	i	
LAwrence's GOldfinch		i		i	
AMerican GOldfinch		i	i	i	
HOuse SParrow		i	i	i	
		i	i	i	
	O	24	13	14	
		i	Σ = 51	i	
		i	i	i	
		i	i	i	
		i	i	i	
		i	i	i	

* Verification Report Form is required. Contact your Regional Coordinator or the Project Coordinator as soon as possible.

BREEDING CRITERIA CODES

Observed (O)

O Species (male or female) **observed** in a block during its breeding season, but no evidence of breeding. Not in suitable nesting habitat. Includes wide ranging species such as vultures or raptors, or colonial nesting species not at the nesting colony.

Possible (PO)

√ Species (male or female) observed in suitable nesting habitat during its breeding season.

X Singing male present in suitable nesting habitat during its breeding season.

Probable (PR)

P **Pair** observed in suitable habitat during its breeding season.

S Permanent territory presumed through **song** at same location on at least two occasions 7 days or more apart.

T Permanent territory presumed through defense of **territory** (chasing individuals of same species).

C **Courtship** behavior or copulation.

N **Visiting** probable **nest-site**.

A **Agitated** behavior or anxiety calls from adult.

B **Nest building** by wrens or excavation of holes by woodpeckers.

B1040.92A

Confirmed (CO)

CN **Carrying nesting** material, such as sticks or other material. Please submit full details including location within the block of the observation.

NB **Nest building** at the actual nest-site.

PE **Physiological evidence** of breeding (i.e. highly vascularised, edematous incubation [brood] patch or egg in oviduct based on bird in hand. To be used by experienced bird banders on local birds during the nesting season).

DD **Distraction display** or injury feigning.

UN **Used nest** or eggshells found. Caution: These must be carefully identified, if they are to be accepted.

PY **Precocial young**. Flightless young of precocial species restricted to the natal area by dependence on adults or limited mobility.

FL **Recently fledged young** (either precocial or altricial) incapable of sustained flight, restricted to natal area by dependence on adults or limited mobility.

ON **Occupied nest**: adults entering or leaving a nest site in circumstances indicating occupied nest. To be used for nests which are too high (i.e. the tops of trees) or enclosed (i.e. chimneys) for the contents to be seen.

CF **Carrying food**: adult carrying food for the young.

FY **Adult feeding** recently **fledged young**.

FS **Adult carrying fecal sac.**

NE **Nest** with **egg(s)**[1].

NY **Nest** with **young** seen or heard[1].

[1] Presence of cowbird eggs or young is confirmation of both cowbird and host species.

Abundance Codes:

1: 1 pair estimated in block.
2: 2-10 pairs estimated in block.
3: 11-100 pairs estimated in block.
4: 101-1,000 pairs estimated in block.
5: 1,001-10,000 pairs estimated in block.

Return the Field Card no later than 1 September.

Santa Clara County Breeding Bird Atlas Field Card

Block Name _Poverty Ridge_ Block Code _1040_
Name _Michael Rogers (also LYR)_ Year _1992_

Trip	Date	Hours	Cum. Hrs.	Cum. Species
1	5/3/92	2.50	2.50	
2	6/19/92	1.25	3.75	
3	7/6/92	3.00	6.75	
4	7/19/92	4.75	11.50	(LYR)
5				
6				
7				
8				
9				
10				
11				
12				

SPECIES	O	PO	PR	CO	A
Pied-Billed GRebe		i	i	i	
EAred GRebe*		i	i	i	
Double-Crested COrmorant*		i	i	i	
AMerican BIttern*		i	i	i	
Great Blue HEron		i	i	i	
GReat EGret		i	i	i	
SNowy EGret		i	i	i	
Little Blue HEron*		i	i	i	
CAttle EGret*		i	i	i	
GReen-backed HEron		i	i	i	
Black-crowned Night HEron		i	i	i	
CAnada GOose		i	i	i	
WOod DUck	4 CH		i		
Green-Winged TEal*		i	i	i	
MALLard	4 CH		i		
northern PINTail		i	i	i	
Blue-Winged TEal*		i	i	i	
CInnamon TEal		i	i	i	
northern SHOVeler		i	i	i	
GADWall		i	i	i	
REDHead*		i	i	i	
LEsser SCaup*		i	i	i	
COmmon MErganser*	4 CH		i		
RUddy DUck		i	i	i	
TUrkey VUlture	3 CH		i	i	
Black-Shouldered KIte		i	i	i	
NOrthern HArrier		i	i	i	
Sharp-Shinned HAwk*		i	i	i	

Figure 5.2a. The Field Card (front side).

by the Block Supplementary List, which provides space for additional breeding records. An additional form, the List Verification Form (not illustrated), was used to document rare species. These block forms were augmented by the Casual Observation Form, which could be used for any block, whether for observations in an atlaser's neighborhood or during casual birding.

We had the Field Card printed on thick paper stock, so that it would hold up under normal field conditions. Information was printed on both sides of 8.5 × 11-inch stock and the card was then folded in three sections so that it would fit in a shirt pocket. Examples of the front and back sides of the Field Card are shown in Figs. 5.2a and 5.2b. On the righthand portion of the front of the Field Card, the atlaser would write the block name, the block number, the atlaser's name, and the year. Below this information is a set of rows where the atlaser recorded the date of each trip along with the hours spent in the field. Columns are also included for cumulative hours and cumulative breeding species evidence, to give the atlaser a gauge of progress in the block. Following the block and trip information is the species list. For each species, there is a column for Observed, double columns for Possible, Probable, and Confirmed evidence, and a column for an abundance code (optional). Definitions of these codes are shown on the front side of the Field Card. For each species for which PO, PR, or CO evidence was obtained, the atlaser would enter the trip number in the first part of the double column and the breeding code in the second part. The reverse side of the Field Card lists most of the other species on the list. Four capital letters were used for each species name, as shown on the Field Card. These four letters are the code used for the atlas database. In most cases, these are the four-letter codes already in use by bird banders at the time the atlas work began, although a few were different (see for example, DIPP, MOCK, and STAR). An asterisk following a species name meant that a record for that species required a List Verification Form. (In the sample in Figs. 5.2a and 5.2b, the atlaser used the database notation CH instead of a √.)

The Block Supplementary List shown in Fig. 5.3 had two purposes. First, the list could be used to provide coordinates and elevations for breeding records (optional). Second, since the Field Card allowed only one entry of confirmed evidence for a species in a block, subsequent breeding records for that block could be entered on the Block Supplementary List (also

SPECIES	O	PO	PR	CO	A
COoper's HAwk		ı	ı	1 CF	2
Red-Shouldered HAwk	ı	ı	ı		
Red-Tailed HAwk	1 CH	ı	ı		
GOlden EAgle	4 CH	ı	ı		
AMerican KEstrel	ı	ı	ı		
PEregrine FAlcon*	ı	ı	ı		
PRairie FAlcon	ı	ı	ı		
Ring-Necked PHeasant	ı	ı	ı		
WIld TUrkey	ı	ı	ı		
CAlifornia QUail	ı	ı	4 PY		
MOuntain QUail*	ı	ı	ı		
CLapper RAil	ı	ı	ı		
VIrginia RAil	ı	ı	ı		
SORA	ı	ı	ı		
COmmon MOorhen	ı	ı	ı		
AMerican COot	ı	ı	ı		
SNowy PLover	ı	ı	ı		
KILLdeer	ı	ı	ı		
Black-Necked STilt	ı	ı	ı		
AMerican AVocet	ı	ı	ı		
SPotted SAndpiper*	ı	ı	ı		
CAlifornia GUll	ı	ı	ı		
WEstern GUll*	ı	ı	ı		
CAspian TErn*	ı	ı	ı		
FOrster's TErn	ı	ı	ı		
LEast TErn*	ı	ı	ı		
ROck DOve	ı	ı	ı		
Band-Tailed PIgeon	ı	ı	ı		
MOurning DOve	2 CH	ı	ı		
greater ROADrunner	ı	ı	ı		
common BArn-OWl	ı	ı	ı		
WEstern screech-OWl	4 CH	ı	ı		3
Great Horned OWl	3 CH	ı	ı		2
northern PYgmy-OWl	ı	ı	ı		
BUrrowing OWl	ı	ı	ı		
Long-Eared OWl*	ı	ı	ı		
Short-Eared OWl*	ı	ı	ı		
northern Saw-Whet OWl*	ı	ı	ı		
LEsser NIghthawk*	ı	ı	ı		
common POORwill	ı	ı	ı		
VAux's SWift*	ı	ı	ı		
White-Throated SWift	ı	ı	ı		
Black-Chin. HUmmingbird*	ı	ı	ı		
ANna's HUmmingbird	2 X	ı	ı		
ALlen's HUmmingbird	ı	ı	ı		
BElted KIngfisher		ı	4 P	ı	2

SPECIES	O	PO	PR	CO	A
LEwis's WOodpecker	ı	ı	ı		
ACorn WOodpecker	ı	ı	ı	2 FL	
NUttall's WOodpecker	2 CH	ı	ı		
DOwny WOodpecker	3 CH	ı	ı	ı	2
HAiry WOodpecker	ı	ı	ı	3 FL	
NOrthern FLicker	2 CH	ı	ı		
PIleated WOodpecker*	ı	ı	ı		
Olive-Sided FLycatcher	ı	ı	ı		
Western Wood-PEwee	ı	ı	3 S	ı	
WIllow FLycatcher*	ı	ı	ı		
WEstern FLycatcher	ı	ı	ı		
BLack PHoebe	ı	ı	ı	4 FL	
SAy's PHoebe	ı	ı	ı		
Ash-Throated FLycatcher	3 CH	ı	ı		
WEstern KIngbird	ı	ı	ı		
HOrned Lark	ı	ı	ı		
PUrple MArtin*	ı	ı	ı		
TRee SWallow	ı	ı	ı		
Violet-Green SWallow	ı	3 P	ı	ı	
nor. Rough-Winged SWallow	ı	ı	ı		
BanK SWallow*	ı	ı	ı		
CLiff SWallow	ı	ı	ı		
BArn SWallow	ı	ı	ı		
STeller's JAy	ı	ı	ı	3 FL	
SCrub JAy	ı	ı	ı	2 FL	
Yellow-Billed MAgpie	ı	ı	ı		
AMerican CRow	ı	ı	ı	2 FL	
COmmon RAven	ı	ı	ı		
Chestnut-Backed CHickadee	4 CH	ı	ı		
PLain TItmouse	2 CH	ı	ı		
BUSHtit	ı	ı	ı	3 FL	2
Red-Breasted NUthatch	ı	ı	ı		
White-Breasted NUthatch	ı	ı	ı	1 CF	
PYgmy NUthatch	ı	ı	ı		
BRown CReeper	1 X	ı	ı		
ROck WRen	ı	ı	ı		
CaNyon WRen	ı	ı	ı	4 FL	2
BEwick's WRen	ı	ı	3 A	ı	3
HOuse WRen	ı	ı	2 A	ı	
Winter WRen	ı	ı	ı		
MArsh WRen	ı	ı	ı		
american DIPPer	4 CH	ı	ı	ı	2
Golden-Crowned KInglet*	ı	ı	ı		
Blue-Gray GNatcatcher	3 CH	ı	ı	ı	1
WEstern BLuebird	ı	ı	ı	2 FL	
SWainson's THrush	ı	ı	ı		

SPECIES	O	PO	PR	CO	A
HErmit THrush*	ı	ı	ı		
AMerican RObin	4 CH	ı	ı		
WRENtit	ı	ı	3 S	ı	3
northern MOCKingbird	ı	ı	ı		
CAlifornia THrasher	ı	ı	3 A	ı	2
PHAInopepla	ı	ı	ı		
LOggerhead SHrike	ı	ı	ı		
european STARling	1 CH	ı	ı		
BEll's VIreo*	ı	ı	ı		
SOlitary VIreo	ı	ı	3 S	ı	
HUtton's VIreo	ı	ı	ı		
WArbling VIreo	2 X	ı	ı		
Orange-Crowned WArbler	ı	ı	1 P	ı	
YEllow WArbler	ı	ı	ı		
Yellow-Rumped WArbler	ı	ı	ı		
Black-thr. GraY WArbler	2 X	ı	ı	ı	1
HErmit WArbler*	ı	ı	ı		
MacGillivray's WArbler*	ı	ı	ı		
COmmon YEllowthroat	ı	ı	ı		
WIlson's WArbler	ı	ı	ı		
Yellow-Breasted CHat*	ı	ı	ı		
WEstern TAnager	ı	2 P	ı	ı	2
Black-Headed GRosbeak	ı	ı	2 FL	ı	
LAzuli BUnting	1 X	ı	ı	ı	2
Rufous-Sided TOwhee	ı	ı	ı	2 FL	
BRown TOwhee	ı	2 P	ı	ı	
Rufous-Crowned SParrow	ı	ı	ı		
CHipping SParrow	ı	ı	ı		
Black-Chinned SParrow	ı	ı	ı		
LArk SParrow	ı	ı	ı		
SaGe SParrow	ı	ı	ı		
SAvannah SParrow	ı	ı	ı		
GRasshopper SParrow	ı	ı	ı		
SOng SParrow	ı	ı	ı		
Dark-Eyed JUnco	ı	3 S	ı	ı	
Red-Winged BLackbird	ı	ı	ı		
TRicolored BLackbird	ı	ı	ı		
WEstern MEadowlark	ı	ı	ı		
Yellow-Headed BLackbird*	ı	ı	ı		
BRewer's BLackbird	ı	ı	ı		
Brown-Headed COwbird	ı	ı	ı		
HOoded ORiole	ı	ı	ı		
NOrthern ORiole	ı	ı	ı		
PUrple FInch	ı	ı	ı		
HOuse FInch	ı	ı	ı		
PIne SIskin	ı	ı	ı		

Figure 5.2b. The Field Card (reverse side).

optional). Active atlasers also used this form to record breeding observations in lieu of the Casual Observation Form.

The Casual Observation Form, shown in Fig. 5.4 was designed to allow an observer to record observed breeding evidence on a casual basis, that is, in a block not being surveyed by that observer. This form was particularly useful for atlasers who noted breeding evidence in their neighborhoods or while casually birding. Casual Observation Forms tended to be used most often to document breeding evidence in urban areas and in county parklands.

The List Verification Form (not shown) was used to document breeding by birds that were either rare breeders in Santa Clara County or for which there had been no known breeding occurrences. The primary purpose of the form was to document, in detail, the observed breeding evidence and the habitat used. Space for the species' description, also included on the form, was particularly useful for female ducks and young, which can

sometimes offer only subtle clues to identification.

We also developed an "atlaser's handbook" for the use of all atlasers. This handbook included all the forms that were needed for atlasing, along with instructions for their use, as well as lessons learned from the pilot year of atlasing. The handbook proved to be a useful syllabus for teaching volunteers the basics of atlasing. Although the atlas protocols were straightforward, a period of training was essential. With the handbook as a basis, all atlasers went through a 2-hour instruction period that covered the basics of atlasing, the atlas protocols, and the use of the data recording forms. Possibly the most useful aspect of the training was a "quiz" that all atlasers were given at the end of the training period. The majority of the questions dealt with ambiguous situations that mimicked realistic field problems that most atlasers encounter, e.g., dealing with breeding evidence at block boundaries, assessing whether a woodpecker was simply at a roosting hole or had a nest, or determining whether a juvenile songbird

Pyramid Rock

Santa Clara County Breeding Bird Atlas
Block Supplementary List

Block 2025 Observer LAUTERBACH & YURCHENCO   Phone 415/494-8062

	Date	Species Observed	CO	East.	Nor.	Elev.	Comments
✓1	3-18-90	Red tailed Hawk	ON	305	150	2640	adult perched 3 ft. from nest
✓5	6-24-90	Red tailed Hawk	NY	360	45	2840	one young at nest, nearly fledged
4	6-3-90	California Quail	PY	360	140	2440	
2	5-20-90	Killdeer	DD	450	105	2680	
2	5-20-90	Mourning Dove	FL	365	145	2640	
4	6-3-90	Acorn Woodpecker	NY	440	100	2720	
2	5-20-90	Nuttall's Woodpecker	NY	300	145	2640	
✓2	5-20-90	Northern Flicker	ON	100	260	2760	
✓5	6-24-90	Northern Flicker	FY	310	75	2920	
5	6-24-90	Western Wood Pewee	ON	325	20	3080	
3	6-2-90	Black Phoebe	ON	170	250	2920	
5	6-24-90	Ash-throated Flycatch	FY	275	75	3000	
4	6-3-90	Violet-Green Swallow	ON	440	110	2720	
5	6-24-90	Stellars Jay	FL	390	55	3160	
✓2	5-20-90	Scrub Jay	FL	345	140	2640	
✓5	6-24-90	Scrub Jay	FY	315	85	2920	
4	6-3-90	Yellow Billed Magpie	UN	200	80	2800	
2		Plain Titmouse	CF			2880	
✓2	5-20-90	Plain Titmouse	CF	380	130	2680	
✓5	6-24-90	Plain Titmouse	CF	320	90	2880	
∅	2/25/90	Bushtit	NB	70	260	2720	
4	6-3-90	White breasted Nuthatch	CF	320	150	2440	
5	6-24-90	Bewicks Wren	FL	110	20	1920	
2	5-20-90	House Wren	NY	285	145	2640	
4	6-3-90	House Wren	FY	350	150	2440	
✓5	6-24-90	House Wren	NY	245	115	2680	
4	6-3-90	Western Bluebird	FY	200	80	2800	
5	6-24-90	American Robin	FY	240	110	2720	
5	6-24-90	Wrentit	CF	160	15	2280	
2	5-20-90	European Starling	ON	280	145	2640	
✓4	6-3-90	European Starling	ON	375	140	2440	
4	6-3-90	Orange Crown Warbler	FY	350	150	2440	
4	6-3-90	Rufous Sided Towhee	CF	440	100	2720	
4	6-3-90	Brown Towhee	CF	200	80	2800	
5	6-24-90	Rufous Crown Sparrow	FL	110	25	2040	
5	6-24-90	Chipping Sparrow	CF	230	100	2720	
5	6-24-90	Lark Sparrow	FY	245	120	2680	

B2025.90A

2025/190

Figure 5.3. An example of the Block Supplementary List.

BLOCK 9540

B9540.91D

Santa Clara County Breeding Bird Atlas
Casual Observation Form

Observer MICHAEL MAMMOSER   Phone 408 248 2288

Address 1250 GARBO WY. #303

SAN JOSE, CA. 95117

B9540.91D

Date	Species Observed	PR	CO	Easting	Northing	Elevation
21 APR 91	ANNA'S HUMMINGBIRD		FL	95.05	43.5	13
"	GREAT BLUE HERON		ON	95.2	44.9	10
4 MAY 91	CHESTNUT BACKED CHICKADEE		CF	95.08	43.43	12
"	BLACK CHINNED HUMMINGBIRD	C		"	"	"
5 MAY 91	" " "		ON	"	"	"
12 MAY 91	" " "		NE	95.05	43.4	"
25 MAY 91	MALLARD		PY	95.32	44.75	10
27 MAY 91	DOWNY WOODPECKER		NY	95.3	44.8	"
25 AUG 91	NORTHERN MOCKINGBIRD		CF	95.15	44.15	10

If possible give nesting locations to the nearest 50 meters relative to the UTM grid. For example, if the block number is 7035, a point in the exact center of the block has Easting = 72.50 and Northing = 37.50. If unable to provide the UTM coordinates please provide a sketch map of the location or the equivalent. The site elevation is in feet above sea level.

Figure 5.4. An example of the Casual Observation Form.

was still dependent and hence whether the fledgling code (FL) was appropriate.

The county atlas blocks were divided into seven regions, these regions corresponding roughly to geographical areas within the county, as shown in Fig. 5.5. Regions 1 and 2 are the northern and southern Santa Cruz Mountains, respectively, the division corresponding approximately to the Los Gatos gap. Region 3 is made up of the bayside blocks. Region 4 is the northern Santa Clara Valley, now largely urban. Region 5, the southern Santa Clara Valley, includes the cities of Morgan Hill and Gilroy as well as agricultural land. Regions 6 and 7 cover the northern and southern reaches of the Diablo Range, respectively. One or more Regional Coordinators managed the atlas coverage for each region. They worked with atlasers in assigning blocks, determined coverage goals (more below), and in many cases did much of the atlasing themselves within their region.

Figure 5.6 shows a map of the county with many of its blocks divided into 1-km "miniblocks," wherever these touch a public highway or road. The open areas, not touched by public roads, are mostly privately held lands. Overlaid on this figure

are the boundaries of Joseph Grant County Park, adjacent to Mt. Hamilton Road, and Henry Coe State Park, in the center of the Diablo Range. From this map, it is immediately apparent that most of the blocks in the western part of the county were accessible, whereas few blocks in the eastern part offered access.

Atlasing problems differed among regions, and the Regional Coordinators developed different strategies to deal with them. Blocks within Regions 1 and 2 in the Santa Cruz Mountains often are accessible from public parklands or public roads. In these regions, the coordinators focused mostly on recruiting volunteers to cover publicly accessible areas. Region 3 consisted of only nine blocks along the Bay, and access was rarely a problem. This region is a rich one for waterbirds, however, and needed repeated fieldwork over the atlas period. For Region 4, largely urban, there was no lack of observers, particularly in residential areas, but the difficulty here lay in contacting these observers and obtaining their records. For this region, the coordinator published a notice in the *Avocet*, the monthly newsletter of the Santa Clara Valley Audubon Society, and asked observers to furnish him with their breeding observations. The coordinator

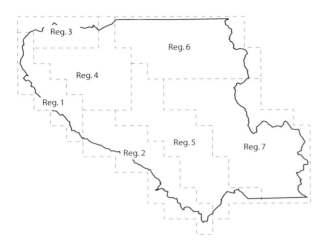

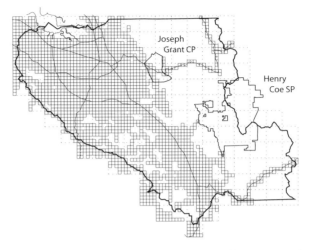

Figure 5.5. The division of Santa Clara County into seven regions, corresponding roughly to geographical areas within the county.

Figure 5.6. The 1-km by 1-km county miniblocks that are accessible by public roads (shown by shading). Boundaries of Henry Coe State Park and Joseph Grant County Park shown as overlays.

then took these reports, mapped the locations, and recorded the data on Casual Observation Forms. Region 5 is a mixture of residential, light industrial, and agricultural lands. Although there is less parkland there than in the Santa Cruz Mountains, public roads provide access to many areas within the region. Regions 6 and 7 are in the Diablo Range. The presence of Henry Coe State Park in the center of the Range afforded atlasers access to many blocks that lie within its boundaries, as seen in Fig. 5.6, but the land outside these boundaries is mostly privately held, and the range has only a few public roads. In these regions, the primary task of the coordinators was obtaining access to privately held lands.

In the western part of the county, individual atlasers worked directly with various land stewards within areas under some form of public ownership. They explained the purpose of the atlas and in all cases were able to obtain access to these lands. Public agencies with land stewardship responsibilities, including the California Department of Parks and Recreation, the Santa Clara County Parks and Recreation Department, the Midpeninsula Regional Open Space District, the Santa Clara Valley Water District, the San Francisco Public Utilities Commission (water department), and the University of California Regents (Lick Observatory), were all generous in granting access to their lands, including those areas normally closed to the public.

Access to private lands was more difficult to obtain. The atlas used a number of approaches, including: (1) cooperation with the U.S. Geological Survey, (2) relationships established through the Mt. Hamilton Christmas Bird Count, (3) new relationships made through personal contacts, and (4) in a few cases, access through direct request.

At the time the atlas got underway, the U.S. Geological Survey had already mapped landowner property lines for all of the 1:100,000 San Jose quadrangle, which covers about three-quarters of the Diablo Range. This work had been done as part of a project for a new geological map of the area. The mapped property lines and an associated database enabled us to identify the landowners of key habitats within unsurveyed blocks. In

a number of cases, geologists at the Survey had already made contact with landowners in the Diablo Range, and had obtained permission to travel on their lands. Often the geologists were able to introduce atlasers to the local landowners, in order to gain them access to these lands. For those areas of the Diablo Range south of the San Jose quadrangle (roughly the Pacheco Creek drainage), where the geologists had done no surveys, atlasers used county records to develop maps of landowner property lines, and to obtain contact information.

The second approach relied on established relationships with landowners within the Mt. Hamilton Christmas Bird Count circle. Donald E. Schmoldt had inaugurated this count in 1977, and over the succeeding ten years had established good relationships with many landowners in the northeastern part of the county. All of these landowners graciously allowed atlasers on their land during the atlas period.

Many blocks in the Diablo Range, however, remained inaccessible. Through maps we developed with the use of public records, it became possible for us to identify property owners with significant holdings in all of the inaccessible blocks. We found that the best approach in these cases was to obtain an introduction to a landowner through mutual acquaintances, family, friends, or other sources. This sort of "warm contact" afforded us the opportunity to discuss the goals of the atlas on a personal basis, and to allay concerns that atlasers would be disruptive to ranching operations, or that the atlas results would somehow endanger the landowner's rights. Moreover, atlasers often agreed to furnish the landowners with a report of the species seen on their property, which the landowners saw as a benefit. This approach was particularly successful in the northern Diablo Range, where once a good relationship had been established, landowners were helpful in providing introductions to adjacent property owners.

Where introductions to a landowner could not be obtained, it was necessary for us to contact them by mail and, if possible, follow up with a phone call. The letter we sent to the landowner described the atlas objectives and procedures and attempted to deal with landowner concerns about unknown atlasers wandering about on their land. The follow-up phone call, when it could be made, attempted to discuss access problems that were worrisome to the landowner. These "cold contacts" had a low success rate compared with the warm contacts, but were successful for several blocks.

Atlasers were encouraged to keep track of their field hours, as well as the cumulative number of species confirmed breeding in each of the blocks they surveyed. An examination of the field hours recorded and the number of breeding species detected gave the atlaser a qualitative impression of the additional effort needed to increase the number of confirmations in a given block, and whether this extra effort was warranted. In the last years of the atlas, the Regional Coordinators tried to assess how well the blocks within their regions had been covered, by comparing the block results with an estimate of the potential number of breeding species in each block. In some cases, the coordinators established a uniform estimate of the potential number of breeding species for the region as a whole. Other coordinators attempted to estimate the potential number of breeding species within each individual block, a huge task. If a Regional Coordinator concluded that the number of species confirmed in a block was too low, then additional time was spent atlasing in that block in the final years.

During the last two years of the atlas, we attempted to obtain uniform coverage in all blocks for which access had been obtained. This major effort focused on blocks completely within the county's borders. Edge blocks with more than 50% of their area within the county were considered of somewhat lower priority, and those with less than 50% within the county were given the lowest priority.

Communication within the community of active atlasers took different forms and evolved over the atlas period. Initially, considerable effort was put into a newsletter sent to all atlasers. This newsletter was used to relate atlaser experiences, describe clues to the breeding of individual species, and examine some of the initial results. The total number of active atlasers in any one year rarely exceeded 30 people, and the use of a newsletter came to be seen as an inefficient means of communication, considering the time and expense of its production. During the middle years of the atlas, a potluck was held early in each season. This allowed atlasers to look at initial results, to sign up for new blocks, and to discuss atlasing experiences and problems. These occasions were also useful to those who were doing the data entry, since they could address particular problems by reference to submitted Field Cards, Block Supplementary Lists, or other data entry forms. Toward the end of the atlas period, communication occurred largely through the Internet. During the height of the breeding season, results of atlasing were posted daily, and updates on coverage goals were posted weekly.

Data entry began at the conclusion of each breeding season, and was mostly complete by the start of the next season. Atlasers were given summaries of all data from blocks in which they had worked, as well as block summaries for blocks that might be of interest to them in the following year. This database information was particularly useful for the blocks closer to urban areas, where a significant portion of the data entered was from Casual Observation Forms. In this way, atlasers could assess the coverage in any block of interest to them, at the start

of each season.

For the most part, atlas database records were drawn from atlasers who surveyed blocks, or from contributors who furnished evidence of breeding in their neighborhoods or in such other locations as they may have visited while birding. Exceptions were records obtained from the Humane Society of Santa Clara Valley (now Humane Society Silicon Valley). People would bring young birds to the Society, sometimes believing they had been abandoned. On other occasions nests were destroyed during gardening operations and the contents were brought to the Society. Staff and volunteers of the Society kept records of the abandoned, injured, or dead birds, and these often included addresses and enough information describing the circumstances that we were able to create records for the atlas database. Joan Priest, an active birder who worked at the Society, granted access to these records. Ann Verdi went through the Humane Society records and, as appropriate, extracted data that were entered into the database. This source provided 175 confirmations for the database, all from urban areas.

Creating the Atlas Database

The atlas database was designed as an ASCII (American Standard Code for Information Interchange) file, one record for each line. The advantage of this approach was that we could access the database with conventional text editors, and no restrictions were caused by the use of proprietary software. Because the operating system saved sequential versions of the database file, there were no problems with accidentally overwriting the database file. FORTRAN programs were written to process the data files.

The initial data structure was based on a 36-character line that defined a record. Some examples are:

```
RSHA9515 42392COON2AVE180440 400
RSHA9520 7 889POCH DLS  -  -  -
```

The first record here is parsed as:

```
RSHA:9515: 42392:COON:2:AVE:180:440:
400:  :
```

The first four characters are the species code (here Red-shouldered Hawk), as defined on the Field Card (see Figs. 5.2a and 5.2b). The next four characters are the block code. This is followed by six characters that give the observation date, in the sequence month-day-year (just five characters were needed here). The next four characters provide the breeding evidence. The first two characters in this sequence describe the basic level of breeding, that is, CO for confirmed, PR for probable, PO for possible, or O for Observed. The second two characters of this sequence describe the specific evidence, such as ON for occupied nest in this example (see the Field Card in Fig. 5.2a for definitions of the specific evidence). A single character, a numeral, conveys the estimated abundance in the block, as explained on the Field Card. (This code is left blank in records when no estimate has been provided.) Following the abundance code is a three-letter code that uniquely identifies the observer or, sometimes, multiple observers. Ten characters, comprising three groups, give the location of the observation in eastings, northings, and elevation. (Location was optional and usually was furnished only for evidence of confirmation.) The first three characters of this sequence are the eastings distance to the observation in tens of meters from the west edge of the block. The next three characters are the northings distance in tens of meters from the south edge. The final four characters (here just three) are the elevation in feet. In cases when no location information was provided, a '–' was used in the last position of the field for the eastings, northings, and elevation. The final two characters of the record relate to the List Verification Form. If a species requires that form, then a disposition code 01 is entered. After evaluation of the List Verification Form, this code is changed either to 02, for accepted, or to 03, for not accepted.

The conversion of the coordinate location in the data record to the conventional NAD 27 datum is straightforward. For the example shown here, the prefix 5 is added to the block easting, 95 (see the discussion above of dropped prefix codes for block designations). To the resulting 595 is added 1.80 km, yielding an easting of 596.80 km (or 596,800 m). Similarly, for the northing, the prefix 41 is added to the block northing, 15, plus 4.40 km, yielding 4,119.40 km (or 4,119,400 m) in the NAD 27 datum.

When the species accounts began to be written, we made a final change to the definition of the record line. Five characters were added to Brown-headed Cowbird records to indicate the host species, if known. The first character was a space, and the next four characters were the code for the host species. Thus, in the final database, the data records are 41 characters long, although the last five characters are used only for the Brown-headed Cowbird records.

To combine all of these records into a database, we sequenced the records by (1) species, (2) block, (3) breeding evidence, and (4) date. The species' order was determined by the American Ornithologists' Union *Check-list of North American Birds* (AOU 1983), with updates through the Thirty-Seventh Supplement (AOU 1989). Within a species, the records were not sequenced numerically by block, but were first sequenced from west to east and then from south to north. Within a block, records were sequenced inversely by the breeding evidence shown on the Field Card. For the same breeding evidence, we sequenced records by date. We defined the basic database structure in this fashion to facilitate editing of the database. Data analysis and plotting programs, however, did not rely on this structure, but examined all database records.

Data entry was a two-step process. We first entered data into a block file, whether from Field Cards, Block Supplementary Lists, or Casual Observation Forms. The naming convention for the block files was based on the block number, year, and entry sequence. For example, the block file B7540.89B was data for Block 7540 for the year 1989, the suffix B indicating that this was the second file entered that year for that block. The second step was to merge the block file into the master database. Line counts of the block file, initial master file, and final master file were checked to ensure a correct merge.

The great majority of the data records were entered each year by just four contributors: the writer (William G. Bousman), Michael M. Rogers, and the team of James Yurchenco and Amy Lauterbach. Each of the contributors followed different approaches for data entry, but in all cases the final result was the same. The benefit, of course, was that this division of labor allowed for faster updates of the database at the close of each

year.

The writer wrote three separate data entry programs, depending upon whether the data were from Field Cards, Block Supplementary Lists, or Casual Observation Forms. These programs, which were interactive at a terminal, asked for appropriate data and then checked the response to ensure that the entered data were of the correct format, and that there were no illegal codes, dates, or whatever. As a final check, for data entry from Field Cards, the output block file was processed to create a facsimile of the Field Card, which could then be compared visually with the original card to identify data entry errors.

Rogers entered the field data in an ASCII file with a text editor. Constant parameters, such as block number, were entered as a heading, and then the individual records for that block were entered by species. The data on one line were sequenced differently than the database record line, but in a way that could be quickly examined for errors. Following data entry, the file was processed by a FORTRAN program that checked for consistency of records, species names, and so forth. Once through with the various checks, Rogers converted the file to the database format with another FORTRAN program and sent it to the writer for merging.

Yurchenco and Lauterbach entered the field data in a spreadsheet. Each column represented a portion of the data record, that is, the species, the block number, the date, the breeding codes, and so forth. In this way, the columns that were constant, such as the block number or the date for a single day's field observations, could be easily entered for all records. Once a block file was complete in the spreadsheet and had been checked, then it was changed to a text file and sent to the writer for merging.

No estimate has been made of the number of errors in the database. Numerous errors were caught on data entry by each of the contributors. Software checks, however, did not catch more subtle errors, such as legal but erroneous block numbers (some cases), legal but erroneous dates, and confirmation coordinates that were not compatible with elevations at those locations. The database review, as discussed below, found some errors not detected by software checks. By and large, these were few, probably well below 1% of all reviewed records, but some errors undoubtedly remain in the database.

After we completed data entry from the 1993 field season, we formed a committee to review the database. The primary purposes of the Review Committee were: (1) to evaluate breeding evidence codes to determine if they were correctly applied, (2) to look for typographic errors in the data records, and, (3) in a few cases, to evaluate documentation for the rare breeding species.

The primary approach to evaluating the accuracy of the data records was to examine our maps of species distribution and our data on breeding phenology. For more common species, such as Mourning Dove, Western Scrub-Jay, and California Towhee, breeding confirmations were obtained in nearly all atlas blocks. For these species there was little review of their distribution, although we did examine their phenology data. For less common species, the maps indicated their basic distribution within the county, but sometimes showed records that were well outside that distribution. These outlying records were examined in detail. In some cases, we detected typographical or other data entry errors, and these were corrected. In other cases, we contacted the original observer and asked for additional information to support the breeding evidence reported. If review of this information supported the record, then it was retained as originally entered. Otherwise, a disposition code (see Table 5.1, below) was added to the end of the record to allow or prevent the mapping, as appropriate.

An example of an unusual outlier on a map was an adult Winter Wren and two fledglings found along San Felipe Creek in the Diablo Range. This location is well away from the Santa Cruz Mountains, where this species normally breeds (see the species account). But extensive details for this unusual record, provided by the original observers, were reviewed and accepted by the committee.

Sometimes, we examined the dates associated with probable or possible evidence of summer residents, that is, birds that nest in the county, but do not winter here. The first sightings of summer residents in early spring (or late winter) are often local birds attempting to establish territories here, rather than birds that will continue their migration to lands farther north. But over the next month or two, we may encounter migrants that sing as they pass through. Safe dates, or windowing criteria, to separate breeding birds from migrants, have been used successfully in more northern atlases, but were problematic for this atlas. We established windowing dates for a limited number of species, and in some cases these were effective in eliminating overwintering birds or late-season dispersants (see Appendix 4). But the Review Committee sometimes found it difficult to assess the status of singing birds that were observed within the breeding window, but appeared to be outside of the species' normal breeding distribution. Wilson's Warbler is an example of this dilemma. This species is a fairly common breeder in wet areas of the Santa Cruz Mountains, but a very rare breeder at the edge of the Diablo Range. It is nonetheless a common migrant and active singer in the Diablo Range through the end of May, and is sometimes found in the same locations for a week or more at a time. We suppressed the majority of these Diablo Range records of likely migrants unless singing birds were found at these locations in June or July.

We also examined percentile data for breeding phenology. For very early or very late breeding records, or when dates were not consistent with the breeding evidence codes, e.g., fledglings seen at the start of the season or nest building at the end, we sought additional information to substantiate the records.

The final decisions of the Review Committee are shown in the database by the disposition codes added at the ends of the records. These codes are defined in Table 5.1.

After the end of the atlas period in 1993, we decided to create a postatlas database. The purpose of this database was to provide a repository for new breeding information gained up to the time the atlas results were published. The data structure used for the atlas database was used here as well. Michael M. Rogers has entered the data for the postatlas database and maintained it.

Analyzing the Atlas Database

Once the review of the database was completed, it was possible for us to analyze it and make valid maps. Database

Table 5.1. Atlas database disposition codes.

Code	Disposition
00	Record valid, no change.
01	Requires List Verification Form and review.
02	List Verification Form reviewed and accepted.
03	List Verification Form reviewed, unaccepted (record not mapped).
04	Status changed to wintering, migrant, or dispersant (record not mapped).
05	Observed code upgraded to POssible/CHeck.
06	Downgraded to Observed.
07	Not used.
08	Not used.
09	Legal COnfirmed code but unsupported; downgraded to POssible/CHeck.
10	Legal PRobable code but unsupported; downgraded to POssible/CHeck.
11	Identification questioned (therefore not mapped).
12	Valid COnfirmed downgraded to POssible/CHeck; location uncertainty.
13	CO/PE code not mapped.
14	Legal COnfirmed code but unsupported; downgraded to PRobable.

analysis fell into three categories: (1) mapping, (2) phenology, and (3) abundance. For the preparation of the maps, we initially used only data for the years from 1987 through 1993, but as new and important records were added to the postatlas database, we decided to include postatlas records on the maps as well, and also to employ them in the analysis of phenology.

Our determination of the mapping symbol used on the species account maps was relatively straightforward. All records for a given species in a given block in the atlas database were examined, and the highest level of breeding evidence was determined. As discussed in Chapter 6, we chose filled circles to represent the atlas data, and the size of the circles defined the level of evidence. That is, confirmations are shown by large circles, probable evidence by medium-sized circles, and possible evidence by small circles. Then, we examined the postatlas database, and if we found a higher level of evidence there, we entered a new symbol. The postatlas symbol is represented by an open circle, in order to visually differentiate these records. For the few species maps that include an observed symbol, "×", there is no differentiation between atlas and postatlas data. The observed symbol is only shown in these cases if there is no higher category of breeding evidence in either the atlas or postatlas database. For each record that carried a disposition code, it was again necessary to take that code into account (see Table 5.1) before determining the level of evidence it represented.

An example phenology graphic (of Common Raven) is shown in Fig. 5.7. For phenology, we analyzed the atlas data via two approaches. The first approach organized the atlas data

ATLAS ORGANIZATION AND METHODS

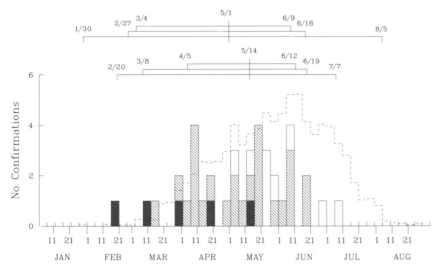

Figure 5.7. Phenology plots for Common Raven (example).

(and sometimes postatlas data) for plotting as a column graph, as shown in Fig. 5.7. The second approach determined the percentiles for the phenology data, and these are shown by the horizontal bars above the column graph in Fig. 5.7.

In preparing the phenology graphics, we used different combinations of data from the atlas and postatlas databases, depending upon the relative proportions of confirmations. We distinguished between the two databases because the atlas database was based on coverage of the entire county (see Fig. 6.2), whereas the postatlas database covered mostly the Santa Clara Valley and nearby areas (see Fig. 6.8). Whether this different coverage would affect the phenology is unknown. Nonetheless, depending upon the number of confirmations in the two databases, we considered four cases. We defined the nominal case (Case 1), which is used for the majority of the phenology graphics, as all species for which the number of postatlas confirmations was less than 70% of the number of atlas confirmations. For this case, we show a column graph and percentile data for only the atlas data. For Case 2, if the number of postatlas confirmations was between 70% and 400% of the number of atlas confirmations, we plotted the column graph based on the atlas confirmations, but included separate percentile bars for both the atlas and postatlas data (as shown in Fig. 5.7). For Case 3, if the number of postatlas confirmations was more than 400% of the atlas confirmations, we combined the two databases and plotted a single column graph and set of percentile bars. In indicating the number of confirmations for this case, we refer to these data as "Combined," rather than "Postatlas" or "Atlas." Finally, for Case 4, if there are no atlas data, we then show a column graph and percentile bars for the postatlas data. If there were fewer than seven confirmations in both databases, only the atlas data were used.

For analysis of the phenology data, all confirmations that included both the month and day were converted to a Julian date. Confirmed data based on the used nest (UN) breeding code were excluded from analysis because the date when a used nest is found bears no relationship to nesting phenology. For the column graph, we separated the confirmation data into stages

based on prenesting evidence, nesting evidence, and postnesting evidence. Prenesting evidence (solid columns) included birds collecting or carrying nest material (CN) and building nests (NB). Nesting evidence (slanted columns) included a bird seen occupying a nest (ON), a nest with eggs (NE), a nest with young (NY), or an adult carrying a fecal sac away from a nest (FS). Postnesting evidence (open columns) included adults feeding young (FY), precocial young (PY), and dependent fledglings (FL). Breeding evidence based on carrying food (CF) and the distraction display (DD) was excluded, since it may occur in more than one stage. We then divided the phenology data into five-day bins, with an arbitrary reference of 1 Jun as the start of a bin, and we divided the atlas period field hours into the same five-day bins, to indicate the time period when atlasers were afield (dotted line). The field hour data were scaled to match the column graph.

In calculating percentile data, we used all of the phenology data (except, again, the used nest data). The number of confirmations used in the analysis is always shown to the right of the phenology graphic. If there are fewer than seven confirmations with phenology data ($n < 7$), then no percentile bars are shown on the graphic. If there are from seven to nine records ($7 \leq n \leq 9$), then a percentile bar is added that shows the first, median, and last records. If the number of records is ten or more, but fewer than twenty ($10 \leq n \leq 19$), then a second percentile bar is added, one comprising the 12.5th to the 87.5th percentiles; that is, it includes 75% of all breeding records. Finally, if there are twenty or more records ($20 \leq n$ as in the Common Raven example), we added a third percentile bar that comprises the 5th to 95th percentiles and thus includes 90% of all breeding records.

Depending upon case, as described previously, we show percentile bars either (1) for the atlas data, (2) one each for the atlas and postatlas data, (3) for combined data, or (4) just for the postatlas data.

Abundance was estimated using two approaches. In the first approach an abundance estimate was derived from the abundance code. In the second approach an abundance index was based on the number of confirmations after excluding duplicate

81

Table 5.2. Abundance estimates.

Abundance Code	Population Estimate		
	Lower	Central	Upper
1	2	2	2
2	4	9	20
3	22	66	200
4	202	636	2,000
5	2,002	6,328	20,000

records. The results of the abundance estimates are discussed in Chapter 6. The estimates are tabulated in Appendix 5.

Estimates of abundance based on the abundance code were obtained from the Field Cards (see Fig. 5.2a). These estimates were made in the manner indicated in Table 5.2. For example, an abundance code of 2 means that between two and ten pairs were estimated to breed within a block. In terms of the number of birds, this indicates a range from four to twenty birds. The low, four birds, was used as a lower bound, and the high, twenty birds, was used as the upper bound. A central estimate was the logarithmic average, about nine birds in this case. To estimate the number of a particular species in Santa Clara County, an average of all abundance codes for the species was computed. Then, using linear interpolation on the logarithmic scale in Table 5.2, we made a central estimate with lower and upper bounds. The estimates based on the average abundance were then multiplied by the number of blocks that had either confirmed, probable, or possible evidence.

The second approach to estimating abundance produced an index of abundance rather than an estimate of the number of birds. This was a count of all confirmations after excluding duplicates. (Duplicate confirmations were identified when multiple confirmations were found in the database at the same location.) For instance, a series of records, such as nest building, occupied nest, nest with young, and fledglings, might be located at one set of coordinates and elevation. In this example, we considered three of the four confirmations to be duplicates, and excluded them from the total number of confirmations. Recording confirmation coordinates and multiple confirmations within a block were both optional, but most active atlasers generally did both. For the atlas database, approximately two-thirds of all confirmations included coordinates and an elevation.

Analyzing the Christmas Bird Count and Summer Bird Count Data

Christmas Bird Count (CBC) and Summer Bird Count (SBC) data are valuable adjuncts to the atlas data, and they have been incorporated in the species accounts. CBC data from the Palo Alto and San Jose count circles extend over roughly 50 years. The Palo Alto CBC data have been recorded continuously from 1959 to the present. The San Jose CBC data extend back as far as 1928. In the early years, this CBC was held as the December field trip of the newly formed Santa Clara Valley Audubon Society (Turner 1962). Multiple parties were first organized about 1940, and the first systematic coverage was undertaken in 1949. (The San Jose circle was shifted a bit in 1972, as will be discussed below.) The San Jose CBC data set used here extends from 1956 to 2004. An additional Christmas Bird Count data set, for the Mt. Hamilton CBC, covers the time period from 1977 to 2004. A Summer Bird Count has been held in the Palo Alto count circle, and data are available from 1981 to 2005. These data, normally obtained in the first week of June, are even more relevant to this breeding bird atlas. Analysis of the Calero-Morgan Hill CBC data, begun in 2000, is not included here, but this new set of data will become increasingly valuable in future years.

The use of CBC data for quantitative purposes remains a difficult problem, and care must be taken in their analysis (Bock and Root 1981, Butcher 1990, Butcher and McCulloch 1990). Analysis of population trends can be based on the number of birds recorded, or the data can be normalized by some measure of level of effort (Butcher 1990). Bock and Root (1981) suggest that in most cases normalization using the number of party-hours is the best approach, although for some species the raw data may be preferable. Figure 5.8 shows the number of Red-tailed Hawks tallied across all years as a function of the number of party-hours for the four data sets used here. In all cases, there is a strong relationship between the party-hours and the number of birds counted. A linear regression line has been fitted to these data, and the slope m, coefficient of determination r^2, and level of significance p are shown in each case. The p values are all less than 0.05, which is the normally accepted value for statistical significance. The relationship is particularly strong for the San Jose and Palo Alto data, and the coefficient of determination of 0.77 indicates that 77% of the variance in hawk numbers depends upon the number of party-hours spent. The data in Fig. 5.8 indicate that normalization by the number of party-hours is appropriate for common birds. Similar analyses have been performed for all the species in the atlas, and, depending upon these results, the data shown are either normalized by the party-hours or left unnormalized.

Errors occur in all CBC data sets. Some of these errors are correctable and some are not. Peterson (1994) has recommended the examination and correction of the party-hour data prior to its use for normalization. If the number of party-hours is divided by the number of parties, the resulting number represents the average number of hours that each party was in the field. In exceptional cases, a few parties may manage 10.5 hours in the field, since this is the extent of daylight hours near Christmas time. An examination of all local count data shows that in most years the average number of hours in the field ranges from 6 to 8 hours per party. In four cases, possible errors in the reported number of party-hours/party have been identified. For the Palo Alto CBC, 12.5 party-hours/party were reported in 1980; for the San Jose CBC, 21.0 party-hours/party were recorded in 1973 and 10.2 party-hours/party in 1980; and for the Mt. Hamilton CBC, 4.0 party-hours/party were reported in 1982. The Palo Alto and San Jose data have been corrected by using the party-hour/party ratio from the adjacent four years to adjust the number of party-hours (the number of parties was assumed to be correct). No change was made to the Mt. Hamilton party-hours.

As mentioned previously, the San Jose count circle was shifted in 1972. The center of the circle was moved 4.3 km

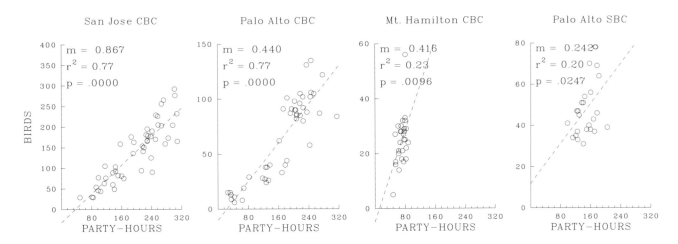

Figure 5.8. Number of Red-tailed Hawks recorded as a function of the number of party-hours spent on three CBCs and the Palo Alto SBC, across all years. Note the differing ordinate scales.

to the north-northwest so as to include more of the Alviso salt ponds and marshes within the count circle. We assume that this shift has affected the number of waterbirds counted but, in most cases, has not influenced the number of landbirds. In calculating trends, as described below, the San Jose CBC data for waterbirds are used only since 1972.

Population trends for the CBC and SBC data have been estimated by log-transforming the number of birds/party-hour (or number of birds in a few cases). A linear regression of the log-transformed data as a function of time was then determined, and the population change, the coefficient of determination, and the level of significance were all computed. In those cases where $p < 0.05$, a trend line is added to the plot of birds/party-hour (or birds), and the population change, the coefficient of determination, and the level of significance are written on the figure.

In a few cases, the population data cannot be log transformed, since the data series includes some years with zero counts. This occurs for rare species and those species showing significant population increases or decreases. In these cases, a pseudo-data set is created by adding a small increment to all of the data prior to log transformation. The increment used is 0.5% of the mean number of birds recorded over the time period.

Assembling Source Materials for the Species Accounts

The species accounts presented in this atlas focus primarily on the atlas breeding data, both the spatial distribution of each species and its phenology, but multiple source materials have been used by the authors in preparing these accounts.

For current or recent information on locally breeding species, our primary source of information has been direct communications with atlasers or other local birders in the area. Much of this information is written in the Santa Clara County notebooks, which in the text are referred to as the "county notebooks." These notebooks were initiated in 1980 and have been maintained since then by the writer. Initially, the county notebooks were physical notebooks with handwritten entries, but since the

summer of 1993 they have been electronic notebooks. Extracts for the breeding season were taken from both the handwritten and electronic notebooks for most species accounts and furnished to the account authors.

We used the postatlas database (abbreviated PADB) as a source of information for many postatlas breeding records of more common species that are not contained in the county notebooks.

Regional information, some of it recent and some stretching over decades, has been obtained from the Regional Editors of the Middle Pacific Coast Region of the journal *North American Birds*. (Note that this region has recently been redesignated the Northern California Region, but the boundaries are unchanged.)

Historical information was available from a variety of sources. There were three initial efforts to extract such information from the ornithological literature: (1) Stephen C. Rottenborn reviewed the local historical literature; (2) Rosalie Lefkowitz reviewed local records published in *Audubon Field Notes* and its successor publications: *American Birds*, *National Audubon Society Field Notes*, and *North American Birds*; and (3) Phyllis M. Browning wrote brief synopses of articles relevant to locally breeding species as published in the *Condor*. In addition, Gloria G. Heller examined egg records for rarer species in the collections at the Western Foundation of Vertebrate Zoology and consolidated these data with other information on egg dates from the ornithological literature.

The Rottenborn compendium comprised extracts from the historical accounts, including Price (1898a-f), Van Denburgh (1899b), Grinnell and Wythe (1927), Grinnell and Miller (1944), and Sibley (1952). He supplemented this compendium with information from old Christmas Bird Counts as published in *Bird-Lore*, and from records in various newsletters of the Santa Clara Valley Audubon Society. These newsletters included the *Wren-Tit*, published from 1929 to 1931, the *Bulletin of the Santa Clara Valley Audubon Society*, published from about 1947 to 1954, and the current newsletter, the *Avocet*, first published in 1954.

The Lefkowitz compendium was made up of extracts of local records relevant to breeding taken from all of the Middle

Pacific Coast Region reports from 1947 to 1995 in *Audubon Field Notes, American Birds,* and *National Audubon Society Field Notes*. Subsequently, the writer revisited this material and added breeding records from nearby counties to the Lefkowitz compendium, so as to provide a regional context. Later, the writer also added records from the region reports from 1995 to 2005 for the *National Audubon Society Field Notes* and *North American Birds*.

The Browning summary included citations and short synopses to all articles pertaining to species in the county or nearby that were published in the *Condor* from 1899 (when it was named the *Bulletin of the Cooper Ornithological Club*) to 1995.

The compendia and summaries mentioned above were consolidated into files organized by species. This information was augmented with additional records from older publications, such as the *Oologist, Ornithology and Oology*, the *Nidiologist*, and *Bird-Lore*, the last of which began including regional records in the 1920s. These combined files were then furnished to the species account authors.

Extensive historical information also exists in egg collections, particularly for the period from 1890 to 1930. As mentioned above, Gloria G. Heller initially visited the Western Foundation of Vertebrate Zoology, at that time in Brentwood, California, and extracted data on local egg records of rarer species. Subsequently, the writer extended that effort to cover more species, and also examined the egg collections at the California Academy of Sciences, San Francisco, and the San Bernardino Natural History Museum, Redlands. I also obtained data online from the Museum of Vertebrate Zoology, Berkeley, and electronic records from the United States National Museum, Washington, D.C. All of this information was then combined in separate species files to support the writing of the species accounts.

6 Atlas Results

ZEV-96

This chapter summarizes the results of atlasing in Santa Clara County for the years 1987 through 1993. The discussion starts with an assessment of the atlas coverage, as the adequacy of this coverage underlies the validity of the results in this chapter and on the individual species maps in Chapter 7. The atlas results are given in terms of the number of breeding species documented (incorporating some postatlas information as well), the distribution of abundance of these species, and the species richness of the county's blocks. The chapter concludes with a brief discussion of postatlas coverage.

Coverage

Although the ideal of atlasing is to obtain uniform coverage of all atlas blocks, this is not always possible, since in some cases not all habitats in a block are accessible or the block is too remote from population centers. In other cases, where a block may offer fewer habitats, we can expect that there are fewer breeding species and less justification for spending time in the block. In the majority of the blocks in the county, the best that can be obtained may be a threshold level of coverage. What follows describes the coverage achieved in Santa Clara County and the temporal progression of the coverage over the atlas years.

The atlas period included the breeding seasons from 1987 to 1993. During this period, atlasers and contributors reported 27,996 breeding records for 165 of the county's 168 atlas blocks. Half of these records, 14,873, were confirmations, the others probables, possibles, or observed. The number of species confirmed breeding in each block is shown in Fig. 6.1. Three edge blocks in the southeast corner of the county, 5090, 5590, and 5015, all on private property, were never accessed, and these blocks are blank in Fig. 6.1 (see Fig. 5.1 in Chapter 5 for an explanation of the block designations). Two blocks on the upper row, 8045 and 8545, have very few confirmations, 2 and 11, respectively. This was not because of a lack of coverage there, per se, but rather because these blocks are mostly water or active salt evaporator ponds. Block 8045 is about 75% open bay, the remainder made up of salt pond edge. Block 8545 is about 10% open bay, the remainder being salt ponds. In some cases, salt pond habitat can hold immense numbers of birds, including a California Gull colony in Block 8545 with thousands of breed-

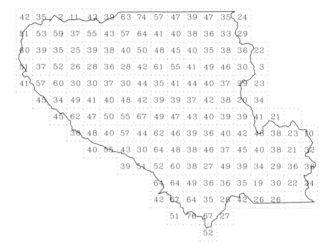

Figure 6.1. Number of species confirmed breeding, 1987 to 1993 in each of 165 county blocks.

ing gulls. But the number of species breeding in these habitats is low.

The average number of species confirmed breeding in the 165 blocks is 41, with a standard deviation of 13. Edge blocks adjacent to Santa Cruz and San Mateo counties on the west and to Alameda County on the north have as many confirmations as in the interior blocks, which is partly a consequence of atlasing in these counties by the respective county atlases as well as our own. But edge blocks on the eastern side of the county, along Stanislaus and Merced counties, and in the southeast along San Benito County, generally show reduced numbers of breeding confirmations, largely a consequence of reduced coverage in these blocks (there was no atlasing in the adjacent counties).

Figure 6.1 provides one measure of how comprehensive the coverage was during the atlas period. A second measure is shown in Fig. 6.2, which shows the total number of species recorded in the 165 atlas blocks surveyed over the atlas period. This number includes not only those species confirmed breeding, which is shown in Fig. 6.1 above, but also species where our evidence was at the probable or possible breeding level. This

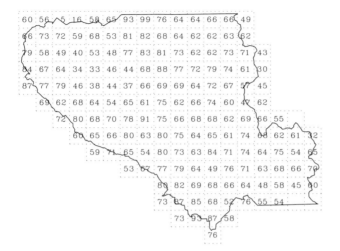

Figure 6.2. Number of species recorded as either confirmed, probable, or possible breeders in each of 165 county blocks, 1987 to 1993.

Figure 6.3. Total numbers of field hours recorded in 165 blocks, 1987 to 1993.

map offers a more realistic estimate of the number of species that breed within each block. In this sense, the map provides a measure of species richness within and across Santa Clara County, which will be discussed in more detail below. Except for a few edge blocks on the Stanislaus, Merced, and San Benito County borders, this figure indicates, at least in a rough sense, the generally good coverage that was obtained during the atlas period.

Another way of looking at the extent of coverage during the atlas period is to examine the number of field hours the atlasers recorded in each block. This number represents a lower bound on the actual field hours, since atlas hours were not always recorded. In some cases, atlasers simply failed to record their field hours, which was an oversight. But for many blocks in urban areas, establishing a satisfactory count of atlasing hours was difficult, since a significant fraction of all confirmations there was recorded on Casual Observation Forms, rather than Field Cards, the primary source for field hours. In the final years of the atlas, some atlasers used the Block Supplementary List rather than a Field Card to record their observations, and they did not always record the hours they spent in fieldwork. (See Chapter 5 for a discussion of these cards and forms.)

Figure 6.3, which tallies the number of field hours recorded in each block, reflects these disparities in recording field hours. The figure shows that there was extensive coverage in many areas of the county, but there are also quite a few blocks where few field hours were recorded. A number of these blocks with low coverage occur in the urbanized area of the northern Santa Clara Valley, as explained above, but apparent low coverage occurred in a number of other blocks, including some of those in the southeastern part of the county.

The different measures of coverage, as represented by breeding evidence (Figs. 6.1 and 6.2), on the one hand, and that represented by effort (Fig. 6.3), on the other hand, are not strongly correlated. Other factors that are important in assessing coverage include the number of species that actually breed in a block (its "richness") and the skill (and sometimes luck) of

the observers. Comparing the number of breeding confirmations with the number of field hours, over all blocks, shows only limited correlation ($r^2 = 0.18$).

One more approach that illustrates the coverage in the county during the atlas period is shown in Fig. 6.4, where all confirmations recorded with coordinates (about two-thirds of them) are shown. As expected, these breeding locations are very dense in the northern Santa Clara Valley and along the edge of the South Bay. The recording of breeding locations by coordinates was optional under the atlas protocols (not always easily done) and was not used by all atlasers. In particular, few breeding locations were recorded in the southern Santa Cruz Mountains in the early years of the atlas. Later, as atlasers moved into the Diablo Range, the recording of confirmation locations became more regular. Thus, this "fly-speck" plot gives a good idea of the extent of coverage in the Diablo Range, an area of

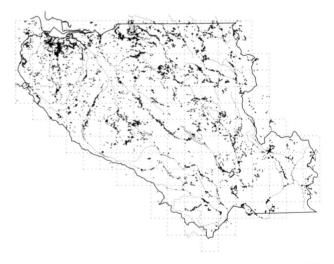

Figure 6.4. Breeding confirmation locations in 165 blocks, 1987 to 1993.

ATLAS RESULTS

Table 6.1. Atlas progress metrics, 1987 to 1993.

Year	No. Atlasers	No. Field Cards	No. Field Hours	No. COs	No. Initial COs
1987	6	8	115	324	283
1988	21	39	801	1,285	1,004
1989	29	60	945	1,906	1,228
1990	31	60	904	2,110	1,058
1991	29	73	937	2,609	1,016
1992	23	88	1,202	3,761	1,518
1993	13	67	608	2,878	689

the county that was largely terra incognita before the start of the atlasing (see Fig. 5.6 in Chapter 5).

A close examination of Fig. 6.4 reflects the fact that the density of breeding confirmations frequently followed the stream courses in the Santa Cruz Mountains, the Diablo Range, and along the valley floor. This is not surprising, because atlasers found that the breeding of birds was generally tied closely to the presence of water or of riparian vegetation, even when the vegetation is adjacent to intermittent streams.

Figures 6.1 to 6.4 illustrate in different ways the breadth of coverage accomplished during the atlas period. This is important for the interpretation of the individual species accounts, because it means that the absence of breeding evidence for a species in various parts of the county is not simply an artifact of lack of coverage.

Table 6.1 presents metrics that show how the coverage progressed during the atlas period. Some of these metrics are imprecise, for the reasons discussed above, but each contributes to an indication of the progress over the atlas period. During the pilot year of 1987, only six atlasers were active, which meant fewer field hours and therefore fewer confirmations (COs). From 1988 to 1992, the number of atlasers in any year varied from 21 to 31. Fewer atlasers were active in 1993, the extended year, and they recorded fewer field hours. For the entire period, 57 different atlasers submitted field cards (see Appendix 1). Because not all atlasers submitted a record of their field hours on their field cards, the number of field hours in Table 6.1 represents a lower bound. From 1988 to 1992, the field hours recorded varied from 801 to 1,202, the high number occurring in 1992, in what was expected to be the final year of the atlas.

The number of confirmations obtained each year is probably the best measure of level of effort. These include not only confirmations recorded on the field cards, but also those entered on Casual Observation Forms, whether from active atlasers or casual contributors. The number of COs increased each year, reaching a peak in 1992. Initial confirmations are those COs that constitute the first confirmation of breeding for a species in a block. For example, the first time breeding evidence was found for a Chestnut-backed Chickadee in a given block, this was then an initial confirmation for that block, and the result was, of course, a new filled full-sized circle on the atlas map. If subsequent visits to the same block found additional breeding evidence for chickadees, such findings were considered subsequent, not initial COs. The number of initial COs did not increase as quickly as all COs, as is to be expected. As more and more COs were found in each block, it became more and more difficult to record an initial or first CO. In 1988, the first full year of the atlas, 79% of all COs were initial ones. By 1993, only 24% were initial COs, and this is a sign of progress.

The progress over the atlas period is portrayed graphically in Fig. 6.5 by comparing the cumulative results for each year with the atlas final results. Thus, for each year, the number of confirmations in each block are tallied, and those numbers are divided by the total number of confirmations, probables, and possibles for the entire atlas period, that is, the totals from Fig. 6.2. If the ratio is greater than 50%, which was our coverage goal, then a filled, full-sized circle is shown on the map in Fig. 6.5. If the ratio is between 25 and 50%, then a medium-sized circle is used, and between 1 and 25%, a small circle is used. (These symbols should not be confused with those used for the species accounts.) The idea was to show, in each block and each atlas year, how nearly that block's coverage had approached our goal. The flatland boundary shown on the maps in Fig. 6.5 outlines the Santa Clara Valley.

Coverage in the 1987 pilot year (Fig. 6.5a) was limited, and the only block that reached the 50% confirmed level was Block 1595 in the southern Santa Cruz Mountains. The next year, 1988 (Fig. 6.5b), was the first full coverage year. The greatest increase in coverage was in blocks in the northwestern part of the county that lie in or adjacent to urban areas. Atlasing was relatively intense in the southern Santa Cruz Mountains that year, and five more blocks reached the coverage goal of >50% confirmed. It can also be seen in Fig. 6.5b that atlasing got underway in the middle of the Diablo Range in Henry Coe State Park, and one block there achieved its coverage goal in 1988. In 1989 (Fig. 6.5c), coverage in the northern Santa Clara Valley continued to increase, and extensive atlasing also took place in the foothills adjacent to the Coyote Narrows. Increased atlasing in that year is also observed in the northern Diablo Range along San Antonio Valley Road, Mines Road, and Del Puerto Road, but extensive areas in the northern and southern Diablo Range still show no coverage.

Coverage of the northern Santa Clara Valley and the northern Santa Cruz Mountains was mostly completed in 1990 (Fig. 6.5d). A number of blocks in the western foothills of the northern Diablo Range were also completed, and coverage continued to improve in the central Diablo Range in or near Henry Coe State Park. The first atlas coverage along Pacheco Creek is observed in this year. In 1991 (Fig. 6.5e), coverage expanded in the Diablo Range. Examination of this map clearly identifies the

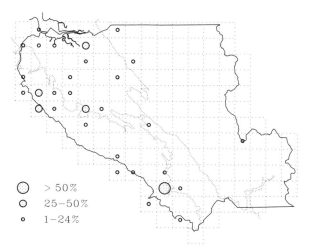

a. 1987

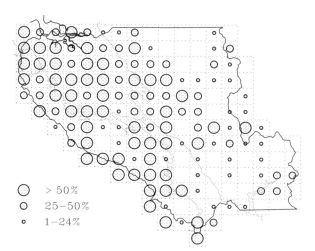

d. 1990

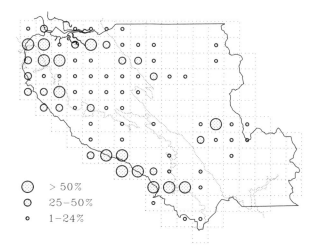

b. 1988

e. 1991

c. 1989

f. 1992

Figure 6.5. Coverage of Santa Clara County atlas blocks, 1987 to 1993. The cumulative numbers of confirmations in each block and year are normalized by the numbers of confirmations, probables, and possibles from 1993 (see Fig. 6.2). (*Continued on next page.*)

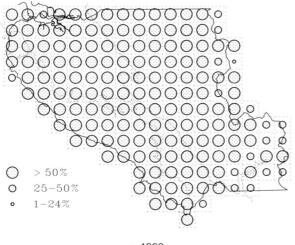

○ > 50%

○ 25-50%

∘ 1-24%

g. 1993

Figure 6.5. (*Concluded.*)

areas that still remained to be covered. These areas included a large region in the center of the northern Diablo Range, scattered areas in the southeastern Diablo Range, a section of blocks in the southern Santa Clara Valley, and a few blocks in the central Santa Cruz Mountains.

On the basis of the original plan, 1992 (Fig. 6.5f) was expected to be the final year of the atlas, and a great deal of effort was focused on the blank areas of the 1991 map. Although the number of active atlasers declined in 1992 from the peak of 31 in 1990, atlas field hours increased by 34% from the average of field hours pursued in 1988–91. The 1992 map demonstrates that at least some coverage was obtained in all but four of the atlas blocks, and that the 50% coverage goals were reached in most of the blocks in the county. After the 1992 year it was decided to extend the atlas by one year, so as to upgrade coverage or extend it to those blocks lacking coverage. The 1993 map (Fig. 6.5g) shows that, by and large, most coverage goals for the county's blocks were met, excepting, of course, the three blocks in the southeast where we never gained access.

Breeding Birds Recorded During the Atlas Period

From 1987 to 1993, atlasers confirmed breeding by 159 species, each of them in one or more of the 165 atlas blocks where access had been granted. Of these 159 species, all but three were observed nesting within the borders of Santa Clara County during this period. The only confirmation of Mountain Quail was in Castle Rock State Park in the Santa Cruz County portion of an edge block, although birds were recorded within Santa Clara County in Stevens Creek Canyon. Probable evidence of Golden-crowned Kinglets breeding was found in a number of Santa Cruz County edge blocks, but the only confirmation was in the Santa Cruz County portion of an edge block. In the postatlas period, 1994 to 2005, however, these kinglets were found breeding within Santa Clara County. One confirmation of breeding by MacGillivray's Warbler was recorded in the Santa Cruz County portion of an edge block, but no confirma-

tions were recorded in Santa Clara County. Species accounts, with graphics, have been prepared for all of the 159 species, and are included in Chapter 7.

Probable breeding evidence was observed for seven additional species during the atlas period, but no confirmation of breeding was obtained in these cases. The seven are Blue-winged Teal, Green-winged Teal, Redhead, Virginia Rail, Greater Roadrunner, Costa's Hummingbird, and Red Crossbill. There are historical breeding records in the county for five of these species: Blue-winged Teal, Green-winged Teal, Redhead, Greater Roadrunner, and Costa's Hummingbird, but no certain historical breeding records for Virginia Rail or Red Crossbill. Greater Roadrunner is a rare resident in Santa Clara County and likely breeds here every year, although its range has contracted in the last 100 years. All seven of these species are considered to be a part of the Santa Clara County breeding avifauna, although, except for Greater Roadrunner, they are considered casual or irregular breeders. Green-winged Teal was found breeding in the Alameda County portion of an edge block in 1997, during the postatlas period. Species accounts have been prepared for each of these seven species.

Following the atlas period, from 1994 to 2005, breeding records were obtained for 11 additional species. These species, with the year when breeding was first observed in parentheses, are: Ring-necked Duck (1997), American Bittern (1997), Osprey (2004), Peregrine Falcon (1996), Black Skimmer (1994), Pileated Woodpecker (1996), Cassin's Kingbird (1997), Bell's Vireo (1997), Cedar Waxwing (2002), Blue Grosbeak (1995), and Great-tailed Grackle (1998). There are historical records for three of these species: American Bittern, Peregrine Falcon, and Bell's Vireo. Species accounts have been prepared for these 11 species, bringing the total of all species accounts to 177. These 177 species, then, are considered the present breeding avifauna of Santa Clara County.

There are ten species that are known to have bred in Santa Clara County prior to the atlas period, but are believed to have been extirpated as breeders within the county. These species, with the date of most recent recorded breeding in parentheses, are: Fulvous Whistling-Duck (1917), Swainson's Hawk (1894), Black Rail (before 1904), Sora (1936), Yellow-billed Cuckoo (1901), Short-eared Owl (1972), Lesser Nighthawk (1937), Willow Flycatcher (1962), Bank Swallow (1931), and Yellow-headed Blackbird (1894). The historical breeding records for each of these species are discussed in Appendix 8.

Four non-native species are grouped with the 177 breeding species discussed previously: Ring-necked Pheasant, Rock Pigeon, European Starling, and House Sparrow. The Ring-necked Pheasant was purposely introduced into Santa Clara County in the last half of the nineteenth century. Rock Pigeons likely arrived with the early Spanish settlers. European Starlings, introduced on the East Coast, invaded western North America on their own wing-power. The House Sparrow was likely introduced into San Francisco in the latter half of the nineteenth century and followed the rail and carriage roads into Santa Clara County. Six additional non-native species have been introduced into Santa Clara County in the last hundred years or so and have established breeding populations, most of which have proved to be ephemeral. These include: Chukar, Northern Bobwhite,

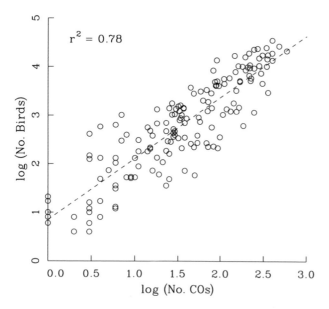

Figure 6.6. Correlation between the log of abundance estimate and the log of the number of confirmations after removing duplicate records (see text).

Mitred Parakeet, Blue-crowned Parakeet, Nutmeg Mannikin, and Orange Bishop. As of 2005, only Mitred Parakeet, Nutmeg Mannikin, and Orange Bishop are believed to be still breeding in Santa Clara County, and it remains unclear whether these populations are established or will be extirpated, as has been the fate of other introduced birds. Breeding by each of these species is discussed in Appendix 9.

Breeding has been recorded in the county in 2006 for two species, Bald Eagle and Virginia Rail, since this book was written, and these records are discussed in Appendix 10.

Abundance

As discussed in Chapter 5, we used two methods to estimate the abundance of individual species nesting in Santa Clara County. The first method was based on the atlasers' estimates of the numbers of birds of each species breeding in a block. We calculated an estimate of the number of birds of a species breeding in the county as a whole by using the average of all block estimates and scaling this average by the total number of blocks in which the species occurred. The abundance estimate thus has a wide error band and is considered approximate. The second method was a total count of breeding confirmations after excluding duplicate records. Atlasers were encouraged to record all breeding confirmations observed, regardless of whether a species had already been confirmed in a block or not. Then, all records with coordinates were searched (two-thirds of all confirmations), and those that were duplicates (had the same coordinates) were not included in the total count of confirmations. The first method provided a direct estimate of the number of birds in the county. Though the second method is an index of abundance, it does not provide a direct estimate of the number of birds in the county.

These two estimates of abundance are related as shown in Fig. 6.6. We calculated the logarithm for each method, and the

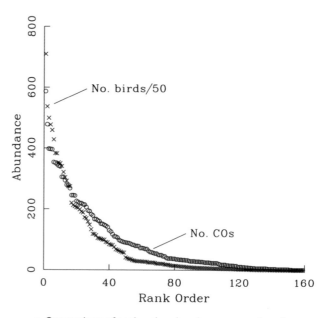

a. Comparison of rank order abundance, normal scale. Number of birds divided by 50.

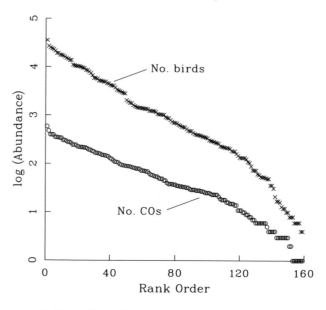

b. Comparison of rank order abundance, log scale.

Figure 6.7. Comparisons of estimates of abundance for confirmed breeding species, 1987 to 1993.

correlation between the log measurements is quite good, with r^2 = 0.79. This correlation suggests that the count of nonduplicate confirmations for the seven-year atlas period can also be used to estimate the actual abundance.

The ranking of species by their frequency of occurrence is a useful way to summarize abundance data (Linsdale 1928), that is, with the most common species ranked first, the second most common second, and so on. This ranking, at least in temperate zones, generally shows a hyperbolic form. Figure 6.7a compares the number of birds (in this case scaled by 50 for com-

Table 6.2. The ten most common species in Santa Clara County, based on the number of birds estimated by using the abundance code from the Field Cards.

Species	No. Birds	Rank
California Towhee	35,457	1
Western Scrub-Jay	26,829	2
House Finch	24,958	3
Mourning Dove	23,846	4
Spotted Towhee	22,960	5
European Starling	21,415	6
Bushtit	19,177	7
Lesser Goldfinch	19,141	8
Oak Titmouse	17,645	9
California Quail	17,511	10

Table 6.3. The ten most common species in Santa Clara County, based on the number of confirmations without duplicates.

Species	No. COs	Rank
European Starling	587	1
Western Scrub-Jay	478	2
Brewer's Blackbird	398	3
California Towhee	397	4
Bushtit	396	5
Black Phoebe	354	6
Oak Titmouse	352	7
Dark-eyed Junco	347	8
American Robin	342	9
House Finch	339	10

Table 6.4. The ten rarest species in Santa Clara County, based on the number of birds estimated by using the abundance code from the Field Cards.

Species	No. Birds	Rank
Hermit Warbler	10	150
Clark's Grebe	8	151
Double-crested Cormorant	8	152
White-faced Ibis	8	153
Golden-crowned Kinglet	6	154
Indigo Bunting	6	155
Long-eared Owl	6	156
MacGillivray's Warbler	6	157
Little Blue Heron	4	158
Western Gull	4	159

Table 6.5. The ten rarest species in Santa Clara County, based on the number of confirmations without duplicates.

Species	No. COs	Rank
Hermit Warbler	3	150
White-faced Ibis	2	151
Western Gull	2	152
Canvasback	1	153
Mountain Quail	1	154
Clark's Grebe	1	155
Purple Martin	1	156
Golden-crowned Kinglet	1	157
MacGillivray's Warbler	1	158
Indigo Bunting	1	159

parison purposes) with the number of nonduplicate confirmations for the 159 species found breeding during the atlas period, based on their frequency of occurrence. Figure 6.7b shows the same information, but on a logarithmic ordinate scale. The data on this log scale show a linear character for the most common birds, that is, the first 75% of all species, whereas the 25% that are the least common are found in lesser numbers than would be predicted by extending the main sequence. The utility of the plots in Fig. 6.7 is to point out that this atlas is most accurate in its abundance assessment of the more common species, whereas the status of the rarest species will always be difficult to assess accurately.

The ten most common breeding species in Santa Clara County are shown in rank order in Tables 6.2 and 6.3 using the two estimates of abundance. Six species appear on both lists: Western Scrub-Jay, Oak Titmouse, Bushtit, European Starling, California Towhee, and House Finch.

The ten rarest breeding species are listed in rank order in Tables 6.4 and 6.5. Seven species appear on both lists: Clark's Grebe, White-faced Ibis, Western Gull, Golden-crowned Kinglet, Hermit Warbler, MacGillivray's Warbler, and Indigo Bunting.

The 159 species confirmed breeding during the atlas period are listed in Appendix 5, with both estimates of their abundance and their position in both rank orders.

Species Richness

Species richness is defined here as the number of species in a block for which we obtained confirmed, probable, or possible evidence during the seven-year atlas period. (The geographical distribution of species richness is shown above in Fig. 6.2.) In discussing species richness, it is useful to divide the blocks into the seven regions we described in Chapter 5 (see Fig. 5.5). Table 6.6 (here) shows statistics that describe the results from the seven regions. The mean values range from 51 in Region 4, the urban region, to 73 in Regions 1 and 2 in the Santa Cruz Mountains. The mean in Region 5, however, in the southern Santa Clara Valley, and that in Region 6, in the northern Diablo Range, is 69, only four species less than that in the Santa Cruz Mountains.

In general, higher species richness is seen in the Santa Cruz Mountains, the Diablo Range, and the southern Santa Clara

Table 6.6. Species richness statistics for seven atlas regions.

	Region	Confirmations, probables, and possibles				No. of blocks
		Mean	Standard deviation	Max	Min	
1	Northern Santa Cruz Mountains	73	9	87	60	13
2	Southern Santa Cruz Mountains	73	10	93	53	24
3	San Francisco Bay edge	52	24	73	5	9
4	Urban (Nor. Santa Clara Valley)	51	12	77	33	20
5	Southern Santa Clara Valley	69	9	91	49	28
6	Northern Diablo Range	69	14	99	30	31
7	Southern Diablo Range	62	9	75	32	40

Valley than along the Bay edge and in urban northern Santa Clara Valley. The species richness along the Bay, however, is biased by Blocks 8045 and 8545, which are mostly water or salt ponds. If these two blocks are excluded, the mean increases to 64 species, the standard deviation is seven species, and the minimum in this case is 56 species. Adjusted in this way, the Bay edge shows species richness that is intermediate between the urban areas and the other regions.

The maximum and minimum numbers of breeding species recorded in the various regions provide some insight into the distribution of species richness. Peak block counts include 99 species in the northern Diablo Range, 93 in the southern Santa Cruz Mountains, and 91 in the southern Santa Clara Valley. In most cases, these high counts are related to the great variety of habitats present there. Often there are large elevation changes in these blocks, and various plant communities are influenced by the amount of insolation. In the Santa Cruz Mountains, shady north-facing slopes are often covered with wet conifer forests, whereas the south-facing slopes will show patches of scrub and chaparral mixed in with broadleaved evergreen forests. In the Diablo Range, the effects of high relief and insolation differences also affect the plant communities, but here the north-facing slopes will have broadleaved evergreen woodlands and some shrub cover, whereas the south-facing slopes are a mixture of chaparral and grasslands. These various habitats are attractive to different species of birds, and even though the Diablo Range receives less rainfall than the Santa Cruz Mountains and supports different bird communities, the species richness of the two is much the same.

The presence of water may promote greater species richness by attracting certain species not found elsewhere. For example, the peak count in the northern Diablo Range was of 99 species in Block 0545, which contains the eastern half of Calaveras Reservoir. The second-highest count in the region was of 93 species in Block 0045, which includes the remainder of Calaveras Reservoir. Similarly, the highest count in the southern Santa Clara Valley was in Block 0515, which includes Calero Reservoir.

The lowest count in the Santa Cruz Mountains was 53 species, whereas the lowest count in the Diablo Range was much lower, at 30 species. In the former case, the edge block had good coverage, and the low richness noted there is probably representative of that region. But the low counts of 30 and 32 species in Regions 6 and 7 were in edge blocks where our coverage was poorer.

The lower species richness in the urban northern Santa Clara Valley may be partly related to urbanization and the resulting lack of diversity of habitats. Those blocks with greater species richness, such as Block 0035, included areas at the edge of the foothills and hence presented greater diversity of habitats. Some urban blocks have parklands associated with the Guadalupe River and Coyote Creek watersheds, and these blocks had increased numbers of species. Even prior to urbanization, northern Santa Clara County may have had a reduced number of species. The combination of a lack of relief and low rainfall probably resulted in fewer plant communities there than are found nearby in the adjacent mountains.

Postatlas Results

The postatlas database includes 9,140 breeding records for the years from 1994 to 2005. Among these are records of 11 species that were not recorded breeding during the atlas period. Of the postatlas records, about 72% are confirmations, and 90% of the confirmations include coordinates and elevations. We made no attempt to obtain uniform coverage of the county for the postatlas database. Rather, the preponderance of records were incidental to other projects or obtained during normal birding excursions. Breeding records in the postatlas database were obtained using the same protocols as for the atlas database.

Figure 6.8 shows the coverage we obtained with the postatlas database. The number of confirmations for that period have been divided by the confirmations, probables, and possibles for the atlas period (Fig. 6.2), using the same format as for Fig. 6.5. The coverage, in general, was very good along the South Bay and in many parts of the northern Santa Clara Valley. Much of the extensive coverage in blocks near the Coyote Narrows was a consequence of Stephen C. Rottenborn's fieldwork for his doctoral thesis (Rottenborn 1997). The coverage in edge blocks in the northern Diablo Range was a result of atlasing carried out for the Alameda County atlas in 1994 and 1995 by Michael M. Rogers. Rogers accessed the southern Alameda County atlas blocks through the same routes he had used in his efforts for the present atlas, and recorded breeding observations in the Alameda County portion of the Santa Clara County edge blocks.

Postatlas coverage can also be examined using the "fly speck" type of plot shown in Fig. 6.4, above, and in Fig. 6.9,

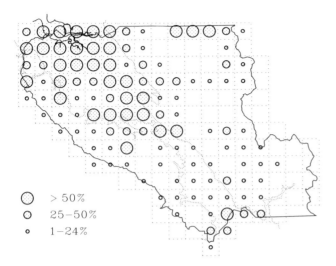

Figure 6.8. Postatlas coverage of Santa Clara County atlas blocks, 1994 to 2005.

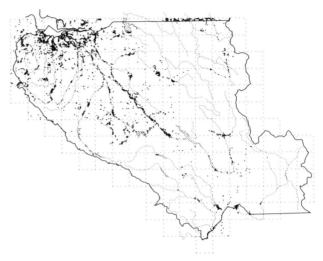

Figure 6.9. Postatlas breeding confirmation locations in 165 blocks, 1994 to 2005.

here. There was extensive coverage in the northern Santa Clara Valley, particularly at the edge of the South Bay. Also notable, as mentioned previously, is Rottenborn's extensive set of breeding records for riparian birds along Coyote Creek and Guadalupe River. In the northern Diablo Range, we see again the extensive set of breeding confirmations recorded by Rogers from the Alameda County portion of the edge blocks there. There is also a scattering of records from the east side of the Santa Cruz Mountains, along Mt. Hamilton, San Antonio Valley, and Del Puerto roads in the northern Diablo Range, and from Henry Coe State Park.

The breeding records in the postatlas database are a valuable addition to the atlas in a number of respects. As mentioned previously, the postatlas database contains the records of 11 breeding species for which no breeding evidence was obtained during the atlas period: Ring-necked Duck, American Bittern, Osprey, Peregrine Falcon, Black Skimmer, Pileated Woodpecker, Cassin's Kingbird, Bell's Vireo, Cedar Waxwing, Blue Grosbeak, and Great-tailed Grackle. (An account is included for each of these species.) In addition, confirmed breeding evidence was found for one species, Green-winged Teal, for which only probable evidence had been obtained during the atlas period. Throughout the species accounts, it will be noted that re-

sults from the postatlas database have been used to add to or "upgrade" the atlas period breeding records. The maps in the species accounts employ different symbols (open circles) for postatlas breeding records, so that atlas and postatlas records are easily differentiated.

For a few species, there have been significant changes in breeding patterns since the atlas fieldwork was completed in 1993. Notable in this regard are the colonially nesting herons. Most of these herons nested only at the Alviso heronry during the atlas period, but with the failure of that heronry in the late 1990s, many species have dispersed to other places along the South Bay and to inland lakes and reservoirs. This movement is well documented in the postatlas data. Another example is the expansion of breeding Dark-eyed Juncos into urban areas, which was just beginning to occur at the end of the atlas period. The further expansion of these new urban birds is documented in the postatlas data.

For some species, the postatlas data have substantially augmented the breeding phenology. In some cases, as discussed above, this is indicated as a second set of percentile bars expressing the postatlas phenology. In other cases, the phenology data from the two databases are combined.

7 Species Accounts

One hundred and seventy-seven species accounts, the heart of this volume, are included here. As discussed in Chapter 6, 159 of these accounts are of birds confirmed breeding in the 165 Santa Clara County atlas blocks surveyed during the atlas period, 1987–93. Eleven additional accounts are of species confirmed breeding here only in the postatlas period, 1994–2005, and seven more are of species considered to be regular elements of the Santa Clara County breeding bird avifauna even though breeding evidence for them was obtained only at the probable level during the atlasing.

Each species account includes a page of text and a facing graphics page. The purpose of what follows is to explain the structure and content of these two pages.

The Text Page

Basically, the text page is designed to cover the following: (1) the distribution of the species, here and elsewhere, (2) its historical status within Santa Clara County, (3) the species' breeding locations and habitats here, as determined during atlasing, (4) the breeding phenology of the species, and (5) relevant information concerning the present status of the species. This basic structure is sometimes modified. For example, Great-tailed Grackle is a species that has only recently begun breeding in Santa Clara County, following a range expansion throughout the southwestern United States. Thus, this grackle has no historical status here, and what is offered instead is a discussion of historical information documenting the range expansion in California, since this provides the appropriate context for Santa Clara County. In other cases, some of the basic information about a species is lacking. For rare species, as an example, there is sometimes not enough information to construct the phenology, and this material may be absent. Finally, the concluding paragraph describing some aspect of a species' local status is not always included. The author of each account is indicated at the end of the account.

In general, the species account does not include information on a species' breeding biology beyond some limited information on habitat preferences and phenology as they apply to Santa Clara County. There is a wealth of such information in the recently completed series of the *Birds of North America* pamphlets. These pamphlets, one per species, can be found in many university libraries as well as in the Santa Clara Valley Audubon Society library in Cupertino. The same information may be accessed on the internet for an annual fee (http://bna.birds.cornell.edu/BNA/). Many of the pamphlets from this series are referenced in the species accounts and, like all sources cited in this volume, are listed in the Literature Cited section at the end of the book. Shuford (1993a) and Roberson and Tenney (1993), in their respective atlases for Marin and Monterey counties, have covered a great deal of the literature concerning the breeding biology of birds found in central California, and both are excellent sources for the reader who wishes to know more about the life histories of these birds.

The first paragraph of the species account typically begins with a sentence or two that attempts to evoke something about the species that is of unique interest. This is followed by a series of sentences that detail the species' worldwide distribution, then its distribution in North America, then in California, finishing with the species' status in Santa Clara County. If the subject species is not monotypic, then there is a limited discussion in this paragraph of the subspecies that occur within Santa Clara County, and sometimes of subspecies found elsewhere.

The second paragraph generally focuses on what is known of the historical status of the species in Santa Clara County. There is a rich history of ornithological exploration in the county, much of which is summarized in Appendix 2. Early authors who recorded species seen in the county include Price (1898a-f), Van Denburgh (1899b), Barlow (1900b), and Fisher (1902). There are also many museums with records of both specimens and egg sets that were collected toward the end of the nineteenth century and in the earlier years of the twentieth century. Later authors offered a more general perspective on California birds. Joseph Grinnell wrote two checklists of California birds, with their status and distribution (Grinnell 1902, Grinnell 1915). In 1927, Grinnell with Margaret W. Wythe published *The Directory to the Bird-Life of the San Francisco Bay Region* (Grinnell and Wythe 1927), which covers the nine counties contiguous to the San Francisco Bay and includes Santa Clara County. Grinnell and Alden H. Miller published *The Distribution of the Birds of California* (Grinnell and Miller 1944), which as with Grinnell's earlier checklists covered all of California. The last of the major historical references is Charles G. Sibley's *The Birds of the South San Francisco Bay Region* (1952). In this mimeographed publication, Sibley treated mostly the birds in the southern San Francisco Bay region, that is, San Francisco, San Mateo, Santa Cruz, Santa Clara, and Alameda counties. For rarer species, however, he included records from Monterey, San Benito, and Contra Costa counties, and sometimes the North Bay counties.

In some cases, the historical paragraph concludes with an examination of Christmas Bird Count (CBC) data from the Palo Alto, San Jose, and Mt. Hamilton count circles, which together cover most of the northern part of Santa Clara County. The time series for the Palo Alto and San Jose circles are particularly extensive, as used here they extend from 1959 to 2004 for the Palo Alto count and 1956 to 2004 for the San Jose count. In addition, a more recent set of data from the Palo Alto count circle, referred to as the Palo Alto Summer Bird Count (SBC), as used here extends from 1981 to 2005 and is useful for covering the most recent 25-year period. When trends are observed in the records of the local count circles, these are sometimes compared to larger regional trends, as reported for the U.S. Government-sponsored Breeding Bird Survey (BBS).

The next one or two paragraphs of the species account discuss the results of atlasing. Generally, there is a description of where a species was found to be breeding in the county, and what habitats the birds used. Data on the elevations where breeding was observed are included when this is considered important. For rare species, there may be a brief mention of individual records, so as to better understand why a species was found in a particular location. In many cases, postatlas information is included, as well as the results from the atlas period. In discussing atlas records, the dates are generally given only as day and month, and the observer's name is not included. But for postatlas records the dates include the year of observation as well, and the observers are normally cited. Postatlas records are sometimes cited as PADB, which refers to the postatlas database.

Most of the species accounts include a paragraph on breeding phenology (calendar dates for nest building, incubation, feeding of young, fledging, and so forth). This paragraph augments the phenology information on the graphics page (discussed below) and provides additional information on the timing of the breeding behaviors that were observed during the atlas period, and sometimes the postatlas period as well.

The species account often ends with a paragraph that discusses some particular circumstance of breeding in the local area. This may refer to unusual behaviors, population trends, or information on the species that is peculiar to its breeding in Santa Clara County. In some cases, however, such information fits better within other paragraphs of the account and in these cases there is no final paragraph of the usual sort.

The Graphics Page

Figure 7.1 is an example of the graphics page (Common Raven). The page includes three sections, as numbered on the figure. The first, or top, section shows population trend data across time, based on the three Christmas Bird Counts (CBCs) and the Summer Bird Count (SBC) in the Palo Alto count circle.

The second, or middle, section shows the atlas map, with symbols that represent the species' breeding status here. (The count circles for the CBC and SBC data shown in the top section are overlaid on the map in the second section.) The third, or bottom, section presents breeding phenology. (See also Fig. 7.3.)

The plot of trend data for each CBC is placed above its respective count circle. The abscissas for all of the trend plots extend from 1955 to 2005, regardless of the timespan of the data series in each circle. The ordinates are normally birds/party-hour, as seen in Fig. 7.1. But there are many cases where the ordinate is the actual number of birds recorded, which is particularly appropriate for rare species, and for nocturnal or secretive species that are hard to detect. For all species the same ordinate is used for each of the trend plots, giving an approximate idea of the relative commonness of a species from one count circle to the next.

Figure 7.1 shows population trend data for the Common Raven in all three count circles, that is, Palo Alto, San Jose, and Mt. Hamilton, but this does not hold for all species. For those that are summer residents (thus not here in December), such as Olive-sided Flycatcher, Blue-gray Gnatcatcher, Yellow Warbler, or Grasshopper Sparrow, only trend data from the Palo Alto SBC are shown. Many resident species, such as the Common Raven, show data from both the SBC and the CBCs, but not all resident species occur in all count circles. Thus, for such Diablo Range residents as Yellow-billed Magpie and Canyon Wren, trend data are shown only for the San Jose and Mt. Hamilton CBCs. A number of species have differing numbers between summer and winter. For example, Yellow-rumped Warbler is abundant in the winter, but very rare in the summer, the only season when they might be county breeders. Thus, only the Palo Alto SBC data are shown for this species. Even some very common species, for example Killdeer and European Starling, have significantly augmented populations in the winter, so again, as with Yellow-rumped Warbler, only the Palo Alto SBC trend data are given.

The computation of population trends is discussed in Chapter 5. If population trend data for a given species are significant at the 0.05 level, then a trend line is added, and the statistics are written out. These statistics include the population change in percent per year, ΔPop; the coefficient of determination, r^2, which shows what fraction of the variation is explained by time; and the value of the level of significance, p. The CBC data are shown with a solid line for all count circles, and if a trend line is included it is dashed. The Palo Alto count circle includes both CBC and SBC data, and it is sometimes difficult to distinguish the two data sets on the graph (a magnifying glass may be helpful). The Palo Alto CBC data extend from 1959 and this may be useful in distinguishing them from the SBC data, which start in 1981. The SBC data are shown with a dashed-dot line and, if a trend line is included, it is also a dashed-dot line. When the trends are significant for both the CBC and SBC data, the CBC numbers are listed first, as in Fig. 7.1.

The San Jose CBC count circle was shifted 4.3 km north-northwest in 1972, as discussed in Chapter 5. For this reason, population trends for waterbirds or other marsh-dependent species are calculated only from 1972 to 2004 for this circle. A good example of this can be seen in the graphic for the Northern Harrier species account.

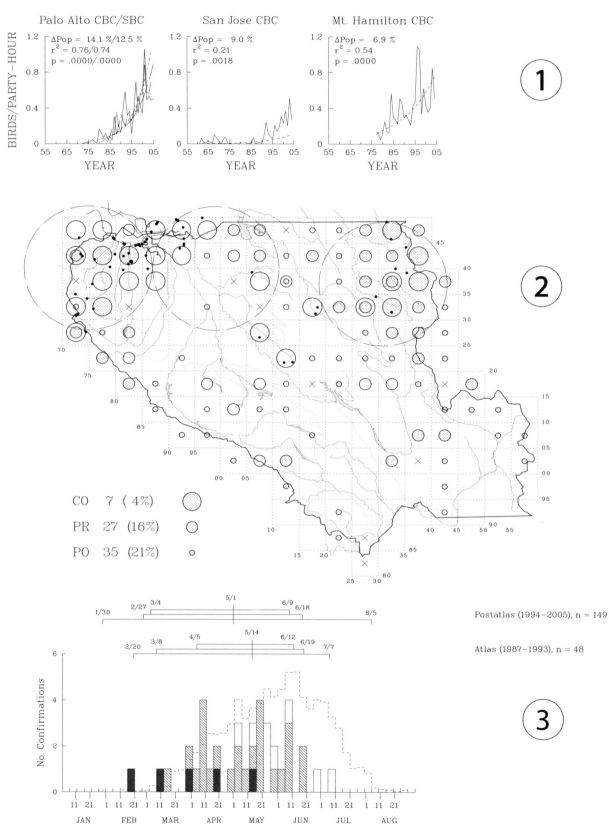

Figure 7.1. Example species account graphic (Common Raven).

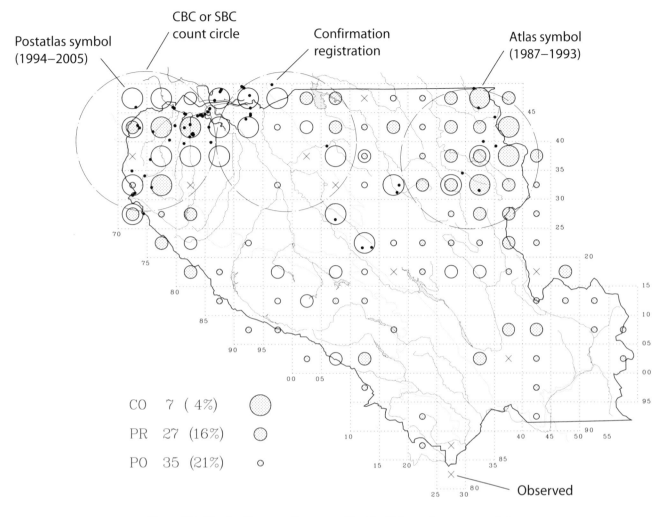

Figure 7.2. Map for Common Raven graphic, identifying various map symbols.

The map for Common Raven is shown at somewhat larger scale in Fig. 7.2, with explanations of the symbols used. In the lower left corner there are three lines that list the number and percentages of county blocks in which confirmations (CO), probable evidence (PR), and possible evidence (PO) were recorded during the atlas period. Included on these lines are the symbols whose sizes contrast the three levels of evidence. Thus, a large filled circle is used for confirmations, a medium filled circle is used for probable evidence, and a small filled circle is used for possible evidence. These three lines of explanation are present on all of the species account graphics.

Various symbols on the map are labeled in Fig. 7.2, for clarification. The atlas data, obtained from 1987 to 1993, are shown with filled circles. The postatlas data, from 1994 to 2005, are shown with open circles. The CBC count circles, which are 24.2 km (15 miles) in diameter, are represented by circles with dashed-dot peripheries. The very small solid black circles are the locations of confirmations; no distinction is made between the atlas and postatlas databases for these symbols.

Observed evidence generally relates to birds that are not in nesting habitat (see the definition in Fig. 5.2) and is included on the atlas maps for only a few wide-ranging species. This evidence is shown with an × symbol and, as with the black dots for confirmation registration, no distinction is made between atlas and postatlas data.

The phenology graphic, which is the third and lowest section of the species account graphic, is shown in Fig. 7.3 with labels illustrating its features. The primary portion of the graphic is a column graph that shows the phenology (temporal distribution) of atlas confirmations obtained from 1987 to 1993. These confirmations are shown in three groups that relate to the nature of the breeding evidence. The first group, representing the nest-building stage (solid-black column portions), includes the codes for carrying nest material (CN) and nest building (NB). The second group, representing the nesting stage (striped column portions), includes the codes for an occupied nest (ON), a nest with eggs (NE), a nest with young (NY), and an adult carrying a fecal sac (FS). The third group, the postnesting stage (clear column portions), includes the codes for precocial young (PY), feeding young (FY), and fledged young (FL). The records are distributed on the graph in five-day bins that are referenced to the date 1 Jun (the bin size and reference date are arbitrary). The

97

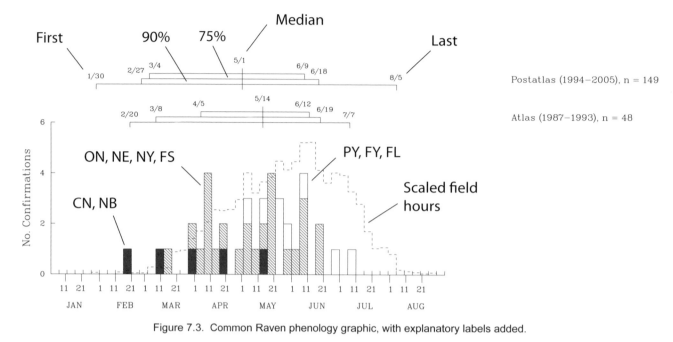

Figure 7.3. Common Raven phenology graphic, with explanatory labels added.

atlas period field hours (unchanged from one species graphic to the next) are shown with a dashed line in the background, using the same five-day bins. (The field hours are scaled to match the column graph ordinate to provide a consistent reference for the species graphics.)

Two sets of percentile bars are shown for the phenology graphic in Fig. 7.3, above the column bars. The lower set of percentile bars, those for the atlas data, corresponds directly to the column graph below. Because the number of dated confirmations for Common Raven is greater than 20 (see discussion in Chapter 5), three sets of percentile bars are illustrated for its graphic: (1) all data, that is, earliest confirmation to latest, including the median or 50th percentile; (2) 5th to 95th percentile, which includes 90% of the data; and (3) 12.5th to 87.5th percentile, which includes 75% of the data. To the right of the percentile bars, the data are labeled to indicate the database and the number of dated confirmations, $n = 48$, in this case. The upper set of percentile bars, those for the postatlas data, is defined in the same fashion as those for the atlas data.

As discussed in Chapter 5, the configuration (and context) of the phenology graphic depends upon both the absolute and the relative sizes of the atlas and postatlas databases. It is important to characterize the phenology associated with the atlas database, since this represents the uniform field coverage that was obtained over the atlas period. The postatlas coverage, in contrast, was incidental and not uniform (compare Figs. 6.5 and 6.8). Hence, the atlas period phenology is the nominal condition and is shown in most of the species accounts. But there are cases where the postatlas data are so extensive relative to the atlas data that it was necessary to include the postatlas phenology in the species graphic.

Four categories or cases are used. Case 1, the nominal case, is used when the number of postatlas records is less than 70% of the number of atlas records. In this case, only the atlas data are shown. An example of a Case 1 phenology graphic, for

Western Kingbird, is shown in Fig. 7.4. This graphic includes a column graph and the associated percentile bars. To the right, the percentile bars are identified as being associated with the atlas period.

The Case 2 phenology graphic has already been shown, in Fig. 7.3, for Common Raven, where the number of dated confirmations in the postatlas database ranges between 70 and 400% of those in the atlas database.

An example of a Case 3 phenology graphic, for Snowy Egret, is shown in Fig. 7.5. Because the number of dated confirmations in the postatlas database exceeds 400% of those in the atlas database, the two sets are combined, and both a column graph and percentile bars are shown. The data are indicated as being "combined" on the right side. The scaled field hour data are shown on the column graph as a reference, even though most of the phenology data in this case is from the postatlas database.

An example of a Case 4 phenology graphic, in this case for Cassin's Kingbird, is shown in Fig. 7.6. Both the column graph and the percentile bars are based on the postatlas data, as indicated to the right. For the column graph, there are no scaled field hours in the background, since all of the phenology data in this case were obtained after the atlas period. The percentile bars in this example include only two bars, the 0th to 100th percentiles and the 12.5th to 87.5 percentiles.

Apparent inconsistencies may appear in the phenology data. These are artifacts of how the data were analyzed, or of how records were supplied by atlasers. One example can be seen in the phenology graphic for Sharp-shinned Hawk. The earliest record in the column graph is for the five-day period starting 6 Jul, although the percentile bar gives the earliest record as 9 Jun. This apparent discrepancy is caused by excluding records of carrying food (CF) from the column graphic, whereas all of these records are used in calculating percentiles. As discussed above, carrying food may reflect prenesting, nesting, or post-

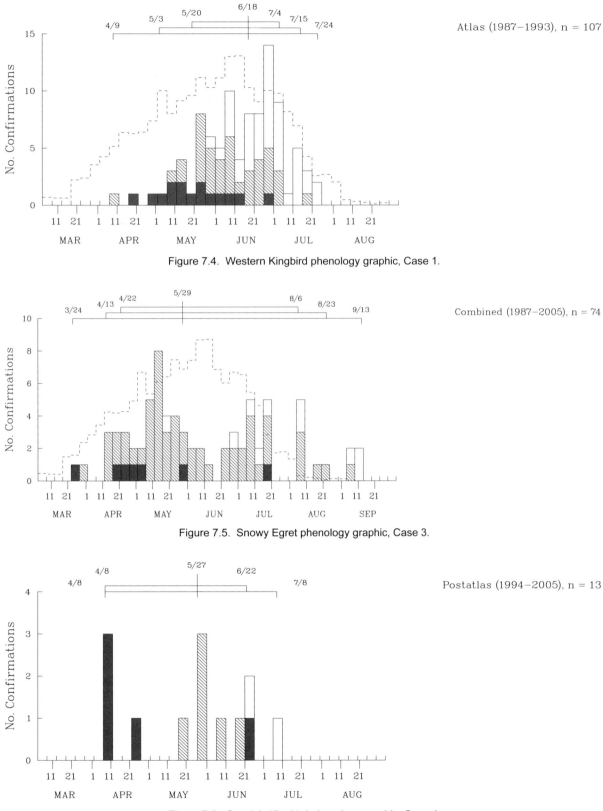

Figure 7.4. Western Kingbird phenology graphic, Case 1.

Atlas (1987–1993), n = 107

Combined (1987–2005), n = 74

Figure 7.5. Snowy Egret phenology graphic, Case 3.

Postatlas (1994–2005), n = 13

Figure 7.6. Cassin's Kingbird phenology graphic, Case 4.

nesting stages, and these records therefore cannot be included on the column graph, which separates the three stages.

Another apparent inconsistency arises in comparing the Ring-necked Pheasant phenology graphic to its map. The phenology graphic indicates that only six dated confirmations were obtained during the atlas period, whereas the map shows that this species was confirmed breeding in eight blocks. The cause of this apparent inconsistency is that confirmations in two bayside blocks were undated, and hence could not be included in the phenology analysis.

Probable evidence of breeding here, but no confirmations, were obtained for seven species during the atlas period: Blue-winged Teal, Green-winged Teal, Redhead, Virginia Rail, Greater Roadrunner, Costa's Hummingbird, and Red Crossbill. During the postatlas period, we recorded one confirmation for Green-winged Teal, and we have therefore included a phenology plot for this species (Case 4). But for the other six species there are no phenology data, and accordingly no phenology graphics are included for these species.

Species Accounts

(beginning on overleaf)

Glossary

Am. Birds. *American Birds*, source of bird records, 1971 to 1994.

Audubon Field Notes. Source of bird records, 1947 to 1970.

Avocet. Newsletter of the Santa Clara Valley Audubon Society, 1954 to 2005.

Bird-Lore. Source of bird records, 1922 to 1941.

CAS. California Academy of Sciences, San Francisco, Cal., egg set or specimen records.

CBC. Christmas Bird Count. Data analyzed from Palo Alto circle (1959 to 2004), San Jose count circle (1956 to 2004), and Mt. Hamilton count circle (1977 to 2004).

Field Notes. Source of bird records, 1994 to 1998.

Gull. Newsletter of the Golden Gate Audubon Society, 1919 to 2005.

MVZ. Museum of Vertebrate Zoology, University of California, Berkeley, egg set or specimen records.

N. Am. Birds. *North American Birds*, source of bird records, 1999 to 2005.

p. Level of significance for population changes in CBC or SBC data (see p. 95).

PADB. Postatlas database, 1994 to 2005.

r^2. Square of correlation coefficient for population trends (see p. 95).

SBC. Summer Bird Count. Data analyzed from Palo Alto count circle (1981 to 2005).

USNM. United States National Museum (Smithsonian), Washington, D.C., egg set or specimen records.

WFVZ. Western Foundation of Vertebrate Zoology, Camarillo, Cal., egg set or specimen records.

ΔPop. Population change in CBC or SBC data, % per year (see p. 95)..

Canada Goose
Branta canadensis

The fall passage of Canada Geese down the midlands of North America once evoked a sense of wildness and images of the distant Arctic. But in a curious turn of fate, this fabled wilderness totem has now shed that wildness and joined us in our urban enclaves. The Canada Goose breeds from Alaska, across Canada, and south to northwestern California and northern Florida (Mowbray et al. 2002). There are additional, disjunct populations of nonmigratory birds south of the historic breeding range, most of them of recent origin and many in urban areas. Seven subspecies are generally recognized, although the number of these and the relationships among them are still unresolved (Mowbray et al. 2002, AOU 2004). A number of western subspecies winter at least occasionally in California, but the subspecies *B. c. moffitti* is the only native subspecies breeding here and is the likely source of our feral populations (Shuford 1993d). Prior to the introduction of feral birds, this goose was an uncommon wintering species in Santa Clara County, most often observed at Calaveras Reservoir. Now, feral birds are increasingly common year-round residents, both near the Bay and in urban areas with lakes and percolation ponds.

Various species of wintering geese were abundant in the South Bay at the time of first settlement (Bryant 1890), but their numbers declined significantly during the era of market hunting (Grinnell et al. 1918). Kobbé (1902) referred to these geese as occurring in the "inner portions" of the San Francisco Bay, whereas Grinnell and Wythe (1927) reported them locally in San Pablo and Suisun bays. It is unclear when Canada Geese first started wintering at the larger reservoirs, such as Crystal Springs and Calaveras, but wintering flocks of 200 to 300 birds were established at Crystal Springs Reservoir by the late 1920s (Moffitt 1931), and Sibley (1952) recorded them wintering at Calaveras Reservoir by 1951.

There are sporadic breeding records from the San Francisco Bay area beginning in the early twentieth century, some assisted by humans, but others thought to be of wild birds. De Groot collected four eggs from a nest in San Francisco on 10 Jun 1915 (WFVZ #96369), but the actual location was not recorded

and the source of the parent stock is unknown. Captive birds from Nevada were transplanted to Alvarado, Alameda County, prior to 1918, and escaped birds nested there (Smith 1918). Over the first two decades of the twentieth century, captive birds of the closely related Cackling Goose were kept at Stow Lake, San Francisco, and these birds nested for the first time in 1920 (D'Evelyn 1920). Two pairs of Canada Geese that apparently nested at Crystal Springs Reservoir in the spring of 1932 were thought to be wild birds (*Bird-Lore 35*:112 1933, Moffitt 1939). In the 1950s, feral birds from captive *moffitti* stock nested at Lake Merritt, Alameda County, and at least four nests were there in 1956 (*Audubon Field Notes 10*:176 1956). Birds found nesting on Brooks Island, Contra Costa County in 1958, were considered to be wild, migratory birds, although their origin is uncertain (Lidicker and McCollum 1979). It appears in any case that feral Canada Geese expanded south along the east side of the Bay in the 1970s. The first evidence of breeding in Santa Clara County was of a pair with three downy young found in Artesian Slough on 23 May 1986 (*S. F. Bay Bird Observ. Newsl. 6*(2) 1986). Shuford (1993d) has argued that the major expansion of breeding Canada Geese into the San Francisco Bay area is based completely on introduced stock rather than wild birds.

Atlasers found Canada Geese breeding in many locations along the edge of the South Bay by 1988 and 1989. As indicated by analysis of Palo Alto CBC and SBC data, the local population has increased by about 30% per year since breeding began. Nesting birds were found in the eastern foothills at Lake Cunningham by 1989 and at Grant Lake by 1990. Breeding farther south occurred at Almaden Lake in 1991, at the Ogier Avenue ponds in 1993, the Parkway Lakes in 1996, and the Los Gatos Creek percolation ponds in 1998. Nesting birds found at San Felipe Lake (close by in San Benito County) in 1992 may have come from the South Bay stock or from birds introduced into Monterey County in 1984 (Weed 1993a). Canada Geese nest in a variety of wetland habitats, ranging from freshwater lakes, reservoirs, and ponds to brackish and saltwater marshes. In most cases they nest on islands, dikes, or drier ground in marshes, where they have protection from ground predators.

During our atlas period, the earliest nesting evidence was a bird on a nest on 30 Mar, but subsequent to the atlas a bird was found on a nest as early as 9 Mar 1999 (Stephen C. Rottenborn, pers. comm.). The latest evidence of nesting during the atlas was fledged young on 21 Jul.

The management of feral Canada Geese in urban areas has now become a major problem for wildlife agencies and other stewardship organizations across the United States and Canada. This species is now a nuisance in over 100 urban areas in 37 states (Mowbray et al. 2002). In some areas feces have been implicated in the eutrophication of small lakes as well as in the contamination of parks, schoolyards, and swimming areas. For feral populations in urban areas, hunting is not a control option, and more expensive techniques, such as removal of birds or addling of eggs, must be employed (Mowbray et al. 2002).

William G. Bousman

CANADA GOOSE

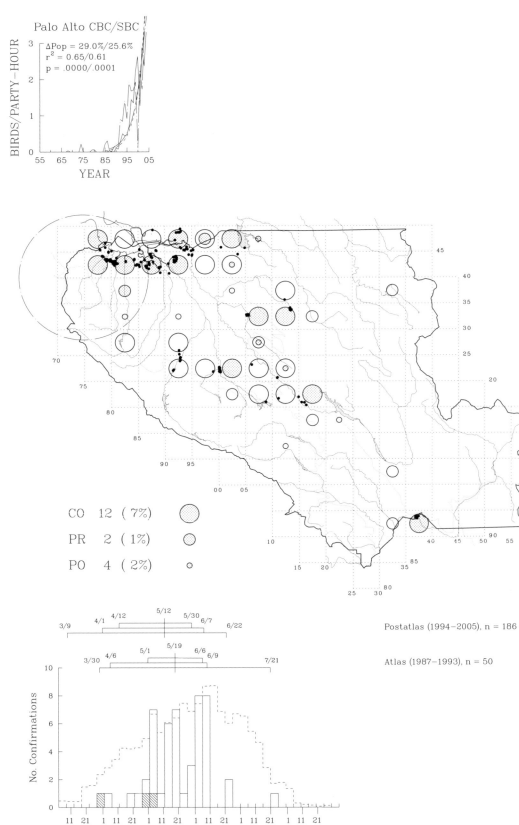

Palo Alto CBC/SBC

ΔPop = 29.0%/25.6%
r^2 = 0.65/0.61
p = .0000/.0001

BIRDS/PARTY–HOUR

YEAR

CO 12 (7%)
PR   2 (1%)
PO   4 (2%)

Postatlas (1994–2005), n = 186

Atlas (1987–1993), n = 50

No. Confirmations

MAR   APR   MAY   JUN   JUL   AUG

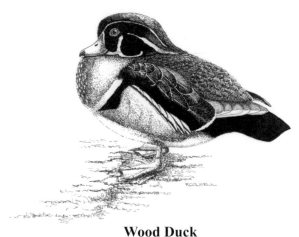

Wood Duck
Aix sponsa

As its name implies, the Wood Duck's favored haunts are quiet wooded streams and backwaters. Here, the richly colored, sleek-crested drake and his more subtly plumaged mate effectively blend into their dappled surroundings. Though Wood Ducks are more common in eastern and central North America, smaller numbers of them occur in the west, from British Columbia through Washington and Oregon, and in California as far south as Santa Barbara. During the breeding season in Santa Clara County, this uncommon species is found almost exclusively along streams, ponds, or reservoir backwaters that are shaded by thick edge growth and mature willow, cottonwood, sycamore, or oak, the trees also providing the nesting cavities required by this species.

Prior to 1870, the Wood Duck was considered common in this part of the state (Sibley 1952), but market hunting and the destruction of riparian woodlands greatly reduced these populations, and by the early 1900s Wood Ducks were considered rare here. In fact, Grinnell and Wythe (1927) knew of no recent records of wild birds in any part of the Bay Area. After 1927 there was a gradual population increase in California, although the paucity of extensive riparian woodland was probably an important factor in limiting this duck's numbers (Sibley 1952). Grinnell and Miller (1944), in documenting the recovery of this species, noted breeding in San Mateo County in 1934 and in Santa Cruz County in 1941–42, but cited no records from Santa Clara County. The first observations of Wood Duck that suggest a repopulation of the county consist of one or more birds seen in Halls Valley in November 1948 and 1949 (*Audubon Field Notes* 3:30 1949, 4:33 1950) and a pair at Almaden Reservoir on 9 Apr 1950 (*Audubon Field Notes* 4:259 1950). Reports of this species in the county increased over the next few years, and three nearly grown young observed on a reservoir 3 miles west of Gilroy on 8 Jul 1955 (*Audubon Field Notes* 9:398 1955) represent the first documented breeding record for the county.

During the atlasing period, successful breeding was confirmed in 40 county blocks, with possible and probable records in 21 additional blocks. In the southern part of the county, this species breeds along many small streams, wherever there is good riparian growth, particularly along those draining eastward

from the Santa Cruz Mountains. Breeding has also been noted along the shaded backwaters of Almaden Reservoir, Chesbro Reservoir, and borrow ponds near Coyote Creek. In the Diablo Range, this species uses stock ponds or other manmade impoundments where there is suitable untrampled edge growth, as well as the streams throughout the range. A few birds are found along San Francisquito Creek in the Palo Alto area, where nesting boxes have probably contributed to successful reproduction in an urban setting. But the absence of breeding along most of the county's urban creeks suggests that this species is vulnerable to urban pressures, and that the San Francisquito Creek records are, therefore, atypical.

Because of the difficulty in locating this species' cavity nests, virtually all confirmations were of adults with precocial or newly fledged young. The only confirmation where Wood Ducks were actually observed using a nesting box was in May 1993 at Chesbro Reservoir. Most sightings of precocial young occurred during May and June, indicating nesting during April and May. Breeding confirmations were noted mainly between 500 and 2,500 feet, but the primary factors limiting breeding distribution and success are probably riparian habitat quality and seclusion rather than elevation.

During the fall and winter, Wood Ducks are more widespread in local ponds and reservoirs, especially at Almaden Reservoir, where wintering numbers of over 100 birds have been noted (pers. obs.). The Wood Duck, however, remains an uncommon breeding species within Santa Clara County; in each block in which breeding was confirmed, atlasers estimated that no more than a few pairs were present. The secretive habits of this species may in part account for the low estimate of breeding population. Suitable nesting conditions for this species have been enhanced in some areas by the placement of nesting boxes along streams and at reservoirs. Even more important to the survival of this species here is the preservation of mature riparian woodlands bordering our ponds, reservoirs, and streams, where a chance encounter with an elegant Wood Duck pair resting in the quiet backwaters or perched high in a sycamore may be likened to the discovery of a hidden treasure.

Ann Verdi

WOOD DUCK

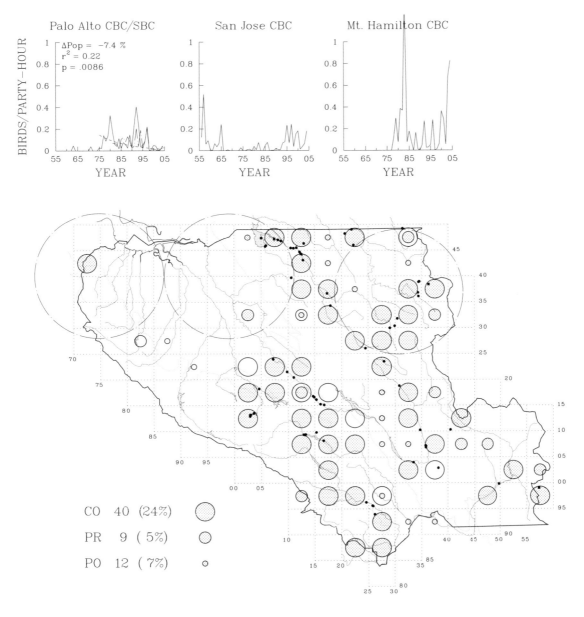

Palo Alto CBC/SBC

ΔPop = −7.4 %
r^2 = 0.22
p = .0086

San Jose CBC

Mt. Hamilton CBC

BIRDS/PARTY−HOUR

YEAR

YEAR

YEAR

CO 40 (24%)

PR 9 (5%)

PO 12 (7%)

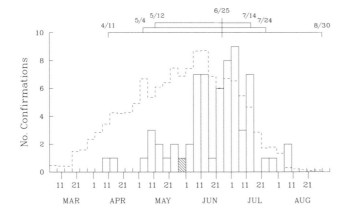

Atlas (1987−1993), n = 69

No. Confirmations

MAR   APR   MAY   JUN   JUL   AUG

ELLEN ARMSTRONG

Gadwall
Anas strepera

Conspicuous in neither plumage nor voice, the Gadwall, once only a rare winter visitor here, has quite surreptitiously become a locally common breeder in Santa Clara County's bayside wetlands. The Gadwall breeds across the mid-northern latitudes throughout much of the Northern Hemisphere, overlapping broadly with the more widely ranging Mallard and Northern Pintail (Madge and Burn 1988). In North America, this duck nests primarily in the western United States, northern Great Plains, and Canada's southern Prairie Provinces, although more local breeding may occur virtually throughout southern Canada and the northern and western states (LeSchack et al. 1997). Gadwalls nest in lowland areas throughout much of California, albeit locally in many areas (Small 1994). In Santa Clara County, the Gadwall is an uncommon to locally common breeder around ponds and wetlands, mostly along the edge of the Bay but also at a few scattered inland locations. Populations are augmented in winter by birds that breed elsewhere, and it is during this season that the Gadwall is most abundant and widespread in the county.

The Gadwall has only recently begun nesting in Santa Clara County. Kobbé (1902) did not include the Gadwall in his list of waterbirds in the San Francisco Bay, and Grinnell and Wythe (1927) considered the species to be only a "rare winter visitant" in the Bay area. In California as a whole, it was breeding at only a few locations in the Sacramento and San Joaquin valleys in 1944, though there were also several historical records of breeding from the southern portion of the state (Grinnell and Miller 1944). Although breeding was confirmed near Elkhorn Slough (Monterey County) in 1950 (*Audubon Field Notes 4*:259 1950), Sibley (1952) considered the Gadwall only an "uncommon winter visitant" in the South Bay.

In Santa Clara County, small numbers were occasionally recorded on San Jose and Palo Alto Christmas Bird Counts from the late 1940s through the 1960s, but oversummering birds remained quite rare in the Bay area during that time. Nevertheless, breeding in several Bay area counties during this period suggested a gradual population increase, and the Gadwall was probably breeding in Santa Clara County before nesting was first reported in 1967. That year, "a maximum of 50 pairs" and confirmed nesting were recorded at the Palo Alto Baylands (*Audubon Field Notes 21*:601 1967). A 1971 survey of South Bay marshes recorded 19 nests and broods and estimated 100-150 pairs of Gadwalls breeding in the region (Gill 1977), although six broods in 1971 and four in 1972 at the Palo Alto Flood Control Basin were still considered sufficiently unusual for mention in *Am. Birds* (*26*:900 1972). But on 11 Jun 1982, the presence of 618 ducklings in at least 61 broods at Moffett Field and Crittenden Marsh (*Am. Birds 36*:1012 1982, William G. Bousman, pers. comm.) indicated that this species had rapidly become quite a common breeder in at least some Santa Clara County locations. The Gadwall's "invasion" of Santa Clara County occurred as part of a largely unexplained, continent-wide range expansion during the latter part of the twentieth century (LeSchack et al. 1997).

Atlasers recorded potentially breeding Gadwalls in 26 of the county's 169 atlas blocks and confirmed breeding in 18 blocks. The majority of these blocks were near sea level at the edge of the San Francisco Bay, where Gadwalls were found breeding commonly near fresh and brackish ponds and marshes, sewage treatment lagoons, tidal sloughs, and salt ponds. Particularly large concentrations of breeding Gadwalls, as evidenced by the abundance of precocial young, were found in impoundments adjacent to fields or levees having abundant cover of grassy or ruderal vegetation, which provided suitable nest sites. At the southern end of the county, breeding was confirmed during the atlas period at San Felipe Lake, just inside San Benito County, and after the atlas period at the South County Regional Waste-Water Authority treatment plant in Gilroy, Santa Clara County (pers. obs.).

The breeding distribution of the Gadwall in the county was found to be much more limited than that of the Mallard. But where these two species co-occurred along the edge of the Bay, breeding Gadwalls seemed at least as abundant as Mallards, and large numbers of both bred together in bayside ponds and marshes. Although Gadwalls were neither as abundant nor as widespread as the Mallard at inland locations, both the Gadwall and the Cinnamon Teal were found breeding more widely at inland locations in the northern Santa Clara Valley than were the rarer Northern Pintail and Northern Shoveler, which seemed more restricted to bayside marshes for breeding.

Atlasers observed flightless young from 10 Apr to 7 Sep. Although the peak in reports of precocial young extended from early June to mid-August, large numbers of flightless broods were still present at the Sunnyvale Water Pollution Control Plant on 25 Aug 1993 (16 broods) and 31 Aug 1996 (nine broods; pers. obs.). The 10 Apr date is quite early for precocial young of this species, which tends to breed later than other dabbling ducks (Bellrose 1976, Palmer 1976a, Shuford 1993g, LeSchack et al. 1997). For example, there were 13 Mallard broods and no Gadwall broods at the Sunnyvale Water Pollution Control Plant on 18 May 1995, whereas no Mallard broods accompanied the nine Gadwall broods observed there on 31 Aug 1996. The 11 nests with eggs found during the atlas and postatlas periods spanned the period 1 May-25 Jun.

Stephen C. Rottenborn

GADWALL

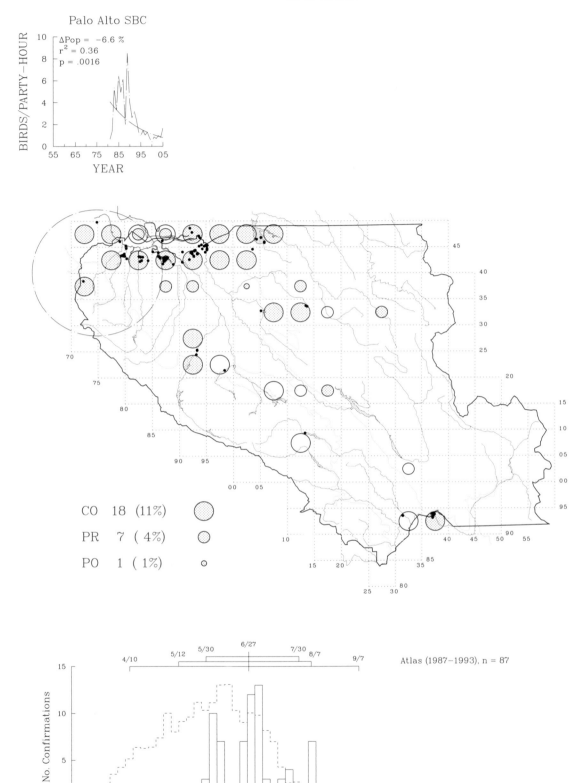

Palo Alto SBC

ΔPop = −6.6 %
r^2 = 0.36
p = .0016

BIRDS/PARTY-HOUR

YEAR

CO 18 (11%)
PR   7 (4%)
PO   1 (1%)

Atlas (1987–1993), n = 87

No. Confirmations

4/10   5/12   5/30   6/27   7/30 8/7   9/7

11 21 1 11 21 1 11 21 1 11 21 1 11 21 1 11 21

MAR   APR   MAY   JUN   JUL   AUG

107

Mallard
Anas platyrhynchos

The Mallard, one of the most widespread and well-studied species of waterfowl in the world, shows an incredible degree of plasticity in its selection of breeding habitat. Throughout much of the Northern Hemisphere, this species seemingly requires little more than cover and slow-moving or standing fresh water for nesting (Bellrose 1976). The Mallard is the most abundant duck in North America, breeding from the Arctic south over most of the northern and western United States (Bellrose 1976), including virtually the entire state of California (Small 1994). Mallards are resident year-round in Santa Clara County, and there is some influx of birds from more northern breeding areas in winter. In summer, this species is the most common and widespread of the county's breeding waterfowl.

The historical breeding status of the Mallard in Santa Clara County is unclear. Grinnell (1902) declared it to be a "common resident in suitable localities throughout the State," but Kobbé (1902) considered it only a "winter visitant" in the San Francisco Bay area marshes. Subsequent authors also stated that the Mallard was a common resident in the Bay area (Grinnell and Wythe 1927, Grinnell and Miller 1944, Sibley 1952), and W. E. Unglish's record of five broods at San Felipe Lake, just south of the Santa Clara/San Benito County line, on 10 May 1934 (Sibley 1952) indicates breeding near the southern part of the county. But even as recently as 1952, the only Santa Clara County nesting locations reported in these references were in San Jose. Furthermore, a nest in Alviso in 1953 was considered sufficiently noteworthy to merit mention in *Audubon Field Notes* 7:324 (1953). Therefore, it appears either that breeding Mallards in the South Bay were not as common as had been reported by these early authors, or that relatively few of the breeding locations known by these authors were published in the literature. Although Small (1994) reported a "precipitous decline" in Mallard populations in California since the 1960s and 1970s, the species increased considerably during this period on both the San Jose and Palo Alto Christmas Bird Counts and on the Palo Alto Summer Bird Count.

Atlasers found the Mallard to be a fairly common breeder in much of Santa Clara County, occurring in most locations offering ponds, lakes, sloughs, or low-gradient streams. This species was recorded in 84% of the county's atlas blocks and confirmed to be breeding in 53% of all blocks during the atlas period. Although breeding was confirmed at elevations ranging from sea level to 2,720 feet, this species was most abundant at low elevations, particularly at ponds and marshes around the edge of the Bay. It was absent primarily from blocks lacking ponds or low-gradient streams in the Santa Cruz Mountains and the Diablo Range. The primary criterion determining suitable breeding habitat was the presence of some relatively slow-moving body of fresh or brackish water, and this species was found breeding in most locations where this requirement was met. Broods of young Mallards have been found in city parks, tidal sloughs, salt ponds, sewage lagoons, percolation ponds, drainage ditches, flooded fields, salt marshes, and a variety of other aquatic habitats. Many Mallards seemed more tolerant of human activity than other breeding waterfowl species, nesting in developed areas and readily accepting food from humans.

Breeding was most frequently confirmed by the observation of precocial young, which were seen primarily from mid-March to August. A noticeable peak in the number of broods in late May and early June is consistent with peak periods of breeding activity reported elsewhere (Bellrose 1976). But the breeding season in Santa Clara County was more protracted, with both earlier and later nesting, than was reported nearby in Monterey County (Weed 1993b) and for most of the North American continent as a whole (Bellrose 1976). A number of broods of flightless young were found in August, particularly in ponds along the edge of the Bay. More than ten broods were observed during the last week of the month, including one as late as 31 Aug 1995 after the atlas period (Tom Grey, pers. comm.). Although these August confirmations indicate that some late breeding takes place in the county on a regular basis, an extremely early record of precocial young accompanying a wild-type female on Adobe Creek in the Palo Alto Flood Control Basin on 13 Jan 1990 (Michael J. Mammoser, pers. comm.) was truly anomalous. Only five dated records of nests with eggs were obtained, all between 5 May and 13 Jun.

Although the destruction of wetland habitats in Santa Clara County may have impacted Mallard populations historically, these populations have benefited from the creation of suitable habitat at ponds and reservoirs, and from the provision of food in some areas. The extent to which these populations have also been augmented by releases is unknown, although the presence of domestic ducks and unusually colored ornamental forms at parks indicates that some releases have occurred. These feral flocks have attracted a number of pairs of wild-type birds to breed in urban areas as well. Hybrids between Mallards and Muscovy Ducks are present in a number of urban parks in the Santa Clara Valley (pers. obs.), indicating either the release of captive-bred hybrids or the hybridization of these species in the wild. Although Johnsgard (1960) reported that Mallard-Muscovy Duck hybrids are "rarely fertile," the wide variety of unusual ducks showing characters of both species suggests that these hybrids may backcross with their parent species.

Stephen C. Rottenborn

MALLARD

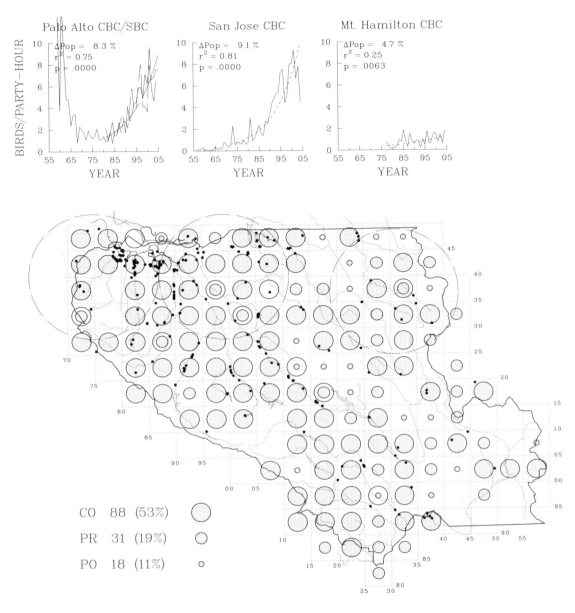

Palo Alto CBC/SBC

ΔPop = 8.3 %
r² = 0.75
p = .0000

San Jose CBC

ΔPop = 9.1 %
r² = 0.81
p = .0000

Mt. Hamilton CBC

ΔPop = 4.7 %
r² = 0.25
p = .0063

BIRDS/PARTY–HOUR

YEAR

CO   88 (53%)

PR   31 (19%)

PO   18 (11%)

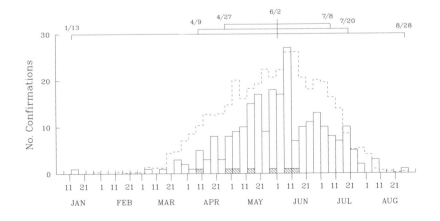

Atlas (1987–1993), n = 246

No. Confirmations

1/13   4/9   4/27   6/2   7/8   7/20   8/28

JAN   FEB   MAR   APR   MAY   JUN   JUL   AUG

109

Blue-winged Teal
Anas discors

The Blue-winged Teal has been confirmed breeding only once in Santa Clara County, and only sporadically elsewhere in central California, where its true status may be confounded by uncertain identification. This elegant teal breeds in North America from central Alaska across Canada to Newfoundland, and south in the United States to northeastern California and New England (Rowher et al. 2002). It nests in small numbers near lakes in northeastern California and occasionally in scattered locations elsewhere in the state (Small 1994). Blue-winged Teal are rare in Santa Clara County, where only a few birds are seen throughout the year, generally along the edge of the South Bay.

At the end of the nineteenth century, the Blue-winged Teal was thought to be rare throughout California. Although it nested as close as northern Nevada, Grinnell et al. (1918) listed only 14 records for the state. In assessing the species' status in the San Francisco Bay area, Grinnell and Wythe (1927) cited only two records, one each from Solano and Napa counties. Fieldwork in the 1930s, however, indicated that this teal was a regular breeder, and locally fairly common, in the northeastern corner of the state (Grinnell and Miller 1944). The 1950s and 1960s saw a general increase in the numbers of Blue-winged Teal west of the Rocky Mountains (Rowher et al. 2002), which resulted in increasing numbers of birds wintering on the central coast of California. In the South Bay, Blue-winged Teal were first recorded in San Mateo County in the winter of 1948-49 and in Santa Clara County in mid-February 1951 (Sibley 1952).

Until the 1970s, Blue-winged Teal occurred only sporadically in the South Bay. The first sighting on the Palo Alto CBC was recorded in 1968, when a single male was observed. But by the mid-1970s, significant numbers—20 to 25 birds each winter from 1974 to 1977—were recorded in the count circle. Breeding on the central coast was first confirmed when a pair and five young were found in a pond in Marina, Monterey County, on 14 Jun 1973 (*Am. Birds* 27:913 1973). And on 21 May the following year, Robert Yutzy observed a pair with eight ducklings in the Palo Alto Flood Control Basin (*Am. Birds* 28:846 1974). Curiously, no further records of extralimital breeding along the central coast were obtained until the last week of May 1997, when a pair with seven ducklings was seen in Olema Marsh, Marin County (*Field Notes* 51:923 1997). More recently, breeding has been reported along the central coast in about one year in three (*N. Am. Birds* 54:420 2000, 58:596 2004).

In Santa Clara County, Blue-winged Teal are present in each month of most years, and are slightly more common in winter than in summer. In contrast, in Monterey County there is a clear spring and fall migration, and few birds are present in either winter or summer (Roberson 2002). Local observations from 1980 to 2003 indicate an average of about eight birds here (ranging from 1 to 19) during the winter months of November through February, whereas about four (ranging from 0 to 14) are observed during the summer period of June through August. The lowest numbers are found in late May, corresponding to the end of the spring migration in the west (Small 1994, Roberson 2002, Rowher et al. 2002). Then, numbers increase through the summer, and a second decline (perhaps related to this duck's period of molt) is observed in August.

Although Blue-winged Teal are present here nearly every summer, paired birds are observed approximately one year out of two. During the atlas period, paired teal were seen in five of the seven years, generally along the edge of the South Bay in such locations as the Palo Alto Flood Control Basin, the Mountain View Forebay, the Sunnyvale Water Pollution Control Plant oxidation ponds, and along Coyote Creek near the Waterbird Management Area below Highway 237. A pair seen near San Felipe Lake, nearby in San Benito County, was the only one found away from the South Bay. Following the atlas period, two pairs were seen at the South County Regional WasteWater Authority treatment ponds in Gilroy on 2 May 2004 (Michael M. Rogers, county notebooks).

Although there are now multiple records of extralimital breeding by Blue-winged Teal on the central coast, documentation of such instances warrants caution (Roberson 1993jj, Shuford 1993f). Blue-winged Teal drakes normally abandon their mates during incubation, although in some cases, early in the season, a male will accompany the female and their brood (Rowher et al. 2002). Thus, a Blue-winged Teal drake seen with a hen and young may not be the parent, and it is essential to determine that the female is in fact a Blue-winged Teal hen, rather than a hen of the similar and more common Cinnamon Teal. Roberson (1993jj) and Shuford (1993f) also warn of the possibility of hybrid Blue-winged × Cinnamon Teal, judging from the frequency of this hybrid pairing. But in Santa Clara County this hybrid appears to be relatively rare. Only 5.0% of male blue-winged-type teal in winter are reported to be hybrids, and this figure drops to 2.6% in the spring (county notebooks). No hybrids have been found locally in summer or fall. Despite the number of paired Blue-winged Teal observed in the summer over the last three decades, it may be that this teal breeds only infrequently in Santa Clara County, if at all.

William G. Bousman

BLUE-WINGED TEAL

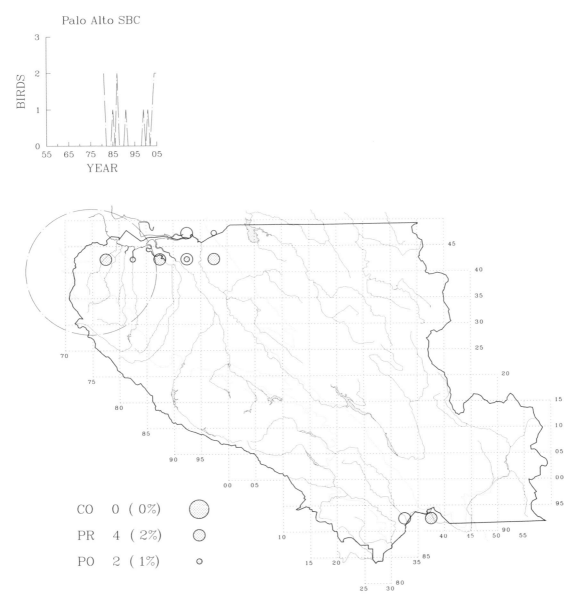

Palo Alto SBC

CO   0 (0%)
PR   4 (2%)
PO   2 (1%)

Cinnamon Teal
Anas cyanoptera

Were it not for the rich cinnamon-red color of the male's nuptial feathering, a pair of small, retiring Cinnamon Teal might go unnoticed in Santa Clara County's bayside wetlands. A bird of North America's western freshwater marshes, the race *A. c. septentrionalium* nests from southern British Columbia and Alberta south through the western United States into Mexico, and four additional races breed in South America (AOU 1957, 1998). Most of North America's Cinnamon Teal winter from California south to northern South America. The Cinnamon Teal nests along freshwater lagoons and marshes and around the borders of ponds and lakes throughout most of California away from the Sierra Nevada, the northern Coast Ranges, and the northern montane regions (Zeiner et al. 1990, Small 1994). It breeds most commonly in the extensive marshlands of the Central Valley and in parts of southern California, and is less common along the coast north of Marin County and in the southeastern desert region. In Santa Clara County, this resident species is a fairly common breeder in freshwater impoundments around the edge of San Francisco Bay, but it breeds much more sparsely elsewhere in the county.

Judging from historical accounts, the Cinnamon Teal has probably never been more than an uncommon breeder in Santa Clara County. In the 1920s, it was "found sparingly as a summer resident on fresh water ponds and sloughs" in the San Francisco Bay area, with breeding noted specifically in Santa Clara County at College Park, near northwestern San Jose (Grinnell and Wythe 1927). In 1932, Unglish found a nest with eggs at San Felipe Lake, in northern San Benito County just south of the Santa Clara County line (Sibley 1952), and the following year, McClintock (unpublished notes) found this species to be fairly common at San Felipe Lake, noting that it was breeding there on 2 Jun 1933. A brood 3 miles west of Gilroy on 8 Jul 1955 furnished the only published breeding record from southern Santa Clara County prior to the atlas project (*Audubon Field Notes* 9:398 1955). In 1967, 75 pairs were reported during the breeding season at the Palo Alto Baylands (*Audubon Field Notes* 21:601 1967). But a 1971 survey of salt marshes throughout much of the South Bay area found only four nests and/or broods of Cinnamon Teal, and the entire South Bay breeding population was estimated to consist of only 75–100 pairs (Gill 1977). Al-

though no significant population trends are evident in Palo Alto Summer Bird Count data, Breeding Bird Survey data suggest that this species has declined throughout much of the southern portion of its North American breeding range since the 1960s (Sauer et al. 2005).

Although Cinnamon Teal generally nest in freshwater marshes (Gammonley 1996), atlasers in Santa Clara County found this species breeding in brackish marshes as well. Cinnamon Teal bred most abundantly near shallow bayside impoundments offering extensive emergent vegetation, such as the Mountain View Forebay and the adjacent Palo Alto Flood Control Basin. Breeding was also confirmed in other nontidal impoundments having adjacent herbaceous cover of ruderal vegetation and grasses, which provide suitable nesting habitat. Such breeding locations included sewage ponds at the San Jose–Santa Clara Water Pollution Control Plant and the Waterbird Management Area along Coyote Creek below Highway 237. A few broods were also found in nontidal ponds and sloughs in pickleweed-dominated salt marsh at New Chicago Marsh in Alviso, and this species has nested in tidal salt marsh along lower Coyote Creek (Anderson and Jennings 1981).

Although Cinnamon Teal were most abundant as breeders along the edge of the Bay, a few pairs nested around the margins of scattered ponds and lakes in inland areas, such as at Calaveras Reservoir, San Felipe Lake, and Grant Lake, as well as at the South County Regional WasteWater Authority treatment ponds in Gilroy. This breeding distribution was similar to that of the Northern Pintail and Gadwall, and the few inland locations where Cinnamon Teal were found breeding usually hosted one or both of these other ducks as well. Throughout the county, however, the Cinnamon Teal was found at fewer locations and in smaller numbers than the Gadwall, though it was more widespread inland than the pintail.

Nearly all atlas breeding confirmations consisted of broods of flightless young. With the exception of single broods seen on 6 and 18 Apr, all were recorded between 4 May and 17 Aug. The number of breeding confirmations in July and August indicates later breeding than was found during the Monterey atlasing, which recorded no broods after 30 Jun (Weed 1993c), but is consistent with later egg dates given by several authors (Bent 1923a, Wheeler and Harris 1970, Bellrose 1976). The 6 Apr brood, however, indicates somewhat earlier nesting than has been reported in these references. The only nest found in the county since the initiation of the atlas project, discovered at Arzino Ranch in Alviso, had eggs on 5 May 1998 (Michael M. Rogers, pers. comm.).

Stephen C. Rottenborn

CINNAMON TEAL

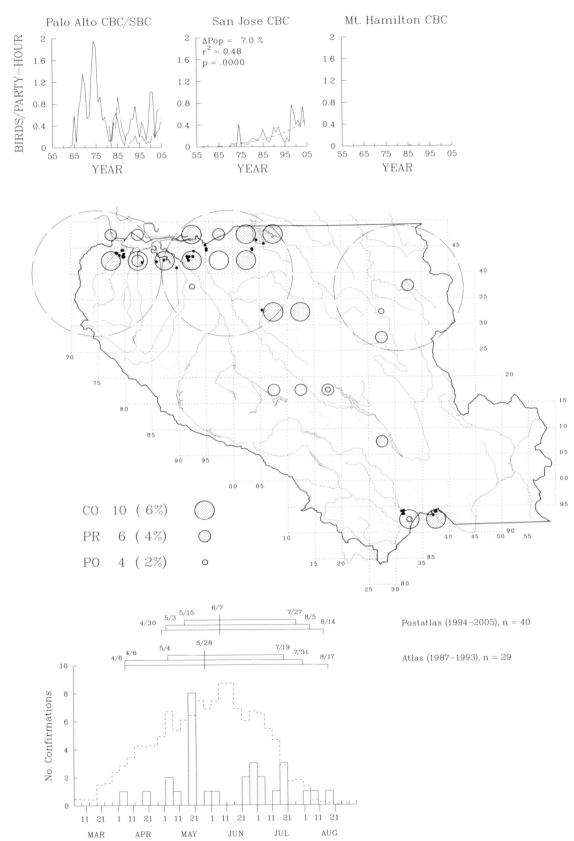

Palo Alto CBC/SBC

San Jose CBC

ΔPop = 7.0 %
r^2 = 0.48
p = .0000

Mt. Hamilton CBC

BIRDS/PARTY-HOUR

YEAR

YEAR

YEAR

CO 10 (6%)

PR   6 (4%)

PO   4 (2%)

Postatlas (1994–2005), n = 40

Atlas (1987–1993), n = 29

No. Confirmations

MAR   APR   MAY   JUN   JUL   AUG

113

...

Northern Shoveler
Anas clypeata

The colorful Northern Shoveler is the most abundant wintering dabbling duck in the South Bay, and in some years a few also remain to breed. In North America, this Holarctic duck breeds from Alaska southeast through the prairie provinces of Canada and into the United States, from northeastern California to southern Minnesota (DuBowy 1996). The shoveler is a fairly common breeder in northeastern California, but fewer nest in the Central Valley (Small 1994), and nesting birds are scarce elsewhere in the state. The Northern Shoveler is an abundant wintering duck in Santa Clara County along the edge of the South Bay, and is common inland on larger lakes and reservoirs. A few remain each summer, and breeding is observed about once every three years.

There are no early records of oversummering or breeding Northern Shovelers in Santa Clara County, but W. O. Emerson collected a set of ten eggs on 28 Mar 1886 near Alvarado, Alameda County (Emerson 1901; CAS #6604). He also found a nest in the same salt marsh on 25 Apr 1901 and stated that this duck was becoming more common in the area (Emerson 1901). Kobbé, however, in assessing the status of waterbirds in the Bay area, described the Northern Shoveler as only a winter visitant (Kobbé 1902). Grinnell et al. (1918), in listing known shoveler breeding records for the state, included Emerson's two Alameda County records, but no others in the San Francisco Bay area. Grinnell and Wythe (1927) included four additional breeding records from Alameda County, as well as a single record from Solano County, but none from Santa Clara County. No further evidence of breeding in the South Bay was reported (Grinnell and Miller 1944, Sibley 1952) until Gill (1977) found a nesting Northern Shoveler in the South Bay during his 1971 breeding surveys. He estimated the local breeding population at one to five pairs, but did not indicate the location of his nesting record.

In the summer of 1967, up to 20 pairs of Northern Shovelers were seen in the Palo Alto Baylands (*Audubon Field Notes* 21:601 1967), and undoubtedly some of these bred. In 1981, R. W. Lowe noted that Northern Shovelers nested on the San Francisco Bay National Wildlife Refuge (*Am. Birds* 35:974 1981), but did not report the county where he observed the breeding.

The earliest certain breeding record for Santa Clara County was of at least four broods observed on 11 Jun 1982 in Crittenden Marsh, the broods including both ducklings and juvenile birds (pers. obs.). Analysis of the Palo Alto SBC data indicates that shovelers were found locally in good numbers in the 1980s (128 tallied in 1987), but have declined significantly in recent years, e.g., 27 in 2003 and 11 in 2004. California-wide, however, summering birds are increasing at 3.8% per year, as recorded in Breeding Bird Survey data for the period 1966 to 2004 (Sauer et al. 2005).

Atlasers confirmed six instances of breeding during the atlas period, each of a female accompanied by precocial or recently fledged young. Four of these records were along the edge of the South Bay. Sites used included a freshwater pond on the Shoreline Golf Course, Crittenden Marsh, New Chicago Marsh near State and Spreckles streets, and a marsh adjacent to Salt Pond A18. Except for the Shoreline Golf Course pond, these marshes were all brackish former tidal marshes that were devoid of tidal action. The confirmations away from the Bay were from San Felipe Lake (San Benito County, in the Pacheco Creek watershed) and a narrow stock pond on the south side of Calaveras Road near the ridge between Calaveras Reservoir and the Bay. The latter breeding record, at an elevation of 1,040 feet, was the only breeding found away from the valley floor. Following the atlas period, two additional breeding confirmations were obtained: one on 25 May 1998 in the South County Regional WasteWater Authority treatment ponds in Gilroy (Stephen C. Rottenborn, pers. comm.) and the other on 7 Jun 2003 in a small pond in San Mateo County, just across San Francisquito Creek from the Palo Alto Municipal Golf Course (Michael M. Rogers, pers. comm.).

Bent (1923b) offered limited egg dates for Northern Shoveler in California and Utah, extending from 28 Mar to 11 Jul. The earliest observation of precocial young during the atlas period was on 6 May, the latest on 30 Jul. Since incubation occurs for 22 to 25 days (Ehrlich et al. 1988), the range of dates for precocial young observed during atlasing is consistent with the range of egg dates listed by Bent.

Unlike those of some of our other dabbling ducks, long-term breeding population estimates for the Northern Shoveler have shown an increase from 1955 to 1995 within the center of the species' range, in the prairie provinces of Canada and the northern United States (DuBowy 1996). Analysis of the Palo Alto and San Jose CBC data shows increases over the last 30 to 40 years of 7.2% per year in Palo Alto and 8.1% per year in San Jose. The increased abundance of this duck may be related in part to its feeding behavior. Because Northern Shovelers generally feed on plankton in the water column, they have been avoided by the gourmands of the past and the hunters of today. During the era of market hunting, shovelers made up only 3.2% of the take (Grinnell et al. 1918); today, they constitute only 2.1% of the annual harvest (DuBowy 1996). And since they are not bottom feeders, they rarely ingest lead and hence avoid lead poisoning (DuBowy 1996).

William G. Bousman

NORTHERN SHOVELER

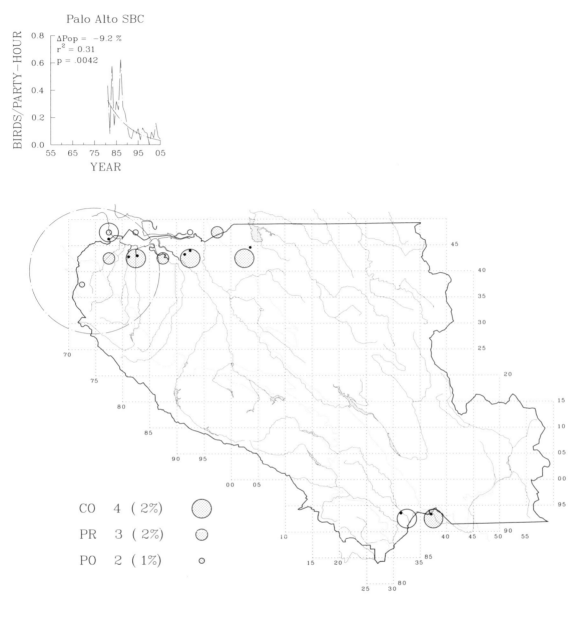

Palo Alto SBC

ΔPop = −9.2 %
$r^2 = 0.31$
p = .0042

BIRDS/PARTY−HOUR

YEAR

CO   4 (2%)
PR   3 (2%)
PO   2 (1%)

Atlas (1987−1993), n = 6

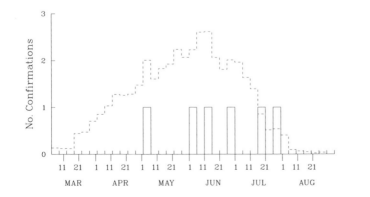

No. Confirmations

MAR   APR   MAY   JUN   JUL   AUG

CJPage ©1987

Northern Pintail
Anas acuta

Subtly patterned but of distinctively slender shape, the Northern Pintail is an elegant member of the avifauna of Santa Clara County's bayside ponds and marshes. This species breeds widely throughout the northern portions of the Northern Hemisphere (Madge and Burn 1988). In North America, it nests from Alaska and Canada south to the northern tier of the United States, extending somewhat farther south in the West (Austin and Miller 1995). Although the Northern Pintail is the most abundant species of waterfowl in California during migration and winter, the state's breeding population is rather small. Most of California's breeding pintails nest in the Great Basin and the northern portion of the state, though small numbers breed at scattered locations south to the Mexican border (Small 1994). In Santa Clara County, the Northern Pintail is plentiful in winter, particularly in ponds and marshes along the Bay, being about as common as the Mallard or Gadwall during this season. In summer, however, the pintail is the least abundant of these three species here, probably numbering fewer than 100 breeding pairs in the county.

Breeding populations of the Northern Pintail in the San Francisco Bay area have always been fairly small. Grinnell and Wythe (1927) considered it to be an uncommon breeder, listing breeding records only from the Hayward/Newark area in Alameda County. Apparently, this status changed little for several decades, for these sites remained the only Bay-area breeding locations listed by Grinnell and Miller (1944) and Sibley (1952), the latter authority stating that only "a few" pintails nested in the South Bay area. A nest in Newark (Alameda County) in 1956 was "one of the few nesting records along San Francisco Bay" (*Audubon Field Notes 10*:359 1956). More recently, a 1971 survey of the breeding birds in South Bay marshes found 21 pintail nests and broods and estimated the breeding population to be 50-100 pairs (Gill 1977). From 1982 to 1985, William G. Bousman (pers. comm.) found pintails breeding each year in the Moffett Field/Crittenden Marsh area, with a high of eight broods (plus 34 fully fledged juveniles) on 11 Jun 1982. These findings suggest either a population increase since the mid-1950s or the discovery of previously undetected breeders. The lack of breeding records in Marin County prior to that county's atlas fieldwork

was attributed to oversight rather than the absence of the pintail as a breeding species (Shuford 1993e). Still, Palo Alto Summer Bird Count data show a significant decline in summering birds in the count circle since the early 1980s, and the pintail is currently an uncommon bird in the South Bay during summer.

Atlasers recorded potentially breeding Northern Pintails in 12 atlas blocks and confirmed breeding in eight of them (following the atlas period, breeding was confirmed in three additional blocks). Atlas work showed that breeding pintails were mostly confined to the blocks immediately bordering the San Francisco Bay. Here, small numbers of them bred at elevations of 0-3 feet in brackish and freshwater marshes and ponds along the Bay's edge. Breeding sites characteristically offered dense herbaceous cover, affording nesting habitat, around the edges of marsh ponds. Sites supporting the largest numbers of breeding pintails included the San Jose-Santa Clara Water Pollution Control Plant vicinity, New Chicago Marsh in Alviso, the Moffett Field/Crittenden Marsh area, and the vicinity of the Mountain View Forebay and Palo Alto Flood Control Basin. Away from the Bay, breeding was confirmed during the atlas period at San Felipe Lake, just south of the county line in San Benito County, and after the atlas period at the South County Regional WasteWater Authority treatment ponds in Gilroy in Santa Clara County (pers. obs.). Otherwise, pintails away from the Bay were represented only by possible breeders at Calaveras Reservoir and at the Ogier Avenue ponds along Coyote Creek north of Morgan Hill. This pattern of distribution closely parallels that found in Marin County, where most breeding confirmations were from the edge of the Bay (Shuford 1993e).

Although differences in breeding habitat use between Northern Pintails and other dabbling ducks have been reported, pintails in Santa Clara County bred where other species, such as Mallards and Gadwalls, were quite common. But throughout much of their range, pintails tend to nest in drier areas, often farther from water, than these species (Bellrose 1976, Palmer 1976a). In Marin County, pintails are thought to breed near larger, shallower bodies of water than the Mallard or Gadwall (Shuford 1993e). In Santa Clara County, the Northern Pintail is a less common breeder and is more restricted to bayside marshes than the Mallard and Gadwall. The number of nests found was insufficient to compare interspecific differences in nesting microhabitats, although broods of young pintails were virtually always found in areas supporting the other two species as well.

A nest with eggs on 27 Apr represented the earliest breeding confirmation during the atlas period, as well as the only Northern Pintail nest found during the atlas, but a record of precocial young on 19 Apr 1996 (pers. obs.), after the atlas period, indicates initiation of nesting as early as late March. Precocial young were observed as late as 29 Jul during the atlas period, with a peak from mid-May through the first week of June. Fledged young were found as late as 10 Aug. Following the atlas period, precocial young were recorded as late as 14 Aug 1999 (Michael M. Rogers, PADB). This breeding period corresponds closely with that reported by Austin and Miller (1995) for North American populations as a whole.

Stephen C. Rottenborn

NORTHERN PINTAIL

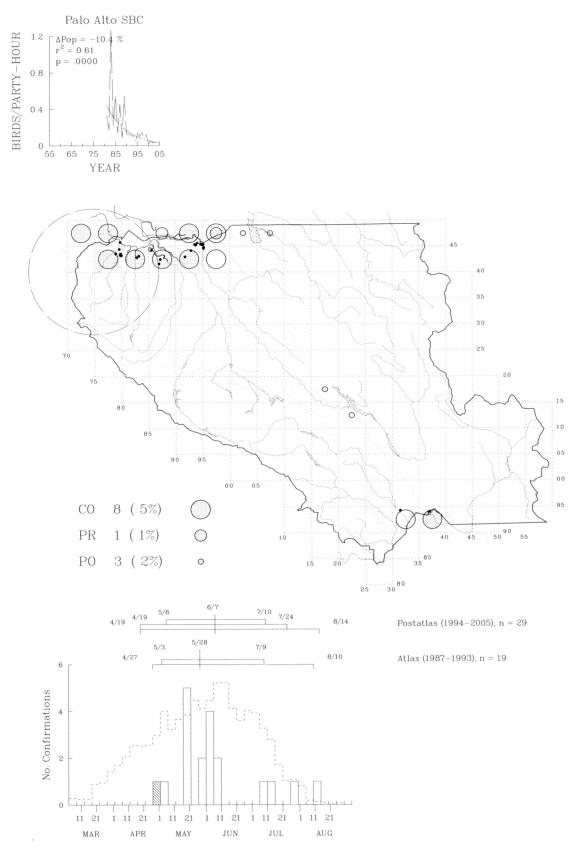

Palo Alto SBC

ΔPop = −10.4 %
r^2 = 0.61
p = .0000

BIRDS/PARTY-HOUR

YEAR

CO   8 (5%)
PR   1 (1%)
PO   3 (2%)

Postatlas (1994−2005), n = 29

Atlas (1987−1993), n = 19

No. Confirmations

MAR   APR   MAY   JUN   JUL   AUG

Green-winged Teal
Anas crecca

Although abundant in Santa Clara County in the winter, this small, graceful teal has been recorded nesting here only once. The Green-winged Teal is a holarctic species, with *A. c. crecca* resident in the Old World, *carolinensis* in the New, and a third subspecies, *nimia*, a nonmigratory population restricted to the Aleutian Islands (Palmer 1976a). In North America, *carolinensis* generally breeds from Alaska across much of northern Canada to Newfoundland, and in the West it occurs south to northern California and northern Nevada (Small 1994, AOU 1998). Although it is found in large numbers in California in the winter, only a few birds remain to breed in the Klamath Basin, the Modoc Plateau, and parts of the northern Sacramento Valley (Small 1994). Green-winged Teal winter in Santa Clara County, generally from September through April, but are rare in the summer. Although, as noted above, there is only one nesting record from Santa Clara County, there is a history of sporadic breeding nearby in Alameda County.

Homer A. Snow, an early oologist, collected a set of Green-winged Teal eggs in a small pond near Newark, in Alameda County, on 4 Apr 1907 (WFVZ #96304). Early observers were often unaware of records in oology collections, so when a female and eggs were collected the next year on the shore of Tulare Lake, Kings County (Goldman 1908), the record was believed to be the first for California. Surprisingly, in the summer of 1915, Dirks (1916) found at least six families of Green-winged Teal in marshes and ponds near Alvarado, Alameda County. On the basis of these records, he judged this teal to be a common breeding species in the San Francisco Bay area. Although there were a number of breeding records from the San Joaquin Valley in the 1920s and 1930s (WFVZ egg sets), nesting was not observed again in the Bay region until the 1980s (*Audubon Field Notes*, *Am. Birds*, Vol. 1-36).

The lone Santa Clara County breeding record was of a pair of Green-winged Teal that nested at Moffett Marsh in 1983 (pers. obs.). Following heavy rains during the winter of 1982-83, seasonal wetlands at Moffett Field became flooded, and water up to 30 cm deep remained on portions of these wetlands into summer. The writer observed a pair of Green-winged Teal in pursuit flight over these wetlands on 3 Jun, and on 8 Jul a female was present with six nearly fledged young. The area used by these teal was in the wettest portion of the wetlands, next to a drainage channel. The channel, covered with a thick growth of cattails, carried a permanent flow of water. The cattails transitioned to a mixture of native wetland grasses and sedges, as well as some non-native weeds spreading across 20 to 50 meters. The maximum expanse of patches of open water in these wetlands was on the order of a meter or two. The female and six young were last seen there on 15 Jul 1983.

Green-winged Teal are rare in the South Bay area in summer. Numbers recorded on the Palo Alto SBC, generally conducted during the first week in June since 1981, have ranged from zero to 13. From 1987 to 1993, pairs of Green-winged Teal were seen in four of the seven years of atlas fieldwork, generally in the Palo Alto Flood Control Basin, the Mountain View Forebay, or the Palo Alto Baylands. In most cases, however, no overt courtship behavior was observed. Subsequent to the atlas fieldwork, a female was found with three small young in a narrow drainage channel north of the Newby Island dump in Alameda County on 22 May 1998 (Stephen C. Rottenborn, pers. comm.). This area was once used as pasture and is now part of the Don Edwards San Francisco Bay National Wildlife Refuge. The teal were found in a storm-drain channel about 3 to 4 meters wide with water about a half-meter deep. This channel drains to Coyote Slough, but the location where the teal were found is above the high-tide line. The herbaceous vegetation in the channel bottom was composed of wetland grasses, sedges, rushes, and a few cattails, while more weedy plants clung to the sloping sides of the channel. The plant growth in the channel was neither dense nor tall, suggesting that it was mowed regularly. Ruderal grasslands were found on both sides of the channel for about a half kilometer.

A general decline has been noted in populations of a number of the dabbling ducks in western North America in the last half of the twentieth century, particularly Northern Pintail, American Wigeon, and Mallard (Banks and Springer 1994). Interestingly, Green-winged Teal numbers have remained stable over this same period, and Johnson (1995) has suggested that this is partly because of this teal's choice of nesting grounds and partly because of its manner of foraging. The Green-winged Teal uses wetlands in boreal forests and adjacent parklands, well removed from the prairie pothole regions favored by the other ducks. Additionally, since this "dabbling" duck feeds at the water line and does not normally tip up to feed on bottom sediments, it is able to avoid ingesting the lead shot found in many wetlands within its winter range.

William G. Bousman

GREEN-WINGED TEAL

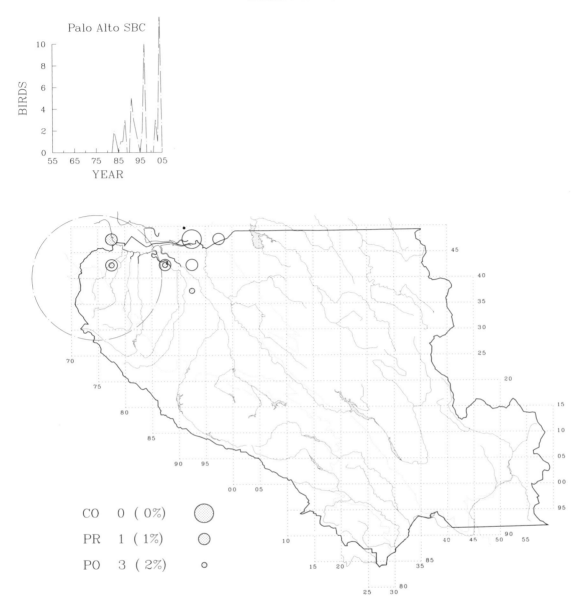

Palo Alto SBC

BIRDS

YEAR

CO   0 (0%)
PR   1 (1%)
PO   3 (2%)

Postatlas (1994−2005), n = 1

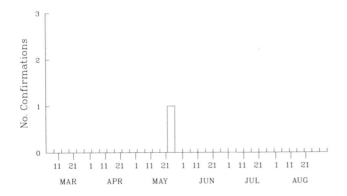

No. Confirmations

11 21 | 1 11 21 | 1 11 21 | 1 11 21 | 1 11 21 | 1 11 21
MAR   APR   MAY   JUN   JUL   AUG

Canvasback
Aythya valisineria

Far from their normal haunts in the prairie-parklands of Canada, a pair of Canvasbacks was found nesting in Santa Clara County in the summer of 1989. These striking ducks breed from western Alaska southeast through the prairies of Canada to Montana and Minnesota (Mowbray 2002). They are also found in smaller numbers at widely scattered sites to the southwest of this range, including south-central Oregon, northeastern California, northern Nevada, and southern Idaho. Canvasbacks are rare breeders in the northeastern portion of California, and there is occasional nesting in scattered locations in the Central Valley (Small 1994). Canvasbacks are a common wintering species in Santa Clara County, normally arriving in significant numbers in mid-October. Throughout the winter, they are found in large flocks on the South Bay, in tidal sloughs, on oxidation ponds, and on salt evaporator ponds. Most wintering birds leave by early April, but some linger to the end of the month. A few Canvasbacks, often injured, are found locally in some summers, but they are generally rare. The 1989 nesting is the sole breeding record for Santa Clara County.

Canvasbacks were known to nest in Oregon and Nevada at the start of the twentieth century (Grinnell et al. 1918), but there were no breeding records for California. Birds were reported summering in California on rare occasions through the 1960s (Grinnell and Miller 1944, *N. Am. Birds* Northern California Region notebooks), but a first nesting record was not obtained until 22 May 1973, when four ducklings were found in the Kesterson National Wildlife Refuge, Merced County (*Am. Birds 27*:814 1973). There are now scattered records of Canvasbacks nesting in the northeastern counties from Siskiyou to Lassen, as well as sporadic records from locations in the Central Valley counties of Yolo, Stockton, Kings, and Kern (Small 1994). Other than the 1989 Santa Clara County record there are no breeding records from the San Francisco Bay estuary, and a pair with three young observed at Paicines Reservoir, San Benito County, in 1998 (*N. Am. Birds 53*:100 1999) is the only record from the coastal ranges of California.

In the summer of 1989, on 17 Jun, observers conducting wildlife surveys along Guadalupe Slough for the San Francisco Bay Bird Observatory were surprised to encounter a male and female Canvasback accompanied by two immature birds. (This confirmation is shown in the phenology graphic.) The immatures were judged "definitely smaller" than the two adults, and when they stretched their wings their primaries appeared half-grown. Although male Canvasbacks tend to leave the female during incubation (Mowbray 2002), this male remained with the family group throughout the development of the young. The group was seen weekly in Guadalupe Slough through 12 Aug. On 20 Aug, only three birds were seen and, subsequently, the family group was no longer encountered. These Canvasbacks used an area of Guadalupe Slough between the Calabazas Creek entrance to the slough and the Moffett Field fuel-loading dock. Within their normal range, Canvasbacks tend to nest in emergent vegetation over water (Mowbray 2002). Presumably, this pair nested either in the tidal marsh along Guadalupe Slough or in vegetation in nearby oxidation or salt ponds. There was no indication that either the drake or the duck was injured.

The size of the immature Canvasbacks found on 17 Jun 1989 allows one to estimate the nest initiation date, using data in Mowbray (2002). Canvasback young fledge about 60 days after hatching. They grow quickly to about 45 days old, when they are about 90% of their size at fledging. Assuming the young were about three-quarters the size of the adults when first observed, then they would have been about 37 days old, and likely had hatched in early May. The incubation period for Canvasbacks is normally 25 days, which argues that the eggs were probably laid in the second week in April. Canvasbacks are considered early nesters, and egg laying starts as early as 6 Apr in Oregon (Mowbray 2002).

There were few records of summering Canvasbacks in Santa Clara County prior to the nesting in 1989. Since then, the number of birds found during the summer months has averaged about four, ranging from zero to twenty. Oversummering birds have been found not only in Guadalupe Slough, but also in other tidal areas from the Palo Alto Baylands to Coyote Slough; in more brackish areas such as the Palo Alto Flood Control Basin, Crittenden Marsh, and Artesian Slough; in the freshwater oxidation ponds at the Sunnyvale Water Pollution Control Plant; and occasionally in salt evaporation ponds. A number of these birds have shown obvious injuries, yet others have appeared healthy. It is unclear, then, whether the single nesting record from 1989 and the modest number of Canvasbacks that have summered here in recent years are harbingers of a trend for the species in central California or just the expected outliers beyond a species' normal range limits.

William G. Bousman

CANVASBACK

Palo Alto SBC

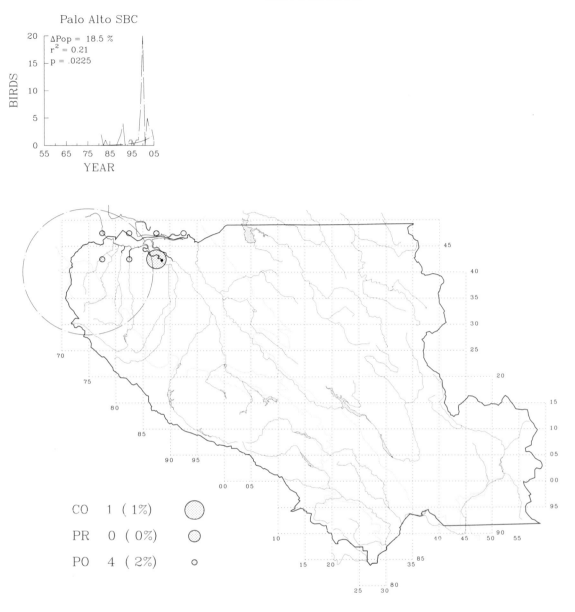

ΔPop = 18.5 %
r^2 = 0.21
p = .0225

BIRDS

YEAR

CO 1 (1%)
PR 0 (0%)
PO 4 (2%)

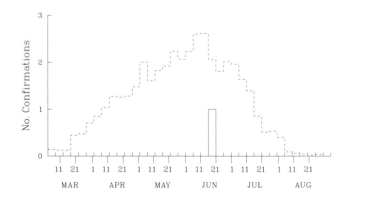

Atlas (1987–1993), n = 1

No. Confirmations

MAR   APR   MAY   JUN   JUL   AUG

Redhead
Aythya americana

This handsome diving duck is seen in Santa Clara County primarily in winter, but a few remain into summer, very rarely breeding. The Redhead breeds primarily in the freshwater marshes of Alaska and western Canada, and in disjunct populations in the western United States through the prairie pothole country of the Midwest and as far south as California and northern Texas (Woodin and Michot 2002). In California there are several scattered breeding locations, largely in the marshes of the northeastern counties, but also in smaller numbers in the Central Valley and at the south end of the Salton Sea (Small 1994). Although Redheads are usually uncommon in Santa Clara County during the winter, concentrations of over a hundred birds have been found in several years. A few birds are noted sporadically during most summers.

Historically, the Redhead was considered a common resident in California. Breeding was confirmed in "the interior valleys" (Grinnell 1902), but, was not recorded by Kobbé (1902) in his list of San Francisco Bay waterbirds. At Alvarado in Alameda County, 12 Redhead eggs taken from a nest by H. C. Bryant on 23 April 1915 hatched four days later at a state game farm (Grinnell et al. 1918). Grinnell and Wythe (1927) reported that the Redhead was also known to have nested in the San Francisco Bay area near Irvington, also in Alameda County, eggs having been noted on 3 Jun and 16 Jun. Grinnell and Miller (1944) stated that the Redhead's statewide breeding population was relatively small, and that it "was formerly common, but now greatly reduced at all seasons." Sibley (1952) described this duck as an uncommon winter visitor and a "rare breeder in marshland" of the south San Francisco Bay area.

Two pairs of Redheads were noted at the Palo Alto Flood Control Basin on 21 May 1974 (Bob Yutzy, Ted Chandik, NAB notebooks), suggesting possible nesting. The first confirmed Santa Clara County breeding was recorded at the same location the following year (*Avocet* 22:6 1975). No additional breeding was reported in the county until 1984, when two different females, both accompanied by duckling broods, the two broods of different ages, were seen in the Palo Alto Flood Control Basin (pers. obs.). The older brood (Class 1B, as described by Bellrose [1976]) was seen on 3 Jun and the younger one (Class 1A) on 8 Jun. A pair seen in nearby Charleston Slough on 7 Jun 1985 suggested the possibility of continued nesting in the area (*Am. Birds* 39:957 1985).

During the atlas period, a pair of Redheads was present 5 May to 12 Jun 1988 at the Palo Alto Flood Control Basin, but there was no additional evidence of breeding within the county. In 1989, a brood of Redhead chicks was reported from the Sunnyvale Water Pollution Control Plant ponds (*Am. Birds* 43:1363 1989), but the record was later retracted when the presumed Redhead chicks feathered up as Lesser Scaup (*Am. Birds* 44:156 1990). In 1993, three ducklings similar in appearance to young Redheads were seen with a brood of typical Mallard ducklings in Sunnyvale and were reported as Redhead chicks (*Am. Birds* 47:450 1993). Brood parasitism, often practiced by Redheads, was presumed to explain this mixed brood. This record, too, was retracted after the same observer later noted similar "mixed" Mallard broods in habitat unlikely to be used by Redheads; it appeared that plumage polymorphism in Mallard broods was responsible for the extensively yellowish coloration of some young (Stephen C. Rottenborn, pers. comm.).

During the postatlas period, one or two Redheads have been present in the bayside marshes in most summers (county notebooks), but they have been recorded on only five of the past 25 Palo Alto SBCs through 2005, and no evidence of breeding has been reported since 1984. It is unclear what factors might be required for successful breeding by this species in the South Bay.

The identification of Redhead ducklings in Santa Clara County is complicated by three factors. First, as mentioned above, the Redhead has a strong propensity for parasitic egglaying (Weller 1959). In one study conducted in Utah, 43% of the Redheads produced at the Farmington Bay Wildlife Management Area were hatched from eggs laid in other species' nests (Joyner 1983). Thus, observers need to be aware that Redhead ducklings may be accompanied by adult females and the young of other species. Second, many local birders are unfamiliar with the typical chick's appearance, both because breeding here has been so infrequent and because most observers do not use the field guides that illustrate ducklings of the various species (e.g., Baicich and Harrison 2005). Third, as pointed out above, some Mallard or feral ducks may produce ducklings with the relatively unmarked pale-yellow coloring of typical Redhead chicks, making the recognition of parasitized broods challenging at best.

Phyllis M. Browning

REDHEAD

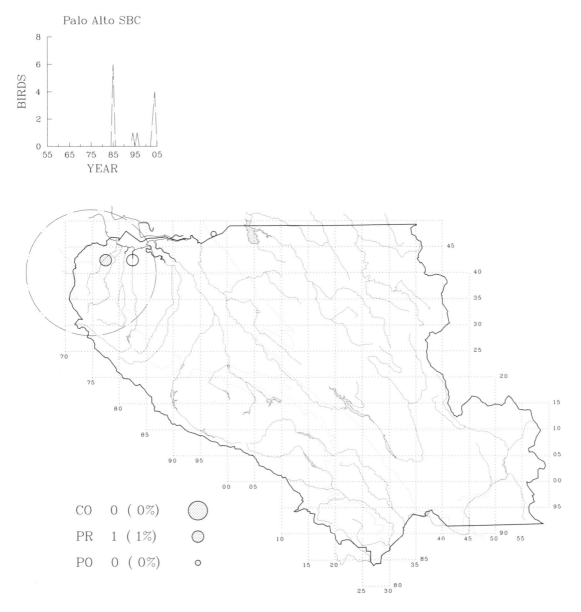

Palo Alto SBC

CO   0 (0%)
PR   1 (1%)
PO   0 (0%)

Ring-necked Duck
Aythya collaris

The Ring-necked Duck is one of the most recent additions to Santa Clara County's breeding avifauna. This species nests in marshes and wooded bogs across much of the northern United States and Canada, from eastern Alaska east to Newfoundland. Scattered breeding populations, particularly in the western United States, can be found as far south as the White Mountains of Arizona (Bellrose 1976, Palmer 1976b). In California, these ducks are uncommon and local breeders in the far northern part of the state and in the Sierra Nevada. The Ring-necked Duck occurs in Santa Clara County primarily as a migrant and winter resident, appearing on freshwater ponds and reservoirs (rarely in saline or brackish waters) throughout the county from late September through March. In recent years, a few have remained in the county through the summer, on scattered ponds and lakes, and there has been one record of confirmed breeding.

Ring-necked Ducks began breeding in significant numbers in California only recently. As of 1944, the only substantiated breeding record in the state was of a juvenile collected at Lake Tahoe in El Dorado County on 24 Aug 1926 (Grinnell and Miller 1944). An earlier breeding record from Eagle Lake in Lassen County in Jun 1905 (Dawson 1923) was considered questionable (Grinnell and Miller 1944). Apparently, no further breeding was noted in the state until 1956, when researchers found 23 nests at Mountain Meadows Reservoir in Lassen County (Hunt and Anderson 1966). Since then, Ring-necked Ducks have been found breeding regularly at various other locations. As of 1994, the species' statewide breeding range included seven counties in far northern California and in the Sierra Nevada south to Crowley Lake in Mono County (*Am. Birds 45*:1157 1991, *47*:1146 1993, Small 1994). Since the early 1970s, small numbers of Ring-necked Ducks have occasionally oversummered away from breeding areas at scattered locations throughout the state, even as far south as Los Angeles and San Diego Counties (Garrett and Dunn 1981, *Am. Birds 35*:978 1981, *39*:962 1985, McCaskie et al. 1988). Breeding, however, was not confirmed away from the northern and mountainous regions until 1997 (more on that below).

In the San Francisco Bay area, Ring-necked Ducks have historically been considered fairly common during migration and winter, but there were no records of oversummering birds until recently. Grinnell and Wythe (1927) knew of no records in the Bay area between 7 Mar and 7 Oct, and neither Grinnell and Miller (1944) nor Sibley (1952) listed any summer records from the region. Since 1940, fewer than ten records of oversummering Ring-necked Ducks in northern California away from known nesting areas have been published in *American Birds* and *Audubon Field Notes*, and prior to the atlas there were no records in Santa Clara County between April and September.

During our atlas period, Ring-necked Ducks were found during midsummer at three locations. Santa Clara County's first summer record was of an apparently healthy male on Kelly Cabin Lake in Henry Coe State Park on 7 Jul 1989. Another male was at the Sunnyvale Water Pollution Control Plant on 17 May and 20 Jun 1992. On 25 June 1992, five Ring-necked Ducks were at the south end of Calaveras Reservoir, and two pairs spent the summer of 1993 there. In 1994, after the atlas period, a female and two males were again at the south end of Calaveras Reservoir, on 23 Jul, and another pair oversummered at the Ogier Avenue Ponds, a collection of borrow pits along Coyote Creek north of Morgan Hill (pers. obs.). A pair of Ring-necked Ducks was again seen at the Ogier Ponds on 26 May and 9 Jul 1996 (pers. obs.), but Calaveras Reservoir was not well surveyed in 1995 or 1996. Despite all these records, no breeding evidence had been observed in the county as of 1996, and some or all of these birds may have been oversummering nonbreeders.

In 1997, on 6 Jul, six males and a female were seen at the south end of Calaveras Reservoir, and on 20 Jul, two males and six females were there (pers. obs.). Then, on 3 Aug that year, the writer observed a brood of three half-grown young closely associated with a female along the south shore of the reservoir, the group representing the first breeding record of Ring-necked Duck in California away from the Sierra Nevada or the far northern part of the state. A total of four adult males and nine females or full-grown immatures were also present there on this date (*Field Notes 51*:1049 1997).

Ring-necked Ducks typically nest in marshy areas, often building their nests on floating vegetation (Mendall 1958), but unlike most other ducks they tend to nest in close proximity to woody vegetation (Bellrose 1976). The combination of emergent herbaceous vegetation and flooded brush at the south end of Calaveras Reservoir apparently provided suitable conditions for nesting. Because breeding site fidelity shown by female Ring-necked Ducks is quite high (Mendall 1958), this species may continue breeding at Calaveras Reservoir if water levels and habitat conditions remain suitable. Similar habitat is present at the Ogier Avenue Ponds and probably at several other locations in Santa Clara County. Given the apparent southward range expansion shown by breeding Ring-necked Ducks in recent years, we may find them breeding on other ponds and reservoirs in the South Bay as well.

Stephen C. Rottenborn

RING-NECKED DUCK

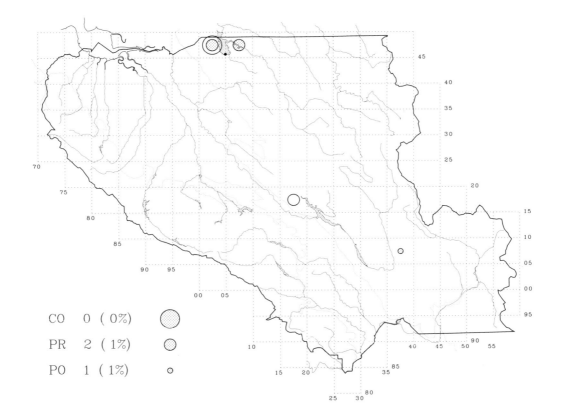

CO 0 (0%)
PR 2 (1%)
PO 1 (1%)

Postatlas (1994−2005), n = 1

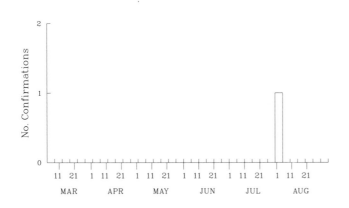

125

Lesser Scaup
Aythya affinis

Usually found breeding in the boreal forests and parklands of Alaska and Canada, the Lesser Scaup now nests along the shores of San Francisco Bay as well. This diving duck breeds primarily from central Alaska east through Canada to Quebec and south in the Rocky Mountains to Colorado, with smaller numbers in scattered locations in the western United States (Austin et al. 1998). In California, Lesser Scaup have nested in Siskiyou and Lassen counties, both in the northeast, and in the San Francisco Bay region (Small 1994). The Lesser Scaup is now an uncommon summer resident in Santa Clara County, nesting near impoundments along the edge of the Bay.

At the end of the nineteenth century, the Lesser Scaup was considered only a winter visitant to San Francisco Bay (Grinnell 1902). Since then, it has nested sporadically in the Bay area, records consisting of a single brood in 1913 at Stow Lake in San Francisco (Schussler 1916) and two to three broods there in 1915 (Mailliard 1915); a single brood in 1915 at Lake Merced in San Francisco (Squires 1915); a nest destroyed by a predator in 1940 in Berkeley (Nichols 1940); and a single brood in 1965 near the Oakland Airport (*Audubon Field Notes 19*:575 1965). Grinnell and Miller (1944) considered the records through 1940 to pertain to crippled birds, although none of the original accounts reported any obvious injuries. No additional breeding records were noted in the Bay area (*Audubon Field Notes*) until the summer of 1980, when a female and at least two young were found on 13 Jul along Adobe Creek in the Palo Alto Flood Control Basin (Joe Morlan, pers. comm.). A female and at least one young were seen there again on 18 Jul that year (Theodore A. Chandik, Jr., pers. comm.). At least two pairs of Lesser Scaup nested again in the Flood Control Basin in 1981 (Theodore A. Chandik, Jr., pers. comm.), although only one nesting record was reported (*Am. Birds 35*:974 1981). Single pairs nested there in 1982 (*Am. Birds 36*:1012 1982) and 1986 (*Am. Birds 40*:1250 1986). Analysis of the data from the Palo Alto SBC indicates a general increase in the local summer population since 1981.

Atlasers did not detect nesting Lesser Scaup in 1987, but in 1988 this duck was found nesting again in the Palo Alto Flood Control Basin, where on 3 Jul a female and one downy young were seen. The following year saw a significant increase in nesting when on 17 Aug ten broods were counted in the Sunnyvale Water Pollution Control Plant oxidation ponds. In the subsequent years of the atlas, these Sunnyvale ponds became the South Bay metropolis of this species: 12 broods were estimated in 1990, seven in 1991, nine in 1992, and five in 1993. Single broods of Lesser Scaup were also found in Charleston Slough in 1990 and 1993. Subsequent to the atlas period, broods of Lesser Scaup have also been observed in the Emily Renzel Wetlands, the Mountain View Forebay, Crittenden Marsh, the New Chicago Marsh, on Salt Pond A18, and in the San Jose-Santa Clara Water Pollution Control Plant drying ponds (county notebooks). But the Sunnyvale ponds continue to be the preferred breeding location, with multiple broods recorded annually (county notebooks).

Both during the atlas period and subsequently, all breeding records of Lesser Scaup have been of precocial young or dependent fledglings. Families of precocial young have been observed on freshwater impoundments, such as the oxidation ponds at the Sunnyvale Water Pollution Control Plant and the Mountain View Forebay; in brackish waters, as found in the Palo Alto Flood Control Basin and Charleston Slough; and in more saline habitats, such as Salt Pond A18. During the atlas period, Lesser Scaup precocial young were recorded from 20 Jun to 28 Aug, with a median date of 28 Jul. Subsequent to the atlas period, a female with a day-old chick was found at the Sunnyvale ponds on 3 Sep 1994 (Peter J. Metropulos, county notebooks). The Lesser Scaup breeds later than our other local nesting ducks. For instance, the median date for Lesser Scaup is later than that for Gadwall (27 Jun, $n = 87$), Mallard (2 Jun, $n = 246$), Cinnamon Teal (28 May, $n = 29$), and Ruddy Duck (3 Jul, $n = 22$). The Santa Clara County phenology, however, corresponds closely with dates recorded for this diving duck in its core nesting area in Alaska and Canada (Austin et al. 1998).

The Lesser Scaup is the most abundant diving duck in North America (Austin et al. 1998). Within its breeding areas it is opportunistic, most pairs breeding in normal years, but few do in drought years (Austin et al. 1998). Perhaps this breeding pattern is related to this duck's recent settlement of our South Bay impoundments in the midst of arid central California—a remarkable contrast to the remote wildernesses of central Alaska and Canada.

William G. Bousman

LESSER SCAUP

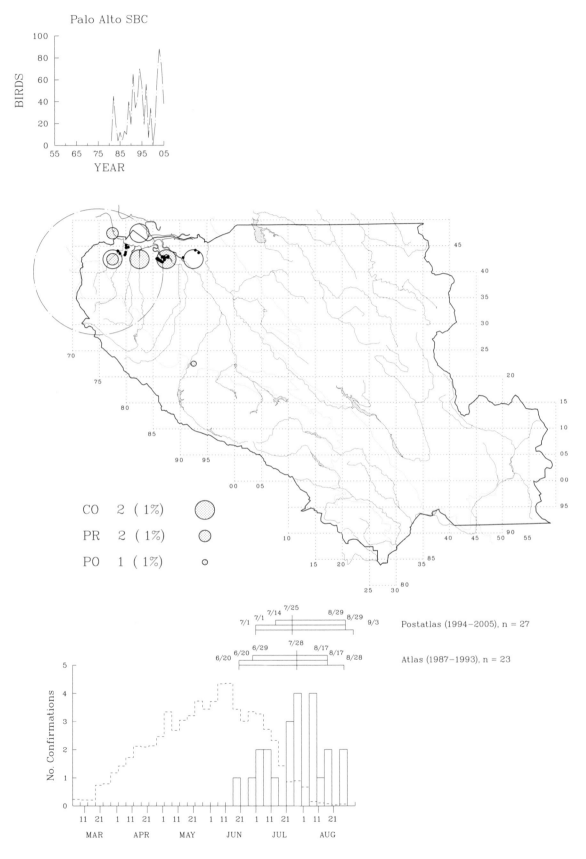

Palo Alto SBC

CO   2 (1%)
PR   2 (1%)
PO   1 (1%)

Postatlas (1994–2005), n = 27

Atlas (1987–1993), n = 23

Common Merganser
Mergus merganser

Breeding Common Mergansers are more at home in Santa Clara County's foothill streams than in the ponds and marshes preferred by most other breeding waterfowl here. This circumpolar breeder nests along wooded streams and lake shores throughout much of the Northern Hemisphere. In North America it breeds across most of Canada and the northern United States, wintering locally throughout the remaining states and south into Mexico (AOU 1998). The Common Merganser is an uncommon breeder in California, nesting primarily in the mountainous northern part of the state, the northern Coast Ranges and Sierra Nevada, and the upper Sacramento River drainages, breeding more locally in the Coast Ranges south to Ventura County (Small 1994). In Santa Clara County, as in the state as a whole, the Common Merganser is most numerous during winter. Flocks of migrant and wintering birds occasionally number in the hundreds on larger reservoirs, and smaller numbers are found on freshwater ponds and streams throughout much of the county, away from the immediate edge of the Bay. In recent years, small numbers have remained to oversummer and breed along the county's foothill and mountain streams.

Historically, the Common Merganser was not known to breed in the San Francisco Bay area. In the 1920s, it was a "winter visitant in fair numbers" in the Bay area (Grinnell and Wythe 1927), but there were no breeding records from the region. Grinnell and Miller (1944) listed breeding localities from the northern third of the state and from the Sierra Nevada, but in the Coast Ranges the species was not known to breed farther south than the Navarro River in Mendocino County. Still, occasional breeding well to the south of this range has been noted, specifically two broods found along the Nacimiento River, Monterey County, in early June 1939 (*Bird-Lore* 41:262 1939) and six eggs collected in San Luis Obispo County on 25 Apr 1941 (MVZ #5130). On 13 Jul 1971, a group of 11 female-plumaged birds thought to be immatures were at Calaveras Reservoir (whether in Santa Clara or Alameda County is unclear), indicating probable nesting there (*Am. Birds* 25:900 1971). The 1980s saw breeding records from Marin, Santa Cruz, and Monterey counties, with probable breeding in San Mateo County as well (*Am. Birds* 35:974 1981, 39:957 1985, 41:483 1987, 41:1482 1987). And on 29 Jun 1986, a female with eight young along upper Coyote Creek near Henry Coe State Park (James Yurchenco

and Amy Lauterbach, pers. comm.) afforded the first record of confirmed breeding for Santa Clara County.

Atlasers found the Common Merganser to be a fairly rare and local breeder in Santa Clara County, gaining confirmations from scattered locations in the Diablo Range and the southern Santa Cruz Mountains. Broods were found on moderately broad streams in well-wooded areas, including the Arroyo Hondo, Arroyo Valle, Alameda Creek, and upper Coyote Creek. One brood in Kelly Cabin Canyon was in the uppermost, intermittent reaches of Coyote Creek. Several broods were also found on large reservoirs, including Lake Elsman and Calaveras, Anderson, Coyote, Almaden, and Uvas reservoirs. Families found on these lakes may have nested in trees around the reservoirs, or they may have nested along tributaries and traveled downstream to the lakes. Common Mergansers were often found in wooded areas, where large snags, fallen trees, and crevices under trees and rocks may have provided suitable nesting sites (although no nests have been found in the county). Although breeding by Common Mergansers was not confirmed in Santa Clara County until 1986, as reported above, the remoteness and inaccessibility of many of the Diablo Range locations where atlasers found breeding mergansers suggests that earlier breeding simply went undetected.

During the atlas period, Common Mergansers were detected breeding only in foothill and mountainous areas, at elevations between 606 and 1,920 feet. Subsequently, two breeding confirmations were noted at lower elevations on the northern valley floor. A female with two flightless young at an elevation of 19 feet along lower Coyote Creek downstream from Montague Expressway, on 22 Jun 1995, was especially surprising (pers. obs.). Though the mature cottonwood riparian habitat along this reach of Coyote Creek provides suitable nesting habitat for these birds, this record was unusual both for being in an urban area and for being so close to the Bay, where few Common Mergansers are seen in any season. Breeding was also confirmed after the atlas period at Almaden Lake Park, at an elevation of 204 feet. Here, an adult accompanying flightless young was observed on 24 Jun 1997 (pers. obs.).

All 44 atlas and post-atlas breeding confirmations were records of flightless or recently fledged young accompanied by adults. Early breeding was signified by records of precocial young on 21 Apr and 9 May. Subsequently, all breeding records fell in the period between 25 May and 20 Jul.

Stephen C. Rottenborn

COMMON MERGANSER

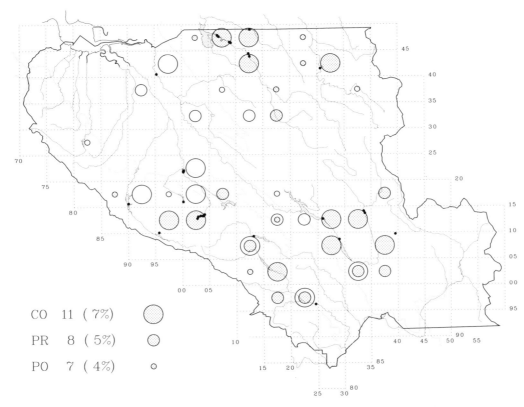

CO 11 (7%)
PR 8 (5%)
PO 7 (4%)

Postatlas (1994–2005), n = 24

Atlas (1987–1993), n = 20

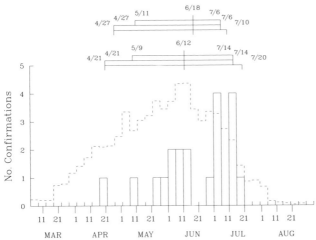

Ruddy Duck
Oxyura jamaicensis

If the male Ruddy Duck's sky-blue bill and rich, rufous plumage do not catch an observer's eye, then surely its outrageous courtship displays will do the trick. The primary breeding range of the Ruddy Duck is the prairie pothole region of North America, from Alberta and Manitoba south to Wyoming and Colorado (Brua 2001). Smaller, disjunct populations are found in wetlands throughout the West, around the Great Lakes, in Mexico, and on the Caribbean islands. These small ducks breed throughout California in freshwater wetlands, the northern populations withdrawing to the south in winter (Small 1994). Ruddies are uncommon but widespread breeders in Santa Clara County, found generally in artificial freshwater ponds. In winter, the number of ruddies increases greatly, and they are found in great abundance in brackish wetlands, on salt evaporator ponds, and on the Bay.

Historically, Ruddy Ducks were common on the San Francisco Bay in the winter, and a few would remain to breed in the South Bay, but there is no evidence of nesting in Santa Clara County until the 1930s. Kobbé (1902) noted that ruddies were found in the Bay area from October to mid-February. C. Stivers collected an egg set in the vicinity of Niles, Alameda County, on 5 May 1888 (MVZ #7518). Grinnell and Wythe (1927) judged Ruddy Ducks to be permanent residents in a few locations in the San Francisco Bay area, mentioning Lake Merced and Golden Gate Park, in San Francisco County, and Alvarado, Irvington, and Niles, in Alameda County, as known breeding locations. H. R. Eschenburg, an egg collector who lived in Gilroy, took a set of six eggs in Santa Clara County on 23 May 1935 (WFVZ #43458), the first breeding record in the county, but he did not note the location on the data slip. Sibley (1952) indicated that the Ruddy Duck was a "common resident" in the South Bay, breeding on freshwater lakes. But although he noted that W. E. Unglish had collected a set of eggs from San Felipe Lake, in adjacent San Benito County, on 30 May 1935, he did not include any records from Santa Clara County. Occasional breeding was noted in the county between the 1950s and the atlas period, including on a pond near Milpitas in 1952 (*Audubon Field Notes*

7:34 1953) and at the Palo Alto Baylands in 1969 (*Audubon Field Notes 23*:690 1969). Gill (1977) considered the South Bay breeding population to be between 50 and 100 pairs.

Ruddy Duck breeding confirmations during atlasing were based mostly on the observation of precocial young (86%), the balance of the confirmations based on fledged young. During the atlas period, these young were found at such bayside locations as the Emily Renzel Wetlands, the Sunnyvale Water Pollution Control Plant oxidation ponds and adjacent channels, the nearby Lockheed Martin ponds, Guadalupe Slough near Salt Pond A4, and the wetlands south of Salt Pond A18. Subsequently, following the atlasing, breeding birds were seen in Charleston Slough, the Calabazas Ponds, sludge-drying ponds at the San Jose-Santa Clara Water Pollution Control Plant, and the Waterbird Management Area along Coyote Creek below Highway 237. Breeding sites away from the Bay on the valley floor during the atlas period included Lake Cunningham and San Felipe Lake; additional sites found subsequently included the percolation ponds along Coleman Road, the Ogier Avenue ponds, and the South County Regional WasteWater Authority treatment ponds in Gilroy. In the Diablo Range, precocial young were seen at Grant Lake, a reservoir in Isabel Valley, a small reservoir north of Mt. Sizer within Henry Coe State Park, and Kelly Cabin Reservoir, also in Coe Park.

In the prairie pothole region, precocial young are normally observed from the middle of June to early September (Brua 2001). The earliest observation of breeding here during the atlas period was precocial young on Lake Cunningham on 16 May, and the latest was precocial young on Grant Lake on 25 Sep. Subsequently, precocial young were seen at the Sunnyvale Baylands Park as early as 9 May 2005 (Michael J. Mammoser, PADB), and at the Ogier Avenue ponds as late as 9 Oct 2002 (Kirsten R. Holmquist, PADB). Presumably, the mild climatic conditions in Santa Clara County permit an extended breeding season here.

Currently, breeding Ruddy Ducks in Santa Clara County are found almost exclusively on artificial or manmade ponds and wetlands. Grinnell and Miller (1944) stated that Ruddy Ducks were "much reduced by reason of disappearance of appropriate breeding conditions." In Santa Clara County, a century ago, there were natural wetlands along the Guadalupe River above San Jose, in the vicinity of present-day Lake Cunningham, in the Coyote Valley, along Llagas and Uvas creeks in the southern reaches of the Santa Clara Valley, and in the Bolsa de San Felipe. The habitat at some of these wetlands, for instance the swamp at Lake Cunningham (Schneider 1893), may have been suitable for ruddies, but there is no nesting evidence from that period. Today, it appears that the construction of impoundments, percolation ponds, borrow pits, and reservoirs over the last hundred years has provided some habitat suitable for this duck, and it has adapted successfully to these manmade sites.

William G. Bousman

RUDDY DUCK

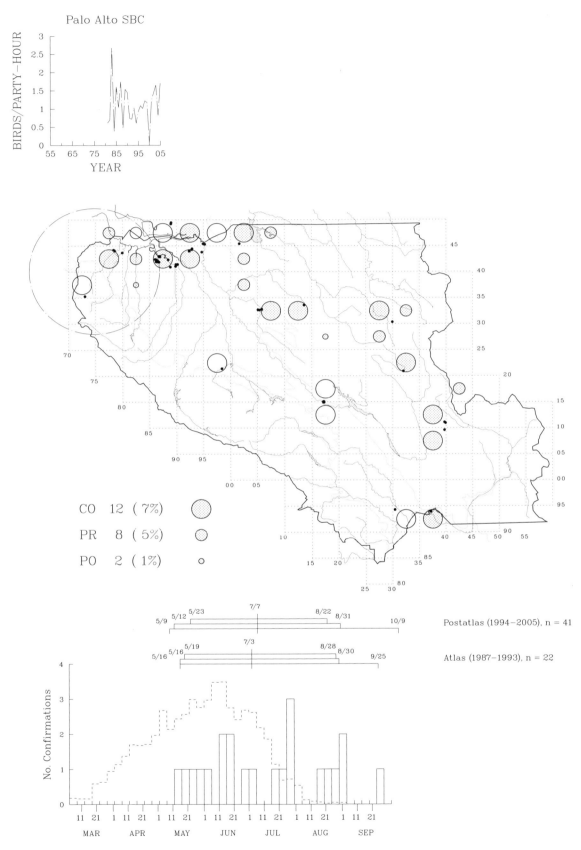

Palo Alto SBC

CO 12 (7%)

PR   8 (5%)

PO   2 (1%)

Postatlas (1994–2005), n = 41

Atlas (1987–1993), n = 22

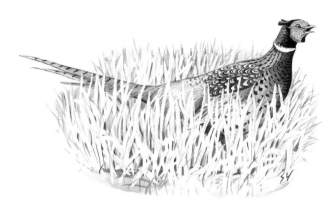

Ring-necked Pheasant
Phasianus colchicus

Introduced into Santa Clara County at the end of the nineteenth century, this striking gamebird is still characteristic of seasonal wetlands and weedy fields along the San Francisco Bay. Native to Asia, from the eastern shores of the Black Sea to Japan and Vietnam, the Ring-necked Pheasant has been introduced widely in North America over the last three centuries, and today is found in middle latitudes from British Columbia across Canada to Nova Scotia, and south to California and Pennsylvania (Giudice and Ratti 2001). It breeds in California and is still widely released in the State, but is largely absent from the coast north of San Francisco and from the southeastern deserts (Small 1994). This pheasant is fairly common in Santa Clara County, particularly near the San Francisco Bay.

In the west, Ring-necked Pheasants were first introduced successfully in the Willamette Valley of Oregon in 1882 (Long 1981). Haphazard efforts to introduce the species in California followed in Santa Cruz County and on the San Francisco Peninsula in the mid-1880s, but with little success (Belding 1890). More organized efforts by the California Fish Commission (now the Department of Fish and Game) began in the 1890s, when significant numbers were released in Santa Clara County and elsewhere (Grinnell et al. 1918). Introductions initially consisted mostly of birds of the *colchicus* and *torquatus* subspecies, *mongolicus* individuals being introduced later (Long 1981). The species was considered well-established in portions of Santa Clara County by 1912. Notable counts from that era include 35 to 40 birds seen between Berryessa and Milpitas in 1914 and a flock of 150 pheasants counted south of Coyote in 1915 (Grinnell et al. 1918). Sibley (1952) considered this species to be common in suitable habitats in the early 1950s, but did not contrast the numbers with earlier abundances. Numbers found today along the edge of the San Francisco Bay, based on CBC data, appear comparable to those recorded in the middle years of the twentieth century. These tallies are quite variable, however; particularly high counts were recorded in the 1980s.

During the atlas period, Ring-necked Pheasants were found principally in areas between the edge of the South Bay and the urban boundary. Confirmations were obtained in eight county blocks, seven of which were adjacent to the Bay. The only confirmation away from the Bay was of a nest with eggs found near Lake Cunningham. Elsewhere in the county, probable and possible evidence was obtained at multiple locations on the Santa Clara Valley floor south of the Coyote Narrows, as well as at a single site in the Santa Cruz Mountains and a few locations in the Diablo Range. All breeding confirmations were below 130 feet, although birds were observed at higher elevations, including some seen above Flint Creek in East San Jose at 660 feet during the atlas period, and others found in Ed Levin County Park at 640 feet after the atlas period (Michael M. Rogers, pers. comm.). Breeding pheasants made extensive use of seasonal wetlands, agricultural fields, and irrigation or stream channels, where there was adequate moisture and a good growth of weeds, grasses, and forbs. But they evidently avoided areas thickly grown with shrubs, or forested riparian habitats adjacent to weedy fields and grasslands.

Ring-necked Pheasant cocks set up their crowing territories in early spring. The earliest breeding evidence found was a nest with eggs on 2 May. All other dated confirmations were of either precocial or fledged young. During the atlas period, the latest breeding evidence obtained was recently fledged young seen on 25 Jun. Following the atlas period, dependent or precocial young were found in July, the latest such record made on 25 Jul 1996 (Michael L. Feighner, pers. comm.).

Ring-necked Pheasants do best in agricultural areas with grains, hayfields, and ample moisture (Grinnell and Miller 1944, Giudice and Ratti 2001). The era of grain farming here was nearly past when pheasants were first introduced into Santa Clara County, but alfalfa and other pasturage crops were still widely planted into the early 1900s, and these provided good habitat for pheasants. As orchards replaced grain fields at the end of the nineteenth century, there remained ample margins of weedy growth and forbs that continued to provide suitable pheasant habitat. Giudice and Ratti (2001) suggest that continental populations of this species likely peaked in the 1930s to 1950s. Since that time there has been a general decline in numbers, largely caused by changes in farming practices and by habitat loss to forest succession and urbanization. Santa Clara County has probably seen a similar pattern, as agricultural lands have been replaced by housing and light industry. We are unlikely ever again to see the large aggregations of Ring-necked Pheasants that were recorded in the early years of the twentieth century. What remains to be determined is whether this handsome non-native bird can continue to thrive along the edge of the South Bay into the future.

William G. Bousman

RING-NECKED PHEASANT

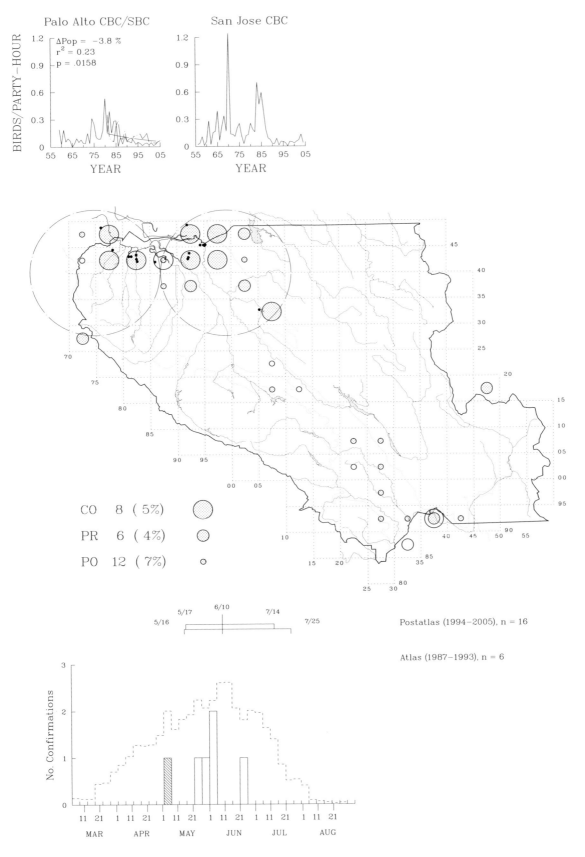

Palo Alto CBC/SBC

ΔPop = −3.8 %
r² = 0.23
p = .0158

San Jose CBC

BIRDS/PARTY-HOUR

YEAR

YEAR

CO   8 (5%)

PR   6 (4%)

PO 12 (7%)

Postatlas (1994−2005), n = 16

Atlas (1987−1993), n = 6

5/17   6/10   7/14

5/16   7/25

No. Confirmations

11 21 1 11 21 1 11 21 1 11 21 1 11 21 1 11 21

MAR   APR   MAY   JUN   JUL   AUG

133

Wild Turkey
Meleagris gallopavo

Moving through one of the county's oak woodlands, a flock of Wild Turkeys, seemingly primeval, is in fact of stock only recently introduced here, and may still retain some barnyard ancestry. The pre-Columbian distribution of Wild Turkeys extended from northern Arizona east through the Great Plains to southern Maine and south through much of the United States to Guerrero, in Mexico (Eaton 1992, AOU 1998). The species' range diminished significantly during the period of European settlement, but birds have been reintroduced within the former range and introduced to areas outside that range, including California (Eaton 1992). Six subspecies of the Wild Turkey are recognized (Eaton 1992). Those introduced in California included *M. g. intermedia*, from the mesquite grasslands of Texas through much of northern Mexico; *merriami*, from Colorado, New Mexico, and Arizona; and *gallopavo*, from southern Mexico (Harper and Smith 1973, Eaton 1992). In California, turkeys have been introduced in the Coast Ranges from Humboldt County to Santa Barbara County, in the foothills of the Sierra Nevada, at scattered locations in the northeast, and in San Diego County (Grenfell and Laudenslayer 1983, Small 1994). The Wild Turkey is now locally fairly common in parts of Santa Clara County, and in some areas the lack of hunting pressure has allowed it to become a nuisance.

Initial attempts to introduce Wild Turkeys into California began as early as 1887, but all were unsuccessful (Grinnell et al. 1918, Grinnell and Miller 1944, Harper and Smith 1973). One difficulty encountered was that wild birds, thought to have been a mixture of *gallopavo* and *merriami*, often did not survive on game farms, and it was sometimes necessary to develop hybrids with domestic birds for use as breeding stock (Harper and Smith 1973). The domestic stock used are believed to have derived from *gallopavo* (Eaton 1992). In California, a major stocking program using hybrid turkeys operated from 1928 to 1951, but most of the introductions failed, though apparently viable populations did persist for at least a few years in Sonoma, Santa Clara, and San Luis Obispo counties (Burger 1954). The Santa Clara County population, centered on the Castro Valley Ranch

southwest of Gilroy, was estimated at 300 birds in 1951 (Burger 1954). At the close of the 1950s, the Department of Fish and Game decided once again to introduce Wild Turkeys into California, but this time to use only wild-trapped birds (Harper and Smith 1973). The new introductions were of turkeys taken from native populations of *intermedia* and *merriami*, and "California hybrids" from San Luis Obispo County (Harper and Smith 1973). Of these new releases (Harper and Smith 1973), only one was in Santa Clara County: in March 1969, 14 hybrids from San Luis Obispo County were released in the Mt. Hamilton Range.

Atlasers found breeding Wild Turkeys widely in the Diablo Range, except in the northeastern corner of the county. Nearly 80% of all confirmations were of precocial young observed in foraging flocks. In the Santa Cruz Mountains, breeding birds were found in the foothills near the Almaden Valley and in a few blocks at the southern terminus of the range, in the vicinity of the Castro Valley Ranch, where game-farm stock had been released in 1939. Following the atlas period, new populations were noted in foothill regions in the Santa Cruz Mountains north of the Los Gatos gap. During the atlas period, breeding confirmations were obtained at elevations from 300 to 2,400 feet. Subsequently, precocial young were found in the Silver Creek Hills at an elevation of 230 feet (Stephen C. Rottenborn, pers. comm.). Most often, turkeys were found in oak woodlands interspersed with grasslands and scrublands. In the Santa Cruz Mountains, they were also seen in grasslands and openings near denser forests of coast redwood and madrone. Turkeys in the county seem to prefer edge habitat of grasslands adjacent to woodlands or forest, and some source of water during the summer dry period appears essential for their survival.

The earliest breeding evidence during the atlas period was of a family group with eight to ten fledged young seen on 4 Apr in Joseph Grant County Park. Fledged or precocial young were more typically found from the middle of May onward. The latest breeding evidence was of precocial young on 27 Jul, also in Joseph Grant County Park. Following the atlas period, precocial young were seen as late as 16 Aug 2005 near Almaden Reservoir (Ann Verdi, PADB).

Wild Turkeys have been introduced into California for the purpose of hunting. Harper and Smith (1973) describe the California hybrid that was released in Santa Clara County as "a hearty, wily bird." Mallette and Slosson (1987) state, "Birds become very wary when hunted, and only the skilled sportsman can coax a bird within range." As of 1990, when the county's population was estimated at between 2,500 and 4,000 birds, only about 20 birds were taken by hunters each year (Foley 1990). A number of our Wild Turkey populations have settled on public lands where they cannot be hunted, and have now become a nuisance. Some aggressive birds in Rancho San Antonio Open Space Preserve have frightened hikers and joggers and have had to be relocated (Gathright 1999). In Calero County Park, large flocks descend on the horse stables each morning for the seven o'clock feeding and compete with the horses there for forage (pers. obs.). Wily, indeed. What we have wrought, unfortunately, is an oak-woodland equivalent of the Canada Goose.

William G. Bousman

WILD TURKEY

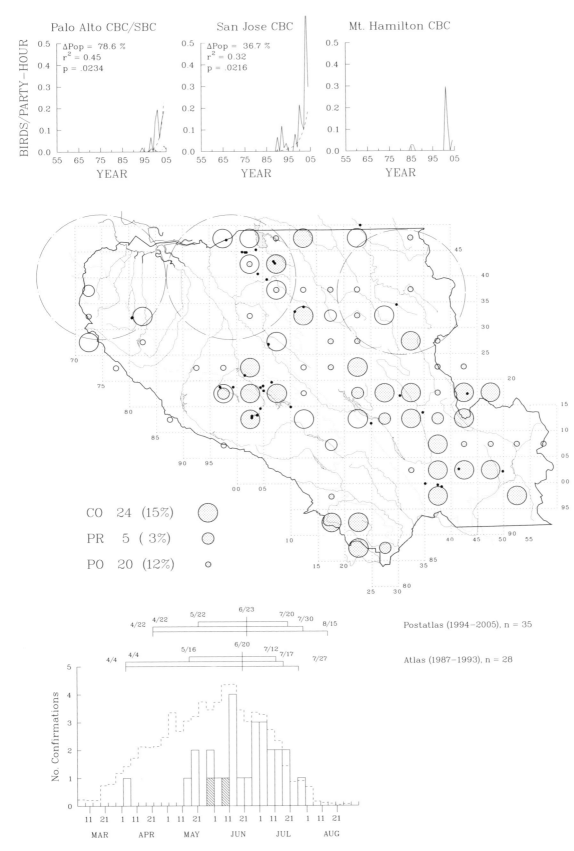

Palo Alto CBC/SBC

ΔPop = 78.6 %
r² = 0.45
p = .0234

San Jose CBC

ΔPop = 36.7 %
r² = 0.32
p = .0216

Mt. Hamilton CBC

BIRDS/PARTY–HOUR

YEAR

CO   24   (15%)
PR   5   (3%)
PO   20   (12%)

Postatlas (1994–2005), n = 35

Atlas (1987–1993), n = 28

No. Confirmations

MAR   APR   MAY   JUN   JUL   AUG

Mountain Quail
Oreortyx pictus

Were it not for the male's far-carrying call, the secretive Mountain Quail might go undetected in Santa Clara County, where few birders have actually seen this species. Mountain Quail range from the Pacific Northwest south through western Nevada and California (including the mountains of the northern and eastern parts of the state and scattered ranges farther south) to northern Baja California (Small 1994, AOU 1998). Mountain Quail are rare and very local residents along the western edge of Santa Clara County.

The historical status of the Mountain Quail in Santa Clara County, and the Santa Cruz Mountains in general, is unclear. As long ago as 1857, Sclater (1857) wrote that this species had been collected by Thomas Bridges in "the Valley of San José." A Mountain Quail egg was collected at "Santa Cruz" on 15 June 1872 (USNM #B21121). McGregor's 1901 summary of the land birds of Santa Cruz County cited reports that the species was "occasionally seen in the Santa Cruz Mountains." Perhaps on the basis of these reports, Grinnell (1902) and Grinnell et al. (1918) described the species as occurring "sparingly" in the Santa Cruz Mountains. In contrast, Grinnell and Wythe's 1927 summary of the Bay Area avifauna did not mention records from these mountains, and Grinnell and Miller (1944) stated that the species was "Of somewhat doubtful occurrence, formerly, in Santa Cruz Mountains," noting specifically that there were no records from Santa Clara County. Sibley (1952) did not mention Mountain Quail in his summary of the South Bay avifauna. Three birds reported at Big Basin, Santa Cruz County, in 1957 represented the only published report from the Santa Cruz Mountains through the first three-quarters of the twentieth century (*Audubon Field Notes 11*:440–41 1957).

In the mid-1970s, the species began to be recorded from the vicinity of Castle Rock State Park, mostly on the Santa Cruz County side of the county line (David L. Suddjian, pers. comm. to William G. Bousman). The first Santa Clara County report since Bridges' nineteenth century record was *circa* 1975, from the end of Stevens Canyon Road (*Am. Birds 39*:345 1985). The only other Santa Clara County records prior to the atlas period were from June 1984, when five birds were seen near Castle

Rock State Park just inside Santa Clara County (David Johnston, pers. comm.), and 20 Apr 1985, when two males were heard at the end of Stevens Canyon Road (*Am. Birds 39*:345 1985).

During the atlas period, Mountain Quail were reported from two edge blocks along the northwestern border of Santa Clara County. Birds were recorded on the Santa Cruz County side of Castle Rock State Park, where the only atlas confirmation (of precocial young at Castle Rock Falls on 16 June 1987) was obtained; and there have been few reports of the species from this area in recent years (David L. Suddjian, pers. comm.). Farther north, Mountain Quail were recorded in the Table Mountain area, from the upper end of Charcoal Road north into the Stevens Creek drainage; reports from there have continued at least through 2004. Since the end of the atlas period, Mountain Quail have been recorded in seven additional blocks. Most recent reports have been from the east side of Monte Bello Ridge in the upper Adobe and Permanente Creek drainages, where up to eight birds have been heard since 1994, although numbers have dwindled in the past few years (county notebooks). A bird heard from Page Mill Road west of Hidden Villa on 21 May 1994 (pers. obs.) represented the northernmost county record. Farther southeast, a bird was heard on the Santa Clara County side of Skyline Boulevard east of Mount Bielawski on 30 May 2003 (Steve Gerow, PADB), and multiple records come from the area from Loma Prieta southeast to Lands End on a number of May and June dates from 1999 to 2005 (Michael M. Rogers, David L. Suddjian, PADB). Santa Clara County records have been from areas dominated by dense chamise or manzanita chaparral, or by live oak/poison oak scrub, at elevations ranging from approximately 1,000 feet west of Hidden Villa to 3,250 feet near Loma Prieta. All Santa Clara County records span the period 10 March to 24 July, when males are giving their advertising calls.

The existence of nineteenth-century Mountain Quail records from the Santa Cruz Mountains suggests that a small population was present there historically. But Grinnell's doubts about the species' occurrence in these mountains (Grinnell and Wythe 1927, Grinnell and Miller 1944), the lack of any mention of the species by Sibley (1952), the existence of only one record (the 1957 Big Basin report) between the late 1800s and mid-1970s, and the sudden occurrence of the species in multiple locations since the mid-1970s all suggest that releases may be responsible for at least the recent records. Although such releases have been rumored (e.g., *Am. Birds 41*:483 1987), details are available for only one such occurrence, when about a dozen Mountain Quail escaped from a backyard pen along Moody Road in Los Altos Hills in the early or mid-1990s (Charles Hirschbeck, pers. comm.). These escapees may be responsible for the records east of Monte Bello Ridge, where birds were first detected in 1994. This species' provenance in the Santa Cruz Mountains thus remains a mystery, and because its future is equally uncertain, all observations of the species in the Santa Cruz Mountains are of great interest.

Stephen C. Rottenborn

MOUNTAIN QUAIL

Palo Alto SBC

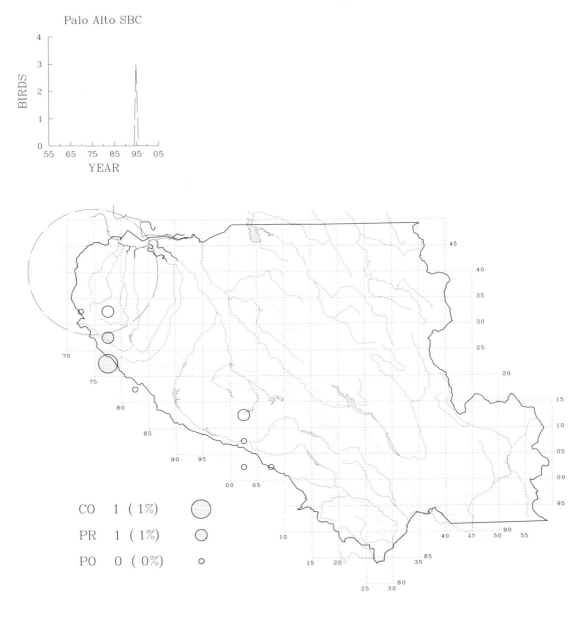

CO 1 (1%)
PR 1 (1%)
PO 0 (0%)

Atlas (1987–1993), n = 1

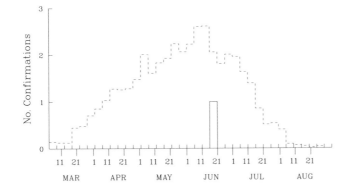

California Quail
Callipepla californica

Frantic rustling in the underbrush, followed by an explosion of quick wingbeats, greets the birder who flushes a covey of California Quail. This ground-dweller roams the west coast of North America from British Columbia to Baja California, although populations north of Oregon and east of California are likely the result of introductions (AOU 1998). The California Quail is resident throughout most of its namesake state, excluding the Mojave Desert and areas of high elevation (Zeiner et al. 1990, Small 1994). In Santa Clara County, the species is common in a variety of habitats, throughout all but the most heavily urbanized parts of the county. Two subspecies breed in the county. *Callipepla c. brunnescens*, which ranges from southern Santa Clara County and Santa Cruz County north along the coast into Oregon, is the form found in most of the county and the Bay area as a whole (Grinnell and Miller 1944). The inland race *californica*, found in the remainder of the state, is thought to reach the southeastern corner of Santa Clara County.

Published records of the California Quail in Santa Clara County date back to 1857, when Sclater (1857) wrote that this species had been collected by Thomas Bridges in "the Valley of San José." Since then, it has apparently been a common resident throughout the county. Osgood (1893) confirmed nesting by California Quail in the county in 1892. Price (1898a) considered it to be "common everywhere" around Stanford University, and Van Denburgh (1899b) wrote that it was "resident in all parts of the county." The large number of nests reported from Santa Clara County around the turn of the century (Hoover 1899, Van Denburgh 1899b, Ray 1900) indicates that this species was a common breeder at that time. Grinnell and Wythe (1927) described the species as abundant in the San Francisco Bay area, and Sibley (1952) wrote that it was a common resident in the brushlands of the South Bay. Although the California Quail

remained common in much of the Bay area prior to the initiation of the atlas, its numbers have likely declined in some urban areas and on intensively cultivated agricultural lands over the years. The numbers seem to agree: quail populations in the rural Mt. Hamilton Christmas Bird Count circle have not shown noticeable declines, whereas data from the Palo Alto and San Jose Christmas Bird Counts, as well as the Palo Alto Summer Bird Count, indicate significant declines at a rate of 4-5% per year in these more urban areas.

During the atlas period, the California Quail was found to be a common, widespread breeder in most of Santa Clara County. It was recorded in 95% of all blocks, and perhaps because the large broods of precocial young so readily attract attention, breeding was confirmed in 86% of all blocks. California Quail frequent a broad array of habitat types, but are most abundant at brushy woodland edges, in open chaparral, and in patches of brush and shrubby vegetation interspersed amid grassland and open woodland. These habitats offer dense low cover, which provides protection for nests and broods, as well as the forbs and seeds on which these birds forage (Bent 1932). California Quail were found to be more sparsely distributed in dense, continuous coniferous forest in the Santa Cruz Mountains, in extensive tracts of heavily farmed land on the Santa Clara Valley floor, and in suburban areas. Most breeding confirmations were obtained at elevations from 200 to 3,000 feet, although breeding was confirmed at elevations as low as 30 feet and as high as 4,000 feet.

In Santa Clara County, California Quail were found to be absent only from the most heavily urbanized blocks on the northern Santa Clara Valley floor. Here, habitat destruction and predation by urban-adapted animals have apparently led to the local extirpation of the species. Even some areas that continue to offer suitable habitat have lost their breeding California Quail in recent years, presumably because these areas have been isolated from source populations by urbanization. For example, coveys present on the Stanford University campus and at the Coyote Creek Field Station have disappeared just within the last decade (pers. obs.; Alvaro Jaramillo, pers. comm.). Although this species was recorded in several atlas blocks on the eastern side of the northern reaches of the Santa Clara Valley and at a few bayside locations, California Quail were quite rare and local in these urban areas, persisting in only a few semi-natural refugia from which they will likely be extirpated in the near future.

Most breeding confirmations during the atlasing were obtained in June and July, later than the peak for most of the county's other resident breeding bird species. But the timespan is great: a record of recently fledged young on 9 Apr implies an egg-laying date of late February or early March. And although this record is earlier than the breeding dates given by Roberson (1993e) for Monterey County, Bent (1932) listed egg dates in California as early as 12 Jan. In our atlasing, precocial young on 27 Apr constituted the only other April confirmation. Records of both precocial young and recently fledged young increased from mid-May to a peak between mid-June and mid-July, and confirmations dropped off abruptly in late July. Records of precocial young on 4 Aug during the atlas and of very small, recently fledged young on 13 Aug 1998 after the atlas (pers. obs.) were our latest breeding confirmations.

Stephen C. Rottenborn

CALIFORNIA QUAIL

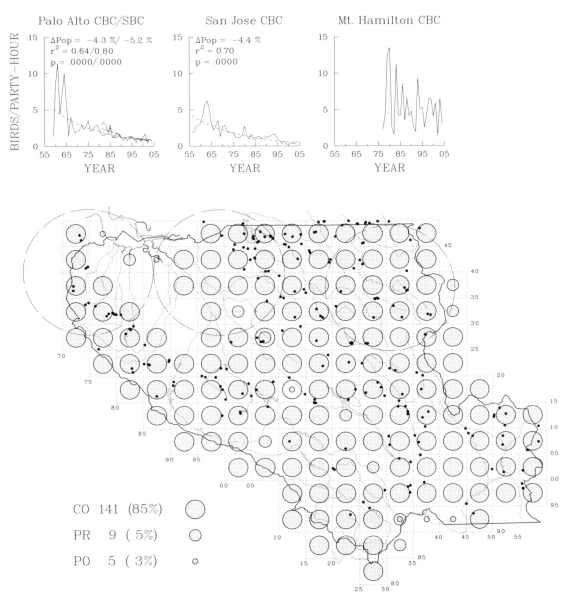

Palo Alto CBC/SBC

ΔPop = −4.3 %/ −5.2 %
r^2 = 0.64/0.80
p = .0000/.0000

San Jose CBC

ΔPop = −4.4 %
r^2 = 0.70
p = .0000

Mt. Hamilton CBC

BIRDS/PARTY-HOUR

YEAR

CO   141   (85%)

PR   9   (5%)

PO   5   (3%)

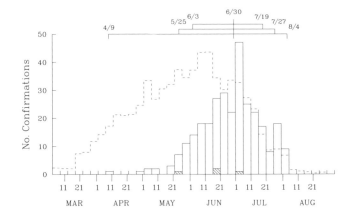

Atlas (1987–1993), n = 301

No. Confirmations

MAR   APR   MAY   JUN   JUL   AUG

SWEBB

Pied-billed Grebe
Podilymbus podiceps

Loud begging calls given by stripe-headed young confirm breeding by the Pied-billed Grebe in Santa Clara County's ponds and marshes. This species breeds throughout much of the New World, from southern Canada through South America (AOU 1998). In California, it nests in suitable habitat throughout most of the state, being absent primarily from elevations above 6,000 feet and breeding only locally in the arid southeastern region (Zeiner et al. 1990, Small 1994). Breeders in the northeastern corner of the state and at higher-elevation lakes subject to freezing leave their breeding areas in winter, and during this season some Pied-billed Grebes may be found in estuarine and coastal saltwater habitats. But most of California's breeding populations, including those in Santa Clara County, are resident. Pied-billed Grebes nest in nontidal marshes and along the margins of ponds and lakes at scattered locations throughout the county. They are also found in salt ponds, tidal waters, and other aquatic habitats during the nonbreeding season.

The historical abundance and distribution of breeding Pied-billed Grebes in Santa Clara County are not well known. Kobbé (1902) noted that this species was common in fall in the San Francisco Bay area and felt that it was "probably resident in favorable situations," but he did not specifically mention breeding. Grinnell and Wythe (1927) indicated that small numbers bred in freshwater habitats in the San Francisco Bay region, listing breeding records at Alvarado (in Alameda County) and in San Francisco. The first mention of breeding in Santa Clara County was a set of seven eggs collected 9 May 1936 by George Brem, Jr., near Gilroy in bulrushes in 3 feet of water (WFVZ #27237). Calling the species a "common resident" in the South Bay, Sibley (1952) noted a brood observed by James B. Rigby on 7 Jun 1947 on Lagunita at Stanford University and a nest with eggs found by W. E. Unglish on 2 May 1936 at San Felipe Lake, just over the county line in San Benito County. A brood of young noted by Emily D. Smith at a reservoir west of Gilroy on 8 Jul 1955 was considered sufficiently noteworthy for publication in *Audubon Field Notes* (9:398 1955). In any case, the Pied-billed Grebe has since proven to be an uncommon to locally common breeder in the county. Whether it was actually less common historically than it is now, or whether earlier breeders were simply not detected or reported by observers, is unclear. Although habi-

tat for this species has likely declined in some lowland areas, owing to wetland conversion, overall the Pied-billed Grebe has probably become somewhat more widespread in the county as a result of the construction of ponds and stream impoundments. Numbers of Pied-billed Grebes recorded on the local Christmas Bird Counts have increased at a rate from 1.2 to 4.4%. But the Breeding Bird Survey data for California as a whole (Sauer et al. 2005) show no significant population changes.

Atlasers found Pied-billed Grebes breeding at locations scattered throughout the county. During the atlas period, this species was recorded during the breeding season in 38% of all atlas blocks, and breeding was confirmed in 31% of all blocks; after the atlas period, breeding was confirmed in eight additional blocks. Most confirmations were from the edge of the Bay, where these grebes nested primarily in nontidal brackish and freshwater marshes, or from the Santa Clara Valley floor, where they nested at the marshy borders of ponds and lakes and along slow-moving streams having suitable emergent vegetation. The species also bred in small reservoirs and stock ponds at scattered locations in the Santa Cruz Mountains and Diablo Range, at elevations up to 2,940 ft. The main criteria determining habitat suitability appeared to be an adequate supply of prey, such as fish or crayfish, and emergent vegetation sufficient for nest construction, nest anchoring, and cover. The highest densities of Pied-billed Grebes occurred where emergent vegetation was abundant, such as along Llagas Creek southeast of Gilroy, and at the Ogier Avenue ponds along Coyote Creek north of Morgan Hill (pers. obs.). Occasionally, the birds built their nests simply by piling up dead vegetation in shallow water, even where there was no live vegetation nearby.

Pied-billed Grebes in Santa Clara County exhibit a protracted breeding period, as shown by a few records of rather early and rather late breeding. During the atlas period, the earliest breeding confirmation was of a nest with eggs on 15 Apr, and the earliest record of precocial young was on 23 Apr. But eight postatlas records of precocial young between 24 Mar and 8 Apr (the earliest in 2001, Robert W. Reiling, PADB) indicate that several clutches were initiated in early March. Records of nests with eggs or occupied nests (presumably having eggs) were found through April, May, and June; late nests were one on 16 Jul during the atlas period and another on 4 Aug 1995 after the atlas period (pers. obs.). Records of precocial young peaked in June and early July, but broods of flightless young were found throughout August and as late as 23 Sep. Recently fledged young still dependent on adults were seen as late as 6 Dec (and postatlas on 7 Dec 2004, Roland Kenner, Patricia L. Kenny, PADB). Such late breeding may be the result of double-brooding (Ehrlich et al. 1988).

Stephen C. Rottenborn

PIED-BILLED GREBE

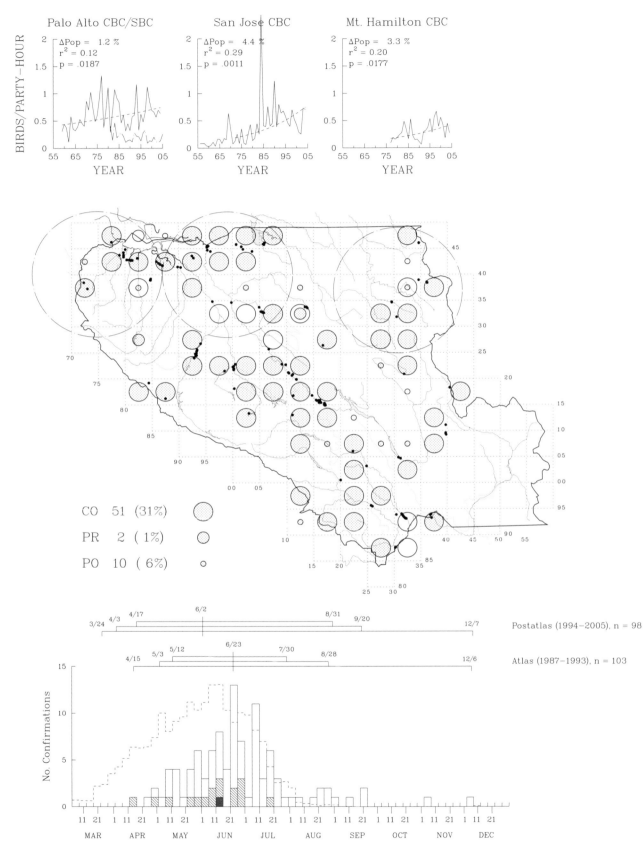

Palo Alto CBC/SBC

ΔPop = 1.2 %
r² = 0.12
p = .0187

San Jose CBC

ΔPop = 4.4 %
r² = 0.29
p = .0011

Mt. Hamilton CBC

ΔPop = 3.3 %
r² = 0.20
p = .0177

BIRDS/PARTY–HOUR

YEAR

CO 51 (31%)
PR   2 (1%)
PO 10 (6%)

Postatlas (1994–2005), n = 98

Atlas (1987–1993), n = 103

No. Confirmations

141

Eared Grebe
Podiceps nigricollis

These small grebes are often seen in the salt ponds and along the Bay in the winter, and a few, transformed into their elegant black breeding plumage with golden ear tufts, remain into the spring and occasionally nest here. The Eared Grebe is a near-cosmopolitan species, with breeding populations in North America, Europe, Asia, and Africa (Cramp 1977). Its North American subspecies, *P. n. californicus*, is found primarily in the interior of the American West during the breeding season, and makes a strong movement to the Pacific coast in winter (Palmer 1962). Although this species is an abundant winter visitor to Santa Clara County, particularly on salt ponds, oversummering Eared Grebes are uncommon and breed here only occasionally, generally following wet winters.

At the start of the twentieth century, Grinnell (1902) described Eared Grebes in California as common breeders on lakes east of the Cascades-Sierra axis, and abundant winter visitors along the coast, with other winter populations inland at low-elevation sites with suitable lakes and reservoirs. Grinnell (1915) also mentioned occasional breeding on lakes and reservoirs in southern California. Grinnell and Wythe (1927), in their survey of birds in the San Francisco Bay region, noted that a few Eared Grebes were found on Lake Merced during the summer, raising the possibility that this species might occasionally breed at this location. But as of the early 1950s this species was not considered to have bred within the South Bay region (Sibley 1952). Apparently overlooked by these regional summaries, a nest with seven eggs had been found in reeds on Lagunita on the Stanford University campus on 14 May 1908 (WFVZ #145157), providing the first record of breeding for Santa Clara County as well as for the San Francisco Bay area.

No further evidence of breeding activity was noted in the San Francisco Bay area until 1982, when 27 alternate-plumaged Eared Grebes were observed in Crittenden Marsh on 11 Jun (pers. obs). A number of these birds were engaged in courtship, giving their Sora-like advertising call (Palmer 1962), but no nesting was observed that year. In the following year, on 28 Mar 1983, many Eared Grebes were heard giving the advertising call in Crittenden Marsh (pers. obs). Nesting in the marsh was

first noted on 22 Jun 1983, when 120 adults and at least ten nests were counted in the western portion of the impoundment (Alan Royer, Lynn Tennefoss, county notebooks). The writer followed the progress of the birds in Crittenden Marsh during the summer of 1983 and observed that nests built on emergent vegetation in the western portion of the marsh were gradually abandoned as the water level dropped. By 15 Jul only one grebe continued to brood in the western portion. By this time, however, the colony had shifted to the eastern portion of the marsh, where 73 birds were brooding and 28 additional birds were building nests. The first young were noted on 31 Jul, and most of the young left Crittenden Marsh for nearby salt ponds shortly after hatching (Tom Rountree, county notebooks). The peak count of juveniles or dependent young in Crittenden Marsh was 39 on 19 Aug, and a juvenile was observed begging from an adult as late as 1 Sep. Four or five alternate-plumaged Eared Grebes were seen in Crittenden Marsh in both 1984 and 1985, but no evidence of breeding was obtained. This species again bred in Crittenden Marsh during 1986, and five adults and 20 young were counted on 29 Aug (Michael M. Rogers, county notebooks).

A few alternate-plumaged birds were seen in various locations during the initial years of the atlas, but no breeding was noted until 1992, when seven nests were counted in Crittenden Marsh on 6 Jun and ten were counted there on 21 Jun. Adults continued to brood there until 17 Jul, but the nests were abandoned by 25 Jul. In 1993, nesting was noted in an inactive salt pond east of Crittenden Marsh, where 12 nests were counted on 11 May. Six juveniles observed there on 5 Jul represented the successful result of the nearby colony. An additional nesting attempt noted in Crittenden Marsh on 24 Jul apparently did not succeed. Following the atlas period, Eared Grebes have been found regularly in a number of locations along the South Bay during the nesting season. Five nests were found on the inactive salt pond east of Crittenden Marsh on 14 May 1995 (Peter J. Metropulos, county notebooks), and two to three young were seen in Crittenden Marsh in the subsequent months (var. obs., county notebooks).

This species is well-known for its opportunistic nesting, particularly at the periphery of its range (Palmer 1962, Cramp 1977), as well as its tendency, in response to wet winters, to breed in the Mediterranean climate of California (Garrett and Dunn 1981). The extensive breeding of this species at Crittenden Marsh in 1983 followed a wet winter in which the rainfall was 130% of normal. Breeding in subsequent years has followed wetter-than-normal winters, except for 1992, which followed a slightly drier-than-normal winter. Further study is needed before we can understand all of the factors that encourage breeding by this grebe in the South Bay area.

William G. Bousman

EARED GREBE

Palo Alto SBC

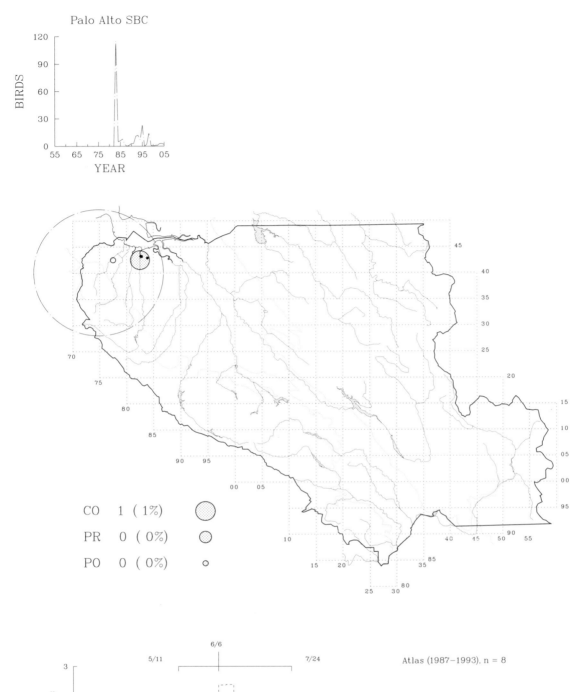

CO 1 (1%)

PR 0 (0%)

PO 0 (0%)

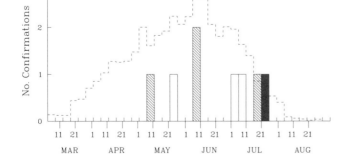

Atlas (1987–1993), n = 8

Western Grebe
Aechmophorus occidentalis

With its neck-arching displays and long tandem sprints across the water, the Western Grebe has one of the most elaborate courtship rituals of Santa Clara County's breeding birds. This species breeds in freshwater lakes and ponds over much of western North America. In California, it breeds primarily east of the Sierra Nevada and Cascades. Although scattered colonies are found at lakes with suitable nesting conditions throughout the rest of the state (Small 1994), Western Grebes are generally most abundant and widespread in California during winter, when they may be found on lakes, estuaries, and the open ocean. This species has long been a common wintering bird on reservoirs and along the Bay in Santa Clara County, but although a few birds oversummer each year, breeding was not detected in the county until 1993.

Because both Western and Clark's Grebes were formally referred to by the name "Western Grebe" until they were separated by the AOU (1985), it is generally impossible to determine whether historical records pertain to Western, Clark's, or both species. In the San Francisco Bay area, "Western" Grebes were first recorded breeding at Lake Merced in San Francisco, where nesting was confirmed in 1885 and again from 1926 to 1933 (Grinnell and Wythe 1927, Sibley 1952). Breeding by *Aechmophorus* grebes was not noted again in the Bay area until 1980, when "Western" Grebes were found breeding at Lake Hennessy in Napa County (Robin Leong, pers. comm.). After these grebes were split in 1985, *occidentalis* was first recorded breeding in the Bay area in 1990, again at Lake Hennessy (*Am. Birds* 45:1156, 1991), and then at San Antonio Reservoir in Alameda County in 1991 (Rusty Scalf, pers. comm.).

Atlas fieldwork found nesting Western Grebes only at the southern end of Calaveras Reservoir. Here, oversummering individuals were present for several years, and courtship was observed during June 1992. On 10 Jun 1993, three occupied nests were found in partially submerged vegetation at the southeastern corner of the reservoir, and by 29 Jun 1993 two of these nests had disappeared and the third had apparently been abandoned. Nonetheless, on 30 Jul that year, a single bird was observed on a nest containing at least two eggs, and four active nests were

present on 21 Aug and 31 Aug. Successful breeding was signaled by a brood of two small young seen on 31 Aug that year, and another brood was seen on 14 Oct and 29 Oct.

Because access to Calaveras Reservoir was granted only during the atlas period, after 1993 our records of nesting grebes were limited to distant observations from Calaveras Road, at the southwest corner of the reservoir. In 1994, the author observed two occupied Western Grebe nests on 24 Jun, and on 23 Jul, three Western Grebe nests, nine nests of unidentified *Aechmophorus* grebes, and a pair of unidentified *Aechmophorus* with large young were observed. A brood of young Western Grebes and another of unidentified *Aechmophorus* were noted on 12 Oct 1994, and on 26 Nov, two broods of Western Grebes (one very young, the other nearly fledged) and a brood of unidentified *Aechmophorus* grebes were observed. On 14 Oct 1996, a pair of Western Grebes was feeding one large young there (Michael M. Rogers, pers. comm.). In 1997, two Western Grebe nests on 6 July had increased to 18 occupied nests (with four additional pairs nest-building) on 3 August (pers. obs.). Nesting was detected again in 1998, with three occupied Western Grebe nests and two nests of unidentified *Aechmophorus* grebes on 13 Aug and a brood of two young on 22 Oct, and in 1999, with two occupied nests and three nests under construction on 22 Jun (pers. obs.). An adult was feeding young on 23 Sep 2000 (Michael M. Rogers, pers. comm.). Observations during the period 2001-2004 were not thorough enough to determine whether breeding occurred in those years, but an adult feeding young was noted at Calaveras Reservoir on 6 Oct 2005 (Michael M. Rogers, pers. comm.)

During the drought that affected most atlas years, water levels at Calaveras Reservoir were low. But after above-average rainfall in the winter of 1992–93 ended the drought, water levels were elevated and, as recounted above, *Aechmophorus* grebes were recorded breeding in the county for the first time. Similar increases in the levels of Lake San Antonio in Monterey County in 1993 stimulated nesting by both Western and Clark's Grebes, for the first time since 1985 (Bailey 1993a). Both there and at Calaveras Reservoir, these grebes used brush that had invaded the margins of the reservoirs during the drought as anchors for their floating nests.

Both the timing and the success of breeding by these grebes were influenced by fluctuations in water levels. In 1993 and 1994, the drawdown of water levels as summer progressed grounded many nests at Calaveras Reservoir, causing their abandonment. For example, nests active on 23 Jul 1994 were abandoned by 24 Aug after water levels dropped, but an increase in water levels by 12 Oct rekindled nesting activity. Apparently, these grebes continued to renest following nest failures, and the very late breeding of some pairs (as evidenced by very small Western Grebe chicks as late as 26 Nov) suggests that a few pairs may have attempted nesting a number of times before they were successful. In any event, few broods were observed relative to the number of nests seen, suggesting that breeding success was quite low.

Stephen C. Rottenborn

WESTERN GREBE

Palo Alto SBC

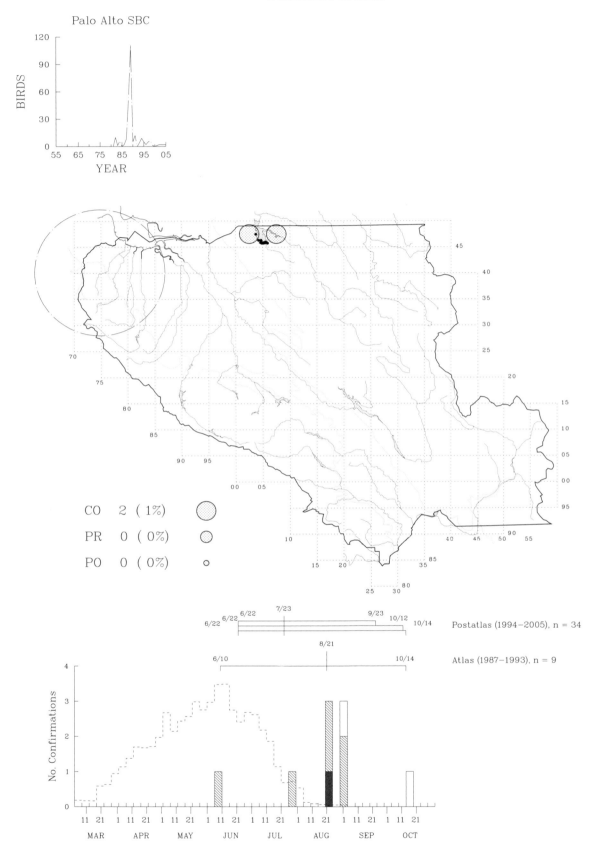

CO 2 (1%)
PR 0 (0%)
PO 0 (0%)

Postatlas (1994–2005), n = 34

Atlas (1987–1993), n = 9

Clark's Grebe
Aechmophorus clarkii

Considered the light morph of the "Western Grebe" prior to 1985, the Clark's Grebe was separated from the Western Grebe by the AOU on the basis of minor differences in plumage, bill color, and vocalizations, as well as the apparent infrequency of hybridization between the two species (AOU 1985, Storer and Nuechterlein 1992). Clark's Grebes breed over most of the range occupied by the Western Grebe, nesting in marshy lakes and ponds throughout much of western North America. In California, the primary breeding areas for this grebe are east of the Sierra Nevada and Cascades, although they breed at scattered lakes throughout the rest of the state as well. Both breeding and wintering populations of this species are less abundant than those of the Western Grebe in California (*Am. Birds 39*:96 1985, *41*:136 1987, Small 1994), and Western Grebes tend to outnumber Clark's Grebes in Santa Clara County during all seasons. In the county, Clark's Grebes are present year-round on reservoirs, salt ponds, and the San Francisco Bay, although they are decidedly less common in summer than during the rest of the year.

Because both Western and Clark's Grebes were formerly referred to by the name "Western Grebe" until they were separated by the AOU (1985), it is generally impossible to determine whether historical records pertain to Western, Clark's, or both species. In the San Francisco Bay area, "Western" Grebes were first recorded breeding at Lake Merced in San Francisco, where nesting was confirmed in 1885 and again from 1926 to 1933 (Grinnell and Wythe 1927, Sibley 1952). A. M. Ingersoll, who collected three sets of eggs there in 1885, specifically referred to them as *A. clarkii* (see the data slip associated with WFVZ #78299), but the other records were not specifically designated as *A. occidentalis* or *A. clarkii*. Breeding by *Aechmophorus* grebes was not noted again in the Bay Area until 1980, when "Western" Grebes were found breeding at Lake Hennessy in Napa County (Robin Leong, pers. comm.). After the Clark's and Western Grebes were split in 1985, the first modern breeding re-

cords of birds definitively identified as Clark's Grebes in the Bay area occurred in 1990, when this species bred at Lake Hennessy in Napa County (*Am. Birds 45*:1156, 1991), and in 1991, when Clark's Grebes nested at San Antonio Reservoir in Alameda County (Rusty Scalf, pers. comm.). In Santa Clara County, this species has occurred regularly in small numbers during summer, but there was no evidence of nesting in the county prior to the atlas project.

During the atlas period, Clark's Grebes were found only at the southern end of Calaveras Reservoir and at San Felipe Lake, the latter in San Benito County just south of the Santa Clara County border. Oversummering individuals were observed at Calaveras Reservoir for several years without evidence of breeding, but on 10 Jun 1993 a pair of Clark's Grebes was seen building a nest among several nests occupied by Western Grebes in the southeastern corner of the reservoir. This nest was later abandoned, and Clark's Grebes apparently did not breed successfully at Calaveras Reservoir in 1993. The single individual at San Felipe Lake, seen on 11 Jun and 28 Jun 1991, was probably a nonbreeder, although high water levels at this lake may provide suitable conditions for breeding.

Because access to Calaveras Reservoir was granted only during the atlas period, after 1993, our records of nesting grebes were limited to distant observations from Calaveras Road, at the southwestern corner of the lake. As a result, it was impossible to identify conclusively all of the grebes breeding in 1994, and some breeding Clark's Grebes may have gone unnoticed. On 23 Jul, the writer saw 16 unidentified *Aechmophorus* grebes, including a pair attending large young, with at least nine nests in submerged vegetation at the southeastern corner of the reservoir. Other broods of unidentified *Aechmophorus* grebes were seen on 12 Oct and 26 Nov 1994. Successful nesting by Clark's Grebes was finally confirmed when a pair of them was seen feeding young on 1 Nov and 26 Nov 1994. The only confirmation in the county since 1994 consisted of an adult on a nest at the south end of Calaveras Reservoir on 3 Aug 1997 (pers. obs.). Few attempts have been made to survey nesting grebes at Calaveras Reservoir in recent years, and whether Clark's Grebes have continued to nest there after 1997 is unknown.

Both Clark's and Western Grebes nested at Calaveras Reservoir in 1993 and 1994, and it is likely that the habitat requirements and response to water-level fluctuations described in the preceding Western Grebe account pertain to this species as well. Because the two species often nest in the same colonies and do interbreed occasionally, atlasers attempted to determine the degree to which interbreeding might have occurred at Calaveras Reservoir. Observations of pairs courting, nest-building, and feeding young allowed observers to document the characters of both members of at least 13 pairs. Of these, only a single mixed pair (courting on 20 May 1993 and 29 Jun 1993 and still closely associated on 30 Jul 1993) was seen, and there was no evidence that this pair actually nested.

Stephen C. Rottenborn

CLARK'S GREBE

Palo Alto SBC

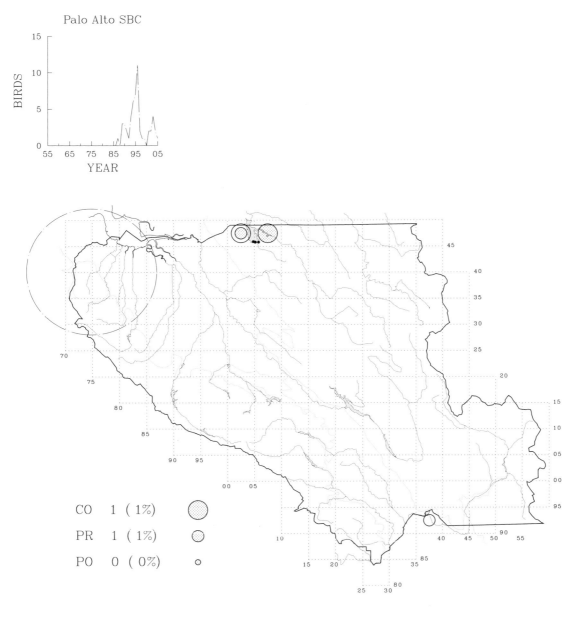

CO   1 (1%)

PR   1 (1%)

PO   0 (0%)

Atlas (1987–1993), n = 1

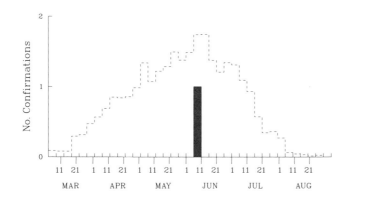

©KLA-C 1986

Double-crested Cormorant
Phalacrocorax auritus

Occurring here only as a winter visitor until recently, the Double-crested Cormorant is now a regular breeding species in Santa Clara County. This cormorant is found across North America, nesting from Alaska to Newfoundland, south through much of Canada and the United States, and into Mexico and Central America (AOU 1998). Of five subspecies, *P. a. albociliatus* is found on the west coast of North America from British Columbia to Baja California and Sinaloa (Hatch and Weseloh 1999). In California, Double-crested Cormorants occur widely along the coast and on inland bodies of water. Major breeding areas include the coast north of Cape Mendocino, inland areas in Siskiyou, Modoc, and Lassen counties, the Farallon Islands, the Channel Islands, and, recently, San Francisco Bay (Small 1994). The Double-crested Cormorant has always been a common wintering species in Santa Clara County, but since the early 1990s the expanding San Francisco Bay population has begun to nest here regularly.

Double-crested Cormorants were considered common in the San Francisco Bay area by early observers (Kobbé 1902, Grinnell and Wythe 1927), but the only known breeding colonies were on the Farallon Islands and on Seal Rocks, off San Francisco (Grinnell and Wythe 1927). These populations were stable through the first half of the twentieth century (Grinnell and Miller 1944, Sibley 1952), but with the introduction of organochlorine pesticides after World War II, cormorant numbers in California began a long-term decline (Small 1994, Carter et al. 1995). By the 1970s, this long-term decline appears to have reversed, and Double-crested Cormorants began nesting within San Francisco Bay. At least 33 nests were counted on 6 Sep 1975 on power transmission towers along Route 37 in Napa and Solano counties (*Am. Birds 30*:118 1976). Five nests were reported on the Richmond-San Rafael Bridge on 3 Jul 1984, and 102 nests were found on the eastern end of the San Francisco-Oakland Bay Bridge on 15 Jul 1984 (*Am. Birds 38*:1057 1984). This breeding population expanded southward in San Francisco Bay, as evidenced by the 12 nests found on the transmission towers along the San Mateo Bridge, in San Mateo County, on 23 Jul

1989 (*Am. Birds 43*:1363 1989). By 1990, the new colony in San Mateo County had grown to 100 nests (*Am. Birds 44*:1181 1990). Concurrently, during the 1980s and 1990s, the number of birds counted on the Palo Alto SBC increased by 42% a year.

During the first five years of the atlas fieldwork, no evidence of breeding by Double-crested Cormorants was noted, although summer birds were found at a number of locations. But the inexorable advance of breeding birds in San Francisco Bay led to the first county breeding records when two nests with young were found 2 Aug 1992 on a transmission tower over Salt Pond A2W, north of Mountain View. In 1993, five nests were found on the same transmission tower, and a single nest was found on a tower a little over a kilometer to the east on Salt Pond B2. Following the atlas period, breeding birds expanded their nesting eastward toward Alviso, most of the new nesting occurring on Salt Pond A18. Maximum nest counts in this period include ten on the Salt Pond A2W towers on 4 Jun 1994 (William Cabot, county notebooks), eight on the Salt Pond B2 towers on 5 Jun 1994 (Peter J. Metropulos, county notebooks), and 27 on six towers on Salt Pond A18 on 6 Jul 1997 (Stephen C. Rottenborn, county notebooks). Following the 1997-98 El Niño year, San Felipe Lake, just south of the Santa Clara County line in San Benito County, flooded well beyond its normal borders. On 25 Apr 1998, four cormorant nests were found in willows and cottonwoods in a Great Blue Heron heronry there, increasing to 11 nests by 25 May (Jan Hintermeister, Stephen C. Rottenborn, county notebooks). Later that year, on 3 Jul, ten ground nests were found on the levee between Salt Ponds A9 and A10 in Alviso, within a California Gull colony (Stephen C. Rottenborn, county notebooks). Although ground nests appear to be preferred by this species (Hatch and Weseloh 1999), predation pressures often cause it to nest in trees and on manmade structures. In the Alviso case, however, predation pressures may have been reduced by the protection offered by the adjacent nesting California Gulls.

The first county breeding records were noted late in the season, but the phenology based on combining these initial records with postatlas records shows an extended breeding period. Birds have been observed on nests as early as 8 Apr 2004 (Michael M. Rogers, Michael J. Mammoser, PADB), and young have remained in nests as late as 26 Sep 1995 (Stephen C. Rottenborn, pers. comm.).

Carter et al. (1995), in documenting the current breeding status of the Pacific Coast subspecies of the Double-crested Cormorant, have speculated about possible causes for the increased numbers of birds in San Francisco Bay, as well as along the coast from British Columbia to southern California. They note that a long-term population decline from the 1800s up through the 1960s occurred for a variety of reasons, including human persecution, egging, destruction of lakes in the interior, and pesticide contamination of the food chain. Since then, the reduction of the organochlorine pesticide burden in the environment, the diminishing of human persecution, and the remarkable ability of this cormorant to use artificial nest sites have all contributed to this population's resurgence.

William G. Bousman

DOUBLE-CRESTED CORMORANT

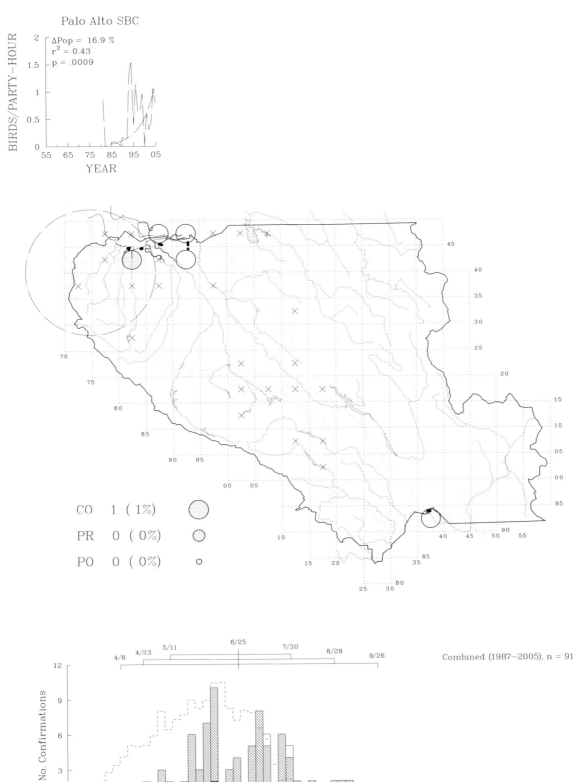

Palo Alto SBC

ΔPop = 16.9 %
r² = 0.43
p = .0009

BIRDS/PARTY–HOUR

YEAR

CO   1 (1%)
PR   0 (0%)
PO   0 (0%)

Combined (1987–2005), n = 91

No. Confirmations

MAR   APR   MAY   JUN   JUL   AUG   SEP

149

American Bittern
Botaurus lentiginosus

Among the most cryptic and reclusive of Santa Clara County's breeding birds, the American Bittern presents a formidable challenge for an observer attempting to confirm its breeding. This species nests in marshes across much of North America, but its distribution is sparse and patchy in many areas, and it is absent as a breeder from higher latitudes in Alaska and Canada and from much of the southern United States (Palmer 1962). In California, American Bitterns nest primarily in freshwater marshes in the northeastern region and in the Central Valley, small numbers breeding at scattered locations elsewhere in the state (Grenfell and Laudenslayer 1983, Small 1994). In Santa Clara County, these birds are uncommon migrants and winter residents, occurring here mostly from September to April, in bayside salt and brackish marshes, and in the county's few remaining freshwater marshes. Only a few remain to breed in the county.

The American Bittern was first recorded in Santa Clara County sometime prior to 1857, when it was collected by Thomas Bridges in "the Valley of San José" (Sclater 1857). In the first half of the twentieth century, authors considered it a fairly common permanent resident in the San Francisco Bay area, found most commonly in freshwater marshes and sloughs, less often in salt marshes (Kobbé 1902, Wheelock 1904, Grinnell and Wythe 1927, Sibley 1952). These authors cited records from Santa Clara County, and noted breeding records from several locations in the Bay area, but the strongest evidence of breeding in Santa Clara County that they mentioned was an individual with "white nuptial patches" in an Alviso salt marsh on 6 May 1951 (Sibley 1952). Santa Clara County's first nest record, apparently unknown to Sibley, was obtained on 1 May 1937, when five eggs were collected from a nest 2 feet above water in dense bulrushes (WFVZ #27154); these eggs were in the collection of H. R. Eschenburg of Gilroy, but the precise location of the nest within the county is unknown.

During intensive surveys of bayside marshes in 1971,

Gill (1977) found American Bitterns near Palo Alto and Alviso on several occasions between March and June. These surveys covered primarily saline and brackish marshes, which are rarely used for nesting by American Bitterns in California (Shuford 1993b), but the presence of birds into June suggests breeding. A nest found in the Palo Alto Flood Control Basin in 1975 (Robert Yutzy, pers. comm. to William G. Bousman) constituted the first modern breeding record of this species in Santa Clara County, but there were no further summer records in the county between 1975 and 1994 (including during the atlas period).

In 1994, an American Bittern was flushed along Artesian Slough in Alviso on 26 Jun (there were several subsequent sightings in August in brackish and salt marshes in that vicinity), and another was observed in a field near Llagas Creek east of Gilroy on 6 Jul (*Am. Birds 48*:984 1994). Subsequently, American Bitterns have been confirmed breeding at two locations in the county. On 13 May 1997, the writer flushed a bittern from a nest containing five eggs in a wet fallow field along Llagas Creek near Bloomfield Avenue, southeast of Gilroy. The nest consisted of a shallow mat of herbaceous vegetation piled on the ground in a field of tall grasses, dock, cattails, and bulrushes. At the time, the mat was only slightly moist (i.e., had no standing water). At least three adult bitterns were present along Llagas Creek on that date, and individuals were observed into May at the same location in 1998, 1999, 2003, and 2004 (county notebooks). On U.S.G.S. topographic quad maps from 1917 and 1939, this area is shown as supporting an extensive freshwater marsh, and it may have been a historical breeding location for bitterns. In contrast, an adult flushed from a nest (not yet containing eggs) at the Ogier Avenue ponds on 23 May 1997 (pers. obs.) was in an area that historically did not provide suitable breeding habitat for American Bitterns. This group of ponds along Coyote Creek north of Morgan Hill was created by gravel mining conducted between the 1950s and 1995. Today this site, part of the Santa Clara County park system, provides emergent marsh vegetation in several areas. The 23 May 1997 nest consisted of a platform of cattail leaves and bulrushes constructed within a broad, dense stand of cattails in a pool 0.5 m deep.

By the early 1900s, the loss of freshwater marshes had begun to take its toll on California populations of this species (Grinnell and Miller 1944), and American Bittern populations have continued to decline, or have been extirpated, in many parts of the state since then (Small 1994). The draining and filling of freshwater and brackish marshes in the South Bay during the late 1800s and early 1900s reduced available breeding habitat in this area considerably. Although the current scarcity of this species' favored nesting habitat clearly limits its abundance within Santa Clara County, recent breeding records (and those in nearby San Benito County [*Field Notes 51*:922–23 1997]) suggest that the American Bittern still maintains a breeding presence in the few South Bay areas where conditions are suitable. The long-term persistence of the American Bittern as a nesting species in Santa Clara County will depend on the preservation, or restoration, of freshwater marshes here, and on the hydrologic conditions that maintain such habitats.

Stephen C. Rottenborn

AMERICAN BITTERN

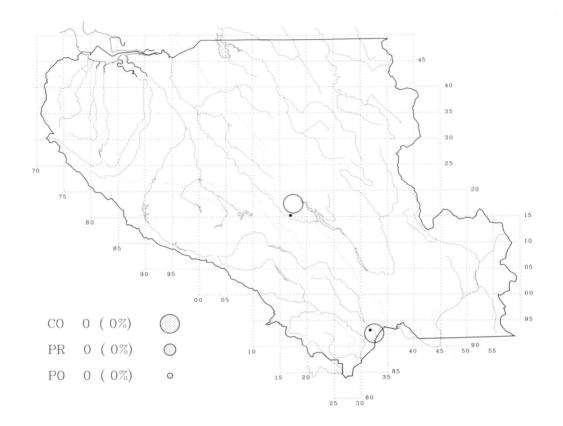

CO   0 (0%)
PR   0 (0%)
PO   0 (0%)

Postatlas (1994–2005), n = 2

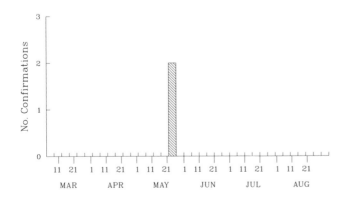

©KLA-C 1986

Great Blue Heron
Ardea herodias

The nesting colonies of these majestic herons aggregate in Santa Clara County wherever suitable foraging exists, but few colonies persist in one location for more than a few years. The Great Blue Heron breeds widely in North America from Alaska and southern Canada south through much of the United States into Mexico and Central America (Butler 1992). At least four subspecies are recognized, and of these *A. h. herodias* is the one found throughout most of North America, including California (Butler 1992). Great Blue Herons are fairly common in California and breed throughout the state, except for the southeastern deserts and the higher mountains (Small 1994). They are common year-round in Santa Clara County, where they can be found near bodies of water of almost any size, and occasionally in upland fields as well.

Most of the early nesting records of Great Blue Herons in Santa Clara County were the work of egg collectors. The earliest egg set was collected from a sycamore in San Jose on 14 Apr 1886 by "S. C. E." (probably Samuel C. Evans, WFVZ #118472), who noted that the tree "contained a large number of other nests." John O. Snyder collected a set of four eggs in a small oak "near Palo Alto" in Santa Clara County on 4 Apr 1896 (WFVZ #95645). The data slip, annotated in different handwriting, states that five or six pairs nested there until the oak was cut down in 1922, at which point the colony moved to a nearby oak. Grinnell and Wythe (1927) reported that this species was resident in the South Bay, and recorded historical colonies near Redwood City in San Mateo County, Alvarado in Alameda County, and Sargent in southern Santa Clara County. Sibley (1952) wrote that Great Blue Herons were common in the South Bay and mentioned recent colonies near Bloomfield Ranch south of Gilroy and at Sargent. In 1952, active colonies included one near Searsville Lake, San Mateo County, and a second in a eucalyptus grove on the Guadalupe River near Agnew. In 1971, the only known colony in the South Bay was on Bair Island, San Mateo County (Gill 1977). Analysis of CBC data shows a decline of 2.1% per year in the Palo Alto count circle and an increase of 4.8% in the San Jose count circle.

Atlasers found Great Blue Herons nesting in 12 blocks (7%) during the atlas period and in an additional seven blocks (4%) following the atlas period. Because Great Blue Herons may forage well over 5 km from their colony sites, all reported probable and possible records were downgraded to observed; each is shown on the map by an ×. Although at least 19 colony sites were recorded during and subsequent to the atlas period, generally only three to eight sites were reported as active in any single year. The records that follow here are documented in the atlas databases, the county notebooks, and San Francisco Bay Bird Observatory files. The largest colony observed was in a large eucalyptus on the Llagas Creek floodplain just south of Watsonville Road, in Morgan Hill. In 1994, following the atlas period, this colony comprised at least 31 nests, and great blues were still nesting there in 2005, despite nearby construction. Few other colonies exceeded five to ten nests, although a eucalyptus on Coyote Creek below Highway 237 held 12 nests in 1995. That eucalyptus was washed away by a storm in the winter of 1996-97, and these herons switched to nearby willows, where ten nests were counted in 2002. Other sizable colonies included one in eucalyptus trees west of Grant Lake with eight nests in 2000, one with eight nests in eucalyptus trees at Vasona Reservoir in 2005, and another in willows at San Felipe Lake that had at least five nests in both 1998 and 2001. Most colonies, however, consisted of fewer than five nests. Along the South Bay these included nests on duck blinds and power transmission towers. In 1991, along Coyote Creek north of Morgan Hill, great blues nested in two sycamores about 1 km apart. As the creek dried up in that fourth year of drought, all these nests were abandoned. Small colonies or single nests were also found in the interior of the Diablo Range, where they were generally placed in foothill pines, the herons apparently foraging in nearby small reservoirs and stock ponds.

Breeding by Great Blue Herons seems to be scattered across many months. The earliest breeding observed during the atlas period was a bird incubating in the colony near Grant Lake on 11 Mar. The earliest local egg record, three eggs collected by George Brem, Jr. at San Felipe Lake, was also on 11 Mar in 1945 (WFVZ #45137). Gill (1977) noted the start of incubation as early as the last week in February on Bair Island, San Mateo County, and Pratt and Winkler (1985), from their 13-year study at Audubon Canyon Ranch, Marin County, recorded the earliest date of egg laying as 13 Feb. Following the atlas period, nesting was noted as early as 11 Jan, at Vasona Reservoir in 2004 (Linda Sullivan, county notebooks), although this early nest failed because of a February storm. The latest breeding evidence obtained during the atlas period was a bird on a nest at Grant Ranch on 8 Jul. Subsequently, young were observed at the Coyote Creek colony below Highway 237, on 26 Aug 1999 (Stephen C. Rottenborn, PADB).

William G. Bousman

GREAT BLUE HERON

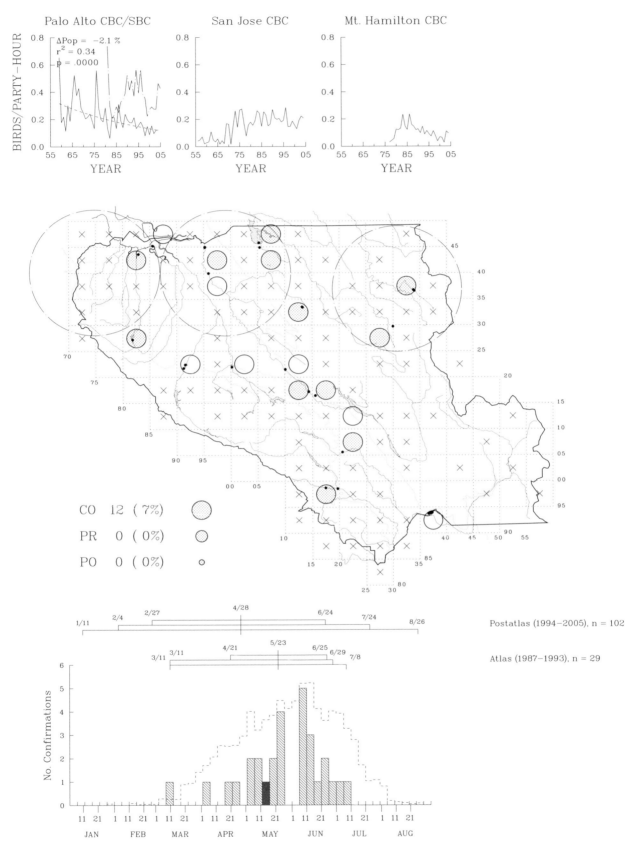

Palo Alto CBC/SBC

San Jose CBC

Mt. Hamilton CBC

ΔPop = −2.1 %
r² = 0.34
p = .0000

BIRDS/PARTY−HOUR

YEAR

CO   12 (7%)
PR   0 (0%)
PO   0 (0%)

Postatlas (1994–2005), n = 102

Atlas (1987–1993), n = 29

No. Confirmations

JAN   FEB   MAR   APR   MAY   JUN   JUL   AUG

153

Great Egret
Ardea alba

This magnificent white egret, found worldwide, survived the onslaught of the plume hunters of the late 1800s to become a symbol of a nascent conservation movement. There are four subspecies of the Great Egret, the subspecies *egretta* occurring in the Americas, from Canada south to Argentina and Chile. In western North America it breeds locally from central Washington south to California and Arizona (AOU 1998, McCrimmon et al. 2001). Great Egrets nest throughout California in suitable habitats, from Humboldt Bay and the northeastern plateau south to the Salton Sea and the lower Colorado River Valley (Small 1994). In Santa Clara County, Great Egrets are year-round residents and breed both along the Bay and at inland sites.

Historically, Great Egrets nested north along the Pacific Coast to Oregon (McCrimmon et al. 2001). Grinnell and Wythe (1927) stated that the species was fairly common in the Bay area in the 1880s, but did not include any breeding records. But two sets of eggs collected by W. A. Burres at Sargent, Santa Clara County, on 4 Apr 1889 (CAS #6697 and #6699) are the only known breeding records in the San Francisco Bay area prior to the Great Egret's recovery from plume hunting. By the beginning of the twentieth century, Great Egrets were considered scarce anywhere in California (Grinnell 1902), as birds were being slaughtered for their spectacular nuptial plumes or "aigrettes." Only with the passage of the Migratory Bird Treaty Act of 1913 did the killing and exploitation of this stunning and graceful heron finally come to a halt. Still, no Great Egrets were found in the Bay area until 1924, when one was seen southwest of Suisun, Solano County, along the railroad (Storer 1931).

By the 1940s, Great Egrets were once again occurring regularly in California and were found in many suitable habitats throughout the state (Grinnell and Miller 1944). Milton S. Ray collected a set of eggs at San Felipe Lake, San Benito County, on 18 May 1940 (MVZ #7400). And by the 1950s, Sibley (1952) considered the species to be the most common ardeid in the South Bay. A colony of Great Egrets (up to 40 nests) and Great

Blue Herons occupied a eucalyptus grove on the Guadalupe River just south of Montague Road from at least as early as 1945 to 1952 (*Audubon Field Notes 1*:187 1947, *2*:213 1948, Sibley 1952, Turner 1962), but was not reported after that. Another colony was in a eucalyptus grove south of Newark, Alameda County, in the 1960s, but had disappeared by 1969 (*Audubon Field Notes 23*:690 1969). Gill (1977) noted that 75 pairs nested on Bair Island, San Mateo County, in 1967, but was unaware of subsequent breeding anywhere in the South Bay. At some point, a new colony appeared along Artesian Slough, north of Alviso. Although the first occupancy dates for this site are uncertain, breeding occurred here as early as 1982 (C.M.S., unpubl. data), and by 1985 this mixed-species colony included at least 50 nests of Great Egrets (Roy W. Lowe, Lee Robinson, county notebooks). At the Alviso heronry, herons and egrets nested in thick bulrushes a few feet off the water. Great Egrets generally nest in trees or shrubs, but in Oregon bulrushes have also been used as a nesting substrate (Palmer 1962).

During the atlas period, Great Egrets nested each year in the Alviso heronry on Artesian Slough. The maximum count recorded during this period was of 28 nests on 13 May 1993. Following the atlas period, birds continued to breed in this colony, 90 nests being recorded there on 17 Apr 1998. The next year, however, only two nests were successful, and for unknown reasons the colony was abandoned by midsummer (county notebooks). Later that year, at least seven pairs, possibly from the Alviso heronry, attempted to nest in willows and cottonwoods along Coyote Creek 4 km to the east, but were unsuccessful. Between 5 and 12 pairs successfully used the willows on Coyote Creek between 2000 and 2002. Two additional colonies were found in the South Bay, one in the Coyote Creek lagoons in 2000, the other on Guadalupe Slough in 2001. Both of these colonies were in thick bulrushes. New colonies have also been found inland, including egrets nesting in giant reeds on the island in Almaden Lake in 1997, in saltbush on an island at Lake Cunningham in 2004, in palms at the Palo Alto Duck Pond in 2004, and in sycamores on Shorebird Way, Mountain View, in 2005.

The earliest evidence of nesting observed during the atlas period was birds carrying nesting material into the Alviso heronry on 4 May. Subsequent to the atlas period, birds were seen occupying nests at Almaden Lake as early as 9 Mar 2005 (Ann Verdi, county notebooks). During the atlas period, the latest evidence of breeding was a nest with young in the Alviso heronry on 7 Aug. Subsequently, young remained at a colony in sycamores in a light industrial area of Mountain View as late as 14 Oct 2005 (Michael M. Rogers, county notebooks).

The Great Egrets nesting at the Alviso colony, from at least 1982 until 1999, appear to have constituted one of the more permanent colonies to form in the South Bay since the recovery of this species. In recent years, nesting egrets have shifted to a number of different sites, both along the Bay edge and inland. So far, all of these South Bay heronries have been relatively short-lived in contrast to the more permanent colonies found in Marin County (Pratt 1983, Shuford 1993c).

William G. Bousman and
Cheryl M. Strong (San Francisco Bay Bird Observatory)

GREAT EGRET

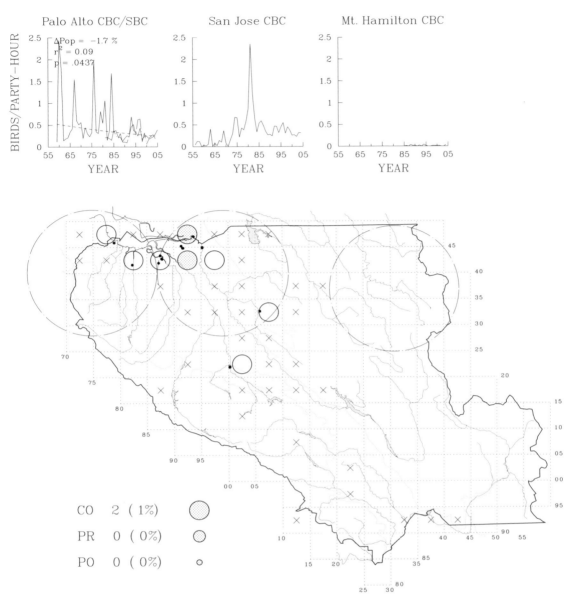

Palo Alto CBC/SBC

ΔPop = −1.7 %
r² = 0.09
p = .0437

San Jose CBC

Mt. Hamilton CBC

BIRDS/PARTY–HOUR

YEAR

CO 2 (1%)
PR 0 (0%)
PO 0 (0%)

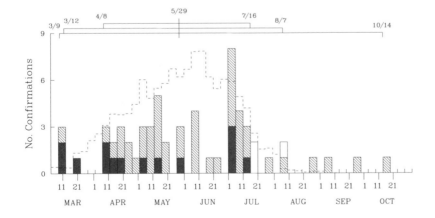

Combined (1987−2005), n = 61

No. Confirmations

Snowy Egret
Egretta thula

Foraging along the margin of a pond, a Snowy Egret shakes its "golden slippers" to startle hidden prey, perhaps reminding us of a time when the "aigrettes" on its back were more valuable than gold. These elegant egrets are primarily coastal nesters in North America, but are found widely in Central and South America as far south as Chile and Argentina (Parsons and Master 2000). In North America, snowies are also found breeding on inland rivers and in wetlands, particularly in the interior western United States, in eastern Texas and Oklahoma, and in the lower Mississippi River Valley. Two poorly differentiated subspecies are recognized, *E. t. brewsteri*, found west of the Rocky Mountains, and the nominate *E. t. thula*, in the remainder of the range (Parsons and Master 2000). In California, Snowy Egrets are found widely, their colonies scattered from Humboldt Bay to the Salton Sea (Small 1994). They are common residents in Santa Clara County, mostly near the San Francisco Bay, but a few individuals are found elsewhere in the county where ponds, streams, or reservoirs provide suitable foraging.

Just as the Great Egret had been, the Snowy Egret was driven nearly to extinction in California following the onset of plume hunting in the 1880s. Although known from southern California, there are no records of Snowy Egrets in the San Francisco Bay area prior to the species' catastrophic decline, except for a group of three stragglers to the Farallon Islands sometime before 1888 (Bryant 1888) and an undated San Mateo County record (Grinnell and Wythe 1927). Grinnell and Miller (1944) believed that the Snowy Egret had become extinct in California by the early 1900s, but noted that birds had begun to reappear by 1908. In 1914, W. L. Dawson (1915) discovered a nest in Merced County, and egg collectors found snowies breeding regularly in the San Joaquin Valley in the 1920s and 1930s. By midcentury, Sibley (1952) described the species as an uncommon winter visitor to the South Bay, where it was not known to breed. The first Snowy Egret record for Santa Clara County was of ten birds found by Emily D. Smith in Alviso on 30 Aug 1954 (*Audubon*

Field Notes 9:51 1955). The first breeding noted in the South Bay was of 150 pairs on Bair Island, San Mateo County, in 1969 (Gill 1977). Santa Clara County's first breeding record was a colony of 150 pairs found by Chris Swarth at the Alviso heronry on 18 Apr 1980 (*Am. Birds 34*:811 1980).

During the atlas period, Snowy Egrets were recorded breeding only in the Alviso heronry, which was situated in a wide area of Artesian Slough, downstream from the outfall of the San Jose-Santa Clara Water Pollution Control Plant. There, the egrets built their nests on bulrushes over water. The peak number of nesting birds at the heronry was recorded prior to the atlas period, when about 350 nests were counted on 22 May 1985 (Roy W. Lowe, Lee Robinson, county notebooks). The number of nesting birds in this colony varied over the next 15 years until, at length, the heronry was abandoned, in 1999. All nonbreeding atlas records were considered "observed" evidence and are shown by ×'s on the map.

Following the atlas period, breeding Snowy Egrets colonized other sites in the South Bay, and this process accelerated once the Alviso heronry was abandoned (San Francisco Bay Bird Observatory; mult. obs., county notebooks). A summary of these colonies follows, including the year of first detection, the span of years in which nesting occurred (possibly including years when birds were absent or not censused), and the peak count of pairs or nests observed. The first pair nesting away from Alviso used an island in a percolation pond at Los Gatos Creek County Park in 1997 (1997–2004, four nests in 1998). In 1998, a single pair nested on a downed eucalyptus amid giant reeds on the island at Vasona Reservoir (1998–2003, eight nests in 2003). In 1999, four pairs nested in giant reeds on the island in Almaden Lake (1999–2005, 15 nests in 2004). In 2000, a colony of 114 nests was found in the Coyote Creek lagoons, an area of heavy marsh vegetation north of Newby Island in Alameda County (2000–2002, 114 nests in 2000). In 2001, a small colony of seven pairs was found nesting in bulrushes along Guadalupe Slough where the Moffett Channel joins the slough (2001–03, seven pairs in 2001). In 2003, at least three pairs of snowies nested in palms at the Palo Alto Duck Pond (2003–05, at least 18 nests in 2004). Also in 2003, a single pair nested in a large eucalyptus (otherwise used by Great Blue Herons) on the Llagas Creek floodplain south of Watsonville Road. And in 2004 and 2005, two pairs nested in saltbush on an island in Lake Cunningham.

The earliest evidence of breeding at the Alviso heronry during the atlas period was adults carrying nest material on 4 May 1991. Subsequent to the atlas period, snowies at the Palo Alto Duck Pond were seen nest-building as early as 24 Mar 2004 (W.G.B., pers. obs.). The latest evidence of breeding during the atlas period was nestlings seen in Alviso on 7 Aug. Following the atlas period, dependent fledged young were seen at the Palo Alto Duck Pond colony as late as 13 Sep 2003 (Michael M. Rogers, pers. comm.).

William G. Bousman and
Cheryl M. Strong (San Francisco Bay Bird Observatory)

SNOWY EGRET

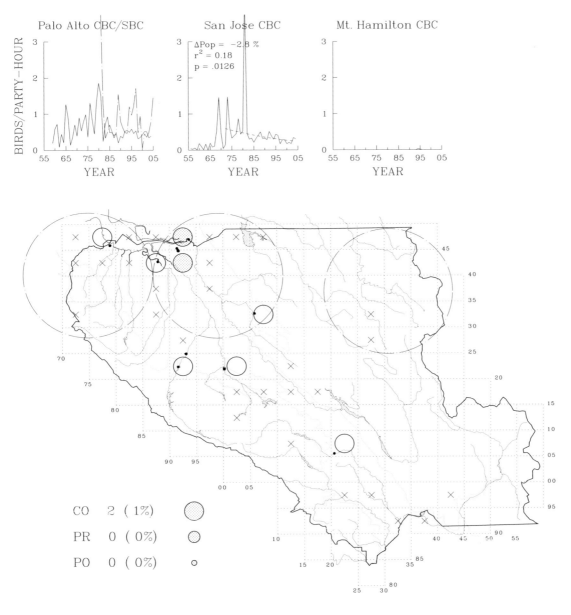

Palo Alto CBC/SBC

San Jose CBC

ΔPop = −2.8 %
r² = 0.18
p = .0126

Mt. Hamilton CBC

BIRDS/PARTY-HOUR

YEAR

YEAR

YEAR

CO   2 (1%)
PR   0 (0%)
PO   0 (0%)

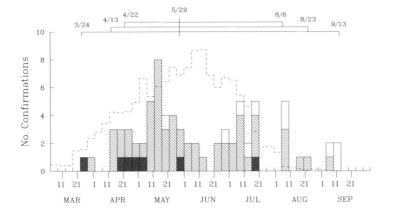

3/24   4/13   4/22   5/29   8/6   8/23   9/13

Combined (1987−2005), n = 74

No. Confirmations

MAR   APR   MAY   JUN   JUL   AUG   SEP

157

Little Blue Heron
Egretta caerulea

In the last decades of the twentieth century, the Little Blue Heron nested in Alviso, well north of its normal subtropical breeding range. This heron is resident on the coasts of the southeastern United States, in the Caribbean, on the coasts of Mexico, and in Central America and northern South America. Summer breeders are regularly found north of this range in North America, from Texas to southern Maine (Rodgers and Smith 1995). Extralimital breeding also occurs in California, Arizona, and the northern Great Plains. In California, this heron is found, depending on location, as a pre- or postbreeding dispersant, a summer visitor, or a very rare and irregular breeder (Unitt 1977, Small 1994). The Little Blue Heron is a very rare summer visitor to Santa Clara County; but it has nested here in at least six different years.

The Little Blue Heron has been found in California only during the last 40 years. The first documented record was of an immature found at Bodega Bay, Sonoma County, on 7 Mar 1964 and collected on 15 Mar (Jeter and Paxton 1964). Earlier sight records from central California remain uncertain (Danby 1936, *Gull 21*:87–88 1939, Watson 1940, *Condor 60*:343 1958). Following the 1964 record, one or two adults were recorded irregularly at the West Marin Island heronry, Marin County, from 1965 to 1971. Although breeding or possible hybridization with Snowy Egrets was suspected, no confirmation of breeding was obtained there (Shuford 1993hh).

The first observations of adult Little Blue Herons in the South Bay were of an adult seen at the Palo Alto Baylands from 30 Apr to 5 Jul 1971 (*Am. Birds 25*:794 1971, pers. obs.). In 1973, an adult was seen in the heronry on Bair Island, San Mateo County, but again without evidence of breeding (*Am. Birds 27*:814 1973). One or two adult Little Blue Herons continued to be seen irregularly in the Palo Alto area throughout the 1970s (Ryan and Hanson, in prep., *Am. Birds 27–34*: 1973–79, county notebooks). A Little Blue Heron × Snowy Egret was found at the Palo Alto Baylands in the winter of 1972–73 (*Am. Birds*

27:814 1973) and similar hybrids were seen locally in 1979 and 1986–91. (These hybrids suggested "calico" immature Little Blue Herons, but differed in having uniformly dark mandibles, yellow lores, mostly slate-gray back, wing, and tail feathers, and mixed coloration on the neck and head.) In April 1980, an adult Little Blue Heron was seen in the new heronry along Artesian Slough at Alviso, and breeding was reported that summer (*Am. Birds 34*:925 1980). Between one and five adult Little Blue Herons were seen at the Alviso heronry throughout the 1980s, although no additional observations of breeding behavior were noted prior to the start of the atlas period (Cheryl M. Strong, San Francisco Bay Bird Observatory, unpubl. data).

In three years during the atlas period, and in two years afterward, Little Blue Herons were found nesting in the Alviso heronry in Artesian Slough (between Salt Ponds A16 and A18). This heronry, which was active from about 1979 to 1999, straddled the boundary between atlas blocks 9040 and 9045, and Little Blue Heron nests were found on both sides of the boundary. The first breeding confirmation during the atlas period was of a newly fledged bird seen with two adults on 8 Aug 1988, and an occupied nest on 19 Jun 1990 offered an additional confirmation. In 1993, two separate nests were found. Four fledglings were seen at the first nest on 26 Jun, and adults were seen brooding young on a second nest on 31 Jul. Following the atlas period, in 1994, a pair was found in one of the nests that had been used in 1993, and on 23 Jul the nest contained two eggs and a newly hatched chick (Peter J. Metropulos, county notebooks). In 1998, a year before the Alviso heronry was abandoned, the last nesting was observed (Cheryl M. Strong, pers. comm.). Nests in the Alviso heronry were built on California and alkali bulrushes, generally about a foot above the high-tide line (Ryan and Hanson, in prep.). Adults were observed foraging in neighboring atlas blocks, as indicated on the map, most often within 2–3 km of the heronry.

During the 1980s and 1990s, the earliest records for returning adult Little Blue Herons were in the last two weeks of April. The earliest nesting evidence was an occupied nest on 1 Jun. The earliest date on which fledglings were observed was 23 Jun, which suggests egg dates as early as 14 Apr, on the basis of brood phenology (Rodgers and Smith 1995). The latest nesting evidence was adults on a nest on 8 Aug. Adult birds were still seen locally in early September, an occasional bird staying until early October.

Little Blue Herons have not nested in the Alviso heronry since 1998. The heronry was largely abandoned in the following year, and the other breeding ardeids moved elsewhere to nest. Two Little Blue Herons were seen in a new heronry along Guadalupe Slough in 1999, but no nesting evidence for them was observed (Cheryl M. Strong, pers. comm.). These herons are still recorded in the county in most summers, but in the six years since 1999, none have been seen earlier than late June or later than the first week in August, suggesting that they are no longer attempting to breed here.

William G. Bousman

LITTLE BLUE HERON

Palo Alto SBC

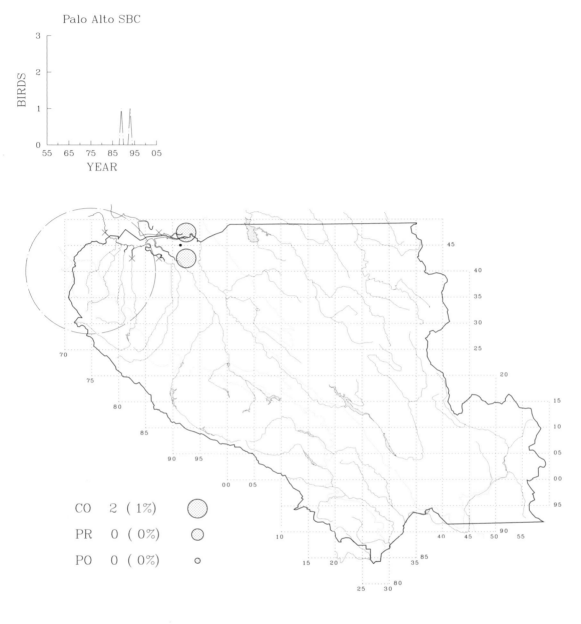

CO 2 (1%)

PR 0 (0%)

PO 0 (0%)

Atlas (1987–1993), n = 5

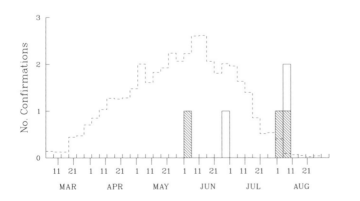

Cattle Egret
Bubulcus ibis

An invader from the Old World, the Cattle Egret has expanded its range to include most of the New World as well. In the Eastern Hemisphere, Cattle Egrets are found from the Iberian Peninsula and Africa east to Japan, Southeast Asia, and Australia. The birds that have invaded the Americas are from the western population, *B. i. ibis* (Telfair 1994, AOU 1998). The Cattle Egret has spread throughout much of the Western Hemisphere, establishing regular breeding colonies from southern California across the United States to Maine, and south through Middle America to northern Argentina and Chile (AOU 1998). In California, this egret breeds abundantly in the vicinity of the Salton Sea, and less commonly in scattered locations as far north as Humboldt Bay (Small 1994). Cattle Egrets are fairly rare in Santa Clara County. They have nested in Alviso on at least six occasions from 1985 to 1997, but not since then.

Telfair (1994) has summarized the invasion of the New World by the Cattle Egret. The species was first recorded in Surinam, in northeastern South America, as early as 1877, and nearby in Guyana in 1911. By 1947 it was considered to be common in those areas. In the Caribbean Region, it was found off Nicaragua by 1933, and in Puerto Rico and Jamaica by 1948. The first sighting in the United States was in southern Florida in 1941, and birds were found nesting there by 1953. The expansion of this species in the New World has been by "widespread, explosive, grenade-like leaps, not concentric waves" (Telfair 1994). Small (1994) records that the first Cattle Egret in California was found in Upper Newport Bay, Orange County, on 27 Dec 1962. The first nest was observed in July 1970 in a large Snowy Egret colony at the Salton Sea. By 1974 there were 850 nests in the Salton Sea colonies, and numbers increased to 5,000 breeding pairs by 1977, and to 25,000 pairs by 1993. In one of Telfair's grenade-like leaps, Cattle Egrets were found suddenly in Northern California in the winter of 1969–70, when 1 to 17 birds were seen in six different counties, from Merced to Humboldt (*Audubon Field Notes 24*:534 1970). This invasion winter

also included a single bird east of Gilroy, the first record for Santa Clara County. The first evidence of Cattle Egrets breeding in northern California was of birds found nesting in three locations in 1978: the Corcoran Irrigation District, Kings County; the Mendota Wildlife Area, Fresno County; and a marsh near Eureka, Humboldt County (*Am. Birds 32*:1204 1978).

After the first observation here in February 1970, Santa Clara County sightings were sporadic in the following decade. Up to seven birds were found in Alviso 7-8 Oct 1979 (mult. obs., county notebooks), 30 were found along Ferguson Road near Gilroy on 23 Mar 1982 (Alan M. Eisner, county notebooks), and 40 were seen in a flooded area north of Bailey Road near Coyote on 10-12 Feb 1984 (Rae Schmuck, county notebooks). The first record of breeding by Cattle Egrets in Santa Clara County was on 22 May 1985, when ten nests were observed in the Alviso heronry by Roy W. Lowe (*Am. Birds 39*:345 1985).

Following the first nesting in Alviso, Cattle Egrets nearly disappeared from Santa Clara County, few birds being found during any season over the next two years. But birds were found in the Alviso area again in the spring of 1989, and two adults were found at a nest with two to three nestlings on 16 May that year. Approximately 17 adults were seen in the heronry at that time. No nesting was observed in the heronry in 1990–92, but nesting was once again observed on 31 Jul 1993, when two nests were found there. One nest contained two large, fledged young and the other held two downy nestlings. Following the atlas period, nesting was observed during surveys of the Alviso heronry from 1995 to 1997 (Cheryl M. Strong, San Francisco Bay Bird Observatory, pers. comm.). Four adults were seen at two nests on 21 May 1995, a nestling was observed in a nest on 12 Jun 1996, and one nest was found on 30 Apr 1997. Although 12 adults were seen in the heronry in 1998, none has been recorded on subsequent surveys there. Away from Alviso, two adults were seen carrying nesting material into willows on the southern shore of San Felipe Lake, south of the county line in San Benito County on 31 May 1998 (Stephen C. Rottenborn, pers. comm.).

An analysis of records in the county notebooks suggests that there have been two invasion periods in the county: from 1982 to 1985 and from 1993 to 1997. Similar variation in numbers of wintering Cattle Egrets has been observed on northern California CBCs (*Audubon Field Notes* and subsequent titles). In recent years, the number of birds recorded on northern California CBCs has been increasing, the majority of these birds observed in the Central Valley and far fewer of them in the San Francisco Bay area. As these Central Valley populations increase, it will be interesting to see whether the South Bay experiences new breeding invasions.

William G. Bousman

CATTLE EGRET

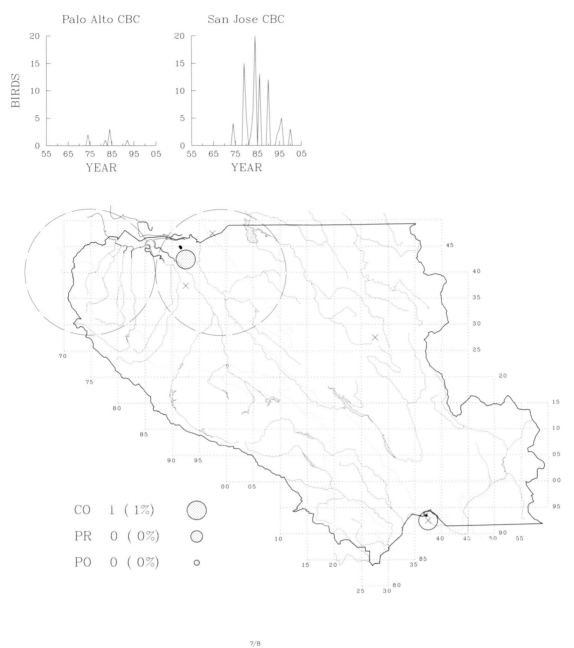

Palo Alto CBC

San Jose CBC

BIRDS

YEAR

YEAR

CO   1 (1%)
PR   0 (0%)
PO   0 (0%)

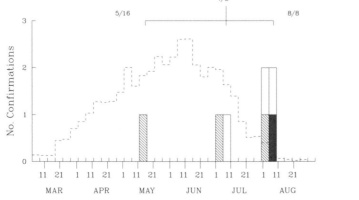

Atlas (1987–1993), n = 7

No. Confirmations

MAR   APR   MAY   JUN   JUL   AUG

R. COLWELL

Green Heron
Butorides virescens

Along the edge of a riparian thicket, a birder may be startled by the loud "skeow" of a Green Heron, disturbed by the unwelcome visitor. Green Herons breed from British Columbia across the southern edge of Canada to Nova Scotia and south through Mexico to Panama, although they are absent from most areas of the mountain west (Davis and Kushlan 1994). Four subspecies are currently recognized, *B. v. anthonyi* being the one found in western North America (Davis and Kushlan 1994). In California, Green Herons are found throughout much of the state, the birds resident in the south and migratory in the north (Small 1994). These herons are uncommon summer residents in Santa Clara County, generally seen along slow-moving streams or lakes near the valley floor. A few birds remain in the county through the winter.

Judging from egg sets collected in the San Francisco Bay area at the end of the nineteenth and beginning of the twentieth centuries, Green Herons were regular, if scarce, breeders throughout the area (WFVZ, CAS, and MVZ egg collections). The first mention of this heron breeding in Santa Clara County was a set of five eggs collected by "I. M. Atkinson" at Lagunita at Stanford on 4 May 1908 (WFVZ #54420). (The data slip is difficult to read, and the name may refer to William M. Atkinson, who attended Stanford and was an active egg collector in the Santa Clara Valley at the end of the nineteenth century.) Grinnell and Wythe (1927) considered Green Herons to be "fairly common in summer locally" in the San Francisco Bay area, but noted breeding records only from Sonoma, Marin, and Alameda counties. From the 1930s to the 1950s, egg collectors in the Gilroy area, including H. R. Eschenburg, W. E. Unglish, and George Brem, Jr., regularly collected egg sets in the south county area (WFVZ egg collections, Sibley 1952), although they rarely specified a precise location for their nest records. Sibley (1952) considered Green Herons to be fairly common summer residents and mi-

grants in the South Bay area, and listed additional nearby breeding records from San Benito and Alameda counties. Analysis of the Palo Alto SBC data shows that these herons have increased in numbers by 6.7% per year since this count was instituted in 1981. This is consistent with increases noted by Davis and Kushlan (1994), who reported a range expansion on the Pacific Coast in recent decades. Analysis of Breeding Bird Survey data from 1966 to 2004 indicates an increase of 4.8% per year on the California BBS routes (Sauer et al. 2005).

During the atlas period, Green Herons were found breeding along low-gradient streams or ponds on the valley floor northwest to central San Jose. Breeding locations ranged in elevation from 120 feet in an urban area near Silver Creek to 720 feet on a small pond just off Uvas Road. The one exception to this valley floor distribution was a fledgling found in the Isabel Valley at an elevation of 2,530 feet. Although Green Herons do not normally nest above 2,000 feet in California (Grinnell and Miller 1944), a few of these herons are found every summer along small reservoirs and low-gradient streams in the San Antonio and Isabel valleys, which are above this elevation, and likely breed each year. Following the atlas period, additional nesting was confirmed farther northwest in the Santa Clara Valley, first at Palo Alto's Arastradero Preserve on 24 May 1995 (Rosalie Lefkowitz, county notebooks), later at Shoreline Lake on 19 Jun 2001 (pers. obs.), and then on the southern edge of Salt Pond A4, at sea level, on 4 Jul 2003 (Jean Myers, county notebooks). Nests found during the atlas period and afterward were generally placed in willows or other riparian trees near or over water, but in a few cases these herons nested in trees in urban areas, 70 to 500 m from the creeks and ponds where they foraged.

Green Herons are known to nest both in loose aggregations among others of their own kind and within nesting colonies of other ardeids (Davis and Kushlan 1994), but most observations of nesting in Santa Clara County were of solitary pairs. One instance of multiple nests was recorded here: two nests along Los Gatos Creek near the Oka percolation ponds on 4 May 1996 (Alan D. Walther, county notebooks). A single instance of Green Herons nesting in a mixed colony was reported: in at least three years they have nested on the island in Almaden Lake along with Great Egrets, Snowy Egrets, and Black-crowned Night-Herons (mult. obs., county notebooks).

The earliest breeding evidence observed during the atlas period was an occupied nest along Uvas Creek on 23 Apr. Subsequent to the atlas period, an occupied nest was found along Pacheco Creek near Casa de Fruta on 4 Apr 2002 (David L. Suddjian, county notebooks). The latest breeding evidence during the atlas period was a nest with young near Silver Creek on 1 Aug. Following the atlas period, an adult was seen feeding a juvenile on the island at Almaden Lake on 6 Aug 2000 (Michael J. Mammoser, PADB).

William G. Bousman

GREEN HERON

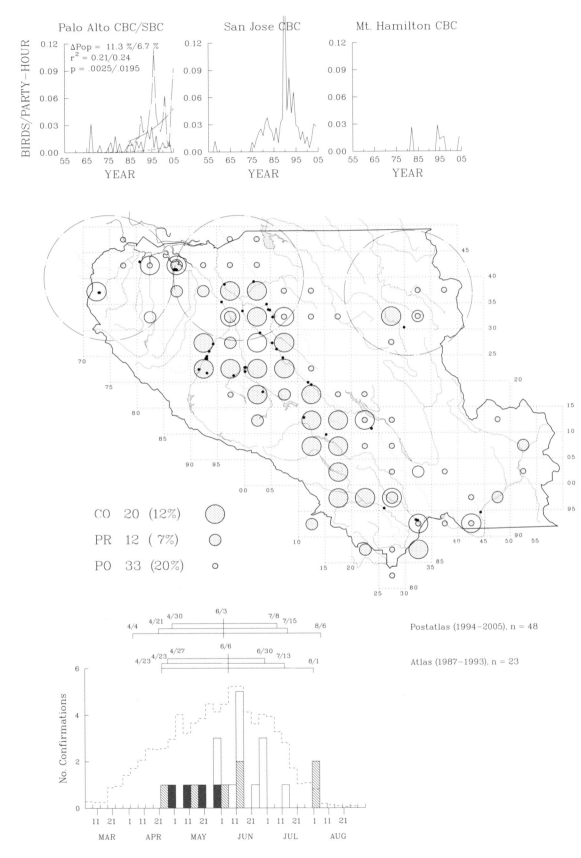

Palo Alto CBC/SBC

ΔPop = 11.3 %/6.7 %
r² = 0.21/0.24
p = .0025/.0195

San Jose CBC

Mt. Hamilton CBC

BIRDS/PARTY–HOUR

YEAR

CO 20 (12%)
PR 12 (7%)
PO 33 (20%)

Postatlas (1994–2005), n = 48

Atlas (1987–1993), n = 23

No. Confirmations

4/4   4/21 4/30   6/3   7/8 7/15   8/6

4/23 4/23 4/27   6/6   6/30 7/13   8/1

MAR   APR   MAY   JUN   JUL   AUG

Black-crowned Night-Heron
Nycticorax nycticorax

At dusk, a strange "quawk" is heard from a night-heron as it flies overhead, announcing the start of another night's foraging. The Black-crowned Night-Heron breeds on every continent except Australia and Antarctica. The subspecies *hoactli* nests from the northern United States and parts of Canada south to Chile and Argentina (Davis 1993). This heron breeds throughout California, excluding the higher mountains and parts of the southeastern deserts (Small 1994). It is a common resident in Santa Clara County, particularly along the edge of the South Bay.

Kobbé (1902), in assessing the status of the Black-crowned Night-Heron in the San Francisco Bay area, noted its presence at Alameda, in Alameda County, and reported breeding near Tiburon, in Marin County. Early egg collectors and other observers, however, found the species to be a more widespread breeder in the Bay area. Daniel A. Cohen (1900) found multiple birds nesting in Alameda in 1898. William L. Finley (1906) described a colony of over 350 nesting birds in the South Bay in 1904, apparently near Alvarado, Alameda County (Grinnell and Miller 1944). In Santa Clara County, William L. Atkinson collected three eggs from a nest 45 feet up in a pine tree near a house in the city of Santa Clara on 18 May 1899 (WFVZ #48922). Chase Littlejohn collected multiple egg sets from a coast live oak on a farm near Menlo Park, San Mateo County, on 28 Apr 1901 (WFVZ #95724 and subsequent). Grinnell and Wythe (1927) were aware of the colonies reported by Cohen and Finley, but mentioned no other records of nesting night-herons in the San Francisco Bay area. By midcentury, there were no active colonies in the South Bay (Sibley 1952), and nesting in the South Bay was not observed again until a heronry that included 200 to 300 Black-crowned Night-Heron nests was discovered at Bair Island, San Mateo County, in 1967 (*Audubon Field Notes 21*:536 1967). Black-crowned Night-Herons again nested in Santa Clara County on 18 Apr 1980, when 150 pairs were discovered in the Alviso heronry (*Am. Birds 34*:811 1980). Analysis of all CBC data from the San Francisco Bay area shows no change in the regional population, although there may be positive or negative trends in individual count circles (Bousman

2000).

During the atlas period, Black-crowned Night-Herons nested only in the Alviso heronry on Artesian Slough. Field observations from the San Francisco Bay Bird Observatory (Cheryl M. Strong, pers. comm.) provide information on the Alviso heronry from 1993 to its abandonment in 1999. In the final year of the atlas period, on 13 May 1993, 106 active nests of this species were counted in the heronry, the birds nesting on bulrushes a foot or two over the water.

Following the atlas period, night-herons continued to use the Alviso heronry, but in the late 1990s expanded to inland sites, as did other heron species (San Francisco Bay Bird Observatory; mult. obs., county notebooks). A summary of these colonies follows, including the year of first detection, the span of years in which nesting occurred (possibly including years when birds were absent or not censused), and the peak count of pairs or nests observed. Breeding Black-crowned Night-Herons were first found at an inland site in 1996, at Almaden Lake (1996–2005, ten nests in 1997). In 1998, two nests were found in giant reeds on an island in Vasona Reservoir (1998–99, two nests both years). In 2000, a colony of 20 nests was found in the Coyote Creek lagoons, an area of heavy marsh vegetation north of Newby Island in Alameda County (2000–2, 20 nests in 2000). In 2001, a single nest was found in the entrance creek at Vasona Reservoir (2001–2002, five nests in 2002). In 2002, 12 nests were found in bulrushes along Guadalupe Slough near the Moffett Channel (2002–2003, 12 pairs in 2002), and at least two nests were being built at San Felipe Lake, San Benito County. In 2003, three nests were found in a eucalyptus along Llagas Creek in Morgan Hill. The same year, night-herons built two nests in palms at the Palo Alto Duck Pond, an incipient colony that eventually expanded into the myoporum around the ranger station (2003–2005, 15 nests in 2004). In 2004, a colony of 13 nesting pairs was found in saltbush on an island in Lake Cunningham (2004–2005, 13 nests in 2004).

The earliest evidence of breeding by Black-crowned Night-Herons during the atlas period was birds carrying nesting material in the Alviso heronry on 2 May. Following the atlas period, night-herons were seen at a nest at Lake Cunningham as early as 6 Mar 2005 (Summer Brasuel, Toni Koenen; county notebooks). The latest breeding evidence observed during the atlas period was a fledgling at the Alviso heronry on 7 Aug. Following the atlas period, fledglings were seen at the Palo Alto Duck Pond still later, on 9 Sep 2005 (pers. obs.).

Black-crowned Night-Herons are primarily crepuscular and nocturnal feeders, although they also feed actively in the daytime during periods of high food demand or availability. Their hunting skills, even in daytime, are apparent. Phyllis M. Browning watched two night-herons in the Palo Alto Flood Control Basin take six downy Gadwall ducklings successively in a period of 30 minutes on 26 Jun 1988 (county notebooks). Each attack was successful. At the same time, a Western Gull attempted to prey on these ducklings, but was not successful.

William G. Bousman

BLACK-CROWNED NIGHT-HERON

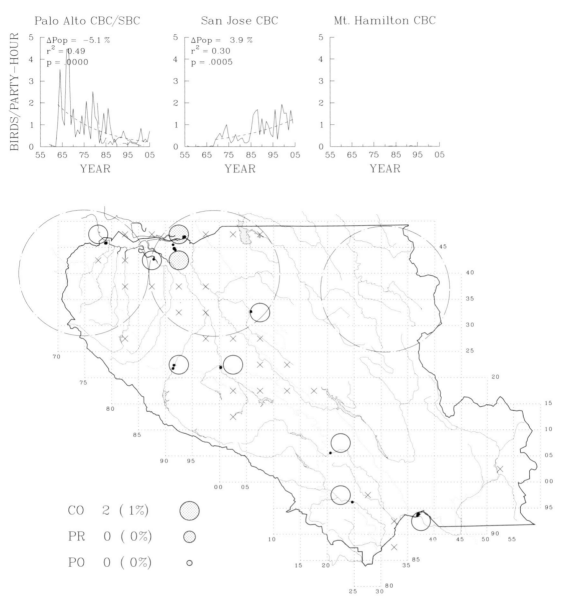

Palo Alto CBC/SBC

ΔPop = −5.1 %
r² = 0.49
p = .0000

San Jose CBC

ΔPop = 3.9 %
r² = 0.30
p = .0005

Mt. Hamilton CBC

BIRDS/PARTY-HOUR

YEAR

CO   2 (1%)
PR   0 (0%)
PO   0 (0%)

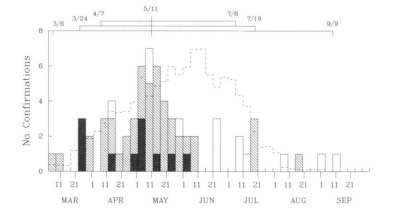

Combined (1987−2005), n = 66

No. Confirmations

MAR   APR   MAY   JUN   JUL   AUG   SEP

White-faced Ibis
Plegadis chihi

This nomadic ibis is well-suited to the dry American West, where "wetlands" can be flooded one year and dry the next. The White-faced Ibis breeds locally from northern California across the Great Basin and Great Plains to North Dakota, south in Mexico to Durango, and along the Gulf Coast of the United States in Louisiana and Texas (Ryder and Manry 1994, AOU 1998). It also nests in South America from Chile and Bolivia south to central Argentina. Nesting populations in California have increased in recent decades, and colonies are found in wetlands in the northeastern part of the state and locally in the Sacramento and San Joaquin valleys (Small 1994). Wintering birds are found as far north as central California. This ibis is a rare visitor to Santa Clara County, primarily in spring and fall, and at least twice has attempted to nest in Alviso.

Grinnell (1902), in his first checklist of the state's birds, considered the White-faced Ibis a common summer visitor in the Central Valley north to Sutter County, and recorded that it also nested in a number of areas on the coastal slope of southern California. The egg collectors at the outset of the twentieth century took egg sets from Central Valley colonies in Merced, Madera, and Kern counties (WFVZ, MVZ, CAS egg collections), but this ibis was rarely observed in the Bay area. Grinnell and Wythe (1927) listed only two occurrences, both in spring: a flock at the Farallon Islands in 1884 and a bird at Irvington, Alameda County, in 1923. Grinnell and Miller (1944) cited no breeding records from California after 1922, nor did they mention additional vagrant occurrences in the Bay area beyond those reported by Grinnell and Wythe. Nonetheless, egg sets were collected in Merced County through 1935, and in Kern County through 1941 (WFVZ egg collections). In his treatment of birds in the South Bay, Sibley (1952) included no records after the single 1923 record from Irvington. By the 1960s, doubt was expressed even about whether the White-faced Ibis continued to breed within California, and it was suggested that the nearest viable colonies were on the Great Salt Lake in Utah (*Audubon Field Notes* 22:473 1968). The first modern records for the San Francisco Bay area were September 1965 in San Rafael, Marin County; 15 Feb 1970 in Fremont, Alameda County; 23 Dec 1975 on Grizzly Island, Solano County; and 2 Jun 1977 at the Palo Alto Baylands, Santa Clara County (*N. Am. Birds* Northern California Region notebooks). Following the initial sighting in Santa Clara County in 1977, birds were seen in the county in four years during the 1980s and in 15 of the 16 years from 1990 to 2003, generally in spring or fall.

Atlasers observed six White-faced Ibis at the Alviso heronry on 16 May 1989, but no evidence of nesting was detected that season. No birds were recorded in the South Bay in 1990, but on 23 and 24 May 1991, two adults in breeding plumage were seen at the Alviso Marina, 2 km southwest of the heronry. Sometime during June 1991, adults were seen carrying nesting material in the heronry (Donald S. Starks, pers. comm.). In early May 1992, flocks of up to 45 birds were seen in the Alviso area, and during the summer one to four birds were spotted in various locations nearby (county notebooks). On 26 Jun 1992, during a survey of the Alviso heronry for the San Francisco Bay Bird Observatory, Peggy J. Woodin and colleagues saw adult birds bringing nesting material to three locations, and also observed nest-site greetings between pairs. The nests were in clumps of California bulrush within the heronry. Under atlas protocols, these observations confirm nesting in Santa Clara County. It is not known whether eggs were laid or young were fledged from these nests, since to avoid disturbance the heronry was not visited regularly during the nesting season.

The timing of nest building observed in the Alviso heronry on 26 Jun is consistent with other nesting records in California. Bent (1926) reported that eggs had been laid from 20 May to 15 Jul, the peak of laying falling between 28 May and 5 Jul. The period from the start of nest construction to the laying of the first egg can be as little as two to four days in this species (Ryder and Manry 1994), suggesting that eggs in the 1992 nests would probably have been laid at the end of June or early in July.

Because of pesticide contamination and loss of habitat, the numbers of nesting White-faced Ibis dropped precipitously in North America in the 1960s and 1970s (Ryder and Manry 1994). Since the 1980s, populations have recovered and expanded, in part because of improved nesting habitat management, increased planting of alfalfa fields (which they use for foraging), and the ban on DDT (Ryder and Manry 1994). In recent years, there has been a westward expansion of breeding White-faced Ibis, as evidenced by birds moving into southeastern Oregon (Ivey et al. 1988), and the many new colonies that were forming in the Central Valley from 1981 to 2001 (*N. Am. Birds* and predecessor publications). The westward expansion and increase in colony numbers may be a result of ibis departing from the large colonies at the Great Salt Lake, Utah, where they had been flooded out in the early 1980s (Ivey et al. 1988, Shuford et al. 1996). The limited nesting observed at Alviso in 1991 and 1992 may have been a part of this westward expansion.

William G. Bousman

WHITE-FACED IBIS

Palo Alto SBC

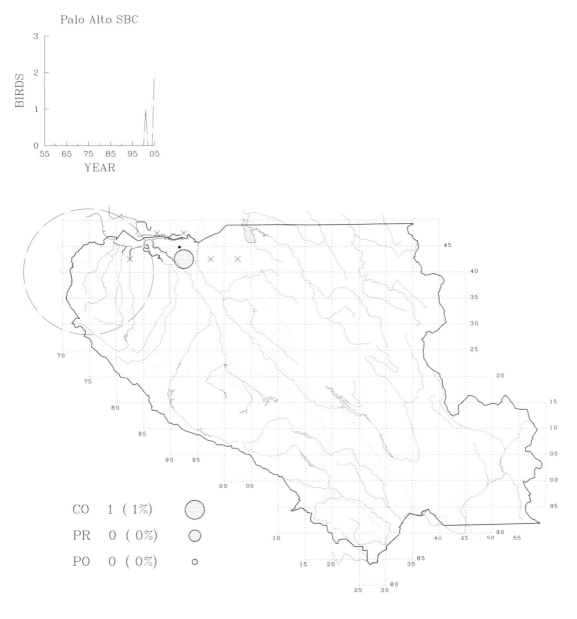

CO 1 (1%)

PR 0 (0%)

PO 0 (0%)

Atlas (1987–1993), n = 1

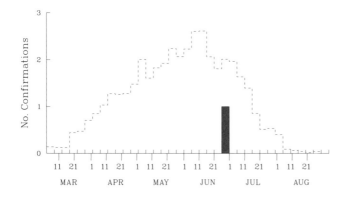

Turkey Vulture
Cathartes aura

As thermals build over the countryside, Turkey Vultures leave their roosts and begin their patient search for carrion, which they recycle as part of the endless chain of life and death. Turkey Vultures breed across North America from southern British Columbia to New England, and south through South America to the Straits of Magellan (Kirk and Mossman 1998, AOU 1998). As many as six subspecies are recognized over this vast range. In the West, *C. a. meridionalis* breeds from southern Canada to California and Texas, the more northern populations moving south in winter as far as Brazil and Paraguay (Kirk and Mossman 1998). Montane and northern birds in California leave their breeding grounds in winter, but lowland and southerly populations appear to be resident (Small 1994). Turkey Vultures are common, widespread, year-round residents in Santa Clara County.

Early observers variably reported Turkey Vultures as either residents or summer visitants in Santa Clara County. Price (1898a) and Van Denburgh (1899b) stated that they were found here year-round, whereas Fisher (1902) and Grinnell and Wythe (1927) considered them to be only summer visitants. Early in the twentieth century, observers in the South Bay recorded fall departure and spring arrival dates for this species, which indicates that they were absent in winter. In 1930, the last departure date was 27 Sep (*Wren-Tit 2(4)* 1930), whereas the earliest arrival date the next spring was 22 Feb (*Wren-Tit 3(2)* 1931). Grinnell and Miller (1944), in discussing the statewide distribution of Turkey Vultures, noted that a "large share" of the population moved southward out of the state in winter. Sibley (1952) also considered this species a common summer resident. Since the 1950s, in any case, the number of Turkey Vultures counted on the San Jose CBC has increased significantly, but the numbers of birds reported on the Palo Alto summer and winter counts are essentially the same, suggesting that this bird is now resident in the lowlands of Santa Clara County.

Turkey Vultures were found widely in Santa Clara County during the atlas fieldwork. The "possible" breeding code was not used for Turkey Vultures because they may cross multiple blocks during their wide-ranging foraging. Hence, all obser-

vations of flying birds were recorded as "observed" and were mapped with an "×." And indeed, nesting evidence for Turkey Vultures is difficult to obtain. Austin (1903) said, "It is seldom one finds a buzzard's nest, seldom that grown-ups find a nest of any sort; it is only children to whom these things happen by right." During the atlas period, nesting evidence was obtained in just five blocks (3%) and, subsequently, in three additional blocks (2%). Observers described four of the nest sites that were found. Three of these were in caves of various shapes and sizes in rock outcrops. The outcrops, in turn, were also of varied size and all occurred within open woodlands. The fourth site was in the hollow base of an oak in an oak woodland. Farther west, on the coastal slope of the Santa Cruz Mountains, vultures typically use hollowed-out redwood logs or stumps for nest sites (David L. Suddjian, pers. comm.), but the limited numbers of nest sites found in Santa Clara County were mostly in caves, as has generally been observed elsewhere in the western United States (Kirk and Mossman 1998). Two confirmations were of nestlings found in urban areas away from their nest sites and unable to fly. A young nestling found in Hellyer County Park one day after an unseasonable rainstorm had probably been washed out of a nearby hillside culvert that had been used as a nest site. The second record was of an older bird found in a concrete-lined portion of Permanente Creek. Perhaps this bird was raised somewhere nearby in a culvert in this urbanized area, but in any case no evidence of a nest site was obtained (Michael M. Rogers, pers. comm.). In our Mediterranean climate, culverts or other openings in portions of urban storm drains may provide suitable nest sites for Turkey Vultures, although they are clearly vulnerable to unseasonal rainstorms. Probable breeding evidence was observed in five blocks during the atlas period and in another six blocks after the atlas fieldwork was complete.

During the atlas period, copulation was observed as early as 11 Mar. The earliest evidence of breeding was the nestling found at Hellyer County Park on 29 May. Subsequent to the atlas period, a nest with eggs was found in a hollowed-out oak near the IBM Almaden facility on 21 Apr 1998 (Charles Tribolet *fide* Michael M. Rogers). Historically, there is an earlier record of nesting, based on a set of eggs collected 9 miles west of Gilroy on 2 Apr 1905 by W. E. Unglish (Sibley 1952). The latest breeding evidence during the atlas fieldwork was a nest with young in nearby Stanislaus County on 9 Jul. After the atlas fieldwork, fledgling birds were seen at the Almaden nest site as late as 7 Aug 1996 (Charles Tribolet *fide* Michael M. Rogers).

Cathartes, from the Greek, means purifier or cleanser. The gut of the Turkey Vulture is able to kill many of the pathogens that occur in carrion, unlike the guts of other scavenging mammals and insects (Kirk and Mossman 1998). Thus, this patient scavenger benefits our local ecosystems, both in the recycling of carrion and in the reduction of infectious bacteria and other pathogens.

William G. Bousman

TURKEY VULTURE

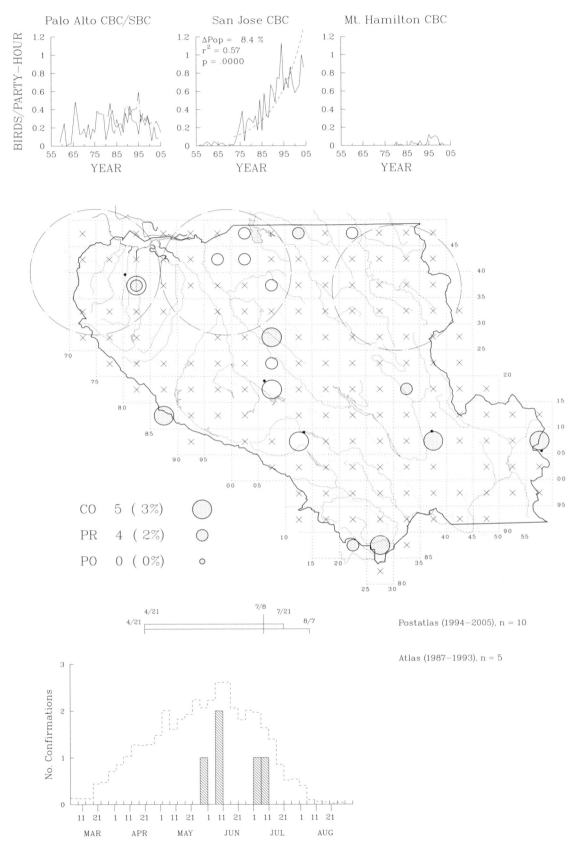

Palo Alto CBC/SBC

San Jose CBC

Mt. Hamilton CBC

BIRDS/PARTY−HOUR

ΔPop = 8.4 %
r^2 = 0.57
p = .0000

YEAR

CO 5 (3%)
PR 4 (2%)
PO 0 (0%)

Postatlas (1994−2005), n = 10

Atlas (1987−1993), n = 5

No. Confirmations

MAR APR MAY JUN JUL AUG

Osprey
Pandion haliaetus

These master fisheaters are expanding their range in central California, and since 2004 have been found nesting in Santa Clara County. The Osprey is a cosmopolitan species with migratory populations in the Nearctic and Palearctic, and resident populations in middle America and the coastal areas of Africa, Asia, and Australia (Poole et al. 2002). In North America, migratory populations are found throughout Alaska and Canada and south along the west coast into northern California and along the east coast into Florida. Farther south, as in Baja California and along the western coast of Mexico, Ospreys are generally nonmigratory. As of 1994, breeding Ospreys were found in northern California as far south in the Coast Ranges as Marin County, and there have been a few recent records of breeding in Inyo and Ventura counties (Small 1994). In the last two decades, Ospreys have been found in increasing numbers in Santa Clara County, and they are now uncommon as winter residents or transients from September to April or May. Over this same time period, summering birds, although rare, have been found with increasing frequency.

Historically, Ospreys in California were known to breed on nearly all the islands, on the mainland near the mouths of major streams, along the Sacramento and San Joaquin rivers in the Central Valley, and beside the lakes on the northeastern plateau (Grinnell and Miller 1944). In central California, Ospreys nested near Santa Cruz prior to 1884 (McGregor 1901), along the Russian River in Sonoma County in 1916 (Squires 1916b), and northeast of Watsonville in 1935 (Unglish 1937). There was a general decline in California's Osprey numbers during the first half of the twentieth century (Grinnell and Miller 1944). More recently, there has been an increase in nesting Ospreys in northern California, mostly associated with reservoirs. In the San Francisco Bay area, Ospreys were found breeding in increased numbers in Sonoma County in 1962 (*Audubon Field Notes 16*:503 1962). They were also found nesting for the first time in Marin County at Point Reyes in 1962, and by 1990 there

were at least 50 pairs throughout that county (Shuford 1993h). By 1986, Ospreys were nest building at Lake Hennessy, Napa County (William T. Grummer, pers. comm.), and by 1990, nesting pairs were found in Solano County (*Am. Birds 44*:1181 1990) and Contra Costa County (*Kite Call 25(1)* 1990). During this expansion period, Donald D. McLean reported that a "pair nested at Calaveras Dam, Santa Clara County 'for a number of years, but Golden Eagles drove them out and took over their nest'" (*Audubon Field Notes 23*:690 1969). The actual location of these records is unclear, since the Calaveras Reservoir dam is in Alameda County, a kilometer north of the Santa Clara County line.

The increasing number of Ospreys noted in Santa Clara County in recent decades is consistent with the upward trend of 6.7% per year that has been recorded on Breeding Bird Survey routes in California for the period 1966 to 2004 (Sauer et al. 2005). Although Ospreys are found year-round in Sonoma, Marin, and Napa counties, fewer birds are seen there in winter (Shuford 1993h, Rudesill 1995, Berner 2003a). It is likely that birds dispersing from these new nesting areas are responsible for the winter influx observed in Santa Clara County in recent years. More northerly birds, such as those nesting in the Columbia River basin, winter along the coast of Mexico (Martell et al. 2001) and are an unlikely source for our wintering birds. Ospreys have recently returned to breed in the Santa Cruz Mountains (David L. Suddjian, pers. comm., *N. Am. Birds 54*:420 2000). The first modern Santa Cruz County breeding record occurred along San Vicente Creek near Davenport in 1997. The San Vicente birds were seen foraging at Loch Lomond, where there was a nesting attempt in 2003, two nesting pairs in 2004, and one or two pairs in 2005.

Prior to breeding in 2004, Ospreys were occasionally seen foraging at reservoirs on the eastern side of the Santa Cruz Mountains and then flying west with their prey. The female of a pair of Ospreys was seen attempting to break off branches at Almaden Reservoir on 3 Apr 1997 (Michael M. Rogers, county notebooks), and a pair was seen carrying sticks over Lexington Reservoir on 27 Mar 2001 (Scott B. Terrill, county notebooks), both sightings suggestive of breeding in Santa Clara County. In 2004, field biologists working in the Los Gatos Creek watershed for Big Creek Lumber Company found an Osprey nest built in a dead-topped Douglas fir southwest of Hooker Gulch (Matt Dias, pers. comm.), establishing the first certain record of Ospreys breeding in Santa Clara County. In 2005, two additional nests were found. The first was built in a Douglas fir snag near Wright's Station Road, and the second was in a flat-topped redwood on the shore of Lake Elsman. The nesting success at these locations is unknown, but on 8 Jul 2004, two adults and two juveniles were seen on Black Road, about 6 km from the nest site near Hooker Gulch (Karen Fishback *fide* Kathryn Parker, county notebooks). If this population increase continues, breeding should be expected at reservoirs elsewhere in Santa Clara County.

William G. Bousman

OSPREY

Palo Alto SBC

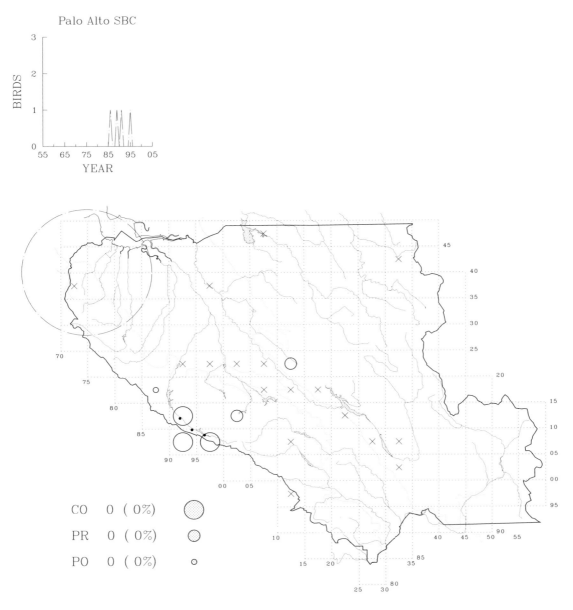

CO   0 (0%)

PR   0 (0%)

PO   0 (0%)

Postatlas (1994–2005), n = 1

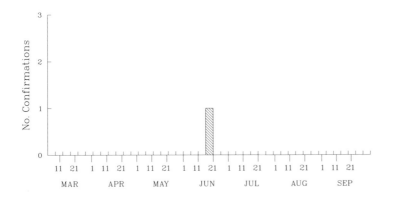

White-tailed Kite
Elanus leucurus

The White-tailed Kite is one of the most distinctive and beautiful of all the raptors we see in Santa Clara County. With a combined range that spans the Americas, populations of this bird are composed of two subspecies, *E. l. leucurus* in South America and *E. l. majusculus* in North and Central America (Dunk 1995). In North America, this raptor is found breeding from extreme southwest Washington, south along the coast of Oregon, through coastal and central California, and into Baja California, Mexico. Other populations breed along coastal and east-central Texas, in a small area of south Florida, and in scattered locations through the south-central United States (AOU 1998). In Santa Clara County, this raptor is a fairly common year-round resident, nesting along the South Bay and in foothill locations.

In Santa Clara County, the White-tailed Kite was considered a common resident around Palo Alto and San Jose before the start of the twentieth century (Van Denburgh 1899b, Grinnell and Wythe 1927). Kite populations suffered a statewide decline in the early decades of the twentieth century (Grinnell 1914a, Dawson 1923), though the Santa Clara Valley may have initially been spared (Pickwell 1930). Pickwell estimated 16 to 20 pairs in the whole of the Santa Clara Valley in 1928, and said that he could ". . . find no evidence of change in kite numbers" here. But within three years he was lamenting the imminent extirpation of these birds in the Valley (Pickwell 1932a). Pickwell's 1928 study of these birds in the Santa Clara Valley indicated that they were found in just four distinct regions. These were the foothills of the Santa Cruz Mountains near Palo Alto and Los Altos in the northwest corner of the valley, the area between San Jose and the Bay, the centrally located Silver Creek Hills, and Arroyo Calero and Llagas Valley in the southwest. By 1930, the kites had vanished from the three foothill regions and persisted only along the bayside. Pickwell wondered whether poisoning of California ground squirrels may have been the cause, but no direct evidence was cited.

By midcentury, White-tailed Kite numbers had begun to recover, the trend attributed by some to an increase in agricultural habitat and a reduction in human persecution, fueled by such advantageous traits as semicolonial breeding and large clutch sizes (Eisenmann 1971). But in fact, the Santa Clara County population may have recovered prior to this time, for an analysis of normalized CBC data from Palo Alto and San Jose shows no significant population change in the northern reaches of the county during the latter half of the twentieth century. Although some North American populations have shown declines during recent decades, the kite's current range on this continent is the most extensive in the known history of the species (Dunk 1995).

During the years of atlas and postatlas fieldwork, these kites were found in 45% of the county's atlas blocks. The species was found breeding across the northern edge of the county from the foothills of the Santa Cruz Mountains near Palo Alto, through the open areas edging the San Francisco Bay, and into the foothills of the Diablo Range east of Milpitas. From there it occurred at scattered locations southward along the western edge of the Diablo Range bordering the Santa Clara Valley. From the Santa Teresa Hills south to the Pajaro River, this raptor was found breeding throughout the foothills of the Santa Cruz Mountains and in a few locations on the valley floor. It was also scattered through the southern Diablo Range north of Pacheco Pass in the southeast section of the county. Kites were generally absent from the higher elevations in both the Santa Cruz Mountains and the Diablo Range. The highest elevation recorded for breeding during the atlas period was 1,760 feet near Pacheco Pass. Following the atlas period, kites were found nesting above 2,200 feet in the Monte Bello Open Space Preserve in both 1999 and 2001 (Les Chibana, pers. obs., PADB). Nesting substrates used by kites varied widely, but included live oak, valley oak, sycamore, willow, eucalyptus, black walnut, English walnut, Monterey pine, Australian pine, elderberry, and coyotebrush (pers. obs.; Stephen C. Rottenborn, pers. comm.). Whatever the substrate used, this species' tendency is to build its nest at the very top of the structure, with the nest cup open to the sky above and generally concealed from below (Pickwell 1930, pers. obs.). Birds were absent from the most heavily urbanized areas of the valley floor and from areas of extensive forest or chaparral.

The earliest evidence of breeding during the atlas period was nest building on 26 Feb. Following the atlas period, nest building was noted earlier, at the Ogier Avenue ponds on 29 Jan 1999 (Thomas P. Ryan, county notebooks). The earliest record for fledged young, near the Ogier Avenue ponds on 16 Apr 1994 (Stephen C. Rottenborn, pers. comm.), would suggest an egg-laying date in mid-February. A review of atlas data shows that it is typical for nesting to conclude by the end of July or beginning of August, and all but one atlas breeding confirmation fell on or before 1 Aug. Following the atlas period, however, a nearly grown young still in a nest along Coyote Creek near the Bay on 10 Oct 1999 (pers. obs.) indicates the extreme lateness of some nestings. The largest percentage of confirmations for this species was of fledged young (43%), which may simply reflect the ease of observing young birds in open habitat once they leave the nest.

Michael J. Mammoser

WHITE-TAILED KITE

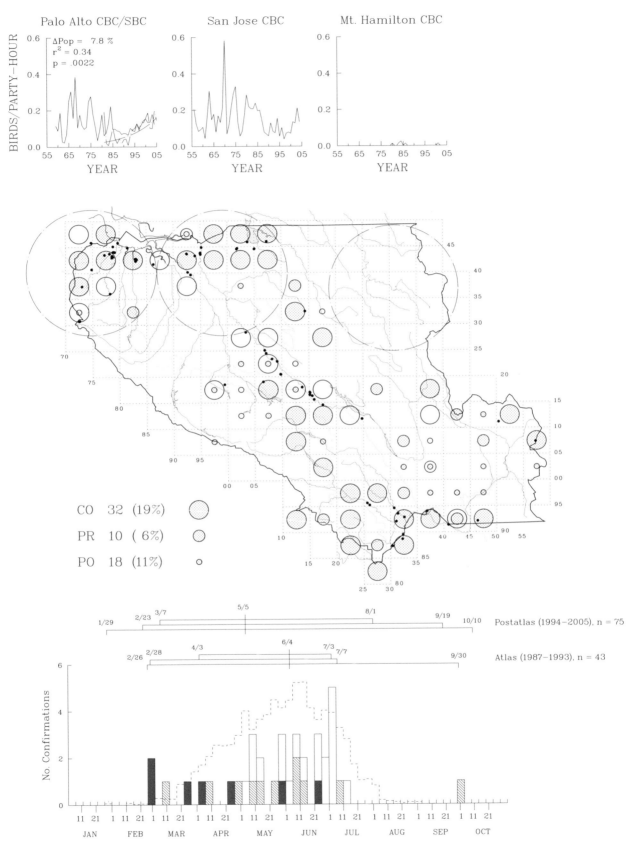

Palo Alto CBC/SBC

San Jose CBC

Mt. Hamilton CBC

BIRDS/PARTY-HOUR

ΔPop = 7.8 %
r² = 0.34
p = .0022

YEAR

CO   32 (19%)

PR   10 (6%)

PO   18 (11%)

Postatlas (1994–2005), n = 75

Atlas (1987–1993), n = 43

No. Confirmations

173

Northern Harrier
Circus cyaneus

A pattern of linked U's, one after the other, traces the courtship "sky-dance" of a male harrier as the nesting season approaches. The Northern Harrier is the most widely distributed member of the genus *Circus*, breeding throughout North America and Eurasia, and is the only member of this genus that nests in North America (MacWhirter and Bildstein 1996). In North America, the subspecies *C. c. hudsonius* breeds from Alaska across Canada to Newfoundland, and thence south along the Pacific Coast to northwestern Baja California and across the interior of the United States to eastern Virginia (MacWhirter and Bildstein 1996). In California, harriers are found nesting in the northern half of the state, but numbers in southern California are much reduced in recent years (Small 1994). Northern Harriers are fairly common in winter in Santa Clara County, generally in salt marshes, wetlands, and old fields along the valley floor, but fewer birds remain to nest, and this raptor is in fact uncommon in the summer.

The Northern Harrier is on Sclater's lists of specimens collected by Thomas Bridges in "the Valley of San José" sometime prior to 1857 (Sclater 1857). Fred A. Schneider mentions finding a harrier's nest in a marsh 7 miles east of San Jose in 1892 (Schneider 1893). This marsh was probably near where Lake Cunningham lies today. Price (1898b) considered this hawk an uncommon permanent resident near Stanford. Barlow (1900b) noted that Rollo H. Beck had found a Northern Harrier nest in the salt marsh at Alviso. Fisher (1902) stated that this harrier was a resident of the marshes around San Francisco Bay. Grinnell and Wythe (1927), in their discussion of birds in the San Francisco Bay area, described the Northern Harrier as a common winter visitant as well as a summer resident locally, mentioning Beck's nest record from Alviso. Sibley (1952) also considered it a common winter visitant, noting that it rarely nested in the South Bay. Analysis of data from the Palo Alto and San Jose Christmas Bird Counts shows a significant increase in the number of wintering birds, from 2.4% per year for Palo Alto to 1.5% per year for San Jose. (Note that the data for San Jose are used only from 1972 onward, following the shift of that count circle to include more of the Alviso marshes.)

For the most part, Northern Harriers were found breeding in just two areas during the atlas period. Most confirmations were obtained along the edge of the South Bay, but additional breeding was found in the Pajaro River drainage, far to the south. Along the edge of the Bay, birds used a variety of habitats for nesting, including salt marsh dominated by pickleweed, brackish marshes with extensive growths of bulrush, and abandoned fields with dense ruderal growth. Nests, when found, were in open areas that allowed the adults unobstructed views. In the southern end of the county, birds nested in fallow fields that include extensive marshy areas along Llagas Creek, open lands north of the Lomerias Muertas, and the Pajaro River floodplain below Chittenden Pass. The only confirmation away from the valley floor consisted of fledged young found at Calaveras Reservoir during the drought years, when the reservoir's southern edge was a kilometer or two north of its normal location, affording broad expanses of weedy habitat apparently suitable for nesting. During the atlas period, harriers were seen in a number of blocks south of the Coyote Narrows, and it may be that in some years they have nested in areas near the Ogier Avenue ponds, or in seasonal wetlands off Bailey Road and Santa Teresa Boulevard (the historical Laguna Seca).

Statewide, Grinnell and Miller (1944) indicated that wintering birds are present from September to April. In Monterey County, Roberson (1993a) noted wintering birds arriving in late August and staying until April. Locally, it is unclear when wintering birds arrive and depart, but our breeding birds appear to be resident. The male harrier's sky-dance has been seen in the county as early as 22 Feb, as was the case in 1981 (pers. obs.), but this spectacular flight is sometimes performed on migration (MacWhirter and Bildstein 1996). The earliest breeding evidence during the atlas period was nest building observed on 27 Mar, and the early stages of nesting were observed throughout April, at a time when migrants may still be passing through. Following the atlas period, earlier evidence of nest building was observed at the Palo Alto Baylands on 6 Mar 2005 (Josh R. Bennett, PADB). The latest nesting evidence was adults feeding young on 23 Aug near Llagas Creek southeast of Gilroy during the atlas period.

Northern Harriers are closely associated with wetlands in Santa Clara County, but these raptors will breed in dry upland situations in the west (MacWhirter and Bildstein 1996). A few birds were also observed at higher elevations in the extensive annual grasslands in the Diablo Range, but no confirmed breeding evidence was obtained in such areas. Future restoration plans for the South Bay bode well for this wetlands hawk at the northern end of the Santa Clara Valley, but it is vulnerable to intense development pressures in the Pajaro River drainage at the valley's southern end. Although the Northern Harrier is just one of the species that use these wetlands habitats, its presence high on the food chain makes it a good indicator of their health.

William G. Bousman

NORTHERN HARRIER

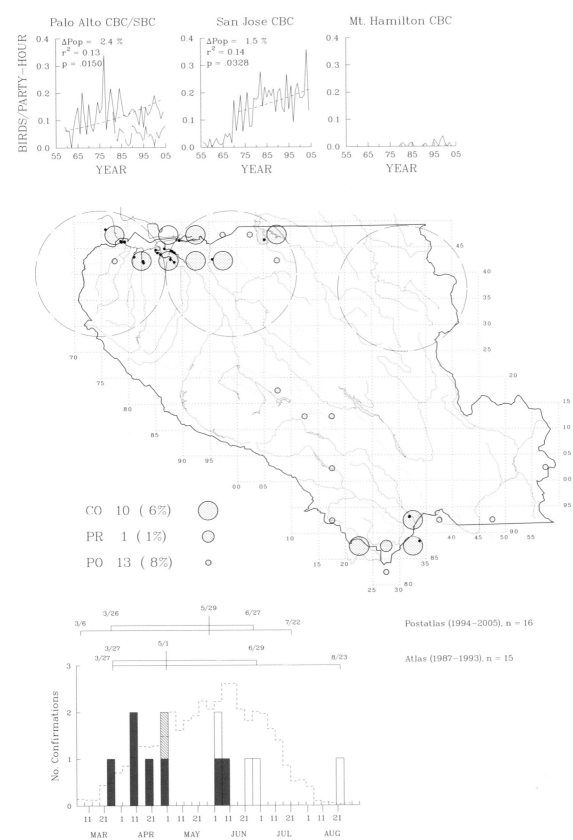

Palo Alto CBC/SBC

$\Delta Pop = 2.4\%$
$r^2 = 0.13$
$p = .0150$

San Jose CBC

$\Delta Pop = 1.5\%$
$r^2 = 0.14$
$p = .0328$

Mt. Hamilton CBC

BIRDS/PARTY–HOUR

YEAR

CO   10 (6%)
PR   1 (1%)
PO   13 (8%)

Postatlas (1994–2005), n = 16

Atlas (1987–1993), n = 15

No. Confirmations

MAR   APR   MAY   JUN   JUL   AUG

Sharp-shinned Hawk
Accipiter striatus

Seldom seen in Santa Clara County in summer, this secretive accipiter conceals its nest well away from human habitation. The Sharp-shinned Hawk breeds from central Alaska east to Newfoundland and south throughout much of the United States and into Central and South America (Bildstein and Meyer 2000). It is absent, however, from large areas of the continental United States, including the humid Pacific Northwest, the interior western plateaus, the Great Plains, and the Southeast. Ten subspecies, most of them resident from Mexico to northern Argentina, have been described. The subspecies *A. s. velox* is found throughout most of North America north of Mexico (Bildstein and Meyer 2000). In California, the Sharp-shinned Hawk is a widespread but scarce breeding species, and the majority of nesting birds are found in the northern half of the state (Grinnell and Miller 1944, Small 1994). Sharp-shins are rare breeders in Santa Clara County, nesting in both the Diablo Range and the Santa Cruz Mountains. Northern birds substantially augment the local population in winter, when the species is widespread and fairly common in the county.

The status of the Sharp-shinned Hawk appears to have changed little in Santa Clara County over the last century and a half. A specimen was obtained by Thomas Bridges in the "Valley of San José" sometime before 1857 (Sclater 1857). Early observers (Price 1898b, Van Denburgh 1899b, Fisher 1902) considered it a common wintering species, but apparently were unaware of local breeding. But on 11 May 1893, Rollo H. Beck collected three eggs near Berryessa (WFVZ #107440), and on 22 Apr 1899, Harold H. Heath collected a set of eggs near Stanford University (MVZ #2699). Later egg sets were taken at Menlo Park, in San Mateo County, on 3 May 1903 (Chase Littlejohn, WFVZ #35187) and at Los Gatos on 1 Mar 1905 (Homer A. Snow, WFVZ #97738). Grinnell and Wythe (1927) judged this hawk to be a common winter visitant in the San Francisco Bay area, but noted only occasional breeding. Sibley, too (1952), considered the sharp-shin to be a common winter visitant that

occasionally nested in the South Bay. Sibley recorded Heath's 1899 breeding record and also eggs collected by W. E. Unglish near Bell Station, east of Gilroy, on 25 Apr 1935. During the 1930s and 1940s, three additional egg sets were taken in the county by Gilroy collectors Steve Brem and George Brem, Jr., but the exact location was not given on the data slips for these eggs (WFVZ egg collections).

Atlasers found breeding evidence for Sharp-shinned Hawks in several areas in the Diablo Range, and at a few locations in the Santa Cruz Mountains, but this small accipiter was largely absent from the valley floor. During the atlas period, breeding confirmations ranged from an elevation of 1,040 feet south of Calaveras Reservoir to 2,960 feet on the slopes of Bollinger Ridge. Following the atlas period, a nest was found above Stevens Creek Reservoir at an elevation of 640 feet (Stephen C. Rottenborn, pers. comm.). In the Diablo Range, sharpies were found in dense, broadleaved evergreen forests of coast live oak and California bay on north-facing slopes with nearly complete canopy closure. One nest in this habitat was 20 to 25 feet above the ground in a California bay. Sharp-shinned Hawks also nested where open oak woodlands included foothill pine. Here the canopy was partly open, and the understory was a mixture of grasses and low shrubs. In the Santa Cruz Mountains, a family group was seen west of Loma Prieta in Douglas firs during the atlas period, although the nest site was not found. The postatlas nest found near Stevens Creek Reservoir was in a dense stand of California bay within a broadleaved evergreen forest of coast live oak and California bay.

Atlasers observed no evidence related to nest building or incubation. The six historical egg dates for Sharp-shinned Hawks from Santa Clara County range from 22 Apr to 13 May (WFVZ, MVZ egg collections, Sibley 1952), which excludes the exceptionally early egg set found by Snow in Los Gatos noted above. During the atlas period, the earliest breeding evidence was of an adult carrying food on 9 Jun; the latest was of fledged young at a nest site on 18 Jul. Subsequent to the atlas period, an adult was seen carrying food on the earlier date of 23 May 1996, and fledged young were seen on the later date of 20 Jul 1997, both on the west side of Calaveras Reservoir (Stephen C. Rottenborn, pers. comm.).

The Sharp-shinned Hawk may be a more common breeding species in Santa Clara County than the few nesting records indicate. Unlike its larger relative, the Cooper's Hawk, which often builds its nests in the open framework of deciduous trees and draws attention to itself by its courtship vocalizations, the sharp-shin is very secretive at its nest. It is easily overlooked early in the season, and nests are not generally discovered until the young are near fledging and are detected by their begging cries. Moreover, unlike the Cooper's Hawk, which has recently settled in urban areas, the sharp-shin appears to avoid human settlement. Although sharpies were confirmed breeding in only ten blocks during and subsequent to the atlas period, probable and possible evidence was obtained in 38 additional blocks over this time span, and they may have bred in most or all of these blocks.

William G. Bousman

SHARP-SHINNED HAWK

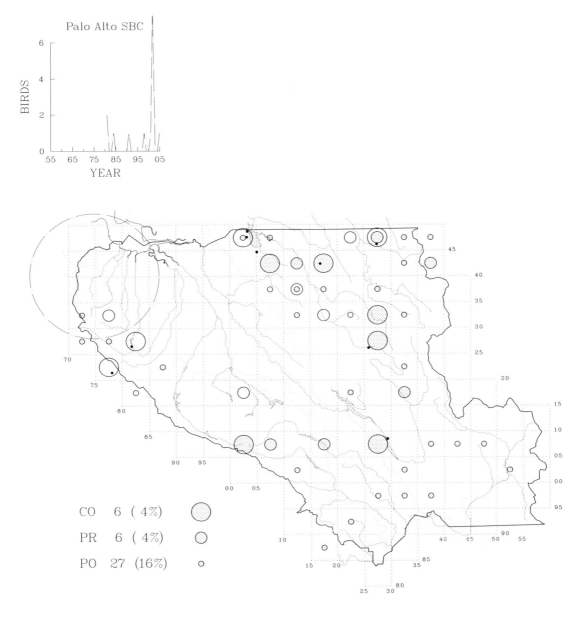

Palo Alto SBC

BIRDS

YEAR

CO 6 (4%)
PR 6 (4%)
PO 27 (16%)

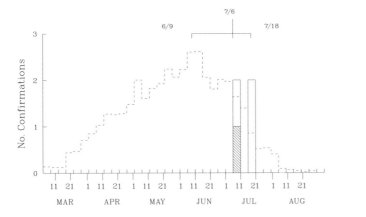

6/9   7/6   7/18

Atlas (1987–1993), n = 7

No. Confirmations

11 21 1 11 21 1 11 21 1 11 21 1 11 21 1 11 21
MAR   APR   MAY   JUN   JUL   AUG

Cooper's Hawk
Accipiter cooperii

This predator of mid-sized birds within California's woodlands and forests has recently adapted to Santa Clara County's urban areas. The Cooper's Hawk breeds across the southern edge of Canada south through the United States and into Mexico. Northern populations move south in winter as far as Guatemala and Honduras (Rosenfield and Bielefeldt 1993). Small (1994) considered this accipiter an uncommon resident in California and noted that it "occurs spottily in the interior valleys and woodlands of the Coast Range." But however spotty its occurrence may be elsewhere, in Santa Clara County this hawk is a fairly common permanent resident.

Although Grinnell (1902) considered the Cooper's Hawk to be a fairly common resident throughout California, early observers in the Santa Clara Valley judged it to be a winter visitor (Price 1898b) or an occasional transient (Fisher 1902). Van Denburgh (1899b) reported seeing only two birds in his years at Los Gatos. H. H. Heath collected a set of eggs 4 miles south of Gilroy on 27 May 1916 (MVZ #2701), but Grinnell and Wythe (1927), who considered Cooper's Hawks to be sparse and local residents in the Bay area, listed no summer records from the Bay area south of Marin County. In the 1930s, W. E. Unglish collected at least four egg sets in the vicinity of Gilroy (Sibley 1952), which suggests that this hawk was not uncommon in the Gilroy area at the time.

Atlasers found Cooper's Hawks breeding widely in the county, obtaining confirmations in 25 blocks (15%), and post-atlas confirmations were made in an additional 19 blocks. Although Grinnell and Miller (1944) emphasized this species' use of riparian areas on flood plains and canyon bottoms, atlasers found a much broader selection of nesting habitats. Within the coniferous-broadleaved evergreen forests, birds were found in relatively mature second-growth forests on steep slopes with extensive canopy cover and moderate undergrowth. Within oak woodlands, nest sites were on slopes with live and deciduous oaks and an understory of grasses and limited shrubs, much as described by Asay (1987) for the oak woodlands on the eastern

side of the Central Valley. Cooper's Hawks nesting in riparian areas frequently used live oaks, as described by Grinnell and Miller (1944), but also used other trees, including shining willow (Stephen C. Rottenborn, pers. comm.). Cooper's Hawks nesting in urban areas used a variety of trees, including coast live oaks, coast redwood, western sycamore, and a variety of non-native trees, including eucalyptus.

Atlasers and other observers reported details on 32 nest sites during and after the atlas period. At six of these sites at least one of the pair was an immature (one-year-old), which is within the range of 6-22% reported in other studies (Rosenfield and Bielefeldt 1993). Surprisingly, both members of a pair found in urban Palo Alto on 26 Apr 1992 were immatures, and the two successfully fledged two young (Phyllis M. Browning, pers. comm.). Five of the nests recorded at the 32 sites were re-used from the previous year, which is comparable to what Asay (1987) found in the Central Valley. One nest was used for three years and another for four.

The density of urban-nesting locations shown on the map is disproportionately high compared with the low density shown for the Santa Cruz Mountains or the Diablo Range. Prior to egg laying, courting Cooper's Hawks are quite vocal, and during the late nestling stage the begging young are often vocal as well. Hence, urban nests were well reported. Within the Santa Cruz Mountains and the Diablo Range, fewer birds were recorded, but this finding is likely a result of more limited coverage. In the oak woodlands on the eastern side of the Central Valley, Asay (1987) recorded Cooper's Hawks nesting within a kilometer of each other, and a similar density may be the norm within the extensive woodlands of the Diablo Range and the Santa Cruz Mountains.

Published atlas efforts on the central California coast indicate that the Cooper's Hawk is an uncommon resident of remote and secluded habitats (Shuford 1993i, Roberson 1993b, Burridge 1995a). The first Cooper's Hawk nest noted from urban areas in Santa Clara County was found on the Stanford University campus in 1987. In subsequent years, there has been an expansion of urban-nesting Cooper's Hawks, and such records are no longer considered unusual. Since the 1950s, numbers recorded on the San Jose CBC have increased by 2.1% a year and on the Palo Alto CBC have increased by 5.6% a year. The Palo Alto SBC data, although of shorter duration, show the same trend. This use of urban habitats, noted elsewhere within this species' range (Rosenfield and Bielefeldt 1993), appears to be a fairly recent phenomenon within the Bay Area. There are now numerous nesting records in urban areas of Alameda County as well (Robert J. Richmond, pers. comm.).

Cooper's Hawks disperse during the winter and return to previous nest sites in late February and early March. Nest building was observed as early as 10 Mar during the atlas period and 17 Feb 2002 after the atlas period (Laurent Droin, PADB). Nesting extends into August: a fledgling was brought to the Santa Clara Valley Humane Society on 4 Aug, during the atlas period; and a late fledgling was observed on 12 Aug 1999 (Michael M. Rogers, pers. comm.) following the atlas period.

William G. Bousman

COOPER'S HAWK

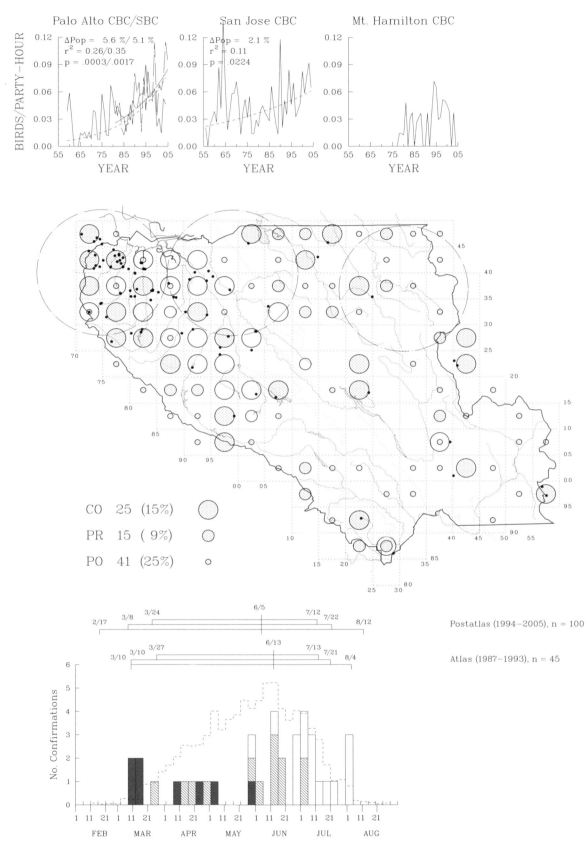

Palo Alto CBC/SBC

ΔPop = 5.6 % / 5.1 %
r² = 0.26/0.35
p = .0003/.0017

San Jose CBC

ΔPop = 2.1 %
r² = 0.11
p = .0224

Mt. Hamilton CBC

BIRDS/PARTY-HOUR

YEAR

CO 25 (15%)
PR 15 (9%)
PO 41 (25%)

Postatlas (1994–2005), n = 100

Atlas (1987–1993), n = 45

No. Confirmations

FEB MAR APR MAY JUN JUL AUG

179

Red-shouldered Hawk
Buteo lineatus

Formerly considered a rare denizen of Santa Clara County's riparian woodlands, the handsome Red-shouldered Hawk is now a fairly common breeder in riparian habitats and in some upland areas as well. This hawk breeds from California east to southern Ontario and south to the northern border of Mexico. The westernmost of the five subspecies, *B. l. elegans*, breeds in lowlands from Baja California north through western and central California to southwestern Oregon (Crocoll 1994). In Santa Clara County, breeding Red-shouldered Hawks are permanent residents, nesting extensively in riparian woodlands from the western foothills of the Diablo Range west to the Santa Cruz Mountains. They also nest in some upland areas (away from streams), where they build their nests primarily in planted eucalyptus and fan palms.

The Red-shouldered Hawk was fairly rare in Santa Clara County at the turn of the twentieth century. The earliest breeding record for the county was a nest with eggs at Sargent in April 1896 (Grinnell and Wythe 1927). Birds were noted in the vicinities of Palo Alto, Santa Clara, and Milpitas around 1900 (Barlow 1900b), and egg sets were collected by A. J. Zschokke near Menlo Park on 2 Apr 1898 (WFVZ #80563) and by N. K. Carpenter at Stanford University on 22 Mar 1908. This hawk apparently remained common in the Gilroy area, where in the early 1930s W. E. Unglish found four sets of eggs (Sibley 1952). But by 1940 this species had declined throughout California as a result of riparian habitat destruction and urbanization (Grinnell and Miller 1944, Henny et al. 1973), and there were few reports of Red-shouldered Hawks in the county from the early 1930s to the late 1950s. Wilbur (1973) considered Red-shouldered Hawks to be sparsely distributed in the South Bay area in 1973, but analyses of Christmas Bird Count data from 1969 to the present indicate annual increases of roughly 13% a year on the Palo Alto CBC and 17% a year on the San Jose CBC, and today this species is fairly common in much of the county.

During the atlas period Red-shouldered Hawks were found to be widespread in lowlands from the northern Santa Clara Valley to the southern edge of the county. This species was also found along streams in the foothills of the Santa Cruz Mountains and at the western edge of the Diablo Range. Although nests were found at elevations of up to 1,600 feet, more than 80% of all atlas confirmations were from elevations below 450 feet, indicating a preference for lowland areas. During the atlas period, Red-shouldered Hawks were recorded in 42% of all blocks and confirmed in 22%, but were conspicuously absent from higher elevations in the Santa Cruz Mountains and from all but the extreme western edge of the Diablo Range.

Postatlas fieldwork found Red-shouldered Hawks in 19 additional atlas blocks and confirmed breeding in 23 additional blocks. Most of these new records were obtained in urban and suburban areas in the vicinity of the northern Santa Clara Valley. In these areas, Red-shouldered Hawks nested where tall, sturdy, nonconiferous trees were present in proximity to open foraging areas such as fields, marshlands, and, in urban areas, lawns and parkland. Some expansion was noted in the Diablo Range: a territorial pair was observed in San Antonio Valley on 17 May 1997 (pers. obs.); and a fledgling and used nest were in Henry Coe State Park on 4 Jul 2002 (Michael M. Rogers, county notebooks).

During a 1994–95 study of Red-shouldered Hawks in northern Santa Clara County (Rottenborn 2000), these hawks were found nesting in exotic eucalyptus and fan palms more frequently than in native trees, in both 1994 (52% in exotics) and 1995 (66% in exotics). In both years, moreover, fledging success was higher for nests in exotic trees than for those in native riparian trees, which consisted primarily of Fremont cottonwoods and western sycamores. Although the reasons are not entirely clear, it may be that the exotic trees were sturdier and provided greater support for nests, and in fact several nests were dislodged from native trees by wind. Most nests were in floodplains, although a surprising number were found in upland areas, up to 1.6 km from the nearest stream. These results indicate that the Red-shouldered Hawk, previously described as being sensitive to human disturbance (Armstrong and Euler 1982, Bosakowski et al. 1992) and nesting only in riparian habitats (Wheelock 1904, Grinnell and Miller 1944), has adapted well to urbanization. Overall, 78% of 1994 nests and 79% of 1995 nests were successful, fledging an average of 2.3 young per successful nest in 1994 and 2.0 young per successful nest in 1995. Six pairs in 1994 and nine pairs in 1995 included a subadult (one-year-old) bird; these pairs had lower nesting success than pairs consisting of two adults.

Red-shouldered Hawks on established territories began nest-building as early as 5 Jan. According to atlas data, most occupied nests were found from mid-April to mid-June. But nests with young were found by atlasers from 4 Apr to 5 Jul, while fledged young still dependent on adults were observed from 9 May to 6 Aug. The dates of fledging from 46 successful nests intensively monitored in 1995, following the atlas period, accorded for the most part with the general pattern of phenology indicated by the atlas data: the nests in the 1995 study began fledging young in early May; and fledging peaked in late May and early June and decreased gradually into July.

Stephen C. Rottenborn

RED-SHOULDERED HAWK

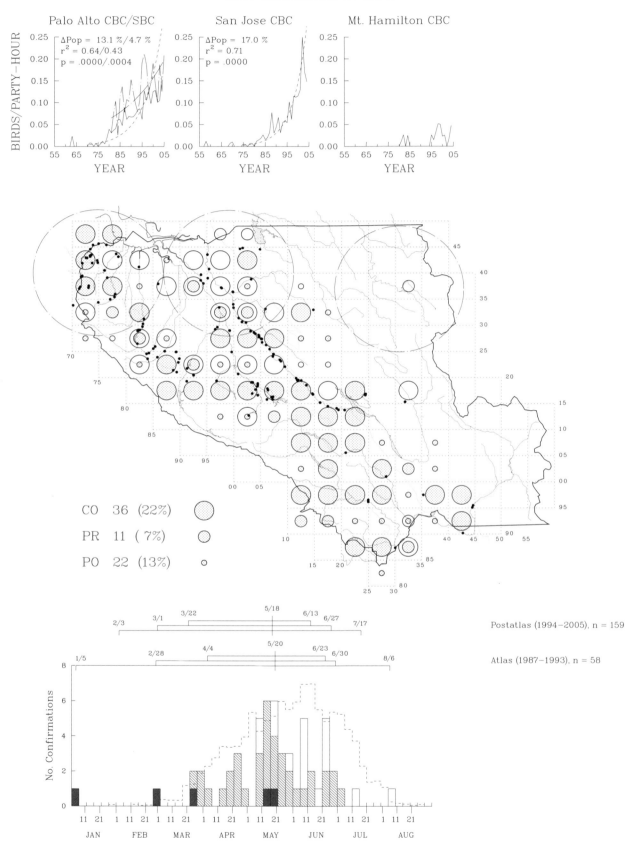

Palo Alto CBC/SBC
ΔPop = 13.1 % / 4.7 %
r^2 = 0.64/0.43
p = .0000/.0004

San Jose CBC
ΔPop = 17.0 %
r^2 = 0.71
p = .0000

Mt. Hamilton CBC

BIRDS/PARTY-HOUR

YEAR

CO   36 (22%)
PR   11 (7%)
PO   22 (13%)

Postatlas (1994-2005), n = 159

Atlas (1987-1993), n = 58

No. Confirmations

JAN   FEB   MAR   APR   MAY   JUN   JUL   AUG

Red-tailed Hawk
Buteo jamaicensis

Requiring little more than a sturdy nest site with open foraging areas nearby, the Red-tailed Hawk is well adapted for life in the mixed landscapes of Santa Clara County. This species breeds more widely in North America than any other diurnal raptor, nesting from Alaska east across most of Canada to the Maritime Provinces and south throughout the continental United States and Mexico to Central America (Preston and Beane 1993). It breeds in a variety of habitats throughout California, including forest edges, open woodlands, savanna, deserts, and agricultural areas, from sea level to montane regions above 12,000 feet (Grinnell and Miller 1944, Small 1994). In Santa Clara County, the Red-tailed Hawk is a widespread permanent resident, most common in open country with scattered trees. Of the 14 subspecies of Red-tailed Hawk currently recognized by the American Ornithologists' Union (1957), the one breeding in Santa Clara County is *B. j. calurus*, which is widespread over much of the western United States and Canada. Other races, including the Harlan's (*B. j. harlani*) and Krider's (*B. j. kriderii*) Red-tailed Hawks, have been recorded in the county as very rare winter visitors.

By all accounts, the Red-tailed Hawk has long been a common breeder in Santa Clara County. Around the turn of the century, Price (1898b) and Fisher (1902) considered it to be common around Stanford and in the Santa Clara Valley, respectively, and Van Denburgh (1899b) proclaimed it "a very common resident in all parts of the county." Grinnell and Wythe (1927) and Sibley (1952) echoed this assessment for the San Francisco Bay area as a whole. This species' abundance and widespread distribution in the area were no doubt encouraged by the vast extent of suitable habitat here, which was described by Grinnell and Miller (1944) as "interspersed woodland and open grassland." Prior to European settlement, such habitat was likely present in oak savanna, riparian habitats, and burned-over forests in much of the county (Clarke 1959), and the fragmentation of formerly continuous forests in the Santa Cruz Mountains by lumber and agricultural interests created additional suitable habitat. Popula-

tions have increased in recent decades throughout most of the species' range, including most of California (Preston and Beane 1993, Sauer et al. 2005), and Christmas and Summer Bird Count data suggest that populations have been increasing in Santa Clara County as well.

As expected, atlasers found the Red-tailed Hawk to be a common breeder throughout most of the county. During the atlas period, this species was recorded in 96% of all atlas blocks and was confirmed breeding in 53% of all blocks. These hawks were probably most abundant in the sparsely wooded foothills along the edges of the Santa Clara Valley, where scattered trees offered nest sites amid extensive open foraging areas. Forest-grassland mosaics in the Santa Cruz Mountains and Diablo Range, agricultural lands with scattered nest trees, and riparian woodlands also supported large numbers of Red-tailed Hawks, and scattered pairs bred in suburban areas offering suitable nest trees and some open foraging habitat with adequate prey. Red-tails were far less common in, or tended to avoid, heavily urbanized areas, dense and continuous closed-canopy forests, and extensive chaparral fields.

Red-tailed Hawks require tall, sturdy nest sites, such as cliffs, power transmission towers, and tall trees with large-diameter branches (Preston and Beane 1993). Of 54 Santa Clara County nests recorded by five active atlasers since the initiation of the atlas project, 11 were on power transmission towers or other artificial structures (including a wind tunnel and a hangar at Moffett Field), 23 were in eucalyptus trees, and the remaining 20 were in eight other tree species. Like the Red-shouldered Hawk, this species nests frequently in eucalyptus in Santa Clara County, probably because of the great height of these trees and the sturdy nesting platforms that their thick branches provide. Most nests in suburban areas were in eucalyptus, and this tree was also used widely in more rural areas, where foothill pines, oaks, and western sycamores also supported a number of nests. At lower elevations, Red-tailed and Red-shouldered Hawks were frequently found in close proximity by atlasers, and the breeding and foraging habitats of these species overlapped to some extent. For example, on two territories, Red-tailed Hawks were recorded using the same nest sites previously used by Red-shouldered Hawks, whereas the opposite was recorded on two other territories (pers. obs.). But the more adaptable Red-tailed Hawk was found breeding over a much broader range of elevations and habitats than was the Red-shouldered Hawk, which was more restricted to lower elevations and more frequently nested near water.

Santa Clara County's breeding Red-tailed Hawks are probably on territory year-round. Their resident status allows some pairs to breed fairly early, as evidenced by a postatlas record of birds carrying nest material on 20 Nov 2003 (Michael M. Rogers, pers. comm.). During the atlas period, nests with young were noted as early as 24 Mar and as late as 1 Jul, with a broad peak in occupied nests between late March and late June. Recently fledged young were observed from 7 May to 2 Aug, with an obvious peak between late June and late July. These phenology data are similar to those reported by Roberson (1993c) in Monterey County.

Stephen C. Rottenborn

RED-TAILED HAWK

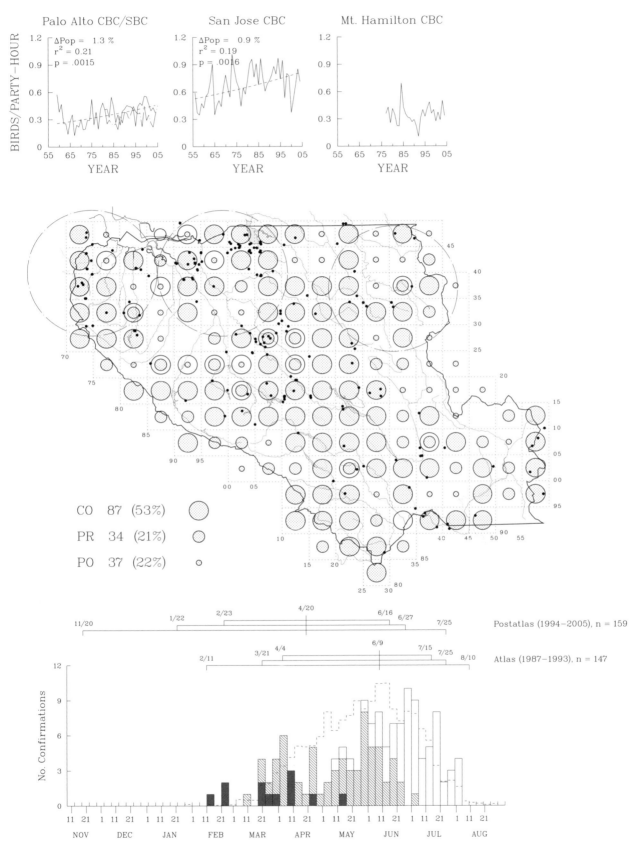

Palo Alto CBC/SBC

San Jose CBC

Mt. Hamilton CBC

BIRDS/PARTY−HOUR

ΔPop = 1.3 %
r² = 0.21
p = .0015

ΔPop = 0.9 %
r² = 0.19
p = .0016

YEAR

CO 87 (53%)
PR 34 (21%)
PO 37 (22%)

11/20   1/22   2/23   4/20   6/16 6/27   7/25   Postatlas (1994−2005), n = 159

2/11   3/21 4/4   6/9   7/15 7/25   8/10   Atlas (1987−1993), n = 147

No. Confirmations

NOV DEC JAN FEB MAR APR MAY JUN JUL AUG

Golden Eagle
Aquila chrysaetos

This great eagle, found in mountains and foothills across the Northern Hemisphere, continues to hunt over the county's sunburnt hills, as it did prior to European settlement. The Golden Eagle's distribution includes North America, northern Eurasia, north Africa, and southwest Asia through the Himalayas to Japan. Five to eight subspecies are recognized worldwide, but only one, *canadensis*, is found in North America (Palmer 1988). This subspecies breeds from Alaska southeast through Canada to Labrador, thence in the western mountains south through the highlands of Mexico to Nuevo León, and in the eastern United States in scattered locations as far south as Tennessee (AOU 1998). In California it is found widely throughout the state, but it is rare on the immediate coast, in deserts, and on agricultural plains (Small 1994). The Golden Eagle is an uncommon but readily visible resident in the mountains and foothills of Santa Clara County.

Golden Eagles may have been more widely distributed in Santa Clara County a century ago, but were perhaps no more numerous than they are today. The earliest record of nesting here is based on a set of three eggs collected by W. A. Burres near Sargent on 5 May 1888 (WFVZ #98674). George Chamberlin, in an early meeting of the Cooper Ornithological Club, discussed the nesting habits of Golden Eagles and noted that he had found a nest in a tree in a wheat field within 10 miles of San Jose in March 1892 (Barlow 1893d). Price (1898b) described these eagles as common around Stanford in the winter. Van Denburgh (1899b) stated that "this eagle breeds abundantly" in the Diablo Range, but added that he had seen it only once in winter at Los Gatos. Fisher (1902) considered the Golden Eagle to be a common resident of the valleys and foothills. From a regional perspective, however, Grinnell and Wythe (1927) categorized it as breeding locally in limited numbers in the inner coast ranges. Sibley (1952) believed it was a fairly common resident, particularly in the Diablo Range. Analysis of the CBC data for the county count circles shows no apparent change in the number of birds since the 1950s.

Golden Eagles were found breeding widely in the Diablo Range during the atlas period. Fewer birds were found in the Santa Cruz Mountains. Breeding birds were confirmed in 17 blocks (10%), but if probable and possible records were to be included, there would be breeding evidence in 107 blocks (65%). Breeding elevations ranged from about 520 feet near Calero Reservoir to 3,500 feet near Loma Prieta. Subsequent to the atlas period, a nest was found just west of Morgan Hill in a dead eucalyptus at an elevation of 380 feet (Deke Descoteaux, PADB). Nests were found in such trees as foothill pine, western sycamore, live oak, eucalyptus, and knobcone pine. Three cliff nests were found in the northern Diablo Range, and one pair nested on transmission towers northwest of Calero Reservoir. Carnie (1954), who studied 17 pairs in the interior coastal range from Mt. Diablo to the Pinnacles from 1947 to 1952, noted that 14 of these pairs nested in trees and three used cliff nests.

Golden Eagles may have multiple nests within their territories and use them alternately or irregularly (Palmer 1988). Courtship and nest building or nest maintenance occur early in the season and were probably missed by most atlasers, who did not start their fieldwork until March. Dated egg sets from Santa Clara County from the Western Foundation of Vertebrate Zoology (67 sets) and the Museum of Vertebrate Zoology (11 sets) have a median date of 20 Mar and an early date of 20 Feb. During the atlas period, the earliest nesting evidence was of a bird on a nest on 18 Mar, and the latest confirmation was of a dependent fledgling observed on 4 Aug. Subsequently, birds have been observed repairing or rebuilding nests as early as 28 Dec 2003 (Ann Verdi, PADB).

James B. Dixon studied breeding Golden Eagles in San Diego County from 1900 to 1936 (Dixon 1937), and much of what he learned applies as well to the birds in Santa Clara County. In the dry coastal hills and valleys facing the Pacific Ocean north of San Diego, Dixon found 27 pairs and mapped their territories. Over the period of the study, he noted a remarkable permanence in the territorial boundaries. At all times, there was a population of nonbreeders, such that if one of a pair died, it was almost immediately replaced. The smallest territories were about 50 km² (two atlas blocks), the largest about 150 km² (six blocks), and the average 93 km² (less than four blocks). The smaller territories were in more mountainous areas, whereas the larger included valleys and limited areas of agriculture. Interestingly, nests were often placed quite close to territory edges where adjacent pairs could keep track of each other. Carnie (1954), who mapped territories in the Diablo Range, also noted this characteristic, and recorded four pairs whose nests were enclosed within a quadrilateral with a longest edge of a little over 3 km, allowing the four nests to fit within one atlas block! It is likely that prior to settlement, Golden Eagle territories included substantial portions of the valley floor, but except for occasional wintering birds these areas are not used by eagles today. On the basis of Dixon's study and an examination of the atlas map herewith, one can estimate that roughly 20 pairs are resident in the Diablo Range portion of the county, whereas only about five pairs reside on the western side of the county.

William G. Bousman

GOLDEN EAGLE

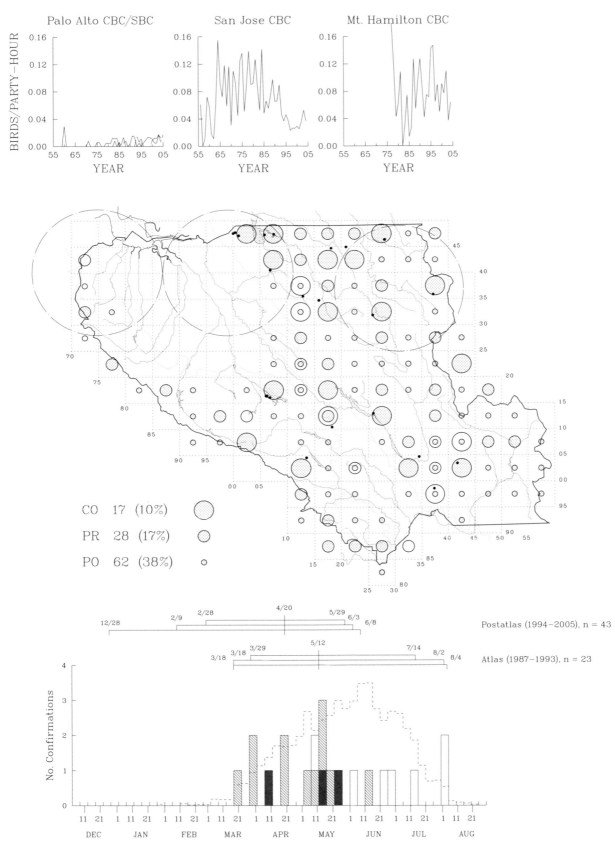

Palo Alto CBC/SBC

San Jose CBC

Mt. Hamilton CBC

BIRDS/PARTY–HOUR

YEAR

CO   17 (10%)
PR   28 (17%)
PO   62 (38%)

Postatlas (1994–2005), n = 43

Atlas (1987–1993), n = 23

No. Confirmations

DEC   JAN   FEB   MAR   APR   MAY   JUN   JUL   AUG

185

American Kestrel
Falco sparverius

Whether perched and bobbing its tail or hovering into the wind, this small falcon is characteristic of open country throughout the Western Hemisphere. American Kestrels breed from central Alaska across Canada to Labrador, and south through the Americas to Tierra del Fuego (AOU 1998, Smallwood and Bird 2002). As many as 17 subspecies have been described, most occurring from Mexico into South America. Only one subspecies, the nominate *sparverius*, is found within Canada and most of the United States (Smallwood and Bird 2002), and it breeds throughout California except for the southeastern deserts (Zeiner et al. 1990). In Santa Clara County, the American Kestrel is a common resident wherever there are suitable grasslands, pastures, or other open spaces.

The earliest mention of the American Kestrel in Santa Clara County was of a bird collected by Thomas Bridges prior to 1857 (Sclater 1857). Local observers considered it a widespread and common resident at the end of the nineteenth century (Price 1898b, Van Denburgh 1899b, Fisher 1902). Grinnell and Wythe (1927) described it as a common resident throughout the Bay area, and Sibley (1952) also considered it a common resident here. Although it is still common in the South Bay, there has been a long-term decline of 1.6 to 3.3% per year on all of our local Christmas Bird Counts.

American Kestrels were found widely during the atlas period, yielding confirmations in 79 blocks (48%) and confirmed, probable, or possible evidence in 145 blocks (88%). Atlasers found these falcons to be common residents throughout most of the Diablo Range, in the eastern foothills of the Santa Cruz Mountains, and on the valley floor. They were much less common or absent altogether from higher areas of the Santa Cruz Mountains. Breeding evidence was found from an elevation of 17 feet at Moffett Field to 3,000 feet along Poverty Ridge, above Arroyo Hondo. Subsequent to the atlas period, this elevational range was extended: fledglings were observed at 7 feet along San

Francisquito Creek, and a nest with young was found at 3,780 feet on Eylar Mountain (Michael M. Rogers, pers. comm.). Kestrels favored a wide variety of open areas, including grasslands, pastures, weedy fields, oak savannas, and mixed areas of low shrubs, brushland, and grasses. They sought out perches on small trees or shrubs, poles, wires, or fence posts, where they could survey open areas for prey. Where suitable perches were lacking they would often hover to find prey, particularly later in the day as afternoon winds developed. These falcons were also found in diverse habitats in suburban or urban areas where vacant lots, open stream channels, or parklands offered foraging opportunities. But they avoided less open woodlands or forests where the understory was well developed, and where only limited open areas were present. Nesting kestrels most often used natural cavities, particularly those occurring in western sycamores and valley oaks. Less often they used woodpecker holes or artificial nest sites, including cavities in house soffits, buildings, and power transmission towers.

The earliest evidence of nesting during the atlas period was birds in a nest cavity on 27 Mar. After this period, birds were seen in nest cavities in two locations on the valley floor on the earlier date of 13 Mar 1994 (Michael M. Rogers, pers. comm.). The latest breeding evidence obtained during the atlas period was a nest with young on 27 Jul. Following the atlas period, dependent fledglings were seen as late as 5 Aug 2001 (Michael M. Rogers, pers. comm.). Bent (1938c) reported egg dates for California extending from 2 Mar to 4 Jun, the majority of the records falling between 12 Apr and 3 May. During the atlas period, the dates of occupied nest (ON) records extended from 27 Mar to 10 Jun, with a median of 3 May. These dates are later than those reported by Bent, but the ON code does not distinguish between egg and nestling stages. The breeding evidence most commonly obtained was of dependent fledglings (47%), and the second most common was adults carrying food (18%).

In some areas of the American Kestrel's range, a restricted availability of nest cavities may limit its population (Smallwood and Bird 2002). Shuford (1993j) considered this kestrel an uncommon breeder in Marin County and noted that it was sparsely distributed even where suitable foraging habitat was at hand. He observed a correspondence between the presence of breeding Northern Flickers and that of breeding American Kestrels, and concluded that an absence of available nest cavities may limit this species' population in Marin County. Roberson (1993d) judged the American Kestrel to be a common resident in Monterey County, and suggested that declines observed there have been caused by the loss of oak woodlands and riparian forests to agriculture and development. But the long-term declines noted locally in Santa Clara County have no obvious explanation. There does not appear to be an absence of large trees with natural cavities suitable for nesting kestrels, and this species appears to be a common breeder here regardless of the presence of Northern Flickers. Urban development has displaced agriculture in the northern Santa Clara Valley over the last 50 years, but whether this shift is responsible for the reduced numbers of this small falcon is unknown. Similar declines have not been observed here for other common raptors, such as the White-tailed Kite and Red-tailed Hawk, which use platform nests.

William G. Bousman

AMERICAN KESTREL

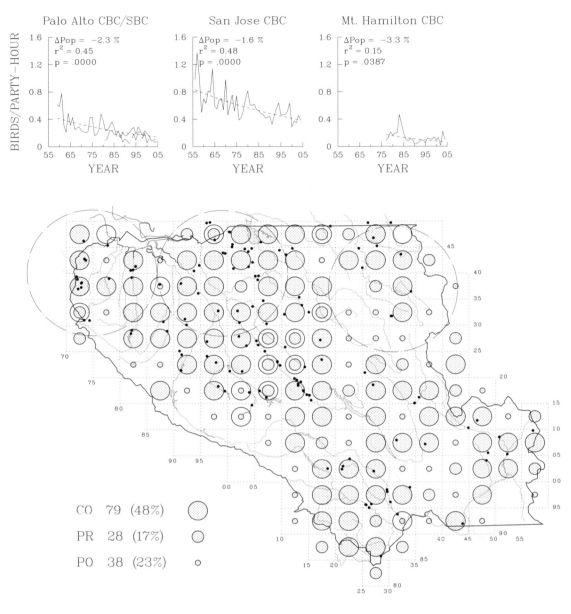

Palo Alto CBC/SBC

ΔPop = −2.3 %
r² = 0.45
p = .0000

San Jose CBC

ΔPop = −1.6 %
r² = 0.48
p = .0000

Mt. Hamilton CBC

ΔPop = −3.3 %
r² = 0.15
p = .0387

BIRDS/PARTY-HOUR

YEAR

CO 79 (48%)
PR 28 (17%)
PO 38 (23%)

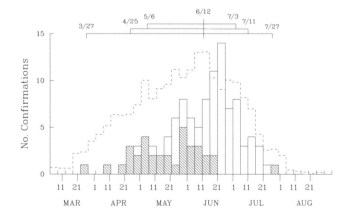

Atlas (1987−1993), n = 131

No. Confirmations

3/27 4/25 5/6 6/12 7/3 7/11 7/27

MAR   APR   MAY   JUN   JUL   AUG

187

Peregrine Falcon
Falco peregrinus

Almost extirpated by the use of organochlorine pesticides following World War II, this magnificent raptor now appears to be recovering, and it is once again breeding in Santa Clara County. The Peregrine Falcon is found widely in northern Europe, Asia, and Africa, and in the Western Hemisphere from northern Alaska to Labrador and south to Chile (AOU 1998). Worldwide, there are 19 subspecies, with *F. p. anatum* breeding in North America from south of the tundra to northern Mexico (White et al. 2002). Historically, this falcon was a rare or uncommon breeder in Santa Clara County, though additional birds from farther north would winter here. Today, Peregrines are increasingly common in the county during all seasons, and at least one pair has nested in the county in recent years.

Egg collectors eagerly sought the eggs of the "Duck Hawk" in the past, but actual nesting information for Santa Clara County is limited, because collectors were sometimes reluctant to discuss the location of their finds. Rollo H. Beck reportedly found this species nesting in Santa Clara County in the late nineteenth century, but no details were published (Barlow 1900b). Grinnell and Wythe (1927) reported that Peregrines had nested in the marshes of San Mateo and Santa Clara counties, but again without dates or specific locations. Chase Littlejohn collected at least four egg sets from ground nests in the marshes near Redwood City from 1896 to 1903 (WFVZ egg sets), but we know of no records of nests from Santa Clara County. Sibley (1952) reported that W. E. Unglish of Gilroy collected a set of eggs "in the Santa Cruz Mts. west of Gilroy" in 1905, but it is unknown whether this location was in Santa Clara County or Santa Cruz County. The first certain breeding record for Santa Clara County was obtained by Ed McClintock and his colleagues, who found a peregrine nesting near Pacheco Pass on 30 Apr 1933 (McClintock's field notes). Nesting within Santa Clara County appears to have occurred up to the 1950s, when Sibley (1952) noted that nests had been found on cliffs near Calaveras Reservoir.

It appears that the population of the Peregrine Falcon in California was stable through the 1940s, but that numbers of breeding birds declined from 1950 to 1970 (Walton et al. 1988).

This local reduction paralleled the worldwide collapse in this falcon's population that followed the introduction of organochlorine pesticides after World War II. The species was very nearly driven to extinction, a calamity almost unnoticed at the time (Kiff 1988). A survey of known nest sites in 1970 (Herman 1971) found only two successful breeding pairs in California, a statewide decline of 95%. The pesticide DDT was banned in 1972, and a recovery program for the species was implemented. The program involved captive breeding, captive incubation of thin-shelled eggs, hacking of young birds near historical aeries, and cross-fostering of young in Prairie Falcon nests (Walton and Thelander 1988). To a substantial degree these efforts have been effective, and populations are recovering.

Following the population's collapse, single birds were found sporadically in winter in Santa Clara County. Between the mid-1950s and 1984, the count of Peregrine Falcons on the Palo Alto and San Jose CBCs never exceeded a single bird. But with the population's recovery, winter numbers in the South Bay have increased substantially in recent years. An unpublished analysis of the nine CBCs that include the San Francisco Bay estuary within their count circles shows an increase in birds per party-hour of 14% per year for the period 1970 to 1994 (level of significance, $p < 0.005$).

Breeding Peregrine Falcons were not detected during the atlas period from 1987 to 1993, even though adult birds were observed irregularly in the breeding season during this period. At least seven adults or immatures were observed in the months of May through July during those years (county notebooks). Following the atlas period, increasing numbers of adults were observed in summer, at least five in 1994 alone. On 9 Jul 1996, an adult female was found attending two fledged young near Lake Elsman in the Santa Cruz Mountains (David L. Suddjian, pers. comm.). The two young were of different sizes, and the larger still showed natal down. The date of this observation, the first modern nesting record for Santa Clara County, suggests that the eggs were laid in the last week in April. The 16th of April is the midpoint of 28 egg dates cited by Bent (1938b) for California.

Currently, Peregrine Falcons are nesting in a number of watersheds in coastal Santa Cruz and San Mateo counties, and also in Alameda County, all in cliffside aeries. These locations include a nesting pair recorded in a Santa Cruz County edge block in 2000 and 2001, as shown on the map. They are also nesting on some of the bridges that cross the Bay, as well as on an office building near the Bay in San Mateo County where a nest box has been provided. It seems likely that nesting will occur in urban Santa Clara County in the future, probably on taller office buildings in areas near the Bay.

William G. Bousman

PEREGRINE FALCON

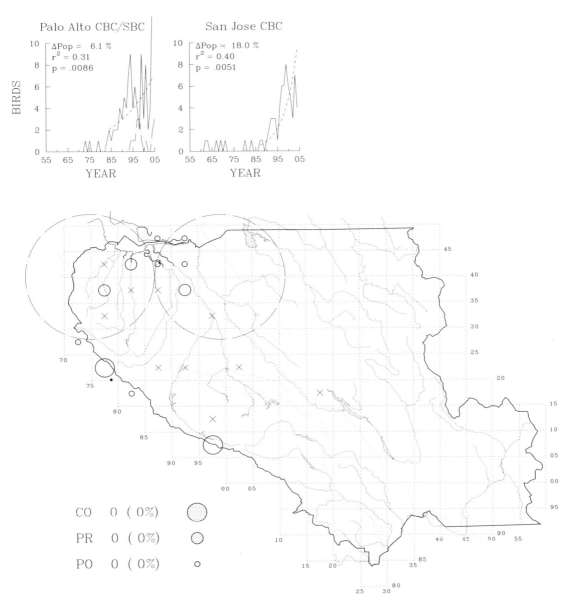

Palo Alto CBC/SBC

ΔPop = 6.1 %
r² = 0.31
p = .0086

BIRDS

San Jose CBC

ΔPop = 18.0 %
r² = 0.40
p = .0051

YEAR

YEAR

CO 0 (0%)

PR 0 (0%)

PO 0 (0%)

Postatlas (1994–2005), n = 3

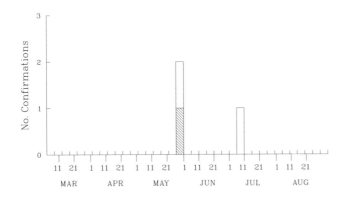

No. Confirmations

MAR   APR   MAY   JUN   JUL   AUG

189

C.C.

Prairie Falcon
Falco mexicanus

Cliffs and rock outcrops adjacent to open country in the Diablo Range are ideal for this falcon of arid habitats. The Prairie Falcon breeds in western North America from south-central British Columbia across southern Canada to North Dakota, and thence south to Baja California, northern Mexico, and Texas (Steenhof 1998). In California, it breeds in suitable habitats throughout the state, except in the humid Coast Ranges from the San Francisco Bay area north (Small 1994). The Prairie Falcon is a rare nesting species in the eastern portion of Santa Clara County, but birds are found more widely in winter.

Most early observations of Prairie Falcons were in fact of wintering birds on the valley floor. Chester Barlow (1900b) recorded that Rollo H. Beck had seen this falcon in winter, and that F. H. Holmes had collected a specimen at Berryessa. Fisher (1902) considered it to be an occasional winter visitant to the valley. Grinnell and Wythe (1927) described Prairie Falcons as resident south and east of the Bay, and reported a record of nesting near Sargent. Along the Pacheco Pass highway, where the cliffs of Lovers Leap rise over the Pacheco Creek valley, Edward McClintock and his friends found both Prairie and Peregrine falcons nesting on 28 Apr 1935 (McClintock's field notes). The Prairie Falcon's nest was on the northeast side, the Peregrine Falcon's on the northwest side. Sibley (1952) considered Prairie Falcons to be uncommon residents in the South Bay area, and noted that they were more numerous in the drier eastern portions of the region. This falcon is generally recorded in low numbers on both the San Jose and Mt. Hamilton CBCs. Within the San Jose count circle there has been a significant increase in wintering birds over the last 30 years. It is unknown whether falcons found locally in the winter have dispersed from areas where they nest in the Diablo Range or are from more northerly areas.

Atlasers found Prairie Falcons nesting in eight county blocks, all within the Diablo Range. Birds were found in blocks with cliffs or outcrops where they could find secure nest sites. These sites generally faced south or east and were in the upper halves of the cliff faces, which is typical for the species (Steenhof 1998). The habitats near the nest sites varied, but generally included extensive grasslands and oak savannas. Some sites also included areas of chaparral, foothill pine, and oak or California

bay woodlands. California ground squirrels and Western Meadowlarks are the most important prey items for Prairie Falcons in central California during the breeding season (Fowler 1931, Steenhof 1998), and the foraging habitats reported by atlasers were generally those that supported good numbers of these prey species.

The highest density of nesting falcons was in the Alameda Creek drainage along the northern border of the county. In 1992, nesting pairs were found in three of the border blocks, another pair was found to the south along Isabel Creek, and a fifth pair was in the Pacheco Creek drainage. Five pairs represents the minimum number of birds nesting each year, since coverage was not uniform within the Diablo Range in any of the atlas years. In the Alameda Creek watershed, available nest sites may limit the total number of birds that can nest there (Michael M. Rogers, pers. comm.). Farther south within Henry Coe State Park, however, previously successful aeries are no longer being used, and it appears that the density of birds in the Coyote Creek and Pacheco watersheds is limited by other factors (James Yurchenco, Amy Lauterbach, pers. comm.). Prairie Falcons forage over great distances while nesting, sometimes as far as 20 km from their nest (Steenhof 1998). It is unclear whether the possible records shown on the map represent foraging birds from known nest sites or birds from unknown aeries. The few summer records classified as observed (marked by "×" on the map) are mostly well away from breeding territories and likely represent nonbreeders.

Wintering birds leave the valley floor by the middle of February (county notebooks), and breeding birds presumably return to their nest sites at about this time. The earliest nesting evidence observed during the atlas period was a nest with eggs on 18 Apr. Of 134 California egg date records compiled by Bent (1938a), half were between 6 and 15 Apr. The latest nesting evidence during the atlas period was an adult carrying food near a known aerie on 27 Jul. Wintering birds are first noted on the valley floor about mid-August (county notebooks).

In the past, conflicts have arisen between conservationists, focused on the health of raptor populations, and falconers, insistent on collecting nestlings for their ancient sport. In the early 1970s, local Audubon Society members guarded a Prairie Falcon nest in Sunol Regional Park, just north of the Santa Clara County border. In both 1972 and 1973, young were successfully fledged from this nest, despite numerous attempts by falconers to remove them (*Am. Birds* 26:901 1972, 27:913–14 1973). Prairie Falcon populations also declined from the effects of the organochlorine pesticide contamination that almost wiped out the Peregrine Falcon. Today, Prairie Falcon populations are stable, and legal falconry probably takes no more than 0.2% of the population annually (Steenhof 1998). Nonetheless, where this falcon is rare and the habitat supports only a few nesting pairs, the collecting of young birds may extirpate these populations.

William G. Bousman

PRAIRIE FALCON

Palo Alto CBC/SBC

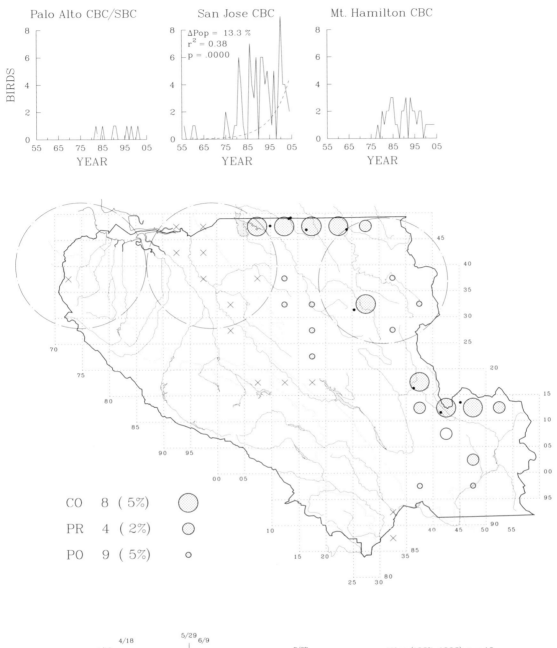

San Jose CBC

ΔPop = 13.3 %
$r^2 = 0.38$
p = .0000

Mt. Hamilton CBC

CO 8 (5%)

PR 4 (2%)

PO 9 (5%)

Atlas (1987–1993), n = 10

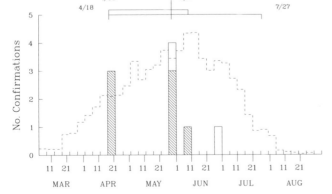

191

Clapper Rail
Rallus longirostris

The ebb and flow of the tides rule the life of the Clapper Rail, struggling to survive in the few remaining salt marshes of San Francisco Bay. Though the species ranges along both coasts of North America and Central America, on the Pacific Coast it is now found in only a few locations north to the San Francisco Bay area. It is this Bay area population, constituting the subspecies *R. l. obsoletus*, that breeds in Santa Clara County. Here it inhabits tidal salt marshes composed primarily of cord grass and pickleweed, as well as brackish sloughs dominated by bulrushes. Owing to declines brought on by habitat loss, predation, and pollution, this population has been listed by both the U.S. Fish and Wildlife Service and the California Department of Fish and Game as endangered.

The subspecies *obsoletus* formerly ranged from Humboldt Bay in northern California south to Morro Bay (Grinnell and Miller 1944). It is now restricted to San Francisco Bay, the southern end of the Bay supporting the greater part of the population (Harding-Smith 1993). For much of the first half of the twentieth century, the construction of salt evaporator ponds began to impact the distribution of this bird. Although extensive salt marshes lay near the town of Alviso in Santa Clara County for most of this time (Applegarth 1938), the eventual conversion of much of them to salt ponds severely reduced the breeding habitat of the Clapper Rail within the county. Sibley (1952) nonetheless still considered it to be a "locally common resident" in the South Bay. A major study of this species at this end of the Bay in 1971 found just 58 active nests in San Mateo, Santa Clara, and Alameda Counties (Gill 1972). And in 1979 its distribution in Santa Clara County was limited to "the marshes of the Palo Alto Baylands Nature Interpretive Center, at the mouth of Charleston Slough, and along the larger fringing marshes of Guadalupe and Alviso sloughs," as well as "the mouth of Alviso slough east to the abandoned town of Drawbridge" (Gill 1979).

During the atlas period, Clapper Rails were found in the marshes just north of the mouth of San Francisquito Creek, in the Palo Alto Baylands marsh that extends from the mouth of San Francisquito Creek to Sand Point, and in the adjacent Palo Alto Yacht Harbor, now abandoned and reverting to tidal marsh. These rails were also found in the fringing marshes along the mouth of Coyote Creek, from Calaveras Point east to Triangle Marsh. The species also ranged well up into the brackish sloughs, away from the edge of the Bay. It was found 1–2 km or more above the mouths of Mountain View Slough and Stevens Creek, and nearly 5 km from the open Bay in the larger marshes along Guadalupe Slough and Alviso Slough.

The earliest atlas breeding confirmation obtained for Clapper Rails was a nest with eggs on 3 Apr, a date near the commencement of the nesting season as reported by Applegarth (1938) and Zucca (1954). Records of nests with eggs, most received through the courtesy of the U.S. Fish and Wildlife Service, were found throughout the breeding season, the last set on 16 Jul. The only other breeding confirmations obtained for the atlas were of family groups seen in mid-July. Downy young were seen on 13 Jul in the Palo Alto Yacht Harbor, and another family with half-grown young was seen on 18 Jul along Stevens Creek, near Crittenden Marsh. After the atlas period, a precocial young was seen near the Palo Alto Flood Control Basin levee as late as 17 Aug 1998 (Richard Carlson, county notebooks). Previous studies indicate that nesting is disrupted by the spring flood tides in June, but that it resumes with a small peak of activity in July (Gill 1972). De Groot (1927) felt that this July burst of nesting indicated double-brooding, but other authors claim that it represents renesting attempts by failed breeders (Applegarth 1938, Zucca 1954).

The Clapper Rail was extensively hunted as a game bird until protective legislation was enacted in 1913 (Grinnell et al. 1918). But despite a short-term recovery, salt pond construction and pollutant accumulation in later years eliminated or degraded the rail's habitat, further reducing its range and numbers. In 1981, the population of *obsoletus* was estimated at 1,200–1,500 birds (T. E. Harvey *fide* Harding-Smith 1993). Declines continued throughout the late 1980s and into the 1990s, culminating in a record low population estimate of 500 birds in the winter of 1991 (Harding-Smith 1993). This latest decline was closely tied to the appearance of the non-native red fox in the East Bay. An intensive predator management program has helped the Clapper Rail recover somewhat, and recent property acquisitions, such as Bair Island, may provide future habitat if the land is restored to tidal salt marsh. It would seem, in any case, that *obsoletus* remains on the brink of extinction, and only concerted management efforts will keep it from going over the edge.

Michael J. Mammoser

CLAPPER RAIL

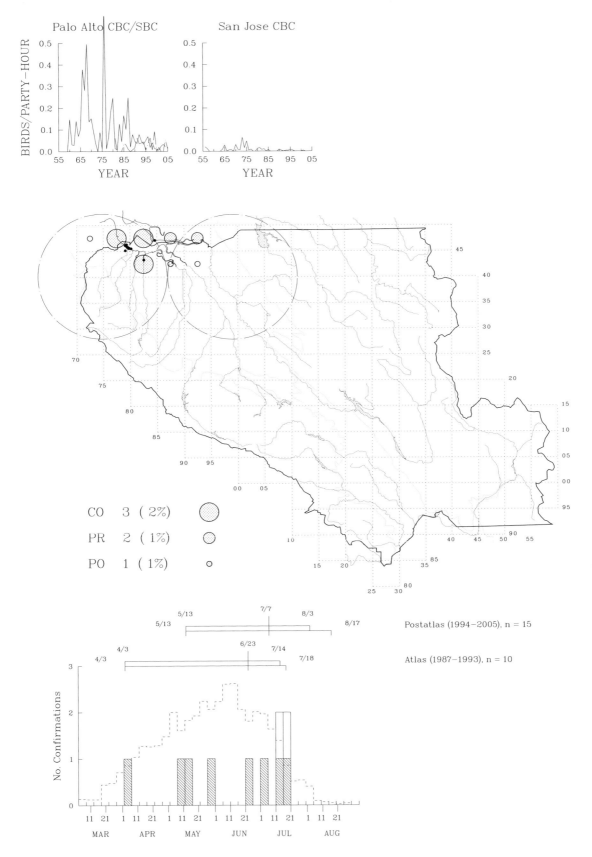

Palo Alto CBC/SBC

San Jose CBC

BIRDS/PARTY–HOUR

YEAR

YEAR

CO 3 (2%)
PR 2 (1%)
PO 1 (1%)

5/13   7/7   8/3
5/13   8/17   Postatlas (1994–2005), n = 15

4/3   6/23   7/14
4/3   7/18   Atlas (1987–1993), n = 10

No. Confirmations

11 21   1 11 21   1 11 21   1 11 21   1 11 21   1 11 21
MAR   APR   MAY   JUN   JUL   AUG

Virginia Rail
Rallus limicola

Although the Virginia Rail probably breeds in Santa Clara County, the true status of this reclusive denizen of our marshes remains an enigma. This rail breeds locally from British Columbia across Canada to Nova Scotia and thence south on the Pacific Coast to Baja California, and in the east to Georgia. Resident populations are found from southern Mexico to Argentina (Ripley 1977, Conway 1995, AOU 1998). The nominate subspecies, *limicola*, is the only one occurring in North America. Virginia Rails are widespread in California, fairly common in northwestern coastal and interior marshes, and less common farther south. They are absent from mountainous areas and the southeastern deserts (Small 1994). This rail is rare in summer in Santa Clara County, being found only occasionally in freshwater wetlands. Numbers increase substantially during migration and in winter, when they are also found in brackish and saltwater marshes.

Not surprisingly, there is little historical information concerning local breeding of Virginia Rails, and much of what does exist is contradictory. Schneider (1893) claimed that rails nested in a freshwater marsh apparently located where Lake Cunningham is today. In the center of that marsh, bulrushes were much taller than a man, whereas at the marsh's edge "rushes grow luxuriantly and in the dead bunches Soras and California Clapper Rails, Gallinules, Coots and others nest." Because Clapper Rails breed only within salt marshes, Schneider probably misidentified the Virginia Rails he saw in this marsh as Clapper Rails. Although he was an active oologist, there is no evidence that he ever collected eggs of the Virginia Rail from this marsh or elsewhere in the county. Kobbé (1902), in his assessment of waterbirds in the San Francisco Bay area, listed this rail only as a fall migrant. Grinnell et al. (1918) considered Virginia Rails to be common throughout California, but mentioned no records from Santa Clara County. Interestingly, however, they did note a Virginia Rail nest at Alvarado, Alameda County, on 23 Apr 1915. Grinnell and Wythe (1927) felt that this rail was a fairly common resident in the San Francisco Bay area, but noted only

four breeding records, including the 1915 record just mentioned. Sibley (1952), in assessing this rail's status in the South Bay region, judged it to be a fairly common resident. Gill (1977), however, knew of no local breeding records, although he suspected nesting at Coyote Hills Regional Park in Alameda County and in freshwater areas in Santa Clara County. During a 1980 Breeding Bird Census of a sector of the salt marsh along Coyote Slough adjacent to Salt Pond A14 in Alviso, the presence of multiple birds was reported (*Am. Birds* 35:102 1981), but these may have been misidentified Clapper Rails.

To date, then, breeding by Virginia Rails has never been confirmed in Santa Clara County. Because migrant Virginia Rails can occur in May and August along the edge of the South Bay, it was necessary for us to limit the records shown on the atlas map to those from the nine-week period from 23 May to 31 Jul, so as not to include nonresident birds. This approach is conservative in the sense that almost 50% of all reported Virginia Rail breeding records from central California involve birds with young before the end of April (*N. Am. Birds* Northern California Region notebooks). The only probable breeding evidence reported during the atlas period was sustained calling and agitated behavior by several Virginia Rails on a sag pond at 2,100 feet in the Monte Bello Open Space Preserve. This ponded area, roughly a hectare in extent, could support multiple pairs of rails, to judge from breeding densities found by telemetry studies in Iowa (Johnson and Dinsmore 1985). Calling birds were heard at the Monte Bello sag pond in at least six of the seven atlas years. In some years, birds were heard giving the *tick-it* call before dawn as well as at midday (pers. obs.). Such sustained calling may be an indicator of unmated males (Conway 1995). Similar calling at this sag pond continued through 1996, but no rails have been reported there since (county notebooks). The San Mateo County Breeding Bird Atlas (Sequoia Audubon Society 2001b) reported confirmed breeding from the same atlas block, but that record has been shown to be in error (Rick Johnson, pers. comm.).

During the atlas period, calling Virginia Rails were heard at a number of freshwater or brackish areas along the South Bay, including the Mountain View Forebay and the abandoned Alviso Marina. Subsequent to the atlas period, calling birds were also heard at the Palo Alto Flood Control Basin, the Stevens Creek Tidal Marsh, and the Calabazas Ponds. Locations of inland records during the atlas period included a different sag pond at Monte Bello at a lower elevation and the upper end of Vasona Reservoir. Subsequently, birds have been heard repeatedly along Llagas Creek, near the South County Regional WasteWater Authority treatment ponds in Gilroy.

Persistent summer calling from freshwater and brackish marshes indicates probable breeding, but to date no confirmation of breeding by Virginia Rails in Santa Clara County has been obtained. In the San Francisco Bay area, recent breeding has been confirmed in every county except San Francisco, Contra Costa, and Santa Clara (Burridge 1995b, Shuford 1993k, Berner 2003c, Sequoia Audubon Society 2001b). But despite the lack of confirmations from Santa Clara County, the preponderance of the evidence suggests that this species is a rare and secretive breeder here.

William G. Bousman

VIRGINIA RAIL

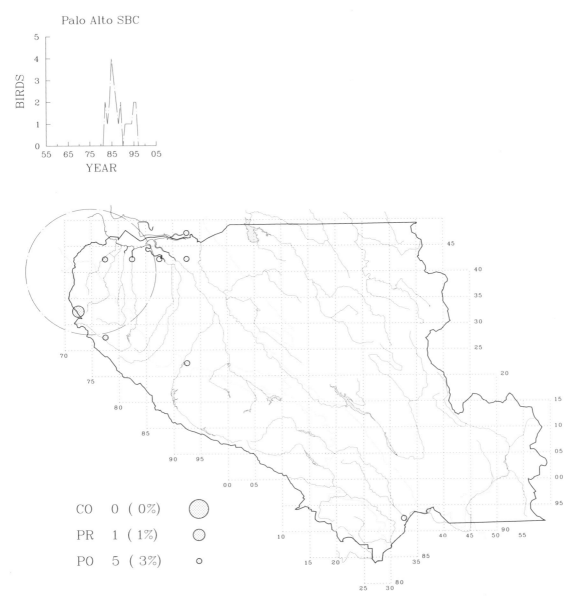

Palo Alto SBC

CO   0 (0%)
PR   1 (1%)
PO   5 (3%)

Common Moorhen
Gallinula chloropus

Rarely found far from the cover of dense emergent vegetation, the shy Common Moorhen usually retreats into the marsh at the first sign of danger. In this respect it is quite different from its less timid cousin, the American Coot, which often nests and forages in more exposed environs. Cosmopolitan in distribution, the Common Moorhen breeds widely over most of the world's continents (AOU 1998). In North America, the species is represented by the race *G. c. cachinnans*, which breeds from the eastern and southwestern United States south to Central America (AOU 1998). The Common Moorhen is an uncommon breeder in California, nesting in freshwater marshes throughout the Central Valley and breeding more sparsely in the coast ranges south of Marin County and in the arid southeastern part of the state (Zeiner et al. 1990, Small 1994). Most breeding populations in California are probably either resident or only partially migratory, although the presence of overwintering birds in areas where breeding does not occur indicates some winter movement (Roberson 1993f, Small 1994). The Common Moorhen is an uncommon and local breeder in Santa Clara County's lowland freshwater marshes, particularly those along the edge of the Bay.

Historically, the Common Moorhen was considered a locally common breeder in parts of the Central Valley, but it was quite a rare bird in the San Francisco Bay area. In 1894, Harry R. Painton collected four sets of eggs within Santa Clara County, although the data slips do not provide a specific location (CAS and WFVZ egg collections). An additional egg set was collected nearby in Alvarado, Alameda County, in 1899 (WFVZ egg collection). These records were unknown to Grinnell and Wythe (1927), who reported only three records from the Bay area: single birds in San Francisco in 1855 and 1916 and two immatures (probably indicating local breeding) near Hayward in Alameda County on 4 Jul 1904. Later, W. E. Unglish (1937) collected eggs on 27 May 1935 and 28 May 1936 at San Felipe Lake, just south of the Santa Clara County line in San Benito County. Only Unglish's egg collections were noted in later summaries (Grinnell and Miller 1944, Sibley 1952), which did not list additional breeding records from the Bay area, or any records specifically from Santa Clara County.

The first published breeding record for the county came in 1957, when several pairs bred "at the intersection of Singleton Road and the Coyote River, 2 miles south of San Jose" (*Audubon Field Notes 11*:427 1957). Most county records prior to the mid-1970s were from the southern reaches of the Santa Clara Valley rather than the Bay edge, and Gill (1977) apparently did not find this species at all along the edge of the South Bay in 1971. Moorhens began to increase on the Palo Alto Christmas Bird Count in the mid-1970s. The first bayside breeding records for the county were from the Palo Alto Baylands in 1977 and Moffett Field in 1979 (William G. Bousman, pers. comm.). Judging from accounts in *Audubon Field Notes* and *Am. Birds*, this species has gradually expanded its breeding range northward and become more common and widespread as a breeder in the Bay area, and on the Central Coast in general, since the 1950s.

Atlasers found the Common Moorhen to be an uncommon breeder in freshwater and brackish marshes along the immediate edge of San Francisco Bay, but a rare and very local breeder elsewhere in the county. Many breeding locations were characterized by fairly shallow, nontidal impoundments having dense emergent vegetation, primarily cattails or bulrushes. Here, moorhens nested in stands of vegetation within ponds or in broad strips of emergent vegetation along the ponds' margins. Moorhens with small young were also observed along the upper reaches of some tidal streams. These birds likely nested in the dense stands of bulrushes present at these locations.

Common Moorhens were present in only a few areas on the valley floor away from the Bay, mostly in small ponds having suitable marshy vegetation. Breeding was confirmed in such ponds at Coleman Road and Almaden Lake near the upper end of the Guadalupe River, at Coyote Ranch and the Ogier Avenue near Coyote Creek, and at the South County Regional WasteWater Authority plant in Gilroy. In addition, a few pairs bred along slow-moving reaches of streams having patches of dense emergent vegetation, such as the Guadalupe River near the San Jose International Airport and Llagas Creek southeast of Gilroy. The sparse distribution of this species in inland areas likely reflects the distribution of suitable nesting habitat on the valley floor. In addition, the drought that persisted during most atlas years probably reduced suitable habitat in inland areas even further, and in fact most breeding records from the southern part of the valley were obtained after the atlas period. All breeding confirmations were from areas below 310 feet in elevation. In contrast to its close relative the American Coot, the Common Moorhen was much less abundant and more local, apparently requiring more extensive emergent vegetation than was present in many of the ponds used by nesting coots.

Only three of the atlas breeding confirmations involved nests, attesting to the relatively secretive nature of nesting Common Moorhens. These records included nest-building on 22 Mar, an occupied nest on 3 May, and a nest with young on 18 May. Otherwise, all breeding confirmations involved flightless or recently fledged young. Flightless young were observed as early as 3 May, and many such records were obtained into late August. A few records of flightless or recently fledged young were obtained as late as 3 Oct.

Stephen C. Rottenborn

COMMON MOORHEN

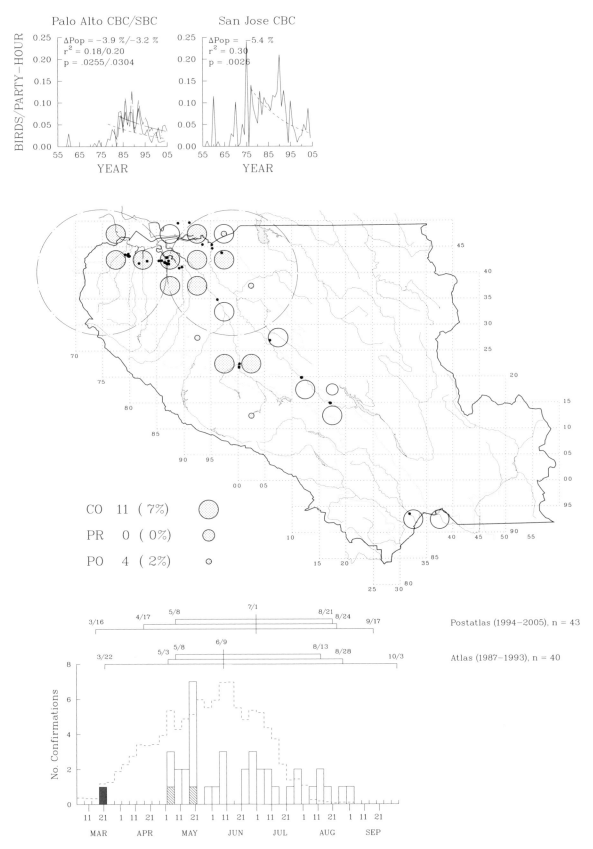

Palo Alto CBC/SBC

ΔPop = −3.9 %/−3.2 %
r² = 0.18/0.20
p = .0255/.0304

San Jose CBC

ΔPop = −5.4 %
r² = 0.30
p = .0026

BIRDS/PARTY-HOUR

YEAR

YEAR

CO   11 (7%)
PR   0 (0%)
PO   4 (2%)

Postatlas (1994−2005), n = 43

Atlas (1987−1993), n = 40

No. Confirmations

MAR   APR   MAY   JUN   JUL   AUG   SEP

197

American Coot
Fulica americana

A coot paddles slowly along the edge of a cattail marsh, its head bobbing back and forth like a child's toy. But everything changes in a moment; its head strains forward as it rushes at a second bird to defend its territory. The American Coot breeds primarily from southern British Columbia to Manitoba, and south through the western United States into Mexico, Central America, and northern South America (Brisbin et al. 2002). Coots also breed locally in the eastern United States, the largest numbers found along the Gulf Coast (Sauer et al. 2005). Two subspecies are recognized, the nominate one, *americana*, found throughout North and Middle America (Brisbin et al. 2002). In California, this coot is found in ponds, marshes, and other wetlands throughout the state, except in the highest mountains and the driest regions of the southeastern deserts (Small 1994). The American Coot is a common resident in Santa Clara County, its numbers augmented significantly by wintering birds between the middle of October and late April.

Among early observers, both Fred A. Schneider (1893) and Chester Barlow (1893b) noted that the American Coot nested in marshes near San Jose. Kobbé (1902) described it as "common everywhere" in the San Francisco Bay area. Grinnell and Wythe (1927) stated that it was an "[a]bundant resident of marshes, lakes and ponds throughout the Bay region." Sibley (1952) considered the coot a common resident throughout the South Bay. Analysis of the Palo Alto SBC data shows no change in the number of resident birds since the start of that count in 1981.

Atlasers found American Coots breeding in scattered locations throughout the county. For breeding, coots generally require thick emergent plant growth, such as cattails and bulrushes, near open fresh water. These preferred habitats were found along the edge of the South Bay in impoundments such as the Palo Alto Flood Control Basin, the Mountain View Forebay, Crittenden Marsh, and the Waterbird Management Area along lower Coyote Creek. Coots also used slow-moving, freshwa-ter channels along the Bay's edge, from Stevens Creek east to Coyote Creek, wherever reasonably thick growths of cattails and other emergent plants were present. Inland in the Santa Clara Valley, birds used percolation ponds, gravel pits, old sewage ponds, slow-moving streams, and lakes for nesting. Permanent reservoirs and stock ponds at higher elevations, where there was a growth of emergent vegetation, were typically used by one or two pairs of birds. In the Diablo Range, such sites included various stock ponds, the Arnold Pond along Arroyo Bayo, Mississippi Lake, and Kelly Cabin Canyon Lake. In the Santa Cruz Mountains and their foothills, ponds and lakes used included Felt Lake, the larger pond at Arastradero Preserve, Horseshoe Lake, the Howell Reservoirs, and Almaden Reservoir. Coots were not found on steep-sided reservoirs with frequent variations in water height and little or no emergent vegetation. During the atlas period, nest elevations ranged from sea level at numerous locations near the edge of the South Bay to an elevation of 2,940 feet on a stock pond in Fenton Canyon, on upper Colorado Creek in the Diablo Range.

American Coots normally conceal their nests in emergent vegetation, but place them within a couple of meters of open water (Brisbin et al. 2002), though they may sometimes build their nests in more open situations. Both before and after the atlas period, coots were observed nesting in bayside impoundments that were without extensive emergent vegetation, their nests thus readily visible. On 15 May 1979, 28 nests were seen in open situations in Crittenden Marsh and adjacent marshes, although some of these nests may have been display platforms (pers. obs). Following the atlas period, one or two pairs of coots nested regularly in a drainage channel west of the Stevens Creek Tidal Marsh, adjacent to a public bike path where little or no emergent vegetation was present (pers. obs).

American Coots breeding in the San Francisco Bay area are considered resident, on the strength of studies of marked birds (Gullion 1954). The great numbers of wintering birds begin to leave in March and April, which is the time that residents begin their breeding activities. The earliest breeding evidence during the atlas period was nest building seen on 20 Mar. Subsequently, earlier breeding was recorded when adults were seen building a nest at the Oka percolation ponds on 18 Feb 2002 (Linda Sullivan, PADB). American Coots appear to be double-brooded in central California (Gullion 1954, Brisbin et al. 2002), and their breeding season consequently extends late in the year. During the atlas period, the latest breeding evidence was precocial young seen on 9 Sep. Following the atlas period, a fledgling was observed as late as 6 Oct 2005 at the Sunnyvale Water Pollution Control Plant (Stephen C. Rottenborn et al., PADB).

William G. Bousman

AMERICAN COOT

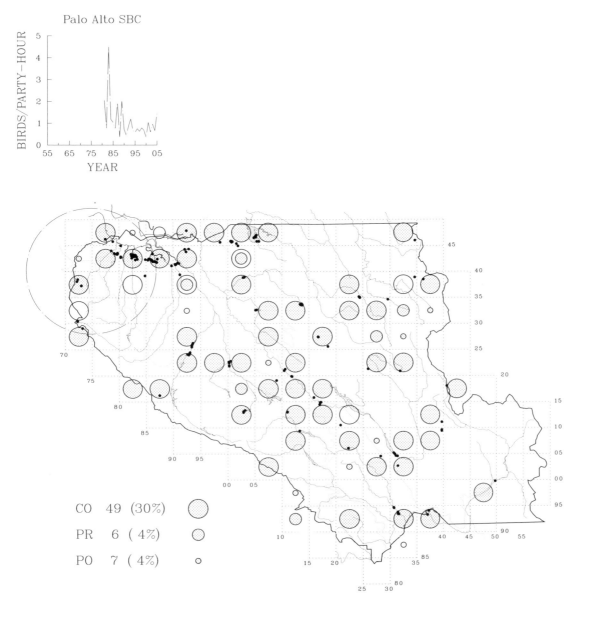

Palo Alto SBC

BIRDS/PARTY-HOUR

YEAR

CO 49 (30%)

PR 6 (4%)

PO 7 (4%)

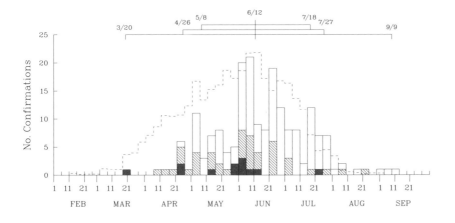

3/20   4/26   5/8   6/12   7/18 7/27   9/9

Atlas (1987–1993), n = 190

No. Confirmations

FEB   MAR   APR   MAY   JUN   JUL   AUG   SEP

199

Snowy Plover
Charadrius alexandrinus

A plaintive alarm call from a flushing bird may be the first indication that one has come across the nest of a Snowy Plover, a species that depends on camouflage and deception to protect its nest and young from predators. In North America, Snowy Plovers typically breed on sandy beaches along the Gulf of Mexico and the Pacific Coast south of Washington, although there are localized populations inland as well, using alkaline wetlands and salt flats. In Santa Clara County this species, listed as threatened in California, is found in the salt evaporators and impoundments along San Francisco Bay, utilizing dried-out pond bottoms and levees with suitable substrate characteristics. Snowy Plovers include a number of subspecies worldwide, the Santa Clara County population consisting entirely of *C. a. nivosus* (AOU 1957).

Although a small amount of natural playa may have existed along the edge of San Francisco Bay prior to the turn of the twentieth century, there is no evidence that Snowy Plovers used these areas for breeding. After development of the salt evaporator system got underway around San Francisco Bay, breeding was first noted here in the summer of 1914 (Grinnell et al. 1918), when nests were reported from the salt pond levees near the town of Alvarado, Alameda County. A general expansion of the salt evaporator system in the 1930s and 1940s (Howard L. Cogswell, pers. comm.) was followed by more widespread reports of Snowy Plover nesting. Fledglings seen on the levees of the old Palo Alto Sports Club in August 1937 (Martin 1939) constituted the first documented Santa Clara County breeding record. Etta Smith reported a nest in Alviso on 27 Apr 1947 (*Bull. SCVAS* August 1947) and regularly reported nesting in this area throughout the 1950s, the most notable report being of 14 nests in 1955 (*Avocet 2(5)*:25–26 1955). Charles Sibley, too, found nests in this vicinity during the early 1950s (Sibley 1952, *Bull. SCVAS* May 1952), all on salt pond levees. A 1971 survey found nine nests along 3 km of levee near the Knapp Gun Club, in the vicinity of Alviso, and seven birds were found just north of Moffett Field (Gill 1972). A decade later, Rigney and Rigney (1981) concluded that the Knapp Gun Club pond was a major nesting area for these birds, and that the southern portion of Salt Pond A8, just west of Alviso, was an incidental nesting area. Birds were also found on Salt Pond A22, north of Coyote Creek

in Alameda County, southwest of Fremont.

The distribution of Snowy Plovers in the county during the atlas period was restricted to the immediate edge of San Francisco Bay and was patchy, even within this limited area. The majority of atlas records were obtained on surveys by the Point Reyes Bird Observatory (Gary Page, pers. comm.) and the San Francisco Bay Bird Observatory (pers. obs.), conducted largely on private property. An apparently mated pair and a few additional individuals were found at the west end of Dumbarton Bridge in San Mateo County, in the salt ponds on either side of Ravenswood Slough. This species' distribution was interrupted by areas of preserved salt marsh, heavily vegetated flood-control impoundments, and human recreational developments from Cooley Landing southeast to Stevens Creek. Breeding was recorded in a dried-out pond north of the Moffett Field runways, and postatlas broods were noted farther north on Salt Pond A3N (Stephen C. Rottenborn, pers. comm.). The old Knapp Gun Club pond, which had been a major nesting site in the past, hosted only a few birds during the atlas period. Since the early 1980s this area has supported an expanding colony of California Gulls, a species known to prey upon plover eggs and chicks (Page et al. 1985). The south end of Salt Pond A8, where many nests and broods were recorded, was undoubtedly the breeding stronghold of this species in the county, during and after the atlas period. No plovers were recorded on the salt ponds immediately north and northeast of Alviso during the atlas years, but postatlas breeding was recorded on an impoundment just north of the former Alviso Marina (Peter J. Metropulos, pers. comm.). Breeding also occurred on Salt Pond A22 in Alameda County, both during and after the atlas period, where birds had been found historically.

Almost all Snowy Plover breeding records were from the month of June, May having yielded only a single record, perhaps owing to the fact that most observations were recorded on scheduled surveys, rather than as a result of an ongoing atlas effort. Postatlas breeding observations found this species sitting on eggs as early as 15 Apr 1995 (pers. obs.), and young chicks were still being attended on 27 Aug 1995 (Michael M. Rogers, pers. comm.).

Surveys by Gill (1972) and by Rigney and Rigney (1981) produced population estimates of 100-150 pairs in San Francisco Bay south of the San Mateo Bridge. A 1978 survey counted 351 adults in this same area (Page and Stenzel 1981). A decade later, surveys of the same areas showed a 35% decline in numbers around South San Francisco Bay (Page et al. 1991). There is no obvious explanation for this decline, but possible causes may include an increase in predator populations and fluctuating water levels in salt ponds, the latter determining the amount of exposed pond bottom available for breeding.

Michael J. Mammoser

SNOWY PLOVER

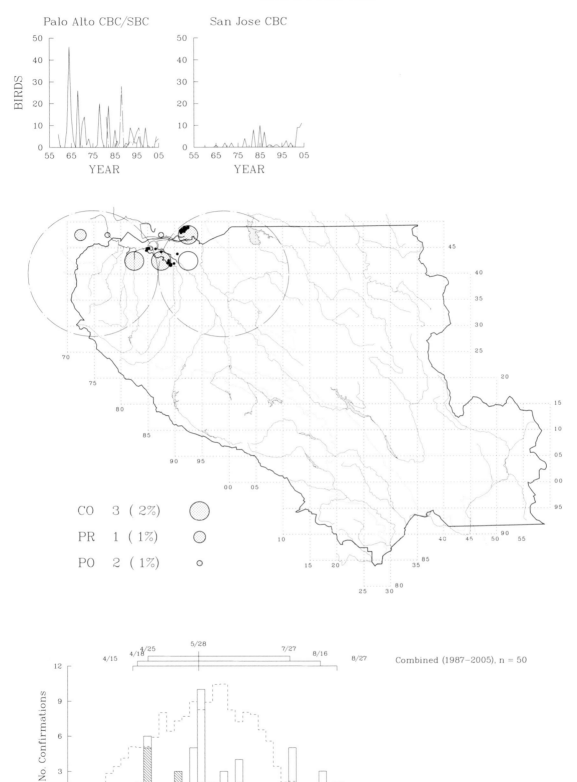

Palo Alto CBC/SBC

San Jose CBC

CO   3 (2%)
PR   1 (1%)
PO   2 (1%)

Combined (1987–2005), n = 50

201

Killdeer
Charadrius vociferus

Spying a predator's approach, a Killdeer feigns injury, dragging one wing along the ground with its tail spread, thus leading the threat away from its vulnerable nest. Killdeer breed from southeast Alaska across northern Canada to Newfoundland, and thence south through the United States into Mexico, with small, disjunct populations in Costa Rica, Ecuador, and Peru (Jackson and Jackson 2000). Three subspecies have been described, the nominate *C. v. vociferus* being the one found throughout North America (Jackson and Jackson 2000). This handsome plover is common and widespread in California (Small 1994), and is a common breeding species in Santa Clara County, found wherever there is open ground and freshwater nearby. Numbers are augmented in winter by birds from northern or higher-elevation regions.

Judging by historical accounts, the Killdeer has long been a common resident in Santa Clara County. The species was included on the list of birds collected by Thomas Bridges in "the Valley of San José" sometime prior to 1857 (Sclater 1857). Kobbé (1902), in his summary of the status of waterbirds in the San Francisco Bay area at the end of the nineteenth century, considered the Killdeer common throughout the year. A quarter of a century later, Grinnell and Wythe (1927) described it as a "common resident locally," and also noted that there was an influx of additional birds to the Bay in winter. In assessing the Killdeer's status in the South San Francisco Bay region, Sibley (1952) judged it a common resident. From 1966 to 2004, Killdeer have declined by 1.9% a year in California (Sauer et al. 2005), but no comparable change has been observed in the numbers recorded on the Palo Alto SBC.

Atlasers confirmed breeding in 91 blocks (55%), and considering probable and possible evidence as well, Killdeer were recorded in 132 blocks (80%). They were found nesting from sea level near the Bay edge to an elevation of 3,120 feet at a stock pond along Valpe Ridge in the Diablo Range. Killdeer laid their eggs on gravel, pebble, or dirt substrates with freshwater nearby and good visibility in all directions. In more remote areas, they sought out the edges of stock ponds and streams. Along permanent streams, they nested either on gravel bars or along their edges. On intermittent streams, they used nest scrapes in the dried-out stream beds, or nested on adjacent flood-scoured gravelly plains. In urban areas and along the valley floor, they also nested adjacent to streams, but often used gravel roads, abandoned quarries or pits, gravel rooftops, and occasionally piles of gravel and crushed rock. In general, nest sites were near open areas that could be used for foraging, such as along streams and ponds, on heavily grazed pastures, in plowed fields, and on human-modified habitats, including urban parks, golf courses, and athletic fields. Some source of freshwater was nearly always present. In the Diablo Range and the Santa Cruz Mountains, the water was often in the form of stock ponds, permanent streams, or small pools along intermittent streams. On the valley floor, water sources included ponds, impoundments, streams, irrigation channels, and even excess water from sprinkler systems.

The most common breeding confirmation obtained by atlasers was the distraction display (40%), but because this display may be used during either the nesting stage or the postnesting stage, these records are not reflected in the phenology graphic. The earliest breeding evidence obtained during the atlas period was a nest with eggs found in the Palo Alto Flood Control Basin on 30 Mar. Subsequent to the atlas period, a nest with eggs was found at the edge of Felt Lake on 20 Feb 1995 (Karen A. Hoyt, county notebooks). The latest breeding evidence during the atlas period consisted of precocial young north of Morgan Hill on 31 Jul. Subsequently, precocial young were observed on a dike beside the western oxidation pond at the Sunnyvale Water Pollution Control Plant as late as 29 Aug 2002 (Michael M. Rogers, PADB).

In the last two centuries, Killdeer have taken advantage of human modifications to South Bay habitats, but some of the benefits thus realized may be countered by human-induced environmental damage. Human modifications that appear to have benefited Killdeer include the addition of gravel roads, levees, and other open gravelly or stony areas that offer nesting substrates. Extensive irrigated lawns in parks and on athletic fields and golf courses have also provided significant year-round food resources for the species. Other human changes, in contrast, primarily pesticide applications on agricultural fields or on grasslands, are detrimental to Killdeer (Jackson and Jackson 2000). Although Jackson and Jackson (2000) state that Killdeer are doing better over most of the United States than at any prior time in their history, this is not the case in California, where there has been a long-term decline, as noted above. In Santa Clara County, it is not clear whether living in association with humans has been a benefit or a detriment in the long run.

William G. Bousman

KILLDEER

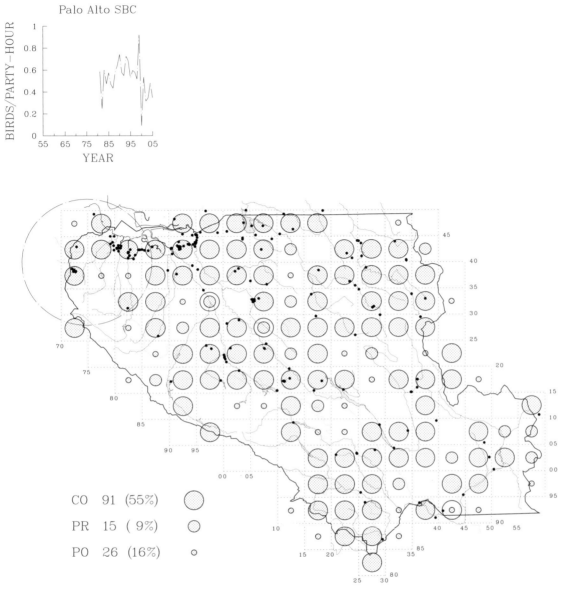

Palo Alto SBC

BIRDS/PARTY–HOUR
YEAR

CO 91 (55%)
PR 15 (9%)
PO 26 (16%)

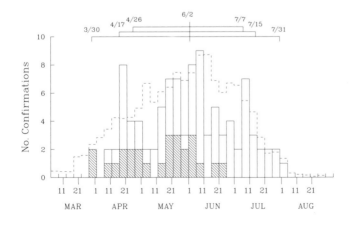

No. Confirmations

MAR   APR   MAY   JUN   JUL   AUG

3/30 4/17 4/26   6/2   7/7 7/15   7/31

Atlas (1987–1993), n = 164

203

Emélie Curtis 1997

Black-necked Stilt
Himantopus mexicanus

This elegant, long-legged shorebird is a picture of grace as it walks and feeds in shallow pools, but during the breeding season it responds to any slight disturbance by becoming a fierce, yapping scourge, defending its nest site or its nearby young. The systematics of stilts worldwide are a subject of much debate (Robinson et al. 1999). Generally, birds in the Western Hemisphere and Oceania are considered one species, *Himantopus mexicanus*, and are divided into three subspecies: *mexicanus* from North America to northern South America, *melanurus* in southern South America, and *knudseni* on the Hawaiian archipelago (Robinson et al. 1999). The nominate *mexicanus* breeds in interior North America from southern Alberta to Missouri and south through Mexico to Ecuador and Brazil (AOU 1998). Birds of this subspecies also nest on the west coast from San Francisco Bay south into Mexico and, more sparingly, on the east coast from southeastern Pennsylvania south through the Caribbean. In California, the Black-necked Stilt breeds locally, with major concentrations on the northeastern plateau, in portions of the Central Valley, in the San Francisco Bay area, and at the Salton Sea (Small 1994). In Santa Clara County, the stilt is a common nesting species along the South Bay and a rare breeder inland at shallow lakes and wetlands.

At the close of the nineteenth century, the Black-necked Stilt was a common summer resident in portions of the Central Valley, the coastal slope of southern California, and areas east of the Sierra, but was only a rare fall and winter visitor to the San Francisco Bay area (Grinnell 1902, Kobbé 1902). The two sets of eggs collected by W. Otto Emerson near Hayward, Alameda County, on 3 May 1908 (CAS #6811) and 11 Jun 1911 (CAS #6820), were the first breeding records for the San Francisco Bay area. Grinnell and Wythe (1927) noted these early records, but commented that the species was found in only limited numbers in summer and fall in the Bay area. The breeding range described by Grinnell and Miller (1944) was much the same as that noted at the end of the preceding century, but they reported a great reduction in numbers in historic breeding areas as wetlands were drained. The first evidence of nesting in Santa Clara

County was a nest with two eggs found by James G. Peterson in Alviso on 26 May 1946 (Sibley 1952). At this time, Sibley (1952) considered the stilt to be an uncommon summer resident and rare winter visitor. Numbers increased in the 1950s and 1960s, and Gill (1977) estimated a South Bay breeding population of 400 to 500 pairs by the early 1970s. Recent surveys in the South Bay (Rintoul et al. 2003) estimate that between 135 and 590 pairs are currently nesting in the South Bay, but within the Palo Alto SBC count circle there has been a decline of 2.6% a year over the last two decades.

During the atlas period, atlasers found the greatest number of Black-necked Stilts breeding in salt evaporation ponds and other impoundments along the edge of San Francisco Bay. Nesting birds or precocial young were observed at the Ravenswood Point salt ponds, the Palo Alto Flood Control Basin, Charleston Slough, Mountain View Forebay, Crittenden Marsh, salt ponds bordering the cities of Mountain View, Sunnyvale, and San Jose, the Sunnyvale Water Pollution Control Plant oxidation ponds, drying ponds at the San Jose-Santa Clara Water Pollution Control Plant, various small wetlands near Alviso, and the Waterbird Management Area along Coyote Creek below Highway 237. Inland, precocial young were found at borrow ponds near Ogier Avenue in Morgan Hill and at San Felipe Lake south of Gilroy. Subsequent to the atlas period, breeding at additional locations was obtained in flooded fields south of Tulare Hill near Coyote (the old Laguna Seca) in 1997 and 1998, southeast of the Ogier Avenue borrow ponds in 1996 and 1997, along Middle Avenue in Morgan Hill in 1998, and at the South County WasteWater Authority treatment ponds in Gilroy in 1998 to 2005 (mult. obs., county notebooks). Habitat use along the edge of the Bay ranged from low-to-moderate-salinity evaporator ponds to freshwater and brackish wetlands. Black-necked Stilts often nested within or adjacent to American Avocet nesting colonies. Inland, breeding birds used freshwater impoundments, flooded fields, and lakes, and nested singly or in loose colonies without avocets.

In the South Bay, Black-necked Stilts are much less common in summer than in winter (Palo Alto CBC and SBC data). Presumably, some of the wintering birds remain to breed, but because this species shows little site fidelity (Robinson et al. 1999) it is unclear whether the local breeding birds are resident or not. The earliest evidence of breeding during the atlas period was a bird on a nest on 23 Apr, and the latest was fledged young observed on 10 Aug. After the atlas period, an incubating bird was recorded on 16 Apr 1994, and precocial young were noted on 2 Sep 1997 (Michael M. Rogers, pers. comm.).

Black-necked Stilts are closely related to American Avocets, and both are commonly found along the edge of the South Bay. Stilts tend to use freshwater or brackish wetlands, particularly where there is some emergent vegetation (Hamilton 1975, Robinson et al. 1999, Rintoul et al. 2003). Avocets are less often found in these habitats and show a preference for saline or alkaline ponds with little vegetation and more expansive views. The two species show slightly different foraging strategies, which may explain these general habitat preferences, but prey are so abundant in the South Bay salt ponds that niche foraging specializations do not offer a significant advantage (Hamilton 1975).

William G. Bousman

BLACK-NECKED STILT

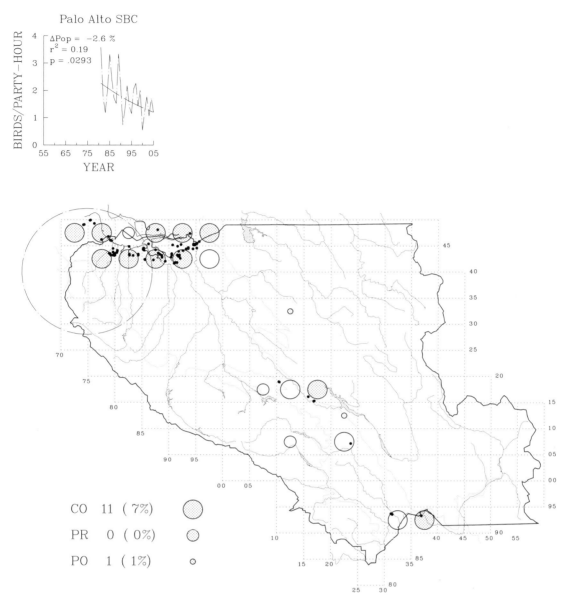

Palo Alto SBC

ΔPop = -2.6 %
r^2 = 0.19
p = .0293

BIRDS/PARTY-HOUR

YEAR

CO   11 (7%)
PR   0 (0%)
PO   1 (1%)

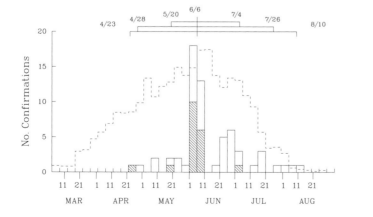

Atlas (1987–1993), n = 71

No. Confirmations

4/23   4/28   5/20   6/6   7/4   7/26   8/10

MAR   APR   MAY   JUN   JUL   AUG

American Avocet
Recurvirostra americana

This elegant shorebird has brought its classic good looks to our modified South Bay habitats. The American Avocet breeds in Canada from southern British Columbia across to western Ontario, south through the United States to California and Texas, and into Mexico (AOU 1998). In California, breeding birds are found most commonly around the lakes in the northeast, at shallow freshwater ponds in the Central Valley, and at salt evaporator ponds in the San Francisco Bay area (Small 1994). In Santa Clara County, the American Avocet is a common nesting species along the edge of the South Bay.

At the end of the nineteenth century, the American Avocet was a common summer resident in California, occurring inland on the Modoc Plateau, in the Central Valley, and in the southern coastal district (Grinnell 1902, Grinnell 1915). In the San Francisco Bay area it was considered at best an irregularly common visitor in the fall and winter, mostly in the South Bay (Grinnell and Wythe 1927). The collection of a downy young in Alvarado, Alameda County, by Ralph E. Ellis, Jr. on 11 May 1926 (MVZ #145184) was the first breeding evidence in the Bay area. Subsequently, Emerson A. Stoner found two nests on 12 May 1934 at a gun club on Island No. 1 on the border between Napa and Solano counties. Unaware of the previous Alameda County specimen, Stoner considered these records to be the earliest evidence of breeding in the San Francisco Bay area (Stoner 1937). Evidence of the first nesting in Santa Clara County was multiple avocet young found by E. W. Martin in June 1937 near the old Palo Alto Sports Club (Martin 1939), now contained within the Palo Alto Flood Control Basin. Grinnell and Miller (1944) considered the avocet to be only an occasional breeder in the San Francisco Bay area at the time they prepared their manuscript. By the late 1940s, however, breeding birds were found more regularly, from Alviso to the Dumbarton Narrows, upwards of 25 to 50 pairs observed in some years (*Audubon Field Notes* 1947–48, *Bull. Santa Clara Valley Audubon Soc.* 1947–49, Sibley 1952). Gill (1977), in his study of breeding birds of the South Bay, found 160 nests in his study area and estimated a total of 1,800 breeding pairs in the South Bay. Recent surveys in the South Bay (Rintoul et al. 2003) estimated a breeding population of between 440 and 1,380 pairs.

The vast majority of breeding American Avocets found during the atlas period were in salt evaporator ponds and other impoundments along the South Bay. The only record away from the Bay edge was of a single family with precocial young along the shore of San Felipe Lake, San Benito County. Following the atlas period, avocets were found nesting inland at the South County WasteWater Regional Authority treatment ponds in Gilroy as well as at San Felipe Lake (mult. obs., PADB). Avocets bred in many of the same locations as Black-necked Stilts, that is, in freshwater or brackish ponds. Relative to stilts, however, they favored moderately saline salt ponds devoid of vegetation. In these habitats, avocets often nested colonially, sometimes intermixed with nesting stilts. Atlasers found avocet nests or precocial young at the Ravenswood Point salt ponds, the Palo Alto Flood Control Basin, Charleston Slough, Mountain View Forebay, Crittenden Marsh, salt ponds bordering the cities of Mountain View, Sunnyvale, and San Jose, the New Chicago Marsh, drying ponds at the San Jose-Santa Clara Water Pollution Control Plant, and the Waterbird Management Area along Coyote Creek below Highway 237.

Although American Avocets winter in large numbers in the South Bay, fewer are found during the nesting season. As with stilts, it is unclear whether our breeding birds are year-round residents. The earliest breeding evidence observed during the atlas period was a nest with eggs and a bird on a nest, both on 29 Mar. Precocial young observed on 7 Aug were the latest evidence. Following the atlas period, a bird was seen on a nest on 26 Mar 2005 (Michael M. Rogers, Michael J. Mammoser, PADB) and precocial young were found on 15 Aug 2003 (Michael M. Rogers, pers. comm.), slightly extending the known breeding period here.

The status of both Black-necked Stilts and American Avocets has undergone significant changes in California in the twentieth century. Formerly, these two recurvirostrids were uncommon or irregularly common nonbreeding visitants to the South Bay during the summer and fall (Grinnell and Wythe 1927), whereas today both are common breeding species. It is likely that the establishment of local breeding populations has been, at least in part, a consequence of the construction of salt evaporator ponds in what had been San Francisco Bay marshes. This change has furnished the food resources needed by these species. The salt ponds in the East Bay, started in the 1850s, had replaced substantial portions of the original salt marsh by the end of the nineteenth century (Ver Planck 1958), but it was not until the middle of the twentieth century that these two species became firmly established as breeders in the San Francisco Bay estuary. At the time of salt pond construction in the Bay area, the wetlands of the Central Valley were being drained for agriculture, yielding a substantial loss of the seasonal wetlands historically used by stilts and avocets. Settlement of these two species in the Bay area may thus have as much to do with loss of historical wetlands as with the gain of salt evaporation ponds (Shuford 1993m, Robinson et al. 1997, Robinson et al. 1999).

William G. Bousman

206

AMERICAN AVOCET

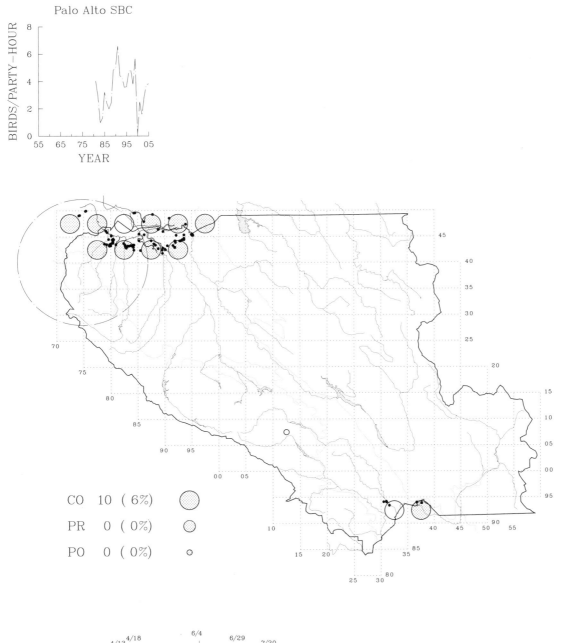

Palo Alto SBC

CO 10 (6%)
PR 0 (0%)
PO 0 (0%)

Atlas (1987–1993), n = 96

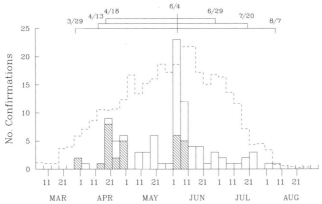

Spotted Sandpiper
Actitis macularius

Well-camouflaged in its preferred gravel-strewn nesting habitat, the Spotted Sandpiper might easily be overlooked but for its distinctive call and incessant bobbing behavior. Among shorebirds, this sandpiper is second only to the Killdeer in the extent of its North American breeding range. Spotted Sandpipers nest along rivers and lake shores throughout the continent north of the southern tier of the United States, most of them wintering in Mexico and Central America (Oring et al. 1997). In California, this species' strongholds are the Sierra Nevada and the mountainous regions of the northern part of the state. The Spotted Sandpiper is an uncommon and local breeder at scattered locations elsewhere in northern and southern California. In the southern part of the state, it breeds primarily west of the Southern Coast Range (Small 1994). In Santa Clara County, the Spotted Sandpiper is an uncommon spring and fall migrant along freshwater streams and lake shores, occasionally also occurring in tidal areas and on salt ponds. Relatively few individuals are present in the county during winter or summer, although this species has recently been found breeding here in small numbers.

Historically, the Spotted Sandpiper was not known to nest in the South Bay. Grinnell (1902) stated that breeding in California was confined to the Sierra Nevada, apparently unaware of an egg set collected 21 May 1899 at Skaggs Spring, Sonoma County, by Milton S. Ray (MVZ #8243). As of 1927, there were no known records of breeding closer to the Bay area than the Russian River in Sonoma County (Grinnell and Wythe 1927). Grinnell and Miller (1944) reaffirmed the breeding range of this species in California as including primarily northern and mountainous areas, with no known breeding in coastal areas south of Sonoma County. An adult with young near Santa Cruz in 1955 (*Audubon Field Notes 9*:398 1955) provided the first breeding confirmation for the central California coast, and over the next three decades Spotted Sandpipers were found nesting in small numbers in several counties along the central coast and in the San Francisco Bay area (*Audubon Field Notes 24*:713 1970, *Am. Birds 25*:901 1971, *32*:1204 1978, Bailey 1993b, Shuford 1993n). During this period, Spotted Sandpipers were occasionally recorded in Santa Clara County in summer as well. It was not clear, however, whether these birds were breeders, oversummering nonbreeders, or migrants, since the spring and fall migrations of this species overlap to some extent (Shuford 1993n).

Prior to the atlas period, the strongest evidence of breeding by Spotted Sandpipers in Santa Clara County consisted of a pair engaged in courtship along the Pajaro River near Sargent on 26 May 1983 (William G. Bousman, pers. comm.).

During the atlas period, Spotted Sandpipers were confirmed breeding in four atlas blocks, and potentially breeding birds were recorded in 11 additional blocks. On 13 Jun 1989, an adult on a nest at Anderson Reservoir represented the first confirmed breeding record in the county. This nest was along the Coyote Creek channel where it passed through the dried-out bed of the reservoir near the Cochrane Bridge. The adult there was accompanied by precocial young on 28 and 29 Jun. Atlasers also found precocial young on 24 Jul 1989, along the Pajaro River near Sargent, and on 27 Jul 1991, along Arroyo Hondo above Calaveras Reservoir. On 4 Jul 1993, an active nest was found on the rocky banks of Chesbro Reservoir. After the atlas period, two broods were seen on small gravel islands at the Ogier Avenue Ponds on 9 Jul 1996, and two deep cup nests, each with a single egg, were found hidden within a bed of clover on an island in these ponds on 23 May 1997 (pers. obs.). Additional postatlas breeding records were of an adult with one young at the upper end of Coyote Reservoir on 16 Jun 2002 (Michael M. Rogers, county notebooks), three adults with one young at San Felipe Lake, in a San Benito County edge block, on 29 Jun 2002 (Michael M. Rogers and Mark Paxton, county notebooks), and an adult with one young at Almaden Lake, 7-16 Jul 2004 (pers. obs.). All of these breeding locations were along fairly broad, low-gradient streams or in the flat beds of lakes or ponds where the substrate consisted of gravel or cobble-sized stones. The elevations of these breeding confirmations ranged from 120 to 770 feet, although there may be ostensibly suitable breeding habitat at higher elevations in some parts of the Diablo Range.

During the atlas period, Spotted Sandpipers were recorded at a number of locations scattered throughout the county, but because of the possibility that migrants may occur in the county virtually throughout the breeding season (Shuford 1993n), it was difficult to distinguish such migrants from breeders in the absence of breeding evidence. Determining the status of the birds involved in these records was therefore problematical. Birds seen in June and July along the edge of the Bay (e.g., at the Palo Alto Flood Control Basin, the Sunnyvale and San Jose-Santa Clara Water Pollution Control Plants, and Coyote Creek below Highway 237) showed no evidence of breeding, and were in habitat presumed to be unsuitable for nesting. Such birds were assumed to have been migrants or nonbreeders, and these records were not mapped for atlas purposes. Given the presence of apparent nonbreeders in some areas during summer, the incidence and distribution of the "possible" and "probable" records should be interpreted with caution.

Stephen C. Rottenborn

SPOTTED SANDPIPER

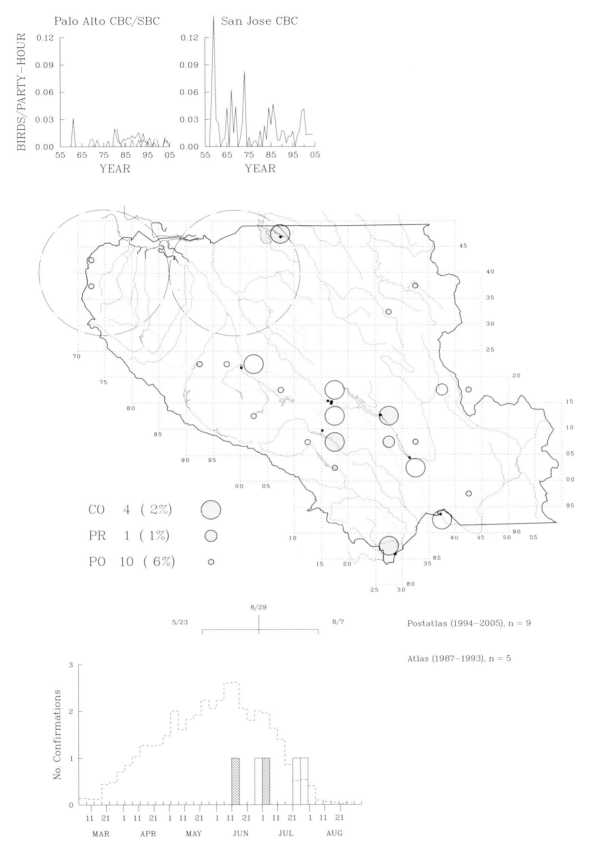

Palo Alto CBC/SBC

San Jose CBC

BIRDS/PARTY-HOUR

YEAR

YEAR

CO   4 (2%)

PR   1 (1%)

PO 10 (6%)

6/29

5/23   8/7

Postatlas (1994–2005), n = 9

Atlas (1987–1993), n = 5

No. Confirmations

11 21   1 11 21   1 11 21   1 11 21   1 11 21   1 11 21

MAR   APR   MAY   JUN   JUL   AUG

California Gull
Larus californicus

Nesting in America's northern prairies and wintering along the Pacific coast, this gull now resides in the South Bay, where it has taken advantage of garbage dumps and other human refuse sources. The California Gull breeds in the prairie provinces of Canada, south into Montana and the Dakotas, and in scattered locations in the arid west from Washington, Oregon, and California east to Colorado (Winkler 1996). In California, this eponymous gull breeds in suitable lakes and reservoirs east of the Cascades-Sierra axis from Siskiyou to Mono counties, in the San Francisco Bay area, and now at the Salton Sea (Shuford and Ryan 2000, Molina 2000). Always a common wintering species, the California Gull is now a common resident in Santa Clara County, breeding at a number of locations along the Bay.

The California Gull was considered a common-to-abundant winter visitant to the San Francisco Bay area at the beginning of the twentieth century, arriving at the end of August and departing by early May (Kobbé 1902, Grinnell and Wythe 1927). At that time, the California Gull nested in natural wetlands in California from Lower Klamath Lake, Siskiyou County, to Mono Lake, Mono County (Shuford and Ryan 2000). These gulls nested sporadically in the Central Valley as well, eggs having been collected along the Sacramento River, Sutter County, in 1910–11 (MVZ and WFVZ egg sets, Grinnell and Miller 1944, Shuford and Ryan 2000) and at Woodward Reservoir, Stanislaus County, in 1925 (Shuford and Ryan 2000). The first breeding of the California Gull in the San Francisco Bay area was detected in 1980 when 12 pairs were found nesting on a system of levees within salt evaporator ponds in the Knapp Tract, between Guadalupe and Alviso sloughs (Jones 1986). The colony here has grown continuously since 1980, 5,741 nests being recorded in 2000 (Shuford and Ryan 2000). Additional colonies have formed nearby in three different salt pond areas in Alameda County (Shuford and Ryan 2000) and at additional sites in Santa Clara County. Data from Shuford and Ryan (2000) show a growth rate in these South Bay colonies of 25.3% a year.

The South Bay nesting sites used by California Gulls in Santa Clara County are either on salt evaporator pond levees or small islands within the salt ponds. The Knapp Tract was originally surrounded by working evaporator ponds, but because these were no longer present after 1993, the area became more susceptible to predators (Shuford and Ryan 2000). Breeding was first noted on levees in the salt ponds northeast of Alviso Slough ("Alviso Pond") in 1984, and numbers there have been variable, the colony in fact abandoned in some years (Shuford and Ryan 2000). Expanding westward, a pair of California Gulls was found nesting on an islet in the northwestern corner of Salt Pond A1 in Mountain View in 1990. That colony has now expanded to well over 200 pairs of birds (pers. obs.). At a nesting colony found in Salt Pond B2 near Moffett Field (the former Jaegel Slough) in 1993, the numbers ranged from 6 to 328 during the late 1990s (Shuford and Ryan 2000). California Gulls were first seen nesting on small islands in Salt Pond A16 in Alviso on 21 Jul 2001 (Ann Verdi, PADB). The most recent expansion of these nesting colonies has been the establishment of breeding on islands in the outer Palo Alto Flood Control Basin noted on 7 Jun 2003 (Michael M. Rogers, county notebooks). It appears that all of the colonies described here were still occupied in 2005, and the numbers of gulls are continuing to increase.

During the atlas period, California Gulls were seen on nests as early as 2 May in the Knapp colony, and dependent fledglings were seen as late as 25 Jul on the island in Salt Pond A1. Subsequently, gulls were seen constructing nests in the Knapp colony as early as 26 Mar 2005, and an adult was seen on a nest as late as 15 Aug 2003 (both records: Michael M. Rogers, Michael J. Mammoser, PADB). Shuford and Ryan (2000) reported the phenology at two colonies in 1998: the dates of first egg-laying were from 18 Apr to 2 May at the Knapp colony and from 5 to 14 May at Salt Pond B2.

Currently, Mono Lake hosts 70-80% of the state's breeding population of California Gulls, and the San Francisco Bay colonies support an additional 11-14% (Shuford and Ryan 2000). The increasing number of breeding birds in the Bay area includes some by way of immigration, since the current rates of population increase cannot be the result of local nesting productivity alone (Shuford and Ryan 2000). In this area, the security of the current nest sites is dependent on both the management of salt evaporator ponds and the control of predation by the non-native red fox. The attractiveness of these nest sites is also tied closely to the abundance of food available at local garbage dumps (Jones 1986). The future of these colonies likely depends on restoration plans for San Francisco Bay as well as the persistence of bayside dumps.

William G. Bousman

CALIFORNIA GULL

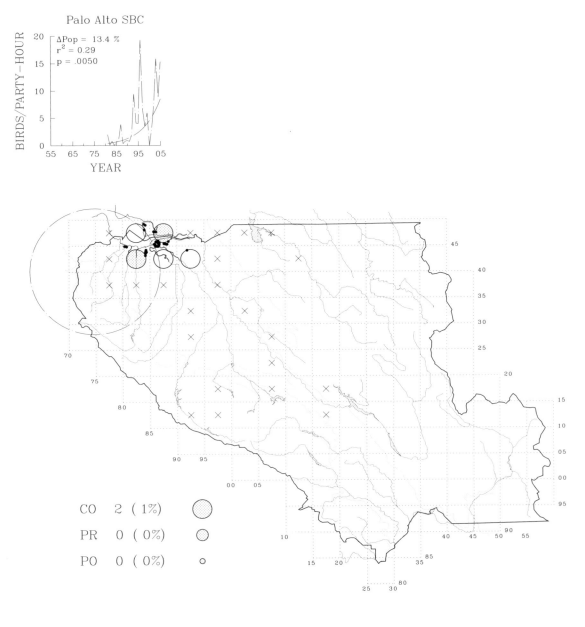

Palo Alto SBC

ΔPop = 13.4 %
r^2 = 0.29
p = .0050

BIRDS/PARTY-HOUR

YEAR

CO   2 (1%)
PR   0 (0%)
PO   0 (0%)

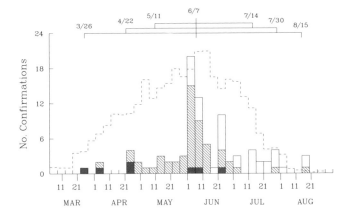

Combined (1987-2005), n = 91

No. Confirmations

MAR   APR   MAY   JUN   JUL   AUG

Western Gull
Larus occidentalis

The typical summer "sea gull" of the California coast, the Western Gull is a common breeding species on coastal islands and sea cliffs, but occasionally nests well inside San Francisco Bay on bridge piers, breakwaters, and dikes or islands of dredge spoil. The Western Gull breeds from coastal Washington south to west-central Baja California (Pierotti and Annett 1995). Two subspecies are recognized: *occidentalis*, which nests in Monterey County and areas farther north, and the darker-mantled *wymani*, found from San Luis Obispo County south (Roberson 2002). Western Gulls have long been considered uncommon winter visitors in Santa Clara County. In recent years, some birds have occasionally remained to nest.

Historically, the Western Gull was known as a common resident of the California coast, breeding on near-shore rocks and on cliffs along headlands. Grinnell and Wythe (1927) reported that in the San Francisco Bay area this species nested only on the Farallon Islands, but by midcentury it was found nesting on the piers of the San Francisco Bay Bridge as well (Grinnell and Miller 1944). Populations of this gull on the Farallons were intentionally reduced by commercial collectors of Common Murre eggs there at the end of the nineteenth century, but by 1959 these populations had largely recovered (Shuford 1993o).

A major expansion of breeding Western Gulls into San Francisco Bay was noted in the mid-1980s. In 1984, nesting Western Gulls were found at six sites in San Francisco, Alameda, and Contra Costa counties (*Am. Birds 38*:1058 1984). In 1986, birds were noted farther inland, at a nest in Benicia, Solano County (*Am. Birds 40*:1251 1986). Surveys in 1988 found 580-650 nests in 27 colonies within the Bay area (*Am. Birds 42*:1337 1988). At the same time, the number of wintering Western Gulls increased significantly in the South Bay. In the period through 1981, the number of Western Gulls tallied on the San Jose CBC averaged 59 birds, whereas in the Palo Alto count circle the average was 20 birds (first recorded there on the 1969 count). On the Palo Alto count, numbers increased to 1,253 in 1982 and further to 3,695 in 1985. For the San Jose circle, 1,120 birds were counted in 1985, and 2,154 in 1988.

The first observation of nesting by Western Gulls in Santa Clara County was in 1983, when four nesting pairs were found within the California Gull colony on the Knapp tract, an abandoned salt evaporator pond between the Alviso and Guadalupe sloughs (Klingmann 1983; Cheryl M. Strong, pers. comm.). During the atlas period, two observations of nesting Western Gulls were recorded. The first was of a nest with two eggs found on 2 Jun 1990, again within the gull colony on the Knapp tract. The second was of a pair of Western Gulls seen carrying sticks and copulating on 8 Jun 1991 in a recently established California Gull colony on a small islet in the northwestern corner of Salt Pond A1 in Mountain View. Following the atlas period, Western Gulls have continued to nest along the margins of the South Bay. One or two nesting pairs are found nearly every year on the Knapp tract (Michael M. Rogers, county notebooks) and on 13 May 1997, three different nests were found (Cheryl M. Strong, pers. comm.). Although this species has not been found in the small Salt Pond A1 California Gull colony again, a pair with nestlings was seen in the Salt Pond B2 colony on 1 Jun 2002 (Michael M. Rogers, county notebooks), and again on 7 Jun 2003 (Michael J. Mammoser, PADB).

The reasons for the recent breeding of Western Gulls in the South Bay are unclear. Three factors appear to be particularly important. First, there seems to be a close chronological correspondence between the initiation of nesting in the South Bay and the general San Francisco Bay expansion of the population discussed previously. Second, the current availability of human refuse as a food resource is in sharp contrast to the meager food availability in the South Bay prior to European settlement. Third, all Western Gull nests here have occurred within much larger California Gull colonies, which are a recent phenomenon. Although the causes of the San Francisco Bay expansion of the early 1980s are also unclear, it may have been related to the El Niño Southern Oscillation (ENSO) event that occurred in the winter and spring of 1982-83, an event that was particularly severe, or perhaps the weaker one of 1977-78. Spear (1988) has reported that dispersing immature Western Gulls tend to develop site fidelity in their first winter, and following a period of particularly poor ocean productivity, as happens during ENSO events, some of these gulls may come to rely on human refuse. Although ENSO events are of regular occurrence, their coinciding with refuse dumps and the newly established California Gull colonies may have provided the impetus for the scattered, irregular breeding that now occurs. In general, successfully nesting Western Gulls feed exclusively in productive oceanic habitats, whereas pairs foraging in less than optimal habitats, for example on human refuse, are unsuccessful (Pierotti and Annett 1995). The South Bay would appear to be a suboptimal habitat for the Western Gull, and it is worth noting that the number of summer birds recorded on the Palo Alto SBC has dropped by about 20% a year since the invasion of the 1980s.

William G. Bousman

WESTERN GULL

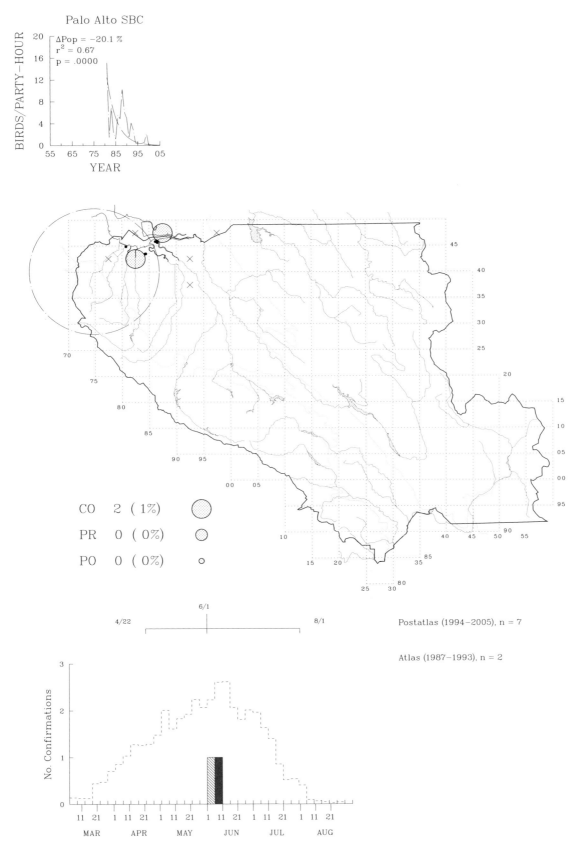

Palo Alto SBC

ΔPop = -20.1 %
r^2 = 0.67
p = .0000

BIRDS/PARTY–HOUR

YEAR

CO   2 (1%)
PR   0 (0%)
PO   0 (0%)

4/22   6/1   8/1

Postatlas (1994–2005), n = 7

Atlas (1987–1993), n = 2

No. Confirmations

MAR   APR   MAY   JUN   JUL   AUG

Caspian Tern
Hydroprogne caspia

This species, largest of the terns, breeds on every continent except Antarctica. In North America, Caspian Terns nest in scattered locations on the Pacific, Atlantic, and Gulf coasts, on lakes and marshes in the western interior, in the prairie provinces of Canada, and around the Great Lakes (Cuthbert and Wires 1999). On the west coast of North America they breed in scattered locations from Alaska south to Sinaloa, Mexico. In California, colonies occur sparingly along the coast from Humboldt to San Diego counties, at the Salton Sea, in the Central Valley from Glenn to Kings counties, and in the wetlands of northeastern California (Small 1994). Caspian Terns are fairly common in Santa Clara County in the summer, nesting in the South Bay and foraging at interior lakes. Only in recent years, however, have they actually nested within the county.

At the end of the nineteenth century, Caspian Terns were considered rare winter visitors or migrants in California (Grinnell 1902, Kobbé 1902, Grinnell 1915). They were first recorded nesting in northeastern California in 1899 and in the Sacramento Valley in 1911 (Gill and Mewaldt 1983). The first colony in the San Francisco Bay area was established by 1916 at the eastern end of the Dumbarton Bridge, Alameda County (De Groot 1931, Grinnell and Miller 1944). A second colony in the Redwood City marshes apparently existed as early as 1923 (Grinnell and Wythe 1927). Although Grinnell and Miller (1944) stated that there was no San Mateo County colony, egg set data at the Western Foundation of Vertebrate Zoology confirm that a colony was active there in the 1920s (Gill 1977). There has been a gradual increase in the number of Caspian Terns in the San Francisco Bay estuary since the first nesting records, an increase that parallels the upward trend in the Pacific Coast population (Gill and Mewaldt 1983, Ryan 2000a).

The only active Caspian Tern colony recorded during the atlas period was on a salt pond levee north of Drawbridge in Alameda County. This colony was just 700 meters north of the Santa Clara County line. Nesting birds were observed there in both 1988 and 1989. In the latter year, 230 nests were counted (L. Richard Mewaldt, pers. comm.), little changed from the 200

recorded at the same location by Gill (1977) in 1971. Following the atlas period, a single nesting pair was found in a Forster's Tern colony on a levee in the Ravenswood Point salt ponds, San Mateo County, on 1 Jun 1996 (Michael J. Mammoser, county notebooks). A nesting pair has been found at this location in at least two subsequent years (county notebooks). A colony found on 6 May 1997 on an island in Salt Pond A7 near Alviso (Thomas P. Ryan, pers. comm.) was the first breeding record for Santa Clara County, and that colony has remained active through 2005.

Caspian Terns may forage far from their breeding colonies. The presence of this tern away from its breeding colonies during the atlas and postatlas periods is indicated on the atlas map by the observed code (shown with an "×"). From these locations it can be seen that adults were found widely in the county during the breeding season, particularly around the larger reservoirs. In 1987 and 1988, records were kept of Caspian Terns flying from the Bay to the coast at Santa Cruz and back over the Santa Cruz Mountains at the Los Gatos gap (David L. Suddjian, pers. comm.). The majority of birds recorded flying south toward Monterey Bay were seen in the morning or around noon, whereas the majority of northbound birds were seen in late afternoon or evening. Whether or not this commute pattern is related to breeding birds is unclear, since only a small number of the northbound birds were observed carrying fish. Most terns at the nesting colonies feed on locally occurring prey species, although some birds forage at nearby reservoirs, as demonstrated by the finding of tagged trout remains from Del Valle and Coyote reservoirs in the Drawbridge colony in Alameda County in 1971 (Gill 1976).

Caspian Terns return to the South Bay between early March and mid-April, with a median arrival date of 2 Apr (county notebooks). The earliest visit to the Drawbridge colony during the atlas period was on 14 May, when the presence of precocial young indicated that nesting had started in early April. Subsequent to the atlas fieldwork, Caspian Terns were found incubating eggs as early as 6 May 1997 (Thomas P. Ryan, pers. comm.). The latest visit to the Drawbridge colony during the atlas period was on 7 Jun, at which time many nesting pairs were still incubating eggs. Following the atlas period, dependent young were seen in the Salt Pond A7 colony as late as 28 Aug 2004 (Michael M. Rogers, Michael J. Mammoser, PADB).

The Pacific Coast population of the Caspian Tern has expanded in range and grown in numbers in the last half century (Gill and Mewaldt 1983). This expansion may be related to a shift in breeding habitat from ephemeral wetlands in the interior to manmade islands and levees along the coast that provide secure nesting areas (Gill and Mewaldt 1983). Numbers of Caspian Terns in the San Francisco Bay estuary have also increased in recent decades, and there has been a northward shift of breeding colonies from the South Bay (Ryan 2000a). The cause of this shift is uncertain. Possible factors include disturbance related to levee maintenance or predation (Ryan 2000a) or nestling fatalities caused by mercury and PCB contamination (Cheryl M. Strong, pers. comm.).

William G. Bousman

CASPIAN TERN

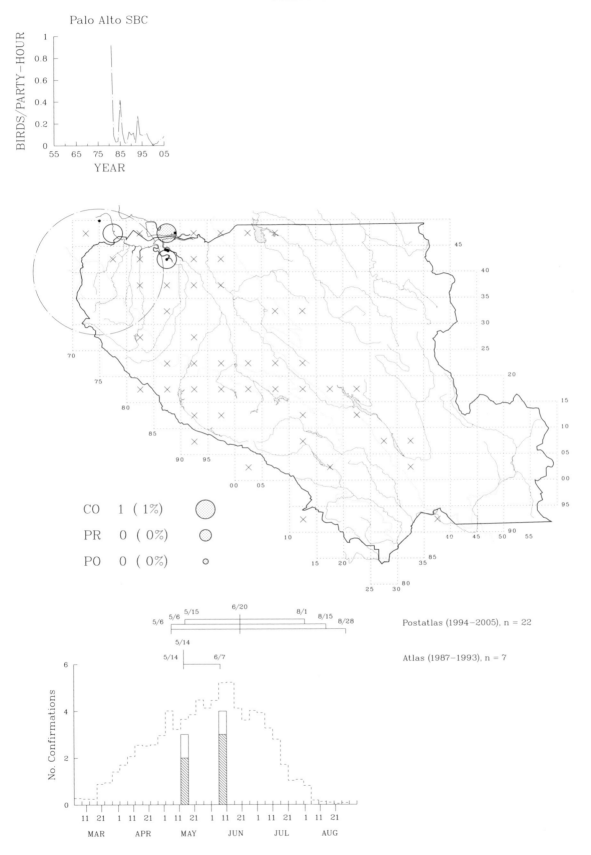

Palo Alto SBC

BIRDS/PARTY-HOUR

YEAR

CO   1   (1%)
PR   0   (0%)
PO   0   (0%)

Postatlas (1994–2005), n = 22

Atlas (1987–1993), n = 7

No. Confirmations

MAR   APR   MAY   JUN   JUL   AUG

S. Web

Forster's Tern
Sterna forsteri

A recent invader here, the Forster's Tern appears to have capitalized on manmade changes to the San Francisco Bay estuary. This tern breeds in the interior of North America across much of southern Canada and the northern United States. It also nests along the Pacific Coast from central California south through Baja California, on the Atlantic Coast from New York's Long Island to South Carolina, and on the Gulf Coast from Alabama to Tamaulipas, Mexico (AOU 1998). Large breeding colonies are found inland in northeastern California and from San Francisco Bay along the coast to San Diego Bay (Small 1994). The Forster's Tern is a common summer resident in Santa Clara County, but uncommon here in winter.

At the beginning of the twentieth century, the Forster's Tern was considered a common breeding species in interior California, but it was found on the coast only as a migrant (Grinnell 1902) or in winter (Kobbé 1902). Grinnell and Wythe (1927) considered this tern a common spring and fall migrant on San Francisco Bay, but noted only one summer record. Nesting occurred on the coast at Monterey by 1932, generally near the Salinas River mouth (MVZ and WFVZ egg sets). Although summer reports of multiple birds within San Francisco Bay near the San Mateo and Dumbarton bridges were more frequent in the 1930s (*Gull 16(9)* 1934, *20*:32 1938), Grinnell and Miller (1944) listed breeding colonies only from northeastern California, the San Joaquin Valley south to the former Buena Vista Lake, and along the coast at Monterey. The first Bay area nesting record was obtained in 1948, when Milton L. Seibert found 110 nests near the eastern end of the San Mateo Bridge in Alameda County (*Audubon Field Notes 2*:187 1948, Sibley 1952). Regular breeding was observed at the Alameda County colonies on the eastern approaches of both the San Mateo and Dumbarton bridges through the 1950s and 1960s (*Audubon Field Notes* records). Nesting in Santa Clara County, however, was not recorded until Gill (1977) observed 100 breeding pairs near the mouth of Alviso Slough on 23 Apr 1971. Gill's South Bay study area, which included portions of San Mateo, Santa Clara, and Alameda counties, supported approximately 1,200 pairs in 1971 and 2,000 pairs in 1972 (Gill 1977).

Atlasers found Forster's Terns nesting in or around salt ponds at the edge of the Bay. Nesting was observed in the north-west corner of Salt Pond 2 in San Mateo County, Charleston Slough, the southeast corner of Salt Pond A1, Salt Ponds B1 and B2, Salt Ponds A6, A7, and A8 (between Guadalupe and Alviso sloughs), the southeast corner of Salt Pond A16, and the southeast corner of Salt Pond A18. At the majority of these sites, the terns used islands of dredge spoil created during construction of the pond levees. In some cases, however, the islands used are high points remaining from the original salt marsh, such as those at Charleston Slough and in Salt Pond B2 (the former Jaegel Slough). Birds foraged extensively in the sloughs and salt ponds and other impoundments adjacent to their nesting colonies, and in San Francisco Bay. Forster's Terns were also seen inland at reservoirs and percolation ponds during the breeding season, as indicated by the "×" symbols on the map. It is unclear, however, whether these inland birds were nesting birds from the salt pond colonies, or nonbreeding visitors to these inland sites.

Although some Forster's Terns are found locally in winter, most birds move south in the fall and return in April. The earliest breeding confirmation was a nest with eggs on 14 May. The peak of nesting was in early June, and precocial young were still at nests as late as 22 Jul. Fledged young were seen being fed by adults at colonies as late as 27 Jul. Following the atlas period, precocial young were seen on an island in Salt Pond B1 as late as 25 Aug 2004 (Michael M. Rogers, PADB).

Gill's original nesting record, near the mouth of Alviso Slough, is close to the Knapp tract (Salt Pond A6), where terns nested during the atlas period. California Gulls started breeding in the Knapp tract in 1980, and as their colony expanded there was a general displacement of nesting terns away from this area. Salt Pond B2 held 834 nesting tern pairs in the summer of 1981 (Roy W. Lowe, county notebooks), but the expanding California Gull population first started using these islands in 1993 (Peter J. Metropulos, county notebooks), and by 1995 only 70 pairs of Forster's Terns were still nesting on the islands at the south end of the pond (Michael M. Rogers, pers. comm.). Farther west, the first report of nesting by terns in Charleston Slough was of two pairs in 1982 (pers. obs.). By 1994, over 200 pairs of terns were nesting here, possibly including some of the birds displaced from Salt Pond B2. Ryan (2000b) noted a general decline in nesting Forster's Terns in the South Bay in recent decades. Known causes of breeding failure here include encroachment by California Gulls, predation by the non-native red fox and feral cats, disturbance by levee maintenance, and fluctuating water levels in the salt ponds (Ryan 2000b). There is a continuing need to monitor these breeding colonies in the future, and to ensure that the management of the complicated South Bay estuary system supports the continued presence of this light and graceful tern.

William G. Bousman

FORSTER'S TERN

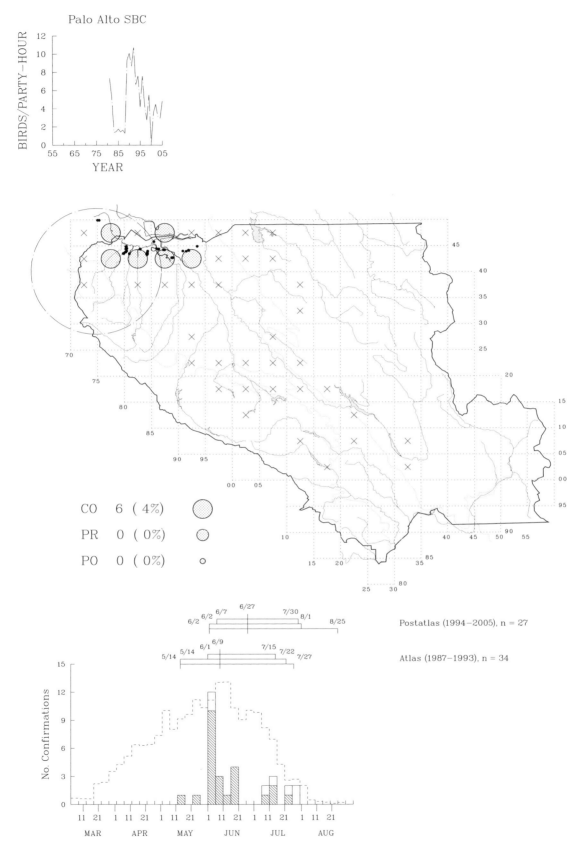

Palo Alto SBC

CO   6   (4%)

PR   0   (0%)

PO   0   (0%)

Postatlas (1994–2005), n = 27

Atlas (1987–1993), n = 34

217

©KLA-C 1986

Black Skimmer
Rynchops niger

The Black Skimmer is the picture of skill and grace as it flies just above the water's surface, its oversized mandible barely cleaving the water, ready to close on an unwary fish. Skimmers breed along the Pacific Coast from San Francisco Bay south to Chile, and on the Atlantic Coast from Massachusetts to northern Argentina (Gochfeld and Burger 1994, AOU 1998). Three subspecies are recognized, only the nominate *R. n. niger* occurring in North America (Gochfeld and Burger 1994). In California, major breeding colonies are located at the Salton Sea and along the coasts of San Diego and Orange counties (Collins and Garrett 1996). Since 1994, a few pairs have also nested along San Francisco Bay. In Santa Clara County, Black Skimmers have increased noticeably in the last decade, and are now considered uncommon residents along the edge of the South Bay.

The Black Skimmer was unknown in California until a single bird was seen at the mouth of the Santa Ana River in Orange County on 8 Sep 1962 (McCaskie and Suffel 1971). There were no subsequent observations until five birds were seen at the Salton Sea on 3 Jul 1968 (McCaskie and Suffel 1971). Subsequently, two to three Black Skimmers were found at the Salton Sea each year. In 1972, at least 19 birds were there, and five nests were discovered at the southern end (McCaskie et al. 1974). Southern California nesting colonies have since been established at San Diego Bay, San Diego County, in 1976; in the Bolsa Chica Ecological Reserve, Orange County, in 1985; in the Upper Newport Bay Ecological Reserve, Orange County, in 1986; at Anaheim Bay, Orange County, in 1987; and at Batiquitos Lagoon, San Diego County, in 1995 (Collins and Garrett 1996).

The first Black Skimmer record in northern California was of a single bird on 24 Jul 1971 at Bodega Bay, Sonoma County (*Am. Birds 25*:902 1971). Later that year, on 26 Aug, two adults were seen flying south past Pt. Pinos, Monterey County (Roberson 1985). The first observations from the south San Francisco Bay were made in 1978, when at least one skim-

mer was seen on three occasions: 29 Jun in the Palo Alto Flood Control Basin (*Avocet 25:7* 1978); 9 Jul, also in the Flood Control Basin (*Avocet 25:7* 1978); and 29 Jul at Alvarado, Alameda County (*Am. Birds 32*:1205 1978). From 1980 to 1984, there were multiple sightings of Black Skimmers in coastal Monterey, coinciding with apparent spring and fall migration (Roberson 1985), as well as observations from April to August in the South Bay (*Am. Birds 35* 1981, *Am. Birds 36* 1982). In the fall of 1984, a juvenile was seen with an adult at Elkhorn Slough in September, indicating successful breeding during the summer, possibly in the South Bay (Roberson 1985). Coastal birds continued to be found in Monterey County in the late 1980s and early 1990s, but there were few records in the South Bay during this period. Documentation of breeding finally occurred when two pairs were seen on 3 Jun 1994 at nest scrapes in Forster's Tern colonies, one on Salt Pond B2 in Santa Clara County, and the other at Hayward Regional Shoreline in Alameda County (Layne et al. 1996).

Following the original breeding records in 1994, Black Skimmers have nested in the South Bay each year, although they were not detected breeding in Santa Clara County in 1996–98. Nesting sites in recent years have included a salt pond west of Flood Slough, an island in Salt Pond 2 on Ravenswood Point, islands in the outer part of the Palo Alto Flood Control Basin, the small island in the southeast corner of Salt Pond A1, the eastern edge of Salt Pond A2W, an island in Salt Pond B1, islands in Salt Pond B2 north of Moffett Field (the original site), and islands in Salt Ponds A7, A8, and A16 in Alviso. As many as three downy young have been seen at some of these sites, but at best only one young bird has been raised to fledging from any of these nests. At nearly all of these sites, skimmers have nested within or adjacent to small colonies of Forster's Terns.

The initial invasion of the South Bay by Black Skimmers appears to have been by birds coming north from the southern California colonies in the spring and returning in the fall (Collins and Garrett 1996, *N. Am. Birds 54*:420 2000, *56*:482 2002). Interestingly, following the 1995 breeding season, a transition of sorts in the wintering behavior of South Bay skimmers was observed. Instead of returning to southern California in September, a few birds remained here into December. In subsequent years, Black Skimmers have remained in the South Bay through the winter, and recently this flock has numbered over 30 birds. There is no obvious explanation for the invasion of California by Black Skimmers over the last 40 years. It has been facilitated, in part, by the construction of salt ponds and the presence of Forster's Tern colonies, a prior invader. Whether the South Bay population will continue to grow, or as sometimes happens with invading species, collapse, is a story to be played out in ensuing years.

William G. Bousman

BLACK SKIMMER

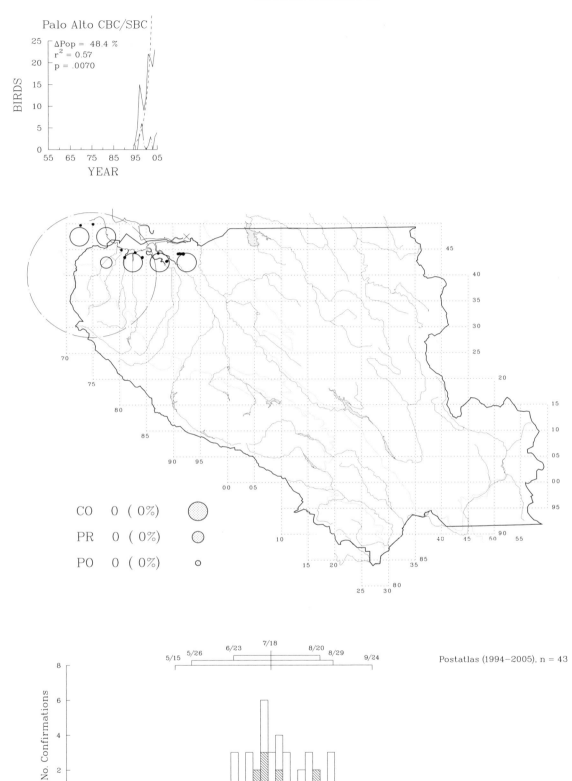

Palo Alto CBC/SBC

ΔPop = 48.4 %
r^2 = 0.57
p = .0070

BIRDS

YEAR

CO   0 (0%)
PR   0 (0%)
PO   0 (0%)

5/15   5/26   6/23   7/18   8/20   8/29   9/24

Postatlas (1994–2005), n = 43

No. Confirmations

MAR   APR   MAY   JUN   JUL   AUG   SEP

Rock Pigeon
Columba livia

If you feel an urge to see Rock Pigeons in Santa Clara County, you need only seek out human habitation, urban parks, or agricultural lands. Rock Pigeons are native to the Old World, but introduced populations in the Western Hemisphere are resident from coastal Alaska across southern Canada to Newfoundland, thence south through the United States, Mexico, Central America, and South America (Johnston 1992). Within this vast range this pigeon is rarely found far from human habitation. In California, it is encountered wherever there is human settlement or agriculture (Small 1994). Rock Pigeons (until recently known as Rock Doves) are common in Santa Clara County as well, mostly on the valley floor and in the nearby foothills.

Wild Rock Pigeons were once resident from England south through northern Africa and into southwestern Asia (Johnston 1992). Wild birds were domesticated 5,000 years ago, and now only a few remnant populations remain that have not interbred with domestic stock (Johnston 1992). Schorger (1952) described the introduction of domesticated Rock Pigeons to the eastern coast of North America early in the seventeenth century. French settlers brought them to Nova Scotia in 1606, and the English introduced them to Virginia in 1621 or 1622. In California, Spanish settlers probably introduced them in the late eighteenth or early nineteenth centuries. Guadalupe Vallejo (1890), writing about the early period of the missions and pueblos, noted that "At many of the Missions there were large flocks of tame pigeons. At the Mission San José the fathers' doves consumed a cental of wheat daily, besides what they gathered in the village. The doves were of many colors, and they made a beautiful appearance on the red tiles of the church and tops of the dark garden walls." A cental is equivalent to 100 pounds, indicating that there must have been a sizable population of domesticated Rock Pigeons around the mission. Presumably, feral populations developed in California soon after the introduction of domesticated pigeons, as they had in the east (Johnston 1992).

The history of Rock Pigeons in California is notable for an absence of information. None of the early state or regional checklists mentions this species (Grinnell 1902, Grinnell 1915, Grinnell and Wythe 1927). Grinnell and Miller (1944) included the Rock Pigeon, but placed it on a supplementary list. Apparently, few oologists collected the eggs of this species, for there is only one record for California at the Western Foundation of Vertebrate Zoology, an egg set found by Franklin J. Smith behind a bar in Eureka, Humboldt County, on 25 Nov 1907 (WFVZ #139081). Even the venerable National Audubon Society Christmas Bird Count did not allow the species to be listed until 1974. Analysis of the Palo Alto CBC data shows a significant increase of 2.8% per year since the species was added, but no significant trend is seen in data from the Palo Alto SBC or the San Jose CBC.

Atlasers confirmed Rock Pigeons breeding throughout the urban areas in the northern Santa Clara Valley, as well as in urban and agricultural areas in the southern reaches of the valley. Breeding confirmations were found from near sea level at Alviso to an elevation of 1,440 feet in a barn in the Hoover Valley on the San Felipe Ranch in the Diablo Range. Most breeding confirmations, however, were at low elevations, 90% of them below 300 feet. For their nest sites, Rock Pigeons selected flat areas with some shelter above, often in relatively confined spaces. Nest sites were on ledges or in crevices in buildings, in protected areas on bridges, in traffic lights and other highway light fixtures, and in barns or covered shelters on farms and ranches. Breeding confirmations were found in a few cases on ranches well away from the major urban areas, including two sites on the San Felipe Ranch northeast of Anderson Reservoir, and on the O'Connor Ranch on the North Fork of Pacheco Creek. Possible or observed evidence was also obtained at more remote locations in the Diablo Range. Although a few birds may nest in these areas, they may have been birds that had escaped from local aviaries, or they were racing or homing pigeons observed in transit. Few nests in natural sites have been reported in Santa Clara County. Two nests were found in a western sycamore in Gilroy in 1993, and they probably nest in crevices in some palm species. They may occasionally nest in natural sites in more remote areas, as indicated by a nest found on Brushy Peak northeast of Livermore in Alameda County on 20 Apr 1996 (*Field Notes 50*:329 1996). In this area of grasslands and sandstone outcrops, both Rock Pigeons and House Sparrows nested in crevices and solution holes in the outcrops near a small ranch. None of the ranch buildings appeared to have nest sites suitable for Rock Pigeons (Stephen C. Rottenborn, pers. comm.).

Rock Pigeons are able to nest throughout the year, because they feed their young on crop milk and regurgitated seeds, and hence the young are not dependent on insect protein for their growth and development (Johnston 1992). Although atlasers were generally active from March through August, breeding confirmations during the atlas period were also obtained in October, November, and December. Following the atlas period, additional confirmations were obtained in all the remaining months of the year.

William G. Bousman

ROCK PIGEON

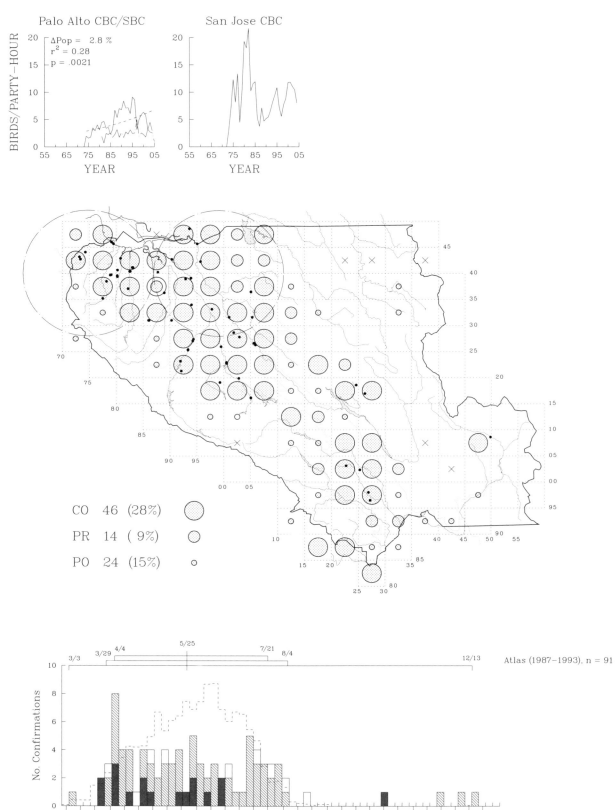

Palo Alto CBC/SBC

ΔPop = 2.8 %
r² = 0.28
p = .0021

San Jose CBC

BIRDS/PARTY-HOUR

YEAR

YEAR

CO 46 (28%)
PR 14 (9%)
PO 24 (15%)

Atlas (1987-1993), n = 91

No. Confirmations

3/3   3/29 4/4   5/25   7/21 8/4   12/13

1 11 21 1 11 21 1 11 21 1 11 21 1 11 21 1 11 21 1 11 21 1 11 21 1 11 21 1 11 21
   MAR   APR   MAY   JUN   JUL   AUG   SEP   OCT   NOV   DEC

Band-tailed Pigeon
Patagioenas fasciata

Highly variable in numbers from year to year, this nomadic pigeon sometimes settles and breeds in areas with a plentiful supply of oak mast, fruits, tender leaves, and buds. The Band-tailed Pigeon nests coastally from British Columbia south to California, and in higher mountain areas from Colorado to northern Argentina (Keppie and Braun 2000). There are approximately six subspecies, but the taxonomy of birds in Middle and South America is not well established. In North America, two subspecies have been described: *monilis* along the Pacific Coast and *fasciata* in the Rocky Mountains and portions of the Southwest. Band-taileds are found widely in California, in both the Upper Sonoran and Transition life zones, with some migratory or dispersive movements away from colder areas in the fall (Small 1994). In Santa Clara County this columbid is fairly common in the Santa Cruz Mountains, but fewer birds are found in the Diablo Range. In some winters, increased numbers of birds are found widely in the county.

At the end of the nineteenth century, the Band-tailed Pigeon was considered a common winter visitant or migrant in Santa Clara County, its numbers varying one year to the next (Price 1898a, Van Denburgh 1899b, Fisher 1902). Grinnell and Wythe (1927) noted that it was resident locally in the coastal belt and reported one nest from Marin County and two from San Mateo County. Atkinson (1899a) reported nesting Band-tailed Pigeons near San Jose in 1895 and 1898, but these records were, for unknown reasons, not included by Grinnell and Wythe. Sibley (1952) considered the Band-tailed to be a fairly common winter visitant but stated that "it is rarely known to nest in the South Bay area." No significant change in winter numbers has been observed on the San Jose and Palo Alto Christmas Bird Counts since the 1950s, although the great variability in these numbers makes the detection of trends difficult.

Atlasers found Band-tailed Pigeons nesting in 19 of the atlas blocks (12%), and birds occurring in a total of 73 blocks (44%). Most of the confirmations were in the Santa Cruz Mountains, where atlasers confirmed breeding in 14 blocks (38% of regional blocks). The remaining breeding confirmations were in the northern Diablo Range (3 blocks, 10%) and the southern Diablo Range (2 blocks, 5%). In the Santa Cruz Mountains, Band-taileds were generally found in extensive stands of dense conifer-dominated forests of coast redwood and Douglas fir mixed with broadleaved evergreens such as tan oak and madrone. They also used smaller patches of coniferous or broadleaved evergreen forest in more open areas, such as along shady drainages within areas of chaparral. Birds breeding in the Diablo Range were generally found in shaded canyons dominated by California bay and live oaks, often with water nearby. An exception was a nest in a live oak on a hot, dry, southwest slope above the Middle Fork of Coyote Creek at 2,400 feet. Breeding elevations in the county ranged from the nest just mentioned down to 500 feet in the Pescadero Creek drainage in the southern Santa Cruz Mountains.

When food resources are adequate, Band-tailed Pigeons exhibit an extended breeding season, with California nesting records for every month of the year (Bailey 1993c, Keppie and Braun 2000). During the atlas period, a nesting Band-tailed Pigeon found in Alum Rock Park on 21 Mar was the earliest breeding evidence observed. Historically, a completed nest was found on the valley floor on 11 Mar 1898 (Atkinson 1899a). The latest breeding record during the atlas period was of a nest with young found on 21 Jul along Summit Ridge south of Loma Prieta.

Judging from Breeding Bird Survey data from 1966 to 2004, the Band-tailed Pigeon has shown a significant decrease of 2.0% a year over its entire range (Keppie and Braun 2000, Sauer et al. 2005), but this decline is not significant for California populations, and the status of this species on the local level is uncertain. Historical accounts of this species' status in the Santa Cruz Mountains are sometimes contradictory. In his summary of land birds in Santa Cruz County, McGregor (1901) indicated that although birds were common in winter, they were rare in summer. W. E. Unglish of Gilroy wrote in 1913 that the species was no longer found locally and that birds were previously "slaughtered by the thousands" (Grinnell et al. 1918). Orr (1942), who studied breeding birds in the Big Basin area over a four-year period in the 1930s, considered them resident in the coast redwood-Douglas fir association and typically found flocks of 10 to 20 individuals. There is no evidence of a decline in the past half century in the Santa Cruz Mountains, but whether this apparent stability has resulted from the maturation of second-growth forest, reduced hunting pressure, or other reasons is unknown.

William G. Bousman

BAND-TAILED PIGEON

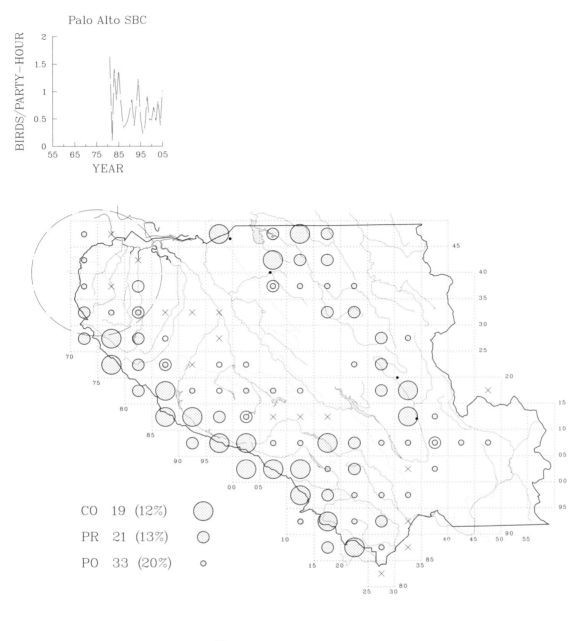

Palo Alto SBC

CO 19 (12%)
PR 21 (13%)
PO 33 (20%)

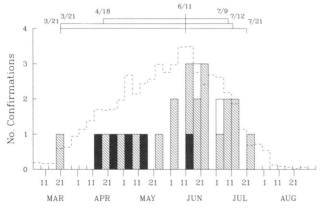

Atlas (1987–1993), n = 27

Mourning Dove
Zenaida macroura

The soft, mournful cooing of this ubiquitous dove is a sign of spring in our towns, parks, and woodlands. The Mourning Dove breeds from southern British Columbia across Canada to eastern Quebec and south throughout the United States and most of Mexico (Mirarchi and Baskett 1994). It is also found throughout the islands of the Caribbean and in isolated populations in Central America. Five subspecies are recognized, *Z. m. marginella* breeding throughout the western United States and most of Mexico (Mirarchi and Baskett 1994). This dove is a fairly common to abundant resident in much of California, with seasonal movements in the fall away from the northwest coast, montane areas, and the northern deserts (Small 1994). The Mourning Dove, a common nesting species in Santa Clara County, is resident at lower elevations but largely retreats from higher elevations in the winter.

The Mourning Dove was considered a common summer resident along the central California coast at the close of the nineteenth century, the first spring arrivals being noted in early April (Belding 1890). Price (1898a) considered it an uncommon species at Stanford in the summer, but Van Denburgh (1899b) judged it to be common on the west side of the valley, arriving at the end of March. Fisher (1902) referred to this dove as a summer visitant, but noted that it was occasionally seen in winter. Grinnell et al. (1918) considered the Mourning Dove to be an abundant breeder in the lowlands of California and described its winter range as extending from Santa Barbara south. Grinnell and Wythe (1927) also considered the Mourning Dove a summer resident and noted the nesting season as extending from 31 Mar to 11 Aug. In the late 1920s and the 1930s, local observers noted spring arrival and fall departure dates in the *Wren-Tit*, the newsletter of the Santa Clara Valley Audubon Society. Apparently, wintering birds were found more regularly in the 1940s, although Sibley (1952) described this dove as a common summer resident, but uncommon in the winter. Since the 1950s, analysis of Christmas Bird Count data shows that wintering

birds have increased by 2.1% per year in the San Jose count circle, but there has been no significant change in the Palo Alto count circle. Analysis of the Palo Alto SBC data shows a recent decline of 2.5% per year. A comparison of the winter and summer data from the Palo Alto count circle suggests that the species is now a year-round resident, at least on the valley floor.

One of our most common birds, Mourning Doves have nested throughout the county, some form of breeding evidence being observed in 163 blocks (99%). Confirmed breeding was recorded in 112 blocks (68%). Breeding birds were uniformly distributed over the county's elevations, from sea level at the Moffett Field golf course to 3,590 feet on a north ridge of Eylar Mountain. In more remote areas of the Diablo Range or the Santa Cruz Mountains, Mourning Doves nested in woodlands, forest openings, and chaparral edge. They generally chose smaller trees with an open framework for nesting, but in areas of extensive grasslands they sometimes nested on the ground. In agricultural areas they nested around barns and houses, in orchards, and in hedgerows. In suburban and urban areas, they nested in both native and non-native trees, on ledges over porches, in flower planters, and on many other manmade structures. The only habitats they avoided were dense, shady forests and marshlands.

Mourning Doves have an extended breeding season. During the atlas period, the earliest breeding evidence obtained was nest building on 2 Mar, the latest evidence fledglings observed on 29 Aug. Following the atlas period, a nest with eggs was found earlier, on 21 Jan 1999, and a dove was seen on a nest on 30 Sep 1996 (both Stephen C. Rottenborn, pers. comm.). Mourning Doves have a short nesting cycle, normally 30 to 34 days (Channing 1979, Mirarchi and Baskett 1994), and in some cases, breeding birds are able to raise six broods a year (Cowan 1952, Channing 1979). Locally, in 2002, pairs produced six broods from a nest on the porch of a house in Mountain View (Karen M. DeMello, pers. comm.) and five broods from a planter at a house in Los Gatos (Jean M. F. Dubois, pers. comm.).

As noted above, early observers considered the Mourning Dove to be a summer resident, although by 1950 this perception had changed. In recent years, at least in the Santa Clara Valley, the winter and summer numbers appear to be equal. At Turlock, in the Central Valley, Channing (1979) banded doves within the town boundaries as well as in the stubble fields of nearby agricultural areas. The birds banded in the town were resident and relatively sedentary, whereas the birds trapped on local fields included local residents, early migrants that moved south into Mexico, and wintering birds from northern breeding populations. Leopold and Dedon (1983) banded Mourning Doves in the Berkeley area in the 1970s. Only one of 42 recoveries, a bird later shot in Yuma, Arizona, was found away from the immediate area. On the basis of these records and Channing's experience in the Central Valley, they concluded that Mourning Doves in the Bay area are largely resident, whereas the major movement of migratory doves in fall and spring occurs inland. Most doves now found in Santa Clara County's lowlands are probably resident as well.

William G. Bousman

MOURNING DOVE

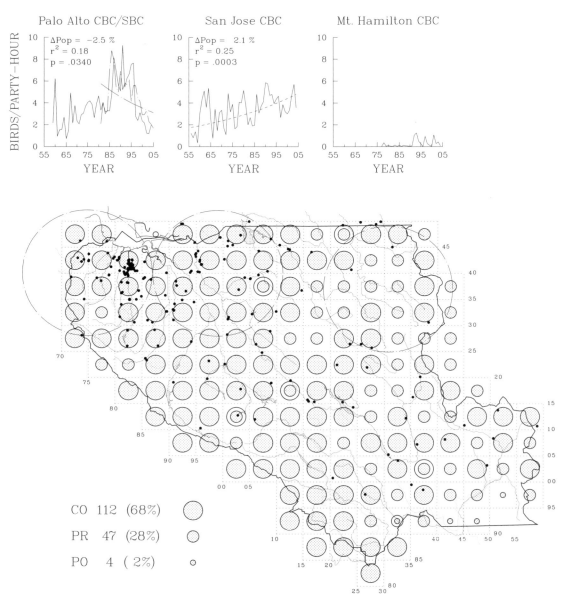

Palo Alto CBC/SBC

ΔPop = −2.5 %
r^2 = 0.18
p = .0340

San Jose CBC

ΔPop = 2.1 %
r^2 = 0.25
p = .0003

Mt. Hamilton CBC

BIRDS/PARTY−HOUR

YEAR

CO 112 (68%)
PR   47 (28%)
PO   4 (2%)

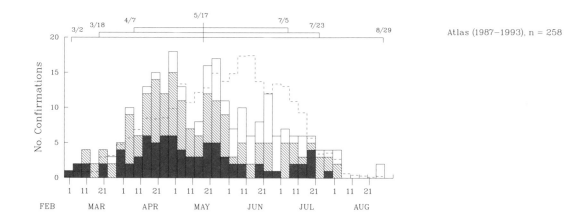

Atlas (1987−1993), n = 258

No. Confirmations

FEB   MAR   APR   MAY   JUN   JUL   AUG

Greater Roadrunner
Geococcyx californianus

Often glimpsed only briefly before disappearing into brushy cover, this strange ground cuckoo is one of our rarest residents. Greater Roadrunners are resident in the southwestern United States from northern California east to southeastern Missouri and south to Baja California, Sinaloa, and Veracruz in Mexico (AOU 1998). In California, the roadrunner is found from the foothills of the northern Sacramento Valley south along both sides of the Central Valley and in adjacent foothills and into the Lower Sonoran Life Zone in southern California, where it is most common (Small 1994). The Greater Roadrunner, rare in Santa Clara County, is found in portions of the Diablo Range and west of the valley floor in the foothills of the Santa Cruz Mountains.

A. J. Grayson, who lived in San Jose from 1853 to 1857 (Stone 1986), describes finding a nest with three young in the lower branches of a California buckeye east of San Jose in the Diablo Range (Bryant 1891), although he provided no specific location or date. Van Denburgh (1899b) described this species as "not very common" by the end of the nineteenth century, but he did find nests in both Los Gatos in 1888 and Palo Alto in 1892. Grinnell (1907), examining the roadrunner's distribution in California, indicated that it was found throughout the Bay area except for the immediate coast. Grinnell and Wythe (1927) judged it to be increasingly rare in the Bay area by the 1920s, but Sibley (1952) considered it to be a fairly common resident in the South Bay in arid, brushy areas. Although roadrunners were once regular along the eastern side of the Santa Cruz Mountains as far north as San Mateo (eggs collected 21 Apr 1907, MVZ #8698), birds are no longer found northwest of the Santa Teresa Hills. The most recent record northwest of the present limit is of a bird found near Stevens Creek Reservoir on 26 Jul 1947 (*Audubon Field Notes 1*:187 1947). Greater Roadrunners are occasionally observed on the San Jose and Mt. Hamilton CBCs, but the detection of this secretive bird has been too infrequent to support inferences of recent population trends.

No breeding confirmations were recorded during the atlas period. The highest level of breeding evidence obtained was of paired birds northwest of the Coyote Narrows in 1989, a male calling above Cochrane Bridge on repeated visits in 1990, and a

pair at the north end of San Antonio Valley in 1993. Following the atlas period, an agitated bird was seen on the Mt. Hamilton Road in 1994, a pair was seen at the south end of the San Antonio Valley in 1995, a bird was apparently building a sham nest in the hills above Alum Rock Park in 1996, and a pair was on Coyote Ridge north of the Kirby Canyon landfill in 2005. The atlas map for this species shows the locations of sightings of Greater Roadrunners from 1987 to 2005 with an "×." The pattern of sightings suggests the general distribution of this rare resident, although to an unknown extent this pattern may be a consequence of accessibility for birders, rather than the actual distribution of this species.

Birds have been found along the western slope of the Diablo Range from the Los Buellis Hills south to Cañada Road, with a gap in observations in the vicinity of Coyote Reservoir. In the eastern Diablo Range, birds have been found along Arroyo Mocho and Colorado Creek, in the San Antonio Valley, and along Arroyo Bayo, all areas in the eastern Alameda Creek watershed. Farther south there are observations in the drier portions of Henry Coe State Park. The species is still found in the Santa Teresa Hills and adjacent to the Almaden Valley, the only locations in the Santa Cruz Mountains where it persists. No birds were found in the southern Santa Cruz Mountains where this range drops to the Pajaro River, but roadrunners are still resident south of the Pajaro River in the Gabilan Hills, Monterey County (Roberson 1993g). Greater Roadrunners appear to use grassland, savanna, open chaparral, and brushy areas, and also require thicker shrubbery or small trees for nesting. Although they may be found along the edges of thicker chaparral stands, they were not detected in dense chaparral fields or in oak or foothill pine woodlands.

Five egg sets have been obtained in Santa Clara County: one March record (28 Mar 1934, Sibley 1952), one April record (16 Apr 1938, Sibley 1952), two May records (14 May 1892 and 31 May 1888, Van Denburgh 1899b), and one June record (3 Jun 1903, WFVZ #4562). The descending "coo-coo-coo" that male Greater Roadrunners give as part of their courtship has been reported from 22 Jan to 1 Aug (mult. obs., county notebooks).

The last century has seen a general contraction of the Greater Roadrunner's range in California (Grinnell 1907, Grinnell and Miller 1944, Small 1994). Although probably always rare in the Bay area, this species once bred in Sonoma County (Burridge 1995d), Marin County (eggs collected 21 Apr 1901, MVZ #8697), and San Mateo County (eggs collected 21 Apr 1907, MVZ #8698). It is no longer found in any of these counties. Greater Roadrunner still reside in the Diablo Range, but it is no longer found in the northern Santa Clara Valley or in the foothills of the Santa Cruz Mountains except perhaps in the Santa Teresa Hills. It appears that this sedentary, ground-dwelling cuckoo is unable to persist where urbanization or agriculture have substantially modified the arid, brushy habitat that it prefers (Small 1994, Hughes 1996).

William G. Bousman

GREATER ROADRUNNER

San Jose CBC

Mt. Hamilton CBC

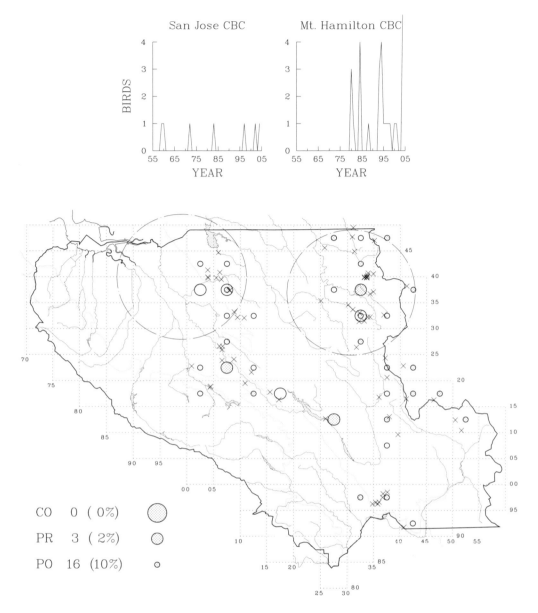

CO   0 (0%)

PR   3 (2%)

PO   16 (10%)

Barn Owl
Tyto alba

A raspy, ascending, unnerving screech at night is often the first sign of a Barn Owl's presence. The most widespread of all owls, this species is found in the Americas, Europe, Africa, southern Asia, and Australia, and on a number of the Pacific Islands (Marti 1992). In North America, Barn Owls are resident from southern British Columbia across the northern tier of states to southern Massachusetts and south throughout the United States, Mexico, and the Caribbean (Marti 1992). As many as 35 subspecies have been described over this owl's near-cosmopolitan range, but in North America only one of these subspecies, *T. a. pratincola*, is found (AOU 1957, Marti 1992). Barn Owls are uncommon to fairly common residents throughout most of California, except in the higher montane areas and the driest deserts (Small 1994). In Santa Clara County, Barn Owls are fairly common residents in lowland areas but are largely absent from heavily forested areas and higher elevations. In healthy riparian areas with adjacent fields for foraging, particularly south of the Coyote Narrows, they are locally common.

Barn Owls were found regularly in Santa Clara County by most of the early observers. The first recorded breeding confirmation was a nest with eggs found by A. L. Parkhurst in San Jose on 25 Jan 1885, which by 8 Feb contained hatched young (Belding 1890). Price (1898b) considered the species resident at Stanford University, and Van Denburgh (1899b) judged it to be common in Palo Alto and San Jose, but absent from Los Gatos. Fisher (1902) considered it to be a common resident in the Santa Clara Valley. Grinnell and Wythe (1927) reported Barn Owls to be common residents in the Bay area, though more numerous east of the Bay, and Sibley (1952) also considered them to be common residents in the South Bay. Little change is apparent in the number of Barn Owls reported on the Palo Alto and San Jose CBCs over the last 40 years, although incomplete and irregular nocturnal coverage on these counts makes the use of these data unreliable for establishing trends for this nocturnal species.

Atlasers found Barn Owls at lower elevations in the county wherever there were grasslands, woodlands with interspersed grasslands, or wetlands. During the atlas period, breeding owls were found from sea level, alongside the Bay, to an elevation of 1,120 feet in the San Felipe Valley east of Anderson Reservoir. Subsequently, on 30 Mar 1997, a nest with eggs was found in a barn in Halls Valley at an elevation of 1,470 feet (James Yurchenco, Amy Lauterbach, pers. comm.) and again in 2002 (David Cook, PADB). Barn Owls were most common on the valley floor where there were ample foraging opportunities in grasslands or agricultural areas, and available nesting cavities. They nested in nearby riparian trees, in outbuildings or old barns, or occasionally in cavities in embankments. They were also found in marshes, in adjacent seasonal wetlands, and in fields with ruderal growth. In such locations, the availability of nest sites was more critical, and birds responded favorably to the placement of nest boxes. Nesting Barn Owls were also found in suburban areas, where they were able to find suitable nest cavities in introduced palm trees or manmade structures. These birds apparently found suitable prey within urban parks and nearby open areas. Barn Owls also nested in foothill areas with a mixture of grasslands and open woodlands. In general, they were scarce or absent from higher elevations, even in locations with high-elevation grasslands and savannas. Although roosting birds were found in the San Antonio Valley at 2,100 feet during a number of summers, nesting evidence was never obtained there.

Barn Owls have an extended nesting period, and in central California may raise two broods (Marti 1992). During the atlas period, the earliest breeding evidence was birds on a nest in Palo Alto on 15 Apr, the latest a nest with young found on 12 Jul in the foothills of the southern Santa Cruz Mountains. Following the atlas period, a nest with young was found off San Felipe Road on 10 Jan 1999 (Karen Hoyt, pers. comm.), and an adult feeding young in Alviso on 30 Aug 1999 (Stephen C. Rottenborn, PADB) extended the nesting period. A nest of downy young found in Livermore, Alameda County, on 9 Sep 1974 (*Am. Birds 29*:115 1975) argues that local breeding may occur even later.

Research on Barn Owls in the San Francisco Bay area in the 1930s showed that nest boxes placed near roosting areas or barns were immediately used by the local owls in every case (Smith and Hopkins 1937). It appears that Barn Owls benefit from the use of nest boxes wherever prey populations are adequate (Marti 1992). That secure sites are necessary is evidenced by the predation on a nesting Barn Owl by a Red-tailed Hawk on the Stanford campus on 16 Apr 1994. The adult owl had laid its eggs in a recess in the Beckman Center, but the site was sufficiently open to the outside so that the hawk was able to fly in and seize the owl (Richard Stovel, pers. comm.).

William G. Bousman

BARN OWL

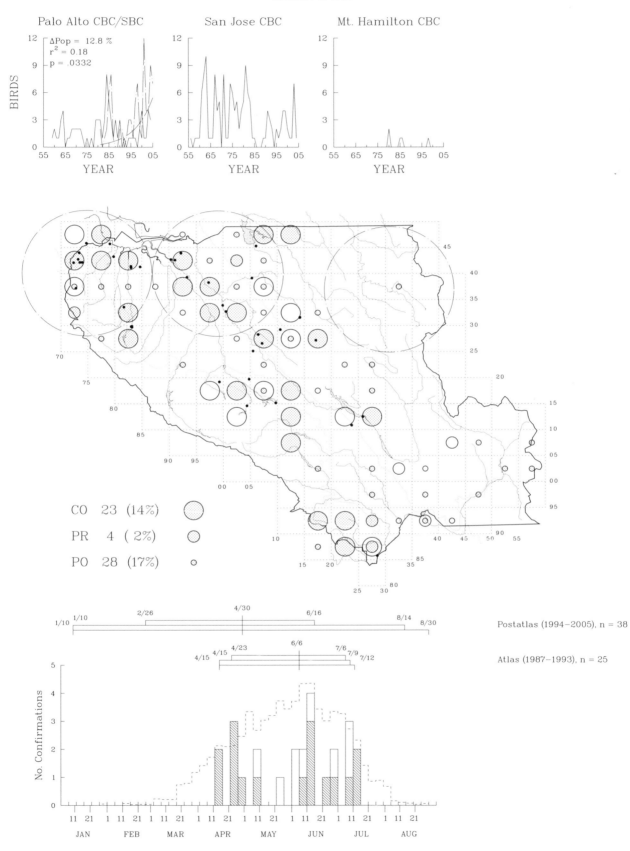

Palo Alto CBC/SBC

San Jose CBC

Mt. Hamilton CBC

ΔPop = 12.8 %
r² = 0.18
p = .0332

CO   23 (14%)

PR   4 (2%)

PO   28 (17%)

Postatlas (1994–2005), n = 38

Atlas (1987–1993), n = 25

229

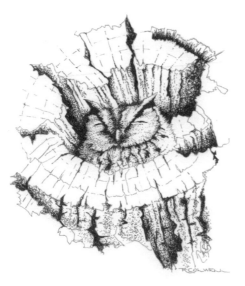

Western Screech-Owl
Megascops kennicottii

As night falls in the oak woodlands, the faint "bouncing ball" calls of the secretive Western Screech-Owl drift softly through the trees. Western Screech-Owls are found from southeastern Alaska, south along the Pacific Coast through Baja California, and east to parts of Colorado and Texas. Eleven subspecies are recognized, and *M. k. bendirei* and *M. k. quercinus* are described as occurring in Santa Clara County (Grinnell and Miller 1944). *M. k. bendirei* ranges from Oregon south to Monterey Bay, excluding the coastal strip in the northwest. *M. k. quercinus* occurs from the Sacramento Valley and the Monterey Bay area south to coastal Baja California. The gradation between *bendirei*, which occupies most of Santa Clara County, and *quercinus*, which is found only in the extreme southern end of the county, is gradual. In Santa Clara County the Western Screech-Owl is widespread, and is usually associated with oaks or mixed broadleaved evergreen forest where there are suitable nesting cavities. It is occasionally found in riparian woodlands along the valley floor.

Historically, the Western Screech-Owl has always been one of our most common owl species. Price (1898b) described this species as the most common owl found on the Stanford University campus and noted that "a few have taken up quarters in campus gymnasiums at times." Van Denburgh (1899b) listed the species as breeding abundantly in all parts of the county, and Grinnell and Wythe (1927) considered it a "common resident of more or less wooded districts throughout the region, showing preference for oak belts." Grinnell and Miller (1944) classified it as common and widespread, with screech-owl populations apparently increasing owing to the "opening-up of heavy forests." Sibley (1952) listed the species as a common resident in the South Bay in woodland areas, being found in oaks, riparian woodland, and urban areas having many trees.

The distribution of breeding Western Screech-Owls observed during the atlas period depended strongly upon the aural detection of this nocturnal species. During a study of owls at the Monte Bello Open Space Preserve in 1986, the writer found

that Western Screech-Owls called primarily during December, January, and February (Noble 1990). For this sedentary species, therefore, such calling provides evidence of possible or probable breeding, and many such records were obtained by atlasers early in the season. Evidence of confirmed breeding, on the other hand, was mostly obtained in July, when the distinctive juvenile begging calls were detected.

During the atlas period, extensive and systematic nocturnal sampling of the Western Screech-Owl was undertaken only in the Santa Cruz Mountains and in the northern Diablo Range. In these areas this species was found breeding in both broadleaved evergreen and deciduous woodlands and showed a decided preference for oaks. The southern parts of the Diablo Range received less concentrated nocturnal efforts and, consequently, yielded fewer confirmations, but the many possibles in this area are, in effect, proof of residency for this sedentary species. There is an almost complete absence of records of this owl in the Pacheco Creek drainage, due largely, it is believed, to the difficulty of night-time access to this area. There were few records on the Santa Clara Valley floor, but it is unclear whether this finding was a consequence of poor coverage or a lack of the necessary habitat. Once common on the Stanford University campus (Price 1898b), this species is largely absent there today. Curiously, this owl was found breeding along Coyote Creek in downtown San Jose after the atlas period, when downy young were observed outside a cavity in a cottonwood on 25 Jun 1995 (Stephen C. Rottenborn, pers. comm.).

The earliest confirmation of breeding by Western Screech-Owls was a bird on a nest on 5 May. The remaining 43 confirmations were of fledged young, most of them detected by their begging calls. These fledgling dates ranged from 15 May through 9 Aug, the month of July having the majority of confirmations. Recorded egg dates in Bent (1938d) range from 7 Mar through 5 Jun, which is consistent with the range of fledgling dates recorded during the atlas period.

The abundance of the Western Screech-Owl here is difficult to determine. The surveying of blocks during the winter months, when calling adults are most vocal, was often hampered by poor weather conditions. Moreover, the secretive nature of these owls makes their detection difficult. These difficulties are responsible for the wide disparity in CBC numbers of Western Screech-Owls from one year to the next. On the 1986 Palo Alto CBC, for example, 58 Western Screech-Owls were detected as a result of a concerted all-night effort by a small cadre of dedicated owlers. In other years, few if any screech-owls were found, owing to poor nocturnal coverage or less than adequate weather conditions.

Paul L. Noble

WESTERN SCREECH-OWL

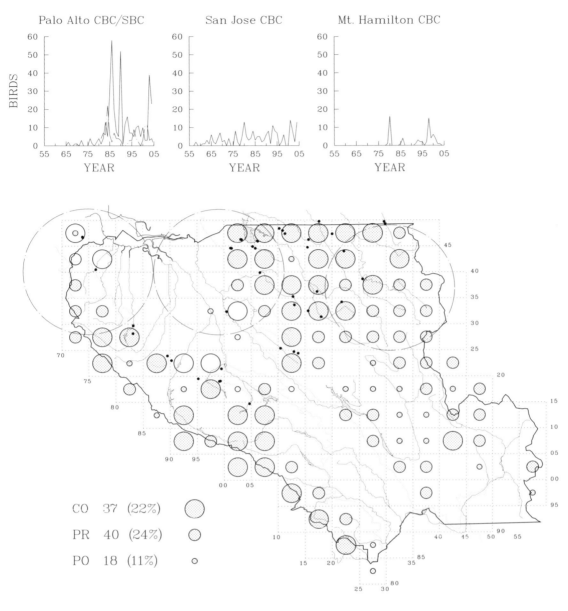

Palo Alto CBC/SBC

San Jose CBC

Mt. Hamilton CBC

CO   37   (22%)
PR   40   (24%)
PO   18   (11%)

Atlas (1987–1993), n = 44

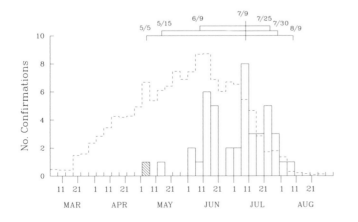

Great Horned Owl
Bubo virginianus

This master predator of the darkness is a generalist, using nearly all of Santa Clara County's habitats. The Great Horned Owl is found throughout North America, from the tundra edge in Alaska, east across arctic Canada and south through the United States and most of Mexico. Populations extend into Central and South America at higher elevations as far south as Tierra del Fuego (Houston et al. 1998). Of 16 subspecies, three are found in California: *B. v. saturatus* along the humid northwest coast, as far south as the coastal forests of San Mateo and Santa Cruz counties; *pacificus* over much of the state from the Oregon border south to northwest Baja California; and *pallescens* in the southeastern deserts and the arid portions of the San Joaquin Valley (Grinnell and Miller 1944, Houston et al. 1998). Within Santa Clara County, all except possibly a few on the western side can be referred to *pacificus* (Grinnell and Miller 1944). The Great Horned Owl is a common resident in Santa Clara County, excluding denser urban areas.

It seems likely that the Great Horned Owl has always been a common resident within Santa Clara County. Both Price (1898b) and Van Denburgh (1899b) considered it to be common in the Palo Alto area. Grinnell and Wythe (1927) considered this owl to occur in "fair numbers" in the San Francisco Bay region, whereas Sibley (1952) judged it to be common. Because nocturnal coverage is more difficult and less satisfactory, population trends based on CBC and SBC data for this species are less reliable than trends determined for diurnal species. There is no significant trend in the San Jose and Mt. Hamilton CBC data, but an examination of the Palo Alto CBC and SBC data for the last two decades suggests a declining population.

Atlasers found Great Horned Owls in 69% of all atlas blocks. This common owl is probably resident in all of the county's blocks, with the exception of blocks close to the Bay and the most densely populated areas of the northern Santa Clara Valley. The locations marked on the map, particularly in the Diablo Range, represent nocturnal coverage by atlasers, rather than the

true distribution of the Great Horned Owl, a problem typical of breeding bird atlases (Roberson 1993h). Atlasers found this owl in a wide variety of habitats, generally characterized by woodland or forest areas with suitable hunting perches and nearby open areas for foraging. Examples of the habitats used include broadleaved evergreen and coniferous forests, oak and foothill pine woodlands, and riparian corridors, all with grasslands or open ground nearby.

Great Horned Owls generally do not construct their own nests, but rely on the used nests of other species, snags or broken trees with suitable cavities, holes in cliffs or earthen banks, and, occasionally, manmade structures (Houston et al. 1998). Atlasers found this owl reusing nests of both Red-tailed and Red-shouldered hawks in a variety of oak woodlands, forests, and riparian areas. The Red-tailed Hawk nests, in particular, were often readily visible in dead trees or snags, and Great Horned Owls were easily observed in these cases. Nor does the Great Horned Owl repair or maintain its nest, and generally abandons stick nests after one season (Houston et al. 1998). Atlasers noted, however, that both Red-tailed and Red-shouldered hawks sometimes rebuilt former owl nests for their own use in subsequent seasons. In 1994, following the atlas period, Great Horned Owls used a Great Blue Heron nest in the San Antonio Valley (Michael J. Mammoser, pers. comm.; Michael M. Rogers, pers. comm.), and historically they have used Golden Eagle nests in Santa Clara County as well (Beck 1901). Great Horned Owls were also observed to use sheltered ledges or cavities in earthen banks and cliffs near suitable foraging habitat. Unlike borrowed stick nests, which tend to disintegrate with time, these cliff nests were sometimes used over multiyear periods.

Great Horned Owls are early nesters. The 106 California egg dates recorded by Bent span the period from 29 Jan to 17 Apr (Bent 1938e), a time of year when few atlasers were afield. Six local egg records (Sibley 1952, MVZ #5930) show a somewhat later span, from 9 Mar to 25 Apr. The earliest nesting evidence obtained during the atlas period was a Great Horned Owl on a used Red-shouldered Hawk's nest in Palo Alto's Arastradero Preserve on 11 Feb. The latest evidence of breeding was an injured fledgling brought to the Humane Society on 10 Aug. The majority of breeding confirmations (59%) were of dependent fledglings, often detected by their begging *screeek* call.

Great Horned Owls are often considered a nocturnal equivalent of the diurnal Red-tailed Hawk (Houston et al. 1998). The two species rely on a similar range of mammal prey and use similar habitats. In this regard, it is interesting to compare the breeding distributions of these two species. Both were found widely in the county, their distribution appearing to differ only within the urbanized northern Santa Clara Valley. Red-tailed Hawks were found in about 91% of these urban blocks, but Great Horned Owls only in 47%. Whether this disparity reflects reduced foraging opportunities for this nocturnal predator, a reduced tolerance to urbanization, or lack of adequate atlas coverage is an unanswered question.

William G. Bousman

GREAT HORNED OWL

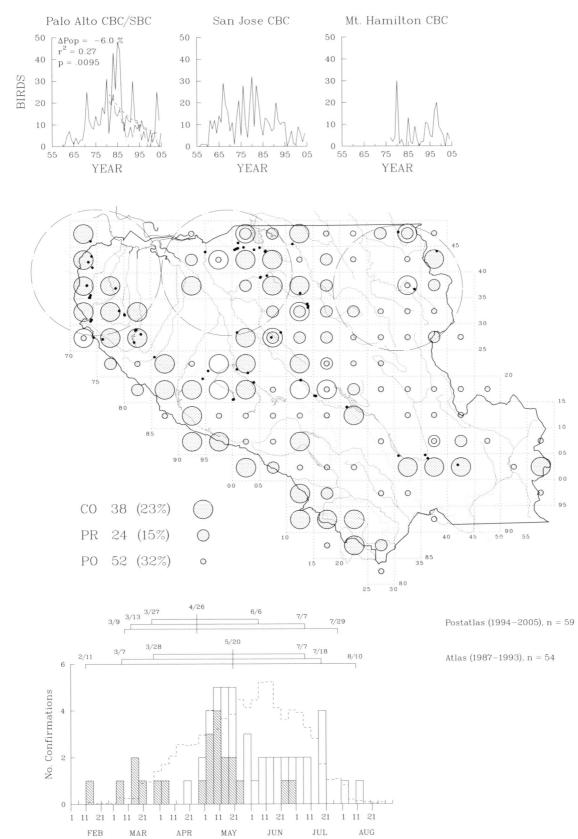

Palo Alto CBC/SBC

San Jose CBC

Mt. Hamilton CBC

ΔPop = −6.0 %
r² = 0.27
p = .0095

CO 38 (23%)

PR 24 (15%)

PO 52 (32%)

Postatlas (1994–2005), n = 59

Atlas (1987–1993), n = 54

233

Northern Pygmy-Owl
Glaucidium gnoma

Observers treasure sightings of this small, fierce diurnal owl, which is far more often heard than seen. The Northern Pygmy-Owl breeds from southeast Alaska, south through the mountains of the western United States into the highlands of Mexico, and thence to Guatemala (Holt and Peterson 2000). Currently, the taxonomy of this species is not fully resolved. But on the basis of the primary call, three groups have been described. The *californicum* group, whose call is a series of single notes, is the only one found north of extreme southeastern Arizona (Holt and Peterson 2000). Three of the four subspecies in the *californicum* group are found in California. Local birds are of the race *grinnelli*, which is found along the coast as far south as Monterey County (Grinnell and Miller 1944, Holt and Peterson 2000). The Northern Pygmy-Owl is apparently a rare-to-uncommon resident in Santa Clara County, found in mixed forests, woodlands, and riparian areas in the Santa Cruz Mountains and the Diablo Range.

The first mention of the Northern Pygmy-Owl locally is in Sclater's list of specimens collected by Thomas Bridges in the "valley of San José" prior to 1857 (Sclater 1857). Price (1898b) considered this species to be a permanent resident in the redwoods near Stanford University. Fisher (1902) stated that it was a "fairly common but inconspicuous resident of the Santa Cruz Mountains." Grinnell and Wythe (1927) reported records from the coastal counties near San Francisco Bay, but they did not characterize the owl's status. In their discussion of its state-wide distribution, Grinnell and Miller (1944) commented that if looked and listened for properly, it was found to be common "for an owl." Sibley (1952) described the pygmy-owl as a fairly common resident in the South Bay. Although the Northern Pygmy-Owl is primarily diurnal, most records on Christmas or Summer Bird Counts are of birds heard calling at dawn or dusk, but not seen. Analysis of the CBC and SBC data shows that calling pygmy-owls are found more often coastally than inland, but are often missed in each of the three counts.

Northern Pygmy-Owls were confirmed breeding in three blocks (2%) during the atlas period. Subsequently, breeding was confirmed in four additional blocks. Confirmed, probable, and possible breeding evidence was found in 26 blocks (16%) during the atlas period, and in a total of 38 blocks (23%) if the postatlas field observations are included. On the basis of the proportion of atlas blocks in which pygmy-owls were recorded, this species was found at the same frequency in both the Santa Cruz Mountains and the northern Diablo Range. But they were less often found in the southern portions of the Diablo Range, which are at the edge of their range (Grinnell and Miller 1944). Pygmy-owls were absent from the Santa Clara Valley floor. Nesting birds were often associated with edge habitats that offered some mixture of forest, woodland, and more open areas such as grasslands or chaparral. In most cases, these habitats also included a stream or creek as a major component. Within the Santa Cruz Mountains, pygmy-owls were found at the edges of Douglas fir forests, broadleaved oak woodlands, and chaparral with a riparian component. They were also observed in mixed broadleaved evergreen woodlands combined with chaparral, and in riparian forests with California bay, coast live oak, and bigleaf maple. In the Diablo Range, they were encountered in shady canyons with California bay and sometimes western sycamore. At higher elevations they were also observed in areas of deciduous oaks and foothill pines along intermittent streams that included a dense layer of manzanita and other shrubs.

The phenology of breeding Northern Pygmy-Owls is poorly defined by the atlas data. A fledgling observed on 11 Jul in the Diablo Range is the only confirmation shown on the phenology graphic, but adults carrying food were seen on 10 Jun and 1 Jul. Subsequent to the atlas period, two additional records of fledglings were obtained, one in Almaden Quicksilver County Park on 12 Jun 2000 (John Mariani, county notebooks) and one along Arroyo Mocho on 23 Jul 1994 (Michael M. Rogers, pers. comm.). Additional instances of carrying food include an adult carrying a mouse in Alum Rock Park on 17 Apr 1999 (Joe Morlan et al., county notebooks) and one with food along Coyote Creek above Coyote Reservoir on 4 May 2004 (Gina Barton, PADB). Historical records that help to define the range of dates for local breeding include an active pygmy-owl nest found in Alum Rock Park on 1 Jun 1970 (*Audubon Field Notes* 23:622 1969) and four fledglings seen in Alum Rock Park on 9 Aug 1950 (*Audubon Field Notes* 4:291 1950).

The actual status of the Northern Pygmy-Owl in Santa Clara County is difficult to assess. Unlike some of our nocturnal owls, pygmy-owls tend to call mostly in the twilight hours at dawn and dusk, and they call throughout the year (Noble 1990). In this sense, this crepuscular or diurnal owl should be more easily detected than other owls, such as the Northern Saw-whet Owl, which calls strictly at night and is seasonal in its vocalizations (Noble 1990). In some areas of the Santa Cruz Mountains, pygmy-owl territories appear quite large and are stable over time, and in such circumstances these owls are fairly common (David L. Suddjian, pers. comm.). But at other locations in apparently identical habitats, they can be variable in their presence or absent altogether. The precise habitat needs of this small predator are thus unclear, and much remains to be learned about its distribution and status in the county.

William G. Bousman

NORTHERN PYGMY-OWL

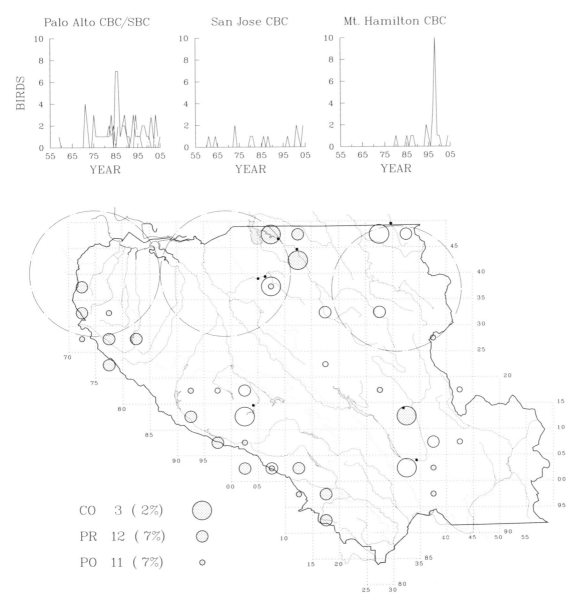

Palo Alto CBC/SBC

San Jose CBC

Mt. Hamilton CBC

CO   3 (2%)
PR 12 (7%)
PO 11 (7%)

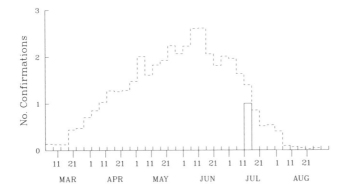

Atlas (1987–1993), n = 3

Burrowing Owl
Athene cunicularia

Originally a common resident of native grasslands on alluvial plains and sinks, this unique, underground-nesting owl has declined in numbers in California in the last 150 years because of habitat loss. It now nests solely in highly altered habitats, such as agricultural or suburban areas. The range of the western subspecies of the Burrowing Owl (*A. c. hypugaea*) extends from the Mississippi River west to the Pacific coast and from the prairie provinces of Canada south into northern Mexico. Throughout most of this range, these birds live in association with colonial rodents, especially ground squirrels and prairie dogs, appropriating burrows dug by the rodents. In Santa Clara County, the owls nest in burrows excavated by California ground squirrels. The native grasslands of the region have been eliminated, and Burrowing Owls now live on fields, airports, golf courses, and other open, short grasslands that offer squirrels and adequate foraging habitat, and freedom from human persecution (Trulio 1997).

At the turn of the twentieth century, the Burrowing Owl was recognized as a common bird of Santa Clara County (Price 1898b, Van Denburgh 1899b, Fisher 1902). Several decades later, Grinnell and Wythe (1927) found that the bird was still a "fairly common resident in the drier, unsettled interior parts of the region," being most abundant in Alameda, Contra Costa, and Santa Clara counties. Grinnell and Miller (1944) noted that Burrowing Owls were becoming scarce in more settled parts of the state, due in some measure to ground squirrel eradication. Since the 1950s there has been additional evidence of a decline in this species' population. The annual Christmas Bird Count (CBC) records from 1954 to 1986 have shown significant Burrowing Owl declines for California as a whole (James and Ethier 1989). Surveys in the last ten years, from Solano County south to Santa Clara County, indicate a loss of approximately 50% of these owls (DeSante et al. 1996). However, no significant population change has been noted for the CBCs in Santa Clara County.

During the atlas period, Burrowing Owls were found in 20 atlas blocks, and breeding was confirmed in 12 of these blocks. All of the breeding records were obtained from locations on the alluvial soils of the valley floor north of the Coyote Narrows. The majority of these records were in a triangle defined by Highway 101, Interstate 880, and the San Francisco Bay. The highest elevation recorded for breeding was 180 feet, but 80% of all confirmations were below 30 feet. The atlas results and those of other researchers (Buchanan 1996, Trulio 1997) found owls

concentrated in the county's remaining open spaces, particularly airports, public parks, vacant lots, and golf courses. Detailed studies of Burrowing Owls independent of the atlas (Buchanan 1996, Trulio 1997) have identified approximately 11 colonies of five pairs or more in Santa Clara County, the largest of which was at Moffett Federal Airfield (Trulio 1994). These results generally show the same distribution of owls as that recorded in the atlas. Subsequent to the atlas fieldwork, breeding birds were found in additional locations farther south. Owls were found in Morgan Hill on alluvial soils in 1995 (pers. obs.) and were confirmed breeding there in 1998 and 1999 (Michael M. Rogers, Stephen C. Rottenborn, PADB). South of the Pajaro River, in northern San Benito County, breeding was confirmed in 1997 (Stephen C. Rottenborn, PADB). In 2004, nesting birds were found less than a kilometer north of the San Benito County line near Highway 152 and Bloomfield Road (Stephen C. Rottenborn, county notebooks).

Burrowing Owls are year-round residents of the Santa Clara Valley, although some migration and/or dispersal occurs in the nonbreeding season. Atlasers found two families with nonflying young at nest burrows as early as 30 Mar near Lake Cunningham and still dependent, fledged young as late as 28 Aug at Moffett Field. This phenology extends the range of egg dates cited by Bent (1938f) of 41 sets collected between 1 Apr and 17 Jun in California. These owls produce one clutch per year and can lay up to 11 eggs, the largest clutch size of any raptor species. In nesting burrows studied in Santa Clara County, however, only two to four chicks generally fledge (Trulio 1994).

Since 1974, the Burrowing Owl has been listed as a Species of Special Concern by the California Department of Fish and Game. The central California population continues to decline as agricultural lands and open fields are converted to urban uses incompatible with use by these owls. Other factors in the decline are ground squirrel poisoning, disking or plowing of fields, and predation by the non-native red fox. In Santa Clara County, efforts have been made to preserve habitat for this owl through exerting public pressure on agencies responsible for land-use decisions, but these efforts have been unsuccessful, and owl habitat continues to be lost. Research and preservation efforts must focus on developing a regional Burrowing Owl conservation plan that will stabilize the population by protecting its preferred habitats.

Lynne A. Trulio

BURROWING OWL

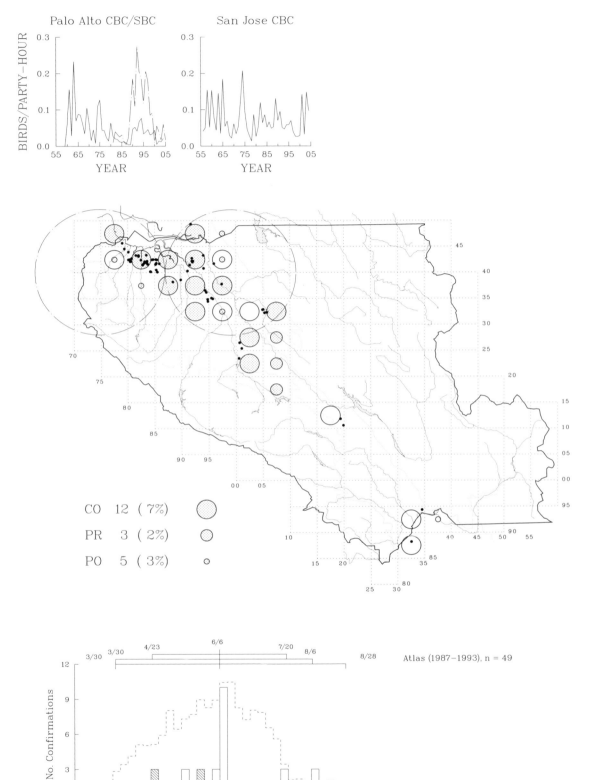

Palo Alto CBC/SBC

San Jose CBC

BIRDS/PARTY–HOUR

YEAR

YEAR

CO 12 (7%)

PR 3 (2%)

PO 5 (3%)

Atlas (1987–1993), n = 49

No. Confirmations

MAR   APR   MAY   JUN   JUL   AUG

Long-eared Owl
Asio otus

Rarely heard and even less often seen, the Long-eared Owl is one of our least known species. This strictly nocturnal owl is widely distributed throughout the Northern Hemisphere. In North America it ranges from British Columbia across Canada to Nova Scotia and south to Baja California and across the middle of the United States to Pennsylvania and the Appalachians (AOU 1998). In California, it breeds sparsely in the Great Basin areas of the northeast and the Modoc plateau, along the western foothills of the Sierra Nevada, and in the Coast Ranges from Sonoma County and southern Lake County south to Santa Barbara County (Small 1994). In Santa Clara County, it is a rare resident and occasional winter visitor.

The first records of the Long-eared Owl in Santa Clara County were of a bird on Black Mountain on 18 Feb 1893 (Van Denburgh 1899b) and of birds shot in willow thickets along San Francisquito Creek (Price 1898f). Rollo H. Beck collected a set of eggs near Berryessa on 6 Apr 1896 (CAS #5968), and D. Bernard Bull collected a set of six eggs in "an old rat nest" in a willow along Silver Creek near Evergreen on 24 Apr 1926 (WFVZ #144976). Grinnell and Wythe (1927) considered Long-eared Owls to be sparse and local residents in the San Francisco Bay area, and reported nest records only from Alameda and Marin counties. Breeding records in the 1930s include young in a nest near Betabel found by W. E. Unglish on 6 Jun 1931, probably in the Pajaro River floodplain (Sibley 1952), and six eggs collected by George Brem, Jr. on 9 Apr 1939 from an old crow's nest in a live oak, although no specific locale in the county is indicated for this record (WFVZ #27242). Sibley (1952) considered this species to be a "fairly common resident" in the South San Francisco Bay region, most often in riparian areas. Since Sibley's account, however, there have only been a few winter records for this species in the county, and no additional evidence of breeding was recorded until the start of the atlasing.

Long-eared Owls were found in only three locations during the atlas period, but in all three locations breeding was confirmed. During 1986 and 1987 the writer made repeated visits to the Monte Bello Open Space Preserve in support of a study of owls (Noble 1990). At that time a pair of Long-eared Owls appeared to be resident, and nesting was confirmed on 14 May 1987 when three fledglings were seen near an old, flattened squirrel's nest in a large California bay tree. This nest tree was at the edge of a small open meadow surrounded by a mixed forest of bay, madrone, and live oak, with a few Douglas firs present. Although no proof of breeding was found after 1987, the owls were seen and heard in every subsequent year through 1996, except 1988. The second nest record during the atlas period was of fledglings found on Rosalia Mountain in Santa Cruz County, just across the Santa Clara County line, on 21 Jul 1988. The third confirmation of Long-eared Owl was recorded in the Uvas Creek area on 4 Jun 1991. As with the Monte Bello birds, nestlings here were observed occupying a large squirrel nest in a bay tree along Uvas Creek, and meadow foraging areas were a short distance away. Following the atlas period, on 11 May 1997, a possible diurnal courtship flight was observed 2 km farther up Uvas Creek from the 1991 nest record (Chris Salander, pers. comm.). The observer saw a Long-eared Owl performing a presumed courtship flight in late afternoon and calling from a copse of fir trees.

During the atlas period, all records were obtained from the Santa Cruz Mountains. No owls were observed in the Diablo Range or on the valley floor. Although owling was not undertaken as intensively in the Diablo Range as in the Santa Cruz Mountains, there was coverage in the spring and summer months, suggesting that at best the Long-eared Owl was very uncommon there. Subsequent to the atlas period, however, an adult and two young were found along Mines Road in the Diablo Range, within Alameda County, on 6 Aug 1995 (*Field Notes 50*:111 1996), and a nest with young was found in Ed Levin County Park, Santa Clara County, on 19 May 2001 (Dusty W. Bleher, county notebooks).

Historically, Long-eared Owls have nested along streams and creeks on the Santa Clara Valley floor, but none were observed there during atlasing. It must be noted, however, that most of these riparian areas received little if any nocturnal sampling during the atlas, and it may be that this highly nocturnal species was overlooked in these areas. Roberson (1993i) indicates that open uncultivated lands must be adjacent to riparian breeding sites for the owl to be successful in its foraging efforts. Such sites are now rare in Santa Clara County, except for a few such areas in the southern part of the county, such as along Pacheco Creek and the Pajaro River. Following the atlas period a Long-eared Owl was heard calling at a possible site along Llagas Creek above Bloomfield Road on 24 Jun 1999 (Thomas P. Ryan, county notebooks). It may be that in some years this seemingly rare owl still returns to nest here.

Paul L. Noble

LONG-EARED OWL

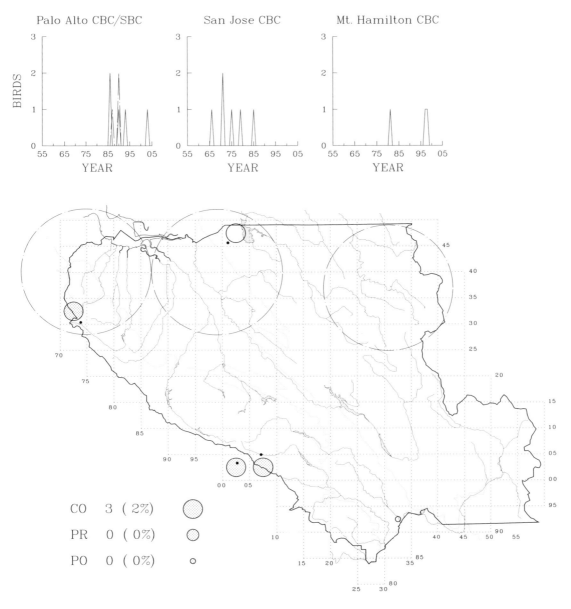

Palo Alto CBC/SBC

San Jose CBC

Mt. Hamilton CBC

BIRDS

YEAR

YEAR

YEAR

CO 3 (2%)
PR 0 (0%)
PO 0 (0%)

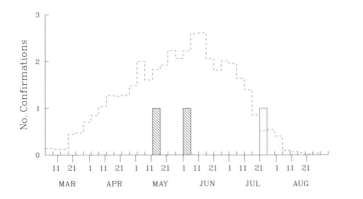

Atlas (1987–1993), n = 3

No. Confirmations

MAR   APR   MAY   JUN   JUL   AUG

239

Northern Saw-whet Owl
Aegolius acadicus

This small nocturnal owl lives a life largely hidden from our diurnal activities. The Northern Saw-whet Owl breeds from Alaska east across the southern provinces of Canada to Nova Scotia, thence on the Pacific Coast south to California, through the northern United States and the Appalachian Mountains south to Tennessee, and locally in the highlands of Mexico south to Oaxaca (Cannings 1993, AOU 1998). In California, saw-whets are found in the Coast Ranges as far south as northern Santa Barbara County, and in the montane forests of the Cascades and Sierra Nevada (Small 1994). Two subspecies have been described, *brooksi* found only on the Queen Charlotte Islands of British Columbia and *acadicus* found elsewhere (Cannings 1993). This owl is a rare resident in the Santa Cruz Mountains of Santa Clara County, although migrants or dispersing birds are occasionally found on the valley floor or in the Diablo Range.

There are few California records of this rare owl from the early years of the twentieth century. Grinnell (1915) considered the Northern Saw-whet Owl an irregular winter visitant in central California, and was aware of only a single breeding record, from the Sierra Nevada. In their survey of the avifauna of the San Francisco Bay region, Grinnell and Wythe (1927) recorded only five observations, four during the winter and one undated. The first definitive evidence of breeding in the Bay area was a female Northern Saw-whet Owl discovered using a nest box in 1937 at the southern end of the Spring Valley Lakes (now Crystal Springs Reservoir), San Mateo County (Granfield 1937, Santee and Granfield 1939). Although Sibley (1952) judged this owl to be an uncommon resident in the Santa Cruz Mountains, he did not list any records for Santa Clara County. The first record of a Northern Saw-whet Owl in Santa Clara County was a juvenile found injured in Stevens Creek County Park in the spring of 1969 and nursed back to health (Ed McClintock, unpubl. field notes). It is possible that the extensive logging in the Santa Cruz Mountains from the 1850s to the end of the century (Jensen 1939, Stanger 1967) reduced or eliminated the moist, coniferous forest used by this species, and that its population is only now recovering as second-growth forests mature. It seems

more likely, however, that this owl has always resided in the Bay area, and was simply missed, because of its nocturnal habits.

The Northern Saw-whet Owl was found in 23 blocks (14%) during the atlas period and was confirmed breeding in seven of these blocks. All confirmations were based on observations of fledged young. Most of these young were found by their incessant begging calls, a coarse "tssshk" (Cannings 1993) or "hissss-t" (David L. Suddjian, pers. comm.). Generally, these owls were found along the crest of the Santa Cruz Mountains, where the wet coastal forest extends into Santa Clara County. This forest is predominantly Douglas fir, with some coast redwood, but also includes tan oak, madrone, and live oaks, often in a midcanopy layer. Breeding saw-whets were also found in adjacent riparian areas with bigleaf maple and willows. Noble (1990) systematically surveyed the upper Stevens Creek watershed in the Monte Bello Open Space Preserve during 1987 and 1988. His study area included Douglas fir forest, broadleaved evergreen forest and woodlands, riparian habitat composed of bigleaf maples, and chaparral and grasslands. Most birds were found in the Douglas fir forest, lesser numbers in the riparian habitat, and a few were in the broadleaved evergreen forest.

The onset of breeding by Northern Saw-whet Owls is marked by their use of advertising calls (Cannings 1993). Noble (1990) found that the local peak of calling was from November to January, although these were responses to taped calls rather than unsolicited advertising calls. Roberson (1993j) has noted that the most active period of calling in Monterey County is from December to March. Early evidence of nesting is difficult to detect, since so much of the activity occurs at night. At two nest sites in Spring Valley in 1937 and 1938, noted above (Granfield 1937, Santee and Granfield 1939), incubation occurred from 18 to 30 Apr, nestlings were present from 30 Apr to 5 Jun, and fledging followed in early June. The seven observations of fledged young during the atlas period extended from 15 Jun to 31 Jul, which is similar to the Spring Valley phenology.

The status of the Northern Saw-whet Owl away from the Santa Cruz Mountains is unclear. From 1986 to 2003, 22 birds were banded on the valley floor along Coyote Creek below Highway 237 from 19 Aug to 5 Mar, (Gina Barton, San Francisco Bay Bird Observatory, pers. comm.), and it seems likely that these were either migrants or wintering birds. During the breeding season in the Diablo Range, owls have been found in Halls Valley, 26 Apr 1981 (*Am. Birds 35*:859 1981); along Smith Creek, 20 Jun 1981 (David Moore, county notebooks); in Mt. Hamilton's Coulter pine forest, 26 Apr 1982 (pers. obs); again at Smith Creek 8 May 1994 (Heather L. Rottenborn et al., county notebooks), and at Coon Hunters Gulch in Henry Coe State Park on 9-10 Jun 2005 (Garth Harwood, county notebooks). Because resident birds should be on territory by February or March, each of these records is suggestive of breeding. Since this owl generally uses only cavities for nesting (Cannings 1993), the 1994 Smith Creek record is particularly interesting, for the owl was indeed found in a cavity in a snag.

William G. Bousman

NORTHERN SAW-WHET OWL

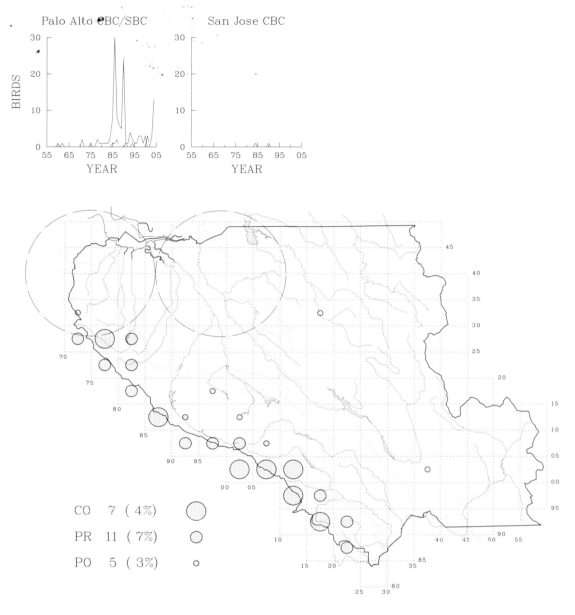

Palo Alto CBC/SBC

San Jose CBC

CO   7 (4%)

PR 11 (7%)

PO   5 (3%)

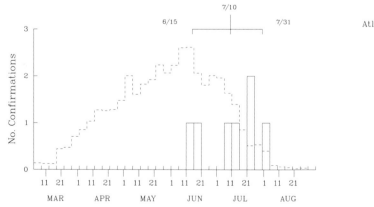

Atlas (1987–1993), n = 7

Common Poorwill
Phalaenoptilus nuttallii

Except when it calls its name during the hours of darkness, the Common Poorwill leads a life hidden from us. This cryptic goatsucker is found breeding from interior British Columbia and western Saskatchewan south through much of western North America to central Mexico (AOU 1998). It is absent, however, from the coastal forests of the Pacific Northwest. Three subspecies are either summer or permanent residents in California. Of these, *P. n. californicus* is found in the Coast Ranges (including Santa Clara County), the foothills of the Sierra, and on the perimeter of the Central Valley (AOU 1957, Grinnell and Miller 1944). In Santa Clara County, the Common Poorwill is a fairly common summer resident of chaparral and open woodlands in the drier portions of the county.

Early observers noted the Common Poorwill's use of less frequented roads in areas of chaparral and open hillsides (Beck 1897, Van Denburgh 1899b). Fisher (1902) considered this species to be an "uncommon resident," but Grinnell and Wythe (1927) recorded only summer records in the Bay area, with earliest arrivals on 1 Mar and the last birds of autumn on 29 Oct. An early summary of nest records from California made no mention of nesting in Santa Clara County (Dixon 1923). The first record of poorwills nesting in the county was of eggs collected along Uvas Creek on 14 Apr 1926 in association with breeding Lesser Nighthawks (Unglish 1929). Sibley (1952) considered the Common Poorwill a fairly common summer resident in the drier parts of the county.

Only three breeding confirmations were obtained during the atlas period, and just two more were detected in the postatlas period. Of these five confirmations, four were associated with nesting and one was a dependent juvenile. During the atlas period, two fledglings flew from a scrape in the shelter of a serpentine rock on a ridge above Calero Reservoir at 1,080 feet elevation on 23 May 1993. In the Diablo Range, a nest was found on 30 May 1992 on an outcrop over Alameda Creek at 2,410 feet elevation. This nest contained an egg and a newly hatched chick. A second Diablo Range nest was found on 15 Jun 1992 on the steep slopes of the east side of Arroyo Valle at 1,800 feet elevation and about 150 feet above the arroyo. This nest,

sheltered by a flat rock, contained two eggs. Following the atlas period, a juvenile was observed at Almaden Quicksilver County Park on 16 Jun 2004 (Ann Verdi, PADB), and two nestlings were found on 1 Jun 1997 at an elevation of 1,570 feet at the base of a rock outcrop above Aguague Creek in Joseph Grant County Park (Lotus Baker, pers. comm.).

Poorwills were generally found in relatively dry, open country, in a mixture of chaparral, grassland, oak woodlands, or foothill pine woodlands. Their basic foraging strategy is to pursue night-flying insects from either a low perch or the ground (Csada and Brigham 1992), and they therefore require openings in the chaparral or woodlands where they can see their prey. Thus, they were not found in dense chaparral or forested areas. As with other nocturnal species, their breeding range, as indicated by the map, is poorly outlined. It is likely that this species was breeding in all of the blocks in which possible or probable breeding evidence was obtained. The absence of poorwill records in most of the drainage of Pacheco Creek and to the northeast of Anderson Reservoir is believed to be a result of inadequate nocturnal coverage of these areas.

The more northerly populations of Common Poorwill are believed to be migratory, although migration in this species is poorly understood (Csada and Brigham 1992). The ability of this species to control its body temperature and respiration by entering a state of torpor provides the Common Poorwill an alternative to migration. Measurements of respiration during torpor suggest that a hibernation period of three months could easily be supported by the fat levels found in fall birds (Bartholomew et al. 1957). Zeiner et al. (1990) suggest that birds are year-round residents from San Luis Obispo County south, but Csada and Brigham (1992) indicate that the line dividing resident and migratory birds is north of Monterey County. Roberson (1993l) also believes that the Monterey population is resident. In Santa Clara County, the status of this species is not clear. There is some evidence of a fall migration, based on banding captures along Coyote Creek north of Highway 237 where the birds do not breed (Coyote Creek Field Station, unpubl. data). Between 1986 and 1997, eight birds were captured with banding dates from 4 to 24 Oct (median date 10 Oct). However, these captures may well represent more northerly populations rather than birds that nest locally. From 1980 to 2005, there were 11 observations of birds in the county from November through February, all of them likely overwintering birds (county notebooks), but the proportion of the actual population that these birds represent is unknown.

William G. Bousman

COMMON POORWILL

Palo Alto SBC

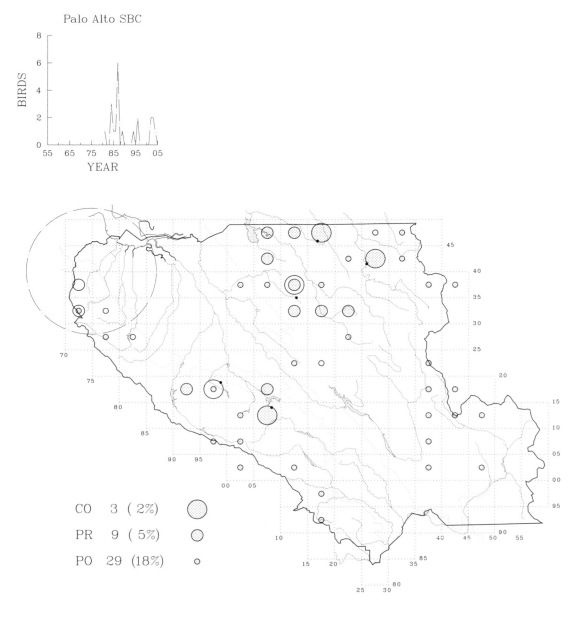

CO 3 (2%)

PR 9 (5%)

PO 29 (18%)

Atlas (1987–1993), n = 5

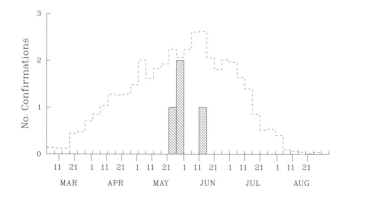

Vaux's Swift
Chaetura vauxi

Vaux's Swifts have long been dependent on the mature coniferous forests of the Pacific Northwest, most of them nesting in the hollows of large snags, usually in old-growth forests (Bull and Collins 1993). Small numbers of Vaux's Swifts, however, including all known Santa Clara County breeders, nest in residential chimneys. Although several races of this species reside in southern Mexico and Central America, the migratory North American populations of the nominate race, *C. v. vauxi*, breed from southeastern Alaska and British Columbia south through the northwestern states to northern California (Bull and Collins 1993). In California, the Vaux's Swift nests at scattered locations in the northern Sierra Nevada south to Tulare County, and along the outer Coast Ranges south to Santa Cruz and Santa Clara counties (Sterling and Paton 1996), with probable breeding in coastal Monterey County as well (Roberson 1993m). The Vaux's Swift occurs in Santa Clara County primarily as a spring and fall migrant, although small numbers breed in a limited portion of the Santa Cruz Mountains near Los Gatos and Saratoga.

The first ornithologists visiting the Santa Cruz Mountains of western Santa Clara County did not confirm breeding by Vaux's Swifts, possibly because the old-growth forests on the eastern side of these mountains had been almost completely logged over by this time (Jensen 1939). On 4 May 1864, Cooper (1870) reported Vaux's Swifts in the Santa Cruz Mountains "12 miles south of Santa Clara" (likely in Santa Cruz County) and suspected nesting in hollow trees within these mountains, although suitable nest trees may have been eliminated by that time. Price (1898b) called the species a "spring and fall transient" around Stanford University. Van Denburgh (1899b) noted Vaux's Swifts in the county and suspected that they nested "among the redwoods" in adjacent Santa Cruz County. Grinnell and Wythe (1927) considered the Vaux's Swift a very local summer resident along the coast, referring to swifts seen in Palo Alto, San Jose, and Los Gatos as migrants. Judging from these accounts, it would seem that any Vaux's Swifts breeding in the Santa Cruz Mountains in the late 1800s and early 1900s probably did so outside Santa Clara County.

No summer records from Santa Clara County were listed in these early references, and no breeding evidence was obtained in the county until June 1948, when a swift nest containing a nestling was found in the chimney of a Los Gatos home (Sibley 1952). Swifts were seen entering another chimney nearby on 29 Jul 1948. Subsequent Los Gatos breeding records include young heard calling in a chimney in 1949 (Sibley 1952), two nests found in 1957 (*Avocet* 4:9–11 1957), a swift carrying twigs into a chimney in 1960 (*Avocet* 7:102–03 1960), and a fledgling banded near its nest in 1963 (*Avocet* 10:74–76 1963). The concentration of breeding confirmations in Los Gatos during this period reflects the excellent coverage of that area by Emily D. Smith, who also confirmed breeding in a chimney in Saratoga each year from 1959 to 1962 (*Audubon Field Notes* 13:397 1959, 16:505 1962). On 10 Jul 1976, young were heard calling from a nest in Cupertino (William G. Bousman, pers. comm.). The logging of suitable nest trees has caused population declines throughout much of this species' North American breeding range over the past few decades (Bull and Collins 1993, Sauer et al. 2005). But in Santa Clara County, a small breeding population has persisted over this time period, possibly owing to the birds' habit of nesting in chimneys instead of hollow trees.

During the atlas period, breeding-season records of Vaux's Swifts in Santa Clara County were concentrated in a relatively small area in the northern Santa Cruz Mountains. Only three breeding confirmations in two blocks were recorded, all consisting of records of nestlings brought to the Santa Clara Valley Humane Society after the birds had fallen out of their nests. After the atlas period, breeding in a new block was recorded when a recently fledged Vaux's Swift was found in a chimney in Los Altos Hills on 23 Jul 1998 (Betty Dale *fide* Garth Harwood). Although swifts were observed foraging widely over various habitats, they were most frequently observed in suburban areas having chimneys suitable for use as nesting sites, such as in Los Gatos, Los Altos, Los Altos Hills, Cupertino, and Campbell. It is possible that some Vaux's Swifts nest in large redwood or Douglas fir snags in western Santa Clara County, but no such nesting was observed or suspected by atlasers. Confirmation of breeding is very difficult, owing to the nature of the birds' nest sites, and there are likely many more nests in these residential areas than are indicated by the above breeding confirmations.

The Vaux's Swifts that Smith observed in Los Gatos in the 1950s and 1960s arrived in their nesting chimneys as early as 6 Apr 1962 (*Avocet* 9:42–44 1962), and were noted carrying nesting material as early as 16 Apr 1960 (*Avocet* 7:102–03 1960). All actual nest records from the county have been from June and July. Prior to the atlas period, nestlings were recorded in several nests between 13 Jun and 25 Jul (Sibley 1952, *Audubon Field Notes* 11:427 1957, 13:397 1959), the young fledging from one nest on 17 Jul 1963 (*Avocet* 10:74–76 1963). The three atlas records of nestlings were dated 28 Jun, 5 Jul, and 11 Jul; postatlas fledglings were found on 18 Jul 2005 (Janna Pauser, PADB), 22 Jul 1999 (Rose Givens *fide* Pat Curtis), and 23 Jul 1998 (as noted above). These dates fall within the date span indicated by historical records.

Stephen C. Rottenborn

VAUX'S SWIFT

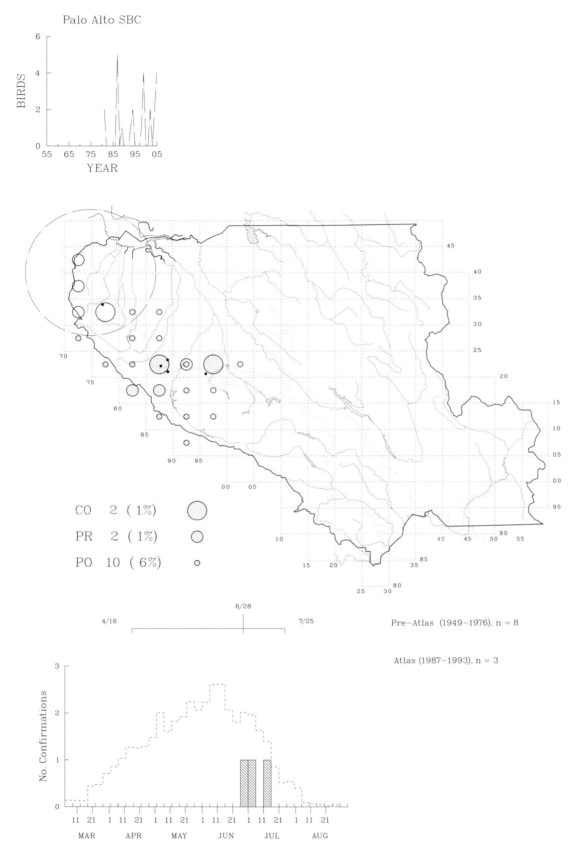

Palo Alto SBC

CO 2 (1%)

PR 2 (1%)

PO 10 (6%)

4/16   6/28   7/25

Pre-Atlas (1949-1976), n = 8

Atlas (1987-1993), n = 3

White-throated Swift
Aeronautes saxatalis

The twittering, descending calls from a flock of White-throated Swifts will quickly raise a birder's eyes to the sky to admire these aerial acrobats. This swift is a summer resident from southeastern British Columbia and northern Montana south into Mexico along the Sierra Madre Occidental to Oaxaca, and birds are also found in the highlands of Central America (Ryan and Collins 2000). In California, it is found year-round as far north as Mendocino County and, in summer, to Humboldt County (Ryan and Collins 2000). Of the two recognized subspecies, *A. s. saxatalis* is the one found in North America. The White-throated Swift is a wide-ranging resident in Santa Clara County and can be fairly common locally.

Historical information on White-throated Swifts suggests that the coastal populations have been expanding slowly northward over the last century. Price (1898b), in summarizing the birds found on the Stanford campus, noted that he had never seen this swift. Barlow (1900b) reported seeing migratory birds, and on one occasion a winter flock over Milpitas. Fisher (1902) considered the White-throated Swift an occasional migrant and reported that it bred at Santa Cruz. Grinnell and Wythe (1927) recorded that the only nest site known in the San Francisco Bay area was in the vicinity of Mt. Diablo, Contra Costa County. A set of eggs collected in Contra Costa in 1878 (Bryant 1894) was probably from this site. On 20 May 1929, Henry W. Carriger found swifts nesting with Bank and Northern Rough-winged swallows in a railroad cut southwest of Sargent and collected three egg sets (WFVZ #34241–34243). In the same spring, R. Schliecker found this species nesting in cliffs at Alum Rock Park (*Wren-Tit 1(3)* 1929). By the late 1930s, nesting was recorded

along the central coast only as far north as San Mateo, Alameda, and Contra Costa counties (Grinnell and Miller 1944). Since then, White-throated Swifts have expanded their range north of the San Francisco Bay. Shuford (1993p) reported breeding along coastal cliffs in Marin County in 1977. The species extended its range into Trinity County by 1997 and Humboldt County by 1998 (Ryan and Collins 2000).

White-throated Swifts were found widely in the county during the atlas period. They were found nesting in crevices in cliffs or buildings that provided protection from predators and suitable support for their nests. These requirements, however, seemed to limit the number of nesting locations. Two-thirds of the breeding records obtained during the atlas period were of birds using manmade structures on the valley floor, or at low elevations adjacent to the flatlands boundary. The other third of the records were of birds found at natural sites in cliff faces in the Diablo Range. On the valley floor, White-throated Swifts used drainage holes in either highway overpasses or bridges over streams, and many of these sites were also used by Northern Rough-winged Swallows and European Starlings. Other nest sites included roof tiles at Stanford and Santa Clara universities, roof tiles in Palo Alto, external cracks in masonry buildings, and internal crevices in the hangars at Moffett Field. Cliff sites used in the Diablo Range ranged in elevation from 740 feet at Alum Rock Park (following the atlas period, Michael M. Rogers, pers. comm.) to 3,600 feet in a cliff below Copernicus Peak on Mt. Hamilton.

Within the Palo Alto count circle, total numbers of White-throated Swifts do not differ significantly from summer to winter, suggesting that this species is largely a permanent resident in Santa Clara County. During the atlas period the earliest evidence of breeding observed was birds on a nest on 8 Apr, and the first young were heard in a nest crevice by 12 Apr. Following the atlas period, birds were found using a nesting cavity on the earlier date of 5 Apr 2005 (Linda Sullivan, PADB). These dates are earlier than the 86 California egg dates recorded by Bent (1940), which ranged from 8 May to 21 Jun. The latest breeding evidence observed was fledglings on 27 Jul.

White-throated Swifts have shown repeated use of nest sites over long periods (Dobkin et al. 1986, Ryan and Collins 2000), perhaps because of the scarcity of suitable crevices in many locations. This pattern of long-term use has also been seen in Santa Clara County. Nesting was observed in Alum Rock Park in 1929 (Smith 1929), and has been noted there regularly since that time (records in *N. Am. Birds* and its predecessor publications). Although specific cliff faces are not identified in these early records, it is interesting to note that birds nested in the cliff face of Eagle Rock on 10 May 1997 (Michael M. Rogers, pers. comm.), following the atlas period. Similarly, at the cliff face east of Cochrane Bridge, at the upper end of Anderson Reservoir, swifts were observed nesting on 18 Jun 1951 by Milton L. Siebert (Sibley 1952), and they were found nesting in this same cliff face during the atlas period. In future years it will be interesting to see if this nest-site fidelity extends to this species' now-extensive use of manmade structures.

William G. Bousman

WHITE-THROATED SWIFT

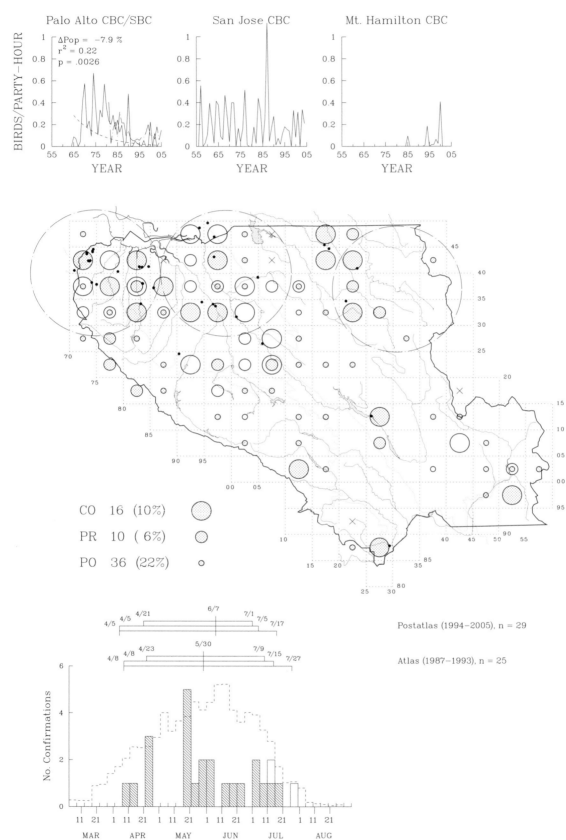

Palo Alto CBC/SBC

San Jose CBC

Mt. Hamilton CBC

BIRDS/PARTY–HOUR

YEAR

ΔPop = −7.9 %
r^2 = 0.22
p = .0026

CO 16 (10%)
PR 10 (6%)
PO 36 (22%)

Postatlas (1994–2005), n = 29

Atlas (1987–1993), n = 25

No. Confirmations

MAR APR MAY JUN JUL AUG

Black-chinned Hummingbird
Archilochus alexandri

The remnants of riparian forest along streams in the urban areas of the Santa Clara Valley host the largest population of Black-chinned Hummingbirds in the San Francisco Bay area. This species is widespread throughout the western United States in summer, and in California it nests in lowland areas over much of the state, except for the humid Coast Ranges north of the San Francisco Bay. Long considered a rare breeder in Santa Clara County at the edge of its range, it has recently been found to be locally common in the northern part of the county, along urban streams dominated by cottonwoods.

W. E. Unglish (1932) provided Santa Clara County's earliest records of Black-chinned Hummingbirds, finding three nests with eggs 4 miles west of Gilroy in 1907. Thereafter, no further evidence of breeding by these hummingbirds was reported in the Gilroy area, although Unglish collected adults there from 1926 to 1933 (Unglish 1933). Despite this species' presence in the southern part of Santa Clara County, it was considered very rare elsewhere in the San Francisco Bay area. As of 1927, there were only three records in the Bay area outside Santa Clara County (Grinnell and Wythe 1927), and Grinnell and Miller (1944) considered Gilroy to be the northernmost breeding location west of the Central Valley. Later, however, Donald McLean discovered Black-chinned Hummingbirds breeding in the San Jose area, observing a female with young in 1966 and again in 1967 (*Audubon Field Notes* 20:597 1966, 21:603 1967). Single individuals in San Jose in 1968–69 (*Audubon Field Notes* 22:573 1968, 23:622 1969) and in 1981–83 (*Am. Birds* 37:1024 1983) suggested continued breeding, but there were no new breeding confirmations prior to the initiation of the atlas project.

During atlas fieldwork, Black-chinned Hummingbirds were detected in six atlas blocks and confirmed breeding in two of those blocks. All records were from the northern reaches of the Santa Clara Valley, except for a single bird observed along Llagas Creek below Chesbro Dam. No Black-chinned Hummingbirds were found closer to the Gilroy area where they had bred in 1907. In 1994 and 1995, surveys of urban riparian habitat in the Santa Clara Valley by the writer found Black-chinned Hummingbirds in seven blocks where they had not been detected during the atlas period, and increased the number of blocks with confirmations to eight. The 1994 surveys yielded at least ten records of confirmed breeding. In 1995, more widespread surveys resulted in a population estimate of at least 155 individuals in lowland riparian habitats in the San Jose area, and 26 cases of confirmed breeding were documented.

Black-chinned Hummingbirds were locally common in these lowland riparian habitats. In 1994 and 1995, this species was found breeding from the Coyote Creek Riparian Station in Alviso upstream to Hellyer Park along Coyote Creek, from Coleman Road upstream to Curtner Road along the Guadalupe River, and from the Guadalupe confluence upstream to the Glen Eyrie Drive area along Los Gatos Creek. Why Black-chinned Hummingbirds were unrecorded in many of these areas during the atlas period, yet seemed so abundant in 1994–95, is unknown. Urban streams in some parts of the Santa Clara Valley are rarely birded, and these birds may have been overlooked in some areas. But because David Suddjian (pers. comm.), on bird surveys in 1989 and 1990, found no Black-chinned Hummingbirds in areas where they were quite common in 1994–95, it may be that the population has increased substantially in recent years, at least in some parts of the northern Santa Clara Valley.

Most Black-chinned Hummingbirds were found in habitats dominated by Fremont cottonwoods. Nests were found in trees of nine different species: 13 of the 25 nests found were in cottonwoods, five were in box elders, and the remaining seven were in trees of seven other species. All nests were composed almost entirely of fibers from cottonwood and willow catkins. Although most Black-chinned Hummingbirds were observed at elevations below 180 feet, where cottonwoods were common, single pairs were seen in 1995 at higher elevations along Coyote Creek near Silicon Valley Boulevard (230 feet), and along Alamitos Creek near McKean Road (320 feet), in riparian habitats dominated by sycamores and oaks. Moreover, the nests found by Unglish in 1907 were also constructed of material from sycamores and were not in areas dominated by Fremont cottonwoods, which argues that the presence of cottonwoods is not a requisite for breeding by these birds. Nesting densities were quite high in some areas, as evidenced by four nests active simultaneously along a 50-meter reach of Los Gatos Creek on 11 May 1994.

Black-chinned Hummingbirds typically arrive in Santa Clara County in mid-April. A completed nest was found as early as 1 May, and eggs as early as 11 May. Nesting activity peaked in mid to late May, but young were observed in the nest as late as 18 Aug, suggesting that some females might have double-brooded. Supporting this hypothesis was a discovery along Los Gatos Creek, where one nest was built less than 10 cm from a nest that had previously fledged young, and the second nest was constructed using all the material from the first nest.

Stephen C. Rottenborn

BLACK-CHINNED HUMMINGBIRD

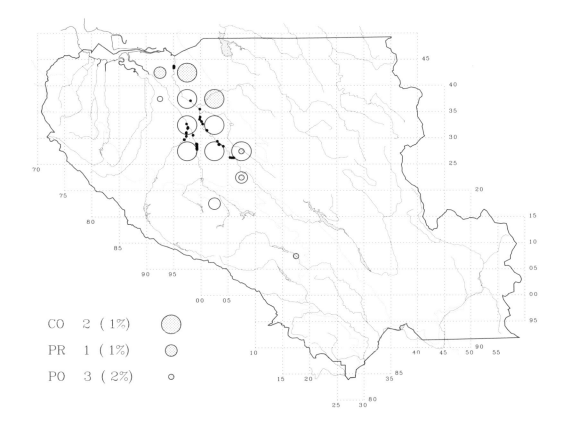

CO 2 (1%)

PR 1 (1%)

PO 3 (2%)

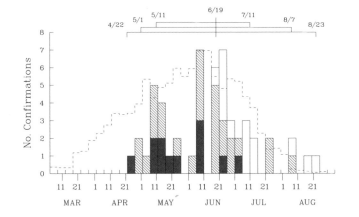

Combined (1987–2005), n = 53

Anna's Hummingbird
Calypte anna

Anna's Hummingbirds return to their breeding territories in late October, and with the onset of the winter rains another nesting season begins. Following a range expansion in the twentieth century, these hummingbirds now breed from Vancouver Island, in British Columbia, south along the Pacific slope to northwestern Baja California, and inland to southern Arizona (Russell 1996, AOU 1998). In California, breeding generally occurs west of the Cascades-Sierra axis, as well as west of the California deserts, and is most frequent in the southern two-thirds of the state (Small 1994). This hummingbird is common in Santa Clara County, and found here throughout the year.

The Anna's Hummingbird was first recorded in Santa Clara County on Sclater's list of birds collected by Thomas Bridges in the "Valley of San José" prior to 1857 (Sclater 1857). Observers at the end of the nineteenth century considered this species to be a common or even abundant resident (Price 1898c, Van Denburgh 1899b, Fisher 1902). Grinnell and Wythe (1927) described the Anna's Hummingbird as a common resident throughout the San Francisco Bay area. Similarly, Sibley (1952) judged this species to be a common resident in the South Bay region. Since the 1950s, winter populations of this hummingbird have increased by 3.2% a year on the Palo Alto CBC and 5.4% a year on the San Jose CBC. A similar trend is seen in the Palo Alto SBC data.

Atlasers found Anna's Hummingbirds throughout the county, with confirmed breeding in 50% of the atlas blocks. Only two blocks next to the San Francisco Bay lacked this common breeding species. During the atlas period, breeding records were obtained from elevations of 2 feet on the lower valley floor to 2,880 feet along Arroyo Mocho. Nesting was somewhat less frequent in the drier areas of the Diablo Range. Generally, wherever nectar-producing flowers were in bloom, males established territories. Females were more often found in shaded, mesic areas or along streams, where they constructed their nests. On the basis of egg set data from the Western Foundation of Vertebrate Zoology, Russell (1996) determined that the nest trees most frequently used by this hummingbird were oaks (34%), eucalyptus (10%), and cypress (10%); and in a study of riparian areas in

the Santa Clara Valley (Stephen C. Rottenborn, pers. comm.), the most common nest trees were Fremont cottonwood (35%), Monterey pine (14%), and coast live oak (11%).

The Anna's Hummingbird is the earliest-nesting species of the county's avifauna (other than Rock Pigeon, which nests year-round). Stiles (1973) defines a prebreeding period from mid-October until the first rains, when birds return to their breeding areas. Breeding then ensues in November and December, when males establish their territories and females begin to nest. Woods (1940) recorded California egg dates from 21 Dec to 17 Aug, and our findings are quite in accord with that timespan. During the atlas period, the earliest observed nesting activity was a female carrying nesting material on 23 Nov, nest building was seen as early as 18 Dec, and a female was seen on a nest on 8 Jan. Subsequent to the atlas period, a female was seen feeding a fledged young near the Coyote Creek Golf Course on 14 Dec 2005 (Robert W. Reiling, county notebooks). Two broods are normal during the season (Russell 1996), and most of the records shown in the phenology graphic are probably related to second broods. During the atlas period, the latest date females were seen on a nest was 30 Jun, and the last date dependent fledglings were observed was 12 Jul. Following the atlas period, a female was found incubating eggs on 22 Aug 2000. This nest was abandoned later, and a single dead nestling was found in the nest (Chris M. Illes, county notebooks).

Since the 1930s there has been a significant expansion of the breeding range of the Anna's Hummingbird (Zimmerman 1973, Russell 1996). Historically, this species bred from the San Francisco Bay area south to northwestern Baja California (Grinnell and Miller 1944, Russell 1996). But as noted above, these hummingbirds now nest as far north as British Columbia, and have also expanded into Arizona. Prior to European settlement, it is believed, they nested coastally in their historical range, and during the summer and fall "minimum food period" the birds dispersed to montane areas where they could better find nectar sources (Stiles 1973). Today, the limiting effect of native nectar resources in summer and early fall has been ameliorated by the introduction of suitable flowering plants into urban areas. Of these plants, probably the most important for hummingbirds are tree tobacco and the various summer- and fall-flowering eucalypts (Grinnell and Miller 1944, Stiles 1973). The expansion of the breeding range of this species, both northward along the Pacific slope and into the Southwest, is likely a result of the new nectar resources associated with urban flowering plants, since Anna's Hummingbirds are found nesting only within the urban portions of this expanded range (Russell 1996).

William G. Bousman

ANNA'S HUMMINGBIRD

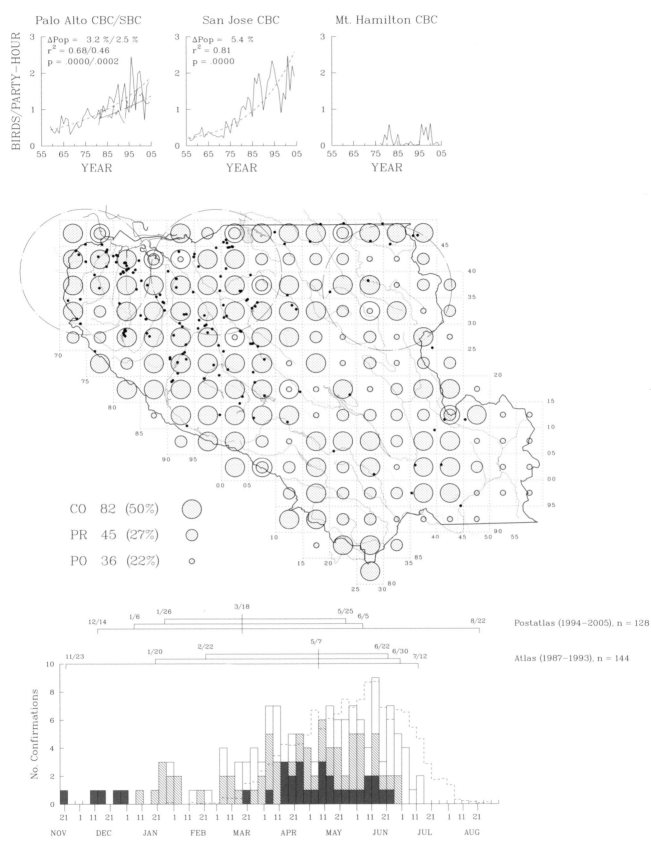

Palo Alto CBC/SBC

ΔPop = 3.2 % / 2.5 %
r² = 0.68/0.46
p = .0000/.0002

San Jose CBC

ΔPop = 5.4 %
r² = 0.81
p = .0000

Mt. Hamilton CBC

BIRDS/PARTY-HOUR

YEAR

CO   82 (50%)
PR   45 (27%)
PO   36 (22%)

Postatlas (1994–2005), n = 128

Atlas (1987–1993), n = 144

No. Confirmations

Costa's Hummingbird
Calypte costae

A prolonged whine emanating from an elliptical flight display confirms the presence of a courting Costa's Hummingbird, a rare breeder in Santa Clara County, which lies at the extreme northwestern edge of the species' breeding range. This hummingbird is primarily a bird of the desert Southwest, breeding from the southern half of California and Nevada south through northwestern Mexico and throughout Baja California (Baltosser and Scott 1996). In California, the species breeds regularly north to western Stanislaus County (Baltosser 1989) and in scattered locations in Monterey and San Benito counties (Roberson 1993n). In Santa Clara County, the Costa's Hummingbird is an extremely rare breeder, only one instance of confirmed breeding having been recorded here; migrants and postbreeding dispersants occur more frequently, but are not detected every year.

Early summaries of Bay Area avifauna listed few records of the Costa's Hummingbird. Grinnell and Wythe (1927) noted single birds at Hayward on 16 May 1875 and at Oakland on 8 May 1890 (both in Alameda County). The same two records were cited by Grinnell and Miller (1944), who noted that the species "nests sparsely on west side of the upper (southern) end of San Joaquin Valley and in inner arid valleys somewhat further westward: due west of Dos Palos, Merced County . . . and north to San Ardo, upper Salinas Valley, Monterey County." Earlier works focusing on Santa Clara County made no mention of this species (Van Denburgh 1899b, Barlow 1900b), and Sibley's (1952) later summary for the South Bay region added no additional records.

McLean (1969) was the first to report a Costa's Hummingbird in Santa Clara County, a female present in his San Jose yard from Apr to Oct 1959. What was likely the same female returned to nest in Apr 1960, successfully fledging a single bird, which fed with the adult in McLean's yard until mid-July. This constitutes the only breeding record for the county. Since 1960, Costa's Hummingbirds have been present, and confirmed to be breeding in some years, in Del Puerto Canyon, Stanislaus County, 20 km east of Santa Clara County (e.g., *Audubon Field Notes*

14:418 1960, *Am. Birds 25*:903 1971, *28*:848 1974).

Probable breeding evidence, based on courting adult males, was found in two locations during the atlas period. Two males were along Peach Tree Creek at about 1,600 feet elevation in upper Del Puerto Canyon in Stanislaus County on 29 May 1993, and another was along Colorado Creek west of Mines Road at 2,080 feet elevation in Santa Clara County on 1 June 1993. The habitat at these locations consisted of open chaparral mixed with foothill pine and manzanita on steep-sided slopes above seasonal creeks. This species is not normally found so far up Del Puerto Canyon, although it occurs regularly at the mouth of the canyon at 400 feet elevation, 19 km to the east, in more xeric habitat along a seasonal creek bordered by grasslands, shrubs, and non-native tree tobacco. After the atlas period, an adult male was found feeding in black sage even farther up the canyon at 2,260 feet elevation, only 300 m from Santa Clara County, on 29 Apr 2003 (Steven A. Glover, pers. comm.). It is likely that this species breeds only irregularly in the area covered by this atlas, as has been opined for peripheral breeding locations in Monterey County (Roberson 1993n).

Subsequent to the atlas period, the first known breeding by Costa's Hummingbirds in Alameda County was confirmed in an extensive southwest-facing chaparral field above the Arroyo Valle north of Devil's Hole, less than 5 km north of the Santa Clara County line (pers. obs.). On 20 May 1995, at least seven birds were found there, including courting males and an agitated female carrying nest material. On a return visit on 19 Jun that year, at least four Costa's Hummingbirds were found, including a female attending two midsized young in a nest in a black sage at 2,000 feet elevation. This timing of breeding accords with that in Del Puerto Canyon, where seven occupied nests have been found, all between 15 Apr and 19 Jun (*fide* Howard L. Cogswell, Arthur L. Edwards, pers. comm., *N. Am. Birds* Northern California Region notebooks). Other breeding-season records of adult Costa's Hummingbirds found in Santa Clara County subsequent to the atlas period include males along Coyote Creek just north of Capitol Expressway on 8 June 1998 (Stephen C. Rottenborn, pers. comm.) and near Eagle Rock in Alum Rock Park on 20 May 2001 (Eric Feuss, pers. comm.). County records of immature males, some displaying, in lowland areas in May or June have not been mapped, since hatching-year males are not known to breed (Baltosser and Scott 1996).

Stiles (1973) suggested that Costa's Hummingbirds may raise a first brood in the desert Southwest and then move to coastal chaparral in mid to late April to raise a second brood, which if true would explain the surprising rarity of documented cases of double-brooding by this species in its core range (Baltosser and Scott 1996). The first arrival dates of breeding birds in Bixby Canyon, Monterey County, span 29 Apr to 2 Jun, consistent with the theory that birds there may not arrive until after completion of breeding elsewhere (Roberson 2002). This timing is similar to that of the Diablo Range records reported above, but arrivals at more inland locations can be much earlier, as evidenced by records from as early as 2 Feb in inland Monterey County (Roberson 2002) and 5 Jan at the mouth of Del Puerto Canyon in Stanislaus County (*Audubon Field Notes 17*:355 1963).

Michael M. Rogers

COSTA'S HUMMINGBIRD

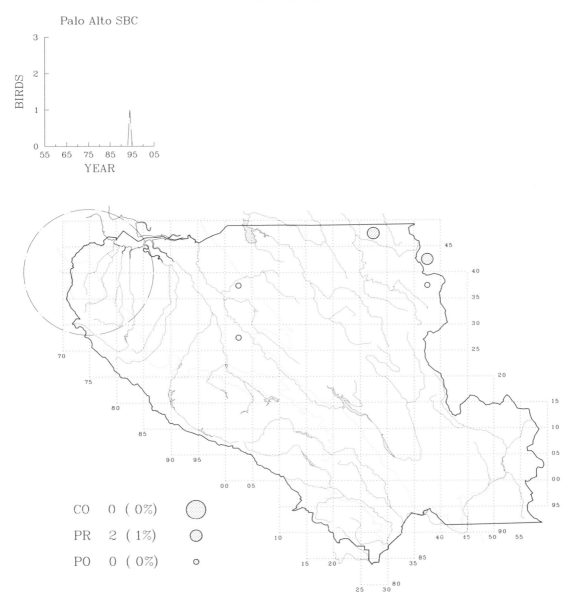

Palo Alto SBC

CO 0 (0%)
PR 2 (1%)
PO 0 (0%)

Allen's Hummingbird
Selasphorus sasin

This most coastal of hummingbirds is never far from the summer fogs that creep over the crest of the Santa Cruz Mountains or build along the South Bay. The Allen's Hummingbird breeds from southwestern Oregon south along the Pacific Coast to Orange County, California (AOU 1998, Small 1994). The subspecies *S. s. sasin* is a summer resident along the coast, and the appropriately named *S. s. sedentarius* is a resident population found on the Channel Islands off southern California, and locally on the Palos Verdes Peninsula in Los Angeles County (AOU 1957, Small 1994). The Allen's Hummingbird is an uncommon summer resident in Santa Clara County in the wetter canyons of the Santa Cruz Mountains, in various riparian areas on the valley floor, and at the western edge of the northern Diablo Range.

Male Allen's Hummingbirds can be confused with males of the closely related Rufous Hummingbird, since some individual Rufous Hummingbirds have extensive green on their backs (McKenzie and Robbins 1999). Moreover, the females and immatures cannot be separated in the field. Observers at the close of the nineteenth century sometimes confused the two species and indicated local breeding by Rufous Hummingbirds. Price (1898c) listed both species as summer visitants to the Stanford campus, and apparently did not understand their different breeding status. Van Denburgh (1899b) found the Allen's Hummingbird to be a regular nesting species in the county, but he referred to all of his observations as Rufous Hummingbird. Grinnell (1901c) clarified the status of local breeding *Selasphorus* species by noting that all California breeding records were of Allen's Hummingbird, and that the Rufous Hummingbirds nested no closer than Oregon. Fisher (1902) described the Allen's Hummingbird as an "[a]bundant summer visitant in the valleys and hills." Grinnell and Wythe (1927) considered it a common summer resident in the Bay area, and noted that it was found only within 25 miles of the seacoast. Sibley (1952) likewise judged this hummingbird to be a common summer resident. To judge from the Palo Alto Summer Bird Count data, there has been a substantial decline in the numbers of this species in recent years, and it is now decidedly uncommon here, although the cause of the decline is unknown. But no significant statewide population change has been detected for the Allen's Hummingbird (Sauer et al. 2005).

Atlasers found breeding Allen's Hummingbirds throughout most of the Santa Cruz Mountains, in healthy riparian areas on the valley floor, and at the western edge of the Diablo Range near the San Francisco Bay. All confirmations were within the coastal boundary described by Grinnell and Miller (1944), who stated "we know of no attested nesting instance farther inland than 20 miles air-line from the sea or coastal bay." The elevations of confirmations ranged from 11 feet on the valley floor to 3,000 feet in the Santa Cruz Mountains northwest of Los Gatos. Ninety percent of these confirmations, however, were at elevations at or below 1,200 feet, which accords with the distribution observed in Monterey County, where all nest records were below 1,600 feet (Roberson 1993o). In Santa Clara County, nesting Allen's Hummingbirds were generally found in moist situations where trees and shrubs provided shade as well as suitable nest locations. In the Santa Cruz Mountains, nesting was observed in broadleaved evergreen-coniferous forests where there were suitable shady conditions. In these circumstances, the species used a variety of trees as nest sites, including redwoods and tan oaks, as well as shrubs in the understory. In riparian areas on the valley floor, atlasers found nests in thickets of blackberry, arroyo willow, box elder, cottonwood, and the occasional planted redwood. Nests in urban areas affording the appropriate moisture and shade were sometimes built in non-native shrubs. One nest was found constructed on an outdoor light structure under the eaves of a building adjacent to the Pajaro River riparian corridor. This case is unusual, however, seeing as only one nest out of the 150 observed by Aldrich (1945) was built on a manmade structure. The lone confirmed breeding record from the edge of the Diablo Range was from Alum Rock Canyon, where a female was attending fledglings in a shaded area of riparian vegetation.

For this atlas it has been assumed that all *Selasphorus* nesting records here apply to the Allen's Hummingbird, since there are no substantiated breeding records of Rufous Hummingbirds closer than the Trinity Mountains in northern California (Zeiner et al. 1990). Ensuring that probable and possible breeding records apply only to the Allen's rather than migrant Rufous Hummingbirds is more difficult, and the records that we have retained should be viewed with caution.

The breeding season for the Allen's Hummingbirds differs from that of most neotropical migrants, because its "spring" migration occurs in our winter, and its "fall" migration occurs in our late spring or early summer (Phillips 1975). Generally, first arrivals are detected in the first two weeks of February, although males are occasionally found as early as the middle of January. During the atlas period, the earliest observation of breeding was of a female seen nest building on 24 Feb, and the latest evidence was dependent fledglings seen on 28 Jun. Following the atlas period, on 15 Feb 1997, nest building was observed in the Arastradero Preserve (Robert W. Reiling, pers. comm.). Allen's Hummingbirds typically raise two broods during a season (Ehrlich et al. 1988). By May or June the adult males start their southward migration; the females move south in June or July after they have fledged their young (Phillips 1975).

William G. Bousman

ALLEN'S HUMMINGBIRD

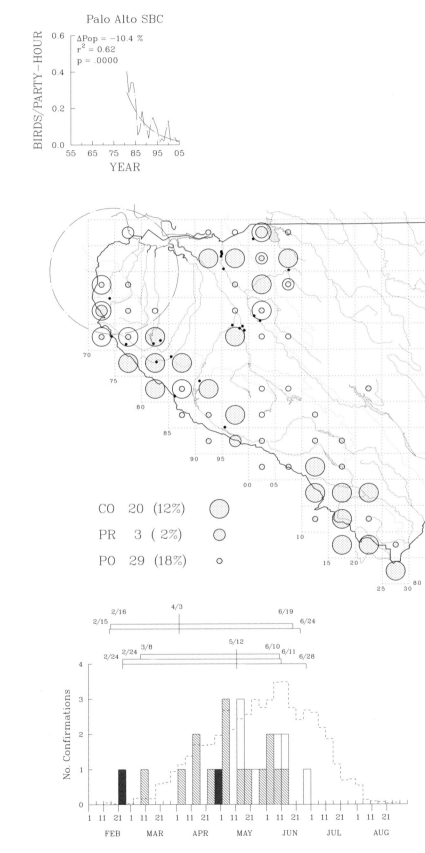

Palo Alto SBC

$\Delta Pop = -10.4\ \%$
$r^2 = 0.62$
$p = .0000$

CO   20 (12%)

PR   3 (2%)

PO   29 (18%)

Postatlas (1994–2005), n = 17

Atlas (1987–1993), n = 23

255

Belted Kingfisher
Megaceryle alcyon

The dry rattle of this shaggy-crested fisherman marks those Santa Clara County streams, reservoirs, and stock ponds having a suitable prey base of fish or arthropods. The Belted Kingfisher breeds widely in North America, from the tundra edge of Alaska and Canada south to California and across the continent to central Florida (Hamas 1994). Two subspecies have been recognized, the westernmost, *C. a. caurina*, being found from Alaska south to California, Arizona, and New Mexico (AOU 1957). This kingfisher is a rare resident in southern California but becomes more common in the northern half of the state (Small 1994). It is fairly common in Santa Clara County, wherever riparian areas provide nesting sites and suitable prey.

Price (1898b) considered the Belted Kingfisher to be a permanent resident near Stanford, and Van Denburgh (1899b) noted that it occasionally nested along larger streams in the county. Grinnell and Wythe (1927) considered it to be fairly common in the Bay area but did not note records for Santa Clara County, other than Van Denburgh's. Sibley (1952) wrote that W. E. Unglish had found adults feeding young on 27 May 1928 and 11 May 1930 at Betabel, presumably along the Pajaro River in either Santa Clara County or San Benito County. Analysis of the San Jose CBC data obtained since the 1950s shows a population increase of about 1.7% a year, whereas numbers have remained fairly constant on the Palo Alto CBC. Numbers detected on the winter and summer Palo Alto counts are similar to one another, suggesting that the birds along these local streams are resident.

Atlasers found the Belted Kingfisher at numerous locations in Santa Clara County, although most breeding records were obtained from streams draining eastward from the Santa Cruz Mountains, from creeks along the valley floor, and in the Alameda Creek drainage in the northern Diablo Range. Birds were also seen along upper portions of Coyote Creek and in the Pacheco Creek drainage, but no proof of nesting was obtained there. The water levels in the upper reaches of both creek systems are intermittent during many summers and may not support the prey base required by nesting kingfishers. (In some cases, atlasers recorded Belted Kingfishers in habitats that they judged unsuitable, and these records are marked with an "×" on the map.) Atlasers recorded breeding birds from elevations as low as 10 feet on the valley floor to as high as 2,320 feet in the northern Diablo Range. Subsequent to the atlas period, on 16 Jul 1994, fledged young were found with a female at a stock pond northeast of Valpe Ridge and Mt. Lewis in the Diablo Range at an elevation of 3,090 feet (Michael M. Rogers, pers. comm.). As expected, atlasers found this kingfisher associated with water, most often along permanent streams, but also at reservoirs and stock ponds.

Belted Kingfisher nest burrows were found at 10 locations during the atlas period, and at 11 additional spots afterward. Most of these burrows were in steep banks over permanent streams, the burrow near the top of the bank, as is typical for this species (Hamas 1994). One burrow, found after the atlas period among tree roots along Coyote Creek, was about 1.5 m above the water (Stephen C. Rottenborn, pers. comm.). Another burrow, along Los Gatos Creek, was near a well-used public footbridge. The most unusual nest site, found after the atlas period on 27 May 1994, was in a dry drainpipe in a 3-m -high concrete wall along San Tomas Aquinas Creek (Stephen C. Rottenborn, pers. comm.).

Most breeding confirmations were based on adults carrying food (54%), and therefore are not reflected in the phenology shown here. Birds were seen at nest burrows as early as 13 Apr during the atlas period, and adults feeding young were seen as late as 12 Jul. After the atlas period, an occupied nest was found on the earlier date of 9 Apr 1997 (Les Chibana, county notebooks) and fledged young were found later, on 22 Jul 2005, at Almaden Reservoir (Ann Verdi, PADB).

Human disturbance of creeks and streams in Santa Clara County, pervasive over the last two centuries, is reflected in the destruction of riparian undergrowth by grazing, the lowering of the water table as a result of groundwater pumping, and the presence of contaminants such as mercury in some of our local streams. Through this period, the Belted Kingfisher appears to have adapted to changes in its prey base. Although native fish continue to dominate at higher elevations or in undisturbed creeks, non-native fishes became established in local streams in the 1950s, and today these assemblages are dominant at lower elevations, where streams and creeks have undergone the greatest modification (Leidy 1984). Despite these changes, the Belted Kingfisher's population remains stable in Santa Clara County.

William G. Bousman

BELTED KINGFISHER

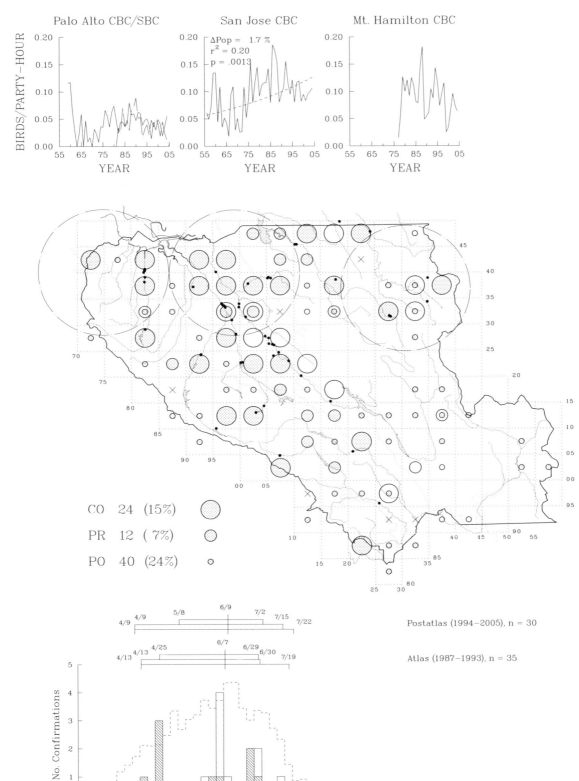

Palo Alto CBC/SBC

San Jose CBC
ΔPop = 1.7 %
r^2 = 0.20
p = .0013

Mt. Hamilton CBC

BIRDS/PARTY–HOUR

YEAR

CO   24 (15%)
PR   12 (7%)
PO   40 (24%)

Postatlas (1994–2005), n = 30

Atlas (1987–1993), n = 35

No. Confirmations

MAR   APR   MAY   JUN   JUL   AUG

257

Lewis's Woodpecker
Melanerpes lewis

The Lewis's Woodpecker is unusual for its crow-like flight style and its propensity for extended flycatching forays. This species breeds very locally from southern British Columbia and Alberta south over most of the western United States in a variety of habitats offering scattered trees, dead wood, and open foraging areas with insects (AOU 1998). Most northern breeders move south in the winter, and during this season the species can be found as far south as northern Mexico. In California, the Lewis's Woodpecker breeds from the northeastern part of the state south along the Sierra Nevada, and along the east slope of the inner Coast Ranges from Tehama County south to San Luis Obispo County (Zeiner et al. 1990, Small 1994). In Santa Clara County, Lewis's Woodpeckers breed primarily in oak savanna and open oak woodland in the northeastern part of the county, occurring elsewhere at scattered locations as a rare migrant or winter visitor. Santa Clara County's populations show considerable interannual fluctuation.

The nomadic nature of Lewis's Woodpecker breeding populations may be responsible for the somewhat contradictory descriptions of this species' historical breeding status in Santa Clara County. Cooper (1870) reported that this species was "quite common near New Almaden, but not elsewhere in the Coast Range southward, during summer." H. C. Benson collected an egg set near Gilroy on 8 May 1894 (USNM #B27038). Price (1898b) considered the bird a permanent resident around Stanford University, and noted that the species might nest in the area. In contrast, Van Denburgh (1899b) wrote that the Lewis's Woodpecker was "not often seen at Palo Alto," and Fisher (1902) considered it only a "winter visitant" in the Santa Clara Valley and the Santa Cruz Mountains. Grinnell and Wythe (1927) called the Lewis's Woodpecker an "erratic winter visitant" in the San Francisco Bay area, listing Palo Alto and New Almaden as areas of occurrence during the nonbreeding season, but indicated that the species was rare as a breeder anywhere in the Bay area. Bolander (1930) suspected nesting in oak savanna near Coyote,

and Unglish considered the Lewis's Woodpecker "erratic in its nesting near Gilroy" in the 1930s (Sibley 1952). Sibley (1952) called it an "uncommon resident, mainly in the drier eastern and southern portions" of the South Bay region.

Since the 1950s, small numbers of Lewis's Woodpeckers have been reported throughout the county during the nonbreeding season, but the vast majority of breeding-season records have been from the interior of the Diablo Range in the San Antonio and Isabel valleys. No statistically significant changes in Lewis's Woodpecker numbers are evident in statewide data from Breeding Bird Surveys (Sauer et al. 2005), or more locally, from the Mt. Hamilton Christmas Bird Count data. But along lower Mines Road in Alameda County, observers noted an apparent decline through the 1970s and 1980s, owing perhaps to competition for nest sites with the European Starling, but perhaps also reflecting the normal population dynamics of a nomadic species at the edge of its range (*Am. Birds* 35:333 1981, 35:975 1981, 36:891 1982).

Atlasers found the Lewis's Woodpecker to be an uncommon breeder in a small section of the northeastern part of Santa Clara County. Its abundance was greatest in the San Antonio Valley, but the species was also confirmed breeding in the surrounding hills and in the Isabel Valley. A single bird at Casa de Fruta on 13 Jun and five at Kelly Cabin Lake in Henry Coe State Park on 18 Jul provided atlas records of possible breeders elsewhere in the Diablo Range. Lewis's Woodpeckers nested most commonly in savanna with scattered mature valley or blue oaks and in open oak woodland. Mature oaks, and occasionally foothill pines, provided nest sites and perches from which these birds launched their aerial sorties for insects. Lewis's Woodpeckers were less common in denser stands and in more extensive tracts of oak woodland. All breeding confirmations were at elevations between 2,020 and 2,500 feet.

Postatlas records show several breeding-season records away from the San Antonio and Isabel valleys (county notebooks), indicating a somewhat broader distribution. Two pairs were confirmed breeding near Eagle Lake at Joseph Grant County Park in 2001; occupied nests discovered on 20 May 2001 had young by 26 May (mult. obs). Birds found north of San Antonio Valley on 17 May 1997 (pers. obs.), northeast of Mt. Lewis on 6 Jul 1995 (Michael M. Rogers, PADB), and on Loma Prieta Road on 1 June 2001 (Robert W. Reiling, Frank Vanslager, county notebooks) presented possible breeding records in additional outlying areas. Other Lewis's Woodpeckers seen at scattered Diablo Range locations in late July and August were likely postbreeding dispersants, whereas individuals recorded away from the northeastern part of the county in April and early May (but not seen later) were considered possible migrants or overwintering birds; such records are not mapped.

During the atlas period, seven nests with young were observed between 22 May and 19 Jun, and single occupied nests with unknown contents were observed on 9 Jun and 7 Jul. Adults were seen carrying food for young on 23 May and 17 Jul. After the atlas period, slightly earlier confirmations included an occupied nest on 3 May 1998 and adults carrying food to a nest on 6 May 2000, both in the San Antonio Valley (Les Chibana, county notebooks).

Stephen C. Rottenborn

LEWIS'S WOODPECKER

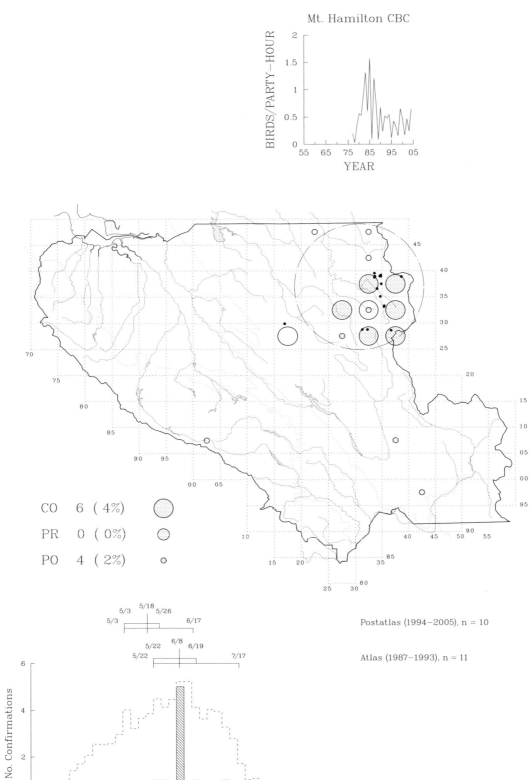

Mt. Hamilton CBC

CO   6 (4%)

PR   0 (0%)

PO   4 (2%)

Postatlas (1994–2005), n = 10

Atlas (1987–1993), n = 11

ROLLWELL 97

Acorn Woodpecker
Melanerpes formicivorus

The noisy, wonderfully colorful Acorn Woodpeckers are seemingly the clowns of the county's oak woodlands. But a closer look reveals birds with complex social behaviors arranged around their amazing acorn granaries. Closely associated with oaks throughout their range, Acorn Woodpeckers are found in separated regions of western North America from Oregon south to Nicaragua (Koenig et al. 1995). In California, they are generally found west of the Cascades-Sierra axis, but are absent from extensive grasslands without oaks in the Central Valley, as well as from the desert regions of the state (Small 1994). Acorn Woodpeckers are common throughout Santa Clara County, except along the edge of the San Francisco Bay and in the urban areas on the valley floor, where oaks and their preferred granary trees are no longer extant.

Early historical records of Acorn Woodpeckers include a specimen collected by James G. Cooper in the Santa Clara Valley on 2 Nov 1855 (USNM #A05957) and another collected by Thomas Bridges in "the Valley of San José" sometime prior to 1857 (Sclater 1857). H. C. Benson collected a set of four eggs near Gilroy on 9 May 1892 (USNM #B25667). Local observers at the close of the nineteenth century considered this species to be a common to abundant resident (Price 1898b, Van Denburgh 1899b, Fisher 1902). Grinnell and Wythe (1927), in assessing the status of birds in the San Francisco Bay area, reported it as common everywhere but San Francisco itself. Sibley (1952) noted that it was a common resident in the South Bay wherever oaks were found. Since the 1950s, analysis of CBC data for the Palo Alto and San Jose count circles shows a decline of 1.3% and 2.7% per year, respectively. But because no significant change has been noted in California as a whole for the period 1966 to 2004 (Sauer et al. 2005), it seems likely that these local declines are related to urbanization.

Atlasers found Acorn Woodpeckers breeding throughout the county, except near the Bay, in denser urban areas, and in three blocks of mostly agricultural land at the edge of the Bolsa de San Felipe. Where found, Acorn Woodpeckers were the most common woodpeckers, generally observed near oak trees where acorn mast was available, the list including valley oaks, coast live oaks, blue oaks, canyon live oaks, and interior live oaks. Inevitably, their breeding territories included one or more granary trees in which acorns were stored. These trees were frequently valley oaks, with holes drilled in the thick bark, but snags in conifers such as coast redwood and Douglas fir were also used. Occasionally, utility poles or other manmade structures were used for granaries. Acorn Woodpeckers most often excavated their nest cavities in oak trees, but on the flatlands they also used various species of introduced palms and occasionally other trees, such as cottonwoods. During the atlas period, breeding was confirmed from an elevation of 70 feet on the Stanford Campus to 3,440 feet at two sites on Black Mountain in the Diablo Range, east of the Calaveras Reservoir. Following the atlas period, breeding was observed on Eylar Mountain at an elevation of 3,780 feet (Michael M. Rogers, PADB).

The earliest evidence of breeding observed during the atlas period was an occupied nest on 15 Apr in the southern Santa Cruz Mountains. Subsequent to the atlas period, an earlier occupied nest was recorded, on 27 Mar 1994 in the foothills of the Diablo Range (Michael M. Rogers, PADB). The latest evidence of breeding was a begging fledgling seen at Stanford University on 20 Nov, probably from an occupied nest that had been seen nearby on 28 Sep. Fall nesting occurs occasionally in Acorn Woodpecker populations in years with good acorn crops (Koenig et al. 1995). Historically, a pair was seen feeding young in Los Gatos on 3 Oct 1930 (Wright and Smith 1930), but in general, late breeding has been noted only rarely in the county. The latest breeding evidence associated with summer nesting was fledged young seen on 10 Aug in the Stevens Creek Canyon in the Monte Bello Open Space Preserve.

The Acorn Woodpecker is often the most abundant woodpecker in areas within its North American range, which has changed little since presettlement times (Koenig et al. 1995). Grinnell and Miller (1944) noted that there were local reductions in its California range as old oak trees were removed, but commented that this was compensated for by the creation of new oak habitat in urban areas that had previously been grassland. As noted above, there has been a slow decline in numbers of Acorn Woodpeckers in urbanized areas of the northern Santa Clara Valley over the last fifty years. Ruth G. Troetschler (1976) made an extensive study of ten groups of Acorn Woodpeckers in parts of Palo Alto, Mountain View, Los Altos, and Los Altos Hills from 1968 to 1974, to examine the effects of nest-hole competition between this woodpecker and the European Starling. Twenty years later, only two of the original ten woodpecker groups remain (Ruth G. Troetschler, pers. comm.). In each case when a group abandoned its territory the cause was the removal of a granary tree. Acorn Woodpeckers are expected to remain common in parklands, preserves, and more remote areas of the county, but are unlikely to remain in urban areas where housing density is increasing.

William G. Bousman

ACORN WOODPECKER

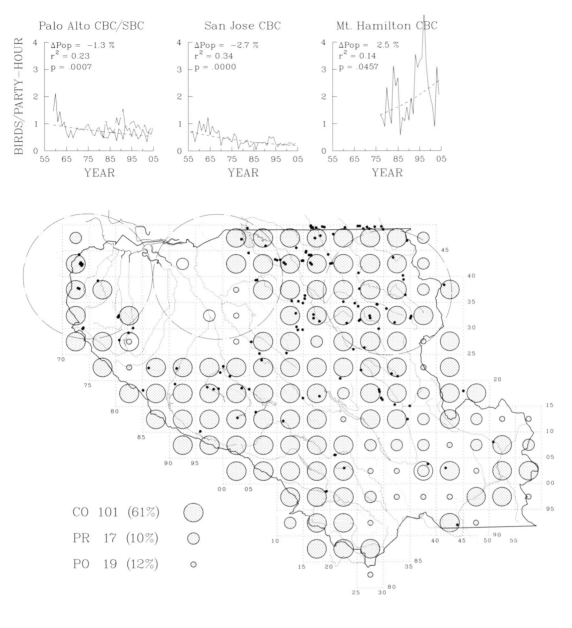

Palo Alto CBC/SBC

ΔPop = −1.3 %
r² = 0.23
p = .0007

San Jose CBC

ΔPop = −2.7 %
r² = 0.34
p = .0000

Mt. Hamilton CBC

ΔPop = 2.5 %
r² = 0.14
p = .0457

BIRDS/PARTY−HOUR

YEAR

CO 101 (61%)
PR   17 (10%)
PO   19 (12%)

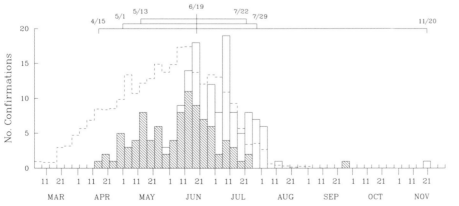

Atlas (1987−1993), n = 182

No. Confirmations

4/15 5/1 5/13 6/19 7/22 7/29 11/20

MAR APR MAY JUN JUL AUG SEP OCT NOV

Nuttall's Woodpecker
Picoides nuttallii

This woodpecker, characteristic of oak woodlands, has expanded its range to fill a variety of habitats in Santa Clara County. A near-endemic to California, the Nuttall's Woodpecker is resident west of both the Cascades-Sierra axis and the southeastern deserts, and occurs south to northwestern Baja California. It is absent, however, from the humid northwest coast (Lowther 2000). In Santa Clara County, this woodpecker is a widespread, common resident.

On his earliest visit to Santa Clara County in November 1855, James G. Cooper collected a Nuttall's Woodpecker (USNM #607238). This woodpecker was also included in Sclater's list of the specimens collected by Thomas Bridges in the "valley of San José" prior to 1857 (Sclater 1857). Its status at the end of the nineteenth century, particularly in the northwestern portion of the county, is unclear. Taylor (1893) found it regularly along the Pajaro River near Sargent, but not elsewhere. Rollo H. Beck, however, collected four eggs at Berryessa on the east side of the Santa Clara Valley on 7 May 1896 (USNM #B28317). Price (1898b) listed it as a permanent resident in the Stanford area, but Van Denburgh (1899b), who lived in both Palo Alto and Los Gatos, reported seeing it only on Mt. Hamilton. Grinnell and Wythe (1927) considered the Nuttall's as "resident in small numbers locally" and cited observations from Palo Alto, Santa Clara, Calaveras Valley, and Mt. Hamilton. By the mid-twentieth century, Sibley (1952) stated that the Nuttall's Woodpecker was common in the drier parts of the South Bay.

Analysis of Christmas and Summer Bird Count data shows an increase in the numbers of Nuttall's Woodpeckers in the northwestern part of the county since the 1950s. In the Palo Alto count circle, it was not recorded prior to 1968, but since then numbers have increased at a rate of 12.7% per year. Although the increase of 2.3% per year in the San Jose CBC circle from 1954 to 2004 is far less than that in Palo Alto, it is still substantial, sufficient for a tripling in numbers over the period. Numbers recorded on the Mt. Hamilton CBC have remained relatively constant since 1977. The dramatic range expansion in northwestern Santa Clara County has continued into adjacent San Mateo County (Sequoia Audubon Society 2001d).

Atlasers found the Nuttall's Woodpecker to be present in nearly all atlas blocks, its breeding confirmed in 134 blocks (81%), and when confirmed, probable, and possible evidence is combined, breeding was likely in 150 blocks (91%). Birds were found nesting from an elevation of 20 feet in riparian woodlands along Coyote Creek to 4,000 feet on Mt. Hamilton. Found most often in oak woodlands, particularly in the Diablo Range, this woodpecker was also found in riparian forests lacking oaks, and in oak woodlands on hillsides adjacent to small riparian areas along intermittent streams. The only blocks where it was not seen were those near the Bay, where potential nest sites were limited, and in the Santa Cruz Mountains, where extensive coniferous and broadleaved evergreen forests were apparently avoided. In oak woodlands, Nuttall's generally nested in blue or valley oaks, sometimes in dead limbs or snags, but also within the trunk when wood could be easily excavated. In riparian areas within oak woodlands these woodpeckers would often use deciduous trees along the stream for nest sites, as noted by Miller and Bock (1972) in Monterey County. In more mesic areas with extensive riparian woodlands and forest, these birds used a variety of trees for nest sites, including live oaks, valley oaks, sycamores, and cottonwoods. They were apparently able to use many habitats, including those modified by man, as long as there were suitable trees nearby for foraging and nesting. During the atlas period, a pair was observed nesting in a eucalyptus grove, and subsequent to the atlasing, a male was found excavating a hole in a roadside utility pole in New Almaden (Michael M. Rogers, pers. comm.).

Miller and Bock (1972) observed that resident male and female Nuttall's Woodpeckers tend to remain separate during fall and winter, but engage in preliminary nesting activities in February. At the Hastings Reservation in Monterey County, active nests were found from 25 Mar to 14 Jun (Miller and Bock 1972). During our atlas period, the earliest nesting evidence was a bird observed at a nest in Stevens Creek County Park on 9 Apr. Subsequent to this period, a pair was found occupying a nest in residential Palo Alto on 24 Mar 1997 (Rosalie Lefkowitz, pers. comm.). The latest nesting evidence was an occupied nest found near Uvas Creek on 12 Jul. Dependent young were found as late as 1 Aug along Arroyo Bayo in the Diablo Range.

Although there is only anecdotal evidence to support the observation, it appears that Nuttall's Woodpeckers were less common in this area a century ago than they are today, and the expansion of this species onto the San Francisco Peninsula over the last half century is now well documented. The reasons for such a rapid expansion are unknown. Have there been subtle changes in climate or human development that have increased prey availability and aided this oak woodland specialist? Or has the Nuttall's Woodpecker simply become a more effective competitor in the more humid northwest portions of the county?

William G. Bousman

NUTTALL'S WOODPECKER

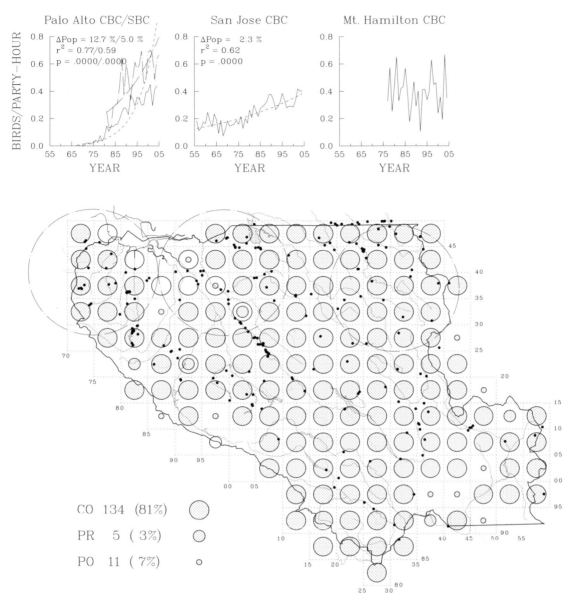

Palo Alto CBC/SBC

ΔPop = 12.7 %/5.0 %
r² = 0.77/0.59
p = .0000/.0000

San Jose CBC

ΔPop = 2.3 %
r² = 0.62
p = .0000

Mt. Hamilton CBC

BIRDS/PARTY-HOUR

YEAR

CO 134 (81%)
PR 5 (3%)
PO 11 (7%)

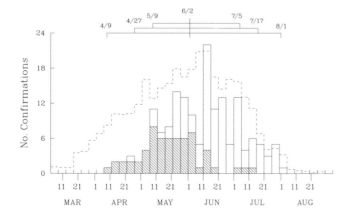

Atlas (1987–1993), n = 225

©KLA-C 1987

Downy Woodpecker
Picoides pubescens

This small, elegant woodpecker is frequently found in its beloved willows and cottonwoods along Santa Clara County's creeks and streams. The Downy Woodpecker breeds from Alaska across Canada to Newfoundland, and south in the United States to southern California and southern Florida (AOU 1988). Of the seven subspecies described, three are found in California (AOU 1957). The subspecies *gairdnerii* is found in the wet coastal forests north of central Mendocino County, and *leucurus* is found in northeastern California (Grinnell and Miller 1944). Formerly called the "Willow Woodpecker," the subspecies *turati* breeds from northern California west of the Sierra Nevada south to San Diego County (Grinnell and Miller 1944). In Santa Clara County, Downy Woodpeckers are fairly common, widespread residents.

A Downy Woodpecker was collected in the "Valley of San José" prior to 1857 by Thomas Bridges (Sclater 1857). Early observers here variously considered this woodpecker uncommon to common (Price 1898b, Van Denburgh 1899b, Fisher 1902). Rollo H. Beck found a nest in Berryessa on 8 Mar 1896 and collected four eggs (USNM #B28316). Grinnell and Wythe (1927) considered this species fairly common locally and mentioned Palo Alto, San Jose, Berryessa, and Los Gatos as locations where it was found within Santa Clara County. Sibley (1952) recorded the Downy Woodpecker as common in local riparian woodlands. Since the 1950s, the numbers of this woodpecker tallied on the local Christmas Bird Counts have remained constant.

During the atlas period, Downy Woodpeckers were found in 126 atlas blocks (76%) and were confirmed breeding in 51 blocks (31%). Nesting birds were found widely in the county, although they were absent from a number of areas, particularly in the Diablo Range, where there are substantial expanses of chaparral and grasslands and a lack of permanent water. Nest sites were found at elevations of 10 feet, along Coyote Creek

near the San Francisco Bay, to an elevation of 2,880 feet on the southwestern side of Eylar Mountain above Colorado Creek, although 90 percent of nest sites were below 1,700 feet. Generally, downies nested in dead limbs or in snags in riparian areas, sometimes over water, but nesting birds were also found away from riparian areas in oak woodlands, as noted by Grinnell and Miller (1944). The high-elevation nest on Eylar Mountain was in an oak in the middle of grasslands on the mountain's southwest slopes.

The earliest nesting evidence observed during the atlas period was a bird occupying a nesting cavity on 17 Apr. Following the atlas period, a pair of downies were seen finishing the excavation of a new nest hole on 16 Mar 1997 (Michael M. Rogers, PADB). The latest breeding evidence obtained was of young being fed on 21 Jul. Bent (1939a) recorded egg dates for nesting Downy Woodpeckers in California as extending from 7 Apr to 9 Jun, with half the records falling between 24 Apr and 13 May. Eleven observations of occupied nests were recorded during the atlas period, and their median date of 6 May agrees well with Bent's egg dates.

The Nuttall's Woodpecker, a congener of the Downy Woodpecker, has expanded its range northwestward in Santa Clara County in the last three decades. Where it was once absent from the Palo Alto count circle, it is now more common than the downy. Although the Downy Woodpecker is considered primarily a riparian species and Nuttall's a bird of oak woodlands, there is a broad overlap in their habitat use. Along Coyote Creek, Rottenborn (1999) found both species to be fairly common, with downies on 53% of his study plots and Nuttall's on 40% of the plots. The Downy Woodpecker tends to forage by drilling, scaling, and prying from limbs and twigs, whereas Nuttall's does more gleaning and probing from the surfaces of limbs and trees (Shuford 1993q). Possibly because of this difference in foraging habits, the invasion of Nuttall's Woodpeckers has had no detectable effect on the local population of Downy Woodpeckers, to judge from an analysis of the two species within the Palo Alto count circle; that is, the numbers are uncorrelated (CBC: $r^2 = 0.07$, $n = 29$; SBC: $r^2 = 0.03$, $n = 18$). Hybridization between these two closely related species is infrequent (Lowther 2000), so the nesting of a male Nuttall's and a female Downy in Palo Alto in 1997 is of interest. This pair was observed during May and June of that year and successfully raised at least one young to fledging (Carlin Otto, county notebooks). It has been hypothesized that hybridization between these species is more likely to occur where one or the other of the two species occurs in low numbers (Unitt 1986), but that is not the case for the Palo Alto hybrid record.

William G. Bousman

DOWNY WOODPECKER

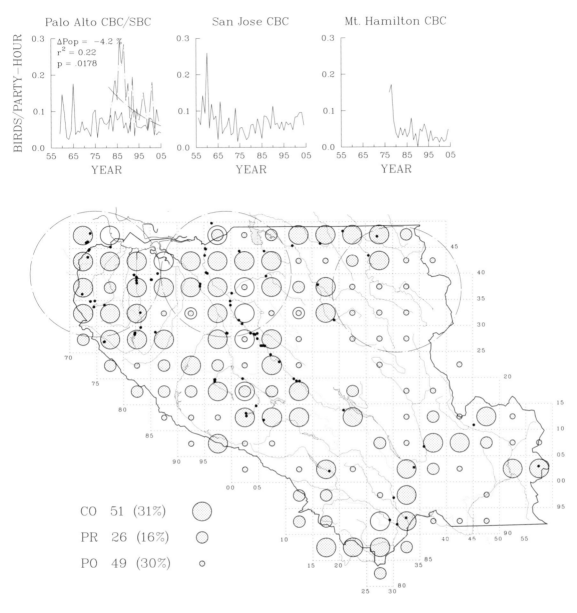

Palo Alto CBC/SBC

ΔPop = −4.2 %
r² = 0.22
p = .0178

San Jose CBC

Mt. Hamilton CBC

BIRDS/PARTY−HOUR

YEAR

CO   51   (31%)
PR   26   (16%)
PO   49   (30%)

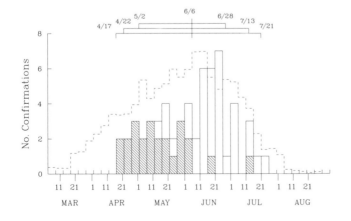

Atlas (1987−1993), n = 70

No. Confirmations

MAR   APR   MAY   JUN   JUL   AUG

Hairy Woodpecker
Picoides villosus

The Hairy Woodpecker, more heavily built than its congener the Downy Woodpecker, is found locally in mature forests and denser woodlands, in contrast to the riparian forest and fragmented woodlands preferred by the downy. The Hairy Woodpecker breeds from central Alaska across Canada to Newfoundland and thence south to Baja California and Florida. Resident populations are also found in the highlands of Mexico and Central America south to Panama, as well as in the Bahamas (Jackson et al. 2002). The species breeds widely throughout the forested areas of California, being absent only from the Central Valley and the deserts of the southeast (Grinnell and Miller 1944, Small 1994). Of seventeen subspecies, four are found in California. Of these, *P. v. hyloscopus* occurs in much of coastal California (including all of Santa Clara County) and in the southern Sierra Nevada (Grinnell and Miller 1944, Jackson et al. 2002). The Hairy Woodpecker is a fairly common resident in Santa Clara County, found generally at higher elevations, although a few nest along lowland streams.

The earliest record of a Hairy Woodpecker in Santa Clara County was a specimen collected by Thomas Bridges in "the Valley of San José" sometime prior to 1857 (Sclater 1857). The type specimen of the subspecies *P. v. hyloscopus*, as described by J. Cabanis and F. Heine in 1863 (AOU 1957), was collected in San Jose. Price (1898b) considered the Hairy Woodpecker a common winter resident along the creeks near Stanford and believed it bred nearby in "the redwoods." Van Denburgh (1899b), however, did not find it either at Los Gatos or at Palo Alto during his days afield. Barlow (1900b) collected a specimen in a valley oak grove near Sargent, but did not describe this species' status in the area. Henry B. Kaeding considered the hairy "not common" in the Santa Cruz Mountains (McGregor 1901), whereas Fisher (1902) said simply that it was resident. Grinnell and Wythe (1927), in examining the status of birds in the San Francisco Bay area, described the Hairy Woodpecker as a fairly common resident in timbered regions. In the South Bay, Sibley

(1952) also judged it to be fairly common. Analysis of CBC and SBC data shows no population changes in the Palo Alto count circle over the last 40 years, but it does show a 3.5% per year decline in the San Jose circle. There has been no change in numbers on the Mt. Hamilton CBC.

Hairy Woodpeckers were found to be widespread throughout the Santa Cruz Mountains and the northern portions of the Diablo Range during the atlas period. In the Santa Cruz Mountains, breeding birds were found in foothill areas on the eastern side, sometimes down to the flatlands boundary. In the Diablo Range, birds bred at higher elevations and were largely absent from the slopes and canyons on the western side. Breeding birds were also found in the southern reaches of the Diablo Range, but in fewer blocks than in the northern portion. During the atlas period, Hairy Woodpeckers were confirmed breeding at elevations ranging from 250 feet in Los Gatos near the Vasona Dam to 3,620 feet on the south slopes of Eylar Mountain. After the atlas period, fledged young were found as low as 96 feet along Coyote Creek below Tully Road (Stephen C. Rottenborn, county notebooks) and as high as 3,730 feet on the northwestern ridge of Eylar Mountain, just over the county line in Alameda County (Michael M. Rogers, PADB). Ninety percent of all atlas breeding records were from elevations above 780 feet. Atlasers generally found Hairy Woodpeckers breeding in forests or dense woodlands. In these areas they appeared to use larger trees, often where there was standing dead timber or live trees with snags. Nest cavities were most often in dead snags or in portions of live trees with extensive rot in the tree center.

Following the atlas period, Hairy Woodpeckers were confirmed nesting in two riparian areas on the valley floor (Stephen C. Rottenborn, pers. comm.). In these areas, they were found in mature cottonwood-dominated forests, generally in broader riparian corridors. A study in the Coyote Creek and Guadalupe River drainage basins in the mid-1990s found Hairy Woodpeckers in only two of 68 circular plots (Rottenborn 1999), whereas Downy and Nuttall's woodpeckers were found on 36 and 27 plots, respectively.

The earliest breeding evidence observed during the atlas period was an occupied nest in the southern Santa Cruz Mountains on 21 Apr. Following the atlas period, an occupied nest was found one day earlier, on 20 Apr 1994, in Stevens Creek County Park (Michael M. Rogers, PADB). The latest breeding evidence observed was fledged young found on 5 Aug southeast of where Guadalupe Creek leaves the foothills in southern San Jose.

Hairy Woodpeckers are largely sedentary in Santa Clara County, and do not show significant seasonal movements. Although Price (1898b) found them along creeks near Stanford during the winter, analysis of recent Palo Alto CBC and SBC data, broken down into eight subregions, indicates that this woodpecker is found in the same mountain and foothill areas in both winter and summer. In Napa County, this woodpecker has invaded forests impacted by fire (Berner 2003e), but in Santa Clara County there were no detailed studies of habitat use following the 1984 Lexington fire, and it is unknown if a similar shift occurred.

William G. Bousman

HAIRY WOODPECKER

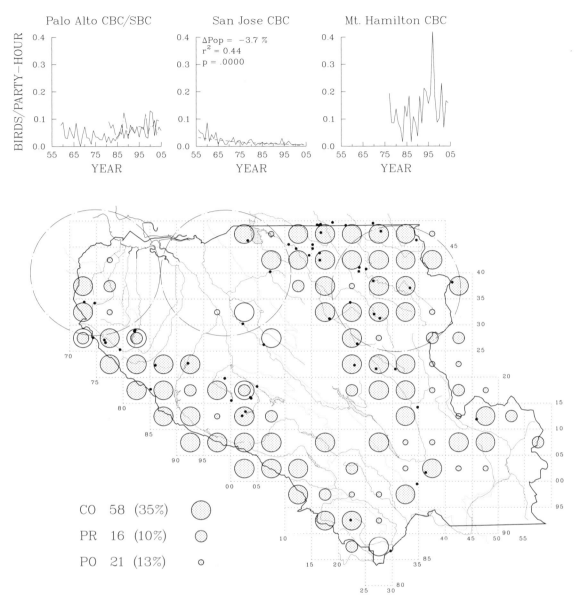

Palo Alto CBC/SBC

San Jose CBC

ΔPop = −3.7 %
r² = 0.44
p = .0000

Mt. Hamilton CBC

BIRDS/PARTY−HOUR

YEAR

CO 58 (35%)
PR 16 (10%)
PO 21 (13%)

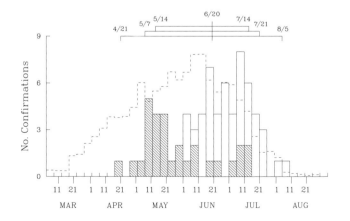

Atlas (1987−1993), n = 80

No. Confirmations

4/21   5/7   5/14   6/20   7/14   7/21   8/5

MAR   APR   MAY   JUN   JUL   AUG

Northern Flicker
Colaptes auratus

An omnivorous forager, this woodpecker with flashing wing linings busies itself on the ground as often as in trees and shrubs. The Northern Flicker breeds from central Alaska, across Canada to Newfoundland, and south throughout the United States and Mexico to Nicaragua (Moore 1995). Specialists place subspecies of this flicker in four groups: *auratus* (Yellow-shafted Flicker) in eastern North America, *cafer* (Red-shafted Flicker) in western North America, *chrysocaulosus* (Cuban Flicker) in Cuba, and *mexicanoides* (Guatemalan Flicker) from Mexico to Nicaragua (AOU 1998). The *cafer* group includes three subspecies, two of which breed in California: *cafer* in the northwestern counties and *collaris* throughout the rest of the state, including Santa Clara County (Grinnell and Miller 1944). The Northern Flicker is a common resident in Santa Clara County, its numbers substantially augmented in the winter by northern and montane birds.

A Northern Flicker collected by Thomas Bridges in "the Valley of San José" prior to 1857 (Sclater 1857) constitutes the first published record of this species in Santa Clara County. An early nesting record was documented by a set of six eggs collected by E. M. Haight in San Jose 8 May 1886 (USNM #B44098). Observers at the end of the nineteenth century considered this woodpecker a common, or even abundant, resident in the local area (Price 1898b, Van Denburgh 1899b, Fisher 1902). Grinnell and Miller (1944) commented that there had been apparently little change in its numbers during the European settlement period. Sibley (1952) regarded the Northern Flicker as a common resident, just as earlier observers had. Since the 1950s, there has been a significant decline in numbers of wintering birds of about 1.4% a year on the San Jose and Palo Alto CBCs, and analysis of the Palo Alto SBC data shows a decline of 2.2% a year. A similar decline of 1.1% a year has been noted for summer residents in California on Breeding Bird Survey routes from 1966 to 2004 (Sauer et al. 2005).

Northern Flickers were found widely in the county during the atlas period. Breeding was confirmed in 65 blocks (39%). Including probable or possible evidence, records were obtained in 133 blocks (81%). Atlasers observed nesting birds from elevations of 100 feet along Coyote Creek in Kelly Park, on the valley floor, to a height of 3,580 feet on the southwest slope of Eylar Mountain in the Diablo Range. Flickers were generally found in more open country offering a mixture of open woodlands and grasslands, forest edges with adjacent grasslands, and along streams with adjacent open areas for foraging. Within this relatively open terrain, they sought out nest sites in dead trees, particularly of softwoods such as cottonwood or pine. Rarely, they were found nesting in dead limbs or snags on living trees. A unique nest site was a utility pole near the summit of Mt. Umunhum. Nesting flickers were uncommon on the valley floor, where most records were from mature riparian forests surrounded by fields or parklands suitable for foraging.

Most of the breeding evidence observed during the atlas period was birds occupying a nesting site or hole (34%) or dependent fledglings (33%). Observations of excavations at nest sites were not generally regarded as breeding confirmations, since this species also excavates holes for roosting. But a bird seen excavating a hole near Anderson Reservoir on 29 Mar later used the same hole successfully for nesting. The earliest evidence of an occupied nest was on 21 Apr, and the latest observation of breeding behavior was adults feeding young on 4 Aug. Bent (1939b) noted records of 75 egg sets in California from 9 Apr to 2 Jul, a span that agrees well with the phenology shown here.

Population declines for the Northern Flicker have been observed throughout North America (Moore 1995) as well as in California (Sauer et al. 2005). Moore (1995) has suggested two hypotheses to explain these declines: competition with European Starlings for nest cavities; and the declining availability of dead trees, snags, or dead limbs suitable for nest-cavity sites. Moore (1995) considers this decline alarming, and states that there have been "no rigorous, focused studies [to] identify the cause of this decline." In Santa Clara County the Northern Flicker continues to be a common breeding species. Nonetheless, the problems this woodpecker is facing regionally demonstrate the need to retain dead trees and snags as an integral element of forest management in our local preserves and parks, not only for the flicker, but for other species that depend upon woodpecker holes for their nesting cavities.

William G. Bousman

NORTHERN FLICKER

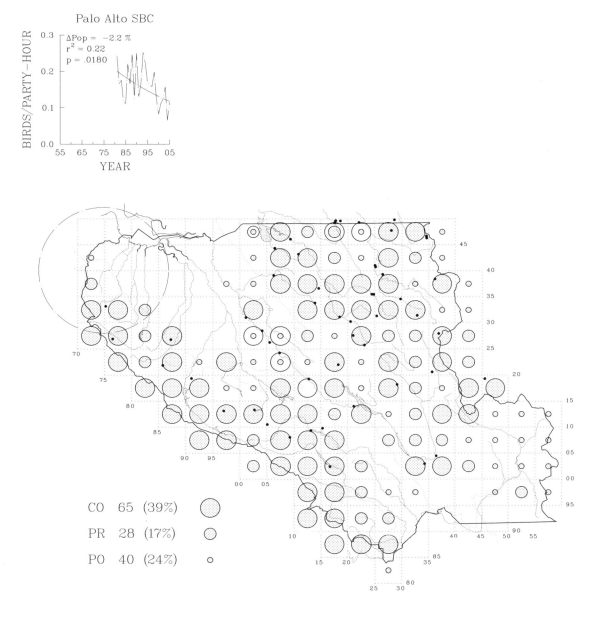

Palo Alto SBC

ΔPop = −2.2 %
$r^2 = 0.22$
p = .0180

BIRDS/PARTY−HOUR

YEAR

CO   65   (39%)
PR   28   (17%)
PO   40   (24%)

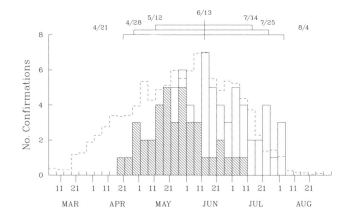

4/21   4/28   5/12   6/13   7/14   7/25   8/4

Atlas (1987–1993), n = 80

No. Confirmations

MAR   APR   MAY   JUN   JUL   AUG

Pileated Woodpecker
Dryocopus pileatus

The breeding range of this large, spectacular woodpecker has expanded southward in the Coast Ranges in recent decades, and a recently established population in the Santa Cruz Mountains is expanding rapidly. The Pileated Woodpecker is resident from British Columbia across Canada to Nova Scotia, and thence south to central California in the west and to Florida in the east (Bull and Jackson 1995). It is absent from extensively treeless areas, such as the Great Plains and the western deserts. Four subspecies have been described, all of the western birds deemed to be *D. p. picinus* (Bull and Jackson 1995). In California, this woodpecker is resident in the northern mountains of the state and is found in scattered locations south through the Coast Ranges to the San Francisco Bay area, and in the Sierra Nevada to Tulare County (Small 1994). In Santa Clara County the Pileated Woodpecker is now a rare resident in the mature Douglas fir and broadleaved evergreen forests of the Santa Cruz Mountains.

Early observers did not find the Pileated Woodpecker in Santa Clara County or nearby areas (Price 1898b, Van Denburgh 1899b, McGregor 1901, Fisher 1902). Cooper (1870) stated that it was rarely seen south of Marin County on the coast, although he had heard of a bird killed on Mt. Diablo in Contra Costa County. Farther out of range, an immature female was collected on 25 Nov 1882 in Hollister, San Benito County, by Henry W. Henshaw (BMNH # 1888.10.10.7525, Grinnell and Miller 1944). In his first state checklist, Grinnell (1902) reported that this woodpecker was found as far south in the Coast Ranges as the mouth of the Eel River in Humboldt County. Sheldon (1908) reported the taking of a specimen farther south, near the Gualala River in Sonoma County. In his second checklist, Grinnell (1915) stated that the species had been found as far south in the Coast Ranges as Seaview and Cazadero in Sonoma County, and Grinnell and Wythe (1927) noted the Sonoma County records as well as sporadic sightings from Marin County. Clark (1930) reported multiple observations of Pileated Woodpeckers on Howell Mountain in Napa County by 1929. But despite the increasing numbers of sight records in the North Bay counties, no breeding was observed in that area until Hemphill (1944) observed fledglings in the Los Posadas State Forest in Napa County, sometime

prior to 1944. The first nest record for Sonoma County was of a pair that fledged a single young at Jack London Ranch on 2 Jun 1963 (*Audubon Field Notes 17*:482 1963). Although observations of this species were regular in Marin County in the 1950s and 1960s, there was no actual observation of breeding evidence until 1976, when a pair was seen nesting at Lake Lagunitas (*Am. Birds 30*:884 1976).

The spread of the Pileated Woodpecker into the South Bay evidently did not begin until the early 1970s, when this species was first observed in the Santa Cruz Mountains (*Am. Birds 26*:805 1972). Curiously, the first record for Santa Clara County was not from the Santa Cruz Mountains, but of a single bird seen west of Calaveras Reservoir on 9 Mar 1980 (Donald E. Schmoldt, James Rosso, county notebooks). The first nesting reported in the Santa Cruz Mountains was from Big Basin Park in Santa Cruz County on 30 Jun 1987 (*Am. Birds 41*:1484 1987). Breeding in San Mateo County was first confirmed on 29 Jul 1988 (Sequoia Audubon Society 2001e). The first sighting of a Pileated Woodpecker on the Santa Clara County side of the Santa Cruz Mountains was on 31 Mar 1989, on Table Mountain (*Am. Birds 43*:533 1989).

During the atlas period, observations of Pileated Woodpeckers recorded in the county notebooks included a bird in Henry Coe State Park on 13 Mar 1987 (Barry Breckling), the Table Mountain record mentioned above, a bird along Gold Mine Creek in the Monte Bello Open Space Preserve on 13 Feb 1993 (Stephen C. Rottenborn, Eric Bjorkstedt), and two birds above Lake Elsman on 26 Nov 1993 (David L. Suddjian). These records were not considered to represent possible breeding, since they were outside of the normal breeding season and there was no history of the species nesting in the county.

Since the atlas period, detections of Pileated Woodpeckers in western Santa Clara County have steadily increased (county notebooks). The first evidence of breeding in the county was an adult female with a dependent fledgling seen near Lake Elsman on 8 Jul 1996 (David L. Suddjian). Subsequently, nesting was observed on Table Mountain on the west side of the Stevens Creek Canyon in 1998 (Nick Lethaby, mult. obs.); dependent fledglings were found farther up Stevens Creek Canyon in 1999 (Les Chibana); and an adult male was feeding young along Los Gatos Creek above Aldercroft Heights in 2003 (pers. obs.). In Santa Clara County, breeding Pileateds have been found in or near dense, mature stands of Douglas fir with smaller amounts of mature broadleaved evergreens. These mature stands have also included numerous snags, dead trees, and downed timber.

Seasonally, the earliest breeding evidence observed in Santa Clara County was a bird in a nest cavity in a dead Douglas fir on Table Mountain on 10 May 1998 (Nick Lethaby, county notebooks). Birds fledged from this nest by 14 Jun (mult. obs., county notebooks; Alan D. Walther, *Field Notes 52*:cover photograph 1998). The latest breeding evidence seen was dependent fledglings observed near the Grizzly Flat Trail in Monte Bello Open Space Preserve on 1 Aug 1999 (Les Chibana, county notebooks).

William G. Bousman

PILEATED WOODPECKER

Palo Alto CBC/SBC

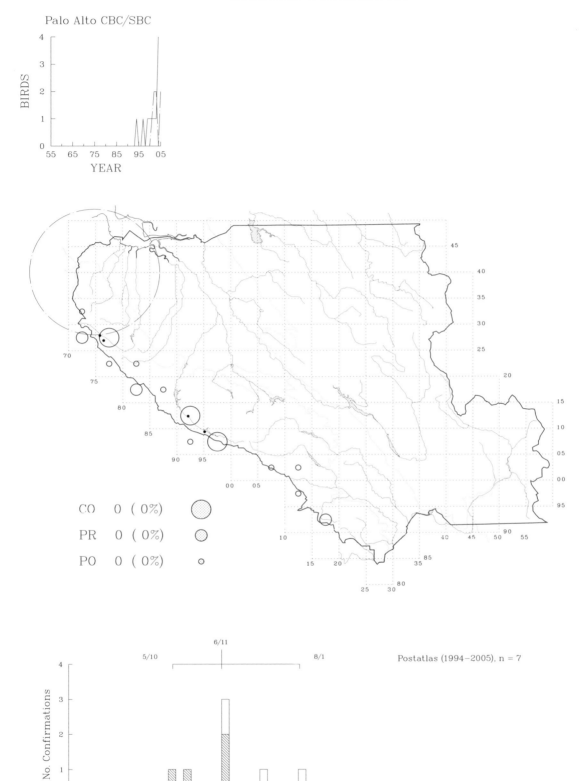

CO 0 (0%)

PR 0 (0%)

PO 0 (0%)

Postatlas (1994–2005), n = 7

Olive-sided Flycatcher
Contopus cooperi

This large flycatcher, fond of exposed perches overlooking the forest edge, is in decline throughout North America. The Olive-sided Flycatcher breeds from Alaska east across Canada to Newfoundland, and thence south in the western United States to northern Baja California, northeastern Arizona, and northern New Mexico, and in the eastern United States to Minnesota, northern New York, and Maine (Altman and Sallabanks 2000). Breeding locations are also scattered south through the Appalachian Mountains to Tennessee. Two subspecies are recognized: *marjorinus*, found in southern California and nearby Baja California; and *cooperi*, over the remainder of the range (Altman and Sallabanks 2000). In California, this flycatcher is found widely in the mountainous areas of the state (Small 1994). It is a fairly common summer resident in the Santa Cruz Mountains on the west side of Santa Clara County, and uncommon to rare in forested portions of the Diablo Range.

Early observers in the Santa Cruz Mountains variously judged this flycatcher to be uncommon or common (Cooper 1870, McGregor 1901). At Stanford, Price (1898d) described it as a rare visitant to the Coast Range. Van Denburgh (1899b) did not record it in Los Gatos, but Barlow (1900b) reported that Joseph Grinnell found a pair apparently nesting at Stanford University in 1900. Fisher (1902) considered it uncommon in the Santa Cruz Mountains. Grinnell and Wythe (1927) described the bird as a summer resident in small numbers in the Bay area, and noted its presence in planted groves of pine, cypress, and eucalyptus as well as in coniferous forests. For the South Bay region, Sibley (1952) judged it to be fairly common in forested areas.

Atlasers found Olive-sided Flycatchers breeding widely in the Santa Cruz Mountains, but only at scattered locations in the northern Diablo Range, and not at all elsewhere. Breeding elevations ranged from 400 feet in Stevens Creek County Park to 3,250 feet on a ridge east of Black Mountain in the Diablo Range. Breeding olive-sideds were generally found in coniferous forests or mixed coniferous and broadleaved evergreen forests, often on relatively steep slopes that included taller trees or snags offering the expansive views they prefer for aerial foraging. In the Santa Cruz Mountains, the coniferous forests where they were found were usually dominated by Douglas fir but included tan oak, live oak, and madrone. In the Diablo Range, atlasers found olive-sideds in open forests of Coulter pines that included black oaks. Nests, when found, were most often in conifers within these forests, but lower than the perches used for foraging. Birds occasionally used less typical habitat: nests were found in an oak within a largely broadleaved evergreen forest near Hicks and Alamitos roads in the Santa Cruz Mountains, and in planted conifers near Smith Creek at the Mt. Hamilton Road in the Diablo Range. Olive-sided Flycatchers also used small groves of eucalyptus trees at lower elevations in moist situations in canyons and arroyos where perches were available for foraging. Typical locations included eucalyptus along Stevens Creek in Stevens Creek County Park and along Penitencia Creek in Alum Rock Park.

Nesting in other types of trees was recorded prior to the atlas. Charles P. Smith (1927a) reported an Olive-sided Flycatcher nest, originally found by Emily D. Smith, that was placed about 50 feet above the ground in a white alder at the base of Monte Bello Ridge. He also described a nest in the upper Los Gatos Creek drainage that was placed 60 feet above the ground in a canyon live oak.

The first Olive-sided Flycatchers generally arrive in Santa Clara County between 9 and 19 Apr. The earliest breeding evidence observed was nest building on 3 May. Olive-sideds have a protracted nesting period (Altman and Sallabanks 2000), and fledglings were observed as late as 15 Aug. Historically, dependent fledglings have been seen as late as 28 Aug 1952 in an unspecified location in the Santa Cruz Mountains (*Audubon Field Notes* 7:35 1953). Following breeding, this flycatcher leaves quickly for its South American wintering grounds, and only a few lingering or migrating birds are encountered in September.

Olive-sided Flycatchers have seen a long-term decline throughout most of their breeding range in North America (Altman and Sallabanks 2000). Analysis of Breeding Bird Survey (BBS) data indicates that the center of abundance for this large flycatcher is in the mountain ranges of the western United States, from British Columbia to southern California, the greatest concentrations in the Sierra Nevada. In California, for the period 1966 to 2004, analysis of the BBS data shows a decline of 3.9% per year (Sauer et al. 2005). A decline of 10.3% per year within the Palo Alto count circle may represent a faster withdrawal of this species from the edge of its range as the overall population declines. Possible causes of these declines are largely conjectural (Altman and Sallabanks 2000), although the widespread nature of the reduction suggests that problems within this flycatcher's wintering range may be a significant factor. On its breeding grounds, the Olive-sided Flycatcher appears to be a burn specialist, succeeding best on the edge of recently burned forests, and decades of fire suppression may have forced this species to use suboptimal habitats associated with clear-cuts in modern managed forests. All of these factors are exacerbated by the reproductive rate of birds of this genus, which is the lowest of all North American passerine genera (Altman and Sallabanks 2000).

William G. Bousman

OLIVE-SIDED FLYCATCHER

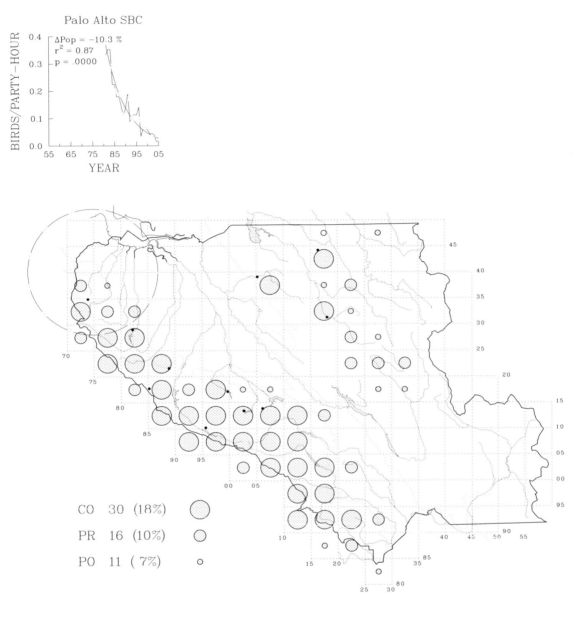

Palo Alto SBC

ΔPop = −10.3 %
r² = 0.87
p = .0000

BIRDS/PARTY−HOUR

YEAR

CO   30 (18%)
PR   16 (10%)
PO   11 (7%)

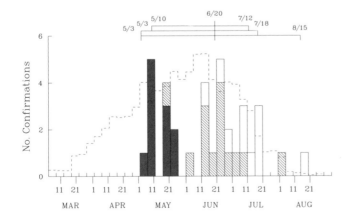

5/3 5/3 5/10   6/20 7/12 7/18   8/15

Atlas (1987−1993), n = 38

No. Confirmations

MAR   APR   MAY   JUN   JUL   AUG

273

©KLA-C 1987

Western Wood-Pewee
Contopus sordidulus

The nasal "pee-eer" of a Western Wood-Pewee, calling from a valley oak, seems as much a part of the open woodland as the insect noises building with the increasing heat of the day. This flycatcher breeds from central Alaska south through most of the western United States to southern Baja California, and south through the Mexican highlands into Guatemala and Honduras (AOU 1998, Bemis and Rising 1999). Four subspecies are generally recognized, although there is some disagreement about their taxonomy (Bemis and Rising 1999). The subspecies that breeds in California, *C. s. veliei*, is found from the northern edge of the state, south through the coastal and interior ranges to Los Angeles County, and south along the Cascades-Sierra axis to Kern County. It is found throughout the mountain ranges of southern California, but is absent from most of the Central Valley (Small 1994). In Santa Clara County, the Western Wood-Pewee is a common summer resident in woodlands and riparian areas in the Santa Cruz Mountains and the Diablo Range, but is less often found at low elevations on the valley floor.

Early observers considered the Western Wood-Pewee to be a common summer resident in Santa Clara County (Price 1898d, Van Denburgh 1899b, Fisher 1902). Price commented that at Stanford it was especially common along the creeks. Grinnell and Wythe (1927) reported it as occurring in varying numbers in most wooded regions of the San Francisco Bay area. Sibley (1952) judged the Western Wood-Pewee to be a common summer resident in almost any type of woodland. Nonetheless, analysis of the Palo Alto SBC data, obtained from the northwestern portion of Santa Clara County, shows a population decline for this species of 6.3% a year since 1981. Analysis of Breeding Bird Survey data within California as a whole shows a decline of 2.0% a year for the period 1966 to 2004 (Sauer et al. 2005).

Atlasers confirmed Western Wood-Pewees breeding in 78 blocks (47%). But considering confirmed, probable, and possible codes together, this pewee showed evidence of breeding in 128 blocks (78%). Observers found it to be a common breeding species in the Santa Cruz Mountains, the Diablo Range, and the southern Santa Clara Valley. It nested in small numbers at the edges of the northern Santa Clara Valley, but was absent from urbanized areas. Pewees nested from an elevation of 55 feet on the west side of the southern Santa Cruz Mountains in a Santa Cruz County edge block to 3,880 feet on Eylar Mountain in the Diablo Range. They were found in a variety of habitats, most birds either in broken woodlands or in riparian areas with a mixture of different tree types and a partially open canopy. Throughout the higher elevations of the Diablo Range and the Santa Cruz Mountains, they were found in open woodlands of oaks and other large trees, particularly where there were adjacent grasslands or other suitable edge habitat. Western Wood-Pewees were often found breeding in riparian areas, particularly where permanent or intermittent streams descended from the foothills of the Santa Cruz Mountains or the Diablo Range. In these riparian areas they selected perches in large trees where there were broad open spaces between trees and an irregular canopy or adjacent grasslands and chaparral. They avoided dense forest habitats where clearings or open space for foraging were lacking. Although they used riparian areas in the foothills, they were less common in such areas on the valley floor. Rottenborn (1999) censused breeding birds on 68 plots in riparian areas along the valley floor in 1995 and found fewer Western Wood-Pewees (7 plots) than Pacific-slope Flycatchers (49 plots) or Black Phoebes (51 plots).

Breeding Western Wood-Pewees arrive in Santa Clara County in mid-to-late April (median arrival date is 19 Apr, county notebooks). The earliest evidence of nesting was a bird constructing a nest near Calaveras Reservoir on 26 Apr. The latest breeding confirmation during the atlas period consisted of fledglings observed on the ridge west of Halls Valley on 1 Aug. After the atlas period, a fledgling was observed being fed by an adult along the Pajaro River near Sargent on 22 Aug 1996 (Stephen C. Rottenborn, pers. comm.).

Bemis and Rising (1999) note that the numbers of Western Wood-Pewees have declined over their entire range, but it is unclear whether this has been caused by riparian habitat losses in the breeding range, unknown changes in the bird's migration or wintering areas, or other factors. Within California, increases have been noted in some areas, such as remnant riparian stretches along the upper Sacramento River (Gaines 1974) and on San Benito Mountain, San Benito County (Johnson and Cicero 1985). Grinnell and Miller (1944) considered this to be one of the most common flycatchers in California, and in Santa Clara County this is still the case. However, the declines seen both locally and regionally are cause for concern, particularly considering how little we know about threats to this species during its annual migrations or on its wintering grounds in South America.

William G. Bousman

WESTERN WOOD-PEWEE

Palo Alto SBC

ΔPop = −6.3 %
r² = 0.79
p = .0000

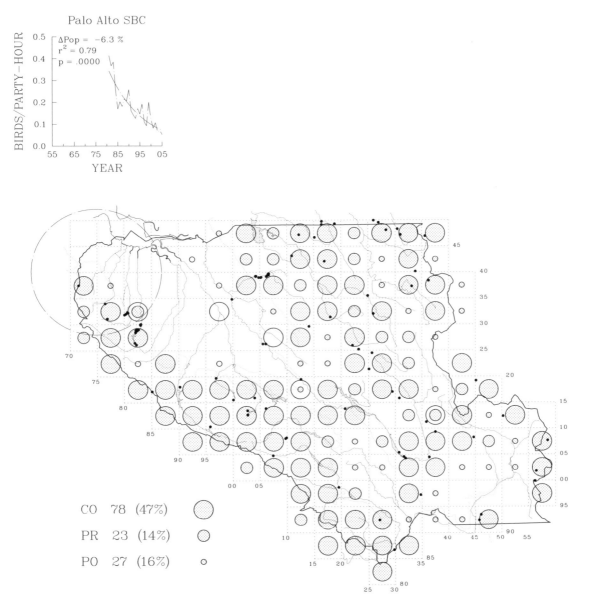

CO 78 (47%)

PR 23 (14%)

PO 27 (16%)

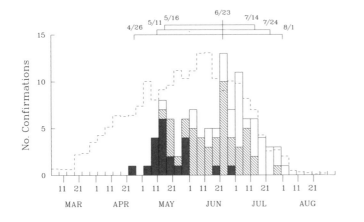

Atlas (1987–1993), n = 116

275

Pacific-slope Flycatcher
Empidonax difficilis

A common summer resident of quiet streamsides and shaded woods, the Pacific-slope Flycatcher is the only *Empidonax* flycatcher that currently nests in Santa Clara County. Until recently, this species and its close relative, the Cordilleran Flycatcher, were considered a single species, the Western Flycatcher. There are, however, differences in vocalizations and morphology between these sibling species (Johnson 1980), and protein electrophoresis has been used to show differences in allozyme frequencies as well (Johnson and Marten 1988). As a consequence of these investigations, the Western Flycatcher was split into two species (AOU 1989). The Pacific-slope Flycatcher breeds from southeastern Alaska to Baja California, and within California is found widely west of the Cascades-Sierra axis (AOU 1998). Of the two subspecies in California, *E. d. difficilis* is found over most of the state, including Santa Clara County; *insulicola* is found only on the Channel Islands off Southern California (Johnson and Marten 1988). The Pacific-slope Flycatcher is a common summer resident in mesic woodlands and forests in the western portion of Santa Clara County, but is less common in the drier Diablo Range.

At the close of the nineteenth century, the Pacific-slope Flycatcher was considered common or very common in Santa Clara County (Price 1898d, Van Denburgh 1899b, Fisher 1902). Grinnell and Wythe (1927) described this flycatcher as an "[a]bundant summer resident" in the San Francisco Bay area and noted its preference for well-shaded situations with a specific attraction to alders and bay trees. Sibley (1952) also considered the Pacific-slope Flycatcher to be common in the local area. There appears to have been little change in this species' status over the last century, and it remains common today in its favored areas.

Pacific-slope Flycatchers were found breeding in 39% of the atlas blocks, and they were summer residents in essentially all of the atlas blocks within the Santa Cruz Mountains. But in the Diablo Range, although found in 72% of the blocks, they were confirmed breeding in only 15% of them. On the valley floor, they were found breeding in streamside habitats, particularly along Coyote Creek and the Guadalupe River, but were absent from urban areas lacking mature vegetation and high-quality riparian habitat. During the atlas period, nesting was found from an elevation of 55 feet along Matadero Creek in urban Palo Alto to 3,580 feet beside a spring on the north slope of Mt. Hamilton. Subsequent to the atlas effort, these flycatchers were found breeding at a slightly lower elevation of 47 feet in wooded Menlo Park (pers. obs.). For nesting, this species prefers well-shaded forest and streamside situations where the canopy is relatively thick and the birds can obtain suitable insect prey. These habitats occur widely in the Santa Cruz Mountains, where this species was found to be common. In the Diablo Range, however, such habitats are more local and less widespread, occurring only in deeper canyons or along north-facing slopes. The reduction in breeding numbers in interior areas lacking dense forests and shade was noted in the Monterey and Marin county atlases as well (Roberson 1993p, Shuford 1993r).

Pacific-slope Flycatchers appear to be both flexible and opportunistic in their nest site selection. Most nests found during the atlas period were constructed on manmade structures, including on a porch light that was used daily by the homeowner. Nests were also found in cavities in stream banks, in tangled roots, and on streamside boulders, and one was built on an abandoned American Robin nest. Following the atlas period, during systematic surveys along the urban riparian corridors of Coyote Creek and Guadalupe River (Rottenborn 1997), most nests were found in shrubs and small trees such as willows, box elders, and small cottonwoods.

Studies of the effects of urbanization on riparian bird communities (Rottenborn 1997) have furnished useful information about the status of this species in the riparian habitats that remain on the valley floor north of the Coyote Narrows. Within 68 study plots in relatively mature and intact cottonwood-willow riparian habitat, the Pacific-slope Flycatcher was the sixth-most abundant species in terms of mean density. The species was widespread and fairly common in plots with increased canopy cover and volume of total vegetation, but numbers of birds declined as measures of urbanization, such as proximity to a bridge, increased.

The first Pacific-slope Flycatchers normally arrive in Santa Clara County in the last two weeks of March. The earliest observation of birds carrying nest material was on 7 Apr. The peak of breeding activity was from May through early July, and the last breeding record during the atlas period (fledged young) occurred on 4 Aug. Subsequent to the atlas period, an adult was seen feeding young on 10 Aug 1995 (Paul L. Noble, pers. comm.). Fall migrants are common from early August through the end of September (unpubl. banding data, Coyote Creek Field Station), and it is assumed that the local nesting birds depart for their Mexican wintering grounds at about this time.

William G. Bousman

PACIFIC-SLOPE FLYCATCHER

Palo Alto SBC

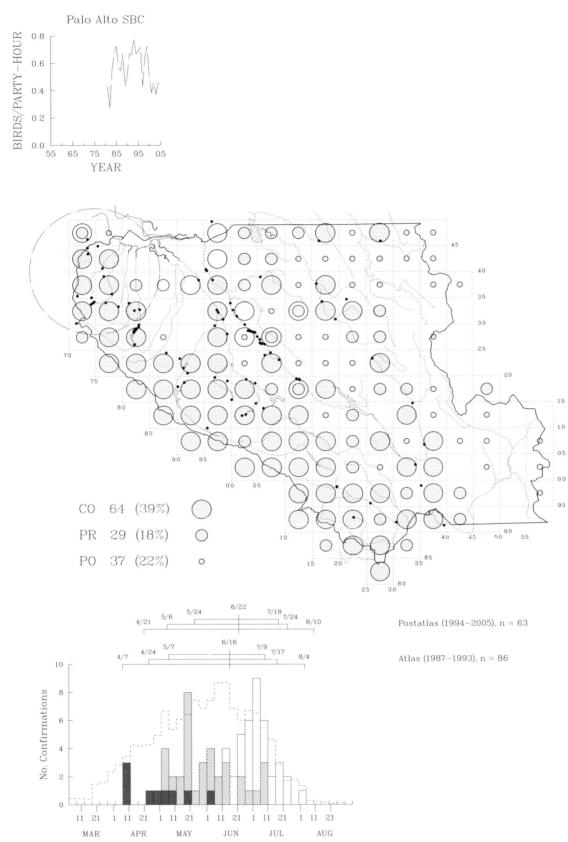

CO 64 (39%)

PR 29 (18%)

PO 37 (22%)

Postatlas (1994–2005), n = 63

Atlas (1987–1993), n = 86

277

Black Phoebe
Sayornis nigricans

The Black Phoebe, our only black-and-white flycatcher, is seen year-round in Santa Clara County, though rarely far from fresh water. This phoebe is resident in California west of the Cascades-Sierra axis, and is also found in Arizona and New Mexico, and south from there into South America. Most populations are resident, but a few, such as those in small areas of northwestern Oregon, central Arizona, and central New Mexico, are migratory (Wolf 1997). Of the six subspecies, only *S. n. semiatra* is found in the United States (Wolf 1997). This phoebe is a common and widespread resident in Santa Clara County wherever there is fresh water and open areas for foraging.

In Santa Clara County, the Black Phoebe was first recorded in the "Valley of San José," in the list of specimens collected by Thomas Bridges prior to 1857 (Sclater 1857). Observers at the end of the nineteenth century considered this flycatcher to be common and widespread in the county and noted its predilection for nesting in barns and sheds (Price 1898c, Van Denburgh 1899b, Fisher 1902). Grinnell and Wythe (1927) observed that nests of this common and widespread species were almost always built near or over water, and were built both on manmade surfaces, such as the beams of bridges, and on natural sites, such as rock ledges and earthen banks. Sibley (1952) characterized the Black Phoebe as a common resident at the midpoint of the twentieth century. Analysis of Palo Alto and San Jose Christmas Bird Count data shows a long-term population increase of 6.5% and 3.5% a year, respectively, since the mid-1950s. That there has been a nearly tenfold increase in the numbers of Black Phoebes in the urban count circles over the last 50 years suggests that this common flycatcher has benefited from urbanization, perhaps because of the large increase in structures available for nesting, as well as the increase in urban watering. For California as a whole, analysis of Breeding Bird Survey data from 1966 to 2004 shows an increase of 1.8% per year (Sauer et al. 2005).

Black Phoebes were confirmed breeding in 85% of the county's blocks, and probable or possible breeding evidence was obtained in another 11% of the blocks. Measured by the number of breeding confirmations, it was the sixth-most common bird species in Santa Clara County, although this high rank results

largely from the ease with which breeding of this species can be confirmed. Black Phoebes were found breeding in most of the major habitats of the county, wherever there was fresh water and a source of mud for nest construction, as well as nearby open areas for foraging. The only blocks without nesting phoebes were those composed largely of bay water, salt marsh, or salt ponds, or blocks in the Santa Cruz Mountains where there were no suitable foraging areas within the mosaic of coniferous and broadleaved evergreen forests, chaparral, and woodlands.

Wolf (1997), in summarizing the use of manmade substrates by Black Phoebes, noted that a study in Santa Barbara County found only 4 of 168 nests on natural substrates, whereas on Santa Cruz Island, 17 of 29 nests were built on such sites. Atlasers in Santa Clara County found that the use of natural nest sites varied widely. In the Santa Cruz Mountains, in the foothills, and on the valley floor, where the density of roads and associated structures is high, most nests were found on manmade structures. Typical nest sites included bridges or large culverts at stream crossings, barns, sheds, outbuildings, and even residences situated near water. In the Diablo Range, however, there are fewer artificial nest sites near permanent or semipermanent streams, but where culverts or bridges did occur, these sites were invariably used by Black Phoebes. In areas of grassland and savanna, where water and mud sources were limited to stock ponds, this phoebe used any available manmade structure, such as the supplemental cattle feeding sheds that can still be found on local ranches. Along permanent streams, however, Black Phoebes constructed their nests directly above the water on natural substrates such as cliffs and boulders. It appears that this species has expanded its habitat by using manmade structures, particularly in locations without natural cliffs, earthen banks, or boulders (Wolf 1997).

In winter, Black Phoebes establish separate territories, and sets of paired birds will often occur on adjacent territories along streams or watercourses (Wolf 1997). Nest site displays begin in mid-February to early March (Wolf 1997). The earliest breeding observed during the atlas period was a bird occupying a nest on 4 Mar. The peak of nesting activity extended from late April to the middle of July. The latest evidence of breeding during the atlas period was fledged young on 1 Aug. In a study of 24 pairs of Black Phoebes along lower Coyote Creek and the sludge drying ponds at the San Jose-Santa Clara Water Pollution Control Plant, Wolf (1991) observed that most pairs were double-brooded, with initial egg dates for the first clutch from 18 Mar to 6 May and dates for the second clutch from 8 to 31 May.

Apparently, in rare circumstances, Black Phoebes may nest unusually late in the year. A pair of phoebes was found feeding a dependent fledgling in downtown San Jose near Highway 101 and I-280 on 25 and 26 Nov 2002 (Eric Feuss, pers. comm.). Both adults fed the fledgling, which showed faint cinnamon wingbars and the remnants of a fleshy gape. But there are few fall records of this species nesting in California, the latest being a nest with young on the Eel River in Humboldt County on 28 Sep 1930 (Jeff N. Davis, pers. comm.).

William G. Bousman

BLACK PHOEBE

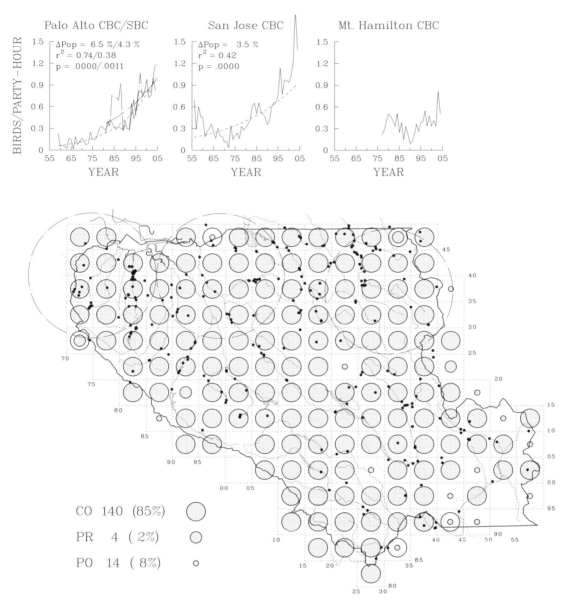

Palo Alto CBC/SBC

ΔPop = 6.5 %/4.3 %
r^2 = 0.74/0.38
p = .0000/.0011

San Jose CBC

ΔPop = 3.5 %
r^2 = 0.42
p = .0000

Mt. Hamilton CBC

BIRDS/PARTY-HOUR

YEAR

CO 140 (85%)
PR 4 (2%)
PO 14 (8%)

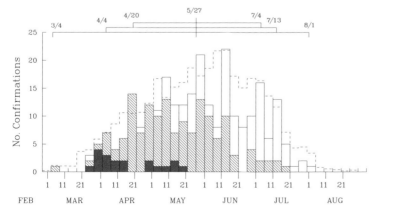

Atlas (1987–1993), n = 280

No. Confirmations

279

Say's Phoebe
Sayornis saya

This phoebe, with its subtle tan and cinnamon plumage, is a resident of the dry interior valleys of California, its breeding range barely edging into Santa Clara County. The Say's Phoebe has two disjunct breeding populations, the northern one in Alaska and the Yukon, the other ranging from southern British Columbia south through the western United States and interior Mexico to Guanajuato (Schukman and Wolf 1998). Of the three subspecies, *S. s. saya* breeds from Alaska to central Mexico; the remaining two nest in Mexico (Schukman and Wolf 1998). In California, this phoebe is resident east of the Cascades-Sierra Nevada axis, in the southeastern deserts, and in the interior Southern Coast Ranges north to Contra Costa County (Small 1994). In Santa Clara County, the Say's Phoebe is a rare resident in scattered locations in the interior of the Diablo Range. It is a fairly common winter visitor in the rest of the county.

The first Say's Phoebe recorded in Santa Clara County was collected in "the Valley of San José" sometime prior to 1857 by Thomas Bridges (Sclater 1857). Price (1898c) recorded it as a winter visitant at Stanford. Van Denburgh (1899b) stated that this phoebe was "not uncommon" as a wintering bird, and Fisher (1902) judged it as "rather common." None of these early observers noted breeding. F. L. Corless, however, collected a set of eggs in Santa Clara County on 2 May 1890, but unfortunately did not record the location (WFVZ #49069). In his first check-list of California birds, Grinnell (1902) noted that breeding birds had been found in the interior of the Southern Coast Ranges as far north as Paicines in San Benito County, but was apparently unaware of Corless's record. Nesting farther north in the Coast Ranges was recorded when Henry W. Carriger collected an egg set at Tesla in eastern Alameda County on 22 Apr 1922 (Grinnell and Wythe 1927). Carriger collected additional egg sets in eastern Alameda County throughout the 1930s (WFVZ egg collections). A nest with eggs was found at St. Mary's College, Moraga, Contra Costa County, on 17 May 1936 (Stephens 1936). Sibley (1952) reported that Albert J. Wool took a set of eggs at Calaveras Dam, just north of the Santa Clara County line, on 24 Apr 1937. Emily D. Smith found a nest and egg at Coyote Reservoir on 1 Apr 1951, thus establishing the first twentieth-century breeding record in Santa Clara County (*Audubon Field Notes* 5:274 1951, Sibley 1952). Breeding in the San Antonio Valley was noted as early as 1952 (*Bull. SCVAS* July-August 1952).

During the atlas period, breeding Say's Phoebes were found in interior Diablo Range locations, such as the San Antonio and Isabel valleys and on Sizer Flat, west of Henry Coe State Park. At the edge of the Santa Clara Valley, a Say's Phoebe was found carrying food near Coyote Reservoir, probably not far from where Smith found her bird nesting in 1951. Breeding elevations ranged from 800 feet near Coyote Reservoir to 2,640 feet on Sizer Flat. Atlasers found only one nest, built on a ledge at an underpass for cattle in the San Antonio Valley. For the most part, these birds nested in the eastern Diablo Range in areas of low rainfall with hot, dry summers. Typically, nesting Say's Phoebes were found in open rangelands edged with oak savanna and dissected by seasonal stream courses. Ranch houses, barns, and other outbuildings were often nearby.

Wintering Say's Phoebes normally arrive in Santa Clara County's lowlands in the last three weeks of September and depart in late March and early April. In breeding areas, however, birds appear to be resident. The earliest breeding evidence observed was a phoebe carrying nest material on 16 Apr. The latest nesting evidence was fledglings seen on 4 Jul. Say's Phoebes are often double-brooded (Schukman and Wolf 1998), but atlasers observed no unequivocal cases of this.

These phoebes are occasionally seen west of the Diablo Range during their breeding season, but there has been no evidence of nesting in Santa Clara County west of the records shown on the map, nor any in San Mateo County. A Say's Phoebe was seen near San Martin on the valley floor on 9 May 1953 (*Audubon Field Notes* 7:289 1953). Two birds were found on the Palo Alto SBC on 1 Jun 1985. The next year, on 14 Jun, two birds were seen on grasslands near I-280 and Edgewood Road in San Mateo County (*Am. Birds* 40:1252 1986). More recently, birds were seen along the Sierra Road summit on 9 and 10 Jun 2001 (Don Ganton, Vivek Tiwari, county notebooks), and one was seen in Almaden Quicksilver County Park on 31 Jul 2005 (Janna L. Pauser, county notebooks). A single breeding record in 1976 for Marin County (Shuford 1993s) suggests that occasionally this dryland phoebe does nest well to the west of its normal breeding range, so extralimital summer birds in Santa Clara County should be watched for evidence of breeding.

William G. Bousman

SAY'S PHOEBE

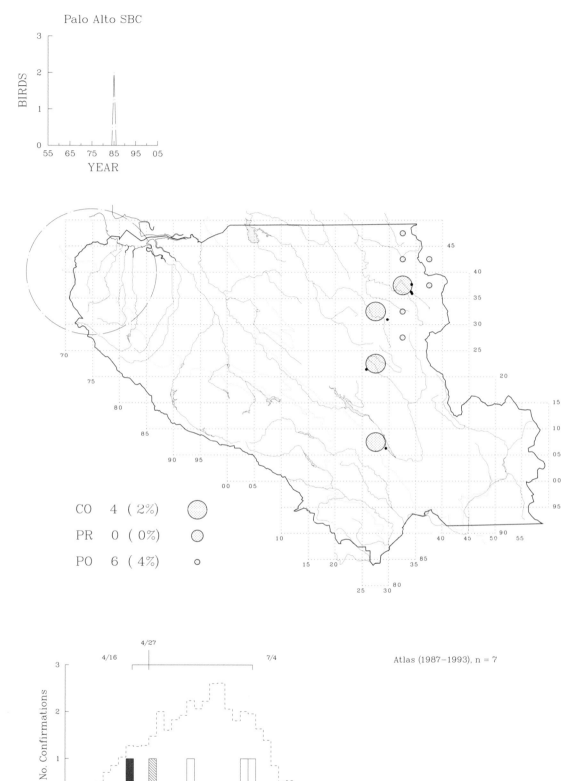

Palo Alto SBC

CO 4 (2%)

PR 0 (0%)

PO 6 (4%)

Atlas (1987–1993), n = 7

Ash-throated Flycatcher
Myiarchus cinerascens

The Ash-throated Flycatcher, our county's only cavity-nesting flycatcher, is found in a multitude of dry-country habitats, including oak woodlands, brushlands, and chaparral. This flycatcher breeds from northwestern Oregon to Kansas and south to Baja California, and in the highlands of Mexico to Jalisco and Guanajuato (AOU 1998). Of the two subspecies, *M. c. cinerascens* is the one found over most of this range, including California (AOU 1957). The Ash-throated Flycatcher is found throughout most of California, excepting only the wetter coastal forests of the northwestern part of the state and the higher mountains of the Cascades-Sierra Nevada axis (Small 1994). Widespread in Santa Clara County, this species is a fairly common or common summer resident, particularly in drier, inland locations.

Observers at the close of the nineteenth century recorded the Ash-throated Flycatcher as a summer visitant in Santa Clara County (Price 1898c, Van Denburgh 1899b, Fisher 1902). In describing its status in the San Francisco Bay area, Grinnell and Wythe (1927) noted that it was a "common summer resident locally of oak-covered hillsides and the drier interior valleys." Sibley (1952) referred to it as a common resident in the South Bay. It appears that there has been little change in the population of this dry-country flycatcher over the last century.

Atlasers confirmed Ash-throated Flycatchers breeding in 115 county blocks (70%). When these birds were present, breeding was easily confirmed; probable and possible records were limited to 18 blocks (11%) and 7 blocks (4%), respectively. During the atlas period, nesting birds were found at elevations from 140 feet beside the Pajaro River to 3,791 feet on Loma Prieta. Subsequent to the atlas period, Ash-throated Flycatchers were found nesting near the Guadalupe River in downtown

San Jose at an elevation of 65 feet (Stephen C. Rottenborn, pers. comm.). This flycatcher breeds in mixed oak and riparian woodlands, often where brushlands and chaparral are nearby. These woodland sites appeared to be selected primarily because of the availability of nesting cavities, while the more open habitats nearby offered additional foraging. This flycatcher was common throughout the Diablo Range, with its mixture of woodlands, scrublands, chaparral, and savanna. It was also widespread in the Santa Cruz Mountains wherever patches of chaparral and more open woodlands were found. And it was generally absent from the urbanized northern Santa Clara Valley, as is typical for species with such habitat requirements.

The cavity-nesting Ash-throated Flycatcher, although not adapted to urban areas, readily uses nest boxes when they are placed in appropriate habitat (Purcell et al. 1997). Studies in Madera County, however, suggest that the use of nest boxes provides no measurable advantage over natural cavities (Purcell et al. 1997). The benefit, therefore, appears to be the use of these artificial sites where natural sites are limited. Ash-throated Flycatchers have also adapted readily to nest boxes in Santa Clara County. Their occasional use of artificial sites other than nest boxes is also well known (Bent 1938g). Van Denburgh described a pair that nested in a tin watering pot in Los Gatos in 1889 (Van Denburgh 1899b), and atlasers reported at least three incidences of nesting in the large metal pipes typically used to support gates in parks or in the back country. The orientation of these pipes varied from horizontal to vertical, and in the latter case the nest was exposed to the sky.

Ash-throated Flycatchers return to Santa Clara County in the first half of April (median 10 Apr, county notebooks). The earliest breeding evidence obtained was on 1 May, which saw separate records of birds carrying nesting material and occupying a nest. These dates correspond to records of first-clutch initiation dates in Madera County, which typically ranged from 2 May to 1 Jun (Purcell et al. 1997). The phenology in Santa Clara County shows nest building and occupied nests extending into July, and these later efforts may be either second broods or renesting attempts. A scattering of breeding records was obtained into early August, the latest breeding evidence being an adult feeding young on 7 Aug. Our local birds appear to leave for their winter quarters in August. Limited banding data along lower Coyote Creek show a median passage date of 21 Aug, some 90% of all birds passing through by 10 Sep (Coyote Creek Field Station, unpubl. data).

Most of the cavity-nesting species that nest in oak woodlands and mixed brushlands in Santa Clara County, such as Oak Titmouse, White-breasted Nuthatch, and Western Bluebird, are resident species. These competitors for nest cavities, along with the early-arriving Violet-green Swallow, would seem to have a significant advantage over the Ash-throated Flycatcher in garnering the most suitable cavities. Nonetheless, this flycatcher appears to be a successful nesting species here, well able to find and defend appropriate nest sites.

William G. Bousman

ASH-THROATED FLYCATCHER

Palo Alto SBC

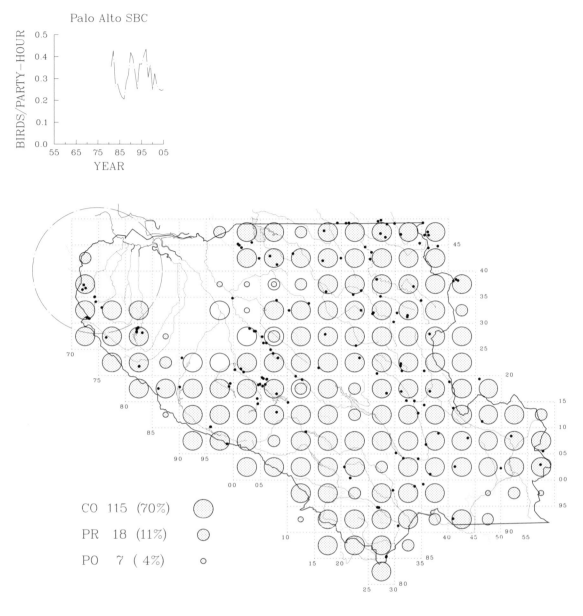

CO 115 (70%)

PR 18 (11%)

PO 7 (4%)

Atlas (1987–1993), n = 206

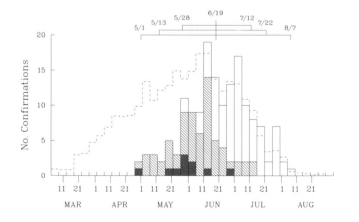

Cassin's Kingbird
Tyrannus vociferans

In recent years, Cassin's Kingbirds have barely edged into Santa Clara County, at the northern periphery of their breeding range. These kingbirds breed from southern Nevada to eastern Colorado and south through interior Mexico to Chiapas (Tweit and Tweit 2000). Disjunct populations extend northeast into Montana and South Dakota, others into California. The center of the Cassin's Kingbird's range in California is in the dry interior valleys of the southern Coast Ranges from San Benito County to Ventura County. Fewer birds are found south into Baja California and along the western edge of the San Joaquin Valley to San Joaquin County (Grinnell and Miller 1944, Small 1994). Cassin's Kingbirds are rare breeding residents at the southern edge of Santa Clara County, though migrants occur elsewhere in the county as well.

James G. Cooper (1870) reported Cassin's Kingbirds in the Santa Clara Valley in 1864. A specimen he collected in the spring of that year is in the Museum of Vertebrate Zoology (MVZ #4299), its locality given as "Santa Cruz Mts." Cooper also noted that Cassin's Kingbirds "winter in small numbers at Santa Cruz." Late in the nineteenth century, the Mailliard brothers described Cassin's Kingbirds as common summer residents at their ranch along the San Benito River at Paicines, approximately 35 km southeast of the Santa Clara County line (Mailliard and Mailliard 1901). This area consistently supports Cassin's Kingbirds to this day, but Grinnell and Wythe (1927) listed no records of this kingbird from the San Francisco Bay area, just a short distance farther north. Sibley (1952), when describing birds in the South Bay, noted one collected near Alvarado, Alameda County, on 27 Mar 1926 (MVZ #145850) and two seen south of Tracy, San Joaquin County, on 15 Jul 1937. The first record of this kingbird in Santa Clara County since Cooper's 1864

record was a bird seen by Donald D. McLean in south San Jose during 8–15 Feb 1967 (*Audubon Field Notes* 21:454 1967).

Cassin's Kingbirds were not found in Santa Clara County at all during the atlas period, but in 1994 the sightings began (the following records are documented in the county notebooks). The first observation in the county since McLean's was of a single bird in Gilroy on 28 May 1994 (Bryan M. Mori). This was followed by a bird along Coyote Creek near the Bay on 14 Sep 1994 (Stephen C. Rottenborn) and then one at Arastradero Preserve, Palo Alto, on 10 Mar 1996 (Theodore A. Chandik, Frank Vanslager). In the spring of 1997, Stephen C. Rottenborn found three pairs of Cassin's Kingbirds in the San Benito County portion of an edge block and was able to confirm breeding by two of the pairs. The nests of both were in small stands of mature eucalyptus that were otherwise in open agricultural areas. Birds found in Santa Clara County in the spring of 1997 included two birds in eucalyptus along San Felipe Road, in the southeastern corner of the county, on 13 Apr (Michael M. Rogers, Michael J. Mammoser), a single bird at the Ogier Avenue ponds on 30 Apr (Michael M. Rogers), and one along the Guadalupe River at Alviso on 2 May (Stephen C. Rottenborn). Repeated observations of Cassin's Kingbirds were made along San Felipe Road following the 13 Apr sighting (mult. obs.). Then, on 27 May, Rottenborn found one bird on a nest in the middle eucalyptus of the three along the road. This was the first breeding record of the species in Santa Clara County.

Cassin's Kingbirds continued to nest in the eucalyptus along San Felipe Road in the summers of 1998, 1999, and 2000, and at least one bird was seen there in 2001 and 2002. It is possible that the Cassin's Kingbirds that nested there from 1997 to 2000 were a single pair. Although year-to-year pair bonds have not been studied for this species (Tweit and Tweit 2000), the closely related Eastern Kingbird will reestablish its pair bonds in subsequent years (Murphy 1996). In any case, breeding by Cassin's Kingbirds was not observed in the county again until 11 May 2005, when a pair was found nesting in a small stand of eucalyptus on private land near Highway 152 and Bloomfield Road (Stephen C. Rottenborn). This location is approximately 7 km northwest of the nest site along San Felipe Road. Cassin's Kingbirds use a variety of tree species for nesting, throughout their range (Tweit and Tweit 2000). In this regard, it is interesting that the four nest sites discussed here were all in eucalyptus trees.

Only limited phenology data are available for the Cassin's Kingbird at the northwestern edge of its range. The earliest nesting evidence was birds building a nest on 8 Apr 1997 in a San Benito County edge block (Stephen C. Rottenborn, county notebooks). The latest evidence observed was an adult feeding a fledgling on 8 Jul 1999 along San Felipe Road (pers. obs.).

One to two birds were present near their nest site along San Felipe Road in the winters of 1998–99 and 1999–2000 (Michael M. Rogers, county notebooks; pers. obs.), but winter presence of this partially migratory species is not unusual. Nearby in San Benito County, a significant number of Cassin's Kingbirds remain through the winter period, although most move south (Debra L. Shearwater, Mark Paxton, pers. comm.).

William G. Bousman

CASSIN'S KINGBIRD

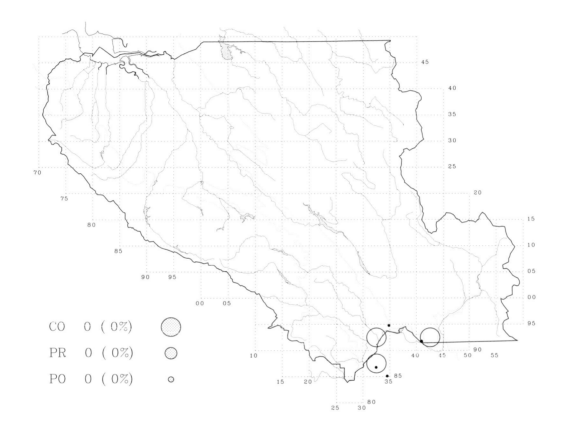

CO   0 (0%)

PR   0 (0%)

PO   0 (0%)

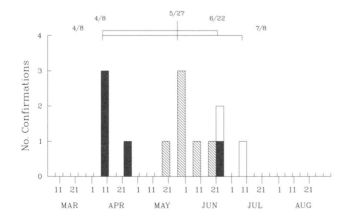

Postatlas (1994–2005), n = 13

Western Kingbird
Tyrannus verticalis

Well before sunrise, in the savanna of the Diablo Range, a Western Kingbird opens the day with a series of *kip* notes followed by a complex series of higher twittering notes. For the atlaser sleeping beneath a nearby tree, this signals that it's time to be up and looking for breeding birds. Western Kingbirds breed from British Columbia across Canada to Manitoba and thence south to Baja California and southern Texas (Gamble and Bergin 1996). In California, they are widespread summer residents, absent only from the immediate coast north of Orange County, the higher mountains of the Cascades and Sierra Nevada, and treeless desert scrub (Small 1994). Western Kingbirds are common summer residents in Santa Clara County east of the Santa Clara Valley and in the southern Santa Cruz Mountains from the Almaden Valley to the Pajaro River. Although fairly common migrants elsewhere in the county, they rarely nest in the northwestern part of the county or near the Bay.

The earliest Western Kingbird record in Santa Clara County was of a bird seen by A. L. Parkhurst in San Jose on 22 Mar 1885 (Belding 1890). Price (1898c) considered it to be "common during the summer" at Stanford at the end of the nineteenth century. Van Denburgh (1899b) noted that it was abundant in the Santa Clara Valley, but not found west of Los Gatos. Fisher (1902) referred to it as a rather common summer visitant. Grinnell and Wythe (1927), in assessing this kingbird's status in the Bay area, recorded that it was "common locally and interiorly." Sibley (1952) described it as a common summer resident in the drier portions of the South Bay.

During the atlas period, Western Kingbirds were found breeding widely in the Diablo Range. They also nested in the eastern foothills of the Santa Cruz Mountains, from the Santa Teresa Hills and the grasslands along McKean Road southeast to the Pajaro River Valley. The elevations of breeding sites ranged from 120 feet in the Pajaro River Valley in a Santa Cruz County edge block to 3,760 feet on the southwestern slopes of Eylar Mountain. Western Kingbirds were generally found in habitats offering a mixture of grasslands and woodlands. These habitats ranged from the grasslands at the edge of most open oak savannas, where there are just a few trees useful for nesting, to woodlands with a grassland understory. Areas of dense woodland with a shrub understory or extensive chaparral were rarely used. Kingbirds were also found in agricultural areas as long as suitable nest sites were nearby. Throughout their range, they built their nests in trees typical of savanna and woodland habitats, including valley oaks, foothill pines, and western sycamores. They also nested in eucalyptus trees in rural farmyards and occasionally on manmade structures such as utility poles and transmission towers.

Following the atlas period, Western Kingbirds were also found nesting in the northern foothills of the Santa Cruz Mountains and along the Bay. From 1994 to 2004 a pair nested, at least in some years, in the Stanford University Academic Reserve in open grasslands near the large radio receiver referred to as "the Dish" (Tom Grey, Grant Hoyt, Karen Hoyt, county notebooks). This area of grasslands, oak savanna, and woodland is similar to habitats used by the species in the Diablo Range. Birds nesting near the Bay edge were much less expected. A pair was seen at an occupied nest at the Palo Alto Municipal Golf Course on 12 Jun 1998 (Scott B. Terrill, county notebooks). Another pair was observed just outside Santa Clara County, building a nest in a grove of planted elms surrounded by wet grasslands at the junction of Auto Mall Parkway and Cushing Road in Fremont, Alameda County, on 22 May 1998, and up to three birds were there again 15-22 Jun 1999 (*Field Notes 52*:387 1998, Stephen C. Rottenborn, pers. comm.).

Western Kingbirds normally first arrive in Santa Clara County between mid-March and mid-April, with a median arrival date of 26 Mar (county notebooks). The earliest breeding evidence during the atlas period was an occupied nest in a Stanislaus County edge block on 9 Apr. The latest breeding evidence during the atlas period was fledglings observed in the southern Santa Cruz Mountains on 24 Jul. Although a few kingbirds are seen locally in September and October, it appears that most of the summer resident birds depart for their wintering grounds during August.

Western Kingbirds appear to be well adapted to the dry grasslands, savannas, and oak woodlands in the eastern portions of Santa Clara County, but they rarely nest in the grasslands and woodlands in the northern Santa Cruz Mountains or in the coastal grasslands to the west. Although Chase Littlejohn considered them common in San Mateo County well before the 1920s (*Gull 4(2)* 1922), they no longer breed within that county (Sequoia Audubon Society 2001f). There are only three breeding records in the last century in Santa Cruz County, all within 20 km of the coast in the Pajaro River Valley (David L. Suddjian, pers. comm.). Shuford (1993t) suggested that the more inland distribution of these kingbirds in Marin County results from a lower availability of the large insects favored by this species within that county's fog-shrouded coastal grasslands. Food preferences may similarly affect their distribution in Santa Clara County.

William G. Bousman

WESTERN KINGBIRD

Palo Alto SBC

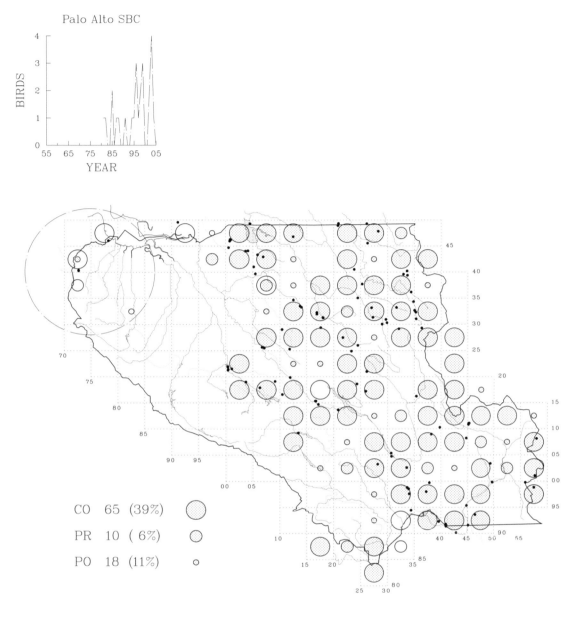

CO 65 (39%)

PR 10 (6%)

PO 18 (11%)

Atlas (1987–1993), n = 107

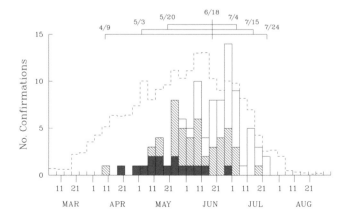

Loggerhead Shrike
Lanius ludovicianus

The Loggerhead Shrike, an adept predator, is the only member of its worldwide family that is endemic to North America. It breeds from northern California to eastern Washington and central Alberta, east to southwestern Quebec and Pennsylvania, and south through Mexico to central Oaxaca and Veracruz (AOU 1998). Five subspecies are recognized in California (AOU 1957), only one of them, *gambeli*, occurring in northern California. This subspecies is found from northeastern California south through the Sacramento and San Joaquin Valleys, and in the Coast Ranges from Sonoma County to southwestern California (Grinnell and Miller 1944, Stafford 1995). The Loggerhead Shrike is an uncommon and local resident in Santa Clara County, its numbers here somewhat augmented in the winter by more northerly birds.

A Loggerhead Shrike was collected in the "Valley of San José" sometime prior to 1857 (Sclater 1857). Observers at the end of the nineteenth century considered it to be a common, or even abundant, resident in the Santa Clara Valley (Van Denburgh 1899b, Atkinson 1901, Fisher 1902). Grinnell and Wythe (1927), in describing this shrike's status in the San Francisco Bay area, considered it to be abundant in the inland counties, but less numerous near the coast. Sibley (1952) described the Loggerhead Shrike as a common resident in open areas of the South Bay. The analysis of Christmas Bird Count data obtained in the Palo Alto and San Jose count circles since the 1950s indicates a population decrease of 3.2% and 2.0% per year, respectively. Although of the two counts, significantly fewer shrikes are recorded in the Palo Alto count circle, there has been no significant change for resident birds there in the last two decades.

During the atlas period, Loggerhead Shrikes were found in 64 blocks in the county (39%), mostly on the Santa Clara Valley floor or on nearby hillsides. Breeding records ranged from an elevation of 3 feet near an abandoned salt pond north of Moffett Field to 1,220 feet on grasslands along Sierra Road, but 90% of all breeding confirmations obtained during the atlas period were below 650 feet. Subsequent to the atlas period, breeding was observed at two locations in the San Antonio Valley, at elevations of about 2,100 feet (Stephen C. Rottenborn, pers.

comm.; Harriet Gerson, pers. comm.). Atlasers found breeding Loggerhead Shrikes in open grasslands with minor components of brushlands, chaparral edge, or open oak woodlands that provided perches and nest sites. Although apparently avoiding the higher ridges on the east side of the Santa Clara Valley, breeding birds were frequently found along open hillsides above the valley and often nested in the shrub and brushlands along small arroyos. In the northern Santa Clara Valley, most breeding birds were found in buffer lands along the South Bay salt evaporator ponds, where they foraged in uplands and ruderal growth and nested in scattered shrubs or even in ornamental plantings in nearby industrial parks. In the southern Santa Clara Valley, birds were confirmed breeding along the valley floor, where they foraged in fallow fields or grazed lands and nested in shrubs along small arroyos.

The earliest breeding evidence obtained during the atlas period was a bird building a nest on 6 Mar at Ed Levin County Park. Loggerhead Shrikes are an early nesting species, however, and it is likely that some of this early activity was missed by atlasers, who did not begin their field activities until March or April. William L. Atkinson (1901), an active egg collector in Santa Clara County, recorded the dates of the first complete clutch he found for a six-year period. The earliest date was 26 Feb 1895, the latest 10 Apr 1899, and the median date was approximately 14 Mar. The latest nesting evidence found during the atlas period was fledged young observed on 28 Jul. Following the atlas period, fledged young were seen on 3 Aug 2005 (Ann Verdi, PADB). This species is normally considered to be single-brooded (Yosef 1996), but occasional second broods are attempted. The extended nesting season shown in the phenology graphic suggests that this species may be double-brooded locally.

The Loggerhead Shrike has undergone a severe decline in the northeastern United States in the last half of the twentieth century (Yosef 1996). Breeding shrikes seem to have moved into the Great Lakes Region and New England following increases in agriculture in the nineteenth century, and their reductions appear to be due, in part, to a combination of reforestation and urbanization (Peterjohn and Sauer 1995). There is no general agreement, however, on the major reasons for this species' population decline (Yosef 1996). In the west, analysis of Breeding Bird Survey data shows a significant decline of 3.4% a year from 1966 to 2004 (Sauer et al. 2005). On the central California coast, too, this species' range appears to be contracting. Stafford (1995) has noted that breeding Loggerhead Shrikes are no longer found north of Healdsburg, Sonoma County, an area where they were found as recently as the early 1970s. On the basis of descriptions from the end of the nineteenth century (Van Denburgh 1899b, Atkinson 1901, Fisher 1902), this species is much less common in Santa Clara County now than it was a century ago. It seems likely that habitat loss caused by more intensive agricultural methods and by the continued spread of urbanization have been detrimental to this species. Locally, however, there appear to be suitable grassland habitats that go unused by Loggerhead Shrikes, and the reasons for their absence from these areas are unclear.

William G. Bousman

LOGGERHEAD SHRIKE

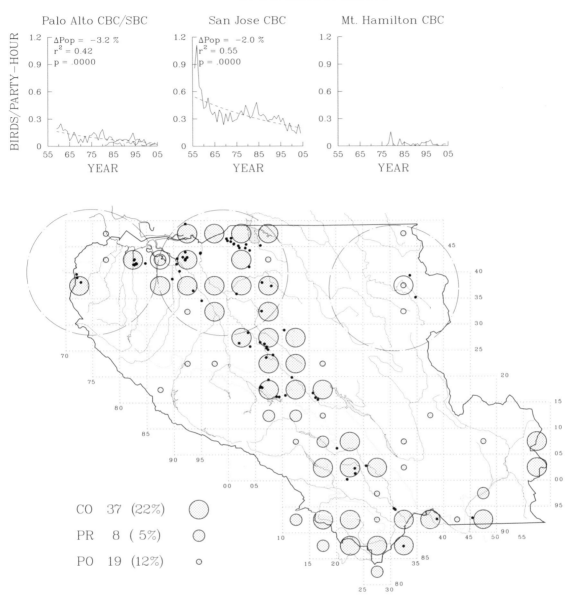

Palo Alto CBC/SBC

ΔPop = −3.2 %
r² = 0.42
p = .0000

San Jose CBC

ΔPop = −2.0 %
r² = 0.55
p = .0000

Mt. Hamilton CBC

BIRDS/PARTY−HOUR

YEAR

CO   37 (22%)
PR   8 (5%)
PO   19 (12%)

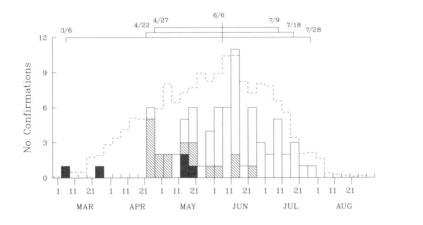

No. Confirmations

3/6   4/22   4/27   6/6   7/9   7/18   7/28

Atlas (1987−1993), n = 84

MAR   APR   MAY   JUN   JUL   AUG

Bell's Vireo
Vireo bellii

After being decimated by both habitat loss and brood parasitism by cowbirds, populations of the Bell's Vireo have increased in response to management efforts, and this species has once again bred in Santa Clara County. Four subspecies of this vireo are recognized (AOU 1957), the three easternmost breeding primarily in riparian woodlands across the Midwest and in arid regions from southeastern California east to Texas and south to north-central Mexico. The race that is (or was historically) most widespread in California, and which has bred in Santa Clara County, is *V. b. pusillus*, the Least Bell's Vireo. Historically, *pusillus* was very common in riparian habitats from Baja California north through southern coastal California and the Central Valley to Red Bluff (Grinnell and Miller 1944, AOU 1957). Severe population declines, however, have been accompanied by a range contraction, and the Least Bell's Vireo currently breeds regularly only as far north as the Santa Ynez River in Santa Barbara County (Roberson 1993y). In Santa Clara County, records of breeding by this species consist of two instances 65 years apart.

Earlier in this century, the Bell's Vireo was considered a common breeder in riparian woodlands throughout the Central Valley and in much of southern California (Grinnell 1902, 1915), but it was not recorded in the San Francisco Bay area until 5 Apr 1905, when a single bird was collected at Redwood City (Grinnell and Wythe 1927). Santa Clara County's first record was of a nest with eggs collected by W. E. Unglish on 19 Apr 1932 in a dense willow thicket along the Pajaro River near Sargent (Unglish 1937). This nest represented the northernmost breeding record of Bell's Vireos west of the Central Valley, although the species bred more commonly from Monterey County southward (Roberson 1993y). The range of Bell's Vireo depicted in Thelander (1994) includes most of eastern Santa Clara County, but this map is in error. The only Santa Clara County record of Bell's Vireo in the Diablo Range (Mewaldt and Kaiser 1988), a migrant, is erroneous (L. R. Mewaldt, pers. comm. to W. G. Bousman).

Over the past two centuries, riparian woodland in California has been reduced to less than 10% of its pre-settlement extent (Smith 1977), resulting in drastic reductions in suitable breeding habitat for the Least Bell's Vireo. Then, from 1900 to 1940, the "Dwarf" Brown-headed Cowbird (*Molothrus ater obscurus*) invaded most of *pusillus*'s range (Laymon 1987) and heavily parasitized this vireo (Franzreb 1987, Goldwasser 1987). The combination of habitat loss and brood parasitism overwhelmed the Least Bell's Vireo populations, which began to decline in the 1930s, particularly in the northern part of the species' range (Grinnell and Miller 1944). This decline continued for half a century. At its low point in the early 1980s, the California breeding population of the Least Bell's Vireo was estimated at only 300 pairs, the majority breeding in far southern California, only a few birds breeding as far north as southern Monterey County (RECON 1989, Roberson 1993y).

Since *pusillus* was listed as "endangered" under the California Endangered Species Act in 1980, and under the federal Endangered Species Act in 1986, riparian habitat restoration and cowbird trapping have resulted in considerable increases in Bell's Vireo populations in southern California (Kus 1996, Griffith and Griffith 1997, Pike and Hays 1997), which now exceed 1,300 pairs (USFWS 1998). A few birds have also begun to appear in more northerly areas. A singing male along the upper Salinas River in Monterey County in June-July 1993 was in an area where this species has occurred sporadically in recent decades (Roberson 1993y), but another along the lower Pajaro River in Monterey and Santa Cruz Counties on 29-30 May 1996 (Jeff N. Davis, pers. comm.) was a pioneering bird just north of the species' historical range limit.

No Bell's Vireos were recorded in Santa Clara County during the atlas period, but on 13 May 1997, the writer observed a pair of Bell's Vireos along Llagas Creek east of Gilroy, only a few kilometers from the county's only previous record. The drab, gray plumage of these birds, presenting virtually no green or yellow tones, is consistent with the expected race *pusillus*. The male was singing incessantly, and both birds were observed repeatedly carrying nesting material (fibers from willow catkins) into the interior of a dense willow surrounded by bulrush. On 17 May, the male was seen courting the female deep within the willow thicket (Michael J. Mammoser, pers. comm.), and the male continued to be seen as late as 28 May 1997. Unfortunately, this area was not visited during June and most of July, and by the time of the next site visit on 27 July, these birds could no longer be found.

This recent breeding attempt by Least Bell's Vireos in southern Santa Clara County is a welcome indication of the increasing health of this subspecies' population in the state. Brown-headed Cowbirds were quite common along Llagas Creek in the summer of 1997, however, and recent studies have demonstrated the importance of cowbird trapping programs for the recovery of populations of rare passerines such as the Bell's Vireo (RECON 1989, Thelander 1994, Stephen A. Laymon and Loren Hays, pers. comm.). Given the paucity of suitable breeding habitat in southern Santa Clara County, and the abundance of cowbirds here, it is questionable whether a viable breeding population of Bell's Vireos can become established in the county without extensive management of both cowbirds and riparian habitat.

Stephen C. Rottenborn

BELL'S VIREO

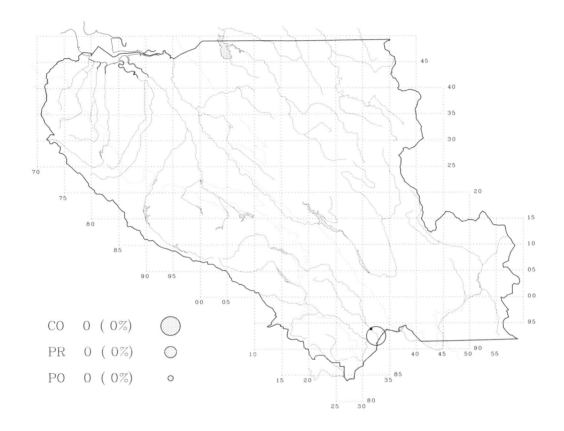

CO   0 (0%)

PR   0 (0%)

PO   0 (0%)

Postatlas (1994−2005), n = 1

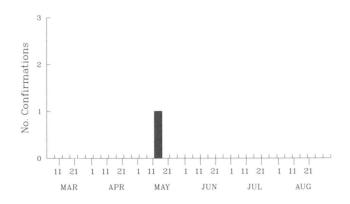

Cassin's Vireo
Vireo cassinii

A rather sedate denizen of Santa Clara County's wooded slopes and canyons, the Cassin's Vireo is less often seen than it is heard, singing from a perch high in an alder or oak. Formerly known as the "Solitary Vireo," this species was split from the other two members of the complex, the Blue-headed Vireo (*V. solitarius*) and Plumbeous Vireo (*V. plumbeus*), on the basis of differences in ecology, voice, and plumage (AOU 1998). Breeding farther west than the other two species, the Cassin's Vireo nests from southern British Columbia, Idaho, and Montana south through Washington and Oregon to Baja California and Nevada, wintering primarily in Mexico (AOU 1998). The California breeding range of the Cassin's Vireo extends from the northern montane regions south through the Sierra Nevada and the Coast Ranges to the mountains of southern California (Zeiner et al. 1990, Small 1994). In Santa Clara County, this species is a fairly common breeder in woodlands of the Santa Cruz Mountains and the Diablo Range, occurring elsewhere in the county as an uncommon to rare transient.

The distribution of the Cassin's Vireo in the county has probably changed little over the past century. On 19 May 1895, Barlow found a nest along the Guadalupe River near Almaden (Barlow 1896, 1900b). Another nest was found near Lexington on 6 Jun 1896 (Ray 1900). Price (1898f) considered the species a summer resident in the vicinity of Stanford University, and in 1929 a nest was reported from Los Gatos (*Wren-Tit 1(3)* 1929). Grinnell and Wythe (1927) wrote that the Cassin's Vireo was a "sparingly transient and summer resident," listing Lexington, Almaden, and Alum Rock among the known breeding locations of this species. Although Grinnell and Wythe may have implied that this species was uncommon in the San Francisco Bay area, Sibley (1952) considered it a common migrant and summer resident in the South Bay. Since then, breeding records reported in *Audubon Field Notes*, *American Birds*, and the *Avocet* indicate that the Cassin's Vireo remained a regular breeder in the county in the years prior to the initiation of atlas fieldwork. Numbers on the Palo Alto Summer Bird Count have declined by 7.3% a year since 1981. Analysis of Breeding Bird Survey data indicate a decline in California since the mid-1960s for BBS routes from the San Francisco Bay and southward (Sauer et al. 2005).

Atlasers found the Santa Clara County breeding range of the Cassin's Vireo to be neatly defined by the two mountain ranges flanking the Santa Clara Valley. This species was found breeding virtually throughout the Santa Cruz Mountains and in most of the Diablo Range, but it was entirely absent from the Valley. Most breeding confirmations were obtained at elevations between 400 and 2,400 feet, with several up to 3,420 feet. Cassin's Vireos bred in a variety of woodland types. Mixed oak woodlands, often with conifers, California bay, and other trees interspersed, were used most frequently. This species also nested along foothill streams in alders, sycamores, and black cottonwoods, and the lower-elevation records of this species around the margins of the valley floor were strictly from such habitats. Unlike the Warbling Vireo, the Cassin's Vireo did not breed in valley riparian habitats dominated by willows and Fremont cottonwoods. Although Cassin's Vireos tend to nest more sparsely where conifers are dominant than in areas having some hardwood component (Shuford 1993bb), some were found breeding in redwood-Douglas fir forests in the Santa Cruz Mountains and in foothill and Coulter pines in the Diablo Range (Michael M. Rogers, pers. comm.). Cassin's Vireos do not necessarily require moist habitats and are often found in relatively dry woodlands (Shuford 1993bb), but in Santa Clara County they tend to avoid very dry habitats. In the Diablo Range and the lower foothills of the Santa Cruz Mountains, for example, they were most frequently encountered on north-facing slopes and along streams, where they often bred in fairly close proximity to Warbling Vireos (Michael M. Rogers, pers. comm.). Cassin's Vireos were not found nesting in open oak savanna, and they were apparently absent from the open woodland and chaparral-dominated landscapes in the eastern and southern Diablo Range. Nevertheless, some mesic woodlands on north-facing slopes south of Pacheco Creek, poorly sampled during atlas fieldwork, might support this species. Cassin's Vireos were recorded by atlasers in 53% of the county's atlas blocks and confirmed in 30% of all blocks.

Cassin's Vireos arrive in their Santa Clara County breeding areas in late March or early April and initiate nesting shortly thereafter. During the atlas period, birds were observed carrying nesting material as early as 5 Apr and as late as 2 Jun, although the peak in nest-building covered the month between late April and late May. Occupied nests, most of which likely contained eggs, were observed from 18 Apr to 20 Jun. Adults carrying food as early as 7 May probably indicated the presence of young in the nest at that time, although the four nests with young found by atlasers were recorded between 3 and 21 Jun. Records of recently fledged young (including those being fed by adults) spanned the period 26 May-25 Jul.

Stephen C. Rottenborn

CASSIN'S VIREO

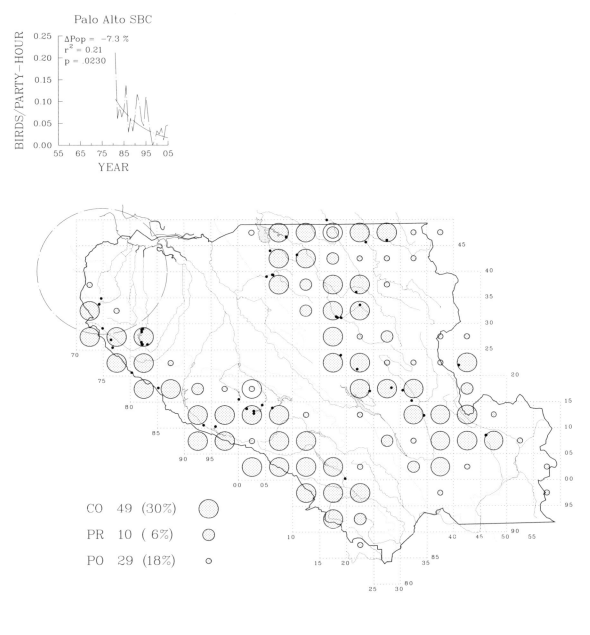

Palo Alto SBC

ΔPop = −7.3 %
r^2 = 0.21
p = .0230

BIRDS/PARTY−HOUR

YEAR

CO 49 (30%)
PR 10 (6%)
PO 29 (18%)

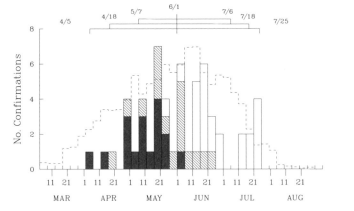

Atlas (1987−1993), n = 72

No. Confirmations

4/5   4/18   5/7   6/1   7/6   7/18   7/25

MAR   APR   MAY   JUN   JUL   AUG

Hutton's Vireo
Vireo huttoni

Our only permanently resident vireo, the Hutton's Vireo is characteristic of forests and shaded canyons dominated by live oaks. Along the west coast of North America, this vireo is found from southwestern British Columbia to northern Baja California, west of the Cascades-Sierra axis. Disjunct populations also occur in southern Baja California, over much of the mountainous regions of Mexico, and south to Chiapas and southwestern Guatemala (Davis 1995). The subspecies of Hutton's Vireo found in California, *V. h. huttoni*, is a bird of live oak forests in the Coast Ranges as well as the foothills of the Sierra Nevada. In Santa Clara County, the Hutton's Vireo is fairly common in broadleaved evergreen forests, generally of coast live oak, but it is also found in woodlands with interior live oak and California bay.

At the end of the nineteenth century, Van Denburgh (1899b) found this species to be fairly common in the Los Gatos area in winter, but thought that it nested along the coast. Fisher (1902), however, considered it to be an abundant resident in the Santa Cruz Mountains. Grinnell and Wythe (1927) reported that the Hutton's Vireo was found most frequently in the oak forests and woodlands of the interior portions of the Bay region. Sibley (1952) considered this vireo to be a fairly common resident of live oak woodlands, although less common in areas with conifers and deciduous trees. Records from the Palo Alto CBC and SBC, and the San Jose CBC, show no significant change in this resident population over the last 50 years.

Hutton's Vireos were found breeding in 27% of the atlas blocks during the atlas period. They were found in all of the atlas blocks in the Santa Cruz Mountains, and breeding evidence was obtained in 70% of them. They were found less often in the Diablo Range and were confirmed in only 21% of these blocks. During the atlas period, nesting elevations ranged from 50 feet at the edge of the valley floor to 3,280 feet near the summit of Mt. Hamilton. Following the atlas period, a nest with young was found along Coyote Creek at 40 feet (Stephen C. Rotten-

born, pers. comm.). Hutton's Vireos were found most often in broadleaved evergreen forests dominated by coast live oaks, particularly so in the Santa Cruz Mountains. They were also found in the Diablo Range on north-facing slopes or in the bottoms of canyons in moist dense forests, often with live oak and California bay. Despite its attraction to live oaks, it appeared that this vireo's habitat needs were more broadly focused on the presence of moist forests with a dense canopy, because they were occasionally found in shaded forests that included coast redwood, Douglas fir, and tan oak. In general, this species was not found nesting on the valley floor, notwithstanding breeding records obtained at two locations along Coyote Creek after the atlas period (Stephen C. Rottenborn, pers. comm.). Two pairs of adults feeding young in Senter Park on the valley floor on 29 May 1998 were in an area of Coyote Creek where live oaks are found, which in this respect was habitat usage like that of birds at higher elevations. A nest found in willows along Coyote Creek near Oakland Road on 17 Jun 1995 was in a dense, closed-canopy forest of willow, cottonwood, and box elder lacking oaks, and in this sense was quite unusual.

Cassin's, Hutton's, and Warbling vireos were all found widely in the Santa Cruz Mountains. In general, Cassin's Vireos were more often found at higher elevations, and when at lower elevations were restricted to alders, sycamores, and black cottonwoods along streams. Warbling Vireos were often found in moist dense forests in habitats similar to those of Hutton's, but appeared to be more adaptable, and unlike Hutton's were fairly common in deciduous riparian forest on the valley floor. Despite these characteristic differences, these species were sometimes found nesting in close proximity, indicating considerable overlap in their habitat use. In the Diablo Range, all three vireos were found less commonly. There, Cassin's tended to occur more often at higher elevations, and in this sense matched more closely the pattern observed for the species in Monterey County (Roberson 1993z). The Warbling Vireo was found more widely in the Diablo Range than the Hutton's, but as in the Santa Cruz Mountains both species were attracted to moist forests in canyon bottoms or along north-facing slopes.

Hutton's Vireos start to nest in February, as evidenced by birds carrying nest materials as early as 2 Feb. But much of this early nesting activity was missed by most atlasers, who did not begin their field activities until late March or April. The latest nesting observation during the atlas period was adults feeding young on 24 Jul. Following the atlas period, in 2002, adults were seen feeding young as late as 3 Aug (Linda Sullivan, PADB). Although nest construction was observed in June, these may have been renesting attempts, since there is no documentation of double-brooding in this species (Davis 1995). The most frequent confirmations obtained during the atlas period were of feeding young (30%), carrying food (28%), and fledged young (24%).

William G. Bousman

HUTTON'S VIREO

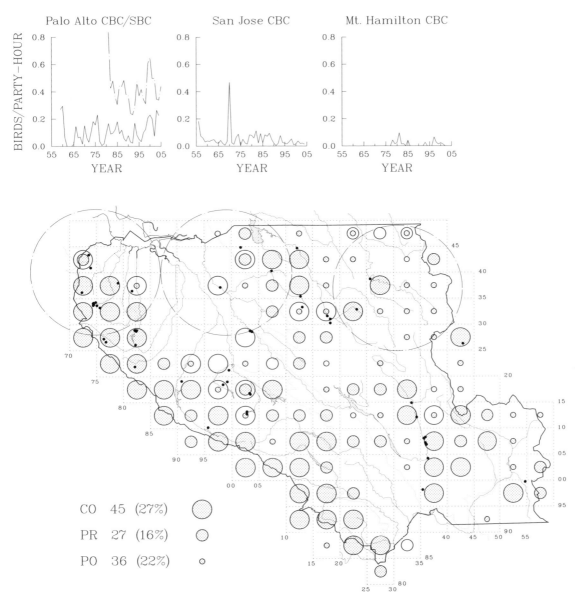

Palo Alto CBC/SBC

San Jose CBC

Mt. Hamilton CBC

BIRDS/PARTY-HOUR

YEAR

CO 45 (27%)

PR 27 (16%)

PO 36 (22%)

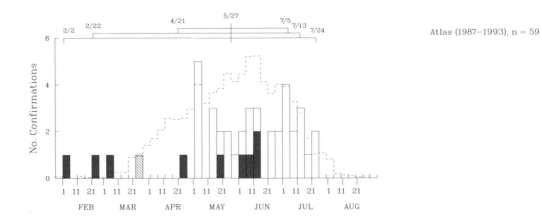

2/2   2/22   4/21   5/27   7/5
                                          7/13
                                             7/24

Atlas (1987–1993), n = 59

No. Confirmations

FEB   MAR   APR   MAY   JUN   JUL   AUG

Warbling Vireo
Vireo gilvus

Even before their nest trees have finished leafing out in spring, Warbling Vireos arrive in Santa Clara County's moist woodlands and begin vociferously establishing their territories. The Warbling Vireo is a locally common breeder over western Canada, most of the United States, and northern Mexico. This neotropical migrant vacates its breeding range in winter, when it is found primarily in Mexico and Central America (AOU 1998). Of the four subspecies recognized by the AOU (1957), the one nesting in Santa Clara County is *V. g. swainsonii*, which breeds throughout most of western North America. The Warbling Vireo is a fairly common breeder in deciduous riparian and moist montane woodlands in California's Coast Ranges, northern montane regions, and the Sierra Nevada, nesting from sea level to the upper limit of deciduous-tree growth at about 10,500 feet (Small 1994). It is less common as a breeder in the mountains of southern California, and it no longer breeds in most of the Central Valley (Gaines 1974, Zeiner et al. 1990, Small 1994). In Santa Clara County, the Warbling Vireo is a common breeder in foothill riparian woodlands and moist montane forests, breeding more locally and in smaller numbers in riparian habitats on the Santa Clara Valley floor.

The occurrence of the Warbling Vireo in Santa Clara County was first cited by Van Denburgh (1899b), who found it breeding at Los Gatos in 1889. Price (1898f) listed the Warbling Vireo as a summer visitor to Stanford, and Fisher (1902) considered it to be common in summer in the Santa Clara Valley and the Santa Cruz Mountains. Grinnell and Wythe (1927) called the Warbling Vireo an "abundant summer resident" breeding in riparian habitats and canyons in the San Francisco Bay area. Grinnell and Miller (1944) reaffirmed its abundance, and Sibley (1952) stated that the Warbling Vireo was a "common summer resident" in deciduous riparian woodlands in the South Bay area. More recently, declines have been noted in several parts of the state (Gaines 1974, Rothstein et al. 1980, Garrett and Dunn 1981, Gaines 1988, Roberson 1993aa), and Breeding Bird Survey data indicate a decline of 1.3% a year since 1966 in California as a whole, particularly in coastal areas (Sauer et al. 2005). Loss of riparian habitat and frequent brood parasitism by Brown-headed Cowbirds have been implicated in declines in

some of these areas. In Santa Clara County, data from the Palo Alto Summer Bird Count indicate an average rate of decline of 6.8% per year since the early 1980s. Curiously, Warbling Vireos in this count circle are found mostly in areas having few cowbirds and little recent habitat alteration, and the reasons for this apparent decline are unknown.

During the atlas period, the Warbling Vireo was recorded in 82% of the atlas blocks and was confirmed breeding in 52% of all blocks. It was found breeding most commonly in the Santa Cruz Mountains, where it bred along streams among willows, alders, and sycamores and in pockets of woodland dominated by California bay and bigleaf maple (and to a lesser extent oaks and conifers) on moist slopes. Warbling Vireos were less abundant in the Diablo Range. Here, they nested fairly commonly in some of the deeper, moister canyons in the western foothills, but were less common and more sparsely distributed in the drier interior of the range. They were also found nesting in sycamores, willows, and cottonwoods on the Santa Clara Valley floor. Although the Warbling Vireo was recorded only sparsely in the northern reaches of the valley during atlas fieldwork, more intensive surveys in the years following the atlasing found it to be a fairly common breeder in mature cottonwood/willow woodlands along much of Coyote Creek, even in urban areas (pers. obs.). In 1995, during breeding-season surveys of riparian bird communities on the urban northern Santa Clara Valley floor, the Warbling Vireo was found at 35 of 68 riparian woodland sites, and breeding was confirmed along Coyote Creek as far downstream as the Coyote Creek Riparian Station (pers. obs.). Postatlas fieldwork confirmed breeding in six additional blocks on the northern Santa Clara Valley floor and in one additional block in the Diablo Range. Breeding was confirmed widely at elevations from 200 to 2,500 feet, although a few records from extreme elevations included confirmations as low as 5 feet and as high as 3,200 feet. Warbling Vireos breeding in the Santa Cruz Mountains and Diablo Range, where Hutton's and Cassin's Vireos also nest, were typically tied more closely to streams and moist slopes than were the other two species, although breeding habitat overlapped among all three species to some extent. On the valley floor, however, the Cassin's Vireo was absent as a breeder, and the few Hutton's Vireos breeding in riparian habitats were far outnumbered by Warbling Vireos.

Warbling Vireos arrive early in Santa Clara County and begin establishing territories in mid-March. Nest-building was noted from 15 Apr to early June, although in one case nest-building was recorded as late as 21 Jun. Atlasers observed 20 occupied nests from 23 Apr to 4 Jul, and nine nests with young from 2 Jun to 11 Jul. Recently fledged young were observed from 6 May to 2 Aug during the atlas period. Subsequently, fledged young were seen as late as 16 Aug 2001 (Michael M. Rogers, PADB). Although later confirmations may have constituted second broods, double-brooding has not been proven to occur in this species (Ehrlich et al. 1988).

Stephen C. Rottenborn

WARBLING VIREO

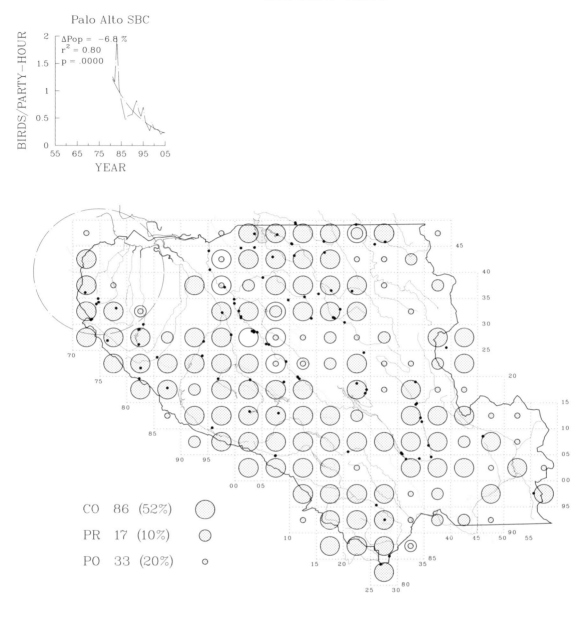

Palo Alto SBC

ΔPop = −6.8 %
r² = 0.80
p = .0000

BIRDS/PARTY–HOUR

YEAR

CO 86 (52%)
PR 17 (10%)
PO 33 (20%)

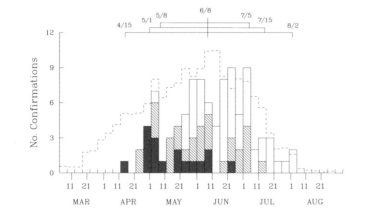

4/15 5/1 5/8 6/8 7/5 7/15 8/2

No. Confirmations

MAR APR MAY JUN JUL AUG

Atlas (1987–1993), n = 127

297

Steller's Jay
Cyanocitta stelleri

A bird of the shadows, the Steller's Jay is rarely found far from the shade of our coniferous and broadleaved evergreen forests. This jay breeds along the Pacific Coast from coastal Alaska south to southern California, and in the Rocky Mountains from Canada to the highlands of Mexico and Central America (Greene et al. 1998). Of 16 subspecies, two are found regularly in California: *C. s. carbonacea* in central California from Marin County south to San Luis Obispo County, including all of Santa Clara County, and *C. s. frontalis* in portions of the Northern and Southern Coast Ranges, the Cascades, and the Sierra Nevada (Grinnell and Miller 1944, Greene et al. 1998). The type specimen of *carbonacea* was collected by Joseph Grinnell in Stevens Creek Canyon on 13 Oct 1900 (Grinnell 1900a). The Steller's Jay is a common resident in Santa Clara County in shaded forests and narrow riparian corridors, but is absent from open oak woodlands, chaparral, and grasslands.

The Steller's Jay was among the specimens collected by Thomas Bridges in "the Valley of San José" sometime prior to 1857 (Sclater 1857). Beck (1895a) collected numerous egg sets near San Jose, presumably in the canyons above Berryessa (USNM egg collections). Price (1898d) found the bird in redwood forests near Stanford and occasionally along the nearby creeks. Van Denburgh (1899b) considered this jay common near Los Gatos over most of the year, but believed it moved into the redwood forests of Santa Cruz County during the breeding season. (Since Van Denburgh's time, others have noted how quiet and secretive this usually noisy species becomes during its nesting season.) Fisher (1902) described the Steller's Jay as an abundant resident in the Santa Cruz Mountains. Grinnell and Wythe (1927) classified *carbonacea* as a common resident in the Bay area. Sibley (1952) also described this jay as a common resident in the South Bay, in areas of coniferous forest or shaded canyons. Analysis of Palo Alto and San Jose CBC data since the 1950s shows an increase of 1.4% per year in the Palo Alto count circle and a decrease of 1.6% per year in the San Jose circle.

Atlasers, too, found the Steller's Jay to be a common and widespread breeding species in the Santa Cruz Mountains. It was also common in the western Diablo Range, in the more mesic arroyos and canyons, but farther east in the Diablo Range, as more open woodlands replaced forests and the reduced rainfall led to drier habitats, Steller's Jays became uncommon, only a few pairs found in the easternmost blocks. With the exception of a few birds that used eucalyptus groves along valley creeks, this jay was generally not found in urban areas or in habitats on the valley floor. Breeding Steller's Jays were found at elevations ranging from 30 feet along Coyote Creek to 4,200 feet on Mt. Hamilton. Ninety percent of all confirmations were from elevations above 400 feet.

Atlasers generally found nesting Steller's Jays in coniferous and broadleaved evergreen forests with a closed canopy. In these forests they used Douglas fir, California bay, and live oaks as nest trees, but also deciduous trees, such as western sycamore, as long as these trees were in the same closed-canopy forest. In the Diablo Range, these mesic forests are less common, and Steller's Jays nested in shaded canyons there, particularly on north-facing slopes with closed-canopy forests of California bay and other species. In drier areas they occasionally nested in foothill pines in mixed chaparral-foothill pine woodlands. An unusual nest site observed during the atlas period was on a ledge on a large boulder in Colorado Creek surrounded by open and fragmented California bay woodland (Michael M. Rogers, pers. comm.). The ledge appeared to be inaccessible to ground predators. Another unusual nest was found after the atlas period in an old barn on the Dowdy Ranch in Henry Coe State Park (James Yurchenco, pers. comm.); the occasional use of buildings has been noted by Greene et al. (1998).

Steller's Jay pairs remain on their territories throughout the year in central California (Brown 1964). The earliest breeding evidence locally was an adult seen carrying nest material on 18 Mar. The earliest nest with eggs was found on 2 May, a typical date for Steller's Jays in California (Bent 1946a). Fledged young were first noted on 9 May. The latest breeding evidence observed was young being fed on 4 Aug. Nest construction and occupation was observed into June. Because the Steller's Jay is single-brooded (Greene et al. 1998), the late records may represent renesting after nest failure.

Over much of the western United States, where Western Scrub-Jays, Steller's Jays, and Clark's Nutcrackers occur, they are separated by elevation, the scrub-jays at lower elevations, the Steller's Jays at middle elevations, and the nutcrackers at higher elevations (Greene et al. 1998). But in central California, Steller's Jays and Western Scrub-Jays are largely sympatric. In Santa Clara County, Steller's Jays are usually the birds of shade and closed-canopy forests, whereas scrub-jays are more likely to be found in open woodlands, scrublands, and chaparral. Yet the two overlap broadly in their use of habitats. Where they do come into contact, the smaller Western Scrub-Jay is nearly always dominant (Brown 1963). More important, however, are their physiological responses to temperature and moisture. The Steller's Jay is much less tolerant of temperature extremes than the scrub-jay, and at high temperatures it must have access to water, whereas the scrub-jay can go for days without water under these same conditions (Mann 1983).

William G. Bousman

STELLER'S JAY

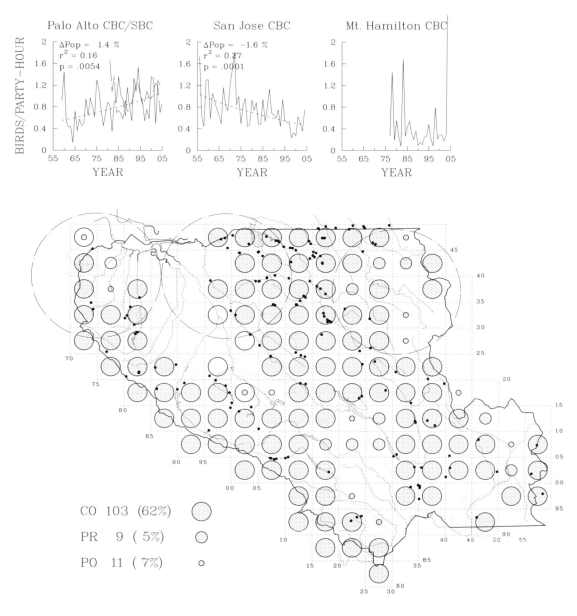

Palo Alto CBC/SBC

ΔPop = 1.4 %
r² = 0.16
p = .0054

San Jose CBC

ΔPop = −1.6 %
r² = 0.27
p = .0001

Mt. Hamilton CBC

BIRDS/PARTY-HOUR

YEAR

CO 103 (62%)

PR   9 (5%)

PO   11 (7%)

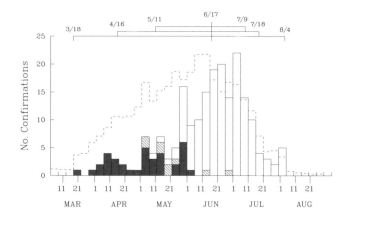

3/18   4/16   5/11   6/17   7/9   7/18   8/4

No. Confirmations

MAR   APR   MAY   JUN   JUL   AUG

Atlas (1987–1993), n = 216

Western Scrub-Jay
Aphelocoma californica

Raucous and without fear, this abundant corvid is conspicuous except while raising its young, when it becomes quiet and furtive. Until recently, the Western Scrub-Jay, the Florida Scrub-Jay, and the Island Scrub-Jay were all considered a single species, the Scrub Jay. But on the basis of genetic, morphological, behavioral, and fossil evidence, the three jays are now considered separate species (AOU 1998). The Western Scrub-Jay is resident widely in the American west from southwestern Washington and southern Idaho south into Mexico as far as Oaxaca. Five subspecies of the Western Scrub-Jay are found in California, *californica* being the subspecies resident in Santa Clara County (AOU 1957). This jay is a widespread and abundant resident in Santa Clara County, making use of most of the county's varied habitats.

Western Scrub-Jays were first recorded in Santa Clara County when Thomas Bridges collected a specimen in the "Valley of San José" prior to 1857 (Sclater 1857). Cooper (1870) regarded this jay as one of the most common birds in the local area, and subsequent observers have agreed with his characterization (Van Denburgh 1899b, Grinnell and Wythe 1927, Sibley 1952). Grinnell and Miller (1944) believed that the number of birds had increased within the prior century because of human settlement. In their judgment, the Western Scrub-Jay's populations were not limited by food resources so much as by a need for large bushes and trees for secure nest sites and overgrown thickets and tangles for roosting. The settlement of open valley lands that had previously lacked these features therefore provided new opportunities for this species. Analysis of Breeding Bird Survey data for California (Sauer et al. 2005) has shown an increase of 0.7% per year for the 1966-2004 period, which indicates that scrub jays are still increasing their population statewide. This increasing trend is supported by data for the Diablo Range from the Mt. Hamilton CBC, but data from the San Jose and Palo Alto CBCs since the late 1950s show a decline in the Western Scrub-Jay's population of 1.0 to 1.3% per year. Both of these count circles include extensive wildlands as well as increasingly urbanized portions of the valley floor, and the cause of the decline there is unknown.

Western Scrub-Jays were confirmed breeding in 94% of

the atlas blocks, and were second only to the European Starling in the number of confirmations obtained by atlasers. They were found in all but two atlas blocks, both with predominantly bayside habitat. A successful generalist, this scrub-jay was found in most of the county's habitats, and nesting was observed during the atlas period from an elevation of 10 feet along San Francisquito Creek up to the highest point in the county at 4,200 feet. Following the atlas period, an adult with nest material was at the Sunnyvale Water Pollution Control Plant at just 5 feet (Stephen C. Rottenborn, PADB). Scrub-jays were most attracted to habitats that provided a mixture of shrubs and trees with substantial foliage cover for nest sites, an understory with thick brush or chaparral for roosting, and open areas nearby for foraging. Thus, habitat edge that included woodlands, chaparral, riparian habitat, or dense urban plantings appeared most suitable. Acceptable habitat for this species appeared to be lacking only along the Bay, where there is no extensive tree or shrub cover, in extensive grasslands, or in continuous tracts of closed-canopy forests. In the Santa Cruz Mountains, dominated by the conifer and broadleaved evergreen forest, this species was missing within the shade of Douglas fir, coast redwood, tan oak, and California bay, habitats preferred by the Steller's Jay. However, patches of chaparral or more open woodlands frequently occur within these forest tracts, and in such areas we often found this jay.

Currently, the Western Scrub-Jay appears to be well adapted to urban life. It shows little fear of man, and is quick to sound the alarm when a cat is found prowling the garden. It benefits from man's largess, consuming smaller fruits and berries in the summer and bird seed in the winter. Possibly the most accomplished of the urban nest robbers, this jay appears equally adept at searching outdoor planters for House Finch nests, shade trees for a prominent American Robin's nest, or even the well-concealed Bushtit nest at the end of a live oak limb. Occasionally, a jay is caught by a Sharp-shinned Hawk (Paul L. Noble, pers. comm.), but on balance the urban habitats appear favorable for this jay.

Western Scrub-Jays were found carrying nest materials as early as 7 Feb during the atlas period, and nest construction was observed as early as 17 Feb. Because this bird is so secretive during nest construction, incubation, and the raising of its nestlings, atlasers found only 24 nests (out of 481 confirmations). The median date for carrying nest material and building nests was in the first week in April, and the period of nest construction may have preceded the bulk of atlaser fieldwork. But although the peak nestling stage occurred in May and early June, when most atlasers were afield, only eight nests were found during that time. Once fledged, there is no noisier young bird than a Western Scrub-Jay, and the observation of fledged young (60%) and fledglings being fed (23%) constituted the bulk of all confirmations. Most fledged young were found from the middle of May to the end of July, but at least a few observations of fledged young were obtained in August, the final record falling on 21 Aug. The phenology data suggest that this species is largely single-brooded.

William G. Bousman

WESTERN SCRUB-JAY

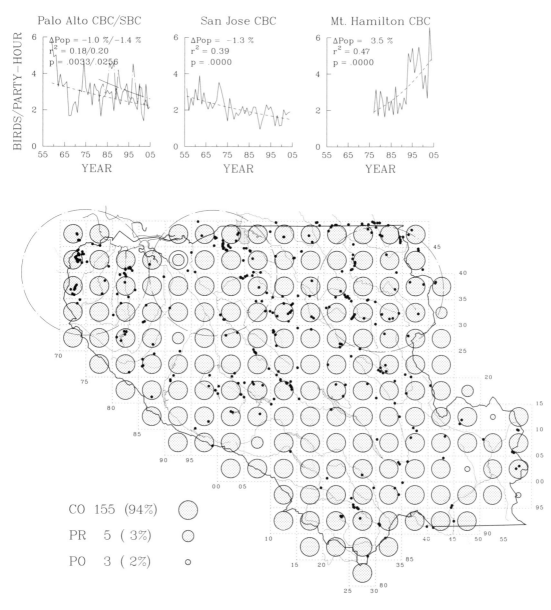

Palo Alto CBC/SBC

ΔPop = −1.0 %/−1.4 %
r^2 = 0.18/0.20
p = .0033/.0256

San Jose CBC

ΔPop = −1.3 %
r^2 = 0.39
p = .0000

Mt. Hamilton CBC

ΔPop = 3.5 %
r^2 = 0.47
p = .0000

BIRDS/PARTY−HOUR

YEAR

CO 155 (94%)
PR   5 (3%)
PO   3 (2%)

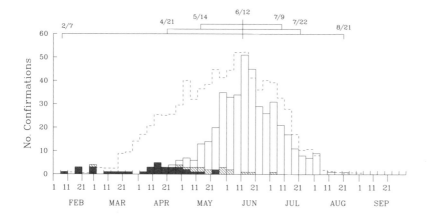

Atlas (1987−1993), n = 481

No. Confirmations

2/7   4/21   5/14   6/12   7/9   7/22   8/21

FEB   MAR   APR   MAY   JUN   JUL   AUG   SEP

Yellow-billed Magpie
Pica nuttalli

California's only endemic bird species, the Yellow-billed Magpie, with its flashing black-and-white pattern, is never far from savannas and grasslands. It is fairly common in the northern Central Valley and adjacent foothills and in the drier parts of the coastal hills from Monterey to Santa Barbara County. But after declines in the last century it is now uncommon and local in the Central Valley south of Madera County. It has been extirpated from Ventura and San Mateo counties, from coastal parts of Monterey County, and portions of Santa Clara County adjacent to the San Francisco Bay (Roberson 1993t, Reynolds 1995). In Santa Clara County, the Yellow-billed Magpie is fairly common in oak savanna, both in the Diablo Range and on the southwestern edge of the Santa Clara Valley.

Historically, the distribution of the Yellow-billed Magpie in Santa Clara County has been tied to oak savannas, grasslands, and ranches. Linsdale (1937) has provided an extensive summary of records from the last half of the nineteenth and the first part of the twentieth century. The distribution shown by these records corresponds closely with the range on the map given here, but there has been an apparent withdrawal of breeding birds from the San Francisco Peninsula. Sibley (1952) considered the magpie to be a common resident in southern and eastern portions of the South Bay area. An analysis of the San Jose and Mt. Hamilton CBCs shows no significant change in winter populations in the last half of the twentieth century. Although magpies have not bred on the San Francisco Peninsula since early in the twentieth century, a few birds lived in urban Los Altos in the early 1980s and nested at least once, fledging a single young in 1980 (Paul L. Noble, pers. comm.). The birds at this small outpost were last seen in 1988.

Breeding by Yellow-billed Magpies was confirmed in 66 blocks (40%) during the atlas period. Most of these confirmations were obtained east of the Santa Clara Valley in the Diablo Range. Breeding magpies were most often found in areas with a mixture of oak savanna and grasslands, generally in valleys with alluvial deposits, or in flat or moderately sloped areas above the alluvial boundary. The grasslands in these areas were often grazed, although birds also used ungrazed areas within Henry Coe State Park. Examination of the atlas map shows gaps in the distribution of breeding Yellow-billed Magpies in the Diablo Range. In some of these areas, as in the northeast corner of the county, portions of the Coyote Creek drainage, and in the upper Pacheco Creek drainage, grasslands and savannas occur only rarely, and these areas are dominated instead by chaparral and blue oak-foothill pine woodlands. The lands south of Pacheco Creek in the southeast seemed suitable for this species, but no nesting was confirmed there. Gaps of this sort were also found, at smaller scale, in blocks where breeding was confirmed. In the southern foothills of the Santa Cruz Mountains west of the Santa Clara Valley, birds nested from the Calero Reservoir at the head of the Almaden Valley southeast to the flatlands where Uvas and Llagas creeks flow onto the valley floor.

Magpies frequently used valley and blue oaks as nest sites, and sycamores along stream courses were also commonly used. Breeding records extended from an elevation of 177 feet at a nest site south of Pacheco Creek, in agricultural land in San Benito County, to 3,600 feet on the southwest slopes of Eylar Mountain. Grinnell and Miller (1944) and Small (1994) have reported that magpies do not normally nest above 1,800 to 2,000 feet, but 26% of all breeding confirmations in Santa Clara County were above 2,000 feet. Linsdale (1937) considered the Yellow-billed Magpie to be limited in its elevation extent by thermal and precipitation effects, but no elevational limit was apparent in Santa Clara County during the atlas period. Rather, breeding magpies appeared at all elevations where suitable habitat was to be found.

The earliest breeding evidence obtained during the atlas period was a bird carrying nest material on 23 Mar near Calaveras Reservoir. Following the atlas period magpies were seen building or repairing a nest in Ed Levin County Park on 15 Feb 1997 (Michael J. Mammoser, pers. comm.). The latest breeding evidence was young birds being fed in the foothills of the southern Santa Cruz Mountains on 27 Jul. Yellow-billed Magpie nests are relatively permanent structures lasting five years or more (Linsdale 1946), and hence are easily observed. Not surprisingly, the majority of breeding confirmations were of used nests (54%). The second most frequent breeding evidence was fledged young (22%).

In the past, Yellow-billed Magpies earned the animosity of ranchers by attacking unguarded stock in winter and pecking through to the entrails (Verbeek 1973). Although direct persecution of this corvid is no longer frequent, it can be an untargeted victim of poisoning for rodent control. In 1984 a magpie colony at the University of California's Hastings Reserve in Monterey County was apparently extirpated after feeding on poisoned ground squirrels (Koenig and Reynolds 1987) and by 1995 had still not been reestablished (Reynolds 1995). There is no documentation of similar losses in Santa Clara County, and magpie populations here appear stable. The greatest threat to this species, however, is continuing urban sprawl, such as along Silver Creek, where oak savanna has been replaced by golf courses and housing. We can hope to continue hearing the jaunty magpie's "qua-qua-qua" if we can preserve the remaining savanna in Santa Clara County.

Charles J. Coston

YELLOW-BILLED MAGPIE

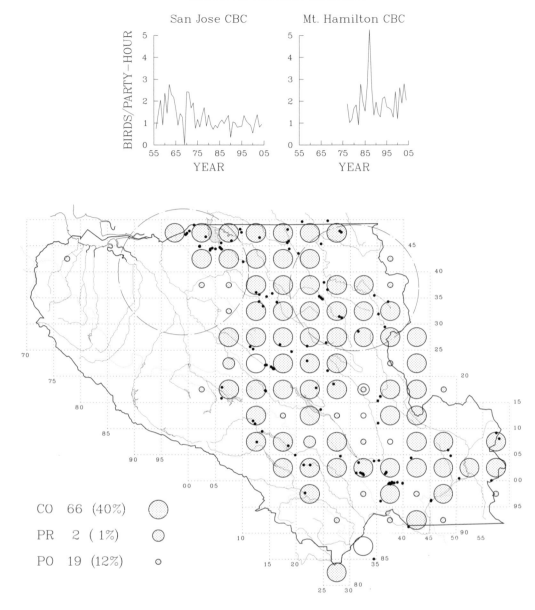

San Jose CBC

Mt. Hamilton CBC

BIRDS/PARTY-HOUR

YEAR

YEAR

CO 66 (40%)

PR 2 (1%)

PO 19 (12%)

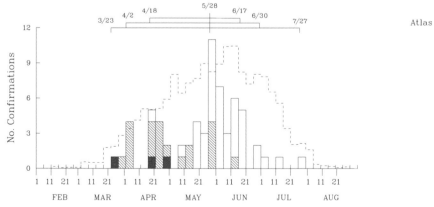

3/23 4/2 4/18 5/28 6/17 6/30 7/27

Atlas (1987–1993), n = 66

No. Confirmations

FEB MAR APR MAY JUN JUL AUG

303

American Crow
Corvus brachyrhynchos

Among the most adaptable of birds, American Crows have moved into our urban areas in recent decades. The American Crow breeds from interior British Columbia across Canada to the southeast coast of Labrador, and south through the United States to northwestern Baja California, Central Texas, and Florida (Verbeek and Caffrey 2002). But it is absent from much of the Great Basin and the deserts from southeastern California to south Texas. Four subspecies have been described, although they are poorly defined (Verbeek and Caffrey 2002). The race *C. b. hesperis* is found along the west coast of North America, but relationships in the mountain west remain controversial. In California, the American Crow is a permanent or summer resident over much of the state, but is absent from the southeastern deserts, the drier portions of the west side of the San Joaquin Valley, and the forested and mountainous areas of the Cascades-Sierra axis (Small 1994). This species is now a common resident in Santa Clara County, including the urban areas, but is absent from heavily forested areas of the Santa Cruz Mountains. Contrary to Verbeek and Caffrey (2002) and Small (1994), this crow is not absent from southeastern Santa Clara County.

Crows were apparently common in the northern Santa Clara Valley in the late 1850s, according to Alfred Doten (Clark 1973), but farmers using poisons such as strychnine for ground squirrels killed many birds. By the end of the century, Price (1898f) stated that crows were rare near Stanford, and Van Denburgh (1899b) noted that he had not observed them in either Palo Alto or Los Gatos. Fisher (1902) stated that they were resident in the southern part of the Santa Clara Valley. Grinnell and Wythe (1927) considered American Crows to be locally common in the San Francisco Bay region, particularly in the counties north of the Bay, and recorded the Calaveras Valley, San Jose, and Gilroy as locations in Santa Clara County where they had been observed. Emlen (1940) systematically surveyed American Crows in California during the winter of 1937–38. He found winter roosts on alluvial soils, including locations in the southern Santa Clara Valley, but commented that none were found in the north-

ern part of the valley, although the habitat seemed suitable. Sibley (1952) considered the crow to be a common resident in the southern and eastern parts of the South Bay. American Crows were rarely observed in the northwestern portion of Santa Clara County in the 1950s and 1960s, as an analysis of Palo Alto CBC data demonstrates. On the Jasper Ridge Biological Preserve, San Mateo County, there were only five sightings between 1954 and 1958, all in the spring (Row 1960). The first crows found on the Palo Alto CBC were seen in the winter of 1966–67. Since then, analysis of the winter and summer count data from the Palo Alto circle shows a robust population increase, varying between 11.6 and 13.2% per year. California-wide, analysis of Breeding Bird Survey data for the years 1966 to 2004 shows an increase of 2.9% per year (Sauer et al. 2005).

American Crows were found breeding widely in the county during the atlas period. Confirmed breeding was observed in 44% of the atlas blocks, and including probable and possible evidence of breeding, records were obtained in 82% of the blocks. Birds were found breeding from an elevation of 3 feet at the Sunnyvale Baylands Park to 3,800 feet at the western edge of Black Mountain, overlooking Arroyo Hondo in the Diablo Range. Habitat selection in urban and nonurban areas appeared to differ. In urban or suburban settings, crows nested in densely foliated trees, generally conifers (such as coast redwood) or palms. Often these nests were near parks or school yards that provided the open areas preferred by this species for foraging, but sometimes nests were located near malls, restaurants, or vacant lots. Apparently, the food resources of our urban setting are sufficient for this omnivorous feeder. Away from urban areas, crows were found nesting in open woodlands, at woodland edges, and in riparian corridors. In these cases grasslands, pastures, agricultural lands, or other open landscapes were available for foraging nearby. Crows were not found in the extensive coniferous and mixed coniferous-broadleaved evergreen forests in the Santa Cruz Mountains, and were also absent from large chaparral fields in the Diablo Range and the Santa Cruz Mountains.

The breeding phenology of the American Crow shows a gap between initial nesting activities, such as carrying nest materials and nest building, and fledged young, which was the most common breeding confirmation (58%). Atlasers obtained few confirmations of incubating birds. The earliest breeding evidence obtained during the atlas period was birds seen carrying nest material on 6 Mar. Following the atlas period, nearly fledged young were seen in a nest on the extraordinarily early date of 27 Feb (Phyllis M. Browning, county notebooks). The latest breeding evidence obtained was young being fed on 9 Aug.

American Crows were once considered a rural species, but their invasion of urban areas, beginning in the late 1950s, has been noted across their breeding range (Verbeek and Caffrey 2002). This expansion is partly a result of reduced shooting within urban areas. Observations of birds nesting in both urban and rural areas near Madison, Wisconsin, have shown that the urban birds stay close to their nests, showing little fear of man, whereas rural birds remain wary and stay outside of gunshot range (Knight et al. 1987). As our communities have become more urban, crows appear to have found sanctuary from rural persecution.

William G. Bousman

AMERICAN CROW

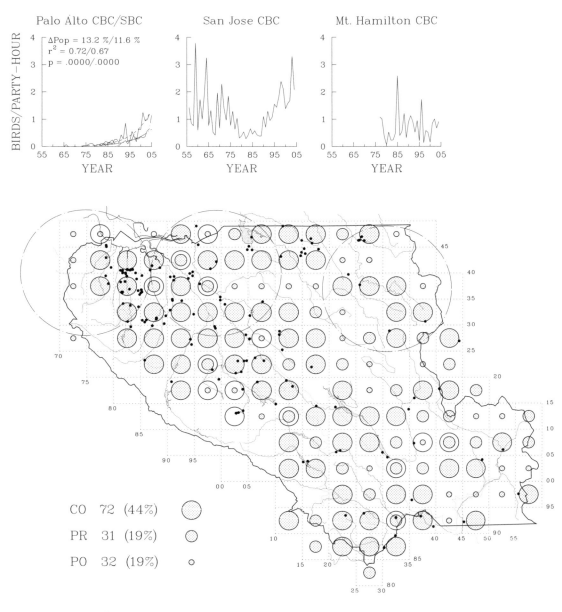

Palo Alto CBC/SBC

ΔPop = 13.2 %/11.6 %
r^2 = 0.72/0.67
p = .0000/.0000

San Jose CBC

Mt. Hamilton CBC

BIRDS/PARTY-HOUR

YEAR

CO 72 (44%)
PR 31 (19%)
PO 32 (19%)

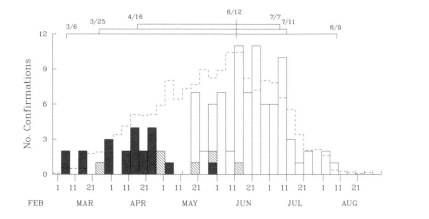

Atlas (1987–1993), n = 117

No. Confirmations

3/6   3/25   4/16   6/12   7/7   7/11   8/9

FEB   MAR   APR   MAY   JUN   JUL   AUG

305

Common Raven
Corvus corax

Bird of mythology and ancient legend, creator and trickster, the imposing Common Raven has readily adapted to our modern world. Its Holarctic distribution extends through the Old World and south to China and North Africa (Boarman and Heinrich 1999). In the New World, it breeds from Alaska across Canada to Newfoundland. East of the Great Plains it is found south into the northern tier of states and in the Appalachian Mountains; west of the Great Plains it is found south through Mexico to Central America. In California, ravens are resident throughout most of the state, but are absent from portions of the Central Valley (Small 1994). The Common Raven is now a fairly common resident in Santa Clara County, particularly near the Bay and in the northern parts of the county.

But the raven appears to be a recent invader of Santa Clara County. In the 1850s, D. S. Bryant reported that ravens "were very common along the roadside from San Francisco to San Mateo" (Bryant 1890). Cooper (1870) considered them regular and widespread in California. By the 1890s, although still found in Marin County, they were largely absent from the rest of central California (Bryant 1890). None of the early observers in Santa Clara County (Price 1898d, Van Denburgh 1899b, Barlow 1900b, Fisher 1902) recorded this species. Grinnell (1915) considered it common in the state, but "scarce or absent in the most thickly settled counties." Grinnell and Wythe (1927) reported that the species was rare in the San Francisco Bay area, except along the coasts of Marin and Sonoma counties. By midcentury, Sibley (1952) described it as an uncommon resident both along the coast and in arid inland areas, but included no records from Santa Clara County. The first mention of the Common Raven in the county was of two birds seen by Anna Richardson in Palo Alto in December 1956 (*Avocet 5*: 42–43 1958). By the 1970s,

it was clear that Common Ravens were increasing in many areas of the United States, including California (Robbins et al. 1986). Analysis of local CBC and SBC data shows a rapid growth in numbers seen in all local count circles starting in the 1970s or 1980s, but at the time the atlas was initiated there were still no breeding records for Santa Clara County.

During the first three years of the atlas period, atlasers observed possible and probable breeding evidence in 15 blocks, mostly along the crest of the Santa Cruz Mountains, but in a few cases in the northeastern part of the county. Included in these records is one of an adult carrying food, although the record is not mapped, since the block where the nest would have been was not determined. The first confirmation of a Common Raven nest was on 28 Mar 1990, when a pair was observed building a nest on the outer structure of the 80- by 120-foot Wind Tunnel at Moffett Field. At least three young were raised in this nest, the last observation on 9 Jun. Near Del Puerto Road, on 13 May 1990, a nest with young was found in a natural cliff site. During the remainder of the atlas period, ravens expanded their breeding range both at the edge of the South Bay, nesting most often on transmission towers, and in the northern Diablo Range, using natural sites, generally in foothill pines. In addition, a nest was found in a large tan oak in the Santa Cruz Mountains on the east side of Black Mountain on 27 May 1991. Following the atlas period, ravens continued to expand into multiple new blocks, as indicated by the open circles on the map. New nest locations were also found farther south in the county, in the Silver Creek Hills and along Metcalf Road.

The earliest breeding evidence during the atlas period was birds carrying nest material near the Moffett Field nest site on 20 Feb. Subsequent to the atlas period, a bird was found working on a nest in the northeastern part of the county as early as 30 Jan 1994 (Michael M. Rogers, PADB). The latest breeding evidence during the atlas period was fledglings observed on 7 Jul. Subsequently, ravens were seen feeding young at the edge of the Palo Alto estuary as late as 5 Aug 2000 (Michael M. Rogers, PADB).

The decline in Common Raven populations in central California noted by Bryant (1890) in the nineteenth century was observed over much of the species' North American range, particularly where there was human settlement (Boarman and Heinrich 1999). Very likely this decline was related directly to the effects of human activities, including shooting, poisoning, trapping, and the extirpation of the American bison (Boarman and Heinrich 1999). Now, Common Ravens are increasing throughout their former range. Kelly et al. (2002) have documented the population growth in the San Francisco Bay area, using roadside surveys as well as CBC and BBS data. The increases are occurring in many habitats, including those in both urban and rural areas. There are several likely causes for these increases, including food resources associated with human refuse and roadside carrion, as well as the decline of human persecution (Boarman and Heinrich 1999). The predation of Snowy Plover nests and young and Clapper Rail nests by Common Ravens has been documented in the South Bay. The impact on these threatened and endangered species is a concern of local refuge personnel (Clyde Morris, pers. comm.).

William G. Bousman

COMMON RAVEN

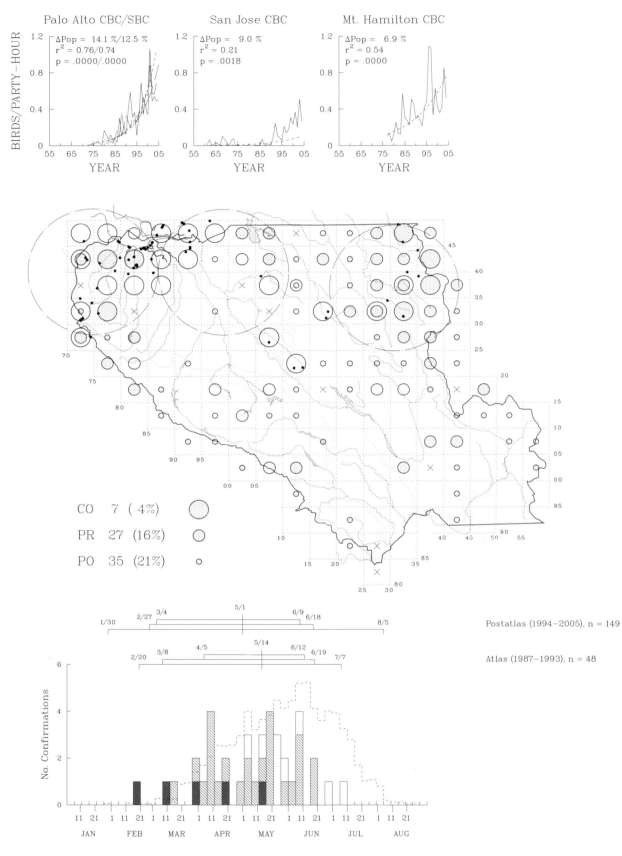

Palo Alto CBC/SBC

ΔPop = 14.1 %/12.5 %
r² = 0.76/0.74
p = .0000/.0000

San Jose CBC

ΔPop = 9.0 %
r² = 0.21
p = .0018

Mt. Hamilton CBC

ΔPop = 6.9 %
r² = 0.54
p = .0000

BIRDS/PARTY-HOUR

YEAR

CO   7 (4%)

PR 27 (16%)

PO 35 (21%)

Postatlas (1994–2005), n = 149

Atlas (1987–1993), n = 48

No. Confirmations

307

Horned Lark
Eremophila alpestris

The Holarctic Horned Lark is the only member of the family Alaudidae that is native to North America. Migratory populations of Horned Larks occur throughout the arctic regions of North America, Europe, and Asia, and south of the arctic the birds are resident. In North America, this lark breeds from Alaska to Newfoundland and south throughout most of the United States into Mexico, wherever barren lands and short-grass prairies are found (Beason 1995). Eight subspecies nest in California. The one breeding in Santa Clara County, *E. a. actia*, is found coastally from Sonoma County to Baja California, and also in the San Joaquin Valley (Grinnell and Miller 1944). The Horned Lark is an uncommon resident in Santa Clara County, most often found in grasslands along the western edge of the Diablo Range.

Egg collectors found nesting Horned Larks in the Santa Clara Valley at the end of the nineteenth century. William L. Atkinson (1895) collected three sets of eggs from a farm and vineyard in 1894 and 1895, presumably near where he lived in San Jose. Chase Littlejohn collected multiple egg sets in Apr 1898 from a pasture east of Redwood City, San Mateo County (WFVZ egg collections). John O. Snyder found a set of three eggs at the edge of the salt marsh near the mouth of San Francisquito Creek (WFVZ #93605) and noted that "Many larks are seen here each year." Price (1898d) reported that a few pairs were found at Stanford near the stock farm, but he did not consider them common. Van Denburgh (1899b) stated that Horned Larks were found in the Valley, not far from Los Gatos. Fisher (1902) wrote that they were "common in the open valley." Grinnell and Wythe (1927) considered them to be fairly common in the San Francisco Bay area on dry plains or hills with short grass. Sibley (1952) stated that the species was a common resident in open country in the South Bay, and noted that it was more widespread in winter. Although Horned Larks are resident, they tend to form large flocks following the breeding season, and to move around among patches of suitable habitat. None were recorded during the early years of the Palo Alto CBC, but during the late 1960s and early 1970s, substantial numbers were found in Redwood City near the cement plant, and in the newly created Bayfront

Park (M. Clark Blake, pers. comm.). Analysis of CBC and SBC data shows a decline of 15.3% per year since 1968 for the CBC and 14.3% per year since 1981 for the SBC within the Palo Alto circle. Analysis of the San Jose CBC data shows no change. In California as a whole, analysis of BBS data shows a decline of 3.5% per year from 1966 to 2004 (Sauer et al. 2005).

Atlasers found Horned Larks breeding widely along the western edge of the Diablo Range and in the Pacheco Creek drainage, but they were scarcer elsewhere in the county. During the atlas period, larks were found breeding at elevations ranging from 145 feet in the Pajaro River floodplain to 3,140 feet on Oak Ridge in the Diablo Range. Following the atlas period, breeding evidence was obtained at an elevation of 8 feet along the Bay in a San Mateo County edge block (Sequoia Audubon Society 2001g). Horned Larks were found in non-native grasslands, particularly in heavily grazed areas with short grasses and bare open areas. They were also found, sometimes at high density, in native serpentine grasslands where many grasses and small forbs were stunted, and in areas where the formation of thin soils with poor nutrients resulted in short grasses and open ground. Only two nests were found during the atlas period, both in the southern Santa Cruz Mountains on heavily grazed lands.

Horned Larks often form large flocks in the winter. These flocks break up in January and February as individual territories are established (Beason 1995). In Santa Clara County and nearby bayside locations in San Mateo County, historical egg dates extend from 18 Apr to 29 Jun (*n* = 10; Atkinson 1895, WFVZ egg collections). The earliest breeding evidence obtained during the atlas period was an adult carrying food on 25 Apr. The two nests found during the atlas period, both with young, were found on 6 and 17 Jun. Horned Larks are normally double-brooded (Beason 1995), and these June nests may be from a second brood. The latest evidence obtained during the atlas period was an adult carrying food on 13 Jul. Subsequently, an adult carrying food was found on the later date of 19 Jul 1997 along the Bay in a San Mateo County edge block (Sequoia Audubon Society 2001g).

Historically, Horned Larks appear to have been a common species on the Santa Clara Valley floor and at the edge of the South Bay. In these locations they were found in pastures, vineyards, and vegetable gardens. These habitats, all related to agriculture, were characterized by a mixture of barren ground and vegetation, either grasses, weeds, or furrow crops. In this sense, Horned Larks benefited from human settlement. They are now rare anywhere in the Valley, in part because so many of these habitats have been displaced by urbanization. And even where agriculture remains, modern farming methods apparently no longer create habitats attractive to this lark.

William G. Bousman

HORNED LARK

Palo Alto CBC/SBC

ΔPop = −15.3 %/−21.8 %
r^2 = 0.44/0.51
p = .0000/.0001

BIRDS/PARTY–HOUR

YEAR

San Jose CBC

YEAR

CO 18 (11%)

PR 12 (7%)

PO 11 (7%)

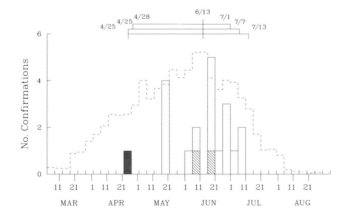

Atlas (1987–1993), n = 29

No. Confirmations

MAR   APR   MAY   JUN   JUL   AUG

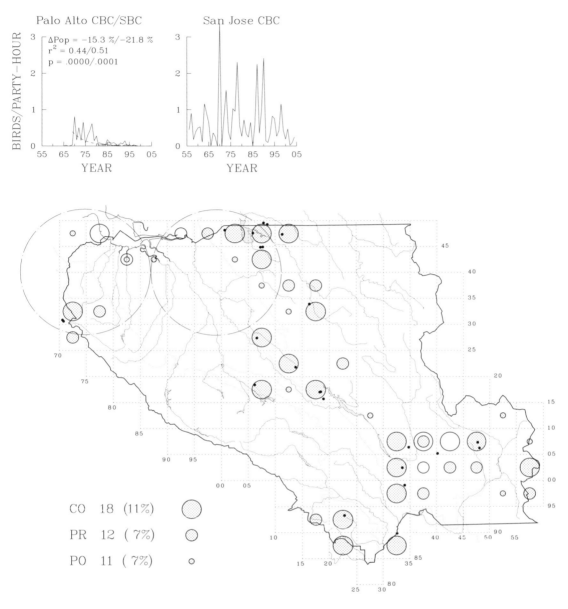

Purple Martin
Progne subis

This largest of the North American swallows is disappearing as a breeding species from the central coast of California, for reasons not completely understood. In western North America, Purple Martins breed in disjunct locations from southwestern British Columbia to southern Baja California; from the Rocky Mountains east, they nest from central Alberta to central Nova Scotia, and south through the United States to southern Texas and Florida (Brown 1997, AOU 1998). Until recently, only two subspecies were described: *hesperia* in Baja California, Arizona, and northwestern Mexico and *subis* over the rest of North America (AOU 1957). More recent work indicates that birds of the Rocky Mountains constitute a third subspecies, *arboricola*, but the subspecific attribution of birds on the Pacific Coast is unclear (Brown 1997). The Purple Martin is a rare-to-uncommon breeder in California, found at scattered sites west of the Cascades-Sierra axis and west of the deserts in southern California (Small 1994). Purple Martins are rare breeders in the Santa Cruz Mountains within Santa Clara County and are rare migrants elsewhere in the county.

The first mention of Purple Martins in the local historical records was of two to three birds in migration observed by A. L. Parkhurst in San Jose on 3 May 1884 (Belding 1890). Price (1898f) considered them to be occasional transients at Stanford, and also noted that they commonly nested around the observatory buildings on Mt. Hamilton. Van Denburgh (1899b) stated that the species "breeds in some numbers on the Mount Hamilton range," but indicated that he had not seen it on the western side of the county. Grinnell and Wythe (1927) recorded no observations of breeding for the San Francisco Bay area, but did state that birds had been observed throughout the nesting season at three sites in Marin and Sonoma counties. Sibley (1952) judged Purple Martins to be uncommon summer residents in the South Bay, citing only two nest records: one near Cedar Mountain, Alameda County, the other on Mt. Hermon, Santa Cruz County.

Only one breeding confirmation was obtained during the atlas period. Two adults were observed coming to a nest cavity in a Douglas fir snag 40 feet above the ground in Barrett Canyon,

north-northwest of Loma Prieta, on 9 Jul 1989. Begging young were heard calling from the cavity. Atlasers observed probable evidence in four additional blocks along Summit Ridge, the crest of the Santa Cruz Mountains in this area. Subsequent to the atlas period, additional confirmations were obtained in that area when adults were seen feeding young on 21 Jul 1995 and dependent fledglings were observed on 24 Jul 1996 (Michael M. Rogers, pers. comm.). Along Summit Ridge, where this breeding evidence has been obtained, there are extensive areas of dense chaparral intermixed with patches of Douglas fir, knobcone pines, and occasionally broadleaved evergreens.

In recent decades, the earliest observation of Purple Martins in the county was a male over Almaden Reservoir on 23 Mar 1997 (Frank Vanslager, county notebooks). Martins have been seen in their breeding areas along Summit Ridge as early as 2 May 1997 and as late as 1 Aug 1995 (Robert W. Reiling, county notebooks). A few martins are seen along the Bay into September, but it is not known if these are dispersing residents or migrants from more northerly areas.

Populations of Purple Martins are declining over much of North America, including California (Small 1994, Brown 1997), a pattern that is particularly true in Santa Clara County. Although subspecific differences are not well established, the birds in western North America nest primarily in abandoned woodpecker holes, whereas eastern birds nest in manmade martin houses or gourds. In the west, birds are loosely colonial, nesting in multiple holes in dead trees, but are never found in the large numbers that are sometimes seen in established martin "apartment houses" in the east. The density of breeding Purple Martins in the west is quite low, the birds found in scattered, widely spaced locations, with much apparently suitable habitat going unused (Brown 1997). Declines in the east have been related to usurpation of nest sites by European Starlings and House Sparrows (Brown 1981, Brown 1997). In the west, the decline has coincided with the westward invasion of European Starlings, which are aggressive competitors for cavity sites (Small 1994). In Monterey County, where Purple Martins were once far more abundant than today, Roberson (1993q) recorded numerous colonies of birds, in both the Upper Sonoran and Transition life zones, that disappeared as starlings invaded the county in the 1950s. Only along the Big Sur Coast, in heavily forested areas where starlings are absent, do a few breeding colonies remain, totaling perhaps 50 to 100 pairs.

Although Purple Martins appear always to have been rare in Santa Clara County, historical records indicate a contraction of their range in the last century. As noted previously, Price (1898f) described them as nesting near the summit of Mt. Hamilton. More recent records of breeding in the Diablo Range include nests on Mt. Hamilton and Mines roads in 1978 (*Avocet 25(6)* 1978) and in the San Antonio Valley in 1982 (*Am. Birds 36*:891 1982). Breeding in the Santa Cruz Mountains was once more extensive, birds having nested in Los Gatos in 1948 (*Audubon Field Notes 3*:31 1949) and at the Lexington Reservoir dam in 1965 (*Avocet 12*:69 1965). Today, the Purple Martin's range in Santa Clara County has contracted to a 15-km segment of Summit Ridge in the Santa Cruz Mountains. If not already extirpated locally, this large swallow's days appear numbered here.

William G. Bousman

PURPLE MARTIN

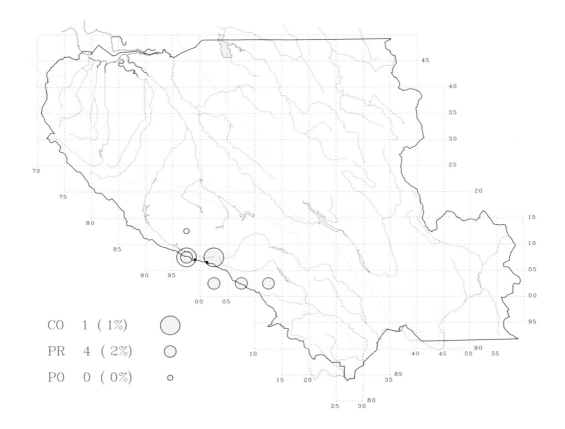

CO 1 (1%)   ●

PR 4 (2%)   ●

PO 0 (0%)   ○

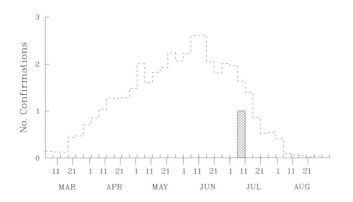

Atlas (1987–1993), n = 1

Tree Swallow
Tachycineta bicolor

Streams, ponds, or marshes with snags that offer suitable nest cavities attract this beautiful iridescent swallow. The Tree Swallow breeds from the treeline in north-central Alaska across Canada to Nova Scotia, and south to the southern United States from California to North Carolina (Robertson et al. 1992). In California, it nests over most of the northern third of the state, in the outer Coast Ranges south to southern Monterey County, in the Central Valley south to Tulare and Kings counties, and at a few locations on the coastal slope of southern California (Zeiner et al. 1990, Small 1994). Tree Swallows are uncommon in Santa Clara County and are generally found breeding only where there are streams or wetlands with suitable dead trees or snags for nesting.

The status of the Tree Swallow in Santa Clara County at the end of the nineteenth century is unclear. Price (1898f) considered it a transient at Stanford, while Van Denburgh (1899b) considered it an abundant breeding species along the western side of the county, noting that it bred "in holes in white oaks." (Currently, nesting in deciduous oaks is more typical of the Violet-green Swallow.) Grinnell and Wythe (1927) considered the Tree Swallow to be a local summer resident in the San Francisco Bay region, mostly north of the Bay, but did mention a successful nest at Palo Alto. Gordon L. Bolander collected eggs at San Felipe Lake, just over the line in San Benito County, on 1 Jul 1930 (MVZ #5038). W. E. Unglish reported many Tree Swallows nesting on San Felipe Lake in 1932 (Sibley 1952) and collected eggs at that location. Sibley (1952) considered the Tree Swallow to be an uncommon summer resident in the South Bay. As of 1960, this species was considered a common summer resident in the Jasper Ridge Biological Preserve (San Mateo County), where more than 20 nests were found (Row 1960).

During the atlas period, Tree Swallows were recorded in 50 county blocks (30%), and confirmations were obtained in 19 blocks (12%). Subsequently, breeding was confirmed in ten additional blocks. (Interestingly, Tree Swallows had not been seen during the atlas period in the majority of these additional blocks.) Nesting swallows generally used cavities in dead snags in more open areas near water, often along streams or manmade reservoirs. Typical locations along streams included Coyote Creek below Highway 237, Coyote Creek above Metcalf Road, Uvas Creek above Gilroy, Pacheco Creek above San Felipe Lake, and the Pajaro River both above and below Highway 101. Birds nesting on Coyote Creek in Kelly Park, San Jose, were in a less typical, partially urban setting. Typical reservoir sites for Tree Swallows included the west shore of Calaveras Reservoir, the Isabel Reservoir in Isabel Valley, and the upper end of Calero Reservoir. In a few places, they used nest boxes that had been placed in open grasslands or scrublands near streams or ponds. Following the atlas period, nest boxes were placed in a number of new areas, including Arastradero Preserve in Palo Alto, Ed Levin County Park, and Joseph Grant County Park, and were successfully used by nesting Tree Swallows. Although these swallows will sometimes nest in close proximity in areas where there are extensive drowned trees with nesting cavities (Roberson 1993r), most atlasers encountered only one or two pairs at the sites indicated on the map. Tree Swallows are less common in Santa Clara County than in the wetter North Bay counties, such as Marin and Sonoma (Shuford 1993u, Burridge 1995c), and also Monterey County, where the Salinas River basin provides suitable wetlands and nest sites (Roberson 1993r). This species is generally absent in the drier interior Coast Ranges south and east of Santa Clara County (Zeiner et al. 1990).

Tree Swallows are found occasionally in Santa Clara County during the winter, but the first spring movement of migrants or summer residents occurs in the last two weeks of February. During the atlas period, the earliest breeding evidence obtained was a nest with eggs along lower Coyote Creek on 22 Apr. Following the atlas period, birds were seen occupying a nest at Ed Levin County Park as early as 9 Mar 2002 (Michael M. Rogers, PADB). The latest confirmation during the atlas period was of adults feeding young in the Isabel Valley on 7 Jul. After the atlas fieldwork, adults were seen feeding fledged young as late as 29 Jul 2005 along Stevens Creek near the Bay (Michael M. Rogers, PADB).

The Tree Swallow's habitat requirements appear to be limiting for this species' populations (Robertson et al. 1992), but the number of Tree Swallows has increased by 4.1% a year in California across the last three decades (Sauer et al. 2005), which is cause for optimism. It is uncertain, however, whether this swallow's numbers have increased in Santa Clara County over the same period. Locally, riparian areas with their mixtures of cottonwood, willow, and oak forests, thick shrub understories, overflow wetlands, and ample dead snags and limbs are in decline wherever these habitats are barriers to encroaching urbanization. The Tree Swallow, therefore, will be a key indicator species of how well we are protecting our remaining riparian forests and wetlands in the coming years.

William G. Bousman

TREE SWALLOW

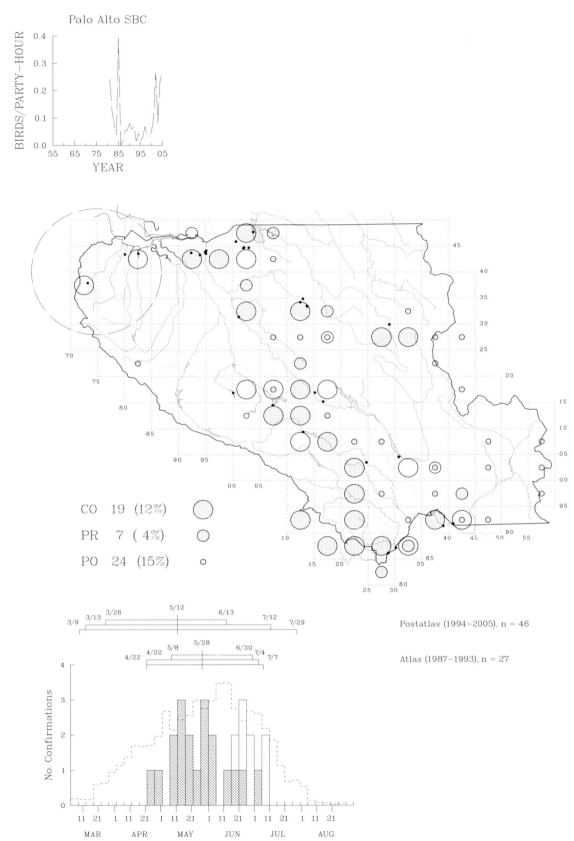

Palo Alto SBC

BIRDS/PARTY–HOUR

YEAR

CO 19 (12%)

PR   7 (4%)

PO 24 (15%)

Postatlas (1994–2005), n = 46

Atlas (1987–1993), n = 27

No. Confirmations

3/9   3/13   3/26   5/12   6/13   7/12   7/29

4/22   4/22   5/8   5/28   6/30   7/4   7/7

MAR   APR   MAY   JUN   JUL   AUG

313

breeding was noted in an additional 63 blocks. The species was most commonly found in the Diablo Range and the Santa Cruz Mountains, and the majority of confirmations were recorded at elevations of 1,000 to 3,000 feet, several nesting records noted above 3,400 feet. The bird was found in open woodlands and forest edges, primarily where oaks were present, but almost any tree cavity was found to be suitable within these general habitats. The species was largely absent as a breeder from the heavily urbanized northern valley floor, and only a few confirmations were noted at elevations below 500 feet. In a few cases, however, Violet-green Swallows did nest in urban, flatland areas. A pair used a nest box in remnant oak woodland in Menlo Park, 12 pairs used the ventilator holes in the Veterans Administration Hospital in Palo Alto, which is located at the flatlands boundary, and, following the atlas period, in 1997, a pair used a large valley oak in Calabazas Park (Stephen C. Rottenborn, pers. comm.).

Violet-green Swallows are found in our area from March through September, beginning their nesting in April and extending it through mid-July. Eighty-five percent of the confirmations were of occupied nests, and most of the confirmations were in May and June. During the atlas period, the earliest breeding confirmation was of an occupied nest on 10 Apr, and the latest was of an occupied nest on 17 Jul. After the atlas period, an occupied nest was observed earlier, on 17 Mar 2004 (Peggy L. Don, PADB), and a later observation of a nest with young was recorded on 22 Jul 1995 (Michael M. Rogers, pers. comm.). Mid- and late-summer observations of Violet-green Swallows throughout the valley floor, including adults still feeding young, are thought to pertain to postbreeding dispersants. By late summer and early fall, hundreds of postbreeders can be seen flying about in mixed swallow flocks or perched on utility wires as they join other swallows in preparation for the fall migration.

The common sight of the Violet-green Swallow in Santa Clara County during the summer months attests to its affinity for our open oak woodlands. As our mature hillside woodlands are increasingly allowed to remain in their natural state for this and other cavity-nesting species, so should this beautiful, ever-active species' presence continue.

Ann Verdi

Violet-green Swallow
Tachycineta thalassina

From dawn to dusk, during the spring and summer months, the Violet-green Swallow swoops and soars over our hillside woodlands. When illuminated just right, this sprightly swallow gleams in stunning emerald and violet iridescence. A bird of the American west, the Violet-green Swallow is a summer resident west of the Rocky Mountains from Alaska south to Baja California. Its geographic range in California includes nearly the entire length of the state, from Siskiyou County to San Diego County, and it breeds widely in the northern two-thirds of the state (Small 1994). In Santa Clara County, breeding Violet-green Swallows are found primarily in oak woodlands and forest edges of the Diablo Range and Santa Cruz Mountains.

At the turn of the century, the Violet-green Swallow was considered a common migrant statewide that bred in the Transition Life Zone in California (Grinnell 1902). Early historical accounts for Santa Clara County are somewhat contradictory, for although Van Denburgh (1899b) considered it an "irregular summer visitant," Fisher (1902) described it as a "common summer visitant" and Price (1898f) noted that it was abundant at times. Egg collectors found this swallow nesting in Redwood City and Menlo Park at that time, with at least three egg sets found from 1900 to 1903 (Chase Littlejohn, E. K. Sopher, WFVZ egg collections). The first proof of breeding in Santa Clara County was a set of eggs collected near Coyote by D. Bernard Bull on 2 Jun 1926 (MVZ #6236). Grinnell and Wythe (1927), however, listed no records of breeding in Santa Clara County, although they did record evidence of nesting in the northern Bay Area counties. In fact, the Tree Swallow, with which the Violet-green Swallow associates in migration, was considered the more common breeder in the San Francisco Bay Area by a number of early observers (Van Denburgh 1899b, Grinnell and Wythe 1927). Grinnell and Miller (1944) considered that the Violet-green Swallow was primarily a Transition Life Zone breeder, although it had been recorded as a frequent nester, locally, in the Upper Sonoran Life Zone. Later, Sibley (1952) noted the bird as a common summer resident in the South Bay, nesting in cavities, usually old woodpecker holes. Today, this species is a common summer resident in much of Santa Clara County.

During the atlas period, Violet-green Swallows were confirmed breeding in 75 atlas blocks, and probable or possible

VIOLET-GREEN SWALLOW

Palo Alto SBC

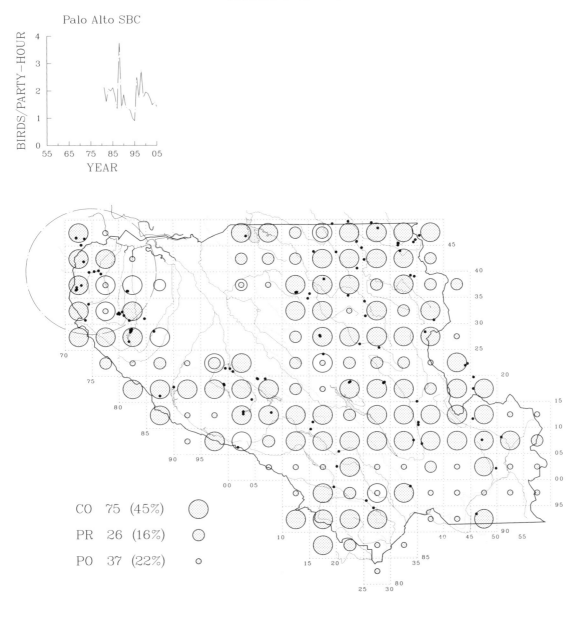

CO 75 (45%)

PR 26 (16%)

PO 37 (22%)

Atlas (1987–1993), n = 110

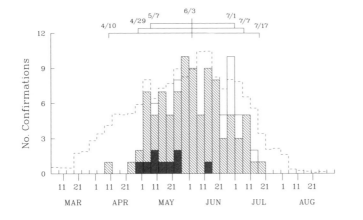

EDWARD ROOKS © 2001

Northern Rough-winged Swallow
Stelgidopteryx serripennis

Just returned from Central America in the spring, a Northern Rough-winged Swallow passes back and forth along a stream, looking for a suitable nest hole in a freshly cut bank. These swallows breed from British Columbia to southern Maine and south throughout the United States (DeJong 1996). Resident populations are found at the southern edge of the United States, and in Mexico south to Costa Rica. Over most of the United States, including California north of the Tehachapi Range, the only subspecies present is *S. s. serripennis* (DeJong 1996). In California, breeding rough-wings are found throughout the state in the Lower and Upper Sonoran life zones, except in the southeastern deserts (Small 1994). Northern Rough-winged Swallows are fairly common summer residents in Santa Clara County, generally at lower elevations.

The earliest mention of the Northern Rough-winged Swallow in Santa Clara County is in Belding's *Land Birds of the Pacific District* (1890), in which A. L. Parkhurst reported the species to be a common summer resident in San Jose and noted a first arrival date of 8 Mar. Chester Barlow collected the first egg set in the county on 9 Jul 1894 (MVZ #332). Van Denburgh (1899b) noted the rough-wing as a breeder in San Jose, but Price (1898f) listed it only as a transient at Stanford. Grinnell and Wythe (1927) thought it "not common" in the San Francisco Bay area and reported only a few localities where it had been found. During the 1930s and 1940s, multiple egg sets were collected from a railroad cut north of the Pajaro River, where White-throated Swifts and Bank Swallows also nested (WFVZ, MVZ egg collections). Rough-wings still nest at this location. Sibley (1952) considered this swallow to be a fairly common summer resident in the South Bay area at midcentury. The numbers of Northern Rough-winged Swallows tallied on the Palo Alto SBC vary, and analysis of the data shows no significant trend. For California as a whole, however, analysis of Breeding Bird Survey data shows a decline of 3.3% per year from 1966 to 2004 (Sauer et al. 2005).

Atlasers found Northern Rough-winged Swallows breeding widely in the Santa Clara Valley and adjacent foothills, gen-

erally along streams or near highway overpasses. During the atlas period, nesting birds were found from an elevation of 14 feet under a freeway overpass in Milpitas to 1,260 feet in an eroded cliff face over the Austrian Gulch arm of Lake Elsman. Ninety percent of all confirmations were at elevations below 780 feet. Following the atlas period, a nesting pair was found using drainage holes in the Summit Road overpass over Highway 17 at 1,805 feet (David L. Suddjian, pers. comm.). Atlasers found Northern Rough-winged Swallows where there were available nest sites and open areas for foraging, but otherwise these swallows were not seen to be associated with any particular habitats.

Two types of nest sites were observed during the atlas period. The first consisted of small holes in the banks of streams. Most of these banks were 2 to 3 meters high, but in a few cases the bank's height was less than a meter from the stream surface to the bank top. Generally, these holes, possibly rodent tunnels or burrows that had been exposed by bank erosion, were about the same size as the swallow. In a few cases, the holes were larger and appeared to have been excavated by Belted Kingfishers. The second type of nest site consisted of ventilation or drainage holes in manmade structures, such as highway overpasses or concrete retaining walls. Some of these holes had vertical entrances, which presumably led to a horizontal section in which the nest could be placed.

Northern Rough-winged Swallows first arrive in Santa Clara County anywhere from the last two weeks of February to the first two weeks of March (median date of 27 Feb, county notebooks). The earliest breeding evidence during the atlas period was birds occupying a nest on 29 Mar. Following the atlas period, nest building was observed as early as 25 Mar 2001 (Michael J. Mammoser, PADB). Breeding evidence based on fledglings is difficult to obtain, because the period of dependency may be quite short (DeJong 1996), and adults with dependent young may range far from where the birds have nested. The earliest observation of fledglings was made on 1 Jun. Breeding by rough-wings during the atlas period was observed as late as 21 Jul, one case being a nest still occupied on this date. Following the atlas period, adults were seen feeding young as late as 6 Aug (Richard G. Jeffers, PADB). This swallow is single-brooded (DeJong 1996), and the later nesting dates shown in the phenology graphic may indicate renesting birds.

Northern Rough-winged Swallows are dependent upon the availability of nest sites, and are unable in most cases to construct their own holes, as Bank Swallows do (DeJong 1996). In Santa Clara County, most breeding occurs at lower elevations, where nesting habitat is created by the scouring of stream banks in alluvial soils on the valley floor, or where there are abundant highway overpasses and other manmade structures. During the atlas period, a few rough-wings seen in the Diablo Range likely bred in locations such as the San Antonio and Isabel valleys, where there are also cut banks in alluvial soils. In these locations, during the atlas period, successful breeding may have been hampered by drought-induced effects, such as limited food resources.

William G. Bousman

NORTHERN ROUGH-WINGED SWALLOW

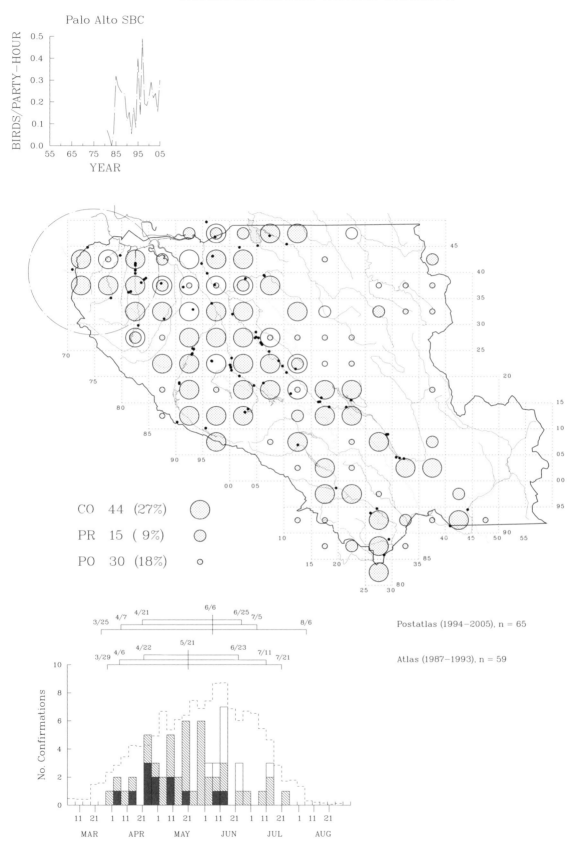

Palo Alto SBC

CO 44 (27%)

PR 15 (9%)

PO 30 (18%)

Postatlas (1994–2005), n = 65

Atlas (1987–1993), n = 59

Cliff Swallow
Petrochelidon pyrrhonota

This abundant swallow's retort-shaped mud nests, packed together in dense colonies, are now most often built on manmade bridges and buildings, showing how completely this species has adapted to human settlement. The Cliff Swallow breeds from Alaska east through Canada to Nova Scotia and New England and thence south through Texas to northwestern Baja California. It also breeds in the interior of Mexico south to central Oaxaca, and in recent decades it has expanded into the southeastern United States (Brown and Brown 1995). Cliff Swallows are found breeding throughout California, except in the higher elevations of the Cascades and the Sierra Nevada, and in the deserts of the southeast (Small 1994). They are abundant breeders in Santa Clara County on the valley floor, but largely avoid the dry interior of the Diablo Range and the more heavily forested areas of the Santa Cruz Mountains.

Judging from early observations, Cliff Swallows appear to have been abundant breeders in the South Bay for more than a century. Price (1898f) noted that this species was the common swallow around the quadrangle at Stanford University. Van Denburgh (1899b) described it as a very common resident in the county, and Fisher (1902) also considered it common. Grinnell and Wythe (1927), in assessing the Cliff Swallow's status in the San Francisco Bay area, referred to it as a common summer resident in rural districts, using the eaves of barns as well as cliff sites for nesting. Sibley (1952) considered it a common summer resident and noted that it nested on "cliffs, walls of buildings, water towers, and other man-made structures which simulate cliffs."

Atlasers found Cliff Swallows nesting widely during the atlas period, but the largest numbers were recorded along the valley floor, fewer birds nesting in the foothills of the Santa Cruz

Mountains and the Diablo Range, and almost none in the drier areas and higher elevations of the Diablo Range. Cliff Swallows bred from sea level in blocks bordering the South Bay to elevations as high as 2,700 feet south of Mt. Lewis between Alameda and Valpe creeks. Half of all confirmations, however, were below 140 feet. Cliff Swallows typically build their nests at the juncture of an overhang and a vertical wall (Brown and Brown 1995). On the valley floor and in nearby foothill areas, they built their nests most frequently on highway and pedestrian bridges over creeks and sloughs. They also used other manmade structures such as substations, pump houses, and abandoned buildings, particularly where these were near the edge of the Bay. Away from the Bay they often used eaves of houses, schools, and large buildings in open areas. In more remote areas they built their nests under the eaves of ranch buildings, but they were also found using cliff sites far from human habitation in the Diablo Range.

Cliff Swallows first arrive in Santa Clara County between 7 Feb and 13 Mar, with a median arrival date of 28 Feb (county notebooks). The variance in the arrival dates between years is probably a consequence of air temperature and its influence on the insect hatches consumed by foraging swallows (Mayhew 1958). Returning birds may make initial visits to previous colony sites, but do not necessarily initiate nest construction immediately upon arrival (pers. obs.). The start of nest construction for various colonies along the San Francisco Bay Trail bike path from Palo Alto to Moffett Field may vary by two to four weeks (pers. obs.), as has been noted for similarly adjacent colonies in the Sacramento Valley (Mayhew 1958). The earliest evidence of nesting during the atlas period was a bird in a nest on 30 Mar. Subsequent to the atlas period, nest construction was observed as early as 1 Mar 1998 (Ann Verdi, PADB). During the atlas period, nest construction (which is highly visible with Cliff Swallows) was noted between 31 Mar and 9 Jun, 75% of the observations between 26 Apr and 16 May. The latest evidence of nesting during the atlas period was a bird in a nest on 2 Aug. Subsequently, adults feeding young were seen as late as 13 Aug 2002 (Michael M. Rogers, PADB). Cliff Swallows disperse or embark on their southbound migration within a few weeks of fledging. A few birds are found until the end of September, but they are rarely encountered later.

Cliff Swallows were largely absent from the interior of the Diablo Range during the atlas period. Prior to this period, small colonies of nesting Cliff Swallows had been observed on ranch buildings in the San Antonio Valley (pers. obs.), but none of these sites was used during the atlas period. In recent years, Cliff Swallows have once again been seen in the valley, although their nest sites have not been located. Most of the atlas period coincided with a severe drought, which may have made the dry interior of the Diablo Range less suitable for nesting swallows. But in the San Antonio Valley during the drought period, water, mud, and suitable substrates for nests were present (pers. obs.). The absence of breeding Cliff Swallows at that time may have been related to a reduction of available insect prey. Cliff Swallows sometimes occupy colony sites erratically, and may be absent altogether from apparently suitable habitats (Brown and Brown 1995).

William G. Bousman

CLIFF SWALLOW

Palo Alto SBC

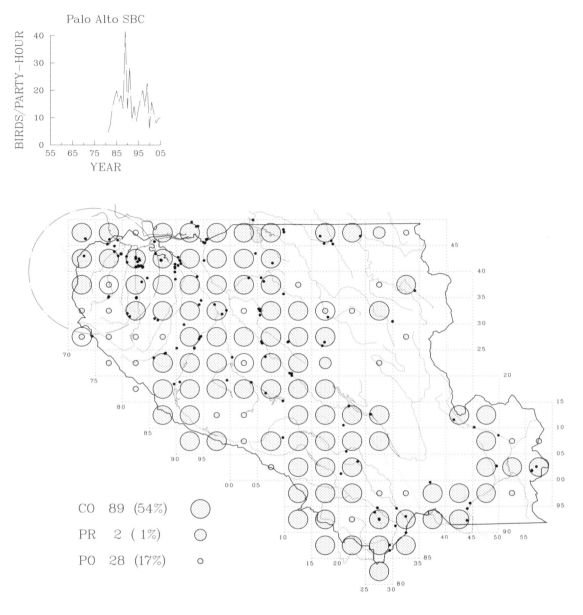

CO 89 (54%)

PR 2 (1%)

PO 28 (17%)

Atlas (1987–1993), n = 210

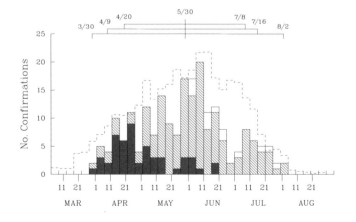

Barn Swallow
Hirundo rustica

Aptly named for its habit of nesting on artificial structures, the Barn Swallow is a characteristic bird of open habitats that offer mud for nest construction and suitable substrates for nest support. This widespread species breeds throughout much of Europe, Asia, northern Africa, and the Americas. The New World race *H. r. erythrogaster* nests from Canada's middle latitudes south into Mexico, and winters primarily in Central and South America (AOU 1957, 1998). In California, the Barn Swallow breeds throughout the northern two-thirds of the state, avoiding only the higher elevations in the Sierra Nevada, and occurs in most of the southern part of the state only as a migrant (Zeiner et al. 1990, Small 1994). These master aviators are common summer residents in suburban and agricultural areas in Santa Clara County. They are absent from, or breed more sparsely in, the drier parts of the county and areas with extensive forest or chaparral.

The historical status of the Barn Swallow in Santa Clara County is unclear. This species was not among those listed by Price (1898f) as occurring at Stanford University around the turn of the twentieth century, even though he listed all the other regularly occurring swallows. Likewise, Van Denburgh (1899b) mentioned only a single "colony" at Alma (near Los Gatos) in his notes of birds in Santa Clara County. But this species may have been more widespread at the turn of the century than these authors indicated, since by 1927 Grinnell and Wythe called the Barn Swallow a "common summer resident throughout the greater part of the Bay region." Grinnell and Miller (1944) and Sibley (1952) also considered this species to be a common breeder in the Bay area. Grinnell and Miller (1944) indicated that breeding Barn Swallows in California had increased both in distribution and in numbers as a result of the spread of irrigation and the construction of bridges and buildings. Since the early 1980s, Barn Swallows have declined at an average rate of 3.1% per year on the Palo Alto Summer Bird Count, although no significant or consistent trend has been noted in Breeding Bird Survey data from California (Sauer et al. 2005).

Atlasers recorded Barn Swallows in 64% of the atlas blocks and confirmed breeding in 46% of all blocks. This species was found to be most common and widespread on the Santa Clara Valley floor, where structures for nest attachment, mud for nest-building, and open foraging areas abound. Here, nests were found on bridges, elevated wooden walkways, and a variety of buildings. Barns, outbuildings, and other structures having wooden beams for nest support, as well as open doors or windows affording the birds easy access, seemed most conducive to nesting. Interestingly, there are no records of Barn Swallow nests on natural substrates in Santa Clara County, indicating this species' dependence on, or at least preference for, artificial structures for nesting. Barn Swallows were sparsely distributed in some heavily urbanized areas lacking open foraging habitats. They also nested in portions of the Santa Cruz Mountains offering suitable habitat, particularly areas having buildings and lacking extensive forest or chaparral. Barn Swallows were common breeders in the more developed western foothills of the Diablo Range, but they were absent from most of the range's interior. Even where barns, mud, and open foraging areas were present in the interior of the Diablo Range, Barn Swallows were not generally confirmed nesting, and they were seldom recorded there in summer at all. Most breeding confirmations were from areas below 800 feet in elevation, although breeding was confirmed as high as 2,640 feet in the Diablo Range.

Barn Swallows were occasionally found nesting amid colonies of Cliff Swallows. But compared to the more gregarious Cliff Swallow, pairs of Barn Swallows usually nested singly or in small, loose groups. As a result, they were less dependent on bridges, cliffs, or other sites providing space for large colonies of birds, and frequently nested on structures that were smaller than those used by Cliff Swallows. Old Barn Swallow nests are occasionally used for nesting by other species. House Finches, House Sparrows, and Black Phoebes are known to use Barn Swallow nests (Ehrlich et al. 1988, pers. obs.), and, in turn, some Barn Swallows are known to use old phoebe nests (Bent 1938h).

Barn Swallows begin arriving at their Santa Clara County breeding areas in March. Nest-building was observed as early as 31 Mar and continued through May. Nests under construction in May probably represented second nestings, as these birds frequently raise two broods in a season (Ehrlich et al. 1988). Nests with young were seen as early as 13 May but were most numerous in June. Although most young had fledged by mid-July, some late-breeding pairs had unfledged young in the nest as late as 25 Aug during the atlas period, and adults were seen feeding young as late as 12 Sep 2004 after this period (Alan M. Eisner, PADB). The breeding phenology constituted by these atlas data is consistent with California egg dates given by Bent (1938h), who indicated a date span of 9 Apr to 24 Jul, with a peak from mid-May to mid-June.

Stephen C. Rottenborn

320

BARN SWALLOW

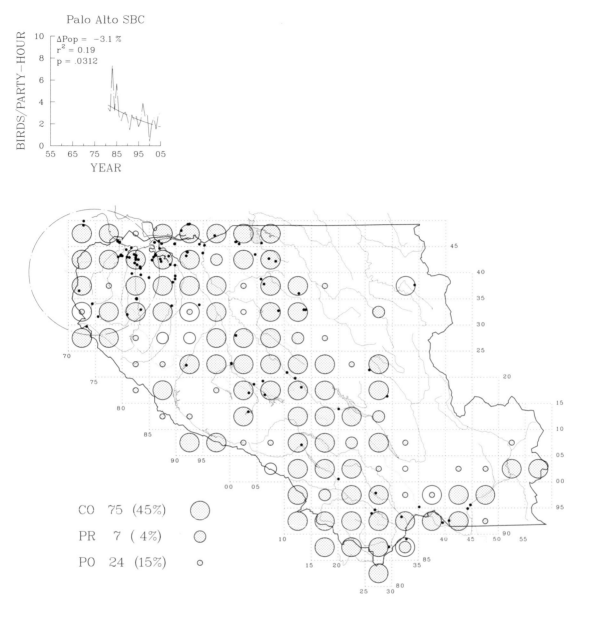

Palo Alto SBC

ΔPop = −3.1 %
$r^2 = 0.19$
p = .0312

BIRDS/PARTY−HOUR

YEAR

CO 75 (45%)
PR   7 (4%)
PO 24 (15%)

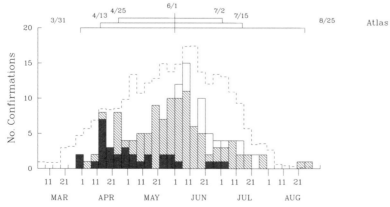

Atlas (1987−1993), n = 142

No. Confirmations

3/31   4/13 4/25   6/1   7/2   7/15   8/25

11 21 1 11 21 1 11 21 1 11 21 1 11 21 1 11 21
MAR   APR   MAY   JUN   JUL   AUG

Chestnut-backed Chickadee
Poecile rufescens

This active, agile parid with its quiet "see-see-see" has undergone a range expansion in the last century throughout western North America, including Santa Clara County. Generally found within 80 km of the coast from southeast Alaska to central California, it is also established well inland in Washington, Idaho, and British Columbia, and in recent decades has expanded into the Sierra Nevada of California as far south as Madera County. Three subspecies are recognized, and the southernmost, *P. r. barlowi*, is the one that resides in Santa Clara County. The range of *barlowi* extends from San Francisco and Oakland south to coastal Santa Barbara County (Garrett and Dunn 1981). The type specimen of *P. r. barlowi* was a male collected by Joseph Grinnell along Stevens Creek in Santa Clara County in October 1900 (Grinnell 1900a). Today, the Chestnut-backed Chickadee is a common resident in the western portions of Santa Clara County wherever there are coniferous or broadleaved evergreen forests or woodlands. It is also fairly common in lowland areas with healthy riparian corridors, as well as in urban habitats with planted conifers and other suitable evergreen trees.

Van Denburgh (1899b) considered this species common near Saratoga, but less so in Los Gatos. Grinnell (1915), in his second distributional list of California birds, noted that the subspecies *barlowi* bred along the coast from San Francisco to the Little Sur River in Monterey County, and placed its easternmost extension on the west shore of the San Francisco Bay near the mouth of San Francisquito Creek. Grinnell and Wythe (1927) considered this distribution little changed at the time of their San Francisco Bay regional survey, and Grinnell and Miller (1944) repeated the earlier range descriptions but also noted breeding in the vicinity of San Jose. By the late 1940s it was apparent that this species was moving into the Berkeley Hills, and this finding led to a series of papers that examined both the range expansion of this chickadee and its ecological interactions with the established parid, the Oak Titmouse (Dixon 1954, Dixon 1960, Root 1964, Hertz et al. 1976). Dixon (1954) tracked the range expansion to Sunol in Alameda County as early as the late 1930s and speculated, plausibly, that the development of orchards in the Santa Clara Valley at the turn of the twentieth century (Broek 1932) had allowed this species to move across the valley and into the Diablo Range. It appears that this chickadee was well established in a number of locations on the east side of the Santa Clara Valley by the late 1920s and early 1930s. Two were recorded on 22 Dec 1928 on a "Christmas census" that covered habitats from Alviso to Berryessa (*Wren-Tit 1(1)* 1929), two families were noted in Alum Rock Park on 23 May 1931 on an SCVAS field trip (*Wren-Tit 3(3)* 1931), and systematic observations compiled from 1929 to 1936 in Alum Rock Park (Linsdale and Rodgers 1937) found these birds to be present on 61% of all trips to the park. Analysis of the Palo Alto and San Jose CBC and SBC data shows that the number of chickadees has been relatively stable over the last three decades, though the Palo Alto CBC has shown a small increase of 1.2% a year.

During atlasing, Chestnut-backed Chickadees were found widely in the county where there were suitable conditions, generally coniferous or broadleaved evergreens that provided shade and a relatively mesic environment. This was an abundant species on the western side of the county on the slopes and canyons of the Santa Cruz Mountains. On the valley floor they were found in lesser numbers, those present generally concentrated along streams with healthy riparian growth where they used evergreens such as coast live oak and California bay as well as deciduous trees such as western sycamore and various willow species. They were also widespread within urban areas offering established tree cover, especially planted evergreens. On the eastern side of the valley the species was found wherever suitable moist woodlands of coast live oak or California bay developed on north-facing slopes or in canyon bottoms. Farther east in the Diablo Range, as woodlands become more open and there are only small patches of broadleaved evergreens, this species was seen less frequently, and there was a remarkably sharp cutoff in its distribution there. It appears that the areas dominated by deciduous oaks, foothill pine, and chaparral in the eastern portion of the county are unsuitable for these birds. Competitive exclusion by the Oak Titmouse, as suggested by Roberson (1993u), may be a significant factor in their absence there as well.

The earliest evidence of nesting during the atlas period was a bird attending a nest in a cavity on 29 Mar. Following the atlas period, excavation of a nesting cavity was seen as early as 20 Feb 1997 (Leda Beth Gray, PADB). The earliest young during the atlas period were detected by their cries in a nest cavity on 10 Apr. A bird found carrying nest material as late as 23 Jun may have represented either a second brood or a renesting attempt. The latest evidence of breeding during the atlas period was fledged young seen on 10 Aug. The most common forms of nesting evidence were adults feeding young (38%) and fledged young (30%).

William G. Bousman

CHESTNUT-BACKED CHICKADEE

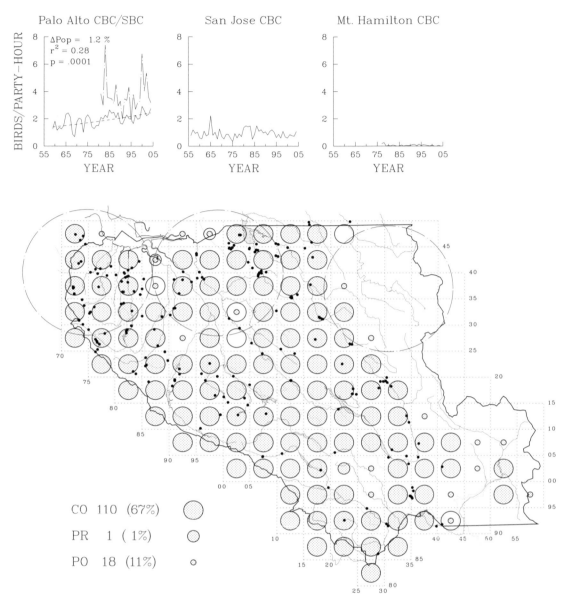

Palo Alto CBC/SBC

$\Delta Pop = 1.2\%$
$r^2 = 0.28$
$p = .0001$

San Jose CBC

Mt. Hamilton CBC

BIRDS/PARTY-HOUR

YEAR

CO 110 (67%)

PR   1 (1%)

PO   18 (11%)

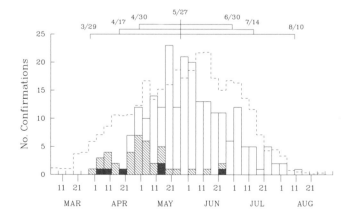

3/29   4/17   4/30   5/27   6/30   7/14   8/10

Atlas (1987-1993), n = 275

No. Confirmations

MAR   APR   MAY   JUN   JUL   AUG

Oak Titmouse
Baeolophus inornatus

Among the oaks of Santa Clara County, this crested sprite announces spring with its ringing call. No other bird, not even White-breasted Nuthatch or Western Bluebird, so strongly associates with the oak woodlands and oak savannas of the county. This titmouse, now considered distinct from the Juniper Titmouse of the interior Southwest, ranges from Oregon to Baja California, generally west of the Sierra Nevada (Cicero 1996, AOU 1997). *B. i. inornatus*, one of the four recognized subspecies, is found in an isolated population in Oregon and nearby northern California, and then continuously from the northern Sacramento Valley south along the San Joaquin Valley foothills to Tulare and Santa Barbara counties (Cicero 1996). It is abundant within the deciduous oak woodlands and savannas of the eastern half of Santa Clara County, but is less common in the western half, where there is a mosaic of coniferous and broadleaved evergreen forests. It is mostly absent from the urban areas of the Santa Clara Valley floor, keeping to the fringes and streamsides where oaks are present.

The Oak Titmouse was considered a common or very common resident in the Santa Clara Valley at the end of the nineteenth century (Van Denburgh 1899b, Fisher 1902). Grinnell and Wythe (1927) noted that it was a common permanent resident "especially characteristic of the oak belt in the Santa Clara and Santa Rosa valleys, and on the Mount Hamilton range." In surveys conducted at Alum Rock Park from 1929 to 1936 (Linsdale and Rodgers 1937), it was found to be the third most common species present. Grinnell and Miller (1944) emphasized its attachment to oak woodlands and noted that where oaks had been cleared for agriculture there had been a retraction in the Oak Titmouse's range. They also noted, however, that this species had occupied new areas on the strength of habitat modifications brought about by tree-planting (species not designated). Analysis of the San Jose CBC data shows a population decline of 4.0% per year, whereas the Palo Alto SBC shows an increase of 1.8% per year. No changes are indicated for the Palo Alto and Mt. Hamilton CBCs.

The Oak Titmouse was one of the most common species found during the atlas. On the basis of total confirmations it ranked seventh, and on the basis of the abundance code it ranked ninth. The highest abundance of breeding titmice was found in the Diablo Range. As with a number of other species typical of oak woodlands, such as Ash-throated Flycatcher, White-breasted Nuthatch, and Western Bluebird, this titmouse was not found in most of the urban area north of the Coyote Narrows, although it did use habitats at the edge of the valley floor as well as urban streams where oaks were present. Studies of riparian bird communities in the northern Santa Clara Valley show that live oak abundance best explains the distribution of this species (Rottenborn 1999). Farther west in the Santa Cruz Mountains, where coniferous and broadleaved forests begin to dominate the habitats and there are fewer oaks, it was less common. Despite its attraction to oaks it is occasionally found well away from these trees, such as along Llagas Creek in the southern Santa Clara Valley in an area of black walnuts and willows (Stephen C. Rottenborn, pers. comm.).

Oak Titmice show a protracted period of nesting, and because little fieldwork was done during February and March, when they are actively courting and nest building, we believe that many breeding records were missed, thus biasing the phenology data. The earliest evidence of nesting during the atlas period was an adult carrying a fecal sac on 5 Mar, indicating recently hatched young. Following the atlas period, on 25 Feb 2001, an adult was seen carrying nesting material (Gloria LeBlanc, PADB). Although Bent (1946b) gives 20 Mar as the earliest egg date for this species in California, birds were noted attending young in Sonoma County on 13 Mar (Ashford 1995) and carrying nesting material in Monterey County on 18 Mar (Tenney 1993a). Even earlier nesting is evidenced by a female with a developing brood patch and an egg in its oviduct that was captured and banded east of Milpitas on 30 Jan 1997 (Rita R. Colwell, pers. comm.). An adult feeding young on 1 Aug was the latest breeding confirmation noted during the atlas period, but an adult carrying food to a nest hole on 18 Oct 1960 (*Avocet* 7:124–25 1960) indicates that nesting occurs late into the fall, at least on rare occasions. Despite the protracted period of nesting shown by the atlas data, a study at Stanford University showed that this species normally has only one brood a season (Price 1936).

William G. Bousman

OAK TITMOUSE

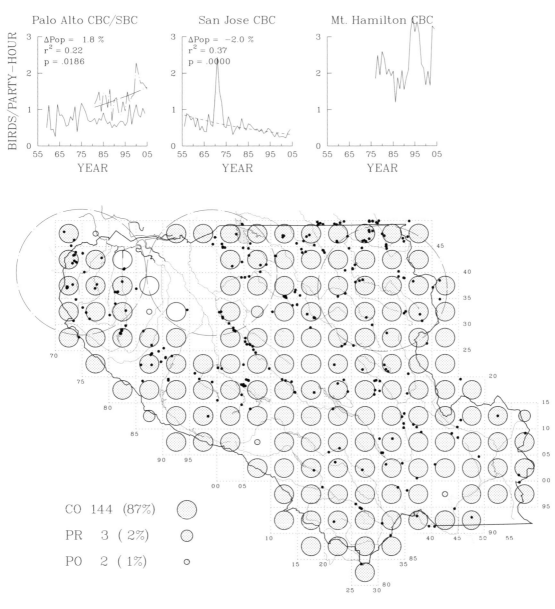

Palo Alto CBC/SBC

ΔPop = 1.8 %
$r^2 = 0.22$
p = .0186

San Jose CBC

ΔPop = −2.0 %
$r^2 = 0.37$
p = .0000

Mt. Hamilton CBC

BIRDS/PARTY-HOUR

YEAR

CO 144 (87%)
PR 3 (2%)
PO 2 (1%)

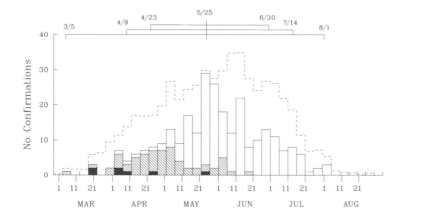

Atlas (1987−1993), n = 348

No. Confirmations

MAR APR MAY JUN JUL AUG

S. WEBB

Bushtit
Psaltriparus minimus

One after another, calling quietly but constantly, these small bits of drab gray fluff cross a gap in the trees on their ever-busy search for insects and spiders. The Bushtit, the only member of the family Aegithalidae found in the New World, is resident in western North America from Vancouver Island south to Baja California on the Pacific Coast, with populations inland from Oregon to New Mexico and south in the highlands of Mexico to Guatemala (Sloane 2001). This common species is found throughout California except in the higher parts of the Sierra Nevada and in the southeastern deserts (Grinnell and Miller 1944, Small 1994). There are nine subspecies, of which four occur in California (Grinnell and Miller 1944, Sloane 2001). *P. m. minimus* is the race found along the coast of California, including all of Santa Clara County, where it is a common resident.

The earliest mention of the Bushtit in Santa Clara County was its inclusion on the list of specimens collected from "the Valley of San José" by Thomas Bridges sometime prior to 1857 (Sclater 1857). Observers at the close of the nineteenth century considered it a common or abundant resident locally (Price 1898b, Van Denburgh 1899b, Fisher 1902). Similarly, Grinnell and Wythe (1927) considered it an abundant resident throughout the Bay area, and Sibley (1952) judged it as common in the South Bay. Analysis of the Palo Alto SBC data shows a decline of 1.6% a year since 1981, whereas the San Jose CBC shows an increase of 1.2% a year since 1956. There are no significant changes in numbers on the Palo Alto or Mt. Hamilton CBCs.

Atlasers found Bushtits breeding throughout Santa Clara County. Breeding was confirmed in 151 blocks (92%) and, including probable and possible evidence, they were recorded in 99% of all atlas blocks. Bushtits bred from sea level, at the edge of the Bay, to an elevation of 4,200 feet near the top of Mt. Hamilton. They were resident wherever broadleaved evergreen shrubs and trees were present, generally where there was some heterogeneity in the pattern of vegetation, such as trees and shrubs of different heights with gaps here and there between. In the Santa Cruz Mountains they were also found in soft chaparral, mostly coyotebrush. In the Diablo Range, Bushtits were commonly found in broadleaved evergreens in wetter canyons and on north-facing slopes, but they also were found in many extensive stands of hard chaparral with manzanitas and other shrubs. Bushtits also nested in riparian corridors, where they were common in cottonwood- and willow-dominated woodlands. In urban areas they also nested in evergreen shrubs and many non-native plants. Although Bushtits used many deciduous trees where these trees were intermixed with broadleaved evergreens, they avoided nesting in extensive tracts of deciduous oak woodlands and grasslands, as are commonly found in parts of the Diablo Range. Bushtits were often found at the edges of coniferous and mixed broadleaved evergreen-coniferous forests, but were not found in dense stands that lacked openings. Their striking pendant nests, frequently constructed within 2 or 3 meters of the ground, were often built in live oaks, but were also built in Douglas fir, Monterey pine, various willow species, and cottonwood, and in non-native trees such as pepper tree and casuarina. They were also found nesting in shrubs such as scrub oak and coyotebrush. Generally, their distinctive nests were well concealed, but atlasers occasionally came upon a nest constructed with little or no concealment.

The earliest breeding evidence obtained during the atlas period was a nest being built in the San Felipe Hills south of Mt. Hamilton on 25 Feb. Following the atlas period, breeding was confirmed on the earlier date of 25 Jan 2003 (Michael J. Mammoser, PADB). Bushtits are very early nesters, and most of this early activity was not observed by atlasers, who were rarely afield before mid-March. Addicott (1938), who studied nesting Bushtits on the Stanford campus in the mid-1930s, noted pairing as early as mid-January and nest building as early as 2 Feb. Construction of these early nests was sometimes delayed during inclement weather, and some were abandoned (Addicott 1938, Sloane 2001). Bushtits normally attempt two broods during the nesting season (Sloane 2001), which may in part explain the extended period of nest construction shown in the phenology graphic. The latest breeding evidence observed during the atlas period was adults feeding young in the northern Santa Cruz Mountains near the Monte Bello Open Space Preserve on 1 Aug. Following the atlas period, adults were observed feeding young at the Stanford Shopping Center on the later date of 23 Aug 1995 (Stephen C. Rottenborn, PADB).

Nest supernumeraries (nest helpers) occur fairly often in inland Bushtit populations in the United States, as well as in Mexico and Guatemala (Sloane 2001), but they occur less commonly in the Pacific Coast populations. Addicott (1938), in her nesting studies at Stanford, observed only one case in which a third adult participated in incubation, feeding of young, and brooding. These birds were not banded, and the relationship of the third adult to the other two is unknown.

William G. Bousman

BUSHTIT

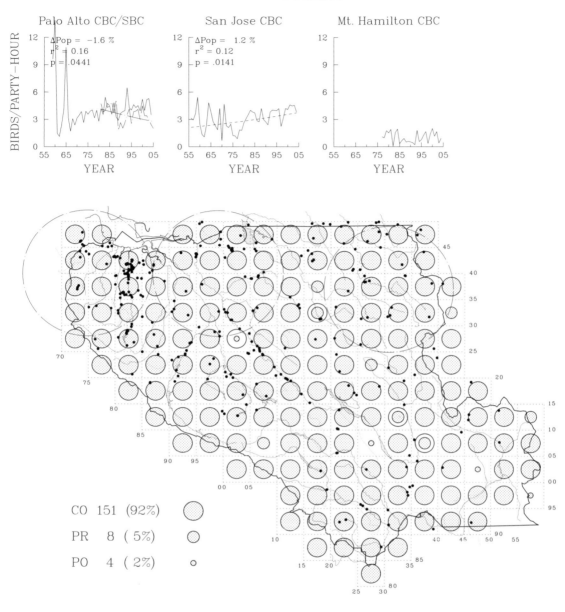

Palo Alto CBC/SBC

ΔPop = −1.6 %
r² = 0.16
p = .0441

San Jose CBC

ΔPop = 1.2 %
r² = 0.12
p = .0141

Mt. Hamilton CBC

BIRDS/PARTY-HOUR

YEAR

CO 151 (92%)
PR   8 (5%)
PO   4 (2%)

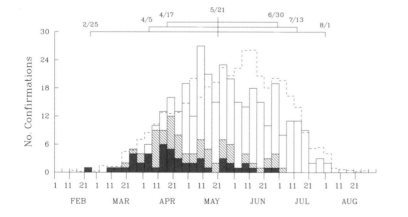

Atlas (1987−1993), n = 387

No. Confirmations

FEB   MAR   APR   MAY   JUN   JUL   AUG

Red-breasted Nuthatch
Sitta canadensis

These sprightly, colorful nuthatches are conifer specialists. At the western edge of Santa Clara County they are sometimes found in the wet, coast redwood forests, but surprisingly, they occupy the dry, knobcone pine forests as well. As its specific name implies, *S. canadensis* is primarily a resident of the boreal forest of Canada (Godfrey 1986). Nonetheless, populations extend southward through coniferous forests on the Pacific slope, the Sierra Nevada, and the Rocky Mountains to southern California, Arizona, and New Mexico, and in the east, they range south through the Appalachians to North Carolina. In California, breeding Red-breasted Nuthatches are fairly common in the Northern Coast Ranges, the Cascades, and the Sierra Nevada, but are less common to the south, where they breed sparingly in portions of the Southern Coast Ranges and isolated ranges in southern California (Small 1994). This nuthatch is a rare and local breeder in Santa Clara County, but is more widely found during winter irruptions.

There is little information regarding the historical distribution of this species in Santa Clara County. Egg collectors active during the early years of the twentieth century left no pertinent records, and neither McGregor (1901), nor Grinnell and Wythe (1927), nor Grinnell and Miller (1944) mentioned breeding in the Santa Cruz Mountains or in Santa Clara County. Robert T. Orr (1942), who made a detailed four-year study of the Big Basin forests in Santa Cruz and San Mateo counties in the 1930s, categorized this species as a winter visitant and remarked that his latest observation was on 1 May. Sibley (1952) considered it a "winter visitor in conifers [and a] rare summer visitor locally." His subsequent statement mentioned verified nesting for Berkeley and Oakland, but since his "locally" was undefined there is uncertainty about the presence of breeding Red-breasted Nuthatches within Santa Clara County at that time. On 14 Jun 1953, Emily Smith observed a pair feeding nestlings at Castle Rock, in Santa Cruz County, about 200 meters from the Santa Clara County line. This was followed by sightings of fledglings near that nest site on 4 and 5 July (*Audubon Field Notes* 7:325 1953). Smith also noted breeding evidence near Castle Rock on 15 Jun 1957 (*Audubon Field Notes* 11:427 1957). A few years

later a nest was found in the Jasper Ridge Biological Preserve, San Mateo County, on 1 May 1960, again not far from the Santa Clara County line (Row 1960). But it was not until the establishment of this atlas in 1987 that documentation of breeding within Santa Clara County was obtained, when adults with dependent young were seen on Table Mountain on 30 May that year.

Red-breasted Nuthatches were found in two different coniferous habitats at higher elevations in the Santa Cruz Mountains, along the western edge of Santa Clara County. In the north, birds were found in the moist coast redwood forests in the vicinity of Table Mountain and Saratoga Summit. These forests are dependent on the coastal fog that often spills over the crest onto the eastern flank of the range (Thomas 1961, Schoenherr 1992). In drier areas farther south, near Loma Prieta and Uvas Canyon, these nuthatches nested in mixed forests of knobcone pine and Douglas fir. Knobcone pines, although growing on rocky, dry ridges, also require summer fog drip (Schoenherr 1992). Breeding was confirmed between 1,500 and 3,080 feet elevation. The western boundary of Santa Clara County, where breeding nuthatches were found, is actually the eastern edge of the species' local range. The range continues westward down the coastal slope into Santa Cruz and San Mateo counties in suitable stands of Douglas fir, coast redwood, knobcone pine, Monterey pine, and ponderosa pine (David L. Suddjian, pers. comm.). Less expected was the occurrence of Red-breasted Nuthatches in the Diablo Range. Breeding was not confirmed there during the atlas period, but three different sightings during the months of April and May suggest either possible breeding or lingering winter visitors. Potential breeding habitats in the Diablo Range include a mixed conifer-oak woodland forest, the conifers in this case being Coulter pine with small pockets of ponderosa pine (Sharsmith 1982).

Sixteen confirmations of breeding were noted between 12 Apr and 21 Jul during the atlas period. Six nest cavities were found, and other confirmations consisted of four instances each of carrying food and feeding young, and one each of nest building and dependent fledglings.

It is unclear whether the Red-breasted Nuthatches that breed in the Santa Cruz Mountains disperse in some years as northern and montane populations do. Irruptions are observed in Santa Clara County about every other year. During weak irruptions, nuthatches are observed even on the valley floor and in the foothills, in late August to early November, and then again the following spring in March and April (county notebooks). But in heavy irruptive years birds are found more widely and are seen all winter. Particularly heavy irruptions have occurred in the winters of 1996–97 and 2004–05.

Gloria G. Heller

RED-BREASTED NUTHATCH

Palo Alto SBC

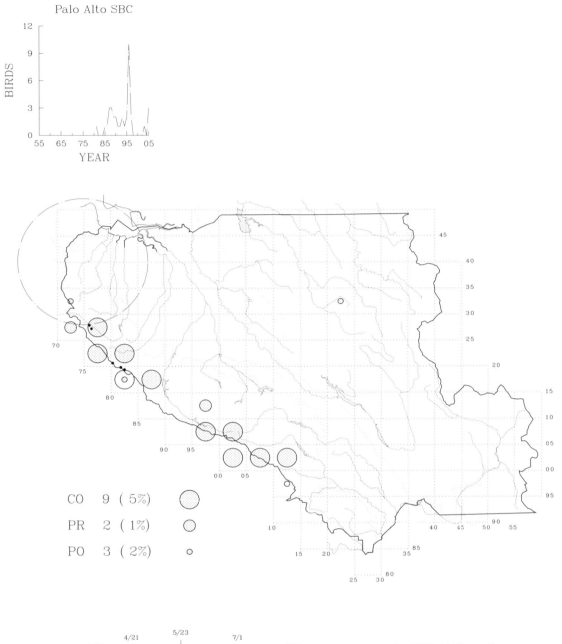

CO   9 (5%)

PR   2 (1%)

PO   3 (2%)

Atlas (1987–1993), n = 16

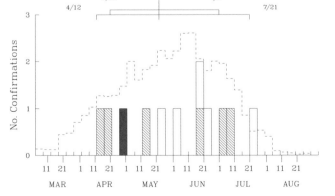

White-breasted Nuthatch
Sitta carolinensis

Wherever there are rough-barked trees, such as deciduous oaks or foothill pines, the White-breasted Nuthatch will be found, usually moving headfirst down their trunks. This nuthatch is resident in North America from southeastern British Columbia across Canada to Nova Scotia, south to northwestern Baja California and northern Florida, and in the highlands of Mexico south to southern Oaxaca (Pravosudov and Grubb 1993). In California, it is found widely in oak woodlands and mixed coniferous forests throughout the state, and is generally absent only from the humid northwest coast, the Central Valley, and the southeastern deserts (Grinnell and Miller 1944, Small 1994). Between 6 and 11 subspecies are recognized (Pravosudov and Grubb 1993), 3 of them found in California: *nelsoni* in the coniferous forests of the northeast, *tenuissima* in the pinyon and limber pines of the White Mountains and nearby ranges, and *aculeata* in oak woodlands throughout most of the state, including Santa Clara County (Grinnell and Miller 1944). The White-breasted Nuthatch is a common resident in the county, generally where deciduous oaks and foothill pines occur.

The first historical reference to the White-breasted Nuthatch here was its inclusion on the list of specimens collected by Thomas Bridges in "the Valley of San José" sometime prior to 1857 (Sclater 1857). Cooper (1870) considered it to be uncommon south of San Francisco, and saw none during his fieldwork near Santa Cruz. Price (1898f) recorded this nuthatch as a permanent resident at Stanford, where he found it in coast redwoods for the most part. Van Denburgh (1899b) did not find the White-breasted Nuthatch in Los Gatos or Palo Alto, but Barlow (1900b) noted it as a common resident in the deciduous oak woodlands in the foothills of the county. Fisher (1902) stated that it was resi-

dent in oaks in the Santa Cruz Mountains. In summarizing the White-breasted Nuthatch's status in the San Francisco Bay area, Grinnell and Wythe (1927) considered it a permanent resident in the interior portions, but largely absent from coastal areas. Sibley (1952) described it as a common resident in oak woodlands in the South Bay, but uncommon in the Santa Cruz Mountains and on the peninsula north of Palo Alto.

Atlasers found White-breasted Nuthatches breeding in 91 blocks (55%), and including probable and possible evidence, they were found in a total of 121 blocks (73%). Breeding elevations ranged from 46 feet in suburban Menlo Park to 3,920 feet along the summit ridge of Eylar Mountain. Breeding birds were widespread and common in oak woodlands throughout the Diablo Range. They were fairly common within the deciduous oak woodlands in the foothills of the Santa Cruz Mountains, but absent from coniferous and mixed coniferous-broadleaved evergreen forests. Nuthatches were also found outside the urban zone in riparian habitats on the valley floor, where they sometimes used coast live oaks as well as deciduous riparian trees such as Fremont cottonwood. White-breasted Nuthatches were most often found in deciduous oaks, particularly blue oak and valley oak, both species having rough, corrugated bark suitable for foraging. At higher elevations in the Diablo Range they were found in black oak and Coulter pine woodlands. Although they were often found in trees at the edges of chaparral and grasslands, they were not found in chaparral expanses or treeless grasslands.

White-breasted Nuthatches live in pairs year-round (Pravosudov and Grubb 1993). The earliest breeding evidence observed during the atlas period was an occupied nest on 9 Mar. Subsequent to the atlas period, one was seen carrying nest material into a nest box on 21 Feb 1997 (Garth Harwood, county notebooks). The latest breeding evidence observed during the atlas period was fledglings seen on 31 Jul. The protracted period of nesting shown in the phenology graph suggests that some birds may nest quite late in the season. A nest with young was found as late as 5 Jul, and a bird was seen in a nest cavity as late as 14 Jul. Pravosudov and Grubb (1993) state that White-breasted Nuthatches are single-brooded, and although there are no reports of renesting after nest failure, it is possible that these late nesting observations are the result of renesting, second broods, or the delayed pairing of resident birds following the loss of a mate.

Nesting White-breasted Nuthatches were found in the eastern foothills of the Santa Cruz Mountains in association with deciduous oaks, but not in the coniferous or coniferous-broadleaved evergreen forest of the crest. But a few kilometers northwest of Saratoga Gap, there are extensive areas of annual grasslands with oak woodlands along their edges, and these areas extend into San Mateo County. Nuthatches were found in these areas along the crest, as well as in the foothills to the east, but were rarely found farther north than the southern edge of Crystal Springs Reservoir in San Mateo County (Sequoia Audubon Society 2001h). In the southern Santa Cruz Mountains, where these hills drop to the Pajaro River, the oak woodlands and oak savanna extend slightly into Santa Cruz County, but this nuthatch is rarely found breeding there or anywhere else in Santa Cruz County (David L. Suddjian, pers. comm.).

William G. Bousman

WHITE-BREASTED NUTHATCH

Palo Alto CBC/SBC   San Jose CBC   Mt. Hamilton CBC

BIRDS/PARTY-HOUR

YEAR   YEAR   YEAR

ΔPop = −1.1 %
r^2 = 0.13
p = .0108

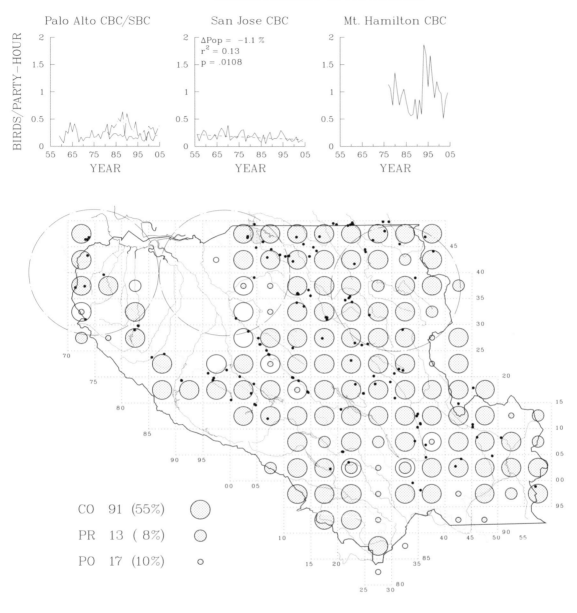

CO 91 (55%)
PR 13 (8%)
PO 17 (10%)

Atlas (1987–1993), n = 148

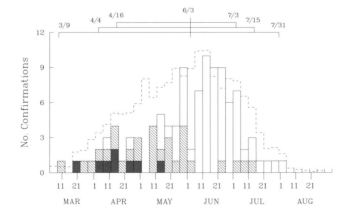

3/9   4/4   4/16   6/3   7/3   7/15   7/31

No. Confirmations

MAR   APR   MAY   JUN   JUL   AUG

R.COLWELL 97

Pygmy Nuthatch
Sitta pygmaea

Staccato, chittering calls from high within the coniferous forest announce a family group of Pygmy Nuthatches, ever busy with their daily foraging. This conifer-loving nuthatch is found in scattered locations from southern British Columbia to Montana, and south in the mountain west to northern Baja California and the highlands of Mexico to Michoacán (Kingery and Ghalambor 2001). Of the six or seven subspecies, three occur in California: *S. p. melanotis* in the Sierra Nevada and adjacent ranges, *leuconucha* from San Jacinto Mountain south, and *pygmaea* locally along the coast from Mendocino County to San Luis Obispo County and including Santa Clara County (Grinnell and Miller 1944, Norris 1958). The Pygmy Nuthatch, although common on the west side of the Santa Cruz Mountains, is uncommon and local in Santa Clara County, occurring mostly in a few forested areas near the crest of this range.

Although the Pygmy Nuthatch was known from the Santa Cruz Mountains near the end of the nineteenth century (McGregor 1901), early observers did not record it in Santa Clara County (Van Denburgh 1899b, Fisher 1902). Grinnell and Wythe (1927) considered it locally fairly common in Marin and Sonoma counties, but included no records from San Mateo or Santa Clara counties. Orr (1942), however, found it to be present in his study area near Big Basin State Park in Santa Cruz and San Mateo counties during the 1930s. He noted it as occurring commonly in knobcone pine forests, less often in the Douglas fir–coast redwood association. Sibley (1952) described this nuthatch as a common resident of the Santa Cruz Mountains, but noted no records specifically from Santa Clara County. The first recorded observation of this species in Santa Clara County was a "small flock" seen near Mt. Madonna on 19 Oct 1947 (Elsie Hoeck, *Bull. SCVAS* November 1947). The first breeding evidence was adults seen feeding young at Aldercroft on 28 Aug 1952 (*Audubon Field Notes* 7:35 1952).

Pygmy Nuthatches were found breeding in only 18 blocks (11%), nearly all of the records occurring along the crest of the Santa Cruz Mountains. The elevations of the breeding records there ranged from 1,400 to 1,840 feet. Birds at these elevations were found in Douglas fir and knobcone pine forests with a fir

component, and also in coast redwood forests that included Douglas fir. Four nest sites were found in the Santa Cruz Mountains during the atlas period. Two of these were described. The first was in a Douglas fir snag in a coniferous forest along Highland Way, west of the Santa Cruz Mountain crest. The second was in a Douglas fir in a coniferous-broadleaved evergreen forest in the Monte Bello Open Space Preserve. Subsequent to the atlas period, three more nest sites were found at Monte Bello, also in Douglas fir snags (Garth Harwood, county notebooks). Breeding confirmations were also obtained well away from the Santa Cruz Mountains along the valley floor in Palo Alto and Menlo Park, at elevations from 35 to 55 feet. These birds were most often in areas with mature Monterey pines, but also in areas with a mixture of native and non-native trees. Two nest sites found during the atlas period were described. In Palo Alto the birds nested in an English walnut along San Francisquito Creek in a mixture of native trees such as valley oak, coast live oak, and western sycamore, and non-native eucalyptus. In Menlo Park, San Mateo County, the nuthatches nested in a mature Monterey pine in an urban area with a mixture of valley oaks, coast live oaks, and other Monterey pines. Following completion of the atlas fieldwork, additional nest locations were found on the valley floor (county notebooks): a nest with young was found in a snag on a eucalyptus along San Francisquito Creek near Stanford (Richard Stovel), two nests were found in palms at the Sacred Heart School in Atherton, San Mateo County (Leda Beth Gray), and adults carried nesting material to a palm tree in Menlo Park (Tate and Curtis Snyder).

The earliest breeding evidence in Santa Clara County during the atlas period was a bird occupying a nest cavity on 12 Apr. The latest was fledged young on 24 Jul. Subsequent to the atlas period, two pairs were seen excavating nesting cavities on the earlier date of 7 Mar 2005 (Garth Harwood, county notebooks). Bent (1948a) records California egg dates as extending from 17 Apr to 27 Jun, which agrees with the limited phenology data obtained during the atlasing. Because family parties foraged together, confirmations were most often obtained when adults were seen feeding young (57%).

Pygmy Nuthatches appear to have expanded their habitat use in the last half century. Grinnell and Miller (1944) noted that the range of the coastal subspecies *pygmaea* coincided closely with the Monterey flora, particularly Monterey and Bishop pines. They observed, however, that other conifers were used as well, including ponderosa pine, Douglas fir, knobcone pine, Monterey cypress, and coast redwood. Shuford (1993v) noted that in Marin County Pygmy Nuthatches breed primarily in native Bishop pines, but that some nest in planted Monterey pines and cypresses as well. Roberson (1993v) describes this nuthatch's use of three different habitats in Monterey County: the native Monterey pine forests of the Monterey Peninsula, the ponderosa and Coulter pine forests at higher elevations in the Santa Lucia Mountains, and planted, mature groves of Monterey pine throughout the county. Kingery and Ghalambor (2001) reported this species' use of non-native eucalyptus and palms in urban areas of the central California coast, and the recent breeding along the valley floor near Palo Alto appears to fit this pattern.

William G. Bousman

PYGMY NUTHATCH

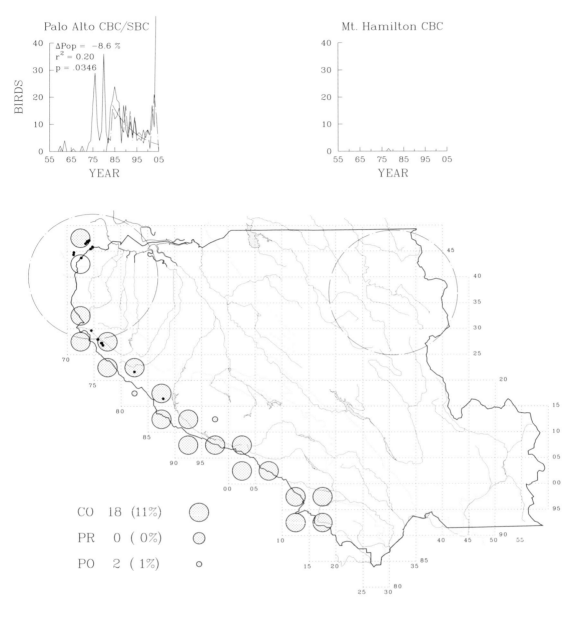

Palo Alto CBC/SBC

ΔPop = −8.6 %
$r^2 = 0.20$
p = .0346

Mt. Hamilton CBC

CO 18 (11%)

PR   0 (0%)

PO   2 (1%)

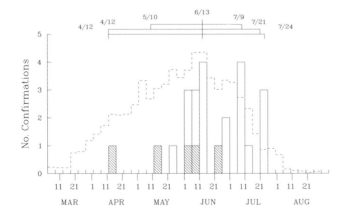

Atlas (1987−1993), n = 28

Brown Creeper
Certhia americana

The Brown Creeper's soft, high-pitched calls and cryptic coloration render it quite inconspicuous within the mature forests it inhabits. This diminutive bark forager breeds in cool, moist woodlands from southern Canada south through parts of the United States and Mexico into the highlands of Central America (AOU 1998). The breeding range of the Brown Creeper in California includes the northern mountainous regions, the Sierra Nevada, the Coast Ranges, and scattered mountain ranges in the southern part of the state (Unitt and Rea 1997). In Santa Clara County, the Brown Creeper is a fairly common resident in the Santa Cruz Mountains, an uncommon resident in the western Diablo Range, and an uncommon to rare visitor elsewhere in winter. Breeders in the Santa Cruz Mountains are considered *C. a. phillipsi* (formerly *occidentalis* in part; AOU 1957), the subspecies that inhabits the outer Coast Ranges from San Francisco south to San Luis Obispo County (Unitt and Rea 1997). The racial identity of Santa Clara County's Diablo Range breeders is unknown, owing to a lack of specimen evidence from this area; these birds may be *phillipsi*, or they may represent the interior race *zelotes* (Rogers 1995, Unitt and Rea 1997).

The Brown Creeper has apparently expanded both in distribution and abundance in Santa Clara County during this century. Although Price (1898f) considered the species resident in redwood-dominated habitats near Stanford University, neither Van Denburgh (1899b) nor Barlow (1900b) reported the species in the county, and it was apparently uncommon in adjacent Santa Cruz County, as well, at the turn of the century (McGregor 1901). Grinnell and Wythe (1927) considered Brown Creepers to be fairly common in mesic coastal forests of the Bay area in the 1920s, but they made no mention of breeding in Santa Clara County. Furthermore, they listed only a single breeding record in the East Bay (from Berkeley in 1918) and mentioned no breeding in the Diablo Range at all. Numerous surveys of Alum Rock Park in east San Jose from 1929 to 1936 resulted in just one record of this species, on 17 Nov 1935 (Linsdale and Rodgers 1937). In the 1940s, this species bred throughout the Santa Cruz Mountains, but on the east side of the San Francisco Bay the subspecies *phillipsi* bred only in a very limited area near Berkeley, and *zelotes* was not known to breed south of Solano County (Grinnell and Miller 1944). Sibley (1952) included only the Santa Cruz Mountains in the South Bay breeding range of this species.

In the spring of 1974, a creeper carrying food along Mines Road (in either Santa Clara County or Alameda County) was thought to be "considerably east of its normal Bay Area range" (*Am. Birds 28*:849 1974). But surveys in Henry Coe State Park that summer found creepers to be "fairly common" (Matthiesen and Mewaldt 1974), and these authors noted that Brown Creepers could also be found at Alum Rock Park and the Wool Ranch in the hills east of Milpitas. Thus, this species was clearly established as a breeder in the Diablo Range by this time. Whether the Diablo Range breeders were derived from *zelotes* expanding southward from Solano County (Rogers 1995) or from *phillipsi* "leapfrogging the Santa Clara Valley" from the Santa Cruz Mountains (Unitt and Rea 1997), as the Chestnut-backed Chickadee had done, is unknown. Analysis of CBC data shows that Brown Creeper numbers have increased by 1.9% per year in the Palo Alto count circle, decreased by 1.9% per year in the San Jose circle, and remain unchanged in the Mt. Hamilton circle.

During the atlas period, the Brown Creeper was found to be a fairly common breeder in the Santa Cruz Mountains, where it was most abundant among the redwoods, Douglas firs, and tan oaks in the most humid areas. These trees provided loose bark in which the Brown Creeper both foraged and nested. It also bred among alders, oaks, and California bays in the Santa Cruz Mountain foothills, most often in canyons or on moist slopes. In the western part of the Diablo Range, creepers bred primarily in oak and bay woodlands on moist north-facing slopes and along streams, some birds also breeding in dense stands of Coulter and foothill pines (Rogers 1995). Creepers were less abundant in most of the Diablo Range than in the Santa Cruz Mountains. Interestingly, the Diablo Range distribution of the Brown Creeper corresponds closely with that of the Chestnut-backed Chickadee, another species that has invaded this mountain range only recently. Atlas breeding confirmations were obtained from elevations between 380 and 3,560 feet, with the exception of a single valley-floor confirmation at 48 feet in Menlo Park, San Mateo County. After the atlas period, breeding was confirmed in several urban atlas blocks on the northern Santa Clara Valley floor, at elevations as low as 65 feet. Most of these birds were nesting in mature cottonwood-dominated riparian habitat along Coyote Creek, although at least two pairs were in cultivated redwoods at Kelley Park (pers. obs.).

Atlasers observed Brown Creepers engaged in nest-building over an extended period between 19 Mar and 10 Jun, the later records possibly indicating second nestings or renestings following failures. Birds were seen carrying food as early as 12 Apr, and fledged young were seen being fed by adults as early as 19 May. Most occupied nests were observed in May and June (although young were recorded in one nest on 23 Jul), whereas records of fledged young showed a broad peak from late May through the end of July.

Stephen C. Rottenborn

BROWN CREEPER

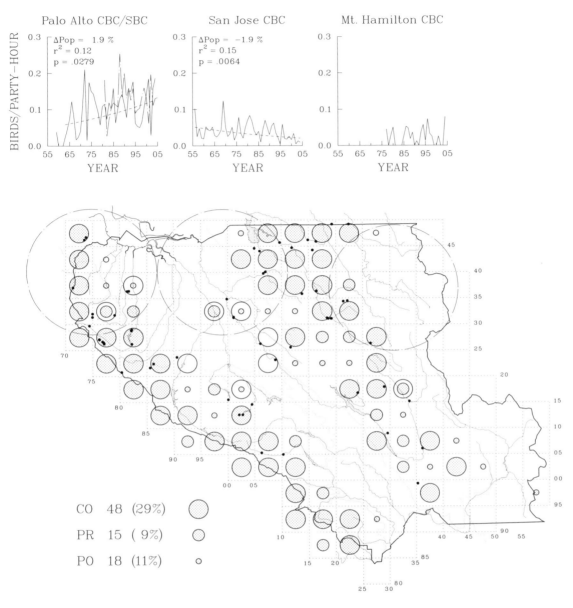

Palo Alto CBC/SBC

ΔPop = 1.9 %
r² = 0.12
p = .0279

San Jose CBC

ΔPop = −1.9 %
r² = 0.15
p = .0064

Mt. Hamilton CBC

BIRDS/PARTY–HOUR

YEAR

CO   48   (29%)
PR   15   (9%)
PO   18   (11%)

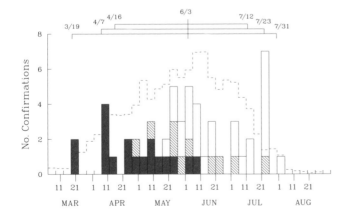

Atlas (1987–1993), n = 66

No. Confirmations

MAR   APR   MAY   JUN   JUL   AUG

Rock Wren
Salpinctes obsoletus

Among the scattered rocky outcrops of an open grassland, the repetitive song phrases of the Rock Wren cleave the air, proclaiming ownership of these seemingly barren grounds. This wren breeds from British Columbia and Saskatchewan south through most of the western United States into Mexico and the highlands of Central America (Lowther et al. 2000). Six to 11 subspecies of the Rock Wren are recognized, the nominate *obsoletus* being found widely throughout the western United States (Lowther et al. 2000). In California this wren occurs statewide in dry, rocky habitats; it is generally absent only from the humid northwest coast (Small 1994). The Rock Wren is a rare permanent resident in Santa Clara County, although it can be locally uncommon in remote areas of the Diablo Range. Wandering birds are occasionally found away from typical habitat.

Rollo H. Beck collected a set of Rock Wren eggs near Berryessa on 19 May 1894 (MVZ #6500), the first documentation of this wren in Santa Clara County. Price (1898f) considered this species to be a rather rare resident in the dry rocky hills above Stanford. Barlow (1900b) noted that it was resident in the rocky foothills of the Diablo Range and near the Coyote Narrows. Fisher (1902) stated that it was a permanent resident in the eastern and southern valley foothills. Grinnell and Wythe (1927) considered the Rock Wren to be "sparingly resident" on rocky hillsides in the interior counties of the San Francisco Bay area, including eastern Alameda and southeastern Santa Clara counties. Sibley (1952) judged it to be a fairly common resident in rocky and arid portions of the South Bay. Rock Wrens are regularly encountered on the San Jose and Mt. Hamilton Christmas Bird Counts.

Rock Wrens were confirmed breeding in 19 county blocks (12%), and probable or possible evidence was found in an additional 19 blocks. Breeding elevations ranged from 440 feet at the old quarry below Anderson Dam to 3,960 feet near the sum-

mit of Eylar Mountain. Most breeding confirmations were obtained in the more remote areas of the Diablo Range, away from highways and public trails. The habitats used by this wren included rolling grasslands with rock outcrops, steeper slopes with outcrops and cliff faces, larger cliffs with extensive fractured rock and talus slopes, abandoned and active quarries, and eroded gullies. The primary characteristics of all of these habitats were the presence of many cracks and crevices within cliffs, outcrops, and highly eroded gullies, as well as high-insolation levels. These wrens were typically found in rocky areas with either poor or serpentine soils, often in association with California ground squirrel colonies. Small numbers of breeding Rock Wrens were found in the Santa Teresa Hills east of the Almaden Valley at the Coyote Narrows, where a foothill spur of the Santa Cruz Mountains lies within a kilometer of the Diablo Range. Most of these birds were in open grasslands with scattered rock outcrops. The only other evidence of breeding obtained in the Santa Cruz Mountains was of two birds at the Hanson Permanente Cement Plant quarry above Cupertino in 1989. Prior to the atlas period, six birds were observed singing in this privately owned quarry in early June 1986 (M. Clark Blake, pers. comm.).

The two earliest breeding confirmations of the Rock Wren recorded during the atlas period were both on 26 Apr: an adult entering an apparent nest site in a cliff at the upper end of Anderson Reservoir, and an adult carrying food on the serpentine ridge between Silver and Coyote creeks. Adults with fledged young were seen as late as 27 Jul on the southwestern side of Oak Ridge above Arroyo Hondo. Nests with eggs have been found in Santa Clara County as early as 7 Apr 1896 (Rollo H. Beck, CAS #5326) and as late as 19 May 1894 (also Beck; see above). Because Rock Wrens are known to be double- or triple-brooded (Lowther et al. 2000), it is possible that a 10 Jul confirmation of birds carrying nest material is related to a second brood.

The fractured rock outcrops of the Diablo Range grasslands where Rock Wrens are often found seem quite different from the shaded canyons sometimes favored by Canyon Wrens. In Santa Clara County, the two wrens do appear to have somewhat separate habitat preferences. The Rock Wren favors rock outcrops within grasslands, small cliffs, and boulder fields, whereas the Canyon Wren is usually found along rock walls in shaded canyons. But this habitat separation does not always hold true, for the Canyon Wren is sometimes found on cliff faces exposed to the full sun and in boulder fields with grasslands and chaparral. And in fact, the two wrens show similar foraging behaviors, with a preference for cracks and crevices within cliffs and rock outcrops, where they prey upon spiders and other arthropods (Jones and Dieni 1995, Lowther et al. 2000). Neither species is known to drink, both apparently obtaining all necessary water from their prey.

William G. Bousman

ROCK WREN

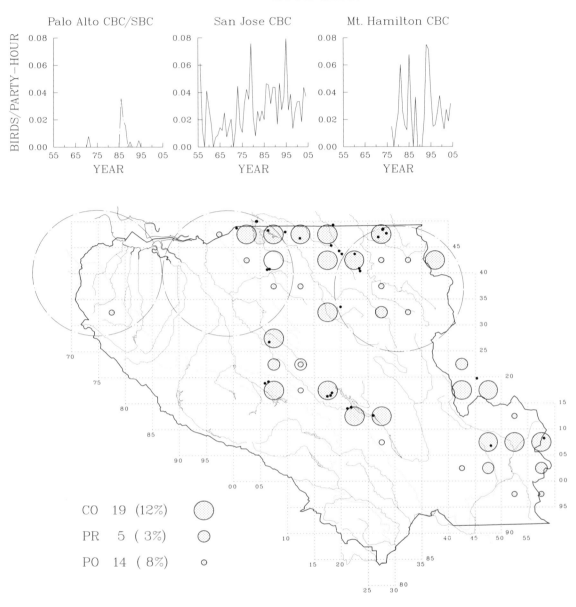

Palo Alto CBC/SBC   San Jose CBC   Mt. Hamilton CBC

BIRDS/PARTY–HOUR
YEAR

CO   19 (12%)
PR   5 (3%)
PO   14 (8%)

Atlas (1987–1993), n = 33

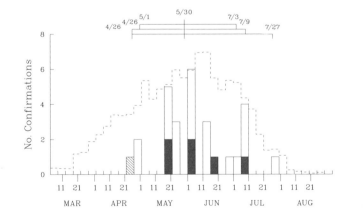

No. Confirmations

4/26 4/26 5/1   5/30   7/3 7/9   7/27

MAR   APR   MAY   JUN   JUL   AUG

337

Canyon Wren
Catherpes mexicanus

A Canyon Wren's descending call of silvery notes, echoing off a water-carved canyon wall deep in the Diablo Range, can hold the listener spellbound. This wren is resident from southern British Columbia, south through much of the western United States, and into Mexico as far south as Oaxaca (Jones and Dieni 1995). Within California it occurs widely in disjunct populations, but is generally absent from the humid northwest coast, the Central Valley, and higher elevations of the Cascades and the Sierra Nevada (Small 1994). This wren is a rare resident in Santa Clara County in some of the more remote canyons and arroyos of the Diablo Range.

Rollo H. Beck (1895b) collected a set of five eggs of a Canyon Wren in a "deep, rocky canyon within 50 miles of San Jose" on 12 (or possibly 19) May 1894 (Barlow 1900b). As was typical of that era, commercial egg collectors like Beck were discrete about disclosing locations where they obtained egg sets of rare species, so it is unknown whether the multiple egg sets he collected were obtained near his home in Berryessa, perhaps along Penitencia Creek, farther afield in the Arroyo Hondo, or elsewhere. Grinnell and Wythe (1927) considered this species a rare and local resident in the interior regions of the San Francisco Bay area, noting Beck's nesting records and eggs collected in Alameda County by Henry W. Carriger. Sibley (1952) recorded this wren as an uncommon resident in the drier, eastern portions of the South Bay. Analysis of San Jose CBC data shows a decline in this species of 10.6% a year since the mid-1950s, and it is no longer found each winter on this count. By contrast, there has been no change in the numbers recorded on the Mt. Hamilton CBC since its inception in the late 1970s.

Canyon Wrens were confirmed breeding in 17 blocks (10%) during the atlas period, and probable and possible evidence was obtained in an additional 15 blocks (9%). All breeding records were from the Diablo Range, and most of these were either in the higher canyons and arroyos of the Alameda Creek drainage to the north, or in lower areas in the Pacheco Creek watershed to the south. Fewer records were obtained in the Coyote Creek watershed. During the atlas period, Canyon Wrens were found nesting from an elevation of 600 feet on the North Fork of Pacheco Creek to 2,860 feet on the southern part of Valpe

Ridge above Alameda Creek. Subsequently, nest building was recorded at 460 feet along Penitencia Creek in Alum Rock Park on 20 Mar 1997 (Kathryn Parker, county notebooks), a location where birds had been present in prior years. Canyon Wrens were normally found along canyons and arroyos with steep rock walls containing cracks, crevices, and broken rock. Often there was permanent water within these canyons, but birds were also found in jumbled boulders and cliffs along intermittent streams offering no water during the breeding season. These wrens also used cliff faces and rock outcrops that were well away from major streams, sometimes with substantial sun exposure.

Five nests were found and described during the atlas period. One was placed in a crack within a 3-meter boulder in a deeply shaded portion of Pacheco Creek. A second was in a crevice in a small cliff face in the Alameda Creek drainage. A third nest was found in an outbuilding at the O'Connor Ranch along the North Fork of Pacheco Creek. And two broods of young were found in Cliff Swallow nests in the northern Diablo Range. Although Canyon Wrens are known to use Cliff Swallow nests for roosting (Brown and Brown 1995), no such use for nesting was recorded by Brown and Brown (1995) or by Jones and Dieni (1995).

The earliest nesting evidence obtained during the atlas period was a wren carrying food for young on 11 May, the latest a nest with young found on 27 Jul in a Cliff Swallow's nest on a remote cliff east of Arroyo Hondo. Subsequent to the atlas period, substantially earlier breeding records were obtained, in one case from nest building in Alum Rock Park on 20 Mar 1997, as noted previously, and in another, birds carrying nest material on 16 Apr 1995 on upper Pacheco Creek (James Yurchenco, Amy Lauterbach, pers. comm.). Bent (1948c) recorded egg dates in California from 28 Mar to 11 Jul.

McGregor (1901) reported that Henry B. Kaeding had observed Canyon Wrens breeding in Santa Cruz County although neither the location nor the dates were recorded. But during the 1970s, singing birds were reported near Castle Rock Falls, Santa Cruz County (David L. Suddjian, pers. comm.), which is suggestive of breeding attempts at that time. There are no records, however, of Canyon Wrens occurring on the Santa Clara County side of the Santa Cruz Mountains, either in historical references or in recent observations.

William G. Bousman

CANYON WREN

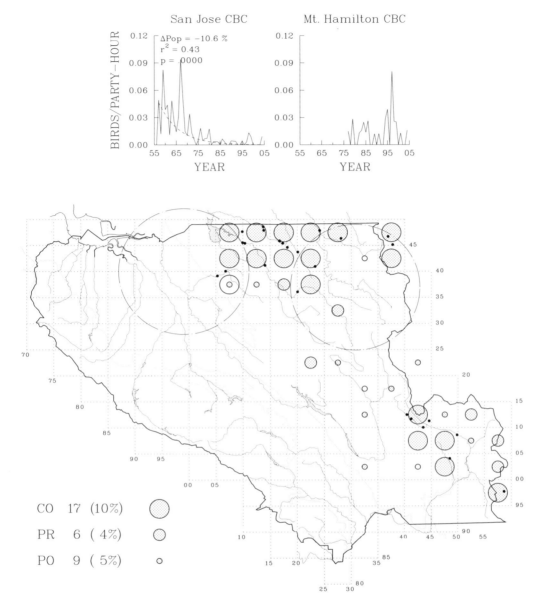

San Jose CBC

ΔPop = −10.6 %
r² = 0.43
p = .0000

Mt. Hamilton CBC

BIRDS/PARTY–HOUR

YEAR   YEAR

CO   17 (10%)
PR   6 (4%)
PO   9 (5%)

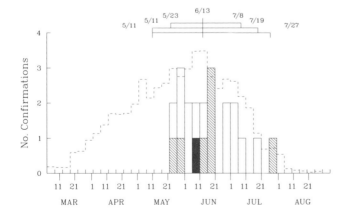

Atlas (1987–1993), n = 26

No. Confirmations

5/11   5/11   5/23   6/13   7/8   7/19   7/27

MAR   APR   MAY   JUN   JUL   AUG

339

Bewick's Wren
Thryomanes bewickii

Rich songs of trills and buzzes are heard year-round as the Bewick's Wren marks its territory. In the westernmost part of its range, this wren breeds from southern British Columbia to Baja California, generally west of the Cascades-Sierra axis (Kennedy and White 1997). Farther east it is found from Colorado to Missouri and south through Arizona, New Mexico, and Texas to southern Mexico. Small relict populations of eastern birds are still found in parts of the Mississippi and Ohio river valleys and in portions of the Appalachians. Twenty subspecies have been described, nine of which are resident in California (Grinnell and Miller 1944, AOU 1957, Kennedy and White 1997). The Bewick's Wren is a common resident throughout most of California, absent only from the higher elevations of the Cascades and the Sierra Nevada, and the southeastern deserts (Small 1994). It is a common resident throughout Santa Clara County, except in the most urban areas of the northern Santa Clara Valley and the marshes adjacent to the San Francisco Bay. Two subspecies occur in the county, *T. b. spilurus* generally on the western side of the Santa Clara Valley and *T. b. drymoecus* on the eastern side (Grinnell and Miller 1944).

Early observers in Santa Clara County considered the Bewick's Wren a common species, much as it is today. Price (1898f) described it as resident near Stanford. Van Denburgh (1899b) considered it moderately to very common, and Fisher (1902) judged it a common resident. Grinnell and Wythe (1927), in assessing the status of the birds in the San Francisco Bay region, described each of the three local subspecies as common residents. Sibley (1952), in his assessment of birds of the South Bay, also described this wren as common. Analysis of CBC and SBC data shows an increase of 1.1% per year for the Palo Alto CBC and 2.8% per year for the SBC, though there is a decline of 1.2% per year for the San Jose CBC. The number of Bewick's Wrens recorded in the Palo Alto count circle is three to four times greater for the SBC than for the CBC, in contrast to most resident species, for which these numbers are generally comparable. This difference may be related to the more vocal nature of this species in summer.

Bewick's Wrens were found widely in the county during the atlas period, with breeding confirmed in 113 blocks (68%). Including probable and possible evidence, breeding was likely in 156 blocks (95%). The only blocks lacking any kind of breeding evidence were six bayside blocks, two highly urbanized blocks, and a block in the northern Diablo Range. Subsequent to the atlas period, breeding was confirmed in the missing northern Diablo Range block, one of the urbanized blocks, and one of the bayside blocks. During the atlas period, confirmed breeding was documented from an elevation of 50 feet along Stevens Creek above Highway 101 to 3,440 feet north of Mt. Boardman in San Joaquin County (an edge block). Subsequently, Bewick's Wrens were found at a lower elevation, nest building near the Alviso Environmental Education Center near sea level (Michael J. Mammoser, PADB) and at a higher elevation of 3,720 feet on a ridge northwest of Eylar Mountain (Michael M. Rogers, pers. comm.). Bewick's Wrens were found in brushy tangles, chaparral, dense shrub understories in woodlands or at forest edges, in bramble thickets along streams, and in urban gardens with heavy shrub cover and undergrowth. In urban or partially rural areas, Bewick's Wrens sometimes nested in bird boxes, sheds or outbuildings, scrap lumber piles, and used fruit boxes. More or less natural nest sites found by atlasers included a ledge or cavity on a steep bank along Stevens Creek concealed by riparian overgrowth, and a manmade brush heap at Stevens Creek County Park.

The earliest evidence of breeding during the atlas period was a Bewick's Wren carrying food for young on 11 Mar. Subsequent to the atlas period, an adult was seen nest building on 6 Feb 2002 (Kathryn Parker, PADB). The latest breeding evidence was a fledgling being fed on 1 Aug. Bewick's Wrens normally are single-brooded (Kennedy and White 1997), and this appears to be consistent with the atlas phenology.

Bewick's Wrens are absent from much of their former range east of the Mississippi River (Kennedy and White 1997). These population losses have coincided with the range expansion of the House Wren, which frequently destroys the nests and eggs of other cavity-nesting species in the eastern United States (Kennedy and White 1997). But although the nesting ranges of Bewick's and House Wrens overlap extensively in the western United States, there is little evidence of territorial displacement or nest destruction by House Wrens in this region (Kroodsma 1973, Kennedy and White 1997). In Santa Clara County, a seven-year study of cavity-nesting species using nest boxes found that the two wrens used these boxes with equal frequency, with no evidence of displacement (Houston 2003). Unlike their eastern relatives, Bewick's Wrens appear to be doing well in Santa Clara County.

William G. Bousman

BEWICK'S WREN

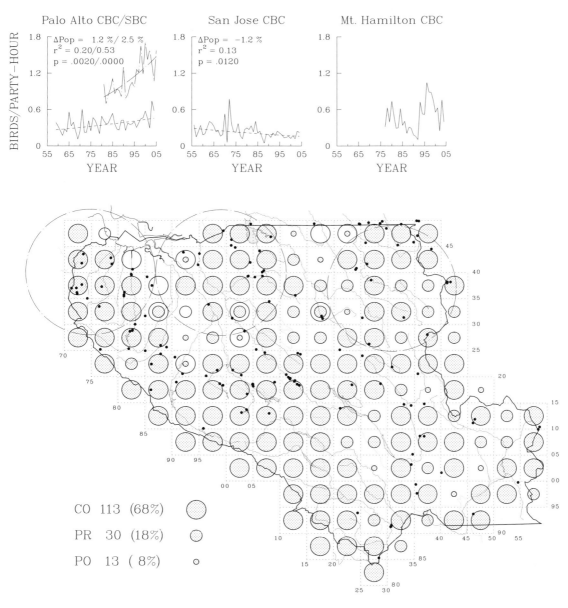

Palo Alto CBC/SBC

ΔPop = 1.2 % / 2.5 %
r² = 0.20/0.53
p = .0020/.0000

San Jose CBC

ΔPop = −1.2 %
r² = 0.13
p = .0120

Mt. Hamilton CBC

BIRDS/PARTY – HOUR

YEAR

CO 113 (68%)
PR 30 (18%)
PO 13 (8%)

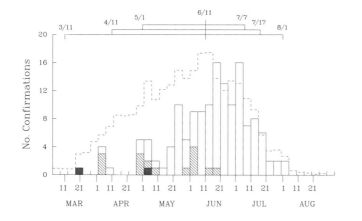

Atlas (1987–1993), n = 191

No. Confirmations

MAR APR MAY JUN JUL AUG

341

House Wren
Troglodytes aedon

The chattering, bubbling, gurgling song of this ebullient wren is a welcome sign of spring in the oak woodlands and streamside sycamores of Santa Clara County. Nesting from northern Saskatchewan south to Tierra del Fuego, the House Wren occupies a greater latitudinal range than any other passerine in North America (Johnson 1998). Among its 30 subspecies, the two belonging to the *aedon* group are found widely in the continental United States. The western subspecies, *T. a. parkmanii*, nests from British Columbia east across Canada to central Ontario, thence south to northwestern Baja California, and east to Missouri and western Kentucky (AOU 1957, Johnson 1998). The House Wren is a common summer resident in California away from the southeastern deserts and the highest mountains (Small 1994). In Santa Clara County, this wren is common in the Diablo Range, less common in the Santa Cruz Mountains and on the valley floor south of the Coyote Narrows, and absent from the northern reaches of the Santa Clara Valley. A few birds are found in winter, generally along streams on the valley floor or at the edges of the Diablo Range.

The status of the House Wren in Santa Clara County does not appear to have changed since the earliest local observations. Van Denburgh (1899b) considered this wren a common summer resident along the eastern edge of the Santa Cruz Mountains in some years, and Fisher (1902) described it as a summer resident among live oaks. Grinnell and Wythe (1927) reported the House Wren as "notably numerous in the oak belts of Santa Clara, Alameda, and Contra Costa counties." Similarly, Sibley (1952) judged the House Wren to be a common summer resident with a decided preference for valley and blue oak woodlands.

The House Wren was found nesting widely in Santa Clara County during the atlas period. Birds were located in 115 blocks (70%) and confirmed breeding in 97 blocks (59%). This wren was found in a variety of habitats, including both deciduous and live oak woodlands, foothill pine-blue oak woodlands, and vegetation along intermittent or permanent streams, generally where sycamores were present. House Wrens appeared to prefer a mixture of plant communities, often with larger trees such as valley oaks, live oaks, and sycamores providing nesting cavities and a shrub understory grading to chaparral or grasslands. Birds were less frequently found in denser oak woodlands transitioning to forest or, at the other extreme, in open oak savannas. They were absent from the wetter, coniferous-broadleaved evergreen forests in the Santa Cruz Mountains, as well as urban habitats. House Wrens were found nesting from an elevation of 150 feet, along Tequisquita Slough in San Benito County (an edge block), to 3,880 feet, near the summit of Eylar Mountain.

House Wrens generally return to Santa Clara County during the last week of March, although birds occasionally arrive on territory as early as the second week in March and are sometimes delayed until early April. Atlasers observed nest building as early as 29 Mar and incubation as early as 16 Apr. Following the atlas period, nest building was seen as early as 17 Mar 2004 (Peggy L. Don, PADB). The latest observation of breeding during the atlas period was of an adult carrying food on 27 Jul. Detailed studies of House Wrens nesting in Madera County in the Sierra foothills (Purcell et al. 1997) have shown mean dates for the first egg of the first clutch to fall from 19 to 23 Apr, with a standard deviation of about six days. The timing of first clutches in Santa Clara County is apparently similar. House Wrens are generally double-brooded (Johnson 1998), and the evidence of later incubation indicated on the phenology graph may reflect second broods or replacement clutches of failed nesters.

Observed differences in nest site selection between the eastern subspecies, *aedon*, and the western subspecies, *parkmanii*, may speak to this species' distribution in Santa Clara County. In the east, *aedon* is often found in close association with manmade structures in suburban or rural areas and has readily adapted to various artificial nest sites, including nest boxes (Johnson 1998). In the west, *parkmanii* has not developed a similar affinity for such structures, although it will readily use nest boxes placed in preferred habitats (Purcell et al. 1997). In Santa Clara County, atlasers generally found House Wrens nesting away from houses or buildings, but it was not clear that this reflected a specific aversion to manmade structures. Instead, it appears that built-up areas here lack habitat characteristics that are important to this species. The tendency of *parkmanii* to nest away from houses has also been noted in Marin and Monterey counties (Shuford 1993w, Tenney 1993b).

House Wrens occasionally destroy the eggs or nestlings of both their own and other species, though the reasons for this are unclear (Johnson 1998). This tendency has been particularly noted for *aedon* in the east, fewer such observations having been noted for *parkmanii* (Johnson 1998). In one example of such aggressive behavior, a House Wren in Los Gatos was observed to cause a Pacific-slope Flycatcher to desert its nest (*Audubon Field Notes* 4:259 1950). But there were no reports of such behavior during the atlas period.

The House Wren is rarely parasitized by the Brown-headed Cowbird (Friedmann and Kiff 1985), so it is of interest that a House Wren was observed feeding a Brown-headed Cowbird fledgling in the southern San Antonio Valley on 18 Jun 1992, in an area of deciduous oaks grading into chaparral.

William G. Bousman

HOUSE WREN

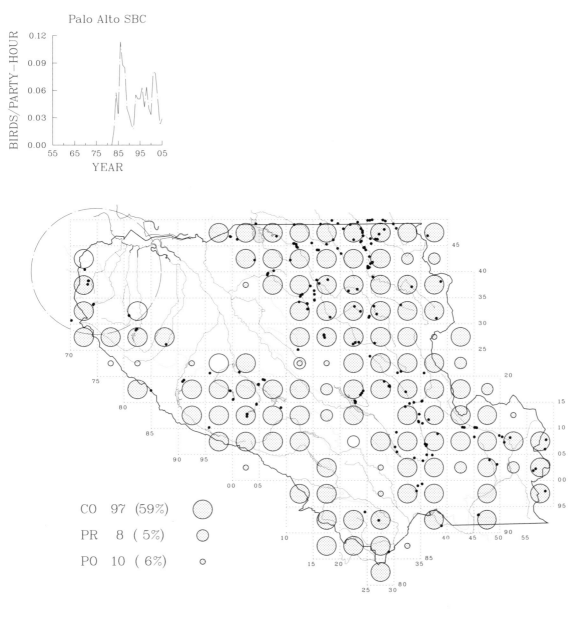

CO 97 (59%)
PR   8 (5%)
PO 10 (6%)

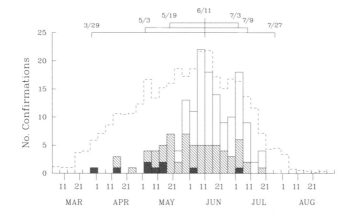

Atlas (1987–1993), n = 226

343

Winter Wren
Troglodytes troglodytes

Moving mouse-like among wet forest tangles, this wren, with its rich brown plumage, blends invisibly into its ancient forest home until suddenly bursting into ebullient, bubbling song. The Winter Wren is a Holarctic species, with anywhere from 35 to 43 recognized subspecies, most of which occur in the palearctic (Hejl et al. 2002). Our local subspecies, *pacificus*, breeds from southeast Alaska south along the Pacific Coast to central California, and inland in regions of the mountain west, including southeast Idaho, northwest Wyoming, and the Sierra Nevada (Hejl et al. 2002). In California, Winter Wrens are most commonly found in the humid forests of the northwest, south along the humid coastal strip to the wet canyons of Monterey County and occasionally San Luis Obispo County, and along the western slope of the Sierra Nevada (Small 1994). In Santa Clara County, they are uncommon residents in wet canyons draining the eastern side of the Santa Cruz Mountains, and also occur as uncommon migrants or winter visitors in the tangled shrubbery along streamsides or other moist tangles in scattered areas throughout the county.

Prior to American settlement, dense forests of coast redwood and Douglas fir occupied the larger canyons on the eastern side of the Santa Cruz Mountains (Stanger 1967). These ancient forests were undoubtedly ideal habitat for the Winter Wren, but by the 1870s most of the timber had been removed and the land burned over (Jensen 1939, Stanger 1967). Nonetheless, Price (1898f) noted that the Winter Wren was found near Stanford along "shaded mountain streams." Fisher (1902) described the species as resident in the Santa Cruz Mountains. Grinnell and Wythe (1927) considered it a fairly common resident of the denser forests near the immediate coast in San Mateo, Marin, and Sonoma counties. Sibley (1952) described the Winter Wren as an uncommon resident of the Santa Cruz Mountains. The edge of the Winter Wren's breeding range in the Santa Cruz Mountains is barely within the Palo Alto count circle, but a few birds are found in most years. There are no significant population trends from analysis of either the winter or the summer count data.

Winter Wrens were found breeding in only 13 blocks (8%) during the atlas period, most confirmations obtained in blocks along the crest of the Santa Cruz Mountains. Atlasers found breeding birds in shaded canyons with mature coniferous and broadleaved evergreen forests, generally within the range of summer fog. Wrens favored areas of permanent water with moss-covered logs and a dense understory of ferns and shrubs. Within these habitats the species was sometimes common, particularly along streams flowing west to the Pacific Ocean. An unusual record away from the Santa Cruz Mountains was an agitated adult found along San Felipe Creek on 15 Jul 1990 with at least two fledglings still exhibiting their rictal flanges. This location, on the upper portion of San Felipe Creek east of Panochita Hill in the Diablo Range, still had flowing water, even in midsummer in a drought year. The wrens were found in an area of low, tangled vegetation and rotting tree stumps, apparently a suitable microhabitat 25 km from their normal breeding locations. Winter Wrens are occasionally found in nearby Henry Coe State Park from October to early April (James Yurchenco, pers. comm.) and have also been seen on the Mt. Hamilton CBC on five occasions. The birds on San Felipe Creek in 1990 may have arrived in the previous winter and remained to nest.

Most of the breeding evidence obtained during the atlas period was fledged young (35%), adults carrying food (29%), or adults feeding young (21%). Two nests were found, both with young, on 4 Jun and 9 Jul. The earliest confirmation obtained was of an adult carrying food on 5 May, the latest date the San Felipe Creek confirmation mentioned above. Judging from egg dates in Bent (1948b), the height of egg-laying lies from 29 Apr to 20 May, which is consistent with the atlas phenology.

Winter Wrens are closely tied to mature or old-growth forests, where creeks descend through fallen logs and tangled vegetation, and summer fog is common. Thus in the Santa Cruz Mountains, this species is found widely in the drainages of streams flowing to the Pacific Ocean. Atlas work in nearby San Mateo County confirmed breeding in 30 blocks (44%) and, when probable and possible evidence is considered, wrens were found in 47 blocks (68%), most of which were in the southern and more mountainous portions of the county (Sequoia Audubon Society 2001i). In Santa Cruz County, birds were recorded in 48 blocks (67%) during that county's atlas period (David L. Suddjian, pers. comm.). Combining the data from the three atlases, Winter Wrens have been found in 92 blocks, or 2,300 km^2, within the Santa Cruz Mountains, which represents the largest contiguous habitat for this species on the central California coast. Winter Wrens are a key indicator of mature, wet coniferous forests, and their extensive distribution in the Santa Cruz Mountains illustrates the importance of this biome.

William G. Bousman

WINTER WREN

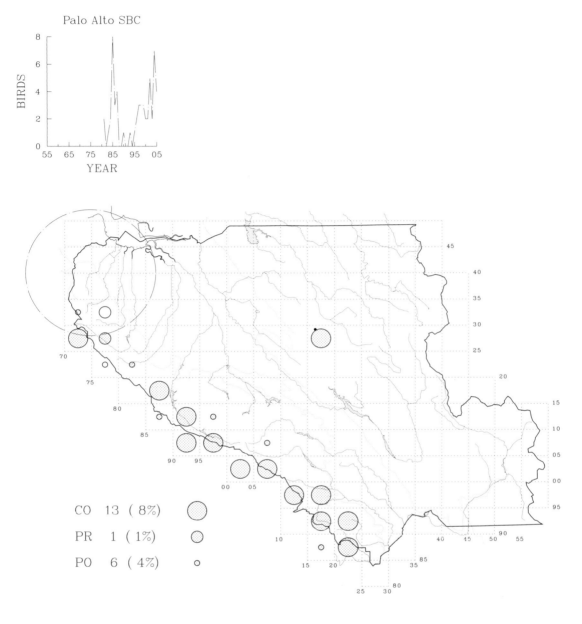

Palo Alto SBC

CO 13 (8%)
PR   1 (1%)
PO   6 (4%)

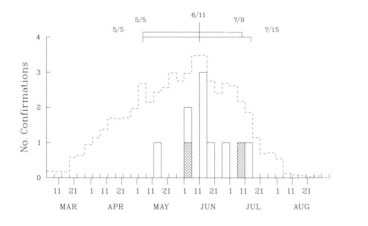

Atlas (1987–1993), n = 14

Marsh Wren
Cistothorus palustris

An exuberant chattering song marks the springtime progress of the male Marsh Wren as it builds nest after nest, all to show its fitness and thereby attract a mate. The Marsh Wren breeds throughout North America from southern British Columbia across Canada to Nova Scotia, south to Baja California and northwestern Sonora, and across to the Gulf Coast of the United States (AOU 1998). Populations found in the western United States are vocally and morphologically distinct from eastern populations and may constitute a separate species (AOU 1998). The subspecies found along the northern and central California coast, *C. p. aestuarinus*, appears to be largely resident (Kroodsma and Verner 1997). The Marsh Wren is a fairly common resident in Santa Clara County in its favored freshwater and brackish marshes. In winter, birds are found more widely, occupying salt marshes along the Bay and, in smaller numbers, other freshwater marshes, where they do not breed.

At the end of the nineteenth century, Price (1898f) noted that the Marsh Wren was found in marshes and tule thickets in the general area of Stanford University. Van Denburgh (1899b) had observed this species nesting in the "marshes south of San Jose," but did not consider it an abundant species. Fisher (1902) believed it was restricted for nesting purposes to areas of bulrush, although he also noted its presence in pickleweed marsh. Within its preferred habitat, however, Grinnell and Wythe (1927) considered it a "common permanent resident." Sibley too (1952) judged it a common resident of marshland.

Marsh Wrens were confirmed breeding in seven blocks during the atlas period, and probable and possible breeding evidence was garnered from an additional five blocks. Most of the confirmations were from blocks adjacent to the edge of the Bay, where there are cattails and bulrushes in freshwater and brackish marshes. In many cases, these marshes border the streams that enter the South Bay, such as Coyote Creek and the Guadalupe River, but birds were also found in effluent-dominated, largely freshwater marshes, such as along Artesian Slough, as well as in wetlands with more or less permanent water, as in the Palo Alto Flood Control Basin. Two confirmations were found away from the Bay edge, one (a nest under construction) at the percola-

tion ponds along Los Gatos Creek, and the second (a nest with young) found higher in the Los Gatos Creek watershed. Following the atlas period, nesting birds away from the Bay edge were found in freshwater marshes lining borrow ponds along Coyote Creek north of Morgan Hill (Stephen C. Rottenborn, PADB) and in marshes south of San Felipe Lake in San Benito County in an edge block (Michael M. Rogers, Mark Paxton, PADB).

Populations of Marsh Wrens are strongly affected by year-to-year fluctuations in water level (Kroodsma and Verner 1997). Because this wren builds its nest over standing water, it abandons ephemeral marshes during drought years. The first four atlas years, 1987–91, had below-average rainfall, and it is likely that birds withdrew from some areas in these years. No birds were noted in the borrow ponds north of Morgan Hill until after the atlas period and the return to average or above-average rainfall. This species shows considerable variation in numbers on the local CBCs and the Palo Alto SBC. As an example, in the three years following the El Niño winter of 1982–83, the Palo Alto SBC recorded 67, 92, and 118 birds. During the atlas (and drought) years from 1987 to 1993, these numbers declined precipitately, to counts of 92, 12, 40, 6, 3, 3, and 6.

The limited number of breeding confirmations affords only a vague outline of the nesting phenology. The earliest record during the atlas period was of a bird carrying nest material on 16 Apr, and under atlas protocols this record may be questioned because the construction of dummy nests does not constitute breeding confirmation for this species. Following the atlas period, nest building was observed as early as 9 Mar 2002 (Louis Beaudet, PADB). Prior to the atlas period, nest surveys in a seasonal wetland adjacent to Crittenden Marsh revealed two active nests in a cattail marsh on 31 Mar 1984, with five and two eggs, respectively (pers. obs.). On 14 Apr 1984, one of these nests held at least three nestlings. Fledged young were recorded through 7 Aug during the atlas period, and a late record of an adult carrying food was subsequently reported on 23 Aug 2004 (pers. obs.).

The Marsh Wren's dependence upon rainfall and marsh habitat makes it a good indicator species for the health of the county's remaining freshwater marshes. Prior to settlement, most of the streams in the Santa Clara Valley drained to seasonal freshwater marshes (*sausals*) rather than to the Bay, and all of these have been drained or filled. Larger marshes, such as Willow Marsh in the Llagas Creek drainage, southwest of Gilroy, and Laguna Seca in the Coyote Creek drainage, were drained for agriculture a century ago. San Felipe Lake, just south of the county line, was a swamp on the Llano del Tequisquita in the nineteenth century. W. E. Unglish found nesting Marsh Wrens there in the 1920s and 1930s (Sibley 1952), but none were observed here until after the atlas period, even though the lake filled following increased rainfall in the early 1990s. Yet marshes still survive in parts of the valley, and more have been created with the development of water supplies. Protection and monitoring of these marshes is necessary for this species' continued health in the county.

William G. Bousman

MARSH WREN

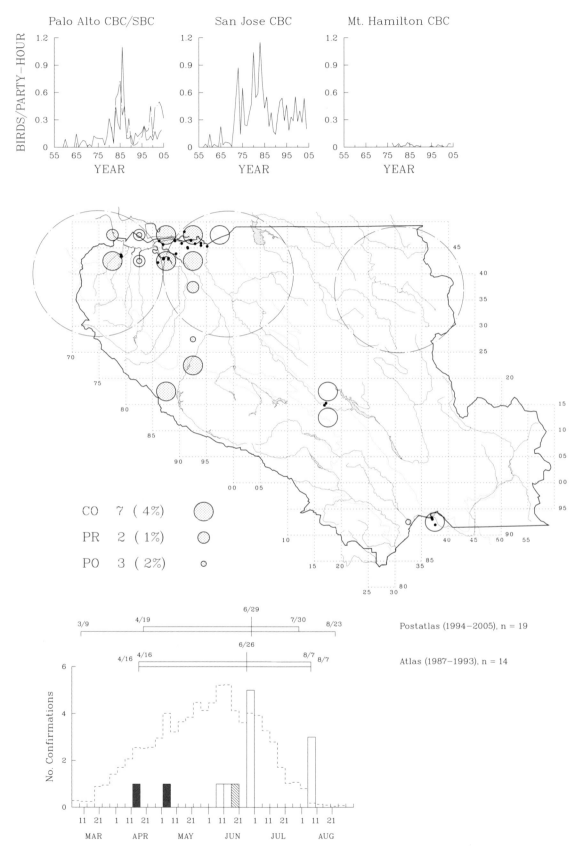

Palo Alto CBC/SBC

San Jose CBC

Mt. Hamilton CBC

BIRDS/PARTY-HOUR

YEAR

CO 7 (4%)

PR 2 (1%)

PO 3 (2%)

Postatlas (1994−2005), n = 19

Atlas (1987−1993), n = 14

No. Confirmations

MAR APR MAY JUN JUL AUG

American Dipper
Cinclus mexicanus

The most aquatic of all passerines, dippers share some of the characteristics of ducks and grebes, namely their dense feathering and a flightless molting period. American Dippers are found from Alaska south through the mountain ranges of western North America, with scattered populations extending into Mexico and Central America as far south as Costa Rica (Kingery 1996). Of the five subspecies that have been described, it is *C. m. unicolor* that occurs in the United States and Canada (Kingery 1996). In California, dippers are found on fast-moving mountain streams throughout much of the state, with most of them resident in the northern mountains and in the Cascades and Sierra Nevada (Small 1994). American Dippers are rare and very local in Santa Clara County, but they reside here along high-gradient, clear-water streams in both the Santa Cruz Mountains and the Diablo Range.

Despite the scarcity of dippers along Santa Clara County's streams, their distribution here appears to have changed little in the last 150 years, to judge from the reports of early ornithologists. James G. Cooper (1870) found dippers nesting in streams flowing out of the Santa Cruz Mountains, including a nest adjacent to a milldam on Los Gatos Creek. Daniel A. Cohen reported finding a nest along Arroyo Hondo in May 1886 (Cohen 1895). Corydon Chamberlin (1893, 1894) found the species nesting along Uvas Creek during the early 1890s. W. E. Unglish collected a set of eggs along Bodfish Creek near Gilroy on 8 May 1905 (Sibley 1952). John W. Mailliard collected a set of eggs along Smith Creek on 19 Apr 1913 (CAS #10145). Grinnell and Wythe (1927) reported dippers resident on both Stevens Creek and Los Gatos Creek. A pair, presumably resident, was observed at Twin Creeks on 21 Feb 1931 (*Wren-Tit 3(2)* 1931, Sibley 1952). Sibley (1952) also reported that dippers nested in Alum Rock Canyon in the late 1940s. Additional breeding records have been obtained in most of these locations during the twentieth century, and birds still nest along all of these drainages, except for Bodfish Creek west of Gilroy.

Atlasers found American Dippers breeding along streams in both the Santa Cruz Mountains and the Diablo Range. In the Santa Cruz Mountains, during the atlas period, breeding dippers were found along Stevens Creek above Mt. Eden Road, often using road bridges for nest sites. Following the atlas period, on 10 May 2003, an adult was found feeding a fledgling about 1 to 2 km upstream of the typical nesting sites on Stevens Creek (Grant Hoyt, PADB). Multiple observations were also made in the area of Twin Creeks, where Herbert Creek and Barrett Canyon join. In 1988, two nests on these creeks were seen to be about 750 meters apart. The remaining Santa Cruz Mountains breeding records were from where Swanson Creek enters Uvas Creek, and in the upper reaches of Soquel Creek in the Santa Cruz County portion of an edge block. In the Diablo Range, during the atlas period, breeding birds were found along a 13-km stretch of Arroyo Hondo and Smith Creek, and in 2004, in the postatlas period, a nesting pair was found along Penitencia Creek in Alum Rock Canyon (mult. obs., county notebooks). All of the Diablo Range nests were on natural sites, such as ledges over water or boulders in streams. During the atlas period, breeding confirmations were recorded from an elevation of 620 feet near Twin Creeks to 1,800 feet on Smith Creek. Following the atlas period, birds were breeding along Stevens Creek at the lower elevation of 560 feet (Les Chibana, county notebooks).

The earliest breeding confirmation during the atlas period was of a bird on a nest on upper Soquel Creek in the Santa Cruz County portion of an edge block on 3 Apr. The latest confirmation was of a nest with young on Swanson Creek on 30 May. Following the atlas period, nest building was observed along Stevens Creek on 21 Feb 2002 (Kristen A. Olson, David E. Quady, county notebooks).

American Dippers are restricted to clear, high-gradient streams that offer abundant aquatic insects and suitable nest sites (Kingery 1996). In the Diablo Range, the streams used by dippers appear to be those with ample natural ledges, crevices within boulders, and recesses in waterfalls where dippers can nest securely. Such sites appear to be scarcer in the Santa Cruz Mountains, where dippers more often used bridges or dam structures for nesting. During the dry season, many of the streams used by dippers in Santa Clara County have reduced flows, but their flows appear to be adequate, since birds are found in these locations year-round. Curiously, American Dippers appear to abandon some of the westward-flowing streams in the Santa Cruz Mountains in Santa Cruz County in late summer as the flows reduce (David L. Suddjian, pers. comm.); this pattern has not been noted for birds in Santa Clara County.

Throughout their range, American Dippers are sensitive to pollution, stream sedimentation, and water diversion (Kingery 1996). Their numbers have declined in the last century in Sonoma, Marin, and Napa counties (Shuford 1993x, Nelson 1995a, Berner 2003f), yet appear stable, though minimal, in Santa Clara County, despite damage to watersheds from logging and grazing. A better understanding of the needs of this charismatic "waterbird" in the county may be necessary if we are to protect the resources on which it depends, and thus allow it to maintain its local populations.

William G. Bousman

AMERICAN DIPPER

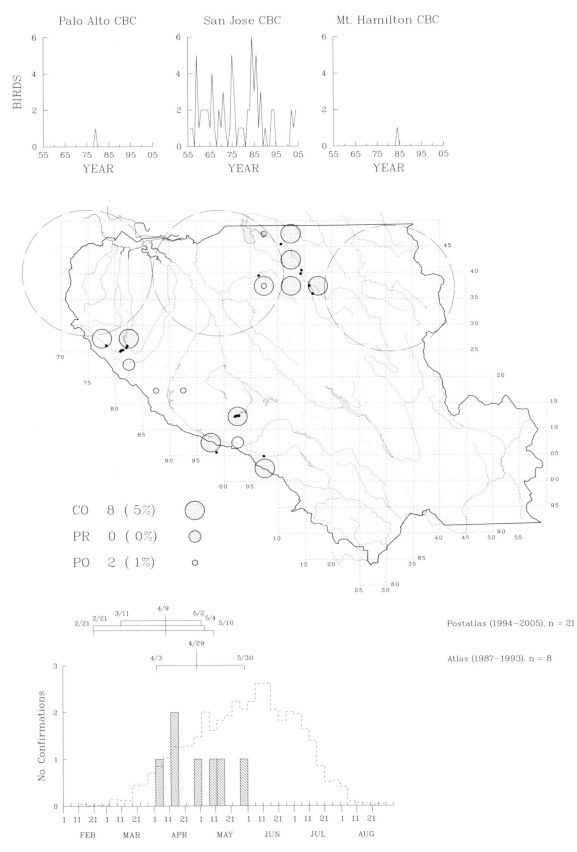

Palo Alto CBC

San Jose CBC

Mt. Hamilton CBC

BIRDS

YEAR

YEAR

YEAR

CO   8 (5%)

PR   0 (0%)

PO   2 (1%)

Postatlas (1994–2005), n = 21

Atlas (1987–1993), n = 8

No. Confirmations

FEB   MAR   APR   MAY   JUN   JUL   AUG

349

Golden-crowned Kinglet
Regulus satrapa

A series of high, thin notes descending from the upper branches of a coast redwood announces the presence of a Golden-crowned Kinglet. This kinglet breeds from coastal Alaska across Canada to Newfoundland, thence south on the Pacific Coast to California, in the Rocky Mountains to southeast Arizona, and in the east into Minnesota, Pennsylvania, and Maine (Ingold and Galati 1997). Disjunct populations are found in the Appalachians as far south as Tennessee, in the central volcanic belt of Mexico, and in mountains from Chiapas, Mexico, to southern Guatemala. In California, it is resident in the humid northwestern forests, in the Coast Ranges south to the Santa Cruz Mountains, in the Cascades and Sierra Nevada, and in some of the higher southern California mountains (Small 1994). Of four or five subspecies, *R. s. apache* is the one resident in California (Ingold and Galati 1997). Golden-crowned Kinglets, very rare breeders in Santa Clara County, nest along the crest of the Santa Cruz Mountains. Migrants and wintering birds occur intermittently in the county, more commonly during irruption years.

Early observers thought the Golden-crowned Kinglet occurred in Santa Clara County solely as a winter visitor (Van Denburgh 1899b, Fisher 1902). In his second state checklist, Grinnell (1915) stated that the Golden-crowned Kinglet bred in the humid coast belt as far south as Marin County, and was found in winter throughout the San Francisco Bay region and south to Monterey County. Grinnell and Wythe (1927), however, noted breeding within the San Francisco Bay area only in northwestern Sonoma County. Subsequently, Donald D. McLean collected an adult male in breeding condition on 10 Jun 1933 about 5 km northwest of the La Honda summit in the Santa Cruz Mountains in San Mateo County, and noted several others of this species at the same location (McLean 1936). Sibley (1952), drawing from McLean's records, indicated that these kinglets might breed in the Santa Cruz Mountains, but recorded no additional observations. On 27 May 1950, Emily D. Smith saw a Golden-crowned Kinglet at Aldercroft Heights south of Los Gatos, the first breeding-season record for Santa Clara County (*Audubon Field Notes* 4:259 1950). From 8 to 14 Jun 1953, Smith observed a female kinglet building a nest at Castle Rock as the male sang nearby

(*Audubon Field Notes* 7:325 1953). This was the first recorded evidence of breeding in the Santa Cruz Mountains, although it is not known on which side of the Santa Cruz-Santa Clara County border the nest was located.

During the atlas period, probable or confirmed breeding evidence was obtained at only three locations along the crest of the Santa Cruz Mountains. A pair was observed near Castle Rock Falls on 16 Jun 1987, not far from where Emily Smith had noted nesting in 1953. To the southeast, a pair was found near Mt. Bielawski on 1 Jul 1991, and on 9 May 1993, nest building was observed in the headwaters of Casserley Creek, just southwest of the crest, not far from Mt. Madonna County Park. But each of these records pertained to birds in Santa Cruz County. Subsequent to the atlas period, in San Mateo County in an edge block, adults were observed carrying food on 21 Jun 1997, their fledglings then seen on 29 Jun (Sequoia Audubon Society 2001j). Certain breeding within Santa Clara County was finally confirmed when adults were seen feeding young on Bodfish Creek, about a kilometer south of the Hecker Pass Highway, on 12 Jul 2001, and a different family south of Los Gatos Creek was observed near the bridge at Wrights Station Road the next day. More recently, a kinglet was found at a nest along Skyline Boulevard, 1.5 km southwest of Lake Ranch Reservoir, on 21 May 2005 (all David L. Suddjian, county notebooks).

Although there are only limited breeding records from the western border of Santa Clara County, the habitat at these locations is similar to that used commonly by nesting Golden-crowned Kinglets in adjacent Santa Cruz and San Mateo counties (David L. Suddjian, pers. comm.). In general, these kinglets breed in coast redwood forests or mixed forests with coast redwood and Douglas fir. They are found in areas with mature trees, and nest sites tend to be in the densest portions of these forests. Tan oak and madrone are often found in these forests as a subcomponent. Breeding elevations for the atlas and postatlas records ranged from 1,000 to 2,700 feet, but elevation per se appears to be unimportant so long as a dense coniferous forest is present (David L. Suddjian, pers. comm.).

How the logging of the original old-growth forests of the Santa Cruz Mountains may have affected the Golden-crowned Kinglet and other species is an unanswered question. By the 1990s, this kinglet was breeding regularly and widely in the second-growth forests on the coastal slope of San Mateo County (Sequoia Audubon Society 2001j) and Santa Cruz County west of the San Lorenzo River (David L. Suddjian, pers. comm.). Were they just as common and widespread in these areas in the 1850s, when the loggers first arrived and began harvesting the timber?

William G. Bousman

GOLDEN-CROWNED KINGLET

Palo Alto SBC

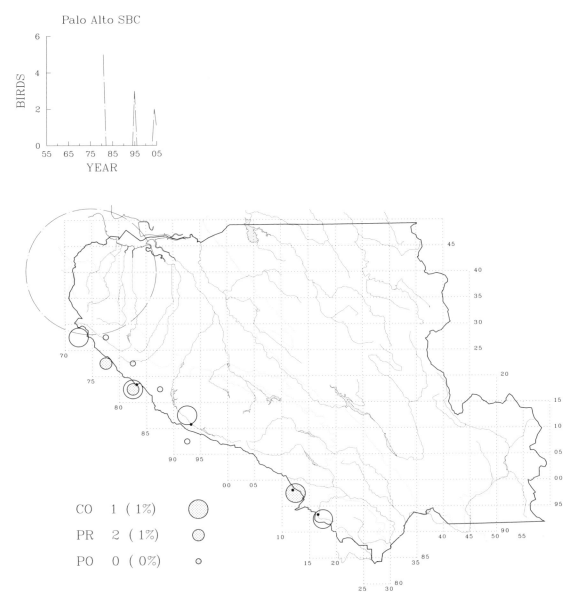

CO   1 (1%)
PR   2 (1%)
PO   0 (0%)

Atlas (1987–1993), n = 1

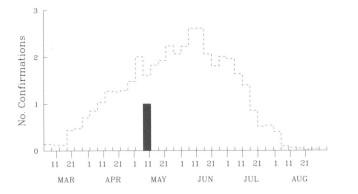

Blue-gray Gnatcatcher
Polioptila caerulea

The energetic tail-flicking of this lively little insectivore is a welcome sign of activity in arid chaparral edges. Blue-gray Gnatcatchers range widely across the eastern and southwestern United States in summer, but most withdraw to Mexico and the southern edge of the United States in winter. In California, they breed in the foothills surrounding the Central Valley, along the coast, and throughout the southern part of the state. Seven subspecies are currently recognized, the birds in Santa Clara County belonging to the race *P. c. amoenissima*, which ranges across the western United States and northwestern Mexico. In Santa Clara County, this bird prefers woodland with brushy undergrowth, often near the edges of chaparral fields, and is found in both the Diablo Range and the Santa Cruz Mountains.

Although not listed on Van Denburgh's (1899b) list of Santa Clara County birds, this gnatcatcher was included in Barlow's (1900b) notes on the basis of observations made by Rollo H. Beck, who suspected breeding in the hills east of Mt. Hamilton after finding this species there in April 1899. Grinnell and Wythe (1927) noted that the Blue-gray Gnatcatcher "occurs in summer, and doubtless nests, rather sparingly in areas of broken chaparral or scrubby oak on the Mount Hamilton Range." Sibley (1952) cited nests with eggs from the San Antonio Valley on 11 May 1946 and two nests, one with small young, along Arroyo Mocho (possibly in nearby Alameda County) on 26 May 1929. On the western side of the county, Price (1898f) listed the species as "resident" at Stanford, and Grinnell and Wythe (1927) cited an April record from Palo Alto. A single bird at Felt Lake on 21 Jun 1947 was considered notable (*Audubon Field Notes* 1:187–88 1947), as was a nest with young near Los Gatos on 17 Jul 1955 (*Audubon Field Notes* 9:401 1955). However, young fledged from nests in Los Altos Hills in June of both 1951 and 1952 (Phyllis M. Browning, pers. comm.), and it may be that this species was under-reported rather than very rare.

Blue-gray Gnatcatchers may have increased in abundance in some areas in recent decades. In 1985, Joe Morlan reported an "explosion" of this species in dry "hard chaparral" in the interior of the East Bay over the previous five years (*Am. Birds* 39:347 1985). Nonetheless, the species drew little comment from observers in the following year (*Am. Birds* 40:521 1986), analysis of Palo Alto SBC data shows a decline of 4.3% a year since 1981.

During the atlas period, Blue-gray Gnatcatchers were found breeding widely away from the valley floor, the highest densities being reported in the drier portions of the Santa Cruz Mountains, where they seemed to prefer chaparral consisting of manzanita and chamise, or knobcone pine forest with manzanita understory. Good numbers were also reported in the Diablo Range in blue oak woodland, typically with chaparral or a brushy understory nearby. Despite extensive coverage in the northwestern reaches of the Diablo Range, very few gnatcatchers were found there, and no confirmations of breeding were noted north or west of Mt. Hamilton, including the adjacent portions of Alameda County (Robert J. Richmond, pers. comm.). Potential breeding habitat (such as chamise chaparral) does exist in this area, and the reason for their absence is unclear. Although a pair was reported from Alum Rock Park in July 1987, atlasing in later years failed to produce any gnatcatchers there, and Linsdale and Rodgers (1937) listed only one summer record (on 29 Jul 1936) of this species out of 50 summer trips to Alum Rock Park. A similar lack of records from the Pacheco Creek drainage in the southeastern part of the county may be attributable to more limited atlas coverage. These gnatcatchers apparently do not use the riparian habitat on the valley floor for breeding in this county, although Bent (1949) noted that they used "groves of cottonwoods in river valleys" for breeding in California, and also used such habitat in the eastern United States. But just as in Santa Clara County, atlasing work in nearby counties did not reveal breeding in riparian habitat away from chaparral (Shuford 1993y, Tenney 1993c).

Nest-building was observed from 3 Apr to 5 Jul, which corresponds very closely to the 5 Apr to 12 Jul range of egg dates given in Bent (1949). The only nest with eggs found during the atlasing was seen on 3 May, and the latest atlas date for an occupied nest was 15 Jul. Fledglings were observed as early as 12 May, and feeding of young was noted until 23 Aug. Nesting was observed at elevations ranging from 200 to 3,920 feet, although most of the breeding confirmations were found between 1,400 and 2,800 feet, as is to be expected of a species absent from the valley floor. Thirty percent of all confirmations were of adults building nests and carrying nest material, and 25% were of adults feeding young. Atlasers found that Blue-gray Gnatcatchers were often surprisingly vocal while nest-building, which may be partly responsible for frequent nest parasitism by Brown-headed Cowbirds. Four of the 24 records of feeding young involved cowbirds, making the gnatcatcher the fourth most common cowbird host in our atlas records.

Michael M. Rogers

BLUE-GRAY GNATCATCHER

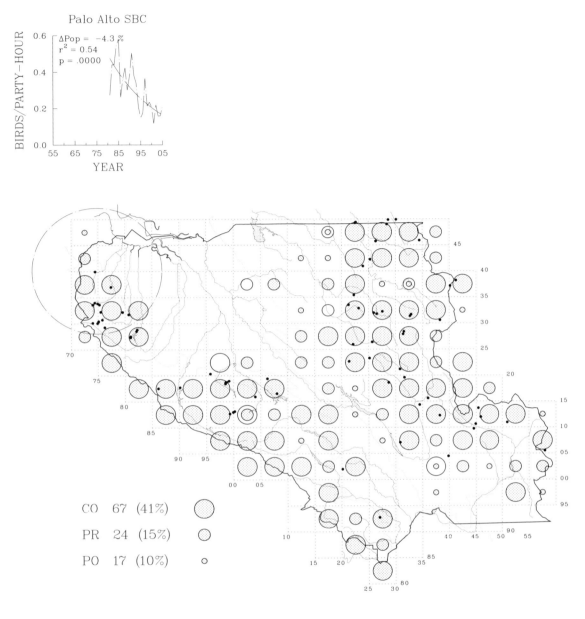

Palo Alto SBC

ΔPop = −4.3 %
r² = 0.54
p = .0000

BIRDS/PARTY-HOUR

YEAR

CO 67 (41%)
PR 24 (15%)
PO 17 (10%)

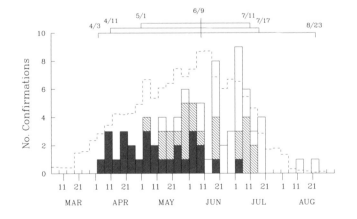

Atlas (1987−1993), n = 94

Western Bluebird
Sialia mexicanus

A common breeder in our oak woodlands and grasslands, the Western Bluebird has recently begun nesting within Santa Clara County's urban habitats as well. Western Bluebirds nest from southern British Columbia, Alberta, and Saskatchewan south through Mexico as far as Michoacán and Veracruz, but they are absent from large portions of the interior west, from central Idaho to northern New Mexico (AOU 1998, Guinan et al. 2000). Six subspecies are recognized, two of which are found in California: *occidentalis*, which occurs over most of the state, and *bairdi*, which breeds only in the southeastern corner (Grinnell and Miller 1944, Guinan et al. 2000). Bluebirds nest widely in California, particularly in foothills and lower montane regions (Small 1994). The Western Bluebird is a fairly common to common resident in the foothill and mountainous regions of Santa Clara County, and a few birds are now found in urban areas.

Western Bluebirds were among the specimens included in Sclater's list of birds collected by Thomas Bridges sometime before 1857 in "the Valley of San José" (Sclater 1857), and an egg set was collected in the county by F. L. Corless on 13 May 1888 (WFVZ #105850). Price (1898f) listed this bluebird as a resident on the Stanford University campus, although not an abundant one. Both Van Denburgh (1899b) and Fisher (1902) judged it to be a common resident. In contrast, Grinnell and Wythe (1927) considered it to be common in winter in the San Francisco Bay area, but noted that it was found only locally and sparingly as a resident south of the Golden Gate, specifically in the oak belts. Sibley (1952), however, described it as a common resident in open country of the South Bay. Analysis of CBC data shows a decline of 1.9% a year in the San Jose CBC circle, although in the Palo Alto circle, which has fewer of these birds, there has been an increase of 1.6% per year in winter and 4.1% per year in summer. No change has been observed for the Mt. Hamilton CBC count circle.

Atlasers found Western Bluebirds nesting throughout the Diablo Range and in most blocks in the Santa Cruz Mountains, but within urban areas this species was largely absent during the atlas period. Breeding was confirmed in 114 blocks (69%), but including probable and possible evidence, breeding was indicated in 128 blocks (78%). During the atlas period, birds were found nesting at elevations from 158 to 4,020 feet, with 90% of the confirmations over 400 feet. Subsequent to the atlas period, birds were observed breeding in the northwestern part of the county at elevations as low as 13 feet (Kristen A. Olson, PADB). Western Bluebirds were found most often in oak and foothill pine woodlands, savannas, and grasslands. They used perches on trees and fences from which they could hunt their insect prey. Farmlands, orchards, and other agricultural areas also provided suitable habitats, with a mixture of trees and fences for perches and adjacent open lands for foraging. The birds built their nests in abandoned woodpecker holes or in natural cavities in a variety of trees, including oaks and fruit trees. They also used nest boxes that had been placed adjacent to oak woodlands and grasslands.

By the end of the atlas period, a few pairs of bluebirds had moved into urban areas that offered parks or athletic fields with suitable oaks nearby for nesting. After the atlas period, this movement of Western Bluebirds into urban areas became more pronounced, especially in the northwestern part of the urban zone. In some cases the movement of these birds into these areas was associated with the placement of nest boxes, but in other cases the birds have managed to find suitable cavities on their own.

The earliest breeding evidence obtained during the atlas period was nest building on 23 Mar. Subsequently, a nest with eggs was observed in a nest box on an earlier date, 10 Mar 2003 (Janna L. Pauser, pers. comm.). Twenty-one egg sets from Santa Clara County (WFVZ, MVZ) span the period 8 Apr to 5 Jun, with a median date of 22 Apr. The latest evidence of breeding was fledged young observed on 20 Aug. Double-brooding by Western Bluebirds is thought not to be common, and studies of a resident population at the Hastings Reservation, Monterey County (Dickinson et al. 1997), showed that fewer than 20% of pairs attempted a second nest after successfully fledging young from the first nest.

Western Bluebirds are cavity nesters and will readily use nest boxes. Comparative studies in Madera County, some of the bluebirds using nest boxes, others using natural cavities, showed a significant advantage in the number of fledged young for birds using the nest boxes rather than a cavity (Purcell et al. 1997). In some cases, however, this advantage in turn results in a disadvantage for other species, particularly open-cup nesters that compete for some of the same food resources (Bock et al. 1992, Guinan et al. 2000).

William G. Bousman

354

WESTERN BLUEBIRD

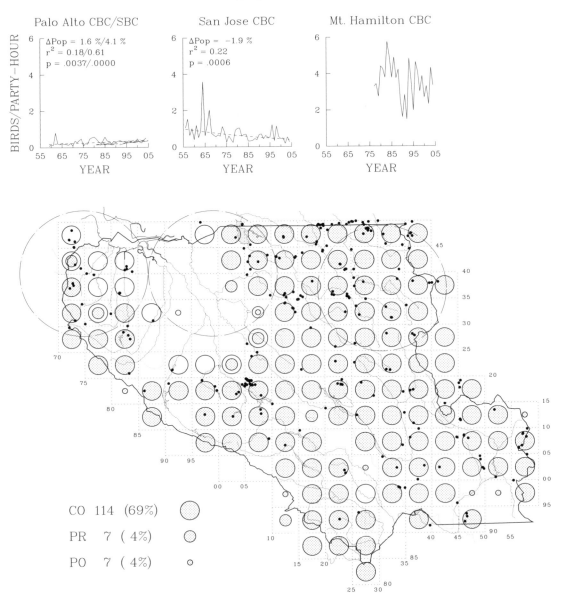

Palo Alto CBC/SBC

ΔPop = 1.6 %/4.1 %
r^2 = 0.18/0.61
p = .0037/.0000

San Jose CBC

ΔPop = −1.9 %
r^2 = 0.22
p = .0006

Mt. Hamilton CBC

BIRDS/PARTY–HOUR

YEAR

CO 114 (69%)
PR 7 (4%)
PO 7 (4%)

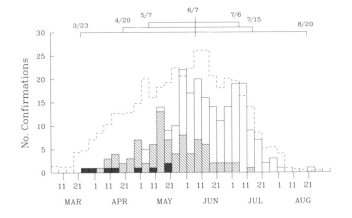

Atlas (1987–1993), n = 298

No. Confirmations

3/23   4/20   5/7   6/7   7/6   7/15   8/20

MAR   APR   MAY   JUN   JUL   AUG

355

Swainson's Thrush
Catharus ustulatus

Owing to its habit of skulking in the shade of dense vegetation, the furtive Swainson's Thrush is heard much more often than seen. It breeds in moist, cool habitats over much of western and northern North America. In northern California, the Swainson's Thrush nests in most mesic mountainous areas, but is conspicuously absent from the Central Valley and adjacent warmer, drier mountains. In the southern part of the state it breeds primarily in the Sierra Nevada and in the Coast Ranges (Small 1994). Of the four races recognized by the AOU (1957), it is the widespread nominate race that breeds in Santa Clara County, nesting in dense vegetation in the moist Santa Cruz Mountains and, more sparsely, in lowland riparian habitats.

The Swainson's Thrush was formerly considered an abundant breeder in riparian habitats in the South Bay, both in mountains and along lowland streams, and it even nested in lowland orchards (Price 1898f, Van Denburgh 1899b, Grinnell and Wythe 1927). Early egg collectors reported nesting birds along the valley floor at numerous locations, including Guadalupe Creek on 26 Jun 1890 (MVZ #1928), College Park on 2 Jul 1890 (USNM #B24350), San Jose on 30 May 1892 (MVZ #256), Palo Alto on 18 May 1901 (MVZ #403), and Alviso on 30 May 1922 (MVZ #10331). Charles P. Smith (1926) described a nest found along Coyote Creek "six feet up in box elder" on 30 Jun 1926, which included a Brown-headed Cowbird egg. Nests were also found in the Santa Cruz Mountains, where one was reported in Los Gatos in 1929 (*Wren-Tit 1(3)* 1929) and another along Stevens Creek in 1950 (*Audubon Field Notes 4*:292, 1950). Although the Swainson's Thrush was apparently not very common at Alum Rock Park, which lies at the western foot of the Diablo Range (Linsdale and Rodgers 1937), it was included in a list of birds found nesting there on 30 May 1929 (*Wren-Tit 1(3)* 1929). Sibley (1952) considered the Swainson's Thrush to be a "common summer resident" in riparian thickets in 1952, and indicated no declines in the South Bay at that time.

Swainson's Thrushes have nonetheless declined throughout North America in recent years (Ehrlich et al. 1988, Terborgh 1989), much of the decline probably owing to habitat degradation on the species' neotropical wintering grounds (Terborgh 1989). Just when Swainson's Thrush populations began to diminish in Santa Clara County is unknown, but since the 1950s this spe-

cies has been nearly extirpated from the Santa Clara Valley floor. The degradation of low-elevation riparian habitats, particularly the loss of extensive willow thickets and dense ground cover, has probably been an important cause of its near disappearance from the Santa Clara Valley. Brood parasitism of Swainson's Thrush nests by Brown-headed Cowbirds, which as mentioned above has been recorded in Santa Clara County, may also have contributed to local declines. This species has also declined dramatically in some portions of the Santa Cruz Mountains, the numbers of Swainson's Thrushes on the Palo Alto Summer Bird Count decreasing at a rate of 8.4% per year from 1981 to 2005.

Atlasers recorded Swainson's Thrushes in 46 atlas blocks and confirmed breeding in 15 of them. Although these thrushes were recorded in riparian habitats in several blocks on the Santa Clara Valley floor, the only lowland breeding confirmations during the atlas period were from the Pajaro River valley, where this species still breeds fairly commonly. All other confirmations during the atlas period were from the species' local breeding stronghold, the Santa Cruz Mountains and their foothills. In these areas, the Swainson's Thrushes were fairly common in moist forests with dense understory vegetation. Where its range overlaps with the similar Hermit Thrush, the Swainson's Thrush tends to nest under broadleaved evergreen tree species (especially along streams) rather than on more open slopes under redwoods and Douglas firs (Shuford 1993z). Breeding Swainson's Thrushes were completely absent from the more xeric Diablo Range.

Following the completion of atlas fieldwork, thorough surveys of some Santa Clara Valley streams produced four breeding confirmations in three blocks along Coyote Creek in 1995: a nest above Oakland Road on 17 Jun, pairs carrying food for young at Kelley Park on 26 Jun and near Hellyer Park on 27 Jun, and recently fledged young on 11 Jul (pers. obs). All of these records were from dense stands of willows with a tangled understory of blackberry vines. Despite these few Santa Clara Valley breeding records, it is clear that Swainson's Thrushes are now extremely rare as breeders in the Valley, where they were formerly quite common.

Swainson's Thrushes typically arrive in Santa Clara County in late April, and a few northbound migrants may still be found away from breeding areas as late as the second week of June. Atlasers observed individuals carrying nesting material on 28 May and 11 Jun, although no nests were found during the atlas period. An observation of a Swainson's Thrush carrying food on 20 May is so early that it may not have been associated with the feeding of young, although it is possible that this record indicates a very early nesting. Most records of adults carrying food and of recently fledged young were obtained from early June to mid-July.

Stephen C. Rottenborn

SWAINSON'S THRUSH

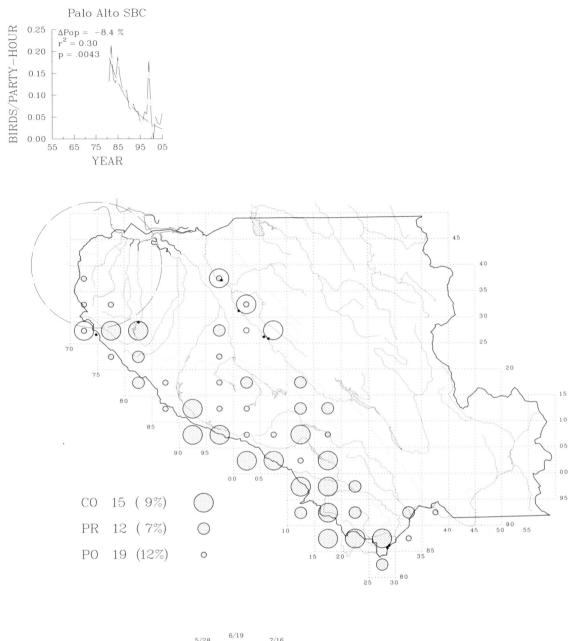

Palo Alto SBC

ΔPop = −8.4 %
$r^2 = 0.30$
p = .0043

BIRDS/PARTY−HOUR

YEAR

CO   15 (9%)
PR   12 (7%)
PO   19 (12%)

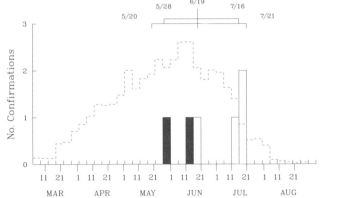

Atlas (1987−1993), n = 18

No. Confirmations

5/20   5/28   6/19   7/16   7/21

MAR   APR   MAY   JUN   JUL   AUG

Hermit Thrush
Catharus guttatus

An ethereal song, each phrase in a different key, drifts through the morning fog along the crest of the Santa Cruz Mountains, bringing an echo of the distant north to coastal California. Hermit Thrushes breed from Alaska across Canada to Newfoundland, thence south in the mountain ranges of the western United States to Baja California and west Texas, and in the eastern United States as far south as North Carolina, in the Appalachian Mountains (Jones and Donovan 1996). The taxonomy of this thrush is controversial, with 8 to 13 subspecies recognized (Jones and Donovan 1996). Five of them are commonly found in California, but two of these, *guttatus* and *nanus*, are present only as common, widespread winter visitors. The other three, *slevini*, *sequoiensis*, and *polionotus*, winter in Mexico and move in spring to their breeding grounds in California and points north. The subspecies *slevini* nests coastally from Monterey County to the Oregon border (a range that thus includes the Santa Cruz Mountains). Hermit Thrushes are common winter visitors throughout Santa Clara County, typically arriving at the end of September and leaving in April, but *slevini* is a rare breeder in western Santa Clara County, arriving in April and departing by September.

At the end of the nineteenth century, breeding Hermit Thrushes were considered uncommon in the Santa Cruz Mountains (McGregor 1901). Van Denburgh (1899b) was aware of their nesting there, but did not believe that they nested in Santa Clara County. He was apparently unaware that F. L. Corless had collected four eggs of a nesting Hermit Thrush in Saratoga on 20 May 1884 (WFVZ #104194), providing the first known breeding record from Santa Clara County. Fisher (1902) described the subspecies *slevini* as a summer visitant in the Santa Cruz Mountains. Grinnell and Wythe (1927) reported that *slevini* was a summer resident in small numbers in the San Francisco Bay area, generally along the immediate coast. Sibley (1952) noted that this subspecies was an uncommon summer resident in the Santa Cruz Mountains. Apparently, *slevini* continued to nest in the Saratoga area, for Emily D. Smith reported that return-ing summer birds were first heard singing there on 9 May 1957 (*Audubon Field Notes 11*:375 1957).

During the atlas period, breeding Hermit Thrushes were found along the Santa Cruz Mountains crest from Castle Rock Ridge to an area southeast of Mt. Madonna County Park, mostly in edge blocks between Santa Clara and Santa Cruz counties. Following the atlas period, breeding birds were found farther northwest, in the Peters Creek drainage in the San Mateo County portion of an edge block (David L. Suddjian, pers. comm.). No Hermit Thrushes were found breeding in the Saratoga area where they had nested historically. In general, they nested where there was moderate to dense vegetation in the shrub layer beneath either coast redwood or, less often, broadleaved evergreen forests (David L. Suddjian, pers. comm.). Breeding birds were sometimes found in brushy gaps in these forests. In other cases they were found in the shrub layer within a closed-canopy forest, suggesting that the shrub layer composition was more important than the amount of canopy closure. The shrub layers used in coast redwood forest sometimes consisted of huckleberry, but in other cases the birds used an understory of tan oak saplings. Three nests were found during the atlas period, two in Santa Clara County blocks and one in a Santa Cruz County edge block. In each case the nests were 70 to 100 cm off the ground in the stems of root crown sprouts from second-growth coast redwoods (David L. Suddjian, pers. comm.).

There is some overlap between the departure of wintering Hermit Thrushes and the arrival of breeding birds. In Santa Cruz County, the median arrival date of breeding birds, as indicated by repeated singing in known breeding areas, is 11 Apr (range 8 to 21 Apr, David L. Suddjian, pers. comm.). The earliest evidence of breeding found during the atlas period was a bird carrying nesting material on 5 May. Singing birds may be heard until mid-July. The latest evidence of breeding was adults feeding young on 18 Jul. Most of the breeding birds appear to leave in August, and probably none remain at the time the wintering birds arrive in September (David L. Suddjian, pers. comm.).

The forests in the Santa Cruz Mountains are occupied by both Hermit and Swainson's thrushes, but in these forests the two species generally breed in separate habitats (David L. Suddjian, pers. comm.). Swainson's Thrushes are normally found nesting in riparian corridors, especially those with extensive deciduous growth. Hermit Thrushes are rarely found in streamside situations, even where the forest is completely evergreen. Occasionally, however, Swainson's Thrushes are found away from streamside forest in the mesic shrub understories of coniferous or broadleaved evergreen forests, and here they share the habitats preferred by Hermit Thrushes.

William G. Bousman

HERMIT THRUSH

Palo Alto SBC

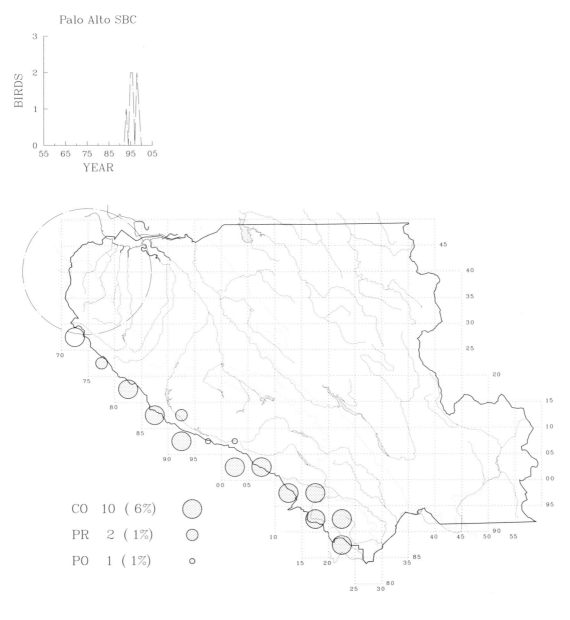

CO 10 (6%)

PR   2 (1%)

PO   1 (1%)

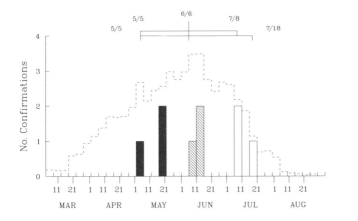

Atlas (1987–1993), n = 14

359

American Robin
Turdus migratorius

One of our most familiar birds, this large thrush appears to be as successful nesting close to humans as it is in the most remote mountain forests. The American Robin breeds across North America from Alaska to Newfoundland in the north and from southern California to northern Florida in the south (Sallabanks and James 1999). It is also resident in the highlands of Mexico south to Oaxaca, and at the southern tip of Baja California. Seven subspecies are recognized, the Santa Clara County breeders belonging to the Pacific Coast race *T. m. propinquus* (Sallabanks and James 1999). Robins nest throughout California west of the Great Basin and the southeastern deserts (Small 1994). In Santa Clara County, the American Robin is common in summer in most of the county, though with reduced numbers in the eastern Diablo Range. In some winters, invading birds from northern areas significantly augment the local population.

An American Robin on the list of specimens collected by Thomas Bridges in "the Valley of San José" prior to 1857 is the earliest record of the species' presence locally (Sclater 1857). James G. Cooper (1870) found it to be numerous at higher elevations in the Santa Cruz Mountains in May 1864 and believed that it nested there. Similarly, W. Otto Emerson noted singing birds on 18 May 1889 along the summit 14 miles from Santa Cruz and also believed that they were nesting (McGregor 1901). A nest found by Mr. Trantham in Los Gatos in 1893, as discussed in a paper read by Fred A. Schneider at the newly formed Cooper Ornithological Club (Barlow 1894a), was the first breeding record for Santa Clara County. Other early observers in the San Francisco Bay area considered the American Robin to be present solely as a winter resident, arriving in October or November and leaving in March or April (Belding 1890, Price 1898f, Van Denburgh 1899b, Fisher 1902, Grinnell 1915). In any event, breeding birds began to invade urban areas by about 1915 (Grinnell and Wythe 1927), and over the next 15 years they became established in settled areas throughout the Bay area, although their status in the more remote areas of the Santa Cruz Mountains and the Diablo Range at that time is unclear. Despite Cooper's and Emerson's statements about probable breeding of American Robins in the Santa Cruz Mountains, Orr (1942), in his studies of the Big Basin area from 1935 to 1939, encountered robins only twice. Similarly, in the Diablo Range, Linsdale and Rodg-

ers (1937) reported American Robins only four times out of 50 summer surveys of Alum Rock Park in the 1930s. Sibley (1952) stated that robins were well established in coastal and urban areas by the 1950s, but made no mention of their nesting in more remote areas.

During the atlas period, American Robins were confirmed breeding in 121 blocks (73%), and including probable and possible evidence they were recorded in 151 blocks (92%). They were found breeding at elevations from 2 feet beside the Bay at Shoreline Lake to 3,360 feet at the southeast end of Oak Ridge in the Diablo Range. Subsequent to the atlas period, breeding evidence was obtained at an elevation of 3,440 feet on a ridge north of Mt. Lewis (Michael M. Rogers, pers. comm.). American Robins generally were found breeding in more mesic areas where moist soils support invertebrate prey and provide mud for nests. They were common along riparian corridors on the valley floor and throughout urban areas, particularly where there were parks and schoolyards with irrigated lawns. In the Santa Cruz Mountains they were found throughout coniferous-broadleaved and coniferous forests, as well as along streams, and in the Diablo Range they were found in many of the arroyos offering some summer moisture, and in woodlands on north-facing slopes with a covering canopy. Fewer birds were found farther east in the Diablo Range, where there is less rainfall and available moisture. Here, however, wet areas with mud and moist soils sometimes occur along intermittent streams well into midsummer, even after the stream flow has ceased, and occasional robin pairs were found in these mostly dry habitats.

It is likely that most of the American Robins breeding in Santa Clara County are resident, although birds from higher elevations in the Diablo Range probably move to lower elevations in winter. Resident birds first start to sing in late January and are in full song by February and March. The earliest evidence of breeding during the atlas period was nest building on 19 Mar near Lake Cunningham. The latest breeding evidence was recently fledged birds observed on 23 Aug. Most robin pairs raise two broods a season, and some occasionally raise three (Sallabanks and James 1999).

American Robins have expanded their range throughout the American Southwest, including much of lowland California, as more mesic habitats have been established through irrigation (Sallabanks and James 1999). In the Bay area, possibly attracted by extensive irrigated lawns and other habitats modified by man, breeding robins appear initially to have settled in suburban habitats and parks. Also interesting, however, is what appears to have been their subsequent expansion into the forests of the Santa Cruz Mountains and the woodlands of the Diablo Range. Many of these more remote areas are little changed from pre-settlement times, yet robins are now nesting successfully in locations where they were previously found only as winter visitors.

William G. Bousman

AMERICAN ROBIN

Palo Alto SBC

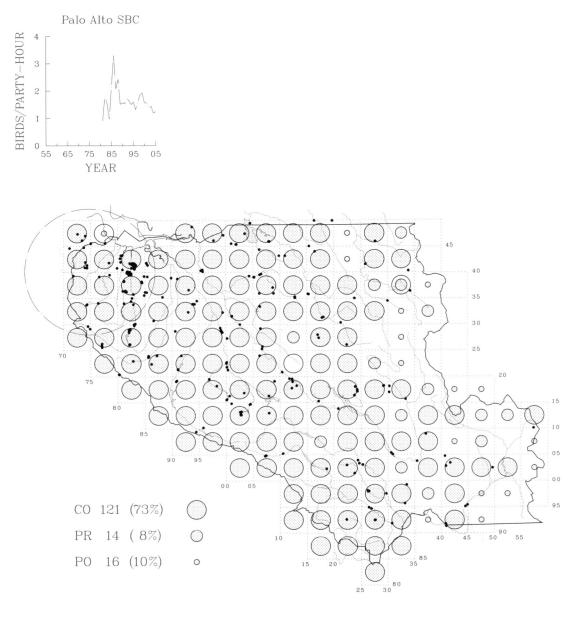

CO 121 (73%)

PR 14 (8%)

PO 16 (10%)

Atlas (1987–1993), n = 331

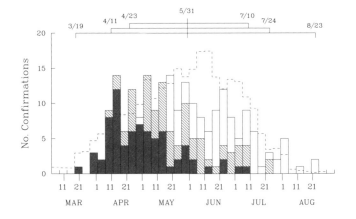

361

Wrentit
Chamaea fasciata

Uniquely among North American birds, the Wrentit is a member of the family *Timaliidae*, the Old World babblers, and is probably of Asiatic origin (Geupel and Ballard 2002). This remarkably sedentary bird's range is largely limited to the west coast of North America, from the Columbia River in Oregon south to northwestern Baja California. It also occurs inland on the slopes of the Cascades and the Sierra Nevada, but is absent from most of the Central Valley and the southeastern deserts of California (Small 1994, Geupel and Ballard 2002). Five subspecies are currently recognized, although the boundaries of their ranges are poorly defined (Geupel and Ballard 2002). In California, *C. f. rufula* is found coastally from Del Norte County to Marin County, *fasciata* occurs in a narrow strip from Lake County to San Luis Obispo County, and *henshawi* is found in the inner Coast Ranges, southwestern California, and inland in the Cascade Mountains and the Sierra Nevada. Wrentits are common residents in Santa Clara County, occurring in chaparral and dense shrublands throughout the county away from urban areas. The subspecies *fasciata* is found through most of the county, although *henshawi* may occur in the southeastern corner (Grinnell and Miller 1944).

Price (1898f) considered Wrentits to be resident in chaparral and thickets along streams around Stanford. Van Denburgh (1899b) described them as very common residents, and noted that he had found eggs on 20 Jun 1890. Fisher (1902) listed this babbler as a common resident in the Santa Cruz Mountains and the Santa Clara Valley. Grinnell and Wythe (1927) considered *fasciata* an abundant resident in the counties south and east of the San Francisco Bay. In discussing the birds of the South Bay, Sibley (1952) described Wrentits as common residents. Analysis of the San Jose CBC data indicates a population decline of 1.7% a year over the last four decades, and a similar decline of 1.5% a year is indicated in the Palo Alto SBC data obtained since 1981.

During the atlas period, Wrentits were found breeding widely in the Santa Cruz Mountains and the Diablo Range, but were largely absent from urban areas in the northern Santa Clara Valley and along the edge of the South Bay. Breeding was recorded from an elevation of 55 feet on the west side of the southern Santa Cruz Mountains (an edge block) to an elevation of 3,560 feet in chaparral on the eastern slopes of Mt. Mocho in the northeastern corner of the county. Ninety per cent of all confirmed breeding elevations were above 400 feet. Typically, Wrentits nested in chaparral dominated by chamise, but including a mixture of manzanita, buck brush, and other chaparral species. This type of "hard" chaparral habitat is found widely in the Diablo Range, as well as on the eastern slopes of the Santa Cruz Mountains. Toward the crest of the Santa Cruz Mountains, Wrentits nested commonly in chaparral consisting mostly of coyotebrush ("soft" chaparral). In the southern portion of the county, streams on the valley floor often have a thick, tangled understory of blackberries, and Wrentits were commonly found breeding there, although they were largely absent from similar thickets in the northern parts of the Santa Clara Valley. Birds occasionally nested in suburban areas where there was sufficient brushland and tangled undergrowth to provide acceptable habitat, but breeding in these locations appeared sporadic.

Wrentits hold their territories year-round (Geupel and Ballard 2002). The earliest breeding evidence during the atlas period was a bird carrying nest material on 26 Mar. After the atlas period, a bird was seen carrying food as early as 22 Mar 1997 (Chris K. Salander, PADB). Fledged young were first found at the end of May, and the latest observation during the atlas period was of an adult carrying food on 25 Jul. Subsequently, a dependent fledgling was observed on 1 Aug 1999 (Gloria Le-Blanc, PADB). Generally, Wrentits are single-brooded (Geupel and Ballard 2002), and the fairly broad span of nest construction dates shown in the phenology graphic likely results from renesting attempts.

In Santa Clara County, Wrentits are generally dependent upon chaparral with suitable cover that provides protection from nest predators, but can also be found in dense riparian thickets in the southern parts of the county. Although they are occasionally found in suburban areas and in thickets along streams elsewhere, they do not appear able to sustain populations within these habitats. Geupel and Ballard (2002) have discussed the effects of urbanization and reduced patch size on breeding success in Wrentits. Large predators, such as coyotes, are reduced or eliminated with increasing urbanization and reduced patches of chaparral. Thus, smaller nest predators increase in numbers, to the detriment of Wrentits. There is also a general increase in corvids with urbanization, and these birds tend to be successful predators of Wrentit nests.

William G. Bousman

WRENTIT

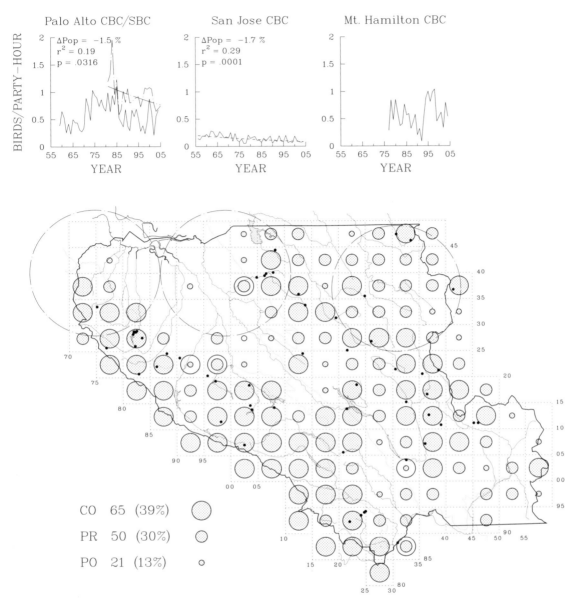

Palo Alto CBC/SBC

ΔPop = −1.5 %
r² = 0.19
p = .0316

San Jose CBC

ΔPop = −1.7 %
r² = 0.29
p = .0001

Mt. Hamilton CBC

BIRDS/PARTY−HOUR

YEAR

CO 65 (39%)

PR 50 (30%)

PO 21 (13%)

Atlas (1987−1993), n = 90

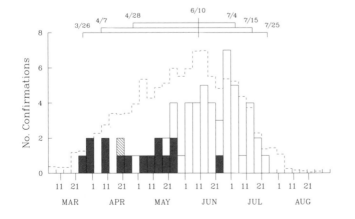

3/26 4/7 4/28 6/10 7/4 7/15 7/25

No. Confirmations

MAR APR MAY JUN JUL AUG

363

Northern Mockingbird
Mimus polyglottos

A varied song, borrowing phrases from various other bird species and emanating from a suburban yard or treetop, announces the presence of a territorial Northern Mockingbird. This conspicuous vocal mimic breeds throughout the United States and most of Mexico, and is resident in most of its range (Derrickson and Breitwisch 1992). Although mockingbird populations have undergone widespread declines in the eastern United States in recent decades, western and northern populations have increased and expanded considerably (Robbins et al. 1986). The Northern Mockingbird currently breeds throughout much of central and southern California, but only scattered populations exist in the extreme northern part of the state, and the species is entirely absent from high elevations (Small 1994). Mockingbirds are present year-round in Santa Clara County, and are most common in developed areas in the Santa Clara Valley.

The Northern Mockingbird was first recorded in Santa Clara County "in the San Jose-Gilroy area" in 1886 (Arnold 1935). Van Denburgh (1899b) listed only one record, of a bird shot at Stanford on 17 Feb 1893. Another was noted at Stanford on 20 Dec 1904 (Fisher 1905). As late as 1911, the mockingbird's breeding range in California was limited to the southern half of the state, and all records north or west of the central San Joaquin Valley were in winter (Arnold 1935). The species' breeding range gradually expanded northward in response to the cultivation of trees and shrubs, but by the mid-1920s it was still known in the San Francisco Bay area strictly as a rare winter visitor (Grinnell and Wythe 1927). But on 12 May 1928, W. E. Unglish found the county's first nest, 2 miles east of Gilroy (Arnold 1935). Nesting was recorded in San Jose the following year (*Wren-Tit 1(3)* 1929), and by the mid-1930s the Northern Mockingbird was recorded widely in the San Francisco Bay area (Arnold 1935). This population increase continued in the South Bay (*Audubon 44*:13–14 1942, Sibley 1952, *Audubon Field Notes 13*:397–98 1959), and remained evident in the county even into the mid-1960s (*Audubon Field Notes 19*:414 1965). But numbers have leveled off in the last half century, as indicated by analysis of the Palo Alto and San Jose CBC data, which shows a decline of 1.2% a year in the Palo Alto count circle and 1.8% a year in the San Jose circle.

Atlasers found Northern Mockingbirds in 50% of the county's atlas blocks and confirmed breeding in 43% of all blocks. They were present throughout the Santa Clara Valley, in the western foothills of the Diablo Range, and in the more highly developed portions of the Santa Cruz Mountains. Mockingbirds showed a strong affinity for developed areas, reaching their highest densities in well-vegetated suburban neighborhoods in the northern Santa Clara Valley. In these areas, mockingbirds were often found singing from wires, television antennas, and rooftops, even at night. They used dense, low ornamental vegetation both for nesting and as a food source. In fact, the provision of fruits and nesting sites by ornamental vegetation and orchards has long been recognized as an influential factor in the range expansion of this species (Arnold 1935, Grinnell and Miller 1944, Arnold 1980). Mockingbirds were also found around ranch houses in some rural areas and, to some extent, even in poorly vegetated residential areas, parks, and industrial sites, indicating that the species' habitat requirements are met by a variety of land-use types.

This species was almost entirely absent as a breeder from the interior of the Diablo Range (where it is an occasional winter visitor), and at higher elevations in the Santa Cruz Mountains. Why it is so abundant within most of its Santa Clara County range yet virtually absent from adjacent regions is not entirely clear. For despite its obvious association with developed areas, the mockingbird was also found in low densities in riparian vegetation and chaparral several miles from human habitation, which argues that it is probably not confined to the Santa Clara Valley solely because of the scarcity of development elsewhere. And indeed, ostensibly suitable habitat was present around human habitations in a number of locations in the Diablo Range and the Santa Cruz Mountains where the species was not recorded in summer. There is another aspect to the puzzle: the Northern Mockingbird is known to have an affinity for lowland areas; it was not found above 400 feet during fieldwork for the Monterey County breeding bird atlas (Roberson 1993w), and it has seldom been found above 3,500 feet anywhere in California (Small 1994). In Santa Clara County, mockingbirds were confirmed breeding at elevations up to 1,700 feet, but 65% of the confirmations were below 200 feet. A lowland affinity or, conversely, an aversion to higher elevations may have influenced the species' distribution in the county, although the mechanism for this relationship is not known.

Northern Mockingbirds have a very protracted breeding period, raising several broods over the course of a breeding season (Derrickson and Breitwisch 1992). Atlasers found mockingbirds building nests as early as 28 Feb, and fledged young were seen as early as 19 Apr. Between late April and late July, there was a broad peak in breeding activity as pairs produced brood after brood of young. Later nesting is indicated by records of nest-building on 20 Jul, a nest with young on 4 Aug, and recently fledged young as late as 13 Sep. After the atlas period, a recently fledged bird was seen along lower Stevens Creek on the even later date of 30 Sep 1996 (pers. obs.).

Stephen C. Rottenborn

NORTHERN MOCKINGBIRD

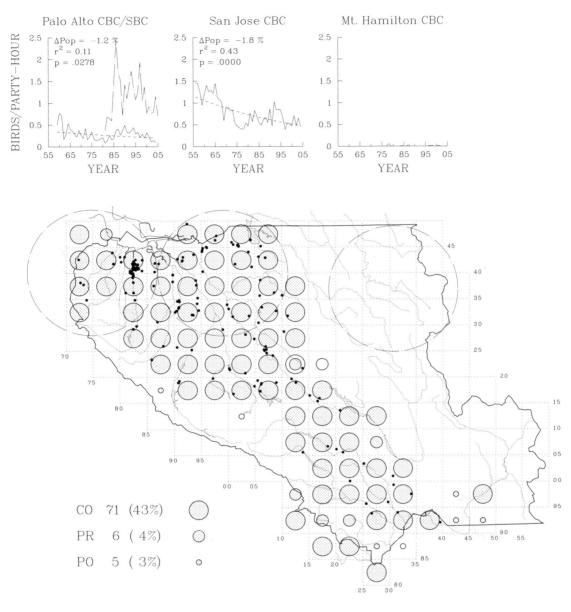

Palo Alto CBC/SBC

ΔPop = −1.2 %
r² = 0.11
p = .0278

San Jose CBC

ΔPop = −1.8 %
r² = 0.43
p = .0000

Mt. Hamilton CBC

BIRDS/PARTY-HOUR

YEAR

CO 71 (43%)
PR 6 (4%)
PO 5 (3%)

Atlas (1987−1993), n = 221

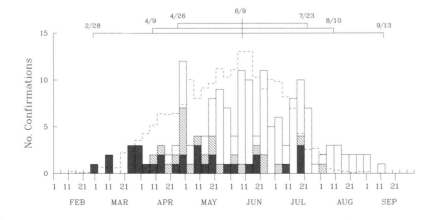

No. Confirmations

2/28   4/9   4/26   6/9   7/23   8/10   9/13

FEB   MAR   APR   MAY   JUN   JUL   AUG   SEP

365

California Thrasher
Toxostoma redivivum

Methodical thrashing in the debris beneath a chaparral thicket betrays the presence of a California Thrasher, which uses its long, curved bill to dig for food in leaf litter and shallow soil. This aptly named species resides entirely within California and northwestern Baja California, with only a single vagrant having been recorded outside this range, in southwestern Oregon (Cody 1998). The nominate race occupies the southern portion of the breeding range, extending north through the Coast Ranges to Monterey, San Benito, and Fresno Counties and along the western slope of the Sierra Nevada north to Mariposa County (Grinnell and Miller 1944, AOU 1957). Intergradation with the northern race *T. r. sonomae*, which breeds north to Humboldt, Trinity, and Siskiyou Counties, apparently occurs near the southern border of Santa Clara County, since our birds are considered *sonomae*. In Santa Clara County, the California Thrasher is a fairly common resident in chaparral, scrub, riparian thickets, and some well-vegetated suburban areas. It breeds throughout most of the Santa Cruz Mountains and Diablo Range, with smaller numbers on the Santa Clara Valley floor.

The distribution and abundance of the California Thrasher in most of its Santa Clara County range has likely changed little since the species was first reported in the county. Sclater (1857) wrote that this species had been collected by Thomas Bridges, sometime prior to his report, in "the Valley of San José." Cooper (1870), who found several nests with eggs in the Santa Clara Valley in May 1864, wrote that the California Thrasher was "common in all the valleys and bushy hillsides south of San Francisco, frequenting chiefly the dense 'chaparral,' or low thickets, which often cover the gravelly sides of valleys for miles." Although much of this chaparral, especially in the northern Santa Clara Valley, had been cleared by the turn of the twentieth century, the California Thrasher was still present in areas where suitable habitat remained. Grinnell and Wythe (1927) considered it a fairly common resident in brushy areas throughout the Bay area, a sentiment that Sibley (1952) echoed for the South Bay in particular. Continued habitat loss and fragmentation resulting from urban and agricultural development have likely displaced

thrashers from parts of the Santa Clara Valley over the past few decades. Analysis of the Palo Alto and San Jose CBC data since the mid-1950s shows declines of 1.6 % per year and 5.3% per year, respectively. On the Palo Alto SBC, the decline since the 1980s has been 4.1% per year. No change has been noted on the Mt. Hamilton CBC. Similar declines have been noted in urban areas elsewhere (Tintle 1993, Cody 1998), and the species has declined on most Breeding Bird Survey routes in the species' range since 1966 (Sauer et al. 2005).

During the atlas period, the California Thrasher was found to be an uncommon to fairly common breeder in many areas offering dense, scrubby vegetation, which provides cover from predators, suitable nesting sites, and leaf litter to support prey populations. Broad expanses of chaparral in the Santa Cruz Mountains and Diablo Range probably supported the highest densities of thrashers in the county. In these mountains, thrashers were also quite common in thickets of manzanita scrub, poison oak, and blackberry having few or no large trees, as well as in more extensive stands of mixed California sagebrush and sticky monkeyflower. They were also found, albeit uncommonly, in some open woodlands having suitable shrub cover, but they were not found in the interior of dense forest. On the southern Santa Clara Valley floor, these thrashers were present primarily in riparian habitats having dense stands of coyotebrush or thickets of blackberry or poison oak, although some were found in willow-dominated habitats with mostly herbaceous understory vegetation. California Thrashers were absent from much of the urban Santa Clara Valley during atlasing, and the few birds present on the floor of the northern reaches of the Valley were mostly confined to riparian corridors surrounded by relatively extensive open space embedded within the urban landscape. Nevertheless, thrashers were fairly common in some suburban areas having suitable ornamental shrubbery or remnant native vegetation, especially in foothill areas. This species was inexplicably absent from, or only sparsely distributed in, large regions of the western and southern Diablo Range that had ostensibly suitable habitat in drainages and on scrubby slopes. Thrashers were confirmed breeding at elevations ranging from 47 feet in Menlo Park to 3,400 feet in the Santa Cruz Mountains.

Most California Thrashers initiate nesting in February or March, as indicated by a 12 Feb bird carrying nest material in San Jose (WFVZ, *fide* Cody 1998). As a result, some breeding had already begun by the time atlasers took to the field in earnest, and the two earliest breeding confirmations were of birds carrying food for young on 30 and 31 Mar. Following the atlas period, a bird carrying nest material was seen on the earlier date of 15 Mar 2005 (Linda Sullivan, PADB). Records of occupied nests and nest-building spanned the broad period between 7 Apr (earlier nests were missed) and 11 Jul. Fledged young were observed as early as 26 Apr. Because this species typically raises two broods in a season (Bent 1948d), numerous records of recently fledged young and of adults carrying food were obtained through mid-July, one record as late as 9 Aug.

Stephen C. Rottenborn

CALIFORNIA THRASHER

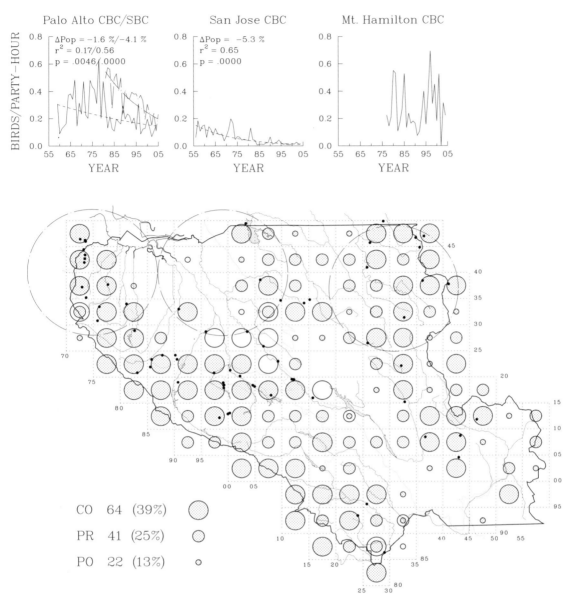

Palo Alto CBC/SBC

ΔPop = −1.6 %/−4.1 %
r² = 0.17/0.56
p = .0046/.0000

San Jose CBC

ΔPop = −5.3 %
r² = 0.65
p = .0000

Mt. Hamilton CBC

BIRDS/PARTY−HOUR

YEAR

CO   64 (39%)

PR   41 (25%)

PO   22 (13%)

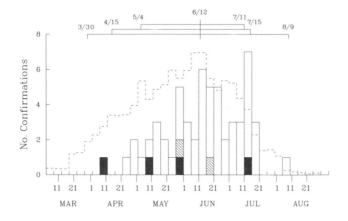

Atlas (1987−1993), n = 87

No. Confirmations

European Starling
Sturnus vulgaris

Able to exploit a variety of nesting sites and food sources, and to challenge all competitors for these provisions, the introduced European Starling is well adapted for Santa Clara County's human-altered landscapes. Following an introduction of 80–100 birds in New York City in 1890–91 (Bent 1950b, Lever 1987), this modest population grew and expanded rapidly. Currently, the starling's Nearctic range includes most of North America, from north-central Canada and Alaska to northern Mexico. This species breeds throughout most of California, and is absent only from very high altitudes and some desert regions (Small 1994). In Santa Clara County this abundant resident breeds most commonly in urban areas, but also nests in more rural areas throughout the county.

After spreading across the United States, populations of the European Starling reached California in January 1942, when a small flock was seen in Siskiyou County (Jewett 1942, Grinnell and Miller 1944). Nesting was first reported in the state in 1949 (Ball and Koehler 1959, *fide* DeHaven 1973). Wintering flocks quickly expanded in the northeastern part of the state and in the Sacramento Valley. But by 1952, the species had been recorded in the San Francisco Bay area solely as a rare winter visitor to Pt. Reyes (Sibley 1952, *Audubon Field Notes* 8:268 1954). Sibley's prediction that this starling would be "one of the most common resident species in the S. F. Bay region within a decade" was realized when its northern California populations surged in the mid-1950s (DeHaven 1973). In 1956, nonbreeding birds on Mt. Hamilton Road and in Palo Alto and Los Altos (*Avocet* 3:9-11 1956) furnished Santa Clara County with its first records of the species, and in 1963, three nests at Stanford provided the first published breeding record for Santa Clara County (*Audubon Field Notes* 17:483 1963). But that same reference stated, "In the San Jose area, where the species has been present for some time, the breeding population has increased several thousandfold since 1959," and Troetschler (1969) suspected breeding as early as 1958 in San Jose and 1960 in Palo Alto. Starling numbers on the San Jose and Palo Alto Christmas Bird Counts increased from the mid-1950s, when the first few birds were recorded, to the mid-1970s, when some counts exceeded 10,000 individuals. This increase was observed in California as a whole (DeHaven 1973). Starling numbers on our local counts then declined more than 50% over the next decade, but neither winter nor summer populations have changed significantly on the local CBCs and the Palo Alto SBC since the mid-1980s.

Atlasers found the European Starling to be a common to abundant breeder throughout most of the county, with records in 92% of all blocks and breeding confirmations in 81%. It was most abundant in urban and suburban areas, where cavities in buildings, bridges, light poles, and fan palm "skirts" provided numerous opportunities for nesting, allowing this species to reach remarkable concentrations. In more rural areas, starlings still nested in highest densities around artificial structures, but woodpecker holes were frequently used where they were available, and starlings bred fairly commonly in some portions of the Diablo Range and Santa Cruz Mountains remote from human activity. Starlings were absent from only a few blocks in these mountain ranges, where extensive chaparral or closed-canopy woodland limited the extent of this species' preferred open foraging areas. Most breeding confirmations were from lower elevations, corresponding with the most intensively human-altered areas, but large numbers were found breeding at elevations up to 3,000 feet, with breeding confirmed as high as 3,940 feet.

The European Starling begins breeding fairly early, allowing it to raise multiple broods (Cabe 1993). A total of 633 breeding confirmations, including 237 nests, afforded an accurate assessment of breeding phenology. There were numerous records of nest building and occupied nests in March, beginning with birds carrying nesting material as early as 2 Mar. Many records of nests with young or of adults carrying food were obtained from early April to mid-June. Likewise, fledged young were seen as early as 4 Apr, although most such records fell between early May and mid-June. Breeding activity fell off sharply in late June. Although occupied nests were found as late as 13 Jul, and adults were seen carrying food on 17 Jul, most starlings were by then in post-breeding flocks, and many Diablo Range birds had dispersed from breeding areas by late June (Michael M. Rogers, William G. Bousman, pers. comm.).

Because European Starlings generally do not excavate their own cavities and therefore often usurp the nests of other cavity nesters, this invader has likely had a detrimental impact on populations of some native species. The starling has been implicated in at least local declines in some native cavity-nesters, including the Acorn Woodpecker (*Am. Birds* 44:493 1990), Purple Martin (Roberson 1993x, Shuford 1993aa), bluebirds (Ehrlich et al. 1988), and others (Weitzel 1988, Cabe 1993). Surprisingly, several studies have found no significant impact on populations of native species (Troetschler 1976, *Am. Birds* 28:849 1974), and despite the starling's abundance and widespread distribution in North America, there have been no convincing studies linking starlings to significant declines in the continental breeding populations of any native species. Nevertheless, the possible effects of European Starlings on populations of native birds should be studied further.

Stephen C. Rottenborn

EUROPEAN STARLING

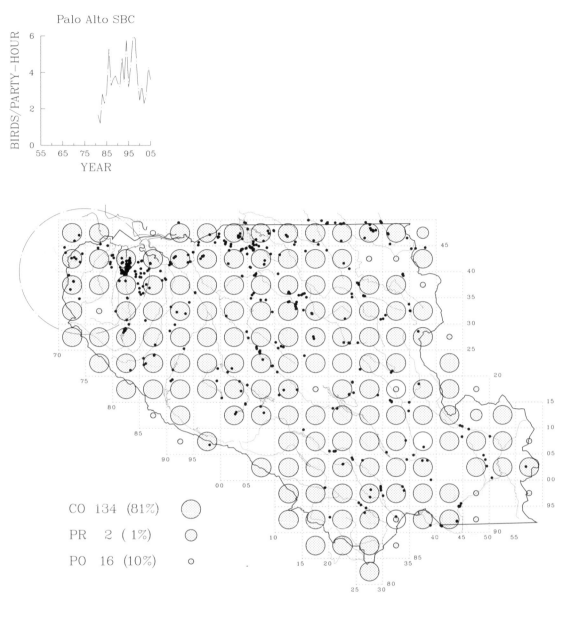

CO 134 (81%)

PR 2 (1%)

PO 16 (10%)

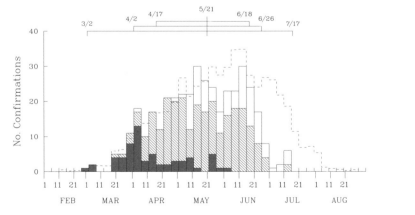

Atlas (1987–1993), n = 633

Cedar Waxwing
Bombycilla cedrorum

Feasting on ripening berries in the fall and winter, this frugivorous passerine typically leaves Santa Clara County for its northern breeding grounds by late May or early June. Cedar Waxwings breed across North America from the central Yukon to Newfoundland and south to northwestern California and Virginia (Witmer et al. 1997). In California, they nest regularly in Del Norte and Humboldt counties, with extralimital breeding on rare occasions in other portions of the state (Small 1994). Cedar Waxwings have long been common wintering birds in Santa Clara County, and some birds have been found casually in the summer months. A breeding record in 2002, however, added this species to the list of Santa Clara County breeding birds.

Early observers considered the Cedar Waxwing to be irregular and sometimes common on the central California coast during winter (Belding 1890, McGregor 1901). Grinnell's first California checklist (1902) categorized it as an irregular, common winter visitant, and he was unaware of any breeding in the state. Fisher (1902) judged it to be an irregular winter visitant. In his second checklist, Grinnell (1915) noted that this species summered "sparingly and locally" along the northwest coast, and that it had nested in Eureka, Humboldt County. Interestingly, he included a record of a fully grown juvenile at Hemet Lake in the San Jacinto Mountains, Riverside County, on 9 Aug 1908, and he thought that this might indicate local breeding in some of the higher ranges of southern California. Grinnell and Wythe (1927) considered the species a common late-winter visitant in the San Francisco Bay area and noted that it was more common east of the Bay, often in city parks or local orchards. Grinnell and Miller (1944) categorized the breeding population in the northwestern counties of California as sparse.

In the last 60 or 70 years, Cedar Waxwings have bred well south of their historical range, but in a sporadic and irregular manner. Eggs were collected in Chester Meadows, Plumas County, by H. P. Davis on 15 Jun 1940 (WFVZ #162767). An adult and three fledglings were found at Dana Point, Orange County, on 7 Jul 1965 (Garrett and Dunn 1981), the southernmost of the California records. Additional extralimital breeding records have subsequently been recorded in Alameda County in 1971 (*Am. Birds 25*:904 1971), in Napa County in 1973 (Glen Clifton *fide* Robin L. C. Leong), in Siskiyou County in 1977 (*Am. Birds 31*:1186 1977), in San Mateo County in 1984 and 2000 (Barry Sauppe *fide* Peter J. Metropulos; *N. Am. Birds 54*:421 2000), in Monterey County in 1987 and 1988 (*Am. Birds 41*:1485 1987, *42*:479 1988), in Santa Cruz County in 1988 (*Am. Birds 42*:479 1988), in Sierra County in 1996 (*Field Notes 50*:994 1996), in Contra Costa County in 2002 (*N. Am. Birds 56*:484 2002), and in Santa Clara County in 2002 (*N. Am. Birds 56*:484 2002), as discussed here.

Cedar Waxwings occur in variable numbers in Santa Clara County each winter. Unlike most other passerines, this species' fall and spring movements are also highly variable. In some years the first fall birds are not observed until mid-September, but in most years they arrive between 22 Aug and 6 Sep (county notebooks). In the spring in some years, the last birds depart in May, but in most years a few linger into June, with departure dates between 2 and 11 Jun. Prior to the breeding record discussed here, there were only five records of their occurring in the county between 12 Jun and 21 Aug. In 1985, a flock of four to eight birds was found in Palo Alto on 9-11 Aug (Paul L. Noble, David L. Suddjian, county notebooks). In 1990, a hatching-year waxwing (which may have been produced by locally breeding birds) was banded at the Coyote Creek Riparian Station on 3 Aug (Bruce Katano, county notebooks). Grinnell and Miller (1944) noted that some birds migrate in juvenal plumage, but Witmer et al. (1997) state that hatching-year birds tend to migrate a month later than the adults. In 1991, five waxwings were seen along Coyote Creek below Highway 237 on 18 Aug (Peter J. Metropulos, county notebooks), and in 1995 a single bird was on Coyote Creek below Berryessa Road on 22 Jun (Stephen C. Rottenborn, county notebooks). The fifth record saw four birds in Sunnyvale on 1 Jul 2001 (Ginger Langdon-Lassagne, county notebooks).

Evidence of breeding by Cedar Waxwings in Santa Clara County was finally obtained on 16 Jun 2002, when two adults were seen with two fledglings in Palo Alto (David L. Suddjian, county notebooks). The fledglings were in fresh juvenal plumage and still retained some bits of down on their auriculars. They begged from the adults, which fed them sweet bracts of pineapple guava flowers. They were seen foraging at this one location for about 20 minutes. They had not been noted there previously in the spring, nor were they observed there again. Adults feed fledged young for 6 to 10 days (Witmer et al. 1997), the incubation period is about 12 days, and the nestling period is 16 days, suggesting that eggs were first laid about 11 May. There are few egg dates prior to June north of California (Witmer et al. 1997, Bent 1950a), although eggs have been collected in Eureka, Humboldt County, as early as 1 May (MVZ #13405). The timing of most extralimital California records agrees with the phenology reported by Witmer et al. (1997), but the extralimital record mentioned previously for Contra Costa County was based on an adult feeding a fledgling on the even earlier date of 4 Jun 2002.

William G. Bousman

CEDAR WAXWING

Palo Alto SBC

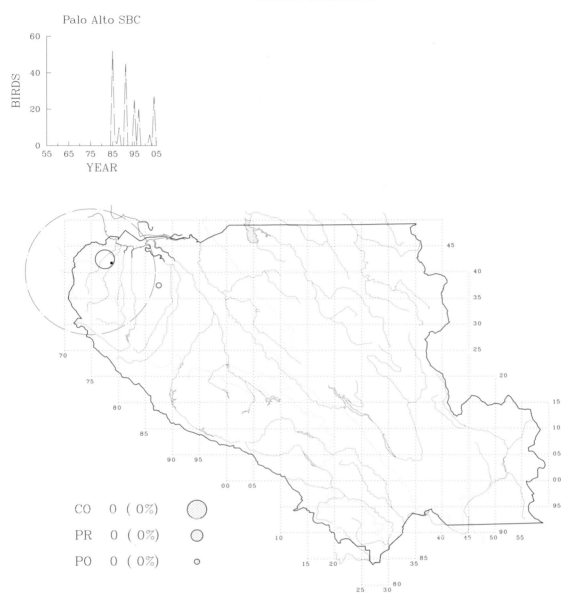

CO 0 (0%)

PR 0 (0%)

PO 0 (0%)

Postatlas (1994–2005), n = 1

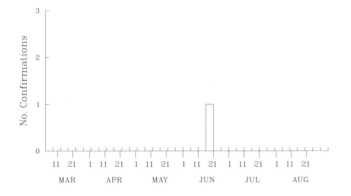

Phainopepla
Phainopepla nitens

The Phainopepla is the only member of the silky-flycatcher family that breeds north of the Mexican border. Phainopeplas nest from the southwestern United States south into Mexico to Oaxaca (Chu and Walsberg 1999). In California, Phainopeplas are generally found in the southern half of the state, breeding in the southeastern deserts in late winter and in coastal and Central Valley areas in summer (Small 1994). Phainopeplas are rare residents in the interior of the Diablo Range, and birds are found infrequently farther west in the foothills on both sides of the Santa Clara Valley.

At the close of the nineteenth century, Phainopeplas were considered casual winter visitors to Santa Clara County. Ernest Adams saw one in the foothills east of San Jose on 28 Oct 1898, and Rollo H. Beck found one in an orchard near Berryessa in November 1899 (Barlow 1900b). In the 1920s and 1930s, the Audubon Association of the Pacific led regular spring field trips to Arroyo Mocho in Alameda County and often reported Phainopeplas in their publication the *Gull*. Grinnell and Wythe (1927) considered the species rare and local in the San Francisco Bay region. In the 1930s, Henry E. Parmenter and his wife saw a Phainopepla east of Saratoga on 21 Jun 1933 (*Gull 15(8)* 1933) and two in Palo Alto on 7 Jun 1934 (*Gull 16(7)* 1934). Sibley (1952) described the species as an uncommon resident in the eastern part of the South Bay area, but cited no breeding records from Santa Clara County. Breeding in the county was not discovered until the unusual invasion years of 1984 and 1985. Virginia Whipple observed a pair in Los Altos Hills in late May 1984, and by early August, there were four birds there, suggesting nesting (county notebooks). The first definite county breeding was confirmed when John Mariani found a female feeding nestlings at the edge of the Santa Teresa Hills on 8 Jul 1985 (*Am. Birds 39*:960 1985). That same summer, a pair nested at the Jasper Ridge Biological Preserve, giving San Mateo County its first breeding record (*Am. Birds 42*:134 1988).

Atlasers found Phainopeplas breeding primarily at the eastern edge of Santa Clara County. Breeding confirmations extended from the Colorado Creek drainage, a few kilometers south of the Alameda County line, southeast to Pacheco Pass. An adult feeding young along Isabel Creek just north of the San Antonio Valley Road bridge was the farthest west of these interior Diablo Range records. Breeding elevations in the interior of the Diablo Range during the atlas period ranged from 1,760 feet, along the North Fork of Pacheco Creek, to 2,200 feet, along Isabel Creek. A postatlas nest northwest of Eylar Mountain in the Alameda County portion of an edge block was at 3,300 feet (Michael M. Rogers, PADB).

Most of the breeding observations in the Diablo Range were in blue oak-foothill pine woodlands with a grassland understory. Sometimes, the understory had some shrub cover and included areas of chaparral. The woodlands used by Phainopeplas were often adjacent to wide expanses of grasslands. Nests, when found, were generally in oaks, typically blue oaks, and were sometimes concealed in clumps of western dwarf mistletoe. During the atlas period, the only breeding confirmation away from the interior of the Diablo Range was from Alum Rock Park, on southwest-facing slopes of Eagle Rock in 1990. Two pairs were also seen there 16-20 Jun 1988 (L. Richard Mewaldt, county notebooks). Subsequent to the atlas period, pairs of Phainopeplas were again found there on 9-15 Jun 2002 (Eric Feuss, Michael M. Rogers, county notebooks), and were observed carrying food for young 3-26 Jun 2004 (Robert W. Reiling, Frank Vanslager, county notebooks).

The dates of breeding confirmations during the atlas period ranged from 25 May, when a Phainopepla was seen carrying nesting material near Mississippi Creek, to 20 Jul, when fledged young were seen near Pacheco Pass. Following the atlas period, breeding evidence was recorded two months earlier, on 16 Mar 1996, when nest construction was observed at two separate locations in San Antonio Valley (Michael J. Mammoser, county notebooks). Young being fed in the southern Diablo Range on 21 Jul 2002 (James Yurchenco, Amy Lauterbach, PADB) provided a breeding confirmation slightly later than those obtained during the atlas period.

Phainopeplas show a curious bimodal breeding cycle in the center of their range in Sonora, Arizona, and southern California (Chu and Walsberg 1999). From early February to early April, they nest in desert areas, whereas from late April to early June, they nest in woodland habitats well away from the deserts. What is unclear is whether this bimodal breeding represents different populations or double-brooding by a single population (Chu and Walsberg 1999). It is also unclear whether Phainopeplas follow this bimodal cycle at the edges of their range (Chu and Walsberg 1999). In Santa Clara County, on the basis of records in the county notebooks, it appears that Phainopeplas in the interior of the Diablo Range are resident, the birds present throughout the year. But the majority of records at the edge of the Santa Clara Valley are from late May to late August, and in this sense match the second breeding cycle observed in the species' core range. Whether the Phainopeplas breeding in Santa Clara County constitute more than one population is unclear.

William G. Bousman

PHAINOPEPLA

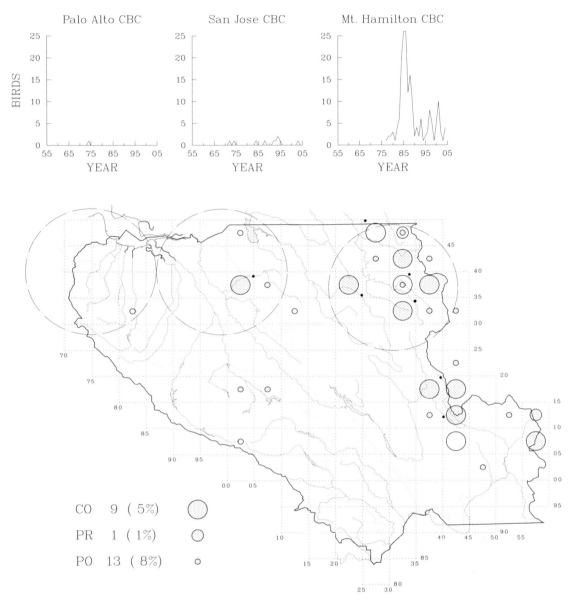

Palo Alto CBC

San Jose CBC

Mt. Hamilton CBC

CO   9 (5%)

PR   1 (1%)

PO 13 (8%)

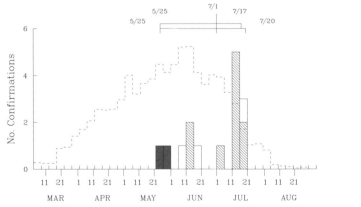

Atlas (1987–1993), n = 15

373

Orange-crowned Warbler
Vermivora celata

In late February, the Orange-crowned Warbler's distinctive, if somewhat colorless, trill is the harbinger of spring in Santa Clara County's chaparral- and shrub-covered hillsides. This warbler breeds from western Alaska across Canada to southeastern Labrador, and south in the western United States to northwestern Baja California (Sogge et al. 1994). In the east it breeds only as far south as the prairie provinces, central Ontario, and central Quebec. In the west it is found widely where there is suitable habitat, but it is absent as a breeder from the deserts and interior plateaus. Four subspecies have been described, three occurring in California (Sogge et al. 1994). Within the state, *orestera* breeds in mountain ranges adjacent to the Great Basin and on the eastern slopes of the Sierra Nevada, *lutescens* breeds west of the Cascades-Sierra axis from the Oregon border to southern California (including Santa Clara County), and *sordida* nests on the Channel Islands and portions of the nearby mainland (Grinnell and Miller 1944, Small 1994). The Orange-crowned Warbler is a common summer resident throughout most of the Santa Clara County, although it is absent as a breeder on the valley floor. It is a somewhat rare winter resident, though often then found in flowering non-native vegetation on the valley floor.

The status of the Orange-crowned Warbler appears to have changed little since the time of the earliest observers. Price (1898f) listed it as a summer resident near Stanford in brushy thickets. Van Denburgh (1899b) recorded it as a regular nesting species, its nestlings found by late April. Fisher (1902) described it as a summer visitant to the chaparral slopes of the Santa Cruz Mountains. Grinnell and Wythe (1927) referred to it as a common summer visitant in the Bay area, and described it as "most plentiful on sparsely wooded canyon sides, or slopes dotted with heavy chaparral." Sibley (1952) also judged the Orange-crowned Warbler to be a common summer resident in the South Bay.

Atlasers found Orange-crowned Warblers breeding widely in the county. Confirmed breeding evidence was obtained in 83 county blocks (50%) and, including probable and possible evidence, breeding records were obtained in 128 blocks (77%). Birds nested throughout the Santa Cruz Mountains and the Diablo Range, but were absent from the valley floor. Confirmed breeding was observed from an elevation of 55 feet, southwest of the southern Santa Cruz Mountains, to 3,200 feet, in the Sierra Azul. Following the atlas period, breeding was confirmed at an elevation of 3,560 feet on the northeastern side of Mt. Boardman (Michael M. Rogers, pers. comm.). Ninety percent of all breeding confirmations were at elevations above 400 feet. In general, Orange-crowned Warblers were found nesting on steep slopes with a thick, tangled shrub understory and some larger shrubs or trees, i.e., habitats that were heterogeneous in structure and offered sufficient light and moisture to allow a thick understory to develop. More specifically, they were found in mixed woodlands of coast live oak, California bay, and California buckeye with a shrub undergrowth of tangled vines, poison oak, and ferns. Orange-crowns were also found on chaparral-covered slopes where small trees and other shrubs, such as scrub oak, were growing within the dense chaparral. Nesting Orange-crowned Warblers were not found on alluvial soils within the flatland boundary, even where the plant associations appeared similar to those that they used on nearby hillsides. This ground-nesting species tends to nest on high-gradient slopes, often where erosion has cut steep banks (Sogge et al. 1994), a habitat rarely found in flatland areas.

The Orange-crowned Warbler is one of the earliest arriving breeders in Santa Clara County, the first males arriving on breeding territories between 22 Feb and 16 Mar (median 2 Mar, county notebooks). The earliest nesting evidence obtained during the atlas period was of adults carrying nest material on 15 Mar. This warbler normally raises a single brood (Sogge et al. 1994), and dispersing juveniles are frequently seen by late May. Nesting records shown in the phenology graphic for June or July are probably the result of renesting attempts. The latest breeding evidence observed was an adult feeding young on 28 Jul.

Orange-crowned Warblers are readily detectable by their song when on their breeding territories, but as singing decreases during the spring the departure of most birds goes unnoticed. In consequence, the departure dates of this warbler are poorly known throughout its range (Sogge et al. 1994). Many birds are captured along lower Coyote Creek at the San Francisco Bay Bird Observatory's banding station, which is well away from breeding areas. Whereas first spring arrivals are found on local breeding territories in early March, the primary spring movement of birds along Coyote Creek is from late March to the first week in May. In the fall, too, there is a clear passage of birds there, from the first of September to the middle of October, and these are likely birds from northerly populations. Dispersing young of the year are captured in small numbers throughout the summer at Coyote Creek, but few adults are captured. Elsewhere in California, this species is known for significant upslope movements following breeding (Gaines 1988, Roberson 1993bb, Small 1994, Steele and McCormick 1995), but in Santa Clara County the dispersal of breeding orange-crowns remains a puzzle.

William G. Bousman

ORANGE-CROWNED WARBLER

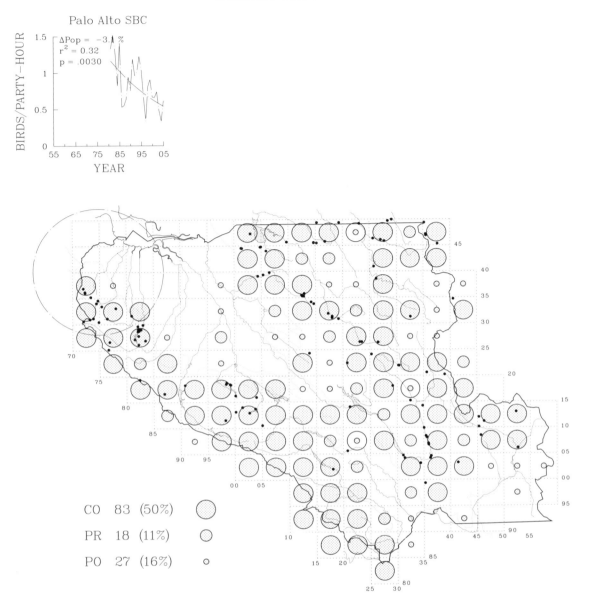

Palo Alto SBC

ΔPop = −3.1 %
r^2 = 0.32
p = .0030

BIRDS/PARTY−HOUR

YEAR

CO 83 (50%)

PR 18 (11%)

PO 27 (16%)

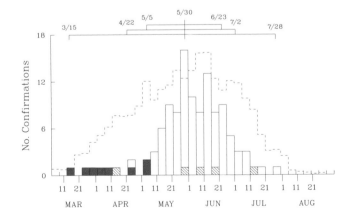

Atlas (1987−1993), n = 160

No. Confirmations

3/15   4/22   5/5   5/30   6/23 7/2   7/28

MAR   APR   MAY   JUN   JUL   AUG

375

Yellow Warbler
Dendroica petechia

The Yellow Warbler, one of North America's most abundant and widespread parulids, is declining in California, at the arid edge of its continental breeding range. Yellow Warbler taxonomy is complex and includes both migratory and sedentary groups within the Americas. The migratory *aestiva* group breeds from Alaska, across Canada to Newfoundland, and thence south on the west coast to Baja California, in the mountain states into central Mexico, and in the east to Georgia and Alabama (AOU 1998). Three subspecies breed in California: *brewsteri* throughout most of northern California and south into Baja California, *morcomi*, the interior subspecies, east of the Sierra Nevada in the Owens Valley, and a few *sonorana* still along the Colorado River (Lowther et al. 1999). Although a common fall migrant, the Yellow Warbler is an uncommon breeding bird in Santa Clara County, where it is found locally in riparian habitats.

Early observers considered Yellow Warblers to be common-to-abundant summer residents in the Santa Clara Valley (Barlow 1893c, Price 1898f, Van Denburgh 1899b, Fisher 1902). These warblers were judged particularly common along streams on the valley floor, but were also found in yards and gardens (Barlow 1893c). Grinnell and Wythe (1927) also noted that the Yellow Warbler was a common summer resident in the Bay region and reported that although it was most common in riparian areas, it was also found in orchards, city parks, and gardens. This warbler's status appeared largely unchanged by the mid-twentieth century, Sibley (1952) judging it to be a common summer resident. Just outside the county, at Stanford University's Jasper Ridge Biological Reserve, the species was still considered common in the early 1960s, when 12 breeding pairs were found (Row 1960), and in the early 1970s, when 20 pairs were counted (*Am. Birds* 25:797–98 1971). A recent decline has been observed, however, an analysis of the Palo Alto SBC showing a reduction of 17% a year since 1981. At Jasper Ridge only one pair nested in 1996 (Stephen C. Rottenborn, pers. comm.). This trend appears to be widespread on the California central coast, with declines also noted in Monterey and Alameda counties (*Am. Birds* 46:1175 1992, Roberson 1993cc, *Field Notes* 49:978 1995).

Atlasers confirmed breeding by Yellow Warblers in 19% of the atlas blocks, which indicates that this is still a widespread species within the county, despite the decline in numbers noted within the Palo Alto count circle. Atlasers found this warbler breeding in riparian habitats, either along foothill streams in the Santa Cruz Mountains, in remnant riparian stretches on the valley floor, or, in a few cases, along streams at higher elevations in the Diablo Range. In the Santa Cruz Mountains, Yellow Warblers were found along foothill streams supporting willow, white alder, and bigleaf maple, with a thick shrub understory. These streams were often found within more mesic coniferous and broadleaved evergreen forests of Douglas fir, coast redwood, and live oaks. On the valley floor, Yellow Warblers were found along riparian corridors, often with an overstory of mature cottonwoods and sycamores, a midstory of willow and box elder, and a substantial shrub understory of vines, blackberries, and forbs. Sections of these creeks, however, where the understory vegetation was reduced because of grazing or urban development, or where the larger trees had been removed, were generally not used by this species. Yellow Warblers were scarce in the Diablo Range, where riparian zones are often limited or discontinuous, because of either the greater aridity there or the consequences of grazing. The riparian areas used there were protected from grazing by either fencing or steep terrain.

Yellow Warblers normally arrive on their breeding ground by the second week in April, and many are found singing on territory by the end of the month. The earliest breeding confirmations obtained during the atlas were of nest building and the carrying of nest material on 30 Apr. Following the atlas period a bird was observed on a nest as early as 26 Apr 1998 (Stephen C. Rottenborn, pers. comm.). Grinnell and Wythe (1927) cited an egg date of 11 May, from Palo Alto, as the earliest in the Bay area. Barlow (1893c), however, described a set of eggs he collected on 5 Apr 1893, a remarkably early date. During the atlas period, fledged young were found as late as 24 Jul. Subsequent to the atlas work, adults were observed feeding young slightly later, on 27 Jul 1997 (Stephen C. Rottenborn, pers. comm.).

In the western United States, 95% of riparian habitats have been lost, altered, or degraded by human-induced change (Ohmart 1994), and it is likely that local habitat losses have severely impacted the Yellow Warbler's population in Santa Clara County. To judge from atlas records, this warbler is frequently parasitized by Brown-headed Cowbirds in Santa Clara County, and it is likely that nest parasitism has significantly contributed to the species' decline. Careful management of a riparian area in Arizona, to allow for the full development of both trees in the overstory as well as a dense understory, has been remarkably successful in increasing the local population of this species (Ohmart 1994). Similar increases have also been obtained through cowbird control programs in Riverside County in California (Gallagher 1997a). Whether similar management efforts will be required in Santa Clara County, if we are to avoid the extirpation of this beautiful warbler, is not yet known.

William G. Bousman

YELLOW WARBLER

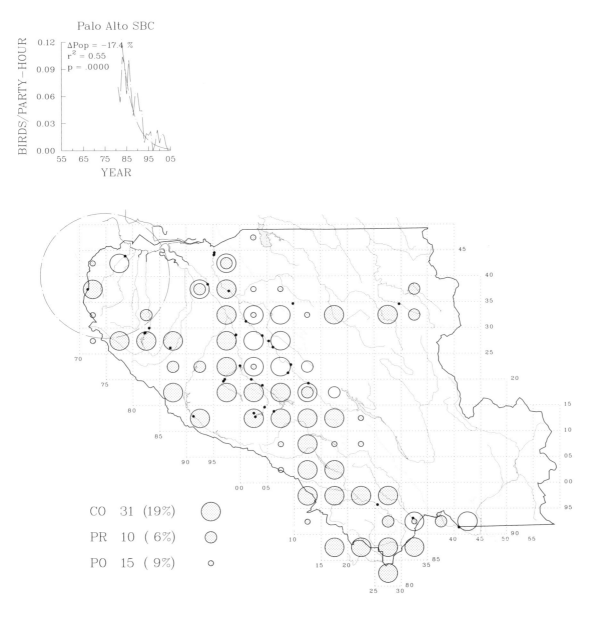

Palo Alto SBC

ΔPop = −17.4 %
r^2 = 0.55
p = .0000

BIRDS/PARTY−HOUR

YEAR

CO   31 (19%)
PR   10 (6%)
PO   15 (9%)

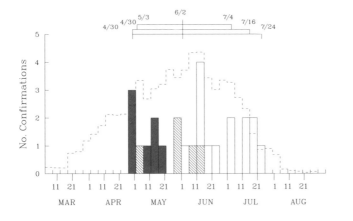

Atlas (1987−1993), n = 36

No. Confirmations

MAR   APR   MAY   JUN   JUL   AUG

Yellow-rumped Warbler
Dendroica coronata

Although it is our most abundant wintering warbler, the Yellow-rumped Warbler is a scarce breeding bird in Santa Clara County. Its five recognized subspecies fall into two groups (Hunt and Flaspohler 1998). The *coronata* group, formerly known as the Myrtle Warbler, breeds from Alaska across Canada to Newfoundland and south to Alberta and New England, and in the Appalachians south to West Virginia. The *auduboni* group, formerly the Audubon's Warbler, breeds from central British Columbia south in the western mountains to California and Arizona, with disjunct resident populations in the highlands of Mexico and Guatemala. Breeding Yellow-rumped Warblers, all of the *D. c. auduboni* subspecies, are found in coniferous forests in the Transition Life Zone and higher in California's mountain ranges (Small 1994). The Yellow-rumped Warbler is an abundant migrant and winter resident at lower elevations in Santa Clara County, *D. c. auduboni* being significantly more common than members of the *coronata* group. In summer, *D. c. auduboni* is a rare breeder in the coniferous forests of the Santa Cruz Mountains and a casual and very rare summer breeder in the Diablo Range.

Yellow-rumped Warblers were considered abundant wintering birds here by early observers, but these observers did not record the presence of breeding birds in the coastal mountains (Belding 1890, Price 1898f, Van Denburgh 1899b, McGregor 1901, Fisher 1902). Joseph Mailliard (1908) found multiple yellow-rumps near Ft. Ross, Sonoma County, in May 1908 and believed that they were breeding at that location. Grinnell and Wythe (1927) considered Mailliard's observation as the only evidence of possible breeding in the Bay area. Harold W. Clark (1930) considered yellow-rumps to be abundant residents on Howell Mountain, Napa County, but did not record his evidence. In that same year, on 22 Jun, Daniel Axlerod observed both adults and young birds at Lokoya, Napa County (H. W. Grinnell 1930b). Proof of breeding in the Bay area was not obtained, however, until Emerson A. Stoner and J. Duncan Graham found a nest with five nestlings about 2 miles north of Cordelia, Solano County, on 28 May 1938 (Stoner 1938). The first nesting record in Santa Clara County consisted of a pair feeding dependent fledglings at Aldercroft Heights on 27 May 1950 (Emily D. Smith, *Audubon Field Notes* 4:259 1950). Shuford (1993cc) has suggested that these initial breeding records were the result of increased ornithological coverage rather than a range expansion, which is probably correct, although the steady increase of second-growth coniferous forests following the logging at the end of the nineteenth century may have enhanced habitats for this species in the Coast Ranges.

The distribution of breeding Yellow-rumped Warblers in the Santa Cruz Mountains during the atlas period was somewhat patchy. Breeding elevations ranged from 1,920 to 3,200 feet, with seven of eight breeding records occurring above 2,500 feet. Along the Santa Cruz Mountains crest, from the intersection of Page Mill Road and Skyline Boulevard to about 3 km southeast of Castle Rock State Park, yellow-rumps used a mixed coniferous-broadleaved evergreen forest dominated by mature Douglas firs, with extensive areas of canyon live oak. Farther southeast, from Barrett Canyon on the northwest side of Loma Prieta southeast to Croy Ridge, nesting birds were found in areas along the crest where stands of mature knobcone pine are mixed with manzanita and other chaparral. Following the atlas period, nesting birds were also found near Mt. Madonna, where they used a different habitat of mixed redwood and tan oak forests between 1,600 and 2,100 feet (David L. Suddjian, pers. comm.). Yellow-rumps also used each of these habitats in Santa Cruz County southwest of the crest, but nesting yellow-rumps are missing from large areas of apparently suitable habitat in that county (David L. Suddjian, pers. comm.).

In the Diablo Range, the only Yellow-rumped Warblers found during the atlas period were on Mt. Hamilton, but no confirmation of breeding was obtained there. Previously, however, breeding was observed on Mt. Hamilton in 1981 and 1982 (*Am. Birds* 35:976 1981, 36:1014 1982). Following the atlas period, a singing bird was found in Coulter pines northwest of Mt. Day on 8 Jun 1996. This record is about 4 km south of where an adult yellow-rump was seen feeding fledglings in Coulter pines in Alameda County on 16 Jul 1994 (both Michael M. Rogers, pers. comm.). No yellow-rumps were found in the ponderosa pine forests to the south, in Henry Coe State Park, during the atlas period, although Milton L. Seibert found two singing males there on 18 Jun 1951 (*Audubon Field Notes* 5:307 1951).

The earliest evidence of breeding was nest building observed in Castle Rock State Park on 7 May. Young birds were seen being fed as early as 28 May, and the latest evidence of nesting was of young being fed on 12 Jul on Croy Ridge. Following the atlas period, fledglings were seen near Mt. Madonna County Park on the later date of 23 Jul 2002 (David L. Suddjian, pers. comm.).

Yellow-rumped Warblers appear to be closely tied to the Transition Life Zone in Santa Clara County, and are rarely found breeding at lower elevations in the Upper Sonoran Life Zone. Nonetheless, a number of higher-elevation sites with mixed coniferous-broadleaved evergreen forests that appear suitable for this species are not occupied, at least not every year. In this sense, even the limited Transition Zone habitat in Santa Clara County is used only irregularly by this montane warbler.

William G. Bousman

YELLOW-RUMPED WARBLER

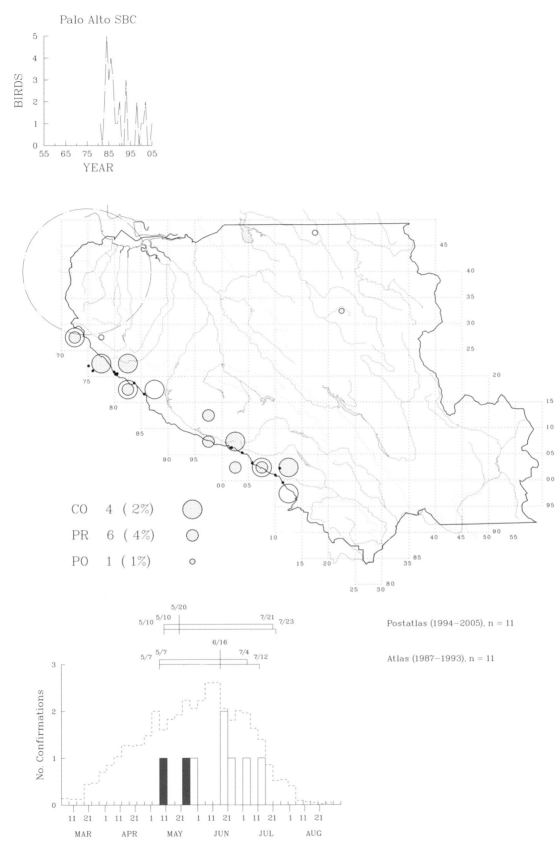

Palo Alto SBC

CO 4 (2%)
PR 6 (4%)
PO 1 (1%)

Postatlas (1994–2005), n = 11

Atlas (1987–1993), n = 11

5/20
5/10   7/21
5/10   7/23

6/16
5/7   7/4
5/7   7/12

Black-throated Gray Warbler
Dendroica nigrescens

This beautiful warbler, with its distinctive black, gray, and white plumage, has strong preferences for woodlands of live oak, black oak, and manzanita. The Black-throated Warbler breeds along the Pacific Coast from British Columbia south to Baja California, and interiorly from Idaho and Wyoming south to Arizona and New Mexico (Guzy and Lowther 1997). Two subspecies are recognized by some authorities, *nigrescens* breeding from northwestern California to British Columbia and *halseii* breeding to the south and east, including Santa Clara County (Guzy and Lowther 1997). The Black-throated Gray Warbler is an uncommon summer resident in Santa Clara County, although in its preferred plant associations it is sometimes locally fairly common.

Little information can be found on the distribution of the Black-throated Gray Warbler in the San Francisco Bay area in the late nineteenth and early twentieth centuries. In part, this may have been a result of limited accessibility to the habitats preferred by this species. Rollo H. Beck reported the species "back of Mt. Hamilton" in April 1899 (Barlow 1900b). Grinnell and Wythe (1927) described this species as an "irregular transient, and possible summer visitant locally." The best evidence of local breeding known to them was John Mailliard's observation of birds of both sexes above Fort Ross in Sonoma County in May 1908 (Mailliard 1908). Although Amelia S. Allen had found a number of Black-throated Gray Warbler nests near Boulder Creek, Santa Cruz County, as early as 1921 (*Gull 3(12)* Dec 1931), the first proof of nesting in the immediate San Francisco Bay area did not occur until Gurnie Wells collected a set of four eggs in the Rincon Valley of Sonoma County on 23 May 1923 (WFVZ #108790). That Grinnell and Wythe were unaware of this and subsequent egg sets collected by Wells (WFVZ egg sets) is not surprising, for there was limited information exchange between the egg collectors and the ornithology professionals in the first part of the twentieth century. Although Sibley (1952) stated that this warbler was a fairly common migrant and summer resident, he did not list any breeding records, other than Allen's from Santa Cruz County. The only Santa Clara County observations he noted were singing males found on Mt. Hamilton on 20 Jun 1948 and May 1950 by Milton L. Seibert and his own sighting of a singing male along Stevens Creek on 13 Apr 1951. There was thus no documentation of this warbler breeding in Santa Clara County until this atlas work.

Black-throated Gray Warblers were confirmed breeding in 26 of the county's blocks (16%) and probable or possible evidence was obtained in an additional 24 blocks (15%). Breeding birds were generally found at higher elevations, 88% of the breeding confirmations at 1,000 feet or above. Atlasers found breeding black-throated grays in mixed plant communities, generally with oaks and chaparral as the dominant components. In all cases these were more xeric habitats, away from shaded canyons or north-facing slopes. In the Santa Cruz Mountains, breeding birds were most often found in broadleaved evergreen forests and woodlands of canyon live oak, coast live oak, and California bay, intermixed with more open areas having chaparral and saplings. Components of the coniferous forest, such as Douglas fir, were occasionally a portion of these drier woodlands. In the Diablo Range, Black-throated Gray Warblers seemed to prefer drier and more open habitats. Birds were found regularly in black oak-manzanita associations with a mixture of canyon live oak, interior live oak, and occasional ponderosa pines. They were also found near drier stream courses in mixed woodland habitats.

In Santa Clara County, as discussed above, Black-throated Gray Warblers appeared to have specific habitat preferences, although these differed between the Santa Cruz Mountains and the Diablo Range. Specific habitat preferences have also been noted in other regional atlases. In Monterey County, this warbler preferred oak-pine woodlands, generally above 2,000 feet (Roberson 1993dd). Although canyon live oak was noted as a component of the Monterey habitat, foothill and ponderosa pine were also commonly found. In Marin County, Douglas fir was a key component within a mixed association of oaks and chaparral (Shuford 1993dd). To the north, in Sonoma County, the Black-throated Gray Warbler preferred either black oak-madrone woodlands, interior live oak-chaparral, or black oak-Douglas fir (Nelson 1995b). The common factor in all of these local habitat preferences is a mixed xeric forest or woodland at higher elevations. These locations are generally remote from water sources, and hence from human settlement. In part, this may explain the scarce historical knowledge of this small and lively harlequin.

Black-throated Gray Warblers arrive in Santa Clara County in early April, with a median arrival date of 5 Apr (county notebooks). The earliest evidence of nesting obtained during the atlas period was an adult carrying nest material on 13 Apr. Most confirmations, however, were of birds out of the nest, either adults feeding young (30%) or dependent fledglings (21%), and the phenology shown here accordingly emphasizes these later nesting stages. The latest breeding evidence obtained was a dependent fledgling observed on 10 Aug.

William G. Bousman

BLACK-THROATED GRAY WARBLER

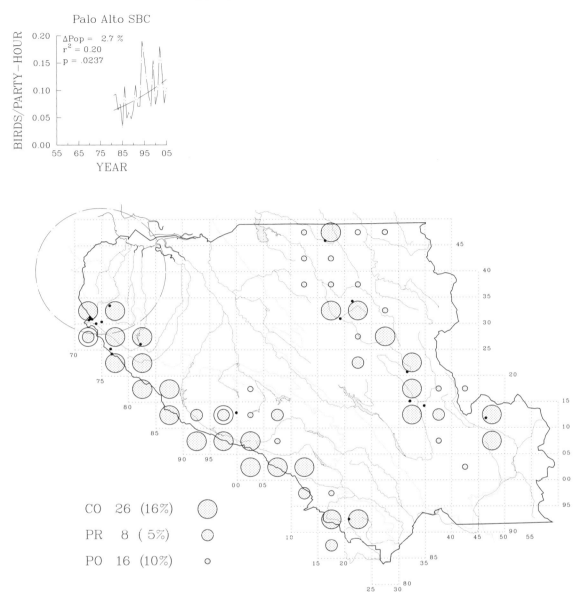

Palo Alto SBC

ΔPop = 2.7 %
r² = 0.20
p = .0237

BIRDS/PARTY–HOUR

YEAR

CO   26 (16%)
PR   8 (5%)
PO   16 (10%)

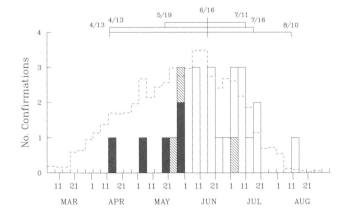

Atlas (1987–1993), n = 33

No. Confirmations

MAR   APR   MAY   JUN   JUL   AUG

Hermit Warbler
Dendroica occidentalis

At the southern edge of its breeding range, the Hermit Warbler is a fairly common summer resident within its preferred habitat in the Santa Cruz Mountains, but only occasionally nests within Santa Clara County. This warbler's limited breeding range extends from southern Washington south through Oregon to Santa Cruz County, California, in the Coast Ranges, and to Tulare County, California, in the Sierra Nevada (Small 1994, Pearson 1997). A very rare summer resident in Santa Clara County, the Hermit Warbler is more common as a spring migrant, and is also occasionally found in fall and winter.

Although Hermit Warblers were encountered at Stanford (Price 1898f) and Berryessa (Barlow 1900b) at the end of the nineteenth century, early observers considered this species to be a rare migrant (Fisher 1902). Similarly, Grinnell and Wythe (1927), in their summary of this warbler's distribution in the San Francisco Bay area, recorded the Hermit Warbler as an irregular migrant, and noted no instances of breeding. The first observation of nesting in the Santa Cruz Mountains was obtained on 22 Jun 1930, when Leslie Hawkins found two adults attending a nest with young, 60 feet up in a coast redwood on Ben Lomond Mountain, Santa Cruz County. Both adults brought food to the nest, and begging cries of the young could be heard. On 10 Jun 1933, Donald B. McLean collected an adult male about 3 miles north of the La Honda summit, San Mateo County (McLean 1936). This male was highly agitated, and other Hermit Warblers were seen nearby. Robert T. Orr (1942), in his extensive summer surveys of the Big Basin area of San Mateo and Santa Cruz counties in the 1930s, found a female on a ridge in the Waddell Creek drainage, Santa Cruz County, on 11 Jun 1935. On the basis of this record and McLean's observations, Orr judged this species to be a "possible resident in small numbers" in the Santa Cruz Mountains. On 29 Jul 1948, Adist Boylan saw three or four fledglings with a pair of adults near her home in Mt. Hermon, Santa Cruz County (Sibley 1952), strongly suggesting that nesting had occurred nearby at this location. Emily D. Smith found a female on a nest at Castle Rock State Park on 30

May 1954 (*Audubon Field Notes 8*:327 1954), but it is uncertain whether this record was in Santa Cruz or Santa Clara County.

Recent fieldwork suggests that the Hermit Warbler is a fairly common summer resident in its preferred habitat in portions of the Santa Cruz Mountains in Santa Cruz and San Mateo counties, generally in mature Douglas fir along the ridges of the western slopes (D.L.S., pers. obs.). Within these areas it is often patchily distributed and difficult to find. Although this species may have suffered some population reduction from logging in the nineteenth century, little change in the population is believed to have occurred during the past century.

Breeding of Hermit Warblers was confirmed in two blocks during the atlas period, and in two additional blocks following the atlasing. During the atlas period, an adult male was seen feeding begging fledglings on 16 Jun 1987 near Summit Meadows, off of Highway 9 and west of the crest of the Santa Cruz Mountains in Santa Cruz County. The second atlas record was a female feeding a newly fledged juvenile on 21 Jul 1993 northeast of the Santa Cruz Mountains crest along Charcoal Road, near Table Mountain in Santa Clara County. Following the atlas period, three additional confirmations were obtained, including breeding records in two new blocks. An adult was seen carrying food at Castle Rock State Park on 25 Jun 1995 (Michael J. Mammoser, pers. comm.), and two adults were seen carrying food about one and a half kilometers southeast of the park on 25 May 2002 (D.L.S., pers. obs.), both records along Skyline Boulevard on the Santa Clara County side. The third confirmation was along Highway 9, about 6 kilometers from Skyline Boulevard, in the Santa Cruz County portion of an edge block (D.L.S., pers. obs.). The habitats associated with these observations were generally a mixed coniferous-broadleaved evergreen forest where the dominant conifer was Douglas fir, occasionally mixed with coast redwood. This sort of mixed forest also included tan oaks, madrone, live oaks, and black oaks.

In the center of its abundance in Washington and Oregon, the Hermit Warbler is generally found in dry, upland sites dominated by Douglas fir (Pearson 1997). Within the Santa Cruz Mountains, this warbler is found in forest stands dominated by Douglas fir, coast redwood forest with a Douglas fir component, and ponderosa pine mixed with Douglas fir. Birds are most consistently found along the ridgelines or in mid-slope areas, and these are also areas where Douglas firs are most numerous. In contrast to Washington and Oregon, where Hermit Warblers reach their greatest densities in younger forests (Pearson 1997), the greatest numbers in the Santa Cruz Mountains are found in old-growth forests or in second-growth forests with a significant component of residual old-growth (D.L.S., pers. obs.).

The peak egg-laying period for this species is from the middle of May to the second week in June, and young are observed from early June to early July (Pearson 1997). California egg dates from Bent (1953) extend from 14 May to 25 June. The limited phenology data from the atlas and postatlas records are generally consistent with these dates.

William G. Bousman and David L. Suddjian

HERMIT WARBLER

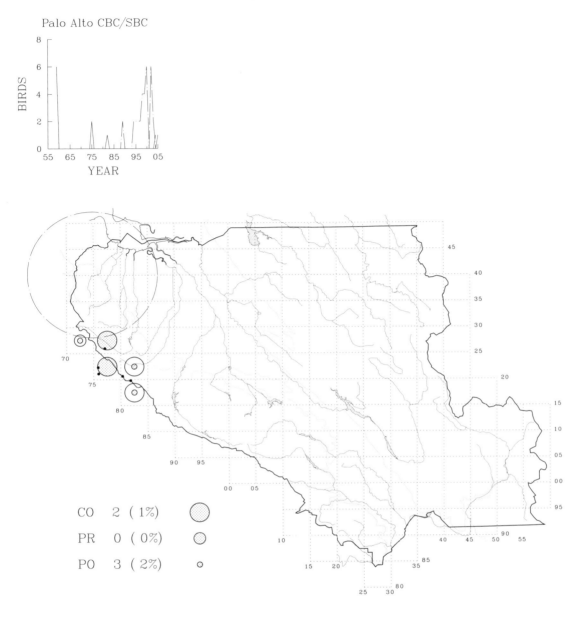

Palo Alto CBC/SBC

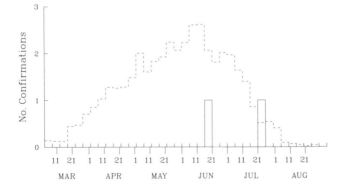

CO   2 (1%)
PR   0 (0%)
PO   3 (2%)

Atlas (1987–1993), n = 2

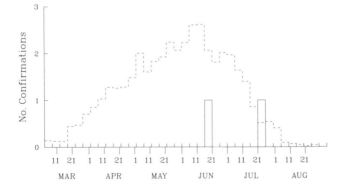

MacGillivray's Warbler
Oporornis tolmiei

A secretive skulker of dense tangles and underbrush, the MacGillivray's Warbler may go undetected until the male delivers his ringing song from a perch within the thicket. This species nests from May to August in low, dense, scrubby vegetation throughout much of western North America (Pitocchelli 1995). It breeds from Alaska and the Yukon south to the mountains of southern California, Arizona, and New Mexico, and it winters in Mexico and Central America (AOU 1998). In California, this species nests across the northern part of the state, extending south through the Sierra Nevada and along the outer Coast Ranges to Marin County, with more local breeding along the coast south to Monterey County (Zeiner et al. 1990, Roberson 1993ee, Small 1994). Although the MacGillivray's Warbler nests at scattered locations in the central and western Santa Cruz Mountains, it is rarer as a breeder in the eastern part of this mountain range. As a result, this species is not known to be nesting currently in Santa Clara County, although it nests within the atlas study area in immediately adjacent portions of Santa Cruz County. The MacGillivray's Warbler occurs as an uncommon to rare transient throughout Santa Clara County, from mid-April to early June and again from mid-August into October.

Although the MacGillivray's Warbler has probably never been more than an uncommon and local breeder in the Santa Cruz Mountains, it has nested in Santa Clara County. Price (1898f) considered it a summer resident around Stanford University, presumably in the adjacent Santa Cruz Mountains. In his summary of birds in Los Gatos and Palo Alto, Van Denburgh (1899b) mentioned a pair seen carrying food to an unseen nest "in the foothills west of Los Gatos" on 24 May 1890. Grinnell and Wythe (1927) stated that the species bred "sparingly" in the San Francisco Bay area, primarily near the coast. On 6 Jun 1931, Carriger and Unglish (1931) found a nest with eggs on the Santa Clara County side of the Pajaro River near Betabel and noted additional birds on the San Benito County side of the river. These authors noted that this location was "far south of the bird's general breeding range in the coast region."

Several breeding records were obtained from the eastern Santa Cruz Mountains in the 1950s, but it is unclear whether these records were from Santa Clara or Santa Cruz County. Emily D. Smith found nestlings "in the Santa Cruz Mts., approximately 7 miles south of Los Gatos" on 26 May 1950 (Sibley 1952) and observed a pair near the "summit of the Los Gatos-Santa Cruz Highway" on 26 May 1951 (*Bull. SCVAS* August 1951). Similarly, a male feeding young on 14 Jul 1952 was reported as being from the Santa Cruz Mountains (*Bull. SCVAS* July-August 1952), although the specific location was not given. Several territorial males were present near Castle Rock Ridge, which straddles the Santa Clara/Santa Cruz County line, in June of 1953 and 1955 (*Audubon Field Notes* 7:325 1953, 9:401 1955). Throughout the 1980s, multiple pairs were present along Langley Hill Road, in San Mateo County approximately 3 km from the county line, but breeding has not been confirmed or suspected in Santa Clara County in recent decades.

Atlas fieldwork by David L. Suddjian confirmed that the MacGillivray's Warbler continues to be a very rare breeder in the eastern Santa Cruz Mountains, with breeding-season records from three atlas blocks and only one breeding confirmation. All atlas records were from the Santa Cruz County portions of these blocks, at elevations of 1,800 feet or more. On 16 Jun 1987, two individuals were recorded in Castle Rock State Park. One of these birds was in Douglas fir forest, the other in mixed Douglas fir-black oak woodland, both sites having a moderately dense understory. On 20 Jul 1989, a female was observed feeding recently fledged young along Spanish Ranch Road, less than a kilometer and a half from the county line southwest of Loma Prieta. These birds were in a draw dominated by mixed Douglas fir, black oak, and California bay, with dense, shrubby understory vegetation. Such dense vegetation close to the ground seems to be a requisite of breeding MacGillivray's Warblers (Grinnell and Miller 1944, Pitocchelli 1995). Suddjian noted similar habitat at somewhat lower elevations in nearby portions of Santa Clara County, but he was not able to find MacGillivray's Warblers in these areas during the atlas period.

The factors underlying the distribution of this species in the Santa Cruz Mountains are not clearly understood. Although the MacGillivray's Warbler is a local breeder in San Mateo and Santa Cruz Counties, recent atlas work has found it breeding more widely and in more diverse habitats there than was previously recognized (*Field Notes* 50:994 1996, 51:925 1997). In addition to its breeding locations in mountain forests, it was recently found breeding in Santa Cruz County in coastal scrub and in riparian habitat along the Pajaro River, downstream from the location where Carriger and Unglish confirmed breeding in 1931 (David L. Suddjian, pers. comm.). An adult with fledglings in Portola Valley on 26 Jun 1996 constituted an unusual low-elevation breeding record on the eastern slope of the Santa Cruz Mountains, in San Mateo County (*Field Notes* 50:994 1996). Perhaps more intensive survey work in the moist, brushy woodlands of western Santa Clara County would find that the MacGillivray's Warbler does still nest somewhere in the county.

Stephen C. Rottenborn

MACGILLIVRAY'S WARBLER

Palo Alto SBC

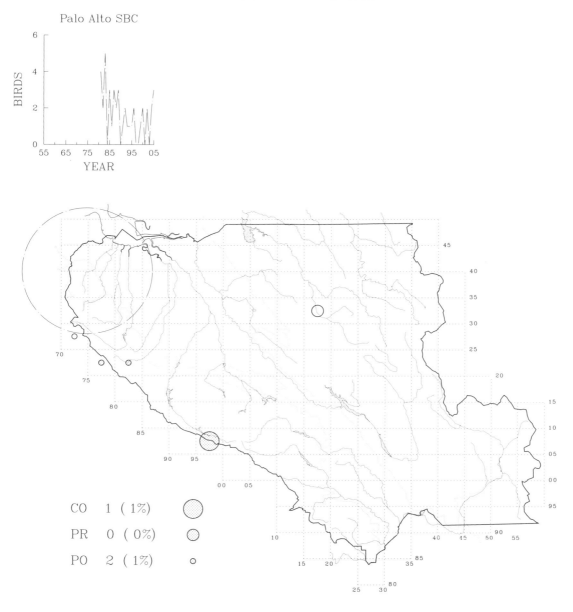

CO   1 (1%)
PR   0 (0%)
PO   2 (1%)

Atlas (1987–1993), n = 1

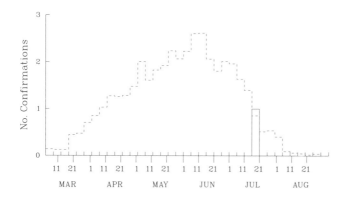

Common Yellowthroat
Geothlypis trichas

A persistent "whichity-whichity-whichity" from a bay-side brackish marsh in early spring indicates that a male Common Yellowthroat is once again establishing his breeding territory. This warbler breeds across North America from Alaska to Newfoundland and south through the United States into Mexico as far as Puebla and Veracruz (Guzy and Ritchison 1999). In this range, 13 subspecies have been recognized, three of which are found in California, and two of those in Santa Clara County (Grinnell and Miller 1944, Guzy and Ritchison 1999). The San Francisco or Salt Marsh Yellowthroat, *G. t. sinuosa*, is found only in the San Francisco Bay area, including Santa Clara County. The Western Yellowthroat, *G. t. arizela*, is found throughout most of northern California, excluding the Bay area, and is the subspecies found in our county in the Pajaro River drainage basin (Grinnell and Miller 1944). The Common Yellowthroat is a locally common resident in brackish and freshwater marshes in Santa Clara County. Wintering birds are found more widely, and are particularly abundant in the salt marshes along the edge of the Bay.

Early observers in the San Francisco Bay area regarded Common Yellowthroats as resident, and most considered them common (Price 1898f, Fisher 1902, Grinnell 1902). Van Denburgh (1899b) recorded that they nested in marshes south of San Jose. Grinnell and Wythe (1927) judged them to be common residents in the immediate vicinity of San Francisco Bay. Grinnell and Miller (1944) later described *sinuosa* as common in the Bay area, with breeding records in Santa Clara County from Palo Alto, Santa Clara, and San Jose. The nearest breeding location noted for *arizela* was from Watsonville, Santa Cruz County. Sibley (1952) considered *sinuosa* to be fairly common in South Bay marshes.

Concern over the status of the Common Yellowthroat in the San Francisco Bay area led to systematic censuses of its breeding populations in the 1970s and 1980s (Foster 1977, Hobson et al. 1986). Foster (1977), who censused birds in 1975, found them breeding within Santa Clara County only at the Palo Alto Baylands (two pairs) and along Coyote Creek near Alviso (14 pairs). Basing her views largely on habitat losses, she concluded that there had been a severe decline in the number of Common Yellowthroats since the end of the nineteenth century. Studies performed in 1985 (Hobson et al. 1986), however, showed significant increases throughout most of the Bay area. In Santa Clara County, the number of pairs increased to 118, compared with the 16 counted in 1975. And an analysis of the Palo Alto SBC data obtained since 1981 shows an increase in the number of Common Yellowthroats of 5.9% a year.

Atlasers found Common Yellowthroats breeding in three general areas during the atlas period. The greatest proportion of breeding records was obtained from brackish or freshwater marshes near the edge of the South Bay. The extensive stands of bulrushes that grow along southern Coyote Slough as it skirts the northern edge of Salt Pond A18 were typical of the brackish marshes used by yellowthroats, whereas the densely growing bed of cattails in the Mountain View Forebay was representative of freshwater marsh habitat. The yellowthroats nesting at these locations were undoubtedly *sinuosa*. The second area where breeding yellowthroats were found was in freshwater marshes at elevations from 130 to 400 feet, on streams draining north into the Bay. The dense marshes of cattails that border Silver Creek by Lake Cunningham and the similar habitat along Calero Creek in the upper Almaden Valley were typical of the central county marshes used by yellowthroats. Occasionally, birds would use areas of dense weeds adjacent to these marshes that were not directly over water. The yellowthroats at these locations are near Grinnell and Miller's (1944) boundary separating the subspecies *sinuosa* and *arizela*, and their racial affinity is unknown. The third area where breeding yellowthroats were found was in the Pajaro River drainage and the coastal slope of the southern Santa Cruz Mountains. Birds along the Pajaro River below Highway 101 used dense tall weeds near deciduous riparian vegetation. The birds at these locations were likely of the subspecies *arizela*.

The earliest evidence of breeding during the atlas period was of nest building on 11 Apr. Following the atlas period, a yellowthroat was seen carrying nest material on 13 Mar 1994 (Michael M. Rogers, PADB). The latest nesting evidence during the atlas period was an adult feeding young on 7 Aug. Subsequently, a dependent fledgling was seen on 18 Aug 1995 (Michael M. Rogers, PADB).

Hobson et al. (1986) found Common Yellowthroats along Coyote Creek and Artesian Slough in many locations where birds were later observed during the atlas period. But they found none on Coyote Creek below the confluence with Mud Slough, along Alviso Slough, or along Guadalupe Slough from about the Calabazas ponds to the Bay. Since their study, many singing birds have been seen in all of these locations (pers. obs.). The increase in Common Yellowthroats along the Bay's tidal tributaries since the 1970s is likely a result of a shift from salt to brackish marsh vegetation in many areas, owing to increased effluent from water treatment plants and other sources as urbanization has intensified.

William G. Bousman

COMMON YELLOWTHROAT

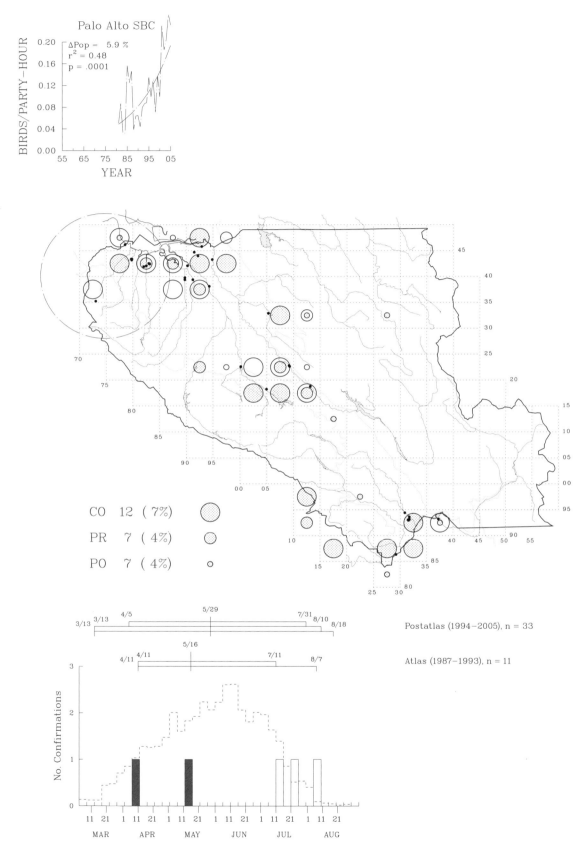

Palo Alto SBC

ΔPop = 5.9 %
r² = 0.48
p = .0001

CO 12 (7%)
PR   7 (4%)
PO   7 (4%)

Postatlas (1994–2005), n = 33

Atlas (1987–1993), n = 11

Wilson's Warbler
Wilsonia pusilla

This bright, lively warbler is at home in the dense tangles of vegetation on the wet western edge of Santa Clara County. The Wilson's Warbler breeds in the boreal forests of North America from Alaska to Labrador, thence south along the Pacific Coast to California, in the Rocky Mountains to Colorado, and in eastern North America to the states along the Canadian border (Ammon and Gilbert 1999). Of the three subspecies, two nest in California, *W. p. chryseola* found widely in the Coast Ranges (including Santa Clara County) and the Sierra Nevada and *W. p. pileolata* occurring at the eastern margin of the state (Grinnell and Miller 1944, Small 1994). In Santa Clara County, the Wilson's Warbler is a fairly common summer resident and a common migrant.

The Wilson's Warbler was apparently more widespread in Santa Clara County a century ago. The first mention of this species was by A. L. Parkhurst, who noted about ten birds arriving in the San Jose area on 22 Mar 1885 (Belding 1890). Egg collectors found Wilson's Warblers breeding in many locations along the valley floor where they are now absent, including College Park on 13 May 1891 (USNM #B31405), Berryessa on 8 May 1896 (USNM #B28270), east of Palo Alto on 21 Apr 1919 (MVZ #11166), Alviso on 17 Jun 1922 (MVZ #11175), and Milpitas on 18 Jun 1922 (MVZ #6800). Barlow (1900b) considered the Wilson's Warbler a "common breeding species along the valley streams near the bay," and Fisher (1902) described it as "common in copses and willow thickets." In the San Francisco Bay area, Grinnell and Wythe (1927) described this warbler as a common summer visitant "wherever are found growths of willow and tangles of other vegetation along stream courses and on shaded canyon sides." Sibley (1952) considered it a common breeder in the South Bay in dense vegetation close to streams.

Atlasers confirmed breeding by Wilson's Warblers in mesic habitats throughout the Santa Cruz Mountains. Breeding evidence was obtained at elevations from 70 feet in the lower Pajaro River Valley to 1,900 feet in Sanborn-Skyline County

Park. This species was generally found in wet forests, often with a mixed canopy of conifers and broadleaved evergreens, but also in stands of Douglas firs, and in dense deciduous riparian forests. In these habitats, Wilson's Warblers normally occurred within a dense understory of shrubs, ferns, and other low vegetation. The only breeding confirmation away from the Santa Cruz Mountains was of an adult feeding young along Las Animas Creek north of Anderson Reservoir. No nests were found during the atlas period, but afterwards, nest building was observed along Corte Madera Creek, and a nest with young was seen near Wrights Station Road. In both cases the nest was built in ferns just a short distance above the ground (Stephen C. Rottenborn, pers. comm.).

The Wilson's Warbler is a common migrant throughout Santa Clara County, the major passage of spring migrants occurring from 13 Apr to 25 May (unpubl. banding data, Coyote Creek Field Station, 5th to 95th percentile dates, $n = 1,275$). The only probable or possible breeding records that have been mapped were those obtained during June and July. In a few cases, these were males that sang persistently in one location, but there was no evidence that they ever attracted a mate. Other records may represent failed nesters or postbreeding dispersants.

The first singing male Wilson's Warblers arrive in Santa Clara County from the second week in March through the first week in April, with a median arrival date of 23 Mar (county notebooks). Males sing persistently until they are paired, and in central California most males are paired within 9 to 15 days (Stewart 1973, Ammon and Gilbert 1999). The earliest breeding evidence noted during the atlasing was the carrying of nest material on 8 Apr. Although a few Wilson's Warblers will raise a second brood even if the first is successful, most are single-brooded (Ammon and Gilbert 1999). The latest breeding evidence during the atlas period was an adult feeding a fledgling on 2 Aug.

Historical data from egg collectors, as well as from early observers, confirm that Wilson's Warblers were found nesting widely along streams on the valley floor in northern Santa Clara County at the beginning of the twentieth century. Although a few birds were found in these areas during and after the atlas period, breeding was not confirmed, and it appears that this species no longer nests on the northern valley floor (although it still breeds along the Pajaro River). In the 1920s, it was considered a common breeder in moister areas of the southern California coastal slope, but urbanization and cowbird parasitism have extirpated the species from this region (Small 1994). Also in the 1920s, Charles P. Smith (1926) described finding a number of nests of Wilson's Warblers in thick riparian growth along Coyote Creek, including two that were parasitized by cowbirds. The absence of breeding Wilson's Warblers from similar habitats on the valley floor during the atlas period may, as in southern California, be a consequence of urbanization and cowbird parasitism. No such parasitism was observed during the atlas fieldwork, but this species will frequently abandon its nest when parasitized (Ammon and Gilbert 1999), which makes such instances more difficult to detect.

William G. Bousman

WILSON'S WARBLER

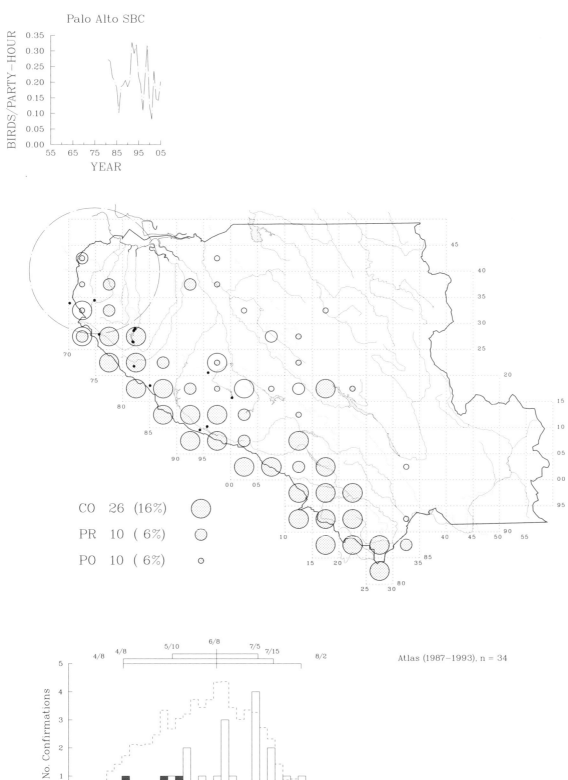

Palo Alto SBC

CO 26 (16%)

PR 10 (6%)

PO 10 (6%)

Atlas (1987–1993), n = 34

Yellow-breasted Chat
Icteria virens

This ragtime singer of rich, throaty songs, with vocal somersaults and occasional bits of whimsy, is a riparian obligate in Santa Clara County, and now occurs only sparingly. Yellow-breasted Chats breed across North America, from southern British Columbia to Ontario, and south into Mexico (AOU 1998). The western subspecies, *auricollis*, breeds locally in California, generally west of the Cascades-Sierra axis in the foothills, in the Coast Ranges, and on the coastal plain in southern California (Small 1994). Once fairly common in Santa Clara County, this warbler is now rare here, and is found breeding only in scattered riparian locations in the Diablo Range and in southern portions of the county.

James G. Cooper collected a male in the "Santa Clara Valley" on 16 May 1864 (MVZ #6424) as a member of the California Geological Survey, but did not provide any details in his published account (Cooper 1870). Van Denburgh (1899b) considered the Yellow-breasted Chat "not uncommon" along streams in the Santa Clara Valley, and Chapman (1907) used the same words in discussing the species' status along the Pajaro River at Sargent. Early oologists collected egg sets from streams in both the northern and southern reaches of the Santa Clara Valley (MVZ and WFVZ egg sets). Grinnell and Wythe (1927) judged this large warbler to be fairly common in the interior of the Bay area. At the midpoint of the twentieth century, Sibley (1952) considered the Yellow-breasted Chat to be an uncommon summer resident, reporting a set of eggs collected at the mouth of Alum Rock Canyon on Penitencia Creek on 12 Jun 1939. Although there have been sporadic records of this bird in the northern Santa Clara Valley since Sibley's summary, there has been no evidence of breeding there, and it appears that the riparian habitats remaining are no longer suitable for this species. Statewide, the population has generally declined, and the species is now considered a local and rare summer visitor in most of the state (Small 1994).

Yellow-breasted Chats were confirmed to be breeding in nine blocks during the atlas period, and subsequently in three additional blocks. Atlasers found breeding chats associated with a variety of riparian habitats. Along the valley floor and in the southern valley, birds were sometimes found along streams with a mature overstory that included Fremont cottonwoods, an understory of willows, and thick tangles of blackberries at the ground level. Other sites lacked the overstory of cottonwoods, but included thick willows and a dense understory of brambles and brush. In the Diablo Range, breeding birds were also found in riparian areas, sometimes intermittently dry, with thick willows and underbrush. In these situations, suitably dense undergrowth occurs in patches of variable size because of the aridity of the region, but chats generally used the thickest patches of willows and brambles. The habitats adjacent to the riparian corridors used by Yellow-breasted Chats varied widely and included grasslands, savannas, fallow fields, pasture, chaparral, and blue oak woodlands. The chats were not observed to use these habitats, however, but remained strictly within the riparian corridor and nearby thick undergrowth.

The first singing males arrive on breeding territories in Santa Clara County as early as 13 Apr, but more typically are first found at the beginning of May (median date 2 May, county notebooks). The earliest breeding evidence recorded was a bird carrying nest material on 10 May near Grant Lake. Birds feeding young have been seen as early as 30 May, and the same evidence has been seen as late as 15 Jul. Locally, birds are seldom seen after July, although presumed migrants are occasionally noted as late as September.

During the atlas period, two of the five Yellow-breasted Chat confirmations that involved eggs or young were parasitized by Brown-headed Cowbirds. In Riverside County, cowbird control efforts have assisted a number of riparian species, but have had little or no effect on chats (Gallagher 1997b), which suggests that cowbirds are probably not the only negative influence on this species. Management efforts in Arizona that have focused on the improvement of riparian habitats have been remarkably successful in increasing the numbers of breeding chats, as well as other riparian species (Ohmart 1994). The complex structure of riparian habitats, often with two levels of tree canopies and a dense undergrowth of shrubs and forbs, depends upon available soil moisture to maintain plant growth throughout arid summers, as well as periodic disturbance from floods, which are natural parts of the life cycle of many riparian plants. The degradation of these habitats by groundwater pumping, the prevention of periodic flooding, overgrazing by cattle, and other human-induced disturbances lead to habitat senescence in these riparian areas. First the forbs and undergrowth are lost, then the shorter-lived trees, and finally the dominant canopy species die, leaving nothing but a dry, barren channel. This process of degradation and extirpation occurs on a time scale of a human life (Ohmart 1994) and hence goes unnoticed. The process is well underway in most of the riparian areas of Santa Clara County, and great efforts will be needed to reverse this degradation.

William G. Bousman

YELLOW-BREASTED CHAT

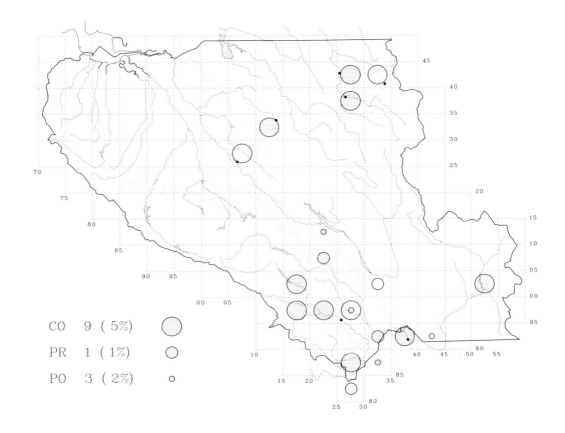

CO 9 (5%)

PR 1 (1%)

PO 3 (2%)

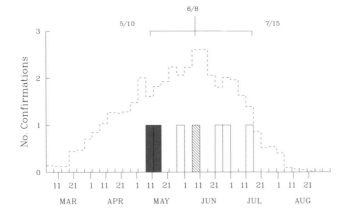

Atlas (1987–1993), n = 9

Western Tanager
Piranga ludoviciana

This spectacularly colorful tanager brings to our temperate woodlands and forests a sample of the beauty of its largely tropical family. The Western Tanager breeds from northern British Columbia and the Northwest Territories south in the mountain west to California, Arizona, and New Mexico, but it is largely absent from the dry plateaus from eastern Washington to northern Nevada (Hudon 1999). In California, it nests in mountain ranges throughout the state, being most common in the Cascades and the Sierra Nevada, and less common in the Coast Ranges (Small 1994). The Western Tanager is a fairly common spring and fall migrant in Santa Clara County, and is an uncommon-to-rare breeder in the Santa Cruz Mountains and the Diablo Range. Occasionally, a few birds are found wintering in the lowlands, usually near flowering eucalypts, where they typically forage on bees or wasps.

Western Tanagers were thought to occur in Santa Clara County solely as spring and fall migrants at the end of the nineteenth century (Price 1898f, Van Denburgh 1899b, Fisher 1902), although according to McGregor (1901), some observers believed that they nested in the Santa Cruz Mountains. Grinnell and Wythe (1927), in assessing the status of the Western Tanager in the San Francisco Bay area, described it as a transient and a local summer resident. They noted two instances of nesting, both in Sonoma County. They also listed other occurrences of birds singing in June in Napa and Sonoma counties, and suggested that these might represent breeding as well. But they overlooked a Santa Clara County record by Storer (1920) of multiple males singing near Alma (where Lexington Reservoir is today) in June 1917. Nesting records became more numerous in Bay area counties in the 1930s, leading Amelia S. Allen to suggest "an extension of range into lower altitudes" (*Bird-Lore* 35:279 1933). The first breeding record in Santa Clara County was obtained on 15 Jun 1935, when James G. Peterson found a nest in a live oak in Alum Rock Park at an elevation of 900 feet (Peterson 1935). Nesting Western Tanagers were found more widely in the 1950s (Sibley 1955), and Sibley (1952) considered the species a fairly common breeder in the Santa Cruz Mountains and uncommon in the Diablo Range.

Atlasers confirmed breeding by Western Tanagers in 25 blocks (15%), and if probable and possible evidence is considered as well, breeding was indicated in 48 blocks (29%). The majority of breeding records were from the Santa Cruz Mountains, where this tanager was found breeding widely, but generally in low numbers. Western Tanagers also nested in scattered locations throughout the Diablo Range. During the atlas period, breeding elevations ranged from 520 feet in urban Los Gatos north of St. Joseph's Hill to 3,530 feet on Bollinger Ridge in the Diablo Range. Prior to the atlas period, nesting had been observed in Stevens Creek County Park in 1984 at an elevation of about 400 feet (Phyllis M. Browning, Paul L. Noble, county notebooks). Atlasers found breeding Western Tanagers in a wide variety of habitats. At higher elevations in the Santa Cruz Mountains, they were often found in mixed forests of Douglas fir, black oak, and tan oak. At lower elevations, they occupied heterogeneous forests containing a mixture of broadleaved evergreens such as coast live oak, canyon live oak, and California bay, and conifers such as Douglas fir. Along streams in the lower foothills they used deciduous trees, such as bigleaf maple, as well as broadleaved evergreens. At higher elevations in the Diablo Range, they were found in mixed Coulter pine and black oak woodlands, ponderosa pine forests, and deciduous oak woodlands dominated by black oaks. They were also found breeding at lower elevations there, using riparian areas along Arroyo Hondo that included broadleaved evergreens such as California bay.

In Santa Clara County, it appears that Western Tanagers prefer a mixture of forest and open areas with considerable variety of tree heights and understory, but avoid both dense forests and open woodlands where trees are too widely spaced. In adjacent Santa Cruz County, they are uncommon or locally fairly common breeders in mixed broadleaved evergreen and Douglas fir forests, usually above 1,000 feet elevation (David L. Suddjian, pers. comm.), habitats similar to those used on the eastern side of the Santa Cruz Mountains in Santa Clara County. Farther north in San Mateo County, however, where persistent summer fog occurs, they had not been found breeding (Sequoia Audubon Society 2001k) until a 2004 record in Long Ridge Open Space Preserve near the crest (David L. Suddjian, pers. comm.). The species' scarcity in these forests suggests an avoidance of the wetter conditions that characterize the coastal slope of the Santa Cruz Mountains north of Waddell Creek.

Migrating Western Tanagers are generally first noted in mid-April, and the peak of their migration occurs in early May. The earliest evidence of breeding during the atlas period was nest building observed on 13 May, and the earliest observation of incubation was on 30 May. Following the atlas period, an adult carrying nest material was seen on an earlier date of 26 Apr 1998 (Ann Verdi, PADB). Prior to the atlas period, a nest with young was found on 19 May 1984 in Stevens Creek County Park (see above), indicating that some birds may nest quite early. The latest evidence of breeding was a fledgling seen on 3 Aug.

William G. Bousman

WESTERN TANAGER

Palo Alto SBC

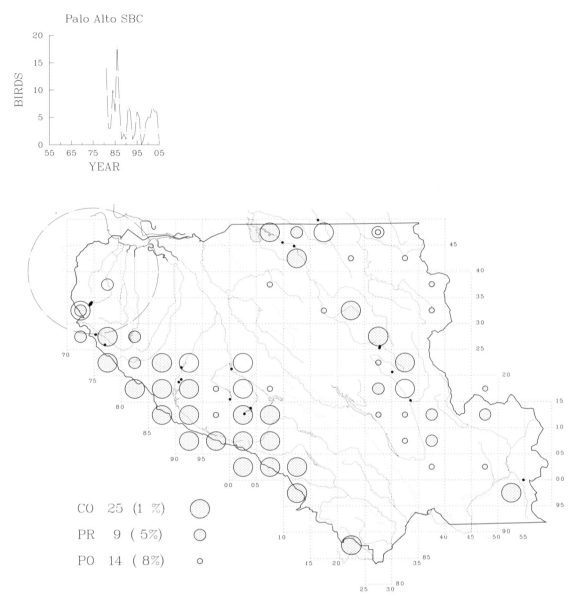

CO 25 (1 %) ⬤

PR 9 (5%) ◔

PO 14 (8%) ○

Atlas (1987–1993), n = 34

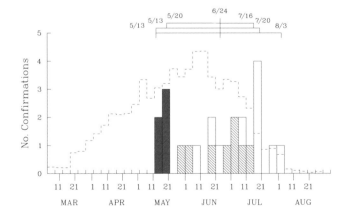

R COLWELL 98

Spotted Towhee
Pipilo maculatus

A persistent trill or a thrashing sound erupting from leaf-littered ground often announces the presence of a Spotted Towhee, whether in chaparral-covered hillsides, brushy riparian thickets, forest and woodland edges, or suburban gardens and parks. Originally described as a separate species, the Spotted Towhee was long considered a subspecies of the Rufous-sided Towhee, on the basis of hybridization of populations on the Great Plains (AOU 1995, Greenlaw 1996). Recent studies, however, have led to the decision to treat this towhee once again as distinct (AOU 1995). The Spotted Towhee is found in North America from the Great Plains west to the Pacific coast and from western Canada south to Mexico. It occurs throughout California except in the southeastern deserts and along the eastern slope of the Sierra Nevada (Grinnell and Miller 1944). The local subspecies, *P. m. falcifer*, occupies coastal areas from the Oregon border to northern Monterey and San Benito counties. It is a breeder and year-round resident throughout Santa Clara County, except where suitable breeding habitat is lacking, as on the lands nearest the San Francisco Bay and in the heavily urbanized portions of the northern Santa Clara Valley.

The Spotted Towhee has long been considered common in Santa Clara County. It was first recorded in "the Valley of San José" by Thomas Bridges sometime prior to 1857 (Sclater 1857). Cooper (1870) described the species as a common resident, favoring thickets and oak groves and foraging "mostly on the ground, scratching among the leaves in the concealment of undergrowth." In towns, he found it about homes and gardens. Van Denburgh (1899b) found the Spotted Towhee in the foothills of Los Gatos, nesting on the ground or, less frequently, in bushes. Grinnell and Wythe (1927) considered it "one of the commonest breeding birds of the San Francisco peninsula." Sibley (1952) also considered this towhee to be common in the South Bay, and that status remains unchanged today.

Atlasers found the Spotted Towhee a possible, probable, or confirmed breeder in 92% of the county's blocks, and confirmed breeding in 76% of those blocks, at virtually all elevations in the county, with records from 48 feet in Palo Alto to 3,560 feet in the Diablo Range. As expected for such a common

species, the Spotted Towhee makes use of a variety of habitats throughout the county. It is primarily a resident of shrub-dominated plant communities, regardless of whether these occur in uniform stands, such as in chaparral fields, or as a component of other habitat types, such as woodlands or closed-canopy forests. It is also resident along riparian corridors with adequate shrub understory, as well as in suburban areas where there is sufficient shrub cover for its foraging needs. Thus it occurs widely in the Santa Cruz Mountains and the Diablo Range, as well as in appropriate habitat on the valley floor. Aggregate numbers may be less in the Diablo Range, where the species eschews grasslands and open-canopy woodlands lacking a shrub understory. But where the appropriate shrub habitats do occur, it is common. Only 45% of the blocks in the northern Santa Clara Valley yielded confirmations of breeding, and these were located primarily along the northwestern and southeastern fringes of the urbanized area and along a few riparian corridors that support suitable shrub cover.

Spotted Towhees were in fact not recorded nesting in the most heavily urbanized portion of the northern Santa Clara Valley during the atlas years. None were found breeding in Santa Clara or central San Jose, despite being recorded in these cities in the 1920s when they were just small towns (Grinnell and Wythe 1927). By contrast, the Spotted Towhee's near relative the California Towhee, with less restrictive habitat requirements (Davis 1957), is a breeder in virtually all of these urban blocks. Urbanization and high-density residential development cause significant habitat destruction for the ground-nesting and leaf-litter-foraging Spotted Towhee, leaving it vulnerable to cat predation even though the parents protect their nests aggressively (Greenlaw 1996). The long-term decline seen on the San Jose CBC is probably due to habitat loss caused by urbanization.

The Spotted Towhee's breeding season as recorded during the seven-year atlas period extends over four months, the earliest confirmation being nest building in Los Altos on 16 Apr, and the latest being adults feeding fledged young on 4 Aug in a block west of Coyote Reservoir. Following the atlas period, fledged young were seen as late as 23 Aug 1995 along San Francisquito Creek below El Camino Real (Stephen C. Rottenborn, PADB). This species comes into breeding condition later than most of the species resident in the county, and the delay agrees generally with the species' phenology elsewhere in the western United States (Greenlaw 1996). Occupied nests recorded in June and July suggest renesting, since this species does not commonly raise a second brood (Greenlaw 1996). In 1931, however, a nesting pair in Palo Alto, did successfully raise three broods in one season, a distinctly unusual occurrence (Stoner 1931, Greenlaw 1996).

Roy S. Cameron

SPOTTED TOWHEE

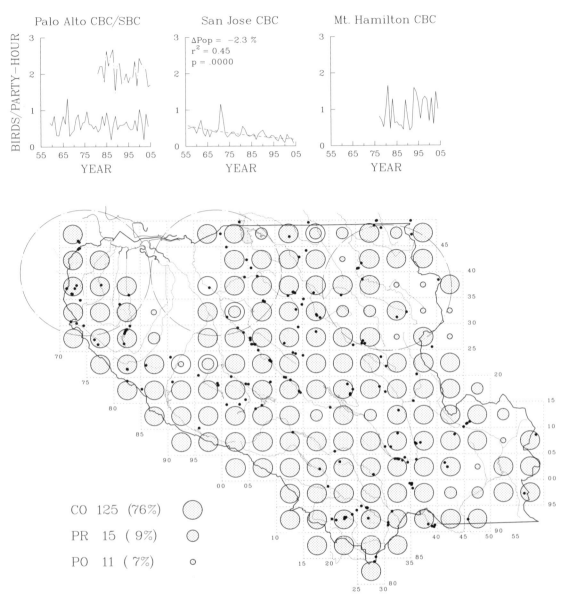

Palo Alto CBC/SBC

San Jose CBC

ΔPop = -2.3 %
r² = 0.45
p = .0000

Mt. Hamilton CBC

BIRDS/PARTY-HOUR

YEAR

CO 125 (76%)
PR   15 (9%)
PO   11 (7%)

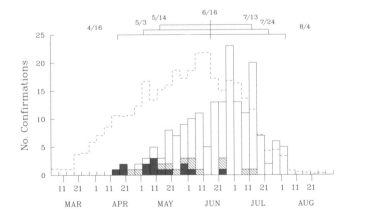

4/16   5/3 5/14   6/16   7/13 7/24   8/4   Atlas (1987–1993), n = 244

No. Confirmations

MAR   APR   MAY   JUN   JUL   AUG

California Towhee
Pipilo crissalis

There is nothing in the somber brown and russet colors of the California Towhee to attract the eye, nor any features of its unremarkable song that linger in the memory, yet this large sparrow long ago mastered the dry woodland edges, scrub, and chaparral of California and now, seemingly, is content at our urban dooryards as well. Until recent years, California Towhees were included in the species previously known as the Brown Towhee, *Pipilo fuscus*. Now, on the strength of studies using genetic markers (Zink 1988), the California Towhee and its inland cousin, the Canyon Towhee, are classified as distinct species (AOU 1989). The California Towhee is resident from southwestern Oregon to Baja California Sur, and within California it is found primarily west of the Cascades-Sierra axis and along the coast from Humboldt County south to the Mexican border (Grinnell and Miller 1944, AOU 1957). Eight subspecies are described (AOU 1957, 1989), the birds in Santa Clara County belonging to the subspecies *petulans* (Grinnell and Swarth 1926). The California Towhee is a common or abundant resident in the majority of habitat types in the county.

This towhee has long been common in Santa Clara County. Thomas Bridges collected it in "the Valley of San José" prior to 1857 (Sclater 1857). Van Denburgh (1899b) considered the California Towhee "a very common resident," and Price (1898f) remarked that it was "found everywhere" on the Stanford campus. Grinnell and Miller (1944) described the species as abundant within California, and judged that its populations had benefited from human development and had increased in numbers since historical times.

Atlasers found California Towhees in 98% of the atlas blocks, and they confirmed breeding in 97% of the blocks where the species was found. They were the fourth-most common species in the county in terms of total confirmations, and the most common species as determined from the abundance codes. California Towhees were found commonly in most of the habitats in the county and were absent only from tracts of continuous coniferous forests, extensive grasslands, and bayside locations lacking a modicum of shrubbery for cover and forage.

California Towhees have an extended breeding period, and many pairs probably have two or three broods. Emily Smith's studies of color-banded birds (*Audubon Field Notes* 9:402 1955) documented cases of double-brooding in Los Gatos in the 1950s. The earliest nesting evidence for the atlas was birds carrying nest material on 16 Mar, nest building on 25 Mar, and a bird on a nest on 10 Apr. Van Denburgh (1899b) noted nesting as early as 16 Apr 1889, and Sibley (1952) reported a nest with a single egg in Los Gatos on 14 Apr 1951. The end of the breeding season was marked by birds carrying nest material on 20 Jul, a nest with young on 4 Aug, adults feeding young on 26 Aug, and an adult carrying food on 29 Aug. Following the atlas period, an adult was observed feeding young on 25 Sep 1994 (Peter J. Metropulos, pers. comm.) for a late-season record. Birds with fledged young (32%) and adults carrying food for young (30%) were the most common breeding evidence obtained for this species.

Although this species is one of our most common birds, analysis of the Palo Alto and San Jose Christmas Bird Count (CBC) data and the Palo Alto Summer Bird Count data show declines of approximately 2 to 3% a year over the last five decades. Because analysis of the Mt. Hamilton CBC data shows a slight increase within that count circle, it seems likely that the Palo Alto and San Jose declines are human-related. Possible explanations include a reduction of foraging areas caused by an increased dwelling density, the effects of an increasing Brown-headed Cowbird population, and predation by domestic and feral cats. Roberson (1993gg) believes that cats are a significant cause of mortality within urban areas, but the true causes of the declines in Santa Clara County are unknown.

In absolute numbers, this species was the most common host for the Brown-headed Cowbird during the atlas, with 23 confirmations involving cowbird young or eggs. Although a slight decline has been noted in urban California Towhee populations, it seems unlikely that cowbird parasitism is a major threat to this species. Nonetheless, this towhee represents a significant host resource for the Brown-headed Cowbird, and in this way may support or assist the increasing population of cowbirds.

William G. Bousman

CALIFORNIA TOWHEE

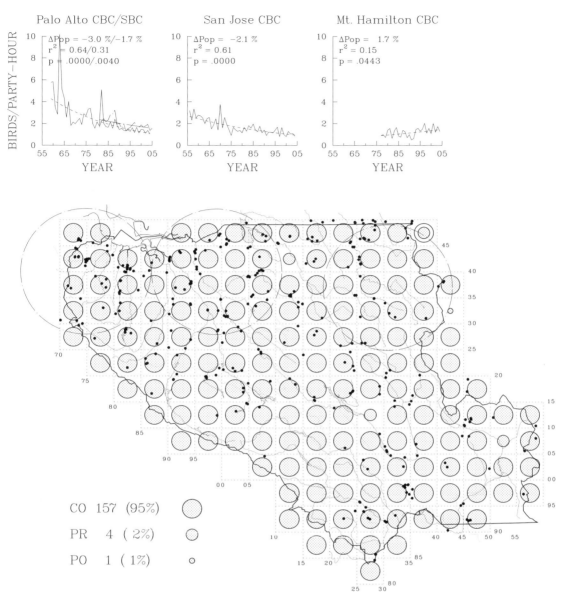

Palo Alto CBC/SBC

ΔPop = −3.0 %/−1.7 %
r² = 0.64/0.31
p = .0000/.0040

San Jose CBC

ΔPop = −2.1 %
r² = 0.61
p = .0000

Mt. Hamilton CBC

ΔPop = 1.7 %
r² = 0.15
p = .0443

BIRDS/PARTY-HOUR

YEAR

CO 157 (95%)
PR 4 (2%)
PO 1 (1%)

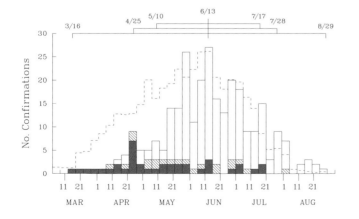

No. Confirmations

3/16   4/25   5/10   6/13   7/17   7/28   8/29

Atlas (1987–1993), n = 406

MAR   APR   MAY   JUN   JUL   AUG

Rufous-crowned Sparrow
Aimophila ruficeps

On the steep slopes of California sagebrush and non-native grasses, this drab, rufous-capped sparrow is often seen for only a moment and then is gone. The Rufous-crowned Sparrow is resident from central California across the southwest to Oklahoma and Arkansas, and south to Oaxaca in Mexico (AOU 1998). Of the seven subspecies that have been described, four are found in California (AOU 1957, Small 1994). The nominate *ruficeps*, the subspecies found in Santa Clara County, occurs from southern Mendocino County south through the Coast Ranges to Santa Barbara County, and then north again in the western foothills of the Sierra Nevada to Shasta County (Small 1994). This sparrow is generally uncommon in Santa Clara County, but can be locally common in its preferred habitat.

Chester Barlow (1900b) considered the Rufous-crowned Sparrow to be a common resident in sagebrush habitats on the eastern side of the Santa Clara Valley. He and Joseph Grinnell studied a "colony" of this species near Milpitas and described a nest that they found (Barlow 1902). In 1904, Grinnell (1905) noted birds on the west side of the Santa Clara Valley at Hidden Villa, low on Black Mountain. Grinnell and Wythe (1927) considered Rufous-crowned Sparrows to be common locally in the San Francisco Bay area on open, sunny hillsides sparsely covered with chaparral. Sibley (1952) described this sparrow as a "sparse resident, sometimes locally common, especially in the more arid portion of the region." Analysis of count data from the San Jose CBC since the 1950s shows variable numbers, but no significant population change.

Atlasers found Rufous-crowned Sparrows in scattered locations in the Diablo Range, as well as in limited portions of the Santa Cruz Mountains. Some level of breeding evidence was found in 56% of the Diablo Range blocks, but birds were absent from many blocks within this range, apparently because of the absence of suitable habitat. Within the Santa Cruz Mountains, birds were found in three areas. In the north they were found (and probably bred in small numbers) along Monte Bello Ridge,

on the eastern side of Black Mountain, and in Stevens Creek County Park. To the southeast, they were locally common in the Santa Teresa Hills and south of the Almaden Valley in the central section of the Santa Cruz Mountains. Breeding birds were also found on steep hillsides in the southern part of the Santa Cruz Mountains, where this range drops to the Pajaro River. Rufous-crowned Sparrows nested from elevations of 300 feet along the edge of the Silver Creek Hills, southeast of Hellyer County Park, to an elevation of 2,480 feet on the hillsides east of Alameda Creek and south of Mt. Lewis.

Atlasers generally found Rufous-crowned Sparrows on steep, grassy hillsides with sparse stands of California sagebrush, a particular habitat preference well-documented for this species (Grinnell and Miller 1944, Cogswell 1968). In some cases, birds were found on grassy hillsides where sagebrush was lacking, but rock outcrops or other scattered chaparral shrubs were present. On occasions this sparrow selected hillside territories that included roadcuts or eroded gullies. The steep hillsides used by Rufous-crowned Sparrows often faced south or west, which provided a microhabitat of intense solar heating. The soils on these hillsides were often thin and poor, which led to the sparse nature of the grasses and scattered shrubs growing on these slopes. No nests were found during the atlas period, but a nest with young was found on 10 Apr 1998 in the Silver Creek Hills (Stephen C. Rottenborn, pers. comm.). This nest was on a 12-inch ledge midway up a 2-m slope in an old gravel pit. The nest was well hidden beneath grasses and forbs in an area dominated by California sagebrush and poison oak.

The phenology documented during the atlas period is biased toward the Rufous-crowned Sparrow's post-nesting activities. Most confirmations were thus of dependent fledged young (58%) or adults seen carrying food for young (30%). (The latter confirmation type is not shown on the graphic, since it cannot be assigned to either the nesting period or postnesting period.) During the atlas period, the earliest nesting evidence encountered was an adult carrying food on 27 Apr. The latest breeding evidence, on 4 Aug, was also of an adult with food. Subsequent to the atlas period, earlier breeding evidence was obtained when an adult was seen with food on 8 Apr 1998 (Michael M. Rogers, pers. comm.) as well as the nest with young mentioned above. Historically, A. J. Wool found nests with young on Mission Ridge on 22 Mar and 1 Aug (Sibley 1952), dates that extend the nesting period shown here.

Barlow (1902) described this species as nesting in colonies, and atlasers, too, observed birds in semicolonial groups. But the plant species preferred by this sparrow, in particular California sagebrush, occur mostly in clumps, and it may be that the semicolonial nesting behavior of this species is more related to the nonuniform distribution of its preferred habitat than to any proclivity for gregariousness.

William G. Bousman

RUFOUS-CROWNED SPARROW

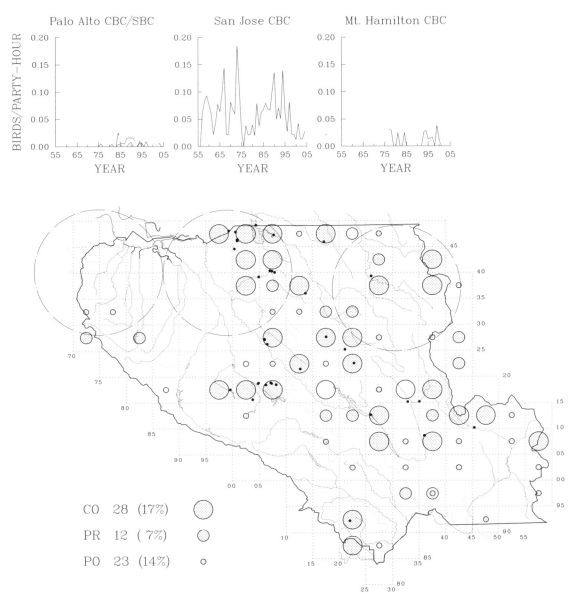

Palo Alto CBC/SBC

San Jose CBC

Mt. Hamilton CBC

BIRDS/PARTY-HOUR

YEAR

CO 28 (17%)

PR 12 (7%)

PO 23 (14%)

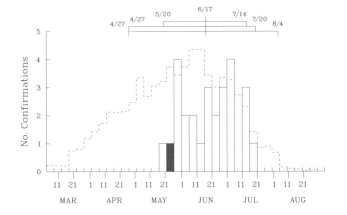

Atlas (1987–1993), n = 38

No. Confirmations

MAR   APR   MAY   JUN   JUL   AUG

Chipping Sparrow
Spizella passerina

This attractive sparrow is now declining throughout California, for reasons that are largely unknown. The Chipping Sparrow breeds from Alaska across Canada to Newfoundland and thence south to Baja California, Texas, and Georgia (Middleton 1998). Resident populations also occur in the highlands of Mexico and south into Nicaragua. Five subspecies are recognized, *S. p. arizonae* being the one found from Alaska to Baja California (Middleton 1998). This sparrow breeds throughout most of California away from the Central Valley, the southern coastal slope, and the desert lowlands (Small 1994). Chipping Sparrows are fairly common summer residents in some areas of the Diablo Range, but elsewhere in Santa Clara County they are uncommon as breeders or absent altogether.

In the 1880s, A. L. Parkhurst considered the Chipping Sparrow to be an abundant summer resident in San Jose (Belding 1890). Other observers at the end of the nineteenth century judged it to be less common, Price (1898f) referring to it as "not abundant" at Stanford, and Van Denburgh (1899b) judging it only "fairly common" near Los Gatos. Fisher (1902) described this sparrow as "not a very common resident" in the Santa Clara Valley and the Santa Cruz Mountains. In the Bay area, Grinnell and Wythe (1927) considered it to be a "common summer resident locally," but described it as less numerous than in prior years. In the South Bay region, Sibley (1952) judged this sparrow to be a fairly common summer resident, particularly on the east side of the Santa Clara Valley. Analysis of the Palo Alto SBC data shows a population decline in the northern Santa Cruz Mountains of 8.5% a year since 1981. Similarly, analysis of Breeding Bird Survey data for California indicates a decline of 4.6% a year over the period 1966 to 2004 (Sauer et al. 2005).

The majority of breeding confirmations obtained during the atlas period were from the Diablo Range. Most of these, however, were from the interior of the range, and few breeding birds were found on the western slope overlooking the Santa Clara Valley. Nesting birds were also found adjacent to grasslands near the crest of the northern Santa Cruz Mountains, in locations such as the Monte Bello Open Space Preserve. Atlasers

generally found breeding Chipping Sparrows in open oak woodlands with annual grasslands as an understory. Breeding birds were more often on the higher ridges, less often in woodlands near arroyos. In the western Diablo Range, these oak woodlands tended to be dominated by valley oaks, whereas to the east there was a transition to blue oak woodlands, where fewer breeding birds were found. Chipping Sparrows used the trees in these open woodlands for song perches and nest sites, and used open or grassy areas, and the sometimes shrubby woodland understory, for foraging. In the northern Santa Cruz Mountains, Chipping Sparrows were found most often at the edge between mixed conifer/broadleaved evergreen woodlands and annual grasslands. This species also used Christmas tree plantations, with their mixture of planted conifers and an understory of annual grasses.

Chipping Sparrows arrive on their breeding grounds in early April, with a median first arrival date of 8 Apr (county notebooks). The earliest breeding evidence was a nest with eggs found on 29 Apr. Egg sets from Santa Clara County include three earlier dates, the earliest on 12 Apr (WFVZ). The latest breeding evidence observed during the atlas period was adults feeding young on 10 Aug. Chipping Sparrows are found in reduced numbers into September and October near breeding areas.

In Santa Clara County, the Chipping Sparrow is now absent from many urban and rural areas where it was apparently common in the nineteenth century. Referring to northern California, James G. Cooper (1870) described these sparrows as coming "about the doorstep to pick up crumbs, and building their nests in low branches of fruit-trees or garden shrubs." Many of the egg sets collected at the beginning of the twentieth century were found in orchards and gardens along the valley floor and in nearby San Mateo County (nest records, WFVZ, MVZ). Today, with an increasing human population, the orchards and truck gardens have been replaced by homes, schools, and shopping centers, and Chipping Sparrows are no longer found in these urban areas. But they are also absent from nearby rural areas in the southern valley and the foothills habitats that would seem to be similar to those of the northern valley of a century ago. Tenney (1993d) has noted a similar disappearance of Chipping Sparrows from the coastal slope of Monterey County, and has suggested that this may be related to landscape management practices that have increased the density of forest canopy and eliminated grassy openings in woodlands. Middleton (1998) has suggested that declines in eastern North America have been caused by a reversion of farmland to forest, parasitism by Brown-headed Cowbirds, and competition with House Finches and House Sparrows. Although this species is considered a frequent host of Brown-headed Cowbirds, none of the 196 incidents of parasitism observed during our atlas period and in the following years have involved the Chipping Sparrow as a host. Whether any of these factors are responsible for the local decline is unclear, and the disappearance of this charming sparrow from much of Santa Clara County remains a mystery.

William G. Bousman

CHIPPING SPARROW

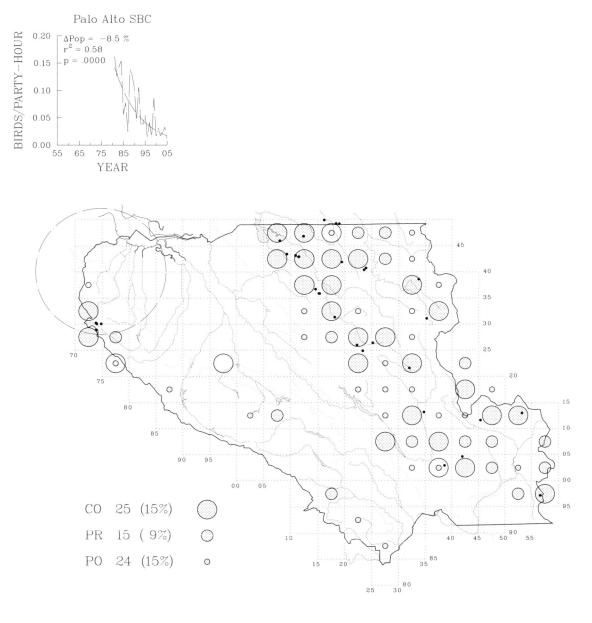

Palo Alto SBC

ΔPop = −8.5 %
r² = 0.58
p = .0000

CO   25 (15%)
PR   15 (9%)
PO   24 (15%)

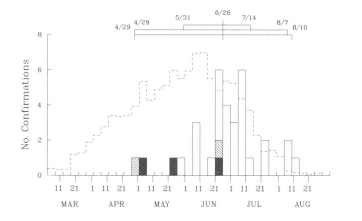

Atlas (1987–1993), n = 35

Black-chinned Sparrow
Spizella atrogularis

The unpredictable Black-chinned Sparrow may breed in small colonies at a location one year, only to be strangely absent there in subsequent seasons. This species ranges throughout the southwestern United States and Mexico, some individuals moving northward into California in summer. In California, the Black-chinned Sparrow breeds from the southern California mountains north through the foothills along the edges of the Central Valley to Lake and Tehama counties (and sporadically to southern Oregon), as well as at scattered locations in the eastern desert ranges (Grenfell and Laudenslayer 1983, Tenney 1997). The isolated population breeding in the inner Coast Ranges from Lake County south through San Benito County belongs to the subspecies *S. a. caurina* (Miller 1929), weakly differentiated from the *S. a. cana* found in southern California (Paynter 1970). In Santa Clara County this uncommon and erratic sparrow breeds in scattered small groups in the chaparral of both the Santa Cruz Mountains and the eastern portions of the Diablo Range. Like the Diablo Range birds, the Santa Cruz Mountain birds are presumed to be *caurina*, although there are no specimens or records to rule out a northward extension of *cana*, which breeds to the south in the Coast Ranges of Monterey County (Chris Tenney, pers. comm.).

Miller (1929) first described the race *caurina* from specimens collected in Contra Costa County on 25 May 1929, following his observations of a "small colony" of at least five pairs in the Berkeley Hills of Alameda County in 1928. Although no specific records were known, Miller (1929) listed the range of *caurina* as "probably" including Santa Clara County. Prior to 1972, the only known records of Black-chinned Sparrows in Santa Clara County consisted of three nests with eggs found by Milton L. Seibert and Henry W. Carriger about a mile north of the San Antonio Junction in the San Antonio Valley, one on 11 May 1941 (Seibert 1942), a second on 10 May 1942 (*Audubon 44*:14 1942), and the third on 11 May 1946 (*Audubon 48:*116 1946). In 1972, an "invasion" of the central coast region result-

ed in records from a variety of San Francisco Bay area counties, including a bird banded at the Wool Ranch west of Calaveras Reservoir on 14 May 1972 (banding data, Mewaldt and Kaiser 1988). Throughout the 1970s, Black-chinned Sparrows were found farther and farther north in California, leading Rich Stallcup and Jon Winter to conclude that the species was "definitely expanding its range in California" (*Am. Birds 29*:906 1975). But data from the Breeding Bird Survey from 1966 to 2004 (Sauer et al. 2005) show a significant decline in California, and England (1993a) concluded that the apparent range expansion "much more likely indicates better coverage by observers." Following this "expansion" in the 1970s, birds were detected for the first time in the Santa Cruz Mountains of Santa Clara County on 18 May 1980, when six birds were found near the summit of Loma Prieta (Don Schmoldt, county notebooks). On 1 Jun 1985, six were noted at the Monte Bello Open Space Preserve, about 30 km farther northwest (Peter LaTourrette, county notebooks). Although birds have been found at Loma Prieta in most years since their discovery, they have been recorded less regularly at Monte Bello (e.g., no reports from 1989 through 1992).

Atlasers found Black-chinned Sparrows in arid chaparral fields in both the Santa Cruz Mountains and the Diablo Range, generally in younger chaparral of varied composition. This habitat preference is consistent with findings elsewhere (England 1993a). Thorough coverage and access to private land resulted in the discovery of several previously unknown breeding locations for this species in the eastern part of the county. Birds were also found just east of the Mt. Hamilton summit in two of those years, and breeding was confirmed farther southeast near Castle Ridge. In addition to these Diablo Range records, birds were found in six blocks in the Santa Cruz Mountains. The records in three of these blocks come from a single south-facing chaparral field west of Black Mountain at the Monte Bello Open Space Preserve (all these records were within about 500 meters of each other). Farther south, breeding was confirmed near Loma Prieta, and single birds were located near Mt. Umunhum and west of Uvas Reservoir, the latter record being of a singing bird at the uncharacteristically low elevation of 560 feet. The majority of atlas records are from elevations between 2,600 and 3,600 feet. Although rare on a countywide scale, Black-chinned Sparrows, when present, may occur in fairly high densities in suitable habitat. In the majority of Diablo Range blocks in which this species was found, it was judged that more than ten pairs were present (pers. obs.). Throughout the county, this species was often found in the company of Sage Sparrows.

Only four breeding confirmations of Black-chinned Sparrow were obtained during the atlas period. Birds were observed carrying food on 1 Jun and 17 Jun, fledged young were seen on 22 Jun, and adults were seen feeding recently fledged young on 9 Jul. Two more confirmations were obtained following the atlas period: a bird carrying nest material on 26 May 1997 (Stephen C. Rottenborn, PADB) and a nest with young on 29 Jun 2002 (Les Chibana, PADB). These dates coincide well with the egg dates recorded in the 1940s from the Diablo Range. Records in Santa Clara County span 24 Apr to 19 Jul, but this sparrow may actually be present later than this, but it is virtually undetectable after singing ceases and breeding is completed in mid-July.

Michael M. Rogers

BLACK-CHINNED SPARROW

Palo Alto SBC

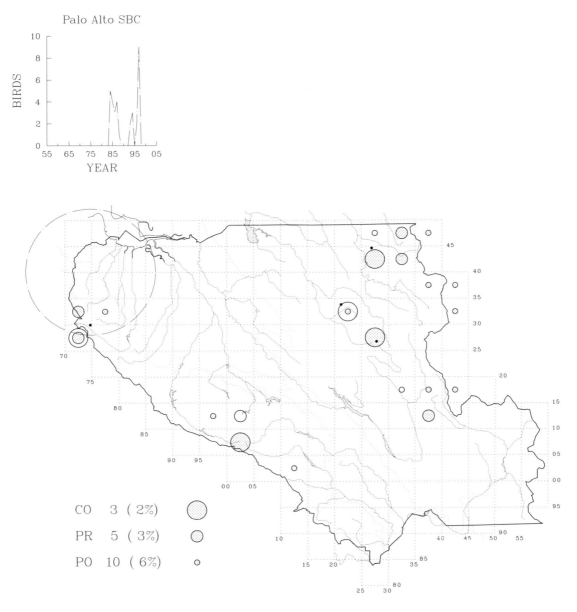

CO   3 (2%)

PR   5 (3%)

PO 10 (6%)

Atlas (1987–1993), n = 4

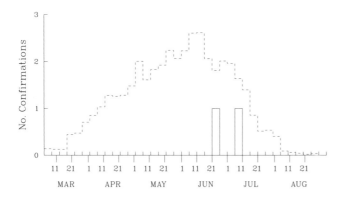

Lark Sparrow
Chondestes grammacus

The ebullient song of this beautifully marked sparrow is one of the spring delights of the mixed oak woodlands and grasslands of the Diablo Range. This sparrow breeds from Oregon, interior Washington, and British Columbia across Canada to central Ontario and thence south to southern California, Mexico, and central Alabama (AOU 1998). The western subspecies *strigatus* is generally common and found widely in the western United States, including California. The Lark Sparrow is common in the Diablo Range, but is less common along the eastern edges of the Santa Cruz Mountains. In winter this sparrow is encountered less frequently, and it is unclear whether this is because some of the local birds winter elsewhere or because it aggregates in large flocks that are patchily distributed.

The earliest evidence of breeding by these sparrows in Santa Clara County is a set of eggs collected at Berryessa by Rollo H. Beck on 6 May 1891 (MVZ #2480). Price (1898e) noted this species near Stanford, at the eastern edge of the Santa Cruz Mountain foothills, at the end of the nineteenth century. Van Denburgh (1899b) considered it a common breeding species in the county, although he noted that it was not found in Los Gatos in the winter. Fisher (1902) reported that Lark Sparrows were more common on the east side of the valley than on the west side. Grinnell and Wythe (1927) considered this sparrow to be a fairly common summer visitant in the San Francisco Bay region, leaving only a few birds to winter in interior areas. Sibley (1952) judged Lark Sparrows to be common residents in open areas with scattered trees.

In recent decades there has been a decline in the number of Lark Sparrows in Santa Clara County. Within the San Jose count circle, there has been a decline of 5.6% a year in the number of wintering Lark Sparrows recorded since the 1950s, but there is no trend in the numbers recorded on the Mt. Hamilton count. Although the number of birds recorded within the Palo Alto count circle is quite small, analysis of the Palo Alto CBC and SBC data shows a declining trend for both counts. A century

ago, egg collectors found nesting Lark Sparrows in many locations on the east side of the Santa Cruz Mountains where none are found today (WFVZ, MVZ egg sets). At the Jasper Ridge Biological Preserve in nearby San Mateo County, this species was considered a common nesting species prior to 1960 (Row 1960), but it is no longer found on the reserve in summer (Richard G. Jeffers, pers. comm.). There also appears to have been a general reduction in the number of nesting birds on the western slope of the Santa Cruz Mountains in Santa Cruz County (David L. Suddjian, pers. comm.).

Lark Sparrows were confirmed breeding in half of the county's blocks, most of these being in the Diablo Range. Breeding birds were also found in three locations in the Santa Cruz Mountains. A small disjunct population was found in fairly extensive grassland areas intermixed with broad-leaved evergreen forests and Christmas tree farms along the crest of the Santa Cruz Mountains west of Palo Alto. This sparrow was also found in dry foothills both south and east of the Almaden Valley. Lastly, in the southern Santa Cruz Mountains, where these hills drop to the Pajaro River, Lark Sparrows were found widely in grasslands that included oak woodlands or chaparral. Confirmation of breeding was obtained from an elevation of 200 feet near Coyote Creek below the Coyote Narrows to 4,000 feet on Eylar Mountain. Birds were largely absent from the valley floor, however, 90% of all confirmations being recorded above 800 feet elevation. Lark Sparrows were generally found in grasslands mixed with other plant communities, usually blue oak woodlands, foothill pine woodlands, or chaparral. Nesting birds appeared to require some heterogeneity in vegetation, nearly always with a grassland component. Generally, these habitats were relatively xeric and away from the denser woodlands on north-facing slopes or from shaded canyons. In all cases where atlasers reported the nesting substrate, nests were placed on the ground, often immediately adjacent to tree trunks, downed limbs, brush, or boulders. Interestingly, a century ago, most egg collectors found Lark Sparrows nesting locally in cypresses, orchard trees, and oaks; only a few of them found birds with ground nests (WFVZ egg sets).

Lark Sparrows begin establishing breeding territories about the end of March. The earliest breeding evidence was of a bird carrying nest material on 5 Apr. The most frequent confirmation was the observation of fledged young (40%); such records peaked in mid-June. The latest confirmation of breeding was of an adult observed carrying food for its young on 2 Aug. Atlasers observed birds carrying nesting material in late June and early July, but this may indicate renesting rather than a second brood. Second broods are considered unusual in this species (Baepler 1968). The phenology derived from the atlas data is consistent with the egg dates reported in Baepler (1968) for California, who listed dates ranging from 4 Apr to 16 Jul (132 records), the peak of egg laying from 1 May to 1 Jun (72 records).

William G. Bousman

LARK SPARROW

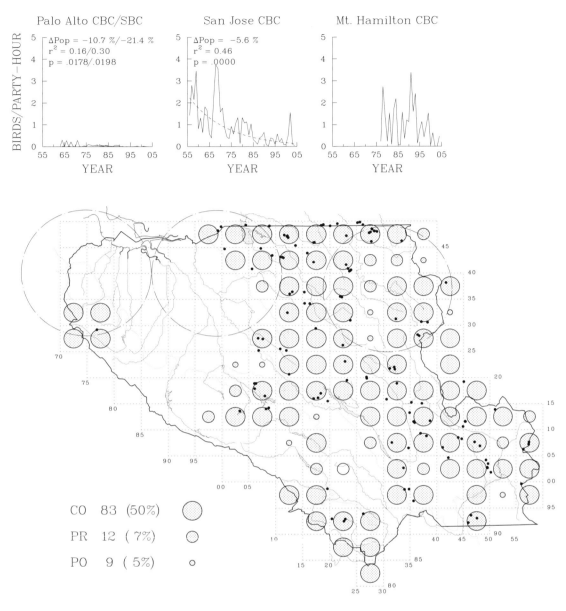

Palo Alto CBC/SBC

ΔPop = −10.7 %/−21.4 %
r² = 0.16/0.30
p = .0178/.0198

San Jose CBC

ΔPop = −5.6 %
r² = 0.46
p = .0000

Mt. Hamilton CBC

BIRDS/PARTY–HOUR

YEAR

CO 83 (50%)
PR 12 (7%)
PO   9 (5%)

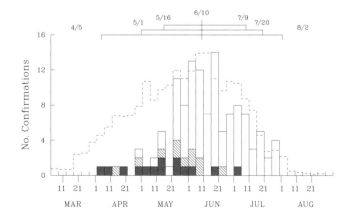

Atlas (1987–1993), n = 168

No. Confirmations

MAR   APR   MAY   JUN   JUL   AUG

Sage Sparrow
Amphispiza belli

Although fairly common in chamise chaparral in parts of the Diablo Range, the Sage Sparrow is infrequently seen by Santa Clara County birders, who rarely venture into its remote breeding areas. The Sage Sparrow breeds throughout the Great Basin of western North America and much of California. Some populations winter south of their breeding areas, from southeastern California to western Texas and northern Mexico (Byers et al. 1995). The subspecies breeding in coastal California, *A. b. belli*, is resident from Trinity and Shasta counties south to northern Baja California, with an isolated population in the western Sierra Nevada (Grinnell and Miller 1944, Rising, pp. 124-127 1996). In Santa Clara County, *belli* is found throughout the eastern Diablo Range where appropriate chamise habitat is available. In similar habitat in the Santa Cruz Mountains, it is rare and occurs irregularly.

Historical records document breeding by Sage Sparrows in both the Santa Cruz Mountains and the Diablo Range in Santa Clara County, although the earliest references mention only birds from chaparral regions within the Santa Cruz Mountains. W. Otto Emerson felt that a bird near "the summit of Loma Prieta" in the 1880s was likely breeding (McGregor 1901). Van Denburgh (1899b) noted a "considerable colony" breeding every year in the mountains west of Los Gatos, where he observed adults feeding young on 23 Jun 1892 and found a nest with eggs on 9 May 1898. A pair in breeding condition was taken near Adobe Creek in the foothills of Black Mountain on 31 Mar 1904 (Jenkins 1904). The first record of this species from the Diablo Range included a nest with eggs found by Milton L. Seibert and Henry W. Carriger on 11 May 1941 in the San Antonio Valley (WFVZ #34856). Through 1947, between 27 Apr and 23 May, these two collectors found at least eight additional nests with eggs in this general area (WFVZ egg set records). Sibley (1952), in his summary of South Bay birds, noted that the Sage Sparrow was a fairly common resident "in the hills bordering the east side of Santa Clara Valley, especially to the east of Mt. Hamilton in the San Antonio Valley region." More recently, breeding has been confirmed at additional locations in the Santa Cruz Mountains: a bird carrying food on 29 Apr 1951 on the road over Mt. Umunhum and Loma Prieta (*Bull. SCVAS* June 1951), and an adult with three juveniles was seen on 1 Aug 1959 on Mt. Umunhum (*Avocet 6:*54 1959). Farther north, breeding was confirmed at Foothills Open Space Preserve, where a bird was photographed carrying food for young on 12 Jun 1982, following the presence of juveniles at the same location in the previous year (Peter LaTourrette, pers. comm.). A bird banded at the Wool Ranch on 29 May 1972 (Mewaldt and Kaiser 1988) and another seen at Alum Rock Park on 8 May 1986 (Jack Cole, pers. comm.) were well west of known Diablo Range breeding areas and may have been late migrants.

During the atlas period, Sage Sparrows were found in chamise chaparral in both the Diablo Range and the Santa Cruz Mountains. Breeding elevations ranged from 1,560 to 3,560 feet. Breeding birds were found widely east of the Mt. Hamilton summit, from areas east of Gilroy Hot Springs and southeast of Mustang Peak north through the San Antonio Valley and into nearby Alameda County. In the southern Diablo Range they were not found south of Pacheco Creek, perhaps owing to less intensive coverage of chamise habitats there. In the Santa Cruz Mountains, breeding locations were more scattered and populations were smaller. Here, breeding was confirmed at Loma Prieta, Mt. Umunhum, Black Mountain in Santa Clara County, and west of Castle Rock in Santa Cruz County. Singing birds were also found in El Sereno Open Space Preserve west of Los Gatos, but no breeding was confirmed there. Although the Santa Cruz Mountains distribution matches the historical range well, no Sage Sparrows were detected in Foothills Open Space Preserve during the atlas years. This absence is not apparently a result of habitat loss, which has caused the disappearance of this species as a breeder from nearby San Mateo County (Peter J. Metropulos, pers. comm.). Sage Sparrows were most strongly associated with younger, somewhat open (often recently burned or dragged) chamise chaparral, choices similar to preferences noted in Marin County (England 1993b). Some Sage Sparrows, however, were found in denser chamise fields as well as in chaparral of more varied composition, sometimes with manzanita or coffeeberry interspersed (David L. Suddjian, pers. comm.; Stephen C. Rottenborn, pers. comm.). High densities were reported in the extreme northeast corner of the county, where an atlaser estimated 50 pairs along an 8-km transect north of Mt. Stakes on 29 May 1993, and still greater densities near Mt. Mocho on 18 Jun 1992 and 13 Jun 1995 (pers. obs.). In the Santa Cruz Mountains, Sage Sparrows were typically not found in the same locations every year, despite the availability of apparently suitable habitat. Such sporadic breeding was also reported in Monterey County (Tenney 1993e). At least during the atlas years, breeding locations in the Diablo Range were more consistently used.

No nests of this species were found during the atlas period, although a single confirmation of a bird carrying nest material was reported on 23 May. All other confirmations were either of adults carrying food for young (as early as 23 May) or of recently fledged young (29 May to 13 Jul). These dates agree with historical nesting dates and with the egg dates given in Bent (1968).

Michael M. Rogers

SAGE SPARROW

Palo Alto CBC/SBC

Mt. Hamilton CBC

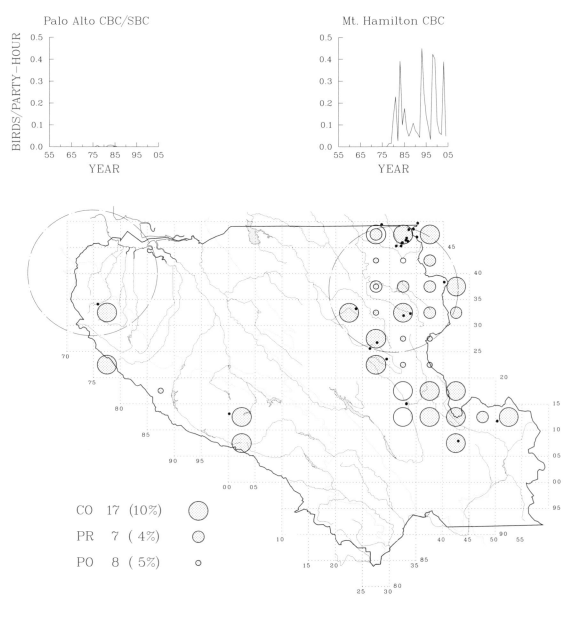

CO   17 (10%)
PR   7 (4%)
PO   8 (5%)

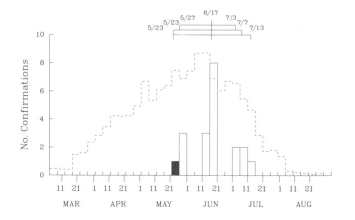

Atlas (1987–1993), n = 27

5/23 5/23 5/27 6/17 7/3 7/7 7/13

Savannah Sparrow
Passerculus sandwichensis

The very different nature of the salt marsh and upland grassland habitats used by Santa Clara County's breeding Savannah Sparrows raises questions regarding their ecology, and possibly their taxonomic status. The Savannah Sparrow breeds in fields, marshes, and tundra throughout much of North America, its northern populations migrating to more southerly areas for the winter (Wheelwright and Rising 1993). In Santa Clara County, this species is a common breeder in bayside salt marshes and an uncommon local breeder in grasslands in the Santa Cruz Mountains. Our resident population is greatly augmented by migrants from the north and east in winter (e.g., the mean abundance is four times greater on Palo Alto's CBC than on its SBC).

Authors at the turn of the twentieth century believed that Savannah Sparrows bred in the Bay area only in the salt marshes. In the South Bay, Price (1898f), Van Denburgh (1899b), and Barlow (1900b) indicated that "*A. s. bryanti,*" or "Bryant's marsh sparrow," resided in salt marshes near Palo Alto, whereas the paler race *alaudinus* was a common winter visitant in upland fields. Later authors, however, established that Savannahs also bred in grassy hills from Humboldt Bay south to San Francisco Bay (Squires 1916a, Mailliard 1917, Bailey 1920, Mailliard and Mailliard 1920, Grinnell and Wythe 1927). Grinnell and Miller (1944) described Savannah Sparrow habitat in the Bay area as "most importantly the salicornia association of tidal marshlands, and secondarily upland grassy slopes in the coastal fog belt." Although Bay area populations have undoubtedly been impacted by the loss of high-marsh habitat around the Bay, no recent population trends are apparent in Santa Clara County's CBC or SBC data, or in BBS data for California as a whole (Sauer et al. 2005).

Atlas work confirmed the variable nature of habitat use by this species in Santa Clara County. Half of the 14 blocks where breeding was confirmed during or after the atlas period are located along the edge of the Bay. Here, Savannah Sparrows were found breeding in pickleweed-dominated salt marsh and in the adjacent transition zone. The shorter vegetation of the high marsh favored by Savannahs overlaps little with the habitat of the salt-marsh-breeding Song Sparrow (*Melospiza melodia*

pusillula) of the South Bay, which favors taller herbaceous vegetation in the lower marsh (Johnston 1968). Gill (1977) found Savannahs nesting in the South Bay on levee sides dominated by pickleweed or on levee tops overgrown with annual grasses. Atlasers reported Savannah Sparrows breeding more sparsely in expanses of short grassland in inland/upland areas. Such areas included "fog belt" locations at the crest of the Santa Cruz Mountains in the vicinity of the Russian Ridge Open Space Preserve (at elevations up to 2,540 feet). Breeders were also noted in the Santa Cruz Mountain foothills just north of the Pajaro River Valley (which are also influenced by summer fog) and warmer, drier areas on the west side of the Coyote Valley farther north. A few atlas records on the valley floor and in the southern Diablo Range may indicate additional breeding locations in these drier areas, although the dates of these records (1 May, 17 May, and 17 July) leave open the possibility that these birds were migrants or dispersants.

During the atlas period, Savannah Sparrows were observed carrying food for young as early as 25 April, a date consistent with eggs collected in an Alviso salt marsh on 15 Apr 1933 by W. E. Unglish (Sibley 1952). Nests with young were found by atlasers on 2, 6, and 10 June. A bird carrying nesting material on 1 July during the atlas period and a postatlas observation of an adult carrying food on 18 August 1998 (Michael M. Rogers, pers. comm.) suggest that some Santa Clara County breeders may produce a second clutch, as has been reported in some populations (e.g., Wheelwright and Rising 1993).

Squires (1916a) suggested that the Savannahs breeding in the San Francisco hills were paler than salt marsh breeders, and that two subspecies might be present. Mailliard (1917) acknowledged "a great likelihood" of two different forms, but later found no consistent differences in plumage or measurements between birds breeding in the hills near Tomales Bay, Marin County, and salt-marsh-breeding birds (Mailliard and Mailliard 1920). Still, Grinnell and Wythe (1927) wrote, "Some doubt is still felt as to whether the upland breeding birds belong to the same subspecies as the salt marsh birds." Most subsequent authorities have recognized only one subspecies breeding in the Bay area (Grinnell and Miller 1944, Sibley 1952, AOU 1957), called *alaudinus* by the AOU (1957), but perhaps more appropriately lumped with the more widespread northern subspecies *anthinus* (Wheelwright and Rising 1993). Rising (pp. 135-142 1996), however, suggested that "the dark Savannah Sparrows that breed in salt marshes in the San Francisco Bay area" might best be considered *beldingi*, "whereas birds in other habitats in that area are probably typical Savannah Sparrows," and the issue of whether salt-marsh-nesting birds are darker than upland breeders in the Bay area has still not been resolved (Rising 2001). Physiological differences in salinity responses, which have been demonstrated between salt-marsh-breeding *beldingi/rostratus* and upland-breeding forms of the Savannah Sparrow (Bartholomew and Cade 1963), may result in segregation of Bay area Savannahs, as has also been demonstrated in the Song Sparrow (Basham and Mewaldt 1987). More study is needed to determine whether there are consistent differences between the Savannah Sparrows breeding in these very different habitats in the South Bay.

Stephen C. Rottenborn

SAVANNAH SPARROW

Palo Alto SBC

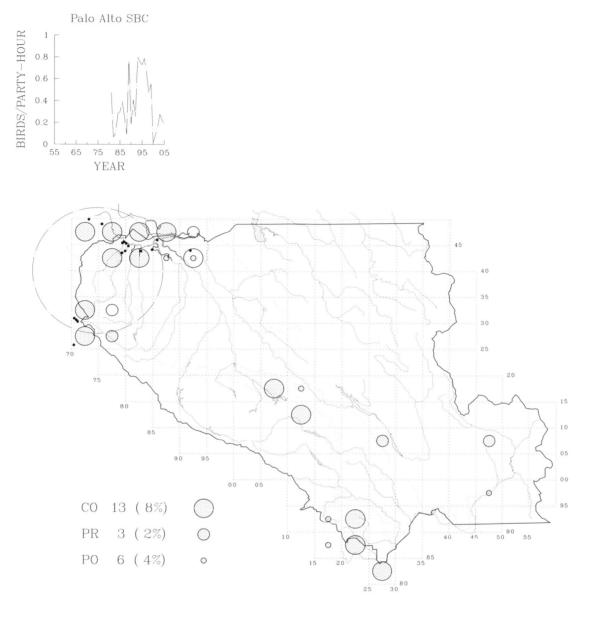

BIRDS/PARTY–HOUR

YEAR

CO 13 (8%)

PR 3 (2%)

PO 6 (4%)

Atlas (1987–1993), n = 18

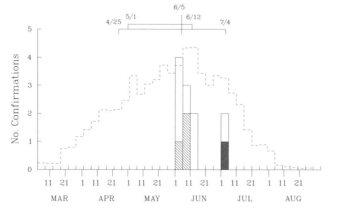

No. Confirmations

4/25 5/1 6/5 6/12 7/4

MAR APR MAY JUN JUL AUG

Grasshopper Sparrow
Ammodramus savannarum

Sharp eyesight and keen hearing are needed to detect the Grasshopper Sparrow in its grassy domain. The common name of this species reflects not only its insect-like song, but also its diet in summer, which consists mainly of grasshoppers. The specific name *savannarum* well describes the rolling grasslands that this secretive species inhabits. Twelve subspecies of the Grasshopper Sparrow are found from southern Canada to northwestern South America, four of them breeding in the United States. The subspecies *A. s. perpallidus* breeds in portions of the Coast Ranges from Del Norte County south to San Diego County (including Santa Clara County), with local populations in the foothills on both sides of the Sacramento Valley (Vickery 1996). In Santa Clara County, Grasshopper Sparrows breed in grasslands in the Santa Cruz Mountains, the Diablo Range, and the low-lying foothills near the Coyote Narrows, wintering sparingly in some of these grasslands as well.

The first mention of Grasshopper Sparrows in the county was of a specimen collected in summer by Rollo H. Beck prior to 1900 near Berryessa, suggesting breeding there (Barlow 1900b). This single record remained our only evidence for this species (Grinnell 1915, Grinnell and Wythe 1927) until Gayle B. Pickwell reported one in the Los Buellis Hills, east of Berryessa, on 19 Apr 1930 (*Wren-Tit 2(2)* 1930). On 20 Apr 1947, three birds were recorded on a Santa Clara Valley Audubon Society field trip to Weller Road (*Bull. SCVAS* July 1947). More southerly observations of Grasshopper Sparrows in the county, including evidence of breeding, were brought to light by Sibley (1952), who reported that R. Smith found a nest with young in the Silver Creek Hills, 10 km southeast of San Jose, in April 1947. Sibley (1952) also reported that Alfred J. Wool found a nest with eggs on Mission Ridge 27 Apr–12 May 1948. In subsequent years, Grasshopper Sparrows were found farther south toward Coyote (*Am. Birds 28*:946 1974) and Gilroy (*Audubon Field Notes 22*:646 1968). Prior to the start of the atlas period, this species was found in additional areas, including three singing birds on

4 Jun 1983 in the Russian Ridge Open Space Preserve in San Mateo County, as well as three singing on 11 Jun 1985 west of Sargent (both William G. Bousman, county notebooks.).

With the initiation of atlasing, a surge of reports made it clear that Grasshopper Sparrows were more common here than previously thought. The present-day distribution includes the historical distribution, but birds were also found more widely in grasslands in the Santa Cruz Mountains and the Diablo Range. Grasshopper Sparrows were reported at altitudes ranging from 200 feet to 2,620 feet, suggesting that altitude was not a limiting factor. In general, breeding Grasshopper Sparrows were found in extensive grasslands where grass heights were from 25 cm to more than a meter. These grasslands often offered some heterogeneity, such as rocks, small shrubs, or fenceposts that males used for song perches. Grasshopper Sparrows were also found in serpentine grasslands where extensive forbs were mixed in with grasses. Within drier grasslands, they were found in wetter swales formed by springs or poor drainage, but there were few records of Grasshopper Sparrows from oak savannas with widely spaced trees, or in heavily grazed areas with short grasses and weeds that provided little cover. In the Santa Cruz Mountains, breeding Grasshopper Sparrows were found in grasslands extending from Monte Bello Open Space Preserve in Santa Clara County to the northwest well into San Mateo County (Sequoia Audubon Society 2001l). Breeding birds were also found in the southeast part of this range, where the hills drop down to the Pajaro River Valley. These sparrows were found in the Santa Cruz Mountains foothills as well, south of the Coyote Narrows. East of the Santa Clara Valley, they were observed most frequently on the west side of the Diablo Range, from Calaveras Reservoir southeast to the hills above Pacheco Creek. Grasshopper Sparrows also occurred in the grasslands both south and north of Pacheco Pass, but they were absent from the drier grasslands in the northeastern part of the county and from the grasslands along the Stanislaus County border south of there. Abundance under appropriate conditions was indicated by a high count of 71 Grasshopper Sparrows seen in the drainage of Sargent Creek in the southern Santa Cruz Mountains on 15 Apr 1989 (David L. Suddjian, pers. comm.).

Ten nests were discovered during the atlas period, seven with eggs and three with young. Nests with eggs were found from 25 Apr to 20 May, and nests with young were found from 2 Jun to 3 Jul. During the atlas period, 50% of the 38 confirmations reported were of recently fledged young or of adults feeding fledglings, with dates spanning 12 Jun through 22 Jul.

Vickery (1996) states that Grasshopper Sparrows in Oregon breed primarily in native bunchgrass, but the bunchgrass in California was disappearing by the middle of the nineteenth century as a result of overgrazing, cultivation, and the introduction of non-native annual grasses (Kozloff and Beidleman 1994). The greatest threat to bunchgrass is competition from the introduced annual grasses, and in Santa Clara County bunchgrass has been almost completely supplanted by invasive European grasses. If Grasshopper Sparrows previously nested in bunchgrass in the county, they have now adapted to weedy exotics as a suitable replacement.

Gloria G. Heller

GRASSHOPPER SPARROW

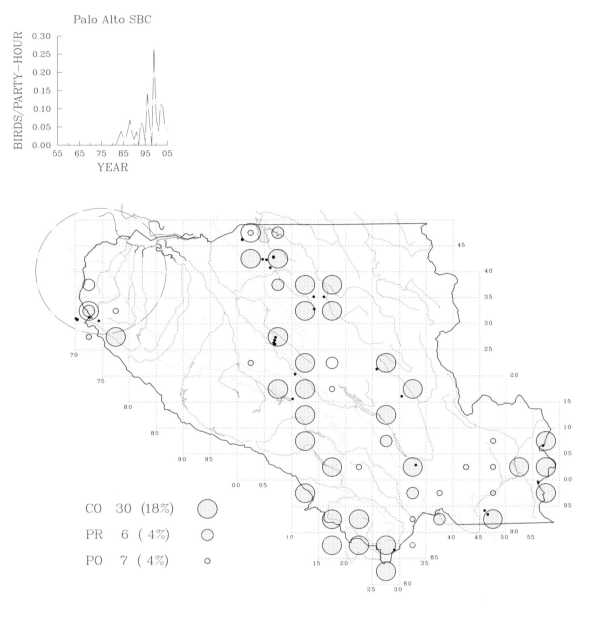

Palo Alto SBC

CO 30 (18%)

PR 6 (4%)

PO 7 (4%)

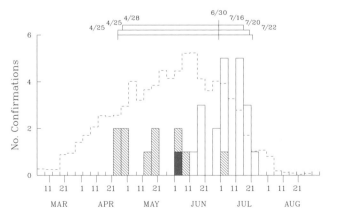

Atlas (1987–1993), n = 38

Song Sparrow
Melospiza melodia

One of the most widespread and geographically variable birds breeding in North America, the Song Sparrow boasts 31 subspecies ranging from the Aleutian Islands east to the Atlantic Ocean and south throughout much of North America to northern Mexico (AOU 1957). Twelve of the subspecies breed in California (Grinnell and Miller 1944, Small 1994), where this species is absent only from the high-altitude Sierran crest and the arid southern deserts. In Santa Clara County, breeding Song Sparrows are represented by two distinct races: *M. m. pusillula*, in tidal salt marshes along the Bay, and *M. m. gouldii*, in riparian habitats and freshwater marshes throughout the portion of the county lying between the western foothills of the Diablo Range and the Santa Cruz Mountains. Though these two subspecies are resident in the county, several other races occur here also, but only in winter (Grinnell and Miller 1944).

Both *gouldii* and *pusillula* have long been considered common in Santa Clara County in their respective habitats (Van Denburgh 1899b, Grinnell and Wythe 1927, Grinnell and Miller 1944, Sibley 1952). Most historical accounts of the county's Song Sparrows have addressed the differentiation between these two races. As early as the turn of the century, Price (1898f) and Barlow (1900b) distinguished the larger, paler Song Sparrows breeding in streamside habitats (*gouldii*) from the smaller, darker birds breeding in Bay marshes (*pusillula*). Grinnell (1901b) found these two races breeding side by side near the mouth of San Francisquito Creek, *gouldii* restricting all its activities in the contact zone to dense willow clumps, while *pusillula* was found only in adjacent salt marsh. The infrequent occurrence of intermediate individuals at the creek mouth indicated that interbreeding between these two races was limited (Grinnell 1901b, Marshall 1948). Several possible mechanisms that promote reproductive isolation have been proposed. *Pusillula* is able to maintain body mass (and therefore survive) in saline environments, whereas *gouldii* cannot (Basham and Mewaldt 1987). This distinction suggests that interbreeding by these races may be inhibited via selection against intergrades that inhabit saline environments but lack *pusillula*'s adaptations. Interbreeding may be further restricted by differences in habitat requirements and breeding phenology, and by the extremely sedentary nature of these birds (Marshall 1948, Johnston 1956, Halliburton and Mewaldt 1976).

Atlasers recorded potentially breeding Song Sparrows in 62% of the county's blocks and confirmed breeding in 50% of all blocks, at elevations ranging from sea level to 2,500 feet. In Santa Clara County, Song Sparrows breed only in areas with abundant moisture and suitably dense ground cover, so it is little surprise that they were found to be quite uncommon and sparsely distributed in the dry interior of the Diablo Range. Attesting to this species' association with water, Song Sparrows were found in 1993 (following a wet winter) along portions of Arroyo Hondo where the species had been absent during the previous drought years (Michael M. Rogers, pers. comm.). Song Sparrows were absent from a few blocks in the Santa Cruz Mountains as well. Apparently, this species avoids streams shaded by dense coniferous canopies, even where ostensibly suitable understory vegetation is present (Shuford 1993ee).

Breeding *gouldii* are most abundant in riparian habitats having dense vegetation near the ground along perennial streams, and in freshwater marshes or the marshy borders of ponds. These birds are less common in more sparsely vegetated riparian habitats, in moist fields having dense stands of charlock, along ephemeral streams, and along high-gradient streams with little herbaceous riparian vegetation. Most nests are within a few feet of the ground in dense herbaceous vegetation. In salt marshes, *pusillula* are most abundant in tall marsh vegetation, particularly in the gum plant/California cord grass association immediately adjacent to tidal sloughs. *M. m. pusillula* are also found in peppergrass in the upper, drier portions of salt marshes (pers. obs.) and in brackish marshes dominated by bulrushes (Marshall and Dedrick 1994). They tend to make limited use of the broad expanses of short pickleweed favored by Savannah Sparrows (Johnston 1956, Collins and Resh 1985). Along several streams in the South Bay, Song Sparrows seem to be distributed continuously from the upper reaches down to tidal salt marsh. This distribution indicates that *gouldii* and *pusillula* come into contact along these streams, probably at the interface of brackish and freshwater habitats, as Grinnell (1901b) found at San Francisquito Creek.

Song Sparrows were observed carrying nesting material as early as 21 Mar during atlasing, but a nest with small young on 29 Mar 1998 (pers. obs.) and an adult feeding fledged young on 1 Apr 1997 (Michael M. Rogers, pers. comm.) indicate even earlier nesting. A broad peak in records of recently fledged young, extending through most of May and June, indicates that peak nesting activity occurs from mid-April to mid-June. Late nesting was evidenced by birds carrying nesting material in late June. Nests with young were found as late as 13 Jul, and adults were seen feeding fledged young as late as 5 Aug during the atlas period. Subsequently, an adult was seen feeding young as late as 30 Aug 1997 (Michael M. Rogers, PADB). Although atlas data provide little information on differences in breeding phenology between *pusillula* and *gouldii*, salt-marsh-breeding Song Sparrows in the Bay area (including *pusillula*) are known to breed about two weeks earlier than *gouldii* (Johnston 1954, 1956). This early breeding by *pusillula* is apparently an adaptation to breeding in a tidal environment, since high tides in late spring and early summer can destroy large numbers of nests.

Stephen C. Rottenborn

SONG SPARROW

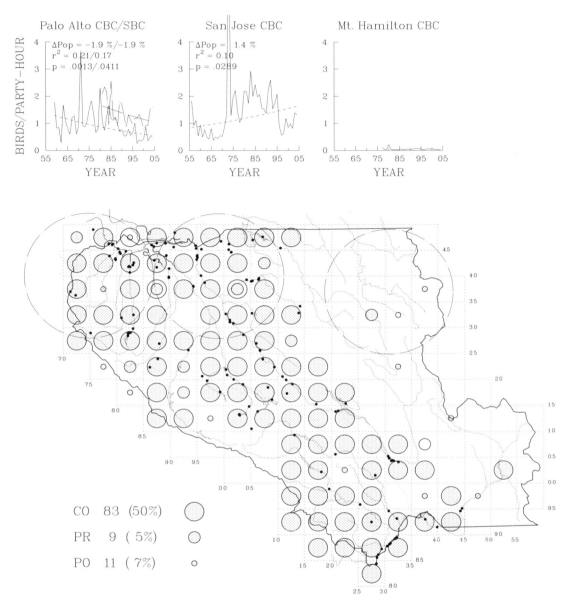

Palo Alto CBC/SBC

ΔPop = −1.9 %/−1.9 %
r² = 0.21/0.17
p = .0013/.0411

San Jose CBC

ΔPop = 1.4 %
r² = 0.10
p = .0289

Mt. Hamilton CBC

BIRDS/PARTY-HOUR

YEAR

CO 83 (50%)
PR   9 (5%)
PO 11 (7%)

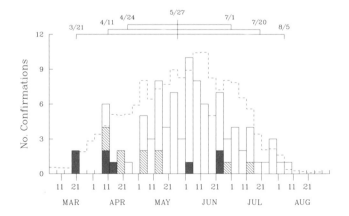

Atlas (1987−1993), n = 163

No. Confirmations

MAR   APR   MAY   JUN   JUL   AUG

413

Dark-eyed Junco
Junco hyemalis

This handsome ground-nesting sparrow, characterized by flashing white outer tail feathers and a musical trill, is typically found foraging under moist undergrowth in the shade of forest and woodland trees. The Dark-eyed Junco is found breeding, wintering, or as a resident throughout North America south of sub-Arctic Alaska and Canada. Fourteen subspecies have been described in this range (AOU 1957), three of which breed in California (Grinnell and Miller 1944). The subspecies *J. h. pinosus*, formerly named *J. oreganus pinosus* or the "Pt. Pinos" Oregon Junco, occurs as a resident breeder in the coastal mountains of California from the San Francisco peninsula and Contra Costa County south to San Benito and San Luis Obispo counties (Grinnell and Miller 1944). In Santa Clara County the Dark-eyed Junco is a common resident of moist forests of the Santa Cruz Mountains and the less arid portions of the Diablo Range.

The Dark-eyed Junco has always been a common species in Santa Clara County. In May 1864, Cooper (1870) found many Dark-eyed Juncos breeding in "the Coast mountains south of Santa Clara." Price (1898f) noted the withdrawal of this species from the Stanford University campus in summer, but believed a few pairs remained to nest. Fisher (1904) subsequently collected a nest, eggs, and a specimen from the campus arboretum. Van Denburgh (1899b) commented that although the juncos bred throughout the redwood region, he found a few of them nesting in the chaparral belt in the hills south of Los Gatos near Alma. A study conducted from 1929 to 1936 at Alum Rock Park in the western foothills of the Diablo Range found that this species was the fourth most abundant bird in that area (Linsdale and Rodgers 1937). Sibley (1952), in his summary of regional records, considered *pinosus* a common resident, especially in the fog belt of the Santa Cruz Mountains, but also in the Diablo Range.

During the atlas period, the Dark-eyed Junco was recorded in 81% of the county's blocks, and confirmed in 71% of the blocks. Breeding juncos were found in the foothills and higher elevations of the Santa Cruz Mountains and the Diablo

Range, and a few were confirmed breeding on the Santa Clara Valley floor. Including records from the postatlas period, juncos bred at elevations ranging from 4 feet in Mountain View east of Highway 101 to 4,000 feet on Eylar Mountain and Mt. Hamilton. The Dark-eyed Junco, predominantly a ground nester and forager, breeds in a great variety of habitats, provided that an understory with some shade and moisture is available. These include redwood canyons, Douglas fir forests, comparatively arid, dense live oak woodlands, and Coulter and foothill pine "forests" (Grinnell and Miller 1944). Atlas observers noted an apparent difference in numbers of breeding birds between the county's two mountain ranges. Abundance was highest in the Santa Cruz Mountains, where suitable habitat with a moist understory is widespread. In the western part of the Diablo Range, where suitable habitats are largely limited to north-facing slopes and canyon bottoms, the abundance was lower. Few birds were found in the dry, eastern Diablo Range, where suitable mesic conditions are uncommon. Small numbers of breeding confirmations were obtained in blocks where the Santa Clara Valley meets the foothills of the Santa Cruz Mountains, such as the Stanford University campus, where pairs nested near campus buildings in English ivy or in low, dense patches of exotic vines. But during the postatlas period, Dark-eyed Juncos were seen to have expanded into the northern Santa Clara Valley as well, where breeding was confirmed in eight additional blocks. By the end of the postatlas period, some birds were breeding within a kilometer of the edge of the Bay. Many of the new breeding records were in mesic habitats associated with landscaping at light industrial parks, particularly the planting of coast redwoods and English ivy as a ground cover. The invasion of breeding birds onto the valley floor is perhaps reflected in the 2.5% per year increase shown by analysis of the Palo Alto SBC data.

The Dark-eyed Junco's breeding season during the atlas period lasted nearly five months, extending from 28 Mar (carrying nesting material on the Stanford campus) to 10 Aug (recently fledged young in the Palo Alto Foothills Park area). Following the atlas period, earlier breeding was evidenced by nest building in Los Gatos on 14 Mar 2000 (Kathryn Parker, PADB), and a later confirmation was furnished by adults feeding fledged young near Great America on 26 Aug 2004 (Michael J. Mammoser, PADB). Nest building and occupancy were most frequently noted from early April to mid-June, and fledglings were found in good numbers from May through July. The protracted breeding period suggests multiple nestings or renestings, not unusual for this species in the southern portion of its range (Ehrlich et al. 1988). Only one instance of cowbird parasitism was noted, out of 273 confirmed nestings during the atlas period, which is consistent with prior findings that *pinosus* is an uncommon host (Ehrlich et al. 1988). But in the postatlas period, 25 instances of parasitism were recorded, all from urban areas, and about half from blocks where no breeding had been observed during the atlas period. Nonetheless, the Dark-eyed Junco continues to be one of the most common birds in the county, reckoned on either total confirmations or the abundance code.

Roy C. Cameron

DARK-EYED JUNCO

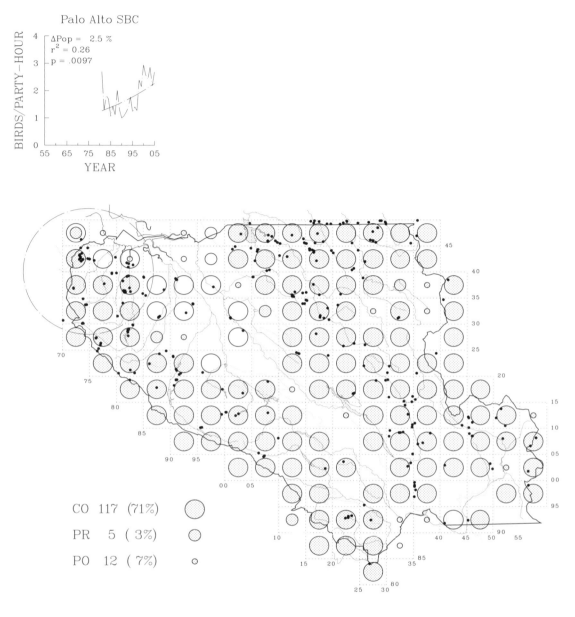

Palo Alto SBC

ΔPop = 2.5 %
$r^2 = 0.26$
p = .0097

BIRDS/PARTY−HOUR

YEAR

CO 117 (71%)
PR 5 (3%)
PO 12 (7%)

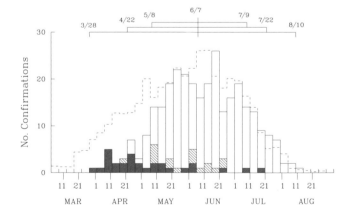

3/28   4/22   5/8   6/7   7/9   7/22   8/10

No. Confirmations

Atlas (1987−1993), n = 351

MAR   APR   MAY   JUN   JUL   AUG

Black-headed Grosbeak
Pheucticus melanocephalus

The male Black-headed Grosbeak presents not only a handsome plumage of black, orange, and flashes of white, but a melodious song as well. As if that were not enough, he seems unable to resist singing from the nest while incubating eggs. Black-headed Grosbeaks breed in western North America from British Columbia east to North Dakota and thence south along the Pacific Coast to Baja California, and south from the Rocky Mountains through the highlands of Mexico to Oaxaca (Hill 1995). Two subspecies are recognized: *P. m. melanocephalus* in the Rocky Mountains and *maculatus* along the Pacific Coast (Hill 1995). In California, Black-headed Grosbeaks breed in forested areas throughout the state (Small 1994). In Santa Clara County, they are common summer residents throughout the county, except in urbanized areas.

The earliest record of the Black-headed Grosbeak in Santa Clara County is an undated specimen collected in San Jose and acquired by the U.S. National Museum sometime prior to 1860 (USNM #33809). This specimen, collected by Andrew J. Grayson, was probably obtained between 1853 and 1857, during which time Grayson lived in San Jose. A set of three eggs collected in Los Gatos on 17 May 1887 by F. H. Corless (USNM #26009) is the earliest breeding record. Early observers remarked on the beauty of this grosbeak's song, and considered the bird common to abundant (Price 1898f, Van Denburgh 1899b, Fisher 1902). Grinnell and Wythe (1927) described it as a common summer resident throughout the San Francisco Bay area, and Sibley (1952) recorded that it was a common summer resident of "riparian woodland, oak woodland, and mixed coniferous forest" in the South Bay. Analysis of the Palo Alto SBC data since 1981 shows a decline of 3.8% per year within that circle. This decline appears local, since no change has been observed in Breeding Bird Survey data for California from 1966 to 2004 (Sauer et al. 2005).

Atlasers found Black-headed Grosbeaks distributed widely in Santa Clara County. Considering confirmed, probable, and possible breeding records, grosbeaks were found in 151 blocks (92%). Breeding was confirmed from an elevation of 20 feet near the Guadalupe River south of Montague Expressway to 3,700 feet near the summit of Black Mountain in the interior of the Diablo Range. Atlasers found Black-headed Grosbeaks along stream courses, in broadleaved evergreen woodlands, and in mixed forests of conifers and broadleaved evergreens. Most birds were found where there was a mixture of trees, shrubs, and understory plants with water nearby. More homogeneous habitats, such as dense broadleaved or coniferous forests without openings or edge habitat, were avoided, as were oak savanna and grasslands. Grosbeaks were often found along the edges of chaparral and grasslands where there was shrub and understory cover along intermittent streams, and even in chaparral on north- and east-facing slopes where a mixture of small tree and shrub species provided the mesic conditions these grosbeaks prefer. Black-headed Grosbeaks tended to avoid suburban or urban areas, except along well-wooded urban creeks. Breeding-season surveys in 1995 found these birds on 54 of 68 study plots in mature cottonwood and willow forest along Coyote Creek, the Guadalupe River, and Los Gatos Creek, though creeks in the most heavily urbanized areas were generally avoided (Rottenborn 1999).

Male Black-headed Grosbeaks begin singing as soon as they arrive on breeding territories in central California (Weston 1947). In Santa Clara County, grosbeaks arrive between 24 Mar and 7 Apr, with a median date of 30 Mar (county notebooks). The earliest breeding evidence during the atlas period was nest building on 3 Apr. Incubation was encountered as early as 13 Apr, and the first fledglings were found by 2 May. The latest breeding evidence was fledglings on 1 Aug. Black-headed Grosbeaks are single-brooded, but will renest following nesting failure through the second week in June (Hill 1995). The males leave breeding areas soon after the young fledge, and the females and juveniles generally depart by August or early September.

Historically, Black-headed Grosbeaks were considered pests in California fruit orchards, particularly for their consumption of cherries (Beal 1910). Early orchardists, using indiscriminate poisons such as strychnine, killed a variety of birds (Daggett 1900). Early ornithologists then undertook a major effort to assess the economic impacts of birds as pests, primarily by the systematic examination of stomach contents (McAtee 1908, Beal 1910). McAtee (1908) pointed out that "for every quart of fruit eaten, more than 3 pints of black olive scales and more than a quart of flower beetles, besides a generous sprinkling of codling moth pupae and cankerworms, fall prey to this grosbeak," indicating the substantial economic benefit of these birds to orchards. The Santa Clara Valley was once a major producer of cherries (Jacobson 1984), but the battle between farmers and birds in the valley is now little more than a memory.

William G. Bousman

BLACK-HEADED GROSBEAK

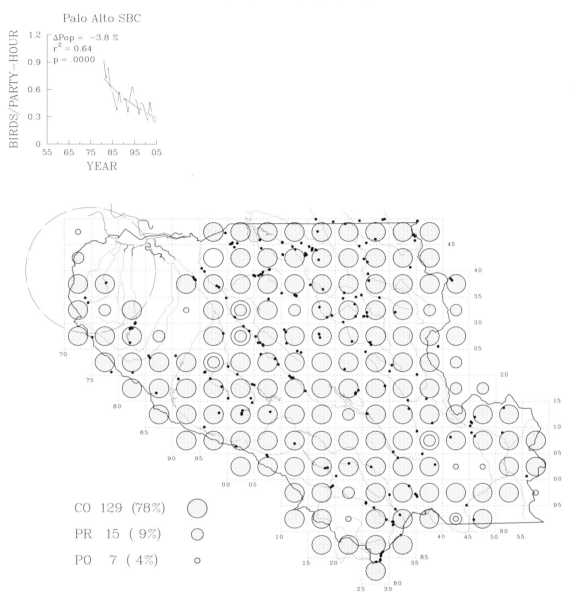

Palo Alto SBC

ΔPop = −3.8 %
r² = 0.64
p = .0000

CO 129 (78%)
PR 15 (9%)
PO 7 (4%)

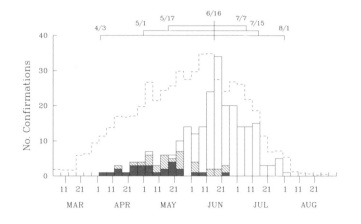

Atlas (1987−1993), n = 275

Blue Grosbeak
Passerina caerulea

This resplendent grosbeak, expanding its range in the western United States, has only recently begun to nest in the Bay area. The Blue Grosbeak breeds from northern California across the Great Plains to Pennsylvania and south through much of the United States into Baja California, Mexico, and Costa Rica (AOU 1998). Two subspecies breed in California, *P. c. salicaria* throughout the Central Valley, southwestern California, and northwestern Baja California, and *interfusa* in the Salton Sink and the Colorado River Valley (Grinnell and Miller 1944). The Blue Grosbeak has recently expanded its range to include Santa Clara County, with breeding records from single locations in both the southern and northern parts of the county.

Price (1898f) stated that the Blue Grosbeak was "rather rare" at Stanford, but he included no details of his observations, and Grinnell and Wythe (1927) knew of only one record in the San Francisco Bay area by the beginning of the twentieth century, a bird seen at Hayward on 1 May 1876. Grinnell and Miller (1944) described *salicaria*'s California breeding range as including coastal southern California, the Sacramento and San Joaquin valleys, and Owens Valley. Although they noted coastal observations extending to the San Francisco Bay region, they were not aware of any breeding west of the Central Valley. Johnson (1994) described a significant northward range expansion from population centers in Arizona and New Mexico, starting in the 1960s. Perhaps coincidentally, breeding well west of the Central Valley was discovered in 1958, when a pair nested south of Hollister, San Benito County, on 1 Jun 1958 (*Audubon Field Notes 13*:398 1959). Although sporadic reports of spring Blue Grosbeaks were obtained subsequently in the San Francisco Bay region, and as far north as Del Norte County, it was not until 1987 that nesting was suspected in eastern Alameda County (*Am. Birds 41*:486 1987), and a repeat nesting occurred in San Benito County (*Am. Birds 41*:1485 1987). Nesting was confirmed in eastern Alameda County and the upper Salinas Valley, Monterey County, in 1990 (*Am. Birds 44*:1183 1990, Roberson

1993ff). On 25 Jul 1995, a pair with at least two fledged young was found near San Pablo Bay in Sonoma County, constituting the first breeding record from the immediate San Francisco Bay region (Burridge 1995e, *Field Notes 49*:978 1995).

The first record of a Blue Grosbeak in Santa Clara County was of a male banded on 22 Jul 1989 at the Coyote Creek Riparian Station (CCRS) near Alviso (L. Richard Mewaldt, pers. comm.). Single second-year males were banded at CCRS on 11 Jun 1992 and 17 Jun 1992 (Gina Barton, pers. comm.), and an atlaser found a male along the Pajaro River at Sargent on 25 Apr 1993. Following the atlas period, a male was found singing in an extensive ruderal area along Coyote Creek north of the Riverside Golf Course in Morgan Hill on 27 Apr 1994 (Stephen C. Rottenborn, Michael M. Rogers; county notebooks). It remained in this area through at least 16 May, but no evidence of nesting was obtained. A male was again found at this location 3-6 May 1995, but again no evidence of nesting was observed (Stephen C. Rottenborn, county notebooks). Finally, on 2 Sep 1995, a female Blue Grosbeak was found in willows along Llagas Creek above Bloomfield Road accompanied by three begging dependent fledglings, one of which was fed by the female (Stephen C. Rottenborn, Michael M. Rogers; pers. comm.). In this agricultural area southeast of Gilroy, Llagas Creek is bordered by levees, and dense growth of willows along the creek bottom and tall, dense, weedy vegetation along the levee sides provided suitable habitat for this first county breeding record.

Since the nesting of Blue Grosbeaks along Llagas Creek in 1995, this species has been found in various locations in the county in every subsequent year. In particular, up to three or four birds have been found in Ed Levin County Park each spring from 1997 to 2001 and again in 2004 (county notebooks). On 3 May 1998, a female was watched as she carried grass stems and mustard stalks to a likely nest site (Michael J. Mammoser, county notebooks). The male continuously guarded the female, but did not participate in nest construction. The nest location was on the slopes above Sandy Wool Lake, in an area of non-native grasses and weeds that had previously been grazed. A small grove of sycamores was within a hundred meters of this location, but otherwise the nest site was located in open grassland with occasional rock outcrops. Subsequent to this observation, however, no further evidence of nesting was obtained.

Typical egg dates for *salicaria*, based on 38 egg sets, range from 18 Apr to 12 Jul (Taber 1968). The carrying of nest material on 3 May 1998 by the bird found in Ed Levin County Park is consistent with these dates. But the observation of fledged young along Llagas Creek on 2 Sep 1995 suggests that these birds hatched from eggs laid in late July or early August, which is late for this species within its historical range. Tyler (1913), for example, considered Blue Grosbeaks to be one of the earliest of fall migrants, with birds departing their breeding areas by early August.

William G. Bousman

BLUE GROSBEAK

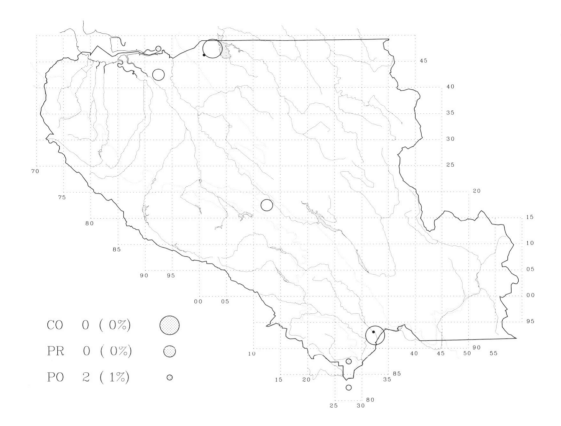

CO   0 (0%)

PR   0 (0%)

PO   2 (1%)

Postatlas (1994−2005), n = 2

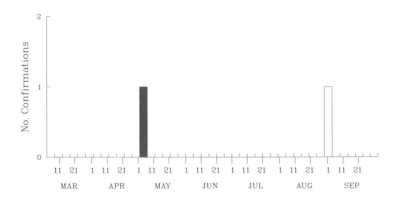

Lazuli Bunting

Passerina amoena

The female Lazuli Bunting is another brush-dwelling little brown bird, but the male decorates the tangles like an orange and turquoise jewel, and wafts a joyous song to the passing breeze. This species is fairly common in dry, brushy edge habitats of the west, breeding from the southern edge of western Canada south through most of the western United States (Greene et al. 1996). In California, it breeds in suitable habitat throughout the state, principally west of the Sierra Nevada and the southeastern deserts (Small 1994). In Santa Clara County, the species breeds sparingly along the Santa Cruz Mountain ridges, but is more common and widespread throughout the drier Diablo range.

Historical records indicate that the Lazuli Bunting has long been considered "common" in broken and edge habitats in the San Francisco Bay area (Price 1898c, Fisher 1902, Grinnell and Wythe 1927, Sibley 1952). In the late nineteenth and early twentieth centuries, egg sets were collected from various locations in Santa Clara County, including College Park, along the Guadalupe River, Almaden, Los Gatos, San Jose, Gilroy, and the Wool Ranch (WFVZ egg collections). The earliest egg set was collected by A. L. Parkhurst on 11 May 1884 (WFVZ #159047), likely from San Jose. Although Lazuli Buntings no longer breed in the northern Santa Clara Valley where they were found historically, there is no indication of population changes in the Palo Alto count circle or in California as a whole in recent decades (Sauer et al. 2005).

Lazuli Buntings were found in more than half of the blocks (86) in the county during the atlas period, and breeding was confirmed in about a quarter of the blocks (39). In the Santa Cruz Mountains, breeding birds were found adjacent to grasslands in the northern part of the range, in broken chaparral and scrublands from Lexington Reservoir south to Loma Prieta, and near the Pajaro River in the southern part of the range. Habitats used in these areas were a mixture of open grasslands, brushy vegetation, and chaparral. In wetter places, dense, herbaceous vegetation added to the mixture of habitats used by Lazuli Bun-

tings. Similar habitats are widespread in the Diablo Range, and possible breeding was found in more than three-quarters (62 of 78) of the blocks east of the Santa Clara Valley, with breeding confirmed in 27 blocks. Breeding birds were also found along the valley floor south of the Coyote Narrows, and in the Pajaro River floodplain. In these valley floor locations, the predominant habitat used by Lazulis was dense, herbaceous vegetation, including poison hemlock and various thistle species. During the atlas period, breeding elevations ranged from 120 feet near the Pajaro River to 2,480 feet south of Colorado Creek in the northern Diablo Range. Following the atlas period, breeding was noted at an elevation of 2,680 feet on Monte Bello Ridge on 9 May 2002 (Les Chibana, PADB) and again on 7 Jun 2003 (Garth Harwood, PADB).

Lazuli Buntings are often attracted to disturbed habitats with new vegetation. The San Diego County Bird Atlas (Unitt 2004) noted a strong association of Lazuli Buntings with recently burned chaparral. Burned areas were uncommon in our county during the atlas period, but new growth was often found in streams or reservoirs where the water table had dropped during the severe drought in the late 1980s. In one of the drought summers ". . . the dried-out bed of Grant Lake was just filled with singing male Lazulis. . ." (William G. Bousman, pers. comm.). In 1991, Arroyo Hondo had dried up by summer, and "singing males about every 100 yards or so" were seen in the herbaceous vegetation along the streambed (Michael M. Rogers, pers. comm.). This observer also noted "many confirmations in streambeds or south-facing fairly steep slopes above streambeds" with "typically dry mixed chaparral and brush with some edge or open areas."

The first Lazuli Buntings generally arrive in Santa Clara County from Mexico in April (median date 18 Apr, county notebooks). During the atlas period, the earliest evidence of breeding was birds carrying nesting material on 13 May; adults were first seen carrying food for young on 22 May. Following the atlas period, birds were seen carrying nesting material on 6 May 1997 (Stephen C. Rottenborn, PADB), and carrying food for young on 9 May 2002 (Les Chibana, PADB). Lazuli Buntings often produce two broods (Ehrlich et al. 1988), the male tending the fledglings while the female renests (Greene et al. 1996). Breeding confirmations from late July and August are possibly second broods. During the atlas period, the latest confirmation was of an adult carrying food on 4 Aug; following the atlas period, a fledgling was observed on 22 Aug 2005 (Garth Harwood, PADB).

In North America, Lazuli Buntings have benefited from successional vegetation following logging, but they no longer nest in urbanized areas (Ehrlich et al. 1988). The breeding status of the Lazuli Bunting in Santa Clara County appears relatively stable, since habitat loss has been largely restricted to the valley floor, and breeding is still widespread, especially in the Diablo Range. Brown-headed Cowbird parasitism of Lazuli Buntings has been a problem elsewhere (Greene et al. 1996, Greene 1999), but no parasitism was detected here during the atlas period or thereafter.

Charles J. Coston

LAZULI BUNTING

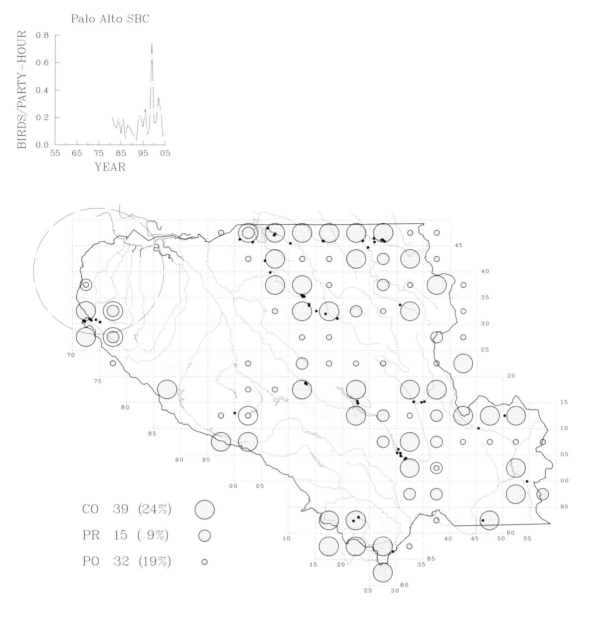

Palo Alto SBC

CO 39 (24%)
PR 15 (9%)
PO 32 (19%)

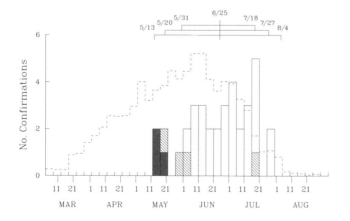

Atlas (1987–1993), n = 63

421

Indigo Bunting
Passerina cyanea

Indigo Buntings, originally limited to the eastern United States, have been detected increasingly in central California in recent decades. These observations include one known breeding attempt in Santa Clara County. Historically, Indigo Buntings have been common summer residents over much of the eastern United States (Payne 1992). In the past century, their summer range has expanded west into the Great Plains states, and since the 1940s this species has been found nesting in the southwestern United States. Indigo Buntings are now regular spring migrants along the eastern border of southern California, and occasional hybrid breeding pairs have been found within the state (Small 1994). In Santa Clara County, Indigo Buntings are still very rare summer visitors, and there are only two winter records, one from November, the other from January. This bunting is found here about once every other year.

There were few records of Indigo Buntings in California prior to their expansion into the southwestern United States. The earliest record in California was of a basic-plumaged male collected by Walter P. Taylor at Mecca, Riverside County, on 11 Apr 1908 (MVZ #811), but misidentified as a Lazuli Bunting (Thompson 1964). First records for northern California occurred in 1939, when birds were reported at three locations in Alameda County: Strawberry Canyon, 24 Jun; near Mills College in Oakland, 3 Aug; and again in Oakland, 26 Aug (Grinnell and Miller 1944). The first record for Santa Clara County was of a singing male found by David DeSante in Foothills Park in the summer of 1975 (*Am. Birds 29*:1029 1975).

From 1987 to 1992, just two male Indigo Buntings were observed during June and July: on Loma Prieta on 22 Jun 1987 (David L. Suddjian, Bryan M. Mori, county notebooks), and in Regnart Canyon, Cupertino, on 17 Jul 1991 (Jo-Ann Gholson, county notebooks). Both records were considered to be of vagrant birds, and neither of the birds was observed subsequently. On 1 Jun 1993, however, while atlasing along Colorado Creek south of Eylar Mountain, Stephen C. Rottenborn and Michael M. Rogers found a male Indigo-like bunting paired with a fe-

male Lazuli Bunting attending a nest with two eggs. The male's plumage was mostly deep blue, but included extensive white on the underparts and white wingbars similar to those of a male Lazuli Bunting. Brown coloration on some wing coverts and tail feathers suggested that this was a second-calendar-year bird. The song seemed similar to that of nearby Lazuli Buntings. Rogers returned to this site on 12 Jun of that year and found the male still present (photograph, *Am. Birds 47*:1148 1993), but no eggs or young were in the nest. Following the atlas period, on 29 May 1994, Rogers returned to the Colorado Creek site and again found a territorial male Indigo-like Bunting at the same location. This bird now lacked the brown hues in the wing coverts and tail feathers seen in 1993, and there were no white wingbars, but there was still extensive white on the abdomen. This time the bird's song was typical of an Indigo Bunting.

Following the atlas period, from 1994 to 2005, additional Indigo Buntings have been found in the county during June and July, all documented in the county notebooks. On 18 Jul 1998, a second-calendar-year male was seen along Coyote Creek below Highway 237 (Alvaro Jaramillo). On 6 Jun 1999, a male was found in the Monte Bello Open Space Preserve (Michael Wienholt). Another second-year bird recorded on 14 Jun 1999 was 5 to 6 kilometers west of this location in the Long Ridge Open Space Preserve in San Mateo County, where it was seen through 15 Jul (Les Chibana, mult. obs.). The next year, a male was found in an area that straddled Page Mill Road in the Los Trancos and Monte Bello open space preserves on 24 May, and it remained at least through 24 Jun (Rosalie Lefkowitz et al., mult. obs.). On 3 Jul 2001, an adult male was seen at the Arastradero Preserve (John Meyer, Lisa Pavey), and on 6 Jun 2004, a female was seen on Summit Road, about 3 kilometers northwest of Highway 17 (David L. Suddjian).

The specific status of the Indigo-like Bunting that was paired with the female Lazuli Bunting near Colorado Creek in 1993 may never be known. The presence of white wingbars and white on the belly is suggestive of a possible hybrid Indigo × Lazuli Bunting (Sibley 2000), but the plumage characteristics of male Indigo Buntings are variable (Kroodsma 1975, Payne 1992). Kroodsma (1975), in his studies in the northern Great Plains, noted that the Indigo Bunting's prenuptial molt is progressive through the season, such that many birds (including full adults) still retain the white underparts of the basic plumage in May, and a significant number of males may still retain these white underparts into August. In contrast, Lazuli Buntings do not have an obvious prenuptial molt (Kroodsma 1975). Payne (1992) described Indigo Bunting alternate plumages as variable, and noted that some adult birds may show different plumages from year to year, including white on the belly. The Colorado Creek male may have been a pure Indigo Bunting or the result of a hybrid pairing. Birds that are hybrids are encountered in central California nearly as often as pure Indigo Buntings, but the Colorado Creek bird, if a hybrid, was not clearly so.

William G. Bousman

INDIGO BUNTING

Palo Alto SBC

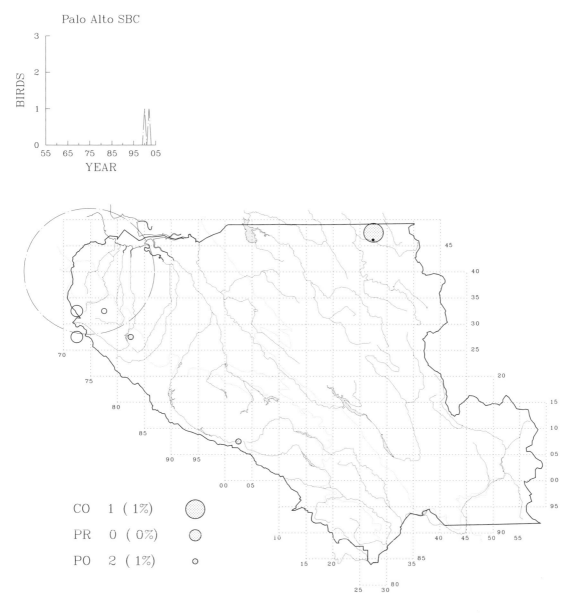

CO 1 (1%)
PR 0 (0%)
PO 2 (1%)

Atlas (1987–1993), n = 1

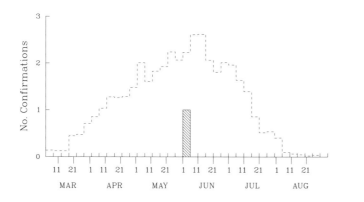

R.COLWELL

Red-winged Blackbird
Agelaius phoeniceus

This blackbird, the male with its fiery red epaulets, is an abundant breeder in South Bay wetlands, both large and small. The Red-winged Blackbird breeds from southern Alaska across Canada to Newfoundland and south through the United States and Mexico to Costa Rica (Yasukawa and Searcy 1995). As many as 26 subspecies have been described, of which 14 occur in North America and seven in California (Small 1994, Yasukawa and Searcy 1995). Curiously, three of the California subspecies are bicolored, lacking the yellowish or buff lower edge to the red shoulder patch. The first of these, *A. p. mailliardorum*, is resident in coastal California from Humboldt County to Monterey County; the second, *californicus*, is found in the Central Valley; and the third, *aciculatus*, is found in the upper Kern River drainage (van Rossem 1926, Grinnell and Miller 1944, Yasukawa and Searcy 1995). In Santa Clara County, *mailliardorum* is a widespread and abundant resident. In winter, other subspecies, with yellowish edges to the wing coverts, are sometimes found mixed into our local flocks.

The Red-winged Blackbird has long been a common resident in Santa Clara County. The species appears on Sclater's list of birds collected by Thomas Bridges in the "Valley of San José" sometime prior to 1857 (Sclater 1857). Chester Barlow collected a set of three eggs in the county on 23 May 1892 (USNM #B44467). Price (1898d) considered the bird a resident at Stanford, and Barlow (1900b) stated that it was abundant in the Santa Clara Valley grainfields and marshes. Fisher (1902) judged it to be an abundant breeder in wet meadows near marshes. Grinnell and Wythe (1927) stated that it was an abundant resident in the San Francisco Bay area. Sibley (1952) considered the redwing a common resident in the South Bay. An analysis of CBC data over the last 50 years indicates that the number of Red-winged Blackbirds has declined by 2.2% per year on the San Jose CBC and by 3.4% per year on the Palo Alto CBC. But analysis of the data from the Palo Alto SBC over the last 25 years shows no significant population trend. For the California region, analysis of the Breeding Bird Survey data showed no significant population trend from 1966 to 2004 (Sauer et al. 2005).

Atlasers found the Red-winged Blackbird to be widely distributed in the county. Breeding confirmations were obtained in 105 blocks (64%), and if probable and possible breeding evidence is included, records were obtained for 135 blocks (82%). Redwings were found nesting from sea level by the Bay to an elevation of 3,280 feet on the slopes of Mt. Hamilton. Grinnell and Miller (1944) stated that most redwings of the subspecies *mailliardorum* breed below 1,000 feet, but nearly 40% of the atlas confirmations were found at elevations higher than that.

Generally, atlasers found redwings nesting near water. Near the Bay and along streams these blackbirds nested in both freshwater and brackish marshes, typically building their nests over water in emergent vegetation such as cattails and bulrushes. In low-lying areas that flood seasonally, they also nested in ruderal growth such as poison hemlock, wild radish, and black mustard. By the time nestlings were hatched, these areas had frequently dried out, and the nests were no longer over water. Similarly, at higher elevations, redwings nested in the emergent vegetation of stock ponds or near seeps that often had dried up by hatching time. These blackbirds appeared to find suitable sites with available water and emergent vegetation throughout the Santa Cruz Mountains and the Diablo Range. Stock ponds in the midst of grasslands or oak savannas in the driest part of the Diablo Range nearly always supported one or two breeding pairs, as long as there was some emergent growth. On the valley floor, most breeding sites were associated with percolation ponds, irrigation channels, borrow ponds, fallow land, and flooded agricultural fields.

During winter there are widespread and erratic movements of large and small Red-winged Blackbird flocks. In February, males once again return to preferred sites on the valley floor and elsewhere and are seen displaying over their territories. The earliest nesting evidence observed was birds engaged in nest building on 23 Mar. The latest breeding confirmation was of dependent fledglings on 25 Jul.

Van Rossem (1926) suggested that *A. p. gubernator*, a bicolored form resident in central Mexico, is the ancestral source of the three bicolored subspecies found in California. The other forms in the west, the Red-winged Blackbirds having yellowish edges on their epaulets, are more recent invaders to the state. Gavin et al. (1991) looked at allozyme variation in ten subspecies from the entire North American range and found almost no differences between subspecies breeding on the Modoc Plateau in northeastern California and those at all locations east of California. The greatest genetic differences were between *nevadensis* redwings on the Modoc Plateau and the bicolored subspecies *mailliardorum* in the San Francisco Bay area. But the bicolored *californicus* subspecies in the Central Valley was found to be more closely related to birds on the Modoc Plateau and in the eastern United States than to *mailliardorum*. These two subspecies have long been in contact in eastern Contra Costa and Alameda counties (Grinnell and Miller 1944) and, to judge from the atlas data, are likely in contact in the eastern Diablo Range. The Red-winged Blackbird is perhaps the most studied avian species in North America (Yasukawa and Searcy 1995), yet the relationships among the California populations remain a puzzle.

William G. Bousman

RED-WINGED BLACKBIRD

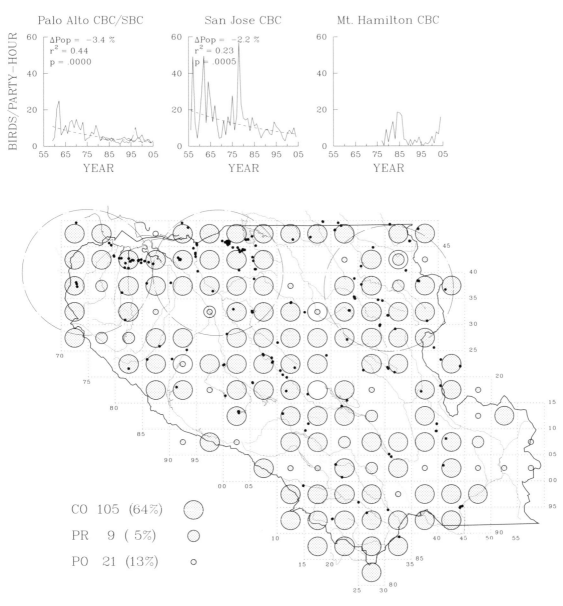

Palo Alto CBC/SBC

ΔPop = −3.4 %
r² = 0.44
p = .0000

San Jose CBC

ΔPop = −2.2 %
r² = 0.23
p = .0005

Mt. Hamilton CBC

BIRDS/PARTY−HOUR

YEAR

CO 105 (64%)
PR 9 (5%)
PO 21 (13%)

Atlas (1987−1993), n = 227

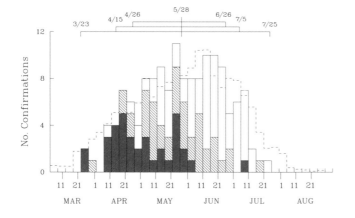

No. Confirmations

3/23 4/15 4/26 5/28 6/26 7/5 7/25

MAR APR MAY JUN JUL AUG

Tricolored Blackbird
Agelaius tricolor

The bustling activity of nest-building females and the cacophony of singing males impart a frenzied atmosphere to a Tricolored Blackbird colony. This gregarious species nests in a variety of densely vegetated freshwater marshes, fields, and thickets, primarily in California. Small numbers also breed in Washington, Oregon, western Nevada, and northern Baja California (Beedy and Hamilton 1999). The heart of the species' range lies in the Sacramento and San Joaquin valleys, with more limited breeding elsewhere in the state (Small 1994). Although most Tricolored Blackbirds are present year-round within this core range, they are anything but sedentary. Flocks occur widely in central and coastal California during the nonbreeding season, and breeding colonies show considerable interannual variation in size and location. The Tricolored Blackbird has bred at a few scattered locations in Santa Clara County, but is absent, or occurs only as a nonbreeder, in most of the county.

The Tricolored Blackbird was first reported in the county by Henry W. Henshaw, who found it breeding in the Santa Clara Valley on 21 Jun 1876 (Belding 1890). Barlow (1900b) discovered a small colony near Sargents, along the Pajaro River in southwestern Santa Clara County, on 26 May 1895. Fisher (1902) called the species rare and local in his list of birds of the Santa Clara Valley and Santa Cruz Mountains. Grinnell and Wythe (1927) suggested that the Tricolored Blackbird was irregular and local in occurrence in the San Francisco Bay region, noting Barlow's breeding record from Sargents and additional observations in San Jose, Santa Clara, and Alviso. In his summary of the birds of the South Bay, Sibley (1952) described the species as an uncommon resident, noting only one additional breeding record—a colony of 2,000 birds on the Wool Ranch, east of Milpitas, on 20 Apr 1947 (*Bull. SCVAS* July 1947, Sibley 1952). Tricolored Blackbirds apparently continued to be uncommon and local breeders in the county over the next few decades, provoking only reports of small colonies from a few scattered Santa Clara County locations prior to the atlas period.

Atlasers confirmed the patchy distribution of the Tricol-ored Blackbird in the county. During the atlas period, this species was recorded in only 29 atlas blocks (17%), and breeding was confirmed in just 15 blocks; subsequently breeding was confirmed in four additional blocks. Breeding sites were almost evenly split between the Santa Clara Valley and the Diablo Range, and there were no breeding-season records in the Santa Cruz Mountains. This species' distribution reflected the patchy nature of its breeding habitat, which was always located near fresh water. Most colonies were in extensive stands of freshwater emergent vegetation (e.g., cattails and bulrushes). Such sites included the Ogier Ponds, an island in Grant Lake, a marsh at the base of Calero Dam, and extensive marshes within scattered stock ponds, mostly in the Diablo Range. Other colonies were in dense, tall herbaceous vegetation such as thistles near lakes (e.g., at Calaveras Reservoir and near San Felipe Lake in a San Benito County edge block) or in mixed bulrush and willow thickets (e.g., at the upper end of Coyote Reservoir). The extensive stands of wetland vegetation favored by Tricolored Blackbirds in Santa Clara County are usually created by disturbance, such as erosion (which may remove woody vegetation), sediment deposition suitable for colonization by cattails and bulrushes, and drawdown of reservoirs. Habitat suitability at breeding locations is often short-lived, owing to livestock grazing, flooding, and succession. Consequently, Santa Clara County colonies have generally not been present at any given location for more than a few years.

Most colonies found by atlasers consisted of hundreds to several thousand individuals. In this respect, the Tricolored Blackbird is much more gregarious than its congener, the Red-winged Blackbird. A few Tricolored occurrences, such as a colony in a small pond at Coyote Ranch, consisted of less than 100 individuals. Tricoloreds generally did not use the narrow wetland fringes around ponds that were so often used by nesting Red-winged Blackbirds, and no breeding was confirmed (despite several bayside blocks offering possible breeding evidence) in any brackish or saltwater marshes during the atlas period. Elevations of breeding confirmations ranged from 15 feet near lower Coyote Creek to 2,720 feet at a Horse Valley stock pond in the upper reaches of Smith Creek; 85% of confirmations were from below 800 feet.

Nest-building was recorded as early as 9 Apr during the atlas period (and 8 Apr subsequently), and Tricolored Blackbirds were recorded carrying nest material as late as 4 Jun. The vast majority of breeding confirmations were of adults carrying food for young, recorded from 13 May to 28 Jun. Adults were observed feeding fledged young as early as 3 May (after the atlas period) and as late as 7 Jul (during the atlas period).

Statewide surveys documented a population decline of more than 50% between 1994 and 2000, the greatest declines observed in the Sacramento Valley (Beedy and Hamilton 1997, Hamilton et al. 1999, Hamilton 2000). Loss of freshwater marsh habitat, modification of flooding regimes, and destruction of nests in agricultural lands by mowing or plowing have contributed to declines of this species in the state (Beedy and Hamilton 1999). Continued breeding in Santa Clara County will likely depend on regular disturbance to create and maintain suitable nesting habitat at inland ponds and lakes.

Stephen C. Rottenborn

TRICOLORED BLACKBIRD

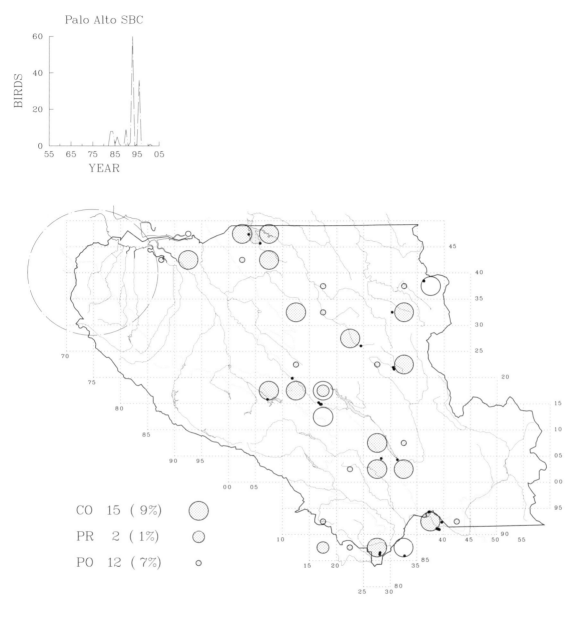

Palo Alto SBC

CO 15 (9%)
PR   2 (1%)
PO 12 (7%)

Atlas (1987−1993), n = 31

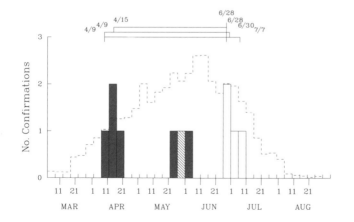

Western Meadowlark
Sturnella neglecta

The vibrant song of the Western Meadowlark rings out in meadows, pastures, and grasslands over much of Santa Clara County. These meadowlarks breed from British Columbia east to Ontario and south to Baja California, Arizona, and through the highlands of Mexico south to Nuevo León (Lanyon 1994). In California, they are found in grasslands and grainfields throughout the state (Small 1994). Meadowlarks are common residents in Santa Clara County, breeding primarily in open grasslands. The species is more widespread in winter, when large flocks form and wander in search of food.

The earliest record of the Western Meadowlark in Santa Clara County is a specimen collected by Thomas Bridges in "the Valley of San José" prior to 1857 (Sclater 1857). Observers at the end of the nineteenth century considered meadowlarks common or abundant in local grasslands and grainfields (Price 1898d, Van Denburgh 1899b, Fisher 1902), but Van Denburgh noted declines in available habitat caused by the "converting of grain fields into orchards." In the San Francisco Bay area, Grinnell and Wythe (1927) stated that the species was an abundant resident in all treeless areas from the coast to the interior. In the South Bay, Sibley (1952) judged it to be a common resident in pastures and grasslands. Analysis of the Palo Alto SBC data since 1981 shows a decline of 3.7% per year within the count circle. In California, analysis of Breeding Bird Survey data from 1966 to 2004 shows a decline of 1.8% per year (Sauer et al. 2005). Both Small (1994) and Berner (2003g) have commented on declines caused by the conversion of agricultural lands and grasslands to suburbs and light industry.

Breeding Western Meadowlarks were found widely in Santa Clara County's grasslands during the atlas period. The greatest numbers of breeding birds were found on the western ridges of the Diablo Range and in the Pacheco Creek drainage.

In the Santa Cruz Mountains, meadowlarks were common in grasslands west of Palo Alto and north of the Pajaro River, but they were largely absent from this mountain range from the upper Stevens Creek Canyon south to Mt. Madonna County Park, where the vegetation consists of forest, woodlands, and chaparral. Breeding birds were also found along the edge of the South Bay in wet grasslands, and in a number of remnant pastures, grainfields, and grasslands on the valley floor. They were found from near sea level in the Palo Alto Flood Control Basin to an elevation of 3,700 feet near the summit of Mt. Day. Western Meadowlarks were most often found breeding in grasslands or grazed pasture offering at least some areas of denser or higher growth or clumps of grasses suitable for nest sites.

In February, when winter flocks of Western Meadowlarks break up, individual pairs begin to form territories. The earliest nesting evidence observed during the atlas period was of a bird carrying nest material on 11 Mar. Fledged young were being fed as early as 16 May. Bryant (1914) noted that Western Meadowlarks in the San Joaquin Valley were double-brooded, the peaks of nesting occurring in April-May and July-August, although Lanyon (1994) stated that few pairs raise a second brood. The latest breeding evidence obtained in Santa Clara County during the atlas period was at Felt Lake on 21 Jul, and no breeding was observed in August, Bryant's observations from the San Joaquin Valley notwithstanding.

Western Meadowlarks and four other grassland specialists—Horned Larks, Lark Sparrows, Savannah Sparrows, and Grasshopper Sparrows—overlap broadly in the use of grassland habitats in Santa Clara County. Differences in habitat use have been observed. Horned Larks favor short grasses and barren ground, whereas the others use grasslands composed of denser and taller grasses. Lark Sparrows, although often associated with grasslands, generally are found where the grasslands are mixed with a scattering of chaparral, shrubs, and trees. Grassland Savannah Sparrows (as opposed to those nesting on the Bay edge) are found most often in more mesic grasslands in the Santa Cruz Mountains, and none have been found breeding in the drier grasslands of the Diablo Range, where meadowlarks are common. Grasshopper Sparrows generally use grasslands at higher elevations, in habitats similar to those used by meadowlarks, but they are occasionally found at lower elevations. Of the five grassland species in Santa Clara County, Western Meadowlarks are the most abundant, Lark Sparrows are less abundant and declining in numbers, and the other three occur in lesser numbers still and at fewer locations.

William G. Bousman

WESTERN MEADOWLARK

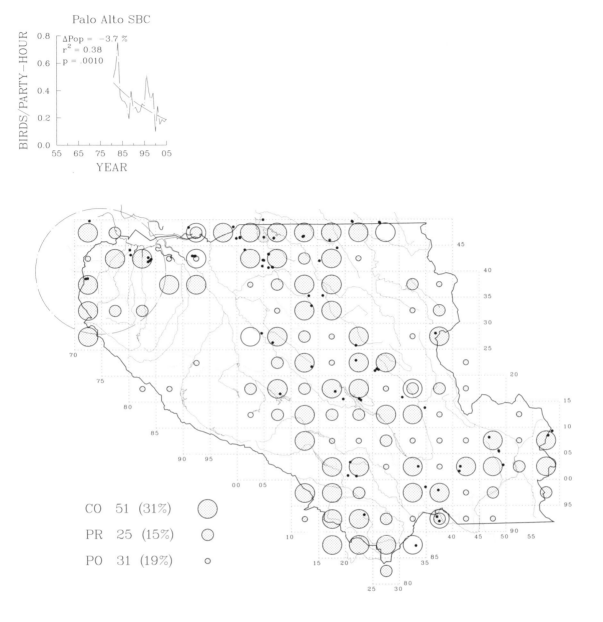

Palo Alto SBC

ΔPop = −3.7 %
r^2 = 0.38
p = .0010

BIRDS/PARTY−HOUR

YEAR

CO 51 (31%)

PR 25 (15%)

PO 31 (19%)

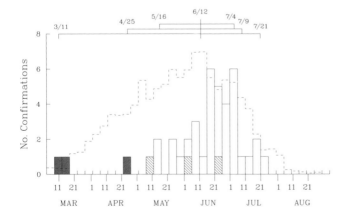

3/11   4/25   5/16   6/12   7/4   7/9   7/21

No. Confirmations

11 21   1 11 21   1 11 21   1 11 21   1 11 21   1 11 21

MAR   APR   MAY   JUN   JUL   AUG

Atlas (1987−1993), n = 85

Brewer's Blackbird
Euphagus cyanocephalus

As males of a local colony preen in the morning sun, there are occasional bursts of song, a nasal, scratching noise that can be surprisingly pleasant when several are given in unison. The Brewer's Blackbird breeds from central British Columbia across the prairies of Canada to southern Ontario and thence south to northwestern Baja California, northern Arizona, and southeastern Colorado, with an expanding eastern population clustered around the Great Lakes (Martin 2002). This blackbird breeds widely in California, absent only from the higher mountains and the southeastern deserts (Small 1994). In Santa Clara County, the Brewer's Blackbird is a common, year-round resident found throughout the county, often in urban areas and parks.

The earliest record of Brewer's Blackbirds in Santa Clara County is a set of five eggs in the United States National Museum, collected in Santa Clara County on 30 Apr 1889 by W. C. Lawrence (USNM #B44467). Price (1898d) listed this species as a permanent resident around Stanford University and considered it "very common about the campus." Van Denburgh (1899b) judged it to be an abundant breeding species, and Fisher (1902) described it as an abundant permanent resident. Grinnell and Wythe (1927) reported that the Brewer's Blackbird was a common resident throughout the San Francisco Bay Region, and was especially common east and south of the Bay. In discussing its status in the state, Grinnell and Miller (1944) judged it to be abundant, and believed that its numbers had increased along with human occupancy of California. Sibley (1952) reported this blackbird to be a common resident in the South Bay area. Analysis of summer and winter bird count data shows a population decline that ranges from 5.4% per year on the Palo Alto SBC to 6.3% per year on the San Jose CBC. Although Brewer's Blackbirds are considered permanent residents in central California, significantly fewer birds are found on the Palo Alto summer bird count than on the winter count (an average of 384 on the summer count and 1,653 on the winter count for the years 1981-2004). Nonetheless, the estimated rate of decline here is the same in both seasons. Analysis of Breeding Bird Survey data show this species to be declining throughout California, with a drop of 1.9% a year over the period 1966-2004 (Sauer et al. 2005).

Brewer's Blackbirds were confirmed breeding in 131 county blocks (79%), and including probable and possible evidence, records were obtained from 150 blocks (91%). These birds nested from sea level beside the Bay to an elevation of 4,000 feet near the summit of Eylar Mountain. Brewer's Blackbirds are colonial nesters, and atlasers found colonies consisting of two to 20 pairs in many parts of the county. The colonies were generally in dense foliage within trees or shrubs. Colony sites were adjacent to open areas that the birds used for foraging and often had streams or small creeks nearby. In urban areas these colonies were in the dense crowns of live oaks, in Monterey and other pines, and in coast redwoods, cypresses, junipers, and evergreen ornamental shrubs. The colonies were frequently near open areas, such as urban parks, golf courses, and school yards that provided areas for foraging. In the Santa Cruz Mountains and the Diablo Range, small colonies occurred near ranches and farms, but they were also found near open areas well away from roads and settlements. Here, nests were built in the dense foliage of native shrubs and trees.

Brewer's Blackbirds were seen nest building as early as 25 Mar, and adults were seen carrying food as late as 21 Aug. As shown in the phenology graphic, the progression of nest-building, incubation, and fledging of young was remarkably uniform. Later nest-building and incubation records are undoubtedly renesting attempts, since this species is normally single-brooded (Martin 2002).

The reduction in the number of Brewer's Blackbirds over the last 40 to 50 years, as evidenced by the CBC data, is surprising, given this bird's apparent tolerance, and even exploitation, of human-altered habitats. Within the San Jose count circle there has been a nearly ten-to-one reduction in numbers, yet because this bird is so common, the decline has gone largely unnoticed. Lesser declines have been noted locally in the other count circles and in California as a whole (Sauer et al. 2005). Within our urban areas, Brewer's Blackbirds seem almost commensal with man, picking up scraps of food from beneath our feet in outdoor cafes and gathering around picnickers in our parks. At first appearance, association with humans would seem to provide them an easy living. But perhaps as our population continues to increase, the reduction in open lands preferred by this species for foraging will result in fewer Brewer's Blackbirds living with us.

William G. Bousman

BREWER'S BLACKBIRD

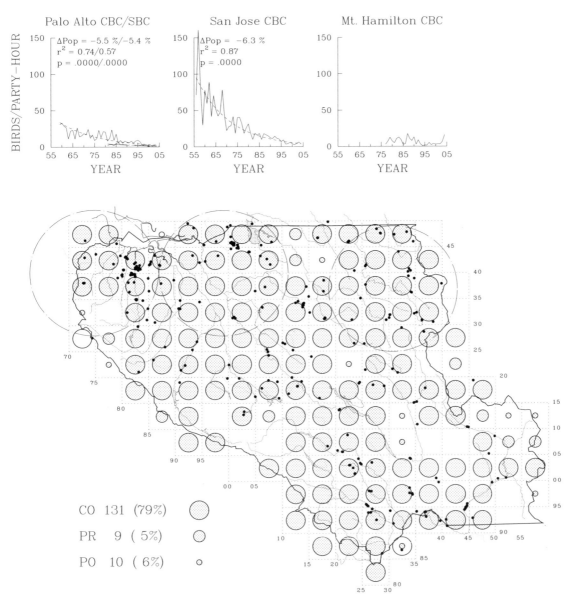

Palo Alto CBC/SBC

ΔPop = −5.5 %/−5.4 %
r^2 = 0.74/0.57
p = .0000/.0000

San Jose CBC

ΔPop = −6.3 %
r^2 = 0.87
p = .0000

Mt. Hamilton CBC

BIRDS/PARTY–HOUR

YEAR   YEAR   YEAR

CO 131 (79%)
PR   9 (5%)
PO 10 (6%)

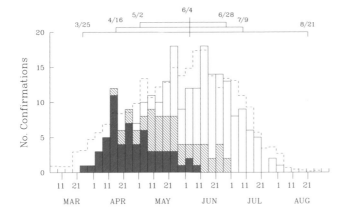

No. Confirmations

Atlas (1987−1993), n = 412

3/25   4/16   5/2   6/4   6/28   7/9   8/21

MAR   APR   MAY   JUN   JUL   AUG

431

Great-tailed Grackle
Quiscalus mexicanus

The massive invasion of this Mexican grackle into the United States in the twentieth century reached Santa Clara County in the 1980s and 1990s. The range of the Great-tailed Grackle now extends from California to Missouri and thence south to northern South America (Johnson and Peer 2001). Eight subspecies have been described, and those on the northern border of Mexico, *Q. m. prosopidicola*, *monsoni*, and *nelsoni*, are responsible for the species' northward invasion (Johnson and Peer 2001). The subspecies *nelsoni*, originally located in Northern Baja California and Sonora, was first found in California in 1964 and is likely the subspecies that now occurs in Santa Clara County. A subsequent invasion of California by *monsoni*, however, has created intergrade populations in southern California (Johnson and Peer 2001). This grackle is an uncommon to fairly common resident in southern California, but it is rare in the northern parts of the state, where the species is still expanding its range (Small 1994). In Santa Clara County, the Great-tailed Grackle is a rare breeding species, normally occurring near inland lakes, reservoirs, and wetlands. Although some birds have been found in winter, it is unclear whether our breeding birds are resident or partially migratory.

Early bird surveys that covered central California (Grinnell and Wythe 1927, Grinnell and Miller 1944, Sibley 1952) made no mention of Great-tailed Grackles. The first record for the state was a female collected near Imperial Dam, Imperial County, on 6 Jun 1964, and the first confirmed breeding occurred near the same location in 1969 (Small 1994). In northern California, the first record was of a male in San Francisco in 1979 (*Am. Birds 33*:895 1979). This male remained through 1991 (*Am. Birds 45*:1160 1991) and was paired with a female from 1980 to at least 1989 (*Am. Birds 44*:326 1990). The pair nested unsuccessfully from 1980 to 1983 (*Am. Birds 43*:1365–66 1989).

The Great-tailed Grackle's invasion of Santa Clara County is documented in the county notebooks as follows. The first observation was of three birds seen flying over residential San Jose on 4 May 1984 (John A. Cole). In 1989, from 9 to 14 Jul, a single bird was found in San Jose (Bruce Barrett). In 1995, a male was seen in Alviso 28 Apr to 6 May (Scott B. Terrill, mult. obs.). Then, in 1998, two males and a female were observed at the northern edge of San Felipe Lake, San Benito County. The female was seen building a nest on 25 May 1998 in bulrushes at the edge of the lake, approximately 8 meters south of the Santa Clara County line (Stephen C. Rottenborn). The males would sometimes sing from perches within Santa Clara County. Three fledglings were seen by the lake on 21 Jul 1998 (Debra L. Shearwater). Two years later, a pair of grackles was seen at Almaden Lake on 22 Jun 2000 (John Mariani). By 16 Jul 2000, both adults were seen carrying food to the presumed nest site on the island in the lake (Michael M. Mammoser), representing the first confirmed breeding in Santa Clara County. Subsequently, successful breeding was observed on the Parkway Lakes in 2002 and 2003 (Michael J. Mammoser, mult. obs.). Although these grackles were observed in a number of places in the county in 2004 and 2005, no further evidence of breeding was obtained. It appears that in each of the three breeding sites used to date, the female Great-tailed Grackles have built their nests in thick stands of bulrushes adjacent to extensive open water. The site used at San Felipe Lake is adjacent to farms and ranches, and the grackles often foraged at a nearby dairy ranch within Santa Clara County. The Almaden Lake site is a city park, where the birds foraged in picnic areas. The Parkway Lakes site is a trout pay-to-fish area that includes fishing and some picnicking.

The records listed previously provide limited information on breeding phenology. The earliest breeding evidence observed in the county atlas blocks was nest building at San Felipe Lake on 25 May 1998 on the San Benito County side of an edge block (Stephen C. Rottenborn, county notebooks). The latest breeding evidence was of three fledglings noted at the same location on 21 Jul 1998 (Debra L. Shearwater, county notebooks).

The most studied Great-tailed Grackle subspecies, *Q. m. prosopidicola*, occupies the northeastern portion of this grackle's range, from Nebraska south to Tamaulipas, Mexico (Johnson and Peer 2001). The male defends a limited territory that contains the nests of one or more females. Although the male will defend nestlings within his territory, he rarely assists with the feeding of the young (Selander 1970, Johnson and Peer 2001). The social behaviors of *nelsoni* and *monsoni*, the subspecies that have invaded California, have been little studied. Observers who watched the pair that nested at Almaden Lake in 2000 saw the male grackle repeatedly forage and return to the nest with apparent food items in his bill (Michael J. Mammoser, county notebooks; pers. obs.). Variation in male parental behavior is not unusual in blackbirds, and it is possible that birds at the edge of an expanding range show behaviors considerably different from those at the center of the range (Alvaro Jaramillo, pers. comm.).

William G. Bousman

432

GREAT-TAILED GRACKLE

Palo Alto SBC

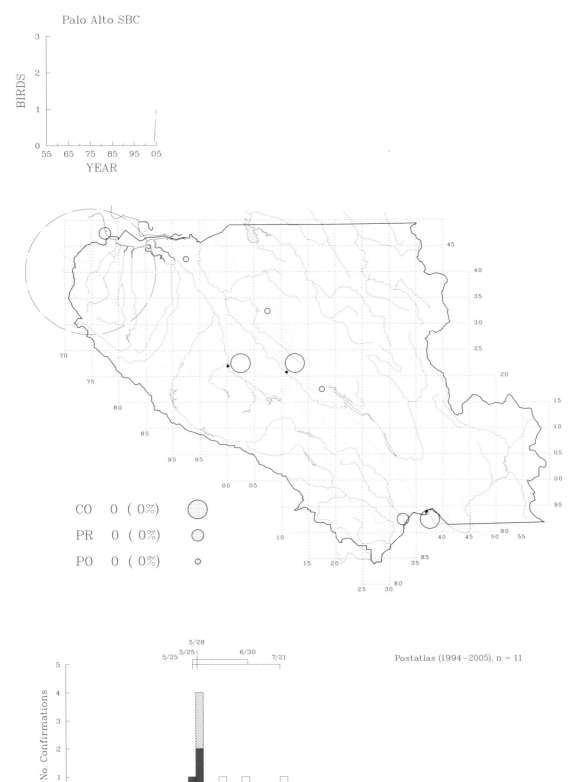

CO   0 (0%)

PR   0 (0%)

PO   0 (0%)

Postatlas (1994–2005), n = 11

433

Brown-headed Cowbird
Molothrus ater

The brood-parasitic Brown-headed Cowbird has taken advantage of anthropogenic habitat modifications and expanded its range over much of the North American continent (Lowther 1993). This species now breeds in most areas where habitats supporting an abundance of hosts occur close to food sources. In Santa Clara County, the species is a fairly common breeder in a variety of habitats, but in winter congregations of flocks at favored feeding areas results in more localized distribution. Of the three recognized subspecies of Brown-headed Cowbird, *M. a. obscurus* is the one that currently occupies most of California, including Santa Clara County (Lowther 1993).

At the turn of the twentieth century, the range of *M. a. obscurus* barely edged into the southeastern corner of California. In the next three decades, this subspecies expanded northward through the state (Dawson 1923, Laymon 1987). Its first appearance in the San Francisco Bay area was marked by ten parasitized nests at Irvington in Alameda County, only a few miles north of Milpitas, in 1922 (La Jeunesse 1923). Charles P. Smith (1926) provided the first records of Brown-headed Cowbird in Santa Clara County, finding single parasitized Wilson's Warbler nests on 13 and 29 Jun 1925 along Coyote Creek in Milpitas. In 1926, he found parasitized nests of Willow Flycatcher, Swainson's Thrush, Common Yellowthroat, and Wilson's Warbler along lower Guadalupe River and Coyote Creek. In the early 1930s, adult cowbirds were repeatedly observed along lower Coyote Creek (*Wren-Tit 2(4)* 1930, *Wren-Tit 3(3)* 1931, Pickwell 1932c), and by 1944 the Brown-headed Cowbird was established throughout the Bay area (Grinnell and Miller 1944).

Atlasers recorded cowbirds in 79% of all county blocks. This species was recorded mostly at lower elevations but was absent from a number of seemingly suitable blocks at higher elevations, one group in the Santa Cruz Mountains and the other a band of contiguous blocks in the Diablo Range. The distribution gap in the Santa Cruz Mountains is associated with extensive evergreen forests, and the scarcity of open ground for foraging in that area may partially explain the absence of cowbirds there. The gap in the Diablo Range, on the other hand, includes some open grassland with free-range cattle interspersed with oak and conifer woodlands and chaparral. This habitat would seem more suitable for cowbirds than that in the Santa Cruz Mountains gap, providing access to both hosts and open foraging areas with livestock.

Interestingly, the males' flight-whistles in the population on the west side of the Diablo Range gap differed from those on the east side. Flight-whistles given by males during the breeding season are important in both male-male and male-female communication (Rothstein et al. 1988). The male cowbirds to the west of this gap gave a "see-you see-ee" whistle, the first phrase descending and the second ascending. This flight-whistle, called the "coastal dialect," has been attributed to all cowbird populations west of the Sierras (Rothstein et al. 1986, Rothstein and Fleischer 1987). But the previously undescribed flight-whistle dialect in the population east of the gap is a higher "see-dee see-dle-ee," both phrases ascending (*RipariaNews 9(3)*:8–9 1994, pers. obs.). The presence of two distinct dialects in the Diablo Range suggests that these two populations have been separated for some time, yet the reason for the absence of cowbirds in the intervening area is unknown.

In Santa Clara County, Brown-headed Cowbirds typically disperse from their wintering areas to breeding localities in March. The earliest nesting evidence detected during the atlas period was a nest containing a cowbird egg on 26 Apr. Following the atlas period, an egg was found on the earlier date of 20 Apr 1997 (Michael M. Rogers, PADB). Similar nest records were obtained through 26 Jun, although the vast majority of breeding confirmations were of recently fledged juveniles (often being fed by their hosts). Records of such fledglings spanned the period 11 May to 10 Aug, with a broad peak from early June until late July. Following the atlas period, a host feeding young was seen as late as 5 Sep 1997 (pers. obs.).

Of the 220+ species known to have been parasitized by Brown-headed Cowbirds over their range (Friedmann and Kiff 1985), 56 were recorded breeding in Santa Clara County during the atlas period. Fifteen of these species were detected being parasitized during this period. For each of these hosts, the accompanying table lists the number and percentage of confirmations that involved parasitism, a crude measure of the impact of parasitism on each species. Following the atlas period, eight additional species were recorded as parasitized: Chestnut-backed Chickadee, Bushtit, Black-throated Gray Warbler, Common Yellowthroat, Spotted Towhee, Hooded and Bullock's orioles, and Lesser Goldfinch. In addition to these species and those reported by Smith (1926), brood parasitism of Wrentit has been observed in the county as well (*Avocet 10*:60–63 1963, pers. obs.).

The species most likely to be threatened by cowbirds are those nesting in low-elevation riparian habitat. Many of these species have already suffered the effects of riparian habitat degradation, and the juxtaposition of high host densities and suitable foraging areas there makes riparian habitats magnets for breeding cowbirds. Although data from the three Santa Clara County Christmas Bird Counts show no significant trends in cowbird abundance in winter, breeding populations have shown an increase of 7.4% annually on the Palo Alto Summer Bird Count since 1981, and the impacts of cowbird parasitism on host populations are likely to continue.

Stephen C. Rottenborn

BROWN-HEADED COWBIRD

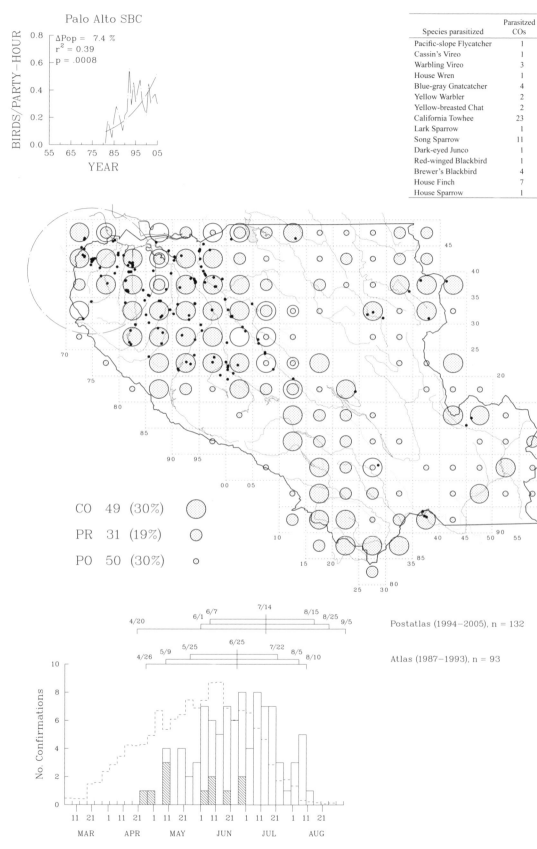

Palo Alto SBC

ΔPop = 7.4 %
r^2 = 0.39
p = .0008

BIRDS/PARTY-HOUR

YEAR

Species parasitized	Parasitzed COs	Total COs	% COs parasitized
Pacific-slope Flycatcher	1	47	2.1
Cassin's Vireo	1	27	3.7
Warbling Vireo	3	59	5.1
House Wren	1	128	0.8
Blue-gray Gnatcatcher	4	40	10.0
Yellow Warbler	2	14	14.3
Yellow-breasted Chat	2	5	40.0
California Towhee	23	244	9.4
Lark Sparrow	1	107	0.9
Song Sparrow	11	91	12.1
Dark-eyed Junco	1	273	0.4
Red-winged Blackbird	1	91	1.1
Brewer's Blackbird	4	161	2.5
House Finch	7	229	3.1
House Sparrow	1	77	1.3

CO   49 (30%)

PR   31 (19%)

PO   50 (30%)

Postatlas (1994–2005), n = 132

Atlas (1987–1993), n = 93

No. Confirmations

MAR   APR   MAY   JUN   JUL   AUG

Hooded Oriole
Icterus cucullatus

The Hooded Oriole has expanded its range into northern California during the twentieth century, following the planting of California fan palms. This brilliantly hued oriole breeds on both coasts of Mexico, from Belize north into Texas in the east and from Sonora to Arizona and northern California in the west (Pleasants and Albano 2001). Five subspecies have been described, one of which, *I. c. nelsoni*, breeds from Sonora, through Arizona, to California (Jaramillo and Burke 1999, Pleasants and Albano 2001). In California, the Hooded Oriole breeds north to Sonoma County, with occasional breeders as far north as Humboldt County, and throughout the Central Valley (Small 1994). In Santa Clara County, the Hooded Oriole is an uncommon summer resident and an irregular and very rare winter visitor in urban areas.

In the early part of the twentieth century, the Hooded Oriole was a common summer resident in southern California, where it was found primarily in riparian areas and oases having fan palms, willows, cottonwoods, and western sycamores (Grinnell 1915). With the planting of fan palms and other decorative trees in urban areas and around farms and ranches, the Hooded Oriole moved into these new "woodlands" (Grinnell and Miller 1944). In Santa Clara County, fan palms had been widely planted in the 1860s and 1870s (Broek 1932), and trees were sufficiently mature for breeding orioles by the turn of the century. At least into the 1920s, however, the northern limit of the Hooded Oriole's range was considered to be Santa Barbara County (Grinnell 1915, Dawson 1923). Initial reports of this oriole in the Bay area, well beyond the southern California range, included a bird likely of this species seen by Leslie Hawkins in the Reliez Valley, Contra Costa County, a second bird seen by Gordon Bolander in Oakland, Alameda County, both about May 1930 (H. W. Grinnell 1930a), and a well-described male in residential San Jose on 21 Jul 1930 (Pickwell 1932b). A Hooded Oriole nest was found in Seabright, Santa Cruz County, as early as 12 Aug 1931 (W. B. Minturn, MVZ #2539), but the first confirmed breeding in the San Francisco Bay area was not in hand until a nest was found in San Leandro, Alameda County, on 17 Jun 1939 (Sibley 1952). The first certain nesting record in Santa Clara County involved a female seen building a nest in a fan palm in downtown San Jose by Emily D. Smith on 24 Apr 1946 (Sibley 1952).

Atlasers found Hooded Orioles breeding throughout most of the Santa Clara Valley during the atlas period, the greatest concentration being in the northern part of the valley. Nesting elevations ranged from 10 feet at two sites in East Palo Alto to 700 feet in the foothills above Saratoga, but 90% of all recorded nest elevations were below 520 feet. When noted, nest sites were generally in fan palms, where the female built a nest beneath a palm frond, suspended from it by palm fibers stripped from the frond edges. This species occasionally bred in other palm species and western sycamores, but even in these instances the nest was generally made with fibers from California fan palms. Detailed studies of nest site use in Marin County (Peake 1993) indicated that most birds used California fan palms for nesting, but that they also used such trees as Mexican fan palm, Canary Island date palm, windmill palm, blue gum eucalyptus, American elm, monkey puzzle tree, northern catalpa, green dracaena, and cypress. According to Peake (1993), "No matter what tree species was selected as a nest site, virtually all Marin nests were made solely from the blond leaf filaments of [*Washingtonia*] fan palms."

Male Hooded Orioles first arrive in Santa Clara County in late March (median date 21 Mar, range 10 Mar to 13 Apr, county notebooks). Males of the subspecies *nelsoni* rarely sing (Jaramillo and Burke 1999), but both sexes are often noticed by their hard *wheet* call note. Females generally arrive a few days later. The earliest nesting evidence was a bird seen at a nest on 28 Mar in Saratoga. Hooded Orioles are double-brooded in parts of their range (Pleasants and Albano 2001), and the phenology shown here suggests possible second nests. The latest breeding evidence found during the atlas period was fledglings in southwest San Jose on 3 Aug. Following the atlas period, 23 later confirmations of dependent fledglings or adults feeding young were obtained, the latest being on 17 Sep 1999 (Michael M. Rogers, PADB).

Populations of Hooded Orioles have been in flux during the twentieth century (Pleasants and Albano 2001). The western subspecies (*nelsoni*) has undergone a range expansion in parts of Arizona and in the Colorado River valley, as well as the northward expansion in California discussed above. The eastern subspecies (*cucullatus*), however, has declined in Texas, particularly in the Rio Grande River valley, where changes in agricultural uses have increased the number of cowbirds and their associated brood parasitism (Pleasants and Albano 2001). Curiously, during the seven years of the atlas period, no instances of Brown-headed Cowbird parasitism were observed in Santa Clara County, but since the completion of the atlas, 16 of 47 Hooded Oriole breeding confirmations of either adults feeding young or of fledged young have involved cowbird parasitism (PADB).

William G. Bousman

HOODED ORIOLE

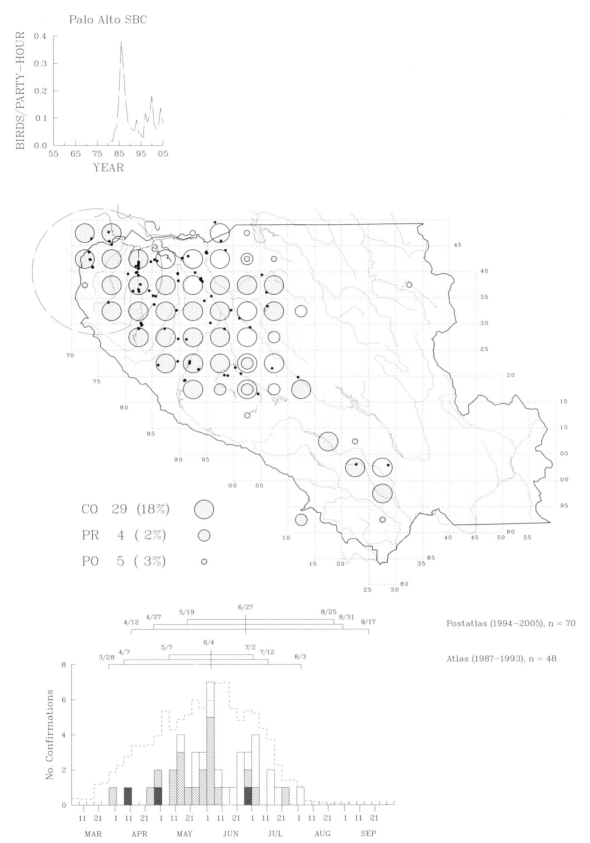

Palo Alto SBC

CO 29 (18%)

PR   4 (2%)

PO   5 (3%)

Postatlas (1994–2005), n = 70

Atlas (1987–1993), n = 48

437

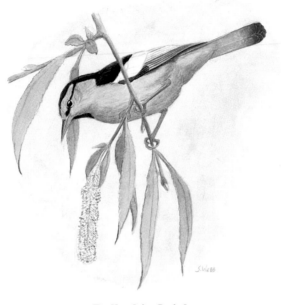

Bullock's Oriole
Icterus bullockii

The chattering scold of the Bullock's Oriole, first heard in late March, marks the return of this brightly colored bird to the county's oak and riparian woodlands. The Bullock's Oriole was formerly merged with the Baltimore Oriole (as the Northern Oriole) because of hybridization in a zone of overlap in the southern Great Plains (AOU 1983), but it is now once again considered a separate species (AOU 1995). This oriole is widely distributed in western North America, from southern British Columbia south to northern Mexico (AOU 1998). Within California it breeds throughout the state except for parts of the Klamath and Siskiyou mountains in the northwest, the Cascades and Sierra Nevada above 8,000 feet, and the southeastern deserts (Small 1994). In Santa Clara County it is a common summer resident of oak and riparian woodlands, as well as urban locations that offer suitable nesting trees. It is absent from higher elevations of the Santa Cruz Mountains.

Historical records indicate that the Bullock's Oriole has always been a common summer resident in Santa Clara County. Van Denburgh (1899b) and Fisher (1902) both considered it common in the summer, but Van Denburgh noted that it was rarely found west of Los Gatos. Grinnell and Wythe (1927) judged it to be common in the drier interior portions of the Bay area and less common in the coastal counties of Marin and San Mateo. Sibley (1952) recorded this oriole as a common summer resident in the South Bay, and noted that it was most abundant in the drier eastern portions of the region. No change in this oriole's population in recent years is apparent from the Palo Alto Summer Bird Count data, although there is an anomalous and puzzling increase in numbers for this species from 1985 to 1987.

Breeding by Bullock's Orioles was easily confirmed because of the conspicuous nature of their pendulous nests and the bright colors of the adults as they flew through the open woodlands carrying food. This species was confirmed breeding in

76% of the atlas blocks, and including records of probable and possible breeding it was found in 88% of all blocks. Nesting birds were found at elevations from 10 to 4,010 feet and were most closely associated with either oak or riparian woodlands. They were found frequently in both valley oak and blue oak woodlands and commonly built their nests in either of these deciduous trees. Typically, they selected nest trees adjacent to open grassland or savanna and used these open areas for foraging. In riparian woodlands, they used closed-canopy riparian forests dominated by Fremont and black cottonwoods and western sycamores, as well as more open, scrublike riparian areas with willows. Many of these riparian woodlands were adjacent to open grasslands or agricultural areas, and both were used for foraging. In urban and suburban habitats, these orioles tended to use many of the same tree species that they used elsewhere, but they occasionally built their nests in non-native trees such as eucalyptus and fan palms. Bullock's Orioles were most common in the Diablo Range, but were also common on the valley floor in suitable habitat, as well as in the southern Santa Cruz Mountains where this range drops down to the Pajaro River. But they were less common or absent entirely in the higher portions of the Santa Cruz Mountains. Although most atlas blocks within these mountains include at least some areas of grassland and the more open woodlands preferred by this species, it appears that the mesic features associated with extensive tracts of broad-leaved evergreen and coniferous forests in these blocks make them unsuitable.

Pairs of Bullock's Orioles sometimes build their nests in close proximity to one another, either in the same tree or in adjacent trees. Each pair defends only a small territory around its nest, and the two share nearby foraging areas (Williams 1993). Examples of this behavior were noted in a variety of habitats by atlasers. For instance, active nests were observed about 25 meters apart in planted Fremont cottonwoods in Santa Clara in an urban setting on 14 May 1997 (Stephen C. Rottenborn, pers. comm.), and at a similar spacing in a grove of valley oaks in San Antonio Valley during the atlas period (pers. obs.).

Bullock's Orioles typically arrive in Santa Clara County in mid-March (median date 19 Mar, county notebooks). Nesting starts in early April, soon after their arrival on breeding territories, and is normally completed by mid- or late July. The earliest evidence of nesting during the atlas period was nest construction on 6 Apr. Late evidence of nesting included adults feeding young on 28 Jul and an adult carrying food on 2 Aug. Subsequently, adults feeding young were seen on 5 Aug 1997 (pers. obs.), slightly extending the late dates. The breeding period observed in the atlas coincides closely with historical egg dates, which range from 22 Apr to 11 Jun (Bent 1958b).

William G. Bousman

BULLOCK'S ORIOLE

Palo Alto SBC

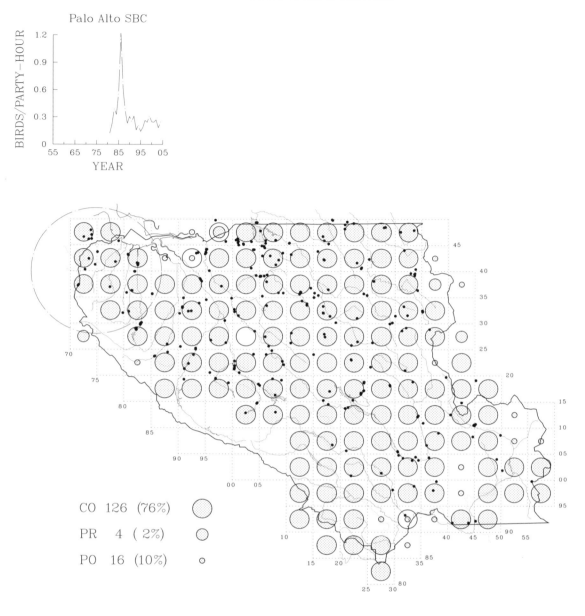

CO 126 (76%)
PR   4 (2%)
PO   16 (10%)

Atlas (1987–1993), n = 282

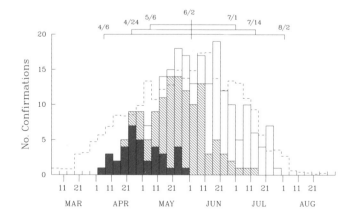

439

Purple Finch
Carpodacus purpureus

Flowing from the top of a conifer, the Purple Finch's soft, warbling song is a common sign of spring in our denser montane forests. This finch breeds from the central Yukon across Canada to Newfoundland. In the west, birds are generally found west of the Cascades-Sierra axis south to northwestern Baja California, whereas in the east they nest south to Wisconsin and New York, and in the Appalachians to West Virginia (Wootton 1996). Two subspecies are generally recognized, *C. p. californicus* being resident in the west and *purpureus* in the east (Wootton 1996). Purple Finches are fairly common in California, breeding in the northern forests of the state, the Coast Ranges, the western slopes of the Sierra Nevada, and the higher mountains of southern California (Small 1994). In Santa Clara County, they are fairly common residents, found widely in the Santa Cruz Mountains, but with a more scattered distribution in the Diablo Range.

A Purple Finch was included in the list of specimens collected by Thomas Bridges from "the Valley of San José" sometime prior to 1857 (Sclater 1857). Although Price (1898d) had seen birds on the Stanford campus in May, he felt that the Purple Finch was only a winter resident locally. Van Denburgh (1899b) observed that this species was resident, but wrote that it was "at no time common." In contrast, Fisher (1902) judged it to be a common resident. Grinnell and Wythe (1927), in describing the Purple Finch's status in the San Francisco Bay area, considered it common in the more humid coastal counties. Sibley (1952) stated that this finch was a fairly common resident in the Santa Cruz Mountains.

The population trend of the Purple Finch since the 1950s, to judge from an analysis of Christmas and Summer Bird Count data, is unclear. Examining the Palo Alto and San Jose CBC data, it would appear that Purple Finches were less common up to the early 1970s, at which point their numbers increased substantially over the next 5 to 10 years. Since that time, there have been declines in winter populations of 5.1% per year in the Palo

Alto count circle and 11.0% per year in San Jose. For the Mt. Hamilton count circle, winter numbers have been quite variable since that count's inception in 1977, but there is no long-term trend. The Palo Alto summer count was begun in 1981, and since then there has been a decline of 2.0% per year. Notably, more birds have been recorded per party-hour in summer than in winter in the Palo Alto circle, perhaps because singing males are easily detected in summer. Within California, a decline of 1.5% a year has been observed in Breeding Bird Survey data obtained from 1966 to 2004 (Sauer et al. 2005).

Purple Finches were found breeding throughout the Santa Cruz Mountains during the atlas period, but although breeding was widespread in the Diablo Range, confirmations were obtained in fewer blocks there. Overall, confirmed breeding was found in 37 blocks (22%), but if probable and possible evidence is included, breeding was suspected in 98 blocks (59%). Breeding evidence was obtained from an elevation of 70 feet in Santa Cruz County, in an edge block on the western side of the Santa Cruz Mountains, to 3,000 feet in the Santa Cruz Mountains west of Saratoga. In the Santa Cruz Mountains, atlasers found this finch in coniferous or mixed coniferous and broadleaved evergreen forests. Nesting birds were often found in more mesic areas, in situations near streams or in the denser areas of forests. In the Diablo Range, nesting Purple Finches were found in foothill pine woodlands and in oak and broadleaved evergreen woodlands, often along intermittent streams. Many of these sites were in the shadier north-facing slopes of canyons, but some were in openings supporting annual grasslands in the foothill pine woodlands. In other parts of California, Purple Finches have been noted to use riparian woodlands (Roberson 1993hh, Small 1994, Berner 2003i), but in Santa Clara County no confirmations were obtained in apparently suitable riparian areas at low elevations.

Purple Finches undertake altitudinal migrations in California (Small 1994). Locally, birds are often found in late winter on the valley floor, where they forage well into March on the opening buds and flowers of trees such as valley oaks before returning to areas where they nest. During the atlas period, the earliest evidence of breeding was a bird on a nest on 23 Apr. Subsequent to the atlas, nest building was seen as early as 31 Mar 1994 (Michael M. Rogers, pers. comm.). Most confirmations were of fledged young. The latest breeding evidence obtained was an adult carrying food on 18 Jul.

The Purple Finch is largely a resident of mesic forests in California's Coast Ranges. In Santa Clara County, however, birds breed widely in the Diablo Range, and sometimes in more xeric habitats in open foothill pine woodlands. As the land becomes drier to the east, Purple Finches no longer nest, and there are no acceptable breeding records from Stanislaus County (*Am. Birds* 43:1366 1989; James Gain, pers. comm.). R. H. Wauer found this finch regularly in May in Henry Coe State Park in the 1950s, but in 1972 it was found there on only two of 69 days during the summer (Matthiesen and Mewaldt 1974). There is evidence that Purple Finches are recent invaders of dry country to the south, on San Benito Mountain (Johnson and Cicero 1985), but it is unclear whether comparable changes have occurred locally in the Diablo Range in the last century.

William G. Bousman

PURPLE FINCH

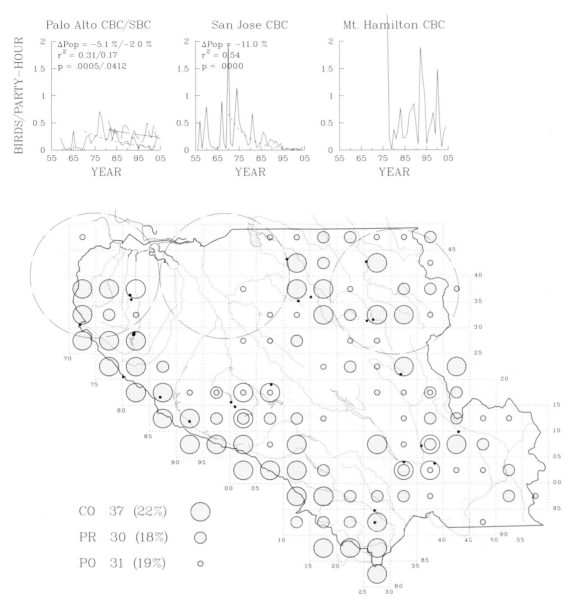

Palo Alto CBC/SBC

ΔPop = −5.1 %/−2.0 %
r² = 0.31/0.17
p = .0005/.0412

San Jose CBC

ΔPop = −11.0 %
r² = 0.54
p = .0000

Mt. Hamilton CBC

BIRDS/PARTY−HOUR

YEAR

CO   37   (22%)
PR   30   (18%)
PO   31   (19%)

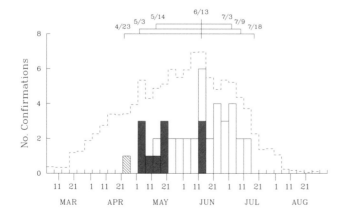

Atlas (1987–1993), n = 49

No. Confirmations

4/23   5/3   5/14   6/13   7/3   7/9   7/18

MAR   APR   MAY   JUN   JUL   AUG

RH'02

House Finch
Carpodacus mexicanus

Its habit of nesting in hanging planters, ornamental shrubbery, and other situations near houses has made the House Finch one of our most familiar birds. The natural breeding range of the House Finch extends from southwestern British Columbia and Montana south through the west and into Mexico as far as Chiapas (Hill 1993). Birds introduced in New York in the 1950s have led to a rapid expansion in recent decades, and breeders are now found from eastern North Dakota across the southern Canadian provinces to New Brunswick and south to Texas and Georgia (Hill 1993, AOU 1998). There is disagreement on the number of House Finch subspecies, particularly in the Mexican populations, but resident birds found on the mainland from Canada to northern Baja California, including those in Santa Clara County, are all of the subspecies *frontalis* (Hill 1993). In California, the House Finch is found statewide except in mountainous areas with dense coniferous forests, in the humid coastal forests, and in the waterless tracts of our deserts (Small 1994). This finch is a widespread and abundant resident in Santa Clara County.

Dr. James G. Cooper, in his first visit to Santa Clara County in late 1855, collected a House Finch on 24 Oct 1855 (USNM #A04487); this is the earliest record of this species in Santa Clara County. The artist Andrew J. Grayson moved to San Jose in 1853 and sometime during his four-year residency made a painting of House Finches, although only a woodcut survives (Stone 1986). Observers at the end of the nineteenth century described the House Finch as abundant (Price 1898d, Van Denburgh 1899b, Fisher 1902), and Grinnell and Wythe (1927) also reported House Finches as abundant residents in the San Francisco Bay area. In the South Bay, Sibley (1952) judged them to be common, and noted that they were particularly abundant east of the Santa Cruz Mountains and around farms and orchards. House Finches have been recorded on the Palo Alto and San Jose Christmas Bird Counts since the 1950s, and analysis of the CBC data shows declines of 4.1 and 3.7% per year in these two circles, respectively. Analysis of Breeding Bird Survey data for California for the period 1966 to 2004 has shown a smaller decline, of 1.8% per year (Sauer et al. 2005). Curiously, analysis of the Palo Alto Summer Bird Count data shows a 3.1% per year

increase since the 1980s. The causes of population declines in California and other western states are not known (Hill 1993), nor are there obvious reasons for the fourfold decline observed on our local CBCs since the 1950s. House Finches are dependent on weed seeds for food, and it may be that the availability of this food is being reduced by urbanization.

Atlasers found it easy to confirm breeding by House Finches, in part because of their abundance but also because fledglings are persistent and noisy as they follow their parents about. Confirmations based on feeding young and dependent fledglings accordingly accounted for 49% of all confirmations. Breeding was confirmed in 138 county blocks (84%) and if the probable and possible evidence is included, breeding evidence was obtained in 158 blocks (96%). Breeding elevations ranged from sea level in atlas blocks near the South Bay to 3,800 feet on Mt. Hamilton. Although the species was found throughout the Diablo Range, the density of breeding birds declined somewhat in the drier eastern portions of the range. House Finches are nonmigratory, but they largely withdraw from the higher portions of the Diablo Range during the winter (they are found just one year in three on the Mt. Hamilton CBC). They were found most often in edge habitats where there are trees and shrubs intermixed with grasses or weedy areas. The only places where they were not found nesting were within the humid, coniferous forests of the Santa Cruz Mountains, in extensive grasslands or chaparral fields devoid of suitable edge, and in marshy areas along the edge of the South Bay where there was an absence of suitable nesting structures. House Finches generally build their nests where there is some supporting structure and overhead cover. The many nooks and crannies found around houses, such as pots, hanging planters, beams, and eaves, are frequently used. House Finches also use the nests of other birds after lining them to suit their needs. They are generally not cavity nesters and were rarely found using partial cavities in dead limbs or nest boxes.

Male House Finches normally start to sing here in late February or early March. The earliest breeding evidence observed during the atlas period was a female carrying nest material on 19 Mar. Nestlings were found as early as 6 Apr. House Finches are multibrooded, and a female may start a new nest after the young from a previous nest fledge, allowing the male to feed and care for the fledglings (Hill 1993). Birds were seen incubating eggs as late as 16 Jul, and the latest breeding evidence was an adult feeding young on 25 Aug.

The House Finch is well adapted for dry and hot conditions and has been very successful in our Mediterranean climate. Metabolic studies have shown that although the House Finch has a high tolerance for these conditions, its metabolism fails under particularly humid conditions (Salt 1952). Its congener, however, the Purple Finch, shows a much greater tolerance for cool and humid conditions, and significantly less tolerance for hot and dry conditions. This difference in tolerance is reflected in the distribution maps for the two species.

William G. Bousman

HOUSE FINCH

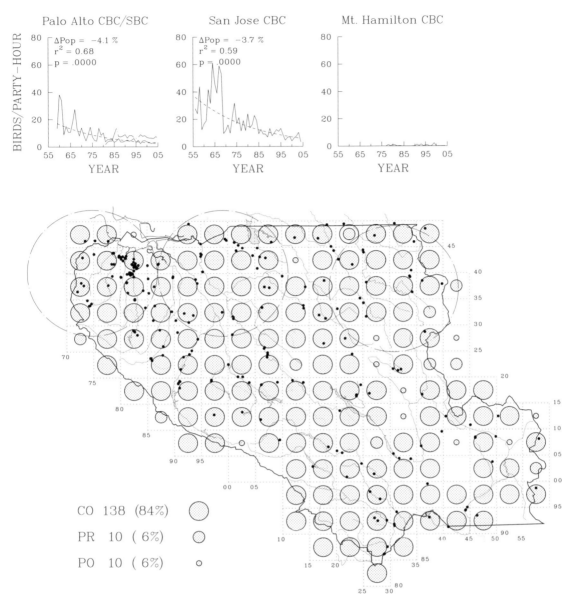

Palo Alto CBC/SBC

ΔPop = −4.1 %
r^2 = 0.68
p = .0000

San Jose CBC

ΔPop = −3.7 %
r^2 = 0.59
p = .0000

Mt. Hamilton CBC

BIRDS/PARTY−HOUR

YEAR

CO 138 (84%)

PR   10 (6%)

PO   10 (6%)

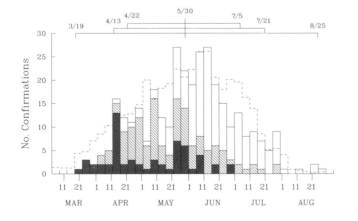

Atlas (1987−1993), n = 352

No. Confirmations

3/19   4/13   4/22   5/30   7/5   7/21   8/25

MAR   APR   MAY   JUN   JUL   AUG

Red Crossbill
Loxia curvirostra

Dependent upon the maturation of its preferred cone crops, the enigmatic Red Crossbill follows this variable resource throughout much of North America. Under favorable conditions this Holarctic species breeds across North America from Alaska to Newfoundland, and south through the Appalachians, the Rocky Mountains, and along the Pacific Coast into Mexico and Nicaragua (Adkisson 1996). At least eight subspecies of this cardueline finch have been proposed in North America (AOU 1957), but as noted by Adkisson (1996), "classification of this species into races has been as diverse as the many authors involved." Red Crossbills are rare and sporadic invaders to Santa Clara County, being found irregularly in the coniferous forests of the Santa Cruz Mountains and even more sporadically in the Diablo Range.

None of the early observers recorded Red Crossbills in Santa Clara County during the nineteenth century or the first half of the twentieth century. From 1878 to 1951, however, about 12 invasion years were noted for the central coast of California, an area from Monterey County to Sonoma County (Kelly 1948, Sibley 1952). On the basis of records in *Audubon Field Notes* and its successor publications, it appears that there have been significant incursions to central California in the years 1960–61, 1973–74, 1984–85, 1987–88, and 1996–97. Small numbers of birds were found in the Santa Cruz Mountains between 1951 and 1960, and breeding was suspected in 1951 and 1955 (*Audubon Field Notes* 5:307 1951, 9:402 1955) in a mixed-coniferous forest of ponderosa pine and Douglas fir (Sibley 1952). The invasion in the fall of 1960 brought birds to the eastern side of the Santa Cruz Mountains, and three birds in Saratoga on 12 Dec 1960 constitute the first record for Santa Clara County (*Avocet* 8:4 1960). Three of the recent invasions, in 1984–85, 1987–88, and 1996–97, have included significant numbers of birds in the local area. High counts during these invasions include 100 birds on Loma Prieta, Santa Clara County, 18 May 1985 (Alan M. Eisner, pers. comm.); 72 in Castle Rock State Park, Santa Cruz County, 6 Nov 1987 (David L. Suddjian, pers. comm.); 93 in the Russian Ridge Open Space Preserve, San Mateo County, 21 Dec 1987 (pers. obs.); and 110 birds in Castle Rock State Park (including 20 in Santa Clara County), 18 Nov 1996 (David L. Suddjian, pers. comm.).

It is probable that Red Crossbills have nested in Santa Clara County during one of the recent invasions, but no proof of breeding has been obtained. The 1987–88 incursion occurred during the atlas period, and the strongest evidence of breeding then was found along the crest of the Santa Cruz Mountains. A male was singing and following a female on 26 Apr 1988 in a redwood-Douglas fir forest near Summit Road and the Soquel-San Jose Road. The Douglas firs were noted to have had a good cone crop that year. Then on 14 May 1988, a pair was feeding in Douglas firs along the ridge above Uvas Creek County Park. Also during the spring of 1988, birds were observed in other forested areas, including knobcone pine forests in the Santa Cruz Mountains and ponderosa pine forest in the Diablo Range. The only confirmed breeding by this species during the 1987–88 incursion consisted of three nest records obtained in stands of Monterey pines along the coast in Santa Cruz County (David L. Suddjian, pers. comm.).

Groth (1993) has noted a correspondence between flight call, morphology, and allozyme frequencies. Eight "types" have been described, and at least four of these, types 2, 3, 4, and 5, have been found in California. The number of races or "types" of Red Crossbills that occur in the Santa Cruz Mountains and the Diablo Range during invasion years is largely a mystery, but during the 1984–85 invasion both specimens and recordings were obtained of birds in the Santa Cruz Mountains (Groth 1993). All four of California's types participated in the invasion, types 2, 3, and 4 being the most common. During the 1996–97 invasion, which extended from Monterey to Humboldt counties, both specimens and tape recordings were obtained, and it appears that all of these were type 2 birds (*Field Notes 51*:117 1997).

The differentiation of the various "types" of Red Crossbills, except by the specialist, requires either specimens or tape recordings of the call notes (Groth 1993). Although specific types favor particular conifer species, this specialization occurs only during nesting (Adkisson 1996). When not nesting, this species uses a wide range of food resources. Understanding this species' true status and life history is an exciting challenge for ornithologists and birders in the future.

William G. Bousman

RED CROSSBILL

Palo Alto CBC/SBC

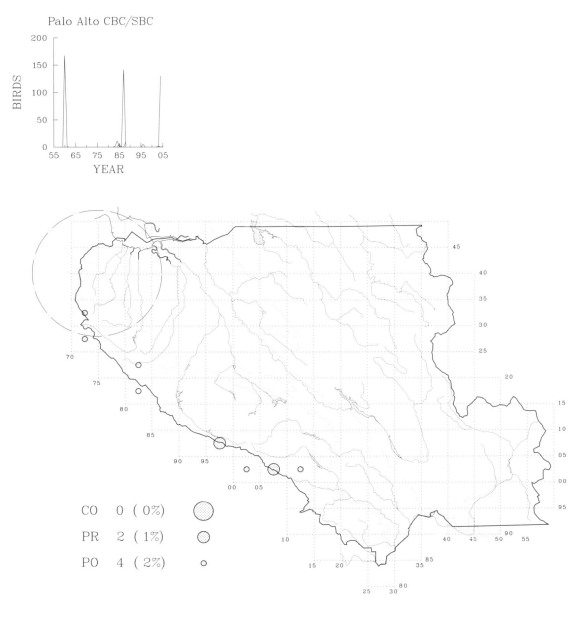

CO	0 (0%)	
PR	2 (1%)	
PO	4 (2%)	

Pine Siskin
Carduelis pinus

Most often seen in winter, this busy streaked "goldfinch" breeds regularly in Santa Clara County only in the coniferous forests along the county's western border. In North America, breeding Pine Siskins are found in the great coniferous forest belt from Alaska to eastern Canada and south in the Rocky Mountains to Mexico, and on the west coast to Baja California (Dawson 1997). Three subspecies have been described, the nominate *C. p. pinus* being the one found throughout North America and northern Mexico (Dawson 1997). In California, Pine Siskins are resident in the humid coastal and montane coniferous forests throughout the state (Small 1994). They are rare residents in western Santa Clara County, but can be fairly common throughout the county during their occasional winter irruptions.

Early observers in Santa Clara County noted Pine Siskins mostly as winter residents. Price (1898e) described "great flocks" at Stanford in the winter months. Van Denburgh (1899b) considered them common in winter, but noted that in some years few were seen. He had not observed siskins during the summer months at either Los Gatos or Palo Alto. Fisher (1902) reported that Pine Siskins were resident in the Santa Cruz Mountains, but were found only as migrants in the Santa Clara Valley. Grinnell and Wythe (1927) described Pine Siskins as common residents in the San Francisco Bay region wherever native or planted conifers were found, and the use of ornamental or planted conifers in urban areas by nesting Pine Siskins was noted by a number of early observers. Van Denburgh (1899b) recorded that an acquaintance, James M. Hyde, had seen a pair nesting in the city of Santa Clara prior to 1899. From 1929 to 1931, Emily D. Smith found siskins nesting at the San Jose State Teachers College and attributed their presence to coast redwoods planted on the valley floor (*Wren-Tit 1(3)* 1929, *2(3)* 1930, *3(3)* 1931). Thomas L. Rodgers (1937) found a pair nesting in a small coast redwood on the same campus in 1934. At midcentury, Sibley (1952) judged Pine Siskins to be common residents in coniferous forests in the South Bay area, but did not report additional observations of siskins nesting on the valley floor.

The only potentially breeding Pine Siskins found during the atlas period were within the coniferous forests of the Santa Cruz Mountains. Records were obtained in 24 county blocks (15%), and breeding confirmations were recorded in just four of those blocks (2%). Breeding was observed from an elevation of 420 feet near Simas Lake in a Santa Cruz County edge block to 1,400 feet in the hills above Saratoga. No breeding or summer birds were observed on the valley floor, notwithstanding the historical records listed above, or in the Diablo Range. When found, Pine Siskins were generally in coniferous forests of Douglas fir, coast redwood, or a mixture of these combined with broadleaved evergreens such as tan oak and madrone. These mixed habitats often included small meadows with a shrub layer at their edge or riparian areas with willows. In some cases a few houses were found within these forest habitats. Nonetheless, Pine Siskins appeared to be absent from a great deal of habitat on the east side of the Santa Cruz Mountains that seemed appropriate for the species.

Our understanding of the breeding phenology of local Pine Siskins is confounded by the presence of northern or montane birds that are still moving through the area in spring following irruptive years. Pine Siskins are occasionally seen into the second week of May in Diablo Range locations where they do not breed. Nearby in San Mateo County, where siskins are more common, activities associated with nest-building have been observed from 13 Apr to 6 Jun (Sequoia Audubon Society 2001m). Carriger and Pemberton (1907) reported egg sets from San Francisco and San Mateo counties that were collected from 10 Apr to 10 Jun. The earliest nesting evidence obtained in Santa Clara County during the atlas period was of adults feeding young on 21 May in Los Gatos. The latest evidence was of adults feeding young on 29 Jul west of the crest of the Santa Cruz Mountains.

Numbers of Pine Siskins appear stable in eastern North America, but analysis of Breeding Bird Survey data demonstrates that they are declining in wide areas of western North America (Dawson 1997). In California, analysis of BBS data shows a decline of 6.8% per year for the period 1966 to 2004 (Sauer et al. 2005), and analysis of Palo Alto SBC data shows a local decline in potentially breeding birds of 15.0% per year. David L. Suddjian (pers. comm.) has noted both a marked decrease in the number of Pine Siskins in the Santa Cruz Mountains in the last 15-20 years and a significant contraction of their range. Since the mid-1990s, they have been absent from most areas where they were found during the atlas period, although there are still pockets of resident birds farther west on the coastal slope in San Mateo and Santa Cruz counties.

William G. Bousman

PINE SISKIN

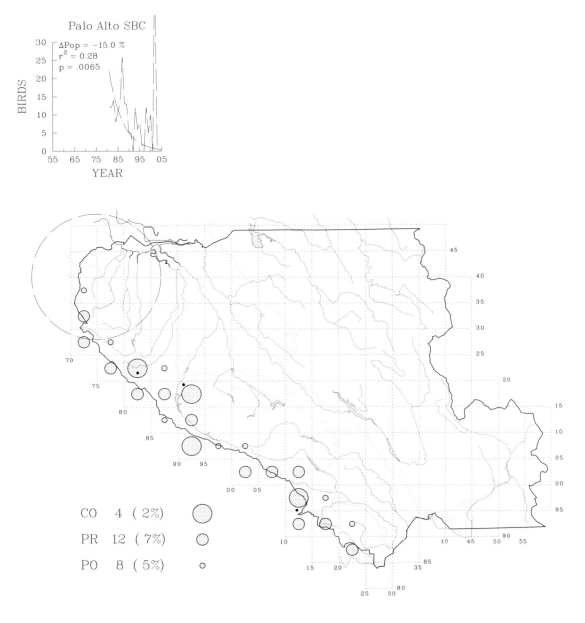

Palo Alto SBC

ΔPop = −15.0 %
r² = 0.28
p = .0065

BIRDS

YEAR

CO   4 (2%)
PR 12 (7%)
PO   8 (5%)

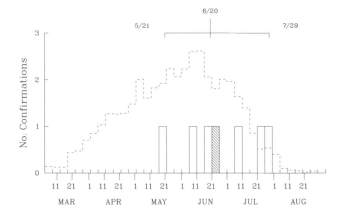

No. Confirmations

5/21   6/20   7/29   Atlas (1987–1993), n = 7

MAR   APR   MAY   JUN   JUL   AUG

Lesser Goldfinch
Carduelis psaltria

With the breeding season over, flocks of these tiny gold-finches gather in fields of grasses and forbs, displaying their acrobatic prowess as they extricate seeds from flower pods on bending stems that seem barely able to support their weight. Smallest of the three North American goldfinches, the Lesser Goldfinch breeds in the western United States from Oregon through Utah to Texas, and south through Mexico to South America from Venezuela to Peru (Watt and Willoughby 1999). Of the five subspecies, *C. p. hesperophila*, sometimes called the "Green-backed Goldfinch," is resident from Oregon to California, Baja California, and Arizona. The Lesser Goldfinch is a widespread and common species found year-round in Santa Clara County.

The first record of Lesser Goldfinch in Santa Clara County was a specimen collected in San Jose by A. J. Grayson prior to 1860 (USNM #B33808). Van Denburgh (1899b) considered this goldfinch to be an abundant breeding species in all areas of the county that he visited, a judgment echoed by Fisher (1902). Grinnell and Wythe (1927) considered it an abundant resident throughout the San Francisco Bay area, although they noted it was less common along the coast than inland. Sibley (1952) reported the Lesser Goldfinch to be a common resident in the South Bay as well. Analysis of Christmas Bird Count data from the Palo Alto and San Jose counts since the mid-1950s shows a population decline of 4.4 to 5.1% per year. A decline of 3.5% per year has been observed in the Palo Alto SBC data, but this trend is not significant ($p = 0.074$). Moreover, an analysis of Breeding Bird Survey data from 1966 to 2004 does not show a significant decline for California routes (Sauer et al. 2005), and thus the decline observed in the Palo Alto and San Jose count circles reflects the influence of local conditions. The increase in mature trees and irrigated gardens that has accompanied urbanization has reduced the acreage of chaparral, grasslands, and brushlands that provide the seed-bearing plants used by this species, and this may be a cause of these declines. A similar change has been described for the Monterey Peninsula (Roberson 1993ii).

The Lesser Goldfinch was recorded in nearly all the blocks in the county (96%), and breeding confirmations were obtained in 127 blocks (77%). Birds were generally found in areas with a mixture of chaparral, grasses, brushlands, oak woodlands, and blue oak-foothill pine woodlands. Essential in all cases was nearby permanent water for drinking and bathing. These habitats are common in the Diablo Range, but are more irregularly distributed in the Santa Cruz Mountains, where coniferous and broadleaved evergreen forests were not used by this species. Breeding Lesser Goldfinches were also found widely on the valley floor. There they were associated with upland growth at the edge of the San Francisco Bay, ruderal growth in undeveloped area, riparian corridors, and city parks.

Wintering Lesser Goldfinches are found into March, when flocks break up as pairs form. The earliest breeding evidence observed during the atlas period was a bird carrying nesting material on 29 Mar. Subsequently, birds were observed gathering nest material on the exceptionally early dates of 28 Jan 1996 (Peter J. Metropulos, pers. comm.) and 28 Jan 2003 (Michael M. Rogers, pers. comm.). The latest breeding evidence in the atlas period was dependent fledglings being fed on 2 Sep. Following the atlas period, the same behavior was observed as late as 14 Sep 1996 (Michael J. Mammoser, pers. comm.). California egg dates extend from 2 Apr to 3 Aug (Linsdale 1968), which shows a general correspondence with the phenology here. It is unclear whether this species is double-brooded (Watt and Willoughby 1999), although the extended breeding season we see here suggests that this is likely.

A Lesser Goldfinch being parasitized by a Brown-headed Cowbird is known from a single instance (Watt and Willoughby 1999). Many of the cardueline finches feed their young regurgitated seeds, and this diet is not adequate for the growth of nestling cowbirds (Kozlovic et al. 1996). Subsequent to the atlas period, a female cowbird was seen to pull an incubating female Lesser Goldfinch from her nest in Ed Levin County Park on 20 Apr 1997 (Michael M. Rogers, pers. comm.). The cowbird stayed in the nest briefly before being chased off by the goldfinches, but it is not known whether she laid an egg.

The three goldfinches, Lesser, Lawrence's, and American, all nest within Santa Clara County. The Lesser Goldfinch, the most widespread of the three, is able to nest successfully in a wide variety of habitats. Lesser and Lawrence's Goldfinches use similar habitats, and there is considerable overlap in the seed resources they use (Linsdale 1957, Coutlee 1968b). The two species show slight differences in their foraging strategies and the size of their nesting territories, but why the Lesser Goldfinch is more widespread than the Lawrence's is unclear (Coutlee 1968a, Coutlee 1968b). Unlike its two relatives, the American Goldfinch shows a preference for riparian habitats, and this preference appears to govern its distribution in Santa Clara County.

William G. Bousman

LESSER GOLDFINCH

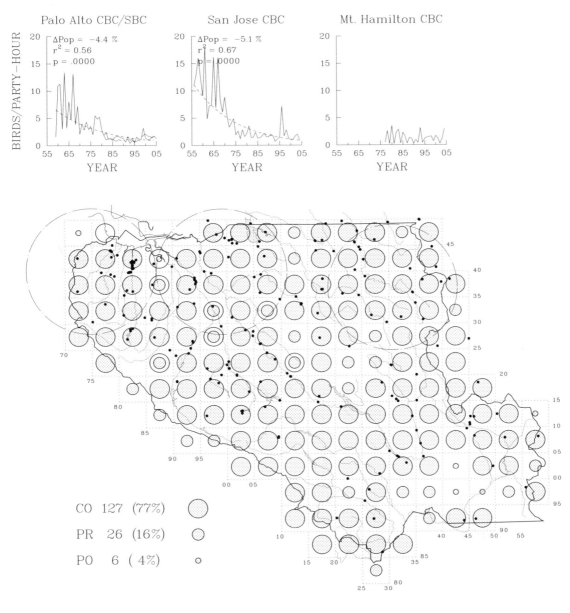

Palo Alto CBC/SBC

ΔPop = −4.4 %
r² = 0.56
p = .0000

San Jose CBC

ΔPop = −5.1 %
r² = 0.67
p = .0000

Mt. Hamilton CBC

BIRDS/PARTY-HOUR

YEAR

CO 127 (77%)
PR 26 (16%)
PO 6 (4%)

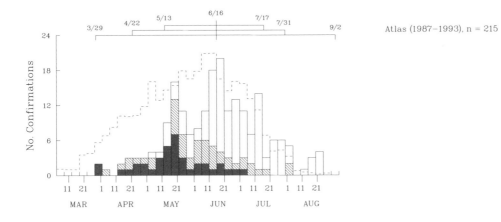

Atlas (1987–1993), n = 215

No. Confirmations

3/29 4/22 5/13 6/16 7/17 7/31 9/2

MAR APR MAY JUN JUL AUG

Lawrence's Goldfinch
Carduelis lawrencei

This nomadic cardueline finch, with its beautiful gray, black, and yellow pattern, continually teases us with its erratic wanderings. The Lawrence's Goldfinch breeds in arid woodlands in Baja California, along the southern California coastal slope, in the southern Coast Ranges, and along the edges of California's Central Valley (Small 1994, Davis 1999). In Santa Clara County, the Lawrence's Goldfinch is an uncommon summer resident in the Diablo Range, and breeders are occasionally found on the valley floor and in the Santa Cruz Mountains. It is an irregular and typically rare fall and winter visitor over this same range, although large winter flocks are occasionally noted.

Nesting in Santa Clara County was first detected on 29 Apr 1894, when Henry R. Taylor collected five eggs near Sargent (WFVZ #116191). The nomadic nature of the Lawrence's Goldfinch was noted by a number of early observers. Price (1898e) recorded it as a summer visitor at Stanford and referred to it as "not abundant." Van Denburgh (1899b) found it nesting in the Santa Cruz Mountains and stated that it was "by no means rare," although not as common as the Lesser Goldfinch. Fisher (1902) judged this goldfinch to be a rare summer resident in the Santa Clara Valley and Santa Cruz Mountains and referred to it as "erratic in its visits." Grinnell and Wythe (1927) considered the Lawrence's Goldfinch to be an irregular and local summer visitor to the San Francisco Bay area, in limited numbers. Sibley (1952) judged it as fairly common but irregular in the South Bay.

Atlasers found Lawrence's Goldfinches breeding throughout the more arid eastern portions of the Diablo Range during the atlas period. Breeding birds were found in blue and valley oak woodlands, blue oak-foothill pine woodlands, and savanna edge throughout these areas, generally near streams where water was available throughout the nesting season. These goldfinches most often built their nests at moderate height in oaks and foothill pines, frequently using the lichens that are so prevalent in these arid woodlands. In a few cases, they used the ornamental conifers that had been planted near ranch houses or other buildings. Farther west, breeding Lawrence's Goldfinches were found irregularly in similar arid oak woodlands along the western front of the Diablo Range. The only breeding confirmation in the Santa Cruz Mountains was of adults feeding young near Loma Prieta on 4 Jul 1987, an irruption year. Two confirmations of adults feeding young were obtained on the valley floor: one near the Pajaro River on 24 Jul 1989, the other in Las

Animas Veterans Park in Gilroy on 16 May 1992. Following the atlas period, additional confirmations were obtained in the northern Diablo Range, as well as on the valley floor at Lake Cunningham, the Ogier Avenue ponds, and two locations near San Felipe Road north of Pacheco Creek. Although breeding was not confirmed in the northern Santa Cruz Mountains within Santa Clara County, multiple breeding records were obtained in four blocks in San Mateo County, west of the county line, from 1989 to 1997 (Sequoia Audubon Society 2001n). Breeding elevations reported during the atlas period ranged from 200 feet at Las Animas Veterans Park to 2,800 feet along upper Arroyo Mocho. Subsequent to the atlas period, breeding birds were found at the lower elevation of 130 feet at Lake Cunningham and at the higher elevation of 3,410 feet along Valpe Ridge just north of the Alameda County line.

In the eastern Diablo Range, in late March and early April each year, small flocks of Lawrence's Goldfinches return to the areas where they breed. The earliest breeding evidence during the atlas period was a female building a nest on 8 Apr in a Stanislaus County edge block. Following the atlas period, nest building was seen on the earlier date of 16 Mar 1996 near San Antonio Junction (Michael J. Mammoser, PADB). Although nest-building activities were seen as late as 25 Jun, the Lawrence's Goldfinch is considered single-brooded (Davis 1999). The latest breeding evidence observed was adults feeding young on 24 Jul near the Pajaro River. Few Lawrence's Goldfinches are found within their normal breeding range after late July, but flocks gather in late September, and in some years they may be encountered almost anywhere until the next breeding season ensues.

Analysis of records in the county notebooks shows differences in the abundance and temporal patterns of Lawrence's Goldfinches between, on the one hand, the center of their population in the Diablo Range and, on the other hand, peripheral areas in the Santa Cruz Mountains and on the valley floor where they are not found every year. In the Diablo Range, again, breeding birds are normally first found at the end of March and remain through the end of July. In fall and winter they are found irregularly, and sometimes in large flocks. In the Santa Cruz Mountains, breeding birds are rarely found before early May, about a month later than their arrival in the Diablo Range, and are less numerous by about a factor of five. Occasional large flocks are found in the Santa Cruz Mountains in fall and early winter, but few are seen again until May. On the Santa Clara Valley floor, breeding birds follow a breeding phenology similar to the Diablo Range birds, but they are less numerous by a factor of 25. Almost no flocks are encountered in the valley in fall and winter.

William G. Bousman

LAWRENCE'S GOLDFINCH

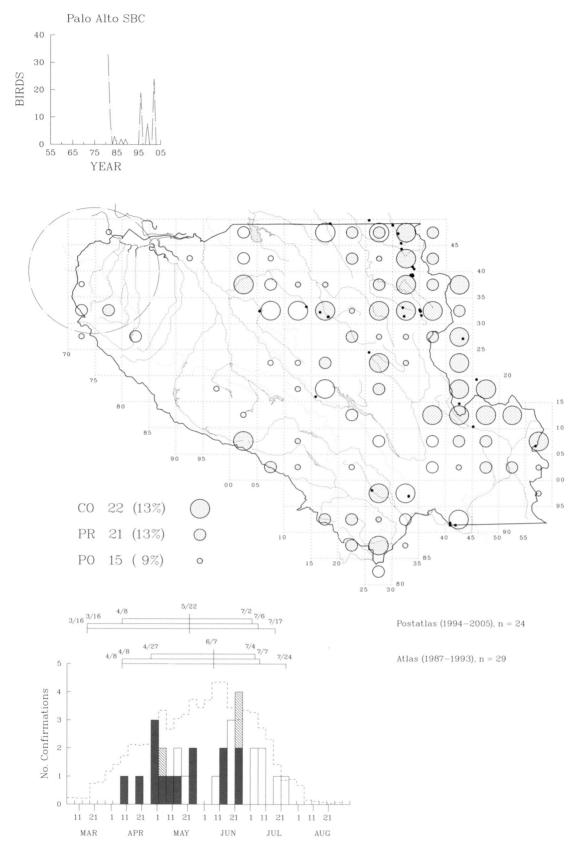

Palo Alto SBC

CO 22 (13%)

PR 21 (13%)

PO 15 (9%)

Postatlas (1994–2005), n = 24

Atlas (1987–1993), n = 29

451

American Goldfinch
Carduelis tristis

Although observed throughout the county, engaged in acrobatic foraging on seed heads or boisterously singing atop a shrub, this small, lively finch is found breeding in only a few of the riparian areas along the Santa Clara Valley floor. The American Goldfinch breeds across North America, the northern limit of its range extending from British Columbia to Newfoundland, the southern limit from southern California to central Georgia (AOU 1998). Within this range, four subspecies have been described (AOU 1957). The central and eastern subspecies show some southward movements in the winter, whereas the two western subspecies tend to be more sedentary, with irregular winter movements. The only subspecies found within California, *C. t. salicamans*, breeds throughout the state west of the Cascades-Sierra axis and the southeastern deserts. Birds that nest north of San Francisco Bay show some movement south in winter (Small 1994). The American Goldfinch is fairly common in Santa Clara County, found widely in winter in a variety of habitats. Fewer birds are present in summer, concentrated in only a few riparian areas on the valley floor.

The distribution of the American Goldfinch appears to have changed little over the last hundred years. In describing the species' California range, Cooper (1870) noted its preference for riparian areas with willow and cottonwoods, and its avoidance of the dry interior hills and forested mountains. Van Denburgh (1899b) commented that it was resident in Palo Alto but appeared in Los Gatos only during the winter. Grinnell and Wythe (1927), in their survey of the avifauna of the San Francisco Bay region, reported that it was locally common, and that breeding birds were found in areas of willow and alder with adjacent weeds and brushy growth for foraging. Sibley (1952) considered the American Goldfinch to be a fairly common resident in riparian willows and alders, noting that it wandered widely to other habitats in the winter.

American Goldfinches were found breeding in only 8% of the county's blocks during the atlas period. These breeding records were from just two locations: the northern Santa Clara Valley near the Bay and along its tributary creeks, and the southern end of the Santa Cruz Mountains in the Pajaro River drainage. Following the atlas period, breeding was confirmed in the middle of the county in the Coyote Valley. Goldfinches were seen feeding young near the Ogier Avenue ponds along Coyote Creek on 9 Jul 1996 and again on 7 Aug 1998 (Stephen C. Rottenborn, county notebooks). Downstream 3 kilometers, birds were seen carrying nest material near the Riverside Golf Course (now the Coyote Creek Golf Course) on 3 May 1997 (Michael J. Mammoser, county notebooks). For the most part, the blocks with breeding goldfinches were those that included riparian areas with willows and cottonwoods in combination with nearby grassy, weedy, or brushy areas that provided the necessary seed resources. Although the geographic extent of these areas was limited, this goldfinch was in many cases common or abundant there. Other riparian areas, however, with seemingly identical vegetation characteristics, supported no breeding American Goldfinches, and the reasons for this disparity are unclear. In coastal Marin County, Shuford (1993gg) concluded that American Goldfinches were most numerous along the immediate coast, where coastal fog increased available moisture. Similarly, Bailey (1993d) found that all breeding locations in Monterey County occurred where summer fog was common. Although Santa Clara County is not directly on the coast, the influence of summer fog is felt both at the south end of San Francisco Bay and along the Pajaro River basin. These are the areas where this finch was commonly found.

Breeding dates for the American Goldfinch during the atlas period extended from 2 May (carrying nesting material) to 13 Aug (feeding young). Following the atlas period, earlier breeding was observed when birds were seen carrying nest material on 12 Apr 2001 (Michael J. Mammoser, PADB), and later breeding was recorded when fledged young were seen on 12 Sep 1994 (Michael M. Rogers, PADB). The breeding phenology shown here agrees with the range of egg dates in California summarized by Tyler (1968), who reported that eggs were found from 10 Apr to 24 Jul, half of the records between 18 May and 14 Jun. In the eastern United States, the American Goldfinch does not begin to nest until July (Middleton 1993), since it feeds its young from the seeds of composites and other plants that do not set seed until midsummer. It appears that the earlier breeding cycle for *salicamans* is a result of the earlier seed set that characterizes the Mediterranean climate in California (Shuford 1993gg).

The American Goldfinch is most common in Santa Clara County in winter, to judge from data from the Palo Alto and San Jose CBCs. Although its winter numbers are highly variable, there has been a long-term decline of 2 to 4% in these winter numbers since the early 1960s. Within the Palo Alto count circle, surprisingly, the number of breeding American Goldfinches has shown a substantial increase over the last 20 years, in stark contrast with the numbers found in winter.

William G. Bousman

AMERICAN GOLDFINCH

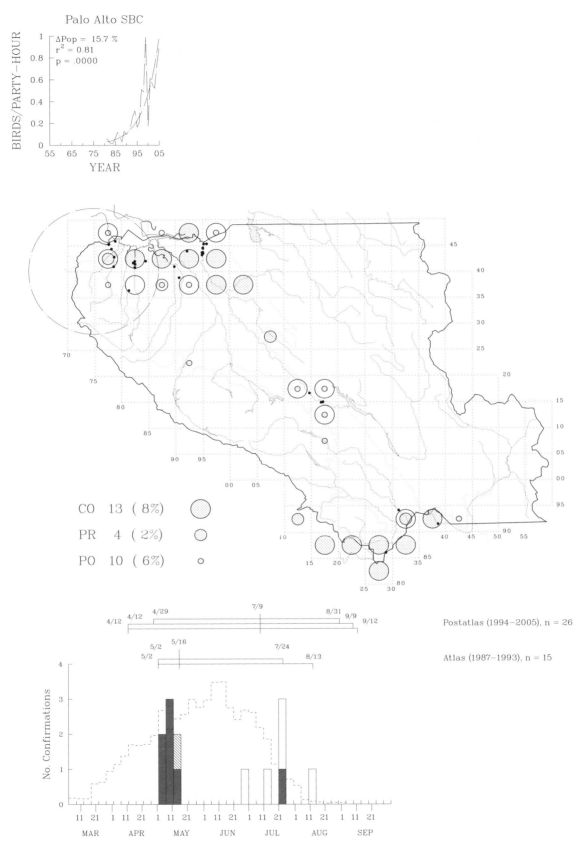

Palo Alto SBC

ΔPop = 15.7 %
$r^2 = 0.81$
p = .0000

CO 13 (8%)
PR 4 (2%)
PO 10 (6%)

Postatlas (1994–2005), n = 26

Atlas (1987–1993), n = 15

House Sparrow
Passer domesticus

Introduced to the Bay area in the nineteenth century, these noisy Eurasian weavers thrived in the days of the horse and buggy, but are declining in our motorized age. The House Sparrow is resident in the Old World from the British Isles east to northern Siberia and south to northern Africa, India, and southeast Asia. In North America, the introduced population now extends from British Columbia east to Newfoundland and south throughout the United States and most of Mexico, with scattered populations in Central America (AOU 1998). This species is found throughout California except in the higher elevations of the Sierra Nevada and in the mountains of northwestern California (Zeiner et al. 1990). In Santa Clara County, it is a common resident in urban areas on the valley floor and in adjacent foothills. It is generally absent from the less settled areas of the Santa Cruz Mountains and the Diablo Range, although a small population resides among the farms and ranches of the San Antonio Valley.

This Old World sparrow was purposely introduced to Brooklyn in 1851 (Lowther and Cink 1992). Grinnell and Miller (1944) have summarized the species' introduction to California. It arrived in San Francisco about 1871 or 1872 apparently, although it is unclear whether this introduction was intentional or coincided with shipments of grain and cattle on the new railroads. By 1886, in any case, it was common in settled areas throughout the Bay area, and birds were also noted in Eureka, Stockton, and Hollister. By 1888, it was found in the Sacramento Valley at Sacramento, Marysville, and Gridley, and was reported in the southern part of the San Joaquin Valley at Bakersfield by 1901. It was found in the Los Angeles Basin by 1905, and had expanded to suitable areas in southeastern California by 1912. Price (1898e) noted that it was well entrenched at Stanford University by 1898. At the midpoint of the twentieth century, it was considered an abundant resident in the South Bay (Sibley 1952).

After its introduction, the House Sparrow rapidly established itself as an urban bird and reached its population peak prior to the introduction of the automobile, because of its ability to find food and shelter in association with horses and stables in towns and cities (Lowther and Cink 1992). At the beginning of the twentieth century, the replacement of horses by automobiles and trucks led to a decline in this sparrow's population and a shift to rural areas with significant cattle operations (Bock 1979, Lowther and Cink 1992). The increase in agricultural efficiency in rural areas in recent decades, particularly on larger farms, has continued this species' population decline (Lowther and Cink 1992, Sauer et al. 2005). Examination of data from the Palo Alto and San Jose CBCs indicates a decline in winter numbers of about 6% per year since the mid-1950s, although House Sparrows continue to be common residents in our urban areas. An examination of the Palo Alto SBC data, collected since 1981, shows no significant change in the population within that count circle, suggesting that the local breeding population is currently stable.

The House Sparrow was confirmed breeding in 49% of the atlas blocks and was considered a probable or possible breeding bird in an additional 4% of the blocks. Of 185 confirmations where elevation was recorded, 90% were below 400 feet. This, however, reflects the species' affinity for urban areas rather than an avoidance of elevation, per se. For instance, birds nesting in the San Antonio Valley were recorded at elevations of 2,050 to 2,290 feet. House Sparrows were found nesting almost anywhere in the urban areas where they could find suitable nest cavities to fill with straw, grass stems, and shreds of paper. Nest sites were most often associated with manmade structures, and typical sites included the cavities formed by clay roof tiles, holes and crevices about the eaves of houses, building vents, and bird houses. Sparrows also used crevices in introduced palms and Cliff Swallow nests on buildings, sometimes displacing the swallows prior to their completion of the nest. House Sparrows are known to use other natural sites, including native coniferous or deciduous trees, or nests of species other than the Cliff Swallow (Lowther and Cink 1992), but atlasers reported no such use.

Birds carrying nest material and building nests constituted 34% of all breeding confirmations. Nesting was noted as early as 14 Feb, with a bird on its nest, and occupied nests were noted through 9 Oct. The main period of nesting shown here, from early March to late July, accords with egg dates recorded from California, e.g., 50 records from 18 Mar to 19 Jul (Bent 1958a).

William G. Bousman

HOUSE SPARROW

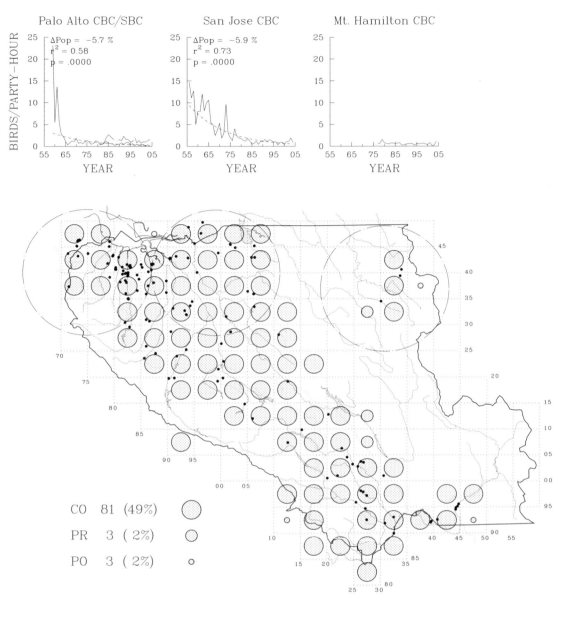

Palo Alto CBC/SBC

ΔPop = −5.7 %
r² = 0.58
p = .0000

San Jose CBC

ΔPop = −5.9 %
r² = 0.73
p = .0000

Mt. Hamilton CBC

BIRDS/PARTY−HOUR

YEAR

CO 81 (49%)
PR   3 (2%)
PO   3 (2%)

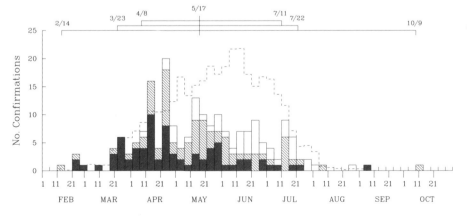

Atlas (1987−1993), n = 224

No. Confirmations

2/14   3/23   4/8   5/17   7/11 7/22   10/9

FEB   MAR   APR   MAY   JUN   JUL   AUG   SEP   OCT

8 The Once and Future County

Sitting on a hillside east of the Santa Clara Valley, I look down on the northern expanse of the valley and the city of San Jose. Wisps of a yellowish photochemical smog are moving among the downtown buildings in the early morning sunshine. Beside me, wild oats and other European grasses are waving in a light breeze. The rains have been heavy this spring and all these grasses have grown tall. Some of the wild oats are over 6 feet tall, and I am reminded of the early ranchers who reported that in a good year the wild oats were so tall you could tie their stalks together across your saddle.

These wild oats and the other grasses here came with the first Spanish explorers and quickly replaced the native grasslands and forbs in this valley, the first of many changes that were to come. We cannot be certain what the native grasslands would have looked like when Portola, Fages, and De Anza rode into the valley. We do know that the Indians had burned the grasses regularly to increase the yield of seed crops. But what else the Indians might have known about the valley's grasslands is lost to us, and their voices too are gone.

I try to imagine what the valley looked like as the Californios settled these lands in the late eighteenth century. Under the Spanish, most lived in the Pueblo of San Jose. Their cattle, which were the basis of their economy, ranged throughout the valley. Later, after the Mexican Revolution, more land grants were issued, and the ranchos spread throughout the valley. The Llano des Robles, or Plain of Oaks, stretched from San Martin to Milpitas, and I try to visualize what it would have looked like with its oak woodlands, savannas, and grasslands, and with cattle grazing everywhere. At Santa Clara, near the mission, there would have been gardens and small fields of wheat, the gardens irrigated with water from the Guadalupe River.

The Californios understood dryland agriculture, the use of irrigation, and the pattern of winter rains and summer drought. After a few winters of heavy rains they learned from the flooding Guadalupe River that they had built the Santa Clara mission too close to the river, and moved it to higher ground. And during the terrible droughts of the late 1820s, they culled their cattle, and particularly the horses, for they knew they could rebuild their herds, but only if the grasslands were not overgrazed.

There must have been a period of rainy years while the

American settlement began to take shape, for the early American ranchers believed the range to be capable of accommodating as many cattle as they wished to stock. That comforting belief, and the profits to be made selling beef in the gold diggings, led to overstocking, and the ensuing dry years, from 1855 to 1865, brought great damage to the range. William H. Brewer, a botanist and geographer with the infant California Geological Survey, described the dust in the summer, blown by the afternoon winds to 2,000 and even 3,000 feet above the valley floor, suggesting a "gauze veil." Travel on the roads pulverized the soils 4 to 6 inches deep, and there was dust everywhere. Every wagon, no matter its slow pace, produced its own dust cloud. In the worst of the drought years, dead cattle were seen everywhere in the valley.

In the meantime, the northern part of the valley had become a center of wheat, barley, and hay production. Farmers cleared the oaks from the land and planted grains. Good yields were obtained from the rich valley soils, and Santa Clara County was a prime area for wheat in the early 1850s. Eventually, new farms in the Central Valley obtained better yields and the wheat farms of the Santa Clara Valley were slowly replaced with orchards. What a prospect it must have been from my hillside, across the changing patchwork of wheat fields and orchards as the years passed. Year by year, the large grain fields were broken up, and more and more fruit trees were planted. What a sight it must have been in early spring when all these fruit trees burst into bloom!

At first, the towns in the valley were modest agricultural centers, but in the twentieth century, more and more of the people who came to live here involved themselves in other businesses. Sometimes they selected homesites away from towns, where they could grow a few fruit trees, or they built homes on smaller lots in town. At midcentury, the pioneering technology industries began to define the county's future, and just as wheat had displaced the cattle ranches, and the orchards had displaced the wheat fields, the orchards began to be supplanted by the houses, research facilities, light industry, and shopping malls that we see today, with block-long parks spotted here and there.

The process of settlement in the Santa Clara Valley, beginning with burning of the native plants by the Indians, grazing

456

and sustenance agriculture during the Spanish-Mexican period, and progressing through increasingly intensive agriculture, leading finally to the urban environment I see from my hillside vantage point, has been the pattern in many developed areas in the world (Foley et al. 2005). Each phase is characterized by an increasing population density and a concomitant increase in the value of the land. For the Californios, cattle raising was sufficient, but today almost all of the valley land is used for housing or commerce. The little that is left for agriculture on the valley floor today is committed to such high-value crops as nursery plants, mushrooms, and cut flowers.

Not all communities have followed the trajectory lineated by Foley et al. (2005), but that is the pattern we have seen in the Santa Clara Valley. In some cases elsewhere, climatic limitations, such as a lack of water or a growing season that suits only a few crops, have prevented the transition to higher-value crops and an increasing population. In other cases, agricultural development has failed: the land may have been exhausted through poor farming techniques, or the groundwater aquifers drained dry (as nearly happened in Santa Clara County), or the land may simply have been unable to support an increasing population (Leopold 1949, Diamond 2005).

The need for water has always been central to communities in the western United States, and Santa Clara County's experience has been typical. The Californios, with their Spanish heritage, were familiar with our Mediterranean climate. They understood dryland agriculture, and irrigated the fruits and vegetables they grew to sustain their communities. In most years the winter rains were sufficient for their needs. With American settlement, new technologies appeared in the valley, and both farmers and city dwellers drilled wells in the aquifer. Some of these wells overflowed from the pressure of the artesian head, and became nuisances as excess water flowed through town. For most wells, however, the water was a few feet down, and windmills were needed to bring it to the surface. Observers in the 1850s described the valley as full of windmills.

At the close of the nineteenth century, boosters for "The Valley of Heart's Delight" touted the perfect weather of the valley, and claimed you could drill a well anywhere and strike water. But by that time, the farmers knew differently. Each year they saw the water table dropping and their pumping costs increasing. It was clear that the aquifer was not being recharged. People did what they could as individuals to slow the drawdown. They built check dams along the valley streams to slow the water and prevent the "loss" or "wastage" of water that otherwise flowed to the Bay. Now we can see that this "wasted water" served the Bay ecosystem well, and that the winter flows of freshwater into the Bay were an essential component of the estuary. But at that time, farmers cared little about the estuary, the fisheries, or the oyster beds.

By the 1910s and '20s, it was clear to many residents and civic officials that something needed to be done about water. The Tibbetts and Kieffer plan of 1921 proposed a large system of reservoirs and percolation ponds that would recharge the aquifer. But the costs that would be incurred with this plan provoked strong opposition. Eventually, the Santa Clara Valley Water District was formed, and the system of reservoirs and ponds we know today was built, largely with Federal money during the

Great Depression.

But it was clear then, even as the new reservoirs and ponds were being built, that this was a temporary solution. The reality was that there was not enough water, no matter how well managed. Over the next three decades the water table continued to drop, and as it did, the ground in the aquifer collapsed, causing subsidence at the surface. This pattern ended only with the advent of imported water, first from the Hetch Hetchy in 1956, then from the South Bay Aqueduct in 1965, and finally from the San Felipe Project in 1987. Today, 57% of all water in the valley is imported. But no longer does this water support farming; all is now used for municipal purposes. And while imported water was coming on line, the drawdown of the aquifer slowed and then ceased, and the water table has recovered. The land subsidence, however, remains.

In an earlier time, we mostly ignored our sewage and other wastes. In the early farming period, trash would be tossed into a local farm dump or the creeks, and outhouses took care of the rest. Indoor plumbing and septic tanks came into use only a century ago, and slowly, as population density increased, these systems were connected by urban drains to sewage plants at the edge of the Bay. Treatment of the sewage was limited at first, but as the harm to the estuarine organisms became evident, laws were passed to require improved sewage treatment. Today, all of the plants remaining at the edge of the Bay use tertiary treatment before discharging their effluent into the Bay. This freshwater effluent, although relatively pure, is still a burden to the San Francisco Bay estuary.

Originally, when the South Bay was salt water, tidal flats, and salt marsh, that rich habitat supported a great variety of birds and animals. Sea otters foraged in the Bay, elk padded through the marshes, and seemingly uncountable Clapper Rails roamed the sloughs and channels. This estuarine ecosystem was ruled by the endless cycles of the daily tides and the winter inflows of freshwater from the nearby hills. Over more than a century, most of the marsh has been replaced by salt evaporator ponds, where no tides flow. Instead of the winter flood of freshwater, the Bay suffers a continuous influx of effluent from our sewage plants. The otters and elk are long gone, and the Clapper Rails barely hang on in the remaining bits of marsh. The salt marsh harvest mouse, too small and seemingly inconsequential to be much of an icon of these once great marshes, remains in only a few areas still salty enough for its particular needs.

So what of the future? We don't know what is to come, any more than we remember what has passed. There are no memories of the grizzlies that once roamed these hills and fed in fields thick with clover on the valley floor. There are books that tell us something of that past, and there are voices—dimly heard by those of us with an excess of imagination—that mourn the passing of a simpler time. But no books tell us what the future will bring, and even imagination fails to envision what is to come.

Foley et al. (2005), in describing the typical trajectory of a region's development, point out that as the wealth of a community accumulates, it begins to go toward the purchase and restoration of the land. In earlier years, as our predecessors were absorbed in earning a living from the land, there was neither time nor money nor even inclination to protect our local habitats. Yet as we gained wealth, we began to realize what was being lost, and we sought to protect those valued places still remaining, and then to restore what we could of other ecosystems.

In the early years of the twentieth century, the concept of parklands in Santa Clara County was of a different character than what we see now. Then, you could walk or ride almost anywhere you wished, and the hills and valley seemed untouched. An occasional farmer would post his land, but most folks didn't mind your trespass, whether you were a young egg collector or a hunter. With time and the increasing numbers of people, more land came to be fenced and trespass was discouraged. The construction of the reservoirs and percolation ponds in the 1920s and 1930s had brought on an era of public lands. The county purchased lands for these new reservoirs, and as construction was completed the adjacent areas were often converted to parks. Private groups, such as the Sempervirens Fund, involved themselves in major land purchases, land that could then be transferred to the county or state government. Descendants of some of the wealthy pioneer families, such as the Henry Coe and Joseph Grant families, donated lands they had acquired, or had inherited during their lifetimes, to local governments, and these generous donations remain a mainstay of our parklands today.

Although thoughtful conservationists like John Muir and Aldo Leopold had long ago discussed our responsibilities for stewardship of the land, their words did not immediately enter our national consciousness. But the 1960s and early 1970s saw a change. The National Environmental Protection Act (NEPA) was enacted in 1969, Earth Day was first celebrated in 1970, the California Environmental Quality Act (CEQA) was passed in 1970, and the Clean Waters Act, originally enacted in 1948, underwent a major expansion in 1972. Legislation for a new wildlife refuge in the South Bay was approved in 1972, and the Don Edwards San Francisco Bay National Wildlife Refuge was the result, opening in 1974.

Just as we have forgotten the grizzly bears, the wheat fields, and the orchards, the memories of the conservation battles of the 1960s and '70s are fading. Originally, much of the South Bay was owned by oyster producers and then the Ideal Cement Company, which harvested old shell deposits for cement. By the 1960s, large corporations had come to own development rights for most of these underwater "lands" and eagerly touted the need to fill them for development. Developers envisioned new Foster Cities encircling the South Bay, whereas conservationists saw a last chance to preserve these lands. The skill and courage of committed conservationists in this battle cannot be too highly praised. Nor should we forget the politicians, at many levels, who supported these actions. This time we won; next time we may not.

In the end, the greatest threat to the land is its division into homesites and the construction of houses. Land can often be restored, even after great injury. Mine sites can be cleaned up, logged forests can be regrown, abandoned farms can revert to a natural state. But once the land is divided into homesites, it remains that way pretty much forever. In the words of the great philosopher Pogo, "We have met the enemy and he is us."

So what will happen in this valley in the future? Many outcomes are possible. Development pressure for homes, businesses, shopping malls, and highways, where none of them belong, will be unending. Conservationists will continue to fight this good fight, and we will sometimes win and sometimes lose. But halting development is only a short-term goal. In the longer term we must protect the land and, where we can, restore it.

We stopped all chance of development of the degraded South Bay marshes in the 1970s, and today we are embarked on an effort to restore them. Converting marshes to salt ponds and industrial sites, as we did in the past, was a simple task, requiring merely some earthmoving machinery and some fill. Restoring these marshes to their ancient state is a different matter. It will require good science, great skill, and some luck. It is something we can all hope to see over the next few decades.

The restoration of the South Bay ecosystem may become one of our great future achievements, although realized at great cost. But there are little things we all can do that are also important. The citizen who takes off a morning or a day to clean trash from a creek, or remove exotic weeds from a local park, or any of hundreds of other tasks is also restoring the earth. The cost and effort may be small, but the returns are great.

But there is more we can do. With the formation of the Midpeninsula Regional Open Space District in the 1970s and the Santa Clara County Open Space Authority in the 1990s, we have taxed ourselves to buy land. What a wonderful thing to do! So we will continue to buy land and restore it. Restoring the South Bay marshes can be a vision for us. Just as these marshes were so harshly degraded, so also have many of our valley wetlands been damaged or destroyed. Those in the northern reaches of the valley are mostly gone, but some remain in the southern valley. Before the seemingly inexorable progress of development marches south, we need to buy and restore as many of these creeks and wetlands as we can. In the northern valley, "buffers" along our creeks are often spread only 5 or 10 meters to each side. We need to insist on buffers in the southern valley of five hundred to a thousand meters on each side. Where we can, we must restore these wonderful creeks and wetlands.

Just as we have taxed ourselves to buy land, we can find ways to buy yet more land and restore it. There is great wealth in this valley. Some of it has been spent frivolously on incongruously pretentious houses on our hillsides and ridges. But the wealth generated by some of the great families of this valley—the Packards, the Hewletts, and the Moores—has gone to foundations that have played a major part in restoring stretches of this land. The battle between conservationists and developers will never end, but we do have many allies among our citizens, and many more will come to support us. In the end, we must do three things: buy land where there is still the promise of healthy ecosystems, restore the earth where it is still possible, and educate our children.

Appendixes

Appendix 1:
Atlasers and Contributors

Atlasers

During the atlas period, from 1987 to 1993, William G. Bousman compiled and maintained the atlas database. About 97% of this database derives from the efforts of 57 atlasers. These atlasers selected blocks to survey, made careful observations in the field, and then filled out the appropriate forms for data entry. The wealth and the depth of the information describing the status of breeding birds in Santa Clara County can be attributed directly to the contributions of the 57 atlasers listed here.

Keith Baker, Lotus H. Baker, Bonnie Bedzin, Barbara Bessey, William G. Bousman, Signe Boyer, Geri A. Brown, Phyllis M. Browning, Roy S. Cameron, Rita Colwell, Charles J. Coston, Derek O. Currall, Maryann Danielson, Alan M. Eisner, Dick Elliott, Michael L. Feighner, Eric Feuss, Shawneen Finnegan, Howard L. Friedman, Ed Frost, Kevin Gilmartin, Jennifer Green, Ed Gustafson, Gloria G. Heller, Grant Hoyt, Karen Hoyt, David Johnson, Dee Kempf, Neil Kernes, Ed Laak, Amy Lauterbach, Briana Lindh, Michael J. Mammoser, Irene Manicci, John Mariani, L. Richard Mewaldt, Bryan M. Mori, Paul L. Noble, Hugh Possingham, Peter Radcliff, Harold M. Reeve, Sherrie Reeve, Elsie Richey, Michael D. Rigney, Michael M. Rogers, Stephen C. Rottenborn, Donald E. Schmoldt, Milton L. Seibert, Dave Sellers, Bonnie Jo Spacek, Jean-Marie Spoelman, David L. Suddjian, Scott Terrill, Ann Verdi, Christine Wolfe, Claire Wolfe, and James Yurchenco.

Atlas Contributors

Atlas contributors furnished less than 4% of the records in the atlas database. Their records, however, were often unique and provided valuable information on breeding birds, particularly within the urban areas. For example, all of the confirmations of breeding Vaux's Swift were obtained from the Humane Society of Santa Clara Valley records of nesting birds in house chimneys. The 102 contributors of these records for the period 1987 to 1993 are listed here.

Alex Aiken, Joy Albertson (U.S. Fish and Wildlife Service), Steve Allison, Eric Baker, Carl Beck, Bonnie Bedford-White, Carol Birch, Steven Birch, Clark Blake, Nick S. Bousman, Barry Breckling, Jeff Brown, Sara Jane Brown, Paulette Burgess, Dave Burnham, William Cabot, Zoe Chandik, Les Chibana, Bob Compton, Jim Corliss, Barbara Costa, Coyote Creek Riparian Station, Emélie Curtis, Robert Dailey, Courtney Dawson-Roberts, Penny Delevoryas, Joe Didonato, Elwyn Dorman, Jean Dubois, Noreen Feuss, Marian Fricano, Jo-Ann Gholson, Helen Gilsdorf, Jay Gilson, Jane Glass, Shirley Gordon, Betty Groce, Anna Hanson, Barbara Harkleroad, Shirley Hawley, Rick

Herder, Majid Hibbard, Vance Hopkins, Jason Hubert, Humane Society of Santa Clara Valley, Richard G. Jeffers, David Jensen, David Johnston, Clay Kempf, Janet Kjelmyr, Bruce LaBar, Earl Lebow, Rosalie Lefkowitz, Jim Liskovec, Sue Liskovec, Jim McCroskey, Al McQueen, Robert Merrill, Peter J. Metropulos, Evelyn Miller, Steve Miller, Steven E. Miller, Joe Morlan, Bill Murphy, Dolores Norton, Olive Gardens Apartments (caretaker), Kristen Olson, Chris Otahal, Gary Page, Kathy Parker, Laurel Paveski, Hans Peeters, Joan Priest, Nadine Redding, Robert W. Reiling, Laurel Rezeau, Robert J. Richmond, Tom Roach, Paul Roberts, Robert S. Rogallo, Ed Rooks, Elizabeth Rush, Leonard Rush, Chris Sanger, Maren Seidler, Kendric C. Smith, Don S. Starks, James H. Stone, Thomas Suftin, Mark Sutherland, Alan K. Thomas, Ron S. Thorn, Janie Tilbury, Ruth Troetschler, Marilyn Vigeant, Alan Walther, Holly Wilkins, Anne Wilson, Peg Woodin, Alan Wray, Betty Wyatt, and Pete Zell.

Postatlas contributors

Following the atlas period, from 1994 to 2005, Michael M. Rogers compiled and maintained the postatlas database. The records included in this database were provided by atlasers and contributors to the original database, as well as new contributors. The 247 contributors to this database are listed here.

Brian Acord, Wally Acree, Linda Adams, Richard J. Adams, Joan Armer, David Armstrong, Mike Azevedo, Lotus H. Baker, Bruce Barrett, Gordon Barrett, Deborah Bartens, Gina Barton, Lou Beaudet, Ginny Becchine, Bonnie Bedford-White, Carol Belew, Josh Bennett, Barbara Bessey, Dick Blaine, Dana Bland, Dusty Bleher, Kim Blythe, Billie R. Bousman, William G. Bousman, Dennis Braddy, Patricia Braddy, Summer Brasuel, Mary Lou Breithaupt, Phyllis M. Browning, Daniel Bump, Trudi Burney, William Cabot, Dotty Calabrese, Richard Carlson, Les Chibana, Mare Chibana, Patty Ciesla, Tom Cochrane, Jack Cole, Rita Colwell, Rob Colwell, Jesse Conklin, Dave Cook, Barbara Costa, Charles J. Coston, Don Crawford, Jill Crawford, Ann Creevy, Julia Curlette, Emélie Curtis, Pat Curtis, Wally Curtis, Betty Dale, Jim Danzenbaker, Jeff N. Davis, Natasha Dehn, Jim Dehnert, Penny Delevoryas, Karen DeMello, Deke Descoteaux, Peggy Descoteaux, Marianne Dieckmann, Vladimir Dinets, Matthew Dodder, Peggy L. Don, Laurent Droin, Jean Dubois, Alan M. Eisner, William Eklund, Michael L. Feighner, Eric Feuss, George Finger, Chris Fischer, Karl Fowler, Linda Fowler, Ed Frost, Don Ganton, Suzanna Gearhart, Steve Gerow, Harriet Gerson, Andy Gibb, Kevin Gilmartin, Rose Givens, Steven A. Glover, Lois Goldfrank, Wally Goldfrank, Darcy Gordon, Phil Gordon, Shirley Gordon, Henrietta Grant-Peterkin, Leda Beth Gray, Tom Grey, Ted Gross, Ed Gustafson, Bobbie Handen, Carl

Handen, Roxie Handler, Janet T. Hanson, Barbara Harkleroad, Garth Harwood, Merry Haveman, Donna Heim, Kristi Hein, Bill Henry, Rick Herder, David Hindin, Jan Hintermeister, Bob Hirt, Kirsten R. Holmquist, Grant Hoyt, Karen Hoyt, Al Huber, Lisa Hug, Humane Society of Santa Clara Valley, Sue Hunt, John B. Hutz, Chris Illes, Alvaro Jaramillo, Richard G. Jeffers, Dorothy Johnson, David Johnston, Alma C. Kali, Pat Kelly, Don Kennedy, Roland Kenner, Pat Kenny, David Kohler, Barbara Kossy, Sue Kruse, Va Landschoot, Barry Langdon-Lassagne, Peter La-Tourrette, Alan Launer, Amy Lauterbach, Valerie Layne, Gloria LeBlanc, Sharon M. Lee, Rosalie Lefkowitz, Nick Lethaby, David B. Lewis, Janet L. Linthicum, Jim Liskovec, Sue Liskovec, Randy Little, Jim Lomax, Lee Lovelady, Bill Lundgren, Bob Lutman, Sharon Lutman, Ian MacGregor, Michael J. Mammoser, Dean Manley, John Mariani, Hugh McDevitt, Larry Mendoza, Peter J. Metropulos, Gary Meyer, John Meyer, Maria Meyer, Anne Miller, Mark Miller, Rebecca Miller, Steven E. Miller, Cheryl Millett, Doug Moran, Bryan M. Mori, Joe Morlan, Mary Murphy, Jean Myers, Lisa Myers, Chuck Nelson, Paul L. Noble, Northern California Rare Bird Alert, Matthew O'Brien, Patrice O'Connell, George Oetzel, Marti Oetzel, Kristen Olson, Kathy Parker, Mike Parker, Janna Pauser, Lisa Pavey, Mark Paxton, Kenneth Petersen, Howard J. Rathlesberger, Robert W. Reiling, Robert J. Richmond, Kathy Robertson, Michael M. Rogers, Edward Rooks, Heather Rottenborn, Stephen C. Rottenborn, Tom Ryan, Jennifer Rycenga, Chris K. Salander, San Francisco Bay Bird Observatory, San Jose State University (students of Lynne Trulio), Eileen Sangster, Ken Schmahl, Debra L. Shearwater, Gina Sheridan, Clint E. Smith, Kendric C. Smith, Tate Snyder, Kathy Speer, Anne Spence, Scott Spencer, Larry Spivak, Don S. Starks, Georgia Stigall, Dick Stovel, Lennie Stovel, Rosalie Strait, David L. Suddjian, Joan Suddjian, Linda Sullivan, Patti Sutch, Nancy Teater, Fred Templin, Scott B. Terrill, Phil Terzian, Dirk Thiele, Ron S. Thorn, Bracey Tiede, Sara Timby, Vivek Tiwari, Jerry Towner, Chuck Tribolet, Ruth Troetschler, James Turley, Frank Vanslager, Ann Verdi, Hannes Vogel, Chuq Von Rospach, Alan Walther, Grant Webb, David C. Weber, David L. Weber, Stuart Weiss, Michael Wienholt, Claire Wolfe, Debbie Wong, Bert Yarborough, Nick Yatsko, Lou Young, James Yurchenco, and Pete Zell.

Appendix 2:
Local Ornithology in the Nineteenth and Early Twentieth Centuries

Before there was even a state or a county here, the earliest ornithologists were the Indians who lived in the Santa Clara Valley and, later, the Spanish who settled here. Excavation of middens reveals that the local Indians hunted a number of bird species, and ethnographers have determined that others were important in ceremonies, particularly the Acorn Woodpecker. European settlement began with Spanish journeys of exploration in the 1760s. The Fathers who accompanied these overland parties often kept detailed diaries, which provided extensive accounts of the country, including descriptions of the hills, rivers, and bays and the kinds of trees and plants they saw. But to a great extent, their focus was on the essentials required for settlement: water, forage for horses and cattle, and wood. Almost none of these journals mention birds. Few of the early California settlers kept diaries, and although they must have known many of the birds that were around them, there are few records of their observations.

California ornithology, of necessity, starts with the written accounts of those who visited California or came to explore it. The earliest accounts were written by naturalists or ship's captains who traveled along the coast of California in the late 1700s and into the 1800s. These visits were often brief, and natural history observations were generally limited to collecting plant and animal specimens. Only a few of these early observers came inland as far as the south San Francisco Bay or visited the Santa Clara Mission or the Pueblo of San Jose.

These visits of exploration were followed by early overland expeditions by collectors such as Thomas Nuttall and William Gambel. Then, following the American settlement of California, these early explorers were followed by other naturalists, such as James G. Cooper and Thomas Bridges. Once the era of initial exploration and collecting passed, a locally based ornithology began to develop, and that is the focus of this appendix. This development is best understood using the comprehensive bibliographies of California ornithological references that Joseph Grinnell put together early in the twentieth century (Grinnell 1909, Grinnell 1924, Grinnell 1939). Figure A2.1 shows the number of such publications per year from 1797 to 1938, the data based on Grinnell's bibliographies. These include books, museum proceedings, reports, journal articles, and ornithological publications. What is most obvious in this figure is the intense new interest in California ornithology that emerged in the 1870s, reflected in an almost exponential increase in the number of works published each year. This sudden flood of information on birds in California provides most of what is known today about local ornithologists at the end of the nineteenth century and the beginning of the twentieth century.

Pacific Voyages of Exploration

From 1785 to 1788, Jean François de Galaup, Compte de la Pérouse, commanded a French expedition to explore the Pacific Ocean, and in 1786 his ships visited Monterey. It was there that the first specimens of California Quail and California Thrasher were collected. From 1792 to 1794 George Vancouver commanded a British expedition that explored the Pacific Coast of North America. He made a number of visits to Monterey and San Francisco during this period, and on one of these visits, the ship's surgeon, Archibald Menzies, collected the first specimen of the California Condor. The descriptions of these specimens, published in 1797 (Grinnell 1909), represent the first publications on California ornithology.

Vancouver wrote a detailed account of his expedition (Vancouver 1798). While his ships were anchored at San Francisco, the Spanish at the garrison provided him horses and a complement of soldiers for a journey down the peninsula to the Santa Clara Mission. Vancouver wrote extensively about this journey, offering many interesting details, but made no mention of vertebrate life beyond the Spanish cattle he saw grazing along the route. (Menzies, an accomplished naturalist, was ill at the time and did not accompany Vancouver to the mission.)

Two visits to the California coast in the 1820s included substantial collections and explorations. Captain Duhaut-Cilly left Le Havre in 1826 on the vessel *Les Heros* for explorations along the Pacific Coast of North America, and visited California ports over the period from January 1827 to July 1828. During his stops in the San Francisco Bay he made some explorations by boat into the southern San Francisco Bay. Duhaut-Cilly's ship's surgeon and naturalist was Dr. Paolo E. Botta, who made limited collections while traveling widely, including a visit to the Santa Clara Mission in July 1827 (Palmer 1917, Palmer 1928). It is not known if Botta made any collections while visiting the Santa Clara Valley.

Captain Frederick W. Beechey, commanding the H.M.S. *Blossom*, also explored along the Pacific Coast, from 1825 to 1828, and made extended visits to San Francisco Bay (Beechey 1831). Dr. Alexander Collie, like Botta a surgeon and naturalist, accompanied Beechey and made extensive natural history collections along with Mr. Lay and Lt. Belcher (Stone 1916). Beechey's account of his expedition offers only a limited discussion of California's natural history (Grinnell 1924), the reporting of which was left to Nicholas A. Vigors (1839).

The natural history collections made on the early voyages were often poorly labeled. Place descriptions were sometimes vague, listing the collection location as "California," which

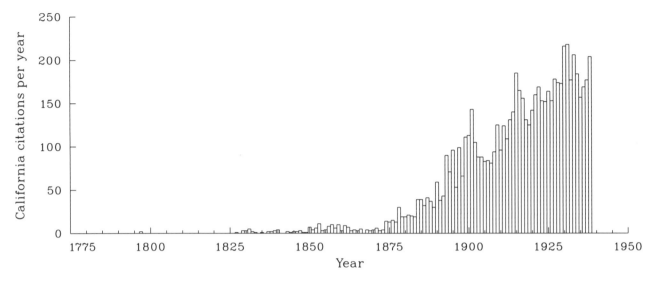

Figure A2.1. Papers and books published per year on California ornithology (Grinnell 1909, Grinnell 1924, Grinnell 1939).

included both upper and lower (Baja) California. Some place names were difficult to interpret for the specialists in European museums, who often ascribed specimens to the wrong location. In particular, many Mexican specimens were erroneously ascribed to California, as described in the appendixes in Grinnell and Miller (1944). The most extreme example, perhaps, is the description of the Red-shafted Flicker by the German zoologist Johann Gmelin (Terres 1980). The specimen he examined was from the Bay of Good Hope in Nootka Sound on Vancouver Island, Canada. Gmelin mistook this as the Cape of Good Hope in Africa and described the species as *cafer*, that is, from the land of the Kaffirs in South Africa. Today, the Red-shafted Flicker is only a subspecies of the Northern Flicker, but its scientific name still indicates that it comes from the land of the Kaffirs.

Early Naturalists in California

A number of naturalists came to California in the early 1800s with the purpose of collecting plants and animals. The Scotsman David Douglas (1798–1834), a medical doctor, traveled widely in the Americas and collected plants in California from 1830 to 1832 (Palmer 1928). He also described a number of species of quail from North America, but is best known for his discovery of the Douglas fir.

Thomas Nuttall (1786–1859), born in England, came to the United States in 1808, where he became a professor of natural history at Harvard. He crossed the continent with John K. Townsend in 1834 and visited Oregon and California (Stone 1916). Near Santa Barbara he collected the first specimens of the Yellow-billed Magpie and Tricolored Blackbird, which were later described by John J. Audubon.

William Gambel (*circa* 1819–1849), a protégé of Thomas Nuttall, came overland to California in either 1841 or 1842 (Stone 1916, Palmer 1928). He was the first ornithologist to make an extended stay in the state. During that time, he described a number of new species, including the Elegant Tern, Nuttall's Woodpecker, Oak Titmouse, Wrentit, Cassin's Auklet, and Mountain Chickadee. During his second visit to the state, he

died of typhoid fever on the Feather River while trying to make a winter crossing of the Sierra Nevada.

The Pacific Railroad Reports

In the 1840s, the selection of the route for a transcontinental railroad became highly politicized (Coan 1982). The northern and southern states both wanted the railroad to start from their own spheres of influence and not serve to support their rivals. Congress passed the Pacific Railroad Survey legislation in early 1853 to obtain information that could be used to determine a practicable route. The primary emphasis of the ensuing surveys was to obtain topographical data that could be used to show the relative merits of the various routes. For the most part, the surveys were performed by the Army Corps of Engineers, but the legislation also provided for the collection of other kinds of information, including specimens of plants and animals, ethnography, and meteorology. Medical doctors with scientific interests were attached to the various survey parties for these purposes.

The initial railroad surveys were carried out in four geographic areas (Coan 1982). The northernmost survey covered areas between the 47th and 49th parallels, from St. Paul, Minnesota, to the Washington Territory. The second followed a line between the 38th and 39th parallels from the headwaters of the Arkansas River to the Great Salt Lake. The third followed a more southerly route along the 35th parallel, and the fourth explored the Central Valley of California to find passes eastward over the Sierra Nevada.

The results of the railroad surveys were published between 1855 and 1860 in 12 volumes entitled *Reports of Explorations and Surveys to Ascertain the Most Practicable and Economical Route for a Railroad from the Mississippi River to the Pacific Ocean* (Fischer 2001). Zoological accounts are found in a number of the volumes, and in some cases include sections written by the physician-naturalists who accompanied the survey parties, such as J. S. Newberry, who was in northern California and Oregon (Newberry 1857), Adolphus L. Heermann, who surveyed in southern and central California (Heermann 1859), C. B. R. Kennerly (1859), who participated in the surveys near the 35th parallel, and James G. Cooper and George Suckley, who worked on the northern route (Cooper and Suckley 1860). Accounts were also prepared by museum scientists in the east, who described the collections that had been made by the field parties (Baird et al. 1858). The 12 volumes of the Pacific Railroad reports were the first detailed descriptions of the geography and zoology of the American West since the expedition of Lewis and Clark (1803–06). The railroad reports, however, covered a much greater area and represent a remarkable documentation of the zoology of the western frontier.

Early Ornithologists in the San Francisco Bay Area

James G. Cooper (1830–1902) was born in New York City, the son of William Cooper, for whom Charles L. Bonaparte named the Cooper's Hawk. William Cooper was a founder of the New York Lyceum of Natural History, and James was exposed to many of the famous zoologists and naturalists of the day. He obtained his medical degree in 1851 and practiced in New York City for the next two years. Spencer F. Baird, who was the Assistant Secretary of the Smithsonian Institution, was able to help Cooper obtain an assignment to the Pacific railroad survey parties working in the Washington Territory. He joined a survey party under Captain George McClellan and worked as a surgeon with the party until April 1854. He was responsible not only for the party's health, but also for natural history collections and meteorological observations.

Cooper was a dedicated naturalist, but did not care much for medical practice (Coan 1982). After leaving the railroad survey party, he continued to collect specimens on the Washington coast, sometimes supporting his activities with a bit of medical practice. Baird was also able to provide him limited support. In 1855 he returned to the East via San Francisco and the Isthmus of Panama. It was during this journey that he first visited Santa Clara County, staying from 19 October to 1 December 1855 in Mountain View (Coan 1982). From Mountain View he traveled in the nearby Santa Cruz Mountains and parts of the Santa Clara Valley. As we know from specimens in the United States National Museum, he collected such typical birds as Common Poorwill (USNM #A05912), Acorn Woodpecker (USNM #A05957), Nuttall's Woodpecker (USNM #A05964), Bushtit (USNM #A05922), and House Finch (USNM #A04487). Less expected, he shot a "Harlan's" Red-tailed Hawk in Mountain View on 11 Nov 1855 (USNM #A08525), the first time this form had been collected.

Back in the East, Cooper worked on his portion of the Pacific Railroad Reports (Cooper and Suckley 1860), spending much of his time in Washington, D.C. He returned to the West in 1860, joining the Blake Expedition, which set out from St. Louis and proceeded up the Missouri River and overland into Idaho and Washington. He again traveled south to San Francisco, and intermittently worked as a contract surgeon for the U.S. Army as well as for Josiah Whitney, head of the California Geological Survey. In between he practiced medicine part-time to meet his expenses. Much of his collecting work was based on promises of payment that were never fulfilled (Coan 1982).

Working part time for Whitney for the California Geological Survey gave Cooper the opportunity to gather together much of his material on birds in the west, and, with the help of Baird, this effort was published as "Ornithology, Volume I, Land Birds" by the California Geological Survey (Cooper 1870). This book was the first significant work on California ornithology.

Cooper married in 1866 and continued his struggle to find a balance between his passion for natural history and the necessity of supporting his family through a medical practice. He attempted to set up a practice in a number of cities, including San Francisco, Santa Cruz, San Mateo, and Oakland. He was often in poor health, and it seemed that places where he could establish a good practice, such as San Francisco, were bad for his health, whereas a city like Santa Cruz, though good for his health, would not support a practice. In 1875, he settled in Hayward (then known as Haywards) and remained there for the rest of his life.

In his letters to Baird, Cooper often seemed despondent, wanting nothing more than to practice science, but instead having to practice medicine. In a letter in 1870 (Coan 1982), he wrote

> In this country, like most others, the pursuit of science as a private business is a losing game. . . . Almost all the "enlightened" people of this city know me as a "naturalist," which is the title of all the taxidermists also, and . . . they avoid employing me professionally as they would a bird-stuffer. The consequence is that . . . my patients are among the poor and ignorant, who don't know much about me and don't pay either. . . . My time is much taken up now in running about trying to raise money enough to pay expenses. . . . As I am not worse off than most other naturalists, I ought not to complain, I suppose, ... Hoping you may not get down to my condition (the best of wishes), I remain, ...

But in other letters, he expresses the simple joy of being out in the field. In a letter to his sister Fan in 1863 (Coan 1982), he wrote

> I have been two weeks visiting my old hunting grounds at Mountain View, and hunting along the Coast Range west of there along Arroyo Quito [Saratoga Creek]. There I found the most lovely scenery I have yet met with in California or anywhere else, and am only sorry that I could not afford to stay longer. It is not as magnificent as that of Yosemite Valley. . . but the details are more beautiful. I should think—groves of tropical looking *Arbutus* with orange-like leaves and red berries, mingled with firs eight feet in diameter and 300 high, redwoods like gigantic yew trees, and many beautiful flowers beneath—altogether make it a most charming picture. Birds were swarming, rich in song and plumage.

Already in 1863 the lumber mills were starting to move up Saratoga Creek. The massive Douglas firs and coast redwoods of that primeval forest that so entranced Cooper were soon gone.

Today, we are remote from James Cooper and the world he lived in. We read the words from his books and papers and try to imagine an earlier time, but only with difficulty. Shortly before Cooper's death, W. Otto Emerson wrote of him (Emerson 1899):

> . . . in memory he is again giving his first field lesson, taking the Rock Wren for an object study as it sits on a huge blue-gray rock singing to us its song of welcome. Here he talked to us of Nature in all of her varied forms; told of the birds, their songs, their flights, plumage and their homelife; of their loves and hates, joys and sorrows! All of this was told in common language, without scientific nomenclature, and thus we saw Nature and her works through the eyes of one who loved and had long questioned and learned many of her secrets, until the setting sun found us yet worshipping in Nature's temple, and the student gaining his first glimpse into that grand arcana. This was our teacher's manner; thus he gathered around him the young ornithologists and in the field taught them the lessons of bird-life.

The only significant tie of Thomas Bridges (1828–1865) to Santa Clara County ornithology is his collection of 33 species of birds in the "Valley of San José," probably made in 1856 or 1857 (Sclater 1857). The botanist William H. Brewer met Bridges near Volcano in August 1863 (Brewer 1966) and described him as

> an old rambler and botanical collector, well known to all botanists. For twenty years he rambled in South America and explored the Andes for plants for the gardens and herbariums of Europe. He first sent seeds of the great Amazon water lily to Europe. He spent three months on the island of Juan Fernandez, came to California, and has been supplying the gardens of England and Scotland with seeds, and the herbariums with plants, from this coast, for the last few years.

In a footnote to Brewer's account, F. P. Farquhar states "Thomas Bridges came to California in 1856, and for the next nine years collected on the coast, much of the time in this State, his collections going mostly to Europe."

A few more details on the life of Thomas Bridges are from the zoologist T. S. Palmer, who has been the source of much historical information regarding the early naturalists (Palmer 1917, Palmer 1928). In a talk to the Audubon Association of the Pacific in August 1927 he gave a short history of ornithology in California (Werner 1927). He stated that Thomas Bridges lived in San Jose while making his collections in the Santa Clara Valley, and refers to him as the "first resident ornithologist of the State." He also noted that Bridges was buried in an unmarked grave in Laurel Hill Cemetery in San Francisco. Subsequently, the Association helped to raise funds for a stone that was placed on Bridges's grave on 21 Oct 1927 (*Gull 9(12)* 1927).

Curiously, at the same time that Cooper and Bridges were making their first visits to the Santa Clara Valley, a self-taught naturalist was living in San Jose and developing his painting skills. Andrew Jackson Grayson (1818–1869) was born in Louisiana and in 1846 traveled overland to California with his wife and young son (Stone 1986). Grayson worked at a number of businesses in the early 1850s, encountering both failure and success. In 1853, his wife Frances told him of a recent purchase of Audubon's *Birds of America* by the Mercantile Library Association in San Francisco. Audubon's magnificent book had a transformative effect on Grayson's life. Long interested in natural history, he determined that he would publish a book on all the birds of the Pacific slope that were not in *Birds of America*. He would both paint these missing species and prepare accounts of their life histories. The Graysons decided to move to San Jose, where he could study birds and develop his skills as an artist. They bought a four-acre site at Fourth and Julian streets, where they built a house and started a garden. They remained at that site, named "Bird's Nest Cottage," until 1857.

Only one of Grayson's paintings from this period is known, a partially leucistic Green-winged Teal that was shot in the Santa Clara Valley in 1853. During the time he lived in San Jose, he sent drawings and accounts of birds to James Mason Hutchings, the publisher of *Hutchings' California Magazine*, and 18 of these appeared in the magazine in 1857 and 1858 (Stone 1986). His observations of Greater Roadrunners, both in the wild and in captivity, were eventually published (Bryant 1891, Stone 1986). Otherwise, little is known of his observations during the years he lived in the Santa Clara Valley.

In 1856 Grayson wrote to the Smithsonian Institution, offering specimens for the new museum, but looking for assistance in identifying birds that he collected. Spencer F. Baird, the Assistant Secretary of the Smithsonian, entered a long correspondence with Grayson and encouraged him in his collections. Although Baird was enthusiastic about the writing of biographies of western species, of which almost nothing was known, he was less supportive of Grayson's attempt to publish a book of paintings to finish Audubon's work. In a letter dated 15 Dec 1856 (Stone 1986), he wrote

> I like very much your idea of writing up the birds of the Pacific Slope, and cheerfully promise all the aid in my power. It is of the greatest importance to have biographies of our birds by persons intimately acquainted with their habits. I cannot tell what support such an undertaking would meet with in California. It would doubtless obtain some subscribers here, and abroad. I will with the greatest pleasure furnish the nomenclature and scientific history of all specimens you may forward to us. Even though you could not afford to publish colored figures of all the species, a contribution to science of little less importance would be this series of biographies, by which you could readily become known in the scientific worlds as the Audubon of the West; the true merit of this man was not in his drawings, but in his masterly delineations of the habits and peculiarities—the life of American birds. Such articles there will be no difficulty in having published; the Institution will see it done, so as to give you the greatest possible credit."

The Graysons moved to Tehuantepec, Mexico, in 1857 and returned to San Francisco the next year. In November 1859 they moved permanently to Mazatlán, Mexico, where he painted Mexican birds, made additional collecting trips for the Smithsonian, and corresponded with Baird. He also strove to have his book published but without success. In 1869, just short of his 51st birthday, he died of yellow fever. Frances Grayson moved back to California and continued to seek a publisher for her husband's work. In 1879 she finally abandoned these efforts and donated the 163 paintings and species accounts to the University of California. Here, this body of work remained until the late 1940s, when Lois C. Stone and Frank Pitelka rediscovered the paintings and struggled to find a publisher who could finally complete this work. In 1986, 117 years after his death, 156 of Grayson's paintings (seven had been lost), the species descriptions, and a biography by Lois C. Stone were published in *Andrew Jackson Grayson, Birds of the Pacific Slope* (Stone 1986).

Early Publications and the American Ornithologists' Union

The first epoch of ornithological discovery in California was by explorers and naturalists who made collections that they dispatched to museums in Europe or the eastern United States. Cooper, Bridges, and Grayson were in many respects part of this first epoch—Cooper and Grayson often collecting for the Smithsonian, and Bridges sending his specimens to Europe.

The second epoch was defined by the native naturalist, someone who lived locally and communicated with fellow workers, sometimes through the auspices of local museums and academies, through publications, or by letters. Where the first generation of naturalists were tied directly to the eastern or foreign museums, the new generation lived in California and studied natural history near where they lived or within a reasonable traveling distance.

Academies, clubs, and publications were central to the growth of ornithology and natural history in California. Tables A2.1 and A2.2, based on Grinnell's bibliography (Grinnell 1909), list publications that included information on California ornithology. It was these publications that were largely responsible for the rapid accumulation of information in the 1870s that is demonstrated in Fig. A2.1 (above). The publications in the tables are grouped into the permanent publications (those that have lasted to the present time) and the transitory publications. The permanent publications are mostly affiliated with professional organizations, such as the American Ornithologists' Union (*Auk*) or conservation organizations, such as the National Audubon Society (*Audubon*). Most of the transitory publications were published by individuals who hoped to sustain publication with a subscription list, although some of the longer-lasting oology magazines were also affiliated with dealers in natural history curios and birds' eggs.

One of the publications in Table A2.1 was the *Bulletin of the Nuttall Ornithological Club*. Then and now, the Nuttall Ornithological Club was based at the Museum of Comparative Zoology at Harvard University. In the late 1870s the *Bulletin* was the de facto publication for ornithology in the United States. With the formation of the American Ornithologists' Union in 1883, the *Bulletin* became the *Auk*, the quarterly of the new na-

Table A2.1. Permanent publications in early ornithology in the United States.

Journal	Dates
American Naturalist	1868–present
Bulletin of the Nuttall Ornithological Club[a]	1876–1883
Auk	1884–present
Wilson Bulletin	1889–present
Condor[b]	1899–present
Bird-Lore/Audubon[c]	1899–present

[a]Predecessor to the *Auk*.
[b]Vol. 1 named *Bull. Cooper Ornithological Club*.
[c]Renamed *Audubon* in 1941.

Table A2.2. Transitory publications in early ornithology in the United States.

Journal	Dates
Forest and Stream	1873–1876?
Oologist/Ornithologist and Oologist[a]	1875–1893
Young Oologist/Oologist[b]	1884–1941
Ridgway Ornithological Club Bulletin	1886–?
Sunny South Oologist	1886
Bay State Oologist	1888
Zoe	1890–1908
Bittern	1890–1891
California Traveller and Naturalist	1892–1893?
Nidiologist/Nidologist[c]	1893–1897
American Magazine of Natural Science	1893-1894
Museum	1894-1900
Oregon Naturalist	1894–1898
Naturalist	1894
Western American Scientist	1885?–1902?
Avifauna	1895–1897
Osprey	1896–1902
Three Kingdoms	1898
Petrel	1901
Warbler	1905–1907

[a]Renamed *Ornithologist & Oologist* in 1881.
[b]Renamed *Oologist* in 1887.
[c]Renamed *Nidologist* in 1896.

tional association of ornithologists.

One of the founding members of the new American Ornithologists' Union (AOU) was Lyman Belding (1829–1917) of Stockton, California. Belding came to California in 1856 and moved to Marysville in 1862 (Fisher 1918). His retirement from business in 1875 gave him more time to engage in fishing and hunting, which were his favorite activities. When, in the spring of 1876, he obtained a copy of James G. Cooper's *Ornithology, Volume I, Land Birds*, the experience was as transformative for him as Audubon's *Birds of America* had been for Grayson. Whereas before, as an active outdoorsman, he believed he knew all of the birds in central California, he could now see that there were many that he had never heard of. Belding became an avid collector of birds and eggs and supplied these to the Smithsonian. By 1878 he had published his first paper in the *Bulletin of the Nuttall Ornithological Club*. He extended his collecting work to Baja California and southern California and worked with the Smithsonian in the description of several new species and subspecies of birds.

An initial project of the new AOU was to establish a system of record keeping where information on bird distribution or migration, obtained by AOU members or like-minded individuals, could be gathered and disseminated. In many respects this effort was similar to the gathering of information that is published today in the quarterly *North American Birds*. Belding agreed to take on the task of gathering this information for California, Oregon, Washington, and British Columbia. The details he assembled were later published as *Land Birds of the Pacific District* (Belding 1890).

Belding continued to work actively through the 1890s in the Central Valley and the Sierra Nevada. He was a Life Member of the California Academy of Sciences and assisted Walter E. Bryant (1861–1905) in building the ornithological collections at the academy, where Bryant was curator from 1886 to 1896. The Cooper Ornithological Club made Belding an Honorary Member in 1896. Fisher (1940) describes with delight one of Belding's few visits to the San Francisco Bay area, where he stopped by to see Chester Barlow:

> On the occasion of one of our visits to Barlow's, Mr. Lyman Belding, the veteran ornithologist, came from his home in Stockton and regaled us with accounts of early days in California, and of his hunting and fishing trips in the Sierras. He was a shy, sensitive, lovable man, patterned for a poet, but fated for rough usage by life. . . .

The Era of Oology

The eastern oologist F. A. Lucas, in a letter to the editor of the *Ornithologist and Oologist* (Lucas 1885), described the typical case of young boys of that era who collected eggs: "In my own class at school were at least eight boys who had pretty good sized collections of eggs. Not one of these boys ever developed into a naturalist, and the eggs—representing many hundreds of birds—eventually 'went to smash.'"

The era of oology, or the study of eggs, ran from about 1880 to 1940 (Kiff 1991). For young boys, the collecting of eggs was a rite of passage, although many of these youthful collections, as noted by Lucas, wound up smashed to pieces and thrown out with the trash. But some of the young men maintained their interest and were serious about collecting as many sets of eggs of as many species as they could. With the growing popularity of egg collecting came opportunities to trade or sell eggs, particularly of less common species, or of those that had a limited nesting range. Dealers printed and sent out catalogs and a number of new publications sprang up in support of the interests of the egg collectors, as well as the dealers. As shown in Table A2.2, many of these publications had a short lifetime. Nationally, the most important were the *Oologist* and the *Ornithologist & Oologist*, and both of these journals included occasional articles written by local egg collectors.

The ornithologists who collected egg sets for museums were careful to document each egg set with a "data slip" that recorded the date and specific location of collection, the condition of the eggs (fresh or partly incubated), details of the nest site, and the name of the collector. Serious amateur oologists also kept careful records, and the egg sets and data slips that have been retained in museum collections provide a wealth of information about birds breeding in California more than a century ago, as well as some information on the ornithologists who made these collections.

With the expansion of ornithological publications and the popularity of egg collecting in the 1880s, records of local ornithologists began to appear in publications. Most notable from this period is probably William Otto Emerson (1856–1940), who came west by wagon train from Illinois in 1870 and eventually settled near Hayward, Alameda County. Emerson became an artist after reaching California, but for ornithologists his extensive writing and large collections of specimens and eggs are of most interest today. Grinnell (1909) lists 63 papers or notes written by Emerson from 1881 to 1907. Most of his writing deals with Alameda County and his observations near his farm, but he also reported from San Francisco, the Farallons, Santa Cruz, Monterey Bay, and farther afield. He collected the first California specimens of the American Redstart at Hayward on 20 Jun 1881; a Black-throated Blue Warbler (with Walter E. Bryant) on the Farallon Islands on 17 Nov 1886; and a Black-and-White Warbler, also on the Farallons, on 28 May 1887 (Grinnell and Wythe 1927). A White-throated Sparrow he collected at Hayward on 20 Nov 1889 is the second record for California (Emerson 1890). As we shall see, he was active in the formation of the Cooper Ornithological Club.

Also active in Alameda County was Henry Reed Taylor of Alameda, who was an egg collector who went on in the 1890s to publish the *Nidiologist*. Taylor made many collecting trips to southern Santa Clara County, particularly in the vicinity of Sargent, at that time a small town on the railroad. Most notable of his collections was a set of Swainson's Hawks' eggs taken in "Ferguson's Swamp" on 30 Apr 1889 (WFVZ #98178), one of only two nesting records from Santa Clara County. (Ferguson's Swamp was likely the name used by Taylor for a swamp along Llagas Creek, near land owned by the Ferguson brothers.) As prolific as Emerson, Taylor wrote 68 articles or notes on California ornithology between 1884 and 1907 (Grinnell 1909).

Active egg collectors in Santa Clara County in the 1880s included A. L. Parkhurst, A. D. Butterfield, Will A. Burres, and F. L. Corless. A. L. Parkhurst lived in San Jose and made collections and observations from 1882 to 1885. He was one of Belding's correspondents in the preparation of *Land Birds of the Pacific District* (1890), and he also wrote a few short articles for the *Ornithologist & Oologist* (Parkhurst 1883, Parkhurst 1884, Parkhurst 1885). He collected an egg set of Yellow-breasted Chat in the Santa Clara Valley on 6 Jun 1882, which is now in the U.S. National Museum (USNM #B26910). His observation of a flock of eight Vaux's Swifts near San Jose on 29 Apr 1883 (Parkhurst 1883) is the earliest mention of this species in the county. A. D. Butterfield of San Jose wrote an article for the *Ornithologist & Oologist* (Butterfield 1883) about collecting Marsh Wren eggs at San Felipe Lake, and his name was sometimes listed in advertisements in the "*O & O*" for egg exchanges, but otherwise nothing is known of him. Eggs collected by F. L (or F. H.) Corless from Los Gatos and Saratoga between 1884 and 1890 are in both the U.S. National Museum and the Western Foundation of Vertebrate Zoology, but as with Butterfield, nothing is known of Corless. Also a mystery is Will A. Burres, who collected eggs in the vicinity of Sargent in 1888 and 1889. Of particular note, he collected two sets of four eggs of the Great Egret (CAS #6697 and #6699) near Sargent on 4 Apr 1889. One data slip notes that the nest was in a cottonwood 60 feet from the ground. This is the only nest record known from the San Francisco Bay area prior to the era of plume hunting and the near extirpation of this species.

Oologists, the Cooper Ornithological Club, and Stanford University

As the number of people interested in ornithology in the San Francisco Bay area increased in the late 1880s there were efforts to organize clubs that would allow interested amateurs to meet and together advance the study of ornithology on the Pacific coast. An early attempt was the California Ornithological Club, organized at the California Academy of Science in early 1889 (*Ornithol. Oologist* 14:29,46 1889). Walter E. Bryant, then curator of birds at the Academy, was the first president, Henry R. Taylor was vice-president, and W. Otto Emerson was secretary and treasurer. In 1890, Bryant initiated the journal *Zoe* to provide a less formal medium for scientific reports from the California Academy of Sciences and from other investigators (the *Pacific Discovery* of its day). In the first volume, it is mentioned that the California Ornithological Club was being reorganized (*Zoe* 1:384 1890), and Henry Taylor was now president, F. O. Johnson was vice-president, and Charles A. Keeler was secretary and treasurer.

At the same time, in the fall of 1890, four students at the University of the Pacific in San Jose, each of them eager egg collectors, formed the Cooper Club for the study of birds, their nests, and their eggs (Evermann 1925, Jennings 1997). These first four members of the Cooper Club included John Van Denburgh and Wilfred H. Osgood, who would both achieve prominence in their chosen fields in zoology. When the Leland Stanford Junior University opened in 1891, Van Denburgh, Osgood, and the others transferred to the new university, in part because of the reputation of its president, the prominent ichthyologist Dr. David Starr Jordan (1851–1931). In the wake of their transfer and new studies, the club was apparently abandoned.

On 22 Jun 1893, the Cooper Ornithological Club was organized in San Jose by Osgood, Harry R. Painton, Chester Barlow, and Fred A. Schneider, Jr. (Barlow 1893e). Osgood (Grinnell 1938) has written of this early period: "Up to that time our small numbers and our consciousness that we were only juvenile egg-collectors gave us a feeling of uncertainty and modesty. We all knew what we wanted to do, but we didn't know how to do it."

Richard C. McGregor entered Stanford in 1893 and quickly became a fast friend of Osgood. Osgood went on to say:

This was at the time the Cooper Ornithological Club was in its infancy, and within a week McGregor was staying the night with me at my home in San José to attend his first meeting. He was slightly older than the rest of us and much more experienced, so he was looked upon as a great acquisition. Largely through him, Walter Bryant, A. W. Anthony, and other still older men became interested in the Club and we began to feel established and confident. . . . McGregor, then, at just the right time, supplied a good deal which none of the rest of us had. Already he was an accomplished bird-skinner and had a considerable private collection of skins, including many species from Colorado and Florida which were unfamiliar to us. Both he and Bryant gave us instruction in making skins and, thereafter, a number of us definitely graduated from the egg-collecting stage of our careers.

The club members produced their first publication, "Bulletin No. 1," in August 1893, basically a statement of the club purposes and an invitation for others to join (Grinnell 1925). About the same time, Henry R. Taylor began publication of the *Nidiologist*, which was an oology magazine focused on the West Coast. He offered to include in the *Nidiologist* a section that would report the club activities, and this would supersede the club bulletin (Barlow 1893a, Grinnell 1925). The fall of 1893 saw the formation of the Southern California Natural History Society in the Los Angeles area, which soon merged to become the Southern Division of the Cooper Ornithological Club (Cogswell 1986, von Bloeker 1993). Membership in the new club grew rapidly with 25 in the first year, 67 by 1896, and 107 by 1900 (Kaeding 1908, [Barlow] 1900a).

The young men who came to Stanford in the 1890s, most of whom had started out as egg collectors, were later referred to by Joseph Grinnell as the "birding boys" (Grinnell 1937). These included not only Van Denburgh, Osgood, and McGregor, but also such students as William W. Price, Walter K. Fisher, and Theodore J. Hoover.

Of the student ornithologists in the early 1890s, Van Denburgh, Osgood, and Fisher are best known for their substantial accomplishments in other areas of zoology. John Van Denburgh (1872–1924) was born in San Francisco (Jennings 1997). His father, a dentist with a practice in San Francisco, bought a 20-acre farm in Los Gatos in 1880. There Van Denburgh was free to ramble, and his first interests were birds and their eggs. At the age of 13, in 1886, he began keeping detailed notes (Van Denburgh 1899b). In 1890 he entered the University of the Pacific in San Jose, and then transferred to Stanford the next year. He obtained his A.B. from Stanford with the first graduating class in 1894, and then took an M.A. in 1895. As an undergraduate, Van Denburgh was drawn to herpetology, and this became his consuming passion. As he was finishing his M.A., the California Academy of Sciences formed a Department of Herpetology, and Van Denburgh was appointed curator. He continued his graduate education and obtained a Ph.D. in Zoology from Stanford in 1897, the first Ph.D. granted by the department.

Van Denburgh's chief desire was to continue his scholarly work on the reptiles of western North America, but he recognized that he could not afford to live on the small stipend available at the Academy. He entered The Johns Hopkins University in the fall of 1898 and graduated with an M.D. degree in 1900. It was during this period that he published two regional papers on California birds (Van Denburgh 1899a, Van Denburgh 1899b). The latter paper, "Notes on some birds of Santa Clara County, California," was meant to be a comprehensive treatment of the land birds of Santa Clara County. Although most of the information was limited to Van Denburgh's observations at either

Los Gatos, where he grew up, or Palo Alto, during his Stanford years, the paper nonetheless provides useful details of the 110 species he discussed. Barlow (1900b) added 32 more species, on the basis of his own observations as well as those of others in the Cooper Club. These two papers thus provide a baseline of what was known of the land birds of Santa Clara County at the end of the nineteenth century.

Van Denburgh established a medical practice in San Francisco (Jennings 1997), spending his mornings curating the herpetology collection at the California Academy of Sciences and his afternoons with his medical practice. He worked aggressively to build up the Academy's collections, particularly following the losses after the 1906 earthquake and fire. Although he retained his early interest in birds, he did no scientific work in this area, since Leverett M. Loomis, the Director of the Academy, was also the curator of ornithology and was jealous of his prerogatives. Once Loomis was replaced by Barton W. Evermann as Director, Van Denburgh again included birds in his field of study.

Van Denburgh was an intensely private man who appears to have repressed his feelings (Jennings 1997). By 1924, he must have been despondent and depressed, but his friends or acquaintances were not aware of the depths of these problems. He left for Hawaii for a vacation in October, and all of his colleagues were glad to see him take a well-earned rest. In Honolulu, on the morning of 24 October, John Van Denburgh slit his carotid arteries with a razor and died. In biographical notes, Jennings (1997) writes

> in the first quarter of the 20th century, John Van Denburgh not only helped build the third largest museum collection of amphibians and reptiles in the New World, but he also found enough spare time away from his medical practice to become an accomplished nature photographer, an authority on reptile poison, and expert on the herpetofauna of the Galápagos Islands and the Far East, as well as a skilled ornithologist and oologist.

His monumental work on the amphibians and reptiles of western North America (Van Denburgh 1922) remains his greatest legacy.

Wilfred H. Osgood (1875–1947) was a founder of the Cooper Ornithological Club and was its first president. He was born in Rochester, New Hampshire, in 1875. In the 1880s, his family moved to a fruit farm in Santa Clara (Schmidt 1950). He entered the University of the Pacific in 1890 with Van Denburgh, and both then transferred to Stanford in 1891. To judge from articles in the *Oologist* (Osgood 1892a, Osgood 1892b) and egg-collection data slips, he was active as a collector in the Santa Clara Valley from 1892 to 1894. In 1897, while still an undergraduate at Stanford, he joined the U.S. Bureau of Economic Ornithology and Mammalogy, which later became the U.S. Biological Survey. He made significant collecting expeditions in northern California and off the coast of Alaska while working for the Survey from 1897 to 1909 and at this time made the first of his lasting contributions to mammalogy (Schmidt 1950). In 1899 he was awarded an A.B. from Stanford in absentia, and in 1909 he left the Survey and joined Chicago's Field Museum of Natural History. He was subsequently involved with numerous

collecting trips to South America and in 1919 obtained a Ph.D. from the University of Chicago, on the basis of his studies of shrew opossums in South America (Schmidt 1950). In 1921, Osgood became the Curator of Zoology at the Field Museum, a job he held until his retirement in 1940.

Richard C. McGregor (1871–1936) entered Stanford in the 1893–94 year and joined the new Cooper Ornithological Club almost immediately. During his early years at Stanford he had particularly close friendships with Van Denburgh, Osgood, and Hoover (Grinnell 1938). He graduated in 1898, not in zoology but in philosophy, possibly because of friction with the zoological faculty (Grinnell 1938). Prior to going to Stanford, while living in Santa Cruz, McGregor had, with E. H. Fiske, prepared a list of the birds of Santa Cruz County for *The Natural History of Santa Cruz County*, published about 1892. Following his graduation, he put together more detailed information on the land birds of Santa Cruz County, and this account was published as the second number in the new *Pacific Coast Avifauna* series of the Cooper Ornithological Club (McGregor 1901). Although McGregor's list deals with Santa Cruz County, many of the comments on birds at the higher elevations of the Santa Cruz Mountains apply to Santa Clara County as well.

In the summers of 1900 and 1901, McGregor was attached to the cutter *Pathfinder*, which allowed him to do some collecting along the coast of Alaska (McGregor 1902, McGregor 1906). After these trips he went on to the Philippines, where he remained for the rest of his life. At first he worked as a collector and eventually was associated with the Philippine Bureau of Science, which appointed him editor of the *Philippine Journal of Science* as well as editor of many department publications. At times he seemed nostalgic, as in a letter to Grinnell in 1907, "I would like to see a Cactus Wren or a Road-runner. These birds here are mostly so wrong I feel uncomfortable" (Grinnell 1938). But on being offered a job with the Brooklyn Museum in 1911, he wrote Grinnell, ". . . it would be fine to be near Washington, Philadelphia, etc.; but I am too long wild; I like to get into new places. Think of the unexplored parts of the Philippine Islands, and the ripe, juicy regions near-by! No U. S. for me. . ." (Grinnell 1938).

Of all the students at Stanford in the 1890s, "Billy" Price was possibly the most interesting. William W. Price (1871–1922) was born in Milwaukee, Wisconsin, on 20 Jan 1871 (Fisher 1923). His mother died when he was two, and Billy was raised by relatives, eventually moving to Riverside, California. His father died when he was 14 and soon after Price left for Arizona, where he explored the southeastern mountains and deserts for a year and a half. He returned to California and completed his secondary education at Oakland High School and then entered Stanford, where he received an A.B. in economics in 1897 and an M.A. in zoology in 1899. During many of his Stanford years, Billy organized summer zoological collecting trips to California, Arizona, and Baja California. During his various Arizona expeditions, Price added the Rose-throated Becard to the list of U.S. birds, and he also found the first nest of the Olive Warbler. At Stanford, Price is best known for a series of articles titled "Birds of the Campus" that were published in the campus magazine, *Sequoia* (Price 1898a-f). Although in most cases Price's comments are limited, his systematic accounts provide insight into the birds present near Stanford a century ago.

Walter K. Fisher (1878–1953) was another of Grinnell's "birding boys." He was the son of Albert K. Fisher (1856–1948), who was a founder of the American Ornithologists' Union. The elder Fisher had worked with C. Hart Merriam, and was instrumental in the formation of the Biological Survey that eventually became part of the U.S. Fish and Wildlife Service. Walter Fisher grew up in the eastern United States and knew all of the famed ornithologists of the time. In describing his and Grinnell's visits to Barlow's house in Santa Clara, Fisher (1940) wrote:

> Often the conversation turned to eastern ornithologists whom Barlow and Grinnell had never seen but whom I had fortunately known since early childhood—Robert Ridgway, Leonhard Stejneger, C. Hart Merriam, Joel Asaph Allen, Frank M. Chapman, Edgar A. Mearns, Edward W. Nelson, William Dutcher, H. W. Henshaw, John H. Sage, Witmer Stone, Charles W. Richmond, Frederick A. Lucas, and especially Charles E. Bendire, the patron saint of oologists. I had *seen* Elliott Coues—and even had *heard* him speak at an A. O. U. meeting; I certainly represented glamour to these avid young men.

Fisher obtained his A.B. from Stanford in 1901, his M.A. in 1903, and a Ph.D. in 1906 (Davis 1958). He was an instructor at Stanford between 1907 and 1909, at which time he became an Assistant Professor. With the formation of Stanford's Hopkins Marine Station in 1917, Fisher became its first director, a job he held until his retirement in 1943.

Even as Fisher's interests became focused on marine biology and invertebrate taxonomy, he maintained an interest in ornithology. Between 1900 and 1940 he published 43 papers or notes in the *Condor* and other journals on ornithology (Davis 1958). His first ornithological paper was a list of species found on Mt. St. Helena, at the north end of the Napa Valley (Fisher 1900), and his last was a note on Clark's Nutcracker on the Monterey Peninsula (Fisher and Fisher 1923). His memoria for various ornithologists (Fisher 1918, Fisher 1923, Fisher 1940) provide a glimpse into the lives of these early workers in the field. In 1902, following Barlow's death, he took over the editorship of the *Condor* and continued as editor until 1905, when he was replaced by Grinnell. He was a skilled artist, as is seen in the cover design of the *Condor* that was used from 1902 to 1946, and in his caricatures of famous ornithologists that were published in the *Condor* in 1901. Locally, Fisher is best known for his list of land birds of the Santa Clara Valley and the Santa Cruz Mountains, which was published in Florence M. Bailey's *Handbook of Birds of the Western United States* (Fisher 1902).

Another student at Stanford at the start of the Grinnell era was Theodore J. Hoover (1871–1955), the older brother of Herbert C. Hoover. Theodore entered Stanford in 1897 and joined the Cooper Club in 1898. He roomed in the same boarding house as McGregor and enjoyed collecting birds and preparing specimens (Hoover 1939). A series of Myrtle Warbler specimens collected by him in 1898 and 1899 was used by McGregor to describe a new subspecies named *Dendroica coronata hooveri* in his honor (McGregor 1899). Hoover also collected an adult male Yellow-billed Cuckoo with eggs along San Francisquito Creek on 22 Jul 1901. At some point the specimen and the egg set were separated and only the location of the specimen is currently known (CAS #14306). This was the last breeding record of this species in Santa Clara County.

Hoover graduated in 1901 with an A.B. in geology and soon became involved in mining ventures in various parts of the world. In 1913 he returned to California and took up a teaching position in mining and metallurgy at Stanford. He became the first Dean of Engineering at Stanford in 1925, a position he held until his retirement in 1936. Hoover was a lifetime member of the Cooper Ornithological Club, but showed little interest in birds in later years. He donated his collection of warbler specimens to the California Academy of Sciences after the San Francisco earthquake and fire (Hoover 1939). Following his return to Palo Alto, he purchased a large portion of the Waddell Creek basin, an area he had first visited in 1898 with some of his Stanford classmates (Hoover 1939, Reese 1997). He named the property Rancho del Oso, and the family often visited the ranch on the weekends. Well after Hoover's death, his children gave the land to the state for the creation of the park that is there today.

The other founders of the Cooper Ornithological Club were local amateurs who had started out as egg collectors, but saw the need for a more broad-based scientific approach to bird study. Foremost of these was Chester Barlow (1874–1902), who was born in San Jose on 9 May 1874. His earliest articles on birds and egg collecting were written in 1892, and over the next ten years he published 73 articles or notes (Grinnell 1909). He worked at the Santa Clara Valley Bank and in his spare time he was able to acquire a large collection of eggs and specimens. Much of this collecting was done in the Santa Clara Valley, but he also made several trips to the Farallon Islands and to the Sierra Nevada. Barlow became ill with tuberculosis in the summer of 1902, but always optimistic, he was certain he would recover (Taylor 1903). He died on the 6th of November that year at the age of 28.

Barlow was the Secretary of the Cooper Ornithological Club for its first nine years. Initially, Henry Taylor's new publication, the *Nidiologist*, was used to report on meetings of the club and to discuss business (Taylor 1903). But when Taylor's magazine failed in 1897, the club needed to find other means to facilitate communication among its members. Barlow promoted the publishing of a club journal, and over the objections of the "graybeards," the *Bulletin of the Cooper Ornithological Club* was published in 1899 with Chester Barlow as editor (Kaeding 1908). The next year, the club renamed their journal *Condor*, the name which it holds today. Barlow's work as Secretary of the club and his new job as Editor of the *Condor* were at the center of this new organization in its early years. Yet it was not so much his considerable efforts that held the club together as it was his spirit and good humor (Taylor 1903). Years later, Fisher (1940) was to write,

> At this time Chester Barlow was secretary of the club, its editor, and psychological center. He had a positive genius for friendship and we were all greatly devoted to him. His untimely death in 1902 brought to a sudden close the pioneer period of the

club. . . . We were young, impressionable. I have often wondered what life would have been like if Barlow had lived his normal span. I think Grinnell felt the same way.

Somewhat less is known of the other founding members of the Cooper Ornithological Club: Harry R. Painton and Fred A. Schneider, Jr. Data slips from egg collections show that Painton was active locally as a collector from 1892 to 1895. Following graduation from Stanford, he entered medical school there, where he obtained his degree (von Bloeker 1993). Painton was no longer active in the Cooper Club, first with his studies and later with an active medical practice. But on his retirement in 1936, Dr. Painton once again took an active role in the Cooper Club, serving as President of the Northern Division in 1940–41 and President of the Board of Governors from 1941 to 1946. The club declared him an Honorary Member in 1947 (von Bloeker 1993). Upon his death in 1955, Painton left an endowment to the Cooper Club. Drawing on this endowment, the club's Board of Governors established the Harry R. Painton Award, granted for the best scientific paper published in the *Condor* over each two-year period (von Bloeker 1993).

As with many of the oologists, Painton often did not include the locations where he collected eggs, which is much to our loss today in trying to understand the distribution of breeding birds a century ago. Within Santa Clara County he collected a number of unusual egg sets, including Common Moorhen (28 Apr 1894, WFVZ #163759; 28 May 1894, CAS #5560; 28 Jun 1894, CAS #5559 and 5561), Willow Flycatcher (College Park, 28 Jun 1892, WFVZ #17816; 16 Jun 1893, CAS #5597), and Yellow-headed Blackbird (5 Jun 1894, CAS #5606). The Yellow-headed Blackbird egg set is the only one known from the county.

Fred A. Schneider, Jr. wrote articles for both the *Oologist* and the *Nidiologist* during the period he was an active egg collector. His description of a freshwater marsh on flatlands where Reid-Hillview Airport and Lake Cunningham are today is one of the few descriptions we have of the historic Laguna Socayre in the Santa Clara Valley, and is thus of particular interest (Schneider 1893, Grossinger et al. 2006). Egg-set data slips indicate he collected locally from 1890 to 1893. It appears that Schneider entered Stanford University about the same time as Van Denburgh and Osgood. A brief notice of his marriage in 1899 indicates that he had become less active as an ornithologist. "Mr. Schneider was formerly among the most active of Californian ornithologists, but for several years past a course at Stanford University has precluded active work in ornithology" (*Bull. Cooper Ornithol. Club* 1:55 1899). As Painton did, he collected a number of unusual egg sets in Santa Clara County, including those of Sora (1 May 1892, CAS #10729) and Willow Flycatcher (9 Jun 1890, San Jose, CAS #4842).

Although ornithology was not their primary field, two of the zoology faculty in the early days at Stanford University, John O. Snyder and Harold H. Heath, had broad interests that included birds. John Otterbein Snyder (1867–1943) came to Stanford in 1892 from Indiana University because of David Starr Jordan, Stanford's President, and Charles H. Gilbert, who was the chairman of the zoology department (Jennings 1997). Snyder was a classmate of Van Denburgh's and just as herpetology had taken hold of Van Denburgh, ichthyology became Snyder's course of study. He also curated the herpetology collection at Stanford after Van Denburgh graduated. Snyder obtained an M.A. from Stanford in 1899 and was hired as an instructor in the department, eventually becoming a full professor. He became head of the department after Gilbert's retirement in 1925, and he in turn retired from Stanford in 1938 (Brittan 1997, Jennings 1997). Data slips from various egg collections show that Snyder was active in the Stanford area from 1893 to 1924. When the Santa Clara Valley Audubon Society was formed in 1925, Snyder was on the organization's first Executive Committee, forerunner of the present Board of Directors (Turner 1962).

Harold Heath (1868–1951) was a professor at Stanford in the late 1890s with a focus on invertebrate zoology (Fisher 1940). As did Snyder, he maintained an interest in ornithology. As an example, Heath traveled to Forrester Island, Alaska, in the summer of 1913 to participate in an avifaunal survey (Heath 1915). He collected eggs in the vicinity of Stanford and nearby in the Diablo Range from 1899 to 1921. Notable is a set of Sharp-shinned Hawk eggs he found near Stanford on 22 Apr 1889 (MVZ #2699).

Many of the local ornithologists at the end of the nineteenth century, such as Van Denburgh, Osgood, and Fisher, started out by collecting eggs and skins, but as they grew older they moved into other aspects of zoology, or sold their collections and went into other lines of work. In this respect, Rollo H. Beck (1870–1950) was unique in that he started out by collecting birds and eggs to satisfy his own curiosity, and then went on to become a professional collector, working for a series of museums (Murphy 1936). Beck was born in Los Gatos on 26 Aug 1870, and the family moved across the valley to Berryessa when he was six. A neighbor, Frank H. Holmes, who had his own extensive collection of bird specimens, taught Beck how to prepare a specimen and how to use Coues's "key" to identify the birds that they collected on their excursions in the field. Although Beck did not graduate from the eighth grade, he appears to have been an apt pupil of Frank Holmes, for at the Smithsonian there is a specimen of an adult female Common Nighthawk that Beck collected at Berryessa on 30 Jun 1885, a few weeks shy of his 15th birthday (USNM #125326). This is one of only a handful of records for this species in Santa Clara County.

Beck collected actively in Santa Clara County through the mid-1890s, mostly in the vicinity of Berryessa, but also in the marshes at Alviso. He collected two specimens of Nelson's Sharp-tailed Sparrow at Alviso, the first on 6 May 1891 (USNM #120310) and the second on 21 Jan 1896 (Grinnell 1902). These were the first records for California. Also in Alviso, he collected two Black Rails on a high tide on 1 Dec 1891, and on a subsequent high tide, on 29 Feb 1892, he took another Black Rail and a Yellow Rail (Beck 1893). A set of Swainson's Hawk eggs collected near Berryessa on 21 Apr 1894 represents one of only two nest records from the county. By this time, Beck was in correspondence with Dr. Robert Ridgway and Captain Charles Bendire at the Smithsonian. In 1894, he joined the American Ornithologists' Union and the newly formed Cooper Ornithological Club.

Beck began to travel more extensively in California with

trips to the Sierra Nevada in 1894 and 1896. On the latter trip he and Wilfred Osgood found the first eggs and nest of Hermit Warbler and Evening Grosbeak, the two within an hour of each other (B[arlow] 1899, Murphy 1936). The next spring he traveled to Santa Barbara and collected in the Channel Islands. Over the next three decades, Beck collected professionally for the California Academy of Sciences, the Museum of Vertebrate Zoology at Berkeley, and the American Museum of Natural History (AMNH). His collecting trips for AMNH ranged over much of the coasts of South America and the islands of the southern Pacific Ocean. Robert Cushman Murphy (1936) of AMNH wrote of Beck:

> [In 1912] Mr. Beck had not only had an extended experience in collecting petrels in the northern Pacific Ocean, at the Galápagos Islands, and elsewhere, but had established a record for field work among sea birds in general which had placed him in a class by himself. Subsequent activities during the Brewster-Sanford Expedition, a later voyage to Alaska, and, finally, the ten years' campaign of the Whitney South Sea Expeditions, have served only to enhance his effectiveness and his reputation. He stands today as the most successful worker in this branch of ornithology that the world has known.

Beck continued to collect specimens to the end of his life. He was 79 when he collected a Yellow-headed Blackbird in Merced on 27 Apr 1950 (MVZ #121680), the last of the many specimens in the Museum of Vertebrate Zoology for which he is responsible.

Many other young men were active oologists in the 1890s, but little is known of their lives. Some joined the Cooper Ornithological Club and occasionally published short notes or were mentioned in its rosters. But others are known only from the brief notations on egg-set data slips.

Ernest Adams was collecting eggs in the South Bay area from 1893 to 1897. He joined the Cooper Ornithological Club in 1896, and their roster shows that he was living in San Jose through 1899 (*Bull. Cooper Ornithol. Club* 1:120 1899). By 1903, he had moved to Placer County (*Condor* 5:29 1903). In 1899 and 1900 he accompanied Rollo Beck on a seven-month collecting expedition to the Galapagos Islands. He was the first of the local ornithologists to find an Evening Grosbeak in Santa Clara County (Adams 1899).

Egg-set data slips indicate that William L. Atkinson collected in the South Bay from 1893 to 1899. He was a prolific contributor to the *Oologist* and provided some notable records to the *Bulletin of the Cooper Ornithological Club* concerning nesting by Band-tailed Pigeons (Atkinson 1899a) and Yellow-billed Cuckoos (Atkinson 1899b). He is pictured with other members of the Cooper Ornithological Club in a photograph taken in 1901 (Fisher 1940). His mailing address was listed as San Francisco in 1904 (*Condor* 6:26–28 1904) and on Hawthorne Way in San Jose in 1918 (*Condor* 20:147–156 1918).

All of H. C. Benson's egg sets, collected so far as is known near Gilroy in the years 1892 to 1894, are in the U.S. National Museum today. Otherwise, nothing is known of Benson.

Corydon and George Chamberlin (presumably brothers) were active egg collectors in the early 1890s. Both wrote articles for the *Oologist* and the *Nidiologist*, and both joined the nascent Cooper Ornithological Club in 1893. As of 1904, Corydon was located in Shasta, and George in San Francisco (*Condor* 6:26–28 1904).

Frank H. Holmes (1865–1924), a resident of Berryessa, has been mentioned as a mentor to Rollo Beck. On the 1899 roster of the Cooper Ornithological Club (*Bull. Cooper Ornithol. Club* 1:120 1899), he is shown as a member, and in that year he published a short note on acquiring the first specimens of Fulvous Whistling-Duck and Long-tailed Duck in Santa Clara County (Holmes 1899). But by 1904, Holmes was no longer listed as a member of the Cooper Club (*Condor* 6:26–28 1904).

During the 1890s and early 1900s, a number of ornithologists from elsewhere visited the South Bay area. Notable among these were two women: Florence Merriam Bailey and Irene Grosvenor Wheelock. Florence Merriam Bailey (1863–1948) was the sister of C. Hart Merriam, whose name today is most often associated with the Life Zone concept. Prior to her marriage to Vernon Bailey in 1899, she had written a number of books that popularized birding and brought the study of nature to a wide audience. Her book the *Handbook of Birds of the Western United States* (F. M. Bailey 1902) was the first systematic publication on western birds. This book is of interest locally, for she included appendixes by Walter K. Fisher on land birds occurring in the Santa Clara Valley and the Santa Cruz Mountains, and by William H. Kobbé on waterbirds in the San Francisco Bay area. Florence Merriam attended Stanford for a brief period in 1894 (Oehser 1952), but there is no indication that she participated in any of the meetings of the newly formed Cooper Club. The only legacy of her brief stay at Stanford is a minor allusion in her account of the Acorn Woodpecker (F. M. Bailey 1902):

> They always have a great deal to say, whether it be in a canyon of the Guadalupe Mountains in New Mexico, where their chatter interrupts the solemn hooting of the band-tailed pigeon, or on the campus of a California university, where much is to be learned by silent listeners.

Her most significant accomplishment relative to western birds (Fischer 2001) was the publication of *Birds of New Mexico* (F. M. Bailey 1928).

Irene Grosvenor Wheelock (1867–1927), a midwesterner, lived in San Jose and made detailed observations in the Santa Clara Valley from October 1894 to July 1902 (Wheelock 1905). Her book, *Birds of California* (Wheelock 1904), summarized the biology and status of California birds as of the turn of the century. From a local perspective, it contains interesting information on the breeding of Black Rails and Yellow-billed Cuckoos in the South Bay. But Wheelock did not generally include the locations of her observations, and when she did provide dates they did not include the year. This lack of documentation of records is frustrating for modern readers. Even at the time of publication, errors in the text were seen as frustrating for readers. Grinnell (*Condor* 6:81 1904) was highly critical of Wheelock's book and suggested that "an occasional resort to the gun would have resulted in a less sweeping generalization in regard to 'regurgitation' than is hurled at the reader in the preface!" Grinnell went on to say that the extent of the errors was such that "detailed criticism seems hardly worth while." J. A. Allen, however, the editor of the *Auk*, was more complimentary in his review (*Auk* 21:299–300 1904). He suggested that her claims regarding regurgitative feeding of young birds provided an interesting area of research. The next year, Wheelock published a piece in the *Auk* that detailed her claims concerning regurgitative feeding (Wheelock 1905). Although she was clearly an active field observer in the six years she lived in the Santa Clara Valley, there is no evidence that she was ever involved with the Cooper Ornithological Club, or that she interacted with local ornithologists.

Joseph Grinnell and a New Era

Walter Fisher (1940) wrote "On a day early in 1900 a red-cheeked, serious young man walked into the zoological laboratory of Stanford University." Fisher goes on to recount Joseph Grinnell's early years in the Bay area. At this time, Grinnell was already an experienced ornithologist, having had 22 publications to his credit, including papers in the *Auk* and the *Condor* (H. W. Grinnell 1940). At 17, in 1894, he had joined both the American Ornithologists' Union and the Cooper Ornithological Club. As Fisher describes this period, Grinnell had a major impact on all around him:

> We all became intensely bird-conscious. When Grinnell arrived at Stanford there were only five local members of the Cooper Club, but by the end of that year there were sixteen, and Palo Alto became a center for meetings, although we met also at Chester Barlow's in Santa Clara, at W. Otto Emerson's, Haywards, and occasionally elsewhere. In January, 1901, Grinnell became president of the club and there is no question that his enthusiasm and talent for leadership did much to promote its rapid growth.

Grinnell was born on Indian lands in the Kansas Territory in 1877, where his father was an agency doctor (H. W. Grinnell 1940). His father was a distant cousin of George Bird Grinnell and the family eventually settled in Pasadena, California, where Grinnell graduated from the Throop Polytechnic Institute in Pasadena (now the California Institute of Technology). He came to Stanford to obtain a doctorate in zoology. President Jordan and Professor C. H. Gilbert, both ichthyologists of renown, sought to steer the best students to their own field (Fisher 1940), but Grinnell was already fixed in his interests in birds and mammals. Nonetheless, Gilbert's remarkable teaching skills and Jordan's continual encouragement were important factors in Grinnell's education. At the time, he and Walter Fisher lived in the same boarding house in Palo Alto,

> which was then a small spread-eagle town with board sidewalks, unpaved streets very muddy in the winter, dim street lights, and stores with false-fronts. Autos were, of course, unknown; 'carriages met all trains.' Everyone, with the price, rode a bicycle. A sumptuous steak cost two-bits. William McKinley was president of the United States; Victoria Regina occupied the throne of England; and in American Ornithology the Age of Coues

had just closed. The Cooper Ornithological Club was seven years old and its 'Bulletin,' entering the second volume, had been named 'The Condor' (Fisher 1940).

Grinnell supported himself by teaching biology and botany at Palo Alto High School and occasionally taught courses at Stanford, but his graduate work ended in the spring of 1903 when he came down with a severe case of typhoid fever (H. W. Grinnell 1940). Grinnell returned to his parents' home in Pasadena to convalesce, intent on returning to Stanford the next year. But he did not return to Stanford as planned, taking, rather, a teaching position in biology at the Throop Polytechnic Institute. It was not until 1912, after writing to Professor Gilbert, that he took up a suggestion that he submit a thesis based on his field research along the lower Colorado River. Grinnell wrote a thesis on his studies there (Grinnell 1914b), took an examination, and obtained his doctorate from Stanford in 1913.

In 1906, Grinnell had married one of his students, Hilda Wood, and they continued to live in Pasadena. In the spring of 1907, Annie M. Alexander visited Grinnell, trying to contact one of his students, Joseph Dixon, whom she wished to employ as a field assistant for a summer expedition to Alaska (H. W. Grinnell 1940). Grinnell was interested in the expedition, recalling his own work in the Kotzebue region of the territory in the late 1890s (Grinnell 1900b). On her return from Alaska, Miss Alexander invited Grinnell to her home in Berkeley over the Thanksgiving holiday. There she told him of her plans to found a museum of vertebrate zoology at the University of California. These plans were of extraordinary interest to Grinnell, and when the museum was formed in 1908 he became its first director, a position he held for the rest of his life. The prestige this museum commands today owes a great deal to Grinnell's foresight and his discipline in the ensuing years, and may well be his greatest legacy.

Of his many contributions, Grinnell's development of a checklist of the birds found in California is probably best known. The idea of preparing a checklist for the state was one of the earliest objectives of the Cooper Ornithological Club. In 1896, in the *Nidologist* (4:8 1896), it was reported that

> The Northern Division met at San Jose September 5, with a large attendance. It has been decided to take up the preparation of a complete annotated list of the Land and Water Birds of California. The work will be begun by County Committees in each county in which the Club is represented by members. Information concerning the work will be sent out during the month and Messrs. Bryant and McGregor have been appointed a committee to receive the county lists when completed.

Subsequently, the plan for a checklist was outlined in more detail (*Nidologist* 4:19 1896):

> The Northern Division met October 3rd at the residence of Walter E. Bryant, in Oakland. Mr. Ernest Adams of San Jose was elected to membership. Mr. A. W. Anthony was added to the State Committee that is to conduct the final work upon the State

list. The following committees were appointed for the counties of Northern California:–Alameda: W. E. Bryant, W. O. Emerson, D. A. Cohen and H. R. Taylor; Amador: Henry B. Kaeding; Lake: A. W. Johnson; Marin: John W. and Jos. Mailliard; Monterey: Oscar P. Silliman and L. W. Brokaw; San Francisco: T. E. Slevin, Claude Fyfe, E. W. Currier; San Luis Obispo: N. M. Moran; San Joaquin: W. B. Sanson and W. F. Sanson; Santa Clara: C. Barlow, W. H. Osgood, R. H. Beck and H. R. Painton; Santa Cruz; Oscar P. Silliman; Sonoma: Henry W. Carriger.

It is unclear whether any draft checklists were ever developed, following these organizational efforts.

Grinnell's plan for a state checklist appears to have been based instead on the Colorado list prepared by W. W. Cooke. In a letter in the *Condor* (Grinnell 1901a), Grinnell described his intentions:

> I have therefore undertaken the compilation of a State List, including an index to all the available literature pertaining strictly to California Birds. This I realize is assuming a very difficult and tedious task, for California is ornithologically, without any doubt, the biggest state in the Union. But even if I cannot bring such a thing to publication myself, I shall keep the bibliography and citations systematically arranged, so that anyone else can take up the work where I leave off.

The bibliography Grinnell prepared was published in volumes of the Pacific Coast Avifauna series (Grinnell 1909, Grinnell 1924, and Grinnell 1939), the last having been finished just before his death (H. W. Grinnell 1940). State checklists were published in the same series as well (Grinnell 1902, Grinnell 1915, and Grinnell and Miller 1944), and the same approach was also used for regional checklists (Grinnell and Wythe 1927). Grinnell's final state checklist was only about half complete upon his death and was finished by his colleague Alden H. Miller (Grinnell and Miller 1944). Sixty years later, the Grinnell and Miller checklist remains a valuable source in ornithology, notable in particular for its precise writing and descriptions.

Grinnell's approach to the development of a checklist was to combine a complete literature search with records of specimens and observations. In addition, he envisioned the use of maps of the state on which observers could indicate certain breeding records

> These maps are 12×15 inches, and printed on paper that will take a light water-color wash. It is our idea that each active member should procure a quantity of these blank maps, and, devoting one map to each species, indicate all points where he knows that species to breed, *from personal experience*. I think the more active collectors would find this very interesting and instructive; and moreover, after a time the maps could be turned into myself, or whoever had charge of the State List work, and from them could be compiled a set of maps to show

our entire knowledge of the distribution of each species in summer within the State.

This part of Grinnell's plan—that is, a qualitative breeding bird atlas—was never carried out. The concept, of course, remains sound. The maps for the state's birds published by Grenfell and Laudenslayer (1983) and Zeiner et al. (1990) are close approximations to what Grinnell was trying to do.

Upon Barlow's death in 1902, the editorship of the *Condor* passed on to Walter K. Fisher. Fisher, although intensely interested in ornithology, found it was not possible for him to continue with the editorship, and Grinnell took over the job in 1905 (H. W. Grinnell 1940).

> The loyal support which was promised to Joseph Grinnell by other Cooper Club members if he would undertake to edit the Condor was so faithfully supplied that he was enabled to carry on the editorial duties through the remaining thirty-three years of his life, assisted by a changing group of associate editors. When he proposed any innovation at one of the annual meetings of the governing board, there was always a hearty "go ahead, Joe, we'll back you up" (H. W. Grinnell 1940).

Grinnell provided continuity and stability for the *Condor* until his death in 1939. This was a period where ornithology was still carried out by amateurs as well as a growing number of professionals. Grinnell was able to integrate these efforts seamlessly, and the *Condor* did much to hold the Cooper Ornithological Society together through war and depression.

Three Paths of the Early Twentieth Century

Interest in ornithology and birds followed three pathways in California in the early twentieth century, sometimes overlapping, sometimes intertwined, but at other times completely separate. The first pathway was that of the oologists, who continued to pursue their hobby of collecting birds' eggs. The second path was that of the amateur and professional scientists who made up the new Cooper Ornithological Club. The third was that taken by a new group of people with strong interests in bird conservation and protection.

The oologists who became so active in the 1880s and 1890s continued to add to their egg collections in the San Francisco Bay area well into the early years of the twentieth century. To judge from the egg collections in the Museum of Vertebrate Zoology in Berkeley, the peak of egg collecting in the San Francisco Bay area was roughly from about 1890 to 1930, as shown in Fig. A2.2. (The data series in Fig. A2.2 was constructed by summing the number of collectors active in the nine counties surrounding the San Francisco Bay for each year. The year's total was then divided by the population in the same counties for that year.)

As we have seen, a number of the early oologists were intent on moving beyond simply collecting eggs, and this led to the formation of the Cooper Ornithological Club in 1893. Once the club started to publish its journal (the *Bulletin* in 1899 and the *Condor* thereafter), many of the club members who were active oologists appear to have been enthusiastic about publishing their observations in the new journal (Carriger 1899, Ray 1899,

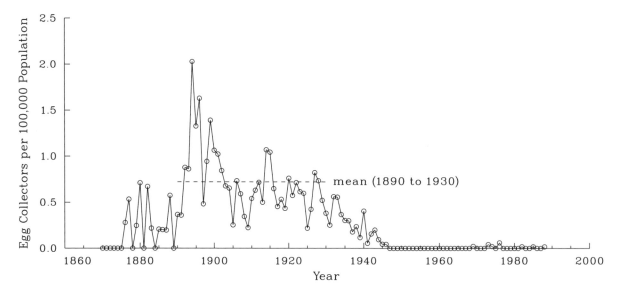

Figure A2.2. Distribution by year of the number of egg collectors whose egg sets are in the Museum of Vertebrate Zoology, Berkeley, California, normalized by population; nine counties of the San Francisco Bay region.

Carriger and Pemberton 1907), whereas before they would probably have sent their papers to the *Ornithologist & Oologist* or the *Oologist*. But other oologists showed little or no interest in the new club or its journal. These oologists appear to have had little contact with the Cooper Club or with Joseph Grinnell, who was preparing both a California state checklist (Grinnell 1902, Grinnell 1915) and regional lists (Grinnell and Wythe 1927). The reasons for the lack of communication between some of the oologists and Grinnell can only be guessed, but it seems likely that there were as many reasons as there were silent oologists. As an example, Harry Painton collected four sets of Common Moorhen eggs in Santa Clara County in 1894 (WFVZ #163759, CAS #5559–5561). Painton was one of the founders of the Cooper Ornithological Club, but it appears that Grinnell was never aware of these records, for he noted breeding no farther north along the coast than Santa Barbara (Grinnell 1915) and knew of no breeding records in the San Francisco Bay area (Grinnell and Wythe 1927). In this case, it appears that Painton had moved away from ornithological interests by the time Grinnell arrived in the Bay area and had probably sold his egg collections, parts of which have been acquired by the Western Foundation of Vertebrate Zoology and the California Academy of Sciences.

Another collector active early in the twentieth century was Will E. Unglish, who lived in Gilroy. It appears that Unglish was unaware of the Cooper Club and Grinnell's work with the new checklists until the publication of the "Directory to the bird-life of the San Francisco Bay region" (Grinnell and Wythe 1927). Unglish had collected egg sets of Lesser Nighthawks along Uvas Creek near Gilroy as early as 1894 (Unglish 1929) and at least three sets of eggs of the Black-chinned Hummingbird (Unglish 1932). That he published these records in the *Condor* not long after the publication of Grinnell and Wythe's "Directory" suggests that he simply was unaware of the Cooper Club and its activities. Yet the channels of communication among local oolo-

gists appear to have been much better. In his Cooper Club paper on the Lesser Nighthawk (Unglish 1929), he mentions that he introduced D. Bernard Bull, another active egg collector, to the Uvas Creek site in 1922, and Bull discovered additional nesting birds on Coyote Creek (where the Parkway Lakes are now) the same year. Another local collector, Charles Piper Smith, also took eggs from the Coyote Creek site and appears to have been a member of the Cooper Club (Smith 1926), but how Unglish and Grinnell finally came together is unclear. Eventually, Unglish published six papers in the *Condor* and made many of his records available to Charles G. Sibley for his *The Birds of the South San Francisco Bay Region* (Sibley 1952).

It appears that other collectors were completely removed from the influence of ornithologists such as Grinnell. Homer A. Snow, who lived in Newark, Alameda County, was an active collector in California. In 1911, he collected multiple egg sets of California Gulls and Caspian Terns in Riego, Butte County, on flooded lands near the Sacramento River (Shuford and Ryan 2000). Yet at the time of his second California checklist, Grinnell (1915) was unaware of either of these nesting records. Eventually, as various egg collections were donated to museums, knowledge of these events entered the ornithological record (Grinnell and Miller 1944).

The second pathway was that of the amateurs and professionals who joined the Cooper Ornithological Club, but had not been egg collectors. Their primary interests at the beginning of the twentieth century were on the taxonomy and life histories of the birds in the western United States. Yet for anyone interested in birds, it was clear that game species were disappearing under the pressure of market hunting, and that many species were being killed in excessive numbers for use by the millinery trade. After its formation in 1883, the American Ornithologists' Union formed the Committee on the Protection of North American Birds. It lobbied intensively to have each state pass a model bird law that would prevent the killing of birds for commerce. The AOU committee was initially successful, but the game distributors and milliners then turned to the recalcitrant states for their supplies. At this point the AOU committee worked for a national law that would prevent interstate trade in game birds and skins. This effort eventually led to the Lacey Act, which did much to reduce the commercial slaughter. The Cooper Club was active in supporting the AOU actions and in lobbying for the passage of a model bird law in California.

The *Condor*, from the beginning, published letters and articles that documented commercial or social activities that were detrimental to birds. Generally, these articles were not a call to arms for political action, but rather a demonstration of facts that could be used to support opposition to the activities. Early examples include a letter from Frank S. Daggett documenting the indiscriminate use of poison by orchardists (Daggett 1900) and a paper by Vernon Bailey on the killing of grebes in northeastern California for their skins (V. Bailey 1902). These types of articles continued over the years and were important in providing a scientific basis for political action. Noteworthy are a well-documented article by Jean Linsdale (1931) on the number of birds killed by thallium poison used for ground squirrel control, and an account by Mary M. Erickson of "sportsman" gatherings to shoot jays and hawks for the supposed benefit of California Quail (Erickson 1937). As conservation groups, such as the local Audubon societies, developed (as we shall see), the need for these activities by the Cooper Club lessened and they eventually disappeared.

The third pathway was the establishment of conservation organizations having a primary interest in birds. In 1886, George Bird Grinnell, editor of the sportsmen's magazine *Forest and Stream*, suggested that an organization be formed for the protection of wild birds (Buchheister and Graham 1973). He volunteered his own staff for the administration of the new organization, to be called the Audubon Society. The response of the public was astonishing. In a year's time 39,000 people had signed up, but Grinnell found the administrative burden too great and eventually relinquished the project.

The failure of Grinnell's project was not that there was no need for bird protection, but that his organizational approach was not appropriate. In 1896, the Massachusetts Audubon Society and the Pennsylvania Audubon Society were formed as statewide organizations, and the next year additional societies were formed in New York, New Hampshire, Illinois, Maine, Wisconsin, New Jersey, Rhode Island, Connecticut, and the District of Columbia. More societies, from other states, followed in subsequent years (Buchheister and Graham 1973). In 1899, Frank M. Chapman started his magazine *Bird-Lore*, which was adopted by the various Audubon societies as their official publication. In 1901, the various state Audubon societies formed a loose federation called the National Committee of Audubon Societies. William Dutcher, who had led the AOU's Committee on the Protection of North American Birds, was selected as the chairman. This organization was incorporated as the National Association of Audubon Societies on 4 Jan 1905 and Dutcher was elected president.

The first Audubon society in Northern California, the Audubon Association of the Pacific, was formed on 15 Jan 1917.

A monthly newsletter, the *Gull*, was first published in January 1919 and continues today with news on conservation topics, reports of field trips, and summaries of unusual bird sightings. Under the present name of the Golden Gate Audubon Society, it was incorporated as a chapter of National Audubon in 1948.

The Santa Clara Valley Audubon Society

The Santa Clara Valley Audubon Society was organized on 8 Jan 1925 (Turner 1962). The first executive committee comprised seven officers and four additional members. At least during the early years, it seemed that the principal interests of the society lay in field trips and bird study (Turner 1962). An extract from the May 1929 meeting minutes reads:

> Miss Yvonne Champreux gave the report of the April field trip.
> A report of the high spots of the recent Ornithology field trip was given.
> Mr. Alton Alderman presented the results from his Killdeer observations.
> Mr. Wilbur Shelley gave a report on a Mockingbird nest that he found.
> Dr. Pickwell gave a brief talk on the Ornithological publications of the West.

When Dr. Gayle B. Pickwell (1899–1949) became president in 1928, he proposed that the society publish a newsletter like the *Gull* that was being published by the Audubon Association of the Pacific. He offered to become the editor, and the first volume of this new publication, the *Wren-Tit*, was issued in 1929. Four numbers were published each year from 1929 to 1931, but then publication ceased (Phyllis M. Browning, pers. comm.). No newsletter was published over the next 15 years, but announcements of meetings and field trips were sent out to individual members (Turner 1962):

> Up to 1947 announcements were sent out each month to each member. These were single sheets containing announcements of field trips, monthly meeting and director's meeting. Beginning in 1947 two or more mimeographed sheets were published giving more details about field trips. Also 'Seasonal Observations' by Emily Smith appeared. Results of Christmas Counts were shown in detail. This new type publication was known as the 'The Bulletin.' By 1949 and 1950 The Bulletin had as many as six or eight or even ten pages especially when Mr. Sibley was editor. It was not until 1954 that the 'The Avocet' was born.

None of the early "bulletins" included volume or number, and they were issued somewhat irregularly (Phyllis M. Browning, pers. comm.). Five were sent out in 1947, 15 in 1948, 16 in 1949, and 13 in 1950. The first title of the newsletter was simply the *Santa Clara Valley Audubon Society*. In 1951, the newsletter was renamed the *Bulletin of the Santa Clara Valley Audubon Society*, and 11 newsletters were published in 1951 and 1952. In 1953, there were again 11 newsletters published, but with the tenth newsletter, November 1953, the title became the *Santa Clara Valley Audubon Society Bulletin*, and the November issue was assigned Vol. 1, No. 1. Ten newsletters were published in 1954. Through June 1954 (Vol. 1, No. 8), the newsletter continued its title, but then, in September 1954 (Vol. 1., No. 9), it was renamed the *Avocet*, the name that it retains today. Over the last 50 years there are numerous errors in publication date, volume, and number (Phyllis M. Browning, pers. comm.).

Records of local observations were published in the *Wren-Tit* series from 1929 to 1931, although the observers' names, as well as other details, were frequently omitted. With the new series of publications in 1947, Emily Smith compiled these records as the "Seasonal Observations" column, and this was followed by Charles Sibley with his "Field Observations" column. The practice of listing local observations of birds continues in the *Avocet* to the present.

A review of the minutes and newsletters of the Santa Clara Valley Audubon Society affords us information on the early Christmas Bird Counts held in the valley (Turner 1962). In the November 1928 minutes it is written that, "Dr. Smith announced that the December field trip would be taken to Alum Rock Park. Miss Emily Smith suggested a Christmas Bird Census be taken on the December trip." Thus, the first San Jose Christmas Bird Count (CBC) was held as part of the monthly Audubon trip. From reports in the *Wren-Tit* and accounts published in *Bird-Lore*, it appears that the San Jose CBC continued to be held each December in conjunction with the monthly trip to Alum Rock Park. The first count on which multiple parties were used appears to have taken place in 1940. The announcement of the December 1940 Christmas count was as follows (Turner 1962):

> Members interested in taking the bird census will meet at the regular corner at San Carlos and South Fifth Streets at 8:00 A.M. One party under the leadership of Mrs. Elizabeth Price will go to the Alviso Marshes; and a second party, under the leadership of Dr. Pickwell and Miss Emily Smith, will go to Alum Rock Park. After the census taking, the parties will return to the home of Mrs. Lester Brubaker at 191 Mt. View Avenue (just off Alum Rock Avenue in the vicinity of the San Jose Country Club, see sketch) at 4 o'clock to compile a report for <u>Bird Lore</u>. Members unable to attend the field trip are invited to come and hear results of the census.

The early CBCs, although held within the modern 15-mile-diameter San Jose count circle, made no attempt to systematically cover the circle. The first attempt at systematic coverage was undertaken on the 1949 CBC, where the count circle was divided into segments (Turner 1962):

> The <u>Bulletin</u> issue of January 1950 contains details of the December 26, 1949 Christmas Count. It was the nineteenth for the Society and was led by James G. Peterson. For the first time San Jose was divided into five segments and each segment was worked to some degree. Center of the count area was the corner of Capitol Avenue and Maybury Road. . . . There were 24 observers in five parties. Total hours on foot 20—total miles on foot 24.6. The following people were mentioned

as participating: Mrs. Grace Brubaker, William Creelman, Curt Dietz, Mrs. W. A. Hillebrand, Miss Elsie Hoeck, Mrs. Emma Miller, Mrs. Harvey Miller, Catherine and Mary Ann Miller, Mrs. Beatrice Nielson, Mrs. Anne Peterson, James Peterson, Sharon and Laurel Jean Peterson, Mr. and Mrs. Clyde Prusman, C. G. Sibley, C. L. Sleeper, Mr. and Mrs. Irving Snow, M. F. Vessel, Albert Wool, Mr. and Mrs. Charles Zwaal. Total 98 species; 19,221 individuals.

At this time the Santa Clara Valley Audubon Society had 100 members.

At the time of the formation of the Santa Clara Valley Audubon Society in 1925, the executive committee included three local ornithologists: John O. Snyder, Charles P. Smith, and Emily D. Smith. Snyder's ornithological contributions have been discussed previously. At the time the new society was created, he had become the head of the Department of Zoology at Stanford (Jennings 1997).

Charles Piper Smith (1877–1955) was born in St. Catharines, Ontario, Canada, and his family moved to Anderson, Indiana, where he graduated from high school in 1897 (Thomas 1956). He went on to Purdue University and earned a B.S., his primary interest being natural history. Smith attended Stanford University from 1904 to 1906 and again from 1907 to 1908, at which time he obtained an M.S. in zoology with a thesis on spiders. His name does not appear in any of the papers or notes published in the *Condor* at this time and it is unclear how active he was in local ornithology.

After leaving Stanford, Smith taught at agricultural colleges in Utah and Maryland and also worked for the Maryland Board of Agriculture and for a seed company in Baltimore (Thomas 1956). Smith had married Edyth G. Menker of San Jose in 1910 and they returned to the San Francisco Bay area in 1920, where Smith took a job teaching biology, at San Jose High School. At this time, his primary interests were in botany, entomology, and ornithology. He appears to have been quite active in the local area, both as an ornithologist and an egg collector (Smith 1926, Smith 1927a) and as a member of the new Audubon Society (Turner 1962). Interestingly, in 1927, he finished a manuscript for "The Birds of Santa Clara County" and was looking for assistance in its publication (Turner 1962). But the manuscript was never published and its whereabouts are unknown.

By this time, Smith's primary interest was in botany, and his particular passion was the lupines. In 1926 he re-entered Stanford to prepare a Ph.D. thesis on the distribution of lupines in western North America, which was accepted in 1927 (Smith 1927b). In 1930, he obtained a grant from the National Research Council to study lupines in herbaria in Europe. While he was gone that summer in Europe, his seven-year-old daughter Rachel died suddenly and, not long after his return in the fall, his wife Edyth also died. Smith remarried the next year and lived in Saratoga for the rest of his life (Thomas 1956). Although he continued to work on issues dealing with the distribution of lupines, which yielded extensive self-publication, it does not appear that he remained active as an ornithologist, for his name is seldom mentioned in local Audubon reports after 1930.

Emily D. Smith (1886–1972), born in Connecticut, came to the Santa Clara Valley in 1913, eventually settling in Los Gatos (Mewaldt 1989). Known to everyone as "Miss Emily," she taught as an instructor at the San Jose State Teachers College in the 1920s and 1930s, where she worked with Gayle Pickwell in developing numerous nature guides and booklets used for science education. Active in the Santa Clara Valley Audubon Society since its beginning, she led field trips, compiled the Christmas Bird Count, and wrote for and sometimes edited the chapter newsletters. She was also a bird-bander and active in the California Native Plant Society. For everyone, she was a reservoir of information on all topics ornithological (Mewaldt 1989). She also found time for two major investigations of rarer species nesting in the San Francisco Bay area, the first on Black Swifts (Smith 1928), the second on Lesser Nighthawks (Pickwell and Smith 1938). She was a meticulous observer, and her records document much of what we know about the status of less common birds in the South Bay.

Pickwell, Sibley, and Mewaldt: The San Jose State University Connection

Local ornithology at the beginning of the twentieth century seemed most closely associated with Stanford University, in part because of the zoological interests of faculty such as John Snyder, Harold Heath, and Walter Fisher, but also because of students such as Joseph Grinnell. From the 1920s on, the scientific side of local ornithology was more closely associated with San Jose State University, then known as San Jose State Teacher's College. Three of the faculty, Gayle Pickwell, Charles Sibley, and Dick Mewaldt, are representative of this connection.

Gayle Benjamin Pickwell (1899–1949) came to San Jose in 1927 or 1928, joining the faculty of the Teacher's College. He had been raised in eastern Nebraska (Pickwell 1948) and to judge from his early publications (Pickwell 1925a, Pickwell 1925b), he appears to have attended the University of Nebraska and, later, Northwestern University. His doctoral work was pursued at Cornell University, where he was granted a Ph.D. in 1927 for his dissertation on Horned Larks (Pickwell 1927), which was later published as a monograph (Pickwell 1931).

Pickwell was active in community activities as well as in research and teaching at the Teacher's College. He became the president of the Santa Clara Valley Audubon Society in 1928 and instituted the publishing of the *Wren-Tit*, the first chapter newsletter (Turner 1962). Over the next two decades he was a frequent leader or participant on field trips. His broad interests in the natural history of birds are reflected in a number of papers in the *Condor* over the next decade (Pickwell 1932a–d, Pickwell 1937a, Pickwell and Smith 1938). Of particular interest was his joint paper with Emily Smith on the nesting behavior of the Lesser Nighthawk in Santa Clara County.

Pickwell was interested in the teaching of ornithology and zoology, and the teaching materials he prepared were widely used (Stone 1935), but his interests extended well beyond ornithology. He wrote texts on a variety of natural history topics, and many were used as part of the basic science curriculum (Pickwell 1937b, Pickwell 1939a,b, and Pickwell 1940). He

also had a particular interest in herpetology, and his basic guide for the Pacific Coast included many of his own photographs and personal observations (Pickwell 1947).

Pickwell's too early death at fifty was mourned by his friends in the Audubon Society (Turner 1962):

> Our beloved Dr. Gayle Pickwell died May 29, 1949. The memory of his rich, inexhaustible enjoyment of birds and his gay comradeship on field trips will be always with those of us who knew him when he was an active member of our Society. A busy professor of ornithology and zoology at San Jose State College and a writer of many books on birds and other nature study subjects, Dr. Pickwell found time to share with the members of the Audubon Society his profound knowledge of birds and his delightful enthusiasm for bird watching.

Charles Gald Sibley (1917–1998) was born in Fresno, California, and was raised in Oakland (Corbin and Brush 1999). He entered the University of California, Berkeley, in the mid-1930s, where he was exposed to Joseph Grinnell and his methods of recording field notes, which Sibley followed for the rest of his life. After graduating from Berkeley with an A.B. in Zoology in 1940, Sibley worked in the Public Health Service for a year and then served in the Navy during World War II. After the war, he returned to Berkeley and obtained a Ph.D. in 1949. His Ph.D. dissertation (Sibley 1949) dealt with speciation and hybridization in the red-eyed towhees of the Mexican highlands. He joined the faculty at the San Jose State College in 1949 as an Assistant Professor of Zoology and held this position until 1953, when he accepted a post at Cornell University (Corbin and Brush 1999). During the period that Sibley lived in San Jose, he was an active member of the Audubon Society, serving as editor of the newsletter, and also compiled observations of local birds in a column titled "Field Observations." Locally, Sibley is best known for his mimeographed notes *The Birds of the South San Francisco Bay Region*, completed in 1952. These notes, which report on all species known from the local areas, are a valuable record of the status of Santa Clara County birds at the midpoint of the twentieth century.

Sibley's Ph.D. dissertation was focused on speciation of birds on the basis of morphometric characters. At Cornell University, and in later years at Yale University, Sibley was a major contributor to the development of molecular systematics in birds, which seeks to determine the relationships and evolution of birds on the basis of their molecular chemistry. A memoriam to Sibley (Corbin and Brush 1999) offered this appreciation:

> He became one of the leading ornithologists during the last half of the 20th century, was one of the founders and a major player in the emerging field of molecular systematics, and contributed significantly to our knowledge of the evolutionary relationships among the higher avian taxa.

Charles Sibley's departure from San Jose State College in 1953 opened up a faculty position in zoology, which was soon filled by Leonard Richard Mewaldt (1917–1990) (L. Richard Mewaldt, pers. comm.). Dick Mewaldt, as he was known by everyone, obtained his B.S. from the University of Iowa in 1940, and served in the U.S. Army from 1942 to 1946 (Ralph 1991). He earned a M.S. at the University of Montana in 1948 and a Ph.D. at Washington State University in 1952 (Mewaldt 1953). Dick became a Master Bander at the age of 19, and his major research interests throughout his career dealt with the cycles of reproduction, molt, and migration in passerines, particularly the White-crowned Sparrow (Ralph 1991). He was one of the founders of the Point Reyes Bird Observatory (now PRBO Conservation Science) in 1965, and was the President of the Board of Directors for many years. Later, in the 1980s, he helped found the San Francisco Bay Bird Observatory in Alviso. Dick was one of the original members of the Santa Clara County Breeding Bird Atlas Committee, and this atlas is dedicated to his memory.

This brief history of local ornithology started with voyages of exploration, which were followed by settlement, population growth, and the decline of natural habitats. Early ornithologists were keen to understand the birds that lived in this area, and that early interest extends to today. The linkage for all, past ornithologists and present alike, has been the discovery of new knowledge and its publication. This linkage, although sometimes fragile, continues to this day with the publication of this atlas.

Appendix 3:
Avifaunal Changes

The purpose of this appendix is to provide a summary of changes to the county's avifauna, species by species, in the years since records were first kept, mostly around the close of the nineteenth century. Because similar data have not been obtained or aggregated previously, the judgments of avifaunal changes made here today are necessarily of a qualitative nature. (The information here is presented in more detail in the species accounts in Chapter 7.)

A variety of approaches can be used to gain some insight into avifaunal changes. To begin with, a review of the early published literature and of data from early egg collections sometimes provides information on the distribution of breeding birds in an earlier time. As discussed in Appendix 2, the written literature was sparse until about the 1870s or 1880s, when articles on birds in California began to be published with greater frequency. Egg collecting also became popular at this time, and the oology magazines are the source of much of the early breeding data. But the status of birds in still earlier times, during the settlement period, is largely unavailable to us.

By 1855, as discussed in Chapter 4, the original perennial grasslands had been almost completely replaced by nonnative grasses, and we will never know the effects that these changes had on the birds in the county's grasslands. The great coniferous forests on the eastern side of the Santa Cruz Mountains were largely cut by the 1870s, and all that we know of the birds in these forests is from limited notes taken by James G. Cooper (Coan 1982). Most of the forest on the western side of the range was cut by the first decade of the twentieth century (Wilson 1937). Few of the early ornithologists had managed to explore these areas prior to the cutting of the old-growth timber (McGregor 1901), and the identities of the inhabitants of those forests will forever remain veiled from our view.

A review of the current literature is a second approach, one that can provide more insight into changes, particularly for species that are undergoing significant range expansions or contractions. In some cases, we can identify when an expanding species was first recorded in California, and we can track the edge of its expanding range as it moves into Santa Clara County. But range contractions are generally more difficult to document.

Quantitative approaches can also provide useful information. The Palo Alto and San Jose Christmas bird counts have been run continuously for 45 to 50 years, and a summer count (SBC) in the Palo Alto count circle has been conducted since 1981. The Mt. Hamilton CBC, in the interior of the Diablo Range, has been held since 1977. The utility of data of this type has been discussed by Butcher (1990) and is also addressed in the discussion of methods in Chapter 5. Trend information is used here only if it is significant at the 5% level. (A 5% level of significance, as indicated by $p = 0.05$, means that the odds of the trend information occurring by chance are 1 in 20.) The three Santa Clara County count circles, each 15 miles (24.1 km) in diameter, cover only a small part of most species' ranges within the county, and extrapolations of trend information to the entire county may not be warranted.

In some cases, quantitative analysis of data from the Breeding Bird Survey (BBS) can be useful. BBS routes are run once a year, usually in early June, and birds are sampled at 50 stations on a 24.5-mile route. Many of these routes have been run since 1966 and thus provide a time series of nearly 40 years. Although there is only one such route in Santa Clara County, the analysis of data from a wider BBS area, such as California, may provide some insight into changes in species' populations.

Below, we present brief summaries of the status of the 177 species that we consider to be the present breeding avifauna in Santa Clara County, as well as the 10 species that have bred here in the past. Change for each species is characterized as (1) showing a population increase, (2) showing a population decrease, or (3) neither: the population is stable, variable, or uncertain. In general, judgments of population increase or decrease are based on known changes in distribution (range). But in some cases, analysis of CBC or SBC data is the basis for the characterization, particularly when the 40- to 50-year time series for both the Palo Alto and San Jose CBCs show similar significant trends.

Table A3.1 provides totals for the three categories of change. Most (59%) are in the category of stable, variable, or uncertain. Forty-three species (23%) are considered to be increasing, and 32 species (17%) are judged to be decreasing. Of the latter group, ten species no longer breed in Santa Clara County and are relegated to the historical avifauna: Fulvous Whistling-Duck, Swainson's Hawk, Black Rail, Sora, Yellow-billed Cuckoo, Short-eared Owl, Lesser Nighthawk, Willow Flycatcher, Bank Swallow, and Yellow-headed Blackbird. Two

Table A3.1. Status of the present and historic species in Santa Clara County.

Present Status	Number of Species
Increasing	43
Decreasing	32
Stable, Variable, or Uncertain	112
TOTAL	187

additional species of this group, considered, for the moment, to be part of our present breeding avifauna, may no longer breed in the county as of this writing: Purple Martin and Pine Siskin.

Fulvous Whistling-Duck (*decrease*). There is one breeding record in the county, from 1917 (Snyder 1919). This species is best considered a sporadic or accidental breeder here during the early twentieth century. It has undergone a significant range contraction in California subsequently (Small 1994), and may no longer breed in California at all (Patten et al. 2003).

Canada Goose (*increase*). Birds from captive stock were likely introduced in the East Bay in the 1950s (Shuford 1993d), although there are a few earlier records of apparently wild birds nearby in San Mateo County (*Bird-Lore 35*:112 1933, Moffitt 1939). The East Bay populations expanded their range and the first nesting was recorded in the county in 1986 (*S. F. Bay Bird Observ. Newsl. 6*(2) 1986). These geese are increasing rapidly in numbers over the last 20 years (Palo Alto CBC and SBC: +29 and +26% per year, respectively).

Wood Duck (*stable, variable, or uncertain*). Grinnell and Wythe (1927) believed this species to be extinct in the Bay area by the 1920s. It began to recover in the 1930s, and the first county breeding record was reported in 1955, west of Gilroy (*Audubon Field Notes 9*:398 1955). Although there are no records of this duck breeding in the county prior to the era of market hunting, it may well have occurred in small numbers. Numbers now appear stable after a period of increase associated with this species' recovery in the post-market-hunting era.

Gadwall (*increase*). Gadwalls did not breed in the Bay area until the 1960s, and the first breeding record in the county was at the Palo Alto Baylands in 1967 (*Audubon Field Notes 21*:601 1967). Following this range expansion, the number of breeding birds has declined in the last 25 years (Palo Alto SBC: −6.6% per year).

Mallard (*increase*). Barlow (1893b) referred to the Mallard as the most common duck in a marsh near San Jose, but found only a single nest there, on 1 May 1893. In the last 30 years this duck, largely resident, appears to be increasing (Palo Alto CBC: +9.0% per year, San Jose CBC: +10.1% per year, and Mt. Hamilton CBC: +4.7% per year).

Blue-winged Teal (*stable, variable, or uncertain*). No trends can be assessed for this rare breeder in central California, which has been recorded nesting only once in Santa Clara County (*Am. Birds 28*:846 1974).

Cinnamon Teal (*stable, variable, or uncertain*). This duck was known to nest in marshes on the valley floor in the late nineteenth century (Schneider 1893) and today it is found primarily along the edge of the South Bay. Although winter numbers on the San Jose CBC have increased by 7.0% a year in the last 35 years, there have been no significant changes in the Palo Alto count circle for either the CBC or the SBC.

Northern Shoveler (*stable, variable, or uncertain*). This species was found breeding in the South Bay as early as 1886 (Emerson 1901). Breeding is detected roughly one year in three in the county. The number of summering birds in the Palo Alto count circle has declined by 9.2% per year in the last 25 years.

Northern Pintail (*stable, variable, or uncertain*). Breeds here every year, but appears to be declining over the last 25 years in the Palo Alto area (Palo Alto SBC: −10.4% per year). Elsewhere along the South Bay there are no obvious trends, and numbers appear stable.

Green-winged Teal (*stable, variable, or uncertain*). This duck is a rare and irregular breeder in the South Bay, and there is only one breeding record from the county (*Am. Birds 37*:1023 1983).

Canvasback (*stable, variable, or uncertain*). A single instance of breeding here in 1989 is the only regional breeding record (*Am. Birds 43*:1363 1989).

Redhead (*stable, variable, or uncertain*). This species is a rare and casual breeder in the South Bay and has been so since the early twentieth century (Grinnell et al. 1918). In Santa Clara County, it has been confirmed breeding only three times, although a few birds are present during most summers.

Ring-necked Duck (*stable, variable, or uncertain*). Prior to the atlas period, 1987–93, no summering birds had been seen in the county. Then, in 1997, following the atlas period, nesting was recorded at Calaveras Reservoir (*Field Notes 51*:1049 1997). Breeding Ring-necked Ducks have been found increasingly in the Cascades and the Sierra Nevada over the last half century, and the increasing numbers locally may be associated with this range expansion.

Lesser Scaup (*increase*). Regular breeding started in the Palo Alto Baylands in 1980 (Joseph Morlan, Theodore A. Chandik, pers. comm.), and represents an expansion of this species' range. This scaup now breeds in the South Bay every year.

Common Merganser (*increase*). First nested here in 1985, in Henry Coe State Park (James Yurchenco, Amy Lauterbach, county notebooks). This first county breeding record is a part of a general southward range expansion in California. The species is now a widespread and established breeder here.

Ruddy Duck (*stable, variable, or uncertain*). Grinnell and Wythe (1927) considered Ruddy Ducks to be permanent residents in the San Francisco Bay area at a few locations. In Santa Clara County they breed mostly in manmade ponds and wetlands. The increase in these artificial wetlands may have benefited these ducks throughout the county. Locally, in the Palo Alto area, numbers have been stable over the last 25 years.

Ring-necked Pheasant (*decrease*). Introduced into the county in the 1890s (Grinnell et al. 1918). This pheasant was formerly more widespread in agricultural areas, but now is found mostly along the edge of the Bay. Within its reduced range, numbers appear fairly stable.

Wild Turkey (*increase*). Introduced unsuccessfully in the 1950s (Burger 1954) and successfully in the 1970s (Harper and Smith 1973). Populations are expanding their range.

Mountain Quail (*stable, variable, or uncertain*). A small population apparently existed in the Santa Cruz Mountains in the late nineteenth century. Whether this population disappeared in the early twentieth century is unclear. The species is now very rare in a few locations in these mountains and some records may be of released birds.

California Quail (*decrease*). This was an abundant and widespread species prior to the era of market hunting (Grinnell et al. 1918). Recent declines, apparent in local areas (Palo Alto CBC and SBC: −4.3 and −5.2% per year respectively, and San Jose CBC: −4.4% per year), may be related to urbanization, since the Mt. Hamilton CBC shows no changes.

Pied-billed Grebe (*stable, variable, or uncertain*). Winter numbers are increasing on local CBCs, but summer numbers show no change. As with many wetland species, this grebe probably declined as wetlands were drained in the late nineteenth and early twentieth centuries, but it has recovered with the development of artificial wetlands.

Eared Grebe (*stable, variable, or uncertain*). This grebe is a rare and sporadic breeder along the edge of the South Bay.

Western Grebe (*stable, variable, or uncertain*). Both Western and Clark's grebes nested in natural lakes, like Lake Merced in San Francisco, during the nineteenth century. With the development of reservoirs, both species have adapted to these manmade wetlands. The Western Grebe is a sporadic breeder at Calaveras Reservoir.

Clark's Grebe (*stable, variable, or uncertain*). As with the Western Grebe, this species is a sporadic breeder at Calaveras Reservoir.

Double-crested Cormorant (*increase*). A century ago, these cormorants nested only on rocky islands along the coast. In the mid-twentieth century, with the introduction of organochlorine pesticides, their populations declined. Starting in the 1970s, this decline reversed, and expanding populations moved into the San Francisco Bay. The first nesting in the county was on the electrical towers in Salt Pond A2W in 1992 (Peter J. Metropulos, county notebooks). Local numbers are increasing (Palo Alto SBC: +17% per year).

American Bittern (*stable, variable, or uncertain*). It seems likely that this secretive marsh resident was present in the few freshwater marshes in Santa Clara County a century ago, but there are no records. Breeding was first recorded here in 1937, and in the last decade we have found it breeding at the Ogier Avenue ponds and in wetlands along Llagas Creek.

Great Blue Heron (*stable, variable, or uncertain*). Widespread breeder, but few colonies persist for more than a decade. Numbers appear stable.

Great Egret (*increase*). A few birds nested in the Pajaro River basin in 1889 (CAS #6697 and #6699), before being extirpated locally during the plume-hunting era. Recovery was signaled by eggs collected at San Felipe Lake in 1940 (MVZ #7400). Now there are a number of colonies in the county.

Snowy Egret (*increase*). No nesting was known prior to the plume-hunting era. The species recovered from the hunting and expanded into the wetlands of the San Joaquin Valley in the 1930s. By the 1950s, it was nesting in the San Francisco Bay area, and by 1980 it first nested in Alviso (*Am. Birds* 34:811 1980). Following this range expansion, colonies now occur in a number of places in the county.

Little Blue Heron (*stable, variable, or uncertain*). This heron was first found in California in the 1960s and was soon found in small numbers around heronries in the Bay area. Breeding was first reported at the Alviso heronry in 1980, and pairs nested there irregularly through about 1998. They no longer nest in the county.

Cattle Egret (*stable, variable, or uncertain*). This Old World ardeid has expanded into the New World in the last 125 years. It was first found in California in 1962 and was first found nesting in 1970. There appear to have been two invasions of Santa Clara County by this egret, one from 1982 to 1985, and the second

from 1993 to 1997. Sporadic breeding was observed from 1985 to 1998, but there have been no breeding records since.

Green Heron (*stable, variable, or uncertain*). On the basis of egg-set data, it appears that locations where Green Herons were found during the atlas period were similar to those where they were reported over the last 100 years. There have been increases on the Palo Alto CBC, but numbers on the San Jose CBC show no trend.

Black-crowned Night-Heron (*stable, variable, or uncertain*). Large colonies were found at the edge of the South Bay at the beginning of the twentieth century (Finley 1906), yet by mid-century no colonies were known from this area (Sibley 1952). Breeding colonies were found on Bair Island in 1967 (*Audubon Field Notes* 21:536 1967) and at Alviso in 1980 (*Am. Birds* 34:811 1980). Currently, these night-herons occupy a number of colonies, both at the Bay edge and inland. Overall, their numbers appear stable in the South Bay.

White-faced Ibis (*stable, variable, or uncertain*). This ibis was a common breeder in the wetlands of the Central Valley in the first half of the twentieth century. In the 1960s and 1970s, the number of nesting ibis dropped precipitously throughout their western range (Ryder and Manry 1994). Subsequently, there has been a recovery in White-faced Ibis populations and it is possible that two nesting attempts noted in 1991 and 1992 at the Alviso heronry were related to a westward expansion of this species that started in the 1980s (Ivey et al. 1988, Shuford et al. 1996).

Turkey Vulture (*stable, variable, or uncertain*). Historically, it appears that the boundary between migratory northern vultures and southern residents was roughly in central California. Interestingly, within the Palo Alto count circle, there has been no change in the winter numbers of vultures over the last 40 to 50 years, whereas in the San Jose circle, birds have been increasing by 8.4% per year. This vulture is widespread and common in the county, a status that is little changed from that noted in historical accounts.

Osprey (*increase*). Although Ospreys were found near river mouths in California in the late nineteenth century, there was a general decline in the first half of the twentieth century (Grinnell and Miller 1944). Since then, there has been an increase in Ospreys in Northern California, with a general range expansion from north to south. Much of this expansion has been associated with reservoirs that have good fish stocks. Birds first returned to nest in the Santa Cruz Mountains in 1997, and nested for the first time in the county in 2004.

White-tailed Kite (*stable, variable, or uncertain*). Numbers declined significantly in the 1920s (Pickwell 1932a), probably from hunting (Eisenmann 1971). This species has recovered since and now nests widely in the county. Winter numbers show little change in the last 40 to 50 years within the Palo Alto count circle, although since 1981 the number of summer birds has increased by 7.8% per year.

Northern Harrier (*stable, variable, or uncertain*). These hawks, associated with wetlands, were probably reduced in numbers with development and drainage of wetlands in the late nineteenth and early twentieth centuries. Currently, winter numbers in the Palo Alto and San Jose count circles have increased, whereas the summer numbers in the Palo Alto count circle are unchanged. Nothing is known of the trends for the harriers found along the Pajaro River.

Sharp-shinned Hawk (*stable, variable, or uncertain*). Egg collectors at the end of the nineteenth and the beginning of the twentieth centuries found a number of nests of this hawk in locations such as Menlo Park, Stanford University, and Los Gatos, where they are not found today. This hawk is still found widely in the county, although no longer on the valley floor, but whether it is more or less common than a century ago is unclear.

Cooper's Hawk (*increase*). Most early observers considered Cooper's Hawks to be transients or wintering birds in Santa Clara County at the beginning of the twentieth century. But in the Gilroy area, a number of egg sets were obtained during the first half of the century. Analysis of the Palo Alto and San Jose CBC data show increases of about 5.6% per year in Palo Alto and 2.1% in San Jose over the last 40 to 50 years. The number of birds recorded on the Palo Alto SBC has increased by 5.1% per year since 1981. Anecdotally, Cooper's Hawks were first noted as breeding in urban areas in the late 1980s, and this change in its breeding patterns, also noted elsewhere (Rosenfield and Bielefeldt 1993), may explain the increase in the Palo Alto and San Jose count circles. No change is noted for the Mt. Hamilton CBC over the last 30 years.

Red-shouldered Hawk (*increase*). This hawk was fairly rare here at the end of the nineteenth century, and that status appears to have been unchanged through the 1960s. Since then, numbers have been increasing (Palo Alto CBC and SBC: +13.1 and +4.7% per year, respectively, and San Jose CBC: +17.0% per year). Elsewhere in the county, birds are now found widely, except for the interior of the Diablo Range. Increasingly, birds appear to be pioneering in areas on the west side of the Diablo Range.

Swainson's Hawk (*stable, variable, or uncertain*). Eggs were collected in the Pajaro River basin in 1889 (WFVZ #9178) and near Berryessa, at the foot of the Diablo Range, in 1894 (MVZ #5227). These records are believed to be extralimital, and this hawk currently nests no closer than the Central Valley in eastern Contra Costa County and San Joaquin County.

Red-tailed Hawk (*increase*). This common hawk is widespread in the county. The species has shown a slow increase in winter numbers in Palo Alto (+1.3% per year) and San Jose (+1.4% per year) over the last 40 to 50 years. To the degree that these changes are adaptations to urban habitats they may not be representative of population changes elsewhere in the county.

Golden Eagle (*stable, variable, or uncertain*). This species has undoubtedly lost some valley floor territories to urbanization in the last 100 years, but within the Diablo Range and the Santa Cruz Mountains, breeding eagles are found at densities that appear similar to historical levels in these ranges (Dixon 1937).

American Kestrel (*decrease*). A common and widespread falcon in the county, but showing long-term declines (Palo Alto CBC: –2.3% per year, San Jose CBC: –1.6% per year, and Mt. Hamilton CBC: –3.3% per year). These declines appear independent of urbanization and remain perplexing.

Peregrine Falcon (*increase*). This falcon was a rare resident here at the end of the nineteenth century, with breeding pairs found from the South Bay to Pacheco Pass. During the period of DDT use following World War II, it was nearly extirpated from California (Small 1994). It is now recovering, with limited breeding in the Santa Cruz Mountains.

Prairie Falcon (*stable, variable, or uncertain*). This falcon presently uses a number of cliff sites in the Diablo Range for nesting, although not all potential sites are used every year. Thus its numbers appear to be close to the carrying capacity of this range, and are perhaps close to the numbers here prior to settlement.

Black Rail (*stable, variable, or uncertain*). Probably has not nested here since the early twentieth century.

Clapper Rail (*decrease*). Once an abundant resident of the South Bay salt marshes, this species has declined because of habitat loss, predation by non-native Norway rats and red foxes, and changes in food resources (including exotic organisms, such as the ribbed mussel, which has invaded the San Francisco Bay estuary).

Virginia Rail (*stable, variable, or uncertain*). There are no satisfactory historical records, but this secretive species has likely nested in some years in small freshwater marshes.

Sora (*stable, variable, or uncertain*). Occasional breeding was recorded up through the 1930s. In central California, now less frequently found nesting than the Virginia Rail.

Common Moorhen (*increase*). Both Schneider (1893) and Barlow (1893b) considered this species to be breeding in freshwater marshes near San Jose, but Grinnell and Wythe (1927) knew of no breeding records in the San Francisco Bay. There has been a general range expansion north in the last 80 years, and birds now nest regularly around the edge of the South Bay and at a number of inland locations.

American Coot (*stable, variable, or uncertain*). Nests widely in the county. No changes in numbers have been observed within the Palo Alto count circle in summer.

Snowy Plover (*increase*). This species probably did not breed in the South Bay prior to the construction of salt ponds. It was first noted breeding on salt pond levees in Alameda County in 1914 (Grinnell et al. 1918), as it still does today. A few birds breed along the edge of the South Bay in Santa Clara County in most years.

Killdeer (*stable, variable, or uncertain*). A common and widespread breeder that sometimes takes advantage of roads, structures, and stock ponds.

Black-necked Stilt (*increase*). A few breeding birds were found along the Bay in Alameda County in the early 1900s, but by the late 1930s this species was still not considered a regular breeder (Grinnell and Miller 1944). The first breeding record in Santa Clara County involved a nest with young found in Alviso in 1946 (Sibley 1952). This species is now found breeding widely in the South Bay and has also moved to inland sites, but in the Palo Alto count circle it has shown a 2.6% per year decline since 1981.

American Avocet (*increase*). Breeding was not observed in the Bay area until 1926, in Alameda County. The first breeding record in Santa Clara County was in 1937 (Martin 1939). The species is now a widespread breeder in the South Bay, and occasionally nests inland in the south county area.

Spotted Sandpiper (*stable, variable, or uncertain*). This sandpiper was known to breed in the Northern Coast Range south to the Russian River in the first half of the twentieth century (Grinnell and Wythe 1927, Grinnell and Miller 1944). It now nests along low-gradient streams in Santa Clara County, but it is such a scarce breeder that it is unclear how long this has been occurring.

California Gull (*increase*). Breeding in the Bay area was first detected in 1980, when 12 pairs were found at Alviso (Jones 1986). Breeding gulls have since expanded beyond the South Bay, with colonies developing in other San Francisco Bay locations (Shuford and Ryan 2000). The number of breeding gulls within the South Bay colonies are currently showing an increase of 25% per year (Shuford and Ryan 2000).

Western Gull (*stable, variable, or uncertain*). Since 1983, a few Western Gulls have been found nesting nearly every year, in California Gull colonies.

Caspian Tern (*increase*). Caspian Terns have expanded their range to include the San Francisco Bay, where they began nesting in 1916. They are now widespread breeders within the estuary, although only a few pairs nest in the Santa Clara County portions of local salt evaporator ponds.

Forster's Tern (*increase*). Forster's Terns nested in the interior of the western United States at the beginning of the twentieth century. They were first found breeding in the Bay area in Alameda County, in 1948 (Sibley 1952). Nesting birds were first found in Santa Clara County in 1971 (Gill 1977), and they now nest widely around the edge of the South Bay.

Black Skimmer (*increase*). Breeding Black Skimmers have been moving north along the Pacific Coast for the last 30 years. The first breeding in the state was noted in 1972 (McCaskie et al. 1974) and the first in Santa Clara County in 1994 (Layne et al. 1996). They have nested locally since then, but it may be too early to know whether this population will continue to spread or will contract and withdraw.

Rock Pigeon (*stable, variable, or uncertain*). This species, introduced with Spanish settlement (Vallejo 1890), continues to be associated with human settlement.

Band-tailed Pigeon (*stable, variable, or uncertain*). Throughout its range, the Band-tailed Pigeon is declining by 2.0% per year over the period 1966 to 2004, but the decline is not statistically significant in California (Sauer et al. 2005). Birds appear to be breeding more widely in the South Bay than had been suggested by Sibley (1952), but this may be an artifact of the exhaustive coverage of this atlas.

Mourning Dove (*stable, variable, or uncertain*). Locally, in the last 30 to 50 years, both declines and increases have been noted (Palo Alto SBC, –2.5% per year, and San Jose CBC, +2.1% per year). Apparently, more birds overwinter than was observed a century ago.

Yellow-billed Cuckoo (*decrease*). At the end of the nineteenth century, this was a rare breeding species in willow thickets near San Francisco Bay, but it is now extirpated. Birds along San Francisquito Creek in 1901 were the last nesting birds found in Santa Clara County. The willow thickets at the mouth of San Francisquito Creek were cut down when the Palo Alto airport and golf course were constructed in the early part of the twentieth century.

Greater Roadrunner (*decrease*). There has been a range contraction of this ground cuckoo in the San Francisco Bay area in the last century. Birds were originally found breeding in the eastern foothills of the Santa Cruz Mountains as far north as San Carlos, San Mateo County, but now are seen only occasionally in the Santa Teresa Hills. In the Diablo Range, there has been some contraction in range (for instance, breeding birds are no longer found along Monument Ridge), but otherwise there is little information on the historical status of this species.

Barn Owl (*stable, variable, or uncertain*). Population trends for nocturnal species are difficult to determine, but birds continue to nest near urban areas, where they were also found over a century ago.

Western Screech-Owl (*stable, variable, or uncertain*). This small owl was considered common a century ago (Price 1898b, Van Denburgh 1899b) and is still common today.

Great Horned Owl (*stable, variable, or uncertain*). This common owl shows no apparent change in status.

Northern Pygmy-Owl (*stable, variable, or uncertain*). This diurnal owl was reported widely in the South Bay a century ago, and is still found widely (although in low numbers) today.

Burrowing Owl (*decrease*). This owl, with its preference for open prairie and agricultural lands, has been forced out of much of its original range in the Santa Clara Valley by urbanization. It continues to nest along the edge of the South Bay and in a few sites with open ground where not disturbed.

Long-eared Owl (*decrease*). To judge from egg collections, this owl was more commonly found in riparian areas on the valley floor than it is today. It is now a rare and infrequent breeder anywhere in the county.

Short-eared Owl (*stable, variable, or uncertain*). The breeding pattern of this diurnal owl is sporadic throughout its range, and is often dependent upon the cycles of its vole prey. Its nesting in the Palo Alto Flood Control Basin in the early 1970s may have been a unique occurrence.

Northern Saw-whet Owl (*stable, variable, or uncertain*). This owl was believed not to breed in the Bay area early in the twentieth century (Grinnell and Wythe 1927). The first evidence of its breeding was a set of eggs found in a nest box in San Mateo County in 1937 (Granfield 1937). Although the atlas map shows this species to be widespread in coniferous and broadleaved evergreen forests in the Santa Cruz Mountains, its prior status there is unknown.

Lesser Nighthawk (*decrease*). Although Grinnell and Wythe (1927) were unaware that this nighthawk nested in Santa Clara County, Unglish (1929) had been collecting its eggs in south county streams since the 1890s. This species' range has contracted about 160 km to the southeast in the last 80 years, in part because of the reduction of flood scouring that produced the habitats most frequently used by this species. It has not been reported nesting in the county at least since 1937.

Common Poorwill (*stable, variable, or uncertain*). It is difficult to detect either population or range changes for this nocturnal species. Observers a century ago noted it in foothill habitats where it is found today, and there have evidently been few changes.

Vaux's Swift (*stable, variable, or uncertain*). This swift has often used chimneys for nesting on the eastern side of the Santa Cruz Mountains. Whether this was a response to the deforestation that began in the 1860s is unknown. The species is sufficiently rare that there is no trend information.

White-throated Swift (*stable, variable, or uncertain*). To some degree, this swift's use of crevices in cliff faces may have limited its distribution prior to human settlement. With the construction of tile roofs and modern bridges with drainage holes, both of which are suitable breeding locations for this resident swift, there may have been an increase in its population. Santa Clara County, however, is near the northern limit of its range, and local birds are sometimes killed by extended periods of cold and rainy weather. It is unclear whether there has been a significant change in numbers or distribution.

Black-chinned Hummingbird (*increase*). This rare hummingbird reaches the northern edge of its range in California's Coast Ranges in Santa Clara County. In the mid-1990s, it was found breeding extensively in urban creeks in the northern Santa Clara Valley, but it had not been seen in some of these area a few years earlier. It is possible that the edge of this species' range expands and contracts variably over time, and that the apparent local increases are only temporary.

Anna's Hummingbird (*increase*). This common hummingbird has responded favorably to the planting of various non-native flowers and trees that provide nectar sources when native plants are not available, particularly in the period of summer drought. Analysis of data shows increases of 3.2 and 2.5% per year for the Palo Alto CBC and SBC, respectively, and an increase of 5.4% per year for the San Jose CBC.

Costa's Hummingbird (*stable, variable, or uncertain*). A casual breeder in the northeastern part of the county.

Allen's Hummingbird (*decrease*). Grinnell and Wythe (1927) believed that this species was rarely found more than 40 kilometers from the coast, and its current distribution in Santa Clara County is consistent with their judgment. No general declines have been noted for this species in California (Sauer et al. 2005), but locally, on the Palo Alto CBC, analysis shows a decline of 10% per year.

Belted Kingfisher (*stable, variable, or uncertain*). Observers a century ago recorded this kingfisher along larger streams (Price 1898b, Van Denburgh 1899b), and Grinnell and Wythe (1927) considered it fairly common in the Bay area. This status appears little changed in the county and elsewhere. The construction of reservoirs early in the twentieth century changed the hydrographic character of many of our local streams, and the introduction of non-native fishes, particularly since the 1950s, has changed the assemblages of fishes found locally (Leidy 1984), but there is no evidence that either of these changes has impacted this species.

Lewis's Woodpecker (*decrease*). This woodpecker appears to have nested in the southern Santa Clara Valley a century ago, but it is now regular only in the alluvial soils of the San Antonio and Isabel valleys of the northeastern part of the county. There appears to have been a contraction of its range in the Arroyo Mocho drainage north of the Santa Clara County line in Alameda County in the last three decades as well.

Acorn Woodpecker (*stable, variable, or uncertain*). This common woodpecker is found widely in Santa Clara County. There has been a reduction in its range in lower foothill areas over the last half century as urbanization continues to destroy native oaks and granary trees, and this is reflected in declines of 1.3% per year on the Palo Alto CBC and 2.7% per year on the San Jose CBC.

Nuttall's Woodpecker (*increase*). The Nuttall's Woodpecker has always been characteristic of the Diablo Range, although perhaps not as common as it is now. Over the last 50 years, there has been an increase in the number of birds found on the San Jose CBC (2.3% per year), and this species began to be found within the Palo Alto count circle in the 1970s. It is now one of the most common woodpeckers in this circle, and analysis shows increases of 13 and 5.0% per year for the CBC and SBC, respectively.

Downy Woodpecker (*stable, variable, or uncertain*). Early observers considered this woodpecker to be uncommon to common (Price 1898b, Van Denburgh 1899b, Fisher 1902), whereas today it is judged to be fairly common. A decline of 4.2% per year over the last 25 years has been noted from the Palo Alto SBC data, but no long-term trends are observed from data of the three winter counts.

Hairy Woodpecker (*stable, variable, or uncertain*). Grinnell and Wythe (1927) described this woodpecker as fairly common in timbered regions of the Bay area, and that status continues to apply at higher elevations in Santa Clara County. Data from the San Jose CBC over the last 50 years show a long-term decline, but birds are quite uncommon within this count circle, and no population changes have been seen in data from the Mt. Hamilton CBC.

Northern Flicker (*stable, variable, or uncertain*). This common species is found widely in the county, and it was also considered common a century ago (Price 1898b, Van Denburgh 1899b, Fisher 1902). A reduction over the last 25 years of 2.2% per year has been determined from the Palo Alto SBC data, but it is not known whether similar changes have occurred elsewhere in the Santa Cruz Mountains, or the Diablo Range.

Pileated Woodpecker (*increase*). This woodpecker has expanded its range southward in the Northern Coast Range in the last 70 years. It was first found in the Santa Cruz Mountains in the 1970s (*Am. Birds 26*:805 1972), and the first observation of breeding there was in 1987 (*Am. Birds 41*:1484 1987). It was first seen in Santa Clara County in 1980, and the first nesting here was observed in 1998. Though nesting is still rare in second-growth forests of the Santa Cruz Mountains, the species appears to be expanding its range there.

Olive-sided Flycatcher (*decrease*). This flycatcher is declining throughout its range (Altman and Sallabanks 2000). In California, for the years 1966 to 2004, analysis of BBS data shows a decline of 3.9% per year (Sauer et al. 2005). Analysis of Palo Alto SBC data shows a local decline of 10% per year.

Western Wood-Pewee (*decrease*). Like the Olive-sided Flycatcher, the Western Wood-Pewee is declining throughout its range (Bemis and Rising 1999). In California, for the years 1966 to 2004, analysis of BBS data indicates a decline of 2.0% per year (Sauer et al. 2005). Analysis of Palo Alto SBC data shows a local decline of 6.3% per year.

Willow Flycatcher (*decrease*). At the end of the nineteenth century, this was an uncommon flycatcher in the San Francisco Bay area, found breeding in thickets along streams in San Mateo, Alameda, and Santa Clara counties. With the destruction of riparian habitat and the expansion of the range of the Brown-headed Cowbird into the Bay area in the 1920s, this species rapidly declined. The last breeding pair noted in the Bay area was along the Guadalupe River in 1962 (*Audubon Field Notes* 16:445 1962).

Pacific-slope Flycatcher (*stable, variable, or uncertain*). A century ago, this flycatcher was considered common or very common (Price 1898d, Van Denburgh 1899b, Fisher 1902). Its present status in the Santa Cruz Mountains is much the same, although it is less common in the Diablo Range. No changes have been observed in numbers in the last 25 years, to judge from the Palo Alto SBC data.

Black Phoebe (*increase*). Black Phoebes were considered a common species by early observers (Price 1898c, Van Denburgh 1899b, Fisher 1902), and they remain so today. This common resident species is showing a general increase locally; analysis of the CBC and SBC data in the Palo Alto count circle shows increases of 6.5 and 4.3% per year, respectively, and for the San Jose CBC, 3.5% per year. Analysis of BBS data from 1966 to 2004 shows an increase of 1.8% per year in California (Sauer et al. 2005).

Say's Phoebe (*stable, variable, or uncertain*). Say's Phoebes nest in scattered locations in the Diablo Range, but are so rare that it is unclear whether there have been changes in range or numbers.

Ash-throated Flycatcher (*stable, variable, or uncertain*). Grinnell and Wythe (1927) considered this flycatcher a common summer resident in drier inland areas, and that remains the case today. But this flycatcher of mixed oaks, chaparrals, and grasslands may once have been more common in the northern Santa Clara Valley, prior to urbanization. No changes have been observed in the last 25 years, to judge from Palo Alto SBC data.

Cassin's Kingbird (*stable, variable, or uncertain*). The range of this kingbird has historically extended to northern San Benito County, but no breeding records were obtained within Santa Clara County until 1997. The records since 1997 are too few to allow judgments concerning numbers or range changes.

Western Kingbird (*stable, variable, or uncertain*). Grinnell and Wythe (1927) judged this kingbird to be common in interior regions. The species was found widely in the Diablo Range during the atlas period and remains common.

Loggerhead Shrike (*decrease*). Loggerhead Shrikes were found commonly in agricultural lands in the northern Santa Clara Valley a century ago, but are less common in these areas today, in part because of urbanization. Analysis of the Palo Alto and San Jose CBC data shows a decline of 3.2 and 2.0% per year, respectively, over the last 50 years. Analysis of BBS data from 1966 to 2004 for California shows a similar decline of 1.6% per year (Sauer et al. 2005).

Bell's Vireo (*stable, variable, or uncertain*). The two breeding records for the county, in 1932 and 1997, were both from the Gilroy area. These records are at the edge of this species' historical range (Grinnell and Miller 1944).

Cassin's Vireo (*stable, variable, or uncertain*). Price (1898f) noted Cassin's Vireos as summer residents at Stanford University. Grinnell and Wythe (1927) considered the species as a "sparing" summer resident, whereas Sibley (1952) judged it as common in summer. Within its present range, it is a fairly common summer resident, but it is unclear if there have been any changes in numbers or range in the last century.

Hutton's Vireo (*stable, variable, or uncertain*). Van Denburgh (1899b) judged this vireo to be fairly common near Los Gatos, whereas Fisher (1902) considered it abundant within the Santa Cruz Mountains. This species is typically found in oak forests and woodlands, as noted by earlier observers (Grinnell and Wythe 1927) and is fairly common today. No changes in winter numbers have been noted over the last 50 years from either the Palo Alto or San Jose CBCs.

Warbling Vireo (*decrease*). Fisher (1902) described this vireo as a common summer resident in the Santa Cruz Mountains, as well as on the valley floor. Grinnell and Wythe (1927) judged it to be an abundant summer resident. Although this species is still common in many areas of the county, analysis of the Palo Alto SBC data shows a decline of 6.8% per year since 1981. Analysis of BBS data for California shows a decline of 1.3% per year for the period 1966 to 2004 (Sauer et al. 2005).

Steller's Jay (*stable, variable, or uncertain*). Fisher (1902) described this jay as an abundant resident in the Santa Cruz Mountains, and Grinnell and Wythe (1927) considered it a common resident in the Bay area. Analysis of CBC data for the Palo Alto and San Jose count circles over the last 50 years shows a slight increase in Palo Alto (+1.4% per year) and a slight decline in San Jose (−1.6% per year). In the last two decades, observers have noted a minor range expansion of this species into urban areas, as planted redwoods and other trees mature. But this range expansion has not been as noticeable as for Bewick's Wren and Dark-eyed Junco.

Western Scrub-Jay (*stable, variable, or uncertain*). Cooper (1870) considered this jay to be one of the most common birds in the local area, and it remains common today, throughout the county.

Yellow-billed Magpie (*stable, variable, or uncertain*). Yellow-billed Magpies once bred along the peninsula as far north as San Bruno in San Mateo County, but declined in the late nineteenth century (Bryant 1890). Once common near Gilroy, they were also gone from that area by the 1880s (Bryant 1890). But within Santa Clara County, there seemed to be a general rebound in the early twentieth century, and the places where they are found today are the places seen in the detailed records of Linsdale (1937).

American Crow (*stable, variable, or uncertain*). According to Alfred Doten, who farmed around Mountain View and Milpitas in the 1850s, American Crows were common on the agricultural land at that time (Clark 1973). Doten, however, noted that poisoned bait was used indiscriminately for California ground squirrels and other supposed pests, and by the time Van Denburgh (1899b) published his notes on Santa Clara County birds, he had never seen a crow in the northern Santa Clara Valley. Emlen (1940), in his studies of wintering crows in California, observed birds in the southern Santa Clara Valley, but was surprised not to find any in the northern valley. By the 1950s, however, American Crows had become common in the San Jose CBC count circle, though they did not expand into urban areas in northwestern Santa Clara County and San Mateo County until the mid-1970s. Analysis of the Palo Alto CBC and SBC data shows increases of 13 and 12% per year, respectively, since that time.

Common Raven (*increase*). Bryant (1890) noted that Common Ravens were common between San Mateo and San Francisco in the 1850s, but disappeared after that time. None were found in

Santa Clara County by early observers, and there is no mention of this species again until 1956 (*Avocet* 5:42–43 1958). Analysis of CBC and SBC data shows an increase of 14 and 13% per year in the Palo Alto circle for the CBC and SBC, respectively, 9.0% per year for the San Jose CBC, and 6.9% per year for the Mt. Hamilton CBC.

Horned Lark (*decrease*). At the end of the nineteenth century, Horned Larks were commonly found along the edge of San Francisco Bay, and in agricultural lands in the Santa Clara Valley. A few birds are still occasionally found in scattered locations along the Bay, but none remain in the urbanized areas of the Santa Clara Valley. They are found in grasslands in the Diablo Range, where they have always presumably been regular nesters, but their range and numbers have contracted in the last century.

Purple Martin (*decrease*). It appears that Purple Martins were always uncommon in Santa Clara County, from the time of settlement. Fifty years ago, birds were still found breeding in a few locations in the Diablo Range, but martins left that range by the 1970s. A few continued to breed in the Santa Cruz Mountains near Loma Prieta, but even these birds appear to be gone now, and this species may be extirpated as a breeder in Santa Clara County.

Tree Swallow (*stable, variable, or uncertain*). Because early observers may have confused Tree and Violet-green swallows, it is unclear how common they were here a century ago. Still, the reduction of riparian habitats over the last century likely had an adverse effect on this species. In the last decade, this species has shown an expansion in range, in part because of the extensive placement of nest boxes.

Violet-green Swallow (*stable, variable, or uncertain*). Early observers (Van Denburgh 1899b, Fisher 1902) differed in how common they judged this swallow to be. Grinnell and Wythe (1927) noted that a few remained through the summer months, but included no breeding records from Santa Clara County. Today, this species is a common summer resident throughout the oak-grassland habitats in the foothills and mountains of the county.

Northern Rough-winged Swallow (*stable, variable, or uncertain*). Grinnell and Wythe (1927) considered this species "not common" in the Bay area. Today, in Santa Clara County, it is considered fairly common. The construction of dams and the resultant reduction in flood scouring has probably reduced the number of available nest sites for this earth-bank nester, but the building of bridges and other structures with drainage and ventilation holes has added a new source of cavities. No changes have been noted over the last 25 years on the basis of data from the Palo Alto SBC.

Bank Swallow (*decrease*). Bank Swallows nested in cutbanks along the Pajaro River through the 1930s, but are no longer found nesting within the county. Elsewhere in the state, flood- and erosion-control projects have reduced the availability of nest sites in many areas where these swallows formerly bred (Small 1994).

Cliff Swallow (*stable, variable, or uncertain*). Early observers considered this swallow to be common to abundant in the county (Price 1898f, Van Denburgh 1899b, Fisher 1902), and it remains common today. Cliff Swallows originally required cliff faces as a substrate for their mud nests, but human habitation and infrastructure have provided new substrates that have benefited this species.

Barn Swallow (*stable, variable, or uncertain*). Grinnell and Wythe (1927) judged this swallow to be a common summer resident throughout the Bay area. It continues to be common today at lower elevations throughout the county, but analysis of Palo Alto SBC data shows a decline of 3.1% per year over the last 25 years. Prior to settlement, this species was restricted to natural ledges such as those found on sea cliffs. Now they universally use manmade structures for their nests, undoubtedly increasing their range since presettlement times.

Chestnut-backed Chickadee (*increase*). A century ago, this chickadee was found in closed-canopy forests of the Santa Cruz Mountains. The species' range expanded into the western Diablo Range in the first part of the twentieth century, probably because of landscape changes brought about by settlement and orchards (Dixon 1954), and has been expanding since. Analysis of Palo Alto CBC data shows that numbers are increasing by 1.2% per year over the last 40 years.

Oak Titmouse (*stable, variable, or uncertain*). This common parid is characteristic of much of the county's oak woodlands. There has been some reduction in numbers in the San Jose CBC count circle, where analysis shows a decline of 2.0% per year in the last half century, but no change is observed in the Palo Alto CBC data. In the last decade, this species has been observed breeding in urban areas away from oaks, where it did not previously nest.

Bushtit (*stable, variable, or uncertain*). Early observers described this species as common or abundant (Price 1898b, Van Denburgh 1899b, Fisher 1902), and it remains so today throughout the county.

Red-breasted Nuthatch (*increase*). Now a rare resident along Santa Clara County's western edge in the Santa Cruz Mountains, the Red-breasted Nuthatch was unknown as a breeder from this range until the 1950s. There has been a general range expansion of the species southward from the Northern Coast Range since the 1930s (Bousman, 2007).

White-breasted Nuthatch (*stable, variable, or uncertain*). A bird of the county's oak woodlands, this species appears to have always been absent in the higher Santa Cruz Mountains and along the valley floor. Barlow (1900b) considered it a common resident in deciduous oak woodlands in the county, and it remains so today.

Pygmy Nuthatch (*stable, variable, or uncertain*). This nuthatch of coastal closed-cone pine forests is found in small numbers in the coniferous forests of the Santa Cruz Mountains crest, and in recent years has expanded its range into lowland areas of Santa Clara County and nearby San Mateo County. Nonetheless, analysis of Palo Alto SBC data shows local declines of 8.6% per year.

Brown Creeper (*increase*). Brown Creepers are found at higher elevations in the Santa Cruz Mountains and the Diablo Range. They appear to have expanded into wetter forests of the Diablo Range in the last century, paralleling the range expansion of Chestnut-backed Chickadees. Analysis of the Palo Alto CBC data shows an increase of 1.9% per year over the last half century, whereas there has been a decline of 1.9% per year in the San Jose count circle, where they are less common.

Rock Wren (*stable, variable, or uncertain*). Early observers found this wren in the Diablo Range foothills and at the Coyote Narrows (Barlow 1900b, Fisher 1902), and occasionally in the foothills near Stanford (Price 1898f). Rock Wren distribution appears little changed in the last century, although there may have been a loss of birds from drier areas of the northern Santa Cruz Mountains foothills. Grinnell and Wythe (1927) referred to it as "sparingly resident," and that is a good characterization today for this uncommon and local wren.

Canyon Wren (*stable, variable, or uncertain*). This wren has always been rare in the Diablo Range. Analysis of data from the San Jose CBC, at the edge of the species' range, shows a decline of 10.6% per year over the last half century.

Bewick's Wren (*stable, variable, or uncertain*). This common wren is found throughout Santa Clara County. Analysis of Palo Alto and San Jose CBC data show only minor changes over the last half century. In the last decade, observers have noted this species' expansion into urban areas and parklands along the Bay not formerly occupied.

House Wren (*stable, variable, or uncertain*). A common wren of riparian areas in the Diablo Range, this wren is less often found in the foothills of the Santa Cruz Mountains. Early observers considered it widespread and numerous (Van Denburgh 1899b, Fisher 1902). Its present numbers and distribution do not appear to have changed in the last century.

Winter Wren (*stable, variable, or uncertain*). It seems likely that this wren's favored habitats were impacted as the forests of the Santa Cruz Mountains were logged from 1850 to 1930, but Grinnell and Wythe (1927) considered it a fairly common resident of the coastal forests in the Bay area. The distribution and numbers of this forest species appear little changed from that period, as the second-growth forest has matured.

Marsh Wren (*stable, variable, or uncertain*). Dependent on freshwater marshes for nesting, this species has likely undergone distributional changes as the natural freshwater marshes of a century ago have been drained, and it now is found in marshes that are largely associated with human-modified habitats. More birds are found after particularly wet winters, when the presence of standing water in seasonal wetlands provides additional habitat.

American Dipper (*stable, variable, or uncertain*). Historical accounts of a century ago mention dippers living along a number of the high-gradient streams in the Santa Cruz Mountains and Diablo Range. Although in some cases breeding birds have withdrawn to higher elevations on these streams, birds are still found at many of these locations.

Golden-crowned Kinglet (*increase*). Early observers judged this kinglet to be solely a winter visitor (Van Denburgh 1899b, Fisher 1902). Grinnell and Wythe (1927) knew of breeding in the Bay area only in northwestern Sonoma County. Like a number of northern coastal forest species, these birds have expanded into the Santa Cruz Mountains over the last 70 or 80 years, possibly in response to the maturing of second-growth forests. The species is now widespread on the coastal slope of the Santa Cruz Mountains, and a few birds are found nesting in wet coniferous forests in adjacent Santa Clara County.

Blue-gray Gnatcatcher (*stable, variable, or uncertain*). Possibly underreported by early observers, this gnatcatcher appears to have expanded in both range and numbers in the 1970s and 1980s. But analysis of Palo Alto CBC data obtained since 1981 shows a decline of 4.3% per year in the scrub and chaparral areas in that circle. It is not known if similar declines have occurred in the southern Santa Cruz Mountains foothills or in the Diablo Range.

Western Bluebird (*stable, variable, or uncertain*). Both Van Denburgh (1899b) and Fisher (1902) considered this bluebird to be a common resident. Today, it is found widely in the county and is generally common. Analysis of the Palo Alto and San Jose CBC data shows only slight changes over the last half century. Notable in the last decade has been an expansion of Western Bluebirds into more urban areas, particularly where there are areas of open grass on playing fields and parks.

Swainson's Thrush (*decrease*). This thrush was common in a number of the riparian habitats on the valley floor a century ago, but with urbanization and the effects of parasitism by the Brown-headed Cowbird, the species has largely withdrawn from these urban streams. Analysis of the Palo SBC data shows a significant decline of 11.4% per year in the foothills of the northern Santa Cruz Mountains.

Hermit Thrush (*stable, variable, or uncertain*). The breeding range of this species, which is more common on the coastal slope of the Santa Cruz Mountains, barely edges into Santa Clara County. Historically, it occasionally bred along some of the east-draining creeks from these mountains, but apparently no longer does so.

American Robin (*increase*). A century ago, the robin was only a wintering bird, but a few birds started to nest in the Bay area early in the twentieth century, generally in urban areas with summer watering. The species appears to have expanded throughout urban portions of the Bay area and then into the foothills and mountains, even in the absence of summer watering. Robins are now found nearly throughout the county, but only a few birds occupy the drier eastern sections.

Wrentit (*stable, variable, or uncertain*). Van Denburgh (1899b) and Fisher (1902) considered Wrentits common or abundant residents in the Santa Cruz Mountains, and that remains true today. Over the last 40 to 50 years, analysis of the San Jose CBC data shows a slight decrease, whereas no change is observed in the Palo Alto CBC data.

Northern Mockingbird (*increase*). Northern Mockingbirds expanded northwest from their southern California range in the 1920s, and 1928 saw the first breeding record in Santa Clara County. Arnold (1935, 1980) concluded that their expansion was related to the planting of trees and shrubs.

California Thrasher (*decrease*). This chaparral thrasher is also found in urban areas where there is a heavy shrub cover, but analysis of the Palo Alto and San Jose CBC data show declines of 1.6 and 3.0% per year, respectively, over the last 40 to 50 years. No changes are seen on the Mt. Hamilton CBC, and it may be that urbanization is related to the declines in the Palo Alto and San Jose count circles. Similar declines have been noted in urban areas elsewhere (Tintle 1993, Cody 1998).

European Starling (*increase*). The European Starling expanded its range from east to west over the last century. The first nest records in the San Francisco Bay area, which included three nests at Stanford University, are from 1963 (*Audubon Field*

Notes 17:483 1963). It is now found throughout the county.

Cedar Waxwing (*stable, variable, or uncertain*). Cedar Waxwings nest sporadically south of their normal range, and this has occurred at least once in Santa Clara County.

Phainopepla (*stable, variable, or uncertain*). This silky-flycatcher is a rare nesting species in the eastern part of the county, and there are occasional records farther west. Scattered nesting has occurred in the northern Diablo Range in Alameda County for nearly a century.

Orange-crowned Warbler (*stable, variable, or uncertain*). Grinnell and Wythe (1927) described this warbler as a common summer resident in the Bay area. Its remains a common breeding species throughout the county on steep slopes of scrub and chaparral. Analysis of the Palo Alto SBC data shows a decline of 3.1% per year over the last 25 years.

Yellow Warbler (*decrease*). Once common along the riparian corridors on the valley floor and at higher elevations (Barlow 1893c, Price 1898f, Van Denburgh 1899b, Fisher 1902), the Yellow Warbler is now an uncommon summer resident. This warbler appears to be decreasing in numbers throughout the Bay area, and analysis of SBC data in the Palo Alto count circle shows a precipitous decline of 17% per year over the last 25 years.

Yellow-rumped Warbler (*stable, variable, or uncertain*). Yellow-rumped Warblers breed in small numbers in coniferous forests along the crest of the Santa Cruz Mountains, and rarely in the Diablo Range. No change in numbers has been observed on the Palo Alto SBC over the last 25 years.

Black-throated Gray Warbler (*stable, variable, or uncertain*). Grinnell and Wythe (1927) considered this warbler to be possibly a local breeder, but listed no breeding records from Santa Clara County. Sibley (1952) described it as a fairly common summer resident, but also listed no breeding records for the county. As shown in this atlas, this uncommon warbler breeds in a variety of habitats in the Santa Cruz Mountains and the Diablo Range. Analysis of the Palo Alto SBC data shows a 2.7% per year increase over the last 25 years.

Hermit Warbler (*stable, variable, or uncertain*). Although Hermit Warblers were not discovered nesting in the Santa Cruz Mountains until the 1930s, they have probably always nested there in very small numbers (David L. Suddjian, pers. comm.).

MacGillivray's Warbler (*stable, variable, or uncertain*). These warblers are uncommon and local breeders in the Santa Cruz Mountains, and there are only a few historical records from Santa Clara County. Breeding birds were found in only three edge blocks during our atlas, all of the locations outside the county.

Common Yellowthroat (*increase*). In recent years, Common Yellowthroats have moved into brackish marshes in the South Bay, where they were not found during previous surveys (Foster 1977, Hobson et al. 1986). Analysis of Palo Alto SBC data shows an increase of 5.9% per year since 1981. It is unclear whether similar changes are occurring in the freshwater marshes in the center of the county or in the Pajaro River drainage.

Wilson's Warbler (*decrease*). A century ago, Wilson's Warblers were common along riparian corridors on the valley floor, where they are now absent. It appears that this range contraction was caused by habitat degradation, cowbird parasitism, and urbanization. Nesting birds are still found in mesic areas at higher

elevations in the Santa Cruz Mountains, and analysis of Palo Alto SBC data shows no change for this species over the last 25 years.

Yellow-breasted Chat (*stable, variable, or uncertain*). Chats have always been rare and sporadic breeders in Santa Clara County, and some sites are used for only a few years. It is unclear whether there have been any significant changes in distribution and numbers over the last century.

Western Tanager (*increase*). These tanagers are thought not to have bred here a century ago (Grinnell and Wythe 1927), although there is contradictory evidence (Storer 1920). An expansion of birds breeding at lower elevations was noted in the 1930s (*Bird-Lore 35*:279 1933), the first county breeding recorded at Alum Rock Park in 1935 (Peterson 1935). Atlas results suggests that this tanager has greatly increased its breeding range in the last 70 years.

Spotted Towhee (*stable, variable, or uncertain*). This common towhee of thickets and scrub is found throughout the county, except for urban areas. Cooper (1870) and Grinnell and Wythe (1927) considered it one of our commonest species, which remains true today. But an analysis of the San Jose CBC data over the last half century shows a decline of 2.3% per year, which may reflect the influence of continuing urbanization.

California Towhee (*stable, variable, or uncertain*). Van Denburgh (1899b) considered this towhee a very common resident a century ago, and that judgment holds today. The California Towhee, one of the commonest birds in the county, is widely distributed. Analysis of Palo Alto and San Jose CBC data shows declines of 3.0 and 2.1% per year, respectively, over the last half century, yet the Mt. Hamilton CBC data, from the interior of the Diablo Range, show an increase of 1.7% per year over the last 30 years, suggesting that the declines in the other counts are related to urbanization.

Rufous-crowned Sparrow (*stable, variable, or uncertain*). This uncommon sparrow is found in grasslands and California sagebrush in the same areas where it was reported a century ago. There are no obvious changes in distribution or numbers.

Chipping Sparrow (*decrease*). Historically, this was a common bird in farms and orchards on the valley floor, but it is no longer found at these low-elevation sites. Although this sparrow is still fairly common in scattered areas in the Diablo Range, there has been a notable range contraction from some locations where it was regular just a few years ago, and significant contractions in the northern Santa Cruz Mountains, where analysis of the Palo Alto SBC data shows a decline of 8.5% per year.

Black-chinned Sparrow (*stable, variable, or uncertain*). This sparrow, rare here, was not known to breed in the Diablo Range until the 1940s, but may simply have been overlooked, considering its small numbers and nomadic habits. There appears to have been an invasion of some coastal mountain sites in the 1970s, but this bird is not found in these locations every year.

Lark Sparrow (*decrease*). Like the Chipping Sparrow, this was a common bird of farms and fruit orchards a century ago, but it is now largely absent from these locations. A small population in the northern Santa Cruz Mountains may now be extirpated. Of more concern are the declines observed in the Diablo Range, where analysis of the San Jose CBC data shows a decline of 5.6% per year over the last half century. But within the more remote Mt. Hamilton count circle, no significant change has been seen in the last 30 years.

Sage Sparrow (*stable, variable, or uncertain*). Early observers found this sparrow nesting in scattered locations on the eastern side of the Santa Cruz Mountains (Van Denburgh 1899b, Jenkins 1904), but birds appear to be absent or less common at these sites more recently, particularly in the last decade. Breeding in the Diablo Range was not observed until the 1940s, although it is suspected that this uncommon sparrow was always resident there. Birds are still found regularly in the interior of the Diablo Range, as indicated on the atlas map.

Savannah Sparrow (*stable, variable, or uncertain*). Early observers considered this species a resident of salt marshes (Price 1898f, Van Denburgh 1899b, Barlow 1900b), although birds nesting in wet grasslands away from the Bay were noted later (Grinnell and Wythe 1927). This sparrow continues to use these same habitats today.

Grasshopper Sparrow (*stable, variable, or uncertain*). This sparrow was not commonly observed here a century ago, but this is thought to be a consequence of observers not looking for it in its favored grasslands. It is now apparent that the species is widely distributed, although it is not clear whether this is a result of recent range expansion or an increase in the birds' numbers. Analysis of Palo Alto SBC data since 1981 shows no change in the number of birds found in the grasslands along the northern Santa Cruz Mountains.

Song Sparrow (*stable, variable, or uncertain*). Two distinct subspecies breed within Santa Clara County. The Salt Marsh Song Sparrow must have undergone a decided reduction in numbers in the county with the development of salt evaporator ponds in the first half of the twentieth century, but numbers appear plentiful along the many channels beside these ponds today. The Upland Song Sparrow was considered common by early observers (Van Denburgh 1899b, Grinnell and Wythe 1927), and remains so today. Analysis of the CBC and SBC data shows a decline of 1.9% per year both winter and summer in the Palo Alto circle, whereas there has been a 1.4% per year increase within the San Jose circle. It is not known whether the two subspecies have been affected equally by these slight trends.

Dark-eyed Junco (*increase*). Dark-eyed Juncos have always been common residents of forested areas throughout Santa Clara County (Price 1898f, Van Denburgh 1899b, Linsdale and Rodgers 1937), and remain so today. In the last 15 years, there has been a local range expansion of this species into urban areas along the valley floor. In these urban areas, they are particularly attracted by planted coast redwoods with ground covers such as ivy.

Black-headed Grosbeak (*stable, variable, or uncertain*). Early observers, such as Price (1898f), Van Denburgh (1899b), and Fisher (1902), considered this grosbeak to be common to abundant. This is still the case over much of the county, but analysis of Palo Alto SBC data since 1981 shows a decline of 3.8% per year.

Blue Grosbeak (*stable, variable, or uncertain*). A rare and sporadic breeder here. The limited breeding in Santa Clara County may be related to a general expansion seen throughout the southwestern United States (Johnson 1994).

Lazuli Bunting (*decrease*). Lazuli Buntings were once common summer residents along the valley floor in fields, orchards, and farms, and they also used the new growth along flood-scoured streams prior to the era of reservoir construction. They are no longer found in these areas, but are still common breeders at higher elevations in the Santa Cruz Mountains and the Diablo Range, and their populations appear stable.

Indigo Bunting (*stable, variable, or uncertain*). One breeding record here, perhaps involving a Lazuli Bunting hybrid. There has been a general movement of this species into the southwestern United States in the last half century (Payne 1992).

Red-winged Blackbird (*stable, variable, or uncertain*). Analysis of Palo Alto and San Jose CBC data over the last half century shows declines of 3.4 and 2.2% per year, respectively, for this abundant and widespread blackbird. It is not known if this trend holds for birds elsewhere in the county.

Tricolored Blackbird (*decrease*). Tricolored Blackbirds nest colonially in a variety of wetlands in the county, sometimes in large numbers. It is difficult to assess their status locally, since they are nomadic and often use a particular nest site for only a few years. Their tendency to abandon a colony site also makes judging trends difficult. In California, they have declined significantly in recent years (Beedy and Hamilton 1999).

Western Meadowlark (*stable, variable, or uncertain*). This species was considered common or abundant in local grasslands and grainfields at the close of the nineteenth century (Price 1898d, Van Denburgh 1899b, Fisher 1902). The transition to orchards and then housing in the northern Santa Clara Valley during the twentieth century has undoubtedly reduced their numbers, but they remain a common species in the county's grasslands. Analysis of Palo Alto SBC data shows a decline of 3.7% per year since 1981.

Yellow-headed Blackbird (*decrease*). A century ago, these blackbirds were found breeding on marshes on the county's valley floor (Barlow 1893b, Van Denburgh 1899b). But Grinnell and Wythe (1927) considered them rare in the Bay area. Santa Clara County's wetlands were mostly drained by the early twentieth century, and unlike other birds, such as Marsh Wrens, which adapted to manmade freshwater wetlands, the Yellow-headed Blackbirds have disappeared as a nesting species.

Brewer's Blackbird (*stable, variable, or uncertain*). Price (1898d), Van Denburgh (1899b), and Fisher (1902) judged this blackbird to be a common permanent resident a century ago. Today, they still remain common in a multitude of habitats, including shopping mall parking lots as well as remote areas of the Diablo Range. But analysis of the Palo Alto and San Jose CBC data shows a decline of 5.5 and 6.3% per year, respectively, over the last half century.

Great-tailed Grackle (*increase*). Great-tailed Grackles first nested in a San Benito County edge block in 1998, and in Santa Clara County in 2000. These birds represent the edge of a massive and ongoing invasion of California (Small 1994).

Brown-headed Cowbird (*increase*). Brown-headed Cowbirds moved northwest through California in the 1920s and 1930s. The first report in the Bay area was of eggs found in Alameda County in 1922 (La Jeunesse 1923), and the first breeding in Santa Clara County was recorded in 1925 (Smith 1926). The species expanded rapidly through urban and agricultural areas. Analysis of the Palo Alto SBC shows that cowbird numbers have increased at a rate of 7.4% per year since 1981.

Hooded Oriole (*increase*). These orioles were not present in the San Francisco Bay area a century ago. There was a general range expansion northwestward in the 1920s, and single birds were found in scattered locations in the Bay area in 1930. A nest was found in Santa Cruz as early as 1931, but the first Santa Clara County breeding was not recorded until 1946 (Sibley 1952). The species generally uses the fronds from the California fan palm to construct its nest, and its expansion has followed the planting of this native palm from southern California.

Bullock's Oriole (*stable, variable, or uncertain*). A century ago, observers judged this oriole to be common here (Van Denburgh 1899b, Fisher 1902), and it remains a common species throughout Santa Clara County.

Purple Finch (*stable, variable, or uncertain*). Historically, Purple Finches were more common in the wetter, coastal forests (Grinnell and Wythe 1927). Winter numbers have been variable over the last half century, judging from the Palo Alto and San Jose CBC data, with fewer birds seen in the 1960s, more in the 1970s, and subsequently another decline in numbers. Since 1981, analysis of the Palo Alto SBC data shows a decrease of 2.0% per year.

House Finch (*stable, variable, or uncertain*). Early observers considered this finch to be abundant here (Price 1898d, Van Denburgh 1899b, Fisher 1902, Grinnell and Wythe 1927), and it remains so today. But analysis of the Palo Alto and San Jose CBC data over the last half century shows declines of 4.1 and 3.7% per year, respectively.

Red Crossbill (*increase*). These nomadic finches are very rare in Santa Clara County, although more common in other areas of the Santa Cruz Mountains. They were first found breeding in coastal areas in Marin County in 1960 (Shuford 1993ff), and are now found breeding irregularly in the Santa Cruz Mountains. The cause of this range expansion is unclear.

Pine Siskin (*decrease*). Analysis of BBS data shows that Pine Siskins have been decreasing over wide areas of western North America in recent decades (Dawson 1997). In California, analysis of BBS data shows a decline of 6.8% per year from 1966 to 2004 (Sauer et al. 2005). Analysis of Palo Alto SBC data shows a local decline of 15% per year, and there has been a significant contraction of this species' range in the Santa Cruz Mountains over the last 10 to 15 years (David L. Suddjian, pers. comm.).

Lesser Goldfinch (*stable, variable, or uncertain*). Both Van Denburgh (1899b) and Fisher (1902) considered this goldfinch to be abundant in Santa Clara County, and it remains common and widespread today. But analysis of the Palo Alto and San Jose CBC data shows declines of 4.4 and 5.1% per year, respectively, over the last half century.

Lawrence's Goldfinch (*stable, variable, or uncertain*). All of the early observers noted the erratic occurrence of this nomadic goldfinch, and none thought it common (Price 1988e, Van Denburgh 1899b, Fisher 1902, Grinnell and Wythe 1927). Today, it breeds regularly in the Diablo Range, where it is nonetheless uncommon, and numbers vary from year to year. There are periodic incursions into the Santa Cruz Mountains, where it is rare.

American Goldfinch (*increase*). Van Denburgh (1899b) noted that this goldfinch was resident in Palo Alto, but that it appeared in Los Gatos only in the winter. Observers generally noted the species' affinity for wetter areas with willows, alders, and cottonwoods. Since 1981, this species has increased significantly in numbers, analysis of the Palo Alto SBC data showing a 16% per year increase.

House Sparrow (*decrease*). Introduced from Europe in the nineteenth century, this sparrow reached its peak populations in North America early in the twentieth century and has been in decline ever since (Lowther and Cink 1992). Analysis of the Palo Alto and San Jose CBC data shows a decline of 5.7 and 5.9% per year, respectively, over the last half century. The species is nonetheless still common in the county's urban areas.

Appendix 4:
Breeding Season Windows for Selected Species

The difficulty an atlaser faces upon encountering a bird, regardless of whether it is singing or not, is determining whether this bird is in nesting habitat during its breeding season, or is a migrating bird that breeds farther north, or is a local bird wintering away from its nesting habitat. As discussed in Chapter 5, the Review Committee used breeding season windows, or safe dates, in a few cases, as a means of discriminating against records that were possibly wintering birds or migrants as opposed to breeding birds. These breeding season windows or safe dates have some value in the application of the possible and probable breeding codes, but do not apply to any of the confirmed codes. For example, the definition of the "X" possible code is "Singing male present in suitable nesting habitat during its breeding season." Similarly, the definition of the "S" probable breeding code is "Permanent territory presumed through song at same location on at least two occasions 7 days or more apart."

A significant difficulty with the use of safe dates is that individuals of many species that are summer residents in Santa Clara County may arrive quite early on their breeding territories here, yet cannot be distinguished from later migrants on their way to Alaska or Canada. Nonetheless, the committee did establish safe dates for 23 species, and these are listed in Table A4.1. The columns shown to the right of the safe dates are the earliest and latest dates of known breeding in the county obtained during the atlas period, each pair based on all codes except used nest (UN). These dates lie mostly within the safe dates, but not always. Breeding evidence for four species in Table A4.1—Peregrine Falcon, Virginia Rail, Sora, and Least Tern—was not obtained during the atlas period (1987 to 1993), and therefore no "Known Dates" are listed.

In a number of cases, additional data obtained during the postatlas period, from 1994 to 2005, showed that these safe dates were often conservative, which is their purpose. This was particularly the case for Double-crested Cormorant (breeding records from 8 Apr to 26 Sep), Great Egret (9 Mar to 14 Oct), and Snowy Egret (24 Mar to 13 Sep). The use of safe dates and

the guesswork this process entails will likely result in errors, both in excluding legitimate breeding evidence and in treating evidence based on nonbreeding birds as legitimate. In the larger sense, the reader of this atlas needs to be cautious in interpreting possible and probable evidence for some species, because of the uncertainty in separating breeding from nonbreeding birds.

Table A4.1. Atlas safe dates for breeding, for selected species.

Species	Safe Dates		Known Dates	
Double-crested Cormorant	1 May	10 Aug	5 Jun	2 Aug
Great Egret	20 Apr	10 Aug	4 May	7 Aug
Snowy Egret	20 Apr	10 Aug	4 May	7 Aug
Black-crowned Night-Heron	10 Apr	10 Aug	6 Mar	9 Sep
Northern Harrier	10 Apr	31 Jul	27 Mar	23 Aug
Sharp-shinned Hawk	20 Apr	15 Aug	9 Jun	18 Jul
Cooper's Hawk	1 May	15 Aug	10 Mar	4 Aug
Peregrine Falcon	15 May	10 Jul	–	–
Prairie Falcon	25 Apr	31 Jul	18 Apr	27 Jul
Virginia Rail	20 May	31 Jul	–	–
Sora	20 May	31 Jul	–	–
American Coot	1 May	31 Jul	20 Mar	9 Sep
Killdeer	1 Apr	31 Jul	30 Mar	31 Jul
Spotted Sandpiper	23 May	18 Jul	13 Jun	27 Jul
California Gull	1 May	31 Jul	26 Mar	15 Aug
Western Gull	1 May	31 Jul	2 Jun	8 Jun
Caspian Tern	1 May	31 Jul	14 May	7 Jun
Forster's Tern	1 May	31 Jul	14 May	27 Jul
Least Tern	1 Jun	30 Jun	–	–
Band-tailed Pigeon	25 Mar	31 Jul	21 Mar	21 Jul
Northern Pygmy-Owl	1 Feb	31 Aug	10 Jun	11 Jul
Vaux's Swift	20 May	31 Jul	28 Jun	11 Jul
Northern Flicker	10 Apr	31 Jul	21 Apr	4 Aug

Appendix 5:
Estimates of Abundance of County Breeding Species

Two measures of a species' abundance in Santa Clara County were used during the atlas period, as described in Chapter 5. The first method derived a population estimate from abundance codes reported on Field Cards. (Forty-two percent of all confirmations included an abundance code.) For each species and each block, an average abundance code was calculated over the atlas period. Then, for each species, an average abundance code was calculated over all blocks in which an abundance code had been provided. Next, the average abundance code was then converted to a central estimate of the number of birds in these blocks (see Table 5.2 in Chapter 5). These numbers were then multiplied by the total number of blocks in the county where either confirmed, probable, or possible breeding evidence had been obtained. That final figure was taken to represent the best estimate of the species' population in Santa Clara County. Upper and lower bounds were also computed, to show the uncertainty in this population estimate.

The second method was to count all nonduplicate confirmations obtained during the atlas period. Under the protocols, atlasers were encouraged to include all confirmations that they observed in each block, even when a species had previously been confirmed in that block. Duplicate confirmations were identified by the coordinates provided by atlasers. If multiple confirmations, whether of nest building, incubation on a nest, of a nest with young, or a fledgling at the nest, were obtained at a single coordinate location, only one of these confirmations was included in the tally of nonduplicate confirmations. Two-thirds of all confirmations recorded included coordinates, which allowed the majority of duplicate confirmations to be identified and removed from the tally. The remaining one-third of all confirmations, those that did not include coordinates, were assumed to be nonduplicates, but in fact a few of these confirmations may have been duplicates. This second method is not a direct estimate of the numbers of birds breeding in the county, as the first method provides, but rather a population index.

The 159 species confirmed breeding in Santa Clara County during the atlas period are listed in Table A5.1. For each species the estimated abundance is shown along with its rank order in columns two through five, and the abundance index for each species (based on nonduplicate confirmations) with its rank order is given in the last two columns.

The estimates and indexes shown in Table A5.1 necessarily entail a number of inaccuracies. On an absolute basis, these estimates are undoubtedly low for many secretive or nocturnal species, including some of the rails, the owls, and Common Poorwill. By contrast, many colonial species were likely underestimated, since often only a few confirmations were included in the database for each colony. It is also likely that many of the rarer species were underestimated. This is caused, in part, because their rarity means they are easily missed. In addition, when a species is recorded in only a few blocks, the average abundance is more sensitive to atlasers' guesses at an abundance code. Another source of inaccuracy may occur for rapidly changing populations. In these cases, the abundance estimates are biased, depending upon whether they were made early in the atlas period or toward the end. As an example, Red-shouldered Hawks have been increasing in numbers and expanding their breeding range over the last 30 years, and the numbers in Table A5.1 are certainly an underestimate of their present status. Pine Siskin is an example of a declining species, and as of 2005 it is uncertain whether there are any breeding birds remaining in the county.

The relative accuracy of the two estimates is also variable. Overall, as shown in Chapter 6, the correlation ($r^2 = 0.78$) between the log of abundance and the log of nonduplicate COs is fairly high, but the level of detectability of some species influences both methods of estimating abundance. For instance, Wrentits are readily detected by their song, and it is likely that atlasers made a reasonable estimate of their abundance, but they are a difficult species to confirm breeding. As a result, the rank of Wrentit using the abundance code is 15, whereas the rank using nonduplicate confirmations is 50.

Table A5.1. Two estimates of abundance: direct population estimate with lower and upper bounds, including rank of central estimate; and index of abundance, from number of nonduplicate COs and rank.

Species	Abundance Estimate				Nonduplicate COs	
	Central	Lower	Upper	Rank	No.	Rank
Canada Goose	59	45	77	132	50	70
Wood Duck	271	176	416	106	69	62
Gadwall	232	104	520	108	83	54
Mallard	1,167	535	2,543	67	245	17

Table A5.1. Two estimates of abundance: direct population estimate with lower and upper bounds, including rank of central estimate; and index of abundance, from number of nonduplicate COs and rank. (*continued.*)

Species	Abundance Estimate				Nonduplicate COs	
	Central	Lower	Upper	Rank	No.	Rank
Cinnamon Teal	162	76	346	118	25	100
Northern Shoveler	31	23	42	141	6	133
Northern Pintail	61	37	101	131	19	108
Canvasback	10	10	10	149	1	155
Lesser Scaup	36	18	73	139	23	103
Common Merganser	109	73	164	125	21	107
Ruddy Duck	186	85	403	115	23	104
Ring-necked Pheasant	181	92	354	117	11	119
Wild Turkey	396	187	840	93	29	90
Mountain Quail	17	8	40	144	1	156
California Quail	17,511	5,749	53,332	10	305	11
Pied-billed Grebe	359	204	631	98	98	46
Eared Grebe	13	5	31	146	6	130
Western Grebe	12	6	22	148	6	131
Clark's Grebe	8	5	12	151	1	154
Double-crested Cormorant	8	4	20	152	4	138
Great Blue Heron	49	33	73	137	25	99
Great Egret	17	8	40	143	4	139
Snowy Egret	132	43	399	123	6	132
Little Blue Heron	4	4	4	158	3	143
Cattle Egret	16	6	39	145	3	144
Green Heron	294	189	456	103	24	102
Black-crowned Night-Heron	132	43	399	121	4	140
White-faced Ibis	8	4	20	153	2	151
Turkey Vulture	74	34	159	128	5	137
White-tailed Kite	262	172	400	107	45	73
Northern Harrier	73	58	92	130	16	112
Sharp-shinned Hawk	105	89	123	126	6	134
Cooper's Hawk	350	231	529	99	38	76
Red-shouldered Hawk	274	189	396	105	54	68
Red-tailed Hawk	1,211	588	2,493	66	152	35
Golden Eagle	473	309	725	88	23	105
American Kestrel	1,227	565	2,664	65	130	40
Prairie Falcon	53	47	61	135	10	122
Clapper Rail	12	12	12	147	3	145
Common Moorhen	73	45	119	129	38	77
American Coot	617	271	1,402	82	183	29
Snowy Plover	397	131	1,199	92	8	126
Killdeer	1,475	638	3,409	55	163	33
Black-necked Stilt	227	91	569	109	72	60
American Avocet	214	84	547	112	93	48
Spotted Sandpiper	49	37	64	138	4	141
California Gull	132	43	399	122	10	123
Western Gull	4	4	4	159	2	152

Table A5.1. Two estimates of abundance: direct population estimate with lower and upper bounds, including rank of central estimate; and index of abundance, from number of nonduplicate COs and rank. (*continued.*)

Species	Abundance Estimate				Nonduplicate COs	
	Central	Lower	Upper	Rank	No.	Rank
Caspian Tern	635	201	1,999	81	6	135
Forster's Tern	1,232	399	3,794	64	33	85
Rock Pigeon	8,477	2,789	25,764	25	82	55
Band-tailed Pigeon	1,778	686	4,616	52	27	93
Mourning Dove	23,846	7,791	72,982	4	268	16
Barn Owl	364	191	694	97	28	94
Western Screech-Owl	3,767	1,355	10,519	42	45	74
Great Horned Owl	912	433	1,920	73	56	67
Northern Pygmy-Owl	148	84	260	119	3	146
Burrowing Owl	223	96	516	110	49	72
Long-eared Owl	6	6	6	156	3	147
Northern Saw-whet Owl	1,021	361	2,902	72	7	128
Common Poorwill	412	181	938	91	3	148
Vaux's Swift	125	56	280	124	3	149
White-throated Swift	701	303	1625	78	23	106
Black-chinned Hummingbird	53	24	120	134	8	127
Anna's Hummingbird	17,035	5,601	51,806	11	145	38
Allen's Hummingbird	1,407	535	3,712	58	25	101
Belted Kingfisher	212	177	253	113	35	81
Lewis's Woodpecker	89	40	200	127	11	120
Acorn Woodpecker	10,222	3,382	30,889	21	179	30
Nuttall's Woodpecker	5,893	2,123	16,435	30	226	20
Downy Woodpecker	1,241	547	2,815	63	71	61
Hairy Woodpecker	1,431	593	3,460	57	79	56
Northern Flicker	2,892	1,136	7,384	47	78	58
Olive-sided Flycatcher	1,435	551	3,746	56	37	79
Western Wood-Pewee	4,517	1,653	12,396	38	110	43
Pacific-slope Flycatcher	4,224	1,564	11,452	39	89	51
Black Phoebe	2,995	1,200	7,493	46	354	6
Say's Phoebe	36	26	50	140	6	136
Ash-throated Flycatcher	9,938	3,291	30,002	22	206	26
Western Kingbird	1,042	450	2,409	69	106	45
Loggerhead Shrike	572	256	1,280	84	79	57
Cassin's Vireo	1,917	752	4,897	50	72	59
Hutton's Vireo	3,139	1,181	8,369	45	59	65
Warbling Vireo	5,911	2,098	16,735	29	126	41
Steller's Jay	11,001	3,628	33,357	17	219	23
Western Scrub-Jay	26,829	8,746	82,293	2	478	2
Yellow-billed Magpie	1,809	715	4,587	51	141	39
American Crow	1,362	598	3,102	61	117	42
Common Raven	436	235	811	90	28	95
Horned Lark	1,063	407	2,786	68	29	91
Purple Martin	21	14	31	142	1	157
Tree Swallow	472	209	1,066	89	29	92

ESTIMATES OF ABUNDANCE

Table A5.1. Two estimates of abundance: direct population estimate with lower and upper bounds, including rank of central estimate; and index of abundance, from number of nonduplicate COs and rank. (*continued.*)

Species	Abundance Estimate				Nonduplicate COs	
	Central	Lower	Upper	Rank	No.	Rank
Violet-green Swallow	5,692	2,036	15,988	31	109	44
Nor. Rough-winged Swallow	742	344	1,597	77	58	66
Cliff Swallow	9,563	3,160	28,938	23	219	22
Barn Swallow	3,264	1,218	8,777	44	151	36
Chestnut-backed Chickadee	15,190	4,983	46,300	13	279	14
Oak Titmouse	17,645	5,788	53,788	9	352	7
Bushtit	19,177	6,291	58,450	7	396	5
Red-breasted Nuthatch	381	144	1,006	95	16	113
White-breasted Nuthatch	7,938	2,653	23,897	26	148	37
Pygmy Nuthatch	520	199	1,365	86	28	96
Brown Creeper	3,377	1,206	9,501	43	69	63
Rock Wren	339	152	760	100	32	87
Canyon Wren	286	128	640	104	26	98
Bewick's Wren	16,046	5,277	48,783	12	193	28
House Wren	5,222	1,842	14,881	32	223	21
Winter Wren	562	212	1,491	85	14	118
Marsh Wren	482	173	1,349	87	15	114
American Dipper	51	30	84	136	9	124
Golden-crowned Kinglet	6	6	6	154	1	153
Blue-gray Gnatcatcher	4,077	1,477	11,303	41	95	47
Western Bluebird	7,428	2,528	21,957	27	294	13
Swainson's Thrush	1,333	502	3,554	62	18	110
Hermit Thrush	181	76	433	116	14	115
American Robin	10,274	3,405	30,992	20	342	9
Wrentit	13,725	4,516	41,714	15	90	50
Northern Mockingbird	6,679	2,206	20,218	28	215	24
California Thrasher	4,122	1,527	11,171	40	88	52
European Starling	21,415	7,002	65,494	6	587	1
Phainopepla	205	92	460	114	15	116
Orange-crowned Warbler	10,465	3,457	31,679	19	160	34
Yellow Warbler	699	297	1,643	79	38	78
Yellow-rumped Warbler	309	116	820	101	11	121
Black-throated Gray Warbler	797	327	1,942	76	33	86
Hermit Warbler	10	10	10	150	3	150
MacGillivray's Warbler	6	6	6	157	1	158
Common Yellowthroat	217	100	468	111	15	117
Wilson's Warbler	1,617	592	4,437	53	34	83
Yellow-breasted Chat	54	36	82	133	9	125
Western Tanager	883	355	2,199	74	34	84
Spotted Towhee	22,960	7,496	70,320	5	244	19
California Towhee	35,457	11,497	109,346	1	397	4
Rufous-crowned Sparrow	869	365	2,075	75	40	75
Chipping Sparrow	1,026	421	2,505	71	35	82
Black-chinned Sparrow	583	216	1,581	83	4	142

APPENDIX FIVE

Table A5.1. Two estimates of abundance: direct population estimate with lower and upper bounds, including rank of central estimate; and index of abundance, from number of nonduplicate COs and rank. (*concluded.*)

Species	Abundance Estimate				Nonduplicate COs	
	Central	Lower	Upper	Rank	No.	Rank
Lark Sparrow	4,958	1,736	14,231	35	167	31
Sage Sparrow	1,039	385	2,817	70	27	97
Savannah Sparrow	135	73	247	120	18	111
Grasshopper Sparrow	1,394	516	3,778	59	37	80
Song Sparrow	5,172	1,797	14,961	33	167	32
Dark-eyed Junco	14,622	4,804	44,504	14	347	8
Black-headed Grosbeak	10,628	3,521	32,081	18	279	15
Lazuli Bunting	2,047	793	5,298	49	63	64
Indigo Bunting	6	6	6	155	1	159
Red-winged Blackbird	381	144	1,006	96	245	18
Tricolored Blackbird	1,539	530	4,490	54	32	88
Western Meadowlark	4,940	1,738	14,111	36	86	53
Brewer's Blackbird	13,718	4,522	41,612	16	398	3
Brown-headed Cowbird	5,093	1,835	14,199	34	91	49
Hooded Oriole	387	169	882	94	54	69
Bullock's Oriole	4,590	1,708	12,381	37	305	12
Purple Finch	2,841	1,070	7,572	48	49	71
House Finch	24,958	8,143	76,495	3	339	10
Pine Siskin	299	127	704	102	7	129
Lesser Goldfinch	19,141	6,277	58,366	8	214	25
Lawrence's Goldfinch	1,363	529	3,520	60	30	89
American Goldfinch	683	266	1,757	80	18	109
House Sparrow	8,639	2,843	26,249	24	195	27

498

Appendix 6:
Mammal, Amphibian, Fish, Invertebrate, and Plant Names

Sara Timby and William G. Bousman

In this atlas, references to animals and plants use their common names. The currently recognized scientific names for birds and often their subspecies are included in the species accounts for the current breeding avifauna in Santa Clara County and in Appendixes 8 and 9 for birds not considered part of the current breeding avifauna. The scientific names of mammals, fishes, amphibians, invertebrates, and plants mentioned by their common names in the text are listed in this appendix, along with alternative common names where they occur. Within each group, names are listed alphabetically by common name.

The taxonomic source we have drawn upon for the common and scientific names of vertebrates and invertebrates is the Integrated Taxonomic Information System (ITIS) database (http://www.itis.gov/). For the native plant botanical names, we have drawn upon the names in Hickman, J. C., ed, 1993. *The Jepson Manual: Higher Plants of California*. Univ. Calif. Press, Berkeley.

Mammals

Common Name	Scientific Name	Family	Other Common Names
American shrew-mole	*Neurotrichus gibbsii*	*Talpidae*	shrew-mole
beaver	*Castor canadensis*	*Castoridae*	
black-tailed jackrabbit	*Lepus californicus*	*Leporidae*	
brush rabbit	*Sylvilagus bachmani*	*Leporidae*	
California ground squirrel	*Spermophilus beecheyi*	*Sciuridae*	
California vole	*Microtus californicus*	*Muridae*	
coyote	*Canis latrans*	*Canidae*	
desert cottontail	*Sylvilagus audubonii*	*Leporidae*	
dusky-footed woodrat	*Neotoma fuscipes*	*Muridae*	
elk	*Cervus elaphus*	*Cervidae*	tule elk
grizzly bear	*Ursus arctos*	*Ursidae*	
mule deer	*Odocoileus hemionus*	*Cervidae*	blacktail deer
Norway rat	*Rattus norvegicus*	*Muridae*	brown rat, house rat
prairie dog spp.	*Cynomys* spp.	*Sciuridae*	
pronghorn	*Antilocapra americana*	*Antilocapridae*	antelope
red fox	*Vulpes vulpes*	*Canidae*	
river otter	*Lontra canadensis*	*Mustelidae*	
ringtail	*Bassariscus astutus*	*Procyonidae*	
salt marsh harvest mouse	*Reithrodontomys raviventris*	*Muridae*	
sea otter	*Enhydra lutris*	*Mustelidae*	
striped skunk	*Mephitis mephitis*	*Mephitidae*	
western gray squirrel	*Sciurus griseus*	*Sciuridae*	

Amphibians

Common Name	Scientific Name	Family	Other Common Names
American bullfrog	*Rana catesbeiana*	*Ranidae*	bullfrog

Fishes

Common Name	Scientific Name	Family	Other Common Names
largemouth bass	*Micropterus salmoides*	*Centrarchidae*	large mouthed bass
salmon spp.	*Oncorhynchus* spp.	*Salmonidae*	
steelhead	*Oncorhynchus mykiss*	*Salmonidae*	

APPENDIX SIX

Fish (continued)

Common Name	Scientific Name	Family	Other Common Names
striped bass	*Morone saxatilis*	*Moronidae*	

Invertebrates

Common Name	Scientific Name	Family	Other Common Names
Atlantic oyster drill	*Urosalpinx cinerea*	*Muricidae*	
bay checkerspot butterfly	*Euphydryas editha bayensis*	*Nymphalidae*	
Douglas-fir beetle	*Dendroctonus pseudotsugae*	*Curculionidae*	
eastern oyster	*Crassostrea virginica*	*Ostreidae*	
Olympia oyster	*Ostrea lurida*	*Ostreidae*	
Pacific oyster	*Crassostrea gigas*	*Ostreidae*	Japanese oyster
red swamp crawfish	*Procambarus clarkii*	*Cambaridae*	red swamp crayfish
ribbed mussel	*Geukensia demissa*	*Mytilidae*	horse mussel
vernal pool fairy shrimp	*Branchinecta lynchi*	*Branchinectidae*	fairy shrimp
vernal pool tadpole shrimp	*Lepidurus packardi*	*Triopsidae*	tadpole shrimp

Plants

Common Name	Scientific Name	Family	Other Common Names
alder spp.	*Alnus* spp.	*Betulaceae*	
alkali bulrush	*Scirpus maritimus*	*Cyperaceae*	cosmopolitan bulrush
alkali heath	*Frankenia salina*	*Frankeniaceae*	alkali seaheath
American elm	*Ulmus americana*	*Ulmaceae*	
arrow grass	*Triglochin concinna*	*Juncaginaceae*	arrow-grass
arroyo willow	*Salix lasiolepis*	*Salicaceae*	
Australian pine	*Casuarina equisetifolia*	*Casuarinaceae*	beach sheoak, common ironwood
barley	*Hordeum* spp.	*Poaceae*	
barnyard grass	*Echinochloa grus-galli*	*Poaceae*	
bedstraw	*Galium aparine*	*Rubiaceae*	goose grass
big squirreltail	*Elymus multisetus*	*Poaceae*	
bigleaf maple	*Acer macrophyllum*	*Aceraceae*	
Bishop pine	*Pinus muricata*	*Pinaceae*	
black cottonwood	*Populus balsamifera*	*Salicaceae*	balsam poplar
black mustard	*Brassica nigra*	*Brassicaceae*	wild mustard
black oak	*Quercus kelloggii*	*Fagaceae*	California black oak
black sage	*Salvia mellifera*	*Lamiaceae*	
black walnut	*Juglans nigra*	*Juglandaceae*	
blackberry spp.	*Rubus* spp.	*Rosaceae*	
blazing star	*Mentzelia laevicaulis*	*Loasaceae*	smoothstem blazingstar
blue elderberry	*Sambucus mexicana*	*Caprifoliaceae*	Mexican elderberry
blue oak	*Quercus douglasii*	*Fagaceae*	
bluegum eucalyptus	*Eucalyptus globulus*	*Myrtaceae*	blue gum
box elder	*Acer negundo*	*Aceraceae*	
buck brush	*Ceanothus cuneatus*	*Rhamnaceae*	
buckwheat	*Eriogonum* spp.	*Polygonaceae*	
bulrush spp.	*Scirpus* spp.	*Cyperaceae*	tule
bur clover	*Medicago polymorpha*	*Fabaceae*	burclover
buttercup	*Ranunculus* spp.	*Ranunculaceae*	
California bay	*Umbellularia californica*	*Lauraceae*	California laurel, bay laurel
California brickellbush	*Brickellia californica*	*Asteraceae*	
California buckeye	*Aesculus californica*	*Hippocastanaceae*	
California buckwheat	*Eriogonum fasciculatum*	*Polygonaceae*	flat-top
California bulrush	*Scirpus californicus*	*Cyperaceae*	tule
California cord grass	*Spartina foliosa*	*Poaceae*	cord grass
California fan palm	*Washingtonia filifera*	*Arecaceae*	California washingtonia

Plants (continued)

Common Name	Scientific Name	Family	Other Common Names
California oatgrass	*Danthonia californica*	*Poaceae*	
California plantain	*Plantago erecta*	*Plantaginaceae*	
California poppy	*Eschscholzia californica*	*Papaveraceae*	California goldenpoppy
California sagebrush	*Artemisia californica*	*Asteraceae*	coast sage, California sage
Canary Island date palm	*Phoenix canariensis*	*Arecaceae*	
canyon live oak	*Quercus chrysolepis*	*Fagaceae*	golden cup oak
casuarina spp.	*Casuarina* spp.	*Casuarinaceae*	
cattail spp.	*Typha* spp.	*Typhaceae*	
ceanothus spp.	*Ceanothus* spp.	*Rhamnaceae*	wild lilac
chamise	*Adenostoma fasciculatum*	*Rosaceae*	greasewood
chaparral pea	*Pickeringia montana*	*Fabaceae*	
charlock	*Sinapis arvensis*	*Brassicaceae*	wild mustard
chinquapin	*Chrysolepis chrysophylla* var. *minor*	*Fagaceae*	
coast live oak	*Quercus agrifolia*	*Fagaceae*	California live oak
coast redwood	*Sequoia sempervirens*	*Taxodiaceae*	redwood
coastal wood fern	*Dryopteris arguta*	*Dryopteridaceae*	
coffeeberry	*Rhamnus californica*	*Rhamnaceae*	coffee berry
common chickweed	*Stellaria media*	*Caryophyllaceae*	
common spikeweed	*Hemizonia pungens*	*Asteraceae*	common tarweed, spikeweed
cottonwood spp.	*Populus* spp.	*Salicaceae*	
Coulter pine	*Pinus coulteri*	*Pinaceae*	
coyotebrush	*Baccharis pilularis*	*Asteraceae*	coyote bush
curly dock	*Rumex crispus*	*Polygonaceae*	dock
currant spp.	*Ribes* spp.	*Saxifragaceae*	gooseberry spp.
cypress spp.	*Cupressus* spp.	*Cupressaceae*	
deerweed	*Lotus scoparius*	*Fabaceae*	common deerweed
dogwood spp.	*Cornus* spp.	*Cornaceae*	
Douglas fir	*Pseudotsuga menziesii*	*Pinaceae*	
Douglas groundsel	*Senecio flaccidus* var. *douglasii*	*Asteraceae*	shrubby butterweed
Douglas iris	*Iris douglasiana*	*Iridaceae*	
dove weed	*Eremocarpus setigerus*	*Euphorbiaceae*	turkey mullein
duckweed	*Lemna* spp.	*Lemnaceae*	common duckweed
elderberry spp.	*Sambucus* spp.	*Caprifoliaceae*	
elm spp.	*Ulmus* spp.	*Ulmaceae*	
English ivy	*Hedera helix*	*Araliaceae*	
English plantain	*Plantago lanceolata*	*Plantaginaceae*	
English walnut	*Juglans regia*	*Juglandaceae*	
eucalyptus spp.	*Eucalyptus* spp.	*Myrtle*	
fan palm spp.	*Washingtonia* spp.	*Arecaceae*	
fathen	*Atriplex patula*	*Chenopodiaceae*	fat-hen, spear scale
filaree	*Erodium cicutarium*	*Geraniaceae*	storksbill, red-stem filaree
filaree spp.	*Erodium* spp.	*Geraniaceae*	
flat-faced downingia	*Downingia pulchella*	*Campanulaceae*	flatfaced calicoflower
foothill pine	*Pinus sabiniana*	*Pinaceae*	gray pine, digger pine
foxtail fescue	*Vulpia myuros* var. *hirsuta*	*Poaceae*	
Fremont cottonwood	*Populus fremontii*	*Salicaceae*	
giant reed	*Arundo donax*	*Poaceae*	
goldfields	*Lasthenia californica*	*Asteraceae*	California goldfields
green dracaena	*Cordyline australis*	*Liliaceae*	
gum plant	*Grindelia hirsutula*	*Asteraceae*	gum weed, marsh gum plant
hardstem bulrush	*Scirpus acutus*	*Cyperaceae*	tule
hazelnut	*Corylus cornuta* var. *californica*	*Betulaceae*	California hazelnut
hedge parsley	*Torilis arvensis*	*Apiaceae*	
hoary nettle	*Urtica dioica* ssp. *holosericea*	*Urticaceae*	

Plants (continued)

Common Name	Scientific Name	Family	Other Common Names
hollyleaf cherry	*Prunus ilicifolia*	*Rosaceae*	
honeysuckle	*Lonicera hispidula*	*Caprifoliaceae*	
huckleberry	*Vaccinium* spp.	*Ericaceae*	
interior live oak	*Quercus wislizenii*	*Fagaceae*	
Italian ryegrass	*Lolium multiflorum*	*Poaceae*	
juniper spp.	*Juniperus* spp.	*Cupressaceae*	
knobcone pine	*Pinus attenuata*	*Pinaceae*	
leather oak	*Quercus durata*	*Fagaceae*	
limber pine	*Pinus flexilis*	*Pinaceae*	
lupine spp.	*Lupinus* spp.	*Fabaceae*	
madrone	*Arbutus menziesii*	*Ericaceae*	Pacific madrone
manzanita spp.	*Arctostaphylos* spp.	*Ericaceae*	
Mexican fan palm	*Washingtonia robusta*	*Arecaceae*	Washington fan palm
miner's lettuce	*Claytonia perfoliata*	*Portulacaceae*	
monkey puzzle tree	*Araucaria araucana*	*Araucariaceae*	
Monterey cypress	*Cupressus macrocarpa*	*Cupressaceae*	
Monterey pine	*Pinus radiata*	*Pinaceae*	
mountain mahogany	*Cercocarpus betuloides*	*Rosaceae*	
mouse barley	*Hordeum murinum* var. *leporinum*	*Poaceae*	farmer's foxtail
mule-fat	*Baccharis salicifolia*	*Asteraceae*	mule's fat
myoporum	*Myoporum laetum*	*Myoporaceae*	ngaio tree
narrow-leaved willow	*Salix exigua*	*Salicaceae*	
nitgrass	*Gastridium ventricosum*	*Poaceae*	
northern catalpa	*Catalpa speciosa*	*Bignoniaceae*	western catalpa
Oregon false goldenaster	*Heterotheca oregona*	*Asteraceae*	
owl's clover	*Castilleja densiflora*	*Scrophulariaceae*	owl's-clover
peppergrass	*Lepidium latifolium*	*Brassicaceae*	
pepper tree	*Schinus molle*	*Anacardiaceae*	American peppertree, California peppertree
pickleweed	*Salicornia virginica*	*Chenopodiaceae*	common pickleweed, saltwort
pineapple guava	*Feijoa sellowiana*	*Myrtaceae*	feijoa
pinyon pine	*Pinus monophylla*	*Pinaceae*	
poison hemlock	*Conium maculatum*	*Apiaceae*	
poison oak	*Toxicodendron diversilobum*	*Anacardiaceae*	
ponderosa pine	*Pinus ponderosa*	*Pinaceae*	yellow pine
prickly sowthistle	*Sonchus asper*	*Asteraceae*	
purple needlegrass	*Nassella pulchra*	*Poaceae*	purple stipa, purple tussockgrass
red berry	*Rhamnus crocea*	*Rhamnaceae*	buck brush
red brome	*Bromus madritensis* ssp. *rubens*	*Poaceae*	
red willow	*Salix laevigata*	*Salicaceae*	
redwood oxalis	*Oxalis oregana*	*Oxalidaceae*	redwood-sorrel
ripgut brome	*Bromus diandrus*	*Poaceae*	
saltbush	*Atriplex* spp.	*Chenopodiaceae*	
saltgrass	*Distichlis spicata*	*Poaceae*	salt grass
saltmarsh dodder	*Cuscuta salina*	*Cuscutaceae*	dodder, goldenthread
scalebroom	*Lepidospartum squamatum*	*Asteraceae*	
Scouler willow	*Salix scouleriana*	*Salicaceae*	
scrub oak	*Quercus berberidifolia*	*Fagaceae*	
sedge	*Carex* spp.	*Cyperaceae*	
shining willow	*Salix lucida* ssp. *lasiandra*	*Salicaceae*	Pacific willow
silktassel	*Garrya* spp.	*Garryaceae*	
silver hairgrass	*Aira caryophyllea*	*Poaceae*	
snowberry	*Symphoricarpos* spp.	*Caprifoliaceae*	
soft chess	*Bromus hordeaceus*	*Poaceae*	soft brome
Spanish brome	*Bromus madritensis*	*Poaceae*	

Plants (continued)

Common Name	Scientific Name	Family	Other Common Names
spikerush spp	*Eleocharis* spp	*Cyperaceae*	
sticky monkeyflower	*Mimulus aurantiacus*	*Scrophulariaceae*	
sword fern	*Polystichum munitum*	*Dryopteridaceae*	
tan oak	*Lithocarpus densiflora*	*Fagaceae*	tanbark oak
tarweed	*Madia* spp., *Hemizonia* spp.	*Asteraceae*	
thimbleberry	*Rubus parviflorus*	*Rosaceae*	
tidytips	*Layia platyglossa*	*Asteraceae*	tidy tips
toyon	*Heteromeles arbutifolia*	*Rosaceae*	Christmas berry
tree tobacco	*Nicotiana glauca*	*Solanaceae*	
trillium	*Trillium* spp.	*Liliaceae*	wakerobin
valley oak	*Quercus lobata*	*Fagaceae*	California white oak
western dwarf mistletoe	*Arceuthobium campylopodum*	*Viscaceae*	mistletoe
western sycamore	*Platanus racemosa*	*Platanaceae*	California sycamore, sycamore
white alder	*Alnus rhombifolia*	*Betulaceae*	
wild mustard	*Brassica* spp.	*Brassicaceae*	
wild oats	*Avena* spp.	*Poaceae*	flaxgrass, oatgrass, wheat oats
wild radish spp.	*Raphanus* spp.	*Brassicaceae*	
willow spp.	*Salix* spp.	*Salicaceae*	
windmill palm	*Trachycarpus fortunei*	*Arecaceae*	fortune palm
yellow star-thistle	*Centaurea solstitialis*	*Asteraceae*	star thistle
yerba santa	*Eriodictyon californicum*	*Hydrophyllaceae*	

Appendix 7:
Local Place Names No Longer in Use

A number of locations in Santa Clara County and nearby areas have undergone name changes over the last 150 years, and the purpose of this appendix is to list and identify archaic place names that appear in the ornithological or natural history literature. In general, the historical paragraphs in the species accounts use place names from the original literature, and where these names are no longer in use this appendix offers their modern equivalents.

Alma. A town above Los Gatos that was flooded after construction of Lexington Reservoir

Alvarado. Now Union City, Alameda County. Originally called New Haven for the city of the same name in Connecticut, it was made the seat of the new county of Alameda in 1853. Later in the year, the name was changed to Alvarado to honor Juan B. Alvarado, governor of California from 1836 to 1842 (Gudde 1998). The town was built on Alameda Creek adjacent to the salt marsh, as shown on the 1899 and 1942 Hayward 15′ topographic maps. It is shown as Union City on the 1959 Hayward 15′ topographic map.

Arroyo Quito. Also known as Campbell Creek after William Campbell, who built a sawmill along the creek in 1846, and as Big Moody Creek and Saratoga Creek (Gudde 1998). It is shown as Campbell Creek on the 1899 and 1940 Palo Alto 15′ topographic maps. It was officially named Saratoga Creek in 1954 (Gudde 1998). Quito refers to a local land grant, which may be from Spanish or a local Indian name (Gudde 1998).

Artesian Slough. A small slough between salt ponds A16 and A17 on the west and A18 on the east that joins Coyote Slough to the north. The slough is also called Mallard Slough and the names appear interchangeable. It now carries the effluent from the San Jose-Santa Clara Water Pollution Control Plant.

Berryessa. The 1899 San Jose 15′ topographic map shows Berryessa as a named crossroads where Capitol Avenue and Berryessa Road meet today. This is about 2.5 km south of where the map shows Berryessa Creek emerging from the hills north of Alum Rock Park and disappearing into the alluvial soil of the valley floor. Rollo H. Beck lived in Berryessa in the late nineteenth century, and many of his specimens and the egg sets he collected are labeled "Berryessa." Nicolás Berryessa obtained a land grant in the Milpitas area in 1834 that included the creek, the town, and the adjacent salt marsh (Gudde 1998). Some of the Berryessa descendants still lived in the area when Beck was growing up (Murphy 1936).

Bloomfield Ranch. About Great Blue Herons, Sibley (1952) wrote "Colony of 60 pairs formerly at Bloomfield Ranch, 3 miles south of Gilroy, now gone." The Thompson and West at-las (1876) shows a Bloomfield Ranch near the present intersection of Highways 101 and 25. Today, you can still see a faded "Bloomfield Ranch" painted on the roof of an outbuilding just off Highway 101 south of there.

College Park. The 1899 San Jose 15′ topographic map shows College Park as a town across the Guadalupe River from San Jose. It was about halfway to Santa Clara along the Alameda. The town was subsumed by San Jose as San Jose and Santa Clara grew together. A College Park station is still along the railroad line.

Evergreen. This name was applied to a post office in this small town on Dry Creek in 1875 (Gudde 1998). The 1899 San Jose 15′ topographic map shows Evergreen as a small town about 2.4 km southeast of the large marsh where Lake Cunningham is today (Laguna Socayre). Both Silver and Dry creeks flowed into this marsh. As of the 1961 San Jose 15′ topographic map, Dry Creek had been named Thompson Creek. Today, Evergreen is part of San Jose.

Ferguson's Swamp. The data slip that accompanies two Swainson's Hawk eggs collected by Henry R. Taylor on 30 Apr 1889 lists the location as 'Ferguson's Swamp' (WFVZ #98178). The Thompson and West (1876) atlas shows marshy lands along Llagas Creek south of Gilroy that are adjacent to land owned by the Ferguson brothers, and it is likely that Ferguson's Swamp refers to this area.

Haywards. Hayward, in Alameda County, was where William Hayward opened a hotel in 1852. The name went through a number of transformations. On 22 Mar 1880, the name was changed to Haywards, which was the name by which it was known when James G. Cooper lived there. It was changed back to Hayward on 11 Jan 1911 (Gudde 1998).

Howell Reservoirs. Two small reservoirs off Black Road above Los Gatos are shown as the Howell Reservoirs on the 1955 Los Gatos 7.5′ topographic sheet, but have been renamed Lake Kittredge and Lake Couzzens on the most recent 7.5′ topographic sheet.

Irvington. Irvington was a town in Alameda County east of Newark. It became part of Fremont in 1956 (Gudde 1998).

Jaegel Slough. The 1899 Palo Alto 15′ topographic map shows Jaegel Slough in the salt marsh north of Mountain View. There were three small landings in this area, Jaegel Landing at the inner end of Jaegel Slough, and Mountain View and Guth landings on the inner portions of Mountain View Slough. Jaegel Slough is now part of the salt ponds being restored immediately north of Moffett Field.

Laguna Seca. Laguna Seca was a natural lake at the northern end of Coyote Valley, where natural levees along Coyote Creek blocked drainage from the western side of the valley (Grossinger et al. 2006). Tulare Hill, just east of the lake, was named for the extensive bulrushes [tules] that grew there. The lake was mentioned as early as 1797 and was part of a land grant in 1834 (Gudde 1998). It was used as a source of irrigation water in the 1830s (Grossinger et al. 2006). The Thompson and West atlas (1876) shows Laguna Seca as a lake a little over a kilometer long. The lake was drained about 1916 (Grossinger et al. 2006) and today only a small portion of the original lake and marsh reappears in wet winters. The marshes here were about a kilometer from the Monterey Highway and may be the "marshes south of San Jose" referred to by early ornithologists.

Laguna Socayre. This seasonal lake was near the present Reid-Hillview Airport and Lake Cunningham. The lake formed on poor soils between the alluvial fans from the Diablo Range and levees along Coyote Creek that blocked drainage (Grossinger et al. 2006). An extensive marsh is shown at this location on the 1899 San Jose 15′ topographic map. This marsh is probably the one described by Schneider (1893), although he did not apply any name to the marsh.

Madrone. The 1917 and 1939 Morgan Hill 15′ topographic maps show Madrone as a stop on the Monterey Highway north of Morgan Hill, halfway between Burnett Avenue and Cochrane Road. It was also a stop on the Southern Pacific Railroad. It is now part of Morgan Hill.

Madrone Soda Springs. These soda springs, now in Henry Coe State Park south of Manzanita Point, were once a resort. Munro-Fraser (1881) describes a "fine road to the Madrone station of the Southern Pacific Railroad . . . making four trips daily." Bird-ers visited this area in the 1930s, but apparently not after the construction of Anderson Reservoir in 1948.

Mallard Slough. See Artesian Slough.

Mayfield. Mayfield was originally a tract of land purchased by Elisha O. Crosby and called Mayfield Farm. Later, a nearby post office and a railroad stop were also named Mayfield, and a town was laid out in 1867. It was annexed to Palo Alto in 1925 (Gudde 1998).

McCarthysville. Founded in 1851 and named for the miller, Martin McCarthy. It was given its present name of Saratoga in 1867 because of the nearby Congress Springs, which reminded people of the famed Saratoga Spring in New York state (Gudde 1998).

Sargents. A railroad stop on the Southern Pacific railroad was named Sargent in 1869 for the local rancher, James P. Sargent. It was commonly called Sargents in the late nineteenth century by egg collectors and ornithologists who rode the train down from the Bay area for birding and collecting excursions (Taylor 1893). At the time, the railroad stop included a livery and a few other buildings. Today, all that is left is a collapsing loading station on the railroad, adorned with graffiti, visible from nearby Highway 101.

Soap Lake. A common name for San Felipe Lake, on the northern edge of the Bolsa de San Felipe. It is completely within San Benito County, but is adjacent to the southern edge of Santa Clara County. Both the 1917 and 1940 Hollister 15′ topographic maps refer to the lake as San Felipe, but local residents and birders have always called it Soap Lake (Sibley 1952).

Appendix 8:
Historical Breeding Species

Fulvous Whistling-Duck
Dendrocygna bicolor

Grinnell (1902), in his first checklist for California, considered the Fulvous Whistling-Duck to be a common summer resident in the San Joaquin and southern Sacramento valleys. Willett (1912) noted that this duck was a common migrant along the coastal slope of southern California, a few birds remaining to breed. In the first quarter of the twentieth century, eggs were frequently collected in Merced, Fresno, Madera, and Kern counties in the San Joaquin Valley (WFVZ, CAS, MVZ egg sets).

One of the most unusual historical breeding records from Santa Clara County involves this species. In the summer of 1917, Miss Ethel Emerson captured several ducklings in a salt marsh near Mountain View. These ducklings were kept in her aviary, where one lived to fledging and was identified as a Fulvous Whistling-Duck by John O. Snyder (Snyder 1919). The surviving whistling-duck escaped about a year later. Grinnell and Wythe (1927) record that the Fulvous Whistling-Duck also nested at least once in marshes near Redwood City, although no date was given. These two records, of apparently wild young, are the only nesting records known from the San Francisco Bay area. The breeding record from Mountain View and a specimen reported by Holmes (1899) are the only records of this duck in Santa Clara County.

There has been a general contraction of the Fulvous Whistling-Duck's range in California in the twentieth century. The last egg set from Merced County was collected in 1937 (WFVZ #37718a). Adults with six unfledged young observed on 5 Oct 1946 on Tulare Lake, Kings County (*Audubon Field Notes 1*:18 1948), constituted the last breeding record from the San Joaquin Valley. Farther south, nesting occurred on the coastal slope of southern California at Playa del Rey, Los Angeles County, until the early 1950s (Garrett and Dunn 1981). Although nonbreeding birds were occasionally recorded north to Merced and Fresno counties in the 1980s, breeding birds were apparently limited to the southern end of the Salton Sea in Imperial County by the early 1990s (Small 1994, Patten et al. 2003). Although a few birds have been found in the Imperial Valley in 2000 through 2003, no breeding has been observed, and this species may now be extirpated as a breeder in California (Patten et al. 2003).

Swainson's Hawk
Buteo swainsoni

In the first part of the twentieth century, the Swainson's Hawk was commonly found on the coastal slope of southern California from San Diego County north to Los Angeles County,

in the coast ranges from Santa Barbara to Monterey County, and in the San Joaquin Valley, particularly in Kern and Fresno counties (WFVZ egg sets, Schlorff and Bloom 1984). Farther north, in San Benito County, it was considered an uncommon summer resident at the end of the nineteenth century (Mailliard and Mailliard 1901).

In Santa Clara County, early observers mentioned Swainson's Hawk only as a rare migrant (Van Denburgh 1899b, Barlow 1900b, Fisher 1902). In their regional survey of the Bay area counties, Grinnell and Wythe (1927) included only one nesting record, that of a nest found in 1915 in the Central Valley between Brentwood and Oakley in eastern Contra Costa County. It appears, however, that this prairie hawk did nest sporadically in Santa Clara County in the late nineteenth century, to judge from records from oological collections. Henry R. Taylor of Alameda collected two eggs of this hawk from "Ferguson's Swamp" on 30 Apr 1889 (WFVZ #98178). The 1876 Thompson and West map of Santa Clara County shows a swampy area along Llagas Creek south of Gilroy that was adjacent to ranch land owned by the Ferguson brothers, and this is probably the swamp referred to by Taylor. The other nest record was a set of eggs collected at Berryessa on 21 Apr 1894 by Rollo H. Beck (MVZ #5227). Although these two egg sets remain in their respective collections, nothing else is known of these early records.

By the latter part of the twentieth century, the Swainson's Hawk had disappeared from most of the locales where it was commonly found a century earlier. In southern California, the Swainson's Hawk is gone from the coastal slope and is a rare and occasional summer resident in a few areas in eastern San Luis Obispo County, in desert washes of San Bernardino County, and in the Owens Valley (Garrett and Dunn 1981, Small 1994). This hawk no longer breeds in the southern coastal ranges (Garrett and Dunn 1981, Roberson 1993kk), but it can be found in the northeastern portion of California and along riparian systems in the Central Valley from south of Fresno north to Chico (Schlorff and Bloom 1984). The Central Valley population, sampled in 1979, is estimated to be just 4 to 17% of the historic population for this area (Schlorff and Bloom 1984).

In recent years, Swainson's Hawks have been recorded as rare spring migrants in Santa Clara County, most of the observations occurring in April and May. Less often, fall migrants are found in August and September. Except for an adult over Metcalf Canyon on 9 Jun 1994 (Stephen C. Rottenborn, county notebooks) and an immature at the Arzino Ranch in Alviso on 27 Jul 2002 (*N. Am. Birds 56*:482 2002), none has been found in Santa Clara County during the summer months of June and July. Thus, it is inexplicable that three nestling Swainson's Hawks have been found in the county from 1999 to 2005. The first nestling, a young bird with extensive natal down, was found on the Summitpointe Golf Course in the hills of eastern Milpitas on 11 Jun 1999 and brought to a rehabilitator. The nestling was presumed to be a Red-tailed Hawk and was not correctly identified as a Swainson's Hawk until September (Karen Hoyt, pers. comm.). The second nestling, nearly fledged, was found in a pool house in Saratoga on 1 Jul 2005 (*N. Am. Birds 59*:650 2005). The third was found north of Tully Road in San Jose on 17 Jul 2005 (*N. Am. Birds 59*:650 2005). The first of these nestlings was eventually identified by an experienced rehabilitator, as noted above, and the 2005 nestlings were photographed and the identifications confirmed by Michael M. Rogers (pers. comm.). No nests were found for any of these birds, and their provenance is unknown. Given the unusual circumstances surrounding all of these records, they are not considered conclusive evidence of breeding by Swainson's Hawks in Santa Clara County.

Black Rail
Laterallus jamaicensis

In the early part of the twentieth century, Black Rails were considered to be fairly common fall and winter visitors to the San Francisco Bay marshes, but breeding in California had not been documented away from the salt marshes of San Diego Bay (Grinnell et al. 1918, Grinnell and Wythe 1927). Irene Wheelock, an amateur ornithologist, conducted fieldwork from October 1894 to July 1902 in Santa Clara County (Wheelock 1905). She stated that this secretive rail nested in the marshes in Alviso (Wheelock 1904), but provided no details of her observations. Grinnell and Wythe (1927) and Grinnell and Miller (1944) either overlooked or discounted her claim, for they included no Santa Clara County records in their regional summaries. Homer A. Snow, an oologist active at the beginning of the twentieth century, collected a set of eight eggs near Newark, Alameda County, on 10 Apr 1911 (WFVZ #99670). The eggs, he stated, were from the nest of a Yellow Rail. Snow's collection was donated to the Oakland Museum after his death, and eventually was transferred to the Western Foundation of Vertebrate Zoology (Kiff 1978). Upon curating this collection, Kiff concluded that Snow's eggs were not those of a Yellow Rail, but instead were Black Rail eggs (Kiff 1978). It would seem, then, that this egg set represents the first concrete evidence of breeding by the Black Rail in the San Francisco Bay marshes.

Most of what we know about the breeding status of Black Rails in California is based on the surveys by Manolis (1978) and Evens et al. (1991). Both these surveys were based on the playing of taped Black Rail calls at marshes in the San Francisco Bay estuary and at coastal marshes from Morro Bay to Bodega Bay. Manolis attracted responses at 14 localities around the San Francisco Bay, but none were south of the Richmond-San Rafael Bridge. Evens et al. detected 608 Black Rails in the San Francisco Bay estuary, but the only responses south of the Richmond-San Rafael Bridge were from two birds heard on 16 Jun 1988 at the east end of the Dumbarton Bridge, Alameda County, in pickleweed-dominated tidal marshes with patches of bulrushes.

Habitat use by Black Rails was reported by both Manolis (1978) and Evens et al. (1991). Manolis (1978) noted that 37 of the 39 rails he heard in the North Bay were in the upper tidal marsh, generally dominated by pickleweed. A few birds were found in marshes with matted saltgrass and cattails rather than pickleweed. Evens et al. (1991) also noted the preference of this species for the upper edge of the tidal marsh, and commented that birds were found in the most pristine of these marshes. But they were not able to explain the absence of this species from other apparently suitable marshes in the North Bay.

The South Bay's pickleweed marshes thus appear to be unsuitable for Black Rails. Even where these pickleweed marshes persist, they lack a transition to upland to provide tidal refugia. Instead, these marshes are bounded by levees that render this rail subject to predation during high tides. Evens and Page (1986) studied predation at two marshes in Marin County and noted that Black Rails suffered high predation rates by herons and egrets at high tide, particularly in the absence of protective vegetation. Similar predation has been noted in the South Bay, as shown in Table A8.1. The records in this table are all from the Palo Alto Baylands, except for the 3 Dec 1994 record of predation by a Ring-billed Gull, which was seen at Cooley Landing, San Mateo County. Groundwater extraction has caused land subsidence of as much as 8 feet in the northern Santa Clara Valley (Poland

Table A8.1. Black Rail predation events in South San Francisco Bay, not all successful.

Date	Predator	Source
12 Dec 1981	Great Egret	Joe Morlan (*Am. Birds 36*:326 1982)
9 Jan 1982	Great Blue Heron	Jeri M. Langham (*Am. Birds 36*:326 1982)
18 Dec 1987	Great Egret	Arianna Rosenbluth (county notebooks)
19 Jan 1992	Great Blue Heron	Alan Walther (county notebooks)
2 Dec 1994	Great Egret	*fide* Michael M. Rogers
3 Dec 1994	Ring-billed Gull	Al DeMartini (*Field Notes 49*:193 1995)
24 Nov 2003	Ring-billed Gull	Ron S. Thorn
11 Dec 2004	Ring-billed Gull	Jennifer Rycenga, Gary Deghi

and Ireland 1988) and this subsidence may have degraded many of the original pickleweed marshes. It is interesting, however, to observe that Snow's original record was of a nest in matted saltgrass about a quarter mile above the marsh line (data slip, WFVZ).

Judging from surveys of recent decades (Manolis 1978, Evens et al. 1991), it seems unlikely that Black Rails nest regularly in the South Bay. But the records of two birds calling on 16 Jun 1988 at the east end of the Dumbarton Bridge mentioned above (Evens et al. 1991) and a single bird heard at the Palo Alto Baylands on 26–27 Apr 1993 (Michael M. Rogers, pers. obs., Stephen C. Rottenborn) suggest that a few birds may occasionally be found in the South Bay during the breeding season. The latter record, from Palo Alto, may represent a late migrant or lingering winter visitant rather than a bird attempting to breed. Nonetheless, the recent discovery of Black Rails breeding at an elevation of about 700 feet in two small foothill marshes north of the Yuba River in the Sierra Nevada foothills (Aigner et al. 1995) and a previous record of a nest in a freshwater marsh in San Bernardino County (Hanna 1935) provide cautionary reminders of how little we truly know about this secretive species.

Sora
Porzana carolina

This stubby-billed rail breeds across Canada from eastern British Columbia to Nova Scotia and south into the United States from California east to Virginia (Melvin and Gibbs 1996). In California, Grinnell (1902) described it as a common resident and recorded it as breeding in "fresh water marshes of the interior valleys." Grinnell and Wythe (1927), in describing the Sora's status in the San Francisco Bay area, stated that it was a "[f]airly common resident on marshlands," but they listed only a single breeding record for the Bay area, that of a nest found by Bryant (1915) near Alvarado, Alameda County, on 23 Apr 1915. Grinnell and Miller (1944), assessing the Sora's status in the state, referred to it as "common and widely distributed," but included no breeding records from the San Francisco Bay area, except for the Alvarado nest found by Bryant. In recent years, Small (1994) has described the Sora as an uncommon to rare breeder in the Central Valley and the greater San Francisco Bay area and a sparse summer visitor east of the Cascades and Sierra Nevada. It is possible that early observers overestimated the numbers of Soras breeding in the state.

There are two records of breeding by Soras in Santa Clara County. The first was based on an egg set collected by Fred A. Schneider on 1 May 1892 at an unspecified location in the county (CAS #10729). Schneider wrote on the data slip "Nest placed in a bunch of dry tulies, one foot from water in a swamp." The location of this swamp is not known, but later Schneider (1893) described a visit to a freshwater marsh that was 7 miles east of where he lived at College Park. This marsh is likely the historic marsh shown on the 1899 San Jose 15′ U.S.G.S. topographic sheet near where Lake Cunningham is located today. He wrote: "Where the water is quite shallow rushes grow luxuriantly and in the dead bunches Soras and California Clapper Rails, Gallinules, Coots and others nest, but very rarely the Cinnamon Teal." As discussed in the Virginia Rail account, Clapper Rails are strictly salt marsh nesters, but Schneider's mention of nesting Soras at the Lake Cunningham marsh suggests that this may be the location where he collected the 1892 egg set. The second nesting record was of an incomplete clutch of two eggs collected by W. E. Unglish in a swamp 3 miles east of Gilroy on 18 Apr 1936 (WFVZ #27051, Sibley 1952). Unglish wrote on the data slip, "Sweet flags broken over and a nest formed on their tops 2 feet above a foot of water in a swamp."

Soras are fairly common migrants and uncommon winter residents in Santa Clara County. Their spring migration extends quite late. The latest date from a wintering site in Arizona is 7 May (Melvin and Gibbs 1996), and the latest date from Monterey County is 8 May (Roberson 2002). Since previous nest records for the South Bay ranged from 18 Apr to 1 May, the

separation of potentially nesting birds from spring migrants remains problematic. Recently, averaging once every three years, Soras have been heard between late May and early July in freshwater wetlands along the Bay, including along Matadero Creek below Highway 101, at the Mountain View Forebay, in marshes near Moffett Field, at the Sunnyvale Water Pollution Control ponds, and at locations near lower Coyote Creek (county notebooks). Adults and juveniles are regularly seen in the county as early as the second week in August, but in some years both are seen as early as the last half of July. Apparent migrants have been detected at the Farallon Islands as early as 21 Jul (Pyle and Henderson 1991) and at a wintering site in Arizona by 22 Jul (Melvin and Gibbs 1996), suggesting that observations in late July may pertain to fall migrants. Tantalizing, nonetheless, were separate observations of an adult and a juvenile Sora at the Mountain View Forebay on 11 Jul 1993 (Stephen C. Rottenborn, county notebooks).

Currently, Soras appear to be decidedly rare breeders in central California. In recent decades, they have been confirmed breeding in Napa County in 1975 (Berner 2003d), in Santa Cruz County in 1976 and 1990 (*Am. Birds 44*:492 1990), in Marin County in 1982 (Shuford 1993l), in Monterey County in 1984 (*Am. Birds 38*:954 1984), in San Mateo County in 1993 (Sequoia Audubon Society 2001c), and in Alameda County in 1993 (*N. Am. Birds* Middle Pacific Coast Region notebooks) and 1994 (*Field Notes 48*:985 1994). Only in Alameda and Santa Cruz counties have birds been found nesting more than once during this time period. In this respect, Soras are less frequent breeders in central California than Virginia Rails, for which there are multiple recent breeding records in many of the Bay area counties.

Yellow-billed Cuckoo
Coccyzus americanus

In his first checklist of California birds, Grinnell (1902) listed the Yellow-billed Cuckoo as a fairly common summer resident in interior valleys with extensive willow bottomlands. A survey of historical breeding records in California (Gaines and Laymon 1984) indicated that it was common or fairly common in areas with extensive willow-cottonwood forests in the Sacramento and San Joaquin valleys, along rivers draining the coastal slope of southern California, and in the Colorado River Valley. Nonetheless, this species appears to have always been uncommon or rare along the central coast (Gaines and Laymon 1984).

There are at least four nesting records from Santa Clara County from the 1890s and 1900s. H. R. Painton collected a set of eggs in about 1890, apparently near San Jose, although the specific location is unclear (*Nidiologist 1*:181 1893). William L. Atkinson described a Yellow-billed Cuckoo nest that he found on a "bank of a running stream about ten miles north of San Jose" on 17 Jun 1899 (Atkinson 1899b). The nest was about 9 feet above the ground in a fork of a small willow and contained three eggs. Although Atkinson was not specific about the location, it is likely that the nest was found along Coyote Creek near where it enters the Bay. Atkinson concluded that the Yellow-billed Cuckoo bred sparingly in this area each year, but did not provide any supporting observations. Theodore J. Hoover collected an adult male on a nest with eggs from the vicinity of Palo Alto on 22 Jul 1901 (CAS #14306). The specimen was donated to the California Academy of Sciences after the earthquake and fire of 1906, but the present location of the egg set is not known (Douglas J. Long, pers. comm.). Irene G. Wheelock made extensive studies of breeding birds in the Santa Clara Valley from October 1894 to July 1902 (Wheelock 1905). During this period she found a Yellow-billed Cuckoo nest in the "Santa Clara Valley" in a willow clump (Wheelock 1904). She noted that the third and last egg in the clutch was laid on 30 May, and that the young successfully fledged from the nest. Beside these nesting records, there are also three sight observations from the late nineteenth century. Belding (1890) reported that A. L. Parkhurst saw and heard a Yellow-billed Cuckoo in San Jose on 6 Jun 1885, a single bird was seen near San Jose on 5 Aug 1893 (*Nidiologist 1*:181 1893), and Grinnell found a bird near Palo Alto in 1900 (Barlow 1900b). Beyond these few records, however, little is known of the Yellow-billed Cuckoo as a historical breeding species in Santa Clara County.

The western breeding range of the Yellow-billed Cuckoo once extended from southwestern British Columbia through Washington, Oregon, California, and the southwest (Laymon and Halterman 1987). There has been a significant range contraction in the past century, the last records of breeding posted in the 1920s in British Columbia, in the 1930s in Washington, and in the 1940s in Oregon (Roberson 1980). Breeding Yellow-billed Cuckoos have declined substantially in California during the last century, undoubtedly because of habitat loss, but also from the effects of pesticides (Gaines and Laymon 1984). Nonetheless, there is extensive habitat within this historical range that appears suitable for Yellow-billed Cuckoos, yet is unoccupied by them (Laymon and Halterman 1987, Hughes 1999).

Before the period of American settlement in the Santa Clara Valley, larger streams here, such as Coyote Creek and San Francisquito Creek, frequently flooded in their lower reaches, resulting in extensive areas of willows, cottonwoods, and open water. Smaller streams such as Permanente, Penitencia, and Stevens creeks did not reach the Bay, sometimes ending in extensive willow thickets and swamps on the valley floor (Cooper 1926). These habitats, as best we can reconstruct them, probably matched the habitats still used by cuckoos along the Sacramento River (Gaines and Laymon 1984). Ditches were constructed in the last half of the nineteenth century to drain these wetlands, and the willow and cottonwood forests were cleared for agriculture, leading to the extirpation of this species from the southern San Francisco Bay area. Yellow-billed Cuckoos are rarely found away from their breeding areas during their migration (Gaines and Laymon 1984), and since the destruction of the willow and cottonwood forests at the end of the nineteenth century, only two birds have been found in Santa Clara County. One flew into a window in Palo Alto in June 1966 (*Avocet 13*:71–74 1966), and the other was found along Coyote Creek 23–31 Jul 1996 (*Field Notes 50*:993 1996). The latter bird was probably within a kilometer or two of Atkinson's 1899 record, but the riparian forest along Coyote Creek today is no more than a shadow of its former glory.

Short-eared Owl
Asio flammeus

Dr. James G. Cooper (1870) considered the Short-eared Owl a winter visitor as far south as the Santa Clara Valley in California. By the end of the nineteenth century it was known to breed occasionally in California's coastal marshes (Grinnell 1902). Grinnell and Wythe (1927) considered the Short-eared Owl a common winter visitor in the San Francisco Bay area and noted that a few remained to breed, citing a nest with eggs found near Redwood City on 20 Apr 1926 by Henry W. Carriger. Local breeding is also indicated by the collection of a nest with ten eggs at the west end of the San Mateo Bridge on 24 Feb 1936 by Chase Littlejohn (WFVZ #48155). Grinnell and Miller (1944) described this owl as common in winter and breeding locally throughout California in very small numbers.

Although wintering Short-eared Owls were reported in Santa Clara County by the earliest observers (Cooper 1870, Price 1898b, Van Denburgh 1899b), breeding evidence was not obtained until the 1960s, when a pair nested in the Palo Alto Baylands for three summers, from 1964 to 1966 (*Audubon Field Notes 20*:597 1966). Subsequently, Gill (1977) reported two nests in the Palo Alto Flood Control Basin in 1972, one of which had in its vicinity two flying young and a pre-fledgling. A pair was seen again in the Palo Alto Flood Control Basin on 3 May 1974 (Theodore A. Chandik, pers. comm.), and one of these birds flew over the observer's head giving raspy notes, possibly related to nest defense. A single bird seen at the Palo Alto Baylands on 29 Jun 1980 (*Am. Birds 34*:926 1980) and two birds there on 5 Jul 1981 (Richard Stovel, county notebooks) are the only subsequent records in Santa Clara County for the period May to August.

Analysis of Christmas Bird Count data shows substantial variation in the numbers of Short-eared Owls wintering in the South San Francisco Bay area over the last half century. Some of the year-to-year fluctuation is likely caused by changes in the number of California voles, which exhibit population swings as great as 300-to-1 over one- to two-year periods in central California (Krebs 1966). Some of the variation in Short-eared Owl numbers may have been caused by these fluctuations, since these owls are particularly dependent upon this prey species (Holt and Leasure 1993). Decadal averages of Short-eared Owls on the Palo Alto CBC were 3.5 birds per year in the 1950s, increasing to 4.7 birds per year in the 1960s, and to 5.1 in the 1970s, both decades being periods when these owls remained to breed. Subsequently, there has been a decline in the number of wintering birds. In the Palo Alto count circle, the decadal average has dropped to 1.9 birds per year in the 1980s and to 0.8 in the 1990s. Other raptors found along the Bay edge, such as Northern Harriers and White-tailed Kites, also depend upon California voles (Dunk 1995, MacWhirter and Bildstein 1996). But over this same period, the numbers of both have remained fairly constant at 24 White-tailed Kites per year and 29 Northern Harriers per year. The stability of these raptors' local populations suggests that the recent decline in Short-eared Owls is not related to a local reduction in its primary prey species.

Lesser Nighthawk
Chordeiles acutipennis

Lesser Nighthawks nested in southern Santa Clara County, at the northern edge of their range, into the 1930s, but disappeared as the species' range contracted. At the end of the nineteenth century, this nighthawk was believed to nest in the California coast ranges as far north as Stanislaus and San Benito counties (Grinnell 1902). Of the early observers, only Price (1898b) recorded nighthawks in the county, noting that near Stanford "the night hawk may be seen during the summer months skimming over meadows and grainfields for insects at sunset or early in the morning." Price identified these nighthawks as *Chordeiles virginianus henryi*, which, unfortunately, was a synonym for both Lesser and Common Nighthawk (Grinnell and Miller 1944). When Grinnell and Wythe (1927) published their directory of the bird life of the San Francisco Bay area, they did not mention Price's records, nor did they include any other observations for the area. But W. E. Unglish, an amateur ornithologist living in Gilroy, had been collecting eggs of this species along Uvas Creek since 1894, and the publication of Grinnell and Wythe's directory prompted him to describe his experiences (Unglish 1929). In 1922, Unglish introduced a friend, D. Bernard Bull, to the nesting areas along Uvas Creek, and Bull collected egg sets there as well. Bull went on to discover an additional nesting area along Coyote Creek (Unglish 1929) as early as 10 Jun 1923 (WFVZ #144648). Unglish continued to collect along Uvas Creek through 1937 (WFVZ #30991), and nesting along Coyote Creek was observed through 1933 (Pickwell and Smith 1938).

Unglish (1929) stated that eight to ten pairs of Lesser Nighthawks nested along 4 miles of Uvas Creek west of Gilroy. He noted that "[w]ell back from the water were dry, rather loose beds of gravel." In these areas birds nested on the gravel, generally on the north side of sparsely distributed blazing star. Pickwell and Smith (1938) studied 12 nests from 1929 to 1933 along a half-mile portion of Coyote Creek north of the narrowest point of the Coyote Narrows. This area of extensive gravel beds was normally dry by summer. The most common plants they noted were mule-fat, Oregon false goldenaster, Douglas groundsel, blazing star, California brickellbush, and black mustard. Less common was scalebroom, an indicator species of the Lower Sonoran Life Zone.

Lesser Nighthawks are common in the southeastern deserts of California (Small 1994), largely within the Lower Sonoran Life Zone. They nest in gravelly areas, foraging on the insects that are adapted to the intense summer heat of these deserts. This species was probably never common in the Santa Clara Valley, but to the south in San Benito County, it was considered abundant at the end of the nineteenth century (Mailliard and Mailliard 1901). Its breeding range in the interior valleys of central California's Coast Ranges has contracted in the last century, and in these valleys it is now found no farther north than the San Lorenzo River and Cholame Valley along the border of Monterey and San Benito counties (Roberson 1993k, Roberson 2002). The reasons for this range contraction are unclear. In Santa Clara County, nesting birds were displaced from the Coyote Creek site when the area was flooded for percolation ponds (the present Parkway Lakes) about 1936 (Pickwell and Smith 1938, D. Bernard Bull, WFVZ #144649 data slip). With the completion of the Coyote Reservoir dam in 1936 and the Anderson Reservoir dam in 1948, the periodic winter flooding and scouring of the gravel beds along the creek ended, and it is unlikely that suitable habitat would have remained. The circumstances of the breeding areas along Uvas Creek are less clear. Bull (WFVZ #144649 data slip) found only two pairs nesting on the creek in 1936 and concluded that the birds were on their way out. The present Uvas Reservoir dam was not completed until 1957, long after the nighthawks had disappeared, but water-control structures were in place on Uvas Creek prior to 1939 (U.S.G.S. Morgan Hill 15′ topographic sheet, 1939). It may be that the scouring associated with winter floods had already been reduced by the mid-1930s, making this area unsuitable for nesting.

Lesser Nighthawks are now very rare visitors to Santa Clara County, yielding only eight observations in the last three decades (county notebooks). Single birds have been seen as early as 18 Apr 1995 east of Gilroy (John A. Cole) and as late as 15 Sep 1986 over Mountain View (David L. Suddjian). Most curious have been two summer records: 12 Jun 1992 over Sunnyvale (Theodore A. Chandik) and 28 Jul 1996 over Coyote Creek at Shady Oaks Park (Stephen C. Rottenborn).

Willow Flycatcher
Empidonax traillii

At the beginning of the twentieth century, the Willow Flycatcher was a locally occurring species in riparian habitats over much of California. By the latter half of the century, however, it was extirpated from most of its former range in California, including Santa Clara County. In his first checklist of California birds, Grinnell (1902) described the Willow Flycatcher as a common summer resident in the Upper Sonoran Life Zone. In Santa Clara County, Barlow (1900b) judged it to breed commonly along creeks flowing into the Bay, and noted a preference for "thick young maple growths." Locally, the first nesting record is of four eggs collected by Fred A. Schneider in San Jose on 9 Jun 1890 (CAS #4242). Multiple egg sets from the South Bay are in various egg collections, but, most unfortunately, offer limited information about nest locations. We know that three sets were collected near the mouth of San Francisquito Creek, San Mateo County, from 1895 to 1901 by Chase Littlejohn (WFVZ #75062–75064), and that one set was collected on Coyote Creek near Milpitas in 1920 by D. Bernard Bull (WFVZ #75065). The dates of these records ranged from 6 to 28 Jun. (The county border in the vicinity of San Francisquito Creek was changed in 1963, and those records may be from present Santa Clara County.) On 3 Jul 1926, Charles P. Smith (1926) found an abandoned Willow Flycatcher nest along the Guadalupe River with single eggs of both the flycatcher and a Brown-headed Cowbird. Grinnell and Wythe (1927) judged the Willow Flycatcher to be a sparse summer resident in the Bay area, with known nesting records only from Alameda and Santa Clara counties. By the mid-twentieth century, Sibley (1952) considered it an uncommon summer resident along willow-bordered streams. Today, the species no longer breeds in coastal central California, but remnant populations of perhaps 140 to 150 pairs of the subspecies *E. t. brewsteri* (the subspecies that nested in Santa Clara County) persist in the Cascades and Sierra Nevada (Small 1994).

The decline and disappearance of the Willow Flycatcher from the Santa Clara Valley went largely unremarked. Near the Agnew heronry, on 19 Jun 1949, Jim Peterson reported looking unsuccessfully "for the Traill's flycatcher which used to nest there" (*Bull. SCVAS,* September 1949). Donald D. McLean noted nesting pairs along the Guadalupe River through 1962 (*Audubon Field Notes 16*:445 1962), but by 1966 they were apparently extirpated (*Audubon Field Notes 20*:544 1966). Possibly the last breeding birds on the central California coast were a pair with four young seen at the Carmel River mouth, Monterey County, on 11 Aug 1974 (*Am. Birds 28*:946 1974).

Although Willow Flycatchers no longer breed in Santa Clara County, they are found more or less regularly along streams on the valley floor in spring and fall. Spring migrants are rare and are not encountered every year, most birds being found between mid-May and about 20 Jun, with a few exceptional records in late April and early May. The majority of the fall migrants occur from mid-August to the first week in October, during which time these birds are uncommon in early successional vegetation, often near riparian corridors. Willow Flycatchers are rarely found in July; there are just four July banding records from Coyote Creek below Highway 237 over the period 1986 to 2003 (San Francisco Bay Bird Observatory, unpubl. data), and these may represent oversummering birds or possibly very early fall migrants. In 1995, there was an exceptional spring movement of Willow Flycatchers, with birds found in multiple locations through the middle of June. One bird, found along the Guadalupe River between Trimble Road and Montague Expressway, was singing from 14 June to 12 July (Stephen C. Rottenborn, county notebooks).

The demise of the Willow Flycatcher in central California was probably brought on by a number of factors. These include habitat destruction and degradation, overgrazing, brood parasitism by Brown-headed Cowbirds, and excessive spraying of broad-scale pesticides (Small 1994, Sedgwick 2000). The descriptions of extensive willow thickets and swamps along many of the streams in the northern Santa Clara Valley at the beginning of the twentieth century suggest a habitat that was ideal for this species, as well as for the Yellow-billed Cuckoo (another species now extirpated from the region). These riparian willow thickets and swamps were long ago bulldozed, cut, burned, and filled; today, there is not even a hint of their former glory. In the southern parts of the county, such as along Llagas Creek, the Pajaro River, and near San Felipe Lake, there are still fairly sizable areas of willows and associated shrubs. Although Willow Flycatchers no longer breed there, these habitats remain valuable for other species dependent upon mature riparian vegetation. These areas remain vulnerable to degradation, however, particularly from excessive groundwater pumping and grazing, both of which destroy the shrub layers and subsequently the willow overstory, thus eliminating their usefulness for riparian species.

Bank Swallow
Riparia riparia

Bank Swallows nested in the Pacheco Creek-Pajaro River basin in the early 1930s, prior to the era of flood- and erosion-control projects in Santa Clara County. None are known to have nested there since the 1930s, and there are no breeding records from other stream basins in the county. Most of the early observers in Santa Clara County did not mention Bank Swallows (Van Denburgh 1899b, Fisher 1902), but Price (1898f) did list them as transients near Stanford University. Grinnell and Wythe (1927) referred to Bank Swallows as locally common summer residents in the San Francisco Bay area, but did not record any colonies within Santa Clara County. Although Grinnell and Miller (1944) noted previous descriptions of this species as fairly common or common locally, they stated that active colony sites were few, and that this species was the least numerous swallow in the state.

Evidence of breeding by Bank Swallows in Santa Clara County is limited. Three sets of eggs were taken along the Pajaro River in Santa Clara County between 1928 and 1931. An observer with initials "NN" collected a set "dug in a sand bank" near Sargent on 27 May 1928 (WFVZ #100200). W. E. Unglish collected four eggs on 28 May 1931 (WFVZ #27946) and five eggs on 6 Jun 1931 (WFVZ #27947) in a "sand cut on railroad" at Betabel. These records probably all refer to the same railroad cut, a mile south of Sargent, that was described by Kelly (1935), who included a photograph. This railroad cut, which is still present today, is currently used only on occasion by Northern Rough-winged Swallows. Apparently, White-throated Swifts and Cliff Swallows also nested in this same railroad cut, and H. R. Eschenburg collected the eggs of the former species on 6 Jun 1933 (WFVZ #66586), noting that the nest was "among [a] colony of bank swallows." Unfortunately, Eschenburg recorded the nest site only as "southern Santa Clara County."

The Bank Swallow no longer breeds in southern California, largely because of the loss of habitat caused by flood- and erosion-control projects, which prevent the establishment and maintenance of the open, vertical earthen or sandy banks required by this species (Small 1994, Garrison 1999). At present, the southernmost colonies in California are along the Salinas River in Monterey County (Roberson 1993s). Extensive colonies existed along the Sacramento River through the 1980s, but because of river-bank stabilization programs the size of these colonies dropped from 16,000 pairs in 1986 to 4,500 pairs in 1990 (Garrison et al. 1987, Small 1994). Today, the only remaining large colonies in California are found in the northeastern part of the state (Small 1994).

It does not appear that Bank Swallows were ever common in Santa Clara County, and the small colony along the Pajaro River described above is the only one that is known with certainty. This swallow is still found in Santa Clara County as a rare migrant in the spring and fall, with occasional midsummer dispersants or nonbreeding birds. The earliest spring date is 4 Apr, and the latest fall date is 29 Sep (county notebooks). There are still a few small colonies in the coastal cliffs of San Mateo and San Francisco counties, but it is not known if the few birds found locally are from these colonies.

Yellow-headed Blackbird
Xanthocephalus xanthocephalus

This spectacular blackbird apparently bred regularly in freshwater marshes on the floor of the Santa Clara Valley at the end of the nineteenth century. Most of these valley marshes were drained for agriculture in the first part of the twentieth century, and there has been no evidence of breeding since. Van Denburgh (1899b) stated that this species "breeds in considerable numbers in the marshes south of San Jose," but he did not mention the location of these marshes or the years in which he recorded breeding. Barlow (1893b) was also vague about the location of a marsh near San Jose where he collected a set of Mallard eggs on 1 May 1893, noting few waterbirds within this marsh except for "a few Coots, Yellow-headed and Bicolored Blackbirds." Harry R. Painton collected a set of four eggs of a Yellow-headed Blackbird on 5 Jun 1894 (CAS #5606) in Santa Clara County, but gave no precise location.

The limited evidence of breeding by Yellow-headed Blackbirds in the Santa Clara Valley at the end of the nineteenth century leaves unanswered questions about colony size, breeding regularity, and the locations of the marshes they occupied. The extensive marsh in Laguna Seca, west of Tulare Hill, has recently been described (Grossinger et al. 2006), but little is known of other historic marshes in the Santa Clara Valley. On the basis of egg collections, it appears that Yellow-headed Blackbirds nested at least irregularly in the San Francisco Bay area into the early part of the twentieth century. Eggs were collected at Pinole, Contra Costa County, on 28 May 1899 (MVZ #3329), and two sets were collected near Hayward, Alameda County, on 21 Apr 1911 (CAS #7797) and 28 May 1911 (CAS #10225). Grinnell and Wythe (1927) also mentioned breeding near Irvington, Alameda County, in 1925, but stated that the Yellow-headed Blackbird was "of rare occurrence in the immediate Bay region."

Today, Yellow-headed Blackbirds appear in Santa Clara County only as rare migrants, generally during spring, 90% of them found from mid-April to mid-May. Occasionally, large numbers have been found. For example, 86 were counted at the Arzino Ranch in Alviso on 9 May 1999 (Michael M. Rogers, county notebooks); this area has produced most of the recent county records. In recent years, these large flocks have been composed of females and first-year males. Adult males migrate in separate flocks and tend to arrive at their breeding grounds a week before the females (Twedt and Crawford 1995). Because comparably sized flocks of adult males have not been found in Santa Clara County, it may be that they use a different route on their spring migration. The fall migration is more protracted in the county, low numbers being found here from early August to late October. For the most part, only single birds are found, but four birds were seen at the Arzino Ranch on 14 Sep 1998 (Stephen C. Rottenborn, county notebooks). There is only one summer record in recent decades, a pair seen near the South County Regional WasteWater Authority treatment plant in Gilroy on 7 Jun 1999 (Thomas P. Ryan, county notebooks). In winter, too, this blackbird is seldom found here, yielding only two recent records, each of a single male: one at Moffett Field on 2 Feb 1980 (pers. obs.), the other in Milpitas on 13 Jan 1988 (Larry Parmeter, county notebooks).

Yellow-headed Blackbirds nest at scattered locations in California, including the northeastern plateau, the wetlands east of the Cascades-Sierra axis, scattered locations in the Central Valley, Clear Lake in Lake County, and near the Salton Sea (Small 1994). Crase and DeHaven (1972) surveyed potential nesting colonies in 1971 and estimated that 2,000 birds were breeding in California, although others have felt this to be a significant underestimate (Small 1994). Casual breeding still occurs in the San Francisco Bay region. Five pairs were found nesting in the American Canyon, Napa County, on 28 Jun 1991, and one or two pairs bred at the Huichica Creek Wildlife Area, Napa County, in 1992 (Berner 2003h). Whether this species will ever again breed in Santa Clara County remains to be seen.

Appendix 9:
Introduced, But Not Established, Breeding Species

Chukar
Alectoris chukar

The Chukar is an Old World partridge that ranges from eastern Greece through Asia Minor, southwest Asia, and India into China (Christensen 1996). Introductions to the United States began as early as 1893, but major importation and breeding did not start until the 1930s (Christensen 1996). The California Department of Fish and Game first purchased Chukars in 1928 (Bade 1937, Harper et al. 1958), from a California breeder. Additional birds were imported from Calcutta the following year. As far as is known, all of the breeding stock were of the subspecies *A. c. chukar* (Harper et al. 1958). By 1937, the game department had 600 breeding stock and had released 4,600 birds in over 80 locations in California (Bade 1937).

Harper et al. (1958) summarized the history of the Chukar in California. In the period from 1932 to 1955, 188 Chukars were released in Santa Clara County, and additional birds were released in nearby counties. In 1952 and 1953, surveys were conducted in all counties where birds had been released, and the species apparently had not become established in the outer Coast Ranges. In particular, birds did not survive in areas with greater than 20 inches of annual rainfall. In mapping the Chukar's range as of 1956, these investigators indicated that there was a breeding population in the Diablo Range of San Benito County north to about 10 to 15 km from the Santa Clara County line.

There is limited evidence that private individuals raised Chukars in Santa Clara County during the initial period of release of farm-raised birds. An egg set at the Western Foundation of Vertebrate Zoology (#33214) was collected near Gilroy from pen-raised birds. But there is no evidence that introduced Chukars have ever nested in Santa Clara County. Today, Chukars are still seen occasionally in various locations in the county. All of these birds are believed to have escaped from breeders who raise the birds for training upland hunting dogs, or for field trials (Paul L. Noble, pers. comm.).

The current range of the Chukar in central California is probably little changed from the 1956 distribution shown by Harper et al. (1958). Coarse mapping by Grenfell and Laudenslayer (1983) suggests that this game bird is resident in eastern Santa Clara County and western Stanislaus County as far north as the Alameda County line, approximately coincident with the 20-inch isohyet. No Chukar, however, have been found in eastern Santa Clara County, nor have they been recorded in nearby Stanislaus County (James Gain, pers. comm.).

Northern Bobwhite
Colinus virginianus

The Northern Bobwhite is native to the eastern United States. It is resident from the river valleys of western Nebraska east to southern New Hampshire and south through the eastern United States to Chiapas, Mexico (Brennan 1999). According to Brennan (1999), the Northern Bobwhite has declined over its eastern range in recent decades, and many local populations have been extirpated. At the same time, introductions of bobwhites have been successful in a number of areas in the West, including the Puget Sound area in Washington, the Willamette Valley in Oregon, and western Idaho (Brennan 1999). Northern Bobwhites of various subspecies have been introduced in California numerous times since the 1870s, but all of these introductions have been unsuccessful (Small 1994).

One of the earliest attempts to import and release bobwhites in California was undertaken by Dr. Newell near Cloverdale, Sonoma County, in the fall of 1872, but the attempt did not succeed (Phillips 1928). Early releases in Santa Clara County met with some initial success, and released birds were known to breed in the county for at least a brief period following their introduction. Belding (1890) reported that birds were placed on the farms of Messrs. Miller, Rea, and J. P. Sargent along Carnadero Creek in Gilroy sometime before 1890, and that they bred successfully in their first year. Henry R. Taylor (1889) noted that quite a few birds were established in the area around Gilroy in 1888 and reported that a boy had found a nest there. He then suggested, tongue in cheek, that it was time to name it the "California Bob-white." Barlow (1900b) also noted that birds were introduced near San Felipe by Charles Culp sometime prior to 1900 and supposedly had done well. The California Fish Commission sponsored introductions in the state from 1904 to 1906, but birds increased in only one of the release areas, the Del Paso Rancho near Sacramento (Grinnell et al. 1918). Even that increase was only temporary, and after four years no birds remained. Attempts to breed bobwhites at the State Game Farm also failed. As of 1944, Grinnell and Miller (1944) knew of no free-living Northern Bobwhites within the state, and this status remains unchanged today.

Northern Bobwhites continue to be released in California for use in the training of hunting dogs (Brennan 1999). In recent years, there have been records of single birds in Morgan Hill, Palo Alto, Sunnyvale, and San Jose. All of these were escaped birds.

Blue-crowned Parakeet
Aratinga acuticaudata

Exotic birds from all over the world have been imported into California. From time to time, some escape and attempt to live on their own in a setting quite different from those of their native lands. The Blue-crowned Parakeet, in its native range, is found in dry woodlands from Colombia and Venezuela south to northern Argentina (Forshaw 2006). Surveys of introduced species (Phillips 1928, Long 1981) make no mention of the introduction or establishment of this species in the United States through the middle of the twentieth century. Garrett (1997) assessed populations of parrots in southern California in the 1990s and estimated that by that time no more than 50 Blue-crowned Parakeets were present in the greater Los Angeles area. Releases of this species probably occurred in the 1980s, when birds were noted sporadically in flocks of Mitred Parakeets in the Los Angeles basin (Johnston and Garrett 1994). On the basis of their head coloration, Garrett (1997) believes that the released birds in the Los Angeles area are of the nominate subspecies, which is found from central Brazil to Argentina.

Within the San Francisco Bay area, mixed flocks of *Aratinga* species have been found in San Francisco and in a number of locations in the South Bay. In the South Bay, flocks have been found in urban areas, as shown on Fig. A9.1, a map of the northern Santa Clara Valley. Small, solid circles on this map indicate sightings of *Aratinga* species (including Blue-crowned, Mitred, Red-masked, and other species). These symbols cluster into roughly two groups, one in the Palo Alto-Mountain View area and the other in the Sunnyvale area, with a few observations in neighboring Cupertino. *Aratinga* were first found in these areas between 1985 and 1990, but their provenance is obscured by the mists of urban legends. The first group of birds was based at St. Mark's Episcopal Church in Palo Alto. On 31 Jul 1994, both banded adult and unbanded juvenile Blue-crowned Parakeets were seen, suggesting the possibility of nesting (Stephen

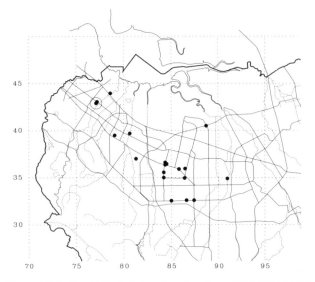

Figure A9.1. Small filled circles show locations of *Aratinga* flocks in the northern Santa Clara Valley. Large circle shows nest location.

C. Rottenborn, county notebooks). The second group of *Aratinga* appears to have been centered around St. Martin's Catholic Church in Sunnyvale. Dead *Aratinga* fledglings were found at St. Martin's in the late 1980s or early 1990s (Peter Frank *fide* Stephen C. Rottenborn, county notebooks). Because multiple *Aratinga* species have been present at St. Martin's, the specific identity of these fledglings is not known.

The maximum count of Blue-crowned Parakeets in the Palo Alto-Mountain View *Aratinga* flock was seven birds on 31 Jul 1994 (Stephen C. Rottenborn, county notebooks). The peak count of blue-crowns in the Sunnyvale flock was three on 23 Aug 1995 (Tom Ryan et al., county notebooks). A mixed *Aratinga* flock of 34 birds in Sunnyvale on 23 Dec 2002 consisted mostly of Mitred Parakeets (Michael M. Rogers, county notebooks).

Introduced populations of birds often show an explosive increase in numbers, followed by a population collapse, either to some sustainable level or to extinction (Phillips 1928). The length of this cycle depends in part on the species' natural longevity. Although psittacids are generally considered to be long-lived, little information is available on the lifespan of the *Aratinga* parakeets (Forshaw 2006). We will continue to observe the status of this species in the Silicon Valley in the years to come.

Mitred Parakeet
Aratinga mitrata

The native range of the Mitred Parakeet, sometimes called the Mitred Conure, extends from central Peru through eastern Bolivia and south to northwestern Argentina, where birds have been collected at elevations from 3,000 to 8,500 feet (Forshaw 2006). Through the first half of the twentieth century (Phillips 1928, Long 1981), no mention was made of this species in surveys of introduced species in the United States. Garrett's (1997) survey of southern California parrot populations in the 1990s estimated that 680 Mitred Parakeets were established in the greater Los Angeles area. He first observed this *Aratinga* species in the Los Angeles basin in the late 1980s, but reported that it had been observed in the Long Beach area as early as 1980.

Mitred Parakeets are the major component of the mixed flocks of *Aratinga* species that have been found in the South Bay. As noted in the Blue-crowned Parakeet account, flocks have been found in two general areas: Palo Alto-Mountain View and Sunnyvale. The parakeets at St. Mark's Episcopal Church in Palo Alto excavated holes in the church gables, and on 18 Aug 1995, adult Mitred Parakeets were seen, and there were at least two nestlings at one of the nest holes (Stephen C. Rottenborn, county notebooks). This breeding confirmation, indicated by a large, open circle in the figure accompanying the Blue-crowned Parakeet account, is the only documented evidence of breeding by this species in the county. The church sealed the nest holes in 1998, and this location no longer appears to be used by the *Aratinga* flock, although birds are still seen occasionally in the Palo Alto-Mountain View area. The second group of *Aratinga* appears to be centered on St. Martin's Catholic Church in Sunnyvale, where the majority of birds are Mitred Parakeets.

The maximum number of Mitred Parakeets seen in the

Palo Alto-Mountain View *Aratinga* flock was 13-14 birds on 10 Jun 1996 (Stephen C. Rottenborn, county notebooks). The peak count of Mitreds in Sunnyvale was seven on 23 Aug 1995 (Stephen C. Rottenborn, county notebooks). A mixed *Aratinga* flock of 34 birds in Sunnyvale on 23 Dec 2002 consisted mostly of Mitred Parakeets (Michael M. Rogers, county notebooks). The number of *Aratinga* found locally is far less than has been observed in Los Angeles.

A group of four *Aratinga* studied in Sunnyvale on 24 Jun 2002 appeared to be Mitred Parakeets, but also showed some characteristics suggesting possible hybridization with both Red-masked and Blue-crowned parakeets (Michael M. Rogers, county notebooks). The *Aratinga* flock in San Francisco includes both Red-masked and Mitred parakeets, and hybrid pairing has occurred at least once (Bittner 2004). In the Los Angeles area, however, these two species are not known to interbreed (Garrett 1997).

Orange Bishop
Euplectes franciscanus

The Orange Bishop, sometimes referred to as the Northern Red Bishop, is found in tall grasses in moist areas in sub-Saharan Africa from Senegal to Kenya (Sibley and Monroe 1990). These brightly colored finches have long been kept as cage birds and widely introduced in various tropical areas of the world (Long 1981, Sibley and Monroe 1990). But none of the earlier surveys of introduced birds recorded this bishop as established in the United States (Phillips 1928, Hardy 1973, Long 1981). Individuals or small groups of Orange Bishops were first observed in the Los Angeles Basin of California in the late 1970s (Garrett 1998). Documentation of breeding was obtained along the Los Angeles River in Los Angeles County in 1991 (Johnston and Garrett 1994). Flocks of 50 to 100 birds are now routinely observed in flood-control basins near Los Angeles (Garrett 1998). A small colony has also been established in Phoenix, Arizona (Gatz 2001).

A male Orange Bishop in breeding plumage is difficult to overlook, but the females, young, and basic-plumaged males are nondescript in plumage, and in fact similar to those of a number of other weavers that are offered in the cage-bird trade. Observations of this exotic finch in Santa Clara County are documented by the county notebooks. The first was a female found along the Stevens Creek channel below La Avenida Avenue in Mountain View on 28 Sep–5 Oct 1993 (Michael M. Rogers, Stephen C. Rottenborn). Nearby, two females or immatures were seen at the Emily Renzel Wetlands on 1 Nov 1993 (Stephen C. Rottenborn). In 1994, a male was found with House Sparrows at the stables at Calero Reservoir County Park on 26 Feb (Michael M. Rogers), but no other bishops were observed until a pair started coming to a Palo Alto feeder on 14 Nov 1994, remaining into March 1995 (Phyllis M. Browning). Orange Bishops were found in a number of widely scattered locations in the county in 1995, but of most interest was the nesting of this species along Matadero Creek in Palo Alto, below Highway 101. On 5 Sep 1995, a male, a female, and two recently fledged juveniles were found along the creek (Stephen C. Rottenborn). The young birds were fed by the female, while the male remained nearby. Birds continued to be

seen in this area in September and October, and two immatures were captured during a banding study nearby on 8 Nov (Rita R. Colwell, pers. comm.). These were hatching-year birds, as shown by their incomplete skull ossification.

Orange Bishops have been seen irregularly in the South Bay since they first nested here in 1995. They have been seen at a number of bayside locations from 1996 to 1999, in 2001, and in 2005. Away from the Bay, single birds have been found in San Jose near Hillsdale and Kirk roads in 1998 (John Delevoryas), along the Guadalupe River near the Santa Clara Valley Water District offices in 1998 and 1999 (Ann Verdi), and at a San Jose feeder in 2001 (Karl Fowler). None was seen nesting in the county again until 2005. On 26 Jun, a pair was seen carrying nest material to a nest site along the Calera and Penitencia Creek channel in Milpitas, and a nest with young was seen on 16 Jul (Michael M. Rogers). This same pair apparently moved 600 meters westward to the Waterbird Management Area on lower Coyote Creek, and there they were seen carrying nest material on 31 Jul (Michael J. Mammoser, PADB) and carrying food on 17 Aug (Robert W. Reiling, PADB).

In southern California, Orange Bishops feed on many of the same seeds used by Nutmeg Mannikins, and particularly on those of barnyard grass (Smithson 2000). The Orange Bishop nests in August and September to take advantage of the ripening of the barnyard grass seeds, and in this regard is less flexible than the Nutmeg Mannikin, which is able to use other grass and weed seeds during a spring breeding peak (Smithson 2000). Clearly, Orange Bishops are able to nest in Santa Clara County, but there is insufficient evidence that they are able to sustain their population. Time will tell.

Nutmeg Mannikin
Lonchura punctulata

Nutmeg Mannikins are common throughout much of southern Asia and the Malay Archipelago (Sibley and Monroe 1990). They are popular cage birds in their native range, and their initial introduction in Europe probably dates back to the early spice trade, hence the alternative name of Spice Finch. There is no evidence of their introduction in the United States in early surveys (Phillips 1928, Hardy 1973, Long 1981). Johnston and Garrett (1994) record that various species of exotic finches have been seen in the Los Angeles Basin since the 1960s, but mention no breeding records for any of these species. Recent studies from the late 1990s, however, show that this mannikin is breeding widely in the Los Angeles Basin in nearly every month of the year (Smithson 2000).

The first evidence of an escaped Nutmeg Mannikin in Santa Clara County was the observation of an adult along Silver Creek above Murtha Drive on 23 Aug and 10 Oct 1994 (Stephen C. Rottenborn, county notebooks; subsequent citations with an observer's name refer to records from these notebooks). The next year a single bird was seen along Stevens Creek near Crittenden Lane on 10 Oct 1995 (Peter J. Metropulos). There were no additional observations in the county until 22 Oct 1997, when four adults and two or three juveniles were seen along the Alamitos Creek Trail above Almaden Lake (Richard J. Adams). Four days later, six birds were found along the Guadalupe River near the Santa Clara Valley Water District ponds (Ann Verdi). The first indication of possible nesting was two birds seen building a nest at Almaden Lake Park on 20 Mar 1999 (Bill Eklund). But because this species commonly constructs nests for roosting (Restall 1997), observations of birds carrying nest material and nest building are not sufficient to confirm breeding. In late July 2001, mannikins were seen carrying food, and young were heard in a nest upstream from Almaden Lake (Pat Kelly *fide* John Meyer). This is the first definitive evidence of nesting in the county. Additional records have followed, including four "voracious" youngsters being fed near Almaden Lake on 21 Mar 2002 (James M. Danzenbaker) and a begging juvenile north of the Santa Clara Valley Water District ponds on 23 Aug 2004 (Janna L. Pauser). Although juvenile birds have been noted on numerous occasions, these three observations are the only certain records of breeding in Santa Clara County.

The map of Fig. A9.2 shows all Nutmeg Mannikin sightings through 2005 (small, filled circles) and the breeding records near Almaden Lake (large, open circles). Except for the initial observation of single birds near Lake Cunningham in 1994 and along Stevens Creek in 1995, all of these observations have been from the vicinity of Almaden Lake. The highest counts to date are of about 20 birds seen upstream from Almaden Lake on 27 Nov 1999 (John Mariani), 19 birds there on 14 Oct 2001 (Don Ganton), and about 20 in Dec 2002 (W. Scott Smithson, pers. comm.). Nutmeg Mannikins have been recorded in double digits in the Almaden Valley in most years since they were first observed in 1997, but there is no discernible population trend.

In southern California there are two peaks of breeding, one in early spring and one in late summer or early fall, and these appear to coincide with the production of exotic grass seeds, par-

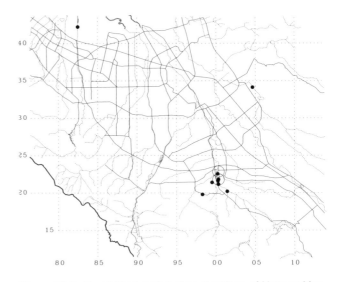

Figure A9.2. Small filled circles show locations of Nutmeg Mannikin sightings in the northern Santa Clara Valley. Large circles show breeding locations.

ticularly from barnyard grass in the fall (Smithson 2000). The foraging habits of the Almaden Valley mannikins have not been studied, nor have we enough data to determine if their breeding phenology is similar to that of the Los Angeles Basin birds. Escaped or introduced birds may become naturalized in an area, increase in numbers, but then die out from disease and predation (Phillips 1928). The future of the Almaden Valley Nutmeg Mannikins remains to be seen.

Appendix 10:
New Breeding Records

The postatlas period was considered complete at the end of the 2005 breeding season. All species accounts and maps were updated to include the 2005 season, and the writing of the atlas was largely completed by the end of that year. During work on this atlas in 2006, two new species were confirmed breeding in Santa Clara County: Bald Eagle and Virginia Rail. These 2006 records are discussed here, amongst some contextual material.

Bald Eagle
Haliaeetus leucocephalus

The Bald Eagle is a widespread nesting species in North America, breeding from Alaska to eastern Canada and south to California, Wisconsin, and Maine. Coastally, it is a common breeder from Delaware to Texas, and there are numerous disjunct populations elsewhere in the United States (Buehler 2000). In California, the Bald Eagle appears to have been more common 150 years ago than it is today. Chase Littlejohn considered it to be common along San Francisco Bay at Redwood City in 1865 (Grinnell and Wythe 1927). By the beginning of the twentieth century, however, this raptor was only a sporadic breeder in California, except on the Channel Islands, where it was still considered common (Grinnell 1915). A nest near La Honda, San Mateo County, in about 1915 (Grinnell and Wythe 1927) was the last evidence of nesting in the Bay area until the species' recent recovery.

Prior to 2006, there had been no concrete evidence that the Bald Eagle had ever nested in Santa Clara County, although a possible nest was reported by the early naturalist Dr. James G. Cooper. After spending six weeks in the Santa Clara Valley in October and November 1855 (Coan 1982), Cooper described his observation of a Bald Eagle in the valley (Cooper and Suckley 1860):

> In Santa Clara county, California, I saw a nest of this bird large enough to fill a wagon. It was built in a large sycamore tree, standing alone in the prairie, and but a short distance from several farm houses. On my shooting a magpie from the tree, one of the eagles came from a distance and flew round to reconnoitre, though, as it was November, they probably had no eggs or young in it. The farmers not having molested it, I suppose the eagles were not troublesome, and probably found enough to eat among the great numbers of cattle dying on those plains.

Grinnell and Wythe (1927) accepted this observation as a valid breeding record. Under current breeding bird atlas protocols, an October or November visit to a used nest does not constitute acceptable breeding evidence. The description of the nest and its surroundings seems to fit better those of Golden Eagles, which had been observed nesting in isolated trees in California valleys early in the settlement period (Barlow 1893d, Dixon 1937). Typically, Bald Eagle nests were, and still are, found in forests or groves near water (Buehler 2000).

Since the use of DDT was banned in 1973, there has been a recovery of Bald Eagle populations in California (Small 1994, Buehler 2000). The first modern Bald Eagle nest record for the San Francisco Bay region was from Lake Berryessa in Napa County. A pair of eagles attempted to nest there in 1989 and finally succeeded in fledging young in 1992 (Berner 2003b). In 1996, a pair of breeding eagles was found at Del Valle Reservoir in Alameda County (*Field Notes* 50:327–28 1996). Releases of captive-raised birds may have contributed to the recurrence of this species, as the female at Del Valle Reservoir that year was a captive-raised bird that had been released in Monterey County.

The Bald Eagle is a rare wintering species in Santa Clara County, typically found near larger reservoirs such as Calaveras, Anderson, Coyote, Isabel, or Calero. Normally, it is found first in early November and may remain until early March. Wintering numbers are variable from year to year, and sometimes the species is entirely absent for a period of years. Although adults predominate, immatures also occur here. The spring and fall migration periods have produced a scattering of records, but from May through August, there have been only four records since 1980 (county notebooks): an adult at Calero Reservoir on 6 May 2003 (Janna L. Pauser et al.), an adult over Casa de Fruta on 18 Jun 1993 (Stephen C. Rottenborn, Michael M. Rogers), an adult near Lexington Reservoir on 1 Jul 2005 (Jean M. Myers), and a second-year bird over Shoreline Park on 27 Jul 2004 (Stephen C. Rottenborn).

Bald Eagles have been breeding in San Benito County, to the south of Santa Clara County, since 2004 (*N. Am. Birds* 58:482 2004, 59:650 2005). Interestingly, these birds are not nesting adjacent to manmade reservoirs, but have built their nest in a deciduous oak in woodlands adjacent to oak savanna. For the most part, it appears that they are feeding on young California ground squirrels. As with the Del Valle Reservoir female in 1996, both adults were captive-raised birds and had been released in adjacent Monterey County (Debra L. Shearwater, pers. comm.).

The first evidence of Bald Eagles breeding in Santa Clara County was obtained in 2006, when a nest with two dead young was found about 13 Jul on the west shore of Calaveras Reservoir in Block 0045 (Hans J. Peeters, pers. comm.). One nestling died at about four to five weeks of age and the other at seven to eight weeks. The carcasses were badly scavenged and the cause of death could not be determined. The nest was placed in a coast live oak along the shoreline, about 30 to 40 feet above the ground. A second Bald Eagle nest was in a second coast live oak about 20 meters from the first. The first nest was clearly layered, suggesting use for at least three years (Hans J. Peeters, pers. comm.). The second nest was older and appeared to have been used at least twice, which suggests that the eagle pair had used these sites since about 2000 or 2001. The nests appeared typical of Bald Eagle nests, being placed prominently in the open, unlike local Golden Eagle nests, which are generally less exposed (Hans J. Peeters, pers. comm.).

Virginia Rail
Rallus limicola

As discussed in Chapter 7, the breeding status of seven species was particularly interesting: although none was confirmed breeding in the county during the atlas period, probable breeding evidence was obtained for all seven (species accounts for all of them are included in this atlas). There is historical breeding evidence for five of the seven species in Santa Clara County, but for two of them, Virginia Rail and Red Crossbill, there had been no proof of breeding here. In 2006, Virginia Rail was confirmed breeding in Santa Clara County, and the documentation below should be read in conjunction with the species account.

While birding in Joseph Grant County Park on 6 May 2006, Michael M. Rogers heard Virginia Rails calling from a freshwater marsh south of the Washburn Trail in a portion of the park within Block 1030 (county notebooks). Following heavy rains in the spring of 2006, this marsh, at an elevation of 1,715 feet, appeared healthy, with many rushes and grasses growing in the shallow water of the marsh. At the edge, up to six adult Virginia Rails, all highly agitated, were observed, though no young were seen at this location. Rogers shifted to a different section of the marsh and found an open alley where rails were visible when they walked along there. At least another four adults were at this location. Eventually, Rogers saw a recently hatched precocial young walk down the alley, and noted that it was downy black with a black band around its short bill, and gave a high-pitched "pee-eet" call.

Later in the season, on 21 May 2006, Rogers and Michael J. Mammoser checked two other Diablo Range marshes where birds had been found earlier (county notebooks). They found two adults in a marsh along Beauregard Creek, beside Mines Road, where the creek enters the San Antonio Valley, about 1.5 km north of the San Antonio Junction in Block 3540. The same day, they heard two birds calling near a reservoir next to Del Puerto Road on another tributary of Beauregard Creek, about 1.1 km east of San Antonio Junction in Block 3535. Although the presence of adults at these marshes suggested possible breeding, no other evidence was obtained.

Literature Cited
and Index

Literature Cited

Prepared by Phyllis M. Browning

Adams, E. 1899. Western Evening Grosbeak in Santa Clara Co., Cal. *Bull. Cooper Ornithol. Club* 1:31.

————. 1900. Notes on the California Clapper Rail. *Condor* 2:31–32.

Addicott, A. B. 1938. Behavior of the Bush-Tit in the breeding season. *Condor* 40:49–63.

Adkisson, C. S. 1996. Red Crossbill (*Loxia curvirostra*). *The Birds of North America*, No. 256 (A. Poole and F. Gill, eds.). Acad. Nat. Sci., Philadelphia; Am. Ornithol. Union, Washington.

Aigner, P. T., J. Tecklin and C. E. Koehler. 1995. Probable breeding population of the Black Rail in Yuba County, California. *West. Birds* 26:157–160.

Albertson, J. D. and J. G. Evens. 2000. California Clapper Rail *Rallus longirostris obsoletus*. *Baylands Ecosystem Species and Community Profiles: Life Histories and Environmental Requirements of Key Plants, Fish and Wildlife*, pp. 332–341. Prepared by the San Francisco Bay Area Wetlands Ecosystem Goals Project (P. R. Olofson, ed.) San Francisco Bay Regional Water Quality Control Board, Oakland, Calif.

Aldrich, E. C. 1945. Nesting of the Allen Hummingbird. *Condor* 47:137–148.

Altman, B. and R. Sallabanks. 2000. Olive-sided Flycatcher (*Contopus cooperi*). *The Birds of North America*, No. 502 (A. Poole and F. Gill, eds.). The Birds of North America, Inc., Philadelphia.

Ammon, E. M. and W. M. Gilbert. 1999. Wilson's Warbler (*Wilsonia pusilla*). *The Birds of North America*, No. 478 (A. Poole and F. Gill, eds.). The Birds of North America, Inc., Philadelphia.

Anderson, J. R. and V. R. Jennings. 1981. Diked coastal salt marsh. *Am. Birds* 35:102.

Anderson, M. K. and D. L. Rowney. 1998. California geophytes: ecology, ethnobotany, and conservation. *Fremontia* 26:12–18.

[AOU] American Ornithologists' Union. 1957. *Check-list of North American Birds*. 5th ed., Lord Baltimore Pr., Baltimore.

————. 1983. *Check-list of North American Birds*. 6th ed., Am. Ornithol. Union, New York.

————. 1985. Thirty-fifth supplement to the American Ornithologists' Union check-list of North American birds. *Auk* 102:680–686.

————. 1989. Thirty-seventh supplement to the American Ornithologists' Union check-list of North American birds. *Auk* 106:532–538.

————. 1995. Fortieth supplement to the American Ornithologists' Union check-list of North American birds. *Auk* 112:819–830.

————. 1997. Forty-first supplement to the American Ornithologists' Union check-list of North American birds. *Auk* 114:542–552.

————. 1998. *Check-list of North American Birds*. 7th ed., Allen Pr., Lawrence, Kans.

————. 2004. Forty-fifth supplement to the American Ornithologists' Union check-list of North American birds. *Auk* 121:985–995.

Applegarth, J. H. 1938. The Ecology of the California Clapper Rail on the South Arm of San Francisco Bay. Master's thesis, Stanford Univ., Stanford, Calif.

Armstrong, E. and D. Euler. 1982. Habitat usage of two woodland *Buteo* species in central Ontario. *Can. Field-Nat.* 97:200–207.

Arnold, J. R. 1935. The changing distribution of the Western Mockingbird in California. *Condor* 37:193–199.

————. 1980. Distribution of the mockingbird in California. *West. Birds* 11:97–102.

Asay, C. E. 1987. Habitat and productivity of Cooper's Hawks nesting in California. *Calif. Fish Game* 73:80–87.

Ashford, D. 1995. Plain Titmouse (*Parus inornatus*). *Sonoma County Breeding Bird Atlas*, p. 117 (B. Burridge, ed.). Madrone Audubon Soc., Santa Rosa, Calif.

Atkinson, W. L. 1895. Some notes on two California birds. *Oologist* 12:186–187.

————. 1899a. Band-tailed Pigeon nesting in Santa Clara County, Cal. *Bull. Cooper Ornithol. Club* 1:57.

————. 1899b. Nesting of the California Cuckoo. *Bull. Cooper Ornithol. Club* 1:95.

————. 1901. Nesting habits of the California Shrike. *Condor* 3:9–11.

Atwater, B. F., C. W. Hedel and E. J. Helley. 1977. Late Quaternary depositional history, Holocene sea-level changes, and vertical crustal movement, southern San Francisco Bay, California. U.S. Geol. Survey Prof. Paper 1014, 15 pp.

Austin, J. E. and M. R. Miller. 1995. Northern Pintail (*Anas acuta*). *The Birds of North America*, No. 163 (A. Poole and F. Gill, eds.). Acad. Nat. Sci., Philadelphia; Am. Ornithol. Union, Washington.

Austin, J. E., C. M. Custer and A. D. Afton. 1998. Lesser Scaup (*Aythya affinis*). *The Birds of North America*, No. 338 (A. Poole and F. Gill, eds.). The Birds of North America, Inc., Philadelphia.

Austin, M. 1903. *The Land of Little Rain.* Houghton Mifflin, Boston. Reissued 1974 by Gordon Pr., New York.

Bade, A. 1937. The Chukar Partridge in California. *Calif. Fish Game* 23:233–236.

Baepler, D. H. 1968. Lark Sparrow (*Chondestes grammacus*). *Life Histories of North American Cardinals, Grosbeaks, Buntings, Towhees, Finches, Sparrows, and Allies*, Pt. 2, p. 901 (O. L. Austin, Jr., comp. & ed.) Smithsonian Inst. U.S. Natl. Museum Bull. 237, Pt.2. Reissued 1968 by Dover Publ., New York.

Baicich, P. J. and C. J. O. Harrison. 2005. *A Guide to the Nests, Eggs, and Nestlings of North American Birds.* 2nd ed., Princeton Univ. Pr., Princeton, N.J.

Bailey, F. M. 1902. *Handbook of Birds of the Western United States.* Houghton, Mifflin, Boston.

———. 1928. *Birds of New Mexico.* New Mexico Dept. Game and Fish, Santa Fe, N. Mex.

Bailey, H. H. 1920. Bryant marsh sparrow in the hills. *Condor* 22:188.

Bailey, S. F. 1993a. Western Grebe (*Aechmophorus occidentalis*) and Clark's Grebe (*Aechmophorus clarkii*). *Atlas of the Breeding Birds of Monterey County, California*, pp. 50–51 (D. Roberson and C. Tenney, eds.). Monterey Peninsula Audubon Soc., Monterey.

———. 1993b. Spotted Sandpiper (*Actitis macularia*). *Atlas of the Breeding Birds of Monterey County, California*, pp. 134–135 (D. Roberson and C. Tenney, eds.). Monterey Peninsula Audubon Soc., Monterey.

———. 1993c. Band-tailed Pigeon (*Columba fasciata*). *Atlas of the Breeding Birds of Monterey County, California*, pp. 148–149 (D. Roberson and C. Tenney, eds.). Monterey Peninsula Audubon Soc., Monterey.

———. 1993d. American Goldfinch (*Carduelis tristis*). *Atlas of the Breeding Birds of Monterey County, California*, pp. 394–395 (D. Roberson and C. Tenney, eds.). Monterey Peninsula Audubon Soc., Monterey.

Bailey, V. 1902. Unprotected breeding grounds. *Condor* 4:62–64.

Baird, S. F., J. Cassin and G. N. Lawrence. 1858. *Pacific Railroad Reports, Vol. 9, Explorations and Surveys for a Railroad Route from the Mississippi River to the Pacific Ocean. Birds*, pp. 1–1005. Washington.

Ball, W. S. and J. W. Koehler. 1959. Bureau of Rodent and Weed Control and Seed Inspection. Calif. Dept. Agr. Bull., 39th Ann. Rep. 49:148–159.

Baltosser, W. H. 1989. Costa's Hummingbird: its distribution and status. *West. Birds* 20:41–62.

Baltosser, W. H. and P. E. Scott. 1996. Costa's Hummingbird (*Calypte costae*). *The Birds of North America*, No. 251 (A. Poole and F. Gill, eds.). The Birds of North America, Inc., Philadelphia.

Banks, R. C. and P. F. Springer. 1994. A century of population trends of waterfowl in Western North America. *A Century of Avifaunal Change in Western North America*, pp. 134–146 (J. R. Jehl, Jr. and N. K. Johnson, eds.). Studies in Avian Biology, No. 15.

Barbier, E. B. 1997. Introduction to the environmental Kuznets curve special issue. *Environ. Dev. Econ.* 2:369–381.

Barbour, M. G. and J. Major, eds. 1988. *Terrestrial Vegetation of California.* New expanded ed. Calif. Native Plant Soc., Spec. Publ. No. 9. Univ. Calif. Davis, Davis.

Barlow, C. 1893a. Cooper Ornithological Club. *Nidiologist* 1:29.

———. 1893b. Nesting of the Mallard Duck. *Nidiologist* 1:38.

———. 1893c. [Minutes of the] Cooper Ornithological Club. *Nidiologist* 1:44.

———. 1893d. Cooper Ornithological Club. *Nidiologist* 1:61.

———. 1893e. Cooper Ornithological Club. *Oologist* 10:230.

———. 1894a. Cooper Ornithological Club. *Nidiologist* 1:95.

———. 1894b. Cooper Ornithological Club. *Nidiologist* 1:122.

———. 1896. Cassin's Vireo in Santa Clara Co., California. *Wilson Bull.* 8:7–8.

B[arlow], C. 1899. Prominent Californian Ornithologists. II. Rollo H. Beck. *Bull. Cooper Ornithol. Club* 1:77–79.

[Barlow, C.]. 1900a. Growth of the Cooper Club. *Condor* 2:116.

Barlow, C. 1900b. Some additions to Van Denburgh's list of land birds of Santa Clara Co., Cal. *Condor* 2:131–133.

———. 1902. Some observations of the Rufous-crowned Sparrow. *Condor* 4:107–111.

Barnes, R. 1993. Riparian forests: rivers of life. *On Behalf of Songbirds; California Planning and Action for the Partners in Flight Initiative.* Point Reyes Bird Observ., Stinson Beach, Calif.

Bartholomew, B. 1970. Bare zone between California shrub and grassland communities; the role of animals. *Science* 170:1210–1212.

Bartholomew, G. A. and T. J. Cade. 1963. The water economy of land birds. *Auk 80*:504–539.

Bartholomew, G. A., T. R. Howell and T. J. Cade. 1957. Torpidity in the White-throated Swift, Anna Hummingbird, and Poor-will. *Condor* 59:145–155.

Basham, M. P. and L. R. Mewaldt. 1987. Salt water tolerance and the distribution of south San Francisco Bay Song Sparrows. *Condor* 89:697–709.

Baumhoff, M. A. 1963. Ecological determinants of aboriginal populations. *Univ. Calif. Publ. Am. Arch. Ethnol. 49*:155–126. Cited in Frenkel, 1970.

Beal, F. E. L. 1907. *Birds of California, in Relation to the Fruit Industry, pt.1.* U.S. Dept. Agric. Biol. Surv. Bull. 30. Washington.

———. 1910. *Birds of California, in Relation to the Fruit Industry, pt. 2.* U.S. Dept. Agric., Biol. Surv., Bull. No. 34. Washington. Quoted in A. C. Bent, 1968, *Pt. 1*, pp. 63–64.

Beason, R. C. 1995. Horned Lark (*Eremophila alpestris*). *The Birds of North America*, No. 195 (A. Poole and F. Gill, eds.). Acad. Nat. Sci., Philadelphia; Am. Ornithol. Union, Washington.

Beck, R. H. 1893. Notes from Berryessa, Cal. *Ornithol. Oologist* 18:131.

———. 1895a. Notes of the Blue-fronted Jay. *Nidiologist* 2:158.

———. 1895b. Notes on the Dotted Canyon Wren. *Nidiologist 3*:3–4.

———. 1897. Watching a Poor-will. *Nidologist 4*:105.

———. 1901. A season with the Golden Eagles of Santa Clara Co., Cal. *Condor 3*:59–64.

Beechey, F. W. 1831. *Narrative of a Voyage to the Pacific and Beering's Strait, To Co-operate with the Polar Expeditions.* 2 vols. Henry Colburn and Richard Bentley, London.

Beedy, E. C. and W. J. Hamilton, III. 1997. Tricolored Blackbird status update and management guidelines. Jones & Stokes Assoc., Inc. 97B099. Prepared for the U.S. Fish and Wildlife Service, Portland, and California Dept. of Fish and Game, Sacramento.

———. 1999. Tricolored Blackbird (*Agelaius tricolor*). *The Birds of North America* No. 423. (A. Poole and F. Gill (eds.). The Birds of North America, Inc. Philadelphia.

Belding, L. 1890. *Land Birds of the Pacific District.* Calif. Acad. Sci., San Francisco.

Bellrose, F. C. 1976. *Ducks, Geese and Swans of North America.* 2nd ed. Stackpole Books, Harrisburg, Pa.

Bemis, C. and J. D. Rising. 1999. Western Wood-Pewee (*Contopus sordidulus*). *The Birds of North America*, No. 451 (A. Poole and F. Gill, eds.). The Birds of North America, Inc., Philadelphia.

Bent, A. C. 1923a. *Life Histories of North American Wild Fowl, Pt. 1*, p. 130. Smithsonian Inst. U.S. Natl. Museum Bull. 126. Reissued in 1962 by Dover Publ., New York.

———. 1923b. *Life Histories of North American Wild Fowl, Pt. 1*, p. 143. Smithsonian Inst. U.S. Natl. Museum Bull. 126. Reissued in 1962 by Dover Publ., New York.

———. 1926. *Life Histories of North American Marsh Birds*, p. 57. Smithsonian Inst. U.S. Natl. Museum Bull. 135. Reissued in 1963 by Dover Publ., New York.

———. 1932. *Life Histories of North American Gallinaceous Birds*, p. 62. Smithsonian Inst. U.S. Natl. Museum Bull. 162. Reissued in 1964 by Dover Publ., New York.

———. 1938a. Life Histories of North American Birds of Prey, Pt. 2, p. 41. Smithsonian Inst. U.S. Natl. Museum Bull. 170. Reissued in 1961 by Dover Publ., New York.

———. 1938b. Life Histories of North American Birds of Prey, Pt. 2, p. 67. Smithsonian Inst. U.S. Natl. Museum Bull. 170. Reissued in 1961 by Dover Publ., New York.

———. 1938c. Life Histories of North American Birds of Prey, Pt. 2, p. 121. Smithsonian Inst. U.S. Natl. Museum Bull. 170. Reissued in 1961 by Dover Publ., New York.

———. 1938d. Life Histories of North American Birds of Prey, Pt. 2, p. 263. Smithsonian Inst. U.S. Natl. Museum Bull. 170. Reissued in 1961 by Dover Publ., New York.

———. 1938e. Life Histories of North American Birds of Prey, Pt. 2, p. 322. Smithsonian Inst. U.S. Natl. Museum Bull. 170. Reissued in 1961 by Dover Publ., New York.

———. 1938f. Life Histories of North American Birds of Prey, Pt. 2, p. 396. Smithsonian Inst. U.S. Natl. Museum Bull. 170. Reissued in 1961 by Dover Publ., New York.

———. 1938g. Life Histories of North American Flycatchers, Larks, Swallows, and Their Allies, p. 130–131. Smithsonian Inst. U.S. Natl. Museum Bull. 179. Reissued in 1963 by Dover Publ., New York.

———. 1938h. Life Histories of North American Flycatchers, Larks, Swallows, and Their Allies, p. 445, p. 458. Smithsonian Inst. U.S. Natl. Museum Bull. 179. Reissued in 1963 by Dover Publ., New York.

———. 1939a. *Life Histories of North American Woodpeckers*, p. 48. Smithsonian Inst. U.S. Natl. Museum Bull. 174. Reissued in 1964 by Dover Publ., New York.

———. 1939b. *Life Histories of North American Woodpeckers*, p. 296. Smithsonian Inst. U.S. Natl. Museum Bull. 174. Reissued in 1964 by Dover Publ., New York.

———. 1940. *Life Histories of North American Cuckoos, Goatsuckers, Hummingbirds and Their Allies, Pt. 2*, p. 319. Smithsonian Inst. U.S. Natl. Museum Bull. 176. Reissued in 1964 by Dover Publ., New York.

———. 1946a. *Life Histories of North American Jays, Crows and Titmice, Pt. 1*, p. 64. Smithsonian Inst. U.S. Natl. Museum Bull. 191. Reissued in 1964 by Dover Publ., New York.

———. 1946b. *Life Histories of North American Jays, Crows and Titmice, Pt. 2*, p. 419. Smithsonian Inst. U.S. Natl. Museum Bull. 191. Reissued in 1963 by Dover Publ., New York.

———. 1948a. *Life Histories of North American Nuthatches, Wrens, Thrashers, and Their Allies*, p. 46. Smithsonian Inst. U.S. Natl. Museum Bull. 195. Reissued in 1964 by Dover Publ., New York.

———. 1948b. *Life Histories of North American Nuthatches, Wrens, Thrashers, and Their Allies*, p. 160. Smithsonian Inst. U.S. Natl. Museum Bull. 195. Reissued in 1964 by Dover Publ., New York.

———. 1948c. *Life Histories of North American Nuthatches, Wrens, Thrashers, and Their Allies*, p. 278. Smithsonian Inst. U.S. Natl. Museum Bull. 195. Reissued in 1964 by Dover Publ., New York.

———. 1948d. *Life Histories of North American Nuthatches, Wrens, Thrashers, and Their Allies*, p. 404. Smithsonian Inst. U.S. Natl. Museum Bull. 195. Reissued in 1964 by Dover Publ., New York.

———. 1949. *Life Histories of North American Thrushes, Kinglets, and Their Allies*, p. 364. Smithsonian Inst. U.S. Natl. Museum Bull. 196. Reissued in 1964 by Dover Publ., New York.

———. 1950a. *Life Histories of American Wagtails, Shrikes, Vireos, and Their Allies*, p. 102. Smithsonian Inst. U.S. Natl. Museum Bull. 197. Reissued in 1965 by Dover Publ., New York.

———. 1950b. *Life Histories of American Wagtails, Shrikes, Vireos, and Their Allies*, p. 183. Smithsonian Inst. U.S. Natl. Museum Bull. 197. Reissued in 1965 by Dover Publ., New York.

———. 1953. *Life Histories of North American Wood Warblers, Pt. 1*, p. 329. Smithsonian Inst. U.S. Natl. Museum Bull. 203. Reissued in 1963 by Dover Publ., New York.

———. 1958a. *Life Histories of North American Blackbirds, Orioles, Tanagers, and Allies*, p. 24. Smithsonian Inst. U.S. Natl. Museum Bull. 211. Reissued in 1965 by Dover Publ., New York.

———. 1958b. *Life Histories of North American Blackbirds, Orioles, Tanagers, and Allies*, p. 280. Smithsonian Inst. U.S. Natl. Museum Bull. 211. Reissued in 1965 by Dover Publ., New York.

———. 1968. *Life Histories of North American Cardinals, Grosbeaks, Buntings, Towhees, Finches, Sparrows, and Allies, Pt. 2*, p. 1013. Smithsonian Inst. U.S. Natl. Museum Bull. 237. Reissued in 1968 by Dover Publ., New York.

Berner, M. 2003a. Osprey (*Pandion haliaetus*). *Breeding Birds of Napa County, California: an Illustrated Atlas of Nesting Birds*, p. 41 (A. Smith, ed.). Napa-Solano Audubon Soc., Vallejo.

———. 2003b. Bald Eagle (*Haliaeetus leucocephalus*). *Breeding Birds of Napa County, California: an Illustrated Atlas of Nesting Birds*, p. 43 (A. Smith, ed.). Napa-Solano Audubon Soc., Vallejo.

———. 2003c. Virginia Rail (*Rallus limicola*). *Breeding Birds of Napa County, California: an Illustrated Atlas of Nesting Birds*, p. 59 (A. Smith, ed.). Napa-Solano Audubon Soc., Vallejo.

———. 2003d. Sora (*Porzana carolina*). *Breeding Birds of Napa County, California: an Illustrated Atlas of Nesting Birds*, p. 60 (A. Smith, ed.). Napa-Solano Audubon Soc., Vallejo.

———. 2003e. Hairy Woodpecker (*Picoides villosus*). *Breeding Birds of Napa County, California: an Illustrated Atlas of Nesting Birds*, p. 91 (A. Smith, ed.). Napa-Solano Audubon Soc., Vallejo.

———. 2003f. American Dipper (*Cinclus mexicanus*). *Breeding Birds of Napa County, California: an Illustrated Atlas of Nesting Birds*, p. 130 (A. Smith, ed.). Napa-Solano Audubon Soc., Vallejo.

———. 2003g. Western Meadowlark (*Sturnella neglecta*). *Breeding Birds of Napa County, California: an Illustrated Atlas of Nesting Birds*, p. 164 (A. Smith, ed.). Napa-Solano Audubon Soc., Vallejo.

———. 2003h. Yellow-headed Blackbird (*Xanthocephalus xanthocephalus*). *Breeding Birds of Napa County, California: an Illustrated Atlas of Nesting Birds*, p. 165 (A. Smith, ed.). Napa-Solano Audubon Soc., Vallejo.

———. 2003i. Purple Finch (*Carpodacus purpureus*). *Breeding Birds of Napa County, California: an Illustrated Atlas of Nesting Birds*, p. 170 (A. Smith, ed.). Napa-Solano Audubon Soc., Vallejo.

Bidwell, J. 1866. Annual address. *Trans. Calif. State Agr. Soc. 1864–1865*, pp. 202–213. Cited in L. T. Burcham, 1957.

Bildstein, K. L. and K. Meyer. 2000. Sharp-shinned Hawk (*Accipiter striatus*). Birds of North America, No. 482 (A. Poole and F. Gill, eds.). The Birds of North America, Inc., Philadelphia.

Bittner, M. 2004. *The Wild Parrots of Telegraph Hill*. Harmony Books, New York.

Blair, R. B. 1996. Land use and avian species diversity along an urban gradient. *Ecol. Appl. 6*:506–519.

Boarman, W. I. and B. Heinrich. 1999. Common Raven (*Corvus corax*). *The Birds of North America*, No. 476 (A. Poole and F. Gill, eds.). The Birds of North America, Inc., Philadelphia.

Bock, C. E. 1979. Joseph Grinnell and the Christmas Bird Count. *Am. Birds 33*:693–694.

Bock, C. E. and T. L. Root. 1981. The Christmas Bird Count and avian ecology. *Estimating Numbers of Terrestrial Birds*, pp. 17–23 (C. J. Ralph and J. M Scott, eds.). Studies in Avian Biology, No. 6.

Bock, C. E., A. Cruz, Jr., M. C. Grant, C. S. Aid and T. R. Strong. 1992. Field experimental evidence for diffuse competition among southwestern riparian birds. *Am. Nat. 140*:815–828.

Bolander, L. P. 1930. Is the Lewis Woodpecker a regular breeder in the San Francisco Region? *Condor 32*:263–264.

Bolton, H. E. 1911. Expedition to San Francisco Bay in 1770. Diary of Pedro Fages. *Publ. Acad. Pac. Coast Hist. 2*:141–159. Univ. Calif., Berkeley.

———. 1930a. *Anza's California Expeditions, Vol. 2: Opening a Land Route to California, Diaries of Anza, Díaz, Garcés, and Palóu.* Univ. Calif., Berkeley.

———. 1930b. *Anza's California Expeditions, Vol. 3: The San Francisco Colony.* Univ. Calif., Berkeley.

———. 1930c. *Anza's California Expeditions, Vol. 4: Font's Complete Diary.* Univ. Calif., Berkeley.

Bonnot, P. 1935. The California oyster industry. *Calif. Fish Game 21*:65–80.

Bosakowski, T., D. G. Smith and R. Speiser. 1992. Status, nesting density, and macrohabitat selection of Red-shouldered Hawks in northern New Jersey. *Wilson Bull. 104*:434–446.

Bousman, W. G. 2000. Black-crowned Night Heron (*Nycticorax nycticorax*). *Baylands Ecosystem Species and Community Profiles: Life Histories and Environmental Requirements of Key Plants, Fish and Wildlife*, pp. 328–331. Prepared by the San Francisco Bay Area Wetlands Ecosystem Goals Project (P. R. Olofson, ed.). San Francisco Bay Regional Water Quality Control Board, Oakland, Calif.

———. 2007. Breeding avifaunal changes in the San Francisco Bay area, 1927–2005. *West. Birds 38*:102–136.

Brabb, E. E., R. W. Graymer and D. L. Jones. 2000. Geologic map and map database of the Palo Alto 30′ × 60′ quadrangle, California. U.S. Geol. Survey Misc. Field Studies Map MF-2332. http://pubs.usgs.gov.mf/2000/mf-2332/.

Breaux, A. M. 2000. Non-native predators: Norway Rat and Roof Rat. *Baylands Ecosystem Species and Community Profiles: Life Histories and Environmental Requirements of Key Plants, Fish and Wildlife*, pp. 249–250. Prepared by the San Francisco Bay Area Wetlands Ecosystem Goals Project (P. R. Olofson, ed.). San Francisco Bay Regional Water Quality Control Board, Oakland, Calif.

Brennan, L. A. 1999. Northern Bobwhite (*Colinus virginianus*). *The Birds of North America*, No. 397 (A. Poole and F. Gill, eds.). The Birds of North America, Inc., Philadelphia.

Brewer, W. H. 1966. *Up and Down California in 1860–1864.* (F. P. Farquhar, ed.). 3rd ed. Univ. Calif. Pr., Berkeley.

LITERATURE CITED

Brisbin, I. L., Jr., H. D. Pratt and T. B. Mowbray. 2002. American Coot (*Fulica americana*) and Hawaiian Coot (*Fulica alai*). *The Birds of North America*, No. 697 (A. Poole and F. Gill, eds.). The Birds of North America, Inc., Philadelphia.

Brittan, M. R. 1997. The Stanford School of Ichthyology: Eighty years (1891–1970) from Jordan (1851–1931) to Myers (1905–1985). *Collection Building in Ichthyology and Herpetology*, pp. 233–263 (T. W. Pietsch and W. D. Anderson, Jr., eds.). Spec. Publ. No. 3. Am. Soc. Ichthyol. Herpetol., Lawrence, Kans.

Broek, J. O. M. 1932. *The Santa Clara Valley, California: a Study in Landscape Changes.* Rikjsuniversiteit te Utrecht, Utrecht.

Brown, A. K. 1966. *Sawpits in the Spanish Redwoods.* San Mateo County Hist. Assoc., San Mateo, Calif.

———. 2001. *A Description of Distant Roads: Original Journals of the First Expeditions into California, 1769–1770.* San Diego State Univ. Pr., San Diego.

———. 2002. Historical oak woodland detected through *Armillaria mellea* damage in fruit orchards. Proc. Fifth Symp. on Oak Woodlands: Oaks in California's Changing Landscape, pp. 651–661. U.S. Forest Serv. Gen. Tech. Rep. PSW-GTR-184. Albany, Calif.

Brown, C. R. 1981. The impact of Starlings on Purple Martin populations in unmanaged colonies. *Am. Birds* 35:266–268.

———. 1997. Purple Martin (*Progne subis*). *The Birds of North America*, No. 287 (A. Poole and F. Gill, eds.). Acad. Nat. Sci., Philadelphia; Am. Ornithol. Union, Washington.

Brown, C. R. and M. B. Brown. 1995. Cliff Swallow (*Hirundo pyrrhonota*). *The Birds of North America*, No. 149 (A. Poole and F. Gill, eds.). Acad. Nat. Sci., Philadelphia; Am. Ornithol. Union, Washington.

Brown, J. L. 1963. Aggressiveness, dominance and social organization in the Steller Jay. *Condor* 65:460–484.

———. 1964. The integration of agonistic behavior in the Steller's Jay, *Cyanocitta stelleri* (Gmelin). *Univ. Calif. Publ. Zool.* 60:223–324.

Brua, R. B. 2001. Ruddy Duck (*Oxyura jamaicensis*). *The Birds of North America*, No. 696 (A. Poole and F. Gill, eds.) The Birds of North America, Inc., Philadelphia.

Bryant, E. 1848. *What I Saw in California.* Appleton, New York.

Bryant, H. C. 1914. A determination of the economic status of the western meadowlark (*Sturnella neglecta*) in California. *Univ. Calif. Publ. Zool.* 11:377–510.

———. 1915. Nesting of Sora and Virginia Rail in Alameda County. *Calif. Fish Game* 1:194.

Bryant, W. E. 1888. Birds and eggs from the Farallon Islands. *Proc. Calif. Acad. Sci.*, 2nd Series, v.1, pp. 25–50.

———. 1890. An ornithological retrospect. *Zoe* 1:289–293.

———. 1891. Andrew Jackson Grayson. *Zoe* 2:34–68.

———. 1894. Eggs of the White-throated Swift. *Nidiologist* 2:7–8.

Buchanan, J. 1996. A spatial analysis of the Burrowing Owl (*Speotyto cunicularia hypugaea*) population in Santa Clara County, California, using a geographic information system. Master's thesis, San Jose State Univ.

Buchheister, C. W. and F. Graham, Jr. 1973. From the swamps and back: a concise and candid history of the Audubon movement. *Audubon* 75:4–43.

Buehler, D. A. 2000. Bald Eagle (*Haliaeetus leucocephalus*). *The Birds of North America*, No. 506 (A. Poole and F. Gill, eds.). The Birds of North America, Inc., Philadelphia.

Bull, E. L. and C. T. Collins. 1993. Vaux's Swift (*Chaetura vauxi*). *The Birds of North America*, No. 77 (A. Poole and F. Gill, eds.). Acad. Nat. Sci., Philadelphia; Am. Ornithol. Union, Washington.

Bull, E. L. and J. E. Jackson. 1995. Pileated Woodpecker (*Dryocopus pileatus*). *The Birds of North America*, No. 148 (A. Poole and F. Gill, eds.). Acad. Nat. Sci., Philadelphia; Am. Ornithol. Union, Washington.

Burcham, L. T. 1957. *California Range Land.* Dept. Natural Resources, Sacramento. Reissued 1981 with a few technical changes by Univ. Calif. Davis, Davis, Calif.

Burger, G. V. 1954. The status of introduced wild turkeys in California. *Calif. Fish Game* 40:123–145.

Burridge, B. 1995a. Cooper's Hawk (*Accipiter cooperi*). *Sonoma County Breeding Bird Atlas*, p. 49, 183 (B. Burridge, ed.) Madrone Audubon Soc., Santa Rosa, Calif.

———. 1995b. Virginia Rail (*Rallus limicola*). *Sonoma County Breeding Bird Atlas*, p. 62 (B. Burridge, ed.) Madrone Audubon Soc., Santa Rosa, Calif.

———. 1995c. Tree Swallow (*Tachycineta bicolor*). *Sonoma County Breeding Bird Atlas*, p. 107 (B. Burridge, ed.) Madrone Audubon Soc., Santa Rosa, Calif.

———. 1995d. Greater Roadrunner (*Geococcyx californianus*). *Sonoma County Breeding Bird Atlas*, pp. 190–191 (B. Burridge, ed.) Madrone Audubon Soc., Santa Rosa, Calif.

———. 1995e. Blue Grosbeak (*Guiraca caerulea*). *Sonoma County Breeding Bird Atlas*, p. 193. (B. Burridge, ed.) Madrone Audubon Soc., Santa Rosa, Calif.

Butcher, G. S. 1990. Audubon Christmas Bird Counts. *Survey Designs and Statistical Methods for the Estimation of Avian Population Trends*, pp. 5–13 (J. R. Sauer and S. Droege, eds.). U.S. Fish Wildl. Serv. Biol. Rep. No. 90(1).

Butcher, G. S. and C. E. McCulloch. 1990. Influence of observer effort on the number of individual birds recorded on Christmas bird counts. *Survey Designs and Statistical Methods for the Estimation of Avian Population Trends*, pp. 120–129 (J. R. Sauer and S. Droege, eds.). U.S. Fish Wildl. Serv. Biol. Rep. No. 90(1).

Butler, R. W. 1992. Great Blue Heron (*Ardea herodias*). *The Birds of North America*, No. 25 (A. Poole and F. Gill, eds.). Acad. Nat. Sci., Philadelphia; Am. Ornithol. Union, Washington.

Butterfield, A. D. 1883. California Long-billed Marsh Wren. *Ornithol. Oologist* 8:64.

Byers, C., J. Curson and U. Olsson. 1995. *Sparrows and Buntings.* Houghton Mifflin, Boston.

Byster, L. A. and T. Smith. 2006. From grassroots to global. *Challenging the Chip: Labor Rights and Environmental Justice in the Global Electronics Industry* (T. Smith, D. A. Sonnenfeld and D. N. Pellow, eds.), pp. 111–119. Temple Univ. Pr., Philadelphia.

LITERATURE CITED

Cabe, P. R. 1993. European Starling (*Sturnus vulgaris*). *The Birds of North America*, No. 48 (A. Poole and F. Gill, eds.). Acad. Nat. Sci., Philadelphia; Am. Ornithol. Union, Washington.

California Resources Agency. 2003. Department of Fish and Game. Habitat Conservation Division. Natural Communities List. www.dfg.ca.gov/whdab/html/natural_communities.html.

California State Commissioners of Fisheries. 1879. Fifth Biennial Report, 1878–79. State Printing Off., Sacramento. Cited in J. E. Skinner, 1962.

Cannings, R. J. 1993. Northern Saw-whet Owl (*Aegolius acadicus*). *The Birds of North America*, No. 42 (A. Poole and F. Gill, eds.). Acad. Nat. Sci., Philadelphia; Am. Ornithol. Union, Washington.

Carnie, S. K. 1954. Food habits of nesting Golden Eagles in the Coast Ranges of California. *Condor* 39:49–56.

Carriger, H. W. 1899. Notes on the nesting of the Slender-billed Nuthatch. *Bull. Cooper Ornithol. Club* 1:83.

Carriger, H. W. and J. R. Pemberton. 1907. Nesting of the Pine Siskin in California. *Condor* 9:18–19.

Carriger, H. W. and W. E. Unglish. 1931. Nesting of the Tolmie Warbler in southern Santa Clara County. *Condor* 31:222.

Carter, H. R., A. L. Sowls, M. S. Rodway, U. W. Wilson, R. W. Lowe, G. J. McChesney, F. Gress and D. W. Anderson. 1995. Population size, trends, and conservation problems of the Double-crested Cormorant on the Pacific Coast of North America. *The Double-crested Cormorant: Biology, Conservation and Management,* pp. 189–215 (D. N. Nettleship and D. C. Duffy, eds.). Colonial Waterbirds 18, Spec. Publ. 1.

Chamberlin, C. 1893. Another California trip. *Oologist* 10:116–118.

———. 1894. The Water Ouzel at home. *Nidiologist* 1:163–165.

Channing, E. 1979. Movements of banded Mourning Doves near Turlock, California. *Calif. Fish Game* 65:23–25.

Chapman, F. M. 1907. *The Warblers of North America.* Appleton, New York.

Cheatham, N. H. and J. R. Haller. 1975. An annotated list of California habitat types. Unpublished report. Univ. Calif. Natural Land and Water Reserves System,

Christensen, G. C. 1996. Chukar (*Alectoris chukar*). *The Birds of North America*, No. 258 (A. Poole and F. Gill, eds.). Acad. Nat. Sci., Philadelphia; Am. Ornithol. Union, Washington.

Chu, M. and G. Walsberg. 1999. Phainopepla (*Phainopepla nitens*). *The Birds of North America*, No. 415 (A. Poole and F. Gill, eds.). The Birds of North America, Philadelphia.

Cicero, C. 1996. Sibling species of titmice in the *Parus inornatus* complex (Aves: Paridae). *Univ. Calif. Publ. Zool.* 128:1–271.

Clark, H. W. 1930. Notes on the avifauna of a Transition island in Napa County, California. *Condor* 32:50–52.

Clark, W. V. T. 1973. *The Journals of Alfred Doten, 1849–1903, Vol. 1.* Univ. Nevada Pr., Reno.

Clarke, W. C. 1959. The vegetation cover of the San Francisco Bay region in the early Spanish Period. Master's thesis, Univ. Calif., Berkeley.

Cleland, R. G. 1941. *The Cattle on a Thousand Hills.* Huntington Library, San Marino, Calif. Quoted in Burcham, 1957.

Coan, E. 1982. *James Graham Cooper, Pioneer Western Naturalist.* Univ. Pr. Idaho, Moscow, Ida.

Cody, M. L. 1998. California Thrasher (*Toxostoma redivivum*). *The Birds of North America*, No. 323 (A. Poole and F. Gill, eds.). The Birds of North America, Inc., Philadelphia.

Cogswell, H. L. 1968. California Rufous-crowned Sparrow. *Life Histories of North American Cardinals, Grosbeaks, Buntings, Towhees, Finches, Sparrows, and Allies,* Pt. 2, pp. 931–940 (O. L. Austen, Jr., comp. & ed.). Smithsonian Inst. U.S. Natl. Museum Bull. 237. Reissued in 1968 by Dover Publ., New York.

———. 1986. Who was 'Cooper'? *Condor* 88:402–403.

Cohen, A. N. and J. T. Carlton. 1998. Acceleration invasion rate in a highly invaded estuary. *Science* 279:555–558.

Cohen, D. A. 1895. Nesting of the Water Ouzel. *Nidiologist* 2:109–110.

———. 1899. California Clapper Rail in Alameda Co. *Bull. Cooper Ornithol. Club* 1:31.

———. 1900. Casual observations on a colony of Black-crowned Night Herons. *Condor* 2:10–12.

Collins, C. T. and K. L. Garrett. 1996. The Black Skimmer in California: an overview. *West. Birds* 27:127–135.

Collins, J. N. and R. M. Grossinger. 2004. Synthesis of scientific knowledge concerning estuarine landscapes and related habitats of the South Bay Ecosystem. SFEI Rep. 308. San Francisco Estuary Inst., Oakland, Calif.

Collins, J. N. and V. H. Resh. 1985. Utilization of natural and man-made habitats by the salt marsh Song Sparrow, *Melospiza melodia samuelis* (Baird). *Calif. Fish Game* 71:40–52.

Conaway, C. H., E. B. Watson, J. R. Flanders and A. R. Flegal. 2004. Mercury deposition in a tidal marsh of south San Francisco Bay downstream of the historic New Almaden mining district, California. *Mar. Chem.* 90:175–184.

Conway, C. J. 1995. Virginia Rail (*Rallus limicola*). *The Birds of North America*, No. 173 (A. Poole and F. Gill, eds.). Acad. Nat. Sci., Philadelphia; Am. Ornithol. Union, Washington.

Cooper, J. G. 1870. *Ornithology, Vol. 1: Land Birds* (S. F. Baird, ed.) Geological Survey of California. University Pr., Cambridge, Mass.

Cooper, J. G. and G. Suckley. 1860. Report upon the birds collected on the survey; land birds. *Report of Explorations and Surveys to Ascertain the Most Practicable and Economical Route for a Railroad from the Mississippi River to the Pacific Ocean*, Vol. 12, Pt. 3. U.S. Senate, 36th Congress, Washington (Thomas H. Ford, Printer).

Cooper, W. S. 1926. Vegetational development upon alluvial fans in the vicinity of Palo Alto, California. *Ecology* 6:1–30.

Corbin, K. W. and A. H. Brush. 1999. In memoriam: Charles Gald Sibley, 1917–1998. *Auk 116*:806–814.

Coutlee, E. L. 1968a. Comparative breeding behavior of Lesser and Lawrence's Goldfinches. *Condor* 70:228–242.

———. 1968b. Maintenance behavior of Lesser and Lawrence's Goldfinches. *Condor* 70:378–384.

LITERATURE CITED

Cowan, J. B. 1952. Life history and productivity of a population of western mourning doves in California. *Calif. Fish Game* 36:505–521.

Cox, A. and Engebretson, D. 1985. Change in motion of Pacific plate at 5 My BP. *Nature* 313:472–474.

Cramp. S., ed. 1977. *Handbook of the Birds of Europe, the Middle East, and North Africa: the Birds of the Western Paleartic, Vol. 1*: Ostriches to Ducks. Oxford Univ. Pr., Oxford.

Crase, F. T. and R. W. DeHaven. 1972. Current breeding status of the Yellow-headed Blackbird in California. *Calif. Birds* 3:39–42.

Crocoll, S. T. 1994. Red-shouldered Hawk (*Buteo lineatus*). *The Birds of North America, No. 107* (A. Poole and F. Gill, eds.). Acad. Nat. Sci., Philadelphia; Am. Ornithol. Union, Washington.

Csada, R. D. and R. M. Brigham. 1992. Common Poorwill (*Phalaenoptilus nuttallii*). *The Birds of North America*, No. 12 (A. Poole and F. Gill, eds.). Acad. Nat. Sci., Philadelphia; Am. Ornithol. Union, Washington.

Cuthbert, F. J. and L. R. Wires. 1999. Caspian Tern (*Sterna caspia*). *The Birds of North America*, No. 403 (A. Poole and F. Gill, eds.). The Birds of North America, Inc., Philadelphia.

Cutler, R. W. P. 2001. *Red Mountain; The Rise and Fall of a Magnesite Mining Empire, 1900–1947*. Morris Publ., Kearney, Nebr.

Daggett, F. S. 1900. A protest against the indiscriminate use of poison by orchardists. *Condor* 2:139.

Danby, D. E. 1936. The Little Blue Heron at Santa Cruz, California. *Condor* 38:88–89.

Dasmann, W. P. and R. F. Dasmann. 1963. Abundance and scarcity in California Deer. *Calif. Fish Game* 49:4–15.

Davis, F. W. and D. M. Stoms. 1999. Gap analysis of mainland California; an interactive atlas of terrestrial biodiversity and land management. Calif. Dept. Fish and Game, Sacramento.

Davis, J. 1957. Comparative foraging behavior of the Spotted and Brown Towhees. *Auk* 74:129–166.

———. 1958. In memoriam: Walter Kenrick Fisher. *Auk* 75:131–134.

Davis, J. N. 1995. Hutton's Vireo (*Vireo huttoni*). *The Birds of North America*, No. 189 (A. Poole and F. Gill, eds.). Acad. Nat. Sci., Philadelphia; Am. Ornithol. Union, Washington.

———. 1999. Lawrence's Goldfinch (*Carduelis lawrencei*). *The Birds of North America*, No. 480 (A. Poole and F. Gill, eds.). The Birds of North America, Inc., Philadelphia.

Davis, W. E., Jr. 1993. Black-crowned Night Heron (*Nycticorax nycticorax*). *The Birds of North America*, No. 74 (A. Poole and F. Gill, eds.). Acad. Nat. Sci., Philadelphia; Am. Ornithol. Union, Washington.

Davis, W. E., Jr. and J. A. Kushlan. 1994. Green Heron (*Butorides virescens*). *The Birds of North America*, No. 129 (A. Poole and F. Gill, eds.). Acad. Nat. Sci., Philadelphia; Am. Ornithol. Union, Washington.

Davis, W. H. 1889. *Sixty Years in California*. A. J. Leary, San Francisco.

Dawson, W. L. 1915. The breeding of Snowy Egret in California. *Condor* 17:97.

———. 1923. *The Birds of California*. South Moulton Co., San Diego.

Dawson, W. R. 1997. Pine Siskin (*Carduelis pinus*). *The Birds of North America*, No. 280 (A. Poole and F. Gill, eds.). Acad. Nat. Sci., Philadelphia; Am. Ornithol. Union, Washington.

De Groot, D. S. 1927. The California Clapper Rail, its nesting habits, enemies and habitat. *Condor* 29:259–270.

———. 1931. History of a nesting colony of Caspian Terns on San Francisco Bay. *Condor* 33:188–192.

DeHaven, R. W. 1973. Winter population trends of the starling in California. *Am. Birds* 27:836–838.

DeJong, M. J. 1996. Northern Rough-winged Swallow (*Stelgidopteryx serripennis*). *The Birds of North America*, No. 234 (A. Poole and F. Gill, eds.). Acad. Nat. Sci., Philadelphia; Am. Ornithol. Union, Washington.

Derrickson, K. C. and R. Breitwisch. 1992. Northern Mockingbird (*Mimus polyglottos*). *The Birds of North America*, No. 7 (A. Poole, P. Stettenheim and F. Gill, eds.). Acad. Nat. Sci., Philadelphia; Am. Ornithol. Union, Washington.

DeSante, D. F., E. Ruhlen, and D. K. Rosenberg. 1996. *The Distribution and Relative Abundance of Burrowing Owls in California: Evidence for a Declining Population*. Institute for Bird Populations, Point Reyes Station, Calif.

D'Evelyn, F. W. 1920. Hutchins Goose breeds in captivity. *Gull* 2(6).

Diamond, J. 2005. *Collapse: How Societies Choose to Fail or Succeed*. Viking, New York.

Dickey, K. E., Jr. 1981. Dams and reservoirs—engineering landmarks. *Water in the Santa Clara Valley: a History*, pp. 45–80 (S. McArthur, ed.). Calif. Hist. Center, De Anza Coll., Cupertino, Calif.

Dickinson, J. L., W. D. Koenig and F. A. Pitelka. 1997. Fitness consequences of helping behavior in the western bluebirds. *Behav. Ecol.* 7:168–177.

Dirks, W. M. 1916. Green-winged Teal nesting in Alameda County. *Cal. Fish Game* 2:46.

Dixon, J. 1923. Nesting records of the Dusky Poor-Will. *Condor* 25:77–85.

Dixon, J. B. 1937. The Golden Eagle in San Diego County, California. *Condor* 39:49–56.

Dixon, K. L. 1954. Some ecological relations of chickadees and titmice in central California. *Condor* 56:113–124.

———. 1960. Additional data on the establishment of the Chestnut-backed Chickadee at Berkeley, California. *Condor* 62:405–408.

Dobkin, D. W., J. A. Holmes and B. A. Wilcox. 1986. Traditional nest-site use by White-throated Swifts. *Condor* 88:252–253.

Donley, M. W., S. Allan, P. Caro and C. P. Patton. 1979. *Atlas of California*. Pacific Book Center, Culver City, Calif.

DuBowy, P. J. 1996. Northern Shoveler (*Anas clypeata*). *The Birds of North America*, No. 217 (A. Poole and F. Gill, eds.). Acad. Nat. Sci., Philadelphia; Am. Ornithol. Union, Washington.

Dunk, J. R. 1995. White-tailed Kite (*Elanus leucurus*). *The Birds of North America*, No. 178 (A. Poole and F. Gill, eds.). Acad. Nat. Sci., Philadelphia; Am. Ornithol. Union, Washington.

Eaton, S. W. 1992. Wild Turkey (*Meleagris gallopavo*). *The Birds of North America*, No. 22 (A. Poole and F. Gill, eds.). Acad. Nat. Sci., Philadelphia; Am. Ornithol. Union, Washington.

Ehrlich, P. R., D. S. Dobkin and D. Wheye. 1988. *The Birder's Handbook*. Simon & Schuster, New York.

Eisenmann, E. 1971. Range expansion and population increase in North and Middle America of the White-tailed Kite. *Am. Birds* 25:529–536.

Ellsworth, R. S. 1931. Reminiscences of a hunter and a collector. *Calif. Fish Game* 31:87–88.

Emerson, W. O. 1890. Birds new or rare in California. *Zoe 1*: 44–46.

————. 1899. Dr. James G. Cooper, a sketch. *Bull. Cooper Ornithol. Club 1*:1–5 and frontispiece.

————. 1901. Nesting of *Spatula clypeata*. *Condor 3*:116.

Emlen, J. T., Jr. 1940. The midwinter distribution of the crow in California. *Condor 42*:287–294.

England, A. S. 1993a. Black-chinned Sparrow (*Spizella atrogularis*). *Marin County Breeding Bird Atlas*, pp. 376–377 (W. D. Shuford, ed.). Bushtit Books, Bolinas, Calif.

————. 1993b. Sage Sparrow (*Amphispiza belli*). *Marin County Breeding Bird Atlas*, pp. 379–380 (W. D. Shuford, ed.). Bushtit Books, Bolinas, Calif.

Erickson, M. M. 1937. A jay shoot in California. *Condor 39*: 111–115.

Evens, J. and G. W. Page. 1986. Predation on Black Rails during high tides in salt marshes. *Condor 93*:107–108.

Evens, J. G., G. W. Page, S. A. Laymon and R. W. Stallcup. 1991. Distribution, relative abundance and status of the California Black Rail in western North America . *Condor 93*: 952–956.

Evermann, B. W. 1915. An attempt to save California Elk. *Calif. Fish Game 1*:85–96.

————. 1925. John Van Denburgh 1872–1924. *Science 61*:508–510.

Finley, W. L. 1906. Herons at home. *Condor 8*:35–40.

Fischer, D. L. 2001. *Early Southwest Ornithologists, 1528–1900*. Univ. Arizona Pr., Tucson.

Fish, K. 1981. Organization for water: rise of economic and political interests. *Water in the Santa Clara Valley: a History*, pp. 20–44 (S. McArthur, ed.). Calif. Hist. Center, De Anza Coll., Cupertino, Calif.

Fisher, A. B., and W. K. Fisher. 1923. The Clark Nutcracker at Pacific Grove, California. *Condor 25*:106.

Fisher, W. K. 1900. A list of birds observed on Mt. St. Helena, California. *Condor 2*:135–138.

————. 1902. List of birds of Santa Clara Valley and Santa Cruz Mountains, exclusive of water birds. *Handbook of Birds of the Western United States*, pp. li–lvi (F. M. Bailey, ed.). Houghton, Mifflin.

————. 1904. Two unusual birds at Stanford University, Cal. *Condor 6*:108–109.

————. 1905. The mockingbird at Stanford University, Cal. *Condor 7*:55.

————. 1918. In memoriam: Lyman Belding. *Condor 20*:50–61.

————. 1923. William Wightman Price. *Condor 25*:50–57.

————. 1940. When Joseph Grinnell and I were young. *Condor 42*:35–38.

Foley, J. 1990. Wild Turkeys thrive in county's hills. *San Jose Mercury News*, p. 1B, Nov. 22.

Foley, J. A., R. DeFries, G. P. Asner, C. Barford, G. Bonan, S. R. Carpenter, F. S. Chapin, M. T. Coe, G. C. Daily, H. K. Gibbs, J. H. Helkoski, T. Holloway, E. A. Howard, C. J. Kucharik, C. Monfreda, J. A. Patz, I. C. Prentice, N. Ramankutty and P. K. Snyder. 2005. Global consequences of land use. *Science 309*:570–574.

Forshaw, J. M. 2006. *Parrots of the World: An Identification Guide*. Princeton Univ. Pr., Princeton, N.J.

Foster, M. L. 1977. Status of the Salt Marsh Yellowthroat (*Geothlypis trichas sinuosa*) in the San Francisco Bay area, California, 1975–1976. Calif. Dept. Fish and Game, Job I-1.12.

Fowler, F. H. 1931. Studies of food and growth of the Prairie Falcon. *Condor 33*:193–201.

Franzreb, K. E. 1987. Endangered status and strategies for conservation of the Least Bell's Vireo (*Vireo bellii pusillus*) in California. *West. Birds 18*:43–49.

Frémont, J. C. 1848. *Geographical Memoir upon Upper California*. Wendell and Van Benthuysen, Washington. Cited in W. C. Clarke, 1959.

Frenkel, R. E. 1970. *Ruderal Vegetation Along Some California Roadsides*. Univ. Calif. Pr., Berkeley.

Friedmann, H. and L. F. Kiff. 1985. The parasitic cowbirds and their hosts. *Proc. West. Found. Vert. Zool. 2(4)*:227–302.

Gaines, D. 1974. A new look at the nesting riparian avifauna of the Sacramento Valley, California. *West. Birds 5*:61–80.

————. 1988. *Birds of Yosemite and the East Slope*. Artemisia Pr., Lee Vining, Calif.

Gaines, D. and S. A. Laymon. 1984. Decline, status and preservation of the Yellow-billed Cuckoo in California. *West. Birds 15*:49–80.

Gallagher, S. R. 1997a. Yellow Warbler. *Atlas of Breeding Birds, Orange County, California*, pp. 179–180 (S. R. Gallagher, ed.). Sea and Sage Audubon Pr., Irvine, Calif.

————. 1997b. Yellow-breasted Chat. *Atlas of Breeding Birds, Orange County, California*, pp. 181–183 (S. R. Gallagher, ed.). Sea and Sage Audubon Pr., Irvine, Calif.

Gamble, L. R. and T. M. Bergin. 1996. Western Kingbird (*Tyrannus verticalis*). *The Birds of North America*, No. 227 (A. Poole and F. Gill, eds.). Acad. Nat. Sci., Philadelphia; Am. Ornithol. Union, Washington.

Gammonley, J. H. 1996. Cinnamon Teal (*Anas cyanoptera*). *The Birds of North America*, No. 209 (A. Poole and F. Gill, eds.). Acad. Nat. Sci., Philadelphia; Am. Ornithol. Union, Washington.

Garrett, K. L. 1997. Population status and distribution of naturalized parrots in southern California. *West. Birds 28*:181–185.

————. 1998. Field separation of bishops (*Euplectes*) from North American emberizids. *West. Birds 29*:231–232.

Garrett, K. and J. Dunn. 1981. *Birds of Southern California*. Los Angeles Audubon Soc., Los Angeles.

Garrison, B. A. 1999. Bank Swallow (*Riparia riparia*). *The Birds of North America*, No. 414 (A. Poole and F. Gill, eds.). The Birds of North America, Inc., Philadelphia.

Garrison, B. A., J. M. Humphrey, and S. A. Laymon. 1987. Bank Swallow distribution and nesting ecology on the Sacramento River, California. *West. Birds* 18:71–76.

Gathright, A. 1999. Hikers do turkey trot on trails. *San Jose Mercury News*, p.1A, March 11.

Gatz, T. A. 2001. Orange Bishops breeding in Phoenix, Arizona. *West Birds 32*:81–82.

Gavin, T. A., R. A. Howard and B. May. 1991. Allozyme variation among breeding populations of Red-winged Blackbirds: the California conundrum. *Auk 108*:602–611.

Geary, G. J. 1934. *The Secularization of the California Missions,* Vol. 17. Catholic University of American Church History. Catholic Univ. Am.,Washington.

Geupel, G. R. and G. Ballard. 2002. Wrentit (*Chamaea fasciata*). *The Birds of North America*, No. 654 (A. Poole and F. Gill, eds.). The Birds of North America, Inc., Philadelphia.

Gill, R., Jr. 1972. South San Francisco Bay breeding bird survey, 1971. Calif. Dept. Fish and Game. Wildlife Management Branch Administrative Rep. 72-6.

———. 1976. Notes on the foraging of nesting Caspian Terns *Hydroprogne caspia* (Pallas). *Calif. Fish Game 62*:155.

———. 1977. Breeding avifauna of the South San Francisco Bay estuary. *West. Birds 8*:1–12.

———. 1979. Status and distribution of the California Clapper Rail. *Calif. Fish Game 65*:36–49.

Gill, R., Jr. and L. R. Mewaldt. 1983. Pacific Coast Caspian Terns: dynamics of an expanding population. *Auk 100*:369–381.

Giudice, J. H. and J. T. Ratti. 2001. Ring-necked Pheasant (*Phasianus colchicus*). *The Birds of North America*, No. 572 (A. Poole and F. Gill, eds.). The Birds of North America, Inc., Philadelphia.

Goals Project. 1999. Baylands Ecosystem Habitat Goals. A report of habitat recommendations prepared by the San Francisco Bay Area Wetlands Ecosystems Goals Project. U.S. Environ. Prot. Agency, San Francisco/S.F. Bay Regional Water Quality Control Board, Oakland, Calif.

Gochfeld, M. and J. Burger. 1994. Black Skimmer (*Rynchops niger*). *The Birds of North America*, No. 108 (A. Poole and F. Gill, eds.). Acad. Nat. Sci., Philadelphia; Am. Ornithol. Union, Washington.

Godfrey, E. W. 1986. *The Birds of Canada.* National Museum of Canada, Ottawa.

Goldman, E. A. 1908. The Green-winged Teal (*Nettion carolinensis*) breeding in California. *Condor 10*:129.

Goldwasser, S. 1987. Distribution, reproductive success and impact of nest parasitism by Brown-headed Cowbirds on Least Bell's Vireos. Fed. Aid Wildl. Res. W-54-R-10, Nongame Wildl. Prog. Job W1.5.1, Final Rep. State of Calif., The Resources Agency, Calif. Dept. Fish and Game, Sacramento.

Granfield, W. M. 1937. Nesting of the Saw-Whet Owl. *Condor 39*:185–187.

Greene, E. 1999. Demographic consequences of Brown-headed Cowbird parasitization of Lazuli Buntings. *Research and Management of the Brown-Headed Cowbird in Western Landscapes*, pp. 144–152. Studies in Avian Biology, No. 18.

Greene, E., V. R. Muehter, and W. Davison. 1996. Lazuli Bunting (*Passerina amoena*). *The Birds of North America* No. 232. (A. Poole and F. Gill, eds.). Acad. Nat. Sci., Philadelphia; Am. Ornithol. Union, Washington.

Greene, E., W. Davison and V. R. Muehter. 1998. Steller's Jay (*Cyanocitta stelleri*). *The Birds of North America*, No. 343 (A. Poole and F. Gill, eds.). Acad. Nat. Sci., Philadelphia; Am. Ornithol. Union, Washington.

Greenlaw, J. 1996. Spotted Towhee (*Pipilo maculatus*). *The Birds of North America*, No. 263 (A. Poole and F. Gill, eds.). Acad. Nat. Sci., Philadelphia; Am. Ornithol. Union, Washington.

Grenfell, W. E., Jr. and W. F. Laudenslayer, Jr., eds. 1983. *The Distribution of California Birds.* California Wildlife/Habitat Relationships Program Publ. No. 4. Calif. Dept. Fish and Game, Sacramento; U.S. Forest Service, San Francisco.

Griffith, J. T. and J. C. Griffith. 1997. Letter/report dated April 16, 1997, to the Fish and Wildlife Service regarding submittal of 1996 reports and report on 1997 activities.

Grinnell, H. W. 1930a. Minutes of the Cooper Club meetings. *Condor 32*:268.

———. 1930b. Minutes of the Cooper Club meetings. *Condor 32*:305–306.

———. 1940. Joseph Grinnell: 1877–1939. *Condor 42*:3–34.

Grinnell, J. 1900a. New races of birds from the Pacific Coast. *Condor 2*:127–129.

———. 1900b. Birds of the Kotzebue Sound Region, Alaska. Pac. Coast Avifauna. No. 1, Cooper Ornithological Club.

———. 1901a. The birds of California. *Condor 3*:83.

———. 1901b. The Santa Cruz Song Sparrow, with notes on the salt marsh Song Sparrow. *Condor 3*:92–93.

———. 1901c. Breeding range of the Allen's and Rufous Hummingbirds. *Condor 3*:127–128.

———. 1902. Check-list of California birds. *Pacific Coast Avifauna*, No. 3. Cooper Ornithol. Club, Berkeley.

———. 1905. Rufous-crowned Sparrow near Stanford University. *Condor 7*:53.

———. 1907. The California distribution of the Roadrunner (*Geococcyx californianus*). *Condor 9*:51–53.

———. 1909. A bibliography of California ornithology. Pac. Coast Avif. No. 5, Cooper Ornithol. Club, Berkeley.

———. 1914a. Occurrence of the White-tailed Kite in Central California in 1913. *Condor 16*:41.

———. 1914b. An account of the mammals and birds of the Lower Colorado Valley with especial reference to the distributional problems presented. *Univ. Calif. Publ. Zool. 12*:51–294.

———. 1915. A distributional list of the birds of California. *Pacific Coast Avifauna*, No. 11. Cooper Ornithol. Club, Berkeley.

———. 1924. Bibliography of California ornithology, second installment to end of 1923. Pac. Coast Avif. No. 16, Cooper Ornithol. Club, Berkeley.

————. 1925. The first Bulletin of the Cooper Ornithological Club. *Condor 27*:161–162.

————. 1937. Notes and news. *Condor 39*:45.

————. 1938. In memoriam: Richard C. McGregor, ornithologist of the Philippines. *Auk 55*:163–175.

————. 1939. Bibliography of California ornithology, third installment to end of 1938. Pac. Coast Avif. No. 26, Cooper Ornithol. Club, Berkeley.

Grinnell, J. and A. H. Miller. 1944. The distribution of the birds of California. *Pacific Coast Avifauna*, No. 27. Cooper Ornithol. Club, Berkeley.

Grinnell, J. and H. S. Swarth. 1926. Systematic review of the Pacific Coast Brown Towhees. *Univ. Calif. Publ. Zool. 21*:427–433.

Grinnell, J. and M. W. Wythe. 1927. Directory to the bird-life of the San Francisco Bay Region. *Pacific Coast Avifauna*, No. 18. Cooper Ornithol. Club, Berkeley.

Grinnell, J., H. C. Bryant and T. I. Storer. 1918. *The Game Birds of California*. Univ. Calif. Pr., Berkeley.

Grossinger, R. M., R. A. Askevold, C. J. Striplen, E. Brewster, S. Pearce, K. N. Larned, L. J. McKee and J. N. Collins. 2006. *Coyote Creek Watershed Historical Ecology Study: Historical Conditions, Landscape Change, and Restoration Potential in the Eastern Santa Clara Valley, California*. SFEI Publ. 426. San Francisco Estuary Inst., Oakland, Calif.

Groth, J. G. 1993. Evolutionary differentiation in morphology, vocalizations, and allozymes among nomadic sibling species in the North American Red Crossbill (*Loxia curvirostra*) complex. *Univ. Calif. Pub. Zool. 127*.

Gudde, E. G. 1998. *California Place Names*. Univ. Calif. Press, Berkeley.

Guinan, J. A., P. A. Gowaty and E. K. Eltzroth. 2000. Western Bluebird (*Sialia mexicana*). *The Birds of North America*, No. 510 (A. Poole and F. Gill, eds.). The Birds of North America, Inc., Philadelphia.

Gullion, G. W. 1954. The reproductive cycle of American Coots in California. *Auk 71*:366–412.

Guzy, M. J. and P. E. Lowther. 1997. Black-throated Gray Warbler (*Dendroica nigrescens*). *The Birds of North America*, No. 319 (A. Poole and F. Gill, eds.). Acad. Nat. Sci., Philadelphia; Am. Ornithol. Union, Washington.

Guzy, M. J. and G. Ritchison. 1999. Common Yellowthroat (*Geothlypis trichas*). The Birds of North America, No. 448 (A. Poole and F. Gill, eds.). The Birds of North America, Inc., Philadelphia.

Halliburton, R. and L. R. Mewaldt. 1976. Survival and mobility in a population of Pacific Coast Song Sparrows (*Melospiza melodia gouldii*). *Condor 78*:499–504.

Hamas, M. J. 1994. Belted Kingfisher (*Ceryle alcyon*). *The Birds of North America*, No. 84 (A. Poole and F. Gill, eds.). Acad. Nat. Sci., Philadelphia; Am. Ornithol. Union, Washington.

Hamilton, J. G. 1997. Changing perceptions of pre-European grasslands in California. *Madroño 44*:311–333.

Hamilton, R. B. 1975. Comparative behavior of the American Avocet and the Black-necked Stilt (*Recurvirostridae*). Ornithol. Monogr. No. 17. Am. Ornithol. Union, Washington.

Hamilton, W. J., III. 2000. Tricolored Blackbird 2000 breeding season census and survey observations and recommendations. Division of Environmental Studies, Univ. Calif., Davis.

Hamilton, W. J., III, L. Cook and K. Hunting. 1999. Tricolored Blackbird 1999 status report. Division of Environmental Studies, Univ. Calif., Davis.

Hanna, W. C. 1935. Farallon Rail nesting inland. *Condor 37*:81–82.

Harding-Smith, E. K. 1993. Summary of California Clapper Rail Winter Populations in the San Francisco Bay, 1989 to 1993. U.S. Fish and Wildlife Service.

Hardy, J. W. 1973. Feral exotic birds in southern California. *Wilson Bull. 85*:506–512.

Harper, H. T. and W. A. Smith. 1973. California's turkey stocking program. *Wild Turkey Management*, pp. 53–63 (G. C. Sanderson and H. C. Schultz, eds.). Univ. Missouri Pr., Columbia.

Harper, H. T., B. H. Harry and W. D. Bailey. 1958. The Chukar Partridge in California. *Calif. Fish Game 44*:5–50.

Harvey, T. E., K. J. Miller, R. L. Hothem, M. J. Rauzon, G. W. Page and R. A. Keck. 1992. Status and trend report on wildlife of the San Francisco Estuary. Prepared by the U.S. Fish and Wildlife Serv. for the San Francisco Estuary Project. U.S. Environ. Prot. Agency, San Francisco.

Hatch, J. J. and D. V. Weseloh. 1999. Double-crested Cormorant (*Phalacrocorax auritus*). *The Birds of North America*, No. 441 (A. Poole and F. Gill, eds.). The Birds of North America, Inc., Philadelphia.

Heady, H. F. 1988. Valley grassland. *Terrestrial Vegetation of California*, pp. 491–514 (M. G. Barbour and J. Major, eds.). New expanded ed. Calif. Native Plant Soc., Spec. Publ. No. 9. Univ. Calif. Davis, Davis.

Heath, H. 1915. Birds observed on Forrester Island, Alaska, during the summer of 1913. *Condor 17*:20–41.

Heermann, A. L. 1859. *Pacific Railroad Reports, Vol. 10, Part 4. Routes in California, to connect with the Routes near the thirty-fifth and thirty-second parallels [etc.] in 1853, No. 2. Report upon the Birds Collected on the Survey*, pp. 29–80. Washington.

Heizer, R. F. 1958. Salt in California Indian culture. *Salt in California*, pp. 101-104, by W. E Ver Planck with a chapter by R. F. Heizer. Bull. 175. Div. of Mines, State of Calif., San Francisco.

Hejl, S. J., J. A. Holmes and D. E. Kroodsma. 2002. Winter Wren (*Troglodytes troglodytes*). *The Birds of North America*, No. 623 (A. Poole and F. Gill, eds.). The Birds of North America, Inc., Philadelphia.

Helley, E. H. and E. E. Brabb. 1971. Geologic map of late Cenozoic deposits, Santa Clara County, California. U.S. Geol. Surv. Misc. Field. Studies Map MF-335, map scale 1:62,500.

Helley, E. H., K. R. Lajoie, W. E. Spangle and M. L. Blair. 1979. Flatland deposits of the San Francisco Bay Region, California—their geology and engineering properties, and their importance to comprehensive planning. U.S. Geol. Surv. Prof. Paper 943, map scale 1:62,300.

LITERATURE CITED

Hemphill, D. V. 1944. Distribution of vertebrate animals in relationship to plant associations on Howell Mountain, Napa County, California. Master's thesis, Univ. Calif., Berkeley.

Hendry, G. W. 1931. The adobe brick as an historical resource. *Agric. Hist.* 5:110–127. Cited in R. E. Frenkel, 1970.

Henny, C J., F. S. Schmidt, E. L. Martin and L. L. Hood. 1973. Territorial behavior, pesticides, and the population ecology of Red-shouldered Hawks in central Maryland, 1943–1971. *Ecology* 54:545–554.

Herman, S. G. 1971. The Peregrine Falcon declines in California. II. Breeding status in 1970. *Am. Birds* 25:818–820.

Hertz, P. E., J. V. Remsen, Jr., and S. L. Jones. 1976. Ecological complementarity of three sympatric parids in a California oak woodland. *Condor* 78:307–316.

Hickman, J. C., ed. 1993. *The Jepson Manual: Higher Plants of California.* Univ. Calif. Pr., Berkeley, Calif.

Hill, G. E. 1993. House Finch (*Carpodacus mexicanus*). *The Birds of North America*, No. 46 (A. Poole and F. Gill, eds.). Acad. Nat. Sci., Philadelphia; Am. Ornithol. Union, Washington.

———. 1995. Black-headed Grosbeak (*Pheucticus melanocephalus*). *The Birds of North America*, No. 143 (A. Poole and F. Gill, eds.). Acad. Nat. Sci., Philadelphia; Am. Ornithol. Union, Washington.

Hobson, K., P. Perrine, E. B. Roberts, M. L. Foster and P. Woodin. 1986. A breeding season survey of Salt Marsh Yellowthroats *Geothlypis trichas sinuosa* in the San Francisco Bay region. San Francisco Bay Bird Observatory. Contract no. 84–57. U.S. Fish and Wildlife Service.

Holland, R. F. 1986. Preliminary description of the terrestrial natural communities of California. Calif. State Dept. Fish Game, Natl. Heritage Div., Resources Agency, Sacramento.

Holmes, F. H. 1899. The Old-Squaw and Fulvous Tree Ducks at Alviso, Cal. *Bull. Cooper Ornithol. Club* 1:51.

Holt, D. W. and S. M. Leasure. 1993. Short-eared Owl (*Asio flammeus*). *The Birds of North America*, No. 62 (A. Poole and F. Gill, eds.). Acad. Nat. Sci., Philadelphia; Am. Ornithol. Union, Washington.

Holt, D. W. and J. L. Peterson. 2000. Northern Pygmy-Owl (*Glaucidium gnoma*). *The Birds of North America*, No. 494 (A. Poole and F. Gill, eds.). The Birds of North America, Inc., Philadelphia.

Hoover, T. J. 1899. The gopher snake as a despoiler of quails' nests. *Condor* 1:126.

———. 1939. Memoranda: being a statement by an engineer. Typescript. Hoover Inst. Library Arch. Stanford Univ., Stanford, Calif.

Hopkins, N. A. 1986. Mycorrhizae in a California serpentine grassland community. *Can. J. Bot.* 65:484–487.

Houston, C. S., D. G. Smith and C. Rohner. 1998. Great Horned Owl (*Bubo virginianus*). *The Birds of North America*, No. 372 (A. Poole and F. Gill, eds.). The Birds of North America, Inc., Philadelphia.

Houston, D. 2003. Bluebird recovery program success continues. *Avocet*, pp. 12–13, Nov.-Dec.

Howell, J. T. 1949. *Marin Flora; Manual of the Flowering Plants and Ferns of Marin County, California.* Univ. Calif. Pr., Berkeley.

Hudon, J. 1999. Western Tanager (*Piranga ludoviciana*). *The Birds of North America*, No. 432 (A. Poole and F. Gill, eds.). The Birds of North America, Inc., Philadelphia.

Hughes, J. M. 1996. Greater Roadrunner (*Geococcyx californianus*). *The Birds of North America*, No. 244 (A. Poole and F. Gill, eds.). Acad. Nat. Sci., Philadelphia; Am. Ornithol. Union, Washington.

———. 1999. Yellow-billed Cuckoo (*Coccyzus americanus*). *The Birds of North America*, No. 418 (A. Poole and F. Gill, eds.). The Birds of North America, Inc., Philadelphia.

Hunt, E. G. and W. Anderson. 1966. Renesting of ducks at Mountain Meadows, Lassen County, California. *Calif. Fish Game* 52:17–27.

Hunt, P. D. and D. J. Flaspohler. 1998. Yellow-rumped Warbler (*Dendroica coronata*). *The Birds of North America*, No. 376 (A. Poole and F. Gill, eds.). The Birds of North America, Inc., Philadelphia.

Ingold, J. L. and R. Galati. 1997. Golden-crowned Kinglet (*Regulus satrapa*). *The Birds of North America*, No. 301 (A. Poole and F. Gill, eds.). Acad. Nat. Sci., Philadelphia; Am. Ornithol. Union, Washington.

Irwin, W. P. 1990. Geology and plate-tectonic development. *The San Andreas Fault System, California*, pp. 60–80 (R. E. Wallace, ed.). U.S. Geol. Surv. Prof. Paper 1515. http://pubs.er.usgs.gov/usgspubs/pp/pp1515.

Ivey, G. L., M. A. Stern and C. G. Carey. 1988. An increasing White-faced Ibis population in Oregon. *West. Birds* 19:105–108.

Jackson, B. J. S. and J. A. Jackson. 2000. Killdeer (*Charadrius vociferous*). *The Birds of North America*, No. 517 (A. Poole and F. Gill, eds.). The Birds of North America, Inc., Philadelphia.

Jackson, J. A., H. R. Ouellet and B. J. S. Jackson. 2002. Hairy Woodpecker (*Picoides villosus*). Birds of North America, No. 702 (A. Poole and F. Gill, eds.). The Birds of North America, Inc., Philadelphia.

Jacobson, Y. 1984. *Passing Farms, Enduring Values.* William Kaufmann, Los Altos, Calif.

James, P. C. and T. J. Ethier. 1989. Trends in the winter distribution and abundance of burrowing owls in North America. *Am. Birds* 43:1224–1225.

Jaramillo, A. and P. Burke. 1999. *New World Blackbirds, the Icterids.* Princeton Univ. Pr., Princeton, N.J.

Jenkins, H. O. 1904. Bell Sparrow (*Amphispiza belli*) in Santa Clara Co., California. *Condor 6:109.*

Jennings, M. R. 1997. John Van Denburgh (1872–1924): Pioneer herpetologist of the American West. *Collection Building in Ichthyology and Herpetology*, pp. 323–250. (T. W. Pietsch and W. D. Anderson, Jr., eds). Spec. Publ. No. 3. Amer. Soc. Ichthyol. Herp., Lawrence, Kans.

Jensen, H. A. 1939. Vegetation types and forest conditions of the Santa Cruz Mountains Unit of California. Forest Survey Release No. 1. U.S. Forest Service, California Forest and Range Experiment Station, Berkeley.

Jeter, H. H. and R. O. Paxton. 1964. Little Blue Heron collected in California. *Condor 66:447.*

Jewett, S. G. 1942. The European Starling in California. *Condor 44:79.*

Johnsgard, P. A. 1960. Hybridization in the Anatidae and its taxonomic implications. *Condor* 62:25–33.

Johnson, K. 1995. Green-winged Teal (*Anas crecca*). *The Birds of North America*, No. 193 (A. Poole and F. Gill, eds.). Acad. Nat. Sci., Philadelphia; Am. Ornithol. Union, Washington.

Johnson, K. and B. D. Peer. 2001. Great-tailed Grackle (*Quiscalus mexicanus*). *The Birds of North America*, No. 576 (A. Poole and F. Gill, eds.). The Birds of North America, Inc., Philadelphia.

Johnson, L. S. 1998. House Wren (*Troglodytes aedon*). *The Birds of North America*, No. 380 (A. Poole and F. Gill, eds.). The Birds of North America, Inc., Philadelphia.

Johnson, N. K. 1980. Character variation and evolution of sibling species in the *Empidonax difficilis-flavescens* complex (Aves: Tyrannidae). *Univ. Calif. Publ. Zool.* 112:1–151.

———. 1994. Pioneering and natural expansion of breeding distributions in western North American birds. *A Century of Avifaunal Change in Western North America*, pp. 27–44 (J. R. Jehl, Jr. and N. K. Johnson, eds.). Studies in Avian Biology, No. 15.

Johnson, N. K. and C. Cicero. 1985. The breeding avifauna of San Benito Mountain, California: evidence of change over one-half century. *West. Birds 16*:1–23.

Johnson, N. K. and J. A. Marten. 1988. Evolutionary genetics of flycatchers. II. Differentiation in the *Empidonax difficilis* complex. *Auk 105*:177–191.

Johnson, R. R. and J. J. Dinsmore. 1985. Brood-rearing and postbreeding habitat use by Virginia Rails and Soras. *Wilson Bull. 97*:551–554.

Johnston, R. F. 1954. Variation in breeding season and clutch size in Song Sparrows of the Pacific Coast. *Condor 56*:268–273.

———. 1956. Population structure in salt marsh Song Sparrows. Pt. 1. Environment and annual cycle. *Condor 50*:24–58.

———. 1968. *Life Histories of North American Cardinals, Grosbeaks, Buntings, Towhees, Finches, Sparrows, and Allies*, Pt. 2, pp. 712–714 (O. L. Austin, Jr., comp. & ed.). Smithsonian Inst. U.S. Natl. Museum Bull. 237, Pt. 2. Reissued in 1968 by Dover Publ., New York.

———. 1992. Rock Dove (*Columba livia*). *The Birds of North America*, No. 13 (A. Poole and F. Gill, eds.). Acad. Nat. Sci., Philadelphia; Am. Ornithol. Union, Washington.

Johnston, R. F. and K. L. Garrett. 1994. Population trends of introduced birds in western North America. *A Century of Avifaunal Change in Western North America*, pp. 221–231 (J. R. Jehl, Jr. and N. K. Johnson, eds.). Studies in Avian Biology, No. 15.

Jones, P. A. 1986. Aspects of the reproductive biology of the California Gull in Alviso, California. Master's thesis, San Francisco State Univ., San Francisco.

Jones, P. W. and T. M. Donovan. 1996. Hermit Thrush (*Catharus guttatus*). *The Birds of North America*, No. 261 (A. Poole and F. Gill, eds.). Acad. Nat. Sci., Philadelphia; Am. Ornithol. Union, Washington.

Jones, S. L. and J. S. Dieni. 1995. Canyon Wren (*Catherpes mexicanus*). *The Birds of North America*, No. 197 (A. Poole and F. Gill, eds.). Acad. Nat. Sci., Philadelphia; Am. Ornithol. Union, Washington.

Joyner, D. E. 1983. Parasitic egg laying in Redheads and Ruddy Ducks in Utah: incidence and success. *Auk 100*:717–725.

Kaeding, H. B. 1908. Retrospective. *Condor 10*:215–218.

Keeley, J. E. 2005. Fire history of the San Francisco East Bay region and implications for landscape patterns. *Int. J. Wildland Fire 14*:285–296.

Kelly, J. P., K. L. Etienne and J. E. Roth. 2002. Abundance and distribution of the Common Raven and the American Crow in the San Francisco Bay area, California. *West. Birds 33*:202–217.

Kelly, J. W. 1935. Geologic factors in the distribution of birds. *Condor 37*:11–15.

———. 1948. A Red Crossbill invasion. *Gull 30*:25–26.

Kennedy, E. D. and D. W. White. 1997. Bewick's Wren (*Thryomanes bewickii*). *The Birds of North America*, No. 315 (A. Poole and F. Gill, eds.). Acad. Nat. Sci., Philadelphia; Am. Ornithol. Union, Washington.

Kennerly, C. B. R. 1859. *Pacific Railroad Reports, Vol. 10, Part 6. Route near the thirty-fifth parallel, explored by Lieutenant A. W. Whipple, topographical engineers, in 1853 and 1854, No. 3. Report on Birds collected on the Route*, pp. 19–35. Washington.

Keppie, D. M. and C. E. Braun. 2000. Band-tailed Pigeon (*Columba* fasciata). *The Birds of North America*, No. 530 (A. Poole and F. Gill, eds.). The Birds of North America, Inc., Philadelphia.

Kiff, L. F. 1978. Probable Black Rail nesting record for Alameda County, California. *West. Birds 9*:169–170.

———. 1988. Commentary. Changes in status of the Peregrine in North America: an overview. *Peregrine Falcon Populations: Their Management and Recovery*, pp. 123–139 (T. J. Cade, J. H. Enderson, C. G. Thelander, and C. M. White, eds.). The Peregrine Fund, Boise, Ida.

———. 1991. The egg came first. *Terra 30(2)*:5–19.

Kingery, H. E. 1996. American Dipper (*Cinclus mexicanus*). *The Birds of North America*, No. 229 (A. Poole and F. Gill, eds.). Acad. Nat. Sci., Philadelphia; Am. Ornithol. Union, Washington.

Kingery, H. E. and C. K. Ghalambor. 2001. Pygmy Nuthatch (*Sitta pygmaea*). *The Birds of North America*, No. 567 (A. Poole and F. Gill, eds.). The Birds of North America, Inc., Philadelphia.

Kirk, D. A. and M. J. Mossman. 1998. Turkey Vulture (*Cathartes aura*). *The Birds of North America*, No. 339 (A. Poole and F. Gill, eds.). The Birds of North America, Inc., Philadelphia.

Klingmann, J. 1983. Flash! Hold the presses!! *San Francisco Bay Bird Observ. Newsl.* No.3.

Knight, R. L., D. J. Grout and S. A. Temple. 1987. Nest-defense behavior of the American Crow in urban and rural areas. *Condor 89*:175–177.

Knudsen, K. L., J. M. Sowers, R. C. Witter, C. M. Wentworth, E. J. Helley, R. S. Nicholson, H. M. Wright and K. M. Brown. 2000. Preliminary maps of Quaternary deposits and liquefaction susceptibility, nine-county San Francisco Bay region, California: a digital database. U.S. Geol. Surv. Open File Rept 00-444. http://publs./gov/of/2000/0f00-444.

Kobbé, W. H. 1902. List of water birds of San Francisco Bay. *Handbook of Birds of the Western United States*, pp. xlvii–1 (F. M. Bailey, ed.). Houghton, Mifflin, Boston.

Koenig, P., B. Stacey, M. T. Stanback and R. L. Mumme. 1995. Acorn Woodpecker (*Melanerpes formicivorus*). *The Birds of North America*, No. 194 (A. Poole and F. Gill, eds.). Acad. Nat. Sci., Philadelphia; Am. Ornithol. Union, Washington.

Koenig, W. D. and M. D. Reynolds. 1987. Potential poisoning of Yellow-billed Magpies by compound 1080. *Wildlife Soc. Bull.* 15:275–276.

Kozloff, E. N. and L. H. Beidleman. 1994. *Plants of the San Francisco Bay Region*. Sagen Pr., Pacific Grove, Calif.

Kozlovic, D. R., R. W. Knapton and Jon C. Barlow. 1996. Unsuitability of the House Finch as a host of the Brown-headed Cowbird. *Condor* 98:253–258.

Krebs, C. J. 1966. Demographic changes in fluctuation populations of *Microtus californicus*. *Ecol. Monogr.* 36:239-273.

Kroodsma, D. E. 1973. Coexistence of Bewick's Wrens and House Wrens in Oregon. *Auk* 90:341–352.

Kroodsma, D. E. and J. Verner. 1997. Marsh Wren (*Cistothorus palustris*). *The Birds of North America*, No. 308 (A. Poole and F. Gill, eds.). Acad. Nat. Sci., Philadelphia; Am. Ornithol. Union, Washington.

Kroodsma, R. L. 1975. Hybridization in buntings (*Passerina*) in North Dakota and eastern Montana. *Auk* 92:66–80.

Kuenzler, E. J. 1961. Phosphorus budget of a mussel population. *Limn. Oceanogr.* 6:400–415.

Kueppers, L. M., M. A. Snyder, L. C. Sloan, E. S. Zavaleta and B. Fulfrost. 2005. Modeled regional climate change and California endemic oak ranges. *Proc. Natl. Acad. Sci. 102*: 16281–16286.

Kus, B. E. 1996. Breeding status of the Least Bell's Vireo in the Tijuana River Valley, California, 1996. Prepared for the Int. Boundary and Water Commission.

La Jeunesse, H. V. 1923. Dwarf cowbird nesting in Alameda County, California. *Condor* 24:31–32.

Langsdorff, G. H. von 1927. *Langsdorff's Narrative of the Rezanov Voyage to Nueva California in 1806*. T. C. Russell, San Francisco. (Cited in W. C. Clarke, 1959.)

Lanyon, W. E. 1994. Western Meadowlark (*Sturnella neglecta*). *The Birds of North America*, No. 104 (A. Poole and F. Gill, eds.). The Birds of North America, Inc., Philadelphia.

Laughlin, S. B. and D. P. Kibbe. 1985. *The Atlas of Breeding Birds of Vermont*. Univ. Pr. New England, Hanover, N.H.

Laymon, S. A. 1987. Brown-headed Cowbirds in California: historical perspectives and management opportunities in riparian habitats. *West. Birds 18*:63–70.

Laymon, S. A. and M. D. Halterman. 1987. Can the western subspecies of the Yellow-billed Cuckoo be saved from extinction? *West. Birds 18*:19–25.

Layne, V. L., R. J. Richmond, and P. J. Metropulos. 1996. First nesting of Black Skimmers on San Francisco Bay. *West. Birds 27*:159–162.

Leidy, R. A. 1984. Distribution and ecology of stream fishes in the San Francisco Bay drainage. *Hilgardia 51(8)*:1–175.

Leopold, A. 1949. *The Sand County Almanac*. Oxford Univ. Pr., New York.

Leopold, A. S. and M. F. Dedon. 1983. Resident Mourning Doves in Berkeley, California. *J. Wildl. Manage. 47*:780–789.

LeSchack, C. R., S. K. McKnight and G. R. Hepp. 1997. Gadwall (*Anas strepera*). *The Birds of North America*, No. 283 (A. Poole and F. Gill, eds.). Acad. Nat. Sci., Philadelphia; Am. Ornithol. Union, Washington.

Lever, C. 1987. *Naturalized Birds of the World*. Longman Sci. Tech. Pr., Essex, England.

Lidicker, W. Z., Jr. and F. C. McCollum. 1979. Canada Goose established as a breeding species in San Francisco Bay. *West. Birds 10*:159–162.

Linsdale, J. M. 1928. A method of showing relative frequency of occurrence of birds. *Condor 30*:180–184.

———. 1931. Facts concerning the use of thallium in California to poison rodents—its destructiveness to game birds, song birds and other valuable wildlife. *Condor 33*:92–106.

———. 1937. *The Natural History of Magpies*. Pacific Coast Avifauna No. 25. Cooper Ornithol. Club, Berkeley.

———. 1946. Yellow-billed Magpie (*Pica nuttalli*). *Life Histories of North American Jays, Crows and Titmice, Pt. 1*, pp. 155–193. Smithsonian Inst. U.S. Natl. Museum Bull. 191. Reissued in 1964 by Dover Publ., New York.

———. 1957. Goldfinches on the Hastings Natural History Reservation. *Am. Midl. Nat. 57*:1–119.

———. 1968. Green-backed Goldfinch (*Spinus psaltria hesperophilus*). *Life Histories of North American Cardinals, Grosbeaks, Buntings, Towhees, Finches, Sparrows, and Allies, Pt. 1*, p. 486. (O. L. Austen, Jr., comp. & ed.). Smithsonian Inst. U.S. Natl. Museum Bull. 237. (Reissued in 1968 by Dover Publ., New York.)

Linsdale, J. M. and T. L. Rodgers. 1937. Frequency of occurrence of birds in Alum Rock Park, Santa Clara County, California. *Condor 39*:108–111.

Long, J. L. 1981. *Introduced Birds of the World*. Universe Books, New York.

Lowther, P. E. 1993. Brown-headed Cowbird (*Molothrus ater*). *The Birds of North America*, No. 47 (A. Poole and F. Gill, eds.). Acad. Nat. Sci., Philadelphia; Am. Ornithol. Union, Washington.

———. 2000. Nuttall's Woodpecker (*Picoides nuttalli*) *The Birds of North America*, No. 555 (A. Poole and F. Gill, eds.). The Birds of North America, Inc., Philadelphia.

Lowther, P. E. and C. L. Cink. 1992. House Sparrow (*Passer domesticus*). *The Birds of North America*, No. 12 (A. Poole and F. Gill, eds.). Acad. Nat. Sci., Philadelphia; Am. Ornithol. Union, Washington.

Lowther, P. E., C. Celada, N. K. Klein, C. C. Rimmer and D. A. Spector. 1999. Yellow Warbler (*Dendroica petechia*). *The Birds of North America*, No. 454 (A. Poole and F. Gill, eds.). The Birds of North America, Inc., Philadelphia.

LITERATURE CITED

Lowther, P. E., D. E. Kroodsma, and G .H. Farley. 2000. Rock Wren (*Salpinctes obsoletus*). *The Birds of North America*, No. 486 (A. Poole and F. Gill, eds.). The Birds of North America, Inc., Philadelphia.

Lucas, F. A. 1885. The destruction of birds for millinery purposes. *Ornithol. Oologist* 10:31–32.

MacWhirter, R. B. and K. L. Bildstein. 1996. Northern Harrier (*Circus cyaneus*). *The Birds of North America*, No. 210 (A. Poole and F. Gill, eds.). Acad. Nat. Sci., Philadelphia; Am. Ornithol. Union, Washington.

Madge, S. and H. Burn. 1988. *Waterfowl: An Identification Guide to the Ducks, Geese and Swans of the World.* Houghton Mifflin, Boston.

Mailliard, J. 1908. Sierra forms on the coast of Sonoma County, California. *Condor* 10:133–137.

———. 1915. Scaup Ducks breeding in Golden Gate Park, San Francisco. *Condor* 17:235.

———. 1917. Concerning the two forms of the Bryant marsh sparrow in California. *Condor* 19:69–70.

Mailliard, J. and J. W. Mailliard. 1901. Birds recorded at Paicines, San Benito Co., California. *Condor* 3:120–127.

———. 1920. Bryant marsh sparrow upon the hills. *Condor* 22:63–66.

Major, J. 1988. California climate in relation to vegetation. *Terrestrial Vegetation of California*, pp. 11–74 (M. G. Barbour and J. Major, eds.). New expanded ed. Calif. Native Plant Soc., Spec. Publ. No. 9. Univ. Calif. Davis, Davis.

Mallette, R. D. and J. R. Slosson. 1987. *Upland Game of California.* 4th ed. California Dept. Fish and Game, Sacramento.

Mankinen, E. A. and C. M. Wentworth. 2003. Preliminary paleomagnetic results from the Coyote Creek Outdoor Classroom drill hole, Santa Clara Valley, California. U.S. Geol. Surv. Open File Rep. 03-187, 32 pp. http://pubs.usgs.gov/of2003/0f03-187/.

Mann, N. J. 1983. Comparative physiology of the Scrub Jay (*Aphelocoma coerulescens*) and Steller's Jay (*Cyanocitta stelleri*). *Comp. Biochem. Physiol.* 76:305–318.

Manolis, T. 1978. Status of the Black Rail in central California. *West. Birds* 9:151–158.

Marshall, J. T. 1948. Ecological races of Song Sparrows in the San Francisco Bay region. Pt. I. Habitat and abundance. *Condor* 50:193–215.

Marshall, J. T. and K. G. Dedrick. 1994. Endemic Song Sparrows and yellowthroats of San Francisco Bay. *A Century of Avifaunal Change in Western North America*, pp. 316–327 (J. R. Jehl, Jr. and N. K. Johnson, eds.). Studies in Avian Biology 15.

Martell, M. S., C. J. Henny, P. E. Nye and M. H. Solensky. 2001. Fall migration routes, timing, and wintering sites of North American Ospreys as determined by satellite telemetry. *Condor* 103:715–724.

Marti, C. D. 1992. Barn Owl (*Tyto alba*). *The Birds of North America*, No. 1 (A. Poole, P. Stettenheim and F. Gill, eds.). Acad. Nat. Sci., Philadelphia; Am. Ornithol. Union, Washington.

Martin, E. W. 1939. Notes from the Palo Alto Sports Club. *Condor* 41:124–125.

Martin, S. G. 2002. Brewer's Blackbird (*Euphagus cyanocephalus*). *The Birds of North America*, No. 616 (A. Poole and F. Gill, eds.). The Birds of North America, Inc., Philadelphia.

Matthiesen, D. G. and W. T. Mewaldt. 1974. A survey of the avifauna. *An ecological base line and human impact study of Henry Coe State Park, Morgan Hill California*, pp. B1–B103 (D. G. Matthiesen and H. G. Weston, Jr., eds.). Biol. Sci. Dept., San Jose State Univ., San Jose, Calif.

Mayer, K. E. and W. F. Laudenslayer, Jr., eds. 1988. *A Guide to Wildlife Habitats of California.* Calif. Dept. Forestry Fire Protection, Sacramento.

Mayhew, W. W. 1958. The biology of the Cliff Swallow in California. *Condor* 60:7–37.

McAtee, W. L. 1908. Food habits of the grosbeaks. *U.S. Dep. Agric., Biol. Surv., Bull. No. 32.* Quoted in A. C. Bent, 1968.

McCarten, N. F. 1993. *Serpentines of the San Francisco Bay Region: Vegetation, Floristics, Disitribution and Soils.* Calif. Dept. Fish Game, Nongame-Heritage Div., Endangered Plant Progr. Sacramento.

McCaskie, G. and S. Suffel. 1971. Black Skimmers at the Salton Sea, California. *Calif. Birds* 2:69–71.

McCaskie, G., P. De Benedictis, R. Erickson and J. Morlan. 1988. *The Birds of Northern California.* Reissued with supplement. Golden Gate Audubon Soc., Berkeley.

McCaskie, G., S. Liston and W. A. Rapley. 1974. First nesting of Black Skimmer in California. *Condor* 76:337–338.

McCrimmon, D. A., Jr., J. C. Ogden and G. T. Bancroft. 2001. Great Egret (*Ardea alba*). Birds of North America, No. 570 (A. Poole and F. Gill, eds.). The Birds of North America, Inc., Philadelphia.

McGarvey, W. P. 1866. [Report of county assessor for 1865], Monterey County. Trans. Calif. State Agric. Soc. *1865–1866*:224–231. Cited in Burcham, 1957.

McGregor, R. C. 1899. The Myrtle Warbler in California and description of a new race. *Bull. Cooper Ornithol. Club 1*:31–33.

———. 1901. A list of the land birds of Santa Cruz County, California. *Pacific Coast Avifauna*, No. 2. Cooper Ornithol. Club, Berkeley.

———. 1902. A list of birds collected in Norton Sound, Alaska. *Condor* 4:135–144.

———. 1906. Birds observed in the Krenitzin Islands, Alaska. *Condor* 8:114–122.

McKenzie, P. M. and M. B. Robbins. 1999. Identification of adult male Rufous and Allen's Hummingbirds, with specific comments on dorsal coloration. *West. Birds* 30:86–93.

McLean, D. D. 1936. Some notable records of birds from California. *Condor* 38:16–17.

———. 1969. Some additional records of birds in California. *Condor* 71:433–434.

Melvin, S. M. and J. P. Gibbs. 1996. Sora (*Porzana carolina*). *The Birds of North America*, No. 250 (A. Poole and F. Gill, eds.). Acad. Nat. Sci., Philadelphia; Am. Ornithol. Union, Washington.

Mendall, H. L. 1958. The Ring-necked Duck in the Northeast. *Univ. Maine Bull. 60(16)*:1–317.

LITERATURE CITED

Mewaldt, L. R. 1953. Reproduction and molt in Clark's Nutcracker, *Nucifraga columbiana*, Wilson. Ph.D. diss., Washington State Univ., Pullman, Wash.

———. 1989. In Memoriam: Emily Dinnin Smith. *Condor* 91:226.

Mewaldt, L. R. and S. Kaiser. 1988. Passerine migration along the inner coast range of central California. *West. Birds 19*:1–23.

Middleton, A. L. A. 1993. American Goldfinch (*Carduelis tristis*). *The Birds of North America*, No. 80 (A. Poole and F. Gill, eds.). Acad. Nat. Sci., Philadelphia; Am. Ornithol. Union, Washington.

———. 1998. Chipping Sparrow (*Spizella passerina*). *The Birds of North America*, No. 334 (A. Poole and F. Gill, eds.). The Birds of North America, Inc., Philadelphia.

Miller, A. H. 1929. A new race of Black-chinned Sparrow from the San Francisco Bay district. *Condor 31*:205–207.

Miller, A. H. and C. E. Bock. 1972. Natural history of the Nuttall Woodpecker at the Hastings Reservation. *Condor* 74:284–294.

Mirarchi, R. E. and T. S. Basket. 1994. Mourning Dove (*Zenaida macroura*). *The Birds of North America*, No. 117 (A. Poole and F. Gill, eds.). Acad. Nat. Sci., Philadelphia; Am. Ornithol. Union, Washington.

Moffitt, J. 1931. The status of Canada Goose in California. *Calif. Fish Game 17*:20–26.

———. 1939. Notes of distribution of Whistling Swan and Canada Goose in California. *Condor 41*:91–97.

———. 1941. Notes on the food of the California clapper rail. *Condor 43*:270–273.

Molina, K. C. 2000. The recent nesting of California and Laughing gulls at the Salton Sea, California. *West. Birds 31*:106–111.

Moore, W. S. 1995. Northern Flicker (*Colaptes auratus*). *The Birds of North America*, No. 166 (A. Poole and F. Gill, eds.). Acad. Nat. Sci., Philadelphia; Am. Ornithol. Union, Washington.

Mowbray, T. B. 2002. Canvasback (*Aythya valisineria*). *The Birds of North America*, No. 659 (A. Poole and F. Gill, eds.). The Birds of North America, Inc., Philadelphia.

Mowbray, T. B., C. R. Ely, J. S. Sedinger and R. E. Trost. 2002. Canada Goose (*Branta canadensis*). *The Birds of North America*, No. 682 (A. Poole and F. Gill, eds.). The Birds of North America, Inc., Philadelphia.

Munro-Fraser, J. P. 1881. *The History of Santa Clara County, California*. Alley, Bowen, San Francisco.

Munz, P. A. and D. O. Keck. 1970. *A California Flora*. Univ. Calif. Pr., Berkeley.

Murphy, M. T. 1996. Eastern Kingbird (*Tyrannus tyrannus*). *The Birds of North America*, No. 253 (A. Poole and F. Gill, eds.). Acad. Nat. Sci., Philadelphia; Am. Ornithol. Union, Washington.

Murphy, R. C. 1936. *Oceanic Birds of South America*. Vol. 1. MacMillan, New York.

Nelson, D. 1995a. American Dipper (*Cinclus mexicanus*). *Sonoma County Breeding Bird Atlas*, pp. 129, 185. (B. Burridge, ed.). Madrone Audubon Soc., Santa Rosa, Calif.

———. 1995b. Black-throated Gray Warbler (*Dendroica nigrescens*). *Sonoma County Breeding Bird Atlas*, p. 148 (B. Burridge, ed.). Madrone Audubon Soc., Santa Rosa, Calif.

Newberry, J. S. 1857. *Pacific Railroad Reports, Vol. 6, Part 4, No. 2. Report upon the Zoology of the Route. Chapter 2. Report upon the Birds*, pp. 73–110. Washington.

Nichols, D. G. 1940. Scaup's nest in Berkeley. *Gull 22*:37–38.

Noble, P. L. 1990. Distribution and density of owls at Monte Bello Open Space Preserve, Santa Clara County, California. *West. Birds 21*:11–16.

Norris, R. T. 1958. Comparative biosystematics and life history of the nuthatches *Sitta pygmaea* and *Sitta pusilla*. *Univ. Calif. Publ. Zool. 56*:119–300.

Oehser, P. H. 1952. In memoriam: Florence Merriam Bailey. *Auk 69*:19–26.

Ogden, A. 1941. The California Sea Otter Trade. Univ. Calif. Publ. Hist., Vol. 26. Univ. Calif. Pr., Berkeley.

Ohmart, R. D. 1994. The effects of human-induced changes on the avifauna of western riparian habitats. *A Century of Avifaunal Change in Western North America*, pp. 273–285 (J. R. Jehl, Jr. and N. K. Johnson, eds.). Studies in Avian Biology, No. 15.

Oring, L. W., E. M. Gray and J. M. Reed. 1997. Spotted Sandpiper (*Actitis macularia*). *The Birds of North America*, No. 289 (A. Poole and F. Gill, eds.). Acad. Nat. Sci., Philadelphia; Am. Ornithol. Union, Washington.

Orr, R. T. 1942. A study of the birds of the Big Basin Region of California. *Am. Midl. Nat. 27*:273–337.

Osgood, W. H. 1892a. After Golden Eagles. *Oologist 9*:134–135.

———. 1892b. The California Bush-Tit. *Oologist 9*:226–227.

———. 1893. Queer places for quails' eggs. *Nidiologist 1*:45.

Page, B. M. 1992. Tectonic setting of the San Francisco Bay Region. *Proc. Second Conf. Earthquake Hazards in the Eastern San Francisco Bay Area* (G. Borchardt and others, eds.). Calif. Div. Mines Geol. Spec. Publ. 113.

Page, B. M., G. A. Thompson and R. G. Coleman. 1998. Late Cenozoic tectonics of the central and southern Coast Ranges of California. *Geol. Soc. Am. Bull. 110*:846–876.

Page, G. W. and L. E. Stenzel. 1981. The breeding status of the Snowy Plover in California. *West. Birds 12*:1–40.

Page, G. W., L. E. Stenzel and C. A. Ribic. 1985. Nest site selection and clutch predation in the Snowy Plover. *Auk 102*:347–353.

Page, G. W., L. E. Stenzel, W. D. Shuford and C. R. Bruce. 1991. Distribution and abundance of the Snowy Plover on its western North American breeding grounds. *J. Field Ornithol. 62*:245–255.

Palmer, R. S., ed. 1962. *Handbook of North American Birds*. Vol. 1: Loons through Flamingos. Yale Univ. Pr., New Haven.

———. 1976a. *Handbook of North American Birds*. Vol. 2: Waterfowl, Pt. 1. Yale Univ. Pr., New Haven.

———. 1976b. *Handbook of North American Birds*. Vol. 3: Waterfowl, Pt. 2. Yale Univ. Pr., New Haven.

———. 1988. *Handbook of North American Birds*. Vol. 5: Diurnal Raptors. Yale Univ. Pr., New Haven.

LITERATURE CITED

Palmer, T. S. 1917. Botta's visit to California. *Condor* 19:159–161.

———. 1928. Notes on persons whose names appear in the nomenclature of California birds. *Condor* 30:261–307.

Parkhurst, A. L. 1883. Notes from San Jose, Cal. *Ornithol. Oologist 8*:79.

———. 1884. Why do shrikes hang up their food? *Ornithol. Oologist 9*:150.

———. 1885. Some Californian raptores, Pt 1 *Ornithol. Oologist 10*:7.

Parsons, K. C. and T. L. Master. 2000. Snowy Egret (*Egretta thula*). *The Birds of North America*, No. 489 (A. Poole and F. Gill, eds.). The Birds of North America, Inc., Philadelphia.

Patten, M. A., G. McCaskie, and P. Unitt. 2003. *Birds of the Salton Sea: Status, Biogeography, and Ecology.* Univ. Calif. Pr., Berkeley.

Pavlik, B. M., P. C. Muick, S. G. Johnson and M. Popper. 1991. *Oaks of California.* Cachuma Pr. and Calif. Oak Fndn., Los Olivos, Calif.

Payne, R. B. 1992. Indigo Bunting (*Passerina cyanea*). *The Birds of North America*, No. 4 (A. Poole and F. Gill, eds.). Acad. Nat. Sci., Philadelphia; Am. Ornithol. Union, Washington.

Paynter, R. A., Jr. 1970. Subfamily Emberizinae. *Check-list of Birds of the World.* Vol. 13, pp. 3–214 (R. A. Paynter, Jr., ed.). Mus. Comp. Zool., Cambridge, Mass.

Peake, H. 1993. Hooded Oriole (*Icterus cucullatus*). *Marin County Breeding Bird Atlas*, pp. 405–408 (W. D. Shuford, ed.). Bushtit Books, Bolinas, Calif.

Pearson, S. F. 1997. Hermit Warbler (*Dendroica occidentalis*). *The Birds of North America*, No. 303 (A. Poole and F. Gill, eds.). Acad. Nat. Sci., Philadelphia; Am. Ornithol. Union, Washington.

Peterjohn, B. G. and J. R. Sauer. 1995. Population trends of the Loggerhead Shrike from the North American Breeding Bird Survey. *Shrikes* (Laniidae) *of the World: Biology and Conservation* (R. Yosef and F. E. Lohner, eds.). *Proc. West. Found. Vert. Zool. 6:(1)*:117–121.

Peterson, A. P. 1994. Erroneous party-hour data and a proposed method of correcting observer effort in Christmas Bird Counts. *J. Field Ornithol.* 66:385–390.

Peterson, J. 1935. Western Tanager nesting at Alum Rock Park, San Jose. *Condor* 37:286.

Phillips, A. 1975. The migrations of Allen's and other hummingbirds. *Condor* 77:196–205.

Phillips, J. C. 1928. Wild birds introduced or transplanted in North America. U.S. Dept. Agric. Tech. Bull. 61.

Pickwell, G. B. 1925a. Some nesting habits of the Belted Piping Plover. *Auk* 42:326–332.

———. 1925b. The nesting of the Killdeer. *Auk 42*:485–496.

———. 1927. The Prairie Horned Lark, Ph.D diss., Cornell Univ.

———. 1930. The White-tailed Kite. *Condor* 32:221–239.

———. 1931. The Prairie Horned Lark. *Trans. St. Louis Acad. Sci. 23*:1–153, figs. 1–18, plates. 1–34.

———. 1932a. Requiem for the White-tailed Kite of Santa Clara Valley. *Condor* 33:44-45.

———. 1932b. The Arizona Hooded Oriole in San Jose, California. *Condor 34*:48.

———. 1932c. A station of frequent observation of the cowbird in the San Francisco Bay region. *Condor 34*:100.

———. 1932d. Swainson Hawks in the Arroyo Calero, Santa Clara County, California. *Condor 34*:139–140.

———. 1937a. Winter habits of the White-throated Swift. *Condor 39*:187–188.

———. 1937b. *Weather.* H. F. Newman, Los Angeles.

———. 1939a. *Deserts.* Whittlesey House, McGraw-Hill, New York.

———. 1939b. *Birds.* Whittlesey House, McGraw-Hill, New York.

———. 1940. *Animals in Action.* Whittlesey House, McGraw-Hill, New York.

———. 1947. *Amphibians and Reptiles of the Pacific States.* Stanford Univ. Pr, Stanford.

———. 1948. Barn Owl growth and behaviorisms. *Auk* 65:359–373.

Pickwell, G. and E. Smith. 1938. The Texas Nighthawk in its summer home. *Condor* 40:193–215.

Pierotti, R. J. and C. A. Annett. 1995. Western Gull (*Larus occidentalis*). *The Birds of North America*, No. 174 (A. Poole and F. Gill, eds.). Acad. Nat. Sci., Philadelphia; Am. Ornithol. Union, Washington.

Pike, J. and L. Hays. 1997. The status and management of the Least Bell's Vireo and Southwestern Willow Flycatcher within the Prado Basin, California, 1986–1996. Unpubl. report. U.S. Fish and Wildlife Service.

Pitocchelli, J. 1995. MacGillivray's Warbler (*Oporornis tolmiei*). *The Birds of North America*, No. 159 (A. Poole and F. Gill, eds.). Acad. Nat. Sci., Philadelphia; Am. Ornithol. Union, Washington.

Pleasants, B. Y. and D. J. Albano. 2001. Hooded Oriole (*Icterus cucullatus*). *The Birds of North America*, No. 568 (A. Poole and F. Gill, eds.). The Birds of North America, Inc., Philadelphia.

Poland, J. F. and R. L. Ireland. 1988. Land subsidence in the Santa Clara Valley, California, as of 1982. U.S. Geol. Survey Prof. Paper 497-F. U.S. Gov. Print. Off., Washington.

Poole, A. F., R. O. Bierregaard and M. S. Martell. 2002. Osprey (*Pandion haliaetus*). *The Birds of North America*, No. 683 (A. Poole and F. Gill, eds.). The Birds of North America, Inc., Philadelphia.

Postel, M. 1988. A lost resource, shellfish in San Francisco. *Calif. Hist.* 67:26–41, 70–72.

Pratt, H. M. 1983. Marin County California heron colonies: 1967–1981. *West. Birds* 14:169–184.

Pratt, H. M. and D. W. Winkler. 1985. Clutch size, timing of laying, and reproductive success in a colony of Great Blue Herons and Great Egrets. *Auk* 102:40–63.

Pravosudov, V. V. and T. C. Grubb, Jr. 1993. White-breasted Nuthatch (*Sitta carolinensis*). *The Birds of North America*, No. 54 (A. Poole and F. Gill, eds.). Acad. Nat. Sci., Philadelphia; Am. Ornithol. Union, Washington.

LITERATURE CITED

Preston, C. R. and R. D. Beane. 1993. Red-tailed Hawk (*Buteo jamaicensis*). *The Birds of North America*, No. 52 (A. Poole and F. Gill, eds.). Acad. Nat. Sci., Philadelphia; Am. Ornithol. Union, Washington.

Price, J. B. 1936. The family relations of the Plain Titmouse. *Condor 38*:108–111.

Price, W. W. 1898a. The birds of the campus, Pt. 1. *Sequoia 7*:297.

———. 1898b. The birds of the campus, Pt. 2. *Sequoia 7*:310–311.

———. 1898c. The birds of the campus, Pt. 3. *Sequoia 7*:327.

———. 1898d. The birds of the campus, 4. *Sequoia 7*:363.

———. 1898e. The birds of the campus, 5. *Sequoia 7*:375.

———. 1898f. The birds of the campus, 6. *Sequoia 7*:386–388.

Priestley, H. I. 1937. *A Historical, Political, and Natural Description of California by Pedro Fages, Soldier of Spain, Dutifully Made for the Viceroy in the Year 1775.* Univ. Calif. Pr., Berkeley.

Purcell, K. L., J. Verner and L. W. Oring. 1997. A comparison of breeding ecology of birds nesting in boxes and tree cavities. *Auk 114*:646–656.

Pyle, P. and R. P. Henderson. 1991. The birds of Southeast Farallon Island: occurrence and seasonal distribution of migratory species. *West. Birds 22*:41–84.

Ralph, C. J. 1991. In memoriam: L. Richard Mewaldt, 1917–1990. *Auk 109*:646–647.

Rantz, S. E. 1971. Mean annual precipitation and precipitation depth-duration-frequency data for the San Francisco Bay Region, California. U.S. Geol. Surv., Water Resources Div., Menlo Park, Calif.

———. 1972. A summary view of water supply and demand in the San Francisco Bay region, California. U.S. Geol. Surv., Water Resources Div., Menlo Park, Calif.

Ray, M. S. 1899. Peculiar eggs of California Shrike and other notes. *Bull. Cooper Ornithol. Club 1*:53.

———. 1900. Notes on some unusual sets of eggs. *Condor 2*:126.

RECON (Regional Environmental Consultants). 1989. Comprehensive species management plan for the Least Bell's Vireo (*Vireo bellii pusillus*). Prepared for San Diego Association of Governments, San Diego.

Reese, J. 1997. A valley of earthly delights. *Stanford Mag.* (Jan./Feb.)

Restall, R. 1997. *Munias and Mannikins.* Yale Univ. Pr., New Haven.

Reynolds, M. D. 1995. Yellow-billed Magpie (*Pica nuttalli*). *The Birds of North America*, No. 180 (A. Poole and F. Gill, eds.). Acad. Nat. Sci., Philadelphia; Am. Ornithol. Union, Washington.

Rickman, D. W. 1981. Farmers unite for water conservation. *Water in the Santa Clara Valley: A History*, pp. 1–19 (S. McArthur, ed.). Calif. History Center, De Anza Coll. Cupertino, Calif.

Rigney, M. and T. Rigney. 1981. A Breeding Bird Survey of the South San Francisco Bay Salt Pond Levee System. South Bay Inst. Avian Studies, Alviso, Calif.

Rintoul, C., N. Warnock, G. W. Page and J. T. Hanson. 2003. Breeding status and habitat use of Black-necked Stilts and American Avocets in South San Francisco Bay. *West. Birds 34*:2–14.

Ripley, S. D. 1977. *The Rails of the World.* David R. Godine, Boston.

Rising, J. D. 1996. *A Guide to the Identification and Natural History of the Sparrows of the United States and Canada.* Academic Pr., San Diego.

———. 2001. *Geographic Variation in Size and Shape of Savannah Sparrows* (Passerculus sandwichensis). Studies in Avian Biology, No. 23.

Robbins, C. S., D. Bystrak and P. H. Geissler. 1986. *The Breeding Bird Survey: Its First Fifteen Years, 1965–1979.* U.S. Dept. Interior Resource Publ. 157, Washington.

Roberson, D. 1980. *Rare Birds of the West Coast*, pp. 225–226. Woodcock Publ., Pacific Grove, Calif.

———. 1985. *Monterey Birds.* Monterey Peninsula Audubon Soc., Carmel, Calif.

———. 1993a. Northern Harrier (*Circus cyaneus*). *Atlas of the Breeding Birds of Monterey County, California*, pp. 90–91 (D. Roberson and C. Tenney, eds.). Monterey Peninsula Audubon Soc., Monterey.

———. 1993b. Cooper's Hawk (*Accipiter cooperi*). *Atlas of the Breeding Birds of Monterey County, California*, pp. 94–95 (D. Roberson and C. Tenney, eds.). Monterey Peninsula Audubon Soc., Monterey.

———. 1993c. Red-tailed Hawk (*Buteo jamaicensis*). *Atlas of the Breeding Birds of Monterey County, California*, pp. 98–99 (D. Roberson and C. Tenney, eds.). Monterey Peninsula Audubon Soc., Monterey.

———. 1993d. American Kestrel (*Falco sparverius*). *Atlas of the Breeding Birds of Monterey County, California*, pp. 102–103 (D. Roberson and C. Tenney, eds.). Monterey Peninsula Audubon Soc., Monterey.

———. 1993e. California Quail (*Callipepla californica*). *Atlas of the Breeding Birds of Monterey County, California*, pp. 112–113 (D. Roberson and C. Tenney, eds.). Monterey Peninsula Audubon Soc., Monterey.

———. 1993f. Common Moorhen. (*Gallinula chloropus*). *Atlas of the Breeding Birds of Monterey County, California*, pp. 120–121 (D. Roberson and C. Tenney, eds.). Monterey Peninsula Audubon Soc., Monterey.

———. 1993g. Greater Roadrunner. (*Geococcyx californianus*). *Atlas of the Breeding Birds of Monterey County, California*, pp. 152–153 (D. Roberson and C. Tenney, eds.). Monterey Peninsula Audubon Soc., Monterey.

———. 1993h. Great Horned Owl (*Bubo virginianus*). *Atlas of the Breeding Birds of Monterey County, California*, pp. 160–161 (D. Roberson and C. Tenney, eds.). Monterey Peninsula Audubon Soc., Monterey.

———. 1993i. Long-eared Owl (*Asio otus*). *Atlas of the Breeding Birds of Monterey County, California*, pp. 168–169 (D. Roberson and C. Tenney, eds.). Monterey Peninsula Audubon Soc., Monterey.

———. 1993j. Northern Saw-whet Owl (*Aegolius acadicus*). *Atlas of the Breeding Birds of Monterey County, California*, pp. 170–171 (D. Roberson and C. Tenney, eds.). Monterey Peninsula Audubon Soc., Monterey.

———. 1993k. Lesser Nighthawk (*Chordeiles acutipennis*). *Atlas of the Breeding Birds of Monterey County, California*, pp. 172–173 (D. Roberson and C. Tenney, eds.). Monterey Peninsula Audubon Soc., Monterey.

———. 1993l. Common Poor-Will (*Phalaenoptilus nuttallii*). *Atlas of the Breeding Birds of Monterey County, California*, pp. 174–175 (D. Roberson and C. Tenney, eds.). Monterey Peninsula Audubon Soc., Monterey.

———. 1993m. Vaux's Swift (*Chaetura vauxi*). *Atlas of the Breeding Birds of Monterey County, California*, pp. 178–179 (D. Roberson and C. Tenney, eds.). Monterey Peninsula Audubon Soc., Monterey.

———. 1993n. Costa's Hummingbird (*Calypte costae*). *Atlas of the Breeding Birds of Monterey County, California*, pp. 186–188 (D. Roberson and C. Tenney, eds.). Monterey Peninsula Audubon Soc., Monterey.

———. 1993o. Allen's Hummingbird (*Selasphorus sasin*). *Atlas of the Breeding Birds of Monterey County, California*, pp. 188–189 (D. Roberson and C. Tenney, eds.). Monterey Peninsula Audubon Soc., Monterey.

———. 1993p. Pacific-slope Flycatcher (*Empidonax difficilis*). *Atlas of the Breeding Birds of Monterey County, California*, pp. 210–211 (D. Roberson and C. Tenney, eds.). Monterey Peninsula Audubon Soc., Monterey.

———. 1993q. Purple Martin (*Progne subis*). *Atlas of the Breeding Birds of Monterey County, California*, pp. 226–227, 250 (D. Roberson and C. Tenney, eds.). Monterey Peninsula Audubon Soc., Monterey.

———. 1993r. Tree Swallow (*Tachycineta bicolor*). *Atlas of the Breeding Birds of Monterey County, California*, pp. 228–229 (D. Roberson and C. Tenney, eds.). Monterey Peninsula Audubon Soc., Monterey.

———. 1993s. Bank Swallow (*Riparia riparia*). *Atlas of the Breeding Birds of Monterey County, California*, pp. 234–235 (D. Roberson and C. Tenney, eds.). Monterey Peninsula Audubon Soc., Monterey.

———. 1993t. Yellow-billed Magpie (*Pica nuttalli*). *Atlas of the Breeding Birds of Monterey County, California*, pp. 244–245, 250 (D. Roberson and C. Tenney, eds.). Monterey Peninsula Audubon Soc., Monterey.

———. 1993u. Chestnut-backed Chickadee (*Parus rufescens*). *Atlas of the Breeding Birds of Monterey County, California*, pp. 254–255 (D. Roberson and C. Tenney, eds.). Monterey Peninsula Audubon Soc., Monterey.

———. 1993v. Pygmy Nuthatch (*Sitta pygmaea*). *Atlas of the Breeding Birds of Monterey County, California*, pp. 264–265 (D. Roberson and C. Tenney, eds.). Monterey Peninsula Audubon Soc., Monterey.

———. 1993w. Northern Mockingbird (*Mimus polyglottos*). *Atlas of the Breeding Birds of Monterey County, California*, pp. 294–295 (D. Roberson and C. Tenney, eds.). Monterey Peninsula Audubon Soc., Monterey.

———. 1993x. European Starling (*Sturnus vulgaris*) *Atlas of the Breeding Birds of Monterey County, California*, pp. 304–306 (D. Roberson and C. Tenney, eds.). Monterey Peninsula Audubon Soc., Monterey.

———. 1993y. Bell's Vireo (*Vireo bellii*). *Atlas of the Breeding Birds of Monterey County, California*, pp. 308–309 (D. Roberson and C. Tenney, eds.). Monterey Peninsula Audubon Soc., Monterey.

———. 1993z. Hutton's Vireo (*Vireo huttoni*). *Atlas of the Breeding Birds of Monterey County, California*, pp. 312–313 (D. Roberson and C. Tenney, eds.). Monterey Peninsula Audubon Soc., Monterey.

———. 1993aa. Warbling Vireo (*Vireo gilvus*). *Atlas of the Breeding Birds of Monterey County, California*, pp. 314–315 (D. Roberson and C. Tenney, eds.). Monterey Peninsula Audubon Soc., Monterey.

———. 1993bb. Orange-crowned Warbler (*Vermivora celata*). *Atlas of the Breeding Birds of Monterey County, California*, pp. 316–317 (D. Roberson and C. Tenney, eds.). Monterey Peninsula Audubon Soc., Monterey.

———. 1993cc. Yellow Warbler (*Dendroica petechia*). *Atlas of the Breeding Birds of Monterey County, California*, pp. 318–319 (D. Roberson and C. Tenney, eds.). Monterey Peninsula Audubon Soc., Monterey.

———. 1993dd. Black-throated Gray Warbler (*Dendroica nigrescens*). *Atlas of the Breeding Birds of Monterey County, California*, pp. 322–323 (D. Roberson and C. Tenney, eds.). Monterey Peninsula Audubon Soc., Monterey.

———. 1993ee. MacGillivray's Warbler (*Oporornis tolmiei*). *Atlas of the Breeding Birds of Monterey County, California*, pp. 324–325 (D. Roberson and C. Tenney, eds.). Monterey Peninsula Audubon Soc., Monterey.

———. 1993ff. Blue Grosbeak (*Guiraca caerulea*). *Atlas of the Breeding Birds of Monterey County, California*, pp. 336–337 (D. Roberson and C. Tenney, eds.). Monterey Peninsula Audubon Soc., Monterey.

———. 1993gg. California Towhee (*Pipilo crissalis*). *Atlas of the Breeding Birds of Monterey County, California*, pp. 342–343 (D. Roberson and C. Tenney, eds.). Monterey Peninsula Audubon Soc., Monterey.

———. 1993hh. Purple Finch (*Carpodacus purpureus*). *Atlas of the Breeding Birds of Monterey County, California*, pp. 380–381 (D. Roberson and C. Tenney, eds.). Monterey Peninsula Audubon Soc., Monterey.

———. 1993ii. Lesser Goldfinch (*Carduelis psaltria*). *Atlas of the Breeding Birds of Monterey County, California*, pp. 388–390 (D. Roberson and C. Tenney, eds.). Monterey Peninsula Audubon Soc., Monterey.

———. 1993jj. Blue-winged Teal (*Anas discors*). *Atlas of the Breeding Birds of Monterey County, California*, pp. 410–411 (D. Roberson and C. Tenney, eds.). Monterey Peninsula Audubon Soc., Monterey.

———. 1993kk. Swainson's Hawk (*Buteo swainsoni*). *Atlas of the Breeding Birds of Monterey County, California*, p. 412 (D. Roberson and C. Tenney, eds.). Monterey Peninsula Audubon Soc., Monterey.

———. 2002. *Monterey Birds*. 2nd ed. Monterey Peninsula Audubon Soc., Carmel.

Roberson, D. and C. Tenney, eds. 1993. *Atlas of the Breeding Birds of Monterey County, California.* Monterey Peninsula Audubon Soc., Monterey.

Robertson, R. J., B. J. Stutchbury and R. R. Cohen. 1992. Tree Swallow (*Tachycineta bicolor*). *The Birds of North America*, No. 11 (A. Poole and F. Gill, eds.). Acad. Nat. Sci., Philadelphia; Am. Ornithol. Union, Washington.

Robinson, J. A., L. W. Oring, J. P. Skorupa and R. Boettscher. 1997. American Avocet (*Recurvirostra americana*). *The Birds of North America*, No. 275 (A. Poole and F. Gill, eds.). Acad. Nat. Sci., Philadelphia; Am. Ornithol. Union, Washington.

Robinson, J. A., J. M. Reed, J. P. Skorupa and L. W. Oring. 1999. Black-necked Stilt (*Himantopus mexicanus*). *The Birds of North America*, No. 449 (A. Poole and F. Gill, eds.). The Birds of North America, Inc., Philadelphia.

Rodgers, J. A., Jr. and H. T. Smith. 1995. Little Blue Heron (*Egretta caerulea*). *The Birds of North America*, No. 145 (A. Poole and F. Gill, eds.). Acad. Nat. Sci., Philadelphia; Am. Ornithol. Union, Washington.

Rodgers, T. L. 1937. Behavior of the Pine Siskin. *Condor* 37:143–149.

Rogers, M. M. 1995. Examples of range expansion. *Riparia-News* 9:6, 8.

Root, R. B. 1964. Ecological interactions of the Chestnut-backed Chickadee following a range extension. *Condor* 66:229–238.

Rosenfield, R. N. and J. Bielefeldt. 1993. Cooper's Hawk (*Accipiter cooperi*). *The Birds of North America*, No. 75 (A. Poole and F. Gill, eds.). Acad. Nat. Sci., Philadelphia; Am. Ornithol. Union, Washington.

Rothstein, S. I. and R. C. Fleischer. 1987. Vocal dialects and their possible relation to honest status signalling in the Brown-headed Cowbird. *Condor* 89:1–23.

Rothstein, S. I., J. Verner and E. Stevens. 1980. Range expansion and diurnal changes in dispersion of the Brown-headed Cowbird in the Sierra Nevada. *Auk* 97:253–267.

Rothstein, S. I., D. A. Yokel and R. C. Fleischer. 1986. Social dominance, mating and spacing systems, female fecundity, and vocal dialects in captive and free-ranging Brown-headed Cowbirds. *Current Ornithology*, Vol. 3, pp. 127–185 (R. H. Johnston, ed.). Plenum Pr., New York.

———. 1988. The agonistic and sexual functions of vocalizations of male Brown-headed Cowbirds, *Molothrus ater. Anim. Behav.* 36:73–86.

Rottenborn, S. C. 1997. The impacts of urbanization on riparian bird communities in central California. Ph.D. diss., Stanford Univ., Stanford, Calif.

———. 1999. Predicting the impacts of urbanization on riparian bird communities. *Biol. Cons.* 88:289–299.

———. 2000. Nest-site selection and reproductive success of urban Red-shouldered Hawks in central California. *J. Raptor Res.* 34:18–25.

Row, R. M. 1960. A check-list of the birds of the Stanford Biological Reserve including Jasper Ridge and Searsville. Unpublished compilation.

Rowher, F. C., W. P. Johnston and E. R. Loos. 2002. Blue-winged Teal (*Anas discors*). *The Birds of North America*, No. 625 (A. Poole and F. Gill, eds.). The Birds of North America, Inc., Philadelphia.

Rudesill, R. 1995. Osprey (*Pandion haliaetus*). *Sonoma County Breeding Bird Atlas*, p. 45 (B. Burridge, ed.). Madrone Audubon Soc., Santa Rosa, Calif.

Russell, S. M. 1996. Anna's Hummingbird (*Calypte anna*). *The Birds of North America*, No. 226 (A. Poole and F. Gill, eds.). Acad. Nat. Sci., Philadelphia; Am. Ornithol. Union, Washington.

Ryan, T. P. 2000a. Caspian Tern (*Sterna caspia*). *Baylands Ecosystem Species and Community Profiles: Life Histories and Environmental Requirements of Key Plants, Fish and Wildlife* (P. R. Olofson, ed.) San Francisco Bay Regional Water Quality Control Board, Oakland, Calif.

———. 2000b. Forster's Tern (*Sterna forsteri*). *Baylands Ecosystem Species and Community Profiles: Life Histories and Environmental Requirements of Key Plants, Fish and Wildlife.* (P. R. Olofson, ed.) San Francisco Bay Regional Water Quality Control Board, Oakland, Calif.

Ryan, T. P. and C. T. Collins. 2000. White-throated Swift (*Aeronautes saxatalis*). *The Birds of North America*, No. 526 (A. Poole and F. Gill, eds.). The Birds of North America, Inc., Philadelphia.

Ryan, T. P. and J. T. Hanson. The Little Blue Heron in Central and Northern California. In prep.

Ryder, R. A. and D. E. Manry. 1994. White-faced Ibis (*Plegadis chihi*). *The Birds of North America*, No. 130 (A. Poole and F. Gill, eds.). Acad. Nat. Sci., Philadelphia; Am. Ornithol. Union, Washington.

Sallabanks, R. and F. C. James. 1999. American Robin (*Turdus migratorius*). Birds of North America, No. 462 (A. Poole and F. Gill, eds.). The Birds of North America, Inc., Philadelphia.

Salt, G. W. 1952. The relationship of metabolism to climate and distribution in three finches of the genus *Carpodacus. Ecol. Monogr.* 22:121–152.

San Francisco Estuary Institute (SFEI). 2005. The pulse of the estuary: monitoring and managing water quality in the San Francisco Estuary. San Francisco Estuary Inst., Oakland, Calif.

Santee, R. and W. Granfield. 1939. Behavior of the Saw-Whet Owl on its nesting grounds. *Condor* 41:3–9.

Sauer, J. R., J. E. Hines and J. Fallon. 2005. *The North American Breeding Bird Survey, Results and Analysis 1966–2004. Version 2005.2.* U.S. Geol. Survey, Patuxent Wildlife Research Center, Laurel, Md.

Sawyer, E. T. 1922. *History of Santa Clara County, California.* Historic Record Co., Los Angeles.

Sawyer, J. O. and T. Keeler-Wolf. 1995. *A Manual of California Vegetation.* Calif. Native Plant Soc., Sacramento.

Schlorff, R. W. and P. H. Bloom. 1984. Importance of riparian systems to nesting Swainson's Hawks in the Central Valley of California. *California Riparian Systems: Ecology, Conservation, and Productive Management*, pp. 23–29 (R. W. Warner and K. M. Hendrix, eds.). Univ. Cal. Pr., Berkeley.

539

Schmidt, K. P. 1950. Wilfred Hudson Osgood, 1875–1947. *Auk* 67:183–189.

Schneider, F. A. 1893. Nesting of the Cinnamon Teal. *Nidiologist 1*:20–22.

Schneider, J. 1992. *Quicksilver, the Complete History of Santa Clara County's New Almaden Mine.* Zella Schneider, San Jose.

Schoenherr, A. A. 1992. *A Natural History of California.* Univ. Calif. Pr., Berkeley.

Schorger, A. W. 1952. Introduction of the domestic pigeon. *Auk 69*:462–463

Schukman, J. M. and B. O. Wolf. 1998. Say's Phoebe (*Sayornis saya*). *The Birds of North America*, No. 374 (A. Poole and F. Gill, eds.). The Birds of North America, Inc., Philadelphia.

Schussler, G. W. 1916. The Pigeon Guillemot nest in San Francisco. *Condor 18*:35.

Sclater, P. L. 1857. List of birds collected by Mr. Thomas Bridges, Corresponding Member of the Society, in the Valley of San Jose, in the State of California. *Proc. Zool. Soc. London 25*:125–127.

Sedgwick, J. A. 2000. Willow Flycatcher (*Empidonax traillii*). *The Birds of North America*, No. 533 (A. Poole and F. Gill, eds.). The Birds of North America, Inc., Philadelphia.

Seibert, M. L. 1942. Occurrence and nesting of some birds in the San Francisco Bay Region. *Condor 44*:71–72.

Selander, R. K. 1970. Parental feeding in a male Great-tailed Grackle. *Condor 38*:238.

Sequoia Audubon Society. 2001a. *San Mateo County Breeding Bird Atlas.* Sequoia Audubon Society.

———. 2001b. Virginia Rail. *San Mateo County Breeding Bird Atlas*, p. 84. Sequoia Audubon Soc.

———. 2001c. Sora. *San Mateo County Breeding Bird Atlas*, p. 85. Sequoia Audubon Society.

———. 2001d. Nuttall's Woodpecker. *San Mateo County Breeding Bird Atlas*, p. 125. Sequoia Audubon Soc.

———. 2001e. Pileated Woodpecker. *San Mateo County Breeding Bird Atlas*, p. 129. Sequoia Audubon Society.

———. 2001f. Western Kingbird. *San Mateo County Breeding Bird Atlas*, p. 135. Sequoia Audubon Society.

———. 2001g. Horned Lark. *San Mateo County Breeding Bird Atlas*, p. 145. Sequoia Audubon Society.

———. 2001h. White-breasted Nuthatch. *San Mateo County Breeding Bird Atlas*, p. 158. Sequoia Audubon Soc.

———. 2001i. Winter Wren. *San Mateo County Breeding Bird Atlas*, p. 164. Sequoia Audubon Soc.

———. 2001j. Golden-crowned Kinglet. *San Mateo County Breeding Bird Atlas*, p. 167. Sequoia Audubon Society.

———. 2001k. Western Tanager. *San Mateo County Breeding Bird Atlas*, p. 190. Sequoia Audubon Society.

———. 2001l. Grasshopper Sparrow. *San Mateo County Breeding Bird Atlas*, p. 199. Sequoia Audubon Society.

———. 2001m. Pine Siskin. *San Mateo County Breeding Bird Atlas*, p. 218. Sequoia Audubon Society.

———. 2001n. Lawrence's Goldfinch. *San Mateo County Breeding Bird Atlas*, p. 220. Sequoia Audubon Society.

Sharsmith, H. K. 1982. *Flora of the Mount Hamilton Range of California.* CNPS Spec. Publ. No. 6. Calif. Native Plant Soc., Grass Valley, Calif.

Sheldon, H. H. 1908. Three nests of note from Northern California. *Condor 10*:120–124.

Shuford, W. D., ed. 1993a. *Marin County Breeding Bird Atlas.* Bushtit Books, Bolinas, Calif.

Shuford, W. D. 1993b. American Bittern (*Botaurus lentiginosus*). *Marin County Breeding Bird Atlas*, pp. 91–92 (W. D. Shuford, ed.). Bushtit Books, Bolinas, Calif.

———. 1993c. Great Egret (*Ardea alba*). *Marin County Breeding Bird Atlas*, pp. 96–97 (W. D. Shuford, ed.). Bushtit Books, Bolinas, Calif.

———. 1993d. Canada Goose (*Branta canadensis*). *Marin County Breeding Bird Atlas*, pp. 104–105 (W. D. Shuford, ed.). Bushtit Books, Bolinas, Calif.

———. 1993e. Northern Pintail (*Anas acuta*). *Marin County Breeding Bird Atlas*, pp. 111–112 (W. D. Shuford, ed.). Bushtit Books, Bolinas, Calif.

———. 1993f. Blue-winged Teal (*Anas discors*). *Marin County Breeding Bird Atlas*, pp. 113–114 (W. D. Shuford, ed.). Bushtit Books, Bolinas, Calif.

———. 1993g. Gadwall (*Anas strepera*). *Marin County Breeding Bird Atlas*, pp. 118–119 (W. D. Shuford, ed.). Bushtit Books, Bolinas, Calif.

———. 1993h. Osprey (*Pandion haliaetus*). *Marin County Breeding Bird Atlas*, pp. 129–132 (W. D. Shuford, ed.). Bushtit Books, Bolinas, Calif.

———. 1993i. Cooper's Hawk (*Accipiter cooperi*). *Marin County Breeding Bird Atlas*, pp. 141–144 (W. D. Shuford, ed.). Bushtit Books, Bolinas, Calif.

———. 1993j. American Kestrel (*Falco sparverius*). *Marin County Breeding Bird Atlas*, pp. 151–153 (W. D. Shuford, ed.). Bushtit Books, Bolinas, Calif.

———. 1993k. Virginia Rail (*Rallus limicola*). *Marin County Breeding Bird Atlas*, pp. 169–170 (W. D. Shuford, ed.). Bushtit Books, Bolinas, Calif.

———. 1993l. Sora (*Porzana carolina*). *Marin County Breeding Bird Atlas*, pp. 171–173 (W. D. Shuford, ed.). Bushtit Books, Bolinas, Calif.

———. 1993m. Black-necked Stilt (*Himantopus mexicanus*). *Marin County Breeding Bird Atlas*, pp. 184–186 (W. D. Shuford, ed.). Bushtit Books, Bolinas, Calif.

———. 1993n. Spotted Sandpiper (*Actitis macularia*). *Marin County Breeding Bird Atlas*, pp. 189–190 (W. D. Shuford, ed.). Bushtit Books, Bolinas, Calif.

———. 1993o. Western Gull (*Larus occidentalis*). *Marin County Breeding Bird Atlas*, pp. 191–193 (W. D. Shuford, ed.). Bushtit Books, Bolinas, Calif.

———. 1993p. White-throated Swift (*Aeronautes saxatalis*). *Marin County Breeding Bird Atlas*, pp. 236–237 (W. D. Shuford, ed.). Bushtit Books, Bolinas, Calif.

———. 1993q. Downy Woodpecker (*Picoides pubescens*). *Marin County Breeding Bird Atlas*, pp. 248–250 (W. D. Shuford, ed.). Bushtit Books, Bolinas, Calif.

———. 1993r. Pacific-slope Flycatcher (*Empidonax difficilis*). *Marin County Breeding Bird Atlas*, pp. 258–260 (W. D. Shuford, ed.). Bushtit Books, Bolinas, Calif.

———. 1993s. Say's Phoebe (*Sayornis saya*). *Marin County Breeding Bird Atlas*, pp. 262–263 (W. D. Shuford, ed.). Bushtit Books, Bolinas, Calif.

————. 1993t. Western Kingbird (*Tyrannus verticalis*). *Marin County Breeding Bird Atlas*, pp. 266–267 (W. D. Shuford, ed.). Bushtit Books, Bolinas, Calif.

————. 1993u. Tree Swallow (*Tachycineta bicolor*). *Marin County Breeding Bird Atlas*, pp. 272–273 (W. D. Shuford, ed.). Bushtit Books, Bolinas, Calif.

————. 1993v. Pygmy Nuthatch (*Sitta pygmaea*). *Marin County Breeding Bird Atlas*, pp. 298–300 (W. D. Shuford, ed.). Bushtit Books, Bolinas, Calif.

————. 1993w. House Wren (*Troglodytes aedon*). *Marin County Breeding Bird Atlas*, pp. 307–308 (W. D. Shuford, ed.). Bushtit Books, Bolinas, Calif.

————. 1993x. American Dipper (*Cinclus mexicanus*). *Marin County Breeding Bird Atlas*, p. 312 (W. D. Shuford, ed.). Bushtit Books, Bolinas, CA.

————. 1993y. Blue-Gray Gnatcatcher (*Polioptila caerulea*). *Marin County Breeding Bird Atlas*, pp. 314–316 (W. D. Shuford, ed.). Bushtit Books, Bolinas, Calif.

————. 1993z. Swainson's Thrush (*Catharus ustulatus*). *Marin County Breeding Bird Atlas*, pp. 318–319 (W. D. Shuford, ed.). Bushtit Books, Bolinas, Calif.

————. 1993aa. European Starling (*Sturnus vulgaris*). *Marin County Breeding Bird Atlas*, pp. 333–336 (W. D. Shuford, ed.). Bushtit Books, Bolinas, Calif.

————. 1993bb. Solitary Vireo (*Vireo solitarius*). *Marin County Breeding Bird Atlas*, pp. 337–339 (W. D. Shuford, ed.). Bushtit Books, Bolinas, Calif.

————. 1993cc. Yellow-rumped Warbler (*Dendroica coronata*). *Marin County Breeding Bird Atlas*, pp. 348–349 (W. D. Shuford, ed.). Bushtit Books, Bolinas, Calif.

————. 1993dd. Black-throated Gray Warbler (*Dendroica nigrescens*). *Marin County Breeding Bird Atlas*, pp. 350–351 (W. D. Shuford, ed.). Bushtit Books, Bolinas, Calif.

————. 1993ee. Song Sparrow (*Melospiza melodia*). *Marin County Breeding Bird Atlas*, pp. 385–387 (W. D. Shuford, ed.). Bushtit Books, Bolinas, Calif.

————. 1993ff. Red Crossbill (*Loxia curvirostra*). *Marin County Breeding Bird Atlas*, pp. 414–416 (W. D. Shuford, ed.). Bushtit Books, Bolinas, Calif.

————. 1993gg. American Goldfinch (*Carduelis tristis*). *Marin County Breeding Bird Atlas*, pp. 422–423 (W. D. Shuford, ed.). Bushtit Books, Bolinas, Calif.

————. 1993hh. Little Blue Heron (*Egretta caerulea*). *Marin County Breeding Bird Atlas*, p. 429 (W. D. Shuford, ed.). Bushtit Books, Bolinas, Calif.

Shuford, W. D. and T. P. Ryan. 2000. Nesting populations of California and Ring-billed gulls in California: recent surveys and historical status. *West. Birds* 31:133–164.

Shuford, W. D., C. M. Hickey, R. J. Safran and G. W. Page. 1996. A review of the status of the White-faced Ibis in winter in California. *West. Birds* 27:169–196.

Sibley, C. G. 1949. Species formation in the Mexican red-eyed towhees, avian genus *Piplio*, Ph.D. diss., Univ. California, Berkeley.

Sibley, C .G. 1952. *The Birds of the South San Francisco Bay Region*. Mimeographed. Available at Santa Clara Valley Audubon Society library, Cupertino, Calif.

Sibley, C. G. 1955. Nesting of the Western Tanager in the Santa Cruz Mountains, California. *Condor* 57:307.

Sibley, C. G. and B. L. Monroe, Jr. 1990. *Distribution and Taxonomy of Birds of the World*. Yale Univ. Pr., New Haven.

Sibley, D. A. 2000. *The Sibley Guide to Birds*. A. A. Knopf, New York.

Sisk, T. D. 1991. Distributions of birds and butterflies in heterogeneous landscapes. Ph.D. diss., Dept. Biol. Sci., Stanford Univ., Stanford, Calif.

Skinner, J. E. 1962. Fish and wildlife resources of the San Francisco Bay area. Calif. Dept. Fish and Game, Water Proj. Br. Rep. 1.

Sloane, S. 2001. Bushtit (*Psaltriparus minimus*). *The Birds of North America*, No. 598 (A. Poole and F. Gill, eds.). The Birds of North America, Inc., Philadelphia.

Small, A. 1994. *California Birds: Their Status and Distribution*. Ibis Publ. Co., Vista, Calif.

Smallwood, J. A. and D. M. Bird. 2002. American Kestrel (*Falco sparverius*). *The Birds of North America*, No. 602 (A. Poole and F. Gill, eds.). The Birds of North America, Inc., Philadelphia.

Smith, C. F. and C. L. Hopkins. 1937. Note on the Barn Owls of the San Francisco Bay region. *Condor* 39:189–191.

Smith, C. P. 1926. Has the cowbird come to stay? *Condor* 28:245.

————. 1927a. The Olive-sided Flycatcher and coniferous trees. *Condor* 29:120–121.

————. 1927b. The lupines of the Pacific States of North America. Ph.D. thesis, Stanford Univ., Stanford, Calif.

Smith, E. 1928. Black Swifts nesting behind a waterfall. *Condor* 30:136–138.

Smith, F. 1977. A short review of the status of riparian forests in California. *Riparian Forests in California: Their Ecology and Conservation*, pp. 1–2 (A. Sands, ed.). Inst. Ecology Publ. 15. Inst. of Ecology, Univ. Calif. Davis, Davis.

Smith, F. B. 1925. (Brochure). Pacific Portland Cement Co. Consol., San Francisco.

Smith, F. M. 1918. Canada Geese bred in Alameda County. *Calif. Fish Game* 4:50–51.

Smithson, W. S. 2000. Breeding biology of the Orange Bishop (*Euplectes franciscanus*) and Nutmeg Mannikin (*Lonchura punctulata*) in southern California. Master's thesis, Cal. State Univ. Long Beach, Calif.

Snyder, J. O. 1904. Notes on the fishes of the streams flowing into San Francisco Bay. Appendix to the Report of the Commissioner of Fisheries to the Secretary of Commerce and Labor of the year ending June 30, 1904, pp. 327–338, plus map. Govt. Print. Off., Washington.

————. 1919. Breeding of the Fulvous Tree-Duck in Santa Clara County. *Calif. Fish Game* 5:43.

————. 1934. Water storage in Santa Clara County. *Calif. Fish Game* 20:390–391.

Sogge, M. K., W. M. Gilbert and C. v. Ripper, III. 1994. Orange-crowned Warbler (*Vermivora celata*). *The Birds of North America*, No. 101 (A. Poole and F. Gill, eds.). Acad. Nat. Sci., Philadelphia; Am. Ornithol. Union, Washington.

Spear, L. B. 1998. Dispersal patterns of Western Gulls from Southeast Farallon Island. *Auk* 105:128–141.

Squires, W. A. 1915. Nesting of wild ducks near San Francisco. *Condor 17*:234–235.

———. 1916a. Are there two forms of the Bryant Marsh Sparrow in San Francisco County? *Condor 18*:228.

———. 1916b. Some field notes from western Sonoma County, California. *Condor 18*:232.

Stafford, L. 1995. Loggerhead Shrike (*Lanius ludovicianus*). *Sonoma County Breeding Bird Atlas,* pp. 139, 185 (B. Burridge, ed.). Madrone Audubon Soc., Santa Rosa, Calif.

Stanger, F. M. 1967. *Sawmills in the Redwoods.* San Mateo Historical Soc., San Mateo, Calif.

Steele, J. and J. McCormick. 1995. Partitioning of the summer grounds by Orange-crowned Warblers into breeding grounds, adult molting grounds and juvenile staging areas. Abstract. *North Am. Bird-bander 20*:152.

Steenhof, K. 1998. Prairie Falcon (*Falco mexicanus*). *The Birds of North America*, No. 346 (A. Poole and F. Gill, eds.). The Birds of North America, Inc., Philadelphia.

Stephens, L. A. 1936. Saint Mary's, Contra Costa County. *Gull 18(6)*.

Sterling, J. and P. W. C. Paton. 1996. Breeding distribution of Vaux's Swift in California. *West. Birds 27*:30–40.

Stewart, R. M. 1973. Breeding behavior and life history of the Wilson's Warbler. *Wilson Bull. 85*:21–30.

Stiles, G. F. 1973. Food supply and the annual cycle of the Anna Hummingbird. *Univ. Calif. Publ. Zool. 97*:1–109.

Stone, L. C. 1986. *Andrew Jackson Grayson; Birds of the Pacific Slope.* Arion Pr., San Francisco.

Stone, W. 1916. Philadelphia to the coast in early days, and the development of western ornithology prior to 1850. *Condor 18*:3–14.

———. 1935. Pickwell's 'Bird Studies'. *Auk 52*:338–339.

Stoner, E. A. 1931. Re-use of its nest by the Spotted Towhee. *Condor 22*:352.

———. 1937. Avocets nesting on San Pablo Bay marsh. *Condor 39*:174.

———. 1938. Audubon Warbler nesting in Solano County, California. *Condor 40*:259.

Storer, R. W. and G. L. Nuechterlein. 1992. Western Grebe (*Aechmophorus occidentalis*), Clark's Grebe (*Aechmophorus clarkii*). *The Birds of North America*, No. 26 (A. Poole and F. Gill, eds.). Acad. Nat. Sci., Philadelphia; Am. Ornithol. Union, Washington.

Storer, T. I. 1920. Western Tanager in Santa Cruz Mountains in summer. *Condor 22*:161.

———. 1931. The American Egret in the Lower Sacramento Valley, California. *Condor 33*:34–35.

Storer, T. I. and L. P. Tevis, Jr. 1955. *California Grizzly.* Univ. Calif. Pr., Berkeley.

Taber, W. 1968. California Blue Grosbeak (*Guiraca caerulea salicaria*). *Life Histories of North American Cardinals, Grosbeaks, Buntings, Towhees, Finches, Sparrows, and Allies,* Pt. 1, p. 80 (O. L. Austin, Jr., comp. & ed.). Smithsonian Inst. U.S. Natl. Museum Bull. 237, Pt.1. Reissued in 1968 by Dover Publ., New York.

Taylor, H. R. 1889. Is it the California Bob-white, A.O.U. 289c? *Ornithol. Oologist 14*:93.

———. 1893. Nesting of Nuttall's Woodpecker. *Nidiologist 1*:7.

———. 1894a. Among the California Clapper Rail. *Nidiologist 1*:153–154.

[Taylor, H. R.] 1894b. Water rats destroying eggs. *Nidiologist 2*:15.

Taylor, H. R. 1903. In memoriam: Chester Barlow. *Condor 5*:2–7.

Telfair, R. C., II. 1994. Cattle Egret (*Bubulcus ibis*). *The Birds of North America*, No. 113 (A. Poole and F. Gill, eds.). Acad. Nat. Sci., Philadelphia; Am. Ornithol. Union, Washington.

Tenney, C. 1993a. Plain Titmouse (*Parus inornatus*). *Atlas of the Breeding Birds of Monterey County, California*, pp. 256–257 (D. Roberson and C. Tenney, eds.). Monterey Peninsula Audubon Soc., Monterey.

———. 1993b. House Wren (*Troglodytes aedon*). *Atlas of the Breeding Birds of Monterey County, California*, pp. 274-275, 307 (W. D. Shuford, ed.). Bushtit Books, Bolinas, Calif.

———. 1993c. Blue-gray Gnatcatcher (*Polioptila caerulea*). *Atlas of the Breeding Birds of Monterey County, California*, pp. 282–283 (D. Roberson and C. Tenney, eds.). Monterey Peninsula Audubon Soc., Monterey.

———. 1993d. Chipping Sparrow (*Spizella passerina*). *Atlas of the Breeding Birds of Monterey County, California*, pp. 346–347 (D. Roberson and C. Tenney, eds.). Monterey Peninsula Audubon Soc., Monterey.

———. 1993e. Sage Sparrow (*Amphispiza belli*). *Atlas of the Breeding Birds of Monterey County, California*, pp. 352–353 (D. Roberson and C. Tenney, eds.). Monterey Peninsula Audubon Soc., Monterey.

———. 1997. Black-chinned Sparrow (*Spizella atrogularis*). *The Birds of North America*, No. 270 (A. Poole and F. Gill, eds.). Acad. Nat. Sci., Philadelphia; Am. Ornithol. Union, Washington.

Terborgh, J. 1989. *Where Have All the Birds Gone?* Princeton Univ. Pr., Princeton, N.J.

Terres, J. K. 1980. *The Audubon Society Encyclopedia of North American Birds.* Alfred A. Knopf, New York.

Thelander, C. G. 1994. *Life on the Edge.* BioSystems Books, Santa Cruz, Calif.

Thomas, J. H. 1956. Charles Piper Smith, 1877–1955. *Botany 8*:41–46.

———. 1961. *Flora of the Santa Cruz Mountains of California; a Manual of the Vascular Plants.* Stanford Univ. Pr., Stanford, Calif.

Thompson and West. 1876. *Historical Atlas Map of Santa Clara County, California.* Thompson and West, San Francisco.

Thompson, W. L. 1964. An early specimen of the Indigo Bunting from California. *Condor 66*:445.

Tibbetts, F. H. and S. E. Kieffer. 1921. Report to Santa Clara Valley Water Conservation Committee on Santa Clara Valley Water Conservation Project. [Publisher unknown.]

Tintle, R. F. 1993. California Thrasher (*Toxostoma redivivum*). *Breeding Birds of Monterey County, California*, pp. 296–297 (D. Roberson and C. Tenney, eds.). Monterey Peninsula Audubon Soc., Monterey.

Townsend, C. H. 1893. Report of observations respecting the oyster resources and oyster fishery of the Pacific Coast of the United States. U.S. Comm. of Fish and Fisheries Report 1889–1891. U.S. Govt. Print. Off., Washington. (Cited in J. E. Skinner, 1962.)

Troetschler, R. G. 1969. The impact of the starling (*Sturnus vulgaris*) on the native hole-nesting species of the San Francisco Bay region. Master's thesis, San Jose State Univ., San Jose.

———. 1976. Acorn Woodpecker breeding strategy as affected by Starling nest-hole competition. *Condor* 78:151–165.

Trulio, L. A. 1994. Study of the Status, Ecology and Distribution of Western Burrowing Owls at Moffett Naval Airfield, Santa Clara County, California. U.S. Navy Contract No. N62474-91-M-0603.

———. 1997. Burrowing Owl demography and habitat use at two urban sites in Santa Clara County, California. *J. Raptor Res.* 9:84–89.

Turner, W. M. 1962. *A History of the Santa Clara Valley Audubon Society.* Mimeographed. Available at Santa Clara Valley Audubon Society library, Cupertino, Calif.

Twedt, D. J. and R. D. Crawford. 1995. Yellow-headed Blackbird (*Xanthocephalus xanthocephalus*). *The Birds of North America*, No. 192 (A. Poole and F. Gill, eds.). Acad. Nat. Sci., Philadelphia; Am. Ornithol. Union, Washington.

Tweit, R. C. and J. C. Tweit. 2000. Cassin's Kingbird (*Tyrannus vociferans*). *The Birds of North America*, No. 534 (A. Poole and F. Gill, eds.). The Birds of North America, Inc., Philadelphia.

Tyler, J. G. 1913. Some birds of the Fresno district, California. *Pac. Coast Avifauna*, No. 9. Cooper Ornithol. Club, Berkeley, Calif.

Tyler, W. M. 1968. *Life Histories of North American Cardinals, Grosbeaks, Buntings, Towhees, Finches, Sparrows, and Allies*, Pt. 1, p. 466 (O. L. Austin, Jr., comp. & ed.). Smithsonian Inst. U.S. Natl. Museum Bull. 237, Pt.1. Reissued in 1968 by Dover Publ., New York.

Unglish, W. E. 1929. The Texas Nighthawk in Santa Clara County, California. *Condor* 31:223.

———. 1932. Nesting of the Black-chinned Hummingbird in Santa Clara County, California. *Condor* 34:228.

———. 1933. A migration of hummingbirds through Santa Clara Co., California. *Condor* 35:237.

———. 1937. A few unusual records from Central California. *Condor* 39:39–40.

Unitt, P. 1977. The Little Blue Heron in California. *West. Birds* 8:151–154.

———. 1986. Another hybrid Downy × Nuttall's Woodpecker from San Diego County. *West. Birds* 17:43–44.

———. 2004. Lazuli Bunting (*Passerina amoena*). *San Diego County Bird Atlas*, pp. 550–552. San Diego Natl. Hist. Museum, San Diego.

Unitt, P. and A. M. Rea. 1997. Taxonomy of the Brown Creeper in California. *The Era of Allan R. Phillips: a Festschrift*, pp. 177–185 (R. W. Dickerman, ed.). Horizon Communications, Albuquerque, N.M.

[USFWS]. U.S. Fish and Wildlife Service. 1998. Draft Recovery Plan for the Least Bell's Vireo. Portland, Oreg.

Vallejo, G. 1890. Ranch and mission days in Alta California. *Century Mag.* 41(2):183–192.

Vancouver, G. 1798. *Voyage of Discovery to the North Pacific Ocean and Round the World. Vol. 2.* G. G. and J. Robinson, London. Reissued in 1967 by Da Capa Pr., Amsterdam.

Van Denburgh, J. 1899a. Birds observed in central California in the summer of 1893. *Proc. Acad. Nat. Sci. Phil. 1898* pp. 206–218.

———. 1899b. Notes on some birds of Santa Clara County, California. *Proc. Am. Philos. Soc. 38(160)*: 157–180.

———. 1922. *The Reptiles of Western North America.* 2 vol., Calif. Acad. Sci., San Francisco.

van Rossem, A. J. 1926. The California forms of *Agelaius phoeniceus* (Linnaeus). *Condor* 28:215–230.

Verbeek, N. A. M. 1973. The exploitation system of the Yellow-billed Magpie. *Univ. Calif. Publ. Zool.* 99:1–58.

Verbeek, N. A. M. and C. Caffrey. 2002. American Crow (*Corvus brachyrhynchos*). *The Birds of North America*, No. 647 (A. Poole and F. Gill, eds.). The Birds of North America, Inc., Philadelphia.

Ver Planck, W. E. 1958. *Salt in California.* With a chapter by R. F. Heizer. Bull. 175. Div. of Mines, State of Calif., San Francisco.

Vickery, P. D. 1996. Grasshopper Sparrow (*Ammodramus savannarum*), *The Birds of North America*, No. 239 (A. Poole and F. Gill, eds.). Acad. Nat. Sci., Philadelphia; Am. Ornithol. Union, Washington.

Vigors, N. A. 1839. *The Zoology of Captain Beechey's Voyage.* Henry G. Bohn, London.

von Bloeker, J. C., Jr. 1993. Who were Harry R. Painton, A. Brazier Howell, and Frances F. Roberts? *Condor* 95:1061–1063.

Wagner, D. L., H. G. Greene, G. J. Saucedo and C. L. Pridmore. 2002. Geologic map of the Monterey 30′ × 60′ quadrangle and adjacent areas, California, a digital database. Calif. Geol. Survey CD 2002-04, map scale 1:100,000.

Walton, B. J. and C. G. Thelander. 1988. Peregrine Falcon management efforts in California, Oregon, Washington, and Nevada. *Peregrine Falcon Populations: Their Management and Recovery,* pp. 587–595 (T. J. Cade, J. H. Enderson, C. G. Thelander and C. M. White, eds.). The Peregrine Fund, Boise, Ida.

Walton, B. J., C. G. Thelander and D. L. Harlow. 1988. The status of Peregrines nesting in California, Oregon, Washington, and Nevada. *Peregrine Falcon Populations: Their Management and Recovery,* pp. 95–104 (T. J. Cade, J. H. Enderson, C. G. Thelander and C. M. White, eds.). The Peregrine Fund, Boise, Ida.

Watson, F. G. 1940. The Little Blue Heron in the San Francisco Bay Region. *Gull* 22:37.

Watt, D. J. and E. J. Willoughby. 1999. Lesser Goldfinch (*Carduelis psaltria*). *The Birds of North America*, No. 392 (A. Poole and F. Gill, eds.). The Birds of North America, Inc., Philadelphia.

Weed, B. J. 1993a. Canada Goose (*Branta canadensis*). *Breeding Birds of Monterey County, California*, pp. 68–69 (D. Roberson and C. Tenney, eds.). Monterey Peninsula Audubon Soc., Monterey.

543

————. 1993b. Mallard (*Anas platyrhynchos*). *Breeding Birds of Monterey County, California*, pp. 72–73 (D. Roberson and C. Tenney, eds.). Monterey Peninsula Audubon Soc., Monterey.

————. 1993c. Cinnamon Teal (*Anas cyanoptera*). *Breeding Birds of Monterey County, California*, pp. 76–77 (D. Roberson and C. Tenney, eds.). Monterey Peninsula Audubon Soc., Monterey.

Weiss, S. B. 1999. Cars, cows, and checkerspot butterflies: nitrogen deposition and management of nutrient-poor grasslands for a threatened species. *Conserv. Biol.* 13:1476–1486.

Weitzel, N. H. 1988. Nest-site competition between the European Starling and native breeding birds in northwestern Nevada. *Condor* 90:515–517.

Welch, W. R. 1931. Game reminiscences of yesteryear. *Calif. Fish Game* 17:255–263.

Weller, M. W. 1959. Parasitic egg laying in the Redhead (*Aythya americana*) and other North American Anatidae. *Ecol. Monogr.* 29:333–365.

Wentworth, C. M. and J. C. Tinsley. 2005. Geologic setting, stratigraphy, and detailed velocity structure of the Coyote Creek borehole, Santa Clara Valley, California. *Blind Comparisons of Shear-wave Velocities at Closely Spaced Sites in San Jose, California* (M. W. Asten and D. M. Boore, eds.). U.S. Geol. Surv. Open File Rep. 2005-1169, Pt. 2_01, 26 pp. http://pubs.usgs.gov/of/2005/1169/

Wentworth, C. M., M. C. Blake, Jr., R. J. McLaughlin and R. W. Graymer. 1998. Preliminary geologic description of the San Jose 30 × 60 minute quadrangle, California. U.S. Geol. Surv. Open File Rep. 98-975. http://pubs.usgs.gov/of/1998/of98-795.

Werner, S. 1927. Proceedings of the August meeting. *Gull* 9(9).

Weston, H. G., Jr. 1947. Breeding behavior of the Black-headed Grosbeak. *Condor* 49:54–73.

Wheeler, R. J. and S. W. Harris. 1970. Duck nesting and production in the Humboldt Bay area of California. *Calif. Fish Game* 56:180–187.

Wheelock, I. G. 1904. *Birds of California*. A. C. McClurg, Chicago.

————. 1905. Regurgitative feeding of nestlings. *Auk* 22:54–71.

Wheelwright, N. T. and J. D. Rising. 1993. Savannah Sparrow (*Passerculus sandwichensis*). *The Birds of North America*, No. 45 (A. Poole and F. Gill, eds.). Acad. Nat. Sci., Philadelphia; Am. Ornithol. Union, Washington.

White, C. M., N. J. Clum, T. J. Cade and W. G. Hunt. 2002. Peregrine Falcon (*Falco peregrinus*). *The Birds of North America*, No. 660 (A. Poole and F. Gill, eds.). The Birds of North America, Inc., Philadelphia.

Wilbur, S. R. 1973. The Red-shouldered Hawk in the western United States. *West. Birds* 4:15–22.

Willett, G. 1912. Birds of the Pacific Slope of Southern California. *Pacific Coast Avifauna*, No. 7, Cooper Ornithol. Club, Berkeley.

Williams, P. L. 1993. Northern Oriole (*Icterus galbula*). *Marin County Breeding Bird Atlas*, pp. 405–408 (W. D. Shuford, ed.). Bushtit Books, Bolinas, Calif.

[Wilson, L. K.] 1931. Ducks in California. [Editorial]. *Calif. Fish Game* 17:66–68.

Wilson, R. C. 1937. Early day lumber operations in the Santa Cruz redwood region. *Timberman* 38(7):12–15.

Winkler, D. W. 1996. California Gull (*Larus californicus*). *The Birds of North America*, No. 259 (A. Poole and F. Gill, eds.). Acad. Nat. Sci., Philadelphia; Am. Ornithol. Union, Washington.

Wirtz, W. O., II. 1991. Avifauna in southern California chaparral: seasonal distribution, habitat association, reproductive phenology. Research paper PSW-RP-209. U.S. Dept. Agric. Forest Serv., Pacific Southwest Res. Station, Berkeley, Calif.

Witmer, M. C., D. J. Mountjoy and L. Elliot. 1997. Cedar Waxwing (*Bombycilla cedrorum*). *The Birds of North America*, No. 309 (A. Poole and F. Gill, eds.). Acad. Nat. Sci., Philadelphia; Am. Ornithol. Union, Washington.

Witter, R. C., K. L. Knudsen, J. M. Sowers, C. M. Wentworth, R. D. Koehler, C. E. Randolph, S. K. Brooks and K. D. Gans. 2006. Maps of Quaternary deposits and liquefaction susceptibility in the central San Francisco Bay Region, California. U.S. Geol. Surv. Open File Rep. 06-1037. http:/pubs.usgs.gov/of/2006/1037/.

Wolf, B. O. 1991. The reproductive biology and natural history of the Black Phoebe (*Sayornis nigricans* Swainson) in central California. Master's thesis, San Jose State Univ.

————. 1997. Black Phoebe (*Sayornis nigricans*). *The Birds of North America*, No. 268 (A. Poole and F. Gill, eds.). Acad. Nat. Sci., Philadelphia; Am. Ornithol. Union, Washington.

Woodin, M. W. and T. C. Michot. 2002. Redhead (*Aythya americana*). *The Birds of North America*, No. 695 (A. Poole and F. Gill, eds.). The Birds of North America, Inc., Philadelphia.

Woods, R. S. 1940. *Life Histories of North American Cuckoos, Goatsuckers, Hummingbirds and Their Allies, Pt. 2*, p. 387. Smithsonian Inst. U. S. Natl. Museum Bull. 176. Republished in 1964 by Dover Publ. Inc, New York, NY.

Wootton, J. T. 1996. Purple Finch (*Carpodacus purpureus*). *The Birds of North America*, No. 208 (A. Poole and F. Gill, eds.). Acad. Nat. Sci., Philadelphia; Am. Ornithol. Union, Washington.

Wright, H. and E. Smith. 1930. Late nesting and puzzling behavior of the California woodpecker. *Wren-Tit* 1(4).

Yasukawa, K. and W. A. Searcy. 1995. Red-winged Blackbird (*Agelaius phoeniceus*). *The Birds of North America*, No. 184 (A. Poole and F. Gill, eds.). Acad. Nat. Sci., Philadelphia; Am. Ornithol. Union, Washington.

Yosef, R. 1996. Loggerhead Shrike (*Lanius ludovicianus*). *The Birds of North America*, No. 231 (A. Poole and F. Gill, eds.). Acad. Nat. Sci., Philadelphia; Am. Ornithol. Union, Washington.

Zeiner, D. C., W. F. Laudenslayer, Jr., K. E. Mayer and M. White. 1990. *California's Wildlife, Vol. 2: Birds*. Calif. Dept. Fish and Game, Sacramento.

Zimmerman, D. A. 1973. Range expansion of Anna's Hummingbird. *Am. Birds* 27:827–835.

Zink, R. M. 1988. Evolution of Brown Towhees: allozymes, morphometrics and species limits. *Condor* 90:79–82.

Zucca, J. J. 1954. A study of the California Clapper Rail. *Wasmann J. Biol.* 12:135–153.

Index

Birds referenced in this atlas are indexed here. Boldfaced page numbers refer to breeding accounts, either for the species accounts in Chapter 7 or for those in Appendixes 8 to 10.